Reading and Writing from Literature

Reading *and*
Writing *from*
Literature

THIRD EDITION

___

JOHN E. SCHWIEBERT
Weber State University

Houghton Mifflin Company　　Boston　New York

"Books are the best of things, well used; abused, among the worst. . . . They are for nothing but to inspire."

—RALPH WALDO EMERSON

Executive Editor: Suzanne Phelps Weir
Sponsoring Editor: Michael Gillespie
Associate Editor: Bruce Cantley
Project Editor: Lindsay Frost
Editorial Assistant: Michelle O'Berg
Manufacturing Coordinator: Carrie Wagner
Senior Marketing Manager: Cindy Graff Cohen

Text credits appear on pages 1214–1220, which constitute an extension of the copyright page.

Cover image credit: Diego Rivera, *Dance in Tehuantepec* (detail), 1935. Charcoal and watercolor. Los Angeles County Museum of Art, Gift of Mr. and Mrs. Milton W. Lipper, from the Milton W. Lipper Estate.

Printed in the U.S.A.

Library of Congress Catalog Card Number: 2003116168

ISBN: 0-618-45412-8

123456789-QUK-09 08 07 06 05

Contents

A Gallery of Pictures
1. Jusepe de Ribera, *Boy with a Clubfoot*
2. Arthur Hughes, *Home from Sea*
3. Unidentified artist, *Running Before the Storm*
4. William T. Wiley, *Detail Study from the Bright Side*
5. Melissa Ann Pinney, *Bat Mitzvah Dance, Chicago, Illinois, 1991*
6. Brian Kershisnik, *Mother and Child with Dogs Vomiting*

Appendices

Preface

Designed for use in literature courses that are also writing courses, *Reading and Writing from Literature* offers a fresh new approach to reading and writing in those classes. The book invokes a "conversation" model of reading and writing that empowers students to interact proactively and constructively with all texts, both literary and their own.

Reading and Writing from Literature presents reading as the primary resource for writing. Rather than only writing *about* literature, student users of this book write *from* literature; they use texts to produce texts. Being personally and culturally diverse, students are encouraged to identify and use those aspects of a text that interest them most as starting points for composing. Throughout the book, the guiding assumption is that, by creating, students also become stronger readers of the literature of past and present.

TEXT FEATURES

Distinctive Features of Reading and Writing from Literature, *Third Edition, That Will Enrich Your AP Class*

The third edition retains all of the unique features of the second edition that have made *Reading and Writing from Literature* unique in the market and popular among teachers and students:

- Treats reading and writing as thoroughly interrelated: rhetoric chapters and other apparatus assure that students are always writing as they read and reading as they write.
- Empowers students both to study literature and to use literature as a springboard for making texts of their own.
- Offers activities and apparatus that get students to look repeatedly at literary texts and their own texts, thereby promoting habits of recursive reading, thinking, and writing.
- Includes an anthology of 171 readings (short stories, poems, essays, and plays) that are weighted toward the contemporary and multicultural to encourage strong responses from students of diverse backgrounds.

- Features a simple and uncluttered apparatus that students can use in class and on their own, without detailed guidance from the teacher.
- Contains numerous examples of student writings in many forms, both creative and analytic.
- Gives students incentives and strategies for continuing to read and write conversationally once this particular course is over.

Features New to the Third Edition

The third edition contains several new features that make it even more versatile:

- The new Chapter 9, "Writing Arguments" helps students to become critical thinkers and to write well-reasoned argumentative essays about literature. It includes a definition of argument, a step-by-step analysis of Barbara Kingsolver's argumentative essay "The One-Eyed Monster, and Why I Don't Let Him In," and a sample student argumentative essay on William Blake's poem "The Clod and the Pebble."
- Responding to the increased emphasis on visual literacy in many literature and composition courses, a new four-color insert, featuring art and other graphics for analysis, has been added. Prompt questions encourage students to respond to the images with creative and analytical writings.
- Chapter 4, "'Hurry Notes:' Keeping a Commonplace Book," is new and expands upon Chapter 3, "Building a Reading Notebook," by encouraging students to write down favorite quotations or jot down ideas for invention and revision. The chapter includes a historic survey of commonplace books treating how writers and other creative individuals have used such books to collect and develop ideas.
- Chapter 5, "Writing in Diverse Forms: The Topic/Form Grid," is also new. The chapter encourages students to use a topic/form grid when deciding which literary form is most appropriate for the topic at hand.
- A new Chapter 10, "Writing Literature-Based Research Papers," and a completely revised Chapter 11, "Documenting Research Essays," present a thorough overview of the research process, including material on keeping a research log, narrowing focus, identifying and keeping track of source information, citing outside sources, and documenting using the latest MLA documentation guidelines. A sample student researched paper is also provided.
- Part V (Chapter 19), "Introduction to Figurative Language," is new, and it places an emphasis on a topic that is oftentimes difficult for students new to literary analysis. The section explains and illustrates all of the major types of figurative language. Students learn how to identify and interpret metaphors, similes, paradoxes, irony, and other figures across literary genres

and other contexts. This section features the most extensive and detailed treatment of figurative language of any composition text on the market.

- A revised Chapter 6, "Ways of Planning: Thinking and Writing Recursively," now includes a new section on "Writing Mini-Essays to Practice Concise Expression," which shows students how to develop their textual annotations and short notes into longer and substantive pieces of writing.
- Chapter 8, "Ways of Revising: Caring and Not Caring," includes a new section on looking critically at a paper draft, and includes a revision checklist.
- Part VI, "A Thematic Anthology of Readings" has been thoroughly revised to include 45 new poems, essays/nonfiction writing, and short stories, all with an emphasis on the contemporary. This section is arranged under the same thematic categories as in the previous edition such as "Gender and Relationships," "Individual and Society," and "People and Cultures in Conflict and Change." This anthology includes a stronger representation of international and multicultural authors than in the previous edition. Among the writers new to the third edition are Antoine de Saint-Exupéry, Derek Walcott, Yusef Komunyakaa, Sei Shōnagon, and Allan Gurganus.

OVERVIEW AND ORGANIZATION OF THE TEXT

Inviting Students to Read and Write Intertextually

The theoretical basis of this book can be distilled into a single word — intertextuality, the primary engine that drives composing. In this book "text" is defined broadly to include all kinds of printed works, such as stories, poems, essays, and plays, as well as non-print phenomena such as movies, pictures, songs, conversations, and experiences. Intertextuality posits that every "text" is related to and evokes other texts, that one text is enmeshed in others. To compose a story poem, or essay is not to invent something out of nothing but to produce a new text out of a complex and interwoven fabric of other texts already "written into" the writer's life.

For a writer, reading is useful because it facilitates getting the texts of one's life on paper. The process begins when the writer reads a springboard text, such as a short story. Some aspect of the story — a character, an image, a phrase, as described incident — resonates with other texts in his or her life, thereby bringing these texts to consciousness. The writer composes a piece of his or her own, and the focus of the resulting composition is not the springboard text but the writer's intertextual web — the intricate and unique fabric of texts that constitutes who that writer is.

Intertextuality provides a rationale for reading and for writing in response to reading: through the process of writing, ideas can be articulated that might not have surfaced if the writer hadn't read and written from that particular text. In addition, intertextuality explains how a person can respond in writing to another text and still produce work that is individual, exciting, and "independent": because each person's intertextual web is unlike anyone else's.

Finally, intertextuality provides a rationale for the student to pursue an ongoing, lifelong program of reading and writing by demonstrating that no text, great or humble, is final, autonomous, or definitive, it validates every act of composing. In addition to being seen as ends-in-themselves, student texts and literary texts alike can be read temporally as parts of a continuing interplay of words and ideas, as "pre-texts" for additional thought, creation, and recreation.

Writing About Literature

This textbook is organized into rhetoric chapters and anthology chapters. The rhetoric chapters introduce students to techniques of reading, writing, and sharing that they can use throughout the term. Chapters are short and accessible enough that students can master most of the material on their own with minimal expenditure of in-class time.

Part I, "A Conversation Model of Writing and Reading" (Chapters 1–5), presents writing and reading as conversational acts in which students "talk back" to the texts they read and use the conversation as a springboard for creating texts of their own. In addition, Part I introduces the "reading notebook," the special kind of journal students can use for collecting their own writings—responses to literary works and creative and analytical writings of many kinds that may be prompted by the texts they read. The reading notebook eliminates the barriers between composing for school and composing for life and a lifetime; while developing techniques for reading and writing that will be useful to them in this course, students also learn strategies for producing meaningful writings of their own independently of this class or this textbook. Finally, Part I shows students how to use a small portable notepad or commonplace book for collecting notes, thoughts, quotations, and ideas for writing, and introduces them to a useful invention resource (the Topic/Form Grid) for composing in a variety of literary forms.

Part II, "Writing Essays About Literature" (Chapters 6–11), emphasizes the intertextual or recursive process of such composing. Students' essays do not materialize out of nothing; they are generated from previous work and from literary texts, the texts in their own notebooks, the texts of lecture and discussion, and the outside resources accessed through primary or secondary research. With strategies described in Part II, students learn how to use these texts to make a new text, i.e., an essay about literature.

Part III, "Creating a Writing Portfolio" (Chapters 12 and 13), shows students how to assemble a portfolio of their best writing for the quarter or semester. A portfolio is the result of a sustained process of recursive reading and writing in which students set aside their failed or mediocre work and concentrate on perfecting their best.

Part IV, "An Introduction to the Major Genres" (Chapters 14–18), introduces students to the genres of literature (short stories, poetry, nonfiction /essays, plays, and notebooks or journals) represented in the anthology. The chapters acquaint students with key literary terms and concepts that will help them to talk and write about short stories, poems, essays, and plays. In addition, Part IV is intended to increase students' technical knowledge of the genres so that they can write in multiple forms themselves.

Part V, "An Introduction to Figurative Language" (Chapter 19), shows students how to identify and interpret metaphors, paradoxes, ironies, and other major figures. Each figure is illustrated with multiple examples from the readings in Part VI and from other sources. Part V emphasizes the important role figures play in making meaning, both in literary texts and in life generally.

The Anthology of Readings

Part VI, "A Thematic Anthology of Readings" (Chapters 20–25), offers an anthology of 171 readings in the four major genres, arranged under six thematic headings: Gender and Relationships, Families, Experience and Identity, Individual and Society, People and Cultures in Conflict and Change, and Work and the Quality of Life. In addition, interspersed among the thematic sections are five interchapters on writers' notebooks and journals; the interchapters include selections from the work of five writers and provide students with practical ideas for creating and sustaining notebooks and journals of their own. I have chosen a thematic arrangement over a genre-based arrangement for two reasons: first, to avoid breaking whole texts into fragmentary "elements" (those of the short story, of poetry, of drama), which is the almost inevitable result of a genre-based organization; and second, to place primary emphasis on issues and experiences that relate intertextually to students' lives.

In making selections I have worked consistently for variety: a mix of familiar authors and less-familiar, of frequently anthologized works and infrequently collected ones. Texts in each thematic grouping represent a diversity of perspectives and experiences, as the Gender and Relationships chapter (Chapter 20) illustrates. Doris Lessing's story about male objectification of the female body ("A Woman on a Roof") is balanced by Scott Russell Sanders's male perspective on the same subject, "Looking at Women." Readings about wounded female and male identity are complemented by passionate and gentle love poems, such as Walt Whitman's "I Heard You Solemn-Sweet Pipes of the Organ" and Liz Rosenberg's "In the End, We Are All Light." Texts that focus on relationships as romance are balanced by Francine du Plessix Gray's discussion of alternative relationships in her essay, "On Friendship."

Finally, in order to encourage strong responses from students of diverse backgrounds and both genders, I have weighted selections toward the modern and contemporary and have included a significant number of multicultural and international selections.

Visual and Aural Literacy

Not only the written word, but *anything*—memories, experiences, dreams, music, nature, pictures—can work upon a writer's mind, shaping thought, encouraging imagination, stimulating reflection and analysis. With that idea in view, the book includes a selection of five paintings and a photograph, along with questions that prompt students to respond to the images with creative and analytical writings. In addition, the companion website includes several activities with links and prompts that ask students to respond to both visuals and music from the Web.

Interchapters on Notebooks and Journals

Interspersed among the thematic chapters in Part VI are five interchapters on writer's notebooks and journals. The interchapters include selections from the notebooks and journals of five writers and provide students with practical ideas for creating and sustaining notebooks and journals of their own. The interchapters can be assigned and discussed in class, assigned but not discussed, or ignored at teacher discretion.

"Literature, So What?"

The book ends with an essay that addresses the question, *Why bother with literature?* Clearly reading and writing from literature equips students with academic and job-related skills. Equally important, in this essay I argue that it intensifies the experience of living by fostering habits of contemplation and empathy in an often hurried world.

Apparatus to Accompany Readings

I believe that students accustomed to making their own texts will also become better readers of others' texts. Accordingly, the book's apparatus is aimed primarily at prompting students to write as well as read. Such apparatus includes:

- Parts I–V of *Reading and Writing from Literature*, described above;
- *Activities for Writing and Discussion* following approximately 60% of the selections. These activities are designed to motivate many kinds of writing in addition to literary analysis. Activities involve students in both creative work and analytic as well as in sharing their work and ideas.
- *Additional Activities for Writing and Discussion* at the end of each thematic section. The Additional Activities encourage students to make connections among the various readings within the section. In addition, they help stu-

dents develop habits of recursiveness as they review and reconsider those readings and the notebook writings they have composed in response to them.

- Numerous examples of student-written texts, both within individual chapters and in the appendices, that will stimulate students in their own composing.

ANCILLARY MATERIALS

In addition to the above-mentioned features within the student text, *Reading and Writing from Literature*, Third Edition, is accompanied by ancillary materials for both students and teachers:

- The ***Reading and Writing from Literature* companion website** has been completely revised to more effectively utilize an online environment to expand upon the text. Features of the student portion of the website include activities that ask students to respond to visuals and music on the Web, advice on keeping notes on a computer and creating an electronic portfolio, an activity focused on evaluating websites when conducting research, links to informational sites to support research and argumentative writing, and helpful quick-reference checklists of topics described in the student text. The teacher portion of the website includes the Instructor's Resource Manual online and a transition guide to help facilitate a smooth transition for teachers moving from the second to this thoroughly revised and updated third edition of the text.
- The **Instructor's Resource Manual** is an excellent resource for both experienced and new teachers, providing an overview of the book, chapter-by-chapter summaries and teaching suggestions, tips for collaboration and grading, and a sample course syllabus.
- The **SMARTHINKING online writing tutoring program**, imbedded in our WriteSpace program, links students to a web-based writing center, staffed by experienced composition teachers. Tutors interact with students in real-time during afternoon and evening homework hours, five days a week, and answer questions and offer helpful feedback on drafts.

ACKNOWLEDGMENTS

I am indebted to Bruce Cantley and Lindsay Frost of Houghton Mifflin Company for their help and support on this edition, and to Mary Dalton-Hoffman for her indefatigable work in securing permissions. Additional thanks to my students and colleagues at Weber State University, and special gratitude to my friends Brian Hare-Diggs and Michael Wutz for their inspiring conversation and invaluable reading suggestions over the years.

A number of reviewers helped immeasurably in preparing for this edition, and I wish to acknowledge them here:

Tracey Gau, University of North Texas
Richard Kaplan, Harper College
Susan Luzzaro, Southwestern College
Kathleen Mollick, Tarleton State University
Donna Rondolone, Drexel University
Paul Rottenberg, Broward Community College
Connie Wasem, Spokane Falls Community College

Some of the most important influences on a book are intangible—ideas gained from reading, daily experiences, the inspirations of literary and personal mentors, meditations, passing thoughts. My best attempt to articulate these influences is the personal essay, "Literature, So What?" that concludes this edition. My wife, Ann Jefferds, and my children, Jack and Elizabeth, have helped me incalculably as a person and writer, as have my parents, Olive Schwiebert and the late Lloyd Schwiebert, to whom I dedicate this book.

—John Schwiebert

A Conversation Model of Writing and Reading

P art I of *Reading and Writing from Literature* presents writing and reading as conversational acts in which you "talk back" to the texts you read, then use the conversation as a springboard for creating works of your own. In addition, Part I introduces you to the "reading notebook," the special kind of journal you will use for collecting your own writings—notes, thoughts, responses to literary works, and creative writings of many kinds that may be prompted by the texts you read. Finally, you will find out how carrying a small 3-by-5-inch notepad can revolutionize your life and how composing in a variety of different forms can stimulate your thought and creativity. As you develop techniques of reading and writing that will be useful to you in this course, you will also learn strategies for producing meaningful writings of your own independently of this class or this textbook. Thus, the ultimate aim of Part I is to make you a strong and independent reader of literature—and an active writer—for life.

Why Don't You
Let It Out Then?

Walt, you contain enough, why don't you let it out then?

—WALT WHITMAN

For only that book can we read which relates to me something that is already in my mind.

—RALPH WALDO EMERSON

Three Writers

Robin wants to write a story about something that has been on his mind a lot lately: husbands and wives. Sitting at his word processor he begins, "Every marriage is improved—or destroyed—by the fires of time." He likes the sound of that and is poised to continue, when inspiration suddenly dies. He searches for something new and profound to say about love; he ransacks his brain for some original characters and situations . . . in vain. Discouraged, he types another sentence or two and gives up.

Robin is anxious about being "original." His anxiety destroys his creativity.

Suppose he approaches the writing task differently. He thumbs through a book of short fiction to find other stories about husbands and wives and discovers "The Story of an Hour" by the nineteenth-century American Kate Chopin. After reading several paragraphs he has become fascinated by the character of its heroine, Louise Mallard. Mrs. Mallard has just learned that her husband has been killed in a railroad accident. Seated by her bedroom window she slips into a reverie about her past and future. Complex emotions beset her. She sobs; then, as she stares blankly at a distant patch of blue sky, an unfamiliar feeling steals over her. Chopin writes:

When she abandoned herself a little whispered word escaped her slightly parted lips. She said it over and over under her breath: "Free, free, free!" The vacant stare and the look of terror that had followed it went from her eyes. They stayed keen and bright. Her pulses beat fast, and the coursing blood warmed and relaxed every inch of her body.

Robin circles this passage and scribbles in the margin, "She *relaxes* at the thought of her husband's death?" Louise's emotions set Robin thinking about fractured relationships, in which one partner prefers freedom to attachment. Thought follows thought, and soon he is remembering his Uncle Jules, who seemed to experience a kind of rebirth following the death of his wife, Aunt Maria. Robin begins writing the story of Uncle Jules and Aunt Maria. "The Story of an Hour" prompts him to write. While his own story is about a husband and wife, it in no way duplicates Chopin's. In short, his work is "original."

Sally keeps a personal diary. Unfortunately, while she thinks of plenty to write when her life is exciting or awful, on most days (which are humdrum) she draws a mental blank. Each day's entry sounds like every other's. Her own writing puts her to sleep.

A friend, Max, suggests her writing may be suffering from egocentrism and that she should seek prompts for writing from her environment. "Writers do it all the time," says Max. "They eavesdrop, look at people, watch movies, hang around shopping malls. . . ." Heeding Max's advice, Sally indulges in one of her favorite activities, watching TV, hoping it will stimulate her imagination. One evening she sees a TV version of Daniel Keyes's "Flowers for Algernon" and learns that this is a short story told entirely in the form of a diary (Algernon's). Inspired, Sally puts her own favorite literary form to work: she writes a story, in diary form, about a would-be writer who "can't" write.

Erica has always loved the sea. Her family vacationed in a seaside town when she was growing up. As a child she built sandcastles and combed the beach for shells. Now, every time she gets near water, she dances or merely stands still, transfixed and staring at the horizon, watching cloud shadows roll over the waves, beholding the most fabulous sunsets imaginable. Erica wants to write about the sea. Every time she tries, however, she gets mired in false and overblown phrases that frustrate and embarrass her.

One day, while reading a biographical note on American playwright Eugene O'Neill, she notices the title of one of O'Neill's plays, *Beyond the Horizon*. The mere title does something to her—and for her. She circles it . . . repeats it to herself a few times out loud. She doodles in the margin: a conch shell, a snail, a long horizontal line. As she thinks, repeats, and doodles, memories and images long dormant rise to consciousness: memories of family trips, of childhood, of her own daughter playing in the sand, of sea-conversations and sea-books. She feels herself transported to those days at the beach and writes the poem she has "always wanted to," about the particular feelings a child-turned-adult has when gazing at the horizon. It turns out to be a poem about love and aging and the integration of child and adult. The poem pleases her.

All three of these writers—Robin, Sally, and Erica—wanted to write but had no "way in" to their writing. All three were stuck—either not moving at all (Robin), or writing in circles (Sally), or producing "false" work that didn't reflect the writer's true feelings (Erica). Each transcended the problem by "reading" another text—a short story, a TV show, the title of a play—and using it to catalyze his or her imagination.

How did Robin, Sally, and Erica use the texts they read?

First, consider what they *didn't* do. They did not:

1. Read the text and slavishly imitate it. Robin does not try writing "like" Chopin because that does not interest him. What does interest him are some similarities between Chopin's characters and people he has known in his own life. Likewise Sally and Erica. "Flowers for Algernon" and *Beyond the Horizon* give them the initial impetus to create but recede in importance as Sally and Erica actually write.

2. Read passively. Robin, Sally, and Erica are not mere consumers of texts; they are also *producers*. They follow their reading by creating texts of their own.

3. Read to "master" the total text. The three writers pick up on particular aspects of the text that interest them at the moment. Robin concentrates on the commitment theme. Sally is indifferent to the themes, characters, and plot of "Flowers for Algernon"; what attracts her are the point of view and form— first-person point of view in diary form. As for Erica, she doesn't even bother to read O'Neill's play, let alone "comprehend" it. The mere title suffices to prompt her memories and imagination and give her momentum for writing.

Robin, Sally, and Erica do not write to comprehend the texts they read; they simply seize upon elements of those texts that they can *use* in order to write themselves. Instead of attempting to understand the texts in total, they converse with those aspects of the text that interest them. Like a participant in a two-way conversation, each of these writers composes something (in this case, a written text rather than a spoken statement) that sustains an ongoing conversation. Because these conversations never end, and because the writer is contributing just one bit more to the discussion, the pressures on the writer to compose "brilliantly" and "profoundly" are greatly reduced.

Robin, Sally, and Erica imagine a particular model—a conversation model— of the relationship between themselves as writers and the texts they use to help them write. The existence of this model is all-important to their success as writers.

A Conversation Model of Writing and Reading

The conversation model says that you interact or *converse* with a text when you read it. Even as you are learning from the text, you yourself are bringing something *to* it, namely, your own background, experiences, thoughts, prior knowledge, biases, and opinions. The conversation model honors your right to *talk back* to the text.

According to the conversation model our minds are not empty receptacles waiting to be filled. As living, sentient beings, each of us brings to a text a history of thoughts, experiences, ideas, and readings. Who you are shapes what meaning you "get" from a text. That is, what essay X "means" is not something intrinsic to the text alone; what it means is largely shaped by the personal and cultural makeup of the reader who reads it.

For example, when I read a short story the "meaning" of the text is partly determined by who I, the reader, am; by what I already know about the subject of the story; by what my feelings, biases, or attitudes are about that subject; and by a whole range of other factors such as my race, gender, previous reading, and personal and cultural experience. In other words, I not only "receive" information, ideas, images, and so on from the story; I also bring my *self* to it. Recall how Robin, for instance, brought his experience of Uncle Jules to his reading of "The Story of an Hour"; his unique individual experience prompted him to read and use Chopin's story in a way that would not have occurred to a different reader. Reading thus becomes a process of negotiation—a sort of conversation—between the distinctive reader "me" and the author and text of the work I am reading.

As an example, imagine you pick up an essay about "the meaning of education." A shudder of insecurity passes through you: "Looks tough. And this writer has a Ph.D. What am *I* going to get out of this?" You are thinking passively. You overlook the fact that you have been in school for many years. Even if you haven't spent your free time reading books and articles on education, you possess another resource that equips you to "converse" with this reading: your dozen or so years as a learner, as a participant in the educational system. You know what it is like to do assignments, and you have encountered all types of teachers, students, and teaching methods. Even though you are not yet ready to read and respond to the text before you as an educational scholar or expert, you do have expertise of a kind. This expertise—your own life and experiences as a student—gives you a way in to any piece of writing about education.

In short: *you know more than you realize.*

This is what American poet Walt Whitman had in mind when he wrote,

> *Walt, you contain enough, why don't you let it out then?*

It's one of the most democratic lines in all literature. Instead of bowing to the Voice of Authority, which says, "You don't know enough yet to write; read some more *first,*" Whitman discovers that he already knows (and you and I know) "enough" to join the conversation *now.*

Of course, you can always know more and write *better*—and reading and writing can be seen as lifelong endeavors to improve your knowledge and verbal dexterity. Whitman, for instance, read voraciously—everything from history and literature to astronomy, mysticism, criticism, human physiology, philosophy, and geology. His notebooks fill six thick volumes. However, he didn't postpone writing as something to be done only *after* reading; he read and wrote simultaneously.

He fused reading and writing into one and treated the whole as a continuous two-way conversation, between himself and the world, himself and the written word, himself and experience.

ACTIVITIES FOR WRITING

1. In your own words, summarize the conversation model. What new understanding, if any, does the conversation model give you of your own habits as a reader and writer? Do you read "conversationally"? How or how don't you? When or when don't you?

2. Practice conversational reading and writing with the following exercise from *Personal Fiction Writing* (New York: Teachers & Writers Collaborative, 1984) by Meredith Sue Willis. Read the dialogue excerpt, below, from Tillie Olsen's novel, *Yonnondio: From the Thirties*. Then write what you imagine might have happened just before or after this dialogue. That is, write a prequel or sequel to the dialogue.

> No one greeted him at the gate—the dark walls of the kitchen enclosed on him like a smothering grave. Anna did not raise her head.
>
> In the other room the baby kept squalling and squalling and Ben was piping an out-of-tune song to quiet her. There was a sour smell of wet diapers and burned pots in the air.
>
> "Dinner ready?" he asked heavily.
>
> "No, not yet."
>
> Silence. Not a word from either.
>
> "Say, can't you stop that damn brat's squallin? A guy wants a little rest once in a while."
>
> No answer.
>
> "Aw, this kitchen stinks. I'm going out on the porch. And shut that brat up, she's driving me nuts, you hear?" You hear, he reiterated to himself, stumbling down the steps, you hear, you hear. Driving me nuts.

3. In the following poem, Gary Soto presents a picture of himself at ten years of age. Allow his poem to stimulate some childhood memories of your own. Then write up those memories (there may be several you wish to write about briefly) or write the story of one particular memory. If you wish, make it a story that ends with a surprise or a sudden confrontation, comic or serious, as "Behind Grandma's House" does. Write in either poetry or prose.

BEHIND GRANDMA'S HOUSE

GARY SOTO

At ten I wanted fame. I had a comb
And two Coke bottles, a tube of Bryl-creem.
I borrowed a dog, one with

Mismatched eyes and a happy tongue,
And wanted to prove I was tough   5
In the alley, kicking over trash cans,
A dull chime of tuna cans falling.
I hurled light bulbs like grenades
And men teachers held their heads,
Fingers of blood lengthening   10
On the ground. I flicked rocks at cats,
Their goofy faces spurred with foxtails.
I kicked fences. I shooed pigeons.
I broke a branch from a flowering peach
And frightened ants with a stream of spit.   15
I said "*Chale,*" "In your face," and "No way
Daddy-O" to an imaginary priest
Until grandma came into the alley,
Her apron flapping in a breeze,
Her hair mussed, and said, "Let me help you,"   20
And punched me between the eyes.

Making New Texts from Old: Intertextuality

Pen, paper, and book make an ideal community.

—Anonymous

In college John took a literature class in which he was assigned to read *Moby-Dick*. *Moby-Dick* is a long novel, and the class spent four days analyzing it. John worked hard, produced a term paper on *Moby-Dick*—and shortly thereafter forgot the book and nearly everything he had learned about it. Then, two years later, something interesting happened. John was writing a short story with a first-person ("I") narrator; his progress was stalled, when suddenly, out of the murk of his subconscious, there returned to him the opening sentence of *Moby-Dick*: "Call me Ishmael." This sentence, in which the novel's narrator introduces himself, echoed in John's consciousness as he resumed and finished his story. A single sentence—a mere three words—suggested a sense of directness that helped him quickly and easily transpose his thoughts to paper.

When he mentioned this experience to a friend who had studied *Moby-Dick* in depth, the friend told him that he had misinterpreted the line "Call me Ishmael"—that it was not about "directness" but about "indirectness and evasion." John thought about this and replied, "You may be right. I only know that that line—whatever it means—helped me produce the best writing I've ever done."

A line from Shakespeare's *King Lear* says, "Nothing will come of nothing." Change the terms in that sentence a bit and you have a truism about the process of writing: *Something will come from something.* Writers have long complained about the dreaded "blank page"; the blank page only exists if you allow it to. Do you want or need to write? Then put something in front of you—a story, a poem, a paragraph—and react to it. Words will come, and sentences will accumulate;

9

and if you react to something that strikes you in a special way the sentences will probably be interesting—or have the potential to be. At its most basic, *writing is reading—reacting.*

What it is about a particular reading that prompts you to write doesn't have to be something major; often—as the examples of John and of Robin, Sally, and Erica in the previous chapter illustrate—it will be something small: a theme, a character, an image, a phrase. The size of the catalyst is not important. What does matter is how powerfully it resonates with your own life and imagination.

A Four-Step Process for Writing from Reading

How can you do as John did and identify the powerful connections you have with a text? How can you then use those connections to produce satisfying writing of your own? Here is a four-step process that builds on the conversation model discussed in Chapter 1. You can apply the process to all your reading—to the short stories, poems, essays, plays, and notebooks and journals in this book and to a range of other texts that you encounter in daily life. Note that you do not have to rigidly follow the steps. Some people prefer to combine Steps One and Two or to skip Step Three. Begin by trying all the steps; then adapt them to your own style and needs.

1. *Do a first reading of the text.* Concentrate on immersing yourself in its rhythms, ideas, conflicts, plot, themes, characters.

2. *On a second reading, annotate passages that strike you.* Perhaps you like an idea, a phrase, a character, or an image, or perhaps you are struck by a section of dialogue, or maybe you are puzzled or mystified by a passage. Underline or bracket any such item. (This assumes, of course, that your copy of the text is your own and not a library's.) Also, in the margins, jot down:

- *Questions* that a passage raises for you
- *Analytical comments,* i.e., what you think about a passage
- *Summaries* of what a passage is saying
- *Connections* that a passage suggests with anything else you have read, thought about, or experienced

The marks you make in a text are called *annotations.* Annotation is as basic to readers and writers as hammers are to carpenters or spoons to cooks. It is your main means of identifying the resonant points of connection you have with a text; these points, in turn, can motivate you to write, as "Call me Ishmael" catalyzed John.

Many great writers and other creative people, past and present, have been annotators, talking back to what they read, using the writings of others to start their own thought processes. Michel de Montaigne, inventor of the personal essay genre (see p. 172), filled the margins of books with his notes. Essayist/poet

Samuel Johnson (see p. 688), who was a devout Anglican Christian, sent his annotations of a religious work to a female friend "so that he could exchange views with a woman he loved."[1] Johnson saw that annotations can be personally revealing, even intimate, because they show how and what you think (and what you think about is largely who you are).

During the late eighteenth and early nineteenth centuries, annotation was actually esteemed as a minor literary genre; people loaned their books to friends for the express purpose of having them mark up the margins. Annotations functioned somewhat like personal letters as annotators exchanged and responded to each other's ideas, suggesting parallels with certain more reflective kinds of e-mail in the twenty-first century. In 1819 the great English critic and poet Samuel Taylor Coleridge published several selections from his marginal notes as "marginalia" (a Latin word for annotations) in a prominent literary magazine. Edgar Allan Poe published his own marginalia in various magazines in the United States during the 1840s. Though annotation has lost most of its status as a literary genre since Poe's time, good readers have never stopped annotating.

One of the more famous examples of an annotator is William Blake, eighteenth-century poet and artist. As he read a book by Sir Joshua Reynolds, a leading artist with whom he disagreed passionately, Blake was furiously taking notes, developing, in a mass of annotations, his own theory of art.

Here are some excerpts from Reynolds's text (*Discourses on Art*) followed by Blake's annotations (the unusual capitalization is Blake's):

Blake: (general comment on the *Discourses*): This Man was Hired to Depress Art.

Reynolds: How incapable of producing anything of their own, those are, who have spent most of their time in making finished copies, is an observation well known to all who are conversant with our art.

Blake: Finished! What does he Mean? Niggling Without the Correct & Definite Outline? If he means That Copying Correctly is a hindrance he is a Liar, for that is the only School to the Language of Art.

Reynolds: But this disposition to abstraction, to generalizing and classification, is the great glory of the human mind.

Blake: To Generalize is to be an Idiot. To Particularize is the Alone Distinction of Merit. General Knowledges are those Knowledges that Idiots possess.

Reynolds: When we read the lives of the most eminent Painters, every page informs us, that no part of their time was spent in dissipation.

Blake: The Lives of Painters say that Rafael died of Dissipation. Idleness is one Thing & Dissipation Another. He who has Nothing to Dissipate Cannot Dissipate. The Weak Man may be Virtuous Enough, but will Never be an Artist. Painters are noted for being Dissipated & Wild.

---

1. H. J. Jackson, *Marginalia: Readers Writing in Books* (New Haven: Yale UP, 2001, p. 65).

Some of the notes Blake jotted down in this fashion resurfaced, verbatim or transformed, as lines in his published work. Blake reread and studied his annotations and used them to develop his own thoughts, which in turn overflowed into his formal writing.

Ralph Waldo Emerson (1803–1882) was another annotator, though he preferred (as you may, also) to write his annotations in separate notebooks rather than in the margins. Emerson thought of himself as a "creative" reader. Some of his notes were strikingly *dissociative* in character; that is, they didn't seem obviously relevant to the texts he was reading but were nevertheless triggered by them. For instance, as a young man a book on reason and revelation inspired him to write a paragraph about the uninhabited parts of the world being perhaps "the abodes of other orders of sentient beings invisible or unexperienced."[2] Emerson's habit of using reading to stimulate writing stuck with him all his life. To a young acquaintance he once summed up his philosophy of reading as follows: "[O]nly read to start your own team."

The key to successful annotating is that you trust the *first thoughts* that occur to you as you read, and write them down. If you are used to doubting the value of your every thought, this requires conscious effort and practice. You may be more accustomed to trusting in second thoughts, those socially acceptable or "correct" thoughts that censor the first ones as "dumb," "ridiculous," or "irrelevant." Reject these second thoughts and cleave to the first. There will be time later for revising and refining your first thoughts.

In a sense good annotating requires *un*learning; often it is less a matter of thinking harder than of thinking *less* hard. Rather than straining to write the "correct" or intellectually "comprehensive" response, you relax, as William Blake did, to write whatever occurs to you. For example, here is how Tyler annotated the opening paragraph of Kate Chopin's "The Story of an Hour" (p. 221):

> Knowing that Mrs. Mallard was afflicted with a <u>heart trouble,</u> great care was taken to break to her as gently as possible the news of her husband's death.
>
> *My good elderly friend had heart trouble too. Jack had a valve replacement.*

At first Tyler's annotation may seem odd and irrelevant; after all, it refers to his "good elderly friend," who isn't even a character in Chopin's story. However, Tyler trusts his first thought enough to write it down and leave questions of relevance till later.

This trust pays off, as the initial memory of his "good elderly friend" stirs other memories. One thought reminds him of another, which reminds him of yet another, and another, and so forth: "Jack Hislop lived next door for the majority of my youth. He was like a grandfather to me. . . . I remembered how Jack would

---

2. Quoted in Robert D. Richardson, Jr., *Emerson: The Mind on Fire* (Berkeley: University of California Press, 1995, p. 11).

joke about his heart, 'I've got a pig valve in my heart, oink-oink.' That would al-ways make me laugh." Shared times with Jack, Jack's appearance and manner-isms, fragments of conversation—all these surface, one after another, in Tyler's consciousness. Ultimately, out of these memories he composes a three-page por-trait entitled "Grandpa Jack." Here is a portion of what he wrote (a copy of the complete portrait can be found in Appendix A):

> As a little boy I would go over to visit [Jack] almost every day after school. One day I ran over to his house and found him lounging on the patio in his back yard. "Take a seat, partner," said Jack as he pulled up a chair for me. He fed me some cold watermelon and a large glass of "sodi water," as he called it. While I was enjoying the fruit Jack told me a story about when he was a young sheepherder. "I was no older than you, partner, maybe eleven years old. . . . Me and Pa and a few of my brothers were high on Durphies' Peak taking the sheep down to a nearby watering hole." His eyes were flashing as he was trying to point out where they were, since the mountain was in a broadside view. "A few sheep took off up a narrow canyon, and I got roped into chasin' after 'em. I rode up the canyon a little way and seen 'em up ahead so I galloped my horse to catch 'em. When I caught those little rascals I started herding 'em back down to the watering hole. On the way down the canyon my horse started to get jittery because some bushes started to shake up ahead, and out charged a huge brown bear." Jack was standing now giving the motions of the incident. Jack blurted, "Holy Shit!" then apologized to me because his wife didn't like him to cuss. "The damn horse started to buck and my two dogs went into a barking frenzy. The bear was huge, it was at least ten feet tall when it reared up on his hind legs. The dogs distracted the bear long enough allowin' me to ride up and around to safety."

If you read "The Story of an Hour," the text that inspired "Grandpa Jack," you will find that it focuses on a woman and her feelings about marriage and her hus-band. Tyler's annotation (and the text it engendered) is about a colorful old friend and has virtually nothing to do with women, husbands, or marriage. What then? Is it merely eccentric and irrelevant? Yes and no. If you take Chopin's text as the central point of reference, then his annotation is indeed irrelevant; however, if you take as the main point of reference the overlap between Chopin's text and the texts of his own life, Tyler's annotation is right on target. After all, it prompts him to articulate an aspect of his life he might never have written about otherwise without the stimulus of Chopin.

A footnote: At home and in class Tyler found enthusiastic readers for his essay. How interesting that so individual a response could have broad appeal to others! At the heart of annotation is a paradox. The more individual it is—the more spon-taneous and intuitive—the more it seems to tap into something *universal* in human experience. "Speak your latent conviction," said Emerson, "and it shall be the universal sense"; or, more simply, if you like it, other people will tend to like it, too.

Here is a second example of annotation. Margaret is a middle-aged wife and mother who has recently entered college. She reads and annotates the following poem by Linda Pastan:

MARKS

My husband gives me an A
for last night's supper,
an incomplete for my ironing,
a B plus in bed.
My son says I am average,
an average mother, but if
I put my mind to it
I could improve.
My daughter believes
in Pass/Fail and tells me
I pass. Wait 'til they learn
I'm dropping out.

*Annotations (left):*
Hard! Anything less than an "A" really hurts

The "typical" family: father, mother, son, daughter. Everyone rates her

*Annotations (right):*
He likes the supper, but anything else? Hm. Sounds like she does all the work— or lots—and then has to get grades for it (pouring salt in the wounds)

More work . . . Is this son shiftless like mine? He should talk!

Wow! She gonna kill herself? get a divorce? take a break? This'll shake 'em up

Note the individuality of Margaret's annotations. Like Tyler, Margaret writes spontaneously and directly about the points at which the literary text speaks to her. By annotating she focuses her attention less on the poem itself than on the overlap between the poem and various aspects of her own life—her own experiences, knowledge, thoughts, and feelings.

3. *Read over your annotations; then take several minutes to list the most powerful thoughts and impressions the text inspires in you.* Here again, trusting your first thoughts is crucial. Instead of writing down the sorts of ideas you think you *ought* to have, put in your list what you *want* to put there. For instance, after Margaret has read and annotated "Marks," she makes the following list:

- I like the phrase "Wait 'til they learn/I'm dropping out." It sounds like an ultimatum.
- Idea: being a wife/mother like being in school. Grades, grades, grades! Always someone grading you.
- I relate to this woman.
- How will she drop out?
- I get a picture of this woman working hard all day and her husband comes home and expects everything to be done for him hand and foot. The son and daughter show up for meals but are always running off to have fun somewhere.
- This house sounds like lots I know. Starting with *mine*.
- Who gets grades? Kids. The mother never gets to grow up!

4. *Review your list; identify your most intense point of response, and compose a text of your own.* To see some of the kinds of texts you can write at this stage, look ahead to the section entitled "Ten Ideas for Writing in a Reading Notebook" in Chapter 3. Margaret reviews her list of thoughts and impressions and finds her

prevailing response is a sense of identification with the speaker in the poem. She explores this identification in a text of her own.

School of Hard Knocks

Grading doesn't begin and end with school. It goes on all our lives. That's what this poem showed me. Wives and mothers especially; we're always being graded!

I got married right out of high school and I thought I was done with getting grades. Little did I know I was just going from one school to another. And I don't mean college. I mean marriage.

There are several classes in this "school."

Marriage 101 is living with a husband. In my case a husband I hardly knew. A nice man and a good provider and all, it turned out, but also a lout who expected me to wait on him hand and foot. Cook the meals, wash the dishes, clean the house, do the errands, entertain the company.

A typical scene: I'm cleaning the bathroom in 95 degree heat, sweat   5
pouring down my face, and he's in the livingroom watching baseball and drinking a beer. His buddies are with him and when the snack tray's empty they yell at me to "please" get more. If I'm a little slow I get a dirty look (that's a "C"). If I yell "Help yourself" and don't come at all I get a growl and some angry comments about "women" (that's an "F"). If I load up the tray and deliver it with a smile it's a "B." To get an "A" I have to do some extra credit—give them their potato chips plus a new round of beers ("A" if the beers are cold, "A—" if they're not).

Marriage 201 is kids. I love my kids, don't get me wrong. They were cute babies and except for the terrible two's the sweetest children I'll ever see. But since they hit their teens it's been a downhill road.

They treat me like their live-in cook and maid. I spend an hour in a hot kitchen making supper—something a little special, chicken cooked a new way—and they shovel it down without a word, it might as well be an old sock fried in batter. No "thank you's" or "This is great"—they're in too big a hurry to get somewhere—a dance, a game, and other places I probably don't want to know about.

I guess they'd give me a "B" for cooking—not good enough for praise, not bad enough to make them throw up (an "F"). If they don't like what I give them you can bet I hear about it. "Mom, what is this?" "Mom, are we supposed to eat this meatloaf or use it for a paperweight?" That's a "C—"— if they even bother to force it down, that is. A grade of "D" means "give it to the Dog."

Kids grade like most of the teachers I had in school. If they like it they don't tell you, and if they hate it they don't let you forget.

Next we come to Marriage 301: middle age. In my generation this   10
means a daughter going on to college and asking you why you became a homemaker and mother instead of getting "a real job." So I could have you and have conversations like this, I say. She looks at me confused like I must be lying. A real job. Boy! I'll tell you about a real job. . . . *This* is a real job. But it's not the job she's interested in.

I'm 45 years old and was on the verge of burnout when I decided to go back to school this fall. I'm a college freshman now at the same school my daughter graduated from a year ago. My son's a sophomore. And I'm getting grades. Am I living my life backwards, or what? I wonder sometimes. I seem to be going back to my childhood: teachers giving me grades. And the teachers get younger and younger. My Math professor's a girl hardly older than my daughter. When she gave me my first test back with a "B" it reminded me of fried chicken! Déjà vu!

Only a mother would understand.

Note that this process of writing from reading leads Margaret to write, as Tyler did, about a number of things that aren't exactly *in* the springboard literary text but are suggested by it. For instance:

- Beliefs traditional in Margaret's culture about appropriate sex roles for men and women—and counterbeliefs that challenge the traditional roles
- The habits and behaviors of her own husband and kids and of other husbands and kids
- Mealtime conversations (those in her own home and perhaps analogous ones she has heard—or heard of—in other homes)
- Memories of various dinners such as chicken and meatloaf
- The particular feelings one has cleaning bathrooms on hot days
- The addiction of some men to TV sports
- The politics of classrooms like grading and teacher-student relations
- Ageism and sexism (both her direct observations of them in life and what she has observed, indirectly, through magazines, books, cosmetics ads, TV shows, movies, and so forth)

You might represent Margaret's reading graphically as follows:

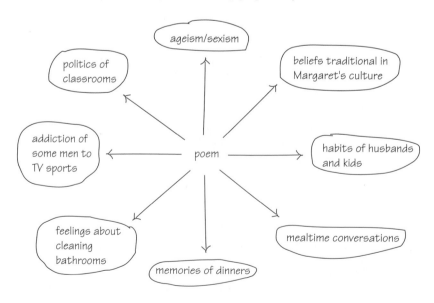

The point in the center is her starting point for writing, i.e., Pastan's poem. The arrows outward lead to the ideas, themes, beliefs, observations, experiences, and memories that she stumbled onto through the process of composing "School of Hard Knocks" and that generated her original focus.

Add a few more lines and you have an image of a web:

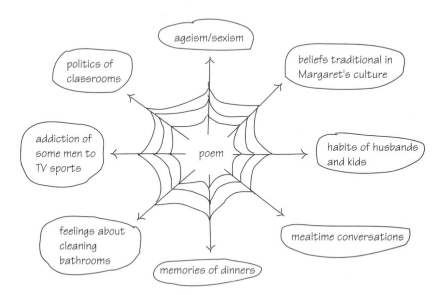

Again, call the circled items "texts"—the texts of Margaret's life. They are texts because they were already present and "written" into her life at the moment she picked up "Marks," and her essay is as much a reading of these texts as it is of Pastan's. Reading and responding to the poem stirs these texts to consciousness, the same as a motion in one strand of a web reverberates through all the other connected strands.

The true focus of Margaret's essay isn't "Marks"; it is the weblike intertextual connections the poem evokes with her own life and imagination.

Language theorists call this phenomenon, of one text activating and talking back and forth with others, *intertextuality*. Intertextuality defines a process of imaginative connecting that is the very pulse beat of writing. It explains how the conversation model creates tremendous momentum for writing. Composing by the conversation model enables you to tap into other texts that are dormant within you—texts that are just "waiting" for some external influence, i.e., another text, to bring them to consciousness.

Applying the Four-Step Process

Now try the Four-Step Process for yourself on the following short poem. Like Tyler and Margaret, strive to focus not on the "meaning" of the work itself but on the overlap of the text with the texts of your own life and imagination. If you wish, do the first three steps collaboratively, with a group or as a class. For Step Four ("compose a text of your own"), strive to write at least three hundred words.

WAITING FOR THE IDIOT TO GO AWAY

PETER SHARPE

The sweet tomato face annealed to itself
in all directions and pressed sloppily
to the car window.
    I sat five years old asking
"why does he do that" and "why is he like that."   5
His name was Benji, he was really
35 or 38 years old and he drooled
and was short. I never got
an answer from my father, who
stared straight ahead, his foot tapping   10
nervously on the accelerator pedal,
lips tight and knuckles whitening
on the wheel, "pretend he isn't there"
he told me.

    I had my first remembered lesson   15
in the social graces: the world
was imperfect, and this was embarrassing.

When you have finished, reflect on the Four-Step Process in your notebook. How did this mode of responding compare with the ways you have written in response to literature in the past? What do you like or dislike about the writing you produced for Step Four? If your piece pleased you, excellent; if not, bear in mind that *no* writer produces great work every time he or she sits down to write. Some of what a writer writes is good, and much—perhaps even most—is "bad" or disappointing. What matters is that out of the patient and continual practice of conversational reading and writing, *good writing will eventually come.*

ACTIVITIES FOR WRITING

1. Use the "Four-Step Process for Writing from Reading" to respond to any one of the texts printed at the end of this chapter, by Ellen Goodman, Barbara Crooker, and Antoine de Saint-Exupéry.

    a. Read through the text a first time without marking it (unless you feel moved to do so).

    b. On a second reading, annotate.

    c. Alone or with a group, create a list of the most powerful thoughts and impressions the piece inspires in you. Don't worry if items on your list seem to go off on a tangent from the text itself.

    d. Identify your favorite item or items in the list of thoughts and impressions and use it/them to create a text of your own that is at least three hundred words long.

2. As mentioned, William Blake incorporated some of his annotations into his published work. As you continue annotating, follow Blake's example by rereading your accumulated annotations periodically and copying any especially striking ones into a notebook. Collect and save these materials for possible use in your other writings—academic or nonacademic. *Note:* If rereading your marginalia prompts any new thoughts—or a revision of your original marginal note—record those in your notebook, too.

3. You can adapt and apply the Four-Step Process to any class or any subject matter. For instance, practice annotating readings assigned in your other classes. You may annotate directly in the margins of the text or follow Emerson's example and record your annotations in a separate notebook. Annotating will help you better comprehend what you read and thus help you study for exams. It will also assist you in preparing term or research papers. Share the results of your efforts in class.

4. You can also apply the Four-Step Process to readings other than literature, such as magazine or newspaper articles, or to nonprint materials such as films, TV programs, conversations, songs, and pictures. Following the texts by Ellen Goodman, Barbara Crooker, and Antoine de Saint-Exupéry you will find two additional items: a series of incident reports and a reproduction of a world-famous painting, Grant Wood's *American Gothic* (1935). If you wish, try the Four-Step Process on either of these items.

    a. For the incident reports, use the Four Steps just as you would on a literary text.

    b. For the Grant Wood painting, do Steps Two through Four on a piece of notebook paper or on a computer. For help with annotation, use any or all of the following questions:

       — Who are these two people, and what is their relationship (father and daughter? mother and son? wife and husband? brother and sister?)?

       — What is the situation in the picture? Why are the two figures standing as they are? Why does he hold a pitchfork?

       — What is the significance of the house in the background? Why are the two figures standing in front of it? What is "gothic" about the house and/or the painting? (Look up *gothic* in a dictionary.)

       — For Step Four consider writing a dialogue between the man and woman.

LIVE-IN MYTHS

ELLEN GOODMAN

"He is not really like that," she said apologetically as her husband left the room.

"Like what?" I asked, wondering which of the many things that had happened that evening she was excusing.

"Well, you know," she said, "cranky."

I thought about that. Cranky. It was typical of the woman that she would choose a gentle, even childish, word for the sort of erratic outbursts of anger which had been her husband's hallmark for the past fifteen years.

He was not really like that. This had been her sentence when they were first dating, when they were living together, and now, since they were married.

When he questioned, minutely, the price tags of her purchases, she would say: "He is really, deep down, very generous." When he disagreed with her politics, veering to the right while she listed to the left, she would cheerily insist that underneath all that he was "basically" liberal.

When he blamed her for the condition of the house, as if he were a lodger, and blamed her for the children's illnesses, as if her negligence had caused their viruses, she would explain, "He is really very understanding."

Even when he was actually his most vital self, amusing and expansive, full of martinis or enthusiasm or himself—and she disapproved—she would forgive him because he wasn't really like that.

This time, dining with them out of town one brief night, I saw that this was the pattern of their lives together—a struggle between realities. His real and her "really."

I had known the wife since college and the husband from their first date. When they met she was a social worker and he was, it seems, her raw material. Was he the case and she the miracle worker? At times she looked at him that way.

Her husband was erratic and difficult, but he had a streak of humor and zaniness as attractive as Alan Arkin's. Over the years, he had grown "crankier" and she more determined in her myth-making.

This trip, for the first time, I wondered what it must be like to be a text living with an interpreter. To be not really like that. And what it must be like for her, living with her myth as well as her man.

I know many other people who live with their ideas of each other. Not with a real person but with a "really." They doggedly refuse to let the evidence interfere with their opinions. They develop an idea about the other person and spend a lifetime trying to make him or her live up to that idea. A lifetime, too, of disappointments.

As James Taylor sings it: "First you make believe / I believe the things that you make believe / And I'm bound to let you down. / Then it's I who have been deceiving / Purposely misleading / And all along you believed in me."

But when we describe what the other person is really like, I suppose we often picture what we want. We look through the prism of our need.

I know a man who believes that his love is really a very warm woman. The belief keeps him questing for that warmth. I know a woman who is sure that her mate has hidden strength, because she needs him to have it.

Against all evidence, one man believes that his woman is nurturing because he so wants her to be. After twenty years, another woman is still tapping hidden wells of sensuality in her mate, which he has, she believes, "repressed."

And maybe they are right and maybe they are wrong, and maybe they are each other's social workers. But maybe they are also afraid that if they let go of their illusions, they will not like each other.

We often refuse to see what we might not be able to live with. We choose distortion.

Leaving this couple, I thought about how much human effort can go into maintaining the "really." How much daily energy that might have gone into understanding the reality—accepting it or rejecting it.

How many of us spend our lives trying to sustain our myths, and how we are "bound to be let down." Because most people are, after all, the way they seem to be.

Really.

You might find yourself particularly drawn to Goodman's reflections in the last several paragraphs, or, just as easily, you might focus your annotations and response on the people and situations portrayed in the first half of the piece. What are this wife and husband like? Do they remind you of any people from your own experience? Do you know—or can you imagine—"people who live with their *ideas* of each other" [italics added] rather than with their authentic selves? These questions suggest just a few of the many points of connection you might find with this text.

PATTY'S CHARCOAL DRIVE-IN

BARBARA CROOKER

First job. In tight black shorts
and a white bowling shirt, red lipstick
and bouncing pony tail, I present
each overflowing tray as if it were a banquet.
I'm sixteen and college-bound,   5
this job's temporary as the summer sun,
but right now, it's the boundaries of my life.
After the first few nights of mixed orders
and missing cars, the work goes easily.
I take out the silver trays and hook them to the windows,   10
inhale the mingled smells of seared meat patties,
salty ketchup, rich sweet malteds.
The lure of grease drifts through the thick night air.
And it's always summer at Patty's Charcoal Drive-In—

carloads of blonde-and-tan girls   15
pull up next to red convertibles,
boys in black tee shirts and slick hair.
Everyone knows what they want.
And I wait on them, hoping for tips,
loose pieces of silver   20
flung carelessly as the stars.
Doo-wop music streams from the jukebox
and each night repeats itself,
faithful as a steady date.
Towards 10 P.M., traffic dwindles.   25
We police the lot, pick up wrappers,
The dark pours down, sticky as Coke,
but the light from the kitchen
gleams like a beacon.
A breeze comes up, chasing papers   30
in the far corners of the darkened lot,
as if suddenly a cold wind had started to blow—
straight at me from the future—
I read that in a Doris Lessing book—
but right now, purse fat with tips,   35
the moon sitting like a cheeseburger on a flat black grill,
this is enough.
Your order please.

Excerpt from *Night Flight*

Antoine de Saint-Exupéry

Thus the three planes of the airmail service, from Patagonia, Chile, and   1
Paraguay, were converging from south, west, and north on Buenos Aires. Their
arrival with the mails would give the signal for the departure, about midnight,
of the Europe postal plane . . .

Then today's work would be over. Worn out, the crews would go to sleep,   2
fresh crews replace them. Rivière alone would have no respite; then, in its
turn, the Europe mail would weigh upon his mind. And so it would always be.
Always. For the first time in his life this veteran fighter caught himself feeling
tired. Never could an arrival of the planes mean for him the victory that ends
a war and preludes a spell of smiling peace. For him it meant just one more
step, with a thousand more to follow, along a straight, unending road. Rivière
felt as though for an eternity he had been carrying a crushing load on his uplifted arms; an endless, hopeless effort.

'I'm ageing.' If he no longer found a solace in work and work alone, surely
he was growing old. He caught himself puzzling over problems which hitherto
he had ignored. There surged within his mind, like a lost ocean murmuring
regrets, all the gentler joys of life that he had thrust aside. Can it be coming on

me—so soon?' He realized that he had always been postponing for his declining years, 'when I have time for it,' everything that makes life kind to men. As if it were ever possible to 'have time for it' one day and realize at life's end that dream of peace and happiness! No, peace there could be none; nor any victory, perhaps. Never could all the airmails land in one swoop once for all.

Rivière paused before Leroux; the old foreman was hard at work. Leroux, too, had forty years of work behind him. All his energies were for his work. When at ten o'clock or midnight Leroux went home it certainly was not to find a change of scene, escape into another world. When Rivière smiled towards him, he raised his heavy head and pointed at a burnt-out axle. 'Jammed it was, but I've fixed it up.' Rivière bent down to look; duty had regained its hold upon him. 'You should tell the shop to set them a bit looser.' He passed his finger over the trace of seizing, then glanced again at Leroux. As his eyes lingered on the stern old wrinkled face, an odd question hovered on his lips and made him smile.

'Ever had much to do with love, Leroux, in your time?'   4

'Love, sir? Well, you see——'   5

'Hadn't the time for it, I suppose—like me.'   6

'Not a great deal, sir.'   7

Rivière strained his ears to hear if there were any bitterness in the reply;   8
no, not a trace of it. This man, looking back on life, felt the quiet satisfaction
of a carpenter who has made a good job of planing down a board. 'There you
are! *That's* done.'

'There you are,' thought Rivière. 'My life's done.'   9

Then, brushing aside the swarm of sombre thoughts his weariness had   10
brought, he walked towards the hangar; for the Chile plane was droning down
towards it.

— Translated by Stuart Gilbert

Humans and Other Animals

A woman called animal control to say she had found a rattlesnake at her home. Asked if she was sure it was a rattlesnake, she said she knew the species because she was from the South. She also called police, who took the snake to the shelter, where it was found to be a common, nonvenomous brown snake. For an unknown reason, the snake was covered with jelly. It was cleaned and transported to a wildlife rehabilitator. . . .

Responding to a report of a fish in an evaporating puddle, an animal-control officer climbed down a wall with a rope, netted the eighteen-inch fish, and released it in deeper water.

A woman called animal control after trying to feed a live rat to her pet snake in its cage. She said the snake would not eat the rat, which attacked the reptile. The woman was afraid to remove the rat, so an animal-control officer took it from the cage. It was euthanized at the shelter.

Responding to a report alleging that a miniature poodle had been hit with a pole, a humane-society officer met with a woman who said a shovel was swung at her thirteen-year-old dog during a fight involving her, a neighbor, and teenage girls. Several people, including the owner, were arrested. The dog was unharmed.

Responding to a report of an opossum "foaming at the mouth" in a tree, an animal-control officer found an apparently healthy animal. Because residents expressed concern that the opossum would attack them, the officer moved it to another area.

A woman called animal control about a kitten stuck for three days in a plastic drainpipe underground outside an apartment building. An animal-control officer ripped a towel into strips, knotted them into a makeshift ladder, and lowered it about three feet down the pipe to the cat, which did not climb up.

The next day, the officer brought a pick and shovel from home and dug to a pipe joint, disconnected it, and unsuccessfully tried to reach the kitten with his hand.

The officer then borrowed a large vacuum cleaner from the building's maintenance crew, sucked the animal against a hose attachment, and grabbed it. The six-week-old male gray tabby was put in foster care.

A woman called animal control asking for help with two cats. When an officer responded, the woman said that she had had the cats for two weeks and that their eyes were turning black. The officer found that the cats were healthy and explained to the woman that cats' pupils dilate in low light.

A woman called animal control after a four-year-old dropped a pet rabbit off the top of a bunk bed. An officer took the rabbit, which appeared to have a broken back and other injuries, to the shelter, where it was euthanized. The mother agreed to wait until the child was much older before considering another pet.

Two youths helped three cats after suffering from injuries in a two-car accident. While they awaited police, they heard a cat trapped in a pillowcase tied to a tree limb. The fifteen-year-old retrieved and opened the pillowcase, which also contained a brick. The cat ran. The youth then reached into a storm drain and rescued two kittens while his aunt held a flashlight. The youths adopted one kitten, and a paramedic adopted another.

A woman called animal control and reported that a dog was tied up outside in the cold and appeared to be frozen to death. An officer went to the scene and found that the "dog" was actually a broom.

AMERICAN GOTHIC

GRANT WOOD

Grant Wood, American, 1891–1942. *American Gothic,* 1930, oil on beaverboard, 74.3 × 62.4 cm. Friends of American Art Collection. All rights reserved by The Art Institute of Chicago and VAGA, New York, NY, 1930.934. Reproduction, The Art Institute of Chicago.

Building a Reading Notebook: Ten Ideas for Writing from Reading

Everything has been said before. There's nothing new to write about—always
the same old things, the same old lies and the same old loves and the same old
tragedy and joy. But you can write about them in a new way, your own way.
—EUGENE O'NEILL

Famous Writers at Work

How do writers produce their finished works? Do their stories, poems, essays,
and plays materialize magically out of nothing? As suggested in the previous
chapter, writers produce texts out of already existing texts. The examples of this
are virtually limitless.

Anton Chekhov (1860–1904) was one of the world's greatest short story writers. Through much of his career he kept notebooks in which he recorded ideas for
stories, brief character sketches, snippets of dialogue, memorable images and
quotations, and thoughts. Many of these items furnished materials for his published stories. Toward the end of his life he said that he had enough ideas stored
up in his notebook "for five years of work."

Playwright Eugene O'Neill (1888–1953) had an enormous impact on the development of modern drama and was awarded the Nobel Prize for Literature in
1936. Behind O'Neill the great dramatist is O'Neill the notebook writer. In his
notebooks O'Neill recorded his "readings" of his own life and of the world
around him. The plays that made him famous evolved out of notes, sketches, and
outlines that he collected in these notebooks. Often this involved a remarkably
slow process of accretion and reworking. For instance, one of his best plays, *The*

Iceman Cometh, evolved from notes he made as many as twenty years before the play was published.

Emily Dickinson (1830–1886), who was all but unpublished during her lifetime, left behind nearly eighteen hundred poems which did not appear in their first complete and scholarly edition until almost seventy years after her death. Rather than pushing to place her work in periodicals or publish them in books, she wove many of her poems into hand-made booklets and shared poems with family and friends in her personal letters. The fact that some poems appear in more than one letter, or in multiple versions, and sometimes in letters that are dated many years apart, suggests that Dickinson amassed large stores of poems and poetic fragments that she regularly mined and reworked for her own satisfaction and for inclusion in her favorite form of publication—the personal letter. Interestingly, Dickinson never made money or gained much public reputation from writing during her lifetime; she loved the process of creation itself.

These are glimpses of writers at work. While the details of habit and behavior differ from one writer to the next, certain commonalities emerge: they collect material; at various times they reread and rework it. Composing is the process of "conversing" with the accumulated notes—reviewing, expanding, revising, and reordering them. The strategy that drives Chekhov's and O'Neill's notebooks and Dickinson's booklets and letters is simple: to accumulate writings that can be reread later and selectively discarded—or reworked and revised into more finished writing. Such is the principle behind the reading notebook.

Using Reading as a Springboard for Writing

Simply defined, a reading notebook is a place where you do as Chekhov, O'Neill, and Dickinson did and "springboard" off texts that you read. These texts may be printed works, such as the stories, poems, essays, plays, and notebooks and journals in Part VI of this book; or they may be unprinted "texts," such as movies, TV programs, pictures, songs, memories, personal relationships, experiences, or conversations. You use these texts, which suffuse your everyday life, as prompts for your own writing.

Ten Ideas for Writing in a Reading Notebook

Use your notebook for producing all kinds of writings that get you involved, personally and imaginatively, in what you read. Here are some suggestions. You can find additional examples of each of these "Ten Ideas" in Appendix A.

1. *Converse with specific points in the text that strike you.* In conversations with other people you do a number of things: agree, disagree, question, comment, joke, continue a point, and so on; you can converse in similar ways with the texts

you read. For example, Stephanie read Ray Bradbury's "[A Story About Love]" (p. 247) and commented on several quotations that were key to her:

> "It's the privilege of old people to seem to know everything. But it's an act and a mask, like every other act and mask. Between ourselves, we old ones wink at each other and smile, saying, How do you like *my* mask, *my* act, *my* certainty? Isn't life a play? Don't I play it well?"

This statement is so very true. Everyone has a mask and plays a part. The only exceptions are children, until they reach a certain age and then they become like the rest of the actors. People play a part and wear a mask because they're afraid of rejection and persecution. No one likes to have their feelings hurt or their egos smashed in.

> "When you're twenty-seven if you still know everything you're still seventeen."

This statement is profound. I think what she means is that if you are 27 and think you know everything, you haven't lived enough, matured enough, or experienced enough to be more than 17. You may have the body of a 27 year-old, but your mind is that of a seventeen year-old.

> "[T]he average man runs helter-skelter the moment he finds anything like a brain in a lady."

This statement strikes me as one spoken by someone who knows. From personal experience, this statement is a fact. I think the key word here is "average." It takes a man who is secure enough in himself and who can see beyond the mask to know when he's got something in a woman with a brain. This is not an average man. That man is an extraordinary man.

> "Kindness and intelligence are the preoccupations of age."

I agree that people become wiser with age, but I don't think that kindness is necessarily a preoccupation of age. Most people try very hard to be kind and spare others' feelings. If she is talking about genuine kindness, then perhaps that is a preoccupation of age. Genuine kindness is a part of the real person; kindness is just another one of the masks we wear.

2. *Write about any personal connections you have with the reading.* Margaret's writing from "Marks," quoted in Chapter 2, is a good example.

3. *Write a letter to the author and/or a return letter from the author to yourself.* This is a good way to gain more confidence in yourself as a reader. Instead of effacing yourself before the author, you address the writer familiarly and person-to-person. You can write to the author about most anything—from your evaluation of the work to your thoughts about a theme, a character or characters, life

issues, or literary technique. Stan read Emily Dickinson's "The Soul Selects Her Own Society" (p. 670) and a few other Dickinson poems, as well as some biographical material. Confused by the poetry but fascinated by the unusual life of its author (see Appendix D), he wrote the following letter:

> Dear Ms. Dickinson:
>
> I hope you won't think I'm disrespectful, but I have a few questions for you. You seem a little unapproachable to me. Your poems are some of the most difficult I've ever seen—they hardly seem to be written in English.
>
> I wonder if there is some connection between the meaning of your poems and your lifestyle.
>
> Why did you shut yourself off from the world? Why, after a certain point in life, did you wear only white? Why did you write so many hundreds of poems without publishing them?
>
> I could go on, but this is probably enough questions for now.
>
> Sincerely,
>
> Stan
>
> P.S.—Please write back in language I can understand.
>
> P.P.S.—I have my own theory of why you shut yourself off. I think you did it as a way to have maximum control over your own life. Live like a recluse and no one will bother you. You get a father who brings home cash, keeps bread on the table, and stays downstairs. You get a sister who can manage the little chores you don't feel like doing and who also stays downstairs—unless you ask her up. You have a servant or two to clean, cook, do the laundry, and you've got it made. You can bake, garden, and do just enough domestic chores to put "experience" into your poems, and you are running the house while everyone else just thinks you are "poor brilliant Emily" who's a little crazy in the head. You shut yourself off, in short, as part of a conscious strategy to control your family and amuse the neighbors so they would leave you alone to do what you wanted to—write.

> Dear friend:
>
> Such bolts of clarity
>
> Inspire your charity—
>
> E. Dickinson

4. *Write an imaginary interview with the author or with a character in a story, novel, or play.* This idea has the same basic advantages as letter writing. The interview format lets you see, hear, and address the author as a flesh-and-blood person. Use your interview to ask the author questions about his or her text, style, characters, ideas, and life, for example.

5. *Compose a prequel or a sequel to a story.* Have you ever felt disappointed to see a story end? Perhaps you enjoyed the plot or identified with the characters and themes and could gladly have inhabited the world of that story—or novel or

play—a while longer. Composing a prequel or sequel is an excellent way to do just that. You can sustain the lives of the characters beyond the author's prescribed ending, or you can imagine what the characters did, thought, and experienced before the story proper begins. This is also a relaxed and pleasurable way of imitating the author's tone, style, and methods of characterization; that is, it is a good way of broadening your own storytelling repertoire.

Helen and Bill, the main characters in Bradbury's "[A Story About Love]," become acquainted one summer day in a drugstore. They fall in love despite a vast difference in age—she is ninety-five and he is thirty-one—and have only a brief relationship before she dies. In the story "reincarnation" is mentioned. This gave Trent the idea to invent a sequel, "written in a Southeast Asian style," that incorporates Buddhist mythology and the idea of reincarnation. "Buddhism," Trent explains, "teaches that human beings can be reincarnated in one of two ways: first, they can improve because of good actions in this life; second, they can regress if they involve themselves in unclean activities."

As William left the house of Helen, she truly desired to be with him. She hoped there was a way because her feelings for him were strong. At this time Buddha looked down and was filled with mercy.

He said to those enlightened about him, "This mortal truly possesses the love necessary to obtain the wish of her heart." He paused, then continued: "But does the other possess the same quality?"

Ong Dia, one of the enlightened, spoke: "We must test the mortal to see if he has this quality."

Buddha replied, "Yes, we must do even as you say, Ong Dia."

Buddha then turned to Tao Quan and said, "Tao Quan, you must go down to the earth and test this mortal. Create a situation in which the mortal voluntarily chooses to do an act of love and mercy; if he chooses not to do this act, then he will not obtain the wish of his heart, and he will have to suffer regression in the great pattern of reincarnation."

The night that Helen died was hard for Bill, and he was having difficulty dealing with it. Just at this moment, a man ran up behind him. The man drew out a knife and demanded Bill's wallet, then ran away. Bill felt as though he had nothing to lose so he chased the man into the woods. They ran for a few minutes, then the thief tripped and fell. The thief was sliding down the edge of a hill which turned out to be a cliff. The bottom appeared to be some twenty feet down. The thief was hanging on to some foliage but was slipping fast.

The thief exclaimed, "Help me, please help me." Bill was scared, he did not know if he should help him. What if the man decided to use the knife and kill him anyway? Bill did not think long, he extended his hand to help the thief up.

Bill pulled the man up, and no sooner had he done so than he witnessed one of the most awesome spectacles he had ever seen. The thief changed form and seemed to float in the air. He then took on his true form, Tao Quan, one of the gods. Light and brilliance shone from his countenance.

Tao Quan spoke to him saying, "Great is the love and mercy possessed by you, mortal. You saved the life of one who had persecuted you and did it with the chance of losing your life; Buddha is smiling upon your action this night. Because of this thing you have done, you will receive the desire of your heart."

That night Bill was full of joy, but he did not know how his wish to be with Helen would be granted. He went to bed. The next morning he awoke and noticed nothing different. However, he felt a need to go to the drugstore.

He went in and everything seem to be the same; so he approached the snow-marble fountain. The man asked, "What'll it be?" Bill responded, "Old fashioned lime-vanilla ice." A shout of joy echoed throughout the store.

A beautiful young woman came running towards Bill. She looked famil- iar to him, and they embraced. He looked into her eyes and saw that it was Helen, except now she was young again. They held each other for a long time, then Bill whispered to Helen, "I love you." She answered, "I've waited for this day for 95 years. I love you too."

6. *Rewrite a text from a point of view different from that presented in the origi- nal text.* "Point of view" refers to the perspective from which a story is told. Any two witnesses to—or participants in—an event are apt to report different ver- sions of what happened. Thus, events or impressions that seem to be definite and "factual" can change more or less drastically depending on who narrates and in- terprets them. (For more on the role of point of view in storytelling, see p. 159.)

Nathan found Chopin's "The Story of an Hour" was "too morose" for his taste, so in his response, he says, he "'livened' it up by taking an outsider's per- spective. Along the way I intertwined a little humor as well." Nathan rewrote "The Story of an Hour" from the point of view of the family physician in Brently and Louise Mallard's hometown. Since the physician appears only briefly in Chopin's short story, Nathan had to invent narrative details out of his own imagination:

"I want my mommy!"

The voices from the exam room could be heard out in the waiting room, making people very nervous. Inside the exam room a doctor struggled with his little patient as the father tried in vain to soothe the child.

Eventually a nurse brought in a lollipop which appeased the child somewhat, and the commotion subsided as the doctor quickly finished the child's checkup.

"There is a slight irritation in his ear due to an earlier rash which has flared up again. It should pass in a day or two," the doctor explained to the now frazzled yet relieved father.

As the father and son in tandem left, the doctor heard the nurse down the hall exclaim, "Next!" Wearily he waited for the next in a never-ending stream of patients, complaints, and anxious mothers of small children. It was always the same, day after day, month after month. Not that he minded, of course. The pay was good, the benefits many, and most of all, he knew it was a vital service he rendered to the people of his community. No, he didn't mind the work; it was just that he had seemingly fallen into a rut. Nothing ever changed. He wished that once in a while something so out of the ordinary would happen that he could get a fresh new perspective on everything.

The next person complained of stomach cramps. He prescribed the correct medication, and told the lady to see him again in a week if the pain still persisted.

Now he thought back to that very morning. He had expressed his feelings to his wife and wondered aloud to her what he could do about it. She had offered some words of encouragement, but said that it was something that he needed to work out for himself. Her last words as he exited the house were, "Maybe this'll be the day things change." He hoped she was right.

Suddenly his thoughts were interrupted by a nurse bringing hurried news of a train crash nearby. He acted quickly, telling the nurse to take over, and dashed out to his car.

When he got to the scene of the accident he was astounded by what he found. He had envisioned hundreds of people screaming, trapped inside a burning train. Instead, what he found was almost comical. The train had hit a herd of cattle while they crossed the tracks. The accident was an hour old when he arrived but appeared as if it had just happened moments ago. The engine had derailed, a fire had started, and the result was a fire that burned several head of cattle. One of the derailed cars contained superglue, and the whole conglomerate mess appeared as the largest, stickiest pile of hamburger the doctor had ever seen.

There were only minor injuries to the people involved, however, so when he got a call about a man involved in the wreck who had wandered home with a head injury he quickly drove to the person's house. When he got to the proper house he discovered the man was perfectly healthy, but his wife had just died. The situation was explained in this manner: the husband "died," the woman rejoiced, the "dead" husband returned, the wife then died, and now the husband rejoiced. The doctor thought it'd make a good Shakespearean play. He then determined the cause of death to be joy from hearing deathly news followed by extreme shock and grief on seeing the dead return. The doctor left satisfied at having his wish fulfilled at seeing the extraordinary.

7. *Rewrite a work into a different genre.* For instance, rewrite all or part of a short story as a poem, or a poem as a play, or a play as a letter, and so forth. Craig,

a new father, was moved by Donald Hall's poem "My Son My Executioner" (p. 378), in which the speaker/father ruminates on the theme of passing time. Hall's speaker glimpses his own mortality in the young life of his infant son. Craig rewrote the poem as a prose meditation by the father:

> I have such strange feelings as I cradle this child. On the one hand, a feeling of joy and happiness to be holding this new life that is bound to me so intimately. On the other hand, this infant child is like a mirror that shows me myself in a new and sudden light: for an instant it seems I am *myself* being cradled, and the large face looking down at me is my own father's. So *this* is what it's all about, I think: My own father is now an old man . . . his father's father is dead . . . life and death. At some level the fact that I am myself dying doesn't bother me because, for this moment, when everything is just an inseparable part of the living and dying, the individual *ME* doesn't matter, doesn't exist. It's a tender feeling I have as I contemplate my son's joyous life, which is all to come, and my own relentless decay. I almost envy myself this tenderness because such moments are so rare . . . moments of perfect wisdom, to be counted on the fingers of one hand.

8. *Borrow an incident or theme from a work to write a piece of your own based on a similar incident or theme.* The train wreck mentioned in Chopin's "The Story of an Hour" reminded JoEllen of a tragedy that occurred in her hometown when she was growing up, when two boys were killed by a train. "Even though I never really knew the family well," she wrote, "the story of these two boys being killed by a train had an impact on me." JoEllen borrowed the incident of the train death to create her own narrative and imagined herself into the story as the narrator/ sister of the two boys.

> Life was casual in the small town of Kaysville. All the necessities were there: a good school, a small grocery store, a bank and the theatre. For such a small place a movie house was a luxury. Many people from neighboring towns came to see the big screen almost weekly. In our family, going to the movies was a monthly ritual. We lived on a farm on the west side of the tracks. Every day was filled to the brim with chores, school, and then chores again. My job was to feed the chickens and slop the pigs. My two brothers helped pa milk the cows and feed the horses. Life was busy, but good.
>
> The summer of '62 is when things changed. . . .
>
> The rains never came that year. The crops were a complete loss and money was very tight. My brothers, now fifteen and sixteen, were looking for jobs off the farm to help ma and pa make ends meet. School was our only outlet from the frustrations we felt at home. One morning as we rode the bus to school we watched the passing train. As it thundered by we talked of its great power and strength. My oldest brother fantasized about

what life would be like engineering a train and traveling all over the country. He felt his future was wide open in front of him. If he only knew. But none of us can predict what will happen in the future.

The day began with the rooster crowing to wake us for our morning chores. Our steps were a little lighter because it was Friday and we knew that we were going to the movies that night. The school day dragged on like most Fridays do, but finally the bell rang and we were out the door into the fresh fall air. We hurried through our chores and met ma in the kitchen fixing our supper. We urged her to hurry for we didn't want to miss a moment of the movie we had been waiting for. Ma and pa opted to stay home that night because of the lack of money or lack of interest—I'm not sure which. My oldest brother could drive, so he got the keys to pa's pickup and the three of us left ready for a break from reality on the farm. As we approached the train tracks my brother flipped on the radio and blasted it in our ears at a level that showed his enthusiasm for life. The night was pitch black with no moon in sight. What happened next was so quick that I can only guess. The powerful train that my brothers had admired only a few days before thundered upon us with no chance of escape. The impact on the driver's side sent me out of the window and to the side of the tracks. My brothers weren't as lucky. As I heard and felt the meshing of metal against metal and the screeching of wheels, I knew my life would never be the same.

9. *Borrow the genre or form of a work to create a piece of your own cast in the same genre or form.* A good example here is Daniel Keyes's story "Flowers for Algernon," which is a narrative related entirely through diary entries. Recall how Sally, mentioned in Chapter 1, borrowed Keyes's form to create a story about a "blocked" writer. While the theme of her story differed totally from Keyes's, the diary form provided a release for emotions and experiences Sally had not been able to articulate in other ways.

Unusual forms like that of "Flowers for Algernon" sometimes generate the most interesting and surprising responses. Eugene O'Neill wrote a one-act play, *Before Breakfast,* which has two characters, only one of whom actually speaks and appears onstage. (The play is a one-way conversation in which a wife, in the kitchen, talks to her husband, who is offstage in the bedroom.) Jean borrowed O'Neill's formal technique to write a short one-way "dialogue" of her own in which a daughter talks on the phone with her mother and the mother herself is never actually heard. Incidentally, O'Neill himself got the idea for *Before Breakfast* from August Strindberg's one-act "monologue" play, *The Stronger.*

10. *Draft a fictional biography or autobiography of a character in a story, poem, or play.* One reason we enjoy literary texts is because they leave much to our own imaginations. Authors reveal selected facts about their characters and leave it to us to "fill in" gaps and missing details. You can use your notebook to reconstruct the life of a character who particularly intrigues you.

This list of "Ten Ideas" is by no means exhaustive. As you compose in your own notebook, you will doubtless discover other ideas for writing. The only rule is to write what you *want* to write, not what you feel you *should* write.

Review List of the Ten Ideas for Writing

1. Converse with specific points in the text that strike you.
2. Write about any personal connections you have with the reading.
3. Write a letter to the author and/or a return letter from the author to yourself.
4. Write an imaginary interview with the author or with a character in a story, novel, or play.
5. Compose a prequel or a sequel to a story.
6. Rewrite a text from a point of view different from that presented in the original text.
7. Rewrite a work into a different genre.
8. Borrow an incident or theme from a work to write a piece of your own based on a similar incident or theme.
9. Borrow the genre or form of a work to create a piece of your own cast in the same genre or form.
10. Draft a fictional biography or autobiography of a character in a story, poem, or play.

ACTIVITIES FOR WRITING

1. On the following pages are two short stories (Elizabeth Bowen's "The Demon Lover" and Katharine Brush's "Birthday Party"), an excerpt from a novel (Sloan Wilson's *The Man in the Gray Flannel Suit*), and an essay (Cullen Murphy's "The Utmost Measures"). Respond to any one of these readings using the Four-Step Process for Writing from Reading described in Chapter 2. For Step Four use one of the "Ten Ideas" in Chapter 3 and compose a response of at least three hundred words.

THE DEMON LOVER

ELIZABETH BOWEN

Towards the end of her day in London Mrs. Drover went round to her shut-up house to look for several things she wanted to take away. Some belonged to herself, some to her family, who were by now used to their country life. It was late August: it had been a steamy, showery day: at the moment the trees down the pavement glittered in an escape of humid yellow afternoon sun. Against the next batch of clouds, already piling up ink-dark, broken chimneys and parapets stood out. In her once familiar street, as in any unused channel, an unfamiliar queerness had silted up; a cat wove itself in and out of railings, but no human eye watched Mrs. Drover's return. Shifting some parcels under her arm, she slowly forced round her latchkey in an unwilling lock, then gave the door, which had warped, a push with her knee. Dead air came out to meet her as she went in.

The staircase window having been boarded up, no light came down into the hall. But one door, she could just see, stood ajar, so she went quickly through into the room and unshuttered the big window in there. Now the prosaic woman, looking about her, was more perplexed than she knew by everything that she saw, by traces of her long former habit of life—the yellow smoke-stain up the white marble mantelpiece, the ring left by a vase on the top of the escritoire; the bruise in the wallpaper where, on the door being thrown open wildly, the china handle had always hit the wall. The piano, having gone away to be stored, had left what looked like claw-marks on its part of the parquet. Though not much dust had seeped in, each object wore a film of another kind; and, the only ventilation being the chimney, the whole drawing-room smelled of the cold hearth. Mrs. Drover put down her parcels on the escritoire and left the room to proceed upstairs: the things she wanted were in a bedroom chest.

She had been anxious to see how the house was—the part-time caretaker she shared with some neighbors was away this week on his holiday, known to be not yet back. At the best of times he did not look in often, and she was never sure that she trusted him. There were some cracks in the structure, left by the last bombing, on which she was anxious to keep an eye. Not that one could do anything—

A shaft of refracted daylight now lay across the hall. She stopped dead and stared at the hall table—on this lay a letter addressed to her.

She thought first—then the caretaker must be back. All the same, who, seeing the house shuttered, would have dropped a letter in at the box? It was not a circular, it was not a bill. And the post office redirected, to the address in the country, everything for her that came through the post. The caretaker (even if he were back) did not know she was due in London today—her call here had been planned to be a surprise—so his negligence in the manner of this letter, leaving it to wait in the dusk and the dust, annoyed her. Annoyed, she picked up the letter, which bore no stamp. But it cannot be important, or they would know. . . . She took the letter rapidly upstairs with her, without a stop to look at the writing till she reached what had been her bedroom, where she let in light. The room looked over the garden and other gardens: the sun had gone in: as the clouds sharpened and lowered, the trees and rank lawns seemed already to smoke with dark. Her reluctance to look again at the letter came from the fact that she felt intruded upon—and by someone contemptuous of her ways. However, in the tenseness preceding the fall of rain she read it: it was a few lines.

Dear Kathleen: You will not have forgotten that today is our anniversary, and the day we said. The years have gone by at once slowly and fast. In view of the fact that nothing has changed, I shall rely upon you to keep your promise. I was sorry to see you leave London, but was satisfied that you would be back in time. You may expect me, therefore, at the hour arranged. Until then . . .

K.

Mrs. Drover looked for the date: it was today's. She dropped the letter on to the bed-springs, then picked it up to see the writing again—her lips, beneath the remains of lipstick, beginning to go white. She felt so much the change in her own face that she went to the mirror, polished a clear patch in it and looked at once urgently and stealthily in. She was confronted by a woman of forty-four, with eyes staring out under a hat-brim that had been rather carelessly pulled down. She had not put on any more powder since she left the shop where she ate her solitary tea. The pearls her husband had given her on their marriage hung loose around her now rather thinner throat, slipping in the V of the pink wool jumper her sister knitted last autumn as they sat around the fire. Mrs. Drover's most normal expression was one of controlled worry, but of assent. Since the birth of the third of her little boys, attended by a quite serious illness, she had had an intermittent muscular flicker to the left of her mouth, but in spite of this she could always sustain a manner that was at once energetic and calm.

Turning from her own face as precipitately as she had gone to meet it, she went to the chest where the things were, unlocked it, threw up the lid and knelt to search. But as rain began to come crashing down she could not keep from looking over her shoulder at the stripped bed on which the letter lay. Behind the blanket of rain the clock of the church that still stood struck six— with rapidly heightening apprehension she counted each of the slow strokes. "The hour arranged. . . . My God," she said, "*what* hour? How should I. . . .? After twenty-five years. . . ."

The young girl talking to the soldier in the garden had not ever completely seen his face. It was dark; they were saying goodbye under a tree. Now and then—for it felt, from not seeing him at this intense moment, as though she had never seen him at all—she verified his presence for these few moments longer by putting out a hand, which he each time pressed, without very much kindness, and painfully, on to one of the breast buttons of his uniform. That cut of the button on the palm of her hand was, principally, what she was to carry away. This was so near the end of a leave from France that she could only wish him already gone. It was August 1916. Being not kissed, being drawn away from and looked at intimidated Kathleen till she imagined spectral glitters in the place of his eyes. Turning away and looking back up the lawn she saw, through branches of trees, the drawing-room window alight: she caught a breath for the moment when she could go running back there into the safe arms of her mother and sister, and cry: "What shall I do, what shall I do? He has gone."

Hearing her catch her breath, her fiancé said, without feeling: "Cold?"

"You're going away such a long way."

"Not so far as you think."

"I don't understand."

"You don't have to," he said, "You will. You know what we said."

"But that was—suppose you—I mean, suppose."

"I shall be with you," he said, "sooner or later. You won't forget that. You need do nothing but wait."

Only a little more than a minute later she was free to run up the silent lawn. Looking in through the window at her mother and sister, who did not for the moment perceive her, she already felt that unnatural promise drive down between her and the rest of all human kind. No other way of having given herself could have made her feel so apart, lost and foresworn. She could not have plighted a more sinister troth.

Kathleen behaved well when, some months later, her fiancé was reported missing, presumed killed. Her family not only supported her but were able to praise her courage without stint because they could not regret, as a husband for her, the man they knew almost nothing about. They hoped she would, in a year or two, console herself—and had it been only a question of consolation things might have gone much straighter ahead. But her trouble, behind just a little grief, was a complete dislocation from everything. She did not reject other lovers, for these failed to appear: for years she failed to attract men— and with the approach of her thirties she became natural enough to share her family's anxiousness on this score. She began to put herself out, to wonder; and at thirty-two she was very greatly relieved to find herself being courted by William Drover. She married him, and the two of them settled down in this quiet, arboreal part of Kensington: in this house the years piled up, her children were born and they all lived till they were driven out by the bombs of the next war. Her movements as Mrs. Drover were circumscribed, and she dismissed any idea that they were still watched.

As things were—dead or living the letter-writer sent her only a threat. Unable, for some minutes, to go on kneeling with her back exposed to the empty room, Mrs. Drover rose from the chest to sit on an upright chair whose back was firmly against the wall. The desuetude of her former bedroom, her married London home's whole air of being a cracked cup from which memory, with its reassuring power, had either evaporated or leaked away, made a crisis—and at just this crisis the letter-writer had, knowledgeably, struck. The hollowness of the house this evening cancelled years on years of voices, habits and steps. Through the shut windows she only heard rain fall on the roofs around. To rally herself, she said she was in a mood—and for two or three seconds shutting her eyes, told herself that she had imagined the letter. But she opened them—there it lay on the bed.

On the supernatural side of the letter's entrance she was not permitting her mind to dwell. Who, in London, knew she meant to call at the house today? Evidently, however, this had been known. The caretaker, *had* he come back, had had no cause to expect her: he would have taken the letter in his pocket, to forward it, at his own time, through the post. There was no other sign that the caretaker had been in—but, if not? Letters dropped in at doors of deserted houses do not fly or walk to tables in halls. They do not sit on the dust of empty tables with the air of certainty that they will be found. There is needed some human hand—but nobody but the caretaker had a key. Under circumstances she did not care to consider, a house can be entered without a key. It was possible that she was not alone now. She might be being waited for, downstairs. Waited for—until when? Until "the hour arranged." At least that was not six o'clock: six had struck.

She rose from the chair and went over and locked the door.

The thing was, to get out. To fly? No, not that: she had to catch her train. As a woman whose utter dependability was the keystone of her family life she was not willing to return to the country, to her husband, her little boys and her sister, without the objects she had come up to fetch. Resuming work at the chest she set about making up a number of parcels in a rapid, fumbling-decisive way. These, with her shopping parcels, would be too much to carry; these meant a taxi—at the thought of the taxi her heart went up and her normal breathing resumed. I will ring up the taxi now; the taxi cannot come too soon: I shall hear the taxi out there running its engine, till I walk calmly down to it through the hall. I'll ring up—But no: the telephone is cut off. . . . She tugged at a knot she had tied wrong.

The idea of flight. . . . He was never kind to me, not really. I don't remember him kind at all. Mother said he never considered me. He was set on me, that was what it was—not love. Not love, not meaning a person well. What did he do, to make me promise like that? I can't remember—But she found that she could.

She remembered with such dreadful acuteness that the twenty-five years since then dissolved like smoke and she instinctively looked for the weal left by the button on the palm of her hand. She remembered not only all that he said and did but the complete suspension of *her* existence during that August week. I was not myself—they all told me so at the time. She remembered—but with one white burning blank as where acid has dropped on a photograph: *under no conditions* could she remember his face.

So, wherever he may be waiting, I shall not know him. You have no time to run from a face you do not expect.

The thing was to get to the taxi before any clock struck what could be the hour. She would slip down the street and round the side of the square to where the square gave on the main road. She would return in the taxi, safe, to her own door, and bring the solid driver into the house with her to pick up the parcels from room to room. The idea of the taxi driver made her decisive, bold: she unlocked her door, went to the top of the staircase and listened down.

She heard nothing—but while she was hearing nothing the *passé* air of the staircase was disturbed by a draught that travelled up to her face. It emanated from the basement: down there a door or window was being opened by some-one who chose this moment to leave the house.

The rain had stopped; the pavements steamily shone as Mrs. Drover let herself out by inches from her own front door into the empty street. The un-occupied houses opposite continued to meet her look with their damaged stare. Making towards the thoroughfare and the taxi, she tried not to keep looking behind. Indeed, the silence was so intense—one of those creeks of London silence exaggerated this summer by the damage of war—that no tread could have gained on hers unheard. Where her street debouched on the square where people went on living, she grew conscious of, and checked, her unnatural pace. Across the open end of the square two buses impassively passed each other: women, a perambulator, cyclists, a man wheeling a barrow signalized, once again, the ordinary flow of life. At the square's most populous corner should be—and was—the short taxi rank. This evening, only one taxi—but this, although it presented its blank rump, appeared already to be alertly waiting for her. Indeed, without looking round the driver started his engine as she panted up from behind and put her hand on the door. As she did so, the clock struck seven. The taxi faced the main road: to make the trip back to her house it would have to turn—she had settled back on the seat and the taxi *had* turned before she, surprised by its knowing movement, recol-lected that she had not "said where." She leaned forward to scratch at the glass panel that divided the driver's head from her own.

The driver braked to what was almost a stop, turned round and slid the glass panel back: the jolt of this flung Mrs. Drover forward till her face was al-most into the glass. Through the aperture driver and passenger, not six inches between them, remained for an eternity eye to eye. Mrs. Drover's mouth hung open for some seconds before she could issue her first scream. After that she continued to scream freely and to beat with her gloved hands on the glass all round as the taxi, accelerating without mercy, made off with her into the hin-terland of deserted streets.

BIRTHDAY PARTY

KATHARINE BRUSH

They were a couple in their late thirties, and they looked unmistakably mar-ried. They sat on the banquette opposite us in a little narrow restaurant, hav-ing dinner. The man had a round, self-satisfied face, with glasses on it; the woman was fadingly pretty, in a big hat. There was nothing conspicuous about them, nothing particularly noticeable, until the end of their meal, when it suddenly became obvious that this was an Occasion—in fact, the husband's birthday, and the wife had planned a little surprise for him.

It arrived, in the form of a small but glossy birthday cake, with one pink candle burning in the center. The headwaiter brought it in and placed it before the husband, and meanwhile the violin-and-piano orchestra played "Happy Birthday to You" and the wife beamed with shy pride over her little surprise, and such few people as there were in the restaurant tried to help out with a pattering of applause. It became clear at once that help was needed, because the husband was not pleased. Instead he was hotly embarrassed, and indignant at his wife for embarrassing him.

You looked at him and you saw this and you thought, "Oh, now, don't *be* like that!" But he was like that, and as soon as the little cake had been deposited on the table, and the orchestra had finished the birthday piece, and the general attention had shifted from the man and the woman, I saw him say something to her under his breath—some punishing thing, quick and curt and unkind. I couldn't bear to look at the woman then, so I stared at my plate and waited for quite a long time. Not long enough, though. She was still crying when I finally glanced over there again. Crying quietly and heartbrokenly and hopelessly, all to herself, under the gay big brim of her best hat.

FROM *THE MAN IN THE GRAY FLANNEL SUIT*

SLOAN WILSON

Before they had gone three blocks the car got caught in a bad traffic jam and could barely crawl. Hopkins put his head back on the soft grey upholstery and closed his eyes. "You've got to slow down!" the doctor had said. It seemed to Hopkins that people had been telling him that all his life.

It had started when he was a boy in public school. He had been editor of the school paper, and though he had been too small to excel at athletics, he had been manager of the football and basketball teams. He had stood at the top of his class scholastically, and whenever there had been a dance or a school play, he had always been chairman of the arrangements committee. "You've got to slow down!" the teachers had told him. "Take it easy, boy—you'll wear yourself out!"

At Princeton, where he had gone on a scholarship, it had been more of the same. He had headed the debating team, managed the football team, and engaged in a dozen other activities in addition to maintaining an almost straight A average in his studies. "You've got to slow down!" his faculty adviser had told him. "Take it easy!"

But he had not slowed down. Summers he had worked at all kinds of jobs, always astonishing his employers with his energy. After college had come a brief stint in the Army, a period during which his friends had kidded him about wanting to be a general. Upon being released from service in 1919, he had worked for a few years at a brokerage house before going to the United Broadcasting Corporation, which had just been started. A year later he had met Helen Perry, who had at the time been a fashionable beauty in New York. He had pursued her with all the zeal he always devoted to anything he wanted, and on June 3, 1921, he had married her. Up to that time, Hopkins had never had a failure in his life.

"You've got to slow down!" Helen had started saying, even before they were married, but unlike the teachers and faculty advisers, she had not let it go at that. As she discovered that it was Hopkins' habit to spend most of his evenings and week-ends at his office, she had become first annoyed, then indignant, and, finally, hurt and bewildered.

"Life isn't worth living like this," she had said. "I never see you! You've got to slow down!"

He had tried. Especially when their first child, Robert, had come, during the second year of their marriage, he had tried. He had come home every evening at six o'clock and conscientiously played with the baby and sat talking with his wife, and he had been genuinely appalled to find that the baby made him nervous, and that while he was talking to his wife, it was almost impossible for him to sit quietly. He had felt impelled to get up and pace up and down the room, jingling his change in his pockets and glancing at the clock. For the first time in his life he had started to drink heavily during those long evenings at home. Gradually he had started staying late at the office again— by that time he had already had a fairly important job at the United Broadcasting Corporation. Helen had remonstrated with him. There had been recriminations, high-pitched arguments, and threats of divorce.

All right, it's a problem, he had said to himself after a particularly bitter scene—it's a problem that must be met head on, like all other problems. To Helen he had said, in a quiet voice, "I don't want to have any more scenes— they wear us both out. I'm prepared to admit that whatever is wrong is entirely my fault. I am preoccupied with my work—I've been that way all my life, and it is nothing for which you should blame yourself."

She had gone pale. "Do you want a divorce?" she had asked.

"No," he had said. "Do you?"

"No."

They had never talked about divorce again, but she had begun to refer to his preoccupation with work as a disease. "You've got to do something about it," she had said, and had suggested a psychiatrist.

For two years Hopkins had submitted to psychoanalysis. Five times a week he had lain on a couch in the psychoanalyst's apartment on Sixty-ninth Street and recalled his childhood. His father had been a cheerful, rather ineffectual man who, each afternoon upon returning from his job as assistant manager of a small paper mill in an upstate New York village, had spent most of his time rocking on the front porch of their shabby but comfortable house. His mother had been disappointed by the modesty of her husband's achievements and aspirations and had been bitterly condescending to him. Leaving her family to fend for itself most of the time, she had thrown all her energy into working for the local garden club and a bewildering variety of social and civic organizations. As she gained positions of leadership in these groups, her resentment at her serenely undistinguished husband had grown. Finally she had established herself in a separate room on the third floor of their house and, throughout most of Ralph's boyhood, had conducted herself like a great lady temporarily forced to live with poor relatives.

Hopkins was not an introspective man, but in recounting all this to the psychoanalyst, he had said, "I always felt sorry for my father because my mother treated him so badly. She never gave me much time, either, except when I did something she thought was outstanding. Whenever I got a particularly good report card, or won anything, she'd take me up to her room to have tea alone with her. 'We're two of a kind,' she used to say. 'We get things done.' I suppose I got the impression from her that achievement means everything."

Hopkins had felt quite proud of his efforts at self-diagnosis and had been surprised when the psychoanalyst had disregarded his suggestions in favour of much more bizarre "explanations of neurosis." He had said that Hopkins probably had a deep guilt complex, and that his constant work was simply an effort to punish and perhaps kill himself. The guilt complex was probably based on a fear of homosexuality, he had said. To Hopkins, who had never consciously worried about homosexuality, or guilt, this had seemed like so much rubbish, but he had tried to believe it, for the psychoanalyst had said it was necessary for him to believe to be cured, and Hopkins had wanted to be cured, in order to make his wife happy.

The trouble had been that every time he left the psychoanalyst's office the temptation to return to his own office and bury himself in work had been irresistible. At the end of two years he had become the youngest vice-president of United Broadcasting and had told his wife he simply wouldn't have time for psychoanalysis any longer.

The Utmost Measures

Cullen Murphy

A word in behalf of subjectivity

About 75 million Americans have taken the SAT for college admission since the Scholastic Aptitude Test (as it was then known) was first administered, in 1926, to 8,040 high school seniors. Last summer the College Board, which oversees the test, announced plans for significant revisions, scheduled to go into effect in the spring of 2005. The biggest change is the addition of an extemporaneous essay. Together with some grammar questions, the essay will constitute a third part of the test, joining the revised math and verbal sections. Students will be given an essay topic; some possibilities mentioned by the College Board include "Nothing requires more discipline than freedom," "The greatest griefs are those we cause ourselves," and "Novelty is too often mistaken for progress."

Educators will argue for years over the wisdom of the specific changes, and over what sorts of students stand to benefit and what sorts stand to lose. But two aspects of the new SAT are welcome developments on their face.

The first is that all those who have ever bragged about their SAT scores will suddenly see their claims undermined. Because there will soon be three sections, worth 800 points apiece, the best possible scores will total 2400; the former gold standard of 1600 appears deeply mediocre by comparison. Supplying an explanatory footnote—as history books do, say, to translate the value of ancient drachmas into modern dollars—will be awkward at best. The entire Baby Boom generation will be in the position of having to make the case to its grandchildren that back in the sixties or seventies an SAT score of 1490 or 1540 was actually not bad—like grandparents today who must patiently explain, to vaguely disbelieving young people, that "five thousand dollars was quite a lot of money in those days."

The second welcome development is the element of subjective judgement, which both the writing and the grading of the essays will require. Subjective judgment has been maligned for decades, on grounds of capriciousness and unfairness, and because it is "unscientific." Standardized testing was, of course, an attempt to get away from subjectivity. But every advance in testing, it seems, elicits the discovery of further flaws. This is the paradox of measurement: the more objective and precise we get, the more nimbly truth manages to keep a certain distance.

Janet L. Norwood, who served as the nation's Commissioner of Labor Statistics for nearly an eternity (well, 12.62 years), once complained, "The real problem is that people often want a number to tell them everything." She was referring to disagreements over the validity of seemingly objective economic measures—the unemployment rate and the poverty rate, the Consumer Price Index and the gross domestic product—but she might as well have been referring to an immutable trait of human character.

By chapter six in the Book of Genesis, three chapters after the expulsion from Eden, human beings must confront the importance of being able to measure things. The Lord commanded Noah to build an ark: "This is how you are to make it: the length of the ark three hundred cubits, its breadth fifty cubits, and its height thirty cubits." To which Noah replied, as recorded on Bill Cosby's first album, "Right. What's a cubit?" (It is the length from the crook of the elbow to the furthest fingertip.) Ever since, measurement has been extended to more and more phenomena—the mass of an electron, the size of the universe—and has become more and more refined.

The number of standardized ways in which a typical person is measured, beginning now with prenatal screening and continuing up through such things as "emotional intelligence" assays and "360-degree" performance reviews, must run into the dozens. Measurements of electrical patterns in the amygdala, a region of the forebrain, may soon reveal our innermost emotions. An automobile designed by Toyota in cooperation with Sony, called the Pod and intended to help control road rage, contains sensors to measure pulse rate and level of perspiration; at the first sign of trouble it begins to play soothing music and warns drivers to calm down. (Memo to Toyota: this will only make them madder.) Measurements are palpated for the subtlest insights. A recent study conducted by clinicians in Toronto explored the relationship between high status and good health by comparing the longevity of Oscar winners with that of other actors and actresses. (Oscar winners live, on average, 3.9 years longer.) In another recent study researchers at the University of California at Berkeley randomly selected 720 people at street festivals in San Francisco, asked them about their sexual orientation, and measured their fingers. Lesbians, the researchers concluded, are more likely to have index fingers that are unusually short relative to their ring fingers.

Everyone knows that many types of measurement are at best crude constructs, especially when it comes to human psychology and well-being. But even the brute physical world remains mysteriously elusive. Fingerprints have been a bedrock of forensic evidence for decades—but the reliability of fingerprint analysis in some circumstances has lately been called into question. If anything ought to stay still long enough to be precisely measured, it is nature's physical "constants." But it turns out that our values for such things as the gravitational constant, the fine-structure constant, and even the speed of light may not be as solid as one would wish. "The constants of nature could be lawless variables," a physicist from London's Imperial College told a conference earlier this year.

In the everyday world, too, standard methods of measurement have been found to fall short. Last year the National Weather Service announced that the formula for the wind-chill factor had been somewhat inaccurate ever since it was adopted, in 1973, and that a new formula would be used in the future. Many meteorologists agree that the heat index, the wind-chill factor's warm-weather counterpart, could also benefit from remedial attention.

No one would argue for scrapping society's vast accumulated infrastructure of measurement. Indeed, there may be some new statistical indices we'd all be grateful to have. For instance, it would be easy enough to devise an accuracy-of-prognostication index for newspaper columnists, perhaps a little number that would appear right after the byline: "by Robert Novak (1.7)"; "by David S. Broder (7.6)." But at the same time, it might be worth giving subjective judgment more weight. Subjective judgment, after all, is what gives us epigrams. It is the methodology that informs such phrases as "gut reaction" and "cut of his jib." It is why NASA still uses noses rather than machines to decide which smells will prove intolerable in space. It often captures truth more fully than any measurement can.

As the College Board has shown, objective measures can easily be supplemented with something more individual and illuminating—namely, a short essay.

Imagine, say, that Albert Camus was a television meteorologist. After reporting the heat index, and maybe comically mopping his brow, he would tell us what being outside in such heat actually felt like:

> I was surprised at how fast the sun was climbing in the sky. I noticed that for quite some time the countryside had been buzzing with the

sound of insects and the crackling of grass. The sweat was pouring down my face . . . The glare from the sky was unbearable. At one point, we went over a section of the road that had just been repaved. The tar had burst open in the sun. Our feet sank into it, leaving its shiny pulp exposed. [*The Stranger*]

Or the meteorologist could be Jack London. After he finished telling us the wind-chill factor, with an affable on-camera shudder and a sideways grin at the news anchor, he might also explain what that terrible degree of cold really did to a person:

It was surprising, the rapidity with which his cheeks and nose were freezing. And he had not thought his fingers could go lifeless in so short a time. Lifeless they were, for he could scarcely make them move together to grip a twig, and they seemed remote from his body and from him. When he touched a twig, he had to look and see whether or not he had hold of it. ["To Build a Fire"]

This approach could usefully augment many types of measured assessment—the latest unemployment figures, an electrocardiogram, a new estimate of the age of the universe. I put it forward with a certain hesitation, aware that novelty is too often mistaken for progress.

"Hurry Notes": Keeping a Commonplace Book

Look sharply after your thoughts. They come unlooked for, like a new bird seen on your trees, and, if you turn to your usual task, disappear; and you shall never find that perception again. . . .

—RALPH WALDO EMERSON (*THE HEART OF EMERSON'S JOURNALS* 333)[1]

What You Think

This chapter originated as a sort of defense against the Information Age, against the exploding quantity of information to which most of us are exposed daily. Several years ago I realized I was ingesting large amounts of information from many sources, yet paying hardly any attention to my own thoughts. Of course, no one would deny that acquiring knowledge from outside is important and necessary for intellectual and personal growth; but unless you sift this material with a thoughtful mind, what good is it? Unsifted information is random information and, however plentiful, finally meaningless. "If a man has read a great number of books, and does not think things through," said the Chinese writer Shu Shuehmou, "he is only a bookcase" (qtd. in Lin Yutang 468). The medieval mystic Meister Eckhart put the problem even more succinctly: "Subtract the mind, and the eye is open to no purpose" (qtd. in Coomaraswamy 43).

Make a list of creative people, past and present, from all areas of human endeavor, and you will not find one who hasn't made a habit, amid even the busiest days and the most intensive researches, of paying close attention to his or her own thoughts. To pay attention to what you think may not be the end of knowledge, but it is the indispensable beginning.

---

1. Since it contains many quotations, I have written this chapter as a research essay using Modern Language Assocation (MLA) documentation style. For more on this style, see Chapter 11, "Documenting Research Essays."

Day and night, year after year, the world "writes" on you—through television, radio, film, the Internet, books, magazines, newspapers and tabloids, songs, pictures, commercial advertisements, and industries and institutions large and small. *You are no "I" if you are only written on. Write back.*

The following is a list of prominent individuals that seems random but isn't: Abraham Lincoln, Joseph Heller, Johann Wolfgang von Goethe, Murasaki Shikibu, Henrik Ibsen, Walt Whitman, Matsuo Bashō, Emily Dickinson, Annie Dillard, Katherine Mansfield, Friedrich Nietzsche, Peter Ilich Tchaikovsky, Richard Wagner, Sir Walter Scott, Igor Stravinsky, Leo Tolstoy, James Joyce, Marianne Moore, Joyce Carol Oates, Charles Darwin, Miguel de Unamuno, Martha Graham, Pete Seeger, John Lennon, Toni Morrison, Jim Morrison, Teddy Roosevelt, Aaron Copland, Ludwig van Beethoven, Mary Oliver, F. Scott Fitzgerald, Joy Harjo, Eugene O'Neill, Joan Didion, Allen Ginsberg, Anton Chekhov, Albert Einstein, Virginia Woolf.[2]

All of these people were notetakers. They all made a practice of carrying a small pad of paper or scraps of paper for making on-the-spot spontaneous notes of their thoughts, ideas, and impressions.

Honor Your Thoughts by Writing Them Down

The point of this chapter is simple. Honor your thoughts. Carry a small notepad or notebook ("commonplace book") at all times for writing down your passing thoughts, impressions, and observations, and any memorable quotations you read or overhear. Copy the contents of your notepad into a larger notebook or into word-processing files periodically for rereading, amusement, and use in other writing.

The practice of keeping commonplace books, small notebooks of thoughts and memorable quotations, has a long and distinguished history. Ancient Greek and Roman philosophers recommended that students collect commonplaces (striking ideas, thoughts, passages from reading or conversation) to help with discovering and constructing logical arguments. When Shakespeare was a schoolboy a popular textbook (by one Roger Ascham) outlined a method for keeping commonplace books, so it is not unreasonable to imagine that the greatest writer in the English language grew up taking and using notes. During the sixteenth and seventeenth centuries the commonplace-book habit spread across Europe and into the North American colonies, and major writers and teachers of the day promoted it as a resource for improving memory and reading comprehension, honing verbal skills, stimulating imagination, and cultivating personal character (Berland, Gilliam, and Lockridge 22–29). In Japan, the commonplace book had its counterpart in the so-called pillow book, "a notebook or collection of notebooks kept in some accessible but relatively private place . . . in which the author

---

2. The notetaking habits of many of these people are described in Vera John-Steiner's excellent *Notebooks of the Mind.* Rev. ed. New York: Oxford UP, 1997.

would from time to time record impressions, daily events, poems, letters, stories, ideas, descriptions of people, etc." (Morris 376n). The most famous example is *The Pillow Book* of Sei Shōnagon, an eleventh-century Japanese courtier whose delightful notes have been edited and translated into English by Ivan Morris (see p. 685 for excerpts).

John Milton (author of *Paradise Lost*), John Locke (widely regarded as the greatest British philosopher), and Thomas Jefferson are just a few well-known writers of the seventeenth and eighteenth centuries who kept commonplace books (Berland, Gilliam, and Lockridge 34; Mohl; Rosenwald 29–30). Writers in the twentieth and twenty-first centuries continue to carry small notebooks for taking notes, though the term "commonplace" for them has generally fallen out of usage.

If you remain skeptical about the value of commonplace books, consider three famous examples.

While dining or drinking with friends, Ludwig van Beethoven was sometimes known to stop conversation, produce a notebook, and scribble down a musical idea. When asked about this unusual behavior, Beethoven explained that he had to record his idea immediately or risk losing it. Later he reviewed the ideas in the notebook and incorporated many of them into his musical compositions (Johnson, Tyson, and Winter 3–6). For all anyone knows, the opening measures of the Fifth Symphony, probably the most famous theme in classical music, may have originated as one of these quickly written notes. "I dread the beginning of these large works," Beethoven once remarked. "Once into the work, and it goes" (Sullivan 102). Quick note taking was one of Beethoven's indispensable ways of "beginning."

Abraham Lincoln was an eloquent and deep political thinker whose Gettysburg Address is among the most influential documents in American political history. He was also an extremely busy man who had to jot down policy plans or ideas for writing or for speeches whenever he could, often hastily. In photographs Lincoln is frequently seen wearing a tall hat. When he wanted to save a thought for later reflection or use, he scribbled it on an envelope or a scrap of paper and stuck it inside the lining of his hat. Later, when he could relax a bit, he would remove the notes from his hat and revise, combine, and expand them. Lincoln's law partner William "Billy" Herndon remarked that his hat was "an extraordinary receptacle. It was his desk and his memorandum book" (Kunhardt, Kunhardt, and Kunhardt 308).

Walt Whitman, nineteenth-century poet, *dressed* for success—at note taking. He wore clothing with large pockets for carrying paper and pencil so that he was ready to write down a good idea whenever one came. Writing even on the run, coming and going, in between other tasks, he took notes on everything. Signs of this appear again and again in his work: in the early notebooks for the first edition of his book *Leaves of Grass* (1855), a line of poetry ("*I am the poet of equality*") appears just below a personal business memo ("Amount rec'd from Mr. V. A."), the inspired and the mundane jumbled together (*Notebooks and Unpublished Prose Manuscripts* 71). In *Specimen Days,* his autobiography, Whitman wrote: "Wherever I go, indeed, winter or summer, city or country, alone at home or traveling, I must take notes. . . ." (82). At one point he considered titling his autobiographical recollections *Abandons. . . Hurry Notes* (167n). During the Civil War, as a volunteer nursing the wounded in military hospitals, he "kept little note-books for impromptu jottings in pencil to refresh my memory of names and circumstances. . . ." (7n). All his life he was dashing off notes and using leisure time to assemble and revise the bits and pieces into poems.

Sometime between 1847 and 1854 Whitman wrote the following note in a 3 ½-by-5 ½-inch notebook:

> Have you supposed it beautiful to be born?
> I tell you I know it is just as beautiful to die;
> For I take my death with the dying
> And my birth with the new-born babes. (*Notebooks and Unpublished Prose Manuscripts* 72–73)

In 1855 these lines appeared, slightly altered and improved, in Whitman's most famous poem, "Song of Myself":

> Has any one supposed it lucky to be born?
> I hasten to inform him or her it is just as lucky to die, and I know it.
> I pass death with the dying, and birth with the new-washed babe
>   . . . and am not contained between my hat and my boots. . . . (*Leaves of Grass* 30–31)

Why Take Notes?

As often as not, sitting down at a desk to *write* or *compose* makes the mind go blank. You sit and stare at the empty screen or paper, and before you know it, an hour may go by with nothing written. On the other hand, many of the best ideas are likely to come when you are away from the workspace and not trying to think: when you are taking a walk, driving, riding the bus, washing dishes, attending a meeting, exercising, mowing the lawn, showering, talking with friends, gardening, or standing in line. Unless you have paper with you for jotting down an idea right away, you may tell yourself, "I'll have to write that down when I get home," but you will probably forget it.

By carrying a notepad and pausing to write in the odd moments of the day, you have less need for long uninterrupted stretches of time for writing. You can write anytime, anywhere, even if for only a few seconds.

This is a significant advantage in the twenty-first century, when everyone seems to be constantly busy, overcommitted, and stressed. The two-hour stretch of free time you wait for never seems to materialize. Writing an idea or impression in your notepad requires no length of unbroken time but just a moment. (For better or for worse, perhaps most of the *best* moments we have anymore are those "odds" moments occurring between this task and that; in fact, we may do most of the things we love in a moment we have to *steal*.)

Carrying a notepad also eliminates the need for "inspiration." "[M]usic is perpetual," wrote Henry David Thoreau. "[O]nly hearing is intermittent" (*Journal* 245). To develop the note-taking habit is to detect the inspiration or music latent in every moment.

Thoreau's sentence is profound. The problem of inspiration, he says, is not that no "music" or idea comes to us from outside; rather, the trouble is that we aren't listening. To test the accuracy of Thoreau's remark, watch yourself as you go from point A to point B, when you are preoccupied with getting to "B": observe how much of anything you see or hear along the way. Your attention seems riveted on B (you are scarcely present *in* the present), on the road, on the driver directly ahead, and on traffic signals.

A woman lamented in her notebook:

> For many years I have collected art. I'm not rich but that's how I spend the little money I manage to save after taking care of my children and mother-in-law. Unfortunately, I am usually racing around my house so fast trying to get things done I don't even notice the pictures on my walls. I don't enjoy them. They might as well not be there.

Good spiritual physician that he was, Thoreau would have quickly diagnosed this woman's problem as "intermittent hearing [or looking]." He might also have prescribed a remedy: *Look and listen continually. Take good notes.*[3]

Finally, if you use a notepad, over time you can accumulate such a large collection of ideas that your primary creative role becomes one of *editing* your old writings rather than of *inventing* new ones; and editing is usually less daunting than inventing. As we saw back in Chapter 2, it is easier to write from something than to write from nothing. Walt Whitman has already been mentioned as someone who jotted down and collected lines of poetry over many years and gradually cut and pasted them together to make a book (*Leaves of Grass*). Another example is Ralph Waldo Emerson, Whitman's contemporary. Emerson spent years gathering ideas in notebooks, eventually filling over 250 volumes, and was able to compose most of his lectures and essays simply by mining, combining, and editing materials already present (and indexed) in his notes (Richardson, *Emerson: The Mind on Fire* 321).

Though you may never write a line of verse, if you habitually record your passing thoughts, impressions, and observations you are, in the broadest sense, a "poet"—that is, a person who approaches the moment mindfully. The German

---

3. Thoreau took his own medicine faithfully. He wrote everywhere, especially during walks, and even kept paper at his bedside at night. Today many naturalists regard him as one of the keenest and most scientific (not to mention poetic) observers of nature who ever lived.

writer Johann Wolfgang von Goethe seems to be using the term "poet" in that sense, in the following quotation:

> The present will have its rights; the thoughts and feelings which daily press upon the poet will and should be expressed. . . . [If the poet] daily seizes the present, and always treats with a freshness of feeling what is offered him, he always makes sure of something good; and, if he sometimes does not succeed, has, at least lost nothing. (*Conversations of Goethe* 7)

Sample Published and Unpublished Notes

G. C. Lichtenberg, eighteenth-century mathematician and physicist. During his student days Georg Lichtenberg began keeping notebooks for collecting scientific jottings as well as miscellaneous reflections on all aspects of life and society— books, learning, religion, politics, philosophy, history, the arts, conversation, manners, human psychology. By the end of his life he had amassed thousands of these notes, which he reread and revised from time to time for his own amusement (Stern 197). Published after his death, Lichtenberg's notebooks have been admired by such writers as Goethe, the philosophers Arthur Schopenhauer, Friedrich Nietzsche, and Søren Kierkegaard, novelist Leo Tolstoy, and physicist Albert Einstein. Here are some excerpts:

> Often when an acquaintance goes past I step back from my window—not so much to spare him the trouble of making me a bow as rather to spare myself the embarrassment of seeing that he has not made me one. (qtd. in Stern 279)
> *Commentary:* In a sentence Lichtenberg strips the curtain from his—and our—vanity.

> We cannot truly know whether we are not at this moment sitting in a madhouse. (Lichtenberg, *Aphorisms* 133)
> *Commentary:* This is a shocking thought that seems eerily accurate: unless we can somehow get outside the world, so long as we are closed within it and indoctrinated into its beliefs, conventions, and ways of knowing, we cannot be certain whether everything in it that passes for "normal" or "sane" among the majority of people isn't in fact the most outrageous insanity. One of Lichtenberg's near contemporaries, Jonathan Swift, believed we *are* in a sort of madhouse which he immortalized in his great satire, *Gulliver's Travels.*

> When a book and a head collide and a hollow sound is heard, must it always have come from the book? (*Aphorisms* 60)

> "What a pity it isn't a sin to drink water," cried an Italian, "how good it would taste." (*Aphorisms* 93)

Waste-book method highly recommended. A note made of every phrase, every expression. Wealth can also be acquired through saving up truths in pennyworths. (*Aphorisms* 104)

The moral Universal inheres in the small penny-events of everyday life no less than in the great ones, as is well known to the few experts there are. There is so much goodness and art in a single raindrop that you wouldn't sell it in a pharmacy for less than half a guilder. . . . (qtd. in Stern 324)

Writing is an excellent means of awakening in every man the system slumbering within him; and everyone who has ever written will have discovered that writing always awakens something which, though it lay within us, we failed clearly to recognize before. (*Aphorisms* 119)
Commentary: Note the words "slumbering" and "awakening." Writing rouses the sleeping knowledge inside us.

Lichtenberg was not a professional writer in the usual sense: he wrote scientific articles but also had a "regular" job, a family, children, and other responsibilities. He could as easily have been a grocery clerk, a custodian, a shoemaker, a student, an engineer, a homemaker, an accountant, unemployed, or retired. Like most of us, he found that thoughts were constantly darting through his mind, often when he was trying to concentrate on other things. "My best ideas always come to me in such a way that I cannot say whence they come" (qtd. in Stern 318). Lichtenberg is proof that anyone can find moments to record his or her thoughts and observations and so live life more attentively.

Elias Canetti, winner of the 1981 Nobel Prize in literature. During the 1940s and '50s Canetti was staggering under the weight of an oppressively long-term project, researching and composing his sociological masterpiece, *Crowds and Power*. He began writing down his thoughts on *other* subjects in a desperate attempt to keep some spontaneity in his life. As he explained in the preface to *The Human Province*, a published volume of his notes, "A safety valve was indispensable, and I found it, at the start of 1942, in my jottings. Their freedom and spontaneity, the conviction that they existed only for their own sake and served no purpose . . . saved me from a fatal paralysis" (v).

Everything one *records* contains a grain of hope, no matter how deeply it may come from despair. (*The Oxford Book of Aphorisms* 290)
Commentary: Is this perhaps the best brief justification ever given for recording sad, "depressing," and horrific stories and experiences—for instance, narratives of the Holocaust? Merely to preserve the story in writing for later generations to read and remember is a life-affirming act, a firm "No" to despair. *I wrote it down; it matters; life matters.*

Whenever you observe an animal closely, you feel as if a human being sitting inside were making fun of you. (*The Oxford Book of Aphorisms* 6)

The process of knowledge consists above all in throwing everything overboard in order to more rapidly and more easily reach a goal that one senses. (*The Human Province* 203)
Commentary: A profound comment about learning. Wise people sometimes say that they have spent the second half of their lives unlearning the prejudices and misconceptions they acquired in the first half.

The first effect of adjusting to other people is that one becomes boring. (*The Human Province* 144)

Only those who can be bothered live. If you can't be bothered, you have already died. (*Notes from Hampstead* 121).
Commentary: We should all remember this the next time we are "bothered"—most likely within the next five minutes.

Malcolm de Chazal, twentieth-century painter and poet. The poet W. H. Auden considered Chazal the best French-language poet of the postmodern (post–World War II) period. Many of Chazal's notes are miniature poems in prose, like these excerpts from his collection, *Plastic Sense.*

The mouth is the starting point of laughter, with the eye its destination. Long after the mouth is exhausted the eye continues to laugh. (21)

Passion cannot survive without an audience. Romeo and Juliet as castaways would have set up petty housekeeping in no time. (24)

A look of indifference is a perpetual goodbye. (28)

Clouds are wind-ribbed umbrellas. (33)

The cat purrs himself to sleep, being the only creature who sings his own lullaby. (52)

All animals are experts, yet we use them merely as help. If only we knew how to get the best out of them, each in his own special capacity, we would be infinitely more successful in holding off the machines that threaten us with creeping destruction. (54)

All in all, the laws represent a minority plot against the best interests of the majority, which is why there are always more policemen patrolling the other side of the railroad tracks than the center of town. (64)

Dag Hammarskjöld, Swedish financier and statesman, Secretary General of the United Nations. Hammarskjöld served as Secretary General from 1953 until his death in a plane crash in 1961. His notebooks were translated into English by W. H. Auden and Leif Sjoberg and published in 1964 under the title of *Markings*. Today *Markings* is still readily available in bookstores. Hammarskjöld spent most of his adult life dealing with international finance, global political crises (present or impending), and obstreperous politicians and dictators; amid all these pressures he found note taking indispensable for maintaining his courage, compassion, and moral poise. Hammarskjöld jotted ideas in many forms: meditations, prayers, poems, aphorisms, annotations of his reading, shorthand descriptions of his dreams. He especially liked haiku poetry, as can be seen in the following examples:

> The trees pant. Silence.
> An irresolute raindrop furrows
> The dark pane. (*Markings* 153)

> In the bare poplar a voice
> Of such well-being
> It burst space open. (155)

> The Lover desires the perfection of the Beloved—which requires, among other things, the liberation of the Beloved from the Lover. (99)

> The only kind of dignity which is genuine is that which is not diminished by the indifference of others. (89)

Other Published Examples

> The ostrich: a giant chick. (Jules Renard 226)
> *Commentary:* Renard (1864–1910) spent much of his life in Paris, where he liked to visit the zoo and observe animals. You can find a larger selection of Renard's animal and other notes in Interchapter IV.

> In the path, the caterpillar plays a soundless little tune on its accordion. (Renard 217)

> To be a boy, and to play alone, in full sunlight, in the square of a little town. (Renard 49)

> My most constant temptation, the one against which I have never ceased fighting to the point of exhaustion: cynicism. (Albert Camus 249)

> Strike a stone
> to see if it's thinking of water. (Rita Dove; qtd. in Kuusisto, Tall, and Weiss 13)

A porcelain cup overturned on a plate: an iridescent igloo. (Dove; qtd. in Kuusisto, Tall, and Weiss 15)

It's better for the heart to break
than not to break. (Mary Oliver; qtd. in Kuusisto, Tall, and Weiss 224)

Something totally unexpected,
like a barking cat. (Oliver; qtd. in Kuusisto, Tall, and Weiss 224)

Unpublished Examples from Various Commonplace Books

Dream: I am not able to find my house. I take the same streets, but all the houses are different.
Commentary: If you can still remember your dreams after you wake up, write them down. The modern British author Grahame Greene wrote an entire book of nothing but his dreams that was published after his death as *A World of My Own: A Dream Diary* (New York: Viking, 1994). In the foreword Yvonne Cloetta describes Greene's method: "[H]e always had a pencil and paper at hand on his bedside table so that when he awoke from a dream . . . he could jot down key words that in the morning would allow him to reconstruct it. He would then transcribe it into his diary" (Cloetta ix). Greene said that some of his short stories were drawn almost in their entirety from his dreams.

March: The pungent smells of spring are the dreams of winter.

There is even a time to hate, says the preacher, but never a time to worry.

January, English class, from another student: "Be yourself, everyone else is taken."

"He who isn't busy being born is busy dying." (Bob Dylan)

An office memorandum: "This project is so important, we can't let things that are more important interfere with it."

[heard/overheard] "I walked past a classroom and heard the professor ask, 'Does anyone in this room have a mother?'"

Collecting Quotations

The last several examples quoted above illustrate one especially useful kind of entry to include in a small notepad—quotations, read or heard. Even though collecting quotations is recording other people's words, it is also a way of recognizing and recording what sings inside yourself. Walt Whitman kept a "well thumb'd common-place book" that he "absorb'd over and over again, when the mood invited." "I find so much," Whitman wrote, "in having a poem or fine suggestion sink into me . . ." (*Specimen Days* 183 – 85). The following are a few quotations Whitman copied into his commonplace book:

> "If you hate a man, don't kill him, but let him live."—Buddhistic.

> The form of oath among the Shoshone Indians is, "The earth hears me. The sun hears me. Shall I lie?"

> "Preach not to others what they should eat, but eat as becomes you, and be silent."—Epictetus. (*Specimen Days* 183n – 85n)

Doubtless Whitman's own poetic voice owes something to his practice of copying, rereading, and memorizing passages of poetry and poetic prose that he liked. Savored and "absorb'd," to use Whitman's word, a favorite quotation is as much your *own* as anything you write yourself.

Michel de Montaigne, a contemporary of Shakespeare's who is regarded as the inventor of the personal essay (see Chapter 16), had fifty-seven of his favorite quotations painted on the ceiling of his personal library so that whenever he wished, he could look up and contemplate them (De Botton 117). You might say he used his ceiling as a commonplace book. Some examples:

> The happiest life is to be without thought.—Sophocles

> Have you seen a man who thinks he is wise? You have more to hope for from a madman than from him.—Proverbs

> There is nothing certain but uncertainty, nothing more miserable and more proud than man.—Pliny

> Everything is too complicated for men to be able to understand. —Ecclesiastes (qtd. in De Botton 118)

Not surprisingly, the quotations address topics and themes—human vanity and skepticism—that are central to Montaigne's own writings. "I quote others," he said, "only the better to express myself" (qtd. in Winokur 272). It is easy to imagine Montaigne using such quotations to spark his own composing.

Kate Chopin, a writer featured prominently in *Reading and Writing from Literature,* copied many striking passages from novels, poetry, and nonfiction works into her commonplace book. She also summarized ideas and facts from her reading that she wanted to remember. Growing to artistic maturity in the man's world of the late nineteenth century, Chopin supplemented quotations with her own opinions and judgments on books, authors, and the topics of the day, gradually honing the strong and independent sensibility detectable in "The Story of an Hour" and other of her short stories and novels (Chopin 9ff.).

Four Ways to Use Your Notes

1. *Enjoy them.* Watching your thoughts is a delight in itself. It requires no further justification. If you date your entries, you can reread them weeks, months, or years later and have the pleasure of observing how your thinking and concerns have changed over time. The modern poet W. H. Auden published his commonplace book (*A Certain World*, 1970) as "a sort of autobiography" and contended that the map it offered of his *mental* world was the best available map of his entire life (Auden vii).

2. *Reread them regularly.* This enables you to commit ideas and passages to memory. As mentioned, Walt Whitman did this, like countless other writers down through the centuries. If you read Thoreau's "Where I Lived, and What I Lived For" (p. 1040) and are struck by his command of quotations, remember that he made a habit of collecting and rereading quotations stored in his journals and "fact books." When you sift ideas repeatedly, you can recall them at will, as Thoreau was able to do, and insert them into your longer writings. The astonishing memory of earlier writers (some carried whole books in their heads) can be traced, in part, to their practice of frequently rereading their notes, along with a discipline of memorization.

3. *Revise your notes—gently. . . .* The *first* thought is usually best. The same rule applies here as to annotation (see p. 10): Honor your first impression and first words, however "dumb," "boring," "unoriginal," or "off the wall" they may seem. What looks unpromising to you at the moment may prove, weeks or years later, to be your best idea.

Here, for example, is a note in its original form: "Note taking is good practice for those who can't write as fast as they think" (September).

And a later revision: "Prose plods. A rickshaw" (late September).

And yet another revision: "Writing is to thought as rickshaw to rocket" (November).

Ideally, the object of such revisions is to express the idea more clearly and exactly, not just to meddle with the words. "It is not my words that I polish, but my ideas" (Joseph Joubert).

4. *Use a note as a center of energy.* From a note, a writer can create a larger piece of writing such as a paragraph, essay, poem, or story. (This, of course, is how Lincoln, Whitman, and many others mentioned in this chapter used their notes.) The crucial point, once again, is to *reread* the notes you collect, not just once but multiple times. As you reread you can revise, expand, and combine them. Through this process a hastily written note, or series of notes, can grow into a finished work.

Much of Henry David Thoreau's classic *Walden* grew out of "seed" notes, in his journal, that he expanded by a kind of layering process through successive rereadings. (Thoreau's writings characteristically grew like trees, from a central idea outward, adding new "rings" with each rereading.) In 1846 Thoreau scribbled the following notes as he was climbing Mount Katahdin in Maine:

> climb tree—torrrent—camping ground—leave party—go up torrent—fir trees—lakes—rocks—clouds—sick and weary—camp—green fish—fire at night—wind up ravine. (qtd. in Richardson, *Henry Thoreau: A Life of the Mind* 180)

He wrote hastily, in shorthand, unwilling to break the spell of the moment, but wrote just enough. Later, rereading these and other jottings brought the whole experience before his mind, and the seed notes matured into the "oak tree" entitled "Ktaadn," one of the great nature essays in English.[4]

On May 14, 1925 English novelist Virginia Woolf scribbled the following in her diary:

> This is going to be fairly short; to have father's character done complete in it; and mother's; and St. Ives; and childhood; and all the usual things I try to put in— life, death, etc. But the centre is father's character, sitting in a boat, reciting We perished each alone, while he crushes a dying mackerel. (*A Writer's Diary* 75)

These quickly written words—a mere two sentences—anticipate the structure of Woolf's major semiautobiographical novel *To the Lighthouse*, which she published two years later, in 1927. The quick sketch defined the original vision that helped her plan the work and carry it to completion.

Works Cited

Auden, W. H. *A Certain World: A Commonplace Book.* New York: Viking, 1970.

Berland, Kevin, Jan Kirsten Gilliam, and Kenneth A. Lockridge, eds. *The Commonplace Book of William Byrd II of Westover.* Chapel Hill: U of North Carolina P, 2001.

Camus, Albert. *Notebooks: 1942–1951.* Trans. Justin O'Brien. New York: Paragon, 1991.

Canetti, Elias. *The Human Province.* Trans. Joachim Neugroschel. New York: Seabury, 1978.

---. *Notes from Hampstead: The Writer's Notes: 1954–1971.* Trans. John Hargraves. New York: Farrar, 1994.

---

4. Thoreau had this to say about short notes: "Each thought that is welcomed and recorded is a nest egg, by the side of which more will be laid. Thoughts accidentally thrown together become a frame in which more may be developed and exhibited" (*A Writer's Journal* 82).

Chazal, Malcolm de. *Plastic Sense.* Trans. Irving J. Weiss. Herder and Herder, 1971.

Chopin, Kate. *Kate Chopin's Private Papers.* Ed. Emily Toth and Per Seyersted. Bloomington: Indiana UP, 1998.

Cloetta, Yvonne. Foreword. *A World of My Own: A Dream Diary.* By Graham Greene. New York: Viking, 1994. vii–xii.

Coomaraswamy, A. K. "The Philosophy of Medieval and Oriental Art." *Selected Papers: Traditional Art and Symbolism.* Ed. Roger Lipsey. Princeton: Princeton UP, 1977. 43–70.

De Botton, Alain. *The Consolations of Philosophy.* New York: Pantheon, 2000.

Emerson, Ralph Waldo. *The Heart of Emerson's Journals.* Ed. Bliss Perry. 1926. New York: Dover, 1995.

Goethe, Johann Wolfgang von. *Conversations of Goethe with Johann Peter Eckermann.* Trans. John Oxenford. 1930. New York: Da Capo, 1998.

Hammarskjöld, Dag. *Markings.* Trans. Leif Sjoberg and W. H. Auden. New York: Ballantine, 1964.

Johnson, Douglas, Alan Tyson, and Robert Winter, eds. *The Beethoven Sketchbooks: History, Reconstruction, Inventory.* Berkeley: U of California P, 1985.

John-Steiner, Vera. *Notebooks of the Mind: Explorations of Thinking.* Rev. ed. New York: Oxford UP, 1997.

Kunhardt, Philip B., Jr., Philip B. Kunhardt III, and Peter W. Kunhardt. *Lincoln: An Illustrated Biography.* New York: Knopf, 1993.

Kuusisto, Stephen, Deborah Tall, and David Weiss, eds. *The Poet's Notebook: Excerpts from the Notebooks of Contemporary American Poets.* New York: Norton, 1995.

Lichtenberg, Georg Christoph. *Aphorisms.* Trans. R. J. Hollingdale. London: Penguin, 1990.

Lin Yutang. *The Importance of Understanding: Translations from the Chinese.* Cleveland: The World Publishing Company, 1960.

Locke, John. *A New Method of Making Common-Place-Books.* London: J. Greenwood, 1706.

Mohl, Ruth, ed. *John Milton and His Commonplace Book.* New York: Ungar, 1969.

Morris, Ivan, ed. and trans. *The Pillow Book of Sei Shōnagon.* New York: Columbia UP, 1991.

The Oxford Book of Aphorisms. Chosen by John Gross. Oxford: Oxford UP, 1983.

Renard, Jules. *The Journal of Jules Renard.* Ed. and trans. Louise Bogan and Elizabeth Roget. New York: George Braziller, 1964.

Richardson, Robert D., Jr. *Emerson: The Mind on Fire.* Berkeley: U of California P, 1995.

———. *Henry Thoreau: A Life of the Mind.* Berkeley: U of California P, 1986.

Rosenwald, Lawrence. *Emerson and the Art of the Diary.* New York: Oxford, 1988.

Stern, J. P., ed. and trans. *Lichtenberg: A Doctrine of Scattered Occasions.* Bloomington, IN: Indiana UP, 1959.

Sullivan, J. W. N. *Beethoven: His Spiritual Development.* 1927. New York: Vintage, 1960.

Thoreau, Henry David. *The Journal of Henry David Thoreau.* Ed. Bradford Torrey and Francis H. Allen. Vol. 9. 1906. New York: Dover, 1962.

---. *A Writer's Journal.* Ed. Laurence Stapleton. New York: Dover, 1960.

Whitman, Walt. *Leaves of Grass: The First (1855) Edition.* Ed. Malcolm Cowley. New York: Penguin, 1986.

---. *Notebooks and Unpublished Prose Manuscripts.* Ed. Edward F. Grier. Vol. 1. New York: New York UP, 1984.

---. *Specimen Days & Collect.* 1882–1883. New York: Dover, 1995.

Winokur, Jon. *Writers on Writing.* Philadelphia: Running P, 1990.

Woolf, Virginia. *A Writer's Diary: Being Extracts from the Diary of Virginia Woolf.* Ed. Leonard Woolf. New York: Harcourt, 1954.

ACTIVITIES FOR WRITING

1. Start your own commonplace book. Buy a small notepad that is easily transportable in a bag, pocket, or purse. For the rest of the quarter or semester, use this notepad for collecting thoughts and observations, quotations read or heard, or other kinds of notes. Concentrate on recording your ideas on-the-spot and in the exact words in which they occur to you, however awkward or strange.

Use the examples in this chapter for inspiration. You can also look ahead to the longer selections of notes in Interchapters I–V on pages 316, 443, 595, 806, and 964.

2. Reread your notes periodically and make any revisions or additions that occur to you.

    a. Reread all or a portion of your notes, with pen or pencil in hand.

    b. Underline or circle phrases, sentences, or ideas that strike you, for whatever reason.

    c. Reread the marked passages and choose one that seems most interesting to you now. Share and discuss the passage with a partner, small group, or friend.

or

In the margins annotate or "talk back" to those notes that strike you. Write about any or all of the following:

- Additional thoughts the item suggests to you
- Why an item interests you
- How you might like, at some point, to expand the item

Writing in Diverse Forms:
The Topic/Form Grid

Beginning writers sometimes suffer from an impoverished sense of the literary forms available to them for composing. They find a good topic, start to write about it by choosing from a repertoire of only one or two forms (for instance, "five-paragraph theme" or "expository essay"), and get bored or lose momentum after a few sentences. The problem may be that the particular topic doesn't "fit" the form chosen. The solution may be to write in a different form, one more suitable for the topic.

The Topic/Form Grid is an invention tool that enables you to observe, in a concise visual format, all your options for writing.

1. Draw a grid and label the vertical axis "topics" and the horizontal "forms," as at right.

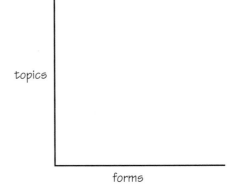

2. Along the "topic" axis list topics for writing that interest you. Along the "form" axis list forms of discourse you could use to write about these topics. Think especially of forms you use most regularly and spontaneously in everyday life. Some typical favorites are "talking to myself," "personal letter," and "conversation."

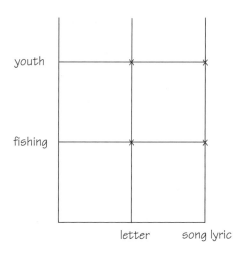

youth

fishing

letter   song lyric

3. Use the diverse topic/form matches available to you to generate writings. For instance, a simple grid like that at left gives you four possible topic/form combinations. You can create a song lyric about youth, a song lyric about fishing, a letter about youth, or a letter about fishing. Increase the number of items along the axes and you increase, exponentially, the combinations available: three topics and three forms yield nine possible combinations; four topics and four forms give you sixteen, and so on.

Virginia is an avid outdoorswoman with a passion for landscaping. Rereading her notebook she discovers the following note:

> Of all things I love landscaping most. I acquired this interest as a small girl from my grandfather, and since then hardly a day passes in the growing season when I don't have my hands in the soil.

She wants to do something with this . . . but what? How can she expand it and say all she would like about her love for landscaping? She consults a Topic/Form Grid she made a few weeks earlier:

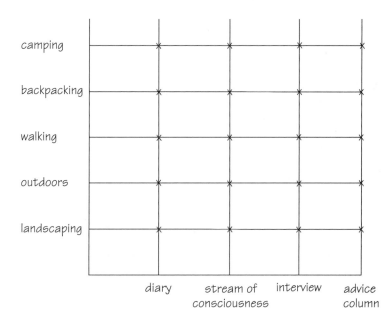

camping

backpacking

walking

outdoors

landscaping

diary   stream of   interview   advice
          consciousness   column

A fan of television interviews, she decides an imaginary interview—with herself—would be a good way of eliciting more information about her passion:

INTERVIEWER (I): Virginia, I am excited to conduct this interview. It will help me and others to get to know you and your interests. Here is my first question. What is something that you enjoy and feel confident doing?

ME (M): I am really interested in landscaping. May I tell you about it?

I: Yes, that would be great.

M: I really take pride in the appearance of my yard. I love to have a well-groomed yard. One that is full of brilliant colors, and a little contrast to emphasize the movement of my lawn. I feel that a yard should be pleasing to the eye.

I: Is this talent close to the imagination of an artist?

M: As a matter of fact, yes. Envision for a minute a blob of clay. Now as a sculptor would begin his piece of work, he plays around with this clay. He or she would place the clay in his or her palm and squeeze it through their fingers. They are creating a picture in their minds of the final piece they are wanting to produce.

I: Hum, interesting.

M: That is basically how I perform my art. As I am out in my yard, doing cultivating, fertilizing, and so on, ideas begin to flow. The colors, types of flowers, trees, and rocks that would best express my love for nature begin to materialize.

I: Tell me, Virginia, how did you get interested in this?

M: My grandfather and a good friend of mine were landscapers. They took great pride in their and others' yards. Even as a little child, as I walked to school I observed yards. I really would be disgusted if a yard was unruly. You know, like the look of your hair in the morning?

I: Are you willing to help others manicure their lawns as well as your own?

M: Yes! I have helped three other families upgrade their yards. It's very rewarding, not only for myself but for the other families also.

I: Well, thanks for your time. Could you come and look at my lawn?

M: Thank you, I would love the challenge.

You can see how remarkably individualized the grid is when you compare Virginia's work with Michelle's. A college sophomore, Michelle is currently preoccupied by issues of love and relationships, interests that are reflected in the "topic" portion of her grid:

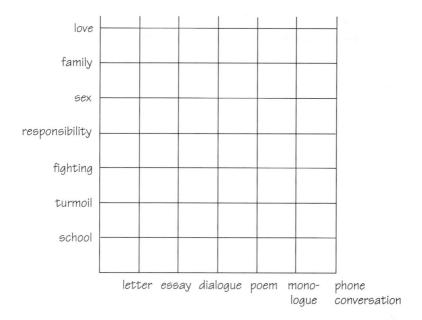

Mulling over her notebook, with its numerous entries about her own experiences of relationships, she discovers how hard it can be to write about them without becoming more personal and confessional than she would like. Her "form" axis gives her an idea: she can use the form of "phone conversation" to render her emotions more objectively. Instead of writing directly about herself, she can invent a conversation between two imaginary lovers experiencing hard times:

Halfway into a long-distance phone conversation:
"John, quit yelling at me! I don't get it. Last week you did the same thing with your friends and I didn't say one word to you!"
"That's not the same thing. When I go to parties with my friends, you know I'm not going to do anything behind your back!"
"So what are you saying, that I can't be trusted? For some reason that doesn't sit right with me!"
"No, Melissa, I'm not trying to say I don't trust you. I just know how you get around other guys when you drink and it makes me worry."
"John, you know how I am around you when I drink and that's because I love you. And it's probably true, I may flirt with guys, but you do the same thing and I know it's harmless. You should know that I would never do anything that might hurt you, no matter how much I've had to drink. I know it's hard living so far away from each other, and if I could change things I would. I hate it every bit as much as you do! But that is no reason not to trust me. I have never been anything but honest with you and I just don't think it's fair when you start coming down on me like this."

"Melissa, I'm sorry. I know you're right. It just kills me to be so far away from you. You know everyone down here teases me about you being away. They all say you're going to find some gorgeous football player and forget all about me. They get me so worried that little things like you going to a party and drinking really set me off. I shouldn't have gotten so upset. I really do trust you. I love you so much and I don't ever want to lose you."

"Quit listening to your friends so much, honey. You know I've never liked football players much. I like the baseball men much better."

"That's not funny, Melissa."

"Okay, I'm sorry. I'm just playing with you. I've told you a million times that you are the one I want to spend the rest of my life with. Nothing is going to change that. I love you. Do you believe me?"

"Yeah, hon. I believe you. I love you too."

"Good! I'll see you as soon as I can, okay? Take care."

"You too. Bye."

"Bye."

One virtue of the grid is its flexibility. Once made, it is never "set in stone"; you can discard old grids and create new ones as your needs and interests change. Moreover, if one topic/form combination fails you, you can shift to a different topic or form on your grid until you find one that works.

Here are a few suggestions for the "form" axis of your grid (certainly not an exhaustive list):

- diary entry or series of diary entries
- personal letter
- unsent letter (e.g., to someone about whom you have strong feelings)
- letter to the editor
- editorial
- monologue
- gossip (a form of dialogue)
- telephone conversation
- e-mail conversation
- song lyrics
- public speech
- cartoon or comic strip (you don't need to limit yourself to verbal forms; drawing can move the imagination in powerful ways)

ACTIVITIES FOR WRITING

1. Use the steps described in this chapter to create your own Topic/Form Grid. Try any of the following options:

   a. Create a *personal* grid, in which the topics are concerns or interests you encounter and think about in your own daily personal life, topics such as "parents," "school," "politics," "work," "friends," "the future," and so on.

b. Create a *course-specific* grid, in which the topics are some of those addressed in a particular college or university class. For example, for an art history class, "modern art," "painting," "expressionism," "tradition and innovation," "Picasso."

c. Create a *task-specific* grid in order to address a specific research assignment or project or to write a particular paper. Here the topics would be germane to the particular assignment.

2. Secure your grid(s) to the inside cover of your notebook for convenient reference. Use them whenever you feel "stuck" in your writing about a particular topic.

3. Use the grid as a revision tool. For instance, if your composition on Flannery O'Connor's "Everything That Rises Must Converge" (p. 632) is boring as a personal essay, try writing it in a different form: for instance, as a dialogue between yourself and one of the characters. Even if the assignment requires that your finished work be a personal or expository essay, writing in the different form can encourage a flow of ideas that will provide the content and momentum for writing the essay.

Part

II

Writing Essays
About Literature

Part I of *Reading and Writing from Literature* showed you ways of producing writings that are sometimes described as "creative" or "imaginative." In Part II we turn to what is probably the most commonly assigned type of composition in literature-based writing courses: the essay about literature. There are some important differences between the kinds of writing addressed in Parts I and II. For example, writings produced in Part I are typically ungraded and may assume a great variety of forms, such as stories, poems, personal memoirs, dialogues, letters, and many others. The kind of writing emphasized in Part II, on the other hand, is normally done for a grade and in some more narrowly prescribed form, generally that of the expository or argumentative essay. (Expository and argumentative essays are short works of nonfiction prose that pose a main point or thesis and support it with evidence and examples.)

How, then, do Parts I and II interconnect? In some ways, the writings you produce as a result of techniques outlined in Part I have a life of their own and can be collected, revised, and enjoyed independently of Part II. Long after you have finished this particular class, you can continue using the "Four-Step Process," the "Ten Ideas," your small notepad/commonplace book, the Topic/Form Grid, and other techniques to build up a body of writings for your intellectual or esthetic pleasure, for sharing, and perhaps even for formal publication. At the same time, Part I prepares you for Part II. Part I strategies enable you to engage literary texts in meaningful ways that will help you when you compose essays about literature. In addition, Part I has introduced you to habits of conversational reading and writing—habits as basic to writing good essays about literature as they are to producing creative and imaginative work.

Ways of Planning: Thinking and Writing Recursively

Look, and look again.

—Ann E. Berthoff

Putting Essays About Literature into Context

Many students get anxious at the thought of writing an essay about literature. Perhaps the phrase "essay about literature" triggers memories of failure, of interpreting a story or poem "incorrectly" and receiving a bad grade, or it may conjure feelings of apathy and distance ("What does this assignment have to do with my life?"). The aim of this part of *Reading and Writing from Literature* is to defuse these feelings and demonstrate strategies for working your way naturally through such essays.

The essay about literature is a diverse genre. It includes essay exams, critical analyses or "explications" of literary texts, argumentative papers (the subject of Chapter 9), personal narratives that are grounded in a reading of a literary text (or texts), and essays that involve outside research (which we will address in Chapters 10 and 11). Sometimes the topics for such essays are assigned by an instructor; other times you, the student, are asked to devise a topic yourself.

Essays about literature have multiple purposes. One function is broadly personal; they can reward you—the writer—by prompting you to discover interconnections among literary texts and the texts of your own life. A second function is pragmatic: essays about literature provide instructors and others with a means of evaluating your ability to write. Being able to write such essays is usually critical for succeeding in class and in school.

Cultivating Recursive Habits of Thinking

One major value of writing essays about literature is this: they help you develop recursive habits of thinking. "Recursive" means "running back again," or, as Ann Berthoff puts it in the epigraph to this chapter, looking and looking again. Recursiveness is the very stuff of thinking, which (in turn) is the stuff of essay writing.

If you paused over the preceding paragraph and reread it to sift its meaning, you were thinking recursively. When you look over a sentence in your small notepad or commonplace book (see Chapter 4) and contemplate or revise it, you are also thinking recursively. For example, Liz wrote,

> Definition of a success: someone whose work is their fun.

Rereading, she revises:

> Definition of a success: someone whose work is their fun. Write a letter about this to Meg?

Emily wrote,

> When you begin to imagine yourself *as* yourself: a good sign.

And revises:

> It's a good sign when you begin to imagine yourself *as* yourself. I know it sounds odd, but a lot of the time I picture myself as having the face of someone else—a celebrity, a friend, someone I've just had a fight with.

When you share your interpretation of a story or a poem in class and then reconsider it on the basis of alternative opinions offered by your instructor or classmates, you are once again working recursively.

Recursiveness provides a powerful term for understanding what you do when you write an essay about literature. Returning to the theme of Part I, you use texts (literary texts, the texts in your notebook, the texts of lecture and discussion, for example) to make a text. Your new thoughts and writings don't come out of nothing; they come from "running back" over previous work or "texts." Thus when you're "stuck" in your writing or your thinking, there is an alternative to panic or to doing nothing: you can go over materials you have already generated and use them to move yourself forward. Writing an essay about literature is not a monolithic task to be accomplished—or irredeemably failed—in a single step. Instead, it is a steady and incremental process that relies on looking and looking again—on rereading, writing, rewriting, and discussing.

Writing Mini-Essays to Practice Concise Expression

Long before you receive any actual assignments to write essays, you can prepare yourself to write them. From the first day of class you begin accumulating materials that can provide you with topics and ideas. These materials include the textual annotations you have made on the assigned stories, poems, essays, and plays anthologized in Part VI of this book; notes from class lectures and discussions; writings, in response to literature, that you have been collecting in your reading notebook; quick notes you have accumulated in your small notepad or commonplace book; and notes on small group discussions (see next section).

One of the best ways you can prepare to write essays is by learning to compose concisely. The temptation to write wordily is easy to understand. Your instructor assigns you to write a five hundred-word essay; you are "written out" at word #250. Rather than risk getting a failing grade, you add another 250 words of "filler" (pausing anxiously every few minutes to see how close you are to the magic number). If this experience is repeated often enough in enough classes, what you mainly learn is not how to write well but how to use words meaninglessly—how to "B.S." This is unfortunate, because a composition or English class ought to achieve the opposite result: helping you learn how to make every word count. As Confucius advised, "Get the meaning across and then *STOP*." In fact, in his classic *Analects* Confucius said, "I'd like to do without words."[1]

Confucius was hinting at a paradox: on the one hand, we must *respect* words by using them accurately and economically, the same way we show respect for any other resource by using it sparingly; on the other hand, we should *despise* words, feel constantly that we are using too many of them and employing them sloppily or perhaps even deceitfully. Confucius, a person of remarkably *few* words, had this paradox always in mind, as did his great modern translator/paraphraser Ezra Pound, who promoted the Confucian ethic of words in his short and excellent book *The ABC of Reading*.

You can practice concise expression every day by making a habit of rereading your collected textual annotations and small notepad entries and revising the best of them into mini-essays—essays ranging from one to a few sentences in length in which you "get the meaning across and stop." The basic process is to identify annotations or notes that catch your eye as you reread but that are vague, undeveloped, or confusing in their present state. The following questions can help you revise:

- What am I really trying to say here? (Oddly enough, we sometimes do say everything *except* what we meant to say.)
- Whom, besides myself, do I have in mind as a reader?
- If I showed this to other people (my intended readers), would they understand it? What do I need to add or change so they would understand?
- Am I using any specialized, obscure, or complicated words or terms (e.g., "reality," "meaning," "transmigration," "ratiocinate") that a reader might not understand and that I need to explain or define?
- My idea looks good to *me*; but will it have more impact on a reader if I illustrate it with a good example or a story?

---

1. Quoted in Confucius, *The Great Digest; The Unwobbling Pivot; The Analects,* translated and with commentary by Ezra Pound (New York: New Directions, 1951, pp. 269, 277).

- As I finish revising my notes into a mini-essay, is it clear and organized? Is it worded memorably to achieve maximum impact?
- *So what?* I like this little essay, but why should anyone else? What's in it for them?

The *So what?* question may be the supreme, all-embracing one to ask about any idea or essay. *Are these words an improvement on nothing? Are they better than silence?*

Here is a sample revision of a note into a mini-essay.

Original note. Celebrity worship is killing me.

Questions: Where does this comment come from? What am I trying to say? I notice my self-esteem goes up when I am away from celebrity for a while—e.g., camping. So what? This cuts to the issue of *what is real?* Celebrity culture is fake.

Mini-essay. It's impossible to say how much my idea of reality has been shaped by 43 years of TV. What if I had never seen a celebrity? Would I feel differently about my modest tasks and achievements? How much more accepting would I be of my own limited life?

Another example:

Life is too short for even a moment's indifference.

This note seems fine as it is. The sentence makes a clear point, and more words might weaken the impact.

A third example:

An original annotation of Emily Dickinson's poem, "'Faith' is a fine invention" (p. 507):

"Faith" is a fine invention
When Gentlemen can *see*—
But *Microscopes* are prudent
In an Emergency.

Annotation. Why is the word "Faith" in quotation marks?

Questions: This poem grabs me. Why? What do I have to say about this? and how, once I figure that out, can I say something that would be intelligible to someone besides myself?

Mini-essay. Curiously, in her poem "'Faith' is a fine invention," Emily Dickinson encloses the word "Faith" in quotation marks. Why? Perhaps she is using the word in a double sense, to refer not just to religious faith, which one would automatically assume to be her subject, but also to other kinds of "faith" that we take so for granted we don't even recognize them as matters of "faith" but as facts. Ironically, she could be including a faith in science, for instance, which people today accept with as little doubt as people a thousand years ago accepted religious doctrine. While subjecting religion to the usual microscopes, perhaps she is saying that today we should also train our microscopes on science (or technology) because we are not seeing them well enough with the naked eye (line 2).

This last mini-essay is unfinished but well begun, on its way to becoming an essay about literature.

As you write or complete a mini-essay, you can share it with a partner or small group in class and receive their feedback as to making any additional revisions.

Sharing and Learning in a Small Group

A small group (typically composed of three to five members) can be among your most stimulating resources in a literature or composition class. Groups embody the rough and surprising spirit of recursiveness. Recursive thinking does not proceed forward in a straight line from brilliance to brilliance; the shape of its movement is more analogous to a web that darts in multiple—even contradictory— directions. Like webs, groups relate and contradict and interconnect. That is what makes them useful and fun. Margaret Fuller, a nineteenth-century essayist, described the group process beautifully. Of her own "conversation" groups she wrote:

> I am so sure that the success of the whole depends on conversation being general that I do not wish any one to join who does not intend, *if possible,* to take an active part. No one will be forced, but those who do not talk will not derive the same advantages with those who openly state their impressions and consent to learn by blundering, as is the destiny of [human beings] here below.

A good group "blunders" its way to understanding, doesn't treat any opinion as "dumb" (so long as the opiner is willing to consider differing opinions and grow from them), and is as lively and various as human thought itself. A small group is an excellent forum for sharing your readings of literary texts and issues. In addition, your group can give you feedback on your mini-essays and at various stages of planning, drafting, revising, and editing your essays.

Your instructor may encourage group sharing as a regular class activity. Here is one rather generic format for sharing that you can relax or modify as you and your group mates become more familiar with each other. For purposes of illustration the focus of group discussion is assumed here to be a literary text. However, a small group can also meet to share opinions about members' writings-in-progress or any other subject of interest to group members and/or the instructor.

1. Form into your group.
2. Share your responses to the assigned literary text for that day. For instance:
   a. Identify a passage in the text that was "most significant" to *you* and explain why,

   or

   b. Read aloud the notebook entry you wrote in response to the text (remembering that you may skip over passages that are too personal or that you are uncomfortable sharing),

   or

   c. Summarize the notebook entry you wrote and share any ways that it enriched your reading of the text.
3. After you have presented, group members can respond by
   a. Pointing out something in your sharing that they found "interesting"
   or
   b. Expressing how they responded to the text differently than you did.
4. Repeat this process, with each member of the group taking a turn as presenter.

Techniques for Note Taking in Small Groups

Make a habit of taking notes on your group discussions, even if some of the ideas presented are ones you disagree with or consider "silly" or "dumb." Note taking improves your listening skills, makes you more conscious of alternative points of view, and provides you with a record of discussion that you can refer to later when writing your essays.

Here are two good ways to develop habits of note taking:

1. *Write while you listen.* Try taking a steady stream of notes as your group mates read their writing or ideas aloud. For instance, here are the notes one student took as he listened to Tyler read the portrait "Grandpa Jack" from Chapter 2 (see p. 13):

Jack—neighbor
visits Jack
Jack "lounges"
Jack down-to-earth
like Jack's talk
tells story
sheepherding incident
"eyes flashing"
colorful
good story/details/suspense

Sometimes writing while you listen can help you to concentrate and to overcome the inertia of not writing (or listening) at all. In addition, of course, you can use items from your list to provide feedback to the writer.

2. *Write after you listen.* Sometimes it's hard to listen and write at the same time—hence this alternative strategy. After a member of your group has read, you and the others can take one minute to jot down reactions to what you just heard. What struck you? What issues does the writing raise for you? Where could you use more information or development? Following the minute of silent writing, group members can hand their written reactions to the author or share their reactions orally.

Finding a Topic: Rereading (and Writing from) the Writing You Have Already Done

As mentioned, when you are assigned to write an essay you do not have to start from scratch. You begin with an already ample storehouse of writings that can provide ideas and prompts for essays. Begin work on your essay by rereading all of your textual annotations, notebook entries, notes on lectures, and notes on class and small-group discussions. Read with pen or pencil in hand. Whenever you find any item that strikes you, for whatever reason, circle or underline it. When you are finished, reread all the items you have marked. In the margin beside each, write yourself a note explaining what it is about this passage that grabs you.

Turning Your Favorite Interest into a Workable Topic

Based on a review of your collected notes and other writings, you can define a workable topic for your essay. Your instructor may introduce you to "brain-storming," "quick-writing" (or "freewriting"), or other activities for coming up with topics. Another good place to begin is with the apparatus included in this book. You can find topics by combing the "Activities for Writing and Discussion" that follow many of the short stories, poems, essays, and plays in Part VI or by looking through the "Additional Activities for Writing and Discussion" that conclude each thematic section in Part VI.

For example, Joe knows that he wants to write something about Doris Lessing's short story "A Woman on a Roof" (p. 240). Lessing's story concerns a woman sunbather whose nakedness stirs complex reactions, e.g., attraction, excitement, anger, in two male roofers named Stanley (in his thirties) and Tom (seventeen). One of Joe's annotations, made in the middle of the story, suggests to him a topic for an essay: "They [Stanley and Tom] have different perspectives—in a sense contradictory." Joe reads the "Activities for Writing and Discussion" that follow the story and decides to write on Activity #5:

Stanley and Tom react to the woman differently. Stanley feels rage toward her, while we are told that Tom feels a "bond between the woman and himself"

(p. 244). Discuss the differences in their reactions. Is Tom (a) "better" or "kinder" than Stanley, (b) simply different from Stanley, or (c) really no different from Stanley?

Developing a "Working Thesis"

A thesis states the main point you are going to make in your essay; it normally appears in the opening paragraph or near the beginning of the essay. A "working thesis" is one you adopt tentatively in order to begin your essay while remaining open to the possibility of revising it in the course of composing.

A clear thesis benefits both writer and readers. First, it gives you—the writer—a manageable focus for your work. A carefully limited thesis can save you from straying off your subject. Second, a thesis helps your readers. A thesis is to an essay as a map is to an unfamiliar city. If you are entering Chicago for the first time, you want a map to show you where you are going. Similarly, a thesis lets your readers know what lies ahead so that they have a context for understanding each of your paragraphs and sentences as the essay unfolds.

You can devise a working thesis in any of several ways. Some writers like to discover a thesis by "quick-writing" (see the following section). Others develop a thesis by using Step Three (list the most powerful thoughts and impressions the text inspires in you) in the "Four-Step Process for Writing from Reading" described in Chapter 2. Start by finding a text or passage that interested you and that you annotated heavily. For example, Sam rereads the following passage in Henry David Thoreau's "Where I Lived, and What I Lived For" (see p. 1040) and the annotations he made in his notebook:

> I went to the woods because I wished to live deliberately, to front only the essential facts of life, and see if I could not learn what it had to teach, and not, when I came to die, discover that I had not lived. I did not wish to live what was not life, living is so dear; nor did I wish to practise resignation, unless it was quite necessary. I wanted to live deep and suck out all the marrow of life, to live so sturdily and Spartan-like as to put to rout all that was not life, to cut a broad swath and shave close, to drive life into a corner, and reduce it to its lowest terms, and, if it proved to be mean, why then to get the whole and genuine meanness of it, and publish its meanness to the world; or if it were sublime, to know it by experience, and be able to give a true account of it in my next excursion. For most men, it appears to me, are in a strange uncertainty about it, whether it is of the devil or of God, and have *somewhat hastily* concluded that it is the chief end of man here to "glorify God and enjoy him forever." . . .

[ANNOTATIONS]

Thoreau went to Walden to experience what life really is, whether that might be good or bad.

doesn't want to waste life but be "deliberate" (= "intentional," "careful in deciding," "slow")

"Spartan-like": scaling life to essentials. What is essential?

beautiful paragraph! something to put on the refrig.

you can only *know* by experience

taking others' opinions without thinking

create story of someone *today* who lives like T.

T. wants to think, to evaluate all he's doing in his life

Noting that his strong response to this passage makes it a promising focus for an essay, Sam then redoes Step Three of the Four-Step Process and comes up with several ideas for a working thesis. Since a thesis is a complete sentence, he tries to phrase each item in his list of thoughts and impressions as a complete sentence.

- I want to save this paragraph, put it somewhere, maybe even memorize it.
- The idea of living deliberately is a good one; we need to slow down, especially in this hectic modern life. Think and examine everything, especially what we do *routinely*. Thesis possibility: Thoreau calls us to examine the way we live, especially what we do routinely without thinking. (Find other passages that support this.)
- Thoreau's point is not about *where* you live but *how*, and *how* is to live deliberately. Thesis possibility: Thoreau's point is not that we must go to the woods as he did but that we must keep the woods—something wild—inside us(?)
- I'm not ready to move to the woods, but I have memories of being in nature and the peace it brings. I could write about this in a personal essay. My own Walden pond is a boulder up Ogden canyon; I go there to "live deliberately."
- Do you go to the woods or do the woods come to you? Do you have to go to the woods to live deliberately or do you just have to get the woods inside your mind? Is Walden a matter of what you do or what you think, or both? Walden in L.A.? New York?
- In *Dead Poets Society* this paragraph was quoted. Seize the day, live life to the full. Thoreau brings back memories of that movie.

You can also develop a thesis by posing a question around some problem:

- "Is Mr. Green's behavior in the story 'A Loaf of Bread' ethical?"
- "Why do Mrs. Hale and Mrs. Peters in Susan Glaspell's *Trifles* conceal the evidence that implicates Minnie Wright in the murder of her husband?"
- "Why does Louise Mallard in 'The Story of an Hour' seem to want to be 'free' of her husband, even though he has always treated her affectionately?"

Then formulate an answer to the question to create a working thesis:

- "Mr. Green is unethical; he consciously exploits customers in the poor (mainly black) neighborhood and then blames society for his own wrongdoing."
- "Mrs. Hale and Mrs. Peters feel an empathy for Minnie Wright that ultimately overrides their sense of obligation to the law."
- "Though her husband is loving toward her, Louise Mallard wants to be 'free' to experience the independence she has never been allowed to have."

These three examples illustrate some important qualities of a "good" or "strong" thesis:

1. A good thesis is nonobvious. The third example would be greatly weakened if it were changed to read, "Mrs. Mallard yearns for freedom." That would merely be stating the obvious since at the story's climax Mrs. Mallard rhapsodizes about being "Free, free, free!"

2. A good thesis makes a worthwhile, interesting contribution to the "conversation" on the topic. Again, the third example illustrates, as it promises to touch on some interesting aspects of "The Story of an Hour," for instance, the rather surprising fact that Mrs. Mallard seems to want to be rid of her husband even though he has been kind to her, and the idea that freedom and self-fulfillment can be quashed by factors, such as marriage, which are normally viewed as self- and life-enhancing. Similarly, the second sample thesis, about *Trifles,* implies a discussion of interesting conflicts between personal conscience and the law.

In Joe's case a question has already been posed for him in the "Activities for Writing and Discussion" after "A Woman on a Roof":

Is Tom (a) "better" or "kinder" than Stanley, (b) simply different from Stanley, or (c) really no different from Stanley?

From the question Joe derives the following working thesis: "Despite his gallant intentions, Tom is essentially no different from Stanley in Doris Lessing's 'A Woman on a Roof.'"

Planning Your Essay: Quick-Writing

The key to planning is flexibility: writers may use different methods to plan different essays. Joe uses a technique called quick-writing. The purpose of a quick-write is simple: to get something—however crude—on paper or screen that can move you forward in your writing and serve as a reference point (perhaps) for instructor or peer feedback. Quick-writing is easy:

- Write for a limited time period (perhaps ten to fifteen minutes) and *stop.*
- Write quickly and continuously.

- Censor nothing; permit yourself to write down everything—brilliant, mediocre, or "dumb"—that occurs to you.
- Do not worry about making grammar, spelling, punctuation, or other sentence-level errors; simply push forward.

Here is Joe's quick-write:

> "Young Tom" in "Woman on a Roof" is really in the same boat as Stanley. "The bond between the woman and himself" is something covert and not outwardly observable. His feelings manifest themselves in the form of elaborate fantasies that he has every evening when he gets home and he somehow imagines that the "woman" has knowledge of these or is somehow informed of his supposed "bond" with her. At the end, young Tom even manages to feel slighted by the woman's apathy towards him as if she has wronged him by reacting in this way. Stanley certainly manifests his feelings in a more direct and observable way.
>
> The woman has made herself unavailable to Stanley who may observe the candor of the relationship Stanley has with Mrs. Pritchett, a woman who has made herself accessible to him and he manages to have a reasonable relationship though it is made possible via the flirtatious nature of their interaction.
>
> Stanley may be capable of dealing with women in only a sexual way and the woman on the roof's uncaring, unmoved manner has been in effect an invalidation of Stanley's sexual persona or merely a rejection— something that Stanley is not accustomed to or perhaps just a rejection in this manner.

Note that quick-writing is a step, not an end in itself; Joe's writing is rather disjointed, but he now has some basic ideas to mull over and develop into a draft. We will come back to these "basic ideas" in a moment.

Also, notice that quick-writing is not only an activity for the "planning" stage of writing; you can quick-write at any time in the course of composing an essay or any other piece of writing. You can quick-write to develop a thesis, to recast an awkward or confusing paragraph, to "rough out" an introduction or conclusion, to regain focus when your mind wanders, or simply to break the inertia of not writing. Quick-writing is a quintessentially recursive activity.

Planning Your Essay: Listing and Sequencing

Another way to plan is by listing the points you want to raise to support your thesis. First, do a brainstorm list; that is, write down any points that occur to you without worrying about their order. Then reread the list and rearrange the items, as necessary, into a logical sequence.

For an example of listing and sequencing, consider Lori's work for an essay on Charlotte Perkins Gilman's story "The Yellow Wallpaper." "The Yellow Wallpaper" is about a married woman in a profound mental and emotional crisis. Her husband, John (a physician), has prescribed complete rest and has moved her to a house in the country, where she is confined to a single garishly wallpapered room. The wife becomes obsessed with the wallpaper, perceiving images in it of a trapped woman trying to escape, and eventually tears the paper from the walls. Critical opinions differ over the end of the story: Has the woman achieved a liberation of some kind, or has she gone insane? In her working thesis and list of supporting points, Lori argues the latter:

> Working thesis: The narrator went insane at the end of the story, but justifiably so.
> Why justifiably?
> John's treatment was that of a Dr. whose last concern is his wife
> John laughs at her—practical—he doesn't believe she's sick
> she admits that he may be the reason she doesn't get better
> he assures friends and relatives she's fine; she's stuck
> doesn't let her work
> she can't be herself around him
> he "takes all care from me" instead of taking care of her
> It's a human characteristic that, when left in one place, alone, people start to think weird things
> She is insane (examples at end)
> insanity was her escape (?)

Lori then rereads and refines her list and classifies related items into groups. Finally (as indicated here by the arrow she has drawn), she arranges the groups into a meaningful sequence:

1. Insane
   examples at end (quotes)
   it was her way of *escape*
2. John's treatment was more like punishment
   left her alone; no variety
   told her she wasn't sick
   didn't let her work
3. It's a human characteristic that, when left in one place, alone, people start to think weird things
   like analyzing wallpaper and giving it a smell
   she has no one to be intimate with/so she becomes intimate with the wallpaper
   she was forced to be in a horrible place and she couldn't deal with it.

Like Joe, Lori now has some ideas with which to work. She follows her list with a quick-write:

> At the first of the story we have a depressed woman. She is slightly depressed and dealing with a mild nervous condition but overall a pretty healthy person. Her husband, John, decides to take his wife away for a while (to hide/rest) and they move into an old abandoned mansion. This could have been a good arrangement. She might have even grown better, but John gave her a cruel schedule to follow. She was told not to work, be around people, or even write. Her eating and sleeping habits were closely monitored, and she got worse. She was kept in a big room with only a heavy bed, bars on the windows and hideous wallpaper. At first she would write her feelings, but after a while she became too weak for that and layed(?) in bed and stared at the wallpaper. She could not grow close to John (in fact, there was a growing gap between them), so she became intimate with this wallpaper. She analyzed its color, texture, patterns, and even gave it a "smell." This woman was forced to live in a horrible place deprived of work, beauty, freedom, and exercise, and she couldn't deal with it.
>
> She is trapped. She is entirely too weak to get out of a world that's destroying her. All she has left is the wallpaper, so she finds a woman in that wallpaper and she displaces/uses her as an avenue to her feelings. The woman is symbolically trying to get out and the narrator is determined to help. She begins stripping the wallpaper off the walls around the room, and in doing so, liberates herself from this mentally torturous reality.
>
> Creeping about, she is finally free. Call it insane, but this is the only "out" she had. Reality didn't hold anything for her. So, she stepped out.

Getting Feedback from a Peer or a Small Group

As they formulate theses and plan their essays, Joe and Lori can benefit from peer feedback. Like quick-writing and listing, feedback is useful at all stages of writing an essay (or any other text). Two common misconceptions about feedback are that its aim is to "tear apart" the other person's paper and that its message is primarily negative. In fact, some of the most helpful and motivating feedback is positive. Its focal aim is not to hurt but to help. In a partnership or small group, the objective is always to assist each other toward better writing.

Different stages of writing call for different kinds of feedback. Here are two general suggestions for feedback during early stages of writing:

1. Offer at least some positive and encouraging comments. What writers most need at this stage is momentum to get all their ideas on paper. Positive comments can help create that momentum. Make your comments as specific as possible. A reaction such as "Joe, I like how you contrast Stanley's treatment of Mrs. Pritchett with his treatment of the woman on the roof, though I'm not sure I understand

it" is quite helpful. It tells Joe that his point is worth developing but needs clarification. On the other hand, a response of "Great piece! Don't change a thing!" is of dubious value. Your feedback, of course, should also be sincere. You don't have to applaud writing that fails to meet the assignment just because you want to be supportive.

2. Since essays often change radically during the drafting, revision, and editing stages, focus on larger issues (appropriateness to the assignment, focus, potential for development) rather than on such sentence-level matters as wording, grammar, and spelling.

Here are a few questions that you and your group might address during the planning stages of writing an essay:

When you have developed a working thesis and are starting to plan your essay:

- Is the thesis appropriate to the assignment? Example: If your assignment says to write on one of the "Activities for Writing and Discussion" at the end of "A Woman on a Roof" and your thesis is on "The Story of an Hour," you need a new thesis.
- Is the thesis nonobvious? Does it promise to make an interesting contribution to the "conversation" about the chosen topic?
- Is the thesis supportable within the prescribed word length for the assignment (e.g., three hundred words, five hundred words, one thousand words)? Example: If your instructor wants an essay of "around one thousand words," you will have trouble covering the following thesis: "Charlotte Perkins Gilman's 'The Yellow Wallpaper' is a critique of nineteenth-century treatments of nervous disorders." Such a thesis would require considerable development and outside research. You would do better to narrow the thesis to something like "John's medical treatment of the narrator helps precipitate her final crisis."

After you have composed one or more quick-writes on your topic:

- Which points relate to and support the thesis? Which, if any, do *not* (and should therefore be cut)?
- Which points seem strongest or most interesting?
- Which points need more explanation or development?

Joe applies these questions to his quick-write on "A Woman on a Roof" and also gets feedback on the questions from his group mates. Then, as shown below, he marks up his quick-write to indicate points for development. With these notes, he begins the transition from quick-write to draft.

"Young Tom" in "Woman on a Roof" is really in the
same boat as Stanley. "The bond between the woman
and himself" is something covert and not outwardly
observable. His feelings manifest themselves in the

form of elaborate fantasies that he has every evening when he gets home and he somehow imagines that the "woman" has knowledge of these or is somehow informed of his supposed "bond" with her. At the end, young Tom even manages to feel slighted by the woman's apathy towards him as if she has wronged him by reacting this way. Stanley certainly manifests his feelings in a more direct and <u>observable</u> way.

Outwardly, Tom and Stanley react differently. Inwardly, their reactions are similar.

The woman has made herself unavailable to Stanley who may observe the candor of the relationship Stanley has with Mrs. Pritchett, a woman who has made herself accessible to him and he manages to have a reasonable relationship though it is made possible via the <u>flirtatious nature</u> of their interaction.

Similarity with Tom's <u>inward</u> fantasies

Stanley may be capable of dealing with women in only a sexual way and the woman on the roof's uncaring, unmoved manner has been in effect an invalidation of Stanley's sexual persona or merely a rejection—something that Stanley is not accustomed to or perhaps just a rejection in this manner.

Compare/contrast their reactions— outward reactions/ inward reactions Conclusion: the nature of unspoken relationships?

ACTIVITY FOR WRITING

1. Practice the art of concise expression. Reread your textual annotations and short notes regularly, and revise the best of them into mini-essays, as demonstrated on pages 72–75. Notice that you can do this quickly, even in short snatches of time. Share your mini-essays with a partner or small group to spark further ideas.

Checklist of Activities for Planning an Essay About Literature

Develop habits of recursive reading and writing:
- Reread your notebook regularly; and mine it for ideas for writing.
- Practice concise expression by turning your favorite textual annotations and short notes into mini-essays.
- Share with your peers to develop your ideas and gain new perspectives.
- Practice habits of note taking and of reviewing and annotating your own notes.

Find a topic:
- Review your notes and notebook.
- Brainstorm or quick-write for possible topics.

- Peruse the "Activities for Writing and Discussion" and the "Additional Activities for Writing and Discussion" that follow many of the reading selections in Part VI.

Develop a working thesis:
- Brainstorm or quick-write your way to a thesis, or
- Use Step Three of the "Four-Step Process for Writing from Reading" (p. 14), to make a list of possible theses, or
- Pose a question around some problem your thesis can answer.

Evaluate your thesis:
- Is it appropriate to the assignment?
- Is it nonobvious, and does it promise to make an interesting contribution to the conversation about the topic?
- Is it supportable within the prescribed word length for the assignment?

Do a quick-write of your essay, or
Make a list of points to support your thesis (and then arrange the points into a logical sequence or outline).

Get feedback at various stages from a partner, small group, and/or your instructor.

7

Ways of Drafting: Building a Barn in a Tornado

I don't give a hoot what the writing's like. I write any sort of rubbish that will cover the main outlines of the story, then I can begin to see it.

—FRANK O'CONNOR

Beginning with Limited Expectations

It's one thing to develop a thesis for an essay, make a list of ideas, and do a quick-write or two; quite another to produce a draft. Somehow a "draft" suggests something *substantial.*

The best way to approach drafting is with limited expectations. Rid yourself of the notion that a draft is a nearly "finished" piece of writing, and think of it, instead, as a *rough approximation* of an essay. When you draft you are trying to get all your ideas on paper (or onscreen) in whatever rough form you can. Concerns about quality and finish are far away.

You may want to keep the following images in mind as you draft:

1. *A safety net.* Spread beneath you as you draft is an immense safety net called "revision," which makes injury impossible, no matter how hard or far you fall. Revision is your invitation to return to your draft and redo it, as much as you'd like, later on.

2. *Building a barn in a tornado.* This was novelist William Faulkner's metaphor for drafting. Imagine yourself in the ultimate race against time. You have to hang on to your hammer and drive the nails *fast* before they blow away.

Two Ways of Drafting

Two basic procedures for drafting are "starting from scratch" and "cutting and pasting." Which approach you use depends on the quality of the writing you have done on your topic so far. If your predraft writings such as notes, lists of ideas to develop, and quick-writes are confused or unsatisfying, you may prefer the "start-from-scratch" method. On the other hand, if your predraft writings read well and already begin to suggest usable "pieces" of a draft, then cutting and pasting is good.

Starting from Scratch: Writing a "Throwaway" or "Rehearsal" Draft

Start from scratch when you have a topic but the preliminary writings you have done for it are too poorly written to include in your essay. First, review your writings, getting the important ideas firmly fixed in your mind. Then write a quick draft. To highlight its tentative nature, call it a "throwaway" draft or, if you prefer, a "rehearsal" draft.

Starting with a fresh sheet of paper (or a clear screen), and without looking back at your preliminary writings, write the draft. Begin by accepting that what you produce will probably be food for the trash bin—compost, waste material, junk. Your main goal in this draft is to *approximate* the shape you want your final text to have.

Here are a few guidelines for throwaway drafting:

- Focus yourself by jotting down your working thesis.
- Write quickly for a limited time period (twenty to thirty minutes works well).
- Make sure the draft has a beginning and an end, however sketchy.
- Do not concern yourself with getting the "correct" phrasing or with providing supporting examples, as fumbling over these matters will break your momentum and disturb your train of thought.
- Whenever you get stuck and can't think of a word, phrase, or sentence, leave a blank and push on. If you are undecided between two different words or phrases, include both and separate them with a slash, e.g., "She loved/enjoyed the book." Aim to achieve an overall shape for the piece, and worry about details later.

Here is the throwaway draft Joe wrote for his essay about "A Woman on a Roof":

Lessing on Men and Women

In Doris Lessing's "A Woman on a Roof," two men/roofers become fascinated with a woman who sunbathes nearby them as they work. While Stanley hoots and ___ angry at the woman, Tom—the younger—sees himself as the woman's protector. Yet, despite his gallant intentions, Tom is essentially no different from Stanley in his treatment of the sunbathing woman.

Outwardly, the two men react quite differently. With the initial sighting of the "woman on a roof" Stanley raises questions about the woman's near-nudity, and, later, he begins acting out at the woman, whistling and hooting at her. Though he is seemingly annoyed at her and her state of near-nudity, he seems inextricably drawn to her and his annoyance deepens with her indifference.

Tom's actions are, at first, little different from Stanley's: he snickers at Stanley's derisive comments about the woman, he goes with Stanley to spy on the woman, and he even stands by Stanley as Stanley hurls epithets at the woman after Tom has come to see himself as the woman's champion. The woman's indifference angers Tom as much as it does Stanley and, ultimately, he comes to feel a resentment in himself toward the woman, even hatred.

Stanley's relationship with the *other* two women of the story, his wife and Mrs. Pritchett, gives us a glimpse of some of his inner motivations. Some of his earlier anger with the "woman on the roof" seems to stem from his feelings about his wife. "If my wife lay about like that, ___" (fill in quote) Stanley says. It seems his annoyance with the sunbathing woman could be related to his inability to control her the way he, probably, controls his wife. Stanley is able to regain that sense of control through his relationship with Mrs. Pritchett and we see him responding positively to her as she seems to be receptive to his physical charms.

Control is also the primary issue in Tom's relationship with the woman on the roof. When he first sees her, he wants to possess her apart from his cohorts, as his own. Tom stands near Stanley as Stanley rages against the woman, hoping that she doesn't associate him with Stanley (reword?); he comes to see himself as having to save the woman from Stanley and even has involved fantasies about becoming the woman's lover. But when the woman does not sunbathe one day, Tom feels betrayed. Her appearance the following day reassures Tom, and the fact she can't be seen by the others makes her seem more like his own. By the end of the story, however, when Tom comes face to face with the woman's indifference, he feels slighted in much the same way that Stanley does.

It is the woman herself who sees Tom, for all his romantic intentions, as no different from Stanley. When Tom finally speaks to her, the woman tells him to go away and that, if he gets a thrill out of "seeing women in bikinis," he should "go to the Lido." Tom feels stung by what he perceives as her mis-perception of his actions and goes away hating the woman, suggesting that the woman saw him with the utmost clarity of all.

What happens to the throwaway draft after you have written it? From its name you might assume it ends up in the wastebasket, and this does occasionally happen. Even then, however, you will not be disappointed because your expectations were modest. You may need to change your topic, do some more preliminary quick-writes, or get feedback from your instructor or classmates about what to do next. On the other hand, like Joe, you may be pleasantly surprised by the quality of your throwaway. Sometimes, when you have low expectations for a draft (telling yourself you're going to "throw it away" when it's done), you end up producing something better, richer, and more exciting than you do when you grit your teeth and say, "This *will* be a masterpiece." Thus, you may end up not "throwing away" the draft at all. You may find that doing a rough draft is basically a matter of filling out and elaborating on the throwaway. Finally, no matter what you do with the draft, you will be going back over it; you will be using it recursively to move your work forward.

Joe reviews his draft in the light of four questions that you might apply to your own throwaways:

1. What are the strengths of the draft, and where is it working well? Identify specific passages.
2. What do you need to do in order to advance to a rough draft? Identify specific passages that need work and why.
3. Which points relate to and support the thesis? Which do not (and therefore should be cut)?
4. Which points could use more explanation or examples?

To observe Joe's next step, see "From Throwaway Draft to Rough Draft," on p. 91.

Cutting and Pasting

Cutting and pasting involves taking various pieces of preliminary writing you have already done on your topic and combining and arranging them to create a draft. You can cut and paste by either of two general methods: onscreen with a word processor or on paper.

As you accumulate a number of entries on a topic that you want to develop into a finished piece of work, e.g., "nonconformity or madness in Ray Bradbury's 'The Murderer'" or "escape themes in 'The Yellow Wallpaper' and 'The Story of an Hour,'" a word processor is enormously helpful. With word processing you can type related notebook items into a word-processing document. That way you can see them all, together and in one place, onscreen. You are "getting all the cards on the table." At this point the "cards" may be extremely disorganized. Nevertheless, you are 51 percent of the way to a finished text because you have all your ideas before you. Now you can begin arranging, rearranging, adding, and deleting materials toward accomplishment of a draft.

To illustrate: suppose the following pages are in your notebook, and the circled parts—"A" and "B"—are passages that please you in their current form:

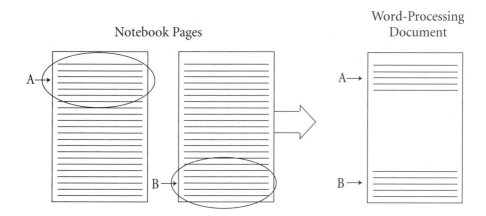

As illustrated, you can "cut" these passages out of your notebook and "paste" them into a *new* word-processing document as parts of a rough draft.

If you lack access to word processing, you can rearrange the pages in your notebook so that entries on your topic are physically juxtaposed. This is where a looseleaf notebook is advantageous. For instance, if entries from October 8 and October 14 talk about "differences between Stanley and Tom in 'A Woman on a Roof,'" put them physically together (within your notebook or in a file folder) so that you can begin to see connections between what you wrote on those two days. This is an excellent way of organizing your ideas, of moving from the notebook writing stage to the draft stage. (I have presented "starting from scratch" and "cutting and pasting" as if they were mutually exclusive activities. They aren't. Often you will end up creating a part of your draft by cutting and pasting and other parts by writing from scratch.)

From Throwaway Draft to Rough Draft

Here is the rough draft that Joe wrote after doing his throwaway. The marginal notes indicate some of the more significant changes he has made from his throwaway draft.

The Clarity of Control:
Lessing on Men and Women

In Doris Lessing's "A Woman on a Roof," two men become fascinated with a woman who sunbathes nearby them as they work. While Stanley hoots and hollers and actually expresses a sense of rage at the woman, Tom, a younger man, comes to see himself as the woman's protector. Yet, despite his gallant intentions, Tom is essentially no different from Stanley in his treatment of the sunbathing woman.

Expands title to be more descriptive

Outwardly, the two men react quite differently. With the initial sighting of the scantily clad woman, Stanley raises questions concerning the woman's state of undress ("Someone'll report her if she doesn't watch out") and, later, begins acting out at the woman, whistling and hooting at her and expressing a great deal of agitation at her subsequent apathy. Though he is seemingly annoyed at her and her state of near-nudity, he seems inextricably drawn to her and his annoyance deepens with her "gesture[s] of indifference."

Here (and elsewhere) adds quotations to illustrate points

Tom's actions are, at first, in conspiracy with Stanley's actions: he snickers at the derisive comments Stanley makes about the woman, he "makes the trip" with Stanley to spy on the woman and, even once he comes to see himself as the woman's champion, he stands by Stanley as Stanley hurls epithets at her. The woman's indifference angers Tom much in the same way it angers Stanley and, ultimately, he comes to feel a resentment in himself toward the woman, even hatred. He feels her "unfairness pale him," and, when it rains at the end of the story, he feels a sense of triumph over her.

Details supplement ideas that were hinted at in throwaway

It is in Stanley's relationship with the other two women of the story, his wife and Mrs. Pritchett, that we glimpse some of his inner motivations. Some of his earlier anger with the "woman on the roof" seems to stem from his feelings about his wife. "If my wife lay about like that," Stanley says, "I'd soon stop her," and it is here that we are able to discern that his annoyance with the sunbathing woman could be related to his inability to control her much in the same way he, no doubt, controls or seeks to control his wife. Stanley is able to regain that sense of control through his relationship with Mrs. Pritchett and we see him responding positively to her as she seems to be receptive to his physical charms.

Expands discussion of Mrs. Pritchett and how Stanley's relationship with her illuminates his relationship with "woman"

Control is the primary issue in Tom's relationship with the woman on the roof, as well. When he first sees her, he wants to possess her apart from his cohorts, to keep her for his own. On one of his trips to spy on the woman, Tom makes the report that "she hadn't moved, but it was a lie. He wanted to keep what he had seen to himself: he had caught her in the act of rolling down the little red pants over her hips. . . ." Tom stands near Stanley as he rages against the woman, hoping that she doesn't associate his proximity with complicity; he comes to see himself as having to save the woman from Stanley and even has involved fantasies about becoming the woman's lover. But when the woman does not sunbathe one day, Tom feels betrayed. Her appearance the following day reassures Tom as does her moving to a part of the roof where the men could not see her, because he feels that she's "more his when the other men couldn't see her." And, by the end of the story, when Tom comes face to face with the woman's indifference, he feels slighted in much the same way that Stanley does.

Extensive expansion of last 2 paragraphs with quotations, examples, and rewording of undeveloped ideas

It is the woman on the roof's perception of Stanley and Tom that is most telling, for she sees Tom, with all his romantic intentions and farflung illusions, as being virtually indivisible from the howling, ranting and hateful Stanley. When Tom finally speaks to her, after he has (in his mind) come to her rescue at the end of the story, the woman tells him to go away and that, if he gets a thrill out of "seeing women in bikinis," he should go somewhere where he'd "see dozens of them, without all this mountaineering." Tom feels stung by what he perceives as her mis-perception of his actions and goes away hating the woman, suggesting that the woman had not mis-perceived the situation at all, but that, perhaps, she had seen Tom with the utmost clarity of all.

Checklist of Activities for Drafting

- **"Start from scratch"** if none of your predraft writings is successful. Write a "throwaway" or "rehearsal" draft.
- Follow your throwaway with a **rough draft.**
- **"Cut and paste"** if portions of your predraft writings are successful. "Cut" the successful portions and "paste" them together. Then add other paragraphs, as needed, to complete your essay.
- **Get feedback** at various stages of drafting from a partner, small group, and/or your instructor.

Ways of Revising: Caring and Not Caring

In composition it is the greatest art to find out as quickly as possible which are the best passages you have written, and tear the rest away to come at them. Even the poorest parts will be most effective when they serve these, as pediments to the column.

—HENRY DAVID THOREAU

Putting Revision into Context

Chapter 7 suggested that you approach drafting with low expectations. Not so revising. The very nature of revision is to revisit, to inspect, and make better. The further along you get in revising a text, the higher your standards of quality become. At the quick-writing stage you have no standards at all. By the time you reach final proofreading, at the other end of the composing spectrum, you ought to be an archperfectionist.

To title this chapter "Revising," as if announcing a new topic in *Reading and Writing from Literature,* is somewhat misleading. Realize it or not, you have been revising constantly throughout this course. To revise means "to look . . . again" (*Oxford English Dictionary*); and "looking again"—that is, "conversing" or being "recursive"—has been a persistent theme of this book. In developing habits of recursiveness, you have automatically developed habits of revision as well. A litany of revision techniques you have already learned and practiced would read like a repetition of the table of contents for Chapters 1–7. Any of the following is, potentially, an act of revision:

- Conversational reading and writing
- Rereading your annotations
- Rereading quick notes you have collected in a small notepad or commonplace book

- Notebook writing and sharing
- Listing and sequencing
- Quick-writing
- Revising from group or instructor feedback
- Reading aloud
- Throwaway/rehearsal drafting
- Cutting and pasting

All of these techniques and habits can help you revise an essay about literature. If it weren't for the problem of redundancy, all could be addressed again in this chapter. The best way to use this book is not to read about these techniques once and never come back to them but—you guessed it—to use the book recursively. "Run back" to these strategies, again and again—at any place, anytime. If one cannot help you in a particular situation, perhaps another can.

Thus, this chapter does not "introduce" revision or presume to confine it to a single chapter; it merely revisits it in the somewhat distinctive context of revising an essay about literature.

Global and Local Revisions

Since revising is a complex task, it is useful to separate revision concerns into "global" and "local." Global concerns include topic selection, thesis, focus, purpose, organization, and clarity. Local concerns involve sentence-level issues of grammar, spelling, punctuation, and usage. Though writers often mix work on the two levels, generally you should deal with global concerns first and local ones later. After all, it doesn't pay to revise sentence X to perfection if you may be throwing it out a few minutes later because it doesn't fit your thesis. Why perform surgery on a toe if you're going to amputate the foot? The strategies in this chapter progress from global to local.

A Checklist of Questions for Looking Critically at Your Draft

Someone once said that writers have two indispensable needs, a passion for what they are writing and an attitude of ruthless objectivity toward their own creations. This is a paradox at the very heart of revising: as a writer you need to care and yet not care; you need to care about what you are creating but be ready—in an instant—to destroy your writing if it's not working.

Most of us feel vulnerable when we revise; we would like a suit of armor to "steel" us for the task and to defend us from the expected "blows" of readers. Together, passion and objectivity constitute this armor. If you are passionate enough about what you are making, if you care enough about the task, the destruction of your text won't matter; you will simply collect yourself and begin again. If you are objective enough, you will never encounter a harsher critic than yourself, so no attack or defeat will astonish you.

Part I of this book dealt mainly with cultivating a passion for writing. Here, now, are some questions to help you see your draft objectively, as another person might see it. Use these questions to look critically at your draft and every paragraph and idea within it.

- Does the draft meet the requirements of the assignment? Is it the appropriate length, and does it address an appropriate topic? Obviously, you should ask this question first, as any further revising will be pointless if you have done the assignment incorrectly.
- What do you really mean (in this essay, paragraph, sentence)? What are you trying to say?
- Is your meaning clear? Will readers understand this?
- Are you using the simplest words possible, and are you being concise without being unclear?
- Are you using any words or terms that may be confusing and need to be defined?
- Who cares?
- *So what?*

As noted back in Chapter 6 (the point is worth repeating), *So what?* is the supreme question to ask of any essay, paragraph, or sentence. Ezra Pound said, "Use no word that under stress of emotion you could not actually say." Excellent advice we all should follow.

Here I am using the checklist of questions to revise an earlier draft of the introduction to this chapter.

By this point in *Reading and Writing from Literature,* you are no stranger to revision. To revise means, literally, "to see again"; and "seeing again"—a.k.a "conversing" or "recursiveness"—has been the constant theme of this book. In developing habits of conversing and recursiveness, you have necessarily developed habits of revision as well. Speaking practically, you have already developed a repertoire of strategies for revising. Refresh your memory of these as often as necessary/Refer back to these as often as necessary. If one cannot help you in a particular situation, perhaps another can.

Margin notes:
EXPAND. *Good ideas but flat*

Good link with earlier chapters

Use a different word? Confusing

Sounds preachy & patronizing(?)

Why should anyone care? So what?

Postdraft Outlining

An outline is a familiar device for planning an essay, but you may not realize that it can be equally useful to do an outline *after* drafting. Postdraft outlining helps you look at your draft closely and objectively. Here are the steps:

1. Read through your whole draft. Then, at the bottom of the last page, write a statement that summarizes what you think the whole paper "does" (that is, what its thesis or purpose is).

2. Reread your draft again, paragraph by paragraph. When you finish reading a paragraph, write in the margin beside it a statement summarizing what you think that paragraph "does," i.e., how it functions in your paper.
3. Beside each paragraph, you can also record your emotional reactions to that paragraph: for instance, "My interest really picks up here," "I find this suspenseful," "I'm feeling bored here," or "I'm losing interest here."
4. When you are finished, review the marginal comments you have written and ask yourself the following questions:
   a. Do my ideas seem to be in a logical order? Does one paragraph and idea follow clearly and logically from another? Draw arrows in the margins to indicate places where you want to rearrange paragraphs or information.
   b. Does each paragraph and idea have a reason for being in the essay? That is, does each paragraph relate to and support the thesis? If not, so indicate.
   c. Are there any places where you need to add more information? or perhaps eliminate some information? or clarify a point? Mark any such places and, if possible, add or delete the information.

Here is Joe's postdraft outline for his paper about "A Woman on a Roof." Skim through the essay, paying particular attention to the "outline" comments in the margins and at the end of the essay.

The Clarity of Control:
Lessing on Men and Women

In Doris Lessing's "A Woman on a Roof," two men become fascinated with a woman who sunbathes nearby them as they work. While Stanley hoots and hollers and actually expresses a sense of rage at the woman, Tom, a younger man, comes to see himself as the woman's protector. Yet, despite his gallant intentions, Tom is essentially no different from Stanley in his treatment of the sunbathing woman.

thesis/intro

Tom is no different from Stanley

Outwardly, the two men react quite differently. With the initial sighting of the scantily clad woman, Stanley raises questions concerning the woman's state of undress ("Someone'll report her if she doesn't watch out") and, later, begins acting out at the woman, whistling and hooting at her and expressing a great deal of agitation at her subsequent apathy. Though he is seemingly annoyed at her and her state of near-nudity, he seems inextricably drawn to her and his annoyance deepens with her "gesture[s] of indifference."

Comparison of outward reactions—Stanley moves from puritanical concern to rage inexorably(?)

Add page #'s for quotations

Tom's actions are, at first, in conspiracy with Stanley's actions: he snickers at the derisive comments

Stanley makes about the woman, he "makes the trip" with Stanley to spy on the woman and, even once he comes to see himself as the woman's champion, he stands by Stanley as Stanley hurls epithets at her. The woman's indifference angers Tom much in the same way it angers Stanley and, ultimately, he comes to feel a resentment in himself toward the woman, even hatred. He feels her "unfairness pale him," and, when it rains at the end of the story, he feels a sense of triumph over her.

It is in Stanley's relationship with the other two women of the story, his wife and Mrs. Pritchett, that we glimpse some of his inner motivations. Some of his earlier anger with the "woman on the roof" seems to stem from his feelings about his wife. "If my wife lay about like that," Stanley says, "I'd soon stop her," and it is here that we are able to discern that his annoyance with the sunbathing woman could be related to his inability to control her much in the same way he, no doubt, controls or seeks to control his wife. Stanley is able to regain that sense of control through his relationship with Mrs. Pritchett and we see him responding positively to her as she seems to be receptive to his physical charms.

Control is the primary issue in Tom's relationship with the woman on the roof, as well. When he first sees her, he wants to possess her apart from his cohorts, to keep her for his own. On one of his trips to spy on the woman, Tom makes the report that "she hadn't moved, but it was a lie. He wanted to keep what he had seen to himself: he had caught her in the act of rolling down the little red pants over her hips. . . ." Tom stands near Stanley as he rages against the woman, hoping that she doesn't associate his proximity with complicity; he comes to see himself as having to save the woman from Stanley and even has involved fantasies about becoming the woman's lover. But when the woman does not sunbathe one day, Tom feels betrayed. Her appearance the following day reassures Tom as does her moving to a part of the roof where the men could not see her, because he feels that she's "more his when the other men couldn't see her." And, by the end of the story, when Tom comes face to face with the woman's indifference, he feels slighted in much the same way that Stanley does.

Tom's outward reaction initially a self-mirroring of Stanley: moves to the end of story. Tom's feelings of hatred

Need to mention that resentment occurs as result of her rejecting him?

Gauging Stanley's internal state via his external relationships with women: it all equals the attempt to gain and maintain control
Clear
Expand?

Control is the catalyst in Tom's motivations re: the woman on the roof as well— speaks in terms of possession—motivation the same as Stanley's

Redundant with end of 3rd paragraph?

It is the woman on the roof's perception of Stanley and Tom that is most telling, for she sees Tom, with all his romantic intentions and farflung illusions, as being virtually indivisible from the howling, ranting and hateful Stanley. When Tom finally speaks to her, after he has (in his mind) come to her rescue at the end of the story, the woman tells him to go away and that, if he gets a thrill out of "seeing women in bikinis," he should go somewhere where he'd "see dozens of them, without all this mountaineering." Tom feels stung by what he perceives as her mis-perception of his actions and goes away hating the woman, suggesting that the woman had not mis-perceived the situation at all, but that, perhaps, she had seen Tom with the utmost clarity of all.

We see that it is the perception of the woman that is illuminating—she views both Tom and Stanley as being the same leering fiend

Despite Tom's intentions, he is driven by the same thing that drives Stanley: control, and the woman perceives this more aptly than either Tom or Stanley.

Joe's draft is already quite strong. The postdraft outline indicates a clear thesis with effective organization and supporting points. Joe does, however, identify a few places for revision. For instance, he raises a question about clarity in the third paragraph, makes a note to "expand" at one point (the end of the fourth paragraph), and locates a possible redundancy between the third and fifth paragraphs.

Having Other People Outline Your Draft

Postdraft outlining enables you to see your draft more objectively. You can also benefit from having other people, particularly a peer or a small group, do outlines of your draft so that you have one or more alternative perspectives to compare with your own. Here's how to do it.

- Bring an extra *clean* copy of your draft with you to class.
- Sit with a partner.
- After you and your partner have finished doing postdraft outlines of your own papers, exchange papers, so you are now looking at your classmate's draft and he or she is looking at yours.
- Now repeat steps 1 through 4 above on your *partner's* draft.
- Finally, with your partner compare how you analyzed each other's papers. This can tell you a lot about how well your paper is working. For instance, if your partner's summary of thesis or purpose for your draft (step #1)

differs from what you intended, you probably need to make your thesis clearer. Similarly, if your partner's analysis of one of your paragraphs suggests that he or she is interpreting it differently from what you meant, then you need to think about revising for greater clarity. If your partner writes, in the margin beside your third paragraph, "I am losing interest here," perhaps you need to revise that paragraph to make it more vivid or exciting, or perhaps you need to consider getting rid of it.

Getting Writer-Initiated Feedback

The postdraft outline is an example of reader-initiated feedback; that is, it involves readers describing their reactions to your work while you—the writer—mainly listen. While such feedback is useful, there may be times when you want input on specific problems or issues that concern you about your draft. Hence the value of *writer*-initiated feedback. This is where you, as writer, indicate to your partner(s) specific kinds of feedback that you want that may not be addressed through postdraft outlining.

Before meeting with your partner or group, take a few moments to answer the following questions:

- What do you feel are the *strengths* of your draft in its current form? Write down the strengths.
- What specific passages in the draft need more work and why? Identify particular passages in the margins.
- Where in the draft would you like suggestions from your partner or small group?

Share your responses to these questions with your partner(s) or group and read your draft aloud to them. Then ask your partner or group members to respond to the specific areas of need you indicated and take notes on their suggestions.

As you request feedback, keep in mind how thick or thin your skin is. If you thrive on tough criticism, you can ask for it. On the other hand, if tough criticism tends simply to destroy your confidence, devise your request for input so that it will elicit gentler comments of the sort that you want and need in order to improve your draft. After all, the ultimate goal of this or any other revision activity is to get the input that will help you move boldly forward toward a better piece of writing.

Developing Your Essay with Illustrative Quotations and Examples

Poet William Stafford once said that he could reduce revision to a single word: "more." Stafford meant that his most frequent response to others' writing was

"Tell me more." Clearly, one of the major defects in many rough drafts is a lack of supporting quotations or examples. The key here is *development:* you can make your ideas clearer and more vivid for readers by illustrating those ideas.

Compare the following two versions of a paragraph in Joe's "The Clarity of Control: Lessing on Men and Women." The first version omits quotations and examples, while the second includes them.

> Control is the primary issue in Tom's relationship with the woman on the roof, as well. When he first sees her, he wants to possess her apart from his cohorts, to keep her for his own. Tom stands near Stanley as he rages against the woman, hoping that she doesn't associate his proximity with complicity; he comes to see himself as having to save the woman from Stanley and even has involved fantasies about becoming the woman's lover. But when the woman does not sunbathe one day, Tom feels betrayed. Her appearance the following day reassures Tom, as does her moving to a part of the roof where the men could not see her.

> Control is the primary issue in Tom's relationship with the woman on the roof, as well. When he first sees her, he wants to possess her apart from his cohorts, to keep her for his own. On one of his trips to spy on the woman, Tom makes the report that "she hadn't moved, but it was a lie. He wanted to keep what he had seen to himself: he had caught her in the act of rolling down the little red pants over her hips. . . ." Tom stands near Stanley as he rages against the woman, hoping that she doesn't associate his proximity with complicity; he comes to see himself as having to save the woman from Stanley and even has involved fantasies about becoming the woman's lover. But when the woman does not sunbathe one day, Tom feels betrayed. Her appearance the following day reassures Tom as does her moving to a part of the roof where the men could not see her, because he feels that she's "more his when the other men couldn't see her." And, by the end of the story, when Tom comes face to face with the woman's indifference, he feels slighted in much the same way that Stanley does.

Notice how the quotations and examples serve to ground discussion more carefully in the text's details. Notice, also, how Joe introduces his quotations; rather than simply insert them without context or explanation, he integrates them seamlessly into his own prose.

To prompt yourself to use more examples in your writing try this: Read over your draft; wherever you introduce a point follow it up with a new sentence beginning, "For example, ____" or "For instance, ____" and fill in the blank. "The woman on the roof is not trying to attract the men's attention. For instance, after the second day she moves to a different part of the roof where the men will not see her." In some cases you may decide that no example is necessary, but the simple phrase "For example," creates a momentum for inserting your illustrations.

Later you can delete some of the "For example" phrases and rework your transitions to eliminate choppiness and redundancy.

Local Revision: Copyediting Your Text

When you draft or do global revisions, imagination is an asset. By contrast, when proofreading, you want to be like a machine that focuses in on individual sentences and words and coldly examines them for errors. The problem is, after rereading your text a dozen times during the drafting and revision stages, you may reach a point where you can no longer "see" it; the words and sentences run together in a confused blur. How can you see your text afresh? Here are two suggestions:

Do a "micro" postdraft outline. While the regular or "macro" postdraft outline described earlier in this chapter focuses on revision at the *paragraph* level, a "micro" outline focuses on *sentences*. Simply follow the directions on page 96 for postdraft outlining, with one difference: wherever you see the word "paragraph" replace it with "sentence." You can apply the "micro" process either to your whole text or to troublesome parts of it.

Proofread your text backward. This is an excellent way of seeing your text objectively.

1. Get a clean hard copy of your text and sit alongside a partner.
2. Turn to the last page of your text and place a sheet of paper over it so that everything is covered except the final sentence.
3. Read the final sentence aloud slowly, with pen or pencil in hand. With your partner, examine the sentence for any of the following:
   • Typographical mistakes, e.g., you typed "teh" for "the"
   • Missing words, e.g., "He bought book"
   • Spelling errors, e.g., you typed "seperate" for "separate"
   • Punctuation errors, e.g., you omitted the apostrophe from the contraction in "She cant"
   • Other errors to which you may be prone, e.g., sentence run-ons, comma splices, mistakes in capitalization.
4. If you or your partner find any errors, correct them. If you are uncertain whether an error exists or how to correct it, consult a good English handbook.
5. Raise your cover sheet so that the second-to-last sentence is exposed and repeat steps 3 and 4 on that sentence.
6. Continue in like manner through the rest of the text so that the last sentence you proofread is the first sentence of your paper.

If this process seems a bit tedious, keep in mind that its larger purpose is to train you to read carefully and with an editor's eye. The reward is a better and more professional-looking text. Over time and as your eye improves, you can modify the steps as appropriate.

"Lightning" Revision: Reading Your Writing Aloud to a Peer or a Small Group

Reading aloud was just recommended as a method of copyediting. In fact, reading aloud is useful at any and all stages of composing an essay about literature (or any other text). You can read your lists of ideas, your notes, your working theses, your quick-writes, your drafts, your revised drafts (or parts of drafts)—anything.

Reading aloud is helpful in at least two ways. First, it can show you whether a particular writing project is worth pursuing. If you are too embarrassed to read a piece aloud, it *may* mean your work is severely flawed and that perhaps you should start over with a different idea. (A poet friend treated this as a litmus: if he hesitated to read his precious poem aloud he knew the poem wasn't precious, and he destroyed it.) Second, reading aloud is an excellent device for "lightning" revision. Often you can make improvements in your work when reading it aloud that you wouldn't when reviewing it silently. You can read aloud to yourself, but it is even better if you read to a partner or small group because the presence of an audience can intensify your concentration. Observe these three simple steps:

1. Begin without apology ("This is really stupid . . .") or introduction ("Well, you know I'd better explain this before I read it . . ."). Simply plunge in and read. It's a fast way to thicken your writer's skin.
2. Read slowly, with pen or pencil in hand. Whenever you come to a place where you want to make a change (correct a typo or spelling error, alter a word or phrase, add or eliminate a phrase or sentence), simply pause and make the revision. Continue thus throughout your text. Remember: this is a method of *rapid* revising, so don't belabor it; only make changes that occur to you spontaneously.
3. When you have finished, congratulate yourself; you have made your work public, and that takes courage. Reading aloud is a mode of instant publication.

Checklist of Activities for Revising

- Focus on global revisions first and local revisions later.
- Use the "Checklist of Questions for Looking Critically at Your Draft" on page 95.
- Do a postdraft outline.
- Have other people do postdraft outlines of your draft.
- Get writer-initiated feedback.
- Develop your essay with illustrative quotations and examples.
- Copyedit your text.
- Do "lightning" revision while reading your writing aloud to a peer or a small group.

Writing Arguments

It is difficult to be muddle-headed, and difficult to be intelligent. It is even
more difficult to graduate from intelligence into muddle-headedness.
— CHENG PANCHIAO, EIGHTEENTH CENTURY

What Is Argument?

The above quotation may seem like a strange epigraph for a chapter on argument. Isn't the purpose of argument to make an intelligent and forceful case
for your opinion on a topic and win? "Muddle-headedness"? What kind of goal is
that? Answer: a goal that is ironic but profound; for Cheng *is* describing a kind of
intellectual progress. If the object of argument is to learn something (and it is),
then the starting point of argument is for us to acknowledge our own limitations
and ignorance; each of us must "graduate," as Cheng says, from being a know-it-
all to becoming a humble questioner who realizes he or she has something to
learn from everyone, because this questioner is aware of being only one mind
among millions. Concisely put, argument is inquiry that grows out of a self-
knowledge like Cheng's.

Good writers of argument possess a sort of split vision that enables them to
hold different or contradictory points of view in mind at the same time. Just as a
visual artist can draw an eyelash while simultaneously keeping the whole head and
figure of the model in view, so a good arguer can see his or her own perspective
while simultaneously viewing alternative points of view. If he or she fails to do so,
the argument will be weak or "wrong," just as the head drawn by an artist who
makes a perfect eyelash while forgetting the form of the whole model will look
odd and misshapen. The greater your capacity to hold contradictory perspectives
in tension, the greater your potential to write effective argument. A "critical
thinker" is someone who can grasp several alternative viewpoints, including those
most opposite his or her own, and use them to reach the best possible conclusion.

The term "argument" can be understood very broadly. Insofar as any writing
is a *search* (an effort to enlarge your understanding through inquiry), writing in

any literary form or **genre** including a novel, short story, poem, or play can be interpreted as an argument. Harriet Beecher Stowe's novel *Uncle Tom's Cabin* (1852) is a famous example of a novel that makes a *conscious* argument. Stowe set out to destroy institutional slavery in the United States and argued powerfully against it through the vehicle of narrative. When President Lincoln met Stowe during the Civil War, he is said to have remarked, "So you're the little woman who wrote the book that made this great war." In his so-called "problem" plays playwright Henrik Ibsen (see p. 1076) addressed many controversial topics of his day, such as divorce, venereal disease, and the hypocrisies of the middle class and was accused by some critics of favoring a "liberal" viewpoint, though Ibsen himself always insisted he was writing as an "objective" artist.

In other imaginative writings an argument may be less conscious; that is, the author's main motive in writing is to tell a good story or write a good poem, essay, or play, and what some readers experience as an argument is largely an incidental by-product of the text, or possibly a creation of the reader's own mind. Gwendolyn Brooks's "Sadie and Maud" (p. 375) depicts two sisters: Maud, a "good" girl who consistently obeys her parents and goes to college but ends up (says Brooks's speaker) as "a thin brown mouse"; and Sadie, who rebels, has two children out of wedlock, and lives hard and dangerously. A person *could* interpret the poem as an argument against "mousy" living as exemplified by Maud. On the other hand, there is no proof that Brooks consciously meant to make this point in her poem.

Thus broadly speaking, any well-crafted text makes an argument; however, in this chapter we focus on explicitly argumentative essays and argumentative essays about literature and how to write them.

Argument Is Dialogic

The word "argument" may suggest an image of two people going at each other with clubs with an aim of victory at any cost. Actually, the aim of authentic argument is not so much victory as knowledge, as even a crude example may illustrate. John Doe, a teacher excessively sensitive about his public image, is debating with himself over whether to stop in the middle of the sidewalk (a very public place) to tie his shoelaces, which have come loose during the walk from the bus stop to his office. If you can imagine two conflicting voices inside Doe, the argument goes something like this:

"Are they OK?"
"Fine."
"They're getting loose—I can feel it."
"Just take big steps. You'll be fine."
"No, no—my left shoe's feeling really loose."
"Who cares?"
"I'm embarrassed at having someone seeing me—a grown man—with shoes untied like a little kid's!"
"Everyone's too busy to notice. Relax."

Doe has no preconceived plan to give the final word to one side or the other; he just wants to decide on the better course of action by hearing both sides of the question (to tie or not to tie). The same motive, of gaining knowledge rather than scoring victory, applies equally to more sophisticated "inner" arguments, the arguments you have with yourself. The following dialogue was composed, after the fact, about a traffic accident in which the student, David, had totaled his wife's car. David detected two voices inside himself ("Me" and "Other Me") debating the question of what to do. Once again, you can see that the aim of the dialogue is not to decide on a preconceived course of action but to sort out the facts. (David composed this dialogue as a creative writing exercise.)

> ME: Ugh! Ugh! I'm delirious. What happened? Geez! The car—it's destroyed! Just look at it! What will Diane say? Ugh! We just unloaded $8000 on this piece of machinery and here it is smashed to smithereens!
>
> OTHER ME: Hey. Just be glad you're alive. You're so materialistic, David. Relax. Look on the bright side. The car may be ruined, but you are sound and in one piece.
>
> ME: Yeah, yeah. . . Some help you are. Your Pollyanna–ish attitude drives me nuts! "Look on the bright side, Look on the bright side"—It's enough to drive a person to drink. Meanwhile, what am I going to do about this mess?
>
> OTHER ME: Hey, insurance will take care of it. Relax. Go home. Watch T.V. Take a nice warm bath. *Sleep.*
>
> ME: Yeah, but what about now, what about now? My wife is gonna kill me, I may never take another bath in my life after she's through with me, she'll put me to sleep for all eternity.
>
> OTHER ME: Hey, cool it, David. You'll give yourself an ulcer. Don't worry. Be happy.

Finally, there is the example of the most famous "arguer" in Western history: the Greek philosopher Socrates. Socrates repeatedly described himself as an ignorant man and insisted that whatever wisdom he had consisted in his awareness of his ignorance. Socrates was always trying to learn more, to hear the other side of the issue, only to gather additional evidence that would raise further questions, and so on. Socrates' position is exemplary for every person who enters into argument. *I am ignorant but curious to know more about this subject of X. I must learn all that I can about X from anyone who is willing to discuss it with me.*

As the examples of Socrates, the shoelaces, and the car wreck show, the engine of argument is always some sort of dialogue, whether inner (with yourself) or outer (with one or more others). Dialogue is basic to good argument because it enables you to identify and understand alternative points of view, assimilate them into what you already know, and move toward a more knowledgeable position on the issue (or perhaps even to change your position). What some people mistake for "argument"—victory at any cost—is the exact opposite of this; the victory-at-any-cost strategy is not dialogic but monologic; one person does all the talking without doing any listening. Its aim is not truth or knowledge but domination, and its result is the perpetuation of ignorance. Commercial advertising is seductive, but it is not argument; it is monologic: the commercial marketers are not interested in "entering into conversation" with you about the merits of the particular goods or services they are trying to sell. They want you to keep quiet and buy now, no questions asked.

All writers of effective argument approach their task dialogically: whatever their own position on the topic, they begin by understanding alternative points of view. Some writers actually *write out* dialogues between themselves and the opposing position(s). In his book *For the Love of It: Amateuring and Its Rivals* (University of Chicago Press, 1999), Wayne Booth (a professor emeritus and also an amateur cellist) makes a case for amateurism in an age that increasingly rewards and prizes "professionalism" and debunks amateur pursuits as unnecessary luxuries. The details of Booth's argument aren't important here, but dialogues crop up often in his book as we see him reasoning through the pros and cons of his position, continually seeking more knowledgeable ground. (It is no coincidence that Wayne Booth has been one of the foremost modern scholars of argument.) Here he is, toward the end of his book, transcribing an actual discussion between himself and the avant-garde composer John Cage. The focus of this particular debate is tradition versus innovation. Booth speaks for tradition, the special province of amateurs; Cage, for innovation.

> **WB** (boldly pushing on): Are you never tempted to compose works again in traditional forms?
>
> **JC:** Yes, of course, but I think it is my responsibility to resist such temptations. My responsibility is to go on pushing myself into what is new.
>
> **WB:** But why is it faulty to use the traditional forms?
>
> **JC:** Because they're old, that's why. Old, old. Only what is new is worth doing or saying.
>
> **WB:** Do you mean that? . . . If I listen to a string quartet now that I heard when I was thirty, surely the most important part of my experience . . . will be identical. There will be additions as life has changed, and subtractions too, probably. But why should I try for a novel listening?
>
> **JC:** Only what is novel in the listening is worth doing. The rest is dead. (qtd. on pp. 201–02)

In conclusion, to say that good argument is dialogic is to say that its purpose (ideally) is to advance or deepen the knowledge of people on all sides of an issue by bringing those people together in conversation. Authentic argument as Socrates practiced it does not produce winners and losers but only winners. Everybody wins. Everybody learns.

Analysis of a Sample Argument: Barbara Kingsolver, "The One-Eyed Monster, and Why I Don't Let Him In"

Barbara Kingsolver's essay (see p. 1068) is a good example of an explicit argumentative essay. Take a few moments to read it. What follows here is not an exhaustive analysis of her piece but an effort to show how she develops three elements that are critical to effective argument—persona, sense of audience, and use of supporting evidence.

Persona

People today have heard plenty of arguments about the benefits and drawbacks of the "one-eyed monster," television. Why read one more? Who is Kingsolver, and what motivates her to write and publish this essay on what some of us may feel is an already exhausted topic?

Kingsolver has to anticipate questions like these, questions that bear on her **persona** as writer. Persona is the Latin word for "mask," and in literature it refers to the particular version of herself a writer chooses to present to her audience in a specific piece of writing. (You can read more about persona in Chapter 15, "Poetry," and Chapter 16, "Essays.") The complete Barbara Kingsolver is a writer, teacher, mother, traveler, activist, biologist, and much more—like any of us, larger than the sum of her parts. In this particular essay, she must offer readers a limited version of herself that is appropriate to her topic (TV) and purpose (to criticize TV).

Sensitive to reader concerns about who she is, Kingsolver identifies herself as a mother and (somewhat tongue-in-cheek) as the "philosopher-king" of her household (p. 1068). The significance of the "mother" persona is obvious enough: she is a parent concerned about the effects of TV on herself and her family. The "philosopher-king" persona is more interesting. Kingsolver alludes to an ancient ideal of a state that is ruled by a philosopher, a seeker and servant of truth. Socrates' pupil Plato elaborated this vision in his classic political work, *The Republic.* The philosopher-king was to be wise and just and, above all, sovereign over his kingdom. In a sense Kingsolver's choice of this persona is ironic, verging on absurd: what twenty-first-century mother in her right mind really believes that she is sovereign over her household and can "rule" or control her children's thoughts and behaviors? Readers may smile at and even pity Kingsolver's "muddle-headedness" on this point. Writer and reader share a jest at the writer's expense, which at least *ought to* make the persona more sympathetic in readers' eyes (you can judge for yourself whether it does).

In another sense, however, Kingsolver seems to be deadly serious about her claim to philosopher-king status and sovereignty. At a time when powerful commercial interests appear to be invading more and more private spaces (notably through the medium of television), Kingsolver asserts the urgency of preserving sovereignty in one's own small sphere, the house, which (she hints) may be among the last strongholds of privacy remaining in the contemporary world. In her persona of philosopher-king she is saying that members of private households *can* exercise sovereignty. No one has found a way to make the "one-eyed monster" a mandatory presence in every house; a person can still choose not to let him in.

Audience

Inseparable from considerations of persona is the author's sense of her audience. To write convincingly, she must recognize her readers as real people with thoughts and opinions of their own, as well as prejudices and emotions. The philosopher Søren Kierkegaard (who wrote many argumentative books) stated: "[I]n my mind's eye I always visualize a reader reading aloud." Good advice. Best of all, visualize a resistant or antagonistic reader who might ask the sorts of probing questions included in the "Checklist of Questions for Looking Critically at Your Draft" on page 95 of Chapter 8. *What's your point? Who cares? So what?*

From the outset we see Kingsolver taking the "dialogic" approach—anticipating and responding to alternative points of view, which are likely to include the following:

- "I'm not a TV *addict* but I have one or two favorite shows that I look forward to watching after a hard day, and what kind of a cultural snob are you to steal my fun?"
- "To call TV a 'monster' that you 'don't let in' is closed-minded. An argument for *less* TV I can understand, but this sounds backward."
- "TV is a great achievement of communications technology. It reaches and connects people around the world. It keeps us informed of the latest up-to-the minute news. Sure it has its flaws, but the benefits far outweigh them."

These are perspectives which Kingsolver needs to acknowledge and respect. She is humble about her own "moral" merit and quickly dispels the label of cultural "snob." "I don't mean to equate my freedom from TV with freedom from sin, or to suggest that it confers on me any special virtue, though others generally interpret the discussion that way" (1069). She adds:

> If you knew me, you'd know there's almost nothing that is categorically beneath my dignity: I can get teary-eyed over a song about family reunions on the country radio station; I love to borrow my teenager's impractical shoes; on a dance floor I'm more at home with salsa and hip-hop than the tango. . . . At a party more recent than I care to admit . . . my friends voted me Most Likely to Dance on the Table. Before I dig this hole any deeper, why don't you just take my word for it? I'm not too high-minded for television. I really just don't like it. (1069–70)

Another audience criticism Kingsolver can anticipate is that she is "backward," failing to change with the times. She takes this charge seriously and does not entirely deny it. On the one hand, she says that "I love to watch movies . . . and we see lots of them at home. We do own a VCR." On the other hand, she admits her identity as a middle-aged woman, even (at one point) as "old and somewhat antiquated" (1072). She says she likes books more than TV programs; she would rather read a history book than "watch the eight-hour docudrama" (1071). But she also persistently deflects attention away from the personal and unimportant question,

Are you individually against change? to a more pragmatic and timely question, *How does TV fit into the economy of a day?*

One passage that especially shows Kingsolver's sensitivity to audience occurs on page 1069, and it concerns this issue of TV and economy or time. The "philosopher-king" answers an appeal from her "serfs" (children), particularly her teenage daughter, to "join the twenty-first century" and purchase cable TV. Rather than saying no, Kingsolver challenges her daughter to draw up an inventory of how she spends each hour of a typical day and then decide whether there is any time remaining for watching cable TV.

> She agreed to this, and at that moment I knew I'd already won. Here is what she does with her time: goes to school, does homework, practices the upright bass, talks with friends on the phone, eats dinner with the family, does more homework, reads for fun, hangs out with friends at their houses or ours, works out, listens to music, jams on the electric bass, tries to form an all-girl band, maintains various pets, participates in family outings, and gets exactly enough sleep. . . . Her time card, in short, is full. Friends, exercise, music—not one minute of these would she give up, nor would I want her to. (1069)

With this story Kingsolver seems to challenge us, her readers, to go through the same exercise as her daughter did. If TV still remains a priority for us after the exercise, so be it; at least the priority will be well reasoned.

Supporting Evidence

Elsewhere in her essay Kingsolver discusses familiar questions about the content of TV and its accuracy and completeness as a vision of human events and life. Whether or not you find her persuasive, notice that she always supports her opinions with *evidence*: relevant facts, examples, stories or experiences, and quotations. Consistent with her essay's title, much of this evidence is personal. The evidence supports her thesis, which is never stated outright but is still clear: that TV has enough drawbacks that she will not "let" it into her house.

Good evidence is critical to any argument. For instance, Chapter 4 of this book ("'Hurry Notes': Keeping a Commonplace Book") makes a simple argument, that we should *honor our thoughts by writing them down,* and supports it with several kinds of evidence:

1. *Facts;* for example, facts about the history of commonplace books, which show that creative people of all kinds have made a habit of writing down their thoughts.
2. *Examples;* for instance, the examples of Beethoven, Lincoln, and Walt Whitman writing down their thoughts.
3. *Relevant stories;* for example, the stories about Henry David Thoreau and Virginia Woolf and how they used short notes to generate their published writings.

4. *Quotations of reputable sources* that lend authority to the thesis. The chapter includes quotations from a variety of successful writers and other creative people, all testifying to the value of collecting "hurry notes."

Kingsolver's story about her daughter and the inventory is only one instance of her using evidence to back up a point. Two other notable examples occur on pages 1073 and 1074. On page 1073 she includes a personal story to support her claim that TV news coverage focuses on the sensational, and thereby gratuitously assaults the mental and emotional well-being of viewers. One day after viewing the "live-camera feed of [the] bloody" victims in the Columbine school massacre, the teachers at her child's school are "jumpy" and confess to "physical panic" that the same sort of bloody attack will occur at their school. While sharing the teachers' horror over the event, Kingsolver points out that "the real probability of our own kids getting shot at school [was] lower than the odds of their being bitten by a rattlesnake while waiting for the bus." She adds: "Obviously, I read verbal accounts of violence and construct from them my own mental pictures, but . . . these self-created images rarely have the same power as external ones to invade my mind and randomly, recurrently, savage my sense of wellbeing."

On page 1074 Kingsolver uses the following dialogue to support her opinion that TV misstates what is and is not newsworthy:

> One summer I was talking on the phone with a friend when she derived from our conversation that I had not yet heard about the tragic crash of the small airplane piloted by John Kennedy, Jr.
>
> "You're *kidding*!" she cried, again and again. "It happened three days ago, and you haven't heard about it yet?"
>
> I hadn't.
>
> My friend was amazed and confused. "People in Turkestan already know about this," she said.
>
> I could have observed that everybody in the world, Turkestanis included, already knows global warming is the most important news on every possible agenda—except here in the United States, where that info has been successfully suppressed.

Steps for Writing an Argument

You can use the following steps to prepare and write an argument. Note that these steps only supplement those already described in Chapters 6–8.

1. If the argument concerns a literary text, choose one to which you have a strong emotional/intellectual reaction, probably a text you annotated heavily. The more complex your reaction, the greater the potential for you to write a good essay. A complex reaction indicates that you have something important to say, and

if you believe what you have to say is important, you are more likely to enjoy writing your essay, even if it means sweating through several drafts.

2. Think about your intended audience. On the basis of class or small-group discussion and your own reflection on the topic, make a list of the different possible positions. As an example look at the bulleted list of likely audience opinions on Kingsolver's piece (p. 109).

3. If it helps, clarify your ideas on the topic by writing a dialogue between yourself and someone (imaginary or real) whose opinion differs from your own.

4. Consider the persona you want to create in your essay. Make it appropriate to your topic and audience. For instance, in writing an argument you will naturally express your personal opinion, so it is entirely appropriate to write in the first person (that is, to use "I"). However, if your main or only audience for your essay is your instructor, and your instructor wants you to produce an academic essay that minimizes the use of "I," you should of course do so.

5. Provide supporting evidence (relevant facts, examples, stories and experiences, quotations) for each point you make. You do not need to come up with all of your evidence at once: use your small notepad (again, see Chapter 4) for jotting down ideas of evidence as they occur to you. Collect evidence over time and insert it into your essay where needed and appropriate.

6. Review each draft and every paragraph within it using the "Checklist of Questions for Looking Critically at Your Draft" on page 95 in Chapter 8.

A Sample Essay

JoLynn reads William Blake's "The Clod & the Pebble" (p. 270). The poem moves her because "I felt challenged by the contrast between the poem's brevity and simple language, on the one hand, and the disturbing conflict it poses, on the other." JoLynn has a complex response to the poem and uses the form of an argumentative essay to plumb this complexity. Interestingly, she begins work not with the aim of arguing down an opponent, but with the idea of arguing with herself toward a clearer understanding of the poem.

As you read JoLynn's essay, note especially her persona, sense of audience, and use of supporting evidence.

Persona. Since JoLynn is writing an academic essay, the "I" is less overtly present in her work than it is in Kingsolver's essay.

Sense of audience. She visualizes her audience as basically friendly and interested (an opinion on Blake's poem is unlikely to incite a riot).

Use of evidence. Her many quotations and examples from the text show that she has read the poem carefully and lend authority and credibility to her interpretation.

JoLynn's title is also well chosen. A title should distill the essence of an essay's content. As you read this piece you will see that "Apocalypse in a Teacup" is a fitting title.

Apocalypse in a Teacup: Blake's "The Clod & the Pebble"

William Blake's "The Clod & the Pebble" is clearly symbolic. Literal clods of clay and pebbles do not "sing" and "warble", and they do not debate about love. Blake's poem offers a disturbing glimpse into a broken and unjust world. The argument of the poem is the more intense because Blake foregoes tidy logic in favor of open-ended symbols that leave readers unsettled, even questioning their own character and ethics.

The two conflicting voices in the dialogue symbolize two radically different kinds of people. The clod is "Trodden," not merely by human beings but by "cattle," beasts of the field; it is the lowest of the low. It is also invisible; more accurately, it exists but is not noticed, being underfoot among countless other clods. The clod could symbolize social outcasts or the poor, or the homeless who are visible enough to people who care to look but unseen by most.

The pebble of the brook is the clod's symbolic opposite: it is smooth, not rough or worn like a rock exposed to the air; nor is it stepped on like a rock in a path or field. Rather, it is securely enveloped by soft liquid water. Nothing endangers the pebble or its comfortable existence. The smooth surface texture associated with a pebble also suggests metaphoric kinds of "smoothness," such as smooth talk or smooth manners which have negative connotations; a smooth talker is a slippery character, a liar and probably a big-time thief. This evokes a symbolic meaning for the pebble as a comfortable, successful, complacent person of material wealth, a captain of industry, perhaps, who profits from the humiliating labor of "clods." The pebble is at the very opposite end of the social-economic scale from the lowly clod. Probably the clod is aware of the pebble's existence, whereas the clod is completely outside the pebble's consciousness, nonexistent.

Clod and pebble express contrasting views of love. (That Blake focuses attention on *love* seems significant, since love and its opposite—hate—are the positive and negative forces in the world.) The clod says love is selfless. Love gives itself entirely for the good of others and rejoices in their happiness and well being; it "builds a Heaven in Hell's despair." In contrast, the pebble offers a perverted vision of love as self-love. The pebble's words sound pleasingly smooth with their alliteration and assonance:

"Love seeketh only Self to please,
To bind another to Its delight,
Joys in another's loss of ease,
And builds a Hell in Heaven's despite."

But the content of the pebble's message is shocking. Particularly disturbing is the second-to-last line: love "Joys in another's loss of ease." This line suggests a dark sadistic side of human consciousness that everyone experiences but few people admit, even to themselves: that we naturally and instinctively rejoice in other people's misfortune. I may offer comforting words to a friend who has just lost her job, even do what I can to help her find another, but only after suppressing a first instinctive thrill of joy that she is now a little worse off than I am. This is how most of us love (maybe Mother Teresa was an exception). I can love as the pebble "loves" and keep a clean conscience; I remain convinced that I am a "good" person. (No doubt the pebble would smile cynically at my hypocrisy.) Perhaps this explains why it *comforts* people to read and hear about murders, wars, natural disasters, and Hollywood divorces. You might suppose such news would be upsetting; but it makes them feel a little better about themselves to be informed of "another's loss of ease" or immorality.

The conflicting content of the clod and the pebble's ethics is unsettling enough, but now we come to what I think is the most ironic aspect of the poem, which is the *way* the two speakers express their views: by singing. The clod "sings" and the pebble "warbles" like a songbird. Looking first at the clod, it is ironic that the oppressed and impoverished outcast from society *sings* of selfless love. Shouldn't he be embittered and angry, shaking a fist or shouting curses at the pebble who is so far above him, and indifferent to his plight, instead of singing? I believe that many people in his circumstances do shake their fists and shout curses; on the other hand, who is more fit to love selflessly than he who has suffered, or is poor, and understands another person's suffering from first-hand experience? Or who is more fit to sing about selfless love than the person who owns so little (in the material sense) that a single coin or one morsel of bread is cause for ecstatic rejoicing? If the clod weren't who he was, he might do like the average comfortable person and sentimentalize love, perverting it just as shamelessly as the pebble does.

It is equally ironic that the pebble, the prosperous person of ease, "warbles" about selfish love. One might expect a rich person to rationalize selfishness as a virtue, but you would think he would keep his self-serving opinion on the subject private, that he would at least *preach* benevolence while *practicing* selfishness. Blake implies that perverted love (selfish love) is beyond shame. It openly sings from the trees and rooftops that hate is love and evil is good. And why not? The pebble "has it all"; nothing can disturb its godlike security and power. There is no indication that the clod and pebble address each other; they sing their views independently, to us readers and to the world, mediated by the voice of the poem's main speaker in the second stanza. This reinforces that the conflict presented in the poem goes beyond two mere individuals, that the clod and the pebble are involved in a contest much larger than themselves.

The clash of visions is not only of the here and now but universal and eternal. Both the pebble and the clod perceive the cosmic range and consequences of the struggle between them. With their different kinds of love, each is busy "building" something, as one pair of hands among many. The clod "builds a Heaven in Hell's despair," while the pebble "builds a Hell in Heaven's despite." The clod builds for Heaven, the pebble builds for Hell.

A final interesting aspect of the poem is the ending. Shouldn't Blake have written a fourth stanza giving his personal opinion on the debate and a hint at which side will win? It would be comforting to know that selfless love will ultimately triumph. As it is, Hell (the pebble) has the last word— for now. However, I believe Blake ended the poem where he should have. He does not present the debate between clod and pebble as a simple morality tale of good versus evil with good ultimately triumphant. Instead, he confronts us with two irreconcilable and cosmic visions of reality, one good and the other evil, and leaves us his readers to choose our own side and live with the consequences of our choice.

Writing Literature-Based Research Papers

In true education, anything that comes to our hand is as good as a book: the prank of a page boy, the blunder of a servant, a bit of table talk—they are all part of the curriculum. . . .

Let our pupil examine every man's talent: a peasant, a bricklayer, a passerby. One may learn something from them all, each in his own line. Nay, the folly and impertinence of others will add to his own wisdom.

—MICHEL DE MONTAIGNE

I hate quotation. Tell me what you know.

—RALPH WALDO EMERSON

Introductory Remarks

This chapter is really an extension of the last one. Everything said about argument in Chapter 9 pertains to research as well, especially the Socratic ideal of understanding ourselves, humbly, as largely ignorant people who can learn something from practically any source, human or other. This is a first important point about research.

A second point is that we are all *natural* researchers. There is no more of a necessary divide between researching and not researching than there is (as we have been seeing throughout this book) between reading and writing. The Montaigne quotation that is an epigraph for this chapter makes that point clearly. Many activities that we don't ordinarily think of as research *are* research. For instance, firsthand experience; listening in a conversation to another person's ideas or opinions; asking someone a question about the interpretation of a story; any kind of reading that adds in some way, large or small, to your knowledge and awareness—all of these have a research element. *Good* researchers have two distinguishing traits: they are curious and they pay attention. Anyone who is curious and pays attention is doing research all the time without necessarily knowing it.

A third important point about research is suggested by the Emerson quotation that is the second epigraph for this chapter: "I hate quotation. Tell me what you know." Doing good research about literature does not mean erasing yourself and turning into an information-gathering machine. (If there is no *I* who wants to know, who does?) Good research keeps a balance between information gathering and paying attention to your own thoughts on your particular topic. One good way of preserving this balance is by keeping a daily log or record of your research.

Keeping a Research Log

You can use a log to keep track of time spent on a project, to work out issues or problems involved in its completion, and to make "to do" lists for the day's (or the next day's) work. For centuries, writers have been keeping logs. For instance, playwright Eugene O'Neill (1888–1953) kept what he called a "work diary" while he was writing his dramatic trilogy, *Mourning Becomes Electra* (a modern remake of the ancient Greek Electra story). Here are two excerpts from O'Neill's log:

Entry for 27 March 1930:

> Read over first draft M.B.E.—scrawny stuff but serves purpose as first draft—parts damned thrilling but lots more lousy—not enough meat . . . reading this first draft I get feeling that more of my idea was left out of play than there is in it!—In next version I must correct this at all costs—run the risk of going to other cluttered-up extreme—use every means to gain added depth and scope—can always cut what is unnecessary afterwards. . . .

Entry for 11 July 1930:

> Finish 2nd draft—feel drained out—have been working morning, afternoon and night every day, without a single let-up—never worked so intensively over such a long period as I have on this damn' trilogy—wish now I'd never attempted the damn' thing—bitten off more than can chew?—Too close to it to see anything but blur of words—discouraged reaction natural now—after all, do know I was deeply moved by each play as I wrote it—that test has always proved valid heretofore—lay it aside now—we are off to Paris tomorrow—nice little vacation in dentist's chair scheduled! Best anodyne for pernicious brooding over one's inadequacies, that!—anything else seems like the best of all possible when your nerves are prancing to sweet and low down of a dental drill!—

Notice that O'Neill's entries are both practical and passionate. He gives himself practical instructions ("use every means to give added depth and scope," "lay [the draft] aside now") and writes in an urgent, determined way that seems certain to intensify his resolve to achieve his aims. As of July 11 O'Neill's draft was in such sorry shape that he was calling it his "damn' trilogy" and a "blur of words." A depressed mood like that, left to work its poison on the mind, is enough to kill any project. If he had not confronted his frustration boldly in his log, O'Neill might have surrendered to the feelings of the moment and given up on the whole task.

Also, note that O'Neill records not just what he has done and is doing but how he *feels* about it. When he is frustrated he vents; when satisfied, he celebrates. The log serves an important psychological purpose: by describing his lousy workday and the despairing feelings he has about it, O'Neill creates something he can look back to, weeks or months later, when he is going through a similar "dry" creative period. He will know then that the earlier awful spell eventually gave way to better workdays and that the later bad spell will give way, too.

Here are some practical suggestions for keeping a log:

- *Record something in your log every day to keep yourself on task.* Even to write "Nothing done" is a hedge against procrastination. It is very hard to write those two words for several days in a row without starting to do some work.
- *Make a habit of describing regularly, in simple and direct language, what you want to create.* This habit is crucial, because it is impossible to create something if you don't have a clear image in your mind of what the something is.
- *Do at least some work on your project every day.* How much you do matters less than that you *do* something—and that you do what you have promised yourself you will. Five minutes of work is infinitely better than zero work ("zero" multiplied a hundred or a thousand times still equals zero). To write one sentence a day every day for a year is better than writing a lot of pages one day, a few on other days, and leaving the other three hundred-odd days to chance.

Plagiarism (p. 126) being the widespread problem that it is, your instructor may require you to keep a log and turn it in along with your research essay, both as a record of your process and as evidence that the work you have done is your own.

Preresearch Steps to Narrow Your Focus and Save Time

Don't begin a research project by doing research. Start by defining, as exactly as you can, what you want to find out. Write down what you already know about your topic.

Like all "steps," the ones below can be adapted to your own needs and situation. Several of these steps echo advice already given in Chapters 6 ("Ways of Planning") and 7 ("Ways of Drafting").

1. Decide on a topic ("men in Kate Chopin's stories," "sources of Naguib Mahfouz's mystical outlook," "Langston Hughes's role in the Harlem Renaissance").

2. Use the methods described on pages 78–80 of Chapter 6 to develop a working thesis.

3. Write an informal preresearch outline or draft of your essay. Whatever your topic, and however little you may know about it in the preresearch stage, you can at least list some points that you hope to address in your essay. If you have a certain working knowledge of your topic already, write a throwaway or rehearsal draft (see p. 88). Of course, there will be many gaps in your current knowledge, but a quick draft can give you momentum to begin research and also enable you to identify particular points or questions that you need to address.

4. Read over your preresearch outline or draft and in the margins, jot down the questions or points that you need to research. Use these questions and points to focus your work. If you don't have very specific ideas to research, you will end up reading far more than you need to and risk being overwhelmed by the task.

An Example of the Preresearch Process

After reading "My Father's Life" (a memoir by Raymond Carver that was reprinted in the second edition of *Reading and Writing from Literature*) and the short story "Kindling" (p. 993), Troy wants to do a paper on point of view in the short stories of Raymond Carver. He writes in his log:

> I want to write on Raymond Carver. I'm especially interested in his use of point of view, of the omniscient narrator. It was mentioned in class that Carver admired Chekhov, who also favored this POV. Why? I think it has something to do with his compassionate stance; he doesn't judge or favor one character over another.

To better define his topic he brainstorms a list of questions based on factors concerning issues he is curious about:

- What was Carver's background? Who or what turned him on to writing? Did he write for any certain purpose?
- Who influenced him? Which writers? What was the influence of Chekhov on Carver? Did Chekhov inspire Carver with the ideal of an omniscient narrator?
- What did he admire in Chekhov?
- Did he have any theories about literature? about the purpose of the short story? What was he trying to do in his work?
- How did Carver himself view the role of the narrator in his stories? Was his choice of omniscient narrators accidental or subconscious or did he talk about clear reasons for liking an omniscient narrator?

These questions help focus Troy's thesis. He decides to write an informative essay investigating "the background behind Carver's use of the omniscient narrator, and why he favored it (with an analysis of how it works in one particular story, 'Kindling')."[1]

Next, he makes an informal list of points to address in his essay, as recommended on page 81 of Chapter 6:

> List of points to raise:
>
> - intro—thesis: informative emphasis: explain Carver's theory and practice of omniscient POV in his stories.
> - a little about his background (short paragraph); what his roots were and how he came into writing. Who or what turned him on to writing? When did he start writing? any ways that his background/roots helped to shape his ideas about narration.
> - influences (focusing on Chekhov)
> - Carver's ideas about POV and "objectivity" in fiction
>   —in general
>   —in his own stories
> - analysis of POV in one short story, "Kindling"
> - conclusion

Finally, he works from this list to write the following throwaway draft (see pp. 88–90). The annotations you see in this draft are Troy's notes about what information he needs in order to complete his essay. Once his draft and these annotations are done, he is ready to begin focused research.

Sample Throwaway Draft

Raymond Carver's Omniscient Narrator

Raymond Carver is one of the great modern writers of the short story. What makes his stories so moving? One factor is his narrators, who <u>are often 3rd person omniscient</u>, and who do not make judgments about the characters in a story but simply report information. In this essay I want to investigate the background of Carver's narrative style, the influences on it, why Carver favored it, and explain how it works in one particular short story, "Kindling."   *True?*

Carver's personal background is important to his handling of narrative, and so I will discuss it briefly. He was born in ____, into a working class family. His father was ____. His mother ____. Growing up, Carver experienced/knew hardship firsthand. Rather than embittering him, this experience seemed to develop his   *Get story of his parents*

What were RC's hardships?

---

1. This is a simplified account of a potentially complex process. Sometimes you may need to do at least some outside reading *before* you can formulate a working thesis. The main point to keep in mind is that you should narrow the research process enough that you can finish your essay by its due date. From that perspective, the closer you can come to defining a thesis before you begin research, the better.

capacities for empathy. This quality of empathy in turn affected his stories.

The specific way it affected them is to give him a nonjudgemental attitude about the characters in his fiction. Rather than judging individual characters, he tells their stories and empathizes with them. This is a form of respect, you might say, for his characters and their lives.

For this reason, Carver often used 3rd person omniscient narration in his stories. In addition to his personal background growing up in an environment where compassion and fellow-feeling were necessary, another factor that affected this choice of narrative POV was literary influence. Here, one of Carver's great models was a Russian writer, Anton Chekhov. Chekhov said that a narrator should ____ [Chekhov's theories—quote.] Carver read and studied Chekhov and commented often? about his influence. [examples/a quote.] What Carver most admired in Chekhov were his ____ and

____.

Read about Chekhov. What did RC admire in him?

Get the quotes

Any interviews? essays by RC?

We can see Carver's narrative technique at work in the story, "Kindling." The protagonist, Myers, is "between lives," and rents a room in the home of a couple named Sol and Bonnie. Relationship that develops— Myers and the couple respect each other's space. All three characters have things wrong with them (Sol's withered arm, Bonnie's fat, Myers's alcoholism) that make them unattractive at first, and we may even expect some meanness or perversion to surface, but it doesn't. Carver's narrator gives the chacters time to unfold and reveal their true selves, which are more attractive than the surface. There are no good guys and bad guys in the story.

How?

Finally, when Myers chops wood he seems through the work to achieve a kind of recovery. By story's end we sense that he is going to make it into a new life, and he has Sol and Bonnie largely to thank for it.

Conclusion: Carver's hands-off narrator doesn't put the characters in a box or judge them and thereby also saves us as readers from making hasty unfair judgements based on surface appearance.

Notice the thought Troy puts into his draft. Though he rarely uses the first-person "I," the sense of him recording *what I think* dominates the draft. This will help both his research and his writing; the more you think for yourself, the more you can narrow the scope of your research, and the more satisfying and efficient the research task will be.

Though Troy could probably spend a happy month reading nothing but writings by and about Raymond Carver, he needs to finish this essay in a hurry. Therefore, to further focus his research he lists several particular subtopics of information that he needs to investigate:

- Upbringing
- What got him into writing
- Literary influences (Chekhov)
- Chekhov's ideas on point of view which Carver admired
- Carver's ideas on point of view

Identifying Useful Sources of Information

When writing an essay about literature, you can use two major types of outside sources: primary texts, which are texts *by* or (in the case of interviews and recordings) *of* the author whom you are studying, and secondary sources, which include writings and other materials (such as tapes or videos) *about* the author or that author's work. For any given author, you may find a large number of both primary and secondary sources, but not all will be of equal quality or relevance to your specific topic.[2]

The following are some of the best resources (after the list, we discuss how to find them):

1. *Relevant primary texts* (your author's published or unpublished stories, poems, essays, plays, personal letters, autobiographical writings, notebooks, private papers, audio- or videorecordings of the writer reading his or her work, recorded or printed interviews). Troy's final essay is supposed to be quite short (about one thousand five hundred to two thousand words), so he has neither the time nor a need to read a lot of Carver's writings. He chooses, initially, to concentrate on one of the Carver stories included in *Reading and Writing from Literature,* "Kindling," and the memoir, "My Father's Life," that was included in the previous edition of this textbook.

2. *A good recent biography.* If the author is no longer living, look for the best and most recent biography. If the author is still alive or recently deceased, consult

---

2. The possibilities for research topics about literature are wide-ranging. Since we cannot address every possibility in this short chapter, it will offer the specific example of an author-centered research project. You should supplement the suggestions in this chapter with help from your instructor, your school or campus reference librarian, and a good book on the research process, such as Joseph Gibaldi's *MLA Handbook for Writers of Research Papers* (6th ed. New York: Modern Language Assocation of America, 2003) or James L. Harner's *Literary Research Guide* (4th ed. New York: Modern Language Association, 2002). Chapter 1 of Gibaldi's book is especially concise and helpful.

Contemporary Authors, which provides brief biographies of writers in many genres, along with bibliographies of works by and about each author. Besides being useful in itself, a good biography will include a comprehensive bibliography of works by and about the author; and the more recent the biography, the more current the bibliography will be. Combing the bibliography will help you find additional titles pertinent to your topic.

3. *Any other book-length critical studies of the author or your topic.*

4. *An edited collection, typically in book form, of critical essays about the author and his or her work.* Such essays are generally reliable sources because the contributors usually have expert knowledge of the subject, and their essays undergo an intensive review process before the book is published.

5. *Articles in scholarly journals.* Articles in academic or scholarly journals are quite reliable as to content and accuracy, though they vary greatly in readability, significance, and interest. One challenge here is to find the journals appropriate to your topic. One respected source to consult is the annual *Modern Language Association International Bibliography (MLAIB),* available both in print form and electronically. If you have access through your library to the electronic version (ask your reference librarian whether you do), you can efficiently locate materials relevant to your topic by conducting author, title, or other searches. If you are using the print version, you may need to search several issues of the *MLAIB* to find precisely the resources you need; start with the most recent issue and work backwards. Newer articles and other studies are not necessarily better written or more insightful than older ones, but they include more current and comprehensive bibliographies that may in turn direct you to additional sources.

6. *Relevant articles in general-interest periodicals.* Publications such as the *New Yorker,* the *New York Review of Books,* the *Atlantic,* and *Harper's* feature short fiction, poetry, and creative nonfiction and may contain writings by or about your author. To find articles on your topic, consult the *Readers' Guide to Periodical Literature* or electronic databases to which your library subscribes (once again, ask your reference librarian for guidance). (For a concise yet detailed introduction to these sources, see Chapter 1 of Gibaldi's *MLA Handbook for Writers of Research Papers.*)

7. *Various sources available electronically.* For example, you may consult reference works available in electronic format, electronic journals, full-text databases, and Internet sites. These sources tend to be more up-to-date and more comprehensive than comparable print sources, and you can access and search them much more efficiently. In the case of Internet sites, however, you need to be especially careful to check sources for accuracy and bias, as the work and opinions included on many sites are not subject to the same sort of review process as scholarly print sources are.

Locating and Keeping Track of Sources

How do you find and use the resources just described? Probably the best place to begin is with your library's online catalog of holdings. Suppose you want to research Gwendolyn Brooks's development as a poet during the 1960s. Type in Brooks's name. Precisely what you see on your screen will vary depending on your library's central information system, but you should be able to find a display of all the library's holdings by and about Gwendolyn Brooks. Since Brooks was a modern/contemporary poet, the number of holdings will be relatively small as compared with, say, the holdings on Shakespeare or Edgar Allan Poe. Scroll through the available titles. Copy the call numbers for as many titles as you see that look pertinent to your topic. (The call number tells you where the work is shelved in the library.) For example, three promising primary sources might be:

- *A Capsule Course in Black Poetry Writing* (Detroit: Broadside, 1975)
- *Primer for Blacks* (Chicago: Third World P, 1980)
- *A Conversation with Gwendolyn Brooks* (videorecording produced for the Library of Congress Information Office)

As is often the case with primary sources, none of these books includes a bibliography of additional materials. To enlarge your search, it is important to find a secondary source or an index that includes a good bibliography of materials by and about Brooks. The online display can direct you to additional Brooks-related subject subheadings; for instance, "American Poetry—African-American" and "Authors—Bio-Bibliography—Dictionaries." Following that link you may find Joyce Owens Pettis's *African American Poets: Lives, Works, and Sources* (Westport, CT: Greenwood P, 2002). This reference book includes both a short biography and a bibliography for Gwendolyn Brooks. If you are unable to access Pettis's book, you can search for a bibliography elsewhere (see p. 125).

For each source you locate, copy the author, title, and full publication information. You can record this information on your computer or on small (e.g., 3- × 5- inch) index cards. For example:

PS3553/.A7894/Z97/1991

Halpert, Sam, ed. ...When We Talk About Raymond Carver: Conversations. Salt Lake City: Peregrine Smith, 1991.

It is important to record all of this bibliographical information (author's full name, the full title, edition, place of publication, publisher, date of publication), along with the library call number (upper right corner), so that you won't have to look it up again when you prepare the "Works Cited" list (see next chapter) for your essay. To be able to access your sources easily as you conduct your research, arrange them alphabetically by author's last name.

Troy looks up Raymond Carver in the online catalog and finds several books among his library's holdings:

Bethea, Arthur F. *Technique and Sensibility in the Fiction and Poetry of Raymond Carver.* New York: Routledge, 2001.

Gentry, Marshall Bruce, and William L. Stull, eds. *Conversations with Raymond Carver.* U of Mississippi P, 1990.

Halpert, Sam, ed. . . . *When We Talk About Raymond Carver: Conversations.* Salt Lake City: Peregrine Smith, 1991.

Meyer, Adam. *Raymond Carver.* New York: Twayne, 1994.

Runyon, Randolph. *Reading Raymond Carver.* Syracuse: Syracuse UP, 1992.

Saltzman, Arthur M. *Understanding Raymond Carver.* Columbia, SC: U of South Carolina P, 1988.

Troy locates the most recently published book, Bethea's *Technique and Sensibility in the Fiction and Poetry of Raymond Carver* (2001) and searches the bibliography at the back for any additional titles that might relate to his research. Once he has perused the bibliography of this fairly recent book-length study, Troy may reasonably assume that he now has most (though probably not all) of the important titles published up through 2000. To find any must-read titles published since then (or any others Bethea may have omitted or missed), he searches the *Modern Language Association International Bibliography* (*MLAIB*), which indexes articles in a wide range of journals, as well as books and other publications, by author and subject.

Another path, besides the online catalog, that will lead you to these and other materials is a good reference work (print or electronic), such as an index, bibliography (like the *MLAIB*), or biographical source. Reference books are legion; to find the ones that pertain to your author or topic, you should once again consult Gibaldi's *MLA Handbook,* Harner's *Literary Research Guide,* or your reference librarian. Logically, Troy looks up Raymond Carver's name in *Contemporary Authors: A Bio-bibliographical Guide to Current Writers in Fiction, General Nonfiction, Poetry, Journalism, Drama, Motion Pictures, Television, and Other Fields,* where he finds a short biography and a bibliography.

If you were pursuing the topic (mentioned earlier) of Gwendolyn Brooks's evolution as poet during the 1960s, Gibaldi, Harner, or your reference librarian might direct you to such reference works as Darwin T. Turner's dated but helpful *Afro-American Writers* (New York: Appleton, 1970), *The Oxford Companion to African American Literature,* edited by William L. Andrews, Frances S. Foster, and Trudier Harris (New York: Oxford UP, 1997), or Joyce Owens Pettis's *African-American Poets* (mentioned earlier). In these works you will find short biographies of the poet as well as bibliographies of primary and secondary sources.

Reading Efficiently: Consult the Table of Contents, Index, and Bibliography

Always begin your review of any source by examining the table of contents and index (if your source is a book) and the bibliography (list of sources the author has cited or consulted in his or her work). First, this will help you evaluate the credibility of the text you are reading. Is the book or article clearly written? well organized? well documented? Second, the table of contents and index will point to the specific pages that pertain to your research topic. For instance, if you have a thick biography of Emily Dickinson, and your purpose is to find out something about the poet's relationship with her mother, do not skim the entire book cover to cover. Instead, first check the table of contents for any promising chapters (e.g., "Family Background" or "Parents"). Then turn to the index and look up "Emily Norcross Dickinson (mother)" or "family," where you will find references to perhaps half a dozen pages. Read those pages to get your information.

All good secondary works of a scholarly nature will include a bibliography or a list of works cited. (Unless you are looking at a general-interest essay in a reputable periodical, such as the *New Yorker* or the *Atlantic*, the lack of a bibliography or a "Works Cited" page is a red flag; treat the source with extreme skepticism.) Even an otherwise mediocre source is useful if it includes a good bibliography— the longer and more recent the better. Read carefully through that bibliography and add any promising-looking entries to your own, once again using your computer or index cards to record complete bibliographical information for each source.

Citing Your Sources: Quoting, Summarizing, and Paraphrasing

Some people think, mistakenly, that writing a research essay means simply copying a lot of paragraphs and pages from various sources and stitching them into an essay. This is *plagiarism*, however, a serious academic offense, and most instructors punish it with a failing grade. As defined by Alexander Lindey in *Plagiarism and Originality* (New York: Harper, 1952), plagiarism is "the false assumption of authorship: the wrongful act of taking the product of another person's mind, and presenting it as one's own" (qtd. in Gibaldi, *MLA Handbook for Writers of Research Papers* 66). Aside from being fraudulent and unethical, plagiarizing deprives you of one of the main pleasures of doing research, which is to read and understand what other people have said or written about your topic. It is intellectually *fun* to read a passage in a book or article, look up from the page to contemplate its meaning, and then put the idea of the passage into your own words; in other words, to paraphrase or summarize. To paraphrase or summarize means to put someone else's text into your own words (a paraphrase usually involves a shorter passage of text; a summary, a longer one).

Putting ideas in a source into your own words is generally preferable to quoting a passage verbatim, for at least three reasons. The first is the objection of plagiarism: it is too easy to quote without giving proper attribution. Second, if you overuse quotations, your essay may read like a patchwork of other people's ideas, and your own presence as author of the essay will suffer. Third, copying ideas word for word from a source is a purely mechanical process that does not even require you to understand what you read. On the other hand, when you summarize or paraphrase, you must sift what the text means. The reward of your effort is that you understand the material much better than you would if you merely copied it.

Summarizing is hard work, but it is not "uncreative." Some of the most imaginative and original writers have honed their creativity and verbal skill, while also broadening their knowledge, by summarizing ideas and passages from other people's writings. As mentioned in Chapter 4, at one time exercises involving summarizing and "translating" were a staple of a good education. Students (some of whom grew up to write now-classic novels, stories, poems, essays, and plays) read short passages in a book and rewrote them as long ones or read long passages and rewrote them in short form. They translated other writers' verse into prose (as well as translating texts from one language into another); and that describes only a beginning to the exercises, which were somewhat like a pianist's practicing scales day after day and year after year—sometimes monotonous and tedious, but always necessary and incalculably beneficial.

How to Paraphrase or Summarize

By now summarizing and paraphrasing should come quite easily to you. You have been practicing annotating throughout this course, and a paraphrase or summary is only a more careful and particular kind of annotation that accurately restates the meaning of an idea or passage in your own words.

1. Read and annotate the passage as usual.
2. Underline or circle key phrases or ideas.
3. Look away from the text and (this is the harder part) restate the idea in your own words, as simply and accurately as you can. Don't worry if your syntax and wording are awkward.
4. As a final step, revise your syntax and wording to convey the meaning of the passage clearly.

Here is an example of using this process to summarize a passage from Wendell Berry's essay "Think Little," page 880:

Original Passage

But the environmental crisis rises closer to <u>home</u>. Every time
we draw a breath, every time we drink a glass of water, every   — *On our doorstep*

time we eat a bite of food we are suffering from it. And more important, every time we indulge in, or depend on, the wastefulness of our economy—and <u>our economy's first principle is waste</u>—we are *causing* the crisis. Nearly every one of us, nearly every day of his life, is contributing *directly* to the ruin of this planet. A protest meeting on the issue of environmental abuse is not a convocation of accusers, it is a convocation of the guilty. That realization ought to clear the smog of <u>self-righteousness</u> that has almost conventionally hovered over these occasions, and let us see the work that is to be done.

True? To waste is the opposite of conservative

Everyone is a part of the problem, we can only hope also to be part of the solution

Angry at self-righteousness, including his own

Summary

Berry says the environmental crisis is everyone's problem and that everyone is contributing to the problem. To <u>recognize</u> this is a first necessary step toward solving the crisis.

<u>Then</u> what? Is he saying we should take some action?

Rewrite

Berry says that the environmental crisis is everyone's problem because every one of us is contributing to it. Unless and until we recognize our shared guilt and reform our own personal behavior to be less wasteful, we won't see the crisis clearly enough to address it effectively (882).

The "(882)" that concludes this summary stands for a particular book-page number and is called a "parenthetical reference." It indicates that the information was taken from page 882 of a text by Berry. In Modern Language Association (MLA) documentation style (the topic of the next chapter), parenthetical references replace traditional footnotes.

Incorporating Outside Sources into Your Essay

As you collect quotations, summaries, and paraphrases of your various sources, how can you keep track of your notes and organize them? While every researcher has his or her own individual method, one of the best introductions to the general process is Chapters 7 ("Making Notes") and 8 ("The Philosophy of Composition") of Richard Altick's *The Art of Literary Research* (3rd ed., New York: Norton, 1981). Old as this book is, it remains an excellent guide to the processes of collecting and organizing notes and integrating them into an original essay.

Though many writers like to take notes on index cards, sheets of paper, or paper slips, my own preferred method is to type them on a computer. For a short research project, such as one you might be assigned, I record all of my notes on a single word-processing file. At the end of the file, I keep an ongoing bibliography or "works cited" list; whenever I add notes from a new source I record the complete bibliographical information for that source in the list. For example, if my topic is "Ralph Waldo Emerson as a Notetaker" (see page 964), I create a file with that name. I type the following summary of a passage from one of my sources:

> Emerson, the "sage of Concord," began life unremarkably, cutting a rather mediocre figure in the eyes of the world. His siblings all looked more promising as children than he did (Richardson 19).

The parenthetical reference, "(Richardson 19)," is extremely important because it tells me exactly where I got the information, on page 19 of "Richardson." At the end of my file, where I keep the "works cited" list, I type in the complete bibliographical information for Richardson as follows:

> Richardson, Robert D., Jr. *Emerson: The Mind on Fire.* Berkeley: U of California P, 1995.

When I write my essay, the combination of parenthetical references and works cited will provide me with all the information I need in order to document my essay properly. It will also enable me to retrieve a source quickly in case I need to double-check the accuracy of my notes.

Documenting Research Essays

[T]he man who thinks for himself becomes acquainted with the authorities for his opinions only after he has acquired them and merely as a confirmation of them, while the book-philosopher starts with his authorities, in that he constructs his opinions by collecting together the opinions of others: his mind then compares with that of the former as an automaton compares with a living man.

—ARTHUR SCHOPENHAUER

This chapter addresses two main questions:

- When and how should you acknowledge your sources?
- What rules should you use for citing your sources and preparing a bibliography or "works cited" page?

Troy's Final Essay

Before we answer the two questions, here is the final version of Troy's essay on Raymond Carver, along with some excerpts from Troy's worklog. Refer to the essay as necessary as you read this chapter or prepare your own research essays. Boxed notes in the margins refer to terms or ideas that are explained in this chapter. For additional examples of documented research essays, see "'The Yellow Wallpaper': A Critical Survey" in Appendix B; Chapter 4 of this book ("'Hurry Notes': Keeping a Commonplace Book"); and Interchapter V ("Your Passing Thoughts: Ralph Waldo Emerson"), on page 964.

130

Detachment and Identity: Narrative Technique in
Raymond Carver's "Kindling"

> Title of essay centered on page

Raymond Carver's short stories are moving, in part, because of the unusual respect he shows for the humanity and mystery of his characters. Rather than exhibiting this respect directly, by exalting his characters, he shows it indirectly, through skillful use of narrative point of view. For example, he uses third-person omniscient narration to allow characters to reveal themselves deeply through speech and action without being prematurely or superficially judged by an intrusive narrator. Carver's own difficult life contributed to his ability to identify with his struggling characters. In this essay I want to discuss the personal and literary influences behind Carver's narrative detachment and show how it promotes empathy for the characters in one particular short story, "Kindling."

> Thesis

Carver's own harsh upbringing foreshadowed the struggles of his characters. He was born to working class parents in the midst of the Great Depression. His father (also named Raymond) was an alcoholic who drifted from job to job and town to town. Home life was generally tense. In his memoir, "My Father's Life," Carver recalled one particular night when his father arrived home drunk. Discovering his wife had locked him out, he climbed through a window, at which point his wife "hit him between the eyes with a colander and knocked him out" (346). Due to alcoholism and related problems, Raymond, Sr., was eventually institutionalized and subjected to electroshock treatments and was unemployable for several years (347).

> Titles of short stories, poems, essays, and other kinds of short works are enclosed in quotation marks

> Example of a parenthetical reference omitting author's last name

Carver's own life had its positive aspects, but for a long time these were overshadowed by failures. On the positive side, he grew up an avid reader and became the first member of his family to graduate from high school (Meyer 3). He also resolved early on to become a professional writer. On the negative side, he had chronic problems with employment, family, and finding time to write. He seemed to inherit his father's bad luck at finding good and steady employment, working at a succession of what he called "crap jobs" which subtracted already scarce time from writing (Meyer 4, 7). Before the age of twenty he had married his teenage sweetheart and fathered two children, whose care

> Example of a paraphrase

> Example of a parenthetical reference using author's last name

made the need for money even more urgent (Carver, "Fires" 22). Carver and his wife worked long hours to support themselves and their children. "I worked sawmill jobs, janitor jobs, delivery man jobs, service station jobs, stockroom boy jobs—name it, I did it" ("Fires" 26). Exhausted by work and family, and unable to write as much and well as he wished, he began drinking heavily in the 1960s. His wife later recalled that he was almost continually drunk from 1971 to 1976. Finally, in June 1977, through a supreme act of will he took his last drink, but by then he and his wife had divorced (Meyer 11–12). Rededicating himself to writing, Carver began what he later described as the best decade of his life, producing much of his best work and achieving widespread fame as a contemporary master of the short story. He died of cancer in 1988 at the tragically young age of 50.

Troy introduces quotations and integrates them into his prose

Example of a summary

Remarkably, Carver seemed to grow stronger though hardship. Rather than embittering him his struggles made him more sympathetic toward "written-off" people, the people of his fiction, whose plight resembled his own (Saltzman 100). "Essentially," he said in a 1984 interview, "I *am* one of those confused, befuddled people, I come from people like that, those are the people I've worked with and earned my living beside for years" (qtd. in Gentry and Stull 112). Carver's capacity for empathy comes through vividly in "My Father's Life," where, instead of blaming his father for being an alcoholic and a "bad" parent, he recalls him with great sensitivity and affection.

Note skillful integration of quotation into Troy's text

To say that Carver sympathizes with his characters does not mean he is easy on them. As interviewer Nicholas O'Connell explains, "Once he gets his hands on [his characters], he can be absolutely pitiless in his examination of [their] nooks and crannies . . . but he does not condemn them. He approaches them with sympathy, and respect for their inherent mystery" (qtd. in Gentry and Stull 133). How he managed to be both "pitiless" *and* sympathetic is through skillful narrative technique which was inspired, in part, by the example of the Russian Anton Chekhov. Carver called Chekhov "the best short story writer who ever lived" (qtd. in Gentry and Stull 139). In addition to liking Chekhov's interest in ordinary people as subjects for fiction, Carver admired Chekhov's narrative detachment.

Carver liked to quote a comment by Chekhov that a writer should feel "as cold as ice" about his characters before he begins to write their stories (Gentry and Stull 154). The writer should be detached. This is not the same as saying he should be indifferent. In fact narrative detachment and indifference are opposites. If you are indifferent to other people you can make snap judgments about them, sum them up falsely based on a first impression. By contrast, if you are detached (disinterested) you will have a patient wait-and-see attitude that gives people time to reveal themselves truthfully, as they deeply are. Indifference means not caring; detachment means the writer/narrator cares enough about the lives of his characters to let them speak and act for themselves, without being blatantly manipulated or judged by himself. Interestingly, the detached "cold as ice" narrator can be "warmer" toward his characters than an intrusive narrator. By refusing to impose himself or his own judgments on his characters, he allows them time to reveal their deep selves fully.

We can see Carver's narrative technique at work in "Kindling," a short story first published a decade after Carver's death. The protagonist, Myers, is "between lives" ("Kindling" 338). His wife has shut him out of the house and gone off with another man. To get his life together, Myers rents a room in the house of a couple named Sol and Bonnie. Myers does not like to intrude into other people's lives or burden them in any way; after checking in and briefly learning about rent and living arrangements, he retires quietly to his room. This begins a pattern, maintained throughout the story, of Myers and the couple respectfully honoring each other's "space."

All three of these characters have obvious weaknesses; none is superficially attractive. Sol has a withered right arm. Bonnie is enormously fat (339). Myers is a recovering alcoholic (he has just spent a month in detox), has had many different jobs (he seems unable to hold on to any), and is evidently a "loser." As readers, we might be repelled by these characters at first or even expect that, since there are physical things "wrong" with them, some sort of perversion will come out in their behavior; but it never does. If we expect any meanness to surface we are surprised. Sol and

Bonnie are totally in love (they touch each other intimately many times in the story) and they are only kind
and considerate toward Myers. For instance, when they
show Myers his room, Bonnie "turn[s] down the covers
on the bed, and this simple gesture almost caused
Myers to weep" (340). There is no dirty secret tucked
away in their lives: what we see is what we get. The
same with Myers. His imperfections are all in the open.
He is working hard to be honest with himself and to
live a better life. He seems to be an aspiring writer. After writing "*Emptiness is the beginning of all things*" in
a notebook he immediately laughs, "Jesus, what rubbish!" and puts his notebook away (341). While we
recognize that Myers must have a problem with self-
deception—he is, after all, an addictive personality—
we also see that he is trying hard to be honest with
himself. He does not *want* lies.

There are no "bad guys" in "Kindling," only ordinary flawed and wounded people trying to live as well
and decently as they can. This is one of the powerful
emotional effects of the story: in contrast to stories that
feature conflicts between good people and bad people,
with a narrator skillfully manipulating our feelings to
favor one character over another, here is a story where
the narrator feels toward his characters as a loving
omniscient god might. Though there are plenty of flaws
he could dwell on in each of these characters, the narrator seems to accent their basic humanity by showing
how kindly and considerately they treat each other.

At the same time, without some sort of conflict the
story would be boring. Where the reader might initially
expect the conflict to occur between Sol/Bonnie and
Myers (maybe Myers won't pay his rent; maybe Bonnie
will try to seduce Myers; maybe Sol will sneak into
Myers's room during the night and rob him), the real
conflict focusses within Myers himself. *He* is the center
of the story. Myers is between lives—like someone
dangling from a bridge between two mountains—and
the question is, will he make it safely to the other
side? A reader could feel indifferent to this question
had Carver's narrator not done such a good job of letting us into Myers's life. When Myers tries to write a
letter of apology to his wife, it is an understated crisis
that could make a sensitive reader weep ("Kindling"
345). Here is a flawed and struggling man who doesn't

blame anyone else for his problems but is shouldering them all himself and almost collapsing under the weight. We want him to make it safely from nowhere to somewhere. We want him to make it out of his "between" status into a new life.

The chance at a new life finally arrives near the end of the story, when a truck drives up and unloads a huge pile of timber in Sol and Bonnie's yard. After finding out from Sol what the timber is for, Myers offers to chop and saw it into kindling. This is another surprising moment in the story. Sol cautions Myers that he had planned to do the work himself and cannot pay Myers to do it, but Myers wants to do it anyway. Myers *must* need money, what with the mess his life is in, and he could try and get a paying job at the local mill or in town; but he would rather chop wood for free. It is not the possibility of money that attracts him but something about the work itself.

The work turns out to be not just a job but something far more important—a lifesaver. Myers works steadily, somehow drawing new and unexpected strength from his tiring physical labor. The sawing and chopping complete the work Sol and Bonnie have begun of saving Myers's life.

The product of Myers's work is "kindling," wood used to make fires, to keep a house warm through the cold winter, and this is plainly symbolic. First, Myers is expressing thanks to Sol and Bonnie for taking him in at a crucial time in his life; he is thanking them by working for free and providing them with a warm house for the winter. Second, the kindling is symbolic because it warms Myers himself. The narrator does not spell out how, but somehow this work gets Myers from the "between" state into the new life. He has taken on a job and seen it through. In his notebook he writes:

> The country I'm in is very exotic. It reminds me of someplace I've read about but never traveled to before now. Outside my window I can hear a river of fast-moving water, and in the valley behind the house there is a forest and precipices and mountain peaks covered with snow. Today I saw a wild eagle, and a deer, and I cut and chopped two cords of wood. (350)

Block-indented quotation (use when a quotation runs to 5 or more typed lines)

In a block-indented quotation, the terminal punctuation precedes the parenthetical reference

Finally, kindling seems to be symbolic of human dignity. The closing phrase of Myers's sentence may be the most important in the paragraph: ". . . I cut and chopped two cords of wood." Eight simple words; but they carry the whole collective weight of Myers's life up until this moment, which, we sense, is a transformative one. He has accomplished this task; he can accomplish others.

The narrator has implied respect for his three characters all through the story by letting them prove themselves to the reader without judgmental interference by himself. He allows us time to see beneath the characters' unattractive surfaces to their essential selves. Myers's surface life was a wreck. Sol and Bonnie's surface life was potentially off-putting. However, as Carver presents them, or allows them to present themselves, these characters are not objects of our pity but of our respect. Myers will move on, he will get back on his feet; and he has Sol and Bonnie largely to thank for that. Carver's detached narrator has heightened the reader's own capacity for empathy and respect that reach beneath superficial appearances.

Works Cited [new page]

The title "Works Cited" is centered at the top of a new page

Carver, Raymond. "Fires." *Fires: Essays, Poems, Stories.* Santa Barbara, CA: Capra, 1983. 19–30.

---. "Kindling." *Prize Stories 2000: The O. Henry Awards.* Ed. Larry Dark. New York: Anchor, 2000. 338–50.

---. "My Father's Life." *Reading and Writing from Literature.* 2nd ed. Ed. John E. Schwiebert. Boston: Houghton, 2001. 344–50.

Gentry, Marshall Bruce, and William L. Stull, eds. *Conversations with Raymond Carver.* Jackson, MS: U of Mississippi P, 1990.

Meyer, Adam. *Raymond Carver.* New York: Twayne, 1994.

Saltzman, Arthur M. *Understanding Raymond Carver.* Columbia, SC: U of South Carolina P, 1988.

Excerpts from Troy's Log

Troy's instructor required him to turn in his worklog and throwaway draft along with his final essay. Here are a few excerpts from his log.

4/16. Write a research essay. Begin work. Thinking of topics, nothing down on paper yet.

4/17. I want to write on Raymond Carver. I'm especially interested in his use of point of view, of the omniscient narrator. It was mentioned in class that Carver admired Chekhov, who also favored this POV. Why? . . .

4/18. Brainstormed a list of questions I'm curious about, then made a short list/outline of points I want to raise in my paper. Excited about this. (Later.) Sat down for half hour to write TA draft, more complete than I expected. My focus will be on the omniscient narrator and how it affects our/readers' feelings towards Carver's characters—namely, it makes us see them as real people, nonjudgmentally. Carver's not intruding on them as narrator seems almost like a sign of respect on his part toward the characters. He (through the narrator) accepts them as they are.

4/20. Looked up Carver in online catalog—I will be able to get plenty of info—interviews, something that looks like a biography, critical books that may be off my topic but worth looking at. Wrote up index cards. 45 min.

4/21. I feel a little overwhelmed. Looked at the books today and some are way over my head. I want to keep my focus and remember what Dr. S. says about not being responsible for all the information out there. Set limited goals. Today—skim through Bethea (2001 book) with long bibliog. Copied info for 8 or 9 more books/articles onto cards.

4/23. I read that many of RC's stories are first-person. Problem?? Did he use 3rd person omniscient POV often? Skim through a book of his stories. Stay focussed!

   When We Talk About Raymond Carver looks interesting—friends reminisce about RC, but has no index. *Exactly* what qualities did RC admire in Chekhov?

   Reading Saltzman, Meyer—I'm getting the most info from the introductions. A lot of Saltzman is just summaries of stories; has useful things to say about RC's simple language style: the words are simple but the characters are complex. Being "between lives" seems to be a common theme in RC's stories.

4/25. Omniscient narrator approach isn't working. Browsing through a lot of RC's stories I see many are first-person. So what is the quality in his works I am trying to write about?? I'm tired!

   Chekhov and Carver; simple language; letting the characters reveal themselves without being limited by a judging narrator. Hands-off detachment. The omniscient narrator is not the only kind RC used, but when he did use it he created special opportunities for himself and readers to empathize with his characters. . . .

When You Need to Cite or Acknowledge a Source

Like Troy, you need to acknowledge any source that you quote, summarize, or paraphrase. Acknowledging sources is important for two main reasons. The first is intellectual honesty. The ideas are someone else's, not your own. Unless you give the other person credit for the idea or words, you are plagiarizing. The second reason for acknowledging sources is *as a courtesy to your readers*. A citation of an outside source shows readers exactly where they can look if they want to learn more about your topic.

MLA Documentation Style

The term "documentation style" refers, in part, to the particular set of rules you follow for citing sources in a research essay. Documentation styles vary from discipline to discipline. If you are writing a paper in an English class, you will probably use the Modern Language Association (MLA) style, which is based on the *MLA Handbook for Writers of Research Papers;* in a psychology class you will use the APA (American Psychological Association) style; and for a paper in biology, the CBE (Council of Biology Editors) style. The important thing is not to memorize the rules for all of these styles but to learn how to understand and follow *a* style consistently. It's like using a cookbook: you don't need to memorize all the steps in a recipe; you just need to know where to look them up and how to read and follow them. If you can read and follow the rules for MLA style, you will be able to learn the rules of style for other subjects and follow them accurately, too.

As pointed out in the last chapter, in MLA style parenthetical references replace traditional footnotes. The following are several common variations of MLA-style parenthetical references:

- **Parenthetical reference including author's last name.** A parenthetical reference usually includes the author's last name and the page number(s) where the information appears:

Finally, in June 1977, through a supreme act of will he took his last drink, but by then he and his wife had divorced (Meyer 11–12).

The reference gives readers all the information they need to find the summarized material in its original source. They merely need to turn to the "Works Cited" page at the end of the essay and run down the alphabetical list of authors till they come to "Meyer." There they will find all the bibliographical data on Meyer:

Meyer, Adam. *Raymond Carver.* New York: Twayne, 1994.

Once they have located Meyer's book, readers can turn to pages 11 and 12 to find the source of the summarized material.

- **Parenthetical reference giving page number(s) only.** If you mention the author's name when introducing your summary or quotation, or if the author's identity is obvious from the context, simply give the page number:

In his memoir, "My Father's Life," Carver recalled one particular night when his father arrived home drunk. Discovering his wife had locked him out, he forced his way through a window, at which point his wife "hit him between the eyes with a colander and knocked him out" (346).

- **Parenthetical reference following a block-indented quotation.** If a quotation exceeds four typed lines, you should block-indent it; this makes it easier for readers to distinguish the quoted passage from the rest of your text. With block-indented quotations, note that the final period or question mark is placed *before,* rather than after, the parenthetical reference:

[Meyers] has taken on a job and seen it through. In his notebook he writes:

> The country I'm in is very exotic. It reminds me of someplace I've read about but never traveled to before now. Outside my window I can hear a river of fast-moving water, and in the valley behind the house there is a forest and precipices and mountain peaks covered with snow. Today I saw a wild eagle, and a deer, and I cut and chopped two cords of wood. (350)

- **Reference to an anonymously authored text.** If a text is authored anonymously, use the title of the source, or an abbreviated version, within your parenthetical reference, as in this example from the *MLA Handbook* (6th ed.):

The nine grades of mandarins were "distinguished by the color of the button on the hats of office" ("Mandarin").

Here "Mandarin" is the title of an anonymously written encyclopedia article.

- **Reference to a work by an author who is listed two or more times in your Works Cited.** If your Works Cited contains two or more works by the same author, use the author's last name and an abbreviated version of the work's title in your parenthetical reference. For example, since Troy's Works Cited includes three works by Raymond Carver, a parenthetical reference will look like this:

Before the age of twenty he had married his teenage sweetheart and fathered two children, whose care made the need for money even more urgent (Carver, "Fires" 22).

Preparing Your List of Works Cited

The Works Cited list begins on a fresh page at the end of your paper and includes all the outside sources you have quoted, paraphrased, or summarized in your work. List sources alphabetically by author's last name, and include the following information, in sequence, for each entry:

- Author (last name first)
- Title of the work
- Title of the larger work, magazine, or journal (if the work you're citing is contained in it).
- Editor, translator, or compiler (if applicable)
- Edition used (if applicable)
- Number of volumes (if applicable)
- Place of publication
- Publisher
- Year of publication
- Page numbers (if the work is only a part of a larger publication, such as a scholarly journal, magazine, or newspaper)

Center the words "Works Cited" (without quotation marks, underlining, or italics) one inch from the top of the page. Double-space down once to begin your first entry. Start the entry flush with the left margin. If the entry goes beyond one line, indent the second and succeeding lines five spaces (this is called a "hanging" indent). Double-space *between* entries as well as *within* an entry.

The following are examples of a few of the more common types of entries you may include in your Works Cited.

- **Book.**
  Saltzman, Arthur M. *Understanding Raymond Carver.* Columbia, SC: U of South Carolina P, 1988.

- **Book with two authors.**
  Rosenthal, M. L., and Sally M. Gall. *The Modern Poetic Sequence: The Genius of Modern Poetry.* New York: Oxford UP, 1983.

- **Book with more than three authors.**
  Britton, James, et al. *The Development of Writing Abilities (11–18).* London: Macmillan Education, 1975.

- **An edited collection of essays.**
  Karpinski, Joanne B., ed. *Critical Essays on Charlotte Perkins Gilman.* New York: G. K. Hall & Co., 1992.

- **A book with an editor and/or translator.**
  Whitman, Walt. *Walt Whitman's Workshop: A Collection of Unpublished Manuscripts.* Ed. Clifton Joseph Furness. Cambridge: Harvard UP, 1928.

Rilke, Rainer Maria. *Letters of Rainer Maria Rilke.* Trans. Jane Bannard Greene and M. D. Herter Norton. 2 vols. New York: Norton Library, 1969.

- **A short story, poem, or essay included in an edited anthology or collection.**

  Faulkner, William. "That Evening Sun." *The Oxford Book of American Short Stories.* Ed. Joyce Carol Oates. New York: Oxford UP, 1992. 334–51.

  Rossetti, Christina Georgina. "Uphill." *The New Oxford Book of English Verse: 1250–1950.* Ed. Helen Gardner. New York: Oxford UP, 1972. 725.

  Carver, Raymond. "Kindling." *Prize Stories 2000: The O. Henry Awards.* Ed. Larry Dark. New York: Anchor, 2000. 338–50.

- **Two or more texts by the same author.** Order the texts alphabetically according to the first word (other than "A" or "The") of the title. For second and successive works, substitute three hyphens and a period for the author's name.

  Carver, Raymond. "Fires." *Fires: Essays, Poems, Stories.* Santa Barbara, CA: Capra, 1983. 19–30.

  ---. "Kindling." *Prize Stories 2000: The O. Henry Awards.* Ed. Larry Dark. New York: Anchor, 2000. 338–50.

- **Article in a professional journal that numbers pages continuously throughout the year.**

  Shumaker, Conrad. "Too Terribly Good to Be Printed: Charlotte Gilman's 'The Yellow Wallpaper.'" *American Literature* 57 (1985): 588–599.

- **Article in a professional journal that begins each issue with page one.**

  Behrens, L. "Writing, reading, and the rest of the faculty: A survey." *English Journal* 67.6 (1978): 54–66.

In the example "6" indicates that this is the sixth issue of the year (1978).

- **Article in an encyclopedia.**

  "Mandarin." *The Encyclopedia Americana.* 1993 ed.

- **An audiorecording.**

  Copland, Aaron. *Symphony No. 3, Quiet City.* Deutsche Grammophon, 1986.

- **A film or videorecording (example borrowed from the *MLA Handbook,* 6th ed.).**

  It's a Wonderful Life. Dir. Frank Capra. Perf. James Stewart, Donna Reed, Lionel Barrymore, and Thomas Mitchell. RKO, 1946.

It's a Wonderful Life. Dir. Frank Capra. Perf. James Stewart, Donna Reed, Lionel Barrymore, and Thomas Mitchell. 1946. DVD. Republic, 2001.

- **A published interview.**
  Davis, Miles. Interview. *Talking Jazz: An Oral History.* By Ben Sidran. Expanded edition. New York: Da Capo, 1995. 7–15.

- **An interview you conducted yourself.**
  James, Richard. Personal interview. 4 April 2003.
  Stephenson, Nancy. Telephone interview. 6 Dec. 2002.

- **Document from an Internet site (example borrowed from *MLA Handbook,* 6th ed.).**
  Stowe, Harriet Beecher. "Sojourner Truth, the Libyan Sibyl." *Atlantic Monthly* Apr. 1863: 473–81. *Electronic Text Center.* Ed. David Seaman. 2002. Alderman Lib., U of Virginia. 19 June 2002 <http://etext.lib.virginia.edu/toc/modeng/public/Sto Sojo.html>.

- **An entire Internet site (example borrowed from *MLA Handbook,* 6th ed.).**
  Electronic Text Center. Ed. David Seaman. 2002. Alderman Lib., U of Virginia. 19 June 2002 <http://etext.lib.virginia.edu/>.

- **An article in an online journal (example borrowed from *MLA Handbook,* 6th ed.).**
  Sohmer, Steve. "12 June 1599: Opening Day at Shakespeare's Globe." *Early Modern Literary Studies* 3.1 (1997): 46 pars. 26 June 2002 <http://www.shu.ac.uk/emls/03-1/sohmjuli.html>.

- **A publication on CD-ROM (example borrowed from *MLA Handbook,* 6th ed.).**
  Braunmuller, A. R., ed. *Macbeth.* By William Shakespeare. CD-ROM. New York: Voyager, 1994.

Part

III

Creating a
Writing Portfolio

A "writing portfolio," as used in this book, is a selection of your best work that you assemble, over a period of time, for presentation to others and for your own use. A portfolio is the result of a sustained process of recursive reading and writing in which you set aside your failed or mediocre writings and concentrate on perfecting your best. Part III suggests strategies for finishing your best work and creating a writing portfolio.

Making the Works:
Twelve Strategies
for Revising

As you can imagine, I have hundreds of new ideas in my head, but the main thing is making, not thinking.

—JOHANN WOLFGANG VON GOETHE

Make *the Works*. . . .

—WALT WHITMAN

T he word "portfolio" means different things in different contexts. As used in this book, a portfolio is a selection of your best work that you assemble, over a period of time, to present to others and to please yourself. In terms of the writing or literature course you are currently taking, your portfolio might be a selection of writings that you submit to your instructor at the end of the quarter or semester for a final grade; in a nonclassroom context, your portfolio might consist of the best work that you assemble, share, and perhaps even publish over a span of years or a lifetime.

A portfolio is the result of a sustained process of recursive reading and writing. No writer writes well consistently; for every piece of writing that succeeds, there may be five or ten or a dozen that fail. Fortunately, professional writers are not evaluated on every scribble they make in the privacy of their workrooms; they are able, instead, to discard the failed texts and present only the worthy ones to their readers. Portfolio evaluation takes into account this unevenness in quality that is common to all writers. Rather than being graded on your failures, a portfolio allows you to be judged on that portion of your cumulative output which is the *best*. You write profusely and get graded on the selected few pieces of work that you revise and polish for inclusion in your portfolio. This process is especially appropriate in a course involving literature because it parallels the composing methods used by the authors in our anthology, who wrote in large quantities and published selectively.

This chapter describes some specific strategies for revising your work. Since revision of essays about literature has already been addressed in Chapter 8, this chapter focuses on revising your writings of a more "creative" nature, such as stories, poems, letters, dialogues, prequels and sequels, or personal memoirs and narratives. Examples of these and related kinds of writing are collected, for your reference, in Appendix A.

What is "good" writing, and how do you know when you've produced it? There is no simple answer to this question because "good" writing means different things to different groups and in different contexts. A "good" piece of writing, e.g., a clear memorandum, an informative report, in a business setting exhibits different qualities from "good" writing in a workshop for science fiction writers; good writing for a popular newspaper differs from good writing for an audience of experts in an academic discipline. Good writing is defined by the community of those among whom and for whom you write. In this course, the community is you and your classmates, the instructor, and others (such as friends or family members) to whom you show your work. Your best way to gauge the quality of your favorite writings is by reworking and sharing them within that community. This chapter shows you some ways of doing that.

Strategies in this chapter are sequenced to move from techniques for more global revision, e.g., starting over from scratch, to more modest revisions. Included are strategies you can do by yourself and ones that involve interaction with a peer or a small group. Treat these ideas as items on a menu; you don't need to use them all. Simply consult the chapter whenever you are revising—at any time during the quarter or semester—and use the particular ideas that fit your needs at that moment.

Finally, your notebook is a repository for all kinds of writings, from one- or two-sentence notes to longer responses to literary texts. In this chapter the word "draft," which usually implies a longer piece of writing, can be used interchangeably with "note," "sketch," or "idea."

1. Start Over: Consult Chapter 3

Perhaps you have selected a notebook text for revision because you like the ideas or issues it addresses, but, as a piece of writing, it is awkward or uninteresting. Review the "Ten Ideas for Writing in a Reading Notebook" in Chapter 3 to find stimulating alternative ways of reworking your draft. For instance, consider recasting your unsatisfying "letter to the author" as a dialogue or rewriting your "character biography" of the husband in "The Yellow Wallpaper" as a prequel to that story.

2. Start Over: Rewrite Using a Topic/Form Grid

See Chapter 5.

3. Use the "Checklist of Questions for Looking Critically at Your Draft"

See Chapter 8, page 95.

4. Do a Postdraft Outline

Postdraft outlining was introduced in Chapter 8 as a tool for revising essays about literature. You can use the same process to revise drafts of a more "creative" nature, such as dialogues, short stories, or personal narratives. Since some creative texts use extremely short individual paragraphs, you may want to summarize *clusters* of related paragraphs (see step #2 on page 97) rather than each individual paragraph.

5. Have Other People Outline Your Draft

See Chapter 8, page 99.

6. Ask Yourself Other Questions Appropriate to the Draft

What questions and problems to address in revision depends on the form (prose narrative, essay, play, poem) of the particular text you are revising. Whatever the form, begin by concentrating on what is working in the draft and on global revisions. From there—and only then—proceed to comments on a more local level. (For a review of the distinction between "global" and "local" revisions, see page 95.) Make your comments *in writing* so you can refer to them as you revise.

For prose narratives such as short fiction texts (stories, prequels, sequels), personal narratives, and plays, respond to the following questions and topics:

- What are two parts of the piece you especially like? Why? Be specific.
- What is one place in the text where you could use more information or detail? Identify the place in the margin.
- Where do the **characters**[1] seem most convincing and alive? Where, if anywhere, are they less so?

---

1. Words in **boldface** are discussed in Part IV, "An Introduction to the Major Genres," or Part V, "An Introduction to Figurative Language," and defined in Appendix C, "Glossary of Literary Terms."

- Does the **dialogue** (if any) sound convincing? At what points does it need revising?
- In what places, if any, might the events of the **plot** be arranged more effectively? Is there adequate conflict to generate and sustain reader interest? Is there a clear climax? How can you strengthen it?
- Where (if at all) does the piece lag for you? Why? Be specific.

If you want, provide a partner or members of your small group with copies of your draft, and have them respond to these questions and topics, too.

For poems address questions and topics such as these (again, you can also get feedback on these questions and topics from a partner or peer group):

- What are two parts of the poem you especially like? Why? Be specific.
- What is one place in the poem where you could use more information or detail?
- Describe the poem's impact on you. How does it make you feel? What does it make you think about?
- Does the poem include examples of **figurative language,** such as **metaphors** or **similes?** Where? How do they affect you? How can they be improved?
- React to the poem's physical shape or appearance—the length of the **stanzas** and lines, the amount of white space on the page, for example. How successfully does this shape work to reinforce the poem's overall effect?
- Identify any images that strike you. Describe in the margins how they affect you.
- If the poem is rhymed, circle **rhyme** words you like; then, jot a marginal note beside each such rhyme that describes how it affects you or why you like it.
- Underline uses of other sound effects, e.g., **assonance, alliteration, consonance,** in the poem that you find effective.
- Note any places where you think the poem is excessively obscure or confusing.

7. Get Writer-Initiated Feedback

See Chapter 8, page 100.

8. "Lightning" Revision: Read Your Writing Aloud to a Peer or a Small Group

See Chapter 8, page 103.

9. Break the Revision Task into Smaller Steps

The difference between timid and bold revision is largely psychological. The timid reviser thinks: "Revision is an overwhelming task, like plunging into freezing waters . . . so do anything you can to avoid it!" By contrast, the bold reviser thinks: "No revision task is too hard because it can always be broken into smaller steps. If I can't 'perfect' my text all at once, I can at least do some small things right now to make it *better.*"

Whenever a particular revision task seems too big, i.e., you are avoiding doing it, break it into smaller parts. Do one part first, then another, and so on—attacking one small bit at a time. Revise what is easiest to revise first—the soft spots—and leave the parts that resist revision—the hard spots—till later. Gradually, the hard spots will soften; return to them a day or two later and suddenly you will see how to improve them. Then, rather than laboring over them for hours, you can revise them quickly.

What are some soft spots you might revise? A soft spot could be a word or a phrase. It could be a sentence. It could be a matter of moving a couple of paragraphs or of expanding an idea by adding some useful bit of supporting information. If you know your piece has an organization problem but cannot yet see how to correct it, do some editing or revise a sentence or the opening or closing paragraph—anything that comes easily. If you can't get the opening paragraph to come right, work on a middle paragraph.

10. Take Advantage of Small Bits of Time

In 1787 the poet and playwright Johann Wolfgang von Goethe was traveling by boat from the Italian mainland to Sicily when he became seasick. Rather than give in to the pain and resign himself to a miserable journey, Goethe got out a draft of one of his plays and began revising it, a bit at a time, as he lay flat on his back. "I remained in my horizontal position," he wrote, "revolving and reviving my play in my mind. The hours passed by and I would not have known what time of day it was if [a friend] had not periodically brought me bread and wine." By journey's end, Goethe reported, he "had almost mastered the whole play."

"I write anywhere," says novelist/attorney Scott Turow. Turow worked out much of his bestselling suspense works, including *Presumed Innocent* and *Pleading Guilty,* while riding the commuter train to work in downtown Chicago. He writes in longhand as the train bumps and rolls along the tracks. Turow utilizes spare moments for writing because he chooses to make time for a life outside that of "author." He has learned to exploit the odd moments of the day for writing.

Novelist Toni Morrison says she is writing all the time, even when she appears to be doing something else. "Writing is a process that goes on all the time," she remarks. "I can find myself in any place, solving some problem in the work that I am at the moment working on. . . . It's just a way of life." The fruits of her habit are impressive, to say the least: over half a dozen novels, two Pulitzer Prizes, a National Book Award, and a Nobel Prize for Literature.

The lesson? Don't wait for huge chunks of time for writing; write in the cracks and crevices of the day. Huge chunks are rare, but the cracks are virtually infinite. Carry around some pages of draft with you and revise when you are:

- Waiting in lines
- Riding the bus
- Cooking
- Cleaning
- Washing dishes
- Just waking up
- Sitting down to eat
- Going to bed

Above all, try writing at "unlikely" times and in unlikely places, when your expectations of success—and the corresponding pressures to succeed—are low. Often you will surprise yourself by accomplishing more than you expect. For some inspiring examples of what writers can accomplish with small bits of time, review Chapter 4 and look ahead to pages 185–186 in Chapter 18.

11. Use Your Small Notepad or Commonplace Book

Use your small notepad or commonplace book (introduced in Chapter 4) as a revision tool. Jot down ideas on the spot as they occur to you during the day. Collect these over time and insert them into your draft where needed and appropriate. A small notepad is one of a writer's most versatile resources. You can use it, with astonishing results, at all stages of the writing process and in all aspects of your daily life.

12. Try Various Miscellaneous Revision Strategies

- Develop as broad a repertoire of revision strategies as possible so that when one fails, you can fall back on another.
- Cultivate an attitude of "I'll try this, and if this doesn't work, I'll try something else." Successful revision depends on risk taking and ingenuity.
- If you get stuck revising one part or aspect of a text, work on a different part or aspect.
- Alternate or diversify your writing tools. If you have been revising at a computer without making satisfactory progress, print a hard copy of your text (or a part of it) and switch to longhand revisions. Conversely, if you are stalling on longhand revisions, change over to computer. If writing at a desk gets tiresome, write in bed or in an easy chair or sit on the floor.
- Alternate between working on details and working on major concepts and structure. When you can't do one, switch to the other. Observe how a painter moves as she creates a painting: she paints up close to do detail

work; then she stands back to get a sense of the whole picture; then she works up close again.

- Revise steadily. Goethe's motto "Without haste, without rest" is excellent advice for revision. On the one hand, you don't need to make "haste" and attempt to revise your work in a single step; on the other hand, you don't want to "rest" staring at the page doing nothing, either. Always act. Always find something to work on, even if it is only the spelling of a word.
- If you are too tired to revise, if the mere sight of your text sickens you, quit. Do something completely different—jog, houseclean, play tennis, sleep, go to a movie, take a walk.

Checklist of Strategies for Revising

- Start over: Consult Chapter 3.
- Start over: Rewrite using a Topic/Form Grid.
- Use the "Checklist of Questions for Looking Critically at Your Draft."
- Do a postdraft outline.
- Have other people outline your draft.
- Ask yourself other questions appropriate to the draft.
- Get writer-initiated feedback.
- "Lightning" revise: Read your writing aloud to a peer or a small group.
- Break the revision task into smaller steps.
- Take advantage of small bits of time.
- Use your small notepad or commonplace book.
- Try various miscellaneous revision strategies.

ACTIVITIES FOR WRITING

1. Use any one of the twelve strategies on one of your drafts. For instance, rewrite using a Topic/Form Grid (Strategy #2), break the revision task into smaller steps (Strategy #9), or revise your work in short stints away from your desk (Strategy #10). Then share the resulting revision with a partner or small group. When you share your revision, also discuss the effectiveness of the strategy you tried, how it helped or didn't help.

2. Repeat Activity #1 with a different strategy.

Assembling Your Final Portfolio

Age sets its house in order, and finishes its works, which to every artist is a supreme pleasure.

—RALPH WALDO EMERSON

Chapter 12 described how to revise selected favorite pieces in your notebook. This chapter shows you how to assemble these revised pieces into a final portfolio for submission to your instructor. This process enables you to synthesize your collected and selected writings from the quarter or semester, to reflect on the whole course and on what you have learned, and to consider how this learning can serve you in other courses and in life.

Your instructor will have specific requirements concerning the contents of your portfolio. Typically, a portfolio might include some combination of the following:

- An introduction to the entire portfolio in which you comment on your selections and reflect on what you have done and learned in the course
- Some sample pages of your annotations of a literary text, along with an analysis of those annotations
- A selection of *shorter* notes—such as thoughts, observations, and quotations read or heard—that you have collected using a small notepad as described in Chapter 4.
- One or more *longer* creative selections
- One or more essays about literature
- Complete process work for one or more of your final selections, along with a "process memorandum" that interprets your process

Writing an Introduction to Your Portfolio

The introduction will be the first item in your portfolio. Since it is difficult, however, to "introduce" a body of materials before the materials themselves are finished and in place, you will want to compose your introduction last. Think of the introduction as a kind of final exam. The difference is, while an exam sometimes seems to draw attention to what you *don't* know (because someone else asks the questions and sets the agenda), the introduction enables *you* to set the agenda and focus attention on what you *do* know. It is an opportunity to show how thoughtfully you have considered the issues of reading, writing, and literature during the course.

One obvious purpose of the introduction is to help the instructor determine your final grade. There are also other, more self-interested reasons for writing an introduction. As an act of summing-up and reflection, composing an introduction gives you a sense of power vis-à-vis the course you have just taken. Rather than simply finishing the class and saying, "Well, that was nice," you assess the course for its current and (likely) long-term value in your life. You see how it fits within your larger life as reader and writer; and you reflect on how you have grown during the course and how you want to continue growing after it's over.

Here are several points to consider in your introduction (you won't be able to do them all; focus on the ones about which you have the most to say):

- Introduce the various selections in your portfolio.
- In what ways do you approach literature differently now than you did at the start of the course? In what ways do you approach reading and writing differently?
- Discuss and illustrate two specific strategies or techniques of writing from reading that you have used during the course and have found especially helpful. (Some possibilities are annotation, conversational reading, rereading, postdraft outlining, any particular forms of writing such as those discussed in Chapter 3.)
- Describe the single *most important* thing you have learned during the course.
- Identify the one aspect of your reading and writing behavior that you would most like to improve.

Examples are crucial for making your ideas clear. Therefore, illustrate your responses to these points with examples from your own notebook and from *Reading and Writing from Literature*. For more on how to add examples, see page 100 in Chapter 8.

Choosing and Interpreting Your Sample Annotations

Annotation is the beginning of response. Each of the finished texts you include in your portfolio originated in some sort of annotation or annotations. Therefore, it is worth reflecting carefully on this process and how you have used it.

Thumb through the annotations you have made in the literary texts included in Part VI of *Reading and Writing from Literature.* Identify a few sample pages (your instructor will tell you how many) that show your use of annotation at its best. (Most likely you will find these pages in a literary text that moved you especially powerfully.) Photocopy those pages for your portfolio. In a preface, attached to the sample:

1. Discuss why you chose these particular pages as your sample.
2. Comment on two or three *specific* annotations in the sample that were especially important to you. How did these annotations enrich your reading of the text? How did they stimulate you to do additional thinking and writing?

Preparing a Selection of Your Favorite Shorter Notes

Compile a selection (your instructor will specify how many pages) of your best or favorite *shorter* notebook entries for the term—thoughts and observations, quotations read or heard, or other kinds of notes you have collected using a small notepad as described in Chapter 4. (*Note:* individual items in this selection would typically be three sentences in length or shorter, as contrasted with the longer entry you revise for the "creative" piece described in the next section.) While you don't need to revise individual items in this selection, you should decide which items to include. If your instructor wishes, attach a preface in which you discuss your experiences with note taking by addressing such questions as the following:

1. What *kinds* of notes did you take—for example, notes of overheard conversation? Of striking images? Of passing thoughts? Quotations?
2. When and where did ideas most frequently occur to you? Be specific. During walks? When you were listening to music? At a coffee shop?
3. What *tools and mechanical process(es)* did you use for recording these ideas, and how well did they work? Did you try alternative tools and processes? Explain.
4. Did you ever reread your notes? When and how often? With what *effects?* For instance, did rereading inspire you to revise or expand a note, to rethink an opinion, or to create a new piece of writing? Share specific examples.
5. How could you integrate this habit of note taking into your life outside of and after college?

Steps for Choosing and Revising a Favorite Longer Creative Text

You may find the following steps helpful:

1. Read through your entire notebook for the quarter or semester.
2. Bracket or underline any pieces that grab or strike you.
3. Reread the marked pieces and choose a favorite. In the margin beside this favorite text, jot down what it is you like about it.

4. If you cannot decide on a favorite text, obtain input on your various options from a partner or small group.
5. Once you have chosen a text, revise it using any of the strategies described in Chapter 12.

Local Revising: Copyediting Your Text

See Chapter 8, page 102.

Preparing a Preface to Your Longer Creative Selection(s)

In order to establish a context for your work, your instructor may want you to attach a preface to your creative selection(s). Here is how:

1. Describe the selection. What kind of text is it? poem? letter to the author? sequel to a play or story? Explain why, out of all the other possibilities available to you, you chose this particular selection for your portfolio.
2. Discuss how the selection originated. What literary text or other source — personal experience, memory, observation, song, movie, photograph — inspired it?
3. Discuss how the piece evolved. Once you got your initial idea, through what sequence of steps did the selection grow into its final form? What challenges or problems did you face during the process of composing, and how did you resolve (or try to resolve) them?
4. If the selection is still not completely satisfactory to you, describe how (given more time) you would change it to improve it.

Be specific and detailed in your preface. The care with which you *reflect* on your work can be as important to your instructor as the work itself.

Preparing a Process Memorandum to Accompany Complete Process Work for One of Your Final Selections

One purpose of a portfolio is to make you more conscious of how you process ideas, from first thoughts to finished work. For at least one of your portfolio selections, save all the writing you did, including first notes, drafts, revisions, and notes on meetings with peers. Turn these in along with the finished text and attach a memorandum (addressed to your instructor) in which you interpret your paper trail and tell the story of your text's evolution.

How did your text originate?

Which parts of the process went well and which posed problems? Why?

At what points did you experience breakthroughs in your development of the piece? Why?

What did you learn through the processes of composing and revising?

Part

IV

An Introduction to the Major Genres

The purpose of Part IV is twofold:
The first purpose is *to increase your technical knowledge of short stories, poetry, essays, plays, and notebooks and journals so that you can write in multiple forms yourself.* For example, if you want to write a personal essay, you can consult Chapter 16 to read about the form and its various components, such as theme, story (or narrative), dialogue, and citation. If you are having trouble deciding how to represent *yourself* in your essay ("How do I want to come across to my readers?"), you can check the paragraphs under the heading "Persona and Voice," which explain that authors construct a persona (or version of a self) to suit the particular context in which they are writing. Then you can peruse or study the essays collected in Part VI to see *how* authors shape their personae.

As another example, imagine that a reading of Susan Glaspell's *Trifles* or Terrence McNally's *Andre's Mother* inspires you to write a short play of your own. You have ideas for a couple of characters, and you know a play centers around dialogue; but there your knowledge ends. How do you represent and punctuate dialogue on the page? How do you incorporate scene descriptions and stage directions to indicate the appearance of the stage and the movements and gestures of your characters? And what do you need in the way of a plot to motivate the characters and actions? Chapter 17, read in conjunction with the plays collected in Part VI, can assist you with these and other questions.

The second purpose is *to introduce you to key literary terms and concepts that will help you talk and write about the short stories, poems, essays, and plays collected in Part VI.* Suppose you read Kate Chopin's "The Story of an Hour" (p. 221), finish the story thinking, "This really grabs me," and decide to write about it for your first essay assignment. You are off to a good start; your excitement suggests the potential for a thoughtful response. In order to write the essay, however, you need to articulate *what* grabs you and *why.* You are fascinated by the story's main character, Louise Mallard. You read the section on "Characters" in Chapter 14 ("Short Stories") to find out ways of discussing characters. There you learn that you can talk about Louise as a "round" character, i.e., one who is individual and complex. In your essay (or in a class discussion) you might analyze this complexity and describe how Mrs. Mallard evolves during the "hour" represented in the story's action. Since the story is told from Mrs. Mallard's perspective, consideration of her character may also lead you to investigate the "Point of View" discussion. In short, the chapter provides you with a vocabulary for articulating your thoughts and feelings about Chopin's story or any of the other stories in Part VI.

Note that, throughout Part IV, literary terms are printed in **boldface.** You can find additional information and references to these terms by consulting Appendix C ("Glossary of Literary Terms") and the Subject Index.

Short Stories

A **short story** is a brief work of prose fiction, shorter than a novel or novella and longer than an anecdote. All short stories include such elements as point of view, characters, plot, theme, and setting that are found in longer works of fiction. Given the great flexibility writers have for manipulating these elements, however, the diversity of stories is enormous.

Point of View

Point of view refers to the perspective from which a story is told. The two basic types of point of view are first-person and third-person.

In the **first-person** point of view the storyteller or **narrator** is a major or minor character within the story who uses the pronoun "I." The first-person narrator is sometimes also called a **persona,** after the Latin word for "mask," to signify a distinction between the author (as a flesh-and-blood individual) and the "mask" that he or she assumes in a particular story. When the youth, naiveté, limited intelligence, or extreme subjectivity of a first-person narrator leads us to question the accuracy of his or her version of characters and events, he or she is called a **naive** or **unreliable** narrator. An example is Sylvia, the young African American girl from the inner city who is the narrator of Toni Cade Bambara's "The Lesson." The story begins:

> Back in the days when everyone was old and stupid or young and foolish and me and Sugar were the only ones just right, this lady moved on our block with nappy hair and proper speech and no makeup. And quite naturally we laughed at her, laughed the way we did at the junk man who went about his business like he was some big-time president and his sorry-ass horse his secretary. . . . Miss Moore was her name. . . . And she was always planning these boring-ass things for us to do.

159

Throughout the story Sylvia reviles and belittles Miss Moore and her "boring" talk and lessons. Miss Moore's actions, however, constantly undercut Sylvia's version of her and of events. Far from wasting Sylvia's time, Miss Moore ends up teaching her profound life lessons and proves to be a strong and remarkable woman.

In the **third-person** point of view the narrator is outside the story and refers to characters as "he," "she," or "they," or by their proper names. A third-person **omniscient** narrator functions as an all-knowing presence who has access to the thoughts, feelings, and actions of any and all of the characters. An **intrusive** omniscient narrator evaluates the actions and motives of characters and inserts other of his/her personal views into a story. An **objective** narrator, on the other hand, merely shows or reports actions and characters without evaluating them. Objective narration is evident in Anton Chekhov's "Gooseberries" (p. 983).

Rather than seeing everything, a narrator in a **third-person limited** point of view relates events from the perspective of one of the characters within the story. An example is Kate Chopin's "The Story of an Hour," in which we perceive events through the consciousness of Louise Mallard, though Louise herself is not the narrator of the story. (Incidentally, Louise Mallard dies at the end of "The Story of an Hour." Thus, if she had written the story in the first person with Louise as narrator, Kate Chopin would have had to change her ending.)

Writers sometimes *mix* various points of view in a single story. For instance, William Faulkner's "Barn Burning" (p. 467) is told, for the most part, from a third-person limited point of view (by a narrator who perceives events through the consciousness of the boy Sarty). At times, however, Faulkner shifts the point of view to first-person and writes *as* Sarty, as in the italicized portions of the following passage:

> They were running a middle buster now, his brother holding the plow straight while he handled the reins, and walking beside the straining mule, the rich black soil shearing cool and damp against his bare ankles, he thought *Maybe this is the end of it. Maybe even that twenty bushels that seems hard to have to pay for just a rug will be a cheap price for him to stop forever and always from being what he used to be;* thinking, dreaming now, so that his brother had to speak sharply to him to mind the mule: *Maybe he even won't collect the twenty bushels. Maybe it will all add up and balance and vanish—corn, rug, fire; the terror and grief, the being pulled two ways like between two teams of horses— gone, done with for ever and ever.*

Sarty's thoughts exemplify a type of narrative technique called **stream of consciousness.** In stream of consciousness a writer seeks to reproduce, without a narrator's intervention, the exact flow of thoughts, feelings, and associations that go through a character's mind as that character moves in the "stream" of time.

Point of view in a story is important for at least two major reasons. First, as writer/teacher James Moffett has noted, "*What* a story is about is a question of *how* it is told." A writer's choice of point of view profoundly affects every other aspect of the story, from its themes and plot structure to its characters and style. For instance, Charlotte Perkins Gilman composed "The Yellow Wallpaper" (p. 224) as a first-person narrative. The narrator is a woman in the midst of a profound mental and emotional crisis who records her fluctuating thoughts and feelings in a diary or journal:

> I don't know why I should write this.
> I don't want to.
> I don't feel able.
> And I know John [the narrator's husband] would think it absurd. But I *must* say what I feel and think in some way—it is such a relief!
> But the effort is getting to be greater than the relief.
> Half the time now I am awfully lazy, and lie down ever so much.

Here the point of view contributes to a sense of urgency (reflected in the short sentences and paragraphs, the sudden shifts in thought, the mood of fear and nagging uncertainty) that would probably be weakened or lost if the story were written from a third-person perspective.

Point of view is also important because it involves us in one of the major functions of imagination, namely, the act of seeing and understanding anew by getting out of our own consciousness and into the consciousness of the "other." Alice Walker writes eloquently about this:

> Writing to me is. . . . about expanding myself as much as I can and seeing myself in as many roles and situations as possible. . . . If I could live as a tree, as a river, as the moon, as the sun, as a star, as the earth, as a rock, I would. Writing permits me to be more than I am. Writing permits me to experience life as any number of strange creations.[1]

Playing with point of view helps a writer understand things (self, culture, life, the world, etc.) *better* or *differently* by knowing them from diverse perspectives. In addition, the possibility of alternative points of view provides a writer with a powerful mode of invention. If the stories you write in your notebook lack vitality, you can bring them to life by manipulating the point of view. You can rewrite your dull first-person narrative about "growing up in the nineties" as a third-person narrative or relate the first-person story that "isn't quite working" from the first-person perspective of a different character in the same story.

Characters

Characters are the imaginary persons who appear in fictional narratives or dramatic works, and characterization is achieved through the depiction of action,

---

1. Quoted in Claudia Tate, ed., *Black Women Writers at Work* (New York: Continuum, 1983, p. 185).

description, and/or dialogue. A **flat character** is one who remains essentially un-changed throughout the story and tends to be less an individual than a type. Akin to flat characters are the merely undeveloped minor characters who appear in many stories and plays. A **round character,** on the other hand, evolves or under-goes change in the course of the story and is more individualized and complex. Good examples of rounded characters are Louise Mallard in Chopin's "The Story of an Hour," whose thoughts and feelings about her life and marriage are shown to fluctuate quite widely, and Sarty in Faulkner's "Barn Burning." As illustrated in the stream of consciousness passage quoted earlier, Sarty has complex thoughts and emotions; by the end of the story he has grown and changed in his relation-ship to his father, his family, and his past.

The main character around whom a narrative or dramatic work centers is called the **protagonist** or **hero/heroine.** The protagonist's main opponent, if any, is the **antagonist.** In Toni Cade Bambara's "The Lesson" the protagonist is Sylvia, a young African American girl from the inner city who would rather fool around than get "educated"; the antagonist is Miss Moore, the neighbor woman who quietly and patiently goes about transforming her. Note that the protagonist's conflict in a story can take many forms; it is not always with a personal opponent bent on his or her destruction. For more about conflict, see the section on "Plot," on page 163.

Dialogue

Dialogue is the spoken conversation that occurs in a story and is a major means both of characterization and of advancing the story's plot. Consider again the wife/protagonist in Charlotte Perkins Gilman's "The Yellow Wallpaper." The wife's illness has prompted her physician husband to take her to a house in the country for a complete "rest" cure. From the wife's point of view, however, the cure is not working, and, in the following dialogue, she approaches her hus-band about leaving the house:

> I thought it was a good time to talk, so I told him that I really was not gain-ing here, and that I wished he would take me away.
> "Why, darling!" said he. "Our lease will be up in three weeks, and I can't see how to leave before.
> "The repairs are not done at home, and I cannot possibly leave town just now. Of course if you were in any danger, I could and would, but you really are better, dear, whether you can see it or not. I am a doctor, dear, and I know. You are gaining flesh and color, your appetite is better, I feel really much easier about you."
> "I don't weigh a bit more," said I, "nor as much; and my appetite may be better in the evening when you are here but it is worse in the morning when you are away!"

"Bless her little heart!" said he with a big hug. "She shall be as sick as she pleases! But now let's improve the shining hours by going to sleep, and talk about it in the morning!"

"And you won't go away?" I asked gloomily.

"Why, how can I, dear? It is only three weeks more and then we will take a nice little trip of a few days while Jennie is getting the house ready. Really, dear, you are better!"

"Better in body perhaps—" I began, and stopped short, for he sat up straight and looked at me with such a stern, reproachful look that I could not say another word.

"My darling," said he, "I beg of you, for my sake and for our child's sake, as well as for your own, that you will never for one instant let that idea enter your mind! There is nothing so dangerous, so fascinating, to a temperament like yours. It is a false and foolish fancy. Can you not trust me as a physician when I tell you so?"

So of course I said no more on that score, and we went to sleep before long.

This bit of dialogue speaks volumes about the two characters and their relationship. That John does nearly all the talking suggests his position of authority over his wife. In saying "I am a doctor, dear, and I know," he uses professional credentials to reinforce this authority. His remark that "*I feel really much easier about you*" [italics added] implies, perhaps, some insensitivity to what *she* feels; and when he exclaims, "Bless her little heart!" he speaks of his wife in the third person, as if she weren't even present with him in the room. The narrator, for her part, is nearly silent (in stark contrast to her effusiveness when she writes). When she does talk it is to utter a feeble protest ("I don't weigh a bit more"), or to ask a question ("And you won't go away?"), or to be cut short by a look from John ("Better in body perhaps—"). The dialogue crystallizes the fundamental conflicts and differences between wife and husband; it *shows* us wife and husband with far more suggestiveness and precision than could any comparably short passage that might merely *tell* us about that relationship.

Plot

Point of view, character, and dialogue interconnect with plot and other features to create a story. The **plot** of a story refers to the pattern of actions and events that combine to produce a total effect in readers. A plot is driven by some sort of conflict (e.g., between the protagonist and his or her antagonist; between the protagonist and outward circumstances—environmental, social, or cosmic; or between opposing impulses within the main character). Traditional plots have a beginning, a middle, and an end and move chronologically. Some critics divide plots into a **rising action,** which introduces the characters and establishes the conflict; a **climax** in which the conflict reaches its height in the form of some decisive action or decision; a **falling action,** in which the conflict moves toward resolution; and a **resolution,** in which the conflicts are resolved. This is only a basic pattern for plot, however, and story writers often generate suspense and surprise by upsetting our conventional expectations about how a story should begin, proceed, and end.

One common departure from straightforward chronology is **flashback.** In a flashback a narrator interrupts the narrative to present or relate some event(s) that occurred at a time chronologically prior to the events of the story itself. James Joyce makes frequent use of this device in "Eveline" (p. 340). The events that happen *in* the story are relatively few: Eveline, a dutiful daughter in conflict with her family and her ordinary life, tries to decide whether to elope with her boyfriend, Frank. Through flashback, however, Joyce acquaints us with details of Eveline's life before the events of the story proper and shows us the motivations and factors that contribute to her final choice between family and Frank.

Theme and Setting

Theme is the basic idea advanced (or implied) in the text. Of course, any group of readers coming from diverse situations and backgrounds will perceive different nuances of theme in the same text, and the more complex and interesting the story, the more diverse the articulations of theme are likely to be. The theme of "The Story of an Hour" could be variously described (broadly) as "marriage" or (more specifically) as "the constraining effects of marriage on individual freedom."

Setting refers to the place, time, and social context in which a story or other narrative takes place. In some stories setting is extremely important. Faulkner's "Barn Burning" would not be the same story if it were set any place other than the Deep South of the post-Civil War period. Charlotte Perkins Gilman's account of a woman's mental crisis is set within a single wallpapered room on a lonely country estate; the room and its wallpaper become symbolic focus points for the narrator's inner turmoil. The narrator/protagonist of Naguib Mahfouz's "Zaabalawi" (p. 481) is dying of an undisclosed illness. His unsuccessful search for the elusive and mysterious Zaabalawi, who is said to possess miraculous powers of healing, takes him through a bewildering maze of "quarters, lanes, alleyways, and squares" in modern Cairo. By evoking feelings of disorientation and helplessness, place intensifies our experience of the narrator's frustrating quest.

15

Poetry

Some students see poetry as the most intimidating form of literature, the form they "love to hate." This may be because of poetry's odd linear appearance on the page or the student's sometimes paralyzing fear of "getting the wrong meaning." It helps, at the outset, to realize that poetry is something broader than a rarified art form; poetry has roots in the ancient past, has flourished among all civilizations and social strata, and is present in popular music, song lyrics, children's verses, and other popular forms. Whether you know it or not, you almost certainly *like* some particular poems even if you profess to *dislike* "poetry" in general.

See for yourself. Before reading the poems in Part VI of *Reading and Writing from Literature,* locate and respond to some song lyrics or other poems that you already know and enjoy. Then:

1. Choose one of these texts that you like the best.
2. Read the text aloud and annotate it.
3. In your notebook make a list of the qualities that make this text beautiful, pleasing, memorable, or meaningful to you. What qualities strike you— the sounds of particular words or phrases? rhymes? images? ideas, themes, or life issues the text raises for you?
4. Share your text and responsive notes with classmates.
5. Working collaboratively with a small group of classmates, make a list of "qualities that make for good poetry."

As another way of overcoming the fears you may have about poems, try approaching poetry with a different psychology. Rather than straining to "get the meaning right"—instead of being on your "best behavior" when you read a poem, assume the role of a "dumb" reader. Follow the advice given in Chapter 2 about trusting your intuitions as you annotate (see pp. 12–13). Reread, again, the example of Margaret's annotations of "Marks" (see p. 14). As you read a poem jot down your uncensored reactions; record the various associations—however strange or far-fetched—that the various words, phrases, or images suggest to you. Share your annotations with others; take notes on your peers' ideas and impressions, and realize the enormous diversity of responses a poem can provoke. This diversity of response is part of what makes poems fun.

Major Types of Poetry

Poems can be divided into **narrative** (poems that tell a story), **epic** (long narrative poems on heroic subjects), and **lyric** (poems in which a speaker expresses a state of mind or feeling). Though most of the poems included in *Reading and Writing from Literature* are lyric, some poems like Robert Frost's "Out, Out—" (p. 1023) and Charles Bukowski's "my old man" (p. 376) relate a story and are short narrative poems. A fourth subclass of poem is the **prose poem.** Prose poems *look* like prose (i.e., they are laid out in paragraphs rather than lines) but display other features of verbal intensity and compression characteristic of poetry. For examples of prose poems, see Julio Cortázar's "Preamble to the Instructions on How to Wind a Watch" (p. 679) and Jack Ridl's "Last Ditch" (p. 1035).

Poems can be further classified as either **traditional** or **free verse.** Traditional poems employ poetic **meter** (see below) and often **rhyme,** and they dominated the Anglo-American tradition of poetry up until the last century. Free verse poems discard meter and usually dispense with rhyme but keep other important poetic elements, such as pronouncedly rhythmic phrasing, various types of patterned sound, and intensive use of **figurative language.**

Speaker and Situation

The "I" in a lyric poem is called the **speaker.** Though the identities of speaker and **author** may seem to be close in some poems, the speaker is normally regarded as a being distinct from the author's self: The "speaker" is a *version* of a self that the author projects in a particular poem, while the "author" is the flesh-and-blood person who wrote the poem. The speaker's situation in a poem is a fundamental part of what the poem means—or more accurately, *how* it means.

Consider Theodore Roethke's "My Papa's Waltz" (p. 373):

> The whiskey on your breath
> Could make a small boy dizzy;
> But I hung on like death:
> Such waltzing was not easy.

We romped until the pans   5
Slid from the kitchen shelf;
My mother's countenance
Could not unfrown itself.

The hand that held my wrist
Was battered on one knuckle;   10
At every step you missed
My right ear scraped a buckle.

You beat time on my head
With a palm caked hard by dirt,
Then waltzed me off to bed   15
Still clinging to your shirt.

The poem's subject is fairly clear: an experience of "rough" love between a child (most likely a son) and his father; but the speaker and situation are at least as interesting as the subject. At the moment he "speaks," how distant is the speaker, in time, from the experience described? The past tense verbs indicate some time has passed, though how much isn't certain. He seems to talk to his father ("The whiskey on your breath . . .") but more as one might "talk to" someone indirectly, as in a letter, than face to face. Most important, perhaps, the whole experience— what happened, the relationship between father (and mother) and son—is filtered and interpreted for us through the consciousness of the son; we don't get *the* story of the experience but the *son's* version of it.

Roethke could keep the same subject but change the speaker or situation to create a radically different poem. For instance, what if he went through the poem and replaced all the second-person pronouns ("you" and "your") with third-person pronouns ("he" and "his")? The poem would become more emotionally detached, less profoundly personal. Or what if he rewrote the poem from either (a) the first-person point of view of the father or mother or (b) the perspective of a third-person narrator who was uninvolved in the events described but heard about them from the son or the mother? These are questions of technique as much as of meaning; and, just as story writers work with point of view, poets work (or play) with such questions constantly.

Poetic Meter

Rhythm refers to a distinct but variable pattern of stressed and lightly stressed sounds in poetry or prose. When the rhythm follows a *regular* repeating pattern of stressed and lightly stressed syllables it is called **meter,** and the poem is said to be metrical. Within a poetic line, meters are measured in **feet,** with each repetition of the pattern comprising a separate foot.

Iambic is by far the most common of meters in traditional poems written in English. An **iambic** foot consists of a lightly stressed followed by a stressed syllable (˘´), as in the following line from Robert Frost's "Out, Out—":

Ănd nóth/ĭng háp/pĕned : dáy/wăs all/bŭt dóne.

The vertical slash marks indicate metrical feet. In this example, each line has five feet and the poem is described as being in iambic **pentameter.** A line of four feet is **tetrameter,** three feet **trimeter,** and two feet **dimeter.**

A less common but important meter is the **trochaic** (´˘), illustrated in these lines from Robert Browning's "Soliloquy of the Spanish Cloister":

Thére's ă / gréat teẋt / iň Ǧa / látiaňs,
Ońce yŏu / tríp ŏn / ít, ĕn / taíls
Twéntў / -níne dĭs / tińct dăm / nátiŏns . . .

Note that the Browning sample exemplifies trochaic tetrameter because it has four metrical feet per line.

Lord Byron's "The Destruction of Sennacherib" provides an example of **anapestic** meter (˘˘´):

Ănd tȟe wíd / oẇs ŏf Aśh / ŭr aře loúd / ĭn thĕir wáil,
Ănd tȟe í / dŏls aře bróke / iň tȟe teḿ / pľe ŏf Báal . . .

Thomas Hardy's "The Voice" illustrates **dactylic** meter (´˘˘):

Wómăn mŭch / míssed, hŏw yŏu / cáll tŏ mĕ, / cáll tŏ mĕ,
Sáyiňg thăt / noẇ yŏu ăre / nót aš yŏu / wére . . .

Using marks to indicate the meter of a poem, as in the above examples, is called a **scansion** of the poem.

Rhyme and Sound Effects

The most familiar sound effect in traditional verse is **end rhyme** (or simply **rhyme**). The example is from "My Papa's Waltz":

The hand that held my wrist
Was battered on one knuckle;
At every step you missed
My right ear scraped a buckle.

In this example, rhymes like "wrist" and "missed," which consist of a single stressed syllable, are called **masculine rhymes.** A rhyme that falls on a final

stressed syllable followed by a lightly stressed one, as in "knuckle" and "buckle,"
is called a **feminine rhyme.** If the rhyming vowel sounds are only approximately
(rather than exactly) alike, the rhyme is called a **slant rhyme** or **partial rhyme.**
The rhyme in the second and fourth lines of the following example (from the
same poem) illustrates:

> The whiskey on your breath
> Could make a small boy dizzy;
> But I hung on like death:
> Such waltzing was not easy.

The following is conventional notation for indicating the rhyme scheme in a
poem:

The whiskey on your breath	a
Could make a small boy dizzy;	b
But I hung on like death:	a
Such waltzing was not easy.	b
We romped until the pans	c
Slid from the kitchen shelf;	d
My mother's countenance	c
Could not unfrown itself.	d
The hand that held my wrist	e
Was battered on one knuckle;	f
At every step you missed	e
My right ear scraped a buckle.	f
You beat time on my head	g
With a palm caked hard by dirt,	h
Then waltzed me off to bed	g
Still clinging to your shirt.	h

The "a" indicates all line endings that rhyme with the first line; "b" indicates a second rhyme sound and its repetitions within the poem; "c" designates a third
rhyme sound; and so on.

   Three other important types of sound effects—alliteration, assonance, and
consonance—involve repetitions of speech sounds in a sequence of nearby
words. These sound effects enrich verbal texture, affect meaning, and enhance the
pleasure experienced in reading. **Alliteration** occurs when consonant sounds are
repeated, particularly at the beginnings of words or of stressed syllables:

> I heard you **s**olemn-**s**weet pipes of the organ as last **S**unday morn I pa**ss**'d the
>   church . . .
>   —Walt Whitman, "I Heard You Solemn-Sweet Pipes of the Organ" (p. 271)

Assonance refers to repeated vowel sounds within words:

> When I have f**ea**rs that I may c**ea**se to b**e**
>> Before my pen has gl**ea**ned my t**ee**ming brain . . .
>> —John Keats, "When I have fears that I may cease to be" (p. 1021)

Consonance refers to repetitions of identical or similar consonant sounds with different intervening vowels:

> Márgarét, are you **gr**ieving Over Golden**gr**ove unleaving? . . .
>> — Gerard Manley Hopkins, "Spring and Fall" (p. 509)

Diction and Syntax

Diction refers to a poet's choice of words and **syntax** to the way those words are put together (e.g., in complex sentences and phrases or simpler sentences and phrases). Persons used to thinking of poetry as always being composed in "high" or rarified language are sometimes surprised to discover the enormous range of vocabularies that poets actually use. Poets can manipulate language to evoke vastly diverse esthetic effects, cultural contexts, and human experiences. This is because the poet's realm is all of personal and cultural experience rather than just some part of it. Thus at one extreme is the *formal* diction and elaborate syntax of Wordsworth's sonnet "The World Is Too Much with Us" (p. 1020):

> The world is too much with us; late and soon,
> Getting and spending, we lay waste our powers:
> Little we see in Nature that is ours;
> We have given our hearts away, a sordid boon!
> This Sea that bares her bosom to the moon. . . .

In this passage words and phrases like "Getting and spending," "sordid boon," and "bares her bosom" convey a sense of formality and magnitude. Syntactically, the speaker's clauses are complex, layered one on the other; it takes him four lines to get through his first sentence, and the fourteen lines of the entire poem are comprised of only three sentences.

At another extreme is the *colloquial* or *informal* diction of Audre Lorde in "Hanging Fire" (p. 512):

> I am fourteen
> and my skin has betrayed me
> the boy I cannot live without
> still sucks his thumb
> in secret
> how come my knees are

always so ashy
what if I die
before morning
and momma's in the bedroom
with the door closed.

A first reaction to this poem might be, "It doesn't even sound like poetry!" No less than Wordsworth, however, Lorde chooses and crafts her words to articulate a particular version of experience. In contrast to Wordsworth's formal language and syntax, Lorde evokes the spontaneous bluntness of the frustrated adolescent in such words and phrases as "I am fourteen," "momma's" (instead of "mother's"), and "how come" (instead of "why"). As for syntax, "Hanging Fire" is almost punctuation-free; where we expect to see commas, periods, and question marks there are none; one thought seems to tumble anxiously into the next, in a way that seems appropriate to the jumpy mental state of Lorde's adolescent speaker.

Diction can also be classified as *abstract* (e.g., Wordsworth writes grandly of "The world") or *concrete* (e.g., Lorde's mention of "ashy" knees); *general* (Wordsworth's generic characterization of our wasted lives as made up of "Getting and spending") or *specific* (Lorde's references to thumbsucking and "skin," for example); and *literal* or *figurative* (see Part V of this book).

Figurative Language

See Part V, page 199.

Symbolism

See Part V, page 212.

16

Essays

Essay is a simple word used to describe a broad variety of writings. The word derives from the French verb "essaier," which means "to attempt," and the Frenchman Michel de Montaigne (1533–1592), the first great essayist, used the genre for the sorts of exploratory, reflective, and personal purposes that are implied by this verb. Generally, "essay" refers to a unified work of nonfiction prose that is relatively short (i.e., shorter than a book). Essays can be classified into **argumentative** essays, which advance an explicit argument and support it with evidence; **expository** essays, which inform an audience or explain a particular subject; and **personal** and **literary** essays. This last group emphasizes elements that are ordinarily associated with "literary" texts—an engaging persona, an intellectual or emotional focus or theme that is usually implied rather than directly stated, artful use of figurative language and of such other "literary" elements as dialogue and narrative. A literary essayist combines and crafts these elements to produce particular emotional and intellectual effects in readers. Most of the essays collected in Part VI of this book are personal or literary essays. Two notable exceptions are Wendell Berry's "Think Little" (p. 880) and Barbara Kingsolver's "The One-Eyed Monster, and Why I Don't Let Him In" (p. 1068), which have a more argumentative emphasis.

Like most texts, essays come into being gradually, through writing and rewriting. The literary essay is latent in journal or notebook entries, personal letters, experimental paragraphs, bits of dialogue, written observations, and portraits of people. Any of these kinds of writing may exhibit the "literary" features characteristic of essays. Thus the texts you compose in your notebook or small notepad/commonplace book can all be viewed as potential essays or parts of essays. As Montaigne would say, they are "attempts"—the attempts that lurk in the evolutionary background of any "finished" work.

Sample Essay: Judith Ortiz Cofer's "Primary Lessons"

Before continuing, take time to read "Primary Lessons" (p. 541), a personal essay by Judith Ortiz Cofer.

Persona and Voice

As mentioned in previous chapters of this book, a persona is the "mask" or version of a self that a writer projects in a particular text. In explicitly autobiographical writings like "Primary Lessons" persona and author may be extremely close, and the authorial presence we perceive in such a text is sometimes called the writer's **voice**. To say that the writer of an essay is "just being herself," however, would be misleading. In important ways the persona is always shaped or *crafted*, for any one essayist will create different personae for different occasions, depending on her subject, purpose, and intended readers. Thus a writer will develop one kind of persona if she is addressing an audience of English professors on the subject of "Metrical Substitutions in the Poems of John Keats" and a very different persona if she is writing for general readers on the subject of "childhood experiences." In the first situation the writer is apt to craft a persona who is authoritative, impersonal, and "scholarly." In the second, the writer will probably want her persona to be personal and "approachable" so as to elicit feelings of empathy or identification in readers.

In "Primary Lessons" Cofer's subject is those "first" or "basic" lessons, learned early, that shape the rest of our lives; her intended audience seems to be adult readers who have experienced similar kinds of "lessons" and who might be interested in revisiting their own childhood experiences by means of this essay. Appropriately, therefore, Cofer crafts a personal and engaging persona who tells a good story. At the same time, she projects a kind of authority—not by marshaling arguments or formidable displays of logic, which might distance her from readers, but by conveying an attitude of simple trust in the facts of her experience:

> My mother walked me to my first day at school at La Escuela Segundo Ruiz Belvis, named after the Puerto Rican patriot born in our town. I remember yellow cement with green trim. All the classrooms had been painted these colors to identify them as government property. This was true all over the Island.

Though in many ways individual and unique, the experience Cofer goes on to relate is apt to resonate in important ways with readers' experiences. Like her, we can recall our "first" school experience, times "of running wild in the sun," or times we didn't want to do what a parent demanded we do. Immediately Cofer establishes a rapport with us, her readers, immersing us in her experiences and making us ready to follow wherever her persona might lead.

Style and Language

A writer's persona in an essay has a shaping effect on his or her style and language.

> "Repeat after me, children: Pollito — Chicken," she [*La Mrs.*] commanded in her heavily accented English that only I understood, being the only child in the room who had ever been exposed to the language. But I too remained silent. No use making waves or showing off. Patiently *La Mrs.* sang her song and gestured for us to join in. At some point it must have dawned on the class that this silly routine was likely to go on all day if we did not "repeat after her." It was not her fault that she had to follow the rule in the teacher's manual stating that she must teach English *in* English, and that she must not translate, but merely repeat her lesson in English until the children "begin to respond" more or less "unconsciously." This was one of the vestiges of the regimen followed by her predecessors in the last generation. To this day I can recite "Pollito — Chicken" mindlessly, never once pausing to visualize chicks, hens, pencils, or pens.

Note how Cofer's language fits and reinforces her candid, "ordinary," and forthright persona. There are no inappropriately "fancy" words here, no abstruse sentences or concepts, nothing that can't be understood and followed by an average attentive reader. The vocabulary and syntax are relatively simple. Note, also, how Cofer shuttles between child and adult perspectives on the experiences she relates. The paragraph opens from the viewpoint of herself as a child, looking on ironically at her teacher's "silly routine"; then the perspective shifts to that of the adult who appreciates the causes behind the teacher's behavior: "It was not her fault that she had to follow the rule in her teacher's manual. . . . This was one of the vestiges of the regimen followed by her predecessors. . . ." We trust this story — as we do others in the rest of the essay — as a truthful account of what Cofer thought and felt as a child; at the same time, we enter into the adult vision that transforms those "experiences" into "lessons."

Theme

Theme refers to what the essay is about, its prevailing idea. One theme in "Primary Lessons" seems to be early experiences and their lasting effects (though Cofer never explicitly traces these effects in her essay). Another theme might center on the whole question of *which* lessons in our lives are the most "primary," "basic," or "important." To articulate or discuss theme is to get at the *what* of the essay (i.e., its content and ideas), while discussions of persona, voice, audience, language, and literary technique immerse us in its *how* (i.e., how it conveys its content and ideas effectively to readers).

Dialogue

Dialogue is a familiar element of fiction that also appears in essays. Writers of personal and literary essays often assume the role of storytellers; therefore, it is not surprising that they make use of this narrative device.

The presence of dialogue in essays raises an interesting question: Since an essay is a form of *non*fiction, must the dialogue be an exact transcription of what was actually said? The answer is a guarded "no." Few people have the kind of memory that can recall a conversation verbatim ten or fifteen years after it occurred. Thus dialogue—even in nonfiction—is usually to some extent shaped or constructed. If you want to include dialogue in an essay of your own, a good way to begin is by getting a sense of what was said, a feeling for the conversation's tone, themes, and conflict (if any) and for the persons who were involved. Then relax and begin writing.

Judith Ortiz Cofer includes three passages of dialogue in "Primary Lessons." One passage begins with the third paragraph and runs through the fifth; a second occurs toward the middle of the essay, where *La Mrs.* instructs her class in the English words for "Pollito," "Gallina," and so on; and a third appears at the end, in the overheard conversation between *La Mrs.* and the other teacher. You can appreciate the rhetorical importance of these dialogues if you imagine what would be lost if they were omitted. For instance, suppose the closing dialogue were replaced with a mere *summary* of what the two teachers said. We would miss the casual jocularity of the teachers' banter, which is made ironic by the references to Lorenzo as the "funny *negrito*" and to his looking "like a fly drowned in a glass of milk." The dialogue renders the speaker's experience with evocative specificity; it *shows* us the two teachers' racial attitudes and outlook and the child's puzzled response, rather than simply *telling* us about them. Finally, note that Cofer exercises selectivity about her dialogue. She could have put in more of the dialogue between the two teachers, but she has included just enough to make her point. As she puts it, "The conversation ends there for me."

Story

Cofer's essay includes several stories, examples of things she said or did or that happened to her during that important seventh year of her life. The stories are a part of the reason we read her essay, with interest, to the end. Like the passages of dialogue, the stories *show* us her experiences instead of merely telling us about them. A weakness of some personal essays is that the writer spends too much time relating abstract information about his ideas and experiences without embodying those ideas and experiences through devices like storytelling. If this is a problem in your own writing, try the following: make a point (e.g., "It was a miserable year for me") and begin the next sentence with the simple word "Once . . ."; then let the story grow from there. Later, of course, you can edit out superfluous repetitions of the word "once" while keeping the stories themselves.

Stories within essays entertain readers while also giving "flesh" to ideas; in other words, the stories are purposeful, and illustrative of the essay's themes. To begin his essay on "Looking at Women" (p. 291), Scott Russell Sanders relates a story about the first time *he* "looked at a woman." Elsewhere in the essay he incorporates other personal stories relevant to his theme. The essay is worth studying for its repeated and skillful blending of narrative (i.e., storytelling) and exposition (i.e., passages where Sanders interprets or comments on his experience or informs us through the writings of others).

Citations of Other Texts; Allusions

The term **citation** signifies a reference to another text. Though more typically associated with academic or research essays, citations also appear in some personal and literary essays. The citation may take the form of a direct quotation or a summary and can be used for various purposes: to illustrate a point or idea, to reinforce a writer's argument or reasoning, to bolster reader trust in the authority of the persona, or to add depth to an essay by expanding its range of literary reference.

Sanders's "Looking at Women" discusses the psychology and cultural implications of how men look at women. While personal storytelling provides Sanders with one means of embodying his ideas, his topic is broad and complex and has been addressed, directly or indirectly, by many social scientists, cultural critics, and other writers. Accordingly, Sanders cites some of these writers and their ideas in his essay. His citations (of D. H. Lawrence, Simone de Beauvoir, John Berger, and others) lend greater authority to his persona, as readers appreciate that "he knows what he's talking about." They also enrich the essay's content by acquainting readers with diverse perspectives on the main theme.

An **allusion** is another particular kind of reference that essayists (and other writers) sometimes use. An allusion is a reference, without explicit identification, to a specific person, place, or other text. Like citations, allusions (appropriately used) can broaden an essay's range of literary and cultural reference and enhance the authority of the persona. Since allusions depend on the reader having a shared frame of reference or knowledge with the writer, however, they must be used with caution. The writer has to be careful to use allusions that will be understood by the essay's intended readers. Scott Sanders's two allusions (to Jimmy Carter and *Playboy*) in the following sentence help ground his ideas about "looking at women" in the worlds of contemporary and popular culture:

> While he was president, Jimmy Carter raised a brouhaha by confessing in a *Playboy* interview, of all shady places, that he occasionally felt lust in his heart for women.

Allusion was a favorite device of Henry David Thoreau, as exemplified in this passage from "Where I Lived, and What I Lived For" (p. 1040):

> All memorable events, I should say, transpire in morning time and in a morning atmosphere. The Vedas say, "All intelligences awake with the morning." Poetry and art, and the fairest and most memorable of the actions of men, date from such an hour. All poets and heroes, like Memnon, are the children of Aurora, and emit their music at sunrise.

The allusions here—to "the Vedas" (sacred and ancient Hindu writings), "Memnon" (a heroic ruler of ancient Ethiopia), and "Aurora" (goddess of the dawn in Roman mythology)—lend a special aura of nobility and heroic precedent to the wakeful life that Thoreau is praising.

17

Plays

While one typically reads short stories, poems, and essays in private and silently, a play is a form of performance art; that is, it is a work normally intended for live performance in a theater. A play relates a story; however, rather than narrating (as in a short story), the writer dramatizes the story by means of characters acting and speaking, within a particular imagined setting, on a stage. **Dialogue** is basic to plays. Other important features of the printed text are **scene descriptions,** which describe what the stage looks like for a particular play; **costume descriptions;** and **stage directions,** which describe the movements or gestures of characters on stage. All three of these, which are typically printed in italics, are illustrated in the opening of Susan Glaspell's *Trifles* (p. 300):

> SCENE: *The kitchen in the now abandoned farmhouse of* JOHN WRIGHT, *a gloomy kitchen, and left without having been put in order—the walls covered with a faded wallpaper. . . . In the rear wall at* R[IGHT], *up two steps is a door opening onto stairs leading to the second floor. In the rear wall at* L[EFT] *is a door to the shed and from there to the outside. Between these two doors is an old-fashioned black iron stove. . . . At the rear the shed door opens and the* SHERIFF *comes in followed by the* COUNTY ATTORNEY *and* HALE. *The* SHERIFF *and* HALE *are men in middle life, the* COUNTY ATTORNEY *is a young man; all are much bundled up and go at once to the stove. They are followed by the two women—the* SHERIFF'S *wife,* MRS. PETERS, *first; she is a slight wiry woman, a thin nervous face.* MRS. HALE *is larger and would ordinarily be called more comfortable looking, but she is disturbed now and looks fearfully about as she enters. The women have come in slowly, and stand close together near the door.*
>
> COUNTY ATTORNEY *(at stove rubbing his hands).* This feels good. Come up to the fire, ladies.
>
> MRS. PETERS *(after taking a step forward).* I'm not—cold.

Note how the italicized text helps you to visualize the action and interpret the characters. For example, the men in the play seem to move around confidently; they enter the kitchen "*and go at once to the stove.*" The women, on the other hand, are described as "*nervous*" and fearful; Mrs. Peters takes one "*step forward*" and stops to deliver a very short and halted speech: "I'm not—cold." Already you get a sense of the contrast between the men characters and the women that will be central to the play. Even if you cannot see a particular play performed, dialogue, scene and costume descriptions, and stage directions enable you to do a good production of it in your head.

Plays can follow a range of structural formats. A main division within a play is called an **act,** and full-length plays are typically composed of two or more acts, which may be further subdivided into **scenes.** Some modern and contemporary plays replace acts altogether with a format of multiple scenes or episodes. For instance, Eugene O'Neill's *The Hairy Ape* (p. 554) is composed of eight scenes.

An important subclass of play is the **one-act play,** which bears somewhat the same relationship to a full-length play as a short story does to a novel. One-acts usually dramatize a single incident and include fewer characters than multiple-act plays. In addition, while a full-length play of two hours may represent actions that are supposed to occur over a period of days, months, or years, the time represented by the onstage action of a one-act play usually corresponds closely to real time; that is, a twenty-minute play corresponds to roughly twenty minutes in the lives of the characters.

Setting

Setting refers to the time and place in which the onstage action of a play is supposed to occur. August Wilson's *Fences* (p. 911) dramatizes the story of Troy Maxson, an African American living in a white man's world. Wilson sets his drama in a specific place (i.e., the yard of "*the Maxson household, an ancient two-story brick house set back off a small alley in a big-city neighborhood*"), and he is also particular about the historical time—1957. In fact, he sets the play against the historical background of migration to America's big cities. While children of European descent found abundant opportunities in the cities, Wilson writes, "*The descendants of African slaves were offered no such welcome or participation. . . . They came strong, eager, searching. The city rejected them and they fled and settled along the riverbanks and under bridges in shallow, ramshackle houses made of sticks and tarpaper.*" This description of setting prepares us to understand and appreciate Troy's struggles and motivations, which develop in a context of historically entrenched racism.

Settings do not have to be realistic. *The Hairy Ape* opens in the stokehole of a transatlantic liner, a loud and cramped environment where men labor under circumstances of inhuman oppression and confinement:

> *The room is crowded with men, shouting, cursing, laughing, singing—a confused, inchoate uproar swelling into a sort of unity, a meaning—the bewildered, furious, baffled defiance of a beast in a cage.*

O'Neill indicates that "*The treatment of this scene . . . should by no means be natu-ralistic*"; that is, the scene is meant to distort reality in order to create particular effects. No less than in *Fences,* however, the setting prepares us for what is to fol-low—the drama of "Yank" Smith (a.k.a. "the Hairy Ape"), whose life and death evoke the ferocity and futility of a defiant "beast in a cage."

Characters and Plot

Like short stories, plays may include **flat characters** and **round characters** (see p. 162); the main character is known as the **protagonist,** and his/her chief oppo-nent in the drama is the **antagonist.**

For purposes of analysis, critics sometimes divide the **plots** of plays into a **ris-ing action,** which introduces the characters and establishes the conflict; a **climax,** in which the conflict reaches its height in the form of some crucial action or de-cision; a **falling action,** in which the conflict moves toward resolution; and a **res-olution,** in which the central conflict is resolved. As this scheme suggests, the es-sential ingredient in any plot is conflict, which may include—but is not limited to—a conflict between protagonist and antagonist. Conflict—physical, per-sonal, social, moral, and/or cosmic—helps to define the characters and themes of the play and to sustain the interest of readers or viewers.

Trifles is set in the farmhouse kitchen of John Wright, who has recently died under mysterious circumstances. Two women and several men (including the women's husbands) are investigating the scene of Wright's death. While the men leave the kitchen and pursue fruitless lines of inquiry, the two women chance upon evidence that both incriminates the dead man's wife (Minnie) and unveils the abusive circumstances under which she lived. Hence the focal conflict: Should the women be law-abiding citizens and turn over the evidence to the men (who remain ignorant of it), or, out of compassion for Minnie, should they conceal the evidence and thus break the law? In plays, as in life, conflict is seldom single and simple but multiple and complex. Thus in *Trifles* one conflict interrelates with others. For instance, one of the women feels an inner conflict of guilt over having neglected Minnie in her unhappy marriage. Additional conflict occurs between the women, who discover evidence among "kitchen things," and the men, who belittle these things as "trifles." At the end of the play the two women make a choice about what to do with their incriminating evidence, and the central conflict is resolved. As in all good plays, however, readers or viewers are left with enough unanswered questions to make discussion or responsive writing interest-ing. What if the women had made a different choice about the evidence? Did they do the "right" thing? Who decides what is or isn't morally "right"?

Dialogue

Dialogue is the primary mode of characterization and of advancing plot in plays. Consider this brief passage of dialogue from *Trifles:*

COUNTY ATTORNEY: . . . [Y]ou and Mrs. Wright were neighbors. I suppose you were friends, too.

MRS. HALE: *(shaking her head)*. I've not seen much of her of late years. I've not been in this house—it's more than a year.

COUNTY ATTORNEY: *(crossing to women U[pper] C[enter])*. And why was that? You didn't like her?

MRS. HALE: I liked her all well enough. Farmers' wives have their hands full, Mr. Henderson. And then—

COUNTY ATTORNEY: Yes—?

MRS. HALE: *(looking about)*. It never seemed a very cheerful place.

COUNTY ATTORNEY: No—it's not cheerful. I shouldn't say she had the homemaking instinct.

MRS. HALE: Well, I don't know as Wright had, either.

COUNTY ATTORNEY: You mean that they didn't get on very well?

MRS. HALE: No, I don't mean anything. But I don't think a place'd be any cheerfuller for John Wright's being in it.

The County Attorney initiates and controls the conversation; confident and aggressive, he presses Mrs. Hale for answers. She, by contrast, maintains a tentative attitude about events and hesitates to interpret them ("I don't mean anything"). The dialogue underscores a broad contrast between the men and women in the play: While the men take an aggressive attitude toward the truth (and achieve nothing), the women take a "wait and see" stance (and discover everything). As for plot, Mrs. Hale's last line is one of many clues in the play that define John Wright as a cold and cruel man who brought on his own demise.

In *Tone Clusters* (p. 407), Joyce Carol Oates departs radically from the kind of *realistic* dialogue used in *Trifles*. Frank and Emily Gulick, "good" citizens and parents, who happen to have a rapist/murderer for a son, are the subjects of an interview for the mass media. Their interviewer, a male voiceover identified simply as "VOICE," never appears on stage. Rather than being realistic, the dialogue is **expressionistic;** that is, Oates exaggerates and distorts reality in order to render the world as we feel it rather than as we literally see it:

VOICE: Of today's pressing political issues   the rise in violent crime most concerns American citizens   Number-one political issue of Mr. and Mrs. Gulick   tell our viewers your opinion?

FRANK: In this state,
the state of New Jersey

EMILY: Oh it's everywhere

FRANK: there's capital punishment supposedly

EMILY: But the lawyers   the lawyers get them off,

FRANK: you bet
There's public defenders the taxpayer pays

EMILY: Oh, it's   it's out of control
(like that, what is it   "acid rain"

FRANK: it can fall on you anywhere,

> EMILY: the sun is too hot too:
> BOTH: the "greenhouse effect") . . .

The characters speak in fractured sentences; the dialogue is unnaturally redundant; syntax or word order is jumbled; and disturbing themes and impressions evoked by the words seem to overshadow the words themselves. The dialogue conveys a sense of the Gulicks as human yet like automatons or puppets, as they mouth, with mechanical predictability, the slogans, fears, and attitudes of their culture.

A **monologue** is a long speech by a single character. For instance, in scene eight of *The Hairy Ape*, Yank (the protagonist) finds himself in "*The monkey house at the Zoo.*" Yank has spent most of the play living down an insinuation that he is a "hairy ape," and now he comes face-to-face with a real-life gorilla, whom he addresses familiarly:

> Say, yuh're some hard-lookin' guy, ain't yuh? I seen lots of tough nuts dat de gang called gorillas, but yuh're de foist real one I ever seen. Some chest yuh got, and shoulders, and dem arms and mits! I bet yuh got a punch in eider fist dat'd knock 'em all silly. . . .

At the end of act two, scene two, of Fences, Troy Maxson feels ultimate disaster closing in upon him. Troy is an African American who has suffered racial injustice but is no mere "victim"; in many ways—physical and other—he is a giant of a man: caring and cruel, magnetic and alienating, powerful yet flawed. Alone on stage, he directs his anger at no ordinary enemy but at the king of enemies— "Mr. Death."

> TROY *(with a quiet rage that threatens to consume him):* All right . . . Mr. Death. See now . . . I'm gonna tell you what I'm gonna do. I'm gonna take and build me a fence around this yard. See? I'm gonna build me a fence around what belongs to me. And then I want you to stay on the other side. See? You stay over there until you're ready for me. Then you come on. Bring your army. Bring your sickle. Bring your wrestling clothes. I ain't gonna fall down on my vigilance this time. You ain't gonna sneak up on me no more. When you ready for me . . . when the top of your list say Troy Maxson . . . that's when you come around here. You come up and knock on the front door. . . .

The monologue reveals to us Troy's inner essence. Powerfully imaginative, he perceives death as no mere idea but as a physical presence poised and ready to attack. He fears death and yet can reduce it to a tangible human shape ("Mr. Death") whom he bosses and bullies as freely as he does his own family ("You stay. . . . Then you come on. . . . Bring your wrestling clothes. . . . You come up. . . ."). Finally, even as he smells his own demise, Troy can taunt and belittle "Mr. Death" for trying to "sneak up" instead of "[knocking] on the front door." The monologue shows us the qualities of imagination, arrogance, and defiance that are at once Troy's sources of power and his defining weaknesses.

18

Notebooks and Journals

There are times when the world so exasperates me that I feel I cannot go on living in it for another moment and I want to disappear for good. But then, if I happen to obtain some nice white paper . . . I decide that I can put up with things as they are a little longer.

—SEI SHŌNAGON

Technically speaking, notebooks and journals are not a literary genre. They adhere to no particular standards of form, structure, or content the way short stories, poems, essays, and plays do. In fact their essence is *freedom*. A *journal* or *notebook* (the two terms are used interchangeably in this book) can include writing in any form (prose or poetry, dialogue or story, simple list or developed analysis) and of any length (from single word to multi-page draft). It can be introspective and outward looking, personal and impersonal, emotional and analytical. It can incorporate drawings, photographs, clippings, musical notations, and memorabilia that complement or relate to the writing. Finally, the material within a notebook can be an end in itself, writing done for the intrinsic pleasure or value of writing; or it can be a means toward some other end, such as drafting and revising work for publication.

Although not all writers keep notebooks and journals, they merit an introductory chapter in this part of *Reading and Writing from Literature* because without them, writing in the other genres might never take place. It is hard to imagine writers producing short stories, poems, essays, or plays without first doing the kind of quick, preliminary, and often rough writing characteristic of notebooks and journals.

This chapter should be read in conjunction with Chapters 3–5, which talk specifically about the kinds of materials you can include in notebook. Looking ahead, in Part VI of this book you will find five interchapters containing selections from the notebooks and journals of prominent writers. These selections should inspire you with ideas for using and developing your own notebooks.

Ralph Waldo Emerson wrote that "[T]he one good in life is concentration; the one evil is dissipation." We live in an age of distraction, and it sometimes seems we want to fill our heads with everything *but* our own thoughts. Notebooks and journals are about the life of the mind, about getting reacquainted with our own thoughts.

An Ideal Democracy of Thoughts

In an ideal political democracy every individual is accepted and has a voice, however personally objectionable he or she may seem to various other members of the society; and as soon as one person is excluded, or the rights of one are denied, the ideal is torn and the whole fabric begins to come undone. It's the same with the entries in a notebook. If the notebook is going to succeed and the fabric hold, it has to be inclusive enough to allow in everything—good, bad, and indifferent, pleasant and unpleasant.

What follows is a sample day's harvest from one notebook:

An old woman with a waltz tied to her back

I look forward to night and to sunrise.

(A sentence from a book): "If you don't take pains, everything is difficult."

in my own limited way

"There's just so much in this head of mine I can't trust."

a heart like a sponge

I saved the money and read the books but forgot to live.

I always tear up when I compliment somebody to their face. Weird.

An article on "Oppositional Defiant Disorder." Every deviation from "normal" behavior in children has a label, a literature, and probably a medication.

A rain-beaten weed plastered in mud. Too much rain.

My muscles are crying out, Have you forgotten us?

Nothing too special here. . . . Then again, who knows? The danger of summarily rejecting a thought that seems uninteresting or "dumb" is twofold. First, by excluding one thought—a "dumb" one—you set a precedent for excluding others that might be wonderful. Second, you may not really know whether a note is "good" or "dumb" until months or even years after you first wrote it down. Literary history is full of examples of writers recording ideas, forgetting them for years, and then suddenly rediscovering them, recognizing their hidden wealth, and working them up into first-rate stories, poems, and other works.

The poet William Stafford began each day by sitting at a window and writing down anything that came to his mind; the phrase or image of the moment became the impetus from which he spun out his poems, sometimes several in a day— good, average, and bad. Stafford worked with an attitude of *welcome anything* and discussed this approach at length in his remarkable book *Writing the Australian Crawl* (University of Michigan Press, 1978):

> There are worthy human experiences that become possible only if you accept successive, limited human commitments, and one such is the sustained life of writing. . . . A writer must write bad poems, as they come, among the better, and not scorn the "bad" ones.

By humbly and conscientiously jotting down even a threadbare idea, something plain or trivial, Stafford enhanced exponentially his prospects for collecting the other, better, ideas that made him one of America's premier poets.

Stafford's example is worth a truckload of books on "inspiration." To be "inspired" means *not to hesitate.* "This thought seems dumb. This idea has been said before." Fine. Acknowledge that, and write it down anyway. Another dumb idea? Write that one down, too. Inspiration is an avalanche that begins with a pebble; *should I write it down* is the little stone that holds the dam.

The Art of the Reflective Pause

Sustained work at a desk is desirable and necessary for good writing; however, to limit writing to the official workspace is, literally, to shut writing inside a room, a *box.* As we saw back in Chapter 4, being a writer is not just a matter of what you do at your desk but of how you work when you are away from it. Writers are people with a singular ability for being *well* interrupted. A poet, or poetic soul, is not so much a person with a special thought or experience as someone who makes a habit of momentarily stopping whatever else he or she is doing at the time to *write the thought or experience down.*

The key concept here is to *pause and reflect in the middle of . . .* , and you can pause to reflect and write in the middle of anything . . . for instance, of walking. William Wordsworth's sister, Dorothy, recalled that the poet conceived some of his best work while strolling up and down in his garden. Henry David Thoreau measured the length of his composing by the length of his walk. ("If shut up in the house," recalled his friend Emerson, "he did not write at all.") People who grew up in William Faulkner's town of Oxford, Mississippi, can remember the great novelist suddenly pausing during a walk to stare up transfixed at an old house or into blank space, quietly contemplating his fictional worlds.

You can also write in the middle of gardening, folding clothes, getting dressed, making the bed, doing dishes, cooking, feeding a baby, stepping out of the car, waiting at a traffic light, standing in a line, riding a bus or train, walking between classes, taking a break on the job, strolling in a park, or lying awake in bed. (The novelist William Saroyan once said he could have become the greatest writer in America with all the ideas he had failed to write down when he was in bed.) Some writers even claim to write *better* amid distractions. John Keats sometimes liked to compose in rooms humming with conversation. So did the philosopher Søren Kierkegaard, who wrote "[M]y imagination works best when I'm sitting by myself in a large gathering, where bustle and noise provide a substrate for my will to hold on to its object . . .".

The Japanese poet Bashō (1644–1694) was a master of the contemplative pause. Bashō liked to travel, and he took writing materials wherever he went. The following is an excerpt from his book *The Narrow Road to the Deep North*, a memoir of interwoven prose and poetry:

I went to a snow-viewing party.

Gladly will I sell
For profit,
Dear merchants of the town,
My hat laden with snow.

I saw a traveller on my way.

Even a horse
Is a spectacle,
I cannot help stopping to see it
On the morning of snow.

I spent the whole afternoon at the beach.

Over the darkened sea,
Only the voice of a flying duck
Is visible—
In soft white.

Bashō's philosophy? *A passing thought is the delight of passing time. . . . Grab it!* One can imagine him rereading his notes, at any time or any place, and revising or adding to them or musing on them for the pleasure of contemplation. There is no moment in a day when a person can't be inspired to pause, think, and write something down. Bashō had a strong *will to reflect* that was on call at all times.

Cultivating the Private Life

"But now," someone might interject, "it's time for a reality check. Packing writing materials, pausing to reflect, recording thoughts and impressions, keeping a notebook. . . . These sound like wonderful ideas in theory, but frankly they leave me exhausted. After all, we live in the twenty-first century, and this is the real world. Who has the time?" These are good objections, and if they can't be answered satisfactorily this whole book is pointless. For that matter, *literature* is pointless, since it takes *time* to make and read good writing. These days it seems as if everyone and everything we meet is laying some sort of claim on our time, attention, and resources. Old realities like private life and leisure time seem dangerously close to extinction; and if *they* go, the writers and audiences for literature will surely vanish along with them.

Fortunately, we do not have to accept this gloomy scenario. If time and solitude are not handed to us (and they aren't), we can, with daily effort, *create* them. Following are sketches of four writers whose lives show that writing and private life can thrive even in the most inhospitable of environments. All four of the writers faced this question: How can you *concentrate* your energies enough to sustain a notebook, or a writing life generally, in a world that constantly tempts and impels you to *dissipate* or scatter them?

Emily Dickinson

Few writers have been more preoccupied with this question than Emily Dickinson (1830–1886). Dickinson lived in Amherst, Massachusetts, a town that frowned on women writing "intellectual" poetry of the sort she composed. Her father believed that for a woman, intellectual life should stop at the end of college, to be replaced by a life of selfless service to the family. Her mother was withdrawn and sickly and in later years required constant attention from her daughter. Though assisted by servants and a sister, Emily was responsible for many other domestic duties as well.

It was not just the demands on her time that threatened to dissipate her energy; it was also what she lacked: chiefly, any significant encouragement to write poetry. During her lifetime hardly anyone knew who Emily Dickinson *was;* those who met her had no idea they were encountering one of the two or three greatest poets in the American literary canon. Only a handful of her poems were published before her death, and those few individuals who read and admired her work generally pronounced it flawed and amateurish. In this context her concentration is perhaps the single most remarkable fact of her life. Living in circumstances that could have scattered the energies of a lesser person, she stuck passionately to her task and wrote, over a span of three decades, some eighteen hundred poems that delineate, like no others, the landscape of the human soul.

How would Emily Dickinson have fared had she lived in our day? Clearly, as a woman she would have more opportunities available to her now than she did over a century ago; but as a poet she would have faced an exponentially greater number of temptations to distraction: telephone, radio, TV cable and satellite, faxes and cell phones, the Internet, videos, cars, shopping malls, the enticements and the means to be a hundred different places quickly or instantaneously, physically or virtually. . . . All good things in themselves; but they complicate the question of how to spend our time. Today we are no longer asking, "Should I do A or B?" (as Emily Dickinson might have) but "Should I do A, B, C, . . . or Z?" And the proliferating choices and opportunities mean that we must learn to say no about twenty times more often than Emily Dickinson ever had to.

Dickinson may have been reflecting on this need of the soul to define and protect its own boundaries when she wrote her poem "The Soul selects her own Society":

> The Soul selects her own Society—
> Then—shuts the Door—
> To her divine Majority—
> Present no more—
>
> Unmoved—she notes the Chariots—pausing—
> At her low Gate—
> Unmoved—an Emperor be kneeling
> Upon her Mat—
>
> I've known her—from an ample nation—
> Choose One—
> Then—close the Valves of her attention—
> Like Stone—

The Soul is "divine." "Chariots"—evoking glitter, speed, and grace, the glamour and accomplishments of mighty nations—do not impress her in the least. An "Emperor"—a powerful personage who could buy her off with wealth, fame, or other mundane riches—cannot turn her head. She is "Unmoved," possessed of an immense inner power that deflects seducers. Ruthlessly selective about what she notices or ignores, she knows how and when to "close the Valves of her attention." When she chooses she becomes impenetrable, "Like Stone."

There may be no better, more succinct affirmation of the private life than this sentence of Dickinson's: "There is always this to be grateful for, that one is oneself and not someone else."

Tillie Olsen

The life of Tillie Olsen (see p. 1192) provides a second example of writing and the private life. The child of poor Russian emigrants, Tillie Olsen had to quit school after the eleventh grade to work. For some twenty years she held a variety of jobs—as a housekeeper, waitress, meat trimmer in a packing house, typist, secretary—while also raising four children. In addition, she helped organize workers in the meatpacking industry (and was jailed for a time for her efforts).

Tillie Olsen also found that she loved to write and *had* to write. So she wrote on the bus going back and forth to work and, as she put it, in "the deep night hours for as long as I could stay awake, after the kids were in bed, after the household tasks were done, sometimes during." Her short story "As I Stand Here Ironing" (see p. 343), in which the narrator "writes" her story while simultaneously pushing an iron, is symbolic of Olsen's own life and writing, which continually overlapped. Tillie Olsen *made* time for the writing that gave her ownership of her own life.

Olsen's experience shows how far removed a private life is from the merely *self-absorbed* one. Her "escape" into writing was not a one-way movement *away from* jobs, tasks, appointments, and responsibilities. Olsen was long active as a labor organizer and later as a feminist. Paradoxically, her insistence on a private life empowered her to *return* to community life as a stronger, more conscious and intentional human being.

Make Your Own Walden

Henry David Thoreau

Walden Pond near Concord, Massachusetts, for the last century and a half has been inseparably linked with the name of Henry David Thoreau. Thoreau built and lived in a small cabin there from 1845 to 1847 and published a classic account of his experiences (*Walden; Or Life in the Woods,* 1854). Thoreau described his time at Walden as an "experiment" in simple economical living during which he did just enough *paid* labor to provide for his basic bodily needs while dedicating most of his time and energies to what he called "the art of living well": thinking, writing in his journal, and enjoying and contemplating, as poet and naturalist, the wonders of nature. As he put it, he "chose to be rich by making [his] wants few." He sensed an urgency about his experiment: "I went to the woods because I wished to live deliberately, to front only the essential facts of life, and see if I could not learn what it had to teach, and not, when I came to die, discover that I had not lived."

Ever since *Walden* was first published people have praised and criticized both Thoreau the man and his experiment; yet neither time nor criticism has tarnished Thoreau's great imaginative achievement, which is the *idea* of Walden: the vision of a life in which contemplation is primary, and working to survive is secondary. Of course, this is not to say that working to survive is unimportant or nonessential; it *is* essential, but it should not be the ultimate or consuming purpose of a human life. The philosopher Aristotle put it well: We are *not-at-leisure* (we work to survive) in order to *be-at-leisure* (to contemplate).[1] According to Thoreau and Aristotle, contemplation should not just be a "break" from work but

---

1. See Joseph Pieper, *Leisure: The Basis of Culture* (South Bend, IN: St. Augustine's Press, 1998, p. 4).

the informing center of our lives that gives meaning to our jobs or employment; and if it is our center, we must claim it immediately and persistently, even if only for a few moments of each day.

As for the meaning of "contemplation," you can define it for yourself by recalling a comment in Chapter 4: "Perhaps some of the best moments we have anymore are 'odd' moments occuring between this task and that; and we may do most of the things we love most in a moment we had to steal." Within the context in which we have just been using it, "contemplation" concerns those "things we love most," which may include writing and much else.

So conceived, the idea of Walden is the same as the idea of a notebook or journal. However tedious your job, however demanding your various commitments, when you write in your notebook, recording what you think or see, you are making your own Walden. Unowned, and temporarily freed from your socioeconomic functionality, you are as much in Walden time as Thoreau himself was 160 years ago.

"I am astonished at the wonderful retirement through which I move," Thoreau wrote in a letter to a friend.[2] If challenged to produce a "pocket" Thoreau, a one-sentence digest of the author's main and persistent message, I would suggest: *Be at least semiretired all your life.* Possibly this could be a one-sentence digest of the message of all great literature. Certainly it is hard to imagine good literature thriving or surviving in a world of total work.

Thoreau understood retirement differently than we usually do. Typically, we treat "retirement" as a *future* event, as something that occurs after you have been gainfully employed for a number of years or when you reach a certain, usually advanced, age. Ironically, retirement thus understood as future event serves to justify its evil twin—workaholism: by working harder and longer hours *now* we seem to assure ourselves of a more carefree and luxurious retirement *then*. Such belief seems misguided. Consider the person who works slavishly till age sixty-five, consoling himself with dreams of a glorious retirement, only to die of a stroke at age sixty-five and two months. By contrast, Thoreau insisted upon retirement as a present reality.

> Keep the time, observe the hours of the universe, not of the cars. What are three-score years and ten hurriedly and coarsely lived to moments of divine leisure in which your life is coincident with the life of the universe? We live too fast and coarsely, just as we eat too fast, and do not know the true savor of our food.[3]

Thoreau's modes of semiretirement were probably too radical for most of us; our commitments and tasks are more multiple and fixed than his. Thoreau's

---

2. Henry David Thoreau, *Letters to Various Persons* (Folcroft Library Editions, 1971, p. 54).
3. Henry David Thoreau, *A Writer's Journal,* ed. Laurence Stapleton (New York: Dover, 1960, p. 93).

desire, however, was not that we imitate his lifestyle literally but that we cultivate a *greater* sense of leisure than we currently enjoy. So how can we be semiretired, starting today—at age eighteen or thirty or fifty? Here are a few ways (not an exhaustive list):

- By developing the habit of deliberately pausing in the middle of tasks to contemplate or enjoy things (with eyes, ears, nose, tongue, skin).
- By making a habit of jotting down our passing thoughts.
- By doing something creative: making a picture, a carving, a sweater, or a poem; by conversing, meditating, dancing, walking for pleasure, making music.
- By playing with children; that is, by learning retirement from the masters of the art.
- By reducing the number of our "affairs." If we can't "let [our] affairs be as two or three," as Thoreau recommends in *Walden,* then why not as five or six, or even nine or ten, as opposed to twenty or thirty?
- By doing nothing. To do nothing in the Thoreauvian sense is to clear out and straighten our often cluttered minds, exert careful control over what we let in and out of them, and leave only the most precious items inside. This is a daily challenge. *Doing nothing* like Thoreau is, paradoxically, a form of exertion; or more precisely, a contemplative pause between hard labors:

  > We must heap up a great pile of doing, for a small diameter of being. Is it not imperative on us that we *do* something, if we only work in a tread-mill? And, indeed, some sort of revolving is necessary to produce a centre and nucleus of being. What exercise is to the body, employment is to the mind and morals.[4]

Heather (high school teacher)

If Thoreau were alive today, he would no doubt respect Heather, a high school teacher in northern Utah. In addition to teaching full-time and parenting three children, Heather is active in several social, civic, and cultural organizations. During most of her waking hours she is occupied with activities that will be scrutinized and judged by others—students, peers and professional colleagues, her principal, her family, and friends. Various parts of herself and of her day are effectively "owned" by diverse people and institutions, and much of the time she seems to enjoy little or no personal autonomy. She doesn't complain about this, however; Heather finds social participation and service of various kinds rewarding and even fun, but she knows they aren't *all* there is to life. She needs a time when she can do, be, and think as she wants to.

---

4. *Letters to Various Persons,* p. 99.

Her solution is to insist on a period of daily retirement. Though it is not a picturesque pond in New England, Heather has her own Walden. At 5:30 every morning she gets up, dresses, and (weather permitting) sits on her front stoop for a few minutes "doing nothing. I don't even try to think, or be creative. I just sit and let the morning work on me." In her notebook she wrote a meditation about these moments of inaction:

> The first requirement of being a thinker is not to insist on having thoughts; the first requirement of being a poet is not to insist on writing poems. Before the thought or the poem there is sitting quietly in a favorite place (for me, it's the front stoop) doing and thinking nothing. The source of all thought and poetry: Life 101.

Next, Heather sits at her desk, lights a scented candle, and writes exactly what she wants to: reflections, poetry, meditations. "I absolutely refuse to write lesson plans or 'to do' lists, grade student papers, or do any practical business during this time. It doesn't matter how messy the day ahead of me looks. This time is *sacred.*" When the rest of the household stirs to life at 7:00, Heather gets up from her desk contented, energized, and "reassured that I still have a soul."

Heather's notebook contains an excellent summary of what Walden time is all about:

> Life fills our heads; it's up to us to clear them.

Generic Ideas for Writing in Response to Published Notebooks and Journals

While great short stories or poems can intimidate us with their polish and perfection and encourage us to leave composing to the masters, a published notebook or journal that you read can have the opposite effect. Few kinds of writing can do more to catalyze thought and writing from you, the reader. Notebook and journal entries are typically preliminary and unfinished; they invite you to shed your inhibitions and participate. The writer delivers the opening conversational gambit, and you build on it. An engaging notebook or journal writer is a sort of master conversationalist who doesn't dominate talk but gets you to "say" the most interesting and surprising things yourself.

Below are ideas for writing to use as you read the selections of published notebooks and journals included as "interchapters" in Part VI of this book. Try the ideas that suit you at a given moment, invent others of your own, and repeat those that work best.

1. Write short commentaries on any notebook entries that strike you. You can use the sample commentaries on G. C. Lichtenberg and Elias Canetti on pages 52–54 of Chapter 4 as models.

2. Record any stray thoughts you have while reading, whether they are related or apparently unrelated to the content of the text. Remember Emerson's observation: "[Y]ou only read to start your own team."

3. Copy down phrases or passages that strike you. Build a collection of favorite quotations that you can reread for amusement, for reflection, or as spurs to additional writing.

Watch your thoughts closely as you copy a favorite passage: the physical process of copying in longhand sometimes suggests unrelated but interesting ideas. For instance, Tom was in the middle of writing out a sentence from Jules Renard's *Journal* (Interchapter IV):

God will often say to us, "You are not in heaven for fun!"

when he thought of the following, which he turned aside to jot down:

Hell would be a completely childproof society.

What Tom wrote is quite different in content—or dissociated—from the sentence he was copying, and his experience illustrates a psychological curiosity: that to look hard at one thing—an object, an idea, a quotation—can point you toward something else. *Seek and you shall find* something different, and perhaps even better, than what you were looking for. If you have a sudden lucky thought as Tom did, pause to jot it down. Take your time. Your accidental thought could be important. To read more about collecting quotations, see pages 56–58 in Chapter 4.

4. Record references to the names of authors, books, or other resources that pique your interest. Notebooks and journals can introduce you to a variety of fascinating writers from diverse time periods, cultures, and languages; and if you like a particular writer's notebook or journal you may also want to read his or her novels, poems, stories, essays, plays, or other works.

5. Note any special and interesting ideas of ways to use a notebook. For instance, if the writer records anecdotes, makes lists of flowers, or writes a dialogue, make a note that you could use your own notebook for similar purposes.

ACTIVITIES FOR WRITING AND DISCUSSION

1. Describe your own history, if any, as a notebook or journal writer. When did you first start keeping a journal or notebook? Why? Did someone inspire you to do so? What physical materials did you use when you first started? Have you kept a journal or notebook consistently since then, or intermittently? Explain

why. How have the physical materials used in your journal keeping changed over time? Have your reasons for keeping a journal changed? Explain.

  a. Do a first draft of this "history" early in the term.
  b. Take notes toward revising the draft periodically during the term.
  c. Prepare a final (for now) version of your story at the end of the term, giving some special attention to how your journal/notebook habits and aims have changed during this class.

2. Do Activity # 1 on page 61 of Chapter 4.

3. Reread your notebook periodically and make any revisions or additions that occur to you.

  a. Reread all or a portion of your notebook, with pen or pencil in hand.
  b. Underline or bracket phrases, sentences, ideas, or passages (long or short) that strike you, for whatever reason.
  c. Reread the marked passages, choose one that seems most interesting to you now, and share and discuss the passage with a partner, small group, or friend.

  or

  In the margins annotate or "talk back" to those passages that strike you. Write about:
  • Additional thoughts the item suggests to you
  • Why an item interests you
  • How you might like, at some point, to expand the item

  d. If you wish, revise a favorite passage or entry by using a Topic/Form Grid (see Chapter 5), one of the revision strategies described in Chapter 12, or some other strategy of your own choosing.

4. Periodically during the quarter or semester, take a few minutes in class to share with a partner or small group some particularly striking entry you have made in your notebook. The entry can be of any length, from a phrase to several pages. Discuss what inspired the entry, why you like it, and what (if anything) else you might like to do with it. If you wish, invite feedback or suggestions from your partner or group.

An Introduction to Figurative Language

The topic of figurative language has inspired a vast literature of books and articles. This part of *Reading and Writing from Literature* is a modest attempt to show how a knowledge of figures of speech, or tropes, can enhance our experience of literature.

A **figure** or **trope** is a word or phrase used in a way that significantly changes its standard or literal meaning; **figurative language** is the term used to describe all nonliteral uses of language. Tropes—metaphors, paradoxes, and ironies, among others—seem to be interwoven into our very processes of thinking and saturate our daily speech and writing. For instance, "Time flies" is an everyday figure which does not mean literally that time sprouts wings like a bird, but rather that it moves swiftly like a bird. Expressive figures or tropes make good writing because they express complex ideas and feelings succinctly and memorably. For example, we know the impact that a cannonball can have, while thoughts may strike us as rather insubstantial. Joseph Joubert's trope "A thought is a thing as real as a cannon ball [*sic*]" reminds us in a remarkably forceful way that a thought is a thing with real and material impact. (It was somebody's thought, after all, that invented the cannonball.) Figurative language tends to abound, as Emerson said, at "the moment our discourse rises above the ground line of familiar facts and is inflamed with passion or exalted by thought." If you want more figures in your writing, you can hardly do better than to live a more concentrated and intentional life.

While tropes are important in many ways, I will single out just three.

First, tropes stimulate thought. The writer of a good trope begins a thought for the reader to "finish." If writing in general can get us to think, figures—which are big ideas in small packages—can prompt us to think especially hard and imaginatively and therefore to write well and imaginatively also.

Second, tropes create mental pictures that make abstract ideas more concrete and memorable. In his notebooks, G. C. Lichtenberg quotes a line from an eighteenth-century magazine, *The Spectator:* "The whole man must move together." Lichtenberg annotates: "To the whole man I reckon head, heart, mouth, and hands, and it is a great art to drive them whole and undivided through wind and weather till they reach the very end, where all movement ceases." Lichtenberg's trope visualizes several parts of a human being—"head, heart, mouth, and hands"—moving through "wind and weather," i.e., all kinds of life trials and troubles. To picture a human being as a collection of parts that have the potential to move in conflicting directions affords a novel and accurate visual image of our contradictory lives; think how often our "head" wills one thing while our "heart" and "hands" do exactly the opposite.

Finally, a knowledge of figurative language gives you a powerful tool for interpreting stories, poems, essays, plays, and all other kinds of discourse, spoken and written. Identifying and understanding an important figure in a text can help clarify the meaning of the whole work. For example, Arthur Schopenhauer's "On Thinking for Oneself" (p. 691) is an intellectually demanding collection of compact statements known as **aphorisms.** One small metaphor in Schopenhauer's text, "the book of the world," can serve as a sort of key to his larger meaning.

Obviously, the metaphor does not mean that the world is a literal book made of paper and binding, but rather that you can in some sense "read" the world and learn from it, the same as you can a literal book. The content of your "reading" would include memories, ideas, experiences, personal relationships, nature, and much more. In addition, since this "book" is as large as the globe, you can read it anywhere and anytime. Schopenhauer's trope is a concise way of saying that learning never stops and that it is not confined to the school or university. This point, in turn, reflects his larger argument that we must make a habit of thinking for ourselves instead of uncritically borrowing our ideas from others.

19

Figurative Language

Metaphor

> We do not think good metaphors are important, but I think a good metaphor is something even the police should keep an eye on. . . .
>
> —G. C. LICHTENBERG

A metaphor is an implicit comparison between dissimilar items that evokes new or vivid ways of perceiving, knowing, and/or feeling. For instance, "Keep an open mind, but don't take off the doors" is a metaphor. Here the "mind" is being compared with something vastly dissimilar to it—something that has doors, like a room or a house. Obviously, viewed literally the mind is not a tangible physical space containing chairs, tables, pictures on the walls, and carpeting. On closer look, however, we see a similarity: like a house, the mind also has its "doors" (eyes, ears, nose, mouth) that can be either opened or shut. If these doors are completely shut, a person is literally senseless and as good as dead; on the other hand, if you "take off the doors" anything whatsoever—the myriad noises and distractions of daily life—can get in and overrun the place, just as nature or robbers (if unobstructed) might lay waste a house. The metaphor suggests that you should keep an open mind while exercising careful control over what you let into it.

The philosopher Aristotle said that metaphor "produces knowledge," and many modern linguists have agreed. In 1980 George Lakoff and Mark Johnson published a fascinating book entitled *Metaphors We Live By* in which they noted that many metaphors are so much a part of our ordinary thinking that we no longer even recognize them as metaphors. For example, we commonly talk about *time as money*, in expressions like "I *spent* a lot of time on that book," "I *wasted* my time," or "*Invest* your time wisely." Another common metaphor is *Love is madness,* reflected in such expressions as "I'm *crazy* about her," "She drives me *out of my mind,*" "He *raves* about her." Or there is the *Love is a patient* metaphor: "This is a *sick* relationship," "They have a *healthy* marriage," "Their relationship is in *good shape.*"

If you pay close attention to your speech and writing, you will notice that metaphors repeatedly surface in your own language. Consider, for instance, these examples from various student notebooks:

> You can only do your best, then *wash* your hands [not *literally* "wash your hands" but *figuratively* forget your mistakes or inadequacies and move on]

> I like to *walk around* an idea before I act on it [not literally "walk on two legs" but ponder the idea from different perspectives]

> We *mask* our true motives [not literally "wear a facial covering" but conceal our purposes through silence or subterfuge]

Other examples underscore how the metaphors we use reflect, and may even help shape, the way we think and view the world. For instance, if we say, "Life is a football game" we imply (without necessarily being conscious of it) a very particular concept of life as competitive (with winners and losers), violent, bruise-ridden, and goal-oriented. On the other hand, if we say, "Life is a dance" we imply that life is friendly, cooperative, peaceful, and enjoyable in and of itself without reference to goals. Of course, the football metaphor, which often goes unspoken but is assumed (many people *feel* that life is a violent competitive sport even if they never actually say so), is much more popular than a dance metaphor would be, and this seems to reflect a widespread societal assumption that we live in a "dog eat dog" world, that "things are nasty out there." Any citizen of a modern industrial society who says or acts as if "life is a dance" is a social anomaly, an idealist and a dreamer, and probably a "poet" in the broadest sense of the word, a childlike or contemplative person.

A literary text that puzzles you now will become clearer if you can identify and interpret its metaphors. Adrienne Rich's essay "A Leak in History" (p. 695) contains a metaphor in its title: Rich compares history with something that develops leaks, i.e., a pipe. Understood literally, "history" and a water pipe are radically dissimilar; but by yoking them together Rich makes us think about how they are alike. She is suggesting that like a pipe that carries a flow of water, history can develop "leaks"—cracks where the water spills out—the "water" being, in this case, cherished traditions or collective historical memory. She could have expressed this idea more literally by saying that we are "losing our connection" with the past, but such a statement is far less complex, visual, and evocative than the one she chose. Amazingly, the four plain words of the title afford a key to the meaning of Rich's whole essay: the body of her text elaborates, with specific arguments and examples, on the title metaphor.

Steps for Analyzing or "Unpacking" a Metaphor

As the Rich example shows, you can go a long way toward understanding a person's meanings and assumptions by identifying and interpreting her metaphors. Therefore it is useful to consider metaphors carefully, to "unpack" them. Here is how:

1. Decide what two things are being compared.
2. List the dissimilarities between the two things being compared.
3. Identify how the two things, which are so dissimilar in literal terms, are on closer view similar.
4. Gauge the power of the metaphor by rephrasing it as a baldly literal statement and comparing the two versions.

Here are analyses of a few metaphors to illustrate this method:

To work is to butt heads with time.

Work and time are compared to two heads colliding, as in a football scrimmage. The metaphor suggests that work is a way of challenging or combatting time and perhaps of overcoming it in some sense, as one linesman overpowers another. A literal translation of the idea—"To work is to overcome time"—is less compelling than the trope, with its visual portrayal of work as heroic and strenuous.

> My son my executioner,
>   I take you in my arms,
> Quiet and small and just astir,
>   And whom my body warms.

This opening stanza of a Donald Hall poem (see p. 378) contains an extremely bold metaphor: an infant son (cuddly, cute, soft, and helpless) and an executioner (large, muscular, and deadly) could not be more dissimilar. Seeing the two joined, we must ask how they are alike; and as we continue reading and finish the poem, we find that this baby, harmless though he is, *is* indeed "executing" his father/speaker, in the sense that every new generation effectively "kills off" the generation before it, by displacing it. Hall phrases this rather commonplace idea unforgettably; no literal restatement of the point could begin to match the impact of his metaphor.

> Grandmother's hips
> bulge from the brush, she's leaning
> into the ice chest, sun through the trees
> printing her dress with soft
> luminous paws.

In this passage from Rita Dove's "Fifth Grade Autobiography" (p. 386) the speaker describes the image of her grandmother in a family photograph. The metaphor in the last three lines evokes the gentleness of the sunlight by likening it to the tangible *weightlessness* one might associate with a cat's paws.

Try unpacking the following metaphors yourself.

Life is a bridge. Cross over it, but build no house on it.
   —Indian proverb

Everybody dies. How he dies is important. Sometimes a death has the weight of the Taishan Mountain; sometimes it is lighter than a feather.
   —Szema Chien, ancient historian

Illnesses are the poor man's travels.
   —Charles-Louis Philippe

Men and women are locked caskets, of which each contains the key to the other.
   —Isak Dinesen

On every summit you are on the brink of an abyss.
   —Stanislaw Lec

It is the art of mankind to polish the world, and every one who works is scrubbing in some part.
   —Henry David Thoreau

Over time I've come to think about my undergraduate students . . . under the metaphor of a train journey. Someone, a parent or other influential adult in their lives, has given them a ticket. On it is stamped medical school, or law school, or business school, or in rarer cases, graduate school. They're on the train and holding this ticket, the countryside is going by very fast, and they're not getting to see much of it. All they know is that when the train arrives at their stop, they'll be getting off.
   —Jane Tompkins

Metaphors of the Human Mind

Since literature is so deeply about the life of the mind, it is interesting to see how the mind has been treated metaphorically in literature.

Many writers have compared the human mind to a material place, such as a house or a room. For example, Emily Dickinson's poem "One need not be a Chamber—to be Haunted" (p. 507), likens the human brain to a haunted house:

One need not be a Chamber—to be Haunted—
One need not be a House—
The Brain has Corridors—surpassing
Material Place—

The word "Corridors," which denotes a network of narrow hallways or passage-ways, is especially striking: the space within one's own brain is being compared to a haunted house, disorienting, with hidden terrors lurking around each corner or ready to pop out from every doorway. While most of us are very good at picking out external enemies—liars, cheats, thieves, hypocrites, potential murderers—Dickinson insists that the most horrifying enemy is always right inside our own heads:

Ourself behind ourself, concealed—
Should startle most—
Assassin hid in our Apartment
Be Horror's least.

Every person, then, is a sort of walking haunted house, populated with its own ghosts, demons, and "assassins"; and at the very instant we point our gun at the enemy outside our "door," the inner enemy is preparing to pounce on us, with what dire results we can only guess:

The Body—borrows a Revolver—
He bolts the Door—
O'erlooking a superior spectre—
Or More—

Here are some other mind-as-place metaphors:

Sir Edward Dyer (1543–1607):

My mind to me *a kingdom* is,
    Such present joys therein I find,
That it excels all other bliss
    That earth affords or grows by kind.
[italics added. The mind is contented and complete, has everything one could
    possibly desire.]

Edmund Burke (1729–1797):

No passion so effectually *robs* the mind of all its powers of acting and reason-
    ing as fear.
[italics added. The mind is a residence or treasury that can be robbed by the
    thief, "passion." Implication: secure the locks.]

William Cowper (1731–1800):

> Absence of occupation is not rest,
> A mind quite *vacant* is a mind distress'd.
> [italics added. The mind is like a vacant or empty room; just as a person liv-
>   ing in an empty room anxiously fills the room with *stuff*, so we quickly fill
>   our empty mind with something. The terrifying question for Cowper
>   seems to be, With *what?*]

Samuel Taylor Coleridge (1772–1834):

> From whatever place I write you will expect that part of my "Travels" will con-
>   sist of *excursions* in my own mind.
> [italics added. The mind is a landscape, apparently a pleasant one, spacious
>   and varied, where you can saunter along at your own pace and enjoy the
>   scenery.]

Walt Whitman (1819–1892):

> In a little house pictures I keep, many pictures
>   hanging suspended—It is not a fixed house,
> It is round—it is but a few inches from one side of it to the other side,
> But behold! it has room enough—in it, hundreds and thousands,—all the
>   varieties. . . .
> For wherever I have been, has afforded me superb pictures,
> And whatever I have heard has given me perfect pictures,
> And every hour of the day and night has given me copious pictures,
> And every rod of land or sea affords me, as long as I live, inimitable
>   pictures.
> [The mind is a gallery of "superb" and "perfect" pictures, i.e., countless im-
>   ages that have impressed themselves on the poet's mind through years of
>   experience and reading.]

Gerard Manley Hopkins (1844–1889)

> O the mind, mind has *mountains*; *cliffs* of fall
> Frightful, sheer, no-man fathomed. Hold them cheap
> May who ne'er hung there.
> [italics added. The mind is a vertical rock to which one clings, barely, for sheer
>   life. Implication: with the least slip of a finger you may lose your grip on
>   your mind, i.e., go mad.]

Francis Thompson (1859–1907)

> I fled Him, down the nights and down the days;
>   I fled him, down the arches of the years;
> I fled Him, down the *labyrinthine ways*
>   *Of my own mind.* . . .

[italics added. The mind is a horrifying place, like a labyrinth from which there
is no escape.]

As these examples show, the metaphors we use to describe our minds cast a
hard light on how we *experience* them. Here are a few more mind metaphors for
you to unpack. What are the implications of each?

- The mind is a mansion.
- The mind is a wilderness.
- The mind is a garden.
- The mind is a public parking lot.
- The mind is a temple.
- The mind is a fire.
- The mind is a prison.
- The mind is a river.

Simile

Closely related to metaphor, a simile makes the comparison between dissimilar
items *explicit* with the word "like" or "as":

A thought is a thing as real as a cannon ball.
    —Joseph Joubert

A poet should be as sensitive as an aching tooth.
    —Anna Swir

Life is like a game of cards. The hand that is dealt you represents determinism;
the way you play it is free will.
    —Jawaharlal Nehru

We are born believing. A man bears beliefs as a tree bears apples.
—Ralph Waldo Emerson

Sharon Olds's poem, "The Elder Sister" (p. 381), contains a striking simile.
Remembering her elder sister's harsh actions toward her (for instance, "sitting
and pissing on me in bed") the speaker reflects:

. . . now I
see I had her before me always
like a shield. [italics added]

A shield is an instrument for blocking and absorbing blows. The simile expresses
the speaker's debt to her sister (the elder sister took the blows that would otherwise have struck the younger one). It also helps explain the elder sister's unusual

hardness: she has been, so to speak, "dented" or "splintered" by life's blows. Therefore, it is no wonder that "her inky eyes have the look of someone who has/been in prison a long time and/knows they can send her back."

William Wordsworth's "I wandered lonely as a cloud" (p. 502) begins:

> I wandered lonely as a cloud
> That floats on high o'er vales and hills,
> When all at once I saw a crowd,
> A host, of golden daffodils;

The opening line is a simile, one very significant to the poem. The poem describes what Wordsworth called a "spot of time"; that is, a moment of transcendent vision experienced in ordinary time that engrafts itself in memory and nurtures a person for future years. According to Wordsworth a person cannot seek out such moments or achieve them through effort; rather, they come as gifts, unsought, when you are alert but humbly receptive before nature. Thus the speaker's comparison of himself to a cloud is especially apt: a cloud is not purposeful; it does not move toward a goal; it "floats" and wanders. If a cloud had eyes, you could say it *contemplated* the "vales and hills" over which it passed.

Paradox

> . . . only great thinkers are prone to what I call paradoxes, which are nothing but grand thoughts still wanting completion.
>
> —SØREN KIERKEGAARD

A paradox is a statement that appears to be contradictory but proves, on further consideration, to make sense. For example, "The first shall be last, and the last shall be first." The apparent contradiction compels us to rethink the statement in order to detect its truth. Like metaphors, paradoxes abound in both speech and writing, in both poetry and prose, reflecting the deeply contradictory nature of experience.

> To lead the people, walk behind them.
> —Lao Tzu

> If the fool would persist in his folly he would become wise.
> —William Blake

> We understand everything; that is why we understand nothing.
> —Stanislaw Lec

> The tragedy of old age is not that one is old, but that one is young.
> —Oscar Wilde

Art is the only way to run away without leaving home.
— Twyla Tharp

Wisdom literature is especially rife with paradoxes. This famous passage from the book of Ecclesiastes presents a deeply paradoxical vision of life:

> To every thing there is a season, and a time to every purpose under the heaven:
> A time to be born, and a time to die; a time to plant, and a time to pluck up
>   that which is planted;
> A time to kill, and a time to heal; a time to break down, and a time to build
>   up;
> A time to weep, and a time to laugh. . . .

Paradox is a major trope in Naguib Mahfouz's short story "Zaabalawi" (p. 481). Slowly dying of an undisclosed illness, Mahfouz's protagonist desperately searches for the elusive and mysterious Zaabalawi, who is said to possess miraculous powers of healing. Though the protagonist's searches are repeatedly frustrated, he persists in his quest, never abandoning hope. As his pain and frustration deepen, one of many people he consults along his journey assures him, "Such suffering is part of the cure!" This casual remark suggests one of many paradoxical questions raised by Mahfouz's story: *Can pain cause healing?*

G. K. Chesterton, a master of paradox, wrote, "Anyone is free at any moment to strike a blow for changing the whole world." At first this sounds like an outlandish claim; after all, we live in a world that seems largely predetermined for us by gigantic and inscrutable forces—big money, big government, the onward "march of progress," and our own unconscious drives and impulses, to name a few. Many of us feel powerless to affect anything. Surely any "blow" for "change" that is struck by an individual or group of individuals is going to be extremely insignificant. But Chesterton's sentence contains an underlying paradox: that properly seen, *small is large and large is small.* Try changing the world in the grandiose sense that most people think of—and see how far you get; mentor a child, feed a street person, or teach an illiterate adult to read, and your impact may be incalculable. So-called "small" actions have the added advantage that opportunities to perform them abound: you are free to do a kind or constructive deed right this minute, wherever you happen to be, in a way that you are not free to be president of the United States or Albert Einstein.

In "A Defence of Humility" (p. 518) Chesterton expands on the *small is large/large is small* paradox. Probably most of us assume that self-assertion is a virtue, and we are taught from an early age to do everything we can to enlarge ourselves with "a triumphant egotism." The problem, says Chesterton, is that the "bigger" you get, the higher you rise above ordinary things, the less you see:

> The most brilliant exponent of the egoistic school, Nietzsche . . . admitted that
> the philosophy of self-satisfaction led to looking down upon the weak, the

cowardly, and the ignorant. Looking down on things may be a delightful experience, only there is nothing, from a mountain to a cabbage, that is really seen when it is seen from a balloon.

According to Chesterton, in order truly to see—that is, know and understand things—we should make ourselves small, "reduc[e] ourselves to a point . . . to a thing with no size at all." Then, from our point's-eye view, we will see the "immeasurable stature" of "the cosmic things." We will recognize that "the grass is an everlasting forest, with dragons for denizens" and "the dandelions are like gigantic bonfires illuminating the lands around. . . ."

Irony

Irony . . . may be defined as what people miss.

—Julian Barnes

Irony is an incongruity (incompatibility or inconsistency). Irony saturates our daily lives, beginning with this basic irony: each of us knows that we will eventually die, yet we generally live and act as if our earthly existence will last forever. Freud noted that "in the unconscious each of us is convinced of his own immortality." Our behavior and emotions are incongruent with our conscious knowledge.

Here are some other everyday ironies:

- A person carries an umbrella to work every day and forgets it on the one day when it actually rains.
- A person works hard without taking time for fun or vacation in order to retire early and dies (of exhaustion) on the brink of retiring.
- A woman introduces her fiancé to her best friend; the fiancé falls in love with the friend and ends up marrying *her* instead.
- A person really begins to live, for the first time, after being diagnosed with a terminal illness.
- Hiking up a mountain, you step cautiously on the steep and slippery parts; no sooner do you reach safe and level ground than you abandon your caution, stumble, and break your leg.
- A liar gives a public lecture on the virtue of honesty.
- A physically disheveled and absent-minded scientist has a perfectly organized mind.
- An "unsinkable" ship (the *Titanic*) sinks.

Given its universality, it is small wonder that irony has supplied poets, novelists, playwrights, songwriters, screenwriters, and other creators with some—if not *most*—of their best material.

Samuel Johnson's essay *The Rambler* #159 (p. 690) takes an ironic view of bashfulness. Though intellectually we may know better, each of us feels that all eyes are watching us; so we may hesitate to show ourselves too much publicly for fear of misstepping and looking "stupid" or foolish. Yet the fact that *each* of us feels this way proves our actual insignificance in the eyes of others, says Johnson, and ought to embolden us:

> While we see multitudes passing before us, of whom perhaps not one appears to deserve our notice, or excites our sympathy, we should remember, that we likewise, are lost in the same throng, that the eye which happens to glance upon us is turned in a moment on him that follows us, and that the utmost we can reasonably hope or fear is to fill a vacant hour with prattle, and be forgotten.

Albert Brock, the hero of Ray Bradbury's "The Murderer" (p. 621) lives in a noise-filled futuristic world of perpetual communication. While everyone else is keeping happily and constantly connected with everyone else via wrist radio (Bradbury's prophetic vision of the cell phone), Brock yearns to be quietly disconnected and alone. At last, overwhelmed by the social din and the nonstop pressures to stay "in touch," he has begun "murdering" wrist radios, intercoms, and other technologies of convenience. For Brock, some of the modern conveniences are, ironically, inconveniences.

The following statements are all ironic. Annotate, interpret, and discuss them.

An imaginary illness is worse than a real one.
   —Yiddish proverb

We carry within us the wonders we seek without.
   —Sir Thomas Browne

He had grown up in a country run by politicians who sent the pilots to fly the bombers to kill the babies to make the world safe for children to grow up in.
   —Ursula K. LeGuin

I give you bitter pills in sugar coating. The pills are harmless; the poison is in the sugar.
   —Stanislaw Lec

Do not walk on the well-trodden path—you may slip.
   —Lec

Normal is getting dressed in clothes that you buy for work and driving through traffic in a car that you are still paying for—in order to get to the job you need to pay for the clothes and the car, and the house you leave vacant all day so you can afford to live in it.
   —Ellen Goodman

How easy to say: find yourself! How scary when it really happens.
   —Elias Canetti

Verbal Irony

The term "verbal irony" refers to a contrast between what a speaker says literally and the meaning that is implied in the larger context of the story, poem, play, essay, or other discourse. In Wole Soyinka's "Telephone Conversation" (p. 866) a black African speaker talks over the phone with a white landlady about renting an apartment:

> The price seemed reasonable, location
> Indifferent. The landlady swore she lived
> Off premises. Nothing remained
> But self-confession. "Madam," I warned,
> "I hate a wasted journey—I am—African."

The word "self-confession"—implying that the speaker has something to be ashamed about—conflicts ironically with our (and Soyinka's) moral sense that no one should have to apologize for the color of his or her skin. The deferential tone of the speaker's address to the woman (in "Madam . . . / . . . I am—African" and elsewhere in the poem) is also ironic, as readers discern the speaker's intellectual and moral superiority to the landlady, whose questions and remarks are ludicrous.

Irony also pervades Carter Revard's poem "Discovery of the New World" (p. 864). The poem reports how the speaker and a force of aliens have conquered and subdued a world that is recognizably planet Earth. The poem's last line ("we will be safe, and rich, and happy here, forever") expresses confidence about the everlasting triumph of the conquerors. That confidence is apt to sound ironic to students of history, who know that civilizations rise and fall and that conquerors are themselves invariably conquered.

Personification

In personification human qualities are ascribed to an abstract concept or inanimate object: "Fortune smiled upon us." Among other uses, personification enables us, temporarily, to reduce abstract or inscrutable realities such as time, fate, nature, and death to human dimensions.

In "Because I could not stop for Death—/He kindly stopped for me—" (p. 506) Emily Dickinson personifies death as a courtly gentleman. Woody Allen's play *Death Knocks* (p. 586) personifies death as an absurd and comical "schlep" (unkempt and clumsy individual). In "To Autumn" John Keats personifies autumn as a sort of drowsy goddess:

> Who hast not seen thee oft amid thy store?
>   Sometimes whoever seeks abroad may find
> Thee sitting careless on a granary floor,
>   Thy hair soft-lifted by the winnowing wind;
> Or on a half-reap'd furrow sound asleep,
>   Drows'd with the fume of poppies. . . .

Though more common in older literary works, personification can be used with striking effect by modern and contemporary writers; for instance by Wislawa Szymborska in her poem "Advertisement" (p. 862). "Advertisement" features a personified object, a tranquilizer, as the speaker of the poem. The tranquilizer is both salesperson and sales product: it is selling itself to a hypothetical "you." The pill understands its market, appealing to the buyer's desire for convenience ("All you have to do is take me,/let me melt beneath your tongue"), self-justification ("Who said/you have to take it on the chin?"), and for a quick and total relief from all problems ("Let me have your abyss,/I'll cushion it with sleep"). But the poem's final three lines imply a heady price to be paid for all these comforts and boldly reveal the speaker's diabolical identity and motives:

Sell me your soul.
There are no other takers.

There is no other devil anymore.

The following are additional examples of personification to read and interpret:

Mother Nature

Shame is Pride's cloke.
  —William Blake

Pleasures are always children, pains always have wrinkles.
  —Joseph Joubert

A mirror has no heart but plenty of ideas.
  —Malcolm de Chazal

Love is the child of illusion and the parent of disillusion.
  —Miguel de Unamuno

The day is like a stranger of divine origin, wishing to pay you his visit. You're fortunate, if he finds you at home.
  —Vilhelm Ekelund

Metonymy and Synecdoche

In **metonymy** the literal term for one thing is used to stand for another with which it is closely associated. In the following lines from Edwin Arlington Robinson's "Richard Cory" (p. 671), "meat" and "bread" signify not just literal animal flesh and baked goods but food and money:

So on we worked, and waited for the light,
And went without the meat, and cursed the bread. . . .

In **synecdoche** a part of something is used to signify the whole, or the whole is used to signify a part; for example, the sailor's expression "All hands on deck." Other examples are the term "jock" to describe an athlete or "suit" to signify a corporate professional (the latter has become less common with the relaxation of corporate dress codes). Sitting in the park on a Sunday afternoon, the title character of Katherine Mansfield's story "Miss Brill" (p. 464) observes a lonely woman, shabby and aging, pathetically seeking out companionship (notably male companionship). The woman is described by the narrator simply as "an ermine toque," i.e., a small close-fitting hat made of weasel fur. Identifying the woman with an item of apparel that she acquired in her youth and still wears, the synecdoche conveys the impoverishment of the woman's life: she has *become* her little hat.

In the examples just given, the impact of synecdoche is reductive: it takes a sailor, an athlete, a businessperson, and a woman and reduces them (respectively) to a "hand," a "jock," a "suit," and a little hat. Another familiar synecdoche that works reductively is the term "consumer." In this case a function or activity (of using up or buying goods or services) is understood to stand for a whole human being. The universality of this term today (in such expressions as "consumer price index," "consumer confidence," departments and offices of "consumer studies" and "consumer affairs") shows, once more, how the tropes we use reflect our sense of ourselves and of life. To say that human beings (who can laugh, weep, compose symphonies, design cities, and write novels) *equal* consumers is to say that their *being* is indistinguishable from their socioeconomic functionality.

Symbolism

Strickly speaking, a **symbol** refers to something that stands for something else. In literary analysis something is said to be symbolic if it evokes a large range of reference beyond itself—the larger and more compelling the range, the better the symbol.

> A stone falls on a pot—woe to the pot; a pot falls on a stone—woe to the pot; in every case, it is bad for the pot.
>   —The Talmud

> The tygers of wrath are wiser than the horses of instruction.
>   —William Blake

> Expect poison from standing water.
>   —Blake

> Monotony is the most beautiful or the most atrocious thing. The most beautiful if it is a reflection of eternity. The most atrocious if it is the sign of an unvarying perpetuity. It is time surpassed or time sterilized.

The circle is the symbol of monotony which is beautiful, the swinging of a
pendulum, monotony which is atrocious.
   —Simone Weil

The fourteenth-century Sufi poet Shams-ud-din Muhammad (also known as
Hafiz) often wrote symbolically. Himself drunk on life, Hafiz looked incredulously
at the ways people waste their lives in pointless busy-ness and idle speculations.
In his poem "What shall we do about that moon?" (p. 657) life is symbolized by
wine spilled from a broken bottle in a field at night, and human beings are symbolized by beetles who can either drink the wine or concern themselves with "such
profoundly useless/Questions" as "What shall we do about that moon?"

   In Walt Whitman's poem "I Saw in Lousiana a Live-Oak Growing" (p. 271)
the speaker comes across a live-oak tree standing "All alone." The oak symbolizes
the speaker's own self: "its look, rude, unbending, lusty, made me think of myself. . . ." Whitman, in fact, often viewed sturdy trees as symbols of "imperturba-
bility and *being*" (qualities he strove to cultivate in himself), "as against the human trait of mere *seeming*." Here, however, the poem takes a curious turn, as the
speaker begins to notice how *unlike* himself the live-oak is: "But I wonder'd how
it could utter joyous leaves standing all alone there without a friend near, for I
knew I could not." Leaving the scene, the speaker carries with him a leafy twig intertwined with moss as a permanent "token" or reminder of the revelation he experienced that day—of his own need for "manly love." Though the poem's point
of view is boldly first-person singular, Whitman's "I" suggestively symbolizes the
condition of every "I": it cannot sing or create ("utter joyous leaves") by itself; it
requires the nurture and affection of friends in order to be fully itself. In fact, all
his life Whitman dreamed of a "city of friends" in which community and individuality alike would thrive. Thus both the live-oak and the speaker in this poem
are symbolic.

   The title character in Katherine Mansfield's short story "Miss Brill" is a lonely
woman whose only excitement in life occurs on Sunday afternoons, when she
walks to the park to listen to a band and watch and eavesdrop on passersby. For
this special occasion she wears a fur neckpiece, a "dear little thing," a "little
rogue" with "dim little eyes," which she treats tenderly, like a child or a pet. When
it is not with her at the park, the fur "lives" inside a box, which suggestively resembles the "cupboard" of a room that Miss Brill herself inhabits. Miss Brill's fur
is an excellent example of a complex symbol. Does it symbolize Miss Brill herself?
a pet animal or a child? a friend or companionship generally? Or does it symbolize something more abstract, such as loneliness, mortality, or human vulnerability (we learn at the story's beginning that the fur is decaying; "the nose . . . wasn't
at all firm")?

   Finally, symbolism need not be limited to persons or things. Animals can be
symbolic—for instance, Edgar Allan Poe's "Black Cat" (p. 815), Susan Glaspell's
canary in *Trifles* (p. 300), or Herman Melville's famous white whale in *Moby-
Dick*. In literature as in life, actions can also be symbols. At the thematic center of
Linda Hogan's essay "Waking Up the Rake" (p. 1064) is a metaphor told her by a

traditional healer: "Our work is our altar." The metaphor connects work with the sacred and informs Hogan's understanding of work as symbolic. Discussing her menial labor at the Birds of Prey Rehabilitation Center, Hogan says, "There is an art to raking . . . one with rhythm in it, and life." For Hogan, the work of raking connects the raker with the natural world and with the natural rhythms of the seasons, of birth and death, and the gathering together and "the turning over of life." Like any art, says Hogan, raking can be done poorly or well, and "On the days I do it well, the rake wakes up. . . . *Everything is there* . . . in the humblest of labor" [italics added].

In his journal Ralph Waldo Emerson writes eloquently about the symbolic character of all human activity. To those who truly see, there is nothing that is *not* symbolic. Emerson urges us to detect poetry everywhere and to pay special attention to *how* we act and see:

> Every thing should be treated poetically—law, politics, housekeeping, money. A judge and a banker must drive their craft poetically as well as a dancer or a scribe. That is, they must exert that higher vision which causes the object to become fluid & plastic. Then they are inventive, they detect its capabilities. If they do not this they have nothing that can be called success, but the work & the workman become blockish & near the point of everlasting congelation. . . . If you would write a code or logarithms or a cookbook you cannot spare the poetic impulse.[1]

Emerson reasserts one of the basic lessons of figurative language and of literature generally: that there are no "walls" anywhere between literature and life.

ACTIVITIES FOR DISCUSSION AND WRITING

1. React to the sample "metaphors of the human mind" on pages 202–205. What kind of space or place is your own mind? Describe it metaphorically.

2. Identify a text (poetry or prose) that you find compelling. Find any tropes in the text and interpret them, using the examples of interpretation in this chapter as models.

3. Comb your own notebook (large or pocket-sized) for tropes, and mark or circle any that seem particularly expressive. Consider using these tropes as centers of energy for creating longer writings, such as stories, poems, or essays.

4. Identify and interpret any figures you find in your own outside reading of books, newspapers, magazines, and so forth, or in other sources such as the Internet, films, commercial advertisements, and television programs.

---

1. From *Emerson in His Journals*, ed. Joel Porte (Cambridge: Harvard UP, 1982, p. 234).

5. Interpret the tropes in the following texts, using the examples of interpretation in this chapter as models. Obviously, this is a selective list of titles. If you prefer, interpret the tropes in other texts, not included in this list.

- Susan Glaspell, *Trifles* (p. 300)
- Gwendolyn Brooks, "Sadie and Maud" (p. 375)
- Sharon Olds, "The Elder Sister" (p. 381)
- Toni Cade Bambara, "The Lesson" (p. 492)
- Emily Dickinson, "Much Madness is divinest Sense" (p. 669)
- Thomas Hardy, "The Ruined Maid" (p. 508)
- Eugene O'Neill, *The Hairy Ape* (p. 554)
- Antonio Machado, *Proverbs and Song-verse* (p. 672)
- Stanislaw Lec, *Unkempt Thoughts* (p. 677)
- Samuel Johnson, *The Rambler* #146 (p. 688)
- Anna Swir, "The Same Inside" (p. 859)
- Sharon Olds, "On the Subway" (p. 868)
- Robert Frost, "Out, Out—" (p. 1023)

Part

VI

A Thematic Anthology of Readings

Parts I through V introduced you to various ideas for conversational reading and writing and to ways of working with the major genres of literature. Now is your chance to apply these ideas to a range of literary works.

Part VI consists of a collection of short stories, poems, essays, and plays for reading and responsive writing. For purposes of convenience, selections have been arranged into several thematic categories: "Gender and Relationships," "Families," "Experience and Identity," "Individual and Society," "People and Cultures in Conflict and Change," and "Work and the Quality of Life." The themes provide a means of classifying related readings into groups of workable size. You will notice, however, that any such arrangement is somewhat arbitrary. Any one story, poem, essay, or play may evoke multiple themes in different readers or in a single reader. For instance, in this book Kate Chopin's "The Story of an Hour" is classified under the theme of "Gender and Relationships"; yet the story prompted Tyler (see Chapter 2) to produce writing that has little to do with the sorts of gender-based "relationships" that are the focus of the particular theme grouping. Tyler created a portrait of a man who served as a surrogate "grandfather" in his life; he produced work that transcends artificially imposed thematic boundaries. You should feel free to do the same. Moreover, if your class is focusing on readings in one thematic section and you want to do additional reading in a different section, do so. Browse, read, enjoy, and write as your individual tastes and instincts dictate.

By referring back to Part I—especially Chapters 2 and 3—you can find ideas for writing in response to *any* of the readings in this anthology. In addition, over half of the individual readings are followed by Activities for Writing and Discussion, which provide ready-made prompts for both "creative" and "analytic" work. The Activities for any particular reading are sequenced to begin with simpler activities and progress toward more complex. Thus, if a particular text puzzles you, you might choose to address Activity #1 rather than one of the later, more demanding activities. Conversely, if a reading affects you powerfully, a later activity may be more appealing. Many readings are also followed by suggestions for research.

The Activities are not meant to be exhaustive or to restrict your options for writing. You can best approach *any* story, poem, essay, or play in the anthology by using the "Four-Step Process for Writing from Reading" described in Chapter 2. Then, for additional writing ideas, either:

1. Consult the Activities (if provided) that follow the selection, or
2. Use one of the "Ten Ideas for Writing" described in Chapter 3, or
3. Use some other mode of response of your own devising.

Each thematic section ends with a set of Additional Activities for Writing and Discussion. The Additional Activities serve a twofold purpose. First, they encourage you to make connections among the various readings within the section. Second, they help you develop habits of recursiveness as you "look again" at those readings and at the notebook writings you did in response to them. You can think and talk more about the readings. You can also rewrite, expand, or otherwise improve your notebook writings as you exercise the habit of "selective revising" that is at the heart of the book.

Finally, in both the Activities for Writing and Discussion and the Additional Activities you will find literary terms printed in **boldface.** These are defined and illustrated in Part IV ("An Introduction to the Major Genres") and Appendix C ("Glossary of Literary Terms").

Gender and Relationships

Short Stories

KATE CHOPIN (1850–1904)

The Story of an Hour

Knowing that Mrs. Mallard was afflicted with a heart trouble, great care was taken 1
to break to her as gently as possible the news of her husband's death.

It was her sister Josephine who told her, in broken sentences, veiled hints that 2
revealed in half concealing. Her husband's friend Richards was there, too, near
her. It was he who had been in the newspaper office when intelligence of the railroad disaster was received, with Brently Mallard's name leading the list of
"killed." He had only taken the time to assure himself of its truth by a second
telegram, and had hastened to forestall any less careful, less tender friend in bearing the sad message.

She did not hear the story as many women have heard the same, with a para- 3
lyzed inability to accept its significance. She wept at once, with sudden, wild abandonment, in her sister's arms. When the storm of grief had spent itself she went
away to her room alone. She would have no one follow her.

There stood, facing the open window, a comfortable, roomy armchair. Into 4
this she sank, pressed down by a physical exhaustion that haunted her body and
seemed to reach into her soul.

She could see in the open square before her house the tops of trees that were 5
all aquiver with the new spring life. The delicious breath of rain was in the air. In
the street below a peddler was crying his wares. The notes of a distant song which
some one was singing reached her faintly, and countless sparrows were twittering
in the eaves.

There were patches of blue sky showing here and there through the clouds 6
that had met and piled one above the other in the west facing her window.

She sat with her head thrown back upon the cushion of the chair, quite mo-   7
tionless, except when a sob came up into her throat and shook her, as a child who
has cried itself to sleep continues to sob in its dreams.

She was young, with a fair, calm face, whose lines bespoke repression and even   8
a certain strength. But now there was a dull stare in her eyes, whose gaze was fixed
away off yonder on one of those patches of blue sky. It was not a glance of reflection, but rather indicated a suspension of intelligent thought.

There was something coming to her and she was waiting for it, fearfully. What   9
was it? She did not know; it was too subtle and elusive to name. But she felt it,
creeping out of the sky, reaching toward her through the sounds, the scents, the
color that filled the air.

Now her bosom rose and fell tumultuously. She was beginning to recognize   10
this thing that was approaching to possess her, and she was striving to beat it back
with her will—as powerless as her two white slender hands would have been.

When she abandoned herself a little whispered word escaped her slightly   11
parted lips. She said it over and over under her breath: "Free, free, free!" The vacant stare and the look of terror that had followed it went from her eyes. They
stayed keen and bright. Her pulses beat fast, and the coursing blood warmed and
relaxed every inch of her body.

She did not stop to ask if it were or were not a monstrous joy that held her. A   12
clear and exalted perception enabled her to dismiss the suggestion as trivial.

She knew that she would weep again when she saw the kind, tender hands   13
folded in death; the face that had never looked save with love upon her, fixed and
gray and dead. But she saw beyond that bitter moment a long procession of years
to come that would belong to her absolutely. And she opened and spread her arms
out to them in welcome.

There would be no one to live for during those coming years; she would live   14
for herself. There would be no powerful will bending her in that blind persistence
with which men and women believe they have a right to impose a private will
upon a fellow-creature. A kind intention or a cruel intention made the act seem
no less a crime as she looked upon it in that brief moment of illumination.

And yet she had loved him—sometimes. Often she had not. What did it mat-   15
ter! What could love, the unsolved mystery, count for in face of this possession of
self-assertion which she suddenly recognized as the strongest impulse of her
being!

"Free! Body and soul free!" she kept whispering.   16

Josephine was kneeling before the closed door with her lips to the keyhole, im-   17
ploring for admission. "Louise, open the door! I beg; open the door—you will
make yourself ill. What are you doing, Louise? For heaven's sake open the door."

"Go away. I am not making myself ill." No; she was drinking in a very elixir of   18
life through that open window.

Her fancy was running riot along those days ahead of her. Spring days, and   19
summer days, and all sorts of days that would be her own. She breathed a quick

prayer that life might be long. It was only yesterday she had thought with a shudder that life might be long.

She arose at length and opened the door to her sister's importunities. There 20 was a feverish triumph in her eyes, and she carried herself unwittingly like a goddess of Victory. She clasped her sister's waist, and together they descended the stairs. Richards stood waiting for them at the bottom.

Some one was opening the front door with a latchkey. It was Brently Mallard 21 who entered, a little travel-stained, composedly carrying his grip-sack and umbrella. He had been far from the scene of accident, and did not even know there had been one. He stood amazed at Josephine's piercing cry; at Richards' quick motion to screen him from the view of his wife.

But Richards was too late.   22

When the doctors came they said she had died of heart disease — of joy that 23 kills.

ACTIVITIES FOR WRITING AND DISCUSSION

1. Louise Mallard's feelings toward her husband are complex. We are told that Brently "never looked save with love upon her," and yet she seems elated over his death. Is there any evidence that Mr. Mallard has treated her cruelly? What reasons might she have for feeling "joy" at his death?

2. Chopin's style is concise, leaving much to her readers' imaginations. In "The Story of an Hour" we get clues about the individual **characters** of Louise and Brently but do not actually see them together. How do you imagine they interact with each other? What is their body language like? What sorts of things do you talk about? Describe a typical day in the marriage of the Mallards, using **dialogue** if you wish, or dramatize their interaction in a specific situation (e.g., "over breakfast," "after dinner," "with friends").

3. Imagine you are Louise Mallard writing in her diary. Compose a diary entry — or entries — in which you reflect on your relationship with Brently.

4. Draft a memoir reflecting on any personal connections you have with the characters or events of this story.

5. Identify and write down two prominent **themes** in this story that interest you. Choose one of them and compare its treatment in this story with its treatment in any other story, poem, essay, or play in this anthology.

6. Research the story of Kate Chopin's life and marriage. In what ways, if any, can "The Story of an Hour" and/or other of her fiction writings be seen as autobiographical?

Charlotte Perkins Gilman (1860–1935)

The Yellow Wallpaper

It is very seldom that mere ordinary people like John and myself secure ancestral halls for the summer.

A colonial mansion, a hereditary estate, I would say a haunted house and reach the height of romantic felicity—but that would be asking too much of fate!

Still I will proudly declare that there is something queer about it.

Else, why should it be let so cheaply? And why have stood so long untenanted?

John laughs at me, of course, but one expects that.   5

John is practical in the extreme. He has no patience with faith, an intense horror of superstition, and he scoffs openly at any talk of things not to be felt and seen and put down in figures.

John is a physician, and *perhaps*—(I would not say it to a living soul, of course, but this is dead paper and a great relief to my mind)—*perhaps* that is one reason I do not get well faster.

You see, he does not believe I am sick! And what can one do?

If a physician of high standing, and one's own husband, assures friends and relatives that there is really nothing the matter with one but temporary nervous depression—a slight hysterical tendency—what is one to do?

My brother is also a physician, and also of high standing, and he says the same   10 thing.

So I take phosphates or phosphites—whichever it is—and tonics, and air and exercise, and journeys, and am absolutely forbidden to "work" until I am well again.

Personally, I disagree with their ideas.

Personally, I believe that congenial work, with excitement and change, would do me good.

But what is one to do?

I did write for a while in spite of them; but it *does* exhaust me a good deal—   15 having to be so sly about it, or else meet with heavy opposition.

I sometimes fancy that in my condition, if I had less opposition and more society and stimulus—but John says the very worst thing I can do is to think about my condition, and I confess it always makes me feel bad.

So I will let it alone and talk about the house.

The most beautiful place! It is quite alone, standing well back from the road, quite three miles from the village. It makes me think of English places that you read about, for there are hedges and walls and gates that lock, and lots of separate little houses for the gardeners and people.

There is a *delicious* garden! I never saw such a garden—large and shady, full of box-bordered paths, and lined with long grape-covered arbors with seats under them.

There were greenhouses, but they are all broken now.   20

There was some legal trouble, I believe, something about the heirs and co-heirs; anyhow, the place has been empty for years.

That spoils my ghostliness, I am afraid, but I don't care—there is something strange about the house—I can feel it.

I even said so to John one moonlight evening, but he said what I felt was a draught, and shut the window.

I get unreasonably angry with John sometimes. I'm sure I never used to be so sensitive. I think it is due to this nervous condition.

But John says if I feel so, I shall neglect proper self-control; so I take pains to 25 control myself—before him, at least, and that makes me very tired.

I don't like our room a bit. I wanted one downstairs that opened on the piazza and had roses all over the window, and such pretty old-fashioned chintz hangings! But John would not hear of it.

He said there was only one window and not room for two beds, and no near room for him if he took another.

He is very careful and loving, and hardly lets me stir without special direction.

I have a schedule prescription for each hour in the day; he takes all care from me, and so I feel basely ungrateful not to value it more.

He said we came here solely on my account, that I was to have perfect rest and 30 all the air I could get. "Your exercise depends on your strength, my dear," said he, "and your food somewhat on your appetite; but air you can absorb all the time." So we took the nursery at the top of the house.

It is a big, airy room, the whole floor nearly, with windows that look all ways, and air and sunshine galore. It was nursery first and then playroom and gymnasium, I should judge; for the windows are barred for little children, and there are rings and things in the walls.

The paint and paper look as if a boys' school had used it. It is stripped off—the paper—in great patches all around the head of my bed, about as far as I can reach, and in a great place on the other side of the room low down. I never saw a worse paper in my life. One of those sprawling flamboyant patterns committing every artistic sin.

It is dull enough to confuse the eye in following, pronounced enough to constantly irritate and provoke study, and when you follow the lame uncertain curves for a little distance they suddenly commit suicide—plunge off at outrageous angles, destroy themselves in unheard-of contradictions.

The color is repellant, almost revolting; a smouldering unclean yellow, strangely faded by the slow-turning sunlight. It is a dull yet lurid orange in some places, a sickly sulphur tint in others.

No wonder the children hated it! I should hate it myself if I had to live in this 35 room long.

There comes John, and I must put this away—he hates to have me write a word.

We have been here two weeks, and I haven't felt like writing before, since that first day.

I am sitting by the window now, up in this atrocious nursery, and there is nothing to hinder my writing as much as I please, save lack of strength.

John is away all day, and even some nights when his cases are serious.

I am glad my case is not serious!   40

But these nervous troubles are dreadfully depressing.

John does not know how much I really suffer. He knows there is no reason to suffer, and that satisfies him.

Of course it is only nervousness. It does weigh on me so not to do my duty in any way!

I mean to be such a help to John, such a real rest and comfort, and here I am a comparative burden already!

Nobody would believe what an effort it is to do what little I am able—to dress   45 and entertain, and order things.

It is fortunate Mary is so good with the baby. Such a dear baby!

And yet I *cannot* be with him, it makes me so nervous.

I suppose John never was nervous in his life. He laughs at me so about this wallpaper!

At first he meant to repaper the room, but afterwards he said that I was letting it get the better of me, and that nothing was worse for a nervous patient than to give way to such fancies.

He said that after the wallpaper was changed it would be the heavy bedstead,   50 and then the barred windows, and then that gate at the head of the stairs, and so on.

"You know the place is doing you good," he said, "and really, dear, I don't care to renovate the house just for a three months' rental."

"Then do let us go downstairs," I said. "There are such pretty rooms there."

Then he took me in his arms and called me a blessed little goose, and said he would go down cellar, if I wished, and have it whitewashed into the bargain.

But he is right enough about the beds and windows and things.

It is as airy and comfortable a room as anyone need wish, and, of course, I   55 would not be so silly as to make him uncomfortable just for a whim.

I'm really getting quite fond of the big room, all but that horrid paper.

Out of one window I can see the garden—those mysterious deep-shaded arbors, the riotous old-fashioned flowers, and bushes and gnarly trees.

Out of another I get a lovely view of the bay and a little private wharf belonging to the estate. There is a beautiful shaded lane that runs down there from the house. I always fancy I see people walking in these numerous paths and arbors, but John has cautioned me not to give way to fancy in the least. He says that with my imaginative power and habit of story-making, a nervous weakness like mine is sure to lead to all manner of excited fancies, and that I ought to use my will and good sense to check the tendency. So I try.

I think sometimes that if I were only well enough to write a little it would relieve the press of ideas and rest me.

But I find I get pretty tired when I try.   60

It is so discouraging not to have any advice and companionship about my work. When I get really well, John says we will ask Cousin Henry and Julia down for a long visit; but he says he would as soon put fireworks in my pillowcase as to let me have those stimulating people about now.

I wish I could get well faster.

But I must not think about that. This paper looks to me as if it *knew* what a vicious influence it had!

There is a recurrent spot where the pattern lolls like a broken neck and two bulbous eyes stare at you upside down.

I get positively angry with the impertinence of it and the everlastingness. Up   65
and down and sideways they crawl, and those absurd unblinking eyes are everywhere. There is one place where two breadths didn't match, and the eyes go all up and down the line, one a little higher than the other.

I never saw so much expression in an inanimate thing before, and we all know how much expression they have! I used to lie awake as a child and get more entertainment and terror out of blank walls and plain furniture than most children could find in a toy-store.

I remember what a kindly wink the knobs of our big old bureau used to have, and there was one chair that always seemed like a strong friend.

I used to feel that if any of the other things looked too fierce I could always hop into that chair and be safe.

The furniture in this room is no worse than inharmonious, however, for we had to bring it all from downstairs. I suppose when this was used as a playroom they had to take the nursery things out, and no wonder! I never saw such ravages as the children have made here.

The wallpaper, as I said before, is torn off in spots, and it sticketh closer than   70
a brother—they must have had perseverance as well as hatred.

Then the floor is scratched and gouged and splintered, the plaster itself is dug out here and there, and this great heavy bed which is all we found in the room, looks as if it had been through the wars.

But I don't mind it a bit—only the paper.

There comes John's sister. Such a dear girl as she is, and so careful of me! I must not let her find me writing.

She is a perfect and enthusiastic housekeeper, and hopes for no better profession. I verily believe she thinks it is the writing which made me sick!

But I can write when she is out, and see her a long way off from these win-   75
dows.

There is one that commands the road, a lovely shaded winding road, and one that just looks off over the country. A lovely country, too, full of great elms and velvet meadows.

This wallpaper has a kind of sub-pattern in a different shade, a particularly irritating one, for you can only see it in certain lights, and not clearly then.

But in the places where it isn't faded and where the sun is just so—I can see a strange, provoking, formless sort of figure that seems to skulk about behind that silly and conspicuous front design.

There's sister on the stairs!

————————

Well, the Fourth of July is over! The people are all gone, and I am tired out. 80 John thought it might do me good to see a little company, so we just had Mother and Nellie and the children down for a week.

Of course I didn't do a thing. Jennie sees to everything now.

But it tired me all the same.

John says if I don't pick up faster he shall send me to Weir Mitchell in the fall.

But I don't want to go there at all. I had a friend who was in his hands once, and she says he is just like John and my brother, only more so!

Besides, it is such an undertaking to go so far. 85

I don't feel as if it was worthwhile to turn my hand over for anything, and I'm getting dreadfully fretful and querulous.

I cry at nothing, and cry most of the time.

Of course I don't when John is here, or anybody else, but when I am alone.

And I am alone a good deal just now. John is kept in town very often by serious cases, and Jennie is good and lets me alone when I want her to.

So I walk a little in the garden or down that lovely lane, sit on the porch un- 90 der the roses, and lie down up here a good deal.

I'm getting really fond of the room in spite of the wallpaper. Perhaps *because* of the wallpaper.

It dwells in my mind so!

I lie here on this great immovable bed—it is nailed down, I believe—and follow that pattern about by the hour. It is as good as gymnastics, I assure you. I start, we'll say, at the bottom, down in the corner over there where it has not been touched, and I determine for the thousandth time that I *will* follow that pointless pattern to some sort of conclusion.

I know a little of the principle of design, and I know this thing was not arranged on any laws of radiation, or alternation, or repetition, or symmetry, or anything else that I ever heard of.

It is repeated, of course, by the breadths, but not otherwise. 95

Looked at in one way, each breadth stands alone; the bloated curves and flourishes—a kind of "debased Romanesque" with delirium tremens—go waddling up and down in isolated columns of fatuity.

But, on the other hand, they connect diagonally, and the sprawling outlines run off in great slanting waves of optic horror, like a lot of wallowing sea-weeds in full chase.

The whole thing goes horizontally, too, at least it seems so, and I exhaust myself trying to distinguish the order of its going in that direction.

They have used a horizontal breadth for a frieze, and that adds wonderfully to the confusion.

There is one end of the room where it is almost intact, and there, when the crosslights fade and the low sun shines directly upon it, I can almost fancy radiation after all—the interminable grotesque seems to form around a common center and rush off in headlong plunges of equal distraction.

It makes me tired to follow it. I will take a nap, I guess.

————————

I don't know why I should write this.

I don't want to.

I don't feel able.

And I know John would think it absurd. But I *must* say what I feel and think in some way—it is such a relief!

But the effort is getting to be greater than the relief.

Half the time now I am awfully lazy, and lie down ever so much.

John says I mustn't lose my strength, and has me take cod liver oil and lots of tonics and things, to say nothing of ale and wine and rare meat.

Dear John! He loves me very dearly, and hates to have me sick. I tried to have a real earnest reasonable talk with him the other day, and tell him how I wish he would let me go and make a visit to Cousin Henry and Julia.

But he said I wasn't able to go, nor able to stand it after I got there; and I did not make out a very good case for myself, for I was crying before I had finished.

It is getting to be a great effort for me to think straight. Just this nervous weakness, I suppose.

And dear John gathered me up in his arms, and just carried me upstairs and laid me on the bed, and sat by me and read to me till it tired my head.

He said I was his darling and his comfort and all he had, and that I must take care of myself for his sake, and keep well.

He says no one but myself can help me out of it, that I must use my will and self-control and not let any silly fancies run away with me.

There's one comfort—the baby is well and happy, and does not have to occupy this nursery with the horrid wallpaper.

If we had not used it, that blessed child would have! What a fortunate escape! Why, I wouldn't have a child of mine, an impressionable little thing, live in such a room for worlds.

I never thought of it before, but it is lucky that John kept me here after all, I can stand it so much easier than a baby, you see.

Of course I never mention it to them any more—I am too wise—but I keep watch for it all the same.

There are things in that paper that nobody knows about but me, or ever will.

Behind that outside pattern the dim shapes get clearer every day.

It is always the same shape, only very numerous.

And it is like a woman stooping down and creeping about behind that pattern. I don't like it a bit. I wonder—I begin to think—I wish John would take me away from here!

————————

It is so hard to talk with John about my case, because he is so wise, and because he loves me so.

But I tried it last night.

It was moonlight. The moon shines in all around just as the sun does.   125

I hate to see it sometimes, it creeps so slowly, and always comes in by one window or another.

John was asleep and I hated to waken him, so I kept still and watched the moonlight on that undulating wallpaper till I felt creepy.

The faint figure behind seemed to shake the pattern, just as if she wanted to get out.

I got up softly and went to feel and see if the paper *did* move, and when I came back John was awake.

"What is it, little girl?" he said. "Don't go walking about like that—you'll get   130 cold."

I thought it was a good time to talk, so I told him that I really was not gaining here, and that I wished he would take me away.

"Why, darling!" said he. "Our lease will be up in three weeks, and I can't see how to leave before.

"The repairs are not done at home, and I cannot possibly leave town just now. Of course if you were in any danger, I could and would, but you really are better, dear, whether you can see it or not. I am a doctor, dear, and I know. You are gaining flesh and color, your appetite is better, I feel really much easier about you."

"I don't weigh a bit more," said I, "nor as much; and my appetite may be better in the evening when you are here but it is worse in the morning when you are away!"

"Bless her little heart!" said he with a big hug. "She shall be as sick as she   135 pleases! But now let's improve the shining hours by going to sleep, and talk about it in the morning!"

"And you won't go away?" I asked gloomily.

"Why, how can I, dear? It is only three weeks more and then we will take a nice little trip of a few days while Jennie is getting the house ready. Really, dear, you are better!"

"Better in body perhaps—" I began, and stopped short, for he sat up straight and looked at me with such a stern, reproachful look that I could not say another word.

"My darling," said he, "I beg of you, for my sake and for our child's sake, as well as for your own, that you will never for one instant let that idea enter your mind! There is nothing so dangerous, so fascinating, to a temperament like yours. It is a false and foolish fancy. Can you not trust me as a physician when I tell you so?"

So of course I said no more on that score, and we went to sleep before long.   140 He thought I was asleep first, but I wasn't, and lay there for hours trying to decide whether that front pattern and the back pattern really did move together or separately.

———

On a pattern like this, by daylight, there is a lack of sequence, a defiance of law, that is a constant irritant to a normal mind.

The color is hideous enough, and unreliable enough, and infuriating enough, but the pattern is torturing.

You think you have mastered it, but just as you get well under way in following, it turns a back-somersault and there you are. It slaps you in the face, knocks you down, and tramples upon you. It is like a bad dream.

The outside pattern is a florid arabesque, reminding one of a fungus. If you can imagine a toadstool in joints, an interminable string of toadstools, budding and sprouting in endless convolutions—why, that is something like it.

That is, sometimes!   145

There is one marked peculiarity about this paper, a thing nobody seems to notice but myself, and that is that it changes as the light changes.

When the sun shoots in through the east window—I always watch for that first long, straight ray—it changes so quickly that I never can quite believe it.

That is why I watch it always.

By moonlight—the moon shines in all night when there is a moon—I wouldn't know it was the same paper.

At night in any kind of light, in twilight, candlelight, lamplight, and worst of   150
all by moonlight, it becomes bars! The outside pattern, I mean, and the woman behind it is as plain as can be.

I didn't realize for a long time what the thing was that showed behind, that dim sub-pattern, but now I am quite sure it is a woman.

By daylight she is subdued, quiet. I fancy it is the pattern that keeps her so still. It is so puzzling. It keeps me quiet by the hour.

I lie down ever so much now. John says it is good for me, and to sleep all I can.

Indeed he started the habit by making me lie down for an hour after each meal.

It is a very bad habit I am convinced, for you see, I don't sleep.   155

And that cultivates deceit, for I don't tell them I'm awake—O no!

The fact is I am getting a little afraid of John.

He seems very queer sometimes, and even Jennie has an inexplicable look.

It strikes me occasionally, just as a scientific hypothesis, that perhaps it is the paper!

I have watched John when he did not know I was looking, and come into the   160
room suddenly on the most innocent excuses, and I've caught him several times *looking at the paper!* And Jennie too. I caught Jennie with her hand on it once.

She didn't know I was in the room, and when I asked her in a quiet, a very quiet voice, with the most restrained manner possible, what she was doing with the paper—she turned around as if she had been caught stealing, and looked quite angry—asked me why I should frighten her so!

Then she said that the paper stained everything it touched, that she had found yellow smooches on all my clothes and John's, and she wished we would be more careful!

Did not that sound innocent? But I know she was studying that pattern, and I am determined that nobody shall find it out but myself!

————

Life is very much more exciting now than it used to be. You see I have something more to expect, to look forward to, to watch. I really do eat better, and am more quiet than I was.

John is so pleased to see me improve! He laughed a little the other day, and   165
said I seemed to be flourishing in spite of my wallpaper.

I turned it off with a laugh. I had no intention of telling him it was *because* of the wallpaper—he would make fun of me. He might even want to take me away.

I don't want to leave now until I have found it out. There is a week more, and I think that will be enough.

————

I'm feeling so much better!

I don't sleep much at night, for it is so interesting to watch developments; but I sleep a good deal during the daytime.

In the daytime it is tiresome and perplexing.   170

There are always new shoots on the fungus, and new shades of yellow all over it. I cannot keep count of them, though I have tried conscientiously.

It is the strangest yellow, that wallpaper! It makes me think of all the yellow things I ever saw—not beautiful ones like buttercups, but old, foul, bad yellow things.

But there is something else about that paper—the smell! I noticed it the moment we came into the room, but with so much air and sun it was not bad. Now we have had a week of fog and rain, and whether the windows are open or not, the smell is here.

It creeps all over the house.

I find it hovering in the dining-room, skulking in the parlor, hiding in the   175
hall, lying in wait for me on the stairs.

It gets into my hair.

Even when I go to ride, if I turn my head suddenly and surprise it—there is that smell!

Such a peculiar odor, too! I have spent hours in trying to analyze it, to find what it smelled like.

It is not bad—at first—and very gentle, but quite the subtlest, most enduring odor I ever met.

In this damp weather it is awful, I wake up in the night and find it hanging   180
over me.

It used to disturb me at first. I thought seriously of burning the house—to reach the smell.

But now I am used to it. The only thing I can think of that it is like is the *color* of the paper! A yellow smell.

There is a very funny mark on this wall, low down, near the mopboard. A streak that runs round the room. It goes behind every piece of furniture, except the bed, a long, straight, even *smooch*, as if it had been rubbed over and over.

I wonder how it was done and who did it, and what they did it for. Round and round and round—round and round and round—it makes me dizzy!

———

I really have discovered something at last.   185

Through watching so much at night, when it changes so, I have finally found out.

The front pattern *does* move—and no wonder! The woman behind shakes it!

Sometimes I think there are a great many women behind, and sometimes only one, and she crawls around fast, and her crawling shakes it all over.

Then in the very bright spots she keeps still, and in the very shady spots she just takes hold of the bars and shakes them hard.

And she is all the time trying to climb through. But nobody could climb 190 through that pattern—it strangles so; I think that is why it has so many heads.

They get through, and then the pattern strangles them off and turns them up-side down, and makes their eyes white!

If those heads were covered or taken off it would not be half so bad.

———

I think that woman gets out in the daytime!

And I'll tell you why—privately—I've seen her!

I can see her out of every one of my windows!   195

It is the same woman, I know, for she is always creeping, and most women do not creep by daylight.

I see her in that long shaded lane, creeping up and down. I see her in those dark grape arbors, creeping all around the garden.

I see her on that long road under the trees, creeping along, and when a car-riage comes she hides under the blackberry vines.

I don't blame her a bit. It must be very humiliating to be caught creeping by daylight!

I always lock the door when I creep by daylight. I can't do it at night, for I 200 know John would suspect something at once.

And John is so queer now that I don't want to irritate him. I wish he would take another room! Besides, I don't want anybody to get that woman out at night but myself.

I often wonder if I could see her out of all the windows at once.

But, turn as fast as I can, I can only see out of one at one time.

And though I always see her, she *may* be able to creep faster than I can turn! I have watched her sometimes away off in the open country, creeping as fast as a cloud shadow in a wind.

———

If only that top pattern could be gotten off from the under one! I mean to try   205
it, little by little.

I have found out another funny thing, but I shan't tell it this time! It does not
do to trust people too much.

There are only two more days to get this paper off, and I believe John is beginning to notice. I don't like the look in his eyes.

And I heard him ask Jennie a lot of professional questions about me. She had
a very good report to give.

She said I slept a good deal in the daytime.

John knows I don't sleep very well at night, for all I'm so quiet!   210

He asked me all sorts of questions, too, and pretended to be very loving and
kind.

As if I couldn't see through him!

Still, I don't wonder he acts so, sleeping under this paper for three months.

It only interests me, but I feel sure John and Jennie are affected by it.

Hurrah! This is the last day, but it is enough. John is to stay in town over night,   215
and won't be out until this evening.

Jennie wanted to sleep with me—the sly thing; but I told her I should undoubtedly rest better for a night all alone.

That was clever, for really I wasn't alone a bit! As soon as it was moonlight and
that poor thing began to crawl and shake the pattern, I got up and ran to help her.

I pulled and she shook, I shook and she pulled, and before morning we had
peeled off yards of that paper.

A strip about as high as my head and half around the room.

And then when the sun came and that awful pattern began to laugh at me, I   220
declared I would finish it today!

We go away tomorrow, and they are moving all my furniture down again to
leave things as they were before.

Jennie looked at the wall in amazement, but I told her merrily that I did it out
of pure spite at the vicious thing.

She laughed and said she wouldn't mind doing it herself, but I must not get
tired.

How she betrayed herself that time!

But I am here, and no person touches this paper but Me—not *alive*!   225

She tried to get me out of the room—it was too patent! But I said it was so
quiet and empty and clean now that I believed I would lie down again and sleep
all I could; and not to wake me even for dinner—I would call when I woke.

So now she is gone, and the servants are gone, and the things are gone, and
there is nothing left but that great bedstead nailed down, with the canvas mattress
we found on it.

We shall sleep downstairs tonight, and take the boat home tomorrow.

I quite enjoy the room, now it is bare again.

How those children did tear about here!   230

This bedstead is fairly gnawed!

But I must get to work.

I have locked the door and thrown the key down into the front path.

I don't want to go out, and I don't want to have anybody come in, till John comes.

I want to astonish him.

I've got a rope up here that even Jennie did not find. If that woman does get out, and tries to get away, I can tie her!

But I forgot I could not reach far without anything to stand on!

This bed will *not* move!

I tried to lift and push it until I was lame, and then I got so angry I bit off a little piece at one corner—but it hurt my teeth.

Then I peeled off all the paper I could reach standing on the floor. It sticks 240 horribly and the pattern just enjoys it! All those strangled heads and bulbous eyes and waddling fungus growths just shriek with derision!

I am getting angry enough to do something desperate. To jump out of the window would be admirable exercise, but the bars are too strong even to try.

Besides I wouldn't do it. Of course not. I know well enough that a step like that is improper and might be misconstrued.

I don't like to *look* out of the windows even—there are so many of those creeping women, and they creep so fast.

I wonder if they all come out of that wallpaper as I did?

But I am securely fastened now by my well-hidden rope—you don't get *me*— 245 out in the road there!

I suppose I shall have to get back behind the pattern when it comes night, and that is hard!

It is so pleasant to be out in this great room and creep around as I please!

I don't want to go outside. I won't, even if Jennie asks me to.

For outside you have to creep on the ground, and everything is green instead of yellow.

But here I can creep smoothly on the floor, and my shoulder just fits in that 250 long smooch around the wall, so I cannot lose my way.

Why there's John at the door!

It is no use, young man, you can't open it!

How he does call and pound!

Now he's crying to Jennie for an axe.

It would be a shame to break down that beautiful door!   255

"John dear!" said I in the gentlest voice. "The key is down by the front steps, under a plantain leaf!"

That silenced him for a few moments.

Then he said—very quietly indeed, "Open the door, my darling!"

"I can't," said I. "The key is down by the front door under a plantain leaf!"

And then I said it again, several times, very gently and slowly, and said it so of- 260 ten that he had to go and see, and he got it of course, and came in. He stopped short by the door.

"What is the matter?" he cried. "For God's sake, what are you doing!"

I kept on creeping just the same, but I looked at him over my shoulder.

"I've got out at last," said I, "in spite of you and Jane[.] And I've pulled off most of the paper, so you can't put me back!"

Now why should that man have fainted? But he did, and right across my path by the wall, so that I had to creep over him every time!

ACTIVITIES FOR WRITING AND DISCUSSION

1. Describe your first impressions of the narrator. Is she an **unreliable narrator,** or do you find her relatively objective? Cite and share particular passages to support your answer.

2. In paragraph 36 the narrator says her husband "hates to have me write a word." Later, in paragraph 105, she declares, "I *must* say what I feel and think in some way—it is such a relief!" Why does she write? What does writing do for her? Identify any passages in the story that relate to writing or imagination. Then produce evidence to support either of the following assertions:

   a. "Writing helps the narrator," or
   b. "Writing and imagination help destroy the narrator."

As you do this exercise, consider what Gilman said of her own experiences with Dr. S. Weir Mitchell:

> [U]sing the remnants of intelligence that remained . . . I cast the noted specialist's advice to the winds and went to work again—work, the normal life of every human being; work, in which is joy and growth and service, without which one is a pauper and a parasite; ultimately recovering some measure of power.

3. The **narrator** expresses ambivalent feelings about John, sometimes challenging his judgments and elsewhere saying "he is so wise, and . . . he loves me so" (paragraph 123). How can you account for such contradictory views? What are the narrator's thoughts and feelings about John? Is John good for her? Why or why not? Cite and analyze two or three passages that provide support for your answer.

4. Read aloud the reported **dialogue** between the narrator and John in paragraphs 130–139.

   a. Underline any words or phrases that seem peculiar or interesting to you. How do these words or phrases illuminate the husband/wife relationship? Discuss your thoughts in class or in a small group.
   b. Read the sentence that concludes the dialogue: "So of course I said no more on that score, and we went to sleep before long" (paragraph 140). How is John able to silence his wife and induce her to sleep?
   c. Write an essay in which you analyze the dialogue and how it helps to characterize the narrator, John, and their relationship.

5. Analyze the story's ending. Has the narrator achieved a greater intellectual and emotional clarity, or has she gone insane? Cite illustrative quotations from the story to support your answer.

6. "The Yellow Wallpaper" is a subjective, **first-person** narrative. As a technical challenge, try rendering the same story in a more objective format. For instance, recast the story as a short play. Provide a **scene description** and **stage directions** to supplement the dialogue of your play.

7. Read the Gilman biography in Appendix D. Then research the story of Gilman's experiences with S. Weir Mitchell and the parallels—and differences—between her own story and that of the protagonist in "The Yellow Wallpaper."

SIDONIE-GABRIELLE COLETTE (1873–1954)

The Other Wife

"Table for two? This way, Monsieur, Madame, there is still a table next to the win- 1
dow, if Madame and Monsieur would like a view of the bay."

Alice followed the maître d'.[1]   2

"Oh, yes. Come on, Marc, it'll be like having lunch on a boat on the water . . ."   3

Her husband caught her by passing his arm under hers. "We'll be more com- 4
fortable over there."

"There? In the middle of all those people? I'd much rather . . ."   5

"Alice, please."   6

He tightened his grip in such a meaningful way that she turned around.   7
"What's the matter?"

"Shh . . ." he said softly, looking at her intently, and led her toward the table 8
in the middle.

"What is it, Marc?"   9

"I'll tell you, darling. Let me order lunch first. Would you like the shrimp? Or 10
the eggs in aspic?"

"Whatever you like, you know that."   11

They smiled at one another, wasting the precious time of an overworked 12
maître d', stricken with a kind of nervous dance, who was standing next to them,
perspiring.

"The shrimp," said Marc. "Then the eggs and bacon. And the cold chicken 13
with a romaine salad. *Fromage blanc?*[2] The house specialty? We'll go with the specialty. Two strong coffees. My chauffeur will be having lunch also, we'll be leaving
again at two o'clock. Some cider? No, I don't trust it . . . Dry champagne."

---

1. **maître d':** Headwaiter.
2. **Fromage blanc:** A mild white cheese, something like cottage cheese.

He sighed as if he had just moved an armoire, gazed at the colorless midday 14
sea, at the pearly white sky, then at his wife, whom he found lovely in her little
Mercury hat[3] with its large, hanging veil.

"You're looking well, darling. And all this blue water makes your eyes look 15
green, imagine that! And you've put on weight since you've been traveling . . . It's
nice up to a point, but only up to a point!"

Her firm, round breasts rose proudly as she leaned over the table.   16

"Why did you keep me from taking that place next to the window?"   17

Marc Seguy never considered lying. "Because you were about to sit next to 18
someone I know."

"Someone I don't know?"   19

"My ex-wife."   20

She couldn't think of anything to say and opened her blue eyes wider.   21

"So what, darling? It'll happen again. It's not important."   22

The words came back to Alice and she asked, in order, the inevitable ques- 23
tions. "Did she see you? Could she see that you saw her? Will you point her out to
me?"

"Don't look now, please, she must be watching us. . . . The lady with brown hair, 24
no hat, she must be staying in this hotel. By herself, behind those children in red . . ."

"Yes, I see."   25

Hidden behind some broad-brimmed beach hats, Alice was able to look at the 26
woman who, fifteen months ago, had still been her husband's wife.

"Incompatibility," Marc said. "Oh, I mean . . . total incompatibility! We di- 27
vorced like well-bred people, almost like friends, quietly, quickly. And then I fell
in love with you, and you really wanted to be happy with me. How lucky we are
that our happiness doesn't involve any guilty parties or victims!"

The woman in white, whose smooth, lustrous hair reflected the light from the 28
sea in azure patches, was smoking a cigarette with her eyes half closed. Alice
turned back toward her husband, took some shrimp and butter, and ate calmly.
After a moment's silence she asked: "Why didn't you ever tell me that she had blue
eyes, too?"

"Well, I never thought about it!"   29

He kissed the hand she was extending toward the bread basket and she 30
blushed with pleasure. Dusky and ample, she might have seemed somewhat
coarse, but the changeable blue of her eyes and her wavy, golden hair made her
look like a frail and sentimental blonde. She vowed overwhelming gratitude to her
husband. Immodest without knowing it, everything about her bore the overly
conspicuous marks of extreme happiness.

They ate and drank heartily, and each thought the other had forgotten the 31
woman in white. Now and then, however, Alice laughed too loudly, and Marc was
careful about his posture, holding his shoulders back, his head up. They waited
quite a long time for their coffee, in silence. An incandescent river, the straggled

---

3. **Mercury hat:** Hat with a feather.

reflection of the invisible sun overhead, shifted slowly across the sea and shone with a blinding brilliance.

"She's still there, you know," Alice whispered.   32

"Is she making you uncomfortable? Would you like to have coffee somewhere   33
else?"

"No, not at all! She's the one who must be uncomfortable! Besides, she does-   34
n't exactly seem to be having a wild time, if you could see her . . ."

"I don't have to. I know that look of hers."   35

"Oh, was she like that?"   36

He exhaled his cigarette smoke through his nostrils and knitted his eyebrows.   37
"Like that? No. To tell you honestly, she wasn't happy with me."

"Oh, really now!"   38

"The way you indulge me is so charming, darling . . . It's crazy . . . You're an   39
angel . . . You love me . . . I'm so proud when I see those eyes of yours. Yes, those
eyes . . . She . . . I just didn't know how to make her happy, that's all, I didn't know
how."

"She's just difficult!"   40

Alice fanned herself irritably, and cast brief glances at the woman in white,   41
who was smoking, her head resting against the back of the cane chair, her eyes
closed with an air of satisfied lassitude.

Marc shrugged his shoulders modestly.   42

"That's the right word," he admitted. "What can you do? You have to feel sorry   43
for people who are never satisfied. But we're satisfied . . . Aren't we, darling?"

She did not answer. She was looking furtively, and closely, at her husband's   44
face, ruddy and regular; at his thick hair, threaded here and there with white silk;
at his short, well-cared-for hands; and doubtful for the first time, she asked herself, "What more did she want from him?"

And as they were leaving, while Marc was paying the bill and asking for the   45
chauffeur and about the route, she kept looking, with envy and curiosity, at the
woman in white, this dissatisfied, this difficult, this superior . . .

ACTIVITIES FOR WRITING AND DISCUSSION

1. Annotate the story. Then react to it using any of the "Ten Ideas for Writing" listed on page 35.

2. Reread the last two paragraphs carefully. What is Alice "doubtful" about,
and why does she look with "envy" at the other wife? (Different readers will answer
these questions differently.) In the **persona** of Alice, write a **stream of consciousness** that expresses your (Alice's) conflicted feelings as you leave the restaurant.

3. Rewrite the story as "The Other Husband" or "The Other Girlfriend/
Boyfriend." Keep the same basic conflict but alter the **point of view, setting,** and
characters as you wish.

4. Write a story of your own, nonfictional or fictional, about a couple who
unexpectedly encounter one or the other's "ex" spouse or girlfriend/boyfriend.

Doris Lessing (b. 1919)

A Woman on a Roof

It was during the week of hot sun, that June.   1

Three men were at work on the roof, where the leads got so hot they had the   2
idea of throwing water on to cool them. But the water steamed, then sizzled; and
they made jokes about getting an egg from some woman in the flats under them,
to poach it for their dinner. By two it was not possible to touch the guttering they
were replacing, and they speculated about what workmen did in regularly hot
countries. Perhaps they should borrow kitchen gloves with the egg? They were all
a bit dizzy, not used to the heat; and they shed their coats and stood side by side
squeezing themselves into a foot-wide patch of shade against a chimney, careful
to keep their feet in the thick socks and boots out of the sun. There was a fine view
across several acres of roofs. Not far off a man sat in a deck chair reading the
newspapers. Then they saw her, between chimneys, about fifty yards away. She lay
face down on a brown blanket. They could see the top part of her: black hair, a
flushed solid back, arms spread out.

"She's stark naked," said Stanley, sounding annoyed.   3

Harry, the oldest, a man of about forty-five, said: "Looks like it."   4

Young Tom, seventeen, said nothing, but he was excited and grinning.   5

Stanley said: "Someone'll report her if she doesn't watch out."   6

"She thinks no one can see," said Tom, craning his head all ways to see more.   7

At this point the woman, still lying prone, brought her two hands up behind   8
her shoulders with the ends of a scarf in them, tied it behind her back, and sat up.
She wore a red scarf tied around her breasts and brief red bikini pants. This being
the first day of the sun she was white, flushing red. She sat smoking, and did not
look up when Stanley let out a wolf whistle. Harry said: "Small things amuse small
minds," leading the way back to their part of the roof, but it was scorching. Harry
said: "Wait, I'm going to rig up some shade," and disappeared down the skylight
into the building. Now that he'd gone, Stanley and Tom went to the farthest point
they could to peer at the woman. She had moved, and all they could see were two
pink legs stretched on the blanket. They whistled and shouted but the legs did not
move. Harry came back with a blanket and shouted: "Come on, then." He sounded
irritated with them. They clambered back to him and he said to Stanley: "What
about your missus?" Stanley was newly married, about three months. Stanley
said, jeering: "What about my missus?"—preserving his independence. Tom said
nothing, but his mind was full of the nearly naked woman. Harry slung the blanket, which he had borrowed from a friendly woman downstairs, from the stem of
a television aerial to a row of chimney-pots. This shade fell across the piece of gutter they had to replace. But the shade kept moving, they had to adjust the blanket, and not much progress was made. At last some of the heat left the roof, and
they worked fast, making up for lost time. First Stanley, then Tom, made a trip to
the end of the roof to see the woman. "She's on her back," Stanley said, adding a

jest which made Tom snicker, and the older man smile tolerantly. Tom's report was that she hadn't moved, but it was a lie. He wanted to keep what he had seen to himself: he had caught her in the act of rolling down the little red pants over her hips, till they were no more than a small triangle. She was on her back, fully visible, glistening with oil.

Next morning, as soon as they came up, they went to look. She was already 9 there, face down, arms spread out, naked except for the little red pants. She had turned brown in the night. Yesterday she was a scarlet-and-white woman, today she was a brown woman. Stanley let out a whistle. She lifted her head, startled, as if she'd been asleep, and looked straight over at them. The sun was in her eyes, she blinked and stared, then she dropped her head again. At this gesture of indifference, they all three, Stanley, Tom, and old Harry, let out whistles and yells. Harry was doing it in parody of the younger men, making fun of them, but he was also angry. They were all angry because of her utter indifference to the three men watching her.

"Bitch," said Stanley.   10

"She should ask us over," said Tom, snickering.   11

Harry recovered himself and reminded Stanley: "If she's married, her old man 12 wouldn't like that."

"Christ," said Stanley virtuously, "if my wife lay about like that, for everyone 13 to see, I'd soon stop her."

Harry said, smiling: "How do you know, perhaps she's sunning herself at this 14 very moment?"

"Not a chance, not on our roof." The safety of his wife put Stanley into a good 15 humour, and they went to work. But today it was hotter than yesterday; and several times one or the other suggested they should tell Matthew, the foreman, and ask to leave the roof until the heat wave was over. But they didn't. There was work to be done in the basement of the big block of flats, but up here they felt free, on a different level from ordinary humanity shut in the streets or the buildings. A lot more people came out on to the roofs that day, for an hour at midday. Some married couples sat side by side in deck chairs, the women's legs stockingless and scarlet, the men in vests with reddening shoulders.

The woman stayed on her blanket, turning herself over and over. She ignored 16 them, no matter what they did. When Harry went off to fetch more screws, Stanley said: "Come on." Her roof belonged to a different system of roofs, separated from theirs at one point by about twenty feet. It meant a scrambling climb from one level to another, edging along parapets, clinging to chimneys, while their big boots slipped and slithered, but at last they stood on a small square projecting roof looking straight down at her, close. She sat smoking, reading a book. Tom thought she looked like a poster, or a magazine cover, with the blue sky behind her and her legs stretched out. Behind her a great crane at work on a new building in Oxford Street swung its black arm across roofs in a great arc. Tom imagined himself at work on the crane, adjusting the arm to swing over and pick her up and swing her back across the sky to drop her near him.

They whistled. She looked up at them, cool and remote, then went on read-   17
ing. Again, they were furious. Or, rather, Stanley was. His sun-heated face was
screwed into a rage as he whistled again and again, trying to make her look up.
Young Tom stopped whistling. He stood beside Stanley, excited, grinning; but he
felt as if he were saying to the woman: Don't associate me with *him,* for his grin
was apologetic. Last night he had thought of the unknown woman before he slept,
and she had been tender with him. This tenderness he was remembering as he
shifted his feet by the jeering, whistling Stanley, and watched the indifferent,
healthy brown woman a few feet off, with the gap that plunged to the street between them. Tom thought it was romantic, it was like being high on two hilltops.
But there was a shout from Harry, and they clambered back. Stanley's face was
hard, really angry. The boy kept looking at him and wondered why he hated the
woman so much, for by now he loved her.

They played their little games with the blanket, trying to trap shade to work   18
under; but again it was not until nearly four that they could work seriously, and
they were exhausted, all three of them. They were grumbling about the weather
by now. Stanley was in a thoroughly bad humour. When they made their routine
trip to see the woman before they packed up for the day, she was apparently
asleep, face down, her back all naked save for the scarlet triangle on her buttocks.
"I've got a good mind to report her to the police," said Stanley, and Harry said:
"What's eating you? What harm's she doing?"

"I tell you, if she was my wife!"   19

"But she isn't, is she?" Tom knew that Harry, like himself, was uneasy at Stan-   20
ley's reaction. He was normally a sharp young man, quick at his work, making a
lot of jokes, good company.

"Perhaps it will be cooler tomorrow," said Harry.   21

But it wasn't; it was hotter, if anything, and the weather forecast said the good   22
weather would last. As soon as they were on the roof, Harry went over to see if the
woman was there, and Tom knew it was to prevent Stanley going, to put off his
bad humour. Harry had grownup children, a boy the same age as Tom, and the
youth trusted and looked up to him.

Harry came back and said: "She's not there."   23

"I bet her old man has put his foot down," said Stanley, and Harry and Tom   24
caught each other's eyes and smiled behind the young married man's back.

Harry suggested they should get permission to work in the basement, and they   25
did, that day. But before packing up Stanley said: "Let's have a breath of fresh air."
Again Harry and Tom smiled at each other as they followed Stanley up to the roof,
Tom in the devout conviction that he was there to protect the woman from Stanley. It was about five-thirty, and a calm, full sunlight lay over the roofs. The great
crane still swung its black arm from Oxford Street to above their heads. She was
not there. Then there was a flutter of white from behind a parapet, and she stood
up, in a belted, white dressing-gown. She had been there all day, probably, but on
a different patch of roof, to hide from them. Stanley did not whistle; he said nothing, but watched the woman bend to collect papers, books, cigarettes, then fold
the blanket over her arm. Tom was thinking: If they weren't here, I'd go over and

say . . . what? But he knew from his nightly dreams of her that she was kind and friendly. Perhaps she would ask him down to her flat? Perhaps . . . He stood watching her disappear down the skylight. As she went, Stanley let out a shrill derisive yell; she started, and it seemed as if she nearly fell. She clutched to save herself, they could hear things falling. She looked straight at them, angry. Harry said, facetiously: "Better be careful on those slippery ladders, love." Tom knew he said it to save her from Stanley, but she could not know it. She vanished, frowning. Tom was full of a secret delight, because he knew her anger was for the others, not for him.

"Roll on some rain," said Stanley, bitter, looking at the blue evening sky.   26

Next day was cloudless, and they decided to finish the work in the basement.   27 They felt excluded, shut in the grey cement basement fitting pipes, from the holiday atmosphere of London in a heat wave. At lunchtime they came up for some air, but while the married couples, and the men in shirt-sleeves or vests, were there, she was not there, either on her usual patch of roof or where she had been yesterday. They all, even Harry, clambered about, between chimney-pots, over parapets, the hot leads stinging their fingers. There was not a sign of her. They took off their shirts and vests and exposed their chests, feeling their feet sweaty and hot. They did not mention the woman. But Tom felt alone again. Last night she had him into her flat: it was big and had fitted white carpets and a bed with a padded white leather head-board. She wore a black filmy negligée and her kindness to Tom thickened his throat as he remembered it. He felt she had betrayed him by not being there.

And again after work they climbed up, but still there was nothing to be seen   28 of her. Stanley kept repeating that if it was as hot as this tomorrow he wasn't going to work and that's all there was to it. But they were all there next day. By ten the temperature was in the middle seventies, and it was eighty long before noon. Harry went to the foreman to say it was impossible to work on the leads in that heat; but the foreman said there was nothing else he could put them on, and they'd have to. At midday they stood, silent, watching the skylight on her roof open, and then she slowly emerged in her white gown, holding a bundle of blanket. She looked at them, gravely, then went to the part of the roof where she was hidden from them. Tom was pleased. He felt she was more his when the other men couldn't see her. They had taken off their shirts and vests, but now they put them back again, for they felt the sun bruising their flesh. "She must have the hide of a rhino," said Stanley, tugging at guttering and swearing. They stopped work, and sat in the shade, moving around behind chimney stacks. A woman came to water a yellow window box opposite them. She was middleaged, wearing a flowered summer dress. Stanley said to her: "We need a drink more than them." She smiled and said: "Better drop down to the pub quick, it'll be closing in a minute." They exchanged pleasantries, and she left them with a smile and a wave.

"Not like Lady Godiva," said Stanley. "She can give us a bit of a chat and a   29 smile."

"You didn't whistle at *her*," said Tom, reproving.   30

"Listen to him," said Stanley, "you didn't whistle, then?"   31

But the boy felt as if he hadn't whistled, as if only Harry and Stanley had. He   32
was making plans, when it was time to knock off work, to get left behind and
somehow make his way over to the woman. The weather report said the hot spell
was due to break, so he had to move quickly. But there was no chance of being
left. The other two decided to knock off work at four, because they were exhausted. As they went down, Tom quickly climbed a parapet and hoisted himself
higher by pulling his weight up a chimney. He caught a glimpse of her lying on
her back, her knees up, eyes closed, a brown woman lolling in the sun. He slipped
and clattered down, as Stanley looked for information: "She's gone down," he
said. He felt as if he had protected her from Stanley, and that she must be grateful
to him. He could feel the bond between the woman and himself.

Next day, they stood around on the landing below the roof, reluctant to climb   33
up into the heat. The woman who had lent Harry the blanket came out and offered them a cup of tea. They accepted gratefully, and sat around Mrs. Pritchett's
kitchen an hour or so, chatting. She was married to an airline pilot. A smart
blonde, of about thirty, she had an eye for the handsome sharp-faced Stanley; and
the two teased each other while Harry sat in a corner, watching, indulgent, though
his expression reminded Stanley that he was married. And young Tom felt envious of Stanley's ease in badinage; felt, too, that Stanley's getting off with
Mrs. Pritchett left his romance with the woman on the roof safe and intact.

"I thought they said the heat wave'd break," said Stanley, sullen, as the time   34
approached when they really would have to climb up into the sunlight.

"You don't like it, then?" asked Mrs. Pritchett.   35

"All right for some," said Stanley. "Nothing to do but lie about as if it was a   36
beach up there. Do you ever go up?"

"Went up once," said Mrs. Pritchett. "But it's a dirty place up there, and it's   37
too hot."

"Quite right too," said Stanley.   38

Then they went up, leaving the cool neat little flat and the friendly   39
Mrs. Pritchett.

As soon as they were up they saw her. The three men looked at her, resentful   40
at her ease in this punishing sun. Then Harry said, because of the expression on
Stanley's face: "Come on, we've got to pretend to work, at least."

They had to wrench another length of guttering that ran beside a parapet out   41
of its bed, so that they could replace it. Stanley took it in his two hands, tugged,
swore, stood up. "Fuck it," he said, and sat down under a chimney. He lit a cigarette. "Fuck them," he said. "What do they think we are, lizards? I've got blisters
all over my hands." Then he jumped up and climbed over the roofs and stood
with his back to them. He put his fingers either side of his mouth and let out a
shrill whistle. Tom and Harry squatted, not looking at each other, watching him.
They could just see the woman's head, the beginnings of her brown shoulders.
Stanley whistled again. Then he began stamping with his feet, and whistled and
yelled and screamed at the woman, his face getting scarlet. He seemed quite mad,
as he stamped and whistled, while the woman did not move, she did not move a
muscle.

"Barmy," said Tom.   42

"Yes," said Harry, disapproving.   43

Suddenly the older man came to a decision. It was, Tom knew, to save some   44
sort of scandal or real trouble over the woman. Harry stood up and began packing
tools into a length of oily cloth. "Stanley," he said, commanding. At first Stanley
took no notice, but Harry said: "Stanley, we're packing it in, I'll tell Matthew."

Stanley came back, cheeks mottled, eyes glaring.   45

"Can't go on like this," said Harry. "It'll break in a day or so. I'm going to tell 46
Matthew we've got sunstroke, and if he doesn't like it, it's too bad." Even Harry
sounded aggrieved, Tom noted. The small, competent man, the family man with
his grey hair, who was never at a loss, sounded really off balance. "Come on," he
said, angry. He fitted himself into the open square in the roof, and went down,
watching his feet on the ladder. Then Stanley went, with not a glance at the
woman. Then Tom, who, his throat beating with excitement, silently promised
her on a backward glance: Wait for me, wait, I'm coming.

On the pavement Stanley said: "I'm going home." He looked white now, so 47
perhaps he really did have sunstroke. Harry went off to find the foreman, who was
at work on the plumbing of some flats down the street. Tom slipped back, not into
the building they had been working on, but the building on whose roof the
woman lay. He went straight up, no one stopping him. The skylight stood open,
with an iron ladder leading up. He emerged on to the roof a couple of yards from
her. She sat up, pushing back her black hair with both hands. The scarf across her
breasts bound them tight, and brown flesh bulged around it. Her legs were brown
and smooth. She stared at him in silence. The boy stood grinning, foolish,
claiming the tenderness he expected from her.

"What do you want?" she asked.   48

"I . . . I came to . . . make your acquaintance," he stammered, grinning, plead- 49
ing with her.

They looked at each other, the slight, scarlet-faced excited boy, and the seri- 50
ous, nearly naked woman. Then, without a word, she lay down on her brown
blanket, ignoring him.

"You like the sun, do you?" he enquired of her glistening back.   51

Not a word. He felt panic, thinking of how she had held him in her arms,   52
stroked his hair, brought him where he sat, lordly, in her bed, a glass of some exhilarating liquor he had never tasted in life. He felt that if he knelt down, stroked
her shoulders, her hair, she would turn and clasp him in her arms.

He said: "The sun's all right for you, isn't it?"   53

She raised her head, set her chin on two small fists. "Go away," she said. He 54
did not move. "Listen," she said, in a slow reasonable voice, where anger was kept
in check, though with difficulty; looking at him, her face weary with anger, "if you
get a kick out of seeing women in bikinis, why don't you take a sixpenny bus ride
to the Lido? You'd see dozens of them, without all this mountaineering."

She hadn't understood him. He felt her unfairness pale him. He stammered: 55
"But I like you, I've been watching you and . . ."

"Thanks," she said, and dropped her face again, turned away from him.   56

She lay there. He stood there. She said nothing. She had simply shut him out. 57
He stood, saying nothing at all, for some minutes. He thought: She'll have to say
something if I stay. But the minutes went past, with no sign of them in her, except
in the tension of her back, her thighs, her arms—the tension of waiting for him
to go.

He looked up at the sky, where the sun seemed to spin in heat; and over the 58
roofs where he and his mates had been earlier. He could see the heat quivering
where they had worked. And they expect us to work in these conditions! he
thought, filled with righteous indignation. The woman hadn't moved. A bit of hot
wind blew her black hair softly; it shone, and was iridescent. He remembered how
he had stroked it last night.

Resentment of her at last moved him off and away down the ladder, through 59
the building, into the street. He got drunk then, in hatred of her.

Next day when he woke the sky was grey. He looked at the wet grey and 60
thought, vicious: Well, that's fixed you, hasn't it now? That's fixed you good and
proper.

The three men were at work early on the cool leads, surrounded by damp driz- 61
zling roofs where no one came to sun themselves, black roofs, slimy with rain.
Because it was cool now, they would finish the job that day, if they hurried.

ACTIVITIES FOR WRITING AND DISCUSSION

1. Working alone or in a small group, brainstorm a list of issues this story
raises for you. Then select one issue that interests you most and relate it (in
writing) to your own or someone else's life experience.

2. Reread and annotate any passages that specifically describe the woman.
Note the items and belongings she carries with her, what she apparently does
(other than sunbathe) while on the roof. Note her various reactions to the men
observing and taunting her. Then, without slavishly following Lessing's plot,
rewrite the story from the woman's **point of view.** Consider composing your piece
in the form of a personal letter (to a recipient of your own imagining), a series of
diary entries, or a **dialogue** between the woman and a friend.

3. Examine Stanley's interactions with Mrs. Pritchett, a woman whom he
likes. How do these interactions differ from those he has with the woman on the
roof, and how might this difference account for his divergent feelings about the
two women?

4. Imagine that, after seeing the woman on the roof for the second or third
time, Stanley describes her behavior to his wife of three months. In what setting
or situation does Stanley broach the subject? What are his unspoken thoughts,
feelings, or words?

    a. Create the conversation between wife and husband.

    b. Share your dialogue with the class or a small group.

c. After hearing the dialogues, write a reaction to your own or someone else's dialogue. What did you hear that surprised you? What do you now understand that you did not when you first read the story?

5. Stanley and Tom react to the woman differently. Stanley feels rage toward her, while we are told that Tom feels a "bond between the woman and himself" (paragraph 32). Discuss the differences in their reactions. Is Tom (a) "better" or "kinder" than Stanley, (b) simply different from Stanley, or (c) really no different from Stanley? Support your analysis with illustrative examples and quotations from the story.

RAY BRADBURY (b. 1920)

[A Story About Love]

And out there in the middle of the first day of August, just getting into his car, was 1 Bill Forrester, who shouted he was going downtown for some extraordinary ice cream or other and would anyone join him? So, not five minutes later, jiggled and steamed into a better mood, Douglas found himself stepping in off the fiery pavements and moving through the grotto of soda-scented air, of vanilla freshness at the drugstore, to sit at the snow-marble fountain with Bill Forrester. They then asked for a recital of the most unusual ices and when the fountain man said, "Old fashioned lime-vanilla ice . . ."

"That's it!" said Bill Forrester. 2

"Yes, sir!" said Douglas. 3

And, while waiting, they turned slowly on their rotating stools. The silver 4 spigots, the gleaming mirrors, the hushed whirl-around ceiling fans, the green shades over the small windows, the harp-wire chairs, passed under their moving gaze. They stopped turning. Their eyes had touched upon the face and form of Miss Helen Loomis, ninety-five years old, ice-cream spoon in hand, ice cream in mouth.

"Young man," she said to Bill Forrester, "you are a person of taste and imagi- 5 nation. Also, you have the will power of ten men; otherwise you would not dare veer away from the common flavors listed on the menu and order, straight out, without quibble or reservation, such an unheard-of thing as lime-vanilla ice."

He bowed his head solemnly to her. 6

"Come sit with me, both of you," she said. "We'll talk of strange ice creams 7 and such things as we seem to have a bent for. Don't be afraid; I'll foot the bill."

Smiling, they carried their dishes to her table and sat. 8

"You look like a Spaulding," she said to the boy. "You've got your grandfather's 9 head. And you, you're William Forrester. You write for the *Chronicle,* a good enough column. I've heard more about you than I'd care to tell."

"I know you," said Bill Forrester. "You're Helen Loomis." He hesitated, then 10
continued. "I was in love with you once," he said.

"Now that's the way I like a conversation to open." She dug quietly at her ice 11
cream. "That's grounds for another meeting. No—don't tell me where or when
or how you were in love with me. We'll save that for next time. You've taken away
my appetite with your talk. Look there now! Well, I must get home anyway. Since
you're a reporter, come for tea tomorrow between three and four; it's just possible
I can sketch out the history of this town, since it was a trading post, for you. And,
so we'll both have something for our curiosity to chew on, Mr. Forrester, you remind me of a gentleman I went with seventy, yes, seventy years ago."

She sat across from them and it was like talking with a gray and lost quivering 12
moth. The voice came from far away inside the grayness and the oldness, wrapped
in the powders of pressed flowers and ancient butterflies.

"Well." She arose. "Will you come tomorrow?"   13
"I most certainly will," said Bill Forrester.   14
And she went off into the town on business, leaving the young boy and the 15
young man there, looking after her, slowly finishing their ice cream.

———————

William Forrester spent the next morning checking some local news items for 16
the paper, had time after lunch for some fishing in the river outside town, caught
only some small fish which he threw back happily, and, without thinking about
it, or at least not noticing that he had thought about it, at three o'clock he found
his car taking him down a certain street. He watched with interest as his hands
turned the steering wheel and motored him up a vast circular drive where he
stopped under an ivy-covered entry. Letting himself out, he was conscious of the
fact that his car was like his pipe—old, chewed-on, unkempt in this huge green
garden by this freshly painted, three-story Victorian house. He saw a faint ghost-
like movement at the far end of the garden, heard a whispery cry, and saw that
Miss Loomis was there, removed across time and distance, seated alone, the tea
service glittering its soft silver surfaces, waiting for him.

"This is the first time a woman has ever been ready and waiting," he said, 17
walking up. "It is also," he admitted, "the first time in my life I have been on time
for an appointment."

"Why is that?" she asked, propped back in her wicker chair.   18
"I don't know," he admitted.   19
"Well." She started pouring tea. "To start things off, what do you think of the 20
world?"

"I don't know anything."   21
"The beginning of wisdom, as they say. When you're seventeen you know 22
everything. When you're *twenty*-seven if you *still* know everything you're still seventeen."

"You seem to have learned quite a lot over the years."   23
"It is the privilege of old people to seem to know everything. But it's an act and 24
a mask, like every other act and mask. Between ourselves, we old ones wink at

each other and smile, saying, How do you like *my* mask, *my* act, *my* certainty? Isn't life a play? Don't I play it well?"

They both laughed quietly. He sat back and let the laughter come naturally 25 from his mouth for the first time in many months. When they quieted she held her teacup in her two hands and looked into it. "Do you know, it's lucky we met so late. I wouldn't have wanted you to meet me when I was twenty-one and full of foolishness."

"They have special laws for pretty girls twenty-one."   26

"So you think I was pretty?"   27

He nodded good-humoredly.   28

"But how can you tell?" she asked. "When you meet a dragon that has eaten a 29 swan, do you guess by the few feathers left around the mouth? That's what it is— a body like this is a dragon, all scales and folds. So the dragon ate the white swan. I haven't seen her for years. I can't even remember what she looks like. I *feel* her, though. She's safe inside, still alive; the essential swan hasn't changed a feather. Do you know, there are some mornings in spring or fall, when I wake and think, I'll run across the fields into the woods and pick wild strawberries! Or I'll swim in the lake, or I'll dance all night tonight until dawn! And then, in a rage, discover I'm in this old and ruined dragon. I'm the princess in the crumbled tower, no way out, waiting for her Prince Charming."

"You should have written books."   30

"My dear boy, I *have* written. What else was there for an old maid? I was a 31 crazy creature with a headful of carnival spangles until I was thirty, and then the only man I ever really cared for stopped waiting and married someone else. So in spite, in anger at myself, I told myself I deserved my fate for not having married when the best chance was at hand. I started traveling. My luggage was snowed under blizzards of travel stickers. I have been alone in Paris, alone in Vienna, alone in London, and, all in all, it is very much like being alone in Green Town, Illinois. It is, in essence, being alone. Oh, you have plenty of time to think, improve your manners, sharpen your conversations. But I sometimes think I could easily trade a verb tense or a curtsy for some company that would stay over for a thirty-year weekend."

They drank their tea.   32

"Oh, such a rush of self-pity," she said good-naturedly. "About yourself, now. 33 You're thirty-one and still not married?"

"Let me put it this way," he said. "Women who act and think and talk like you 34 are rare."

"My," she said seriously, "you mustn't expect young women to talk like me. 35 That comes later. They're much too young, first of all. And secondly, the average man runs helter-skelter the moment he finds anything like a brain in a lady. You've probably met quite a few brainy ones who hid it most successfully from you. You'll have to pry around a bit to find the odd beetle. Lift a few boards."

They were laughing again.   36

"I shall probably be a meticulous old bachelor," he said.   37

"No, no, you mustn't do that. It wouldn't be right. You shouldn't even be here   38
this afternoon. This is a street which ends only in an Egyptian pyramid. Pyramids
are all very nice, but mummies are hardly fit companions. Where would you like
to go, what would you really like to do with your life?"

"See Istanbul, Port Said, Nairobi, Budapest. Write a book. Smoke too many   39
cigarettes. Fall off a cliff, but get caught in a tree halfway down. Get shot at a few
times in a dark alley on a Moroccan midnight. Love a beautiful woman."

"Well, I don't think I can provide them all," she said. "But I've traveled and I   40
can tell you about many of those places. And if you'd care to run across my front
lawn tonight about eleven and if I'm still awake, I'll fire off a Civil War musket at
you. Will that satisfy your masculine urge for adventure?"

"That would be just fine."   41

"Where would you like to go first? I can take you there, you know. I can weave   42
a spell. Just name it. London? Cairo? Cairo makes your face turn on like a light.
So let's go to Cairo. Just relax now. Put some of that nice tobacco in that pipe of
yours and sit back."

He sat back, lit his pipe, half smiling, relaxing, and listened, and she began to   43
talk. "Cairo . . ." she said.

The hour passed in jewels and alleys and winds from the Egyptian desert. The   44
sun was golden and the Nile was muddy where it lapped down to the deltas, and
there was someone very young and very quick at the top of the pyramid, laughing, calling to him to come on up the shadowy side into the sun, and he was
climbing, she putting her hand down to help him up the last step, and then they
were laughing on camel back, loping toward the great stretched bulk of the
Sphinx, and late at night, in the native quarter, there was the tinkle of small hammers on bronze and silver, and music from some stringed instruments fading
away and away and away. . . .

William Forrester opened his eyes. Miss Helen Loomis had finished the ad-   45
venture and they were home again, very familiar to each other, on the best of
terms, in the garden, the tea cold in the silver pourer, the biscuits dried in the
latened sun. He sighed and stretched and sighed again.

"I've never been so comfortable in my life."   46

"Nor I."   47

"I've kept you late. I should have gone an hour ago."   48

"You know I love every minute of it. But what you should see in an old silly   49
woman . . ."

He lay back in his chair and half closed his eyes and looked at her. He squinted   50
his eyes so the merest filament of light came through. He tilted his head ever so
little this way, then that.

"What are you doing?" she asked uncomfortably.   51

He said nothing, but continued looking.   52

"If you do this just right," he murmured, "you can adjust, make allowances. . . ." 53 To himself he was thinking, You can erase lines, adjust the time factor, turn back the years.

Suddenly he started. 54

"What's wrong?" she asked. 55

But then it was gone. He opened his eyes to catch it. That was a mistake. He 56 should have stayed back, idling, erasing, his eyes gently half closed.

"For just a moment," he said, "I saw it." 57

"Saw what?" 58

"The swan, of course," he thought. His mouth must have pantomimed the 59 words.

The next instant she was sitting very straight in her chair. Her hands were in 60 her lap, rigid. Her eyes were fixed upon him and as he watched, feeling helpless, each of her eyes cupped and brimmed itself full.

"I'm sorry," he said, "terribly sorry." 61

"No, don't be." She held herself rigid and did not touch her face or her eyes; 62 her hands remained, one atop the other, holding on. "You'd better go now. Yes, you may come tomorrow, but go now, please, and don't say any more."

He walked off through the garden, leaving her by her table in the shade. He 63 could not bring himself to look back.

Four days, eight days, twelve days passed, and he was invited to teas, to sup- 64 pers, to lunches. They sat talking through the long green afternoons—they talked of art, of literature, of life, of society and politics. They ate ice creams and squabs and drank good wines.

"I don't care what anyone says," she said. "And people are saying things, aren't 65 they?"

He shifted uneasily. 66

"I knew it. A woman's never safe, even when ninety-five, from gossip." 67

"I could stop visiting." 68

"Oh, no," she cried, and recovered. In a quieter voice she said, "You know you 69 can't do that. You know you don't care what they think, do you? So long as we know it's all right?"

"I don't care," he said. 70

"Now"—she settled back—"let's play our game. Where shall it be this time? 71 Paris? I think Paris."

"Paris," he said, nodding quietly. 72

"Well," she began, "it's the year 1885 and we're boarding the ship in New York 73 harbor. There's our luggage, here are our tickets, there goes the sky line. Now we're at sea. Now we're coming into Marseilles. . . ."

Here she was on a bridge looking into the clear waters of the Seine, and here 74 he was, suddenly, a moment later, beside her, looking down at the tides of summer flowing past. Here she was with an apéritif in her talcum-white fingers, and here he was, with amazing quickness, bending toward her to tap her wineglass with his. His face appeared in mirrored halls at Versailles, over steaming *smörgas-börds* in Stockholm, and they counted the barber poles in the Venice canals. The things she had done alone, they were now doing together.

————————

In the middle of August they sat staring at one another one late afternoon.   75

"Do you realize," he said, "I've seen you nearly every day for two and a half   76 weeks?"

"Impossible!"   77

"I've enjoyed it immensely."   78

"Yes, but there are so many young girls . . ."   79

"You're everything they are not—kind, intelligent, witty."   80

"Nonsense. Kindness and intelligence are the preoccupations of age. Being   81 cruel and thoughtless is far more fascinating when you're twenty." She paused and drew a breath. "Now, I'm going to embarrass you. Do you recall that first afternoon we met in the soda fountain, you said that you had had some degree of—shall we say affection for me at one time? You've purposely put me off on this by never mentioning it again. Now I'm forced to ask you to explain the whole uncomfortable thing."

He didn't seem to know what to say. "That's embarrassing," he protested.   82

"Spit it out!"   83

"I saw your picture once, years ago."   84

"I never let my picture be taken."   85

"This was an old one, taken when you were twenty."   86

"Oh, that. It's quite a joke. Each time I give to a charity or attend a ball they   87 dust that picture off and print it. Everyone in town laughs; even *I*."

"It's cruel of the paper."   88

"No. I told them, If you want a picture of me, use the one taken back in 1853.   89 Let them remember me that way. Keep the lid down, in the name of the good Lord, during the service."

"I'll tell you all about it." He folded his hands and looked at them and paused   90 a moment. He was remembering the picture now and it was very clear in his mind. There was time, here in the garden to think of every aspect of the photograph and of Helen Loomis, very young, posing for her picture the first time, alone and beautiful. He thought of her quiet, shyly smiling face.

It was the face of spring, it was the face of summer, it was the warmness   91 of clover breath. Pomegranate glowed in her lips, and the noon sky in her eyes. To touch her face was that always new experience of opening your window one December morning, early, and putting out your hand to the first white cool powdering of snow that had come, silently, with no announcement, in the night. And all of this, this breath-warmness and plum-tenderness was held forever in one miracle of photographic chemistry which no clock winds could blow upon to change one hour or one second; this fine first cool white snow would never melt, but live a thousand summers.

That was the photograph; that was the way he knew her. Now he was talking   92 again, after the remembering and the thinking over and the holding of the picture in his mind. "When I first saw that picture—it was a simple, straightforward picture with a simple hairdo—I didn't know it had been taken that long ago. The item in the paper said something about Helen Loomis marshalling the Town Ball that night. I tore the picture from the paper. I carried it with me all that day. I intended going to the ball. Then, late in the afternoon, someone saw me looking at the picture, and told me about it. How the picture of the beautiful girl had been taken so long ago and used every year since by the paper. And they said I shouldn't go to the Town Ball that night, carrying that picture and looking for you."

They sat in the garden for a long minute. He glanced over at her face. She was looking at the farthest garden wall and the pink roses climbing there. There was no way to tell what she was thinking. Her face showed nothing. She rocked for a little while in her chair and then said softly, "Shall we have some more tea? There you are." 93

They sat sipping the tea. Then she reached over and patted his arm. "Thank you." 94

"For what?" 95

"For wanting to come to find me at the dance, for clipping out my picture, for everything. Thank you so very much." 96

They walked about the garden on the paths. 97

"And now," she said, "it's my turn. Do you remember, I mentioned a certain young man who once attended me, seventy years ago? Oh, he's been dead fifty years now, at least, but when he was very young and very handsome he rode a fast horse off for days, or on summer nights over the meadows around town. He had a healthy, wild face, always sunburned, his hands were always cut and he fumed like a stovepipe and walked as if he were going to fly apart; wouldn't keep a job, quit those he had when he felt like it, and one day he sort of rode off away from me because I was even wilder than he and wouldn't settle down, and that was that. I never thought the day would come when I would see him alive again. But you're pretty much alive, you spill ashes around like he did, you're clumsy and graceful combined, I know everything you're going to do before you do it, but after you've done it I'm always surprised. Reincarnation's a lot of milk-mush to me, but the other day I felt, What if I called Robert, Robert, to you on the street, would William Forrester turn around?" 98

"I don't know," he said. 99

"Neither do I. That's what makes life interesting." 100

August was almost over. The first cool touch of autumn moved slowly through the town and there was a softening and the first gradual burning fever of color in every tree, a faint flush and coloring in the hills, and the color of lions in the wheat fields. Now the pattern of days was familiar and repeated like a penman beautifully inscribing again and again, in practice, a series of *l*'s and *w*'s and *m*'s, day after day the line repeated in delicate rills. 101

William Forrester walked across the garden one early August afternoon to find Helen Loomis writing with great care at the tea table. 102

She put aside her pen and ink.   103

"I've been writing you a letter," she said.   104

"Well, my being here saves you the trouble."   105

"No, this is a special letter. Look at it." She showed him the blue envelope,   106
which she now sealed and pressed flat. "Remember how it looks. When you receive this in the mail, you'll know I'm dead."

"That's no way to talk, is it?"   107

"Sit down and listen to me."   108

He sat.   109

"My dear William," she said, under the parasol shade. "In a few days I will be   110
dead. No." She put up her hand. "I don't want you to say a thing. I'm not afraid.
When you live as long as I've lived you lose that, too. I never liked lobster in my
life, and mainly because I'd never tried it. On my eightieth birthday I tried it. I
can't say I'm greatly excited over lobster still, but I have no doubt as to its taste
now, and I don't fear it. I dare say death will be a lobster, too, and I can come to
terms with it." She motioned with her hands. "But enough of that. The important
thing is that I shan't be seeing you again. There will be no services. I believe that a
woman who has passed through that particular door has as much right to privacy
as a woman who has retired for the night."

"You can't predict death," he said at last.   111

"For fifty years I've watched the grandfather clock in the hall, William. After   112
it is wound I can predict to the hour when it will stop. Old people are no different. They can feel the machinery slow down and the last weights shift. Oh, please
don't look that way—please don't."

"I can't help it," he said.   113

"We've had a nice time, haven't we? It has been very special here, talking every   114
day. It was that much-overburdened and worn phrase referred to as a 'meeting of
the minds.'" She turned the blue envelope in her hands. "I've always known that
the quality of love was the mind, even though the body sometimes refuses this
knowledge. The body lives for itself. It lives only to feed and wait for the night. It's
essentially nocturnal. But what of the mind which is born of the sun, William, and
must spend thousands of hours of a lifetime awake and aware? Can you balance
off the body, that pitiful, selfish thing of night against a whole lifetime of sun and
intellect? I don't know. I only know there has been your mind here and my mind
here, and the afternoons have been like none I can remember. There is still so
much to talk about, but we must save it for another time."

"We don't seem to have much time now."   115

"No, but perhaps there *will* be another time. Time is so strange and life is twice   116
as strange. The cogs miss, the wheels turn, and lives interlace too early or too late.
I lived too long that much is certain. And you were born either too early or too
late. It was a terrible bit of timing. But perhaps I am being punished for being a
silly girl. Anyway, the next spin around, wheels might function right again. Meantime you must find a nice girl and be married and be happy. But you must promise me one thing."

"Anything."   117

"You must promise me not to live to be too old, William. If it is at all conve-   118
nient, die before you're fifty. It may take a bit of doing. But I advise this simply because there is no telling when another Helen Loomis might be born. It would be
dreadful, wouldn't it, if you lived on to be very, very old and some afternoon in
1999 walked down Main Street and saw me standing there, aged twenty-one, and
the whole thing out of balance again? I don't think we could go through any more
afternoons like these we've had, no matter how pleasant, do you? A thousand gallons of tea and five hundred biscuits is enough for one friendship. So you must
have an attack of pneumonia some time in about twenty years. For I don't know
how long they let you linger on the other side. Perhaps they send you back immediately. But I shall do my best, William, really I shall. And everything put right
and in balance, do you know what might happen?"

"You tell me."   119

"Some afternoon in 1985 or 1990 a young man named Tom Smith or John   120
Green or a name like that, will be walking downtown and will stop in the drugstore and order, appropriately, a dish of some unusual ice cream. A young girl the
same age will be sitting there and when she hears the name of that ice cream,
something will happen. I can't say what or how. *She* won't know why or how, as-
suredly. Nor will the young man. It will simply be that the name of that ice cream
will be a very good thing to both of them. They'll talk. And later, when they know
each other's names, they'll walk from the drugstore together."

She smiled at him.   121

"This is all very neat, but forgive an old lady for tying things in neat packets.   122
It's a silly trifle to leave you. Now let's talk of something else. What shall we talk
about? Is there any place in the world we haven't traveled to yet? Have we been to
Stockholm?"

"Yes, it's a fine town."   123

"Glasgow? Yes? Where then?"   124

"Why not Green Town, Illinois?" he said. "Here. We haven't really visited our   125
own town together at all."

She settled back, as did he, and she said, "I'll tell you how it was, then, when I   126
was only nineteen, in this town, a long time ago. . . ."

It was a night in winter and she was skating lightly over a pond of white moon   127
ice, her image gliding and whispering under her. It was a night in summer in this
town of fire in the air, in the cheeks, in the heart, your eyes full of the glowing and
shutting-off color of fireflies. It was a rustling night in October, and there she
stood, pulling taffy from a hook in the kitchen, singing, and there she was, running on the moss by the river, and swimming in the granite pit beyond town on
a spring night, in the soft deep warm waters, and now it was the Fourth of July
with rockets slamming the sky and every porch full of now red-fire, now blue-fire,
now white-fire faces, hers dazzling bright among them as the last rocket died.

"Can you see all these things?" asked Helen Loomis. "Can you see me doing   128
them and being with them?"

"Yes," said William Forrester, eyes closed. "I can see you."   129

"And then," she said, "and then . . ."   130

Her voice moved on and on as the afternoon grew late and the twilight deep-   131
ened quickly, but her voice moved in the garden and anyone passing on the road,
at a far distance, could have heard its moth sound, faintly, faintly. . . .

———————

Two days later William Forrester was at his desk in his room when the letter   132
came. Douglas brought it upstairs and handed it to Bill and looked as if he knew
what was in it.

William Forrester recognized the blue envelope, but did not open it. He sim-   133
ply put it in his shirt pocket, looked at the boy for a moment, and said, "Come on,
Doug; my treat."

They walked downtown, saying very little, Douglas preserving the silence he   134
sensed was necessary. Autumn, which had threatened for a time, was gone. Summer was back full, boiling the clouds and scouring the metal sky. They turned in
at the drugstore and sat at the marble fountain. William Forrester took the letter
out and laid it before him and still did not open it.

He looked out at the yellow sunlight on the concrete and on the green awnings   135
and shining on the gold letters of the window signs across the street, and he
looked at the calendar on the wall. August 27, 1928. He looked at his wrist watch
and felt his heart beat slowly, saw the second hand of the watch moving moving
with no speed at all, saw the calendar frozen there with its one day seeming forever, the sun nailed to the sky with no motion toward sunset whatever. The warm
air spread under the sighing fans over his head. A number of women laughed by
the open door and were gone through his vision, which was focused beyond them
at the town itself and the high courthouse clock. He opened the letter and began
to read.

He turned slowly on the revolving chair. He tried the words again and again,   136
silently, on his tongue, and at last spoke them aloud and repeated them.

"A dish of lime-vanilla ice," he said. "A dish of lime-vanilla ice."   137

ACTIVITIES FOR WRITING AND DISCUSSION

1. Respond to the story using the "Four-Step Process for Writing from Reading" described in Chapter 2.

2. Describe the love that binds Bill and Helen together. Is it physical? spiritual? social? emotional? intellectual? all or some of the above? which? Elaborate
with examples from the text.

3. Reflecting the perspective of ninety-five years of life, Helen's conversation
is marvelously witty and perceptive. Annotate any remarks by her that strike you.
Then, in your notebook, reflect on these remarks.

4. Bill and Helen fantasize themselves to be together in various exotic places
around the globe. Imagine that through a wrinkle in time, a young William meets

a young Helen. What happens? What sort of relationship do they form? How does this relationship evolve over the next ten, twenty, or fifty years?

5. The **setting** of the story is memorable: the 1920s, summertime, a small average town in Middle America. Write a story or memoir of your own in which you emphasize the setting (whether pleasant or unpleasant), describing time and place in vivid and evocative terms.

Claire Kemp (b. 1936)

Keeping Company

William wakes me with water. He sprays me through the window screen and I am 1
introduced to morning under tangled sheets, sprinkled damp and rolled like laundry ready for the iron. He's whistling. When he sings, "Lazy Mary, will you get up?", I do and go outside in my nightdress to stand barefoot on the cool wet cement close to William. "Hello, wife," he says.

Two men walking to the beach smile and wave a hand in greeting. I raise my 2
hand to wave to them but William checks me with a look. He aims the hose at the street but the pressure is down and the water falls short. "Missed by a mile," he says. "I'm losing my touch."

"They're not bothering anyone. What do you care?"   3

"They're bothering me and I care." A small muscle in his cheek keeps an angry 4
beat.

"You'll be late for work," I tell him and run inside to make his eggs, soft boiled 5
on white toast.

"Never happen," he says. The hose, a fat green snake, uncoils and follows obe- 6
diently wherever he walks.

———

Mornings I go to the beach. I go alone because William won't. Certain young 7
men come to stroll on this beach. Their walk is a slow dance, graceful and sure. They glide on pewter sand like skaters do on ice. In their brief suits, satin bands of azure blue, magenta, yellow, emerald green, they appear as exotic flowers blooming in the desert. I am taken with their beauty and don't mind sitting in their shade. Not unkindly they dismiss me with their eyes, unencumbered souls walking free at water's edge with perhaps a scarlet towel over one tanned shoulder or a small cloth bag worn around the neck to hold the treasures of the moment. They have smiles for each other but not for me. I'm a cabbage in their garden, a woman large with child, a different species altogether. Next year, I'll have someone to keep me company. I'll teach her how to make castles with turrets from paper cups and wet sand. Swizzle sticks will make a fine bridge to span the moat. Perhaps we'll place cocktail parasols for color in the sand palace courtyard. And I'll take her home before the tide comes in to take it down. She's with me

now, tumbling and turning in her water bed and dancing on my ribs with tiny heels and toes. She's coming to term and letting me know. It won't be long.

Afternoons I tend my flowers. Today, I see an open truck parked next door. 8 And a piano on the porch. Two men are discussing how to get it through the door. One goes inside to pull; the other stays out to push. I think of the piano as a stubborn horse, its mahogany rump splendid in the sun. "Perhaps, if you offer it sugar," I suggest. The outside man grins. "Hello," he says and vaults over his porch rail. I brush potting soil from my hands and reach to shake his hand.

"I'm James," he says. His eyes are gray blue and direct. When he smiles his fea- 9 tures merge brightly like a photograph in focus. He has a good face. He says, "Dennis is inside. He might come out or he might not. He's shy." Behind him, someone parts the lace curtain at one window and lets it fall.

I tell James my name and he says, "It's nice to meet you, Nora. Your flowers 10 are lovely." But he's not looking at my flowers. Just at me. He nods in affirmation of some private thought and says, "Moving's more work than I bargained for. I'd better get back to it."

"Yes, see you again" I reply and bend to the task of breaking off the blooms 11 gone by. The aroma of geranium is so strong it seems to leave a taste on my tongue. When I go inside to make myself a cup of tea, the piano has made it through the door and there is no one in sight.

After dinner, I tell William we have neighbors and he tells me he's not blind. 12 He uncaps a beer and tilts the bottle to his lips. He wipes foam from his beard with the back of his hand and gives me a long look I'm meant to pay attention to. "Don't bother with them, Nora. They're not our kind." From next door I hear a tentative chord or two. I listen for more but the night air is still, not another note. I listen for sounds from their house over the sounds of our house all evening long. I don't know why I would. After a while the heat leaves the house and it's cool enough for sleep and still I listen.

James brings me a croissant sprinkled with cinnamon and sugar. I put down 13 my watering can and take it from his hand. Dennis is practicing scales and I remember how it felt to play, my eyes on the page, not on the keys.

"What are you hoping for?" James asks shyly. 14

"It's a girl. We already know. Doctors can tell in advance now. We've named 15 her Sara."

"Imagine," he says but his eyes are worried as if he marvels at giving credibil- 16 ity to someone who can't yet breathe on her own. "She's like a present, as yet unwrapped," he says. Abruptly the music stops. I picture Dennis closing the piano, covering the keys and going to another part of his house.

"Dennis is tired," James explains. He has already turned from me toward the 17 silence and I am left holding the still warm pastry in one hand and nothing in the other.

I hang the wash, William's work shirts, dish cloths and towels, heavy sheets 18
that pull on my arms. Next door, James and Dennis talking, always talking. Their
voices rise and fall and blend together. They have so much to say. They never seem
to tire of talk. Their screen door opens and shuts throughout the day as they come
and go. When they are out of each other's sight, one calls out and the other
answers.

Late in the day, I take in the dry clothes, stripping the line and folding as I go 19
along, leaving the clothespins to bob like small wooden birds. Dennis and James
head for the beach. Dennis wears a light jacket zipped to the neck as if he is cold.
His short sandy hair curls up around his cap, leaving the back of his neck bare,
like a young boy's. I can tell James would walk faster if he was alone. Perhaps he
would run. As it is, he holds back to keep the pace that Dennis sets but his energy
shows itself in the enthusiastic swing of his arms and the quick, attentive way he
inclines his head to catch the words that Dennis speaks. When they're out of sight
beyond the dunes, I go inside to wait for William.

James is teaching me backgammon. We sit on his patio under the Cinzano 20
umbrella and drink iced tea with lemon slices on the rim of tall oddly shaped amber glasses, no two alike. Dennis will not play but once he points out a move for
me and seems quietly pleased when I take that game from James. I do not tell
William where I spend my summer afternoons. I'm where I belong when he gets
home. He slides his arms around me and rubs my face with his beard and says
proudly, "Nora, I swear, you're as big as a house." "I am," I agree, laughing. "I'm
Sara's house." He does not ask me what I do all day and I would not tell him if he
did. I know something about myself that I didn't know before. I'm successful at
sins of omission, never really lying, never telling truth. I hoard secrets like a dog
who buries bones to relish at some future time. I wonder if when that time comes,
I will remember why or where I dug the holes.

William comes home early, tires spinning in the sand on the lane between our 21
house and theirs. I'm caught and stand up fast from James' table and hurry home
leaving James in the middle of a play.

"I don't want you over there," William tells me. "Is that clear?" 22

"But why? They're good company." 23

"They can keep each other company. Not you. I'm your good company. The 24
only company you'll ever need."

William sighs when he looks at me as though I'm a chore he must complete. 25

Dennis gives a concert in my honor, all my favorite pieces played perfect, 26
without flaw or fault. I sit on my front step as evening falls to dark and listen till
he's done.

William is building a wall. To make certain he's within his rights, he engages a 27
surveyor to determine the exact boundaries of our land. After supper and on

Saturdays he works on his wall. There are guidelines he must follow as to height. I know if permitted he would make it six feet high, five inches taller than the top of my head, but the law won't allow it. Its purpose is to keep me in my place. When he's done, he calls me out to admire his work and I do. I tell him it's a fine wall which is what he wants to hear. James, on his porch, raises his glass in a silent toast. I send him my best smile, an apology big enough for both William and myself.

William has gone south to deliver a boat and won't be home before midnight 28 at least. James invites me for dinner. I'm invited, so I go. Their kitchen is yellow and blue, quaint, like a woman's sitting room. There are many plants I can't begin to name in clay pots and hanging baskets. I sit on paisley cushions in a wicker chair by the window watching James make stew from scratch. While James chops vegetables, his hand on the knife making quick, precise cuts, Dennis copies the recipe in his spidery script on a card for me to take home. I set the table, lace cloth from Ireland, tall rose colored candles in crystal, linen napkins in shell rings and sterling silver by the plates. James holds my chair and seats me as if I am a lady and not a country girl in faded shorts and one of William's shirts. Dennis searches the yard for hibiscus blooms. He floats them in a shallow blue bowl for a centerpiece. I have gone over the wall.

Unlike Cinderella, I'm home well before midnight in my own kitchen, with a 29 bowl of stew for William over a low flame on my stove. He eats out of the pan. "What are these yellow things?" he asks, poking with his fork.

"Parsnips."   30

"OK," he says. "Next time peas. Otherwise, not bad at all."   31

I let him think I made the stew myself which of course I could have done. And 32 maybe will someday. The recipe is out of sight in the bottom of my sewing box.

We are in a tropical depression. Hot steady rain for a week and thick humid 33 air that leaves me worn out and sleepy. I stay inside, an idle woman, changing in spite of myself like a mushroom growing at a furious rate in this damp and fertile season. We lose our power and Dennis brings candles. He hands the bag to William and runs off without a proper thank you. William hands it quick to me as if its contents are not candles but sticks of dynamite that could go off at any minute. He follows me like the tail of a kite as I place lighted candles on waxed saucers in each room of our house. "The wall is holding," he says. "Can you believe it?" I say, "Yes, I believe it."

In September, Sara will be born.   34

When the storms give in to sun I'm glad, but it reigns in the sky like a lion. Its 35 heat is fierce. I have not seen Dennis or James. The piano does not play. I knock on their door and finally James is there behind the screen. He doesn't lift the latch. I say, "How are you? I miss you two." "Not to worry," he assures me without meeting my eyes. When I ask for Dennis, James shrugs as if Dennis is someone he's lost track of somehow and can't be bothered getting back, which I know for sure is not the truth. He laughs then, a short harsh sound like a bark. "Sorry," he says. "Dennis is in the hospital. I don't know that he'll be coming home." He says this like he's asking a question, like he's asking me for an answer. I put my hand on my side of the screen and James touches it briefly with his. We stand for a moment, like visitors in prison before he closes the inside door and shuts me out. I wish I could take back the days.

I go home where I belong. There is laundry to fold, chores to do, an entire 36 house to put to order. I do a proper job of every task, a proper penance. Before bed, I tell William. I know as I begin to speak that it will not go well but I'm bound to tell it, to lay it out like a soiled cloth on our clean table.

"Dennis is sick," I say and at just that moment I know that this truth is another 37 bone I buried.

William says, "Yes, he is. Very sick. Have you been over there again? I told you 38 to stay away from them. I warned you. But, knowing you. . . ."

"You don't." 39

"Don't what?" 40

"Know me." I stand up. There is a knot of sorrow that drops in me like a 41 sinker in a tidal pool. I walk out the door and away from William. At the jetty, I climb the slick black rocks, heedless of the cruel pockets of stone that could snap a limb as easy as not. I find a smooth stone that makes a good seat. I'm surprised to know I'm crying. Our porch light comes on and there is William, his pale hair like a halo under its glow. He calls me. "Nora, come home," but the tide takes his voice and swallows my name. When I'm thoroughly chilled and empty of anger, I leave my perch and travel north on the wet sand, close to the cool fingers of incoming tide. I'm a small but competent ship sailing the coast line. I set my own course. I hear someone running in my wake and it's William, breathless from the chase. He passes me on fast feet, then turns, dancing backward like a boxer until I stop just shy of the circle of his arms. He carries my sweater, which he puts around my shoulders with great care, as if it is a precious fur he wraps me in and I too am precious. He buttons one button under my chin with clumsy fingers. "Let's go back," he says, so we do. We do not talk about anything, simply walk forward in silence, which is the way it is between husbands and wives, with married people.

RAYMOND CARVER (1938–1988)

Call If You Need Me

We had both been involved with other people that spring, but when June came 1 and school was out we decided to let our house for the summer and move from Palo Alto to the north coast country of California. Our son, Richard, went to Nancy's grandmother's place in Pasco, Washington, to live for the summer and work toward saving money for college in the fall. His grandmother knew the situation at home and had begun working on getting him up there and locating him a job long before his arrival. She'd talked to a farmer friend of hers and had secured a promise of work for Richard baling hay and building fences. Hard work, but Richard was looking forward to it. He left on the bus in the morning of the day after his high school graduation. I took him to the station and parked and went inside to sit with him until his bus was called. His mother had already held him and cried and kissed him good-bye and given him a long letter that he was to deliver to his grandmother upon his arrival. She was at home now finishing last-minute packing for our own move and waiting for the couple who were to take our house. I bought Richard's ticket, gave it to him, and we sat on one of the benches in the station and waited. We'd talked a little about things on the way to the station.

"Are you and Mom going to get a divorce?" he'd asked. It was Saturday morn- 2 ing, and there weren't many cars.

"Not if we can help it," I said. "We don't want to. That's why we're going away 3 from here and don't expect to see anyone all summer. That's why we've rented our house for the summer and rented the house up in Arcata. Why you're going away, too, I guess. One reason anyway. Not to mention the fact that you'll come home with your pockets filled with money. We don't want to get a divorce. We want to be alone for the summer and try to work things out."

"You still love Mom?" he said. "She told me she loves you." 4

"Of course I do," I said. "You ought to know that by now. We've just had our 5 share of troubles and heavy responsibilities, like everyone else, and now we need time to be alone and work things out. But don't worry about us. You just go up there and have a good summer and work hard and save your money. Consider it a vacation, too. Get in all the fishing you can. There's good fishing around there."

"Water-skiing, too," he said. "I want to learn to water-ski." 6

"I've never been water-skiing," I said. "Do some of that for me too, will you?" 7

We sat in the bus station. He looked through his yearbook while I held a news- 8 paper in my lap. Then his bus was called and we stood up. I embraced him, and said again, "Don't worry, don't worry. Where's your ticket?"

He patted his coat pocket and then picked up his suitcase. I walked him over 9 to where the line was forming in the terminal, then I embraced him again and kissed him on the cheek and said good-bye.

"Good-bye, Dad," he said, and turned from me so that I wouldn't see his tears. 10

I drove home to where our boxes and suitcases were waiting in the living 11 room. Nancy was in the kitchen drinking coffee with the young couple she'd found to take our house for the summer. I'd met the couple, Jerry and Liz, grad-uate students in math, for the first time a few days before, but we shook hands again, and I drank a cup of coffee that Nancy poured. We sat around the table and drank coffee while Nancy finished her list of things they should look out for or do at certain times of the month, the first and last of each month, where they should send any mail, and the like. Nancy's face was tight. Sun fell through the curtain onto the table as it got later in the morning.

Finally, things seemed to be in order and I left the three of them in the kitchen   12
and began loading the car. It was a furnished house we were going to, furnished
right down to plates and cooking utensils, so we wouldn't need to take much with
us from this house, only the essentials.

I'd driven up to Eureka, 350 miles north of Palo Alto, on the north coast of   13
California, three weeks before and rented us the furnished house. I went with Susan, the woman I'd been seeing. We stayed in a motel at the edge of town for three
nights while I looked in the newspaper and visited real estate agents. She watched
me as I wrote out a check for the three months' rent. Later, back at the motel, in
bed, she lay with her hand on her forehead, and said, "I envy your wife. I envy
Nancy. You hear people talk about 'the other woman' always and how the incumbent wife has the privileges and the real power, but I never really understood or
cared about those things before. Now I see. I envy her. I envy her the life she will
have with you in that house this summer. I wish it were me. I wish it were us. Oh,
how I wish it were us. I feel so crummy," she said. I stroked her hair.

Nancy was a tall, long-legged woman with brown hair and eyes and a gener-   14
ous spirit. But lately we had been coming up short on generosity and spirit. The
man she had been seeing was one of my colleagues, a divorced, dapper, three-
piece-suit-and-tie fellow with graying hair who drank too much and whose
hands, some of my students told me, sometimes shook in the classroom. He and
Nancy had drifted into their affair at a party during the holidays not too long after Nancy had discovered my own affair. It all sounds boring and tacky now—it
is boring and tacky—but during that spring it was what it was, and it consumed
all of our energies and concentration to the exclusion of everything else. Sometime in late April we began to make plans to rent our house and go away for the
summer, just the two of us, and try to put things back together, if they could be
put back together. We each agreed we would not call or write or otherwise be in
touch with the other parties. So we made arrangements for Richard, found the
couple to look after our house, and I had looked at a map and driven north from
San Francisco and found Eureka, and an agent who was willing to rent a furnished house to a respectable middle-aged married couple for the summer. I
think I even used the phrase second honeymoon to the real estate agent, God forgive me, while Susan smoked a cigarette and read tourist brochures out in the car.

I finished storing the suitcases, bags, and cartons in the trunk and back seat   15
and waited while Nancy said a final good-bye on the porch. She shook hands with
each of them and turned and came toward the car. I waved to the couple, and they
waved back. Nancy got in and shut the door. "Let's go," she said. I put the car in
gear and we headed for the freeway. At the light just before the freeway we saw a
car ahead of us come off the freeway trailing a broken muffler, the sparks flying.
"Look at that," Nancy said. "It might catch fire." We waited and watched until the
car managed to pull off the road and onto the shoulder.

We stopped at a little café off the highway near Sebastopol. EAT AND GAS, the   16
sign read. We laughed at the sign. I pulled up in front of the café and we went inside and took a table near a window in the back of the café. After we had ordered
coffee and sandwiches, Nancy touched her forefinger to the table and began

tracing lines in the wood. I lit a cigarette and looked outside. I saw rapid movement, and then I realized I was looking at a hummingbird in the bush beside the window. Its wings moved in a blur of motion and it kept dipping its beak into a blossom on the bush.

"Nancy, look," I said. "There's a hummingbird." 17

But the hummingbird flew at this moment, and Nancy looked, and said, "Where? I don't see it." 18

"It was just there a minute ago," I said. "Look, there it is. Another one, I think. It's another hummingbird." 19

We watched the hummingbird until the waitress brought our order and the bird flew at the movement and disappeared around the building. 20

"Now, that's a good sign, I think," I said. "Hummingbirds. Hummingbirds are supposed to bring luck." 21

"I've heard that somewhere," she said. "I don't know where I heard that, but I've heard it. Well," she said, "luck is what we could use. Wouldn't you say?" 22

"They're a good sign," I said. "I'm glad we stopped here." 23

She nodded. She waited a minute, then she took a bite of her sandwich. 24

We reached Eureka just before dark. We passed the motel on the highway where Susan and I had stayed and had spent the three nights some weeks before, then turned off the highway and took a road up over a hill overlooking the town. I had the house keys in my pocket. We drove over the hill and for a mile or so until we came to a little intersection with a service station and a grocery store. There were wooded mountains ahead of us in the valley, and pastureland all around. Some cattle were grazing in a field behind the service station. "This is pretty country," Nancy said. "I'm anxious to see the house." 25

"Almost there," I said. "It's just down this road," I said, "and over that rise." "Here," I said in a minute, and pulled into a long driveway with hedge on either side. "Here it is. What do you think of this?" I'd asked the same question of Susan when she and I had stopped in the driveway. 26

"It's nice," Nancy said. "It looks fine, it does. Let's get out." 27

We stood in the front yard a minute and looked around. Then we went up the porch steps and I unlocked the front door and turned on the lights. We went through the house. There were two small bedrooms, a bath, a living room with old furniture and a fireplace, and a big kitchen with a view of the valley. 28

"Do you like it?" I said. 29

"I think it's just wonderful," Nancy said. She grinned. "I'm glad you found it. I'm glad we're here." She opened the refrigerator and ran a finger over the counter. "Thank God, it looks clean enough. I won't have to do any cleaning." 30

"Right down to clean sheets on the beds," I said. "I checked. I made sure. That's the way they're renting it. Pillows even. And pillowcases, too." 31

"We'll have to buy some firewood," she said. We were standing in the living room. "We'll want to have a fire on nights like this." 32

"I'll look into firewood tomorrow," I said. "We can go shopping then too and see the town." 33

She looked at me, and said, "I'm glad we're here."   34

"So am I," I said. I opened my arms and she moved to me. I held her. I could feel 35 her trembling. I turned her face up and kissed her on either cheek. "Nancy," I said.

"I'm glad we're here," she said.   36

We spent the next few days settling in, taking trips into Eureka to walk around and 37 look in store windows, and hiking across the pastureland behind the house all the way to the woods. We bought groceries and I found an ad in the newspaper for firewood, called, and a day or so afterward two young men with long hair delivered a pickup truckload of alder and stacked it in the carport. That night we sat in front of the fireplace after dinner and drank coffee and talked about getting a dog.

"I don't want a pup," Nancy said. "Something we have to clean up after or that 38 will chew things up. That we don't need. But I'd like to have a dog, yes. We haven't had a dog in a long time. I think we could handle a dog up here," she said.

"And after we go back, after summer's over?" I said. I rephrased the question. 39 "What about keeping a dog in the city?"

"We'll see. Meanwhile, let's look for a dog. The right kind of dog. I don't know 40 what I want until I see it. We'll read the classifieds and we'll go to the pound, if we have to." But though we went on talking about dogs for several days, and pointed out dogs to each other in people's yards we'd drive past, dogs we said we'd like to have, nothing came of it, we didn't get a dog.

Nancy called her mother and gave her our address and telephone number. 41 Richard was working and seemed happy, her mother said. She herself was fine. I heard Nancy say, "We're fine. This is good medicine."

One day in the middle of July we were driving the highway near the ocean and 42 came over a rise to see some lagoons that were closed off from the ocean by sand spits. There were some people fishing from shore, and two boats out on the water.

I pulled the car off onto the shoulder and stopped. "Let's see what they're 43 fishing for," I said. "Maybe we could get some gear and go ourselves."

"We haven't been fishing in years," Nancy said. "Not since that time Richard 44 was little and we went camping near Mount Shasta. Do you remember that?"

"I remember," I said. "I just remembered too that I've missed fishing. Let's 45 walk down and see what they're fishing for."

"Trout," the man said, when I asked. "Cutthroats and rainbow trout. Even 46 some steelhead and a few salmon. They come in here in the winter when the spit opens and then when it closes in the spring, they're trapped. This is a good time of the year for them. I haven't caught any today, but last Sunday I caught four, about fifteen inches long. Best eating fish in the world, and they put up a hell of a fight. Fellows out in the boats have caught some today, but so far I haven't done anything today."

"What do you use for bait?" Nancy asked.   47

"Anything," the man said. "Worms, salmon eggs, whole kernel corn. Just get it 48 out there and leave it lay on the bottom. Pull out a little slack and watch your line."

We hung around a little longer and watched the man fish and watched the 49 little boats chat-chat back and forth the length of the lagoon.

"Thanks," I said to the man. "Good luck to you."   50

"Good luck to you," he said. "Good luck to the both of you."   51

We stopped at a sporting goods store on the way back to town and bought li-   52
censes, inexpensive rods and reels, nylon line, hooks, leaders, sinkers, and a creel.
We made plans to go fishing the next morning.

But that night, after we'd eaten dinner and washed the dishes and I had laid a   53
fire in the fireplace, Nancy shook her head and said it wasn't going to work.

"Why do you say that?" I asked. "What is it you mean?"   54

"I mean it isn't going to work. Let's face it." She shook her head again. "I don't   55
think I want to go fishing in the morning, either, and I don't want a dog. No, no
dogs. I think I want to go up and see my mother and Richard. Alone. I want to be
alone. I miss Richard," she said, and began to cry. "Richard's my son, my baby,"
she said, "and he's nearly grown and gone. I miss him."

"And Del, do you miss Del Shraeder, too?" I said. "Your boyfriend. Do you   56
miss him?"

"I miss everybody tonight," she said. "I miss you too. I've missed you for a   57
long time now. I've missed you so much you've gotten lost somehow, I can't explain it. I've lost you. You're not mine any longer."

"Nancy," I said.   58

"No, no," she said. She shook her head. She sat on the sofa in front of the fire   59
and kept shaking her head. "I want to fly up and see my mother and Richard tomorrow. After I'm gone you can call your girlfriend."

"I won't do that," I said. "I have no intention of doing that."   60

"You'll call her," she said.   61

"You'll call Del," I said. I felt rubbishy for saying it.   62

"You can do what you want," she said, wiping her eyes on her sleeve. "I mean   63
that. I don't want to sound hysterical. But I'm going up to Washington tomorrow.
Right now I'm going to go to bed. I'm exhausted. I'm sorry. I'm sorry for both of
us, Dan. We're not going to make it. That fisherman today. He wished us good
luck." She shook her head. "I wish us good luck too. We're going to need it."

She went into the bathroom, and I heard water running in the tub. I went out   64
and sat on the porch steps and smoked a cigarette. It was dark and quiet outside.
I looked toward town and could see a faint glow of lights in the sky and patches
of ocean fog drifting in the valley. I began to think of Susan. A little later Nancy
came out of the bathroom and I heard the bedroom door close. I went inside and
put another block of wood on the grate and waited until the flames began to move
up the bark. Then I went into the other bedroom and turned the covers back and
stared at the floral design on the sheets. Then I showered, dressed in my pajamas,
and went to sit near the fireplace again. The fog was outside the window now. I
sat in front of the fire and smoked. When I looked out the window again, something moved in the fog and I saw a horse grazing in the front yard.

I went to the window. The horse looked up at me for a minute, then went back   65
to pulling up grass. Another horse walked past the car into the yard and began to
graze. I turned on the porch light and stood at the window and watched them.
They were big white horses with long manes. They'd gotten through a fence or an
unlocked gate from one of the nearby farms. Somehow they'd wound up in our

front yard. They were larking it, enjoying their breakaway immensely. But they were nervous too; I could see the whites of their eyes from where I stood behind the window. Their ears kept rising and falling as they tore out clumps of grass. A third horse wandered into the yard, and then a fourth. It was a herd of white horses, and they were grazing in our front yard.

I went into the bedroom and woke Nancy. Her eyes were red and the skin 66 around the eyes was swollen. She had her hair up in curlers and a suitcase lay open on the floor near the foot of the bed.

"Nancy," I said. "Honey, come and see what's in the front yard. Come and see 67 this. You must see this. You won't believe it. Hurry up."

"What is it?" she said. "Don't hurt me. What is it?" 68

"Honey, you must see this. I'm not going to hurt you. I'm sorry if I scared you. 69 But you must come out here and see something."

I went back into the other room and stood in front of the window and in a few 70 minutes Nancy came in tying her robe. She looked out the window, and said, "My God, they're beautiful. Where'd they come from, Dan? They're just beautiful."

"They must have gotten loose from around here somewhere," I said. "One of 71 these farm places. I'll call the sheriff's department pretty soon and let them locate the owners. But I wanted you to see this first."

"Will they bite?" she said. "I'd like to pet that one there, that one that just 72 looked at us. I'd like to pat that one's shoulder. But I don't want to get bitten. I'm going outside."

"I don't think they'll bite," I said. "They don't look like the kind of horses 73 that'll bite. But put a coat on if you're going out there; it's cold."

I put my coat on over my pajamas and waited for Nancy. Then I opened the 74 front door and we went outside and walked into the yard with the horses. They all looked up at us. Two of them went back to pulling up grass. One of the other horses snorted and moved back a few steps, and then it too went back to pulling up grass and chewing, head down. I rubbed the forehead of one horse and patted its shoulder. It kept chewing. Nancy put out her hand and began stroking the mane of another horse. "Horsey, where'd you come from?" she said. "Where do you live and why are you out tonight, Horsey?" she said, and kept stroking the horse's mane. The horse looked at her and blew through its lips and dropped its head again. She patted its shoulder.

"I guess I'd better call the sheriff," I said. 75

"Not yet," she said. "Not for a while yet. We'll never see anything like this 76 again. We'll never, never have horses in our front yard again. Wait a while yet, Dan."

A little later, Nancy was still out there moving from one horse to another, pat- 77 ting their shoulders and stroking their manes, when one of the horses moved from the yard into the driveway and walked around the car and down the driveway toward the road, and I knew I had to call.

In a little while the two sheriff's cars showed up with their red lights flashing 78 in the fog and a few minutes later a fellow with a sheepskin coat driving a pickup with a horse trailer behind it. Now the horses shied and tried to get away, and the man with the horse trailer swore and tried to get a rope around the neck of one horse.

"Don't hurt it!" Nancy said.   79

We went back in the house and stood behind the window and watched the   80
deputies and the rancher work on getting the horses rounded up.

"I'm going to make some coffee," I said. "Would you like some coffee, Nancy?"   81

"I'll tell you what I'd like," she said. "I feel high, Dan. I feel like I'm loaded. I   82
feel like, I don't know, but I like the way I'm feeling. You put on some coffee and
I'll find us some music to listen to on the radio and then you can build up the fire
again. I'm too excited to sleep."

So we sat in front of the fire and drank coffee and listened to an all-night ra-   83
dio station from Eureka and talked about the horses and then talked about Richard, and Nancy's mother. We danced. We didn't talk about the present situation
at all. The fog hung outside the window and we talked and were kind with each
other. Toward daylight I turned off the radio and we went to bed and made love.

The next afternoon, after her arrangements were made and her suitcases packed,   84
I drove her to the little airport where she would catch a flight to Portland and then
transfer to another airline that would put her in Pasco late that night.

"Tell your mother I said hello. Give Richard a hug for me and tell him I miss   85
him," I said. "Tell him I send love."

"He loves you too," she said. "You know that. In any case, you'll see him in the   86
fall, I'm sure."

I nodded.   87

"Good-bye," she said, and reached for me. We held each other. "I'm glad for   88
last night," she said. "Those horses. Our talk. Everything. It helps. We won't forget that," she said. She began to cry.

"Write me, will you?" I said. "I didn't think it would happen to us," I said. "All   89
those years. I never thought so for a minute. Not us."

"I'll write," she said. "Some big letters. The biggest you've ever seen since I   90
used to send you letters in high school."

"I'll be looking for them," I said.   91

Then she looked at me again and touched my face. She turned and moved   92
across the tarmac toward the plane.

Go, dearest one, and God be with you.   93

She boarded the plane and I stayed around until its jet engines started and, in   94
a minute, the plane began to taxi down the runway. It lifted off over Humboldt
Bay and soon became a speck on the horizon.

I drove back to the house and parked in the driveway and looked at the hoof-   95
prints of the horses from last night. There were deep impressions in the grass, and
gashes, and there were piles of dung. Then I went into the house and, without
even taking off my coat, went to the telephone and dialed Susan's number.

Po-Chu-I (ninth century)

Rejoicing at the Arrival of Ch'ên Hsiung

When the yellow bird's note was almost stopped,
And half formed the green plum's fruit—
Sitting and grieving that spring things were over,
I rose and entered the Eastern Garden's gate.
I carried my cup and was dully drinking alone;   5
Suddenly I heard a knocking sound at the door.
Dwelling secluded, I was glad that someone had come;
How much the more, when I saw it was Ch'ên Hsiung!
At ease and leisure—all day we talked;
Crowding and jostling—the feelings of many years.   10
How great a thing is a single cup of wine!
For it makes us tell the story of our whole lives.

William Shakespeare (1564–1616)

Sonnet 18

Shall I compare thee to a summer's day?[1]
Thou art more lovely and more temperate:[2]
Rough winds do shake the darling buds of May,
And summer's lease[3] hath all too short a date;[4]
Sometime too hot the eye of heaven shines,   5
And often is his gold complexion dimm'd,
And every fair from fair[5] sometime declines,
By chance or nature's changing course untrimm'd:[6]
But thy eternal summer shall not fade,

---

1. **a summer's day:** i.e. the summer season.
2. **temperate:** of even temperature.
3. **lease:** allotted time.
4. **date:** duration.
5. **fair . . . fair:** beautiful thing . . . beauty.
6. **untrimm'd:** divested of beauty.

Nor lose possession of that fair thou ow'st,[7]   10
Nor shall Death brag thou wand'rest in his shade,
When in eternal lines to time thou grow'st.[8]
 So long as men can breathe or eyes can see,
 So long lives this, and this gives life to thee.

WILLIAM BLAKE (1757–1827)

The Clod & the Pebble

"Love seeketh not Itself to please,
Nor for itself hath any care;
But for another gives its ease,
And builds a Heaven in Hell's despair."

 So sang a little Clod of Clay,   5
 Trodden with the cattle's feet;
 But a Pebble of the brook,
 Warbled out these metres meet:

"Love seeketh only Self to please,
To bind another to its delight;   10
Joys in another's loss of ease,
And builds a Hell in Heaven's despite."

ACTIVITIES FOR WRITING AND DISCUSSION

1. Read the poem aloud, or better, memorize it. Enjoy its sound. Identify the rhyme scheme, using the notation described on page 169. Mark any instances of **assonance**, **alliteration**, and **consonance**.

2. What contrasting visions of love do the clod and the pebble present? In what ways is each vision appropriate to the nature of the speaker? In what ways do the clod and the pebble seem to be **symbolic?**

3. Which vision of love strikes you as more true or accurate? Explain, using examples from life.

---

7. **ow'st:** ownest.
8. **to . . . grow'st:** you become inseparably engrafted upon time.

WALT WHITMAN (1819–1892)

I Heard You Solemn-Sweet Pipes of the Organ

I heard you solemn-sweet pipes of the organ as last Sunday morn I pass'd the
    church,
Winds of autumn, as I walk'd the woods at dusk I heard your long-stretch'd
    sighs up above so mournful,
I heard the perfect Italian tenor singing at the opera, I heard the soprano in the
    midst of the quartet singing;
Heart of my love! you too I heard murmuring low through one of the wrists
    around my head,
Heard the pulse of you when all was still ringing little bells last night under   5
    my ear.

I Saw in Louisiana a Live-Oak Growing

I saw in Louisiana a live-oak growing,
All alone stood it and the moss hung down from the branches,
Without any companion it grew there uttering joyous leaves of dark green,
And its look, rude, unbending, lusty, made me think of myself,
But I wonder'd how it could utter joyous leaves standing alone there without   5
    its friend near, for I knew I could not,
And I broke off a twig with a certain number of leaves upon it, and twined
    around it a little moss,
And brought it away, and I have placed it in sight in my room,
It is not needed to remind me as of my own dear friends,
(For I believe lately I think of little else than of them,)
Yet it remains to me a curious token, it makes me think of manly love;   10
For all that, and though the live-oak glistens there in Louisiana solitary in a
    wide flat space,
Uttering joyous leaves all its life without a friend a lover near,
I know very well I could not.

ACTIVITIES FOR WRITING AND DISCUSSION

1. It has been said that no verse is entirely "free" (that is, without verbal or
rhythmic patterning of some sort). What sorts of patterning does Whitman use to
replace the **rhyme** and **meter** of **traditional verse?** To answer this question, begin
by making a list of everything that strikes you in "I Heard You Solemn-Sweet
Pipes of the Organ" and "I Saw in Louisiana a Live-Oak Growing": words and
phrases, images, and feelings. Then review the poems and identify the pattern(s).

Finally, consider how Whitman's type of pattern supplants traditional rhyme and meter.

2. Whitman believed that the function of a poem is to impel readers along individual paths of thought and growth. Thus he wrote that a poem "is no finish to a man or woman" and that "the reader . . . must himself or herself construct indeed the poem . . . the text furnishing the hints, the clue, the start or frame-work." Taking the poet at his word, treat "I Heard You Solemn-Sweet Pipes of the Organ" or "I Saw in Louisiana a Live-Oak Growing" as a "start" to some reflective or imaginative writing of your own. For instance:

    a. Use either poem as a pathway to meditation. Begin by memorizing the poem, reciting it to yourself, and living with it a while. Keep a written record of any thoughts or feelings that occur to you as a result of this process.

    b. Write a poem of your own that employs the long and flowing lines of "I Heard You Solemn-Sweet Pipes of the Organ" and "I Saw in Louisiana a Live-Oak Growing." Afterward reflect on what was challenging about imitating Whitman's style.

3. Though each poem contains several independent clauses, each poem is punctuated as a single sentence. How would the effect of either poem be changed if more terminal punctuation, e.g., periods, were added (for instance, periods could be inserted at the ends of lines 1, 2, and 4 in "I Saw in Louisiana a Live-Oak Growing")?

Christina Rossetti (1830–1894)

Margery

What shall we do with Margery?
    She lies and cries upon her bed,
    All lily-pale from foot to head,
Her heart is sore as sore can be;
Poor guileless shamefaced Margery.   5

A foolish girl, to love a man
    And let him know she loved him so!
She should have tried a different plan;
    Have loved, but not have let him know:
    Then he perhaps had loved her so.   10

What can we do with Margery
    Who has no relish for her food?
We'd take her with us to the sea—

Across the sea—but where's the good?
She'd fret alike on land and sea.   15

Yes, what the neighbours say is true:
    Girls should not make themselves so cheap.
But now it's done what can we do?
    I hear her moaning in her sleep.
    Moaning and sobbing in her sleep.   20

I think—and I'm of flesh and blood—
    Were I that man for whom she cares
    I would not cost her tears and prayers
To leave her just alone like mud,
    Fretting her simple heart with cares.   25

A year ago she was a child,
    Now she's a woman in her grief;
    The year's now at the falling leaf,
At budding of the leaves she smiled;
Poor foolish harmless foolish child.   30

It was her own fault? so it was.
    If every own fault found us out
    Dogged us and snared us round about,
What comfort should we take because
    Not half our due we thus wrung out?   35

At any rate the question stands:
    What now to do with Margery,
A weak poor creature on our hands?
    Something we must do: I'll not see
    Her blossom fade, sweet Margery.   40

Perhaps a change may after all
    Prove best for her: to leave behind
    Those home-sights seen time out of mind;
To get beyond the narrow wall
Of home, and learn home is not all.   45

Perhaps this way she may forget,
    Not all at once, but in a while;
May come to wonder how she set
    Her heart on this slight thing, and smile
    At her own folly, in a while.   50

Yet this I say and I maintain:
    Were I the man she's fretting for
    I should my very self abhor
If I could leave her to her pain,
Uncomforted to tears and pain.   55

In an Artist's Studio

One face looks out from all his canvases,
    One selfsame figure sits or walks or leans;
    We found her hidden just behind those screens,
That mirror gave back all her loveliness.
A queen in opal or in ruby dress,   5
    A nameless girl in freshest summer-greens,
    A saint, an angel;—every canvass means
The same one meaning, neither more nor less.
He feeds upon her face by day and night,
    And she with true kind eyes looks back on him   10
Fair as the moon and joyful as the light:
    Not wan with waiting, not with sorrow dim;
Not as she is, but was when hope shone bright;
    Not as she is, but as she fills his dream.

THOMAS HARDY (1840–1928)

At Tea

The kettle descants in a cosy drone,
And the young wife looks in her husband's face,
And then at her guest's, and shows in her own
Her sense that she fills an envied place;
And the visiting lady is all abloom,   5
And says there was never so sweet a room.

And the happy young housewife does not know
That the woman beside her was first his choice,
Till the fates ordained it could not be so. . . .
Betraying nothing in look or voice   10
The guest sits smiling and sips her tea,
And he throws her a stray glance yearningly.

In the Room of the Bride-Elect

"Would it had been the man of our wish!"
Sighs her mother. To whom with vehemence she
In the wedding-dress—the wife to be—
"Then why were you so mollyish
As not to insist on him for me!"   5
The mother, amazed: "Why, dearest one,
Because you pleaded for this or none!"

"But Father and you should have stood out strong!
Since then, to my cost, I have lived to find
That you were right and that I was wrong;   10
This man is a dolt to the one declined. . . .
Ah!—here he comes with his button-hole rose.
Good God—I must marry him I suppose!"

Outside the Window

"My stick!" he says, and turns in the lane
To the house just left, whence a vixen voice
Comes out with the firelight through the pane,
And he sees within that the girl of his choice
Stands rating her mother with eyes aglare   5
For something said while he was there.

"At last I behold her soul undraped!"
Thinks the man who had loved her more than himself;
"My God—'tis but narrowly I have escaped.—
My precious porcelain proves it delf." [1]   10
His face has reddened like one ashamed,
And he steals off, leaving his stick unclaimed.

ACTIVITIES FOR WRITING AND DISCUSSION

1. Hardy originally published "At Tea," "In the Room of the Bride-Elect,"
and "Outside the Window" in a collection entitled *Satires of Circumstance*. "Satire" is related to **irony** and refers to "A literary work that attacks human vice or
folly through irony, derision, or wit" (*American Heritage College Dictionary*). Describe the "circumstance" depicted in each poem and what makes the circumstance satiric or ironic.

---

1. **proves it delf:** shows itself to be ordinary pottery (delft).

2. Each poem suggests a miniature story or drama complete with the elements of **characters, conflict, dialogue** (actual or implied), **setting,** and the hint at least of a **plot.** Choose one of the poems and reread and annotate it, paying close attention to each of these elements. Then either:

    a. Recast the poem as a story in prose or a short play;

    or

    b. Respond to the poem using one of the "Ten Ideas for Writing" that are described in Chapter 3 and summarized on page 35.

3. Draft an essay in which you draw some conclusions about the nature of marriage as portrayed in these three poems.

Ezra Pound (1885–1972)

The River-merchant's Wife: A Letter

While my hair was still cut straight across my forehead
Played I about the front gate, pulling flowers.
You came by on bamboo stilts, playing horse,
You walked about my seat, playing with blue plums.
And we went on living in the village of Chōkan: 5
Two small people, without dislike or suspicion.

At fourteen I married My Lord you.
I never laughed, being bashful.
Lowering my head, I looked at the wall.
Called to, a thousand times, I never looked back.   10

At fifteen I stopped scowling,
I desired my dust to be mingled with yours
Forever and forever and forever.
Why should I climb the look out?

At sixteen you departed,   15
You went into far Ku-tō-en, by the river of swirling eddies,
And you have been gone five months.
The monkeys make sorrowful noise overhead.

You dragged your feet when you went out.
By the gate now, the moss is grown, the different mosses,   20
Too deep to clear them away!
The leaves fall early this autumn, in wind.

The paired butterflies are already yellow with August
Over the grass in the West garden;
They hurt me. I grow older.   25
If you are coming down through the narrows of the river Kiang,
Please let me know beforehand,
And I will come out to meet you
      As far as Chō-fū-Sa.

—By Rihaku (Li T'ai Po)

ROBERT BLY (b. 1926)

In Rainy September

In rainy September, when leaves grow down to the dark,
I put my forehead down to the damp, seaweed-smelling sand.
The time has come. I have put off choosing for years,
perhaps whole lives. The fern has no choice but to live;
for this crime it receives earth, water, and night.   5

We close the door. "I have no claim on you."
Dusk comes. "The love I have had with you is enough."
We know we could live apart from one another.
The sheldrake floats apart from the flock.
The oaktree puts out leaves alone on the lonely hillside.   10

Men and women before us have accomplished this.
I would see you, and you me, once a year.
We would be two kernels, and not be planted.
We stay in the room, door closed, lights out.
I weep with you without shame and without honor.   15

ADRIENNE RICH (b. 1929)

Living in Sin

She had thought the studio would keep itself;
no dust upon the furniture of love.
Half heresy, to wish the taps less vocal,
the panes relieved of grime. A plate of pears,

a piano with a Persian shawl, a cat   5
stalking the picturesque amusing mouse
had risen at his urging.
Not that at five each separate stair would writhe
under the milkman's tramp; that morning light
so coldly would delineate the scraps   10
of last night's cheese and three sepulchral bottles;
that on the kitchen shelf among the saucers
a pair of beetle-eyes would fix her own—
envoy from some village in the moldings . . .
Meanwhile, he, with a yawn,   15
sounded a dozen notes upon the keyboard,
declared it out of tune, shrugged at the mirror,
rubbed at his beard, went out for cigarettes;
while she, jeered by the minor demons,
pulled back the sheets and made the bed and found   20
a towel to dust the table-top,
and let the coffee-pot boil over on the stove.
By evening she was back in love again,
though not so wholly but throughout the night
she woke sometimes to feel the daylight coming   25
like a relentless milkman up the stairs.

Novella

Two people in a room, speaking harshly.
One gets up, goes out to walk.
(That is the man.)
The other goes out into the next room
and washes the dishes, cracking one.   5
(That is the woman.)
It gets dark outside.
The children quarrel in the attic.
She has no blood left in her heart.
The man comes back to a dark house.   10
The only light is in the attic.
He has forgotten his key.
He rings at his own door
and hears sobbing on the stairs.
The lights go on in the house.   15
The door closes behind him.
Outside, separate as minds,
the stars too come alight.

ACTIVITIES FOR WRITING AND DISCUSSION

1. After consulting Part V of this book, identify and interpret any **metaphors** or **similes** in either of Rich's poems. In each case explain how the metaphor or simile contributes to the overall impact or meaning.

2. A novella is "a short novel" (*American Heritage College Dictionary*). Why has Rich chosen this title and not, for instance, "Short Story" or "Novel"?

3. Describe the narrative **point of view** in "Novella." Why do you think Rich chose the point of view she did? Explain. Then:
   a. Retell the story from the point of view of "the man," "the woman," or one of the children; or
   b. Retell all or a part of the story in any manner you wish, embellishing with imaginative details of your own.

DEREK WALCOTT (b. 1930)

The Young Wife
(FOR NIGEL)

Make all your sorrow neat.
Plump pillows, soothe the corners
of her favourite coverlet.
Write to her mourners.

At dusk, after the office,   5
travel an armchair's ridge,
the valley of the shadow in the sofas,
the drapes' dead foliage.

Ah, but the mirror—the mirror
which you believe has seen   10
the traitor you feel you are—
clouds, though you wipe it clean!

The buds on the wallpaper
do not shake at the muffled sobbing
the children must not hear,   15
or the drawers you dare not open.

She has gone with that visitor
that sat beside her, like wind
clicking shut the bedroom door;
arm in arm they went,   20

leaving her wedding photograph in
its lace frame, a face smiling at
itself. And the telephone
without a voice. The weight

we bear on this heavier side   25
of the grave brings no comfort.
But the vow that was said
in white lace has brought

you now to the very edge
of that promise; now, for some,   30
the hooks in the hawthorn hedge
break happily into blossom

and the heart into grief.
The sun slants on a kitchen floor.
You keep setting a fork and knife   35
at her place for supper.

The children close in the space
made by a chair removed,
and nothing takes her place,
loved and now deeper loved.   40

The children accept your answer.
They startle you when they laugh.
She sits there smiling that cancer
kills everything but Love.

ACTIVITIES FOR WRITING AND DISCUSSION

1. What do you imagine is the relationship of the poem's speaker to the grieving husband? Would you describe his or her advice to the husband ("Make all your sorrows neat . . .") as good? bad? ironic? Explain, drawing upon your own experience (direct or indirect) of grief.

2. Line 41 says, "The children accept your answer." What was the question? Reconstruct the scene at the kitchen table and the dialogue between the husband and his children.

3. Respond to the poem using any of the "Ten Ideas for Writing" on page 35.

4. Research the topic of "grief" and the grieving process. Then discuss how the process is reflected or dramatized in Walcott's poem.

Tomioka Taeko (b. 1935)

Just the Two of Us

You'll make tea,
I'll make toast.
While we're doing that,
at times, early in the evening,
someone may notice the moonrise dyed scarlet   5
and at times visit us
but that'll be the last time the person comes here.
We'll shut the doors, lock them,
make tea, make toast,
talk as usual about how   10
sooner or later
there will be a time
you bury me,
and I bury you, in the garden,
and go out as usual to look for food.   15
There will be a time
either you or I
bury either me or you in the garden
and the one left, sipping tea,
then for the first time, will refuse fiction.   20
Even your freedom
was like a fool's story.

—*Translated by Burton Watson and Hiroaki Sato*

ACTIVITIES FOR WRITING AND DISCUSSION

1. Who are the "you" and the "I" in "Just the Two of Us"? How would you characterize their relationship? their lives?

2. Underline or circle any words or phrases that are repeated in the poem. Why are they repeated, and to what effect?

3. What is the "fiction" referred to in line 20? In the context of this poem, is living by "fiction" a virtue or a weakness? How do you interpret the last two lines?

4. Using details in the poem and your own imagination, tell the story of a typical day in the lives of this couple, or, writing from the **point of view** of the surviving partner, narrate the events of the day on which one partner dies.

Diane Wakoski (b. 1937)

Belly Dancer

Can these movements which move themselves
be the substance of my attraction?
Where does this thin green silk come from that covers my body?
Surely any woman wearing such fabrics
would move her body just to feel them touching every part of her.   5

Yet most of the women frown, or look away, or laugh stiffly.
They are afraid of these materials and these movements in some way.
The psychologists would say they are afraid of themselves, somehow.
Perhaps awakening too much desire—
that their men could never satisfy?   10

So they keep themselves laced and buttoned and made up
in hopes that the framework will keep them stiff enough not to feel
the whole register.
In hopes that they will not have to experience that unquenchable desire
for rhythm and contact.   15

If a snake glided across this floor
most of them would faint or shrink away.
Yet that movement could be their own.
That smooth movement frightens them—
awakening ancestors and relatives to the tips of the arms and toes.   20

So my bare feet
and my thin green silks
my bells and finger cymbals
offend them—frighten their old-young bodies.
While the men simper and leer—   25
glad for the vicarious experience and exercise.
They do not realize how I scorn them:
or how I dance for their frightened,
unawakened, sweet
women.   30

Activities for Writing and Discussion

1. Circle any lines, images, or other features that make "Belly Dancer" sensual. What senses (other than sight) are evoked? In which lines and phrases? To what effect(s)?

2. In lines 16–18 the **speaker** imagines the movement of "a snake" and suggests that the women both fear it (they "would faint or shrink away") and desire it ("that movement could be their own"). How do you explain this apparent contradiction?

3. Imagine you are a woman in the dancer's audience. Borrowing details from the poem and writing in a **stream of consciousness** mode, express the emotions and conflicts you have as you watch the dancer dance.

4. As an alternative to Activity #3, imagine yourself to be an audience member of a different sexual orientation, or disabled, or of a different cultural/racial identity. From any of these **points of view,** what do you celebrate or denounce in what you see? What voices from your culture do you hear influencing your voice and the content of your writing?

SHARON OLDS (b. 1942)

Sex Without Love

How do they do it, the ones who make love
without love? Beautiful as dancers,
gliding over each other like ice-skaters
over the ice, fingers hooked
inside each other's bodies, faces   5
red as steak, wine, wet as the
children at birth whose mothers are going to
give them away. How do they come to the
come to the   come to the   God   come to the
still waters, and not love   10
the one who came there with them, light
rising slowly as steam off their joined
skin? These are the true religious,
the purists, the pros, the ones who will not
accept a false Messiah, love the   15
priest instead of the God. They do not
mistake the lover for their own pleasure,
they are like great runners: they know they are alone
with the road surface, the cold, the wind,
the fit of their shoes, their over-all cardio-   20
vascular health—just factors, like the partner
in the bed, and not the truth, which is the
single body alone in the universe
against its own best time.

LIZ ROSENBERG (b. 1958)

In the End, We Are All Light

I love how old men carry purses for their wives,
those stiff light beige or navy wedge-shaped bags
that match the women's pumps,
with small gold clasps that click open and shut.
The men drowse off in medical center waiting rooms,   5
with bags perched in their laps like big tame birds
too worn to flap away. Within, the wives slowly undress,
put on the thin white robes, consult, come out
and wake the husbands dreaming openmouthed.
And when they both rise up   10
to take their constitutional,
walk up and down the block, her arms are free as air,
his right hand dangles down.

So I, desiring to shed this skin
for some light silken one,   15
will tell my husband, "Here, hold this,"
and watch him amble off into the mall among the shining
cans of motor oil, my leather bag
slung over his massive shoulder bone,
so prettily slender-waisted, so forgiving of the ways   20
we hold each other down, that watching him
I see how men love women, and women men,
and how the burden of the other comes to be
light as a feather blown, more quickly vanishing.

ACTIVITIES FOR WRITING AND DISCUSSION

1. Underline images in "In the End, We Are All Light" that strike you. In your notebook, react to one or two of these images by doing some writing or by drawing a realistic or cartoon picture based on the image(s). What sorts of feelings do the images evoke in you? How would you describe the relationship that is suggested between the "old men"/husbands and their wives?

2. How would the poem change if the "old men" were replaced by "young men" with young wives? Does the poem imply any differences between "old" couples and young? If so, what differences?

3. Interpret the last several lines. How or why *does* "the burden of the other [come] to be/light as a feather blown"?

FRANCINE DU PLESSIX GRAY (b. 1930)

On Friendship

I saw Madame Bovary[1] at Bloomingdale's the other morning, or rather, I saw many incarnations of her. She was hovering over the cosmetic counters, clutching the current issue of *Cosmopolitan,* whose cover line read "New Styles of Coupling, Including Marriage." Her face already ablaze with numerous products advertised to make her irresistible to the opposite sex, she looked anguished, grasping, over-wrought, and terribly lonely. And I thought to myself: Poor girl! With all the reams of literature that have analyzed her plight (victimized by double standards, by a materialistic middle-class glutting on the excess of romantic fiction), notwithstanding all these diagnoses, one fact central to her tragic fate has never been stressed enough: Emma Bovary had a faithful and boring husband and a couple of boring lovers—not so intolerable a condition—but she did not have a friend in the world. And when I think of the great solitude which the original Emma and her contemporaries exude, one phrase jumps to my mind. It comes from an essay by Francis Bacon, and it is one of the finest statements ever penned about the human need for friendship: "Those who have no friends to open them-selves unto are cannibals of their own hearts."

In the past years the theme of friendship has been increasingly prominent in our conversations, in our books and films, even in our college courses. It is evi-dent that many of us are yearning with new fervor for this form of bonding. And our yearning may well be triggered by the same disillusionment with the reign of Eros that destroyed Emma Bovary. Emma was eating her heart out over a fantasy totally singular to the Western world, and only a century old at that: the notion that sexual union between men and women who believe that they are passionately in love, a union achieved by free choice and legalized by marriage, tends to offer a life of perpetual bliss and is the most desirable human bond available on earth. It is a notion bred in the same frenzied climate of the romantic epoch that caused countless young Europeans to act like the characters of their contemporary liter-ature. Goethe's *Werther* is said to have triggered hundreds of suicides. Numerous wives glutted on the fantasies of George Sand's heroines demanded separations because their husbands were unpoetic. And Emma Bovary, palpitating from that romantic fiction which precurses our current sex manuals in its outlandish hopes for the satiation of desire, muses in the third week of her marriage: Where is "the felicity, the passion, the intoxication" that had so enchanted her in the novels of Sir Walter Scott?

---

1. Title character in the novel by Gustave Flaubert (1821–1880)

This frenzied myth of love which has also led to the downfall of Cleopatra, Juliet, Romeo, and King Kong continues to breed, in our time, more garbled thinking, wretched verse, and nonsensical jingles than any emotion under the sun: "All You Need Is Love," or as we heard it in our high-school days. "Tell me you'll love me forever, if only tonight." As Flaubert put it, we are all victims of romanticism. And if we still take for granted its cult of heterosexual passion, it is in part because we have been victimized, as Emma was, by the propaganda machine of the Western novel. It was the power and the genius of the novel form to fuse medieval notions of courtly love with the idealization of marriage that marked the rise of the eighteenth-century middle class. (By "romantic love," I mean an infatuation that involves two major ingredients: a sense of being "enchanted" by another person through a complex process of illusion, and a willingness to totally surrender to that person.)

One hardly needs a course in anthropology to realize that this alliance of marriage and romantic love is restricted to a small segment of the Western world, and would seem sheer folly in most areas of this planet. The great majority of humans—be it in China, Japan, Africa, India, the Moslem nations—still engage in marriages prearranged by their elders or dictated by pragmatic reasons of money, land, tribal politics, or (as in the Socialist countries) housing shortages. Romantically motivated marriage as the central ingredient of the good life is almost as novel in our own West. In popular practice, it remained restricted to a narrow segment of the middle class until the twentieth century. And on the level of philosophical reflection, it was always friendship between members of the same sex, never any bonding of sexual affection, which from Greek times to the Enlightenment was held to be the cornerstone of human happiness. Yet this central role allotted to friendship for two thousand years has been progressively eroded by such factors as the nineteenth-century exaltation of instinct; science's monopoly on our theories of human sentiment; the massive eroticizing of society; and that twentieth-century celebration of the body that reaches its peak in the hedonistic solitude of the multiple orgasm.

To Aristotle, friendship can be formed only by persons of virtue: a man's capacity for friendship is the most accurate measure of his virtue; it is the foundation of the state, for great legislators care even more for friendship than they care for justice. To Plato, as we know, passionate affection untainted by physical relations is the highest form of human bonding. To Cicero, *Amicitia* is more important than either money, power, honors, or health because each of these gifts can bring us only one form of pleasure, whereas the pleasures of friendship are marvelously manifold; and friendship being based on equity, the tyrant is the man least capable of forming that bond because of his need to wield power over others. Montaigne's essay, along with Bacon's, is the most famous of many that glorify our theme in the Renaissance. And like the ancients, he stresses the advantages of friendship over any kind of romantic and physical attachment. Love for members of the opposite sex, in Montaigne's words, is "an impetuous and fickle flame, undulating and variable, a fever flame subject to fits and lulls." Whereas the fire of friendship produces "a general and universal warmth, moderate and

5

even," and will always forge bonds superior to those of marriage because marriage's continuance is "constrained and forced, depending on factors other than our free will."

A century later, even La Rouchefoucauld, that great cynic who described the imperialism of the ego better than any other precursor of Freud, finds that friendship is the only human bond in which the tyrannical cycle of our self-love seems broken, in which "we can love each other even more than love ourselves." One of the last classic essays on friendship I can think of before it loses major importance as a philosophical theme is by Ralph Waldo Emerson. And it's interesting to note that by mid-nineteenth century, the euphoric absolutes which had previously described this form of bonding are sobered by many cautious qualifications. A tinge of modern pragmatism sets in. Emerson tends to distrust any personal friendship unless it functions for the purpose of some greater universal fraternity.

Yet however differently these thinkers focused on our theme, they all seemed to reach a consensus on the qualities of free will, equity, trust, and selflessness unique to the affection of friendship. They cannot resist comparing it to physical passion, which yearns for power over the other, seeks possession and the state of being possessed, seeks to devour, breeds on excess, can easily become demonic, is closely allied to the death wish, and is often a form of agitated narcissism quite unknown to the tranquil, balanced rule of friendship. And rereading the sagas of Tristan and Iseult, Madame Bovary, and many other romantic lovers, it is evident that their passions tend to breed as much on a masturbatory excitement as on a longing for the beloved. They are in love with love, their delirium is involved with a desire for self-magnification through suffering, as evidenced in Tristan's words, "Eyes with joy are blinded. I myself am the world." There is confrontation, turmoil, aggression, in the often militaristic language of romantic love: Archers shoot fatal arrows or unerring shafts; the male enemy presses, pursues, and conquers; women surrender after being besieged by amorous assaults. Friendship on the other hand is the most pacifist species in the fauna of human emotions, the most steadfast and sharing. No wonder then that the finest pacifist ideology in the West was devised by a religious group—the Quakers—which takes as its official name the Religious Society of Friends; the same temperate principle of fraternal bonding informs that vow demanded by the Benedictine Order—the Oath of Stability—which remains central to the monastic tradition to this day. No wonder, also, that the kind of passionate friendship shared by David and Jonathan has inspired very few masterpieces of literature, which seem to thrive on tension and illicitness. For until they were relegated to the dissecting rooms of the social sciences, our literary views of friendship tended to be expressed in the essay form, a cool, reflective mode that never provided friendship with the motive, democratic, propagandistic force found by Eros in novel, verse, and stage. To this day, friendship totally resists commercial exploitation, unlike the vast businesses fueled by romantic love that support the couture, perfume, cosmetic, lingerie, and pulp-fiction trades.

One should note, however, that most views of friendship expressed in the past twenty centuries of Western thought have dealt primarily with the male's capacity for affection. And they tend to be extremely dubious about the possibility of women ever being able to enjoy genuine friendships with members of their own sex, not to speak of making friends with male peers. Montaigne expressed a prejudice that lasts well into our day when he wrote, "The ordinary capacity of women is inadequate for that communion and fellowship which is the nurse of that sacred bond, nor does their soul feel firm enough to endure the strain of so tight and durable a knot." It is shocking, though not surprising, to hear prominent social scientists paraphrase that opinion in our own decades. Konrad Lorenz and Lionel Tiger, for instance, seem to agree that women are made eminently unsociable by their genetic programming; their bondings, in Lorenz's words, "must be considered weak imitations of the exclusively male associations." Given the current vogue for sociobiology, such assertions are often supported by carefully researched papers on the courtship patterns of Siberian wolves, the prevalence of eye contact among male baboons, and the vogue for gangbanging among chimpanzees.

Our everyday language reflects the same bias: "Fraternity" is a word that goes far beyond its collegiate context and embraces notions of honor, dignity, loyalty. "Sorority" is something we might have belonged to as members of the University of Oklahoma's bowling team in the early 1950s. So I think it is high time that the same feminist perspective that has begun to correct the biases of art history and psychoanalysis should be brought to bear on this area of anthropology. We have indeed been deprived of those official, dramatically visible rites offered to men in pub, poolroom, Elks, hunting ground, or football league. And having been brought up in a very male world, I'm ashamed to say it took me a decade of feminist consciousness to realize that the few bonding associations left to twentieth century women—garden clubs, church suppers, sewing circles (often derided by men because they do not deal with power)—have been activities considerably more creative and life-enhancing than the competition of the poolroom, the machismo of beer drinking, or the bloodshed of hunting.

Among both sexes, the rites and gestures of friendship seemed to have been   10 decimated in the Victorian era, which brought a fear of homosexuality unprecedented in the West. (They also tended to decrease as rites of heterosexual coupling became increasingly permissive). Were Dr. Johnson and James Boswell gay, those two men who constantly exhibited their affection for each other with kisses, tears, and passionate embraces? I suspect they were as rabidly straight as those tough old soldiers described by Tacitus begging for last kisses when their legion broke up. Since Freud, science has tended to dichotomize human affection along lines of deviance and normalcy, genitality and platonic love, instead of leaving it as a graduated spectrum of emotion in which love, friendship, sensuality, sexuality, can freely flow into each other as they did in the past. This may be another facet of modern culture that has cast coolness and self-consciousness on our gestures of friendship. The 1960s brought us some hope for change, both in its general emotional climate and in our scientists' tendency to relax their definitions of normalcy and deviance. For one of the most beautiful signs of that decade's renewed yearning for friendship and community, particularly evident among the groups who marched in civil-rights or anti-war demonstrations, was the sight of men clutching, kissing, embracing each other as unabashedly as Dr. Johnson and James Boswell.

Which leads me to reflect on the reasons why I increasingly turn to friendship in my own life: In a world more and more polluted by the lying of politicians and the illusions of the media, I occasionally crave to hear and to tell the truth. To borrow a beautiful phrase from Friedrich Nietzsche, I look upon my friend as "the beautiful enemy" who alone is able to offer me total candor. I look for the kind of honest friend Emma Bovary needed: one who could have told her that her lover was a jerk.

Friendship is by its very nature freer of deceit than any other relationship we can know because it is the bond least affected by striving for power, physical pleasure, or material profit, most liberated from any oath of duty or of constancy. With Eros the *body* stands naked, in friendship our *spirit* is denuded. Friendship, in this sense, is a human condition resembling what may be humanity's most beautiful and necessary lie—the promise of an afterlife. It is an almost celestial sphere in which we most resemble that society of angels offered us by Christian theology, in which we can sing the truth of our inner thoughts in relative freedom and abundance. No wonder then that the last contemporary writers whose essays on friendship may remain classics are those religiously inclined, scholars relatively unaffected by positivism or behaviorism, or by the general scientificization of human sentiment. That marvelous Christian maverick, C. S. Lewis, tells us: "Friendship is unnecessary, like philosophy, like art, like the universe itself (since God did not *need* to create). It has no survival value; rather it is one of those things that give value to survival." And the Jewish thinker Simone Weil focuses on the classic theme of free consent when she writes: "Friendship is a miracle by which a person consents to view from a certain distance, and without coming any nearer, the very being who is necessary to him as food."

The quality of free consent and self-determination inherent in friendship may be crucial to the lives of twentieth-century women beginning their vocations. But in order to return friendship to an absolutely central place in our lives, we might have to wean ourselves in part from the often submissive premises of romantic passion. I suspect that we shall always need some measure of swooning and palpitating, of ecstasy and trembling, of possessing and being possessed. But, I also suspect that we've been bullied and propagandized into many of these manifestations by the powerful modern organism that I call the sexual-industrial complex and that had an antecedent in the novels that fueled Emma Bovary's deceitful fantasies. For one of the most treacherous aspects of the cult of romantic love has been its complex idealization and exploitation of female sexuality. There is now a new school of social scientists who are militantly questioning the notion that Western romantic love is the best foundation for human bonding, and their criticism seems much inspired by feminist perspectives. The Australian anthropologist Robert Brain, for instance, calls romantic love "a lunatic relic of medieval passions . . . the handmaiden of a moribund capitalistic culture and of an equally dead Puritan ethic."

What exactly would happen if we women remodeled our concepts of ideal human bonding on the ties of friendship and abandoned the premises of enchantment and possession? Such a restructuring of our ideals of happiness could be extremely subversive. It might imply a considerable de-eroticizing of society. It could bring about a minor revolution against the sexual-industrial complex that brings billions of dollars to thousands of men by brainwashing us into the roles of temptress and seductress, and estranges us from the plain and beautiful Quaker ideal of being a sister to the world. How topsy-turvy the world would be! Dalliance, promiscuity, all those more sensationalized aspects of the Women's Movement that were once seen as revolutionary might suddenly seem most bourgeois and old-fashioned activities. If chosen in conditions of rigorous self-determination, the following values, considered up to now as reactionary, could suddenly become the most radical ones at hand: Virginity. Celibacy. Monastic communities. And that most endangered species of all, fidelity in marriage, which has lately become so exotically rare that it might soon become very fashionable, and provide the cover story for yet another publication designed to alleviate the seldom-admitted solitude of swinging singles: "Mick Jagger Is into Fidelity."

Activities for Writing and Discussion

1. Read and annotate the essay. Then respond to it in your notebook using Idea #1 from the "Ten Ideas for Writing from Reading" found on page 35. (For a sample using Idea #1 in response to a different text see pages 27–28.)

2. Reread your annotations of "On Friendship." Then identify *one* sentence or paragraph that is *most* significant or provocative to you.
   a. Share your annotations of the sentence or paragraph with a partner or small group.
   b. Use the passage (supplemented by feedback from your partner or group) as a springboard for composing a notebook entry of at least three hundred words.

3. In paragraph 13 Gray introduces the term "sexual-industrial complex." Reread the paragraph carefully. Then, working alone or collaboratively:
   a. Explain (in writing) what Gray means by this term.
   b. Draw upon your knowledge and experience to identify, discuss, and write about some particular manifestations of the sexual-industrial complex in society at large and in your own life. Share examples and, where possible, specific stories.
   c. Examine Gray's conclusion in paragraph 14 that an "ideal human bonding" based on friendship "could be extremely subversive" to the sexual-industrial complex. First explain how she reaches this conclusion; how does the ideal of friendship subvert "the premises of enchantment and possession"? Then agree or disagree with the conclusion, supporting your position with examples from your own knowledge, reading, or experience.

4. Supplement your work on Activity #3 with outside research.

Scott Russell Sanders (b. 1945)

Looking at Women

On that sizzling July afternoon, the girl who crossed at the stoplight in front of our car looked, as my mother would say, as though she had been poured into her pink shorts. The girl's matching pink halter bared her stomach and clung to her nubbin breasts, leaving little to the imagination, as my mother would also say. Until that moment, it had never made any difference to me how much or little a girl's clothing revealed, for my imagination had been entirely devoted to other mysteries. I was eleven. The girl was about fourteen, the age of my buddy Norman who lounged in the back seat with me. Staring after her, Norman elbowed me in the ribs and murmured, "Check out that chassis."

His mother glared around from the driver's seat. "Hush your mouth."

"I was talking about that sweet Chevy," said Norman, pointing out a souped-up jalopy at the curb.

"I know what you were talking about," his mother snapped.

No doubt she did know, since mothers could read minds, but at first I did not ⁵ have a clue. Chassis? I knew what it meant for a car, an airplane, a radio, or even a cannon to have a chassis. But could a girl have one as well? I glanced after the retreating figure, and suddenly noticed with a sympathetic twitching in my belly the way her long raven ponytail swayed in rhythm to her walk and the way her fanny jostled in those pink shorts. In July's dazzle of sun, her swinging legs and arms beamed at me a semaphore I could almost read.

As the light turned green and our car pulled away, Norman's mother cast one more scowl at her son in the rearview mirror, saying, "Just think how it makes her feel to have you two boys gawking at her."

How? I wondered.

"Makes her feel like hot stuff," said Norman, owner of a bold mouth.

"If you don't get your mind out of the gutter, you're going to wind up in the state reformatory," said his mother.

Norman gave a snort. I sank into the seat, and tried to figure out what power ¹⁰ had sprung from that sashaying girl to zap me in the belly.

Only after much puzzling did it dawn on me that I must finally have drifted into the force-field of sex, as a space traveler who has lived all his years in free fall might rocket for the first time within gravitational reach of a star. Even as a bashful eleven-year-old I knew the word *sex,* of course, and I could paste that name across my image of the tantalizing girl. But a label for a mystery no more explains a mystery than the word *gravity* explains gravity. As I grew a beard and my taste shifted from girls to women, I acquired a more cagey language for speaking of desire, I picked up disarming theories. First by hearsay and then by experiment, I learned the delicious details of making babies. I came to appreciate the urgency for propagation that litters the road with maple seeds and drives salmon up waterfalls and yokes the newest crop of boys to the newest crop of girls. Books in their killjoy wisdom taught me that all the valentines and violins, the waltzes and

glances, the long fever and ache of romance, were merely embellishments on biology's instructions that we multiply our kind. And yet, the fraction of desire that
actually leads to procreation is so vanishingly small as to seem irrelevant. In his
lifetime a man sways to a million longings, only a few of which, or perhaps none
at all, ever lead to the fathering of children. Now, thirty years away from that July
afternoon, firmly married, twice a father, I am still humming from the power un-
leashed by the girl in pink shorts, still wondering how it made her feel to have two
boys gawk at her, still puzzling over how to dwell in the force-field of desire.

———————

How should a man look at women? It is a peculiarly and perhaps neurotically
human question. Billy goats do not fret over how they should look at nanny goats.
They look or don't look, as seasons and hormones dictate, and feel what they feel
without benefit of theory. There is more billy goat in most men than we care to
admit. None of us, however, is pure goat. To live utterly as an animal would make
the business of sex far tidier but also drearier. If we tried, like Rousseau, to peel
off the layers of civilization and imagine our way back to some pristine man and
woman who have not yet been corrupted by hand-me-down notions of sexuality,
my hunch is that we would find, in our speculative state of nature, that men regarded women with appalling simplicity. In any case, unlike goats, we dwell in
history. What attracts our eyes and rouses our blood is only partly instinctual.
Other forces contend in us as well: the voices of books and religions, the images
of art and film and advertising, the entire chorus of culture. Norman's telling me
to relish the sight of females and his mother's telling me to keep my eyes to myself are only two of the many voices quarreling in my head.

If there were a rule book for sex, it would be longer than the one for baseball
(that byzantine sport), more intricate and obscure than tax instructions from the
Internal Revenue Service. What I present here are a few images and reflections
that cling, for me, to this one item in such a compendium of rules: How should a
man look at women?

———————

Well before I was to see any women naked in the flesh, I saw a bevy of them
naked in photographs, hung in a gallery around the bed of my freshman roommate at college. A *Playboy* subscriber, he would pluck the centerfold from its
staples each month and tape another airbrushed lovely to the wall. The gallery
was in place when I moved in, and for an instant before I realized what I was looking at, all that expanse of skin reminded me of a meat locker back in Newton Falls,
Ohio. I never quite shook that first impression, even after I had inspected the pinups at my leisure on subsequent days. Every curve of buttock and breast was news
to me, an innocent kid from the Puritan back roads. Today you would be hard
pressed to find a college freshman as ignorant as I was of female anatomy, if only
because teenagers now routinely watch movies at home that would have been
shown, during my teen years, exclusively on the fly-speckled screens of honky-
tonk cinemas or in the basement of the Kinsey Institute. I studied those alien

shapes on the wall with a curiosity that was not wholly sexual, a curiosity tinged with the wonder that astronomers must have felt when they pored over the early photographs of the far side of the moon.

The paper women seemed to gaze back at me, enticing or mocking, yet even in my adolescent dither I was troubled by the phony stare, for I knew this was no true exchange of looks. Those mascaraed eyes were not fixed on me but on a camera. What the models felt as they posed I could only guess — perhaps the boredom of any numbskull job, perhaps the weight of dollar bills, perhaps the sweltering lights of fame, perhaps a tingle of the power that launched a thousand ships.

Whatever their motives, these women had chosen to put themselves on display. For the instant of the photograph, they had become their bodies, as a prizefighter does in the moment of landing a punch, as a weightlifter does in the moment of hoisting a barbell, as a ballerina does in the whirl of a pirouette, as we all do in the crisis of making love or dying. Men, ogling such photographs, are supposed to feel that where so much surface is revealed there can be no depths. Yet I never doubted that behind the makeup and the plump curves and the two dimensions of the image there was an inwardness, a feeling self as mysterious as my own. In fact, during moments when I should have been studying French or thermodynamics, I would glance at my roommate's wall and invent mythical lives for those goddesses. The lives I made up were adolescent ones, to be sure, but so was mine. Without that saving aura of inwardness, these women in the glossy photographs would have become merely another category of objects for sale, alongside the sports cars and stereo systems and liquors advertised in the same pages. If not extinguished, however, their humanity was severely reduced. And if by simplifying themselves they had lost some human essence, then by gaping at them I had shared in the theft.

What did that gaping take from me? How did it affect my way of seeing other women, those who would never dream of lying nude on a fake tiger rug before the million-faceted eye of a camera? The bodies in the photographs were implausibly smooth and slick and inflated, like balloon caricatures that might be floated overhead in a parade. Free of sweat and scars and imperfections, sensual without being fertile, tempting yet impregnable, they were Platonic ideals of the female form, divorced from time and the fluster of living, excused from the perplexities of mind. No actual woman could rival their insipid perfection.

The swains who gathered to admire my roommate's gallery discussed the pinups in the same tones and in much the same language as the farmers back home in Ohio used for assessing cows. The relevant parts of male and female bodies are quickly named — and, the *Kamasutra* and Marquis de Sade notwithstanding, the number of ways in which those parts can be stimulated or conjoined is touchingly small — so these studly conversations were more tedious than chitchat about the weather. I would lie on my bunk pondering calculus or Aeschylus and unwillingly hear the same few nouns and fewer verbs issuing from one mouth after another, and I would feel smugly superior. Here I was, improving my mind, while theirs wallowed in the notorious gutter. Eventually the swains would depart, leaving me in peace, and from the intellectual heights of my bunk I would glance across at those photographs — and yield to the gravity of lust. Idiot flesh! How stupid that a counterfeit stare and artful curves, printed in millions of copies on glossy paper, could arouse me. But there it was, not the first proof of my body's automatism and not the last.

Nothing in men is more machinelike than the flipping of sexual switches. I have never been able to read with a straight face the claims made by D. H. Lawrence and lesser pundits that the penis is a god, a lurking dragon. It more nearly resembles a railroad crossing signal, which stirs into life at intervals to announce, "Here comes a train." Or, if the penis must be likened to an animal, let it be an ill-trained circus dog, sitting up and playing dead and heeling whenever it takes a notion, oblivious of the trainer's commands. Meanwhile, heart, lungs, blood vessels, pupils, and eyelids all assert their independence like the members of a rebellious troupe. Reason stands helpless at the center of the ring, cracking its whip.

While he was president, Jimmy Carter raised a brouhaha by confessing in a 20 *Playboy* interview, of all shady places, that he occasionally felt lust in his heart for women. What man hasn't, aside from those who feel lust in their hearts for other men? The commentators flung their stones anyway. Naughty, naughty, they chirped. Wicked Jimmy. Perhaps Mr. Carter could derive some consolation from psychologist Allen Wheelis, who blames male appetite on biology: "We have been selected for desiring. Nothing could have convinced us by argument that it would be worthwhile to chase endlessly and insatiably after women, but something has transformed us from within, a plasmid has invaded our DNA, has twisted our nature so that now this is exactly what we *want* to do." Certainly, by Darwinian logic, those males who were most avid in their pursuit of females were also the most likely to pass on their genes. Consoling it may be, yet it is finally no solution to blame biology. "I am extremely sexual in my desires: I carry them everywhere and at all times," William Carlos Williams tells us on the opening page of his autobiography. "I think that from that arises the drive which empowers us all. Given that drive, a man does with it what his mind directs. In the manner in which he directs that power lies his secret." Whatever the contents of my DNA, however potent the influence of my ancestors, I still must direct that rebellious power. I still must live with the consequences of my looking and my longing.

———————

Aloof on their blankets like goddesses on clouds, the pinups did not belong to my funky world. I was invisible to them, and they were immune to my gaze. Not so the women who passed me on the street, sat near me in classes, shared a table with me in the cafeteria: it was risky to stare at them. They could gaze back, and sometimes did, with looks both puzzling and exciting. It only complicated matters for me to realize that so many of these strangers had taken precautions that men should notice them. The girl in matching pink halter and shorts who set me humming in my eleventh year might only have wanted to keep cool in the sizzle of July. But these alluring college femmes had deeper designs. Perfume, eye shadow, uplift bras (about which I learned in the Sears catalog), curled hair, stockings, jewelry, lipstick, lace—what were these if not hooks thrown out into male waters?

I recall being mystified in particular by spike heels. They looked painful to me, and dangerous. Danger may have been the point, since the spikes would have made good weapons—they were affectionately known, after all, as stilettos. Or danger may have been the point in another sense, because a woman teetering along on such heels is tipsy, vulnerable, broadcasting her need for support. And who better than a man to prop her up, some guy who clomps around in brogans wide enough for the cornerstones of flying buttresses? (For years after college, I felt certain that spike heels had been forever banned, like bustles and foot-binding, but lately they have come back in fashion, and once more one encounters women teetering along on knife points.)

Back in those days of my awakening to women, I was also baffled by lingerie. I do not mean underwear, the proletariat of clothing, and I do not mean foundation garments, pale and sensible. I mean what the woman who lives in the house behind ours—owner of a shop called "Bare Essentials"—refers to as "intimate apparel." Those two words announce that her merchandise is both sexy and expensive. These flimsy items cost more per ounce than truffles, more than frankincense and myrrh. They are put-ons whose only purpose is in being taken off. I have a friend who used to attend the men's-only nights at Bare Essentials, during which he would invariably buy a slinky outfit or two, by way of proving his serious purpose, outfits that wound up in the attic because his wife would not be caught dead in them. Most of the customers at the shop are women, however, as the models are women, and the owner is a woman. What should one make of that? During my college days I knew about intimate apparel only by rumor, not being that intimate with anyone who would have tricked herself out in such finery, but I could see the spike heels and other female trappings everywhere I turned. Why, I wondered then and wonder still, do so many women decorate themselves like dolls? And does that mean they wish to be viewed as dolls?

On this question as on many others, Simone de Beauvoir has clarified matters for me, writing in *The Second Sex:* "The 'feminine' woman in making herself prey tries to reduce man, also, to her carnal passivity; she occupies herself in catching him in her trap, in enchaining him by means of the desires she arouses in him in submissively making herself a thing." Those women who transform themselves into dolls, in other words, do so because that is the most potent identity available to them. "It must be admitted," Beauvoir concedes, "that the males find in woman more complicity than the oppressor usually finds in the oppressed. And in bad faith they take authorization from this to declare that she has *desired* the destiny they have imposed on her."

Complicity, oppressor, bad faith: such terms yank us into a moral realm 25 unknown to goats. While I am saddled with enough male guilt to believe three-quarters of Beauvoir's claim, I still doubt that men are so entirely to blame for the turning of women into sexual dolls. I believe human history is more collaborative than her argument would suggest. It seems unlikely to me that one-half the species could have "imposed" a destiny on the other half, unless that other half were far more craven than the females I have known. Some women have expressed their own skepticism on this point. Thus Joan Didion: "That many women are victims of condescension and exploitation and sex-role stereotyping was scarcely news, but neither was it news that other women are not: nobody forces women to buy the package." Beauvoir herself recognized that many members of her sex refuse to buy the "feminine" package: "The emancipated woman, on the contrary, wants to be active, a taker, and refuses the passivity man means to impose on her."

Since my college years, back in the murky 1960s, emancipated women have been discouraging their unemancipated sisters from making spectacles of themselves. Don't paint your face like a clown's or drape your body like a mannequin's, they say. Don't bounce on the sidelines in skimpy outfits, screaming your fool head off, while men compete in the limelight for victories. Don't present yourself to the world as a fluff pastry, delicate and edible. Don't waddle across the stage in a bathing suit in hopes of being named Miss This or That.

A great many women still ignore the exhortations. Wherever a crown for beauty is to be handed out, many still line up to stake their claims. Recently, Miss Indiana Persimmon Festival was quoted in our newspaper about the burdens of possessing the sort of looks that snag men's eyes. "Most of the time I enjoy having guys stare at me," she said, "but every once in a while it makes me feel like a piece of meat." The news photograph showed a cheerleader's perky face, heavily made-up, with starched hair teased into a blond cumulus. She put me in mind not of meat but of a plastic figurine, something you might buy from a booth outside a shrine. Nobody should ever be seen as meat, mere juicy stuff to satisfy an appetite. Better to appear as a plastic figurine, which is not meant for eating, and which is a gesture, however crude, toward art. Joyce described the aesthetic response as a contemplation of form without the impulse to action. Perhaps that is what Miss Indiana Persimmon Festival wishes to inspire in those who look at her, perhaps that is what many women who paint and primp themselves desire: to withdraw from the touch of hands and dwell in the eye alone, to achieve the status of art.

By turning herself (or allowing herself to be turned) into a work of art, does a woman truly escape men's proprietary stare? Not often, says the British critic John Berger. Summarizing the treatment of women in Western painting, he concludes that—with a few notable exceptions, such as works by Rubens and Rembrandt—the woman on canvas is a passive object displayed for the pleasure of the male viewer, especially for the owner of the painting, who is, by extension, owner of the woman herself. Berger concludes: "Men look at women. Women watch themselves being looked at. This determines not only most relations between men and women but also the relation of women to themselves. The surveyor of woman in herself is male: the surveyed female. Thus she turns herself into an object—and most particularly an object of vision: a sight."

That sweeping claim, like the one quoted earlier from Beauvoir, also seems to me about three-quarters truth and one-quarter exaggeration. I know men who outdo the peacock for show, and I know women who are so fully possessed of themselves that they do not give a hang whether anybody notices them or not. The flamboyant gentlemen portrayed by Van Dyck are no less aware of being *seen* than are the languid ladies portrayed by Ingres. With or without clothes, both gentlemen and ladies may conceive of themselves as objects of vision, targets of envy or admiration or desire. Where they differ is in their potential for action: the men are caught in the midst of a decisive gesture or on the verge of making one; the women wait like fuel for someone else to strike a match.

I am not sure the abstract nudes favored in modern art are much of an ad- 30 vance over the inert and voluptuous ones of the old school. Think of two famous examples: Duchamp's *Nude Descending a Staircase* (1912), where the faceless woman has blurred into a waterfall of jagged shards, or Picasso's *Les Demoiselles d'Avignon* (1907), where the five angular damsels have been hammered as flat as cookie sheets and fitted with African masks. Neither painting invites us to behold a woman, but instead to behold what Picasso or Duchamp can make of one.

The naked women in Rubens, far from being passive, are gleefully active, exuberant, their sumptuous pink bodies like rainclouds or plump nebulae. "His nudes are the first ones that ever made me feel happy about my own body," a woman friend told me in one of the Rubens galleries of the Prado Museum. I do not imagine any pinup or store-window mannequin or bathing-suited Miss Whatsit could have made her feel that way. The naked women in Rembrandt, emerging from the bath or rising from bed, are so private, so cherished in the painter's gaze, that we as viewers see them not as sexual playthings but as loved persons. A man would do well to emulate that gaze.

I have never thought of myself as a sight. How much that has to do with being male and how much with having grown up on the back roads where money was scarce and eyes were few, I cannot say. As a boy, apart from combing my hair when I was compelled to and regretting the patches on my jeans (only the poor wore patches), I took no trouble over my appearance. It never occurred to me that anybody outside my family, least of all a girl, would look at me twice. As a young man, when young women did occasionally glance my way, without any prospect of appearing handsome I tried at least to avoid appearing odd. A standard haircut and the cheapest versions of the standard clothes were camouflage enough. Now as a middle-aged man I have achieved once more that boyhood condition of invisibility, with less hair to comb and fewer patches to humble me.

Many women clearly pass through the world aspiring to invisibility. Many others just as clearly aspire to be conspicuous. Women need not make spectacles of themselves in order to draw the attention of men. Indeed, for my taste, the less paint and fewer bangles the better. I am as helpless in the presence of subtle lures as a male moth catching a whiff of pheromones. I am a sucker for hair ribbons, a scarf at the throat, toes leaking from sandals, teeth bared in a smile. By contrast, I have always been more amused than attracted by the enameled exhibitionists whom our biblical mothers would identify as brazen hussies or painted Jezebels or, in the extreme cases, as whores of Babylon.

To encounter female exhibitionists in their full glory and variety, you need to go to a city. I never encounted ogling as a full-blown sport until I visited Rome, where bands of Italian men joined with gusto in appraising the charms of every passing female, and the passing females vied with one another in demonstrating their charms. In our own cities the most notorious bands of oglers tend to be construction gangs or street crews, men who spend much of their day leaning on the handles of shovels or pausing between bursts of riveting guns, their eyes tracing the curves of passersby. The first time my wife and kids and I drove into Boston we followed the signs to Chinatown, only to discover that Chinatown's miserably congested main street was undergoing repairs. That street also proved to be the city's home for X-rated cinemas and girlie shows and skin shops. LIVE SEX ACTS ON STAGE. PEEP SHOWS. PRIVATE BOOTHS. Caught in a traffic jam, we spent an hour listening to jackhammers and wolf whistles as we crept through the few blocks of pleasure palaces, my son and daughter with their noses hanging out the windows, my wife and I steaming. Lighted marquees peppered by burnt-out bulbs announced the titles of sleazy flicks; life-size posters of naked women flanked the doorways of clubs: leggy strippers in miniskirts, the originals for some of the posters, smoked on the curb between numbers.

After we had finally emerged from the zone of eros, eight-year-old Jesse inquired, "What was *that* place all about?"   35

"Sex for sale," my wife Ruth explained.

That might carry us some way toward a definition of pornography: making flesh into a commodity, flaunting it like any other merchandise, divorcing bodies from selves. By this reckoning, there is a pornographic dimension to much advertising, where a charge of sex is added to products ranging from cars to shaving cream. In fact, the calculated imagery of advertising may be more harmful than the blatant imagery of the pleasure palaces, that frank raunchiness which Kate Millett refers to as the "truthful explicitness of pornography." One can leave the X-rated zone of the city, but one cannot escape the sticky reach of commerce, which summons girls to the high calling of cosmetic glamor, fashion, and sexual display, while it summons boys to the panting chase.

You can recognize pornography, according to D. H. Lawrence, "by the insult it offers, invariably, to sex, and to the human spirit." He should know, Millet argues in *Sexual Politics*, for in her view Lawrence himself was a purveyor of patriarchal and often sadistic pornography. I think she is correct about the worst of Lawrence, and that she identifies a misogynist streak in his work; but she ignores his career-long struggle to achieve a more public, tolerant vision of sexuality as an exchange between equals. Besides, his novels and stories all bear within themselves their own critiques. George Steiner reminds us that "the list of writers who have had the genius to enlarge our actual compass of sexual awareness, who have given the erotic play of the mind a novel focus, an area of recognition previously unknown or fallow, is very small." Lawrence belongs on that brief list. The chief insult to the human spirit is to deny it, to claim that we are merely conglomerations of molecules, to pretend that we exist purely as bundles of appetites or as food for the appetites of others.

Men commit that insult toward women out of ignorance, but also out of dread. Allen Wheelis again: "Men gather in pornographic shows, not to stimulate desire, as they may think, but to diminish fear. It is the nature of the show to reduce the woman, discard her individuality, her soul, make her into an object, thereby enabling the man to handle her with greater safety, to use her as a toy. . . . As women move increasingly toward equality, the felt danger to men increases, leading to an increase in pornography and, since there are some men whose fears cannot even so be stilled, to an increase also in violence against women."

Make her into an object: all the hurtful ways for men to look at women are vari- 40 ations on this betrayal. "Thus she turns herself into an object," writes Berger. A woman's ultimate degradation is in "submissively making herself a thing," writes Beauvoir. To be turned into an object—whether by the brush of a painter or the lens of a photographer or the eye of a voyeur, whether by hunger or poverty or enslavement, by mugging or rape, bullets or bombs, by hatred, racism, car crashes, fires, or falls—is for each of us the deepest dread; and to reduce another person to an object is the primal wrong.

Caught in the vortex of desire, we have to struggle to recall the wholeness of persons, including ourselves. Beauvoir speaks of the temptation we all occasionally feel to give up the struggle for a self and lapse into the inertia of an object: "Along with the ethical urge of each individual to affirm his subjective existence, there is also the temptation to forgo liberty and become a thing." A woman in particular, given so much encouragement to lapse into thinghood, "is often very well pleased with her role as the *Other.*"

Yet one need not forgo liberty and become a thing, without a center or a self, in order to become the Other. In our mutual strangeness, men and women can be doorways one for another, openings into the creative mystery that we share by virtue of our existence in the flesh. "To be sensual," James Baldwin writes, "is to respect and rejoice in the force of life, of life itself, and to be *present* in all that one does, from the effort of loving to the breaking of bread." The effort of loving is reciprocal, not only in act but in desire, an *I* addressing a *Thou,* a meeting in that vivid presence. The distance a man stares across at a woman, or a woman at a man, is a gulf in the soul, out of which a voice cries, *Leap, leap.* One day all men may cease to look on themselves as prototypically human and on women as lesser miracles; women may cease to feel themselves the targets for desire; men and women both may come to realize that we are all mere flickerings in the universal fire; and then none of us, male or female, need give up humanity in order to become the *Other.*

Ever since I gawked at the girl in pink shorts, I have dwelt knowingly in the force-field of sex. Knowingly or not, it is where we all dwell. Like the masses of planets and stars, our bodies curve the space around us. We radiate signals constantly, radio sources that never go off the air. We cannot help being centers of attraction and repulsion for one another. That is not all we are by a long shot, nor all we are capable of feeling, and yet, even after our much-needed revolution in sexual consciousness, the power of eros will still turn our heads and hearts. In a world without beauty pageants, there will still be beauty, however its definition may have changed. As long as men have eyes, they will gaze with yearning and confusion at women.

When I return to the street with the ancient legacy of longing coiled in my DNA, and the residues from a thousand generations of patriarchs silting my brain, I encounter women whose presence strikes me like a slap of wind in the face. I must prepare a gaze that is worthy of their splendor.

ACTIVITIES FOR WRITING AND DISCUSSION

1. Sanders's essay is quite long, complex, and suggestive. To begin establishing a connection with the piece, review your annotations—questions, reactions, personal associations—of the essay. Select two or three that strike or affect you the most and write about them for a few minutes. Then share those selected annotations in class or in a small group.

2. Several paragraphs into his essay Sanders poses the question that becomes his focus: "How should a man look at women?" Is it significant that he uses the word "should" and not "does"? What sorts of cultural influences on sexual attitudes and behavior are implied by "should"? Draw on Sanders's essay and your own experience to make a list of such influences.

3. The essay includes quotations from various writers (Simone de Beauvoir, John Berger, Kate Millett, Allen Wheelis, and others). Reread and annotate these passages. Then select one passage that particularly strikes you and write an objective summary of it. (See p. 127 for some suggestions on summarizing.) Finally, discuss ways in which you agree and/or disagree with the writer quoted in the passage.

4. Sanders relates several experiences from his own past in which he looked at women. Tell the story of a time when *you* "looked at women" (or at men, or were yourself looked at). Then, like Sanders, analyze ways in which the experience reflects wider cultural influences on sexual attitudes and behavior.

Plays

SUSAN GLASPELL (1882–1948)

Trifles

SCENE: *The kitchen in the now abandoned farmhouse of* JOHN WRIGHT, *a gloomy kitchen, and left without having been put in order—the walls covered with a faded wallpaper.* D. R. *is a door leading to the parlor. On the* R. *wall above this door is a built-in kitchen cupboard with shelves in the upper portion and drawers below. In the rear wall at* R., *up two steps is a door opening onto stairs leading to the second floor. In the rear wall at* L. *is a door to the shed and from there to the outside. Between these two doors is an old-fashioned black iron stove. Running along the L. wall from the shed door is an old iron sink and sink shelf, in which is set a hand pump. Downstage of the sink is an uncurtained window. Near the window is an old wooden rocker. Center stage is an unpainted wooden kitchen table with straight chairs on either side. There is a small chair D. R. Unwashed pans under the sink, a loaf of bread outside the breadbox, a dish towel on the table—other signs of incompleted work. At the rear the shed door opens and the* SHERIFF *comes in followed by the* COUNTY ATTORNEY *and* HALE. *The* SHERIFF *and* HALE *are men in middle life, the* COUNTY ATTORNEY *is a young man; all are much bundled up and go at once to the stove. They are followed by the two women—the* SHERIFF'S *wife,* MRS. PETERS, *first; she is a slight wiry woman, a thin nervous face.* MRS. HALE *is larger and would ordinarily be called more comfortable looking, but she is disturbed now and looks fearfully about as she enters. The women have come in slowly, and stand close together near the door.*

COUNTY ATTORNEY (*at stove rubbing his hands*). This feels good. Come up to the fire, ladies.

MRS. PETERS (*after taking a step forward*). I'm not—cold.

SHERIFF (*unbuttoning his overcoat and stepping away from the stove to right of table as if to mark the beginning of official business*). Now, Mr. Hale, before we move things about, you explain to Mr. Henderson just what you saw when you came here yesterday morning.

COUNTY ATTORNEY (*crossing down to left of the table*). By the way, has anything been moved? Are things just as you left them yesterday?

SHERIFF (*looking about*). It's just the same. When it dropped below zero last night I thought I'd better send Frank out this morning to make a fire for us—(*sits right of center table*) no use getting pneumonia with a big case on, but I told him not to touch anything except the stove—and you know Frank.

COUNTY ATTORNEY: Somebody should have been left here yesterday.

SHERIFF: Oh—yesterday. When I had to send Frank to Morris Center for that man who went crazy—I want you to know I had my hands full yesterday. I knew you could get back from Omaha by today and as long as I went over everything here myself——

COUNTY ATTORNEY: Well, Mr. Hale, tell just what happened when you came here yesterday morning.

HALE (*crossing down to above table*). Harry and I had started to town with a load of potatoes. We came along the road from my place and as I got here I said, "I'm going to see if I can't get John Wright to go in with me on a party telephone." I spoke to Wright about it once before and he put me off, saying folks talked too much anyway, and all he asked was peace and quiet—I guess you know about how much he talked himself; but I thought maybe if I went to the house and talked about it before his wife, though I said to Harry that I didn't know as what his wife wanted made much difference to John——

COUNTY ATTORNEY: Let's talk about that later, Mr. Hale. I do want to talk about that, but tell now just what happened when you got to the house.

HALE: I didn't hear or see anything; I knocked at the door, and still it was all quiet inside. I knew they must be up, it was past eight o'clock. So I knocked again, and I thought I heard somebody say, "Come in." I wasn't sure, I'm not sure yet, but I opened the door—this door (*indicating the door by which the two women are still standing*) and there in that rocker—(*pointing to it*) sat Mrs. Wright. (*They all look at the rocker* D. L.)

COUNTY ATTORNEY: What—was she doing?

HALE: She was rockin' back and forth. She had her apron in her hand and was kind of—pleating it.

COUNTY ATTORNEY: And how did she—look?

HALE: Well, she looked queer.

COUNTY ATTORNEY: How do you mean—queer?

HALE: Well, as if she didn't know what she was going to do next. And kind of done up.

COUNTY ATTORNEY (*takes out notebook and pencil and sits left of center table*). How did she seem to feel about your coming?

HALE: Why, I don't think she minded—one way or other. She didn't pay much attention. I said, "How do, Mrs. Wright, it's cold, ain't it?" And she said, "Is it?"—and went on kind of pleating at her apron. Well, I was surprised; she didn't ask me to come up to the stove, or to set down, but just sat there, not even looking at me, so I said, "I want to see John." And then she—laughed. I guess you would call it a laugh. I thought of Harry and the team outside, so I said a little sharp: "Can't I see John?" "No," she says, kind o' dull like. "Ain't he home?" says I. "Yes," says she, "he's home." "Then why can't I see him?" I asked her, out of patience. "'Cause he's dead," says she. "*Dead?*" says I. She just nodded her head, not getting a bit excited, but rockin' back and forth. "Why—where is he?" says I, not knowing what to say. She just pointed upstairs—like that. (*Himself pointing to the room above*). I started for the stairs, with the idea of going up there. I walked from there to here—then I says, "Why, what did he die of?" "He died of a rope round his neck," says she, and just went on pleatin' at her apron. Well, I went out and called Harry. I thought I might—need help. We went upstairs and there he was lyin'—

COUNTY ATTORNEY: I think I'd rather have you go into that upstairs, where you can point it all out. Just go on now with the rest of the story.

HALE: Well, my first thought was to get that rope off. It looked . . . (*stops, his face twitches*) . . . but Harry, he went up to him, and he said, "No, he's dead all right, and we'd better not touch anything." So we went back downstairs. She was still sitting that same way. "Has anybody been notified?" I asked. "No," says she, unconcerned. "Who did this, Mrs. Wright?" said Harry. He said it business-like—and she stopped pleatin' of her apron. "I don't know," she says. "You don't *know*?" says Harry. "No," says she. "Weren't you sleepin' in the bed with him?" says Harry. "Yes," says she, "but I was on the inside." "Somebody slipped a rope round his neck and strangled him and you didn't wake up?" says Harry. "I didn't wake up," she said after him. We must 'a' looked as if we didn't see how that could be, for after a minute she said, "I sleep sound." Harry was going to ask her more questions but I said maybe we ought to let her tell her story first to the coroner, or the sheriff, so Harry went fast as he could to Rivers' place, where there's a telephone.

COUNTY ATTORNEY: And what did Mrs. Wright do when she knew that you had gone for the coroner?

HALE: She moved from the rocker to that chair over there (*pointing to a small chair in the* D. R. *corner*) and just sat there with her hands held together and looking down. I got a feeling that I ought to make some conversation, so I said I had come in to see if John wanted to put in a telephone, and at that she started to laugh, and then she stopped and looked at me—scared. (*The* COUNTY ATTORNEY, *who has had his notebook out, makes a note*). I dunno, maybe it wasn't scared. I wouldn't like to say it was. Soon Harry got back, and then Dr. Lloyd came, and you, Mr. Peters, and so I guess that's all I know that you don't.

COUNTY ATTORNEY (*rising and looking around*). I guess we'll go upstairs first— and then out to the barn and around there. (*To the* SHERIFF). You're convinced that there was nothing important here—nothing that would point to any motive?

SHERIFF: Nothing here but kitchen things. (*The* COUNTY ATTORNEY, *after again looking around the kitchen, opens the door of a cupboard closet in* R. *wall. He brings a small chair from* R.—*gets up on it and looks on a shelf. Pulls his hand away, sticky.*)

COUNTY ATTORNEY: Here's a nice mess. (*The women draw nearer* U. C.)

MRS. PETERS (*to the other woman*). Oh, her fruit; it did freeze. (*To the* LAWYER). She worried about that when it turned so cold. She said the fire'd go out and her jars would break.

SHERIFF (*rises*). Well, can you beat the women! Held for murder and worryin' about her preserves.

COUNTY ATTORNEY (*getting down from chair*). I guess before we're through she may have something more serious than preserves to worry about. (*Crosses down* R.C.)

HALE: Well, women are used to worrying over trifles. (*The two women move a little closer together.*)

COUNTY ATTORNEY (*with the gallantry of a young politician*). And yet, for all their worries, what would we do without the ladies? (*The women do not unbend. He goes below the center table to the sink, takes a dipperful of water from the pail and pouring it into a basin, washes his hands. While he is doing this the* SHERIFF *and* HALE *cross to cupboard, which they inspect. The* COUNTY ATTORNEY *starts to wipe his hands on the roller towel, turns it for a cleaner place*). Dirty towels! (*Kicks his foot against the pans under the sink*). Not much of a housekeeper, would you say, ladies?

MRS. HALE (*stiffly*). There's a great deal of work to be done on a farm.

COUNTY ATTORNEY: To be sure. And yet (*with a little bow to her*) I know there are some Dickson County farmhouses which do not have such roller towels. (*He gives it a pull to expose its full length again.*)

MRS. HALE: Those towels get dirty awful quick. Men's hands aren't always as clean as they might be.

COUNTY ATTORNEY: Ah, loyal to your sex, I see. But you and Mrs. Wright were neighbors. I suppose you were friends, too.

MRS. HALE (*shaking her head*). I've not seen much of her of late years. I've not been in this house—it's more than a year.

COUNTY ATTORNEY (*crossing to women U. C.*). And why was that? You didn't like her?

MRS. HALE: I liked her all well enough. Farmers' wives have their hands full, Mr. Henderson. And then——

COUNTY ATTORNEY: Yes——?

MRS. HALE (*looking about*). It never seemed a very cheerful place.

COUNTY ATTORNEY: No—it's not cheerful. I shouldn't say she had the home-making instinct.

MRS. HALE: Well, I don't know as Wright had, either.

COUNTY ATTORNEY: You mean that they didn't get on very well?

MRS. HALE: No, I don't mean anything. But I don't think a place'd be any cheerfuller for John Wright's being in it.

COUNTY ATTORNEY: I'd like to talk more of that a little later. I want to get the lay of things upstairs now. (*He goes past the women to U. R. where steps lead to a stair door.*)

SHERIFF: I suppose anything Mrs. Peters does'll be all right. She was to take in some clothes for her, you know, and a few little things. We left in such a hurry yesterday.

COUNTY ATTORNEY: Yes, but I would like to see what you take, Mrs. Peters, and keep an eye out for anything that might be of use to us.

MRS. PETER: Yes, Mr. Henderson. (*The men leave by U. R. door to stairs. The women listen to the men's steps on the stairs, then look about the kitchen.*)

MRS. HALE (*crossing L. to sink*). I'd hate to have men coming into my kitchen, snooping around and criticizing. (*She arranges the pans under sink which the LAW-YER had shoved out of place.*)

MRS. PETERS: Of course it's no more than their duty. (*Crosses to cupboard U. R.*)

MRS. HALE: Duty's all right, but I guess that deputy sheriff that came out to make the fire might have got a little of this on. (*Gives the roller towel a pull*). Wish I'd thought of that sooner. Seems mean to talk about her for not having things slicked up when she had to come away in such a hurry. (*Crosses R. to MRS. PETERS at cupboard.*)

MRS. PETERS (*who has been looking through cupboard, lifts one end of a towel that covers a pan*). She had bread set. (*Stands still.*)

MRS. HALE (*eyes fixed on a loaf of bread beside the breadbox, which is on a low shelf of the cupboard*). She was going to put this in there. (*Picks up loaf, then abruptly drops it. In a manner of returning to familiar things*). It's a shame about her fruit. I wonder if it's all gone. (*Gets up on the chair and looks*). I think there's some here that's all right, Mrs. Peters. Yes—here; (*holding it toward the window*) this is cherries, too. (*Looking again*). I declare I believe that's the only one. (*Gets down, jar in her hand. Goes to the sink and wipes it off on the outside*). She'll feel awful bad after all her hard work in the hot weather. I remember the afternoon I put up my cherries last summer. (*She puts the jar on the big kitchen table, center of the room. With a sigh, is about to sit down in the rocking chair. Before she is seated realizes what chair it is; with a slow look at it, steps back. The chair which she has touched rocks back and forth.* MRS. PETERS *moves to center table and they both watch the chair rock for a moment or two.*)

MRS. PETERS (*shaking off the mood which the empty rocking chair has evoked. Now in a businesslike manner she speaks*). Well, I must get those things from the front room closet. (*She goes to the door at the* R., *but, after looking into the other room, steps back*). You coming with me, Mrs. Hale? You could help me carry them. (*They go in the other room; reappear,* MRS. PETERS *carrying a dress, petticoat and skirt,* MRS. HALE *following with a pair of shoes*). My, it's cold in there. (*She puts the clothes on the big table, and hurries to the stove.*)

MRS. HALE (*right of center table examining the skirt*). Wright was close. I think maybe that's why she kept so much to herself. She didn't even belong to the Ladies' Aid. I suppose she felt she couldn't do her part, and then you don't enjoy things when you feel shabby. I heard she used to wear pretty clothes and be lively, when she was Minnie Foster, one of the town girls singing in the choir. But that— oh, that was thirty years ago. This all you was to take in?

MRS. PETERS: She said she wanted an apron. Funny thing to want, for there isn't much to get you dirty in jail, goodness knows. But I suppose just to make her feel more natural. (*Crosses to cupboard*). She said they was in the top drawer in this cupboard. Yes, here. And then her little shawl that always hung behind the door. (*Opens stair door and looks*). Yes, here it is. (*Quickly shuts door leading upstairs.*)

MRS. HALE (*abruptly moving toward her*). Mrs. Peters?

MRS. PETERS: Yes, Mrs. Hale? (*At* U. R. *door.*)

MRS. HALE: Do you think she did it?

MRS. PETERS (*in a frightened voice*). Oh, I don't know.

MRS. HALE: Well, I don't think she did. Asking for an apron and her little shawl. Worrying about her fruit.

MRS. PETERS (*starts to speak, glances up, where footsteps are heard in the room above. In a low voice*). Mr. Peters says it looks bad for her. Mr. Henderson is awful sarcastic in a speech and he'll make fun of her sayin' she didn't wake up.

MRS. HALE: Well, I guess John Wright didn't wake when they was slipping that rope under his neck.

MRS. PETERS (*crossing slowly to table and placing shawl and apron on table with other clothing*). No, it's strange. It must have been done awful crafty and still. They say it was such a—funny way to kill a man, rigging it all up like that.

MRS. HALE (*crossing to left of* MRS. PETERS *at table*). That's just what Mr. Hale said. There was a gun in the house. He says that's what he can't understand.

MRS. PETERS: Mr. Henderson said coming out that what was needed for the case was a motive; something to show anger, or—sudden feeling.

MRS. HALE (*who is standing by the table*). Well, I don't see any signs of anger around here. (*She puts her hand on the dish towel which lies on the table, stands looking down at table, one-half of which is clean, the other half messy*). It's wiped to here. (*Makes a move as if to finish work, then turns and looks at loaf of bread outside the breadbox. Drops towel. In that voice of coming back to familiar things*).

Wonder how they are finding things upstairs. (*Crossing below table to* D. R.). I hope she had it a little more red-up up there. You know, it seems kind of *sneaking*. Locking her up in town and then coming out here and trying to get her own house to turn against her!

MRS. PETERS: But, Mrs. Hale, the law is the law.

MRS. HALE: I s'pose 'tis. (*Unbuttoning her coat*). Better loosen up your things, Mrs. Peters. You won't feel them when you go out. (MRS. PETERS *takes off her fur tippet, goes to hang it on chair back left of table, stands looking at the work basket on floor near* D. L. *window*.)

MRS. PETERS: She was piecing a quilt. (*She brings the large sewing basket to the center table and they look at the bright pieces,* MRS. HALE *above the table and* MRS. PETERS *left of it.*)

MRS. HALE: It's a log cabin pattern. Pretty, isn't it? I wonder if she was goin' to quilt it or just knot it? (*Footsteps have been heard coming down the stairs. The* SHERIFF *enters followed by* HALE *and the* COUNTY ATTORNEY.)

SHERIFF: They wonder if she was going to quilt it or just knot it! (*The men laugh, the women look abashed.*)

COUNTY ATTORNEY (*rubbing his hands over the stove*). Frank's fire didn't do much up there, did it? Well, let's go out to the barn and get that cleared up. (*The men go outside by* U. L. *door*.)

MRS. HALE (*resentfully*). I don't know as there's anything so strange, our takin' up our time with little things while we're waiting for them to get the evidence. (*She sits in chair right of table smoothing out a block with decision*). I don't see as it's anything to laugh about.

MRS. PETERS (*apologetically*). Of course they've got awful important things on their minds. (*Pulls up a chair and joins* MRS. HALE *at the left of the table.*)

MRS. HALE (*examining another block*). Mrs. Peters, look at this one. Here, this is the one she was working on, and look at the sewing! All the rest of it has been so nice and even. And look at this! It's all over the place! Why, it looks as if she didn't know what she was about! (*After she has said this they look at each other, then start to glance back at the door. After an instant* MRS. HALE *has pulled at a knot and ripped the sewing.*)

MRS. PETERS: Oh, what are you doing, Mrs. Hale?

MRS. HALE (*mildly*). Just pulling out a stitch or two that's not sewed very good. (*Threading a needle*). Bad sewing always made me fidgety.

MRS. PETERS (*with a glance at door, nervously*). I don't think we ought to touch things.

MRS. HALE: I'll just finish up this end. (*Suddenly stopping and leaning forward*). Mrs. Peters?

MRS. PETERS: Yes, Mrs. Hale?

MRS. HALE: What do you suppose she was so nervous about?

MRS. PETERS: Oh—I don't know. I don't know as she was nervous. I sometimes sew awful queer when I'm just tired. (MRS. HALE *starts to say something, looks at* MRS. PETERS *then goes on sewing*). Well, I must get these things wrapped up. They may be through sooner than we think. (*Putting apron and other things together*). I wonder where I can find a piece of paper, and string. (*Rises.*)

MRS. HALE: In that cupboard, maybe.

MRS. PETERS (*crosses* R. *looking in cupboard*). Why, here's a bird-cage. (*Holds it up*). Did she have a bird, Mrs. Hale?

MRS. HALE: Why, I don't know whether she did or not—I've not been here for so long. There was a man around last year selling canaries cheap, but I don't know as she took one; maybe she did. She used to sing real pretty herself.

MRS. PETERS (*glancing around*). Seems funny to think of a bird here. But she must have had one, or why would she have a cage? I wonder what happened to it?

MRS. HALE: I s'pose maybe the cat got it.

MRS. PETERS: No, she didn't have a cat. She's got that feeling some people have about cats—being afraid of them. My cat got in her room and she was real upset and asked me to take it out.

MRS. HALE: My sister Bessie was like that. Queer, ain't it?

MRS. PETERS (*examining the cage*). Why, look at this door. It's broke. One hinge is pulled apart. (*Takes a step down to* MRS. HALE'S *right.*)

MRS. HALE (*looking too*). Looks as if someone must have been rough with it.

MRS. PETERS: Why, yes. (*She brings the cage forward and puts it on the table.*)

MRS. HALE (*glancing toward* U. L. *door*). I wish if they're going to find any evidence they'd be about it. I don't like this place.

MRS. PETERS: But I'm awful glad you came with me, Mrs. Hale. It would be lonesome for me sitting here alone.

MRS. HALE: It would, wouldn't it? (*Dropping her sewing*). But I tell you what I do wish, Mrs. Peters. I wish I had come over sometimes when she was here. I—(*looking around the room*)—wish I had.

MRS. PETERS: But of course you were awful busy, Mrs. Hale—your house and your children.

MRS. HALE (*rises and crosses* L.). I could've come. I stayed away because it weren't cheerful—and that's why I ought to have come. I—(*looking out* L. *window*)—I've never liked this place. Maybe because it's down in a hollow and you don't see the road. I dunno what it is, but it's a lonesome place and always was. I wish I had come over to see Minnie Foster sometimes. I can see now——(*Shakes her head.*)

MRS. PETERS (*left of table and above it*). Well, you mustn't reproach yourself, Mrs. Hale. Somehow we just don't see how it is with other folks until—something turns up.

MRS. HALE: Not having children makes less work—but it makes a quiet house, and Wright out to work all day, and no company when he did come in. (*Turning from window*). Did you know John Wright, Mrs. Peters?

MRS. PETERS: Not to know him; I've seen him in town. They say he was a good man.

MRS. HALE: Yes—good; he didn't drink, and kept his word as well as most, I guess, and paid his debts. But he was a hard man, Mrs. Peters. Just to pass the time of day with him—— (*Shivers*). Like a raw wind that gets to the bone. (*Pauses, her eye falling on the cage*). I should think she would 'a' wanted a bird. But what do you suppose went with it?

MRS. PETERS: I don't know, unless it got sick and died. (*She reaches over and swings the broken door, swings it again, both women watch it.*)

MRS. HALE: You weren't raised round here, were you? (MRS. PETERS *shakes her head*). You didn't know—her?

MRS. PETERS: Not till they brought her yesterday.

MRS. HALE: She—come to think of it, she was kind of like a bird herself—real sweet and pretty, but kind of timid and—fluttery. How—she—did—change. (*Silence; then as if struck by a happy thought and relieved to get back to everyday things. Crosses* R. *above* MRS. PETERS *to cupboard, replaces small chair used to stand on to its original place* D. R.). Tell you what, Mrs. Peters, why don't you take the quilt in with you? It might take up her mind.

MRS. PETERS: Why, I think that's a real nice idea, Mrs. Hale. There couldn't possibly be any objection to it, could there? Now, just what would I take? I wonder if her patches are in here—and her things. (*They look in the sewing basket.*)

MRS. HALE (*crosses to right of table*). Here's some red. I expect this has got sewing things in it. (*Brings out a fancy box*). What a pretty box. Looks like something somebody would give you. Maybe her scissors are in here. (*Opens box. Suddenly puts her hand to her nose*). Why—— (MRS. PETERS *bends nearer, then turns her face away*). There's something wrapped up in this piece of silk.

MRS. PETERS: Why, this isn't her scissors.

MRS. HALE (*lifting the silk*). Oh, Mrs. Peters—it's—— (MRS. PETERS *bends closer.*)

MRS. PETERS: It's the bird.

MRS. HALE: But, Mrs. Peters—look at it! Its neck! Look at its neck! It's all—other side to.

MRS. PETERS: Somebody—wrung—its—neck. (*Their eyes meet. A look of growing comprehension, of horror. Steps are heard outside.* MRS. HALE *slips box under quilt pieces, and sinks into her chair. Enter* SHERIFF *and* COUNTY ATTORNEY. MRS. PETERS *steps* D. L. *and stands looking out of window.*)

COUNTY ATTORNEY (*as one turning from serious things to little pleasantries*). Well, ladies, have you decided whether she was going to quilt it or knot it? (*Crosses to* C. *above table.*)

MRS. PETERS: We think she was going to—knot it. (SHERIFF *crosses to right of stove, lifts stove lid and glances at fire, then stands warming hands at stove.*)

COUNTY ATTORNEY: Well, that's interesting, I'm sure. (*Seeing the bird-cage*). Has the bird flown?

MRS. HALE (*putting more quilt pieces over the box*). We think the—cat got it.

COUNTY ATTORNEY (*preoccupied*). Is there a cat? (MRS. HALE *glances in a quick covert way at* MRS. PETERS.)

MRS. PETERS (*turning from window takes a step in*). Well, not *now*. They're superstitious, you know. They leave.

COUNTY ATTORNEY (*to* SHERIFF PETERS, *continuing an interrupted conversation*). No sign at all of anyone having come from the outside. Their own rope.

Now let's go up again and go over it piece by piece. (*They start upstairs*). It would have to have been someone who knew just the—— (MRS. PETERS *sits down left of table. The two women sit there not looking at one another, but as if peering into something and at the same time holding back. When they talk now it is in the manner of feeling their way over strange ground, as if afraid of what they are saying, but as if they cannot help saying it.*)

MRS. HALE (*hesitatively and in hushed voice*). She liked the bird. She was going to bury it in that pretty box.

MRS. PETERS (*in a whisper*). When I was a girl—my kitten—there was a boy took a hatchet, and before my eyes—and before I could get there——(*Covers her face an instant*). If they hadn't held me back I would have—(*catches herself, looks upstairs where steps are heard, falters weakly*)—hurt him.

MRS. HALE (*with a slow look around her*). I wonder how it would seem never to have had any children around. (*Pause*). No, Wright wouldn't like the bird—a thing that sang. She used to sing. He killed that, too.

MRS. PETERS (*moving uneasily*). We don't know who killed the bird.

MRS. HALE: I knew John Wright.

MRS. PETERS: It was an awful thing was done in this house that night, Mrs. Hale. Killing a man while he slept, slipping a rope around his neck that choked the life out of him.

MRS. HALE: His neck. Choked the life out of him. (*Her hand goes out and rests on the bird-cage.*)

MRS. PETERS (*with rising voice*). We don't know who killed him. We don't know.

MRS. HALE (*her own feeling not interrupted*). If there'd been years and years of nothing, then a bird to sing to you, it would be awful—still, after the bird was still.

MRS. PETERS (*something within her speaking*). I know what stillness is. When we homesteaded in Dakota, and my first baby died—after he was two years old, and me with no other then——

MRS. HALE (*moving*). How soon do you suppose they'll be through looking for the evidence?

MRS. PETERS: I know what stillness is. (*Pulling herself back*). The law has got to punish crime, Mrs. Hale.

MRS. HALE (*not as if answering that*). I wish you'd seen Minnie Foster when she wore a white dress with blue ribbons and stood up there in the choir and sang. (*A look around the room*). Oh, I *wish* I'd come over here once in a while! That was a crime! That was a crime! Who's going to punish that?

MRS. PETERS (*looking upstairs*). We mustn't—take on.

MRS. HALE: I might have known she needed help! I know how things can be—for women. I tell you, it's queer, Mrs. Peters. We live close together and we live far apart. We all go through the same things—it's all just a different kind of the same thing. (*Brushes her eyes, noticing the jar of fruit, reaches out for it*). If I was you I wouldn't tell her her fruit was gone. Tell her it *ain't*. Tell her it's all right. Take this in to prove it to her. She—she may never know whether it was broke or not.

MRS. PETERS (*takes the jar, looks about for something to wrap it in; takes petticoat from the clothes brought from the other room, very nervously begins winding this around the jar. In a false voice*). My, it's a good thing the men couldn't hear us. Wouldn't they just laugh! Getting all stirred up over a little thing like a—dead canary. As if that could have anything to do with—with—wouldn't they *laugh!* (*The men are heard coming downstairs.*)

MRS. HALE (*under her breath*). Maybe they would—maybe they wouldn't.

COUNTY ATTORNEY: No, Peters, it's all perfectly clear except a reason for doing it. But you know juries when it comes to women. If there was some definite thing. (*Crosses slowly to above table.* SHERIFF *crosses* D. R. MRS. HALE *and* MRS. PETERS *remain seated at either side of table*). Something to show—something to make a story about—a thing that would connect up with this strange way of doing it—— (*The women's eyes meet for an instant. Enter* HALE *from outer door.*)

HALE (*remaining* U. L. *by door*). Well, I've got the team around. Pretty cold out there.

COUNTY ATTORNEY: I'm going to stay awhile by myself. (*To the* SHERIFF). You can send Frank out for me, can't you? I want to go over everything. I'm not satisfied that we can't do better.

SHERIFF: Do you want to see what Mrs. Peters is going to take in? (*The* LAWYER *picks up the apron, laughs.*)

COUNTY ATTORNEY: Oh, I guess they're not very dangerous things the ladies have picked out. (*Moves a few things about, disturbing the quilt pieces which cover the box. Steps back*). No, Mrs. Peters doesn't need supervising. For that matter a sheriff's wife is married to the law. Ever think of it that way, Mrs. Peters?

MRS. PETERS: Not—just that way.

SHERIFF (*chuckling*). Married to the law. (*Moves to* D. R. *door to the other room*). I just want you to come in here a minute, George. We ought to take a look at these windows.

COUNTY ATTORNEY (*scoffingly*). Oh, windows!

SHERIFF: We'll be right out, Mr. Hale. (HALE *goes outside. The* SHERIFF *follows the* COUNTY ATTORNEY *into the other room. Then* MRS. HALE *rises, hands tight together, looking intensely at* MRS. PETERS, *whose eyes make a slow turn, finally meeting* MRS. HALE'S. *A moment* MRS. HALE *holds her, then her own eyes point the way to where the box is concealed. Suddenly* MRS. PETERS *throws back quilt pieces and tries to put the box in the bag she is carrying. It is too big. She opens box, starts to take bird out, cannot touch it, goes to pieces, stands there helpless. Sound of a knob turning in the other room.* MRS. HALE *snatches the box and puts it in the pocket of her big coat. Enter* COUNTY ATTORNEY *and* SHERIFF, *who remains* D. R.)

COUNTY ATTORNEY (*crosses to* U. L. *door facetiously*). Well, Henry, at least we found out that she was not going to quilt it. She was going to—what is it you call it, ladies?

MRS. HALE (*standing* C. *below table facing front, her hand against her pocket*). We call it—knot it, Mr. Henderson.

CURTAIN

ACTIVITIES FOR WRITING AND DISCUSSION

1. Do a "readers' theater" performance of the play. Form into groups of five or six, assign character roles, and read the play aloud. Since **scene descriptions** and **stage directions**—printed in italics—are important, you may want to assign one person to read the italicized text. As you are performing:

    a. Mark any words, lines, stage directions, or other things that strike you—for whatever reason, and

    b. Note any ways that your interpretation of a character changes as you hear the play performed.

When you are finished, share with the class or your group any new perspectives you have on the play as a result of hearing it performed.

2. Imagine you are Minnie Wright, and you have kept a diary of your experiences since girlhood. After consulting details of Minnie's life story as revealed in the play, compose several of the entries you believe she might have written in her diary. You might include your (Minnie's) thoughts and feelings about life, music, John, and the canary, among other things.

3. Based on evidence in the play, determine whether Minnie Wright murdered her husband and how she might have done it. Then, writing in the **first person** as Minnie Wright or as a **third-person narrator,** tell the story of how John Wright died.

4. Sometimes you can obtain interesting perspectives on a story or play by assuming the **point of view** of an involved inanimate object or animal. Imagine you are the unfortunate canary in *Trifles*. Tell your story, paying particular attention to your life and witness in the Wright household.

5. Read the Glaspell biography in Appendix D. Then research the history of *Trifles* and of Glaspell's involvement in the Provincetown Players, who also premiered the earliest one-act plays of Eugene O'Neill (see page 554).

TERRENCE McNALLY (b. 1939)

Andre's Mother

Characters

Cal, a young man
Arthur, his father
Penny, his sister
Andre's Mother

Time: Now
Place: New York City, Central Park

Four people—Cal, Arthur, Penny, and Andre's Mother—enter. They are nicely dressed and each carries a white helium-filled balloon on a string.

CAL: You know what's really terrible? I can't think of anything terrific to say. Goodbye. I love you. I'll miss you. And I'm supposed to be so great with words!

PENNY: What's that over there?

ARTHUR: Ask your brother.

CAL: It's a theatre. An outdoor theatre. They do plays there in the summer. Shakespeare's plays. (*To Andre's Mother.*) God, how much he wanted to play Hamlet again. He would have gone to Timbuktu to have another go at that part. The summer he did it in Boston, he was so happy!

PENNY: Cal, I don't think she . . . ! It's not the time. Later.

ARTHUR: Your son was a . . . the Jews have a word for it. . .

PENNY (*quietly appalled*): Oh my God!

ARTHUR: Mensch, I believe it is, and I think I'm using it right. It means warm, solid, the real thing. Correct me if I'm wrong.

PENNY: Fine, Dad, fine. Just quit while you're ahead.

ARTHUR: I won't say he was like a son to me. Even my son isn't always like a son to me. I mean . . . ! In my clumsy way, I'm trying to say how much I liked Andre. And how much he helped me to know my own boy. Cal was always two handsful but Andre and I could talk about anything under the sun. My wife was very fond of him, too.

PENNY: Cal, I don't understand about the balloons.

CAL: They represent the soul. When you let go, it means you're letting his soul ascend to Heaven. That you're willing to let go. Breaking the last earthly ties.

PENNY: Does the Pope know about this?

ARTHUR: Penny!

PENNY: Andre loved my sense of humor. Listen, you can hear him laughing. (*She lets go of her white balloon.*) So long, you glorious, wonderful, I-know-what-Cal-means-about-words . . . *man*! God forgive me for wishing you were straight every time I laid eyes on you. But if any man was going to have you, I'm glad it was my brother! Look how fast it went up. I bet that means something. Something terrific.

ARTHUR (*lets his balloon go*): Goodbye. God speed.

PENNY: Cal?

CAL: I'm not ready yet.

PENNY: Okay. We'll be over there. Come on, Pop, you can buy your little girl a Good Humor.

ARTHUR: They still make Good Humor?

PENNY: Only now they're called Dove Bars and they cost twelve dollars.

(*Penny takes Arthur off. Cal and Andre's Mother stand with their balloons.*)

CAL: I wish I knew what you were thinking. I think it would help me. You know almost nothing about me and I only know what Andre told me about you. I'd always had it in my mind that one day we would be friends, you and me. But if you didn't know about Andre and me . . . If this hadn't happened, I wonder if he would have ever told you. When he was sick, if I asked him once I asked him a thousand times, tell her. She's your mother. She won't mind. But he was so afraid of hurting you and of your disapproval. I don't know which was worse. (*No response. He sighs.*) God, how many of us live in this city because we don't want to hurt our mothers and live in mortal terror of their disapproval. We lose ourselves here. Our lives aren't furtive, just our feelings toward people like you are! A city of fugitives from our parents' scorn or heartbreak. Sometimes he'd seem a little down and I'd say, "What's the matter, babe?" and this funny sweet, sad smile would cross his face and he'd say, "Just a little homesick, Cal, just a little bit." I always accused him of being a country boy just playing at being a hotshot, sophisticated New Yorker. (*He sighs.*)

It's bullshit. It's all bullshit. (*Still no response.*)

Do you remember the comic strip *Little Lulu*? Her mother had no name, she was so remote, so formidable to all the children. She was just Lulu's mother. "Hello, Lulu's Mother," Lulu's friends would say. She was almost anonymous in her remoteness. You remind me of her. Andre's mother. Let me answer the questions you can't ask and then I'll leave you alone and you won't ever have to see me again. Andre died of AIDS. I don't know how he got it. I tested negative. He died bravely. You would have been proud of him. The only thing that frightened him was you. I'll have everything that was his sent to you. I'll pay for it. There isn't much. You should have come up the summer he played Hamlet. He was magnificent. Yes, I'm bitter. I'm bitter I've lost him. I'm bitter what's happening. I'm bitter even now, after all this, I can't reach you. I'm beginning to feel your disapproval and it's making me ill. (*He looks at his balloon.*) Sorry, old friend. I blew it. (*He lets go of the balloon.*)

Good night, sweet prince, and flights of angels sing thee to thy rest! (*Beat.*) Goodbye, Andre's mother.

(*He goes. Andre's Mother stands alone holding her white balloon. Her lips tremble. She looks on the verge of breaking down. She is about to let go of the balloon when she pulls it down to her. She looks at it awhile before she gently kisses it. She lets go of the balloon. She follows it with her eyes as it rises and rises. The lights are beginning to fade. Andre's Mother's eyes are still on the balloon. The lights fade.*)

GENDER AND RELATIONSHIPS: ADDITIONAL ACTIVITIES FOR WRITING AND DISCUSSION

1. Reread all or a portion of your notebook. Mark any passages, however long or short, that strike you, for whatever reason. Beside each passage, write a note explaining its significance for you. Finally, pick a favorite passage and either:
    a. Expand it into a new piece of writing, or

    b. Make notes on how you *could* expand or use it at some future date, or

    c. Rewrite it in a different form (e.g., poem, dialogue, letter, memoir).

For a list of strategies for expanding or revising, see Chapter 12.

    2. Following the death of her husband, Minnie Wright (*Trifles*) sits in her jail cell. Several women **characters** and **speakers** in this section of readings might have things to say to her. Imagine that one or more of the following visit Minnie in her cell: the unnamed narrator of "The Yellow Wallpaper," one of the women in the Thomas Hardy poems, Christina Rossetti's Margery, Pound's river-merchant's wife, Wakoski's belly dancer. After selecting your visitor(s), draft a list of subjects she/they might raise with Minnie. Then dramatize her/their encounter with Minnie in the form of a dialogue or a short play (including, if you wish, a **scene description** and **stage directions**).

    3. Several readings in this section take what could be seen as a "dim" view of men. As an alternative to Activity #2, bring together two or more male characters or speakers from these texts and create a dialogue or short play about their encounter.

    4. What ground do the gay couple James and Dennis ("Keeping Company") and Cal (*Andre's Mother*) occupy in the "gender wars"? Conduct an interview with one or more of these characters, inviting his/their opinion(s) on any of the characters or conflicts featured in the other readings within this thematic section.

    5. The death of a spouse occurs (or is implied) in both Chopin's "The Story of an Hour" and Tomioka Taeko's "Just the Two of Us." Both texts also highlight the notion of "freedom" (note the next-to-last line of Taeko's poem and Louise Mallard's thoughts in "The Story of an Hour"). Write a notebook entry or essay assessing these and/or any other connections you see between these two texts and the characters whose lives they dramatize. If you wish, as an alternative, contrast either Chopin's or Taeko's text with Derek Walcott's "The Young Wife," which depicts a husband mourning the loss of his wife.

    6. Imagine you are Kate Chopin's Louise Mallard, Colette's Alice, the narrator in Claire Kemp's "Keeping Company," or one of the other women characters, speakers, or personae included in the readings in Chapter 20. Then read Francine du Plessix Gray's "On Friendship" and

    a. Annotate the essay as that particular character/speaker/persona might.

    b. Still in character, respond to "On Friendship" in an essay or a letter to the author. If you wish, pay special attention to ideas and issues raised in the paragraph that begins, "The quality of free consent . . ." (paragraph #13).

    7. Near the end of "Looking at Women," Scott Russell Sanders writes:

To be turned into an object—whether by the brush of a painter or the lens of a photographer or the eye of a voyeur, whether by hunger or poverty or enslavement, by mugging or rape, bullets or bombs, by hatred, racism, car crashes, fires, or falls—is for each of us the deepest dread; and to reduce another person to an object is the primal wrong.

Reread the paragraph in which this sentence appears and any other passages that discuss how women—or people generally—turn themselves (or are turned) into objects. If you have not already done so, annotate those passages. Then, in an essay:

    a. Summarize the process of objectification to which Sanders and others (e.g., John Berger, Allen Wheelis) are referring. By what means do women/human beings become "objects," and in what respects is being thus objectified bad or harmful?

    b. Apply the process of objectification you have just summarized in an analysis of "A Woman on a Roof," "Keeping Company," "Sex Without Love," or some other story or poem you have read thus far in the course.

8. Review your entire notebook; as you do, make a running list of memorable or striking topics, e.g., "women as objects," "friendship," "marriages," "kinds of love." Then choose a favorite topic, make a Topic/Form Grid (see Chapter 5), and use one of the forms on your grid to create a new notebook entry about the topic. If your chosen form does not work, do a Topic/Form Shift to a different form on your grid.

Interchapter on Notebooks and Journals (I)

The Notebook As "Pure" Poetry: Joseph Joubert

Joseph Joubert once wrote, "And perhaps there is no advice to give a writer more important than this:—Never write anything that does not give you great pleasure." Joubert followed his own advice: uninterested in money, publication, or fame, for some four decades he wrote for no other apparent reason than the pleasure of it.

Joubert had an outwardly uneventful life. Born in Montignac (Dordogue), France, in 1754, the second of eight surviving children, in his twenties he moved to Paris, where he became a secretary to the great French encyclopedist and man of letters Denis Diderot, and a member of French literary and artistic circles. He served a term as a rural justice of the peace but withdrew from politics in the bloody wake of the French Revolution, which he had initially welcomed. During his fifties he returned to public service as an education inspector. Living in the small town of Villeneuve in Burgundy, the family home of his wife (a member of the moneyed middle class), he died in 1824, at the age of 70.

From the late 1780s on Joubert's notebooks were his absorbing passion. As he wrote: "These thoughts form not only the foundation of my work, but of my life." Insatiably curious, he read widely in all subjects and was an ardent practitioner of what Ralph Waldo Emerson would later call "read[ing] to start your own team": Joubert darkened the margins of the books he read with annotations, which he subsequently reread and used to inspire reflections and observations of his own.

His friends repeatedly urged him to publish his work, but Joubert declined. After his death his widow found his notes—many of them scribbled on the backs of envelopes or on fragments of scrap paper held together by safety pins—inside a large trunk he had used for storing papers. The first published selection from the notebooks, edited by the French writer and statesman Chateaubriand (who had been a friend of Joubert's), did not appear until 1838. Other editions followed, in French and in translation, and by the latter part of the nineteenth century Joubert had become posthumously famous in Europe and America.

Why Joubert refused to publish remains a mystery. Having married a woman of means, he didn't need to write for money, and he wasn't interested in fame. The future of his writings didn't concern him. To have recorded a thought and worded it accurately was reward enough. When friends saw him they probably learned to ask, not, "What have you been doing, Joseph?" but "What have you been *thinking*?"

If such a thing exists, you could almost call Joubert a "pure" poet. Not that his writing is "poetry" in the technical sense: many of his reflections seem more philosophic than poetic, and his words aren't formatted as verse. But Joubert engages life with a purely poetic spirit. Every moment is a package; inside is the gift. "All reflection," he writes, "is art."

Joubert in his notebooks is far removed from a purely *functional* orientation toward life. The functional outlook holds that everything has to have a use to be meaningful, that simply to *be* is not enough. A man or woman is made meaningful by a job; every idea has to be developed and applied, or it wasn't worth having; every poem or story has to be finished and published, or it has been a waste of time. Even a vacation, perhaps, is only "successful" if it has resulted in the conquest of "X" many cities or "Y" many popular landmarks. The functional outlook emphasizes action and minimizes reflection; one acts without necessarily pausing to question *why* (or without considering the possible advantages of doing nothing). . . . The functionality of our actions, of course, is important and necessary; if we rejected it outright—if we stopped doing jobs or developing ideas—we would probably starve. The issue is one of balance.

Early in life Joubert seems to have decided that the poetry of a thing is that you don't have to *do* anything with it. The poetry of an idea is the idea itself—a thing to be recorded and contemplated without necessarily turning it to public use. The poetry of a rose or a river is what you get by perceiving it—looking, listening, smelling, touching. Trees are poetic not as building materials or as shelter against rain—both valuable *functions* of trees—but because you enjoy being in their presence.

As far as words are concerned, with the thought, "I could *do* something with this," poetry recedes and rhetoric takes over. Published writers hammer and caress their words into shape for public consumption without (they hope) compromising the artistic qualities. In this respect the poems of Shakespeare, Mary Oliver, Wislawa Szymborska, and Gary Soto—to name just a few of the poets anthologized in this book—are the result of poetry and rhetoric working *together*. For reasons known only to himself, Joubert was content to pitch his tent inside the initial hunch or intuition and never stir from the spot. He seems to say, *Why try to round or finish what isn't? Effort lies.*

Joubert writes about anything and everything—weather, astronomy, music, silence and sound, the nature of memory, politics, time, imagination, theology, parents and children, love, body and soul—whatever hooks his attention at the moment. "The thoughts that come to us are worth more than the ones we seek," he writes. His observations are typically no more than a sentence or two in length, aiding the rapid shift from topic to topic:

One would say that in such dark eyes there is a flame without light.

Pleasures are always children, pains always have wrinkles.

Everything is a game except what makes the soul better or worse.

Our arms are canes of flesh with which the soul reaches out and touches.

The weather strikes me on the head. I feel it rattle my teeth.

Some notes are not even complete grammatical sentences:

. . . passing their life in contradicting their childhood,—in erasing it.

Abuse of words, foundation of ideology.

Children. Need models more than critics.

This brevity and fragmentariness should not be mistaken for laziness or incompetence. Joubert habitually reread his notes and painstakingly revised those that interested him most . . . or, more accurately, he revised his *thoughts*. In a brilliant sentence about literary style he remarks, "It is not my words that I polish, but my ideas." For instance, he could have edited the last note above to make a single complete sentence ("Children need models more than critics"); however, the revision weakens the point of the note. It seems that he wants to give the word "Children" added weight by assigning it its own sentence, thereby emphasizing the "weighty" importance of children as a topic of private and public concern.

Focusing his energies on phrases and sentences, Joubert is forever striving "to put a whole book in a page, a whole page in a sentence, and this sentence in a word." For him style is perfected in the sentence or nowhere; and the sentence is only perfected in the idea.

In an age like our own that is saturated with images of celebrity, Joubert reminds us that the main pleasure of writing is the act of writing itself; and while *having written*—achieving commercial success or getting published—is desirable and gratifying, it is the *least interesting* part of composing. If this weren't so, why would we find that the best writers continually start new works even as they are finishing with the old? To "enjoy" a success is to put it behind you. Creation itself is the fruit of composing, says Joubert, success and notoriety the rind.

For further reading:
Joubert, Joseph. *The Notebooks of Joseph Joubert: A Selection.* Ed. and trans. Paul Auster. San Francisco: North Point P, 1983.

Excerpts from *The Notebooks of Joseph Joubert*

I imitate the dove, and often I throw a blade of grass to the drowning ant.   1

———

Thought forms in the soul in the same way clouds form in the air.   2

———

Through memory we travel against time, through forgetfulness we follow its   3
course.

———

We are in the world as words are in a book. Each generation is like a line, a phrase.   4

———

Let heaven forgive the wicked, after they have been punished.   5

———

Pleasures are always children, pains always have wrinkles.   6

———

There are truths that cannot be apprehended in conversation.   7

———

God is the place where I do not remember the rest.   8

———

Lovers. Whoever does not have their weaknesses cannot have their strengths.   9

———

Our arms are canes of flesh with which the soul reaches and touches.   10

———

What good is modesty?—It makes us seem more beautiful when we are beautiful,   11
and less ugly when we are ugly.

———

Children. Need models more than critics.   12

———

Everything is a game except what makes the soul better or worse.   13

———

One would say that in such dark eyes there is a flame without light.   14

———

The weather strikes me on the head. I feel it rattle my teeth.   15

―――――

The natural pace of the mind. And how it should move so as not to get worn out   16
by quickness or bogged down and made impatient by slowness.

―――――

The thoughts that come to us are worth more than the ones we seek.   17

―――――

Lightning flashes that cross the mind and illuminate so quickly they are hardly   18
noticed. In such cases, more is seen than retained. Thus, whoever does not observe himself carries within him some experience he does not know about.

―――――

Anger. Its fermentation is necessary to the maturing of certain soft and peaceful   19
feelings. But if the crisis does not take place, if the fermentation leads only to its
own bitterness, the operation has not borne fruit and the natural course of things
has not been followed.

―――――

Those useless phrases that come into the head. The mind is grinding its colors.   20

―――――

These thoughts form not only the foundation of my work, but of my life.   21

―――――

It is not my words that I polish, but my ideas.   22

―――――

Of those who feel God as rules, as light, and of those who feel him as love.   23

―――――

. . . passing their life in contradicting their childhood,—in erasing it.   24

―――――

All reflection is art.   25

―――――

And, in fact, when we speak, we write what we are saying in the air.   26

―――――

My dreams are more amorous than my actions have ever been.   27

―――――

The little cat and the piece of paper he turns into a mouse. He touches it lightly, 28
for fear of unmasking his illusion.

Little people have few passions, they hardly have anything but needs.   29

To want to express such subtle ideas faithfully is to want to capture an object that 30
endlessly escapes and reappears, that shows itself only for a moment. You must
wait, in spite of yourself, you must look.

Properly speaking, man inhabits only his head and his heart. All other places are 31
vainly before his eyes, at his sides, and under his feet: he himself is not there at all.

Freedom. The freedom to do something well. There is no need of any other kind. 32

Truths. The truths that teach us to act well and to live well. There is no need of 33
any other kind.

Abuse of words, foundation of ideology.   34

I am like Montaigne: "unsuited to continuous discourse."   35

More than once I have brought the cup of abundance to my lips; but it is a water 36
that has always escaped me. (Another version: I have often brought to my lips the
cup that holds abundance; it is a water that has always escaped me.)

There is in each man a divine part that is born with him, and a human and even 37
animal part that grows with time. The first must be conserved and carefully cultivated within ourselves, the other thrives without help.

Retreat often into your sphere, rest yourself in your center, plunge yourself into 38
your element: good advice, which must be remembered.

Tormented by the cursed ambition always to put a whole book in a page, a whole 39
page in a sentence, and this sentence in a word. I am speaking of myself.

And perhaps there is no advice to give a writer more important than this: — 40
Never write anything that does not give you great pleasure.

— Translated by Paul Auster

ACTIVITIES FOR WRITING AND DISCUSSION

1. Review your own notebook and/or your textual annotations. Are there any items that you could describe as "nonfunctional" or "purely" poetic in the Joubertian sense? Share any such items with a partner or small group. If these pieces are not "functional," what value, if any, do they have?

2. Thinking of your own experiences of writing, does writing always have to serve a *function?* If it doesn't serve a function, does the time spent on it seem to you to have been wasted? Can you write "nonfunctionally," as Joubert did, and at the same time excel at the functional kinds of composing emphasized in classes, on the job, and in other public settings? Are the two kinds of writing complementary or at odds with each other? Explain, and, if possible, illustrate your answers with some personal stories or examples.

3. Joubert used his notebooks, in part, to develop his literary style. Try using your own notebook for the same purpose. Jot down "the thoughts that come to" you in single phrases and sentences. Reread these thoughts periodically, identifying those that most intrigue you, and revise them so that they reflect more accurately and forcefully your initial thoughts.

4. Do any of the "Generic Ideas for Writing" on page 192.

Families

Guy de Maupassant (1850–1893)

The Olive Grove

When the longshoremen of Garandou, a little port of Provence, situated in the 1 bay of Pisca, between Marseilles and Toulon, perceived the boat of the Abbé Vilbois entering the harbor, they went down to the beach to help him pull her ashore.

The priest was alone in the boat. In spite of his fifty-eight years, he rowed with 2 all the energy of a real sailor. He had placed his hat on the bench beside him, his sleeves were rolled up, disclosing his powerful arms, his cassock was open at the neck and turned over his knees, and he wore a round hat of heavy, white canvas. His whole appearance bespoke an odd and strenuous priest of southern climes, better fitted for adventures than for clerical duties.

He rowed with strong and measured strokes, as if to show the southern sailors 3 how the men of the north handle the oars, and from time to time he turned around to look at the landing point.

The skiff struck the beach and slid far up, the bow plowing through the sand; 4 then it stopped abruptly. The five men watching for the abbé drew near, jovial and smiling.

"Well!" said one, with the strong accent of Provence, "have you been suc- 5 cessful, Monsieur le Curé?"

The abbé drew in the oars, removed his canvas headcovering, put on his hat, 6
pulled down his sleeves, and buttoned his coat. Then having assumed the usual
appearance of a village priest, he replied proudly: "Yes, I have caught three red-
snappers, two eels, and five sunfish."

The fishermen gathered around the boat to examine, with the air of experts, 7
the dead fish, the fat red-snappers, the flat-headed eels, those hideous sea-
serpents, and the violet sunfish, streaked with bright orange-colored stripes.

Said one: "I'll carry them up to your house, Monsieur le Curé."   8

"Thank you, my friend."   9

Having shaken hands all around, the priest started homeward, followed by the 10
man with the fish; the others took charge of the boat.

The Abbé Vilbois walked along slowly with an air of dignity. The exertion of 11
rowing had brought beads of perspiration to his brow and he uncovered his head
each time that he passed through the shade of an olive grove. The warm evening
air, freshened by a slight breeze from the sea, cooled his high forehead covered
with short, white hair, a forehead far more suggestive of an officer than of a priest.

The village appeared, built on a hill rising from a large valley which descended 12
toward the sea.

It was a summer evening. The dazzling sun, traveling toward the ragged crests 13
of the distant hills, outlined on the white, dusty road the figure of the priest, the
shadow of whose three-cornered hat bobbed merrily over the fields, sometimes
apparently climbing the trunks of the olive-trees, only to fall immediately to the
ground and creep among them.

With every step he took, he raised a cloud of fine, white dust, the invisible 14
powder which, in summer, covers the roads of Provence; it clung to the edge of
his cassock turning it grayish white. Completely refreshed, his hands deep in his
pockets, he strode along slowly and ponderously, like a mountaineer. His eyes
were fixed on the distant village where he had lived twenty years, and where he
hoped to die. Its church—his church—rose above the houses clustered around
it; the square turrets of gray stone, of unequal proportions and quaint design,
stood outlined against the beautiful southern valley; and their architecture suggested the fortifications of some old château rather than the steeples of a place of
worship.

The abbé was happy; for he had caught three red-snappers, two eels, and five 15
sunfish. It would enable him to triumph again over his flock, which respected
him, no doubt, because he was one of the most powerful men of the place, despite
his years. These little innocent vanities were his greatest pleasures. He was a fine
marksman; sometimes he practiced with his neighbor, a retired army provost
who kept a tobacco shop; he could also swim better than anyone along the coast.

In his day he had been a well-known society man, the Baron de Vilbois, but 16
had entered the priesthood after an unfortunate love-affair. Being the scion of an
old family of Picardy, devout and royalistic, whose sons for centuries had entered
the army, the magistracy, or the Church, his first thought was to follow his
mother's advice and become a priest. But he yielded to his father's suggestion that
he should study law in Paris and seek some high office.

While he was completing his studies his father was carried off by pneumonia; 17 his mother, who was greatly affected by the loss, died soon afterward. He came into a fortune, and consequently gave up the idea of following a profession to live a life of idleness. He was handsome and intelligent, but somewhat prejudiced by the traditions and principles which he had inherited, along with his muscular frame, from a long line of ancestors.

Society gladly welcomed him and he enjoyed himself after the fashion of a 18 well-to-do and seriously inclined young man. But it happened that a friend introduced him to a young actress, a pupil of the Conservatoire, who was appearing with great success at the Odéon. It was a case of love at first sight.

His sentiment had all the violence, the passion of a man born to believe in 19 absolute ideas. He saw her act the romantic rôle in which she had achieved a triumph the first night of her appearance. She was pretty, and, though naturally perverse, possessed the face of an angel.

She conquered him completely; she transformed him into a delirious fool, 20 into one of those ecstatic idiots whom a woman's look will forever chain to the pyre of fatal passions. She became his mistress and left the stage. They lived together four years, his love for her increasing during the time. He would have married her in spite of his proud name and family traditions, had he not discovered that for a long time she had been unfaithful to him with the friend who had introduced them.

The awakening was terrible, for she was about to become a mother, and he 21 was awaiting the birth of the child to make her his wife.

When he held the proof of her transgressions—some letters found in a 22 drawer—he confronted her with his knowledge and reproached her with all the savageness of his uncouth nature for her unfaithfulness and deceit. But she, a child of the people, being as sure of this man as of the other, braved and insulted him with the inherited daring of those women, who, in times of war, mounted with the men on the barricades.

He would have struck her to the ground—but she showed him her form. As 23 white as death, he checked himself, remembering that a child of his would soon be born to this vile, polluted creature. He rushed at her to crush them both, to obliterate this double shame. Reeling under his blows, and seeing that he was about to stamp out the life of her unborn babe, she realized that she was lost. Throwing out her hands to parry the blows, she cried:

"Do not kill me! It is his, not yours!"   24

He fell back, so stunned with surprise that for a moment his rage subsided. He 25 stammered:

"What? What did you say?"   26

Crazed with fright, having read her doom in his eyes and gestures, she re- 27 peated: "It's not yours, it's his."

Through his clenched teeth, he stammered: 28

"The child?"   29

"Yes."   30

"You lie!"   31

And again he lifted his foot as if to crush her, while she struggled to her knees 32
in a vain attempt to rise. "I tell you it's his. If it was yours, wouldn't it have come
much sooner?"

He was struck by the truth of this argument. In a moment of strange lucidity, 33
his mind evolved precise, conclusive, irresistible reasons to disclaim the child of
this miserable woman, and he felt so appeased, so happy at the thought, that he
decided to let her live.

He then spoke in a calmer voice: "Get up and leave, and never let me see you 34
again."

Quite cowed, she obeyed him and went. He never saw her again.   35

Then he left Paris and came south. He stopped in a village situated in a valley, 36
near the coast of the Mediterranean. Selecting for his abode an inn facing the sea,
he lived there eighteen months in complete seclusion, nursing his sorrow and despair. The memory of the unfaithful one tortured him; her grace, her charm, her
perversity haunted him, and withal came the regret of her caresses.

He wandered aimlessly in those beautiful vales of Provence, baring his head, 37
filled with the thoughts of that woman, to the sun that filtered through the grayish-
green leaves of the olive-trees.

His former ideas of religion, the abated ardor of his faith, returned to him 38
during his sorrowful retreat. Religion had formerly seemed a refuge from the unknown temptations of life, now it appeared as a refuge from its snares and tor-
tures. He had never given up the habit of prayer. In his sorrow, he turned anew
to its consolations, and often at dusk he would wander into the little village
church, where in the darkness gleamed the light of the lamp hung above the altar, to guard the sanctuary and symbolize the Divine Presence.

He confided his sorrow to his God, told Him of his misery, asking advice, pity, 39
help, and consolation. Each day, his fervid prayers disclosed stronger faith.

The bleeding heart of this man, crushed by love for a woman, still longed for 40
affection; and soon his prayers, his seclusion, his constant communion with the
Savior who consoles and cheers the weary, wrought a change in him, and the mystic love of God entered his soul, casting out the love of the flesh.

He then decided to take up his former plans and to devote his life to the 41
Church.

He became a priest. Through family connections he succeeded in obtaining a 42
call to the parish of this village which he had come across by chance. Devoting a
large part of his fortune to the maintenance of charitable institutions, and keeping only enough to enable him to help the poor as long as he lived, he sought refuge in a quiet life filled with prayer and acts of kindness toward his fellow-men.

Narrow-minded but kind-hearted, a priest with a soldier's temperament, he 43
guided his blind, erring flock forcibly through the mazes of this life in which every
taste, instinct, and desire is a pitfall. But the old man in him never disappeared
entirely. He continued to love out-of-door exercise and noble sports, but he hated
every woman, having an almost childish fear of their dangerous fascination.

II

The sailor who followed the priest, being a southerner, found it difficult to refrain 44
from talking. But he did not dare start a conversation, for the abbé exerted a great
prestige over his flock. At last he ventured a remark: "So you like your lodge, do
you, Monsieur le Curé?"

This lodge was one of the tiny constructions that are inhabited during the 45
summer by the villagers and the town people alike. It was situated in a field not
far from the parish-home, and the abbé had hired it because the latter was very
small and built in the heart of the village next to the church.

During the summer time, he did not live altogether at the lodge, but would re- 46
main a few days at a time to practice pistol-shooting and be close to nature.

"Yes, my friend," said the priest, "I like it very well." 47

The low structure could now be seen; it was painted pink, and the walls were 48
almost hidden under the leaves and branches of the olive-trees that grew in the
open field. A tall woman was passing in and out of the door, setting a small table
at which she placed, at each trip, a knife and fork, a glass, a plate, a napkin, and a
piece of bread. She wore the small cap of the women of Arles, a pointed cone of
silk or black velvet, decorated with a white rosette.

When the abbé was near enough to make himself heard, he shouted: 49

"Eh! Marguerite!" 50

She stopped to ascertain whence the voice came, and recognizing her master: 51
"Oh! it's you, Monsieur le Curé!"

"Yes. I have caught some fine fish, and want you to broil this sunfish immedi- 52
ately, do you hear?"

The servant examined, with a critical and approving glance, the fish that the 53
sailor carried.

"Yes, but we are going to have a chicken for dinner," she said. 54

"Well, it cannot be helped. Tomorrow the fish will not be as fresh as it is now. 55
I mean to enjoy a little feast—it does not happen often—and the sin is not great."

The woman picked out a sunfish and prepared to go into the house. "Ah!" she 56
said, "a man came to see you three times while you were out, Monsieur le Curé."

Indifferently he inquired: "A man! What kind of man?" 57

"Why, a man whose appearance was not in his favor." 58

"What! a beggar?" 59

"Perhaps—I don't know. But I think he is more of a 'maoufatan.'" 60

The abbé smiled at this word, which, in the language of Provence means a 61
highwayman, a tramp, for he was well aware of Marguerite's timidity, and knew
that every day and especially every night she fancied they would be murdered.

He handed a few sous to the sailor, who departed. And just as he was saying: 62
"I am going to wash my hands"—for his past dainty habits still clung to him—
Marguerite called to him from the kitchen where she was scraping the fish with a
knife, thereby detaching its blood-stained, silvery scales:

"There he comes!" 63

The abbé looked down the road and saw a man coming slowly toward the 64
house; he seemed poorly dressed, indeed, so far as he could distinguish. He could

not help smiling at his servant's anxiety, and thought, while he waited for the stranger: "I think, after all, she is right; he does look like a 'maoufatan.'"

The man walked slowly, with his eyes on the priest and his hands buried deep 65 in his pockets. He was young and wore a full, blond beard; strands of curly hair escaped from his soft felt hat, which was so dirty and battered that it was impossible to imagine its former color and appearance. He was clothed in a long, dark overcoat, from which emerged the frayed edge of his trousers; on his feet were bathing shoes that deadened his steps, giving him the stealthy walk of a sneak thief.

When he had come within a few steps of the priest, he doffed, with a sweep- 66 ing motion, the ragged hat that shaded his brow. He was not bad-looking, though his face showed signs of dissipation and the top of his head was bald, an indication of premature fatigue and debauch, for he certainly was not over twenty-five years old.

The priest responded at once to his bow, feeling that this fellow was not an or- 67 dinary tramp, a mechanic out of work, or a jail-bird, hardly able to speak any other tongue but the mysterious language of prisons.

"How do you do, Monsieur le Curé?" said the man. The priest answered sim- 68 ply, "I salute you," unwilling to address this ragged stranger as "Monsieur." They considered each other attentively; the abbé felt uncomfortable under the gaze of the tramp, invaded by a feeling of unrest unknown to him.

At last the vagabond continued: "Well, do you recognize me?"   69

Greatly surprised, the priest answered: "Why, no, you are a stranger to me."   70

"Ah! you do not know me? Look at me well."   71

"I have never seen you before."   72

"Well, that may be true," replied the man sarcastically, "but let me show you 73 some one whom you will know better."

He put on his hat and unbuttoned his coat, revealing his bare chest. A red sash 74 wound around his spare frame held his trousers in place. He drew an envelope from his coat pocket, one of those soiled wrappers destined to protect the sundry papers of the tramp, whether they be stolen or legitimate property, those papers which he guards jealously and uses to protect himself against the too zealous gendarmes. He pulled out a photograph about the size of a folded letter, one of those pictures which were popular long ago; it was yellow and dim with age, for he had carried it around with him everywhere and the heat of his body had faded it.

Pushing it under the abbé's eyes, he demanded: 75

"Do you know him?"   76

The priest took a step forward to look and grew pale, for it was his own 77 likeness that he had given Her years ago.

Failing to grasp the meaning of the situation he remained silent.   78

The tramp repeated: 79

"Do you recognize him?"   80

And the priest stammered: "Yes."   81

"Who is it?"   82

"It is I."   83

"It is you?"   84

"Yes."   85

"Well, then, look at us both—at me and at your picture!"   86

Already the unhappy man had seen that these two beings, the one in the pic- 87
ture and the one by his side, resembled each other like brothers; yet he did not understand, and muttered: "Well, what is it you wish?"

Then in an ugly voice, the tramp replied: "What do I wish? Why, first I wish 88
you to recognize me."

"Who are you?"   89

"Who am I? Ask anybody by the roadside, ask your servant, let's go and ask   90
the mayor and show him this; and he will laugh, I tell you that! Ah! you will not
recognize me as your son, papa curé?"

The old man raised his arms above his head, with patriarchal gesture, and   91
muttered despairingly: "It cannot be true!"

The young fellow drew quite close to him.   92

"Ah! It cannot be true, you say! You must stop lying, do you hear?" His   93
clenched fists and threatening face, and the violence with which he spoke, made
the priest retreat a few steps, while he asked himself anxiously which one of them
was laboring under a mistake.

Again he asserted: "I never had a child."   94

The other man replied: "And no mistress, either?"   95

The aged priest resolutely uttered one word, a proud admission: 96

"Yes."   97

"And was not this mistress about to give birth to a child when you left her?" 98

Suddenly the anger which had been quelled twenty-five years ago, not quelled, 99
but buried in the heart of the lover, burst through the wall of faith, resignation,
and renunciation he had built around it. Almost beside himself, he shouted:

"I left her because she was unfaithful to me and was carrying the child of an- 100
other man; had it not been for this, I should have killed both you and her, sir!"

The young man hesitated, taken aback at the sincerity of this outburst. Then   101
he replied in a gentler voice:

"Who told you that it was another man's child?"   102

"She told me herself and braved me."   103

Without contesting this assertion the vagabond assumed the indifferent tone   104
of a loafer judging a case:

"Well, then, mother made a mistake, that's all!"   105

After his outburst of rage, the priest had succeeded in mastering himself   106
sufficiently to be able to inquire:

"And who told you that you were my son?"   107

"My mother, on her deathbed, M'sieur le Curé. And then—this!" And he held   108
the picture under the eyes of the priest.

The old man took it from him; and slowly, with a heart bursting with anguish, 109
he compared this stranger with his faded likeness and doubted no longer—it was
his son.

An awful distress wrung his very soul, a terrible, inexpressible emotion in- 110
vaded him; it was like the remorse of some ancient crime. He began to understand a little, he guessed the rest. He lived over the brutal scene of the parting. It
was to save her life, then, that the wretched and deceitful woman had lied to him,
her outraged lover. And he had believed her. And a son of his had been brought
into the world and had grown up to be this sordid tramp, who exhaled the very
odor of vice as a goat exhales its animal smell.

He whispered: "Will you take a little walk with me, so that we can discuss these 111
matters?"

The young man sneered: "Why, certainly! Isn't that what I came for?"   112

They walked side by side through the olive grove. The sun had gone down and 113
the coolness of southern twilights spread an invisible cloak over the country. The
priest shivered, and raising his eyes with a familiar motion, perceived the trembling gray foliage of the holy tree which had spread its frail shadow over the Son
of Man in His great trouble and despondency.

A short, despairing prayer rose within him, uttered by his soul's voice, a prayer 114
by which Christians implore the Savior's aid: "O Lord! have mercy on me."

Turning to his son he said: "So your mother is dead?"   115

These words, "Your mother is dead," awakened a new sorrow; it was the tor- 116
ment of the flesh which cannot forget, the cruel echo of past sufferings; but
mostly the thrill of the fleeting, delirious bliss of his youthful passion.

The young man replied: "Yes, Monsieur le Curé, my mother is dead."   117

"Has she been dead a long while?"   118

"Yes, three years."   119

A new doubt entered the priest's mind. "And why did you not find me out be- 120
fore?"

The other man hesitated.   121

"I was unable to, I was prevented. But excuse me for interrupting these 122
recollections—I will enter into more details later—for I have not had anything
to eat since yesterday morning."

A tremor of pity shook the old man and holding forth both hands: "Oh! my 123
poor child!" he said.

The young fellow took those big, powerful hands in his own slender and fever- 124
ish palms.

Then he replied, with that air of sarcasm which hardly ever left his lips: "Ah! 125
I'm beginning to think that we shall get along very well together, after all!"

The curé started toward the lodge.   126

"Let us go to dinner," he said.   127

He suddenly remembered, with a vague and instinctive pleasure, the fine fish 128
he had caught, which, with the chicken, would make a good meal for the poor
fellow.

The servant was in front of the door, watching their approach with an anxious 129
and forbidding face.

"Marguerite," shouted the abbé, "take the table and put it into the dining- 130
room, right away; and set two places, as quick as you can."

The woman seemed stunned at the idea that her master was going to dine with 131
this tramp.

But the abbé, without waiting for her, removed the plate and napkin and car- 132
ried the little table into the dining-room.

A few minutes later he was sitting opposite the beggar, in front of a soup- 133
tureen filled with savory cabbage soup, which sent up a cloud of fragrant steam.

III

When the plates were filled, the tramp fell to with ravenous avidity. The abbé had 134
lost his appetite and ate slowly, leaving the bread in the bottom of his plate. Suddenly he inquired:

"What is your name?" 135

The man smiled; he was delighted to satisfy his hunger. 136

"Father unknown," he said, "and no other name but my mother's, which you 137
probably remember. But I possess two Christian names, which, by the way, are
quite unsuited to me—Philippe-Auguste."

The priest whitened. 138

"Why were you named thus?" he asked. 139

The tramp shrugged his shoulders. "I fancy you ought to know. After mother 140
left you, she wished to make your rival believe that I was his child. He did believe
it until I was about fifteen. Then I began to look too much like you. And he dis-
claimed me, the scoundrel. I had been christened Philippe-Auguste; now, if I had
not resembled a soul, or if I had been the son of a third person, who had stayed
in the background, today I should be the Vicomte Philippe-Auguste de Pravallon,
son of the count and senator bearing this name. I have christened myself 'No-
luck.'"

"How did you learn all this?" 141

"They discussed it before me, you know; pretty lively discussions they were, 142
too. I tell you, that's what shows you the seamy side of life!"

Something more distressing than all he had suffered during the last half hour 143
now oppressed the priest. It was a sort of suffocation which seemed as if it would
grow and grow till it killed him; it was not due so much to the things he heard as
to the manner in which they were uttered by this wayside tramp. Between himself and this beggar, between his son and himself, he was discovering the existence
of those moral divergencies which are as fatal poisons to certain souls. Was this
his son? He could not yet believe it. He wanted all the proofs, every one of them.
He wanted to hear all, to listen to all. Again he thought of the olive-trees that
shaded his little lodge, and for the second time he prayed: "O Lord! have mercy
upon me."

Philippe-Auguste had finished his soup. He inquired: "Is there nothing else, 144
abbé?"

The kitchen was built in an annex. Marguerite could not hear her master's 145
voice. He always called her by striking a Chinese gong hung on the wall behind
his chair. He took the brass hammer and struck the round metal plate. It gave a

feeble sound, which grew and vibrated, becoming sharper and louder till it finally died away on the evening breeze.

The servant appeared with a frowning face and cast angry glances at the 146 tramp, as if her faithful instinct had warned her of the misfortune that had befallen her master. She held a platter on which was the sunfish, spreading a savory odor of melted butter through the room. The abbé divided the fish lengthwise, helping his son to the better half: "I caught it a little while ago," he said, with a touch of pride in spite of his keen distress.

Marguerite had not left the room.   147

The priest added: "Bring us some wine, the white wine of Cape Corse."   148

She almost rebelled, and the priest, assuming a severe expression was obliged 149 to repeat: "Now, go, and bring two bottles, remember," for, when he drank with anybody, a very rare pleasure, indeed, he always opened one bottle for himself.

Beaming, Philippe-Auguste remarked: "Fine! A splendid idea! It has been a 150 long time since I've had such a dinner." The servant came back after a few minutes. The abbé thought it an eternity, for now a thirst for information burned his blood like infernal fire.

After the bottles had been opened, the woman still remained, her eyes glued 151 on the tramp.

"Leave us," said the curé.   152

She intentionally ignored his command.   153

He repeated almost roughly: "I have ordered you to leave us."   154

Then she left the room.   155

Philippe-Auguste devoured the fish voraciously, while his father sat watching 156 him, more and more surprised and saddened at all the baseness stamped on the face that was so like his own. The morsels the abbé raised to his lips remained in his mouth, for his throat could not swallow; so he ate slowly, trying to choose, from the host of questions which besieged his mind, the one he wished his son to answer first. At last he spoke:

"What was the cause of her death?"   157

"Consumption."   158

"Was she ill a long time?"   159

"About eighteen months."   160

"How did she contract it?"   161

"We could not tell."   162

Both men were silent. The priest was reflecting. He was oppressed by the mul- 163 titude of things he wished to know and to hear, for since the rupture, since the day he had tried to kill her, he had heard nothing. Certainly, he had not cared to know, because he had buried her, along with his happiest days, in forgetfulness; but now, knowing that she was dead and gone, he felt within himself the almost jealous desire of a lover to hear all.

He continued: "She was not alone, was she?"   164

"No, she lived with him."   165

The old man started: "With him? With Pravallon?"   166

"Why, yes."   167

And the betrayed man rapidly calculated that the woman who had deceived   168
him, had lived over thirty years with his rival.

Almost unconsciously he asked: "Were they happy?"   169

The young man sneered. "Why, yes, with ups and downs! It would have been   170
better had I not been there. I always spoiled everything."

"How, and why?" inquired the priest.   171

"I have already told you. Because he thought I was his son up to my fifteenth   172
year. But the old fellow wasn't a fool, and soon discovered the likeness. That created scenes. I used to listen behind the door. He accused mother of having deceived him. Mother would answer: 'Is it my fault? you knew quite well when you
took me that I was the mistress of that other man.' You were that other man."

"Ah! They spoke of me sometimes?"   173

"Yes, but never mentioned your name before me, excepting toward the end,   174
when mother knew she was lost. I think they distrusted me."

"And you—and you learned quite early the irregularity of your mother's   175
position?"

"Why, certainly. I am not innocent and I never was. Those things are easy to   176
guess as soon as one begins to know life."

Philippe-Auguste had been filling his glass repeatedly. His eyes now were be-   177
ginning to sparkle, for his long fast was favorable to the intoxicating effects of the
wine. The priest noticed it and wished to caution him. But suddenly the thought
that a drunkard is imprudent and loquacious flashed through him, and lifting the
bottle he again filled the young man's glass.

Meanwhile Marguerite had brought the chicken. Having set it on the table,   178
she again fastened her eyes on the tramp, saying in an indignant voice: "Can't you
see that he's drunk, Monsieur le Curé?"

"Leave us," replied the priest, "and return to the kitchen."   179

She went out, slamming the door.   180

He then inquired: "What did your mother say about me?"   181

"Why, what a woman usually says of a man she has jilted: that you were hard   182
to get along with, very strange, and that you would have made her life miserable
with your peculiar ideas."

"Did she say that often?"   183

"Yes, but sometimes only in allusions, for fear I would understand; but never-   184
theless I guessed all."

"And how did they treat you in that house?"   185

"Me? They treated me very well at first and very badly afterward. When   186
mother saw that I was interfering with her, she shook me."

"How?"   187

"How? very easily. When I was about sixteen years old, I got into various   188
scrapes, and those blackguards put me into a reformatory to get rid of me." He
put his elbows on the table and rested his cheeks in his palms. He was hopelessly
intoxicated, and felt the unconquerable desire of all drunkards to talk and boast
about themselves.

He smiled sweetly, with a feminine grace, an arch grace the priest knew and   189
recognized as the hated charm that had won him long ago, and had also wrought
his undoing. Now it was his mother whom the boy resembled, not so much because of his features, but because of his fascinating and deceptive glance, and the
seductiveness of the false smile that played around his lips, the outlet of his inner
ignominy.

Philippe-Auguste began to relate: "Ah! Ah! Ah!—I've had a fine life since I left   190
the reformatory! A great writer would pay a large sum for it! Why, old Père Dumas's Monte Cristo has had no stranger adventures than mine."

He paused to reflect with the philosophical gravity of the drunkard, then he   191
continued slowly:

"When you wish a boy to turn out well, no matter what he has done, never   192
send him to reformatory. The associations are too bad. Now, I got into a bad
scrape. One night about nine o'clock, I, with three companions—we were all a
little drunk—was walking along the road near the ford of Folac. All at once a
wagon hove in sight, with the driver and his family asleep in it. They were people
from Martinon on their way home from town. I caught hold of the bridle, led the
horse to the ferryboat, made him walk into it, and pushed the boat into the middle
of the stream. This created some noise and the driver awoke. He could not see in
the dark, but whipped up the horse, which started on a run and landed in the water with the whole load. All were drowned! My companions denounced me to the
authorities, though they thought it was a good joke when they saw me do it. Really, we didn't think that it would turn out that way. We only wanted to give the
people a ducking, just for fun. After that I committed worse offenses to revenge
myself for the first one, which did not, on my honor, warrant the reformatory. But
what's the use of telling them? I will speak only of the latest one, because I am sure
it will please you. Papa, I avenged you!"

The abbé was watching his son with terrified eyes; he had stopped eating.   193

Philippe-Auguste was preparing to begin. "No, not yet," said the priest, "in a   194
little while."

And he turned to strike the Chinese gong.   195

Marguerite appeared almost instantly. Her master addressed her in such a   196
rough tone that she hung her head, thoroughly frightened and obedient: "Bring
in the lamp and the dessert, and then do not appear until I summon you."

She went out and returned with a porcelain lamp covered with a green shade,   197
and bringing also a large piece of cheese and some fruit.

After she had gone, the abbé turned resolutely to his son.   198

"Now I am ready to hear you."   199

Philippe-Auguste calmly filled his plate with dessert and poured wine into his   200
glass. The second bottle was nearly empty, though the priest had not touched it.

His mouth and tongue, thick with food and wine, the man stuttered: "Well,   201
now for the last job. And it's a good one. I was home again—stayed there in spite
of them, because they feared me—yes, feared me. Ah! you can't fool with me, you
know—I'll do anything, when I'm roused. They lived together on and off. The
old man had two residences. One official, for the senator, the other clandestine,

for the lover. Still, he lived more in the latter than in the former, as he could not get along without mother. Mother was a sharp one—she knew how to hold a man! She had taken him body and soul, and kept him to the last! Well, I had come back and I kept them down by fright. I am resourceful at times—nobody can match me for sharpness and for strength, too—I'm afraid of no one. Well, mother got sick and the old man took her to a fine place in the country, near Meulan, situated in a park as big as a wood. She lasted about eighteen months, as I told you. Then we felt the end to be near. He came from Paris every day—he was very miserable—really.

"One morning they chatted a long time, over an hour, I think, and I could not   202 imagine what they were talking about. Suddenly mother called me in and said:

"'I am going to die, and there is something I want to tell you before-hand, in   203 spite of the Count's advice.' In speaking of him she always said 'the Count.' 'It is the name of your father, who is alive.' I had asked her this more than fifty times— more than fifty times—my father's name—more than fifty times—and she always refused to tell. I think I even beat her one day to make her talk, but it was of no use. Then, to get rid of me, she told me that you had died penniless, that you were worthless and that she had made a mistake in her youth, an innocent girl's mistake. She lied so well, I really believed you had died.

"Finally she said: 'It is your father's name.'   204

"The old man, who was sitting in an armchair, repeated three times, like this: 205 'You do wrong, you do wrong, you do wrong, Rosette.'

"Mother sat up in bed. I can see her now, with her flushed cheeks and shining   206 eyes; she loved me, in spite of everything; and she said: 'Then you do something for him, Philippe!' In speaking to him she called him 'Philippe' and me 'Auguste.'

"He began to shout like a madman: 'Do something for that loafer—that   207 blackguard, that convict? Never!'

"And he continued to call me names, as if he had done nothing else all his life   208 but collect them.

"I was angry, but mother told me to hold my tongue, and she resumed: 'Then   209 you must want him to starve, for you know that I leave no money.'

"Without being deterred, he continued: 'Rosette, I have given you thirty-five   210 thousand francs a year for thirty years—that makes more than a million. I have enabled you to live like a wealthy, a beloved, and I may say, a happy woman. I owe nothing to that fellow, who has spoiled our late years, and he will not get a cent from me. It is useless to insist. Tell him the name of his father, if you wish. I am sorry, but I wash my hands of him.'

"Then mother turned toward me. I thought: 'Good! now I'm going to find my   211 real father—if he has money, I'm saved.'

"She went on: 'Your father, the Baron de Vilbois, is today the Abbé Vilbois,   212 curé of Garandou, near Toulon. He was my lover before I left him for the Count!'

"And she told me all, except that she had deceived you about her pregnancy.   213 But women, you know, never tell the whole truth."

Sneeringly, unconsciously, he was revealing the depths of his foul nature. With 214
beaming face he raised the glass to his lips and continued:

"Mother died two days—two days later. We followed her remains to the 215
grave, he and I—say—wasn't it funny?—he and I—and three servants—that
was all. He cried like a calf—we were side by side—we looked like father and son.

"Then he went back to the house alone. I was thinking to myself: 'I'll have to 216
clear out now and without a penny, too.' I owned only fifty francs. What could I
do to revenge myself?

"He touched me on the arm and said: 'I wish to speak to you.' I followed him 217
into his office. He sat down in front of the desk and, wiping away his tears, he told
me that he would not be as hard on me as he had said he would to mother. He
begged me to leave you alone. That—that concerns only you and me. He offered
me a thousand-franc note—a thousand—a thousand francs. What could a fellow like me do with a thousand francs?—I saw that there were very many bills in
the drawer. The sight of the money made me wild. I put out my hand as if to take
the note he offered me, but instead of doing so, I sprang at him, threw him to the
ground and choked him till he grew purple. When I saw that he was going to give
up the ghost, I gagged and bound him. Then I undressed him, laid him on his
stomach and—ah! ah! ah!—I avenged you in a funny way!"

He stopped to cough, for he was choking with merriment. His ferocious, 218
mirthful smile reminded the priest once more of the woman who had wrought
his undoing.

"And then?" he inquired.   219

"Then—ah! ah! ah!—There was a bright fire in the fireplace—it was in the 220
winter—in December—mother died—a bright coal fire—I took the poker—I
let it get red-hot—and I made crosses on his back, eight or more, I cannot
remember how many—then I turned him over and repeated them on his stomach. Say, wasn't it funny, papa? Formerly they marked convicts in this way. He
wriggled like an eel—but I had gagged him so that he couldn't scream. I gathered
up the bills—twelve in all—with mine it made thirteen—an unlucky number. I
left the house, after telling the servants not to bother their master until dinner-
time, because he was asleep. I thought that he would hush the matter up because
he was a senator and would fear the scandal. I was mistaken. Four days later I was
arrested in a Paris restaurant. I got three years for the job. That is the reason why
I did not come to you sooner." He drank again, and stuttering so as to render his
words almost unintelligible, continued:

"Now—papa—isn't it funny to have one's papa a curé? You must be nice to 221
me, very nice, because you know, I am not commonplace—and I did a good
job—didn't I—on the old man?"

The anger which years ago had driven the Abbé Vilbois to desperation rose 222
within him at the sight of this miserable man.

He, who in the name of the Lord, had so often pardoned the infamous secrets 223
whispered to him under the seal of confession, was now merciless in his own behalf. No longer did he implore the help of a merciful God, for he realized that no
power on earth or in the sky could save those who had been visited by such a
terrible disaster.

All the ardor of his passionate heart and of his violent blood, which long years 224
of resignation had tempered, awoke against the miserable creature who was his
son. He protested against the likeness he bore to him and to his mother, the
wretched mother who had formed him so like herself; and he rebelled against the
destiny that had chained this criminal to him, like an iron ball to a galley-slave.

The shock roused him from the peaceful and pious slumber which had lasted 225
twenty-five years; with a wonderful lucidity he saw all that would inevitably ensue.

Convinced that he must talk loud so as to intimidate this man from the first, 226
he spoke with his teeth clenched with fury:

"Now that you have told all, listen to me. You will leave here tomorrow morn- 227
ing. You will go to a country that I shall designate, and never leave it without my
permission. I will give you a small income, for I am poor. If you disobey me once,
it will be withdrawn and you will learn to know me."

Though Philippe-Auguste was half dazed with wine, he understood the threat. 228
Instantly the criminal within him rebelled. Between hiccoughs he sputtered: "Ah!
papa, be careful what you say—you're a curé, remember—I hold you—and you
have to walk straight, like the rest!"

The abbé started. Through his whole muscular frame crept the unconquer- 229
able desire to seize this monster, to bend him like a twig, so as to show him that
he would have to yield.

Shaking the table, he shouted: "Take care, take care—I am afraid of nobody." 230

The drunkard lost his balance and seeing that he was going to fall and would 231
forthwith be in the priest's power, he reached with a murderous look for one of
the knives lying on the table. The abbé perceived his motion, and he gave the table
a terrible shove; his son toppled over and landed on his back. The lamp fell with
a crash and went out.

During a moment the clinking of broken glass was heard in the darkness, then 232
the muffled sound of a soft body creeping on the floor, and then all was silent.

With the crashing of the lamp a complete darkness spread over them; it was 233
so prompt and unexpected that they were stunned by it as by some terrible event.
The drunkard, pressed against the wall, did not move; the priest remained on his
chair in the midst of the night which had quelled his rage. The somber veil that
had descended so rapidly, arresting his anger, also quieted the furious impulses of
his soul; new ideas, as dark and dreary as the obscurity, beset him.

The room was perfectly silent, like a tomb where nothing draws the breath of 234
life. Not a sound came from outside, neither the rumbling of a distant wagon, nor
the bark of a dog, nor even the sigh of the wind passing through the trees.

This lasted a long time, perhaps an hour. Then suddenly the gong vibrated! It 235
rang once, as if it had been struck a short, sharp blow, and was instantly followed
by the noise of a falling body and an overturned chair.

Marguerite came running out of the kitchen, but as soon as she opened the 236
door she fell back, frightened by the intense darkness. Trembling, her heart beating as if it would burst, she called in a low, hoarse voice: "M'sieur le Curé! M'sieur
le Curé!"

Nobody answered, nothing stirred. 237

"*Mon Dieu, mon Dieu,*" she thought, "what has happened, what have they   238
done?"

She did not dare enter the room, yet feared to go back to fetch a light. She felt   239
as if she would like to run away, to screech at the top of her voice, though she knew
her legs would refuse to carry her. She repeated: "M'sieur le Curé! M'sieur le Curé!
it is me, Marguerite."

But, notwithstanding her terror, the instinctive desire of helping her master   240
and a woman's courage, which is sometimes heroic, filled her soul with a terrified
audacity, and running back to the kitchen she fetched a lamp.

She stopped at the doorsill. First, she caught sight of the tramp lying against   241
the wall, asleep, or simulating slumber; then she saw the broken lamp, and then,
under the table, the feet and black-stockinged legs of the priest, who must have
fallen backward, striking his head on the gong.

Her teeth chattering and her hands trembling with fright, she kept on repeat-   242
ing: "My God! My God! what is this?"

She advanced slowly, taking small steps, till she slid on something slimy and   243
almost fell.

Stooping, she saw that the floor was red and that a red liquid was spreading   244
around her feet toward the door. She guessed that it was blood. She threw down
her light so as to hide the sight of it, and fled from the room out into the fields,
running half crazed toward the village. She ran screaming at the top of her voice,
and bumping against the trees she did not heed, her eyes fastened on the gleaming lights of the distant town.

Her shrill voice rang out like the gloomy cry of the night-owl, repeating con-   245
tinuously, "The maoufatan—the maoufatan—the maoufatan"—

When she reached the first house, excited men came out and surrounded her;   246
but she could not answer them and struggled to escape, for the fright had turned
her head.

After a while they guessed that something must have happened to the curé,   247
and a little rescuing party started for the lodge.

The little pink house standing in the middle of the olive grove had grown   248
black and invisible in the dark, silent night. Since the gleam of the solitary window had faded, the cabin was plunged in darkness, lost in the grove, and unrec-
ognizable for anyone but a native of the place.

Soon lights began to gleam near the ground, between the trees, streaking the   249
dried grass with long, yellow reflections. The twisted trunks of the olive-trees assumed fantastic shapes under the moving lights, looking like monsters or infernal serpents. The projected reflections suddenly revealed a vague, white mass, and
soon the low, square wall of the lodge grew pink from the light of the lanterns.
Several peasants were carrying the lamps, escorting two gendarmes with re-
volvers, the mayor, the *garde-champêtre,* and Marguerite, supported by the men,
for she was almost unable to walk.

The rescuing party hesitated a moment in front of the open, gruesome door.   250
But the brigadier, snatching a lantern from one of the men, entered, followed by
the rest.

The servant had not lied, blood covered the floor like a carpet. It had spread 251 to the place where the tramp was lying, bathing one of his hands and legs.

The father and son were asleep, the one with a severed throat, the other in a 252 drunken stupor. The two gendarmes seized the latter and before he awoke they had him handcuffed. He rubbed his eyes, stunned, stupefied with liquor, and when he saw the body of the priest, he appeared terrified, unable to understand what had happened.

"Why did he not escape?" said the mayor.   253

"He was too drunk," replied the officer.   254

And every man agreed with him, for nobody ever thought that perhaps the 255 Abbé Vilbois had taken his own life.

ACTIVITIES FOR WRITING AND DISCUSSION

1. What do you see as the major themes of the story? Orally or in writing, explain and illustrate the themes with examples, events, or passages from the text.

2. Maupassant is known for his skillful **plot** construction. What central conflicts (see p. 163) keep you reading this story? Where do you locate the climax? Is the end of the story forshadowed in any ways, and, if so, how? Support your thoughts with references to specific passages in the text.

3. In paragraph 224 the narrator states that "[The abbé] protested against the likeness [his son] bore to him and to his mother, the wretched mother who had formed him so like herself." Is the character of Philippe-Auguste purely his mother's creation, or does it bear qualities of the father he has never met till now? Explain your answer with evidence to support your view.

4. Working with a small group or as a class, reconstruct the details of what happens between the time the lamp crashes (paragraph 231) and the last sentence of the story.

5. The Abbé Vilbois meets his son for the first time and dies just a few hours later. During those few hours, however, he is forced to remember his whole unhappy life. We witness his "fury" and his determination to intimidate Philippe-Auguste but are privy to few details of what passes through his mind as he tries to process the sordid revelations presented him. After the lamp crashes and the room has gone dark father and son sit still and silent for "perhaps an hour." Reread this part of the story. Then:
   a. Recreate, in a **stream of consciousness** form, the "new ideas" that "beset" the abbé (what is your, i.e., the abbé's, plan?); or
   b. Imagine that Philippe-Auguste has fled the room and, as the priest, write a suicide note or a murder-suicide note that explains what you are about to do next.

6. Rewrite the ending any way you wish. Then discuss whether Maupassant's ending is the only possible satisfactory ending, or whether there are others equally good or better.

James Joyce (1882–1941)

Eveline

She sat at the window watching the evening invade the avenue. Her head was 1
leaned against the window curtains and in her nostrils was the odour of dusty cretonne. She was tired.

Few people passed. The man out of the last house passed on his way home; she 2
heard his footsteps clacking along the concrete pavement and afterwards crunching on the cinder path before the new red houses. One time there used to be a field
there in which they used to play every evening with other people's children. Then
a man from Belfast bought the field and built houses in it—not like their little
brown houses but bright brick houses with shining roofs. The children of the avenue used to play together in that field—the Devines, the Waters, the Dunns, little
Keogh the cripple, she and her brothers and sisters. Ernest, however, never played:
he was too grown up. Her father used often to hunt them in out of the field with
his blackthorn stick; but usually little Keogh used to keep *nix* and call out when he
saw her father coming. Still they seemed to have been rather happy then. Her father was not so bad then; and besides, her mother was alive. That was a long time
ago; she and her brothers and sisters were all grown up; her mother was dead.
Tizzie Dunn was dead, too, and the Waters had gone back to England. Everything
changes. Now she was going to go away like the others, to leave her home.

Home! She looked round the room, reviewing all its familiar objects which 3
she had dusted once a week for so many years, wondering where on earth all the
dust came from. Perhaps she would never see again those familiar objects from
which she had never dreamed of being divided. And yet during all those years she
had never found out the name of the priest whose yellowing photograph hung on
the wall above the broken harmonium beside the coloured print of the promises
made to Blessed Margaret Mary Alacoque. He had been a school friend of her
father. Whenever he showed the photograph to a visitor her father used to pass
it with a casual word:

—He is in Melbourne now.   4

She had consented to go away, to leave her home. Was that wise? She tried to 5
weigh each side of the question. In her home anyway she had shelter and food; she
had those whom she had known all her life about her. Of course she had to work
hard both in the house and at business. What would they say of her in the Stores
when they found out that she had run away with a fellow? Say she was a fool, perhaps, and her place would be filled up by advertisement. Miss Gavan would be
glad. She had always had an edge on her, especially whenever there were people
listening.

—Miss Hill, don't you see these ladies are waiting?   6
—Look lively, Miss Hill, please.   7
She would not cry many tears at leaving the Stores.   8
But in her new home, in a distant unknown country, it would not be like that. 9
Then she would be married—she, Eveline. People would treat her with respect

then. She would not be treated as her mother had been. Even now, though she was over nineteen, she sometimes felt herself in danger of her father's violence. She knew it was that that had given her the palpitations. When they were growing up he had never gone for her, like he used to go for Harry and Ernest, because she was a girl; but latterly he had begun to threaten her and say what he would do to her only for her dead mother's sake. And now she had nobody to protect her. Ernest was dead and Harry, who was in the church decorating business, was nearly always down somewhere in the country. Besides, the invariable squabble for money on Saturday nights had begun to weary her unspeakably. She always gave her entire wages—seven shillings—and Harry always sent up what he could but the trouble was to get any money from her father. He said she used to squander the money, that she had no head, that he wasn't going to give her his hard-earned money to throw about the streets, and much more, for he was usually fairly bad of a Saturday night. In the end he would give her the money and ask her had she any intention of buying Sunday's dinner. Then she had to rush out as quickly as she could and do her marketing, holding her black leather purse tightly in her hand as she elbowed her way through the crowds and returning home late under her load of provisions. She had hard work to keep the house together and to see that the two young children who had been left to her charge went to school regularly and got their meals regularly. It was hard work—a hard life—but now that she was about to leave it she did not find it a wholly undesirable life.

She was about to explore another life with Frank. Frank was very kind, manly, 10 open-hearted. She was to go away with him by the night-boat to be his wife and to live with him in Buenos Ayres where he had a home waiting for her. How well she remembered the first time she had seen him; he was lodging in a house on the main road where she used to visit. It seemed a few weeks ago. He was standing at the gate, his peaked cap pushed back on his head and his hair tumbled forward over a face of bronze. Then they had come to know each other. He used to meet her outside the Stores every evening and see her home. He took her to see *The Bohemian Girl* and she felt elated as she sat in an unaccustomed part of the theatre with him. He was awfully fond of music and sang a little. People knew that they were courting and, when he sang about the lass that loves a sailor, she always felt pleasantly confused. He used to call her Poppens out of fun. First of all it had been an excitement for her to have a fellow and then she had begun to like him. He had tales of distant countries. He had started as a deck boy at a pound a month on a ship of the Allan Line going out to Canada. He told her the names of the ships he had been on and the names of the different services. He had sailed through the Straits of Magellan and he told her stories of the terrible Patagonians. He had fallen on his feet in Buenos Ayres, he said, and had come over to the old country just for a holiday. Of course, her father had found out the affair and had forbidden her to have anything to say to him.

—I know these sailor chaps, he said. 11

One day he had quarrelled with Frank and after that she had to meet her lover 12 secretly.

The evening deepened in the avenue. The white of two letters in her lap grew 13
indistinct. One was to Harry; the other was to her father. Ernest had been her
favourite but she liked Harry too. Her father was becoming old lately, she noticed;
he would miss her. Sometimes he could be very nice. Not long before, when she
had been laid up for a day, he had read her out a ghost story and made toast for
her at the fire. Another day, when their mother was alive, they had all gone for a
picnic to the Hill of Howth. She remembered her father putting on her mother's
bonnet to make the children laugh.

Her time was running out but she continued to sit by the window, leaning her 14
head against the window curtain, inhaling the odour of dusty cretonne. Down far
in the avenue she could hear a street organ playing. She knew the air. Strange that
it should come that very night to remind her of the promise to her mother, her
promise to keep the home together as long as she could. She remembered the last
night of her mother's illness; she was again in the close dark room at the other side
of the hall and outside she heard a melancholy air of Italy. The organ-player had
been ordered to go away and given sixpence. She remembered her father strutting
back into the sickroom saying:

—Damned Italians! coming over here! 15

As she mused the pitiful vision of her mother's life laid its spell on the very 16
quick of her being—that life of commonplace sacrifices closing in final craziness.
She trembled as she heard again her mother's voice saying constantly with foolish
insistence:

—Derevaun Seraun! Derevaun Seraun! 17

She stood up in a sudden impulse of terror. Escape! She must escape! Frank 18
would save her. He would give her life, perhaps love, too. But she wanted to live.
Why should she be unhappy? She had a right to happiness. Frank would take her
in his arms, fold her in his arms. He would save her.

She stood among the swaying crowd in the station at the North Wall. He held 19
her hand and she knew that he was speaking to her, saying something about the
passage over and over again. The station was full of soldiers with brown baggages.
Through the wide doors of the sheds she caught a glimpse of the black mass of the
boat, lying in beside the quay wall, with illumined portholes. She answered nothing. She felt her cheek pale and cold and, out of a maze of distress, she prayed to
God to direct her, to show her what was her duty. The boat blew a long mournful
whistle into the mist. If she went, tomorrow she would be on the sea with Frank,
steaming towards Buenos Ayres. Their passage had been booked. Could she still
draw back after all he had done for her? Her distress awoke a nausea in her body
and she kept moving her lips in silent fervent prayer.

A bell clanged upon her heart. She felt him seize her hand: 20
—Come! 21

All the seas of the world tumbled about her heart. He was drawing her into 22
them: he would drown her. She gripped with both hands at the iron railing.

—Come! 23

No! No! No! It was impossible. Her hands clutched the iron in frenzy. Amid 24
the seas she sent a cry of anguish!

—Eveline! Evvy!   25

He rushed beyond the barrier and called to her to follow. He was shouted at 26
to go on but he still called to her. She set her white face to him, passive, like a helpless animal. Her eyes gave him no sign of love or farewell or recognition.

Activities for Writing and Discussion

1. Joyce's story uses the device of **flashback** rather than straightforward
chronology. Collaboratively, reconstruct the complex details of Eveline's life
story, family, and relationships with her father and mother. For what reasons,
ultimately, does she choose to stay with her family rather than elope with Frank?

2. Assuming the **character** of Eveline, compose a series of diary entries that
articulate your divided feelings for Frank and your family. Where appropriate, incorporate details from Joyce's story into your entries.

3. Eveline's conflict (self-development versus social duty or duty to family) is
shared by countless sons and daughters. Tell the story of a real-life (or imagined)
son or daughter whose experience is analogous to Eveline's.

4. Joyce's *Dubliners,* from which "Eveline" is excerpted, is among the most
important and influential short story collections in modern literature. Research
the history of *Dubliners* and the specific innovations Joyce brought to the art of
the short story.

Tillie Olsen (b. 1912/1913)

I Stand Here Ironing

I stand here ironing, and what you asked me moves tormented back and forth 1
with the iron.

"I wish you would manage the time to come in and talk with me about your 2
daughter. I'm sure you can help me understand her. She's a youngster who needs
help and whom I'm deeply interested in helping."

"Who needs help." Even if I came, what good would it do? You think because 3
I am her mother I have a key, or that in some way you could use me as a key? She
has lived for nineteen years. There is all that life that has happened outside of me,
beyond me.

And when is there time to remember, to sift, to weigh, to estimate, to total? 4
I will start and there will be an interruption and I will have to gather it all together
again. Or I will become engulfed with all I did or did not do, with what should
have been and what cannot be helped.

She was a beautiful baby. The first and only one of our five that was beautiful 5 at birth. You do not guess how new and uneasy her tenancy in her now-loveliness. You did not know her all those years she was thought homely, or see her poring over her baby pictures, making me tell her over and over how beautiful she had been—and would be, I would tell her—and was now, to the seeing eye. But the seeing eyes were few or non-existent. Including mine.

I nursed her. They feel that's important nowadays. I nursed all the children, 6 but with her, with all the fierce rigidity of first motherhood, I did like the books then said. Though her cries battered me to trembling and my breasts ached with swollenness, I waited till the clock decreed.

Why do I put that first? I do not even know if it matters, or if it explains any- 7 thing.

She was a beautiful baby. She blew shining bubbles of sound. She loved mo- 8 tion, loved light, loved color and music and textures. She would lie on the floor in her blue overalls patting the surface so hard in ecstasy her hands and feet would blur. She was a miracle to me, but when she was eight months old I had to leave her daytimes with the woman downstairs to whom she was no miracle at all, for I worked or looked for work and for Emily's father, who "could no longer endure" (he wrote in his good-bye note) "sharing want with us."

I was nineteen. It was the pre-relief, pre-WPA world of the depression. I would 9 start running as soon as I got off the streetcar, running up the stairs, the place smelling sour, and awake or asleep to startle awake, when she saw me she would break into a clogged weeping that could not be comforted, a weeping I can hear yet.

After a while I found a job hashing at night so I could be with her days, and it 10 was better. But it came to where I had to bring her to his family and leave her.

It took a long time to raise the money for her fare back. Then she got chicken 11 pox and I had to wait longer. When she finally came, I hardly knew her, walking quick and nervous like her father, looking like her father, thin, and dressed in a shoddy red that yellowed her skin and glared at the pockmarks. All the baby love-liness gone.

She was two. Old enough for nursery school they said, and I did not know 12 then what I know now—the fatigue of the long day, and the lacerations of group life in the nurseries that are only parking places for children.

Except that it would have made no difference if I had known. It was the only 13 place there was. It was the only way we could be together, the only way I could hold a job.

And even without knowing, I knew. I knew the teacher that was evil because 14 all these years it has curdled into my memory, the little boy hunched in the cor-ner, her rasp, "why aren't you outside, because Alvin hits you? that's no reason, go out, scaredy." I knew Emily hated it even if she did not clutch and implore "don't go Mommy" like the other children, mornings.

She always had a reason why she should stay home. Momma, you look sick, 15 Momma. I feel sick. Momma, the teachers aren't there today, they're sick. Momma, we can't go, there was a fire there last night. Momma, it's a holiday today, no school, they told me.

But never a direct protest, never rebellion. I think of our others in their three-, four-year-oldness—the explosions, the tempers, the denunciations, the demands—and I feel suddenly ill. I put the iron down. What in me demanded that goodness in her? And what was the cost, the cost to her of such goodness?

The old man living in the back once said in his gentle way: "You should smile at Emily more when you look at her." What *was* in my face when I looked at her? I loved her. There were all the acts of love.

It was only with the others I remembered what he said, and it was the face of joy, and not of care or tightness or worry I turned to them—too late for Emily. She does not smile easily, let alone almost always as her brothers and sisters do. Her face is closed and sombre, but when she wants, how fluid. You must have seen it in her pantomimes, you spoke of her rare gift for comedy on the stage that rouses a laughter out of the audience so dear they applaud and applaud and do not want to let her go.

Where does it come from, that comedy? There was none of it in her when she came back to me that second time, after I had had to send her away again. She had a new daddy now to learn to love, and I think perhaps it was a better time.

Except when we left her alone nights, telling ourselves she was old enough.

"Can't you go some other time, Mommy, like tomorrow?" she would ask. "Will it be just a little while you'll be gone? Do you promise?"

The time we came back, the front door open, the clock on the floor in the hall. She rigid awake. "It wasn't just a little while. I didn't cry. Three times I called you, just three times, and then I ran downstairs to open the door so you could come faster. The clock talked loud. I threw it away, it scared me what it talked."

She said the clock talked loud again that night I went to the hospital to have Susan. She was delirious with the fever that comes before red measles, but she was fully conscious all the week I was gone and the week after we were home when she could not come near the new baby or me.

She did not get well. She stayed skeleton thin, not wanting to eat, and night after night she had nightmares. She would call for me, and I would rouse from exhaustion to sleepily call back: "You're all right, darling, go to sleep, it's just a dream," and if she still called, in a sterner voice, "now go to sleep, Emily, there's nothing to hurt you." Twice, only twice, when I had to get up for Susan anyhow, I went in to sit with her.

Now when it is too late (as if she would let me hold and comfort her like I do the others) I get up and go to her at once at her moan or restless stirring. "Are you awake, Emily? Can I get you something?" And the answer is always the same: "No, I'm all right, go back to sleep, Mother."

They persuaded me at the clinic to send her away to a convalescent home in the country where "she can have the kind of food and care you can't manage for her, and you'll be free to concentrate on the new baby." They still send children to that place. I see pictures on the society page of sleek young women planning affairs to raise money for it, or dancing at the affairs, or decorating Easter eggs or filling Christmas stockings for the children.

They never have a picture of the children so I do not know if the girls still wear 27 those gigantic red bows and the ravaged looks on the every other Sunday when parents can come to visit "unless otherwise notified"—as we were notified the first six weeks.

Oh it is a handsome place, green lawns and tall trees and fluted flower beds. 28 High up on the balconies of each cottage the children stand, the girls in their red bows and white dresses, the boys in white suits and giant red ties. The parents stand below shrieking up to be heard and the children shriek down to be heard, and between them the invisible wall "Not To Be Contaminated by Parental Germs or Physical Affection."

There was a tiny girl who always stood hand in hand with Emily. Her parents 29 never came. One visit she was gone. "They moved her to Rose College," Emily shouted in explanation. "They don't like you to love anybody here."

She wrote once a week, the labored writing of a seven-year-old. "I am fine. 30 How is the baby. If I write my leter nicly I will have a star. Love." There never was a star. We wrote every other day, letters she could never hold or keep but only hear read—once. "We simply do not have room for children to keep any personal possessions," they patiently explained when we pieced one Sunday's shrieking to-gether to plead how much it would mean to Emily, who loved so to keep things, to be allowed to keep her letters and cards.

Each visit she looked frailer. "She isn't eating," they told us. 31

(They had runny eggs for breakfast or mush with lumps, Emily said later, I'd 32 hold it in my mouth and not swallow. Nothing ever tasted good, just when they had chicken.)

It took us eight months to get her released home, and only the fact that she 33 gained back so little of her seven lost pounds convinced the social worker.

I used to try to hold and love her after she came back, but her body would stay 34 stiff, and after a while she'd push away. She ate little. Food sickened her, and I think much of life too. Oh she had physical lightness and brightness, twinkling by on skates, bouncing like a ball up and down up and down over the jump rope, skimming over the hill; but these were momentary.

She fretted about her appearance, thin and dark and foreign-looking at a time 35 when every little girl was supposed to look or thought she should look a chubby blonde replica of Shirley Temple. The doorbell sometimes rang for her, but no one seemed to come and play in the house or be a best friend. Maybe because we moved so much.

There was a boy she loved painfully through two school semesters. Months later 36 she told me how she had taken pennies from my purse to buy him candy. "Licorice was his favorite and I brought him some every day, but he still liked Jennifer bet-ter'n me. Why, Mommy?" The kind of question for which there is no answer.

School was a worry to her. She was not glib or quick in a world where glibness 37 and quickness were easily confused with ability to learn. To her overworked and exasperated teachers she was an overconscientious "slow learner" who kept try-ing to catch up and was absent entirely too often.

I let her be absent, though sometimes the illness was imaginary. How differ- 38
ent from my now-strictness about attendance with the others. I wasn't working.
We had a new baby, I was home anyhow. Sometimes, after Susan grew old enough,
I would keep her home from school, too, to have them all together.

Mostly Emily had asthma, and her breathing, harsh and labored, would fill the 39
house with a curiously tranquil sound. I would bring the two old dresser mirrors
and her boxes of collections to her bed. She would select beads and single earrings, bottle tops and shells, dried flowers and pebbles, old postcards and scraps,
all sorts of oddments; then she and Susan would play Kingdom, setting up landscapes and furniture, peopling them with action.

Those were the only times of peaceful companionship between her and Susan. 40
I have edged away from it, that poisonous feeling between them, that terrible balancing of hurts and needs I had to do between the two, and did so badly, those
earlier years.

Oh there are conflicts between the others too, each one human, needing, 41
demanding, hurting, taking—but only between Emily and Susan, no, Emily toward Susan that corroding resentment. It seems so obvious on the surface, yet it
is not obvious. Susan, the second child, Susan, golden- and curly-haired and
chubby, quick and articulate and assured, everything in appearance and manner
Emily was not; Susan, not able to resist Emily's precious things, losing or sometimes clumsily breaking them; Susan telling jokes and riddles to company for applause while Emily sat silent (to say to me later: that was *my* riddle, Mother, I told
it to Susan); Susan, who for all the five years' difference in age was just a year behind Emily in developing physically.

I am glad for that slow physical development that widened the difference be- 42
tween her and her contemporaries, though she suffered over it. She was too vulnerable for that terrible world of youthful competition, of preening and parading,
of constant measuring of yourself against every other, of envy, "If I had that copper hair," "If I had that skin. . . ." She tormented herself enough about not looking like the others, there was enough of the unsureness, the having to be conscious of words before you speak, the constant caring—what are they thinking of
me? without having it all magnified by the merciless physical drives.

Ronnie is calling. He is wet and I change him. It is rare there is such a cry now. 43
That time of motherhood is almost behind me when the ear is not one's own but
must always be racked and listening for the child cry, the child call. We sit for a
while and I hold him, looking out over the city spread in charcoal with its soft
aisles of light. "*Shoogily,*" he breathes and curls closer. I carry him back to bed,
asleep. *Shoogily.* A funny word, a family word, inherited from Emily, invented by
her to say: *comfort.*

In this and other ways she leaves her seal, I say aloud. And startle at my saying 44
it. What do I mean? What did I start to gather together, to try and make coherent?
I was at the terrible, growing years. War years. I do not remember them well. I was
working, there were four smaller ones now, there was not time for her. She had to
help be a mother, and housekeeper, and shopper. She had to set her seal. Mornings of crisis and near hysteria trying to get lunches packed, hair combed, coats

and shoes found, everyone to school or Child Care on time, the baby ready for transportation. And always the paper scribbled on by a smaller one, the book looked at by Susan then mislaid, the homework not done. Running out to that huge school where she was one, she was lost, she was a drop; suffering over the unpreparedness, stammering and unsure in her classes.

There was so little time left at night after the kids were bedded down. She would struggle over books, always eating (it was in those years she developed her enormous appetite that is legendary in our family) and I would be ironing, or preparing food for the next day, or writing V-mail to Bill, or tending the baby. Sometimes, to make me laugh, or out of her despair, she would imitate happenings or types at school. 45

I think I said once: "Why don't you do something like this in the school amateur show?" One morning she phoned me at work, hardly understandable through the weeping: "Mother, I did it. I won, I won; they gave me first prize; they clapped and clapped and wouldn't let me go." 46

Now suddenly she was Somebody, and as imprisoned in her difference as she had been in anonymity. 47

She began to be asked to perform at other high schools, even in colleges, then at city and statewide affairs. The first one we went to, I only recognized her that first moment when thin, shy, she almost drowned herself into the curtains. Then: Was this Emily? The control, the command, the convulsing and deadly clowning, the spell, then the roaring, stamping audience, unwilling to let this rare and precious laughter out of their lives. 48

Afterwards: You ought to do something about her with a gift like that—but without money or knowing how, what does one do? We have left it all to her, and the gift has as often eddied inside, clogged and clotted, as been used and growing. 49

She is coming. She runs up the stairs two at a time with her light graceful step, and I know she is happy tonight. Whatever it was that occasioned your call did not happen today. 50

"Aren't you ever going to finish the ironing, Mother? Whistler painted his mother in a rocker. I'd have to paint mine standing over an ironing board." This is one of her communicative nights and she tells me everything and nothing as she fixes herself a plate of food out of the icebox. 51

She is so lovely. Why did you want me to come in at all? Why were you concerned? She will find her way. 52

She starts up the stairs to bed. "Don't get me up with the rest in the morning." "But I thought you were having midterms." "Oh, those," she comes back in, kisses me, and says quite lightly, "in a couple of years when we'll all be atom-dead they won't matter a bit." 53

She has said it before. She *believes* it. But because I have been dredging the past, and all that compounds a human being is so heavy and meaningful in me, I cannot endure it tonight. 54

I will never total it all. I will never come in to say: She was a child seldom smiled at. Her father left me before she was a year old. I had to work her first six years when there was work, or I sent her home and to his relatives. There were 55 years she had care she hated. She was dark and thin and foreign-looking in a world where the prestige went to blondeness and curly hair and dimples, she was slow where glibness was prized. She was a child of anxious, not proud, love. We were poor and could not afford for her the soil of easy growth. I was a young mother, I was a distracted mother. There were the other children pushing up, demanding. Her younger sister seemed all that she was not. There were years she did not want me to touch her. She kept too much in herself, her life was such she had to keep too much in herself. My wisdom came too late. She has much to her and probably nothing will come of it. She is a child of her age, of depression, of war, of fear.

Let her be. So all that is in her will not bloom—but in how many does it? 56 There is still enough left to live by. Only help her to know—help make it so there is cause for her to know—that she is more than this dress on the ironing board, helpless before the iron.

ACTIVITIES FOR WRITING AND DISCUSSION

1. Respond to the story using the "Four-Step Process for Writing from Reading" described in Chapter 2.

2. Read other of Tillie Olsen's writings, particularly her 1978 work, *Silences*. In an essay discuss how "I Stand Here Ironing" articulates major themes of her other work.

TOBIAS WOLFF (b. 1945)

The Rich Brother

There were two brothers, Pete and Donald.   1

Pete, the older brother, was in real estate. He and his wife had a Century 21 2 franchise in Santa Cruz. Pete worked hard and made a lot of money, but not any more than he thought he deserved. He had two daughters, a sailboat, a house from which he could see a thin slice of the ocean, and friends doing well enough in their own lives not to wish bad luck on him. Donald, the younger brother, was still single. He lived alone, painted houses when he found the work, and got deeper in debt to Pete when he didn't.

No one would have taken them for brothers. Where Pete was stout and hearty 3 and at home in the world, Donald was bony, grave, and obsessed with the fate of his soul. Over the years Donald had worn the images of two different Perfect Masters around his neck. Out of devotion to the second of these he entered an ashram in Berkeley, where he nearly died of undiagnosed hepatitis. By the time Pete finished paying the medical bills Donald had become a Christian. He drifted from church to church, then joined a pentecostal community that met somewhere in the Mission District to sing in tongues and swap prophecies.

Pete couldn't make sense of it. Their parents were both dead, but while they 4 were alive neither of them had found it necessary to believe in anything. They managed to be decent people without making fools of themselves, and Pete had the same ambition. He thought that the whole thing was an excuse for Donald to take himself seriously.

The trouble was that Donald couldn't content himself with worrying about his 5 own soul. He had to worry about everyone else's, and especially Pete's. He handed down his judgments in ways that he seemed to consider subtle: through significant silence, innuendo, looks of mild despair that said, *Brother, what have you come to?* What Pete had come to, as far as he could tell, was prosperity. That was the real issue between them. Pete prospered and Donald did not prosper.

At the age of forty Pete took up sky diving. He made his first jump with two 6 friends who'd started only a few months earlier and were already doing stunts. They were both coked to the gills when they jumped but Pete wanted to do it straight, at least the first time, and he was glad that he did. He would never have used the word *mystical*, but that was how Pete felt about the experience. Later he made the mistake of trying to describe it to Donald, who kept asking how much it cost and then acted appalled when Pete told him.

"At least I'm trying something new," Pete said. "At least I'm breaking the 7 pattern."

Not long after that conversation Donald also broke the pattern, by going to 8 live on a farm outside of Paso Robles. The farm was owned by several members of Donald's community, who had bought it and moved there with the idea of forming a family of faith. That was how Donald explained it in the first letter he sent. Every week Pete heard how happy Donald was, how "in the Lord." He told Pete that he was praying for him, he and the rest of Pete's brothers and sisters on the farm.

"I only have one brother," Pete wanted to answer, "and that's enough." But he 9 kept this thought to himself.

In November the letters stopped. Pete didn't worry about this at first, but 10 when he called Donald at Thanksgiving Donald was grim. He tried to sound upbeat but he didn't try hard enough to make it convincing. "Now listen," Pete said, "you don't have to stay in that place if you don't want to."

"I'll be all right," Donald answered.   11

"That's not the point. Being all right is not the point. If you don't like what's 12 going on up there, then get out."

"I'm all right," Donald said again, more firmly. "I'm doing fine."   13

But he called Pete a week later and said that he was quitting the farm. When 14 Pete asked him where he intended to go, Donald admitted that he had no plan. His car had been repossessed just before he left the city, and he was flat broke.

"I guess you'll have to stay with us," Pete said.   15

Donald put up a show of resistance. Then he gave in. "Just until I get my feet 16
on the ground," he said.

"Right," Pete said. "Check out your options." He told Donald he'd send him 17
money for a bus ticket, but as they were about to hang up Pete changed his mind.
He knew that Donald would try hitchhiking to save the fare. Pete didn't want him
out on the road all alone where some head case could pick him up, where anything could happen to him.

"Better yet," he said, "I'll come and get you." 18

"You don't have to do that. I didn't expect you to do that," Donald said. He 19
added, "It's a pretty long drive."

"Just tell me how to get there." 20

But Donald wouldn't give him directions. He said that the farm was too de- 21
pressing, that Pete wouldn't like it. Instead, he insisted on meeting Pete at a service station called Jonathan's Mechanical Emporium.

"You must be kidding," Pete said. 22

"It's close to the highway," Donald said. "I didn't name it." 23

"That's one for the collection," Pete said. 24

The day before he left to bring Donald home, Pete received a letter from a man 25
who described himself as "head of household" at the farm where Donald had
been living. From this letter Pete learned that Donald had not quit the farm, but
had been asked to leave. The letter was written on the back of a mimeographed
survey form asking people to record their response to a ceremony of some kind.
The last question said:

What did you feel during the liturgy?
   a) Being
   b) Becoming
   c) Being and Becoming
   d) None of the Above
   e) All of the Above

Pete tried to forget the letter. But of course he couldn't. Each time he thought 26
of it he felt crowded and breathless, a feeling that came over him again when he
drove into the service station and saw Donald sitting against a wall with his head
on his knees. It was late afternoon. A paper cup tumbled slowly past Donald's feet,
pushed by the damp wind.

Pete honked and Donald raised his head. He smiled at Pete, then stood and 27
stretched. His arms were long and thin and white. He wore a red bandanna across
his forehead, a T-shirt with a couple of words on the front. Pete couldn't read
them because the letters were inverted.

"Grow up," Pete yelled. "Get a Mercedes." 28

Donald came up to the window. He bent down and said, "Thanks for coming. 29
You must be totally whipped."

"I'll make it." Pete pointed at Donald's T-shirt. "What's that supposed to say?" 30

Donald looked down at his shirt front. "Try God. I guess I put it on back- 31
wards. Pete, could I borrow a couple of dollars? I owe these people for coffee and
sandwiches."

Pete took five twenties from his wallet and held them out the window.   32

Donald stepped back as if horrified. "I don't need that much."   33

"I can't keep track of all these nickels and dimes," Pete said. "Just pay me back 34
when your ship comes in." He waved the bills impatiently. "Go on—take it."

"Only for now." Donald took the money and went into the service station 35
office. He came out carrying two orange sodas, one of which he gave to Pete as he
got into the car. "My treat," he said.

"No bags?"   36

"Wow, thanks for reminding me," Donald said. He balanced his drink on the 37
dashboard, but the slight rocking of the car as he got out tipped it onto the passenger's seat, where half its contents foamed over before Pete could snatch it up
again. Donald looked on while Pete held the bottle out the window, soda running
down his fingers.

"Wipe it up," Pete told him. "Quick!"   38

"With what?"   39

Pete stared at Donald. "That shirt. Use the shirt."   40

Donald pulled a long face but did as he was told, his pale skin puckering 41
against the wind.

"Great, just great," Pete said. "We haven't even left the gas station yet."   42

Afterwards, on the highway, Donald said, "This is a new car, isn't it?"   43

"Yes. This is a new car."   44

"Is that why you're so upset about the seat?"   45

"Forget it, okay? Let's just forget about it."   46

"I said I was sorry."   47

Pete said, "I just wish you'd be more careful. These seats are made of leather. 48
That stain won't come out, not to mention the smell. I don't see why I can't have
leather seats that smell like leather instead of orange pop."

"What was wrong with the other car?"   49

Pete glanced over at Donald. Donald had raised the hood of the blue sweat- 50
shirt he'd put on. The peaked hood above his gaunt, watchful face gave him the
look of an inquisitor.

"There wasn't anything wrong with it," Pete said. "I just happened to like this 51
one better."

Donald nodded.   52

There was a long silence between them as Pete drove on and the day darkened 53
toward evening. On either side of the road lay stubble-covered fields. A line of low
hills ran along the horizon, topped here and there with trees black against the grey
sky. In the approaching line of cars a driver turned on his headlights. Pete did
the same.

"So what happened?" he asked. "Farm life not your bag?"   54

Donald took some time to answer, and at last he said, simply, "It was my 55
fault."

"What was your fault?"   56

"The whole thing. Don't play dumb, Pete. I know they wrote to you." Donald   57
looked at Pete, then stared out the windshield again.

"I'm not playing dumb."   58

Donald shrugged.   59

"All I really know is they asked you to leave," Pete went on. "I don't know any   60
of the particulars."

"I blew it," Donald said. "Believe me, you don't want to hear the gory details."   61

"Sure I do," Pete said. He added, "Everybody likes the gory details."   62

"You mean everybody likes to hear how someone else messed up."   63

"Right," Pete said. "That's the way it is here on Spaceship Earth."   64

Donald bent one knee onto the front seat and leaned against the door so that   65
he was facing Pete instead of the windshield. Pete was aware of Donald's scrutiny.
He waited. Night was coming on in a rush now, filling the hollows of the land.
Donald's long cheeks and deep-set eyes were dark with shadow. His brow was
white. "Do you ever dream about me?" Donald asked.

"Do I ever dream about you? What kind of a question is that? Of course I don't   66
dream about you," Pete said, untruthfully.

"What do you dream about?"   67

"Sex and money. Mostly money. A nightmare is when I dream I don't have   68
any."

"You're just making that up," Donald said.   69

Pete smiled.   70

"Sometimes I wake up at night," Donald went on, "and I can tell you're   71
dreaming about me."

"We were talking about the farm," Pete said. "Let's finish that conversation   72
and then we can talk about our various out-of-body experiences and the interesting things we did during previous incarnations."

For a moment Donald looked like a grinning skull; then he turned serious   73
again. "There's not that much to tell," he said. "I just didn't do anything right."

"That's a little vague," Pete said.   74

"Well, like the groceries. Whenever it was my turn to get the groceries I'd blow   75
it somehow. I'd bring the groceries home and half of them would be missing, or
I'd have all the wrong things, the wrong kind of flour or the wrong kind of chocolate or whatever. One time I gave them away. It's not funny, Pete."

Pete said, "Who did you give the groceries to?"   76

"Just some people I picked up on the way home. Some fieldworkers. They had   77
about eight kids with them and they didn't even speak English—just nodded
their heads. Still, I shouldn't have given away the groceries. Not all of them, anyway. I really learned my lesson about that. You have to be practical. You have to be
fair to yourself." Donald leaned forward, and Pete could sense his excitement.
"There's nothing actually wrong with being in business," he said. "As long as
you're fair to other people you can still be fair to yourself. I'm thinking of going
into business, Pete."

"We'll talk about it," Pete said. "So, that's the story? There isn't any more to it 78 than that?"

"What did they tell you?" Donald asked.   79

"Nothing."   80

"They must have told you something."   81

Pete shook his head.   82

"They didn't tell you about the fire?" When Pete shook his head again Donald 83 regarded him for a time, then said, "I don't know. It was stupid. I just completely lost it." He folded his arms across his chest and slumped back into the corner. "Everybody had to take turns cooking dinner. I usually did tuna casserole or spaghetti with garlic bread. But this one night I thought I'd do something differ- ent, something really interesting." Donald looked sharply at Pete. "It's all a big laugh to you, isn't it?"

"I'm sorry," Pete said.   84

"You don't know when to quit. You just keep hitting away."   85

"Tell me about the fire, Donald."   86

Donald kept watching him. "You have this compulsion to make me look 87 foolish."

"Come off it, Donald. Don't make a big thing out of this."   88

"I know why you do it. It's because you don't have any purpose in life. You're 89 afraid to relate to people who do, so you make fun of them."

"Relate," Pete said softly.   90

"You're basically a very frightened individual," Donald said. "Very threatened. 91 You've always been like that. Do you remember when you used to try to kill me?"

"I don't have any compulsion to make you look foolish, Donald—you do it 92 yourself. You're doing it right now."

"You can't tell me you don't remember," Donald said. "It was after my opera- 93 tion. You remember that."

"Sort of." Pete shrugged. "Not really."   94

"Oh yes," Donald said. "Do you want to see the scar?"   95

"I remember you had an operation. I don't remember the specifics, that's all. 96 And I sure as hell don't remember trying to kill you."

"Oh yes," Donald repeated, maddeningly. "You bet your life you did. All the 97 time. The thing was, I couldn't have anything happen to me where they sewed me up because then my intestines would come apart again and poison me. That was a big issue, Pete. Mom was always in a state about me climbing trees and so on. And you used to hit me there every chance you got."

"Mom was in a state every time you burped," Pete said. "I don't know. Maybe 98 I bumped into you accidentally once or twice. I never did it deliberately."

"Every chance you got," Donald said. "Like when the folks went out at night 99 and left you to baby-sit. I'd hear them say good night, and then I'd hear the car start up, and when they were gone I'd lie there and listen. After a while I would hear you coming down the hall, and I would close my eyes and pretend to be asleep. There were nights when you would stand outside the door, just stand there, and then go away again. But most nights you'd open the door and I would hear you in the room with me, breathing. You'd come over and sit next to me on the bed—you remember, Pete, you have to—you'd sit next to me on the bed and pull the sheets back. If I was on my stomach you'd roll me over. Then you would lift up my pajama shirt and start hitting me on my stitches. You'd hit me as hard as you could, over and over. And I would just keep lying there with my eyes closed. I was afraid that you'd get mad if you knew I was awake. Is that strange or what? I was afraid that you'd get mad if you found out that I knew you were trying to kill me." Donald laughed. "Come on, you can't tell me you don't remember that."

"It might have happened once or twice. Kids do those things. I can't get all ex- 100 cited about something I maybe did twenty-five years ago."

"No maybe about it. You did it." 101

Pete said, "You're wearing me out with this stuff. We've got a long drive ahead 102 of us and if you don't back off pretty soon we aren't going to make it. You aren't, anyway."

Donald turned away. 103

"I'm doing my best," Pete said. The self-pity in his own voice made the words 104 sound like a lie. But they weren't a lie! He was doing his best.

The car topped a rise. In the distance Pete saw a cluster of lights that blinked 105 out when he started downhill. There was no moon. The sky was low and black.

"Come to think of it," Pete said, "I did have a dream about you the other 106 night." Then he added, impatiently, as if Donald were badgering him, "A couple of other nights too. I'm getting hungry," he said.

"The same dream?" 107

"Different dreams. I only remember one of them well. There was something 108 wrong with me, and you were helping out. Taking care of me. Just the two of us. I don't know where everyone else was supposed to be."

Pete left it at that. He didn't tell Donald that in this dream he was blind. 109

"I wonder if that was when I woke up," Donald said. He added, "I'm sorry I 110 got into that thing about my scar. I keep trying to forget it but I guess I never will. Not really. It was pretty strange, having someone around all the time who wanted to get rid of me."

"Kid stuff," Pete said. "Ancient history." 111

They ate dinner at a Denny's on the other side of King City. As Pete was pay- 112 ing the check he heard a man behind him say, "Excuse me, but I wonder if I might ask which way you're going?" and Donald answer, "Santa Cruz."

"Perfect," the man said. 113

Pete could see him in the fish-eye mirror above the cash register: a red blazer 114 with some kind of crest on the pocket, little black moustache, glossy black hair combed down on his forehead like a Roman emperor's. A rug, Pete thought. Definitely a rug.

Pete got his change and turned. "Why is that perfect?" he asked. 115

The man looked at Pete. He had a soft ruddy face that was doing its best to ex- 116 press pleasant surprise, as if this new wrinkle were all he could have wished for, but the eyes behind the aviator glasses showed signs of regret. His lips were moist and shiny. "I take it you're together," he said.

"You got it," Pete told him.   117

"All the better, then," the man went on. "It so happens I'm going to Santa   118
Cruz myself. Had a spot of car trouble down the road. The old Caddy let me down."

"What kind of trouble?" Pete asked.   119

"Engine trouble," the man said. "I'm afraid it's a bit urgent. My daughter is   120
sick. Urgently sick. I've got a telegram here." He patted the breast pocket of his blazer.

Pete grinned. Amazing, he thought, the old sick daughter ploy, but before he   121
could say anything Donald got into the act again. "No problem," Donald said. "We've got tons of room."

"Not that much room," Pete said.   122

Donald nodded. "I'll put my things in the trunk."   123

"The trunk's full," Pete told him.   124

"It so happens I'm traveling light," the man said. "This leg of the trip anyway.   125
In fact I don't have any luggage at this particular time."

Pete said, "Left it in the old Caddy, did you?"   126

"Exactly," the man said.   127

"No problem," Donald repeated. He walked outside and the man went with   128
him. Together they strolled across the parking lot, Pete following at a distance. When they reached Pete's car Donald raised his face to the sky, and the man did the same. They stood there looking up. "Dark night," Donald said.

"Stygian," the man said.   129

Pete still had it in mind to brush him off, but he didn't do that. Instead he un-   130
locked the door for him. He wanted to see what would happen. It was an adventure, but not a dangerous adventure. The man might steal Pete's ashtrays but he wouldn't kill him. If Pete got killed on the road it would be by some spiritual person in a sweatsuit, someone with his eyes on the far horizon and a wet Try God T-shirt in his duffel bag.

As soon as they left the parking lot the man lit a cigar. He blew a cloud of   131
smoke over Pete's shoulder and sighed with pleasure. "Put it out," Pete told him.

"Of course," the man said. Pete looked into the rearview mirror and saw the   132
man take another long puff before dropping the cigar out the window. "Forgive me," he said. "I should have asked. Name's Webster, by the way."

Donald turned and looked back at him. "First name or last?"   133

The man hesitated. "Last," he said finally.   134

"I know a Webster," Donald said. "Mick Webster."   135

"There are many of us," Webster said.   136

"Big fellow, wooden leg," Pete said.   137

Donald gave Pete a look.   138

Webster shook his head. "Doesn't ring a bell. Still, I wouldn't deny the con-   139
nection. Might be one of the cousinry."

"What's your daughter got?" Pete asked.   140

"That isn't clear," Webster answered. "It appears to be a female complaint of 141
some nature. Then again it may be tropical." He was quiet for a moment, and
added: "If indeed it *is* tropical, I will have to assume some of the blame myself. It
was my own vaulting ambition that first led us to the tropics and kept us in the
tropics all those many years, exposed to every evil. Truly I have much to answer
for. I left my wife there."

Donald said quietly, "You mean she died?"   142

"I buried her with these hands. The earth will be repaid, gold for gold."   143

"Which tropics?" Pete asked.   144

"The tropics of Peru."   145

"What part of Peru are they in?"   146

"The lowlands," Webster said.   147

Pete nodded. "What's it like down there?"   148

"Another world," Webster said. His tone was sepulchral. "A world better 149
imagined than described."

"Far out," Pete said.   150

The three men rode in silence for a time. A line of trucks went past in the other 151
direction, trailers festooned with running lights, engines roaring.

"Yes," Webster said at last, "I have much to answer for."   152

Pete smiled at Donald, but Donald had turned in his seat again and was gaz- 153
ing at Webster. "I'm sorry about your wife," Donald said.

"What did she die of?" Pete asked.   154

"A wasting illness," Webster said. "The doctors have no name for it, but I do." 155
He leaned forward and said, fiercely, "*Greed.*" Then he slumped back against his
seat. "My greed, not hers. She wanted no part of it."

Pete bit his lip. Webster was a find and Pete didn't want to scare him off by 156
hooting at him. In a voice low and innocent of knowingness, he asked, "What
took you there?"

"It's difficult for me to talk about."   157

"Try," Pete told him.   158

"A cigar would make it easier."   159

Donald turned to Pete and said, "It's okay with me."   160

"All right," Pete said. "Go ahead. Just keep the window rolled down."   161

"Much obliged." A match flared. There were eager sucking sounds.   162

"Let's hear it," Pete said.   163

"I am by training an engineer," Webster began. "My work has exposed me to 164
all but one of the continents, to desert and alp and forest, to every terrain and season of the earth. Some years ago I was hired by the Peruvian government to search
for tungsten in the tropics. My wife and daughter accompanied me. We were the
only white people for a thousand miles in any direction, and we had no choice but
to live as the Indians lived—to share their food and drink and even their culture."

Pete said, "You knew the lingo, did you?"   165

"We picked it up." The ember of the cigar bobbed up and down. "We were 166
used to learning as necessity decreed. At any rate, it became evident after a couple
of years that there was no tungsten to be found. My wife had fallen ill and was

pleading to be taken home. But I was deaf to her pleas, because by then I was on the trail of another metal—a metal far more valuable than tungsten."

"Let me guess," Pete said. "Gold?"   167

Donald looked at Pete, then back at Webster.   168

"Gold," Webster said. "A vein of gold greater than the Mother Lode itself. Af-   169
ter I found the first traces of it nothing could tear me away from my search—not the sickness of my wife nor anything else. I was determined to uncover the vein, and so I did—but not before I laid my wife to rest. As I say, the earth will be repaid."

Webster was quiet. Then he said, "But life must go on. In the years since my   170
wife's death I have been making the arrangements necessary to open the mine. I could have done it immediately, of course, enriching myself beyond measure, but I knew what that would mean—the exploitation of our beloved Indians, the bru-tal destruction of their environment. I felt I had too much to atone for already." Webster paused, and when he spoke again his voice was dull and rushed, as if he had used up all the interest he had in his own words. "Instead I drew up a pro-gram for returning the bulk of the wealth to the Indians themselves. A kind of trust fund. The interest alone will allow them to secure their ancient lands and rights in perpetuity. At the same time, our investors will be rewarded a thou-sandfold. Two-thousandfold. Everyone will prosper together."

"That's great," Donald said. "That's the way it ought to be."   171

Pete said, "I'm willing to bet that you just happen to have a few shares left. Am   172
I right?"

Webster made no reply.   173

"Well?" Pete knew that Webster was on to him now, but he didn't care. The   174
story had bored him. He'd expected something different, something original, and Webster had let him down. He hadn't even tried. Pete felt sour and stale. His eyes burned from cigar smoke and the high beams of road-hogging truckers. "Douse the stogie," he said to Webster. "I told you to keep the window down."

"Got a little nippy back here."   175

Donald said, "Hey, Pete. Lighten up."   176

"Douse it!"   177

Webster sighed. He got rid of the cigar.   178

"I'm a wreck," Pete said to Donald. "You want to drive for a while?"   179

Donald nodded.   180

Pete pulled over and they changed places.   181

Webster kept his counsel in the back seat. Donald hummed while he drove,   182
until Pete told him to stop. Then everything was quiet.

Donald was humming again when Pete woke up. Pete stared sullenly at the   183
road, at the white lines sliding past the car. After a few moments of this he turned and said, "How long have I been out?"

Donald glanced at him. "Twenty, twenty-five minutes."   184

Pete looked behind him and saw that Webster was gone. "Where's our friend?"   185

"You just missed him. He got out in Soledad. He told me to say thanks and   186
good-bye."

"Soledad? What about his sick daughter? How did he explain her away?" Pete 187
leaned over the seat. Both ashtrays were still in place. Floor mats. Door handles.

"He has a brother living there. He's going to borrow a car from him and drive 188
the rest of the way in the morning."

"I'll bet his brother's living there," Pete said. "Doing fifty concurrent life sen- 189
tences. His brother and his sister and his mom and his dad."

"I kind of liked him," Donald said. 190

"I'm sure you did," Pete said wearily. 191

"He was interesting. He'd been places." 192

"His cigars had been places, I'll give you that." 193

"Come on, Pete." 194

"Come on yourself. What a phony." 195

"You don't know that." 196

"Sure I do." 197

"How? How do you know?" 198

Pete stretched. "Brother, there are some things you're just born knowing. 199
What's the gas situation?"

"We're a little low." 200

"Then why didn't you get some more?" 201

"I wish you wouldn't snap at me like that," Donald said. 202

"Then why don't you use your head? What if we run out?" 203

"We'll make it," Donald said. "I'm pretty sure we've got enough to make it. 204
You didn't have to be so rude to him," Donald added.

Pete took a deep breath. "I don't feel like running out of gas tonight, okay?" 205

Donald pulled in at the next station they came to and filled the tank while Pete 206
went to the men's room. When Pete came back, Donald was sitting in the passenger's seat. The attendant came up to the driver's window as Pete got in behind the
wheel. He bent down and said, "Twelve fifty-five."

"You heard the man," Pete said to Donald. 207

Donald looked straight ahead. He didn't move. 208

"Cough up," Pete said. "This trip's on you." 209

Donald said, softly, "I can't." 210

"Sure you can. Break out that wad." 211

Donald glanced up at the attendant, then at Pete. "Please," he said. "Pete, I 212
don't have it anymore."

Pete took this in. He nodded, and paid the attendant. 213

Donald began to speak when they left the station but Pete cut him off. He said, 214
"I don't want to hear from you right now. You just keep quiet or I swear to God I
won't be responsible."

They left the fields and entered a tunnel of tall trees. The trees went on and on. 215
"Let me get this straight," Pete said at last. "You don't have the money I gave you."

"You treated him like a bug or something," Donald said. 216

"You don't have the money," Pete said again. 217

Donald shook his head. 218

"Since I bought dinner, and since we didn't stop anywhere in between, I as- 219
sume you gave it to Webster. Is that right? Is that what you did with it?"

"Yes."   220

Pete looked at Donald. His face was dark under the hood but he still managed 221
to convey a sense of remove, as if none of this had anything to do with him.

"Why?" Pete asked. "Why did you give it to him?" When Donald didn't an- 222
swer, Pete said, "A hundred dollars. Gone. Just like that. I *worked* for that money,
Donald."

"I know, I know," Donald said.   223

"You don't know! How could you? You get money by holding out your hand."   224

"I work too," Donald said.   225

"You work too. Don't kid yourself, brother."   226

Donald leaned toward Pete, about to say something, but Pete cut him off 227
again.

"You're not the only one on the payroll, Donald. I don't think you understand 228
that. I have a family."

"Pete, I'll pay you back."   229

"Like hell you will. A hundred dollars!" Pete hit the steering wheel with the 230
palm of his hand. "Just because you think I hurt some goofball's feelings. Jesus,
Donald."

"That's not the reason," Donald said. "And I didn't just *give* him the money."   231

"What do you call it, then? What do you call what you did?"   232

"I *invested* it. I wanted a share, Pete." When Pete looked over at him Donald 233
nodded and said again, "I wanted a share."

Pete said, "I take it you're referring to the gold mine in Peru."   234

"Yes," Donald said.   235

"You believe that such a gold mine exists?"   236

Donald looked at Pete, and Pete could see him just beginning to catch on. 237
"You'll believe anything," Pete said. "Won't you? You really will believe anything
at all."

"I'm sorry," Donald said, and turned away.   238

Pete drove on between the trees and considered the truth of what he had just 239
said—that Donald would believe anything at all. And it came to him that it would
be just like this unfair life for Donald to come out ahead in the end, by believing
in some outrageous promise that would turn out to be true and that he, Pete,
would reject out of hand because he was too wised up to listen to anybody's pitch
anymore except for laughs. What a joke. What a joke if there really was a blessing
to be had, and the blessing didn't come to the one who deserved it, the one who
did all the work, but to the other.

And as if this had already happened Pete felt a shadow move upon him, dark- 240
ening his thoughts. After a time he said, "I can see where all this is going, Donald."

"I'll pay you back," Donald said.   241

"No," Pete said. "You won't pay me back. You can't. You don't know how. All 242
you've ever done is take. All your life."

Donald shook his head.   243

"I see exactly where this is going," Pete went on. "You can't work, you can't 244 take care of yourself, you believe anything anyone tells you. I'm stuck with you, aren't I?" He looked over at Donald. "I've got you on my hands for good."

Donald pressed his fingers against the dashboard as if to brace himself. "I'll 245 get out," he said.

Pete kept driving.   246

"Let me out," Donald said. "I mean it, Pete."   247

"Do you?"   248

Donald hesitated. "Yes," he said.   249

"Be sure," Pete told him. "This is it. This is for keeps."   250

"I mean it."   251

"All right. You made the choice." Pete braked the car sharply and swung it to 252 the shoulder of the road. He turned off the engine and got out. Trees loomed on both sides, shutting out the sky. The air was cold and musty. Pete took Donald's duffel bag from the back seat and set it down behind the car. He stood there, facing Donald in the red glow of the taillights. "It's better this way," Pete said.

Donald just looked at him.   253

"Better for you," Pete said.   254

Donald hugged himself. He was shaking. "You don't have to say all that," he 255 told Pete. "I don't blame you."

"Blame me? What the hell are you talking about? Blame me for what?"   256

"For anything," Donald said.   257

"I want to know what you mean by blame me."   258

"Nothing. Nothing, Pete. You'd better get going. God bless you."   259

"That's it," Pete said. He dropped to one knee, searching the packed dirt with 260 his hands. He didn't know what he was looking for; his hands would know when they found it.

Donald touched Pete's shoulder. "You'd better go," he said.   261

Somewhere in the trees Pete heard a branch snap. He stood up. He looked at 262 Donald, then went back to the car and drove away. He drove fast, hunched over the wheel, conscious of the way he was hunched and the shallowness of his breathing, refusing to look at the mirror above his head until there was nothing behind him but darkness.

Then he said, "A hundred dollars," as if there were someone to hear.   263

The trees gave way to fields. Metal fences ran beside the road, plastered with 264 windblown scraps of paper. Tule fog hung above the ditches, spilling into the road, dimming the ghostly halogen lights that burned in the yards of the farms Pete passed. The fog left beads of water rolling up the windshield.

Pete rummaged among his cassettes. He found Pachelbel's Canon and pushed 265 it into the tape deck. When the violins began to play he leaned back and assumed an attentive expression as if he were really listening to them. He smiled to himself like a man at liberty to enjoy music, a man who has finished his work and settled his debts, done all things meet and due.

And in this way, smiling, nodding to the music, he went another mile or so 266 and pretended that he was not already slowing down, that he was not going to turn back, that he would be able to drive on like this, alone, and have the right an-swer when his wife stood before him in the doorway of his home and asked, Where is he? Where is your brother?

ACTIVITIES FOR WRITING AND DISCUSSION

1. Why, despite their many differences, do Pete and Donald remain con-nected? Do they have anything in common besides blood? Explain. Drawing on experiences in your own family or in other families, share any stories of siblings who are similarly "opposite" in character or temperament. In those instances has the opposition been a source of alienation or of a stronger relationship?

2. Donald is described as intensely introspective, as "bony, grave, and ob-sessed with the fate of his soul" (paragraph 3). Review the key events in Donald's story and his opinions about Pete, money, work, and the meaning of life. Then write a series of diary entries, in his **persona,** that cover some portion of his life—for instance, his stint at the farm commune he was asked to leave.

3. Donald accuses Pete of trying to "kill" him when they were children.
    a. Reread and annotate the paragraphs where this accusation is discussed.
    b. In your notebook recreate the story of this attempted "killing." Narrate from either Donald's or Pete's **point of view,** or from a third-person perspective, inventing background and details as necessary.
    c. Use your fictional version of the event to discuss *why* this episode is in Wolff's story.

4. Write a sequel in which Pete (a) returns and picks up Donald; or (b) con-tinues on home without Donald. If you do (b) write the dialogue that occurs when Pete encounters his wife.

5. Interpret paragraphs 260–262.

GLORIA NAYLOR (b. 1950)

Kiswana Browne

From the window of her sixth-floor studio apartment, Kiswana could see over the   1
wall at the end of the street to the busy avenue that lay just north of Brewster Place. The late-afternoon shoppers looked like brightly clad marionettes as they moved between the congested traffic, clutching their packages against their bod-ies to guard them from sudden bursts of the cold autumn wind. A portly mailman had abandoned his cart and was bumping into indignant window-shoppers as he puffed behind the cap that the wind had snatched from his head. Kiswana leaned

over to see if he was going to be successful, but the edge of the building cut him off from her view.

A pigeon swept across her window, and she marveled at its liquid movements 2 in the air waves. She placed her dreams on the back of the bird and fantasized that it would glide forever in transparent silver circles until it ascended to the center of the universe and was swallowed up. But the wind died down, and she watched with a sigh as the bird beat its wings in awkward, frantic movements to land on the corroded top of a fire escape on the opposite building. This brought her back to earth.

Humph, it's probably sitting over there crapping on those folks' fire escape, 3 she thought. Now, that's a safety hazard. . . . And her mind was busy again, creating flames and smoke and frustrated tenants whose escape was being hindered because they were slipping and sliding in pigeon shit. She watched their cussing, haphazard descent on the fire escapes until they had all reached the bottom. They were milling around, oblivious to their burning apartments, angrily planning to march on the mayor's office about the pigeons. She materialized placards and banners for them, and they had just reached the corner, boldly sidestepping fire hoses and broken glass, when they all vanished.

A tall copper-skinned woman had met this phantom parade at the corner, and 4 they had dissolved in front of her long, confident strides. She plowed through the remains of their faded mists, unconscious of the lingering wisps of their presence on her leather bag and black fur-trimmed coat. It took a few seconds for this transfer from one realm to another to reach Kiswana, but then suddenly she recognized the woman.

"Oh, God, it's Mama!" She looked down guiltily at the forgotten newspaper in 5 her lap and hurriedly circled random job advertisements.

By this time Mrs. Browne had reached the front of Kiswana's building and 6 was checking the house number against a piece of paper in her hand. Before she went into the building she stood at the bottom of the stoop and carefully inspected the condition of the street and the adjoining property. Kiswana watched this meticulous inventory with growing annoyance but she involuntarily followed her mother's slowly rotating head, forcing herself to see her new neighborhood through the older woman's eyes. The brightness of the unclouded sky seemed to join forces with her mother as it highlighted every broken stoop railing and missing brick. The afternoon sun glittered and cascaded across even the tiniest fragments of broken bottle, and at that very moment the wind chose to rise up again, sending unswept grime flying into the air, as a stray tin can left by careless garbage collectors went rolling noisily down the center of the street.

Kiswana noticed with relief that at least Ben wasn't sitting in his usual place on 7 the old garbage can pushed against the far wall. He was just a harmless old wino, but Kiswana knew her mother only needed one wino or one teenager with a reefer within a twenty-block radius to decide that her daughter was living in a building seething with dope factories and hang-outs for derelicts. If she had seen Ben, nothing would have made her believe that practically every apartment contained a family, a Bible, and a dream that one day enough could be scraped from those meager Friday night paychecks to make Brewster Place a distant memory.

As she watched her mother's head disappear into the building, Kiswana gave 8 silent thanks that the elevator was broken. That would give her at least five minutes' grace to straighten up the apartment. She rushed to the sofa bed and hastily closed it without smoothing the rumpled sheets and blanket or removing her nightgown. She felt that somehow the tangled bedcovers would give away the fact that she had not slept alone last night. She silently apologized to Abshu's memory as she heartlessly crushed his spirit between the steel springs of the couch. Lord, that man was sweet. Her toes curled involuntarily at the passing thought of his full lips moving slowly over her instep. Abshu was a foot man, and he always started his lovemaking from the bottom up. For that reason Kiswana changed the color of the polish on her toenails every week. During the course of their relationship she had gone from shades of red to brown and was now into the purples. I'm gonna have to start mixing them soon, she thought aloud as she turned from the couch and raced into the bathroom to remove any traces of Abshu from there. She took up his shaving cream and razor and threw them into the bottom drawer of her dresser beside her diaphragm. Mama wouldn't dare pry into my drawers right in front of me, she thought as she slammed the drawer shut. Well, at least not the *bottom* drawer. She may come up with some sham excuse for opening the top drawer, but never the bottom one.

When she heard the first two short raps on the door, her eyes took a final flight 9 over the small apartment, desperately seeking out any slight misdemeanor that might have to be defended. Well, there was nothing she could do about the crack in the wall over that table. She had been after the landlord to fix it for two months now. And there had been no time to sweep the rug, and everyone knew that off-gray always looked dirtier than it really was. And it was just too damn bad about the kitchen. How was she expected to be out job-hunting every day and still have time to keep a kitchen that looked like her mother's, who didn't even work and still had someone come in twice a month for general cleaning. And besides . . .

Her imaginary argument was abruptly interrupted by a second series of 10 knocks, accompanied by a penetrating, "Melanie, Melanie, are you there?"

Kiswana strode toward the door. She's starting before she even gets in here. 11 She knows that's not my name anymore.

She swung the door open to face her slightly flushed mother. "Oh, hi, Mama. 12 You know, I thought I heard a knock, but I figured it was for the people next door, since no one hardly ever calls me Melanie." Score one for me, she thought.

"Well, it's awfully strange you can forget a name you answered to for twenty- 13 three years," Mrs. Browne said, as she moved past Kiswana into the apartment. "My, that was a long climb. How long has your elevator been out? Honey, how do you manage with your laundry and groceries up all those steps? But I guess you're young, and it wouldn't bother you as much as it does me." This long string of questions told Kiswana that her mother had no intentions of beginning her visit with another argument about her new African name.

"You know I would have called before I came, but you don't have a phone yet. 14
I didn't want you to feel that I was snooping. As a matter of fact, I didn't expect to
find you home at all. I thought you'd be out looking for a job." Mrs. Browne had
mentally covered the entire apartment while she was talking and taking off her
coat.

"Well, I got up late this morning. I thought I'd buy the afternoon paper and 15
start early tomorrow."

"That sounds like a good idea." Her mother moved toward the window and 16
picked up the discarded paper and glanced over the hurriedly circled ads. "Since
when do you have experience as a fork-lift operator?"

Kiswana caught her breath and silently cursed herself for her stupidity. "Oh, 17
my hand slipped—I meant to circle file clerk." She quickly took the paper before
her mother could see that she had also marked cutlery salesman and chauffeur.

"You're sure you weren't sitting here moping and daydreaming again?" Am- 18
ber specks of laughter flashed in the corner of Mrs. Browne's eyes.

Kiswana threw her shoulders back and unsuccessfully tried to disguise her 19
embarrassment with indignation.

"Oh, God, Mama! I haven't done that in years—it's for kids. When are you go- 20
ing to realize that I'm a woman now?" She sought desperately for some womanly
thing to do and settled for throwing herself on the couch and crossing her legs in
what she hoped looked like a nonchalant arc.

"Please, have a seat," she said, attempting the same tones and gestures she'd 21
seen Bette Davis use on the late movies.

Mrs. Browne, lowering her eyes to hide her amusement, accepted the invita- 22
tion and sat at the window, also crossing her legs. Kiswana saw immediately how
it should have been done. Her celluloid poise clashed loudly against her mother's
quiet dignity, and she quickly uncrossed her legs. Mrs. Browne turned her head
toward the window and pretended not to notice.

"At least you have a halfway decent view from here. I was wondering what lay 23
beyond that dreadful wall—it's the boulevard. Honey, did you know that you can
see the trees in Linden Hills from here?"

Kiswana knew that very well, because there were many lonely days that she 24
would sit in her gray apartment and stare at those trees and think of home, but
she would rather have choked than admit that to her mother.

"Oh, really, I never noticed. So how is Daddy and things at home?" 25

"Just fine. We're thinking of redoing one of the extra bedrooms since you chil- 26
dren have moved out, but Wilson insists that he can manage all that work alone.
I told him that he doesn't really have the proper time or energy for all that. As it
is, when he gets home from the office, he's so tired he can hardly move. But you
know you can't tell your father anything. Whenever he starts complaining about
how stubborn you are, I tell him the child came by it honestly. Oh, and your
brother was by yesterday," she added, as if it had just occurred to her.

So that's it, thought Kiswana. That's why she's here. 27

Kiswana's brother, Wilson, had been to visit her two days ago, and she 28
had borrowed twenty dollars from him to get her winter coat out of layaway. That

son-of-a-bitch probably ran straight to Mama—and after he swore he wouldn't say anything. I should have known, he was always a snotty-nosed sneak, she thought.

"Was he?" she said aloud. "He came by to see me, too, earlier this week. And   29
I borrowed some money from him because my unemployment checks hadn't cleared in the bank, but now they have and everything's just fine." There, I'll beat you to that one.

"Oh, I didn't know that," Mrs. Browne lied. "He never mentioned you. He   30
had just heard that Beverly was expecting again, and he rushed over to tell us."

Damn. Kiswana could have strangled herself.   31

"So she's knocked up again, huh?" she said irritably.   32

Her mother started. "Why do you always have to be so crude?"   33

"Personally, I don't see how she can sleep with Willie. He's such a dishrag."   34

Kiswana still resented the stance her brother had taken in college. When   35
everyone at school was discovering their blackness and protesting on campus, Wilson never took part; he had even refused to wear an Afro. This had outraged Kiswana because, unlike her, he was dark-skinned and had the type of hair that was thick and kinky enough for a good "Fro." Kiswana had still insisted on cutting her own hair, but it was so thin and fine-textured, it refused to thicken even after she washed it. So she had to brush it up and spray it with lacquer to keep it from lying flat. She never forgave Wilson for telling her that she didn't look African, she looked like an electrocuted chicken.

"Now that's some way to talk. I don't know why you have an attitude against   36
your brother. He never gave me a restless night's sleep, and now he's settled with a family and a good job."

"He's an assistant to an assistant junior partner in a law firm. What's the big   37
deal about that?"

"The job has a future, Melanie. And at least he finished school and went on   38
for his law degree."

"In other words, not like me, huh?"   39

"Don't put words into my mouth, young lady. I'm perfectly capable of saying   40
what I mean."

Amen, thought Kiswana.   41

"And I don't know why you've been trying to start up with me from the mo-   42
ment I walked in. I didn't come here to fight with you. This is your first place away from home, and I just wanted to see how you were living and if you're doing all right. And I must say, you've fixed this apartment up very nicely."

"Really, Mama?" She found herself softening in the light of her mother's ap-   43
proval.

"Well, considering what you had to work with." This time she scanned the   44
apartment openly.

"Look, I know it's not Linden Hills, but a lot can be done with it. As soon as   45
they come and paint, I'm going to hang my Ashanti print over the couch. And I thought a big Boston Fern would go well in that corner, what do you think?"

"That would be fine, baby. You always had a good eye for balance."   46

Kiswana was beginning to relax. There was little she did that attracted her 47 mother's approval. It was like a rare bird, and she had to tread carefully around it lest it fly away.

"Are you going to leave that statue out like that?"   48

"Why, what's wrong with it? Would it look better somewhere else?"   49

There was a small wooden reproduction of a Yoruba goddess with large pro- 50 truding breasts on the coffee table.

"Well," Mrs. Browne was beginning to blush, "it's just that it's a bit suggestive, 51 don't you think? Since you live alone now, and I know you'll be having male friends stop by, you wouldn't want to be giving them any ideas. I mean, uh, you know, there's no point in putting yourself in any unpleasant situations because they may get the wrong impressions and uh, you know, I mean, well . . ." Mrs. Browne stammered on miserably.

Kiswana loved it when her mother tried to talk about sex. It was the only time 52 she was at a loss for words.

"Don't worry, Mama." Kiswana smiled. "That wouldn't bother the type of 53 men I date. Now maybe if it had big feet . . ." And she got hysterical, thinking of Abshu.

Her mother looked at her sharply. "What sort of gibberish is that about feet? 54 I'm being serious, Melanie."

"I'm sorry, Mama." She sobered up. "I'll put it away in the closet," she said, 55 knowing that she wouldn't.

"Good," Mrs. Browne said, knowing that she wouldn't either. "I guess you 56 think I'm too picky, but we worry about you over here. And you refuse to put in a phone so we can call and see about you."

"I haven't refused, Mama. They want seventy-five dollars for a deposit, and I 57 can't swing that right now."

"Melanie, I can give you the money."   58

"I don't want you to be giving me money—I've told you that before. Please, 59 let me make it by myself."

"Well, let me lend it to you, then."   60

"No!"   61

"Oh, so you can borrow money from your brother, but not from me."   62

Kiswana turned her head from the hurt in her mother's eyes. "Mama, when I 63 borrow from Willie, he makes me pay him back. You never let me pay you back," she said into her hands.

"I don't care. I still think it's downright selfish of you to be sitting over here 64 with no phone, and sometimes we don't hear from you in two weeks—anything could happen—especially living among these people."

Kiswana snapped her head up. "What do you mean, *these people*. They're my 65 people and yours, too, Mama—we're all black. But maybe you've forgotten that over in Linden Hills."

"That's not what I'm talking about, and you know it. These streets—this 66 building—it's so shabby and rundown. Honey, you don't have to live like this."

"Well, this is how poor people live."   67

"Melanie, you're not poor."   68

"No, Mama, *you're* not poor. And what you have and I have are two totally dif-   69
ferent things. I don't have a husband in real estate with a five-figure income and
a home in Linden Hills—*you* do. What I have is a weekly unemployment check
and an overdrawn checking account at United Federal. So this studio on Brewster
is all I can afford."

"Well, you could afford a lot better," Mrs. Browne snapped, "if you hadn't   70
dropped out of college and had to resort to these dead-end clerical jobs."

"Uh-huh, I knew you'd get around to that before long." Kiswana could feel   71
the rings of anger begin to tighten around her lower backbone, and they sent her
forward onto the couch. "You'll never understand, will you? Those bourgie
schools were counterrevolutionary. My place was in the streets with my people,
fighting for equality and a better community."

"Counterrevolutionary!" Mrs. Browne was raising her voice. "Where's your   72
revolution now, Melanie? Where are all those black revolutionaries who were
shouting and demonstrating and kicking up a lot of dust with you on that campus? Huh? They're sitting in wood-paneled offices with their degrees in mahogany frames, and they won't even drive their cars past this street because the
city doesn't fix potholes in this part of town."

"Mama," she said, shaking her head slowly in disbelief, "how can you—a   73
black woman—sit there and tell me that what we fought for during the Movement
wasn't important just because some people sold out?"

"Melanie, I'm not saying it wasn't important. It was damned important to   74
stand up and say that you were proud of what you were and to get the vote and
other social opportunities for every person in this country who had it due. But
you kids thought you were going to turn the world upside down, and it just was-
n't so. When all the smoke had cleared, you found yourself with a fistful of new
federal laws and a country still full of obstacles for black people to fight their way
over—just because they're black. There was no revolution, Melanie, and there
will be no revolution."

"So what am I supposed to do, huh? Just throw up my hands and not care   75
about what happens to my people? I'm not supposed to keep fighting to make
things better?"

"Of course, you can. But you're going to have to fight within the system, be-   76
cause it and these so-called 'bourgie' schools are going to be here for a long time.
And that means that you get smart like a lot of your old friends and get an important job where you can have some influence. You don't have to sell out, as you
say, and work for some corporation, but you could become an assemblywoman
or a civil liberties lawyer or open a freedom school in this very neighborhood.
That way you could really help the community. But what help are you going to be
to these people on Brewster while you're living hand-to-mouth on file-clerk jobs
waiting for a revolution? You're wasting your talents, child."

"Well, I don't think they're being wasted. At least I'm here in day-to-day con-   77
tact with the problems of my people. What good would I be after four or five years
of a lot of white brainwashing in some phony, prestige institution, huh? I'd be like

you and Daddy and those other educated blacks sitting over there in Linden Hills with a terminal case of middle-class amnesia."

"You don't have to live in a slum to be concerned about social conditions, 78 Melanie. Your father and I have been charter members of the NAACP for the last twenty-five years."

"Oh, God!" Kiswana threw her head back in exaggerated disgust. "That's be- 79 ing concerned? That middle-of-the-road, Uncle Tom dumping ground for black Republicans!"

"You can sneer all you want, young lady, but that organization has been work- 80 ing for black people since the turn of the century, and it's still working for them. Where are all those radical groups of yours that were going to put a Cadillac in every garage and Dick Gregory in the White House? I'll tell you where."

I knew you would, Kiswana thought angrily.   81

"They burned themselves out because they wanted too much too fast. Their 82 goals weren't grounded in reality. And that's always been your problem."

"What do you mean, my problem? I know exactly what I'm about."   83

"No, you don't. You constantly live in a fantasy world—always going to 84 extremes—turning butterflies into eagles, and life isn't about that. It's accepting what is and working from that. Lord, I remember how worried you had me, putting all that lacquered hair spray on your head. I thought you were going to get lung cancer—trying to be what you're not."

Kiswana jumped up from the couch. "Oh, God, I can't take this anymore. Try- 85 ing to be something I'm not—trying to be something I'm not, Mama! Trying to be proud of my heritage and the fact that I was of African descent. If that's being what I'm not, then I say fine. But I'd rather be dead than be like you—a white man's nigger who's ashamed of being black!"

Kiswana saw streaks of gold and ebony light follow her mother's flying body 86 out of the chair. She was swung around by the shoulders and made to face the deadly stillness in the angry woman's eyes. She was too stunned to cry out from the pain of the long fingernails that dug into her shoulders, and she was brought so close to her mother's face that she saw her reflection, distorted and wavering, in the tears that stood in the older woman's eyes. And she listened in that stillness to a story she had heard from a child.

"My grandmother," Mrs. Browne began slowly in a whisper, "was a full- 87 bloodied Iroquois, and my grandfather a free black from a long line of journey-men who had lived in Connecticut since the establishment of the colonies. And my father was a Bajan who came to this country as a cabin boy on a merchant mariner."

"I know all that," Kiswana said, trying to keep her lips from trembling.   88

"Then, know this." And the nails dug deeper into her flesh. "I am alive be- 89 cause of the blood of proud people who never scraped or begged or apologized for what they were. They lived asking only one thing of this world—to be allowed to be. And I learned through the blood of these people that black isn't beautiful and it isn't ugly—black is! It's not kinky hair and it's not straight hair—it just is.

"It broke my heart when you changed your name. I gave you my grand- 90
mother's name, a woman who bore nine children and educated them all, who
held off six white men with a shotgun when they tried to drag one of her sons to
jail for 'not knowing his place.' Yet you needed to reach into an African dictionary
to find a name to make you proud.

"When I brought my babies home from the hospital, my ebony son and my 91
golden daughter, I swore before whatever gods would listen—those of my
mother's people or those of my father's people—that I would use everything I had
and could ever get to see that my children were prepared to meet this world on its
own terms, so that no one could sell them short and make them ashamed of what
they were or how they looked—whatever they were or however they looked. And
Melanie, that's not being white or red or black—that's being a mother."

Kiswana followed her reflection in the two single tears that moved down her 92
mother's cheeks until it blended with them into the woman's copper skin. There
was nothing and then so much that she wanted to say, but her throat kept closing
up every time she tried to speak. She kept her head down and her eyes closed, and
thought, Oh, God, just let me die. How can I face her now?

Mrs. Browne lifted Kiswana's chin gently. "And the one lesson I wanted you 93
to learn is not to be afraid to face anyone, not even a crafty old lady like me who
can outtalk you." And she smiled and winked.

"Oh, Mama, I . . ." and she hugged the woman tightly. 94

"Yeah, baby." Mrs. Browne patted her back. "I know." 95

She kissed Kiswana on the forehead and cleared her throat. "Well, now, I bet- 96
ter be moving on. It's getting late, there's dinner to be made, and I have to get off
my feet—these new shoes are killing me."

Kiswana looked down at the beige leather pumps. "Those are really classy. 97
They're English, aren't they?"

"Yes, but, Lord, do they cut me right across the instep." She removed the shoe 98
and sat on the couch to massage her foot.

Bright red nail polish glared at Kiswana through the stockings. "Since when 99
do you polish your toenails?" she gasped. "You never did that before."

"Well . . ." Mrs. Browne shrugged her shoulders, "your father sort of talked me 100
into it, and, uh, you know, he likes it and all, so I thought, uh, you know, why not,
so . . ." And she gave Kiswana an embarrassed smile.

I'll be damned, the young woman thought, feeling her whole face tingle. 101
Daddy's into feet! And she looked at the blushing woman on her couch and suddenly realized that her mother had trod through the same universe that she herself was now traveling. Kiswana was breaking no new trails and would eventually
end up just two feet away on that couch. She stared at the woman she had been
and was to become.

"But I'll never be a Republican," she caught herself saying aloud. 102

"What are you mumbling about, Melanie?" Mrs. Browne slipped on her shoe 103
and got up from the couch.

She went to get her mother's coat. "Nothing, Mama. It's really nice of you to 104
come by. You should do it more often."

"Well, since it's not Sunday, I guess you're allowed at least one lie." 105

They both laughed. 106

After Kiswana had closed the door and turned around, she spotted an enve- 107
lope sticking between the cushions of her couch. She went over and opened it up;
there was seventy-five dollars in it.

"Oh, Mama, darn it!" She rushed to the window and started to call to the 108
woman, who had just emerged from the building, but she suddenly changed her
mind and sat down in the chair with a long sigh that caught in the upward draft
of the autumn wind and disappeared over the top of the building.

ACTIVITIES FOR WRITING AND DISCUSSION

1. React to the paragraph near the end of the story that begins, "I'll be
damned . . ."

> And she looked at the blushing woman on her couch and suddenly realized
> that her mother had trod through the same universe that she herself was now
> traveling. Kiswana was breaking no new trails and would eventually end up
> just two feet away on that couch. She stared at the woman she had been and
> was to become.

    a. In what ways *is* Kiswana's mother "the woman she [Kiswana] had been
    and was to become"? Jot down some ways and discuss them with a part-
    ner or group.

    b. Compose a sequel in which you sketch out Kiswana's subsequent life.
    What choices does she make about family, career, politics, and social
    causes? How does the middle-aged Kiswana/Melanie resemble or dif-
    fer from her middle-aged mother?

2. Make a list of similarities and differences between you and your own
mother or father. Then, in a notebook entry, explore how *you* have become
more—or less—like your own mother or father as you have grown older.

3. Recall a conflict in your relationship with your own mother or father.
Brainstorm a list of memories of that conflict. Then create a dialogue between you
and your parent that dramatizes the conflict and its resolution—if there was one.

Poems

WILLIAM CARLOS WILLIAMS (1883–1963)

The Last Words of My English Grandmother

There were some dirty plates
and a glass of milk
beside her on a small table
near the rank, disheveled bed—

Wrinkled and nearly blind   5
she lay and snored
rousing with anger in her tones
to cry for food,

Gimme something to eat—
They're starving me—   10
I'm all right I won't go
to the hospital. No, no, no

Give me something to eat
Let me take you
to the hospital, I said   15
and after you are well

you can do as you please.
She smiled, Yes
you do what you please first
then I can do what I please—   20

Oh, oh, oh! she cried
as the ambulance men lifted
her to the stretcher—
Is this what you call

making me comfortable?   25
By now her mind was clear—
Oh you think you're smart
you young people,

she said, but I'll tell you
you don't know anything.   30
Then we started.
On the way

we passed a long row
of elms. She looked at them
awhile out of   35
the ambulance window and said,

What are all those
fuzzy-looking things out there?
Trees? Well, I'm tired
of them and rolled her head away.   40

ACTIVITIES FOR WRITING AND DISCUSSION

1. How would you describe the **speaker's** feelings about his grandmother? What clues in the poem help you with your description?

2. Look at the poem's **free verse** form. Try rewriting a few of Williams's sentences in *prose* form. What, if anything, is lost by not having the text laid out in lines and **stanzas?** How does Williams's visual layout affect your experience of the poem?

3. Think of elderly men or women you have met or known. List some of their characteristics; for instance, their personalities, appearance, gestures, speech, or favorite topics of conversation. Then, assuming the character of an elderly person in the midst of some urgent situation such as death, illness, a move, or some other change in lifestyle, write out your thoughts in a **stream of consciousness** form.

THEODORE ROETHKE (1908–1963)

My Papa's Waltz

The whiskey on your breath
Could make a small boy dizzy;
But I hung on like death:
Such waltzing was not easy.

We romped until the pans   5
Slid from the kitchen shelf;
My mother's countenance
Could not unfrown itself.

The hand that held my wrist
Was battered on one knuckle;   10
At every step you missed
My right ear scraped a buckle.

You beat time on my head
With a palm caked hard by dirt,
Then waltzed me off to bed   15
Still clinging to your shirt.

ACTIVITIES FOR WRITING AND DISCUSSION

1. Considering the title alone, what expectations do you have for the poem's tone and content? How and where are these expectations met or undercut as you read the poem itself?

2. Working in a small group or as a class, read the poem aloud twice. During the second reading, pause after each line or two to discuss any associations that are triggered for you by individual words or phrases. How, if at all, do any of these words or phrases affect your sense of the poem's meaning?

3. The poem offers a concise sketch of a family unit—father, mother, and child. Supplementing clues in the text with your own imagination and experience of families, try to describe this family—its members and their interrelationships—in as much detail as you can. Then show how your finished description is consistent with the spare details provided in the poem.

Anna Swir (1909–1984)

I Wash the Shirt

For the last time I wash the shirt
of my father who died.
The shirt smells of sweat. I remember
that sweat from my childhood,
so many years   5
I washed his shirts and underwear,
I dried them
at an iron stove in the workshop,
he would put them on unironed.

From among all bodies in the world,   10
animal, human,
only one exuded that sweat.
I breathe it in
for the last time. Washing this shirt
I destroy it   15
forever.
Now
only paintings survive him
which smell of oils.

— *Translated from the Polish by Czeslaw Milosz and Leonard Nathan*

The Greatest Love

She is sixty. She lives
the greatest love of her life.

She walks arm-in-arm with her dear one,
her hair streams in the wind.

Her dear one says: 5
"You have hair like pearls."

Her children say:
"Old fool."

— *Translated from the Polish by Czeslaw Milosz and Leonard Nathan*

Gwendolyn Brooks (b. 1917)

Sadie and Maud

Maud went to college.
Sadie stayed at home.
Sadie scraped life
With a fine-tooth comb.

She didn't leave a tangle in.   5
Her comb found every strand.
Sadie was one of the livingest chits
In all the land.

Sadie bore two babies
Under her maiden name.   10
Maud and Ma and Papa
Nearly died of shame.

When Sadie said her last so-long
Her girls struck out from home.
(Sadie had left as heritage   15
Her fine-tooth comb.)

Maud, who went to college,
Is a thin brown mouse.
She is living all alone
In this old house.   20

Activities for Writing and Discussion

1. Largely through skillful use of **metaphor,** "Sadie and Maud" tells the story of a family in five compact stanzas. Identify and "unpack" the metaphors in the poem, explaining how they articulate the contrasting characters of the two sisters and the interrelationships among the sisters and parents.

2. Gwendolyn Brooks's writing career spanned several decades. Research her role in the evolution of modern and contemporary African American poetry.

CHARLES BUKOWSKI (1920–1994)

my old man

16 years old
during the depression
I'd come home drunk
and all my clothing—
shorts, shirts, stockings—   5
suitcase, and pages of
short stories
would be thrown out on the
front lawn and about the
street.   10

my mother would be
waiting behind a tree:
"Henry, Henry, don't
go in . . . he'll
kill you, he's read   15
your stories . . ."

"I can whip his
ass . . ."

"Henry, please take
this . . . and   20
find yourself a room."

but it worried him
that I might not
finish high school
so I'd be back   25
again.

one evening he walked in
with the pages of
one of my short stories
(which I had never submitted   30
to him)

and he said, "this is
a great short story."
I said, "o.k.,"
and he handed it to me   35
and I read it.
it was a story about
a rich man
who had a fight with
his wife and had   40
gone out into the night
for a cup of coffee
and had observed
the waitress and the spoons
and forks and the   45
salt and pepper shakers
and the neon sign
in the window
and then had gone back
to his stable   50
to see and touch his
favorite horse
who then
kicked him in the head
and killed him.   55

somehow
the story held
meaning for him
though
when I had written it   60
I had no idea
of what I was
writing about.

so I told him,
"o.k., old man, you can   65
have it."
and he took it
and walked out
and closed the door.
I guess that's   70
as close
as we ever got.

ACTIVITIES FOR WRITING AND DISCUSSION

1. How does this piece change—or what does it lose—if you reformat it as prose and transform each grouping of lines into a prose paragraph?

2. The father objects to his son's short stories. Why?

3. The father liked *one* of the **speaker's** short stories. From the little you know of the father, what "meaning" could that story have "held" for him? What do you make of the word "close" in the next-to-last line? Do you take the word literally or as an example of **verbal irony?** What kind of closeness did this father and son have?

4. Drawing on details in the poem and on your own imagination, reconstruct the speaker's early life with his parents. Tell the story of his life from the **point of view** of the son or of either parent.

DONALD HALL (b. 1928)

My Son My Executioner

My son my executioner,
　　I take you in my arms,
Quiet and small and just astir,
　　And whom my body warms.

Sweet death, small son, our instrument   5
　　Of immortality,
Your cries and hungers document
　　Our bodily decay.

We twenty-five and twenty-two,
　　Who seemed to live forever,   10
Observe enduring life in you
　　And start to die together.

ACTIVITIES FOR WRITING AND DISCUSSION

1. Read the poem aloud. Plot out the **rhyme** scheme. Indicate sound patterns using a single underline for examples of **alliteration** and a double underline for examples of **assonance** or **consonance.**

2. Who are the "our" and the "we" in the poem?

3. Working alone or in a group, explicate the poem's dominant metaphor, which identifies "my son" as "my executioner."

    a. What images come to mind when you think of an "executioner"? Make a list of these images or of any other **connotations** the word has for you.

    b. Describe any ways in which the son *is* his father's "executioner." Are all sons or daughters executioners of their fathers or mothers? As an experiment, carry the metaphor to an extreme: Create a short dialogue between parent and child in which the child is a *literal* executioner. Finally, with the class or your group, discuss how a literal executioner differs from a metaphoric one.

A. K. Ramanujan (1929–1993)

Self-Portrait

I resemble everyone
but myself, and sometimes see
in shop-windows,
    despite the well-known laws
    of optics,   5
the portrait of a stranger,
date unknown,
often signed in a corner
by my father.

Ted Kooser (b. 1939)

Father

Theodore Briggs Kooser
May 19, 1902–December 31, 1979

You spent fifty-five years
walking the hard floors
of the retail business,
first, as a boy playing store

in your grandmother's barn,   5
sewing feathers on hats
that the neighbors threw out,
then stepping out onto

the smooth pine planks
of your uncle's grocery—
SALADA TEA in gold leaf   10
over the door, your uncle

and father still young then
in handlebar mustaches,
white aprons with dusters   15
tucked into their sashes—

then to the varnished oak
of a dry goods store—
music to your ears,
that bumpety-bump   20

of bolts of bright cloth
on the counter tops,
the small rattle of buttons,
the bell in the register—

then on to the cold tile   25
of a bigger store, and then one
still bigger—gray carpet,
wide aisles, a new town

to get used to—then into
retirement, a few sales   30
in your own garage,
the concrete under your feet.

You had good legs, Dad,
and a good storekeeper's eye:
asked once if you remembered   35
a teacher of mine,

you said, "I certainly do;
size ten, a little something
in blue." How you loved
what you'd done with your life!   40

Now you're gone, and the clerks
are lazy, the glass cases
smudged, the sale sweaters
pulled off on the floor.

But what good times we had   45
before it was over:

after those stores had closed,
you posing as customers,

strutting in big flowered hats,
those aisles like a stage,   50
the pale manikins watching;
we laughed till we cried.

SHARON OLDS (b. 1942)

The Elder Sister

When I look at my elder sister now
I think how she had to go first, down through the
birth canal, to force her way
head-first through the tiny channel,
the pressure of Mother's muscles on her brain,   5
the tight walls scraping her skin.
Her face is still narrow from it, the long
hollow cheeks of a Crusader on a tomb,
and her inky eyes have the look of someone who has
been in prison a long time and   10
knows they can send her back. I look at her
body and think how her breasts were the first to
rise, slowly, like swans on a pond.

By the time mine came along, they were just
two more birds on the flock, and when the hair   15
rose on the white mound of her flesh, like
threads of water out of the ground, it was the
first time, but when mine came
they knew about it. I used to think
only in terms of her harshness, sitting and   20
pissing on me in bed, but now I
see I had her before me always
like a shield. I look at her wrinkles, her clenched
jaws, her frown-lines—I see they are
the dents on my shield, the blows that did not reach me.   25
She protected me, not as a mother
protects a child, with love, but as a
hostage protects the one who makes her
escape as I made my escape, with my sister's
body held in front of me.   30

Linda Hogan (b. 1947)

Heritage

From my mother, the antique mirror
where I watch my face take on her lines.
She left me the smell of baking bread
to warm fine hairs in my nostrils,
she left the large white breasts that weigh down   5
my body.

From my father I take his brown eyes,
the plague of locusts that leveled our crops,
they flew in formation like buzzards.

From my uncle the whittled wood   10
that rattles like bones
and is white
and smells like all our old houses
that are no longer there. He was the man
who sang old chants to me, the words   15
my father was told not to remember.

From my grandfather who never spoke
I learned to fear silence.
I learned to kill a snake
when you're begging for rain.   20

And grandmother, blue-eyed woman
whose skin was brown,
she used snuff.
When her coffee can full of black saliva
spilled on me   25
it was like the brown cloud of grasshoppers
that leveled her fields.
It was the brown stain
that covered my white shirt,
my whiteness a shame.   30
That sweet black liquid like the food
she chewed up and spit into my father's mouth
when he was an infant.
It was the brown earth of Oklahoma
stained with oil.   35
She said tobacco would purge your body of poisons.
It has more medicine than stones and knives
against your enemies.

That tobacco is the dark night that covers me.

She said it is wise to eat the flesh of deer   40
so you will be swift and travel over many miles.
She told me how our tribe has always followed a stick
that pointed west
that pointed east.
From my family I have learned the secrets   45
of never having a home.

ACTIVITIES FOR WRITING AND DISCUSSION

1. React to the poem's images. How do they make you feel? Are they pleasant? unpleasant? perplexing? disturbing? Why? Be specific, and share your reactions in class or in a small group.

2. How would you characterize the **speaker's** attitude toward her heritage? Does she regard it fondly? bitterly? with mixed emotions? Cite words or lines in the poem to support your answers.

3. Create a poem about your own heritage. Consider imitating Hogan's form by beginning each section with the words "From my [grandmother/uncle/father/mother" and so on] and following with the particular legacy you have from that ancestor or relative.

YUSEF KOMUNYAKAA (b. 1947)

My Father's Love Letters

On Fridays he'd open a can of Jax
After coming home from the mill,
& ask me to write a letter to my mother
Who sent postcards of desert flowers
Taller than men. He would beg,   5
Promising to never beat her
Again. Somehow I was happy
She had gone, & sometimes wanted
To slip in a reminder, how Mary Lou
Williams' "Polka Dots & Moonbeams"[1]   10
Never made the swelling go down.
His carpenter's apron always bulged
With old nails, a claw hammer

---

1. Recording by jazz pianist and composer Mary Lou Williams (1910–1981).

Looped at his side & extension cords
Coiled around his feet.   15
Words rolled from under the pressure
Of my ballpoint: Love,
Baby, Honey, Please.
We sat in the quiet brutality
Of voltage meters & pipe threaders,   20
Lost between sentences . . .
The gleam of a five-pound wedge
On the concrete floor
Pulled a sunset
Through the doorway of his toolshed.   25
I wondered if she laughed
& held them over a gas burner.
My father could only sign
His name, but he'd look at blueprints
& say how many bricks   30
Formed each wall. This man,
Who stole roses & hyacinth
For his yard, would stand there
With eyes closed & fists balled,
Laboring over a simple word, almost   35
Redeemed by what he tried to say.

TIMOTHY YOUNG (b. 1949)

The Thread of Sunlight

Where the thread of sunlight crossed the top bunk,
I touched the rough-cut rafter,
and watched two spiders approach
on the lumber's vertical plane.

Just when my heart condensed to arachnid size   5
the great wounds of war opened before me.
One spider limped on,
with the other's head in its mouth.

When I asked my mother about war,
she told me, "You're thinking too much and . . ."   10
Before her sentence ended my father rushed in,
chattering about the chores we'd accomplish.
The magneto for the mill saw needed repair,
the window trim should be painted,
the outboard motors could be tuned,   15

and if the work gets done,
we might go fishing in the evening.

The sunlight reflected off the flat lake
and I stood, between my mother
and father, thinking.   20

Activities for Writing and Discussion

1. On the basis of the poem's sparse details, characterize the mother and father. What conflicts or differences, if any, do you see between them and their child (the speaker)?

2. Expand on the poem's last two lines—that is, write what the speaker/child is "thinking."

3. Neither the mother nor the father seems to respond directly to the questions or needs of the child. Taking the dialogue in your poem as your cue:
   a. Imagine (and write up) a typical mealtime conversation among the mother, father, and child; or
   b. Write up a similar dialogue between a parent (or parents) and child of your own invention; or
   c. Write a sequel to the poem. Do the father and child end up "fishing in the evening"?

4. Research the topic of parent/child communications. Do parents and children communicate with each other? How much or how often, by what means, and how well? Where communication is deficient, what are some suggestions offered for improvement?

Deb Casey (b. 1950)

ZOOOOOOOM

A Familiar Story: Drop-off/Pick–up Panic
ZOOOM: morning frenzy, the held-breath beginning to each work day. (Zip past the entire get-up, dress-feed-comb/brush-assemble struggle, the tension between adults as to who is doing what, and who isn't.) **BEGIN** at the car: load, fasten, dash back for forgotten items. Check watch: two minutes past the sure parking spot. Accelerate. Stay calm. Sing, babble, wiggle, jounce, offer a finger to chew, look at the "*Look*" commands: back, sideways; **DRIVE.** Five miles to campus. **Park.** (First spot easy.) Unbelt, gather children (*stay close!* to the oldest), deliver one: sign in, situate, converse with Lead Teacher (casual mother), glance to clock, *Ooops!: Got to go . . .* Be thankful: almost past the tearful goodbyes with this daughter. **Resituate:** baby into seat (again), kiss the sweet lips, eager eyes (careful not to bend

legs backward in haste). Turn around. Now the real struggle. Twenty minutes gone in that drop-off (and the center opens no earlier). Circle. Lot after lot. Seethe. No parking. No options—no *good* options. Give up. **Park** on the fringe. Prepare for the hike. Gather bags, umbrella, baby stuff, books. Adjust Baby in the front pack, distribute weight. **Stride!** (And be thankful the umbrella isn't necessary, no hand left.) Trudge. **DELIVER** baby to grad-student in father's office. (Take advantage of his morning-empty space.) Whisk out the baby decor: padded play place, fur, jump-seat, chewables. Nurse. Insistently: here. Now. Greet care taker. Make fast small-talk. Say goodbyes. Breathe—no, not yet. Ignore the sudden squawk, tears, of a baby who wants you. No, don't: acknowledge the uneasiness. **Return.** Console. Promise. Leave again. NOW breathe. Find a bathroom—forget it: late. Run. (Forget, too, figuring how on earth you'll regroup bodies with the car, where it is compared to all three of our stations. **Skip** the logistics of breastfeeding connections and so on. Get to the day's close.) **DEPARTURE:** Get edgy as meeting runs late. **Fidget.** Lose all train of thought. Try not to be obvious as you pack-up, already overdue. Dash across the quad, and up three flights (fast!), present the breast, **FEED,** hear her contented warble, relax, sooth her moist cheek, soft fontanel, **marvel** again: how wide her *feed-me*-bird-mouth glomps around the nipple (See: we working mothers are not oblivious), keep her attached as you try to move smoothly, quickly (the easy minute up), **gather** her pieces. Sweater her snug, hug closely as you run to the car, urging all the bulk of you to advance a bit faster, imagining you'll find your older daughter parked on the curb: *"her time was up."* Don't exaggerate. No guilt: you called apologizing, think no more of it. Get to the car. Strap Baby in. Try to hush her yelps. Promise (again): *soon*... Remember what you should have brought home from the office. Try not to catch your mind sliding forward, backward. Don't think what you'd like is a drink. A moment... Watch the road, **shift, sing, juggle, jiggle,** fingerrub the baby's gums. Zoom. Grab Baby (gently!): up and over (watch the head). Find Older Daughter. Apologize to Lead Teacher. Concentrate on this reunion time: **focus**—while urging Daughter toward her cubby and out of the action. (And don't wrinkle the painting.) Keep Baby from the breast position temptation. **Give up:** sling Baby over hip, guide to nipple, button Older Daughter's sweater, one-handed, gather other drawings, praise (sincerely), pat, burp, sign-out (Don't forget!), get them out and loaded (again) into the car and belted and grinning, or grumbling (whatever), **DRIVE.** Sing. (What's in the fridge?) Shift.

Rita Dove (b. 1952)

Fifth Grade Autobiography

I was four in this photograph fishing
with my grandparents at a lake in Michigan.
My brother squats in poison ivy.

His Davy Crockett cap
sits squared on his head so the raccoon tail   5
flounces down the back of his sailor suit.

My grandfather sits to the far right
in a folding chair,
and I know his left hand is on
the tobacco in his pants pocket   10
because I used to wrap it for him
every Christmas. Grandmother's hips
bulge from the brush, she's leaning
into the ice chest, sun through the trees
printing her dress with soft   15
luminous paws.

I am staring jealously at my brother;
the day before he rode his first horse, alone.
I was strapped in a basket
behind my grandfather.   20
He smelled of lemons. He's died—

but I remember his hands.

ACTIVITY FOR WRITING AND DISCUSSION

1. Find a childhood photograph of you and your family. Writing in the present tense, describe the photograph's visual details. In your description, incorporate the thoughts that were likely going through your mind—and/or the minds of others in the picture—at the moment the picture was taken.

SHARON HASHIMOTO (b. 1953)

Eleven A.M. on My Day Off, My Sister Phones Desperate for a Babysitter

Sitting in sunlight, the child
I sometimes pretend is my own
fingers the green weave of the rug
while the small shadow of her head falls over
a part of my lap and bent knee. At three,   5
she could be that younger part of myself, just beginning
to remember how the dusty warmth feels on her back.
"Are you hungry?" I ask. Together we open
the door of the refrigerator. One apple sits
in the vegetable bin but she gives it to me,   10

repeating her true mother's words "to share."
Turning the round fruit under the faucet,
the afternoon bright in my face, I look down
at a smile in the half moons of her eyes
and for a moment, I'm seven, looking up   15
at my childless aunt in Hawaii,
her hands and the long knife peeling
the mango I picked off the tree, rubbing my arms
from the stretch on the back porch
to an overhead branch. Plump   20
with the island's humidity, it tasted tart
like the heavy clatter of rain on a June Sunday.
"Careful," my niece warns as I slice the apple sideways
to show her the star in the middle.
She eats the core but saves the seeds   25
to plant in the soft earth of my yard.

Debra Kang Dean (b. 1955)

Taproot

Stooping to pull up a weed,
I think of my father
who made of weeding an art.

After work, he'd take a bucket
and his weeder from the toolshed   5
and clear an area of a yard he knew

would never look manicured,
whose quality would, at best,
be like something homemade.

He'd set the bucket upside down   10
and sit on it. Plotting a route
he'd shift the bucket, a move

so deft you might think he was just
leaning out to extend his reach.
He knew exactly where and what angle   15

to drive the weeder down,
north and south of the weed,
without severing its taproot.

When my father worked like this,
making small mounds he'd later   20
gather up in his bucket,

the dog would sniff at his bare feet
then lie down in the shade his body made.
Grounded there, he was most himself,

his hunger for perfection and control   25
giving way, finally, to the work itself.
It was easy to love him then.

ACTIVITIES FOR WRITING AND DISCUSSION

1. What is a taproot? Explain any possible **symbolism** the word "taproot" may have in this poem.

2. Two kinds of "work" are mentioned, the father's paying job (line 4) and his "work" of weeding. What sort of paying job do you imagine the father has? What differences, if any, are implied between the two kinds of work and the father's experience of them?

3. Read closely the poem's last six lines. Underline what are for you the most important words and phrases, and explain and discuss their importance with a partner or small group. Look especially at the final line and the final word "then." Then:

    a. Write a character description or biography of the father; or
    b. Write the story of the father and daughter's (speaker's) relationship.

Nonfiction/Essays

Joy Harjo (b. 1951)

The Place of Origins

for my cousin John Jacobs (1918–1991), who will always be with me

I felt as if I had prepared for the green corn ceremony my whole life. It's nothing I can explain in print, and no explanation would fit in the English language. All I can say is that it is central to the mythic construct of the Muscogee people (otherwise known as "Creek"), a time of resonant renewal, of forgiveness.

The drive to Tallahassee Grounds in northeastern Oklahoma, with my friends Helen and Jim Burgess and Sue Williams, was filled with stories. Stories here are thick as the insects singing. We were part of the ongoing story of the people.

Helen and I had made a promise to participate together in a ceremony that ensures the survival of the people, a link in the epic story of grace. The trees and tall, reedlike grasses resounded with singing.

There's nothing quite like it anywhere else I've been, and I've traveled widely. The most similar landscape is in Miskito country in northeastern Nicaragua. I thought I was home again as I walked with the Miskito people whose homeland had suffered terrible destruction from both sides in the war. The singing insects provided a matrix of complex harmonies, shifting the cells in the body that shape imagination. I imagine a similar insect language in a place I've dreamed in West Africa. In summer in Oklahoma it's as if insects shape the world by songs. Their collective punctuation helps the growing corn remember the climb to the sun.

Our first stop was Holdenville, to visit one of my favorite older cousins, John Jacobs, and his wife Carol. They would join us later at the grounds. We traded gifts and stories, ate a perfectly fried meal at the Dairy Queen, one of the few restaurants open in a town hit hard by economic depression. I always enjoy visiting and feasting with these, my favorite relatives, and I feel at home in their house, a refuge surrounded by peacocks, dogs, and well-loved cats, guarded by giant beneficent spirits disguised as trees.

Across the road an oil well pumps relentlessly. When I was a child in Oklahoma, the monster insect bodies of the pumping wells terrified me. I would duck down in the car until we passed. Everyone thought it was funny. I was called high-strung and imaginative. I imagined the collapse of the world, as if the wells were giant insects without songs, pumping blood from the body of Earth. I wasn't far from the truth.

Marsie Harjo and Family. (Courtesy Joy Harjo.)

MARSIE HARJO AND KATIE MENAWE HARJO. (Courtesy Joy Harjo.)

My cousin John, who was more like a beloved uncle, gave me two photographs he had culled for me from family albums. I had never before seen my great-grandparents on my father's side. As I held them in my hand, reverberations of memory astounded me.

I believe stories are encoded in the DNA spiral and call each cell into perfect position. Sound tempered with emotion and meaning propels the spiral beyond three dimensions. I recognized myself in this photograph. I saw my sister, my brothers, my son and daughter. My father lived once again at the wheel of a car, my father who favored Cadillacs and Lincolns—cars he was not always able to afford but sacrificed to own anyway because he was compelled by the luxury of well-made vehicles, the humming song of a finely constructed motor. He made sure his cars were greased and perfectly tuned. That was his favorite music.

I was shocked (but not surprised) to recognize something I must always have known—the images of my great-grandmother Katie Menawe, my great-grandfather Marsie Harjo, my grandmother Naomi, my aunts Lois and Mary, and my uncle Joe. They were always inside me, as if I were a soul catcher made of a blood-formed crystal. I had heard the names, the stories, and perhaps their truths had formed the images, had propelled me into the world. My grandchildren and great-grandchildren will also see a magnification of themselves in their grandparents. It's implicit in the way we continue, the same way as corn plants, the same way as stars or cascades of insects singing in the summer. The old mystery of division and multiplication will always lead us to the root.

I think of my Aunt Lois's admonishments about photographs. She said that they could steal your soul. I believe it's true, for an imprint remains behind forever, locked in paper and chemicals. Perhaps the family will always be touring somewhere close to the border, dressed in their Sunday best, acutely aware of the soul stealer that Marsie Harjo hired to photograph them, steadying his tripod on the side of the road. Who's to say they didn't want something left to mark time in that intimate space, a space where they could exist forever as a family, a world drenched in sepia?

Nothing would ever be the same again. But here the family is ever-present, as 10 is the unnamed photographer through his visual arrangement. I wonder if he was surprised to see rich Indians.

The parents of both my great-grandparents made the terrible walk of the Muscogee Nation from Alabama to Indian Territory. They were settled on land bordered on the north by what is now Tulsa—the place my brothers, my sister, and I were born. The people were promised that if they made this move they would be left alone by the U.S. government, which claimed it needed the tribal homelands for expansion. But within a few years, white settlers were once again crowding Indian lands, and in 1887 the Dawes Act, better known as the Allotment Act, was made law. Private ownership was forced on the people. Land that supposedly belonged in perpetuity to the tribe was divided into plots, allotted to individuals. What was "left over" was opened for white settlement. But this did not satisfy the settlers, who proceeded, by new laws, other kinds of trickery, and raw force, to take over allotments belonging to the Muscogee and other tribes. The Dawes Act undermined one of the principles that had always kept the people together: that land was communal property which could not be owned.

On December 1, 1905, oil was struck in Glenpool, Oklahoma. This was one of the richest lakes of oil discovered in the state. At its height it produced forty million barrels annually. Marsie Harjo's allotted land was in Glenpool. He was soon a rich man, as were many other Indian people whose allotted land lay over lakes of oil. Land grabs intensified. Many tribal members were swindled out of their property, or simply killed for their money. It's a struggle that is still being played out in the late twentieth century.

Oil money explains the long elegant car Marsie Harjo poses in with his family. In the stories I've been told, he always loved Hudsons. The family was raised in luxury. My grandmother Naomi and my Aunt Lois both received B.F.A. degrees in art and were able to take expensive vacations at a time when many people in this country were suffering from economic deprivation. They also had an African-American maid, whose name was Susie. I've tried to find out more about her, but all I know is that she lived with the family for many years and made the best ice cream.

There are ironies here, because Marsie Harjo was also half or nearly half African-American, and in more recent years there has been racism directed at African-Americans by the tribe, which originally accepted Africans and often welcomed them as relatives. The acceptance of slavery came with the embrace of European-American cultural values. It was then that we also began to hate ourselves for our own darkness. It's all connected: ownership of land has everything to do with the ownership of humans and how they are treated, with the attitude toward all living things.

This picture of my great-grandparents' family explodes the myth of being In- 15
dian in this country for both non-Indian and Indian alike. I wonder how the image of a Muscogee family in a car only the wealthy could own would be interpreted by another Muscogee person, or by another tribal person, or by a
non-Indian anywhere in this land. It challenges the popular culture's version of
"Indian"—an image that fits no tribe or person. By presenting it here, I mean to
question those accepted images that have limited us to cardboard cut-out figures,
without blood or tears or laughter.

There were many photographs of this family. I recently sent my cousin Donna
Jo Harjo a photograph of her father Joe as a child about five. He was dressed in a
finely tailored suit and drove a child's-size model of a car. His daughter has never
lived in this kind of elegance. She lives on her salary as a sorter for a conglomerate
nut and dried fruit company in northern California. She loves animals, especially
horses and cats. (Our clan is the Tiger Clan.) I wonder at the proliferation of photographs and the family's diminishment in numbers to this present generation.

The second photograph is a straight-on shot of the same great-grandparents
standing with two Seminole men in traditional dress, wearing turbans. They are
in stark contrast to my great-grandparents—especially Marsie Harjo, who is
stately and somewhat stiff with the fear of God in his elegant white man's clothes,
his Homburg hat.

Marsie Harjo was a preacher, a Creek Baptist minister, representing a coun-
terforce to traditional Muscogee culture. He embodied one side in the split in our
tribe since Christianity was introduced and the people were influenced by European cultural values; the dividing lines remain the same centuries later. He was
quite an advanced thinker, and I imagine he repressed what he foresaw for the
Muscogee people, who probably would not have believed him anyway.

My great-grandfather was in Stuart, Florida, as he was every winter, to "save"
the souls of the Seminole people. He bought a plantation there, and because he
hated pineapples, he had every one of the plants dug up and destroyed. I've also
heard that he owned an alligator farm. I went to Stuart this spring on my way to
Miami and could find no trace of the mission or the plantation anywhere in the
suburban mix of concrete, glass, and advertisements. My memories are easier to
reach in a dimension that is as alive and living as anything in the three dimensions
we know with our five senses.

My great-grandmother Katie Menawe is much more visible here than in the 20
first photograph, where she is not up front, next to the driver, but in the very back
of the car, behind her four children. Yet she quietly presides over everything as she
guards her soul from the intrusive camera. I sense that Marsie boldly entered the
twentieth century ahead of most people, while Katie reluctantly followed. I doubt
if she ever resolved the split in her heart between her background and foreground.

I don't know much about her. She and her siblings were orphaned. Her sister
Ella, a noted beauty, was my cousin John's mother. They were boarded for some
time at Eufaula Indian School. I don't know how old Katie was when she married
Marsie Harjo. But the name Monahwee* is one of those Muscogee names that is

---

* His name is sometimes spelled Menawe or Menewa, but on his gravestone in Okmulgee, Oklahoma, it
is spelled Monahwee. [Author's note]

charged with memory of rebellion, with strength in the face of terrible adversity. Tecumseh came looking for Monahwee when he was building his great alliance of nations in the 1800s. Monahwee was one of the leaders of the Red Stick War, an armed struggle against the U.S. government to resist Andrew Jackson's demand for the removal of the tribes from their Southeastern homelands. Creeks, Seminoles, and Africans made up the fighting forces. Most of those who survived went to Florida, where the Seminoles successfully resisted colonization by hiding in the swamps. They beat the United States forces, who were aided by other tribes, including other Creeks who were promised land and homes for their help. The promises were like others from the U.S. government. Those who assisted were forced to walk west to Indian Territory like everyone else.

Monahwee stayed in Alabama and was soon forced west, but not before he joined with Jackson's forces to round up Seminoles for removal to Oklahoma. My cousin John said he died on the trail. I know that he died of a broken heart. I have a McKenney Hall portrait print of Monahwee, an original hand-colored lithograph dated 1848. Katie has the same eyes and composure of this man who was her father.

By going to Tallahassee Grounds to take part in a traditional tribal ceremony, I was taking my place in the circle of relatives, one more link in the concatenation of ancestors. Close behind me are my son and daughter, behind them, my granddaughter. Next to me, interlocking the pattern, are my cousins, my aunts and my uncles, my friends. We dance together in this place of knowing beyond the physical dimensions of space, much denser than the chemicals and paper of photographs. This place is larger than mere human memory, than the destruction we have walked through to come to this ground.

Time can never be stopped, rather it is poised so we can make a leap into knowing or into a field of questions. I understood this as we stompdanced in the middle of the night, as the stars whirred overhead in the same patterns as when Katie, Marsie, and the children lived beneath them. I heard time resume as the insects took up their singing again, to guide us through memory. The old Hudson heads to the east of the border of the photograph. For the Muscogee, East is the place of origins, the place the People emerged from so many hundreds of years ago. It is also a place of return.

ACTIVITIES FOR WRITING AND DISCUSSION

1. In paragraph 15 Harjo says, "This picture of my great-grandparents' family explodes the myth of being Indian in this country for both non-Indian and Indian alike." What is this "myth"? Why should Harjo be concerned to "explode" it?

2. What do the photographs add to this essay? How would the text be weakened, strengthened, or changed if the photos were eliminated?

3. Following Harjo's example, compose an essay about your own family in which you include one or more family photographs that serve as springboards for your writing. If you wish, select photographs that reveal both your family and some aspects of a culture to which you and your family belong.

4. Harjo sees family and culture as closely interconnected. Consider a culture (racial, religious, ethnic, social, avocational, or professional) with which you yourself identify. In an essay, describe some myths or beliefs about the culture that are held by outsiders. Then show how you, your family, or others close to you exemplify and/or belie those myths.

5. As an alternative to Activity #4, focus on a culture with which you do *not* identify instead of one with which you do. If possible, interview some members of that culture or do other outside research on it. Then, in an essay, discuss the stereotypes you and others have of that culture and show how the stereotypes are exemplified and/or belied by individuals.

FENTON JOHNSON (b. 1953)

The Limitless Heart

It is late March—the Saturday of Passover, 1991, to be exact—and I am driving an oversize rented car through West Los Angeles. This side of the city I have never seen except in the company of my lover Larry Rose, who died of AIDS in a Paris hospital some six months earlier.

He was an only child, who asked more than once that I promise to visit his parents after his death. Youngest son of a large family and a believer in brutal honesty, I'd refused. I have too much family already, I told him. There are limits to how much love I can give.

Now I am driving along one of the lovelier streets of Santa Monica, San Vicente Boulevard, west from Wilshire to the Pacific. The street is divided by a broad green median lined with coral trees, which the city has seen fit to register as landmarks. They spread airy, elegant crowns against a movie-set heaven, a Maxfield Parrish blue. Each branch bleeds at its tip an impossibly scarlet blossom, as if the limbs themselves had pierced the thin-skinned sky.

Larry's parents, Fred and Kathy Rose, are too old to get about much. They are German Jews, who spent the war years hiding in a Dutch village a few miles from Germany itself. Beaten by Nazis before the war, Fred hid for three years with broken vertebrae, unable to see a doctor. When he was no longer able to move, Kathy descended to the street to find help, to see falling from the sky the parachutes of their liberators. After the war they married and came to California, promised land of this promised land. Like Abraham and Sarah,[1] in their advanced years they had a single son; proof that it is possible, in the face of the worst, to pick up sticks and start again.

Fred greets me at the door of their small bungalow. Even in mourning he 5 wears his customary suit and tie, but he seems smaller than in my earlier visits. In

---

1. In the Old Testament, Abraham and Sarah gave birth to a son, Isaac, in their old age.

his bent and shrunken frame I understand that Larry was a shield against his memories, and now Larry is gone.

Fred, Kathy, and I sit to talk, but Fred is reserved; he does not talk about Larry with the women of his life—his wife or his surviving sister. No doubt he fears giving way before his grief, and his life has not allowed for much giving way. This much he and I share: a gay man who grew up in the rural South, I am no stranger to hiding.

Kathy always goes to bed early—partly by way of coping with grief—but this evening Fred all but asks her to retire. After she leaves, he begins talking of Larry, and I listen and respond with gratefulness. We are two men in control, who permit ourselves to speak to each other of our loss because we subscribe implicitly, jointly, unconditionally to this code of conduct.

Fred tells a familiar story, of the day when Larry, then eight years old, wanted to go fishing. The quintessential urban Jew, Fred nonetheless bought poles and hooks and drove fifty miles to Laguna Beach. There they dropped their lines from a pier to discover the hooks dangled some ten feet above the water. "Thank God," Fred said. "Otherwise we might have caught something." A passerby scoffed, "What the hell do you think you're trying to catch?" Fred shrugged, unperturbed. "Flying fish," he said.

I respond with my most vivid memory of my time with Larry. A wiser man than I, he spoke many times of his great good luck, his great good fortune. "I'm so lucky," he said again and again. Denial pure and simple, or so I told myself in our first years together. AZT, ddI, ACT-UP, CMV, DHPG, and what I came to think of as the big "A" itself—he endured this acronymed life, while I listened and participated and helped with I could.

Until our third and final trip to Paris, when on our last night to walk about 10 the city, we sat in the courtyard of the Picasso Museum. There under a dusk-deep sky I turned to him and said, "I'm so lucky," and it was as if the time allotted to him to teach me this lesson, the time allotted to me to learn it had been consumed, and there was nothing left but the facts of things to play out.

A long pause after this story—I have ventured beyond what I permit myself, what I am permitted.

I change the subject, asking Fred to talk of the war years. He speaks not of his beating or of murdered family and friends but of moments of affection, loyalty, even humor, until he speaks of winters spent confined to bed, huddled in Kathy's arms, their breaths freezing on the quilt as they sang together to pass time, to stay warm, to distract him from his pain, to ward off their fear.

Another silence. Now he has ventured too far. "I have tried to forget these stories," he says in his halting English.

In the presence of these extremes of love and sorrow I am reduced to cliché. "It's only by remembering them that we can avoid repeating them," I say.

"They are being repeated all the time," Fred says. "It is bad sometimes to 15 watch too much television. You see these things and you know we have learned nothing."

Are we so dense that we can learn nothing from all this pain, all this death? Is it impossible to learn from experience? The bitterness of these questions I can taste, as I drive east to spend the night at a relative's apartment.

Just south of the seedier section of Santa Monica Boulevard I stop at a bar recommended by a friend. I need a drink, I need the company of men like myself—survivors, for the moment anyway, albeit of a very different struggle.

The bar is filled with Latino drag queens wearing extraordinary clothes. Eighty years of B movies have left Hollywood the nation's most remarkable supply of secondhand dresses, many of which, judging from this evening, have made their ways to these men's closets.

I am standing at the bar, very Anglo, very out of place, very much thinking of leaving, when a tiny, wizened, gray-haired Latina approaches the stage, where under jerry-built lights (colored cellophane, Scotch tape) a man lip-synchs to Brazilian rock. His spike heels raise him to something more than six feet; he wears a floor-length sheath dress slit up the sides and so taut, so brilliantly silver, so lustrous that it catches and throws back the faces of his audience. The elderly Latina raises a dollar bill. On tottering heels he lowers himself, missing not a word of his song while half-crouching, half-bending so that she may tuck his dollar in his cleavage and kiss his cheek.

"*Su abuelita,*" the bartender says. "His grandmother."   20

One A.M. in the City of Angels—the streets are clogged with cars. Stuck in traffic, I am visited by voices and visions: by the high, thin songs of Fred and Kathy as they huddle under their frozen quilt, singing into their breaths; by a small boy and his father sitting on a very long pier, their baitless fishhooks dangling above the vast Pacific; by the face of *su abuelita*, uplifted and adoring, mirrored in her grandson's dress.

Somewhere a light changes; the traffic unglues itself. As cars begin moving, I am visited by two last ghosts—myself and Larry Rose, sitting in the courtyard of the Hôtel Salé, transfigured by the limitless heart.

BARBARA KINGSOLVER (b. 1955)

Letter to My Mother

I imagine you putting on your glasses to read this letter. *Oh, Lord, what now?* You tilt your head back and hold the page away from you, your left hand flat on your chest, protecting your heart. "Dear Mom" at the top of a long, typed letter from me has so often meant trouble. Happy, uncomplicated things—these I could always toss you easily over the phone: I love you, where in the world is my birth certificate, what's in your zuchini casserole, happy birthday, this is our new phone number, we're having a baby in March, my plane comes in at seven, see you then, I love you.

The hard things went into letters. I started sending them from college, the kind of self-absorbed epistles that usually began as diary entries and should have stayed there. During those years I wore black boots from an army surplus store and a five-dollar haircut from a barbershop and went to some trouble to fill you in on the great freedom women could experience if only they would throw off the bondage of housewifely servitude. I made sideways remarks about how I couldn't imagine being anybody's wife. In my heart I believed that these letters—in which I tried to tell you how I'd become someone entirely different from the child you'd known—would somehow make us friends. But instead they only bought me a few quick gulps of air while I paced out the distance between us.

I lived past college, and so did my hair, and slowly I learned the womanly art of turning down the volume. But I still missed you, and from my torment those awful letters bloomed now and then. I kept trying; I'm trying still. But this time I want to say before anything else: Don't worry. Let your breath out. I won't hurt you anymore. We measure the distance in miles now, and I don't have to show you I'm far from where I started. Increasingly, that distance seems irrelevant. I want to tell you what I remember.

I'm three years old. You've left me for the first time with your mother while you and Daddy took a trip. Grandmama fed me cherries and showed me the secret of her hair: Five metal hairpins come out, and the everyday white coil drops in a silvery waterfall to the back of her knees. Her house smells like polished wooden stairs and soap and Granddad's onions and ice cream, and I would love to stay there always but I miss you bitterly without end. On the day of your return I'm standing in the driveway waiting when the station wagon pulls up. You jump out your side, my mother in happy red lipstick and red earrings, pushing back your dark hair from the shoulder of your white sleeveless blouse, turning so your red skirt swirls like a rose with the perfect promise of *you* emerging from the center. So beautiful. You raise one hand in a tranquil wave and move so slowly up the driveway that your body seems to be underwater. I understand with a shock that you are extremely happy. I have been miserable and alone waiting in the driveway, and you were at the beach with Daddy and *happy*. Happy without me.

I am sitting on your lap, and you are crying. *Thank you, honey, thank you,* you keep   5 saying, rocking back and forth as you hold me in the kitchen chair. I've brought you flowers: the sweet peas you must have spent all spring trying to grow, training them up the trellis in the yard. You had nothing to work with but abundant gray rains and the patience of a young wife at home with pots and pans and small children, trying to create just one beautiful thing, something to take you outside our tiny white clapboard house on East Main. I never noticed until all at once they burst through the trellis in a pink red purple dazzle. A finger-painting of colors humming against the blue air: I could think of nothing but to bring it to you. I climbed up the wooden trellis and picked the flowers. Every one. They are gone already, wilting in my hand as you hold me close in the potato-smelling kitchen, and your tears are damp in my hair but you never say a single thing but *Thank you.*

Your mother is dead. She was alive, so thin that Granddad bought her a tiny dark-blue dress and called her his fashion model and then they all went to the hospital and came home without her. Where is the dark-blue dress now? I find myself wondering, until it comes to me that they probably buried her in it. It's under the ground with her. There are so many things I don't want to think about that I can't bear going to bed at night.

It's too hot to sleep. My long hair wraps around me, grasping like tentacles. My brother and sister and I have made up our beds on cots on the porch, where it's supposed to be cooler. They are breathing in careless sleep on either side of me, and I am under the dark cemetery ground with Grandmama. I am in the stars, desolate, searching out the end of the universe and time. I am trying to imagine how long forever is, because that is how long I will be dead for someday. I won't be able to stand so much time being nothing, thinking of nothing. I've spent many nights like this, fearing sleep. Hating being awake.

I get up, barefoot and almost nothing in my nightgown, and creep to your room. The door is open, and I see that you're awake, too, sitting up on the edge of your bed. I can make out only the white outline of your nightgown and your eyes. You're like a ghost.

Mama, I don't want to die.

You don't have to worry about that for a long, long time.   10

I know. But I'm thinking about it now.

I step toward you from the doorway, and you fold me into your arms. You are real, my mother in scent and substance, and I still fit perfectly in your lap.

You don't know what Heaven is like. It might be full of beautiful flowers.

When I close my eyes I discover it's there, an endless field of flowers. Columbines, blue asters, daisies, sweet peas, zinnias: one single flower bed stretching out for miles in every direction. I am small enough to watch the butterflies come. I know them from the pasture behind our house, the butterflies you taught me to love and name: monarchs, Dianas, tiger swallowtails. I follow their lazy zigzag as they visit every flower, as many flowers as there are stars in the universe. We stay there in the dark for a long time, you and I, both of us with our eyes closed, watching the butterflies drift so slowly, filling as much time as forever.

I will keep that field of flowers. It doesn't matter that I won't always believe in   15
Heaven. I will suffer losses of faith, of love and confidence, I will have some bitter years, and always when I hurt and can't sleep I will close my eyes and wait for your butterflies to arrive.

Just one thing, I'm demanding of you. It's the middle of summer, humid beyond all reason, and I am thirteen: a tempest of skinned knees and menarche. You are trying to teach me how to do laundry, showing me how to put the bluing in with the sheets. The swampy Monday-afternoon smell of sheets drowning under the filmy, shifting water fills me with pure despair. I want no part of that smell. No future in white sheets and bluing. *Name one good thing about being a woman,* I say to you.

There are lots of good things. . . . Your voice trails off with the thin blue stream that trickles into the washer's indifferent maw.

In a rare flush of adrenaline or confidence, I hold on, daring you: *OK, then. If that's true, just name me one.*

You hesitated. I remember that. I saw a hairline crack in your claim of a homemaker's perfect contentment. Finally you said, *The love of a man. That's one thing. Being taken care of and loved by a man.*

And because you'd hesitated I knew I didn't have to believe it.   20

At fifteen I am raging at you in my diary, without courage or any real intention, yet, of actually revealing myself to you. *Why do you want to ruin my life? Why can't you believe I know how to make my own decisions? Why do you treat me like a child? No makeup or nail polish allowed in this house—you must think I am a baby or a nun. You tell me if I forget to close the curtains when I get undressed the neighbor boy will rape me. You think all boys are evil. You think if I go out with my girlfriends I'll get kidnaped. You think if I'm in the same room with a boy and a can of beer, I'll instantly become a pregnant alcoholic.*

Halfway through the page I crumble suddenly and write in a meeker hand, *I have to learn to keep my big mouth shut and not fight with Mom. I love her so much.*

I am a young woman sliced in two, half of me claiming to know everything and the other half just as sure I will never know anything at all. I am too awkward and quiet behind my curtain of waist-length hair, a girl unnoticed, a straight-A schoolmouse who can't pass for dumb and cute in a small-town, marry-young market that values—as far as I can see—no other type.

I understand this to be all your fault. You made me, and I was born a girl. You trained me to be a woman, and regarding that condition I fail to see one good thing.

The woodsmoke scent in the air puts me in mind of raked leaves, corduroy   25 jumpers and new saddle shoes, our family's annual trip to Browning's orchard for apples and cider: a back-to-school nostalgia altogether too childish for me now, and yet here I am, thrilled to the edge of all my senses to be starting college. You and Dad have driven three hundred miles in our VW bus, which is packed like a tackle box with my important, ridiculous stuff, and now you have patiently unloaded it without questioning my judgment on a single cherished object—the plants, the turtle-shell collection, the glass demijohn, the huge striped pillow, the hundred books. You're sitting on my new bed while Dad carries in the last box. To you this bed must look sadly institutional compared with the furniture lovingly lathed for us from red cherrywood by your father before he died. To me the new metal bed frame looks just fine. Nothing fussy; it will do. I am arranging my plants in the windowsill while you tell me you're proud of the scholarship I won, you know I'll do well here and be happy, I should call if I need anything, call even if I don't.

I won't need anything, I tell you.

I am visited suddenly by a peculiar photographic awareness of the room, as if I were not really in it but instead watching us both from the doorway. I understand we are using up the very last minutes of something neither of us can call, outright, my childhood. I can't wait for you to leave, and then you do. I close the door and stand watching through my yellow-curtained window and the rust-orange boughs of a maple outside as you and Dad climb into the VW and drive away without looking back. And because no one can see me I wipe my slippery face with the back of my hand. My nose runs and I choke on tears, so many I'm afraid I will drown. I can't smell the leaves or apples or woodsmoke at all. I feel more alone than I've ever felt in my life.

———

At the Greencastle Drive-In on a double date, I am half of the couple in the backseat. We have the window open just a crack to accommodate the hissing metal speaker, and the heater is on full blast. Outside our happy island of steamy heat, frost is climbing the metal poles and whitening the upright bones of the surrounding cornfields; it's nearly Thanksgiving, surely the end of drive-in season as we know it. Tomorrow I have a midterm exam. Surprisingly, I don't even care. I feel heady and reckless. Truth be told, I will probably ace the exam, but even if I don't, so what? I'll live. Finally I have a genuine social life and the privilege of giving in to peer pressure: I threw *Heart of Darkness* over my shoulder at the first bark of temptation and went out on a date.

The movie is *Cabaret.* Sally Bowles, with her weird haircut and huge, sad eyes, is singing her heart out about being abandoned by her mother.

With a physical shock I wake up to what's been tugging at my ear all day: November 20 — it's your birthday! I've never forgotten your birthday, not since I was old enough to push a crayon around in the shape of a heart on a folded piece of construction paper. How can it be that this year I didn't even think to send a card? I sit bolt upright and open my mouth, preparing to announce that I have to go home immediately and call my mother. My friend and her boyfriend in the front seat are deeply involved in each other. I imagine them staring at me, hostile under rumpled hair, and feel myself shrinking into my former skin, the vessel of high school misery. I despise that schoolmouse. The happiness of my new adulthood is so precarious that I have to be careful not to wreck it like a ship. I sigh, settle back, shut my mouth, and watch Sally Bowles ruin her life.

———

I am nineteen, a grown woman curled like a fetus on my bed. Curled in a knot so small I hope I may disappear. I do not want to be alive.

I've been raped.

I know his name, his address—in fact I will probably have to see him again on campus. But I have nothing to report. Not to the police, not to you. The telephone rings and rings and I can't pick it up because it may be you. My mother. Everything you ever told me from the beginning has come home to this knot of nothingness on my bed, this thing I used to call me. I was supposed to prevent what happened. Two nights ago I talked to him at a bar. He bought me a drink and told my friends he thought I was cute. *That girl with the long hair,* he said. *What's her name?* Tonight when he came to my door I was happy, for ten full seconds. Then. My head against a wall, suffocation, hard pushing and flat on my back and screaming for air. Fighting an animal twice my size. My job was to stop him, and I failed. How can I tell you that? *You met him in a bar. You see?*

From this vantage point, a dot of nothingness in the center of my bed, I understand the vast ocean of work it is to be a woman among men, that universe of effort, futile whimpers against hard stones, and oh God I don't want it. My bones are weak. I am trapped in a room with no flowers, no light, a ceiling of lead so low I can never again straighten up. I don't want to live in this world.

I will be able to get up from this bed only if I can get up angry. Can you understand there is no other way? I have to be someone else. Not you, and not even me. Tomorrow or someday soon I will braid my long hair for the last time, go to my friend's house with a pair of sharp scissors, and tell her to cut it off. All of it. Tomorrow or someday soon I will feel that blade at my nape and the weight will fall.

Summer light, Beaurieux, France. At twenty-three I'm living in an enormous, centuries-old stone farmhouse with a dozen friends, talkative French socialists and a few British expatriates, all of us at some loose coupling in our lives between school and adulthood. We find a daily, happy solace in one another and in the scarlet poppies that keep blooming in the sugar-beet fields. We go out to work together in the morning and then come home in the evening to drink red table wine and make ratatouille in the cavernous stone-floored kitchen. This afternoon, a Saturday, a gaggle of us have driven into town to hang out at the village's only electrified establishment, a tiny café. We are entrenched in a happy, pointless argument about Camus when the man wiping the counter answers the phone and yells, *"Mademoiselle Kingsolver? Quelque'un des États Unis!"*

My heart thumps to a complete stop. Nobody from the United States can possibly know where I am. I haven't written to my parents for many months, since before I moved to France. I rise and sleepwalk to the telephone, knowing absolutely that it will be you, my *mother,* and it is. I still have no idea how you found me; I can hardly even remember our conversation. I must have told you I was alive and well, still had all my arms and legs—what else was there for me to say? You told me that my brother was getting married and I ought to come home for the wedding.

Ma mère! This is what I tell my friends, with a shrug, when I return to the table. I tell them you probably called out the French Foreign Legion to find me. Everybody laughs and declares that mothers are all alike: They love us too much, they are a cross to bear, they all ought to find their own things to do and leave us alone. We pay for our coffee and amble toward somebody's car, but I decide on impulse I'll walk back to the farm. I move slowly, turning over and over in my mind the telephone's ringing, the call that was for me. In France, a tiny town, the only café, a speck of dust on the globe. Already it seems impossible that this really happened. The roadside ditch is brilliant with poppies, and as I walk along I am hugging myself so hard I can barely breathe.

———————

I'm weeding the garden. You admired my garden a lot when you came to visit me here in Tucson, in this small brick house of my own. We fought, of course. You didn't like my involvement with Central American refugees, no matter how I tried to talk you through the issues of human rights and our government's support of a dictatorship in El Salvador. Even more, you didn't like it that I was living in this little brick house with a man, unmarried. But you did admire my vegetable garden, and the four-o' clocks in the front yard, you said, were beautiful. The flowers were our common ground. They'll attract hummingbirds, you told me, and we both liked that.

On this day I am alone, weeding the garden, and a stranger comes to the door. 40 He doesn't look well, and he says he needs a glass of water, so I go to the kitchen. When I turn around from the sink, there he is, with a knife shoved right up against my belly.

Don't scream or I'll kill you.

But I do scream. Scream, slap, bite, kick, shove my knee into his stomach. I don't know what will happen next, but I know this much: It's not going to be my fault. You were partly wrong and partly right; bad things are bound to happen, but this hateful supremacy that sometimes shoves itself against me is *not* my fault. You've held on to me this long, so I must be someone worth saving against the odds. When I can finally tell you that, I know you will agree with me. So this time I scream. I scream for all I'm worth.

———————

I'm somewhere between thirty and a hundred, and I've written a book. My first novel, but to me it seems more like the longest letter to you I've ever written. Finally, after a thousand tries, I've explained everything I believe in, exactly the way I always wanted to: human rights, Central American refugees, the Problem That Has No Name, abuse of the powerless, racism, poetry, freedom, childhood, motherhood, Sisterhood Is Powerful. All that, and still some publisher has decided it makes a good story.

But that doesn't matter right now, because you are on my front-porch glider turning the pages one at a time, and it's only a stack of paper. The longest typed letter ever, a fistful of sweet peas, the world's largest pile of crayoned hearts. I'm supposed to be cooking dinner but I keep looking out the window, trying to see what page you're on now, trying to read your thoughts from the back of your head. All I can see is that you're still reading, and your hair is gray. In another few minutes mine will be, too. My heart is pounding. I boil water and peel the potatoes but forget to put them in the pot. I salt the water twice. At last you come in with tears in your eyes.

Barb, honey, it's beautiful. So good.   45

You fold me into your arms, and I can't believe it: I still fit. Or I fit once again.

I'm thirty-two, with my own daughter in my arms. I've sent you a picture of her, perfect and gorgeous in her bassinette. Her tiny hand is making a delicate circle, index finger to thumb, pinkie extended as if she were holding a teacup. How could my ferocious will create such a delicate, feminine child? *This one is all girl,* I write on the back, my daughter's first caption. You send back a photo of me at the same age, eight weeks, in my bassinette. I can't believe it: I am making a delicate circle with my hand, index finger to thumb, pinkie extended.

We've flown back to Kentucky for Christmas. I'm thirty-seven but feeling weirdly transported backward. For all the years I've been away from my hometown, Main Street is perfectly unchanged. The commercial district is set off by a stoplight on either end of a single block: hardware store, men's clothing, five-and-dime, drugstore, county jail. An American flag made of red, white, and blue light bulbs (some of them burned out) blinks to life on the courthouse's peeling silver dome at dusk. Who on earth was I, in the years I called this place home?

I've come into town to run a few errands, and to tell the truth, it's a relief to take a few hours' respite from a house overstuffed with Christmas decorations and sugary fruitcakes, a kitchen stifling from an overworked oven, and hugs at every turn. How did I ever live *there?* My own life is so different now. So pared down. In fact, I haven't found a way to tell you this, but my marriage is slowly dying, and I will soon be on my own again—this time next year I'll be a single mother. I am handling this, I cope. I stop in at Hopkins' Drug to get something for my daughter's cough. The bell over the door jingles, and I wave a leather-gloved hand at Mr. Hopkins, still filling prescriptions at the back of the store. I tell him yes, I'm home visiting, and ask what he recommends for my daughter. She picked up a cold on the trip; she hasn't been sick many times in her life, so I'm worried, but only a little. In my tweed winter coat and convenient shoulder-length haircut I feel competent and slightly rushed, as usual. A woman of my age.

An elderly woman I don't recognize stops me with an arthritic hand across my   50 wrist as I'm about to leave the drugstore. Her eyes swim toward me like dark fish as she eyes me through thick glasses, up and down. *You must be Virginia Kingsolver's daughter. You look exactly like her.*

My nine-year-old daughter comes home from a summer slumber party with painted nails, and I mean *painted.* Day-Glo green on the fingers, purple on the toes. We drive to the drugstore for nail-polish remover.

Please! All the girls my age are doing this.

How can every nine-year-old on the planet possibly be painting her toenails purple?

I don't know. They just are.

School starts in a week. Do you want to be known by your teacher as the girl with 55 *the green fingernails?*

Yes. But I guess you *don't.*

Do you really?

She looks down at her nails and states: *Yes.* With her porcelain skin and long, dark lashes, she is a Raphael cherub. Her perfect mouth longs to pout, but she resists, holds her back straight. A worthy vessel for her own opinions. Despite myself, I admire her.

OK, we'll compromise. The green comes off. But keep the purple toenails.

At forty, I'm expecting my second child. Through my years of being coupled and 60 then alone, years of accepting my fate and then the astonishing chance of remarriage, I've waited a lifetime for this gift: a second child. But now it is past due, and I am impatient. I conceived in late September and now it's July. I have dragged this child in my belly through some portion of every month but August. In the summer's awful heat I am a beached whale, a house full of water, a universe with ankles. It seems entirely possible to me that the calendar will close and I will somehow be bound fairy-tale-wise to a permanent state of pregnancy.

During these months you and I have talked more often than ever before. Through our long phone conversations I've learned so many things: that you fought for natural childbirth all three times, a rebel against those patronizing doctors who routinely knocked women out with drugs. In the fifties, formula was said to be modern and breast-feeding crude and old-fashioned, but you ignored the wagging fingers and did what you and I both know was best for your babies.

I've also learned that ten-month pregnancies run in our family.

When your sister was two weeks overdue, I made Wendell drive over every bumpy road in the country.

Did it work?

No. With you, we were in Maryland. We drove over to see the cherry blossoms on 65 *the Capitol Mall in April, and Wendell said, "What if you go into labor while we're hours away from home?" I told him, "I'll sing Hallelujah."*

A week past my due date you are calling every day. Steven answers the phone, holds it up, and mouths, "Your mother again." He thinks you may be bugging me. You aren't. I am a woman lost in the weary sea of waiting, and you are the only one who really knows where I am. Your voice is keeping me afloat. I grab the phone.

She is born at last. A second daughter. I cry on the phone, I'm so happy and relieved to have good news for you, finally. I promise you we'll send pictures right away. You will tell me she looks just like I did. She looks like her father, but I will believe you anyway.

Later on when it's quiet I nurse our baby, admiring her perfect hands. Steven is in a chair across the room, and I'm startled to look up and find he is staring at us with tears in his eyes. I've seen him cry only once before.

What's wrong?

Nothing. I'm just so happy.   70

I love him inordinately. I could not bear to be anyone but his wife just now. I could not bear to be anyone but the mother of my daughters.

I was three years old, standing in the driveway waiting for the car to bring you back from Florida. You arrived glowing with happiness. *Because of me.* I felt stung, thinking you could carry on your life of bright-red lipstick smiles outside of my presence, but I know now I was wrong. You looked happy *because of me.* You hadn't seen me for more than a week, hadn't nursed me for years, and yet your breasts tingled before you opened the car door. The soles of your feet made contact with the ground, and your arms opened up as you walked surefooted once again into the life you knew as my mother. I know exactly how you felt. I am your happiness. It's a cross I am willing to bear.

ACTIVITIES FOR WRITING AND DISCUSSION

1. Near the start of her letter Kingsolver states her purpose: "I want to tell you what I remember," and her letter is a sequence of memories chronologically arranged. Begin a letter to your own mother, father, or other parental figure with the same line; then write what *you* remember. (Suggestion: You might compose this letter over a period of days, using a small notepad to record "shorthand" recollections that you later expand into paragraphs.)

2. Essays can be written for anonymous audiences or (as in Kingsolver's case) primarily for a specific personal audience. Having the "right" personal audience can be a strong stimulant to creativity; writers like Henry David Thoreau and Emily Dickinson, to name just two, have produced some of their best writing as personal letters. Practice writing short essays to various personal audiences (friends, family members, mentors) to see which elicits your best thinking and storytelling. For topic ideas, try using a Topic/Form Grid as described in Chapter 5.

3. Respond to Kingsolver's essay using Idea #1, #2 or #8 of the Ten Ideas for Writing on page 35.

4. Identify a favorite author of yours and find a published collection of his or her letters. Read the letters. How, if at all, do the letters complement or inform the author's essays, poems, plays, or fiction?

Joyce Carol Oates (b. 1938)

Tone Clusters

A Play in Nine Scenes

CHARACTERS

FRANK GULICK: fifty-three years old
EMILY GULICK: fifty-one years old
VOICE: male, indeterminate age

These are white Americans of no unusual distinction, nor are they in any self-evident way "representative."

Tone Clusters *is not intended to be a realistic work, thus any inclination toward the establishment of character should be resisted. Its primary effect should be visual (the dominance of the screen at center stage, the play of lights of sharply contrasting degrees of intensity) and audio (the* VOICE, *the employment of music—"tone clusters" of Henry Cowell and/or Charles Ives, and electronic music, etc.). The mood is one of fragmentation, confusion, yet, at times, strong emotion. A fractured narrative emerges which the audience will have no difficulty piecing together even as—and this is the tragicomedy of the piece—the characters* MR. *and* MRS. GULICK *deny it.*

In structure, Tone Clusters *suggests an interview, but a stylized interview in which questions and answers are frequently askew. Voices trail off into silence or may be mocked or extended by strands of music. The* VOICE *is sometimes overamplified and booming; sometimes marred by static; sometimes clear, in an ebullient tone, like that of a talk-show host. The* VOICE *has no identity but must be male. It should not be represented by any actual presence on the stage or within view of the audience. At all times, the* VOICE *is in control: the principals on the stage are dominated by their interrogator and by the screen, which is seemingly floating in the air above them, at center stage. Indeed the screen emerges as a character.*

The piece is divided into nine uneven segments. When one ends, the lights dim, then come up again immediately. (After the ninth segment the lights go out completely and darkness is extended for some seconds to indicate that the piece is ended: it ends on an abrupt cutoff of lights and images on the screen and the monitors.)

By degree the GULICKS *become somewhat accustomed to the experience of being interviewed and filmed, but never wholly accustomed: they are always slightly disoriented, awkward, confused, inclined to speak slowly and methodically or too quickly, "unprofessionally," often with inappropriate emotion (fervor, enthusiasm, hope, sudden rage) or no emotion at all (like "computer voices"). The* GULICKS *may at*

times speak in unison (as if one were an echo of the other); they may mimic the qual-
ities of tone-cluster music or electronic music (I conceive of their voices, and that of
the VOICE, *as music of a kind); should the director wish, there may be some clear-cut*
relationship between subject and emotion or emphasis—but the piece should do no
more than approach "realism," and then withdraw. The actors must conceive of
themselves as elements in a dramatic structure, not as "human characters" wishing to
establish rapport with an audience.

Tone Clusters *is about the absolute mystery—the* not knowing—*at the core of*
our human experience. That the mystery is being exploited by a television documen-
tary underscores its tragicomic nature.

Scene 1.

Lights up. Initially very strong, near-blinding. On a bare stage, middle-aged FRANK
and EMILY GULICK *sit ill-at-ease in "comfortable" modish cushioned swivel chairs,*
trying not to squint or grimace in the lights (which may be represented as the lights
of a camera crew provided the human figures involved can be kept shadowy, even in-
distinct). They wear clip-on microphones, to which they are unaccustomed. They are
"dressed up" for the occasion, and clearly nervous: they continually touch their faces,
or clasp their hands firmly in their laps, or fuss with fingernails, buttons, the micro-
phone cords, their hair. The nervous mannerisms continue throughout the piece but
should never be too distracting and never comic.

Surrounding the GULICKS, *dominating their human presence, are the central*
screen and the TV monitors and/or slide screens upon which, during the course of the
play, disparate images, words, formless flashes of light are projected. Even when the
GULICKS' *own images appear on the screens they are upstaged by it: they glance at it*
furtively, with a kind of awe.

The rest of the time, the monitors always show the stage as we see it: the GULICKS
seated, glancing uneasily up at the large screen. Thus there is a "screen within a
screen."

The employment of music is entirely at the director's discretion. The opening
might be accompanied by classical tone cluster piano pieces—Henry Cowell's "Ad-
vertisement," for instance. The music should never be intrusive. The ninth scene
might well be completely empty of music. There should certainly be no "film-music"
effect. (The GULICKS *do not hear the music.)*

The VOICE *too in its modulations is at the discretion of the director. Certainly at*
the start the VOICE *is booming and commanding. There should be intermittent au-*
dio trouble (whistling, static, etc.); the VOICE, *wholly in control, can exude any num-*
ber of effects throughout the play—pomposity, charity, condescension, bemusement,
false chattiness, false pedantry, false sympathy, mild incredulity (like that of a televi-
sion emcee), affectless "computer talk." The GULICKS *are entirely intimidated by the*
VOICE *and try very hard to answer its questions.*

Screen shifts from its initial image to words: IN A CASE OF MURDER—*large*
black letters on white.

VOICE: In a case of murder   (taking murder as an abstraction)   there is always a sense of the Inevitable   once the identity of the murderer   is established. Beforehand there   is   a sense   of disharmony.

And humankind fears and loathes disharmony,
Mr. and Mrs. Gulick of Lakepointe, New Jersey, would you comment?

FRANK: . . .Yes I would say,   I think that

EMILY: What is that again, exactly?   I . . .

FRANK: My wife and I, we . . .

EMILY: Disharmony . . . ?

FRANK: I don't like disharmony.   I mean, all the family,
we are a law-abiding family.

VOICE: A religious family   I believe?

FRANK: Oh yes.   Yes,
We go to church every

EMILY: We almost never miss a,   a Sunday
For a while,   I helped with Sunday School classes
The children,   the children don't always go but they believe,
our daughter Judith for instance she   and Carl

FRANK: oh yes   *yessir*

EMILY: and Dennis,   they do believe they were raised to
believe in God and, and Jesus Christ

FRANK: We raised them that way because   we were raised that way,

EMILY: there *is* a God whether you agree with Him   or not.

VOICE: "Religion" may be defined as   a sort of adhesive matter invisibly
holding together   nation-states, nationalities, tribes, families
   for   the   good   of   those   so
                              held together,
                           would you comment?

FRANK: Oh,   oh yes.

EMILY: For the good of . . .

FRANK: Yes I would say so,   I think so.

EMILY: My husband and I, we were married in church, in

FRANK: In the Lutheran Church.

EMILY: In Penns Neck.

FRANK: In New Jersey.

EMILY: All our children,

BOTH: they believe.

EMILY: God sees into the human heart.

VOICE: Mr. and Mrs. Gulick   from your experience would you   theorize for
our audience: is the Universe "predestined"   in every particular
or   is   man   capable   of   acts   of   "freedom"?

BOTH: . . .

EMILY: . . . I would say,   that is hard to say.

FRANK: Yes. I believe that man is free.

EMILY: If you mean like, I guess   choosing good and evil?   Yes

FRANK: I would have to say   yes.   You would have to say
mankind is free.
Like moving my hand. *(moves hand)*
    EMILY: If nobody is free   it wouldn't be right would it
to punish anybody?
    FRANK: There is always   Hell.
I believe in Hell.
    EMILY: Anybody at all
    FRANK: Though I am not free to, to   fly up in the air am I? *(laughs)*
because   Well I'm not built right for that am I? *(laughs)*
    VOICE: Man is free.   Thus man is   responsible for his acts.
    EMILY: Except, oh   sometime if,   maybe for instance if
A baby born without
    FRANK: Oh one of those "AIDS" babies
    EMILY: poor thing
    FRANK: "crack" babies
Or if you were captured   by some enemy, y'know   and tortured
Some people never have a chance.
    EMILY: But God sees into the human heart,
God knows who to forgive   and who not.

Lights down.

Scene 2.

Lights up. Screen shows a suburban street of lower-income homes; the GULICKS *stare at the screen and their answers are initially distracted.*

    VOICE: Here we have Cedar Street   in Lakepointe, New Jersey   neatly kept
homes (as you can see)   American suburb   low crime rate,
single-family homes   suburb of Newark, New Jersey
    population twelve thousand   the neighborhood of
    Mr. and Mrs. Frank Gulick the parents of   Carl Gulick
    Will you introduce yourselves to our audience please?
    (House lights come up.)
    FRANK: . . . Go on, you first
    EMILY: I, I don't know what to say
    FRANK: My name is   Frank Gulick, I   I am fifty-three years old
that's our house there   2368 Cedar Street
    EMILY: My name is Emily Gulick, fifty-one years old,
    VOICE: How employed,   would you care to say?   Mr. Gulick?
    FRANK: I work for the post office,   I'm a supervisor for
    EMILY: He has worked for the post office for twenty-five years
    FRANK: . . . The Terhune Avenue branch.
    VOICE: And how long have you resided   in your attractive home   on Cedar
Street?

(House lights begin to fade down.)

FRANK: . . . Oh I guess, how long   if this is
this is 1990?

EMILY: (oh just think: 1990!)

FRANK: we moved there in, uh   Judith wasn't born yet so

EMILY: Oh there was our thirtieth anniversary a year ago,

FRANK: wedding
no that was two years ago

EMILY: was it?

FRANK: or three, I   twenty-seven years, this is 1990

EMILY: Yes: Judith is twenty-six,   now I'm a grandmother

FRANK: Carl is twenty-two

EMILY: Denny is seventeen, he's a senior in high school
No none of them are living at home now

FRANK: not now

EMILY: Right now poor Denny is staying with my sister in

VOICE: Frank and Emily Gulick you have been happy here in Lakepointe
raising your family like any   American couple   with your
hopes and aspirations
                                    until recently?

FRANK: . . .Yes, oh yes.

EMILY: Oh for a long time we *were*

FRANK: oh yes.

EMILY: It's so strange to,   to think of
The years go by so

VOICE: You have led a   happy family life   like so many millions
                              of Americans

EMILY: Until this,   this terrible thing

FRANK: *Innocent until proven guilty*—that's a laugh!

EMILY: Oh it's a, a terrible thing

FRANK: Never any hint beforehand of   the meanness of people's hearts.
I mean the neighbors.

EMILY: Oh now don't start that,   this isn't the

FRANK: Oh God you just try to   comprehend

EMILY: this isn't the place, I

FRANK: Like last night: this carload of kids
drunk, beer-drinking   foul language in the night

EMILY: oh don't, my hands are

FRANK: Yes but you know it's the parents   set them going
And telephone calls   our number is changed now, but

EMILY: my hands are shaking so
we are both on medication   the doctor says,

FRANK: oh you would not believe, you would not   believe   the hatred
like Nazi Germany

EMILY: Denny had to drop out of school,   he loved school he is
an honor student

FRANK: everybody turned against us

EMILY: My sister in Yonkers, he's staying with

FRANK: Oh he'll never be the same boy again.
none of us will.

VOICE: In the development of   human identity   there's the element
of chance,   and there is genetic determinism.

Would you comment please?

FRANK: The thing is,   you try your best.

EMILY: oh dear God yes.

FRANK: Your best.

EMILY: You give all that's in your heart

FRANK: you
can't do more than that can you?

EMILY: Yes but there is certain to be   justice.
There *is* a, a sense of things.

FRANK: Sometimes there is a chance, the way they   turn out
but also   what they *are.*

EMILY: Your own babies

VOICE: Frank Gulick   and Mary   what is your assessment of
American civilization   today?

EMILY: . . . it's Emily.

FRANK: My wife's name is,

EMILY: it's
Emily.

VOICE: Frank and EMILY   Gulick.

FRANK: . . . The state of the   civilization?

EMILY: It's so big,

FRANK: We are here to   tell our side of,

EMILY: . . . I don't know: it's a,   a Democracy

FRANK: the truth is,   do you want the truth?
the truth is where we live
Lakepointe
it's changing too

EMILY: it has changed

FRANK: Yes but it's all over, it's
terrible, just terrible

EMILY: Now we are grandparents we fear for

FRANK: Yes what you read and see on TV

EMILY: You don't know what to think,

FRANK: Look: in this country   half the crimes
are committed by the,   by half the population against
the other half.   *(laughs)*
You have your law-abiding citizens,

EMILY: taxpayers

FRANK: and you have the   rest of them
Say you went downtown into a city like   Newark, some night
    EMILY: you'd be crazy if you got out of your car
    FRANK: you'd be dead.   That's what.
    VOICE: Is it possible,   probable   or in your assessment *im*probable
that the slaying of   fourteen-year-old   Edith Kaminsky
    on February 12, 1990   is related to
            the social malaise
      of which you speak?
    FRANK: . . . "ma-lezz"?
    EMILY: . . . oh it's hard to,   I would say yes
    FRANK: . . . whoever did it, he
    EMILY: Oh it's terrible the things that
keep happening
    FRANK: If only the police would arrest the right person,
    VOICE: Frank and Emily Gulick   you remain adamant in your belief
in your faith in your twenty-two-year-old son   Carl
    that he is innocent   in the death of
      fourteen-year-old Edith Kaminsky
        on February 12, 1990?
    EMILY: Oh yes,
    FRANK: oh yes that is
the single thing we are convinced of.
    EMILY: On this earth.
    BOTH: With God as our witness,
    FRANK: yes
    EMILY: Yes.
    FRANK: The single thing.

Lights down.

Scene 3.

Lights up. Screen shows violent movement: urban scenes, police patrol cars, a fire burning out of control, men being arrested and herded into vans; a body lying in the street. The GULICKS *stare at the screen.*

    VOICE: Of today's pressing political issues   the rise in violent crime
most concerns American citizens   Number-one political issue of
    Mr. and Mrs. Gulick   tell our viewers your opinion?
    FRANK: In this state,
the state of New Jersey
    EMILY: Oh it's everywhere
    FRANK: there's capital punishment supposedly
    EMILY: But the lawyers   the lawyers get them off,

FRANK: you bet
There's public defenders the taxpayer pays
    EMILY: Oh, it's   it's out of control
(like that, what is it   "acid rain"
    FRANK: it can fall on you anywhere,
    EMILY: the sun is too hot too:
    BOTH: the "greenhouse effect")
    FRANK: It's a welfare state by any other name
    EMILY: Y'know who pays:
    BOTH: the taxpayer
    FRANK: The same God damn criminal, you pay for him   then he
That's the joke of it *(laughs)*
the same criminal who slits your throat *(laughs)*
He's the one you pay bail for, to get out.
But it sure isn't funny.   *(laughs)*
    EMILY: Oh God.
    FRANK: It sure isn't funny.
    VOICE: Many Americans have come to believe   this past decade that
capital punishment is one of the   answers: would you
comment please?
    FRANK: Oh in cases of actual, proven   murder
    EMILY: Those drug dealers
    FRANK: Yes *I* would have to say, definitely   yes
    EMILY: I would say so yes
    FRANK: You always hear them say   opponents of the death penalty
"The death penalty doesn't stop crime"
    EMILY: Oh that's what they say!
    FRANK: Yes but *I* say, once a man is dead   he sure ain't gonna commit
any more crimes, is he.   *(laughs)*
    VOICE: The death penalty *is* a deterrent to crime   in those cases
when the criminal has been   executed
FRANK: But you have to find the right,
the actual murderer.
EMILY: Not some poor innocent*   some poor innocent*

Lights down.

Scene 4.

Lights up. Screen shows a grainy magnified snapshot of a boy about ten. Quick jump to a snapshot of the same boy a few years older. Throughout this scene images of "Carl Gulick" appear and disappear on the screen though not in strict relationship to what is being said, nor in chronological order. "Carl Gulick" in his late teens and early

---

*"Innocent" is an adjective here, not a noun. [Author's note].

twenties is muscular but need not have any other outstanding characteristics: he may look like any American boy at all.

VOICE: Carl Gulick, twenty-two years old   the second-born child of Frank and Emily Gulick of Lakepointe, New Jersey   How would you describe your son, Frank and Emily

FRANK: D'you mean how he looks or . . .?

EMILY: He's a shy boy, he's   shy   Not backward just

FRANK: He's about my height I guess   brown hair, eyes

EMILY: Oh! no I think   no he's much taller Frank he's been taller than you   for years

FRANK: Well that depends on how we're both standing. How we're both   standing Well in one newspaper it said six feet one inch, in the other six feet three inches, that's the kind of

EMILY: accuracy

FRANK: reliability of the news media you can expect!

EMILY: And oh that terrible picture of, in the paper that face he was making   the police carrying him against his will   laying their hands on him

FRANK: handcuffs

EMILY: Oh that isn't *him*

BOTH: that isn't our son

(GULICKS *respond dazedly to snapshots flashed on screen.*)

EMILY: Oh! that's Carl   age I guess about

FRANK: four?

EMILY: that's at the beach one summer

FRANK: only nine or ten, he was big for

EMILY: With his sister Judith

FRANK: that's my brother George

EMILY: That's

FRANK: he loved Boy Scouts,

EMILY: but Oh when you are the actual parents it's a different

FRANK: Oh it is so different! from something just on TV.

VOICE: In times of disruption   of fracture   it is believed that human behavior moves   in unchartable leaps   History is a formal record of such   leaps   but in large-scale demographical   terms in which the   individual   is   lost Frank and Emily Gulick it's said your son   Carl   charged in the savage slaying of   fourteen-year-old   shows no sign of

remorse   that is to say, *awareness* of the act:
thus the question we pose to you   Can guilt reside in those
    without conscience,
or is memory   conscience, and conscience memory?
    can "the human" reside in those
      devoid of "memory"
    EMILY: . . . Oh the main thing is,
he is innocent.
    FRANK: . . . Stake my life on it.
    EMILY: He has always been   cheerful, optimistic
    FRANK: a good boy, of course he has not
forgotten
    BOTH: He is innocent.
    EMILY: How could our son "forget" when he has nothing to
    BOTH: "forget"
    FRANK: He took that lie detector test voluntarily didn't he
    EMILY: Oh there he is   weight-lifting, I don't remember
who took that picture?
    FRANK: When you are the actual parents you see them every day,
you don't form judgments.
    VOICE: And how is your son employed, Mr. and Mrs. Kaminsky?
Excuse me: GULICK.
    FRANK: Up until Christmas he was working in
This butcher shop in East Orange
    EMILY: . . . it isn't easy, at that age
    FRANK: Before that, loading and unloading
    EMILY: at Sears at the mall
    FRANK: No: that was before, that was before the other
    EMILY: No: the job at Sears was
    FRANK: . . . Carl was working for that Italian, y'know that
    EMILY: the lawn service
    FRANK: Was that before?   or after
Oh in this butcher shop   his employer
    EMILY: yes there were hard feelings, on both sides
    FRANK: Look: you can't believe a single thing   in the newspaper
or TV
    EMILY: it's not that they lie
    FRANK: Oh yes they lie
    EMILY: not that they lie, they just   get everything wrong
    FRANK: Oh they do lie!   And it's printed and you can't stop them.
    EMILY: In this meat shop, I never wanted him to work there
    FRANK: In this shop there was pressure on him
to join the union.
    EMILY: Then the other side, his employer
did not want him to join.

He's a sensitive boy,   his stomach and nerves
He lost his appetite for weeks, he'd say "oh if you could see
some of the things I see"   "the insides of things"
and so much blood
    VOICE: There was always a loving   relationship   in the household?
    EMILY: . . . When they took him away he said,   he was so brave
he said Momma I'll be back soon
I'll be right back,   I am innocent he said
I don't know how she came to be in   our house
I don't know,   I don't know he said
I looked into my son's eyes and saw   truth shining
His eyes have always been   dark green,
like mine.
    VOICE: On the afternoon of   February 12 you have told police that
no one was home   in your house?
    EMILY: I, I was . . . I had a doctor's appointment,
My husband was working, he doesn't get home until
    FRANK: Whoever did it,   and brought her body in
    EMILY: No: they say she was   they say it,   it happened there
    FRANK: No I don't buy that,   He brought her in   carried her
whoever that was,
I believe he tried   other houses
seeing who was home and who   wasn't
and then he
    EMILY: Oh it was like lightning striking
    VOICE: Your son Dennis   was at Lakepointe High School attending a
meeting of the yearbook staff,   your son Carl has told police he
    was   riding   his   motor scooter
      in the park,
    FRANK: They dragged him like   an animal
put their hands on him like
Like Nazi Germany,
    EMILY: it couldn't be any worse
    FRANK: And that judge
it's a misuse of power, it's
    EMILY: I just don't understand
    VOICE: Your son Carl on and after   February 12   did not exhibit
(in your presence) any unusual sign of   emotion?
    agitation? guilt?
    EMILY: Every day in a house,   a household
is like the other days.   Oh you never step back,   never *see*.
Like I told them, the   police,   everybody. *He did not.*

Lights down.

Scene 5.

Lights up. Screen shows snapshots, photographs, of the murdered girl Kaminsky. Like Carl Gulick, she is anyone at all of that age: white, neither strikingly beautiful nor unattractive.

VOICE: Sometime in the evening of February 12 of this year forensic
reports say   fourteen-year-old Edith Kaminsky daughter of   neighbors
2361 Cedar Street, Lakepointe, New Jersey   multiple stab wounds,
sexual assault   strangulation
An arrest has been made but   legally or otherwise,   the absolute
identity of the murderer has yet to be
    EMILY: Oh it's so unjust,
    FRANK: the power of a single man
That judge
    EMILY: Carl's birthday is   next week
Oh God he'll be in that terrible   cold place
    FRANK: "segregated" they call it
How can a judge refuse to set bail
    EMILY: oh I would borrow a million dollars
if I could
    FRANK: Is this America or   Russia?
    EMILY: I can't stop crying
    FRANK: . . . we are both under medication you see but
    EMILY: Oh it's true he wasn't himself   sometimes.
    FRANK: But that day when it happened, that wasn't one of the times.
    VOICE: You hold out for the possibility that   the true murderer
    carried Edith Kaminsky into your house,   into your basement
thus meaning to throw suspicion on your son?
    FRANK: Our boy is guiltless that's the main thing, I will never doubt that.
    EMILY: Our body is innocent . . .   What did I say?
    FRANK: Why the hell do they make so much of
Carl lifting weights, his   muscles
He is not a freak.
    EMILY: There's lots of them   and women too, today   like that,
    FRANK: He has other interests he used to collect stamps   play baseball
    EMILY: Oh there's so much misunderstanding
    FRANK: actual lies
Because the police do not know who the murderer *is*
of course they will blame   anyone they can.

Lights down.

Scene 6.

Lights up. Screen shows the exterior of the Gulick house seen from various angles; then the interior (the basement, evidently, and the "storage area" where the young girl's body was found).

VOICE: If, as is believed, "premeditated" acts arise   out of a
mysterious sequence of neuron discharges   (in the brain)
out of what source   do
    "unpremeditated"   acts   arise?
EMILY: Nobody was down in,   in the basement
until the police came.   The storage space is behind the
water heater,   but
FRANK: My God if my son is   so shiftless   like people are saying
just look: he helped me paint the house last summer
EMILY: Yes Carl and Denny both,
FRANK: Why are they telling such   lies, our neighbors?   We have never
wished them harm,
EMILY: I believed a certain neighbor was my friend,   her and I, we
we'd go shopping together   took my car
Oh my heart is broken
FRANK: It's robin's-egg blue,   the paint turned out brighter than
when it dried, a little brighter than we'd   expected
EMILY: *I* think it's pretty
FRANK: Well.   We'll have to sell the house,   there's no choice
the legal costs   Mr. Filco our attorney has said
EMILY: He told us
FRANK: he's going to fight all the way, he believes Carl is   innocent
EMILY: My heart is broken.
FRANK: *My* heart isn't,
I'm going to fight this all the way
EMILY: A tragedy like this,   you learn fast who is your friend and who
is your enemy
FRANK: Nobody's your friend.
FRANK: The Gulicks and Kaminskys were   well acquainted?
EMILY: We lived on Cedar first,   when they moved in I don't remember:
my mind isn't right these days
FRANK: Oh yes   we knew them
EMILY: I'd have said Mrs. Kaminsky   was my friend, but
that's how people are
FRANK: Yes
EMILY: Carl knew her,   Edith
I mean, we all did
FRANK: but not well,
EMILY: just neighbors
Now they're our declared enemies, the Kaminskys
FRANK: well,   so be it.
EMILY: Oh! that poor girl   if only she hadn't,
I mean, there's no telling who   she was with,   walking home
walking home from school I guess
FRANK: Well she'd been missing overnight,
EMILY: yes overnight
FRANK: of course we were aware

FRANK: The Kaminskys came around ringing doorbells,
EMILY: then the police,
FRANK: then
they got a search party going,   Carl helped them out
EMILY: Everybody said how much he helped
FRANK: he kept at it for hours
They walked miles and miles,
he's been out of work for a while,
EMILY: he'd been looking
in the *help wanted* ads but
FRANK: . . . He doesn't like to use the telephone.
EMILY: People laugh at him he says,
FRANK: I told him no he was imagining it.
EMILY: This neighborhood:
FRANK: you would not believe it.
EMILY: Call themselves Christians
FRANK: Well   some are Jews.
EMILY: Well it's still white isn't it   a white neighborhood,   you expect
better.
VOICE: The murder weapon   has yet to be found?
FRANK: One of the neighbors had to offer an opinion,   something sarcastic
I guess
EMILY: Oh don't go into *that*
FRANK: the color of the paint   on our house
So Carl said, You don't like it, wear sunglasses.
EMILY: But,
he was smiling.
VOICE: A young man with a sense of   humor.
FRANK: Whoever hid that poor girl's
body
in the storage space of our
basement well clearly it
obviously it was   to deceive
to cast blame on our son.
EMILY: Yes   if there were fingerprints down there,
BOTH: that handprint they found on the wall
FRANK: well for God's sake it was from when Carl
was down there
BOTH: helping them
FRANK: He cooperated with them,
EMILY: Frank wasn't home,
FRANK: Carl led them downstairs
EMILY: Why they came to our house, I don't know.
Who was saying things   I don't know,
it was like everybody had gone   crazy
casting blame on all sides.

VOICE: Mr. and Mrs. Gulick   it's said that from your son's room
Lakepointe police officers confiscated   comic books, military
magazines, pornographic magazines   a cache of more than one dozen
    knives including switchblades   plus
a U.S. Army bayonet (World War II)   Nazi memorabilia
    including a "souvenir" SS helmet   (manufactured in Taiwan)
a pink plastic skull   with lightbulbs in eyes
    a naked Barbie doll, badly scratched   bitten
        numerous pictures of naked women
    and women in fashion magazines,   their eyes
breasts   crotches   cut out with a scissors
    (pause)
Do you have any comment   Mr. and Mrs. Gulick?
    FRANK: . . . .
Mainly they were hobbies,
    EMILY: I guess I don't,
    FRANK: we didn't know about
    EMILY: Well   he wouldn't allow me in his room,   to vacuum, or
    FRANK: You know how boys are
    EMILY: Didn't want his mother
    FRANK: poking her nose in
    EMILY: So . . .
    (EMILY upsets a glass of water on the floor.)
    VOICE: Police forensic findings   bloodstains, hairs, semen
    and DNA "fingerprinting"   constitute a tissue of
        circumstance   linking your son to
    EMILY: *(interrupting)*: Mr. Filco says   it's all pieced together
"Circumstantial evidence," he says   not proof
    FRANK: *I* call it bullshit   *(laughs)*
    EMILY: Oh Frank
    FRANK: *I* call it bullshit   *(laughs)*
    VOICE: Eyewitness accounts disagree,   two parties report
having seen Carl Gulick and Edith Kaminsky   walking together
    in the afternoon, in the alley   behind Cedar Street
        a third party   a neighbor   claims to have seen
the girl   in the company of a   stranger   at approximately
        4:15 p.m.   And Carl Gulick insists
he was "riding his motor scooter"   all afternoon
    FRANK: He is a boy
    EMILY: not capable of lying
    FRANK: Look: I would have to discipline him sometimes,
    EMILY: You have to, with boys
    FRANK: Oh yes you have to, otherwise
    EMILY: He was always a good eater   didn't fuss
    FRANK: He's a quiet boy

EMILY: You can't guess his thoughts
FRANK: But he loved his mother and father   respected
EMILY: Always well behaved at home
That ugly picture in the paper, oh
FRANK: THAT WASN'T HIM
EMILY: You can't believe   the cruelty in the human heart
FRANK: Giving interviews! his own teachers from the school
EMILY: Telling lies   cruel   nasty
FRANK: His own teachers from the   school
VOICE: Mr. and Mrs. Gulick   you had no suspicion
                                        no   awareness
you   had   no   sense   of   the   fact
    that the battered   raped   mutilated body of
                fourteen-year-old Edith Kaminsky
        was hidden in your basement   in a storage space
                wrapped in plastic garbage bags
for approximately   forty   hours
GULICKS: . . . .
VOICE: No consciousness of   disharmony
in your household?
FRANK: It was a day like
EMILY: It *was,*   I mean, it wasn't
FRANK: I keep the cellar clean, I   There's leakage
EMILY: Oh
Last week at my sister's   where we were staying,
we had to leave   this terrible place
in Yonkers I was crying,   I could not stop   crying
downstairs in the kitchen   three in the morning
I was standing by a window and there was suddenly   it looked
like snow!
it was moonlight moving in the window and there came a   shadow I
guess
like an eclipse?   was there an eclipse?
Oh I felt so, I felt   my heart stopped   Oh but I, I wasn't scared
I was thinking   I was seeing how the world is
how the universe *is*
it's so hard to say, I feel like a   a fool
I was gifted by this, by   seeing   how the world *is* not
how you see it   with your eyes, or talk   talk about it
I mean names you give to,   parts of it   No I mean how it *is*
when there is nobody there.
VOICE: A subliminal conviction of disharmony   may be nullified by   a
    transcendental leap of   consciousness;   to a "higher plane"
                of celestial harmony.
        would you comment   Mr. and Mrs. Gulick?

EMILY: Then Sunday night it was,
FRANK: this last week
EMILY: they came again
FRANK: threw trash on our lawn
EMILY: screamed
Murderers! they were drunk, yelling   in the night *Murderers!*
FRANK: There was the false report that Carl was released on   bail
that he was home with us,
EMILY: Oh dear God if only that was true
FRANK: I've lost fifteen pounds since February
EMILY: Oh Frank has worked so hard   on that lawn,
it's his pride and joy and in the neighborhood   everybody knows,
they compliment him,   and now
Yes he squats right out there, he pulls out crabgrass   by hand
Dumping such such ugly nasty disgusting things
Then in the A&P a woman followed me   up and down the aisles
I could hear people   *That's her, that's the mother of*
the murderer   I could hear them   everywhere in the store
Is that her,   is that the mother of the murderer? they were saying
Lived in this neighborhood, in this town for   so many years
we thought we were welcome here and now
Aren't you ashamed to show your face!   a voice screamed
What can I do with my face,   can I hide it forever?
FRANK: And all this when our boy is   innocent.
VOICE: Perceiving the inviolate nature of   the Universe   apart from human
suffering   rendered you happy, Mrs. Gulick   is this so?
    for some precious moments?
EMILY: Oh yes, I was crying but
not because of
no   I was crying because
I was happy I think.

Lights down.

Scene 7.

Lights up. Screen shows neurological X-rays, medical diagrams, charts as of EEG and CAT-scan tests.

VOICE: Is it possible that in times of   fracture, of evolutionary
unease   or, perhaps, at any time   human behavior mimics that
of minute   particles   of light?   The atom is primarily emptiness
    the neutron dense-packed
The circuitry of the human brain   circadian rhythms   can be tracked
but never,   it's said comprehended.   And then   in descent

from "identity"—(memory?)   to tissue to cells to cell-particles
   electrical impulses   axon-synapse-dendrite
         and beyond, be-
            neath
         to subatomic bits
      Where is "Carl Gulick"?
   (GULICKS *turn to each other in bewilderment. Screen flashes images: kitchen
interior; weightlifting paraphernalia; a shelf of trophies; photographs; domestic
scenes, etc.)*
      VOICE: Mr. and Mrs. Gulick you did not notice anything   unusual   in
your son's behavior on the night of February 12   or the following
day,   to the best   of your recollection?
      EMILY: . . . Oh we've told the police this so many   many times
      FRANK: Oh you forget what you remember,
      EMILY: That night, before we knew there was anyone missing   I mean, in
the neighborhood   anyone we knew
      FRANK: I can't remember.
      EMILY: Yes but Carl had supper with us like always
      FRANK: No I think,   he was napping up in his room
      EMILY: he was at the table with us:
      FRANK: I remember   he came down around nine o'clock,   but he did
eat.
      EMILY: Him and Denny, they were at the table with us
      FRANK: We've told the police this so many times, it's
I don't know any longer
      EMILY: I'm sure it was Denny too.   Both our sons.
We had meatloaf   ketchup baked on top, it's the boys'
favorite dish just about   isn't it?
      FRANK: Oh anything with hamburger and ketchup!
      EMILY: Of course he was at the table with us,   he had his usual appetite.
      FRANK: . . . he was upstairs, said he had a touch of   flu
      EMILY: Oh no he was there.
      FRANK: It's hard to speak of your own flesh and blood,   as if
they are other people
it's hard   without giving false testimony against your will.
      VOICE: Is the intrusion of the "extra-ordinary"   into the dimension of the
"ordinary"   an indication that such Aristotelian categories are
invalid?   If one day fails to resemble the preceding
      what does it resemble?
      FRANK: . . . He has sworn to us, we are his parents
He did not touch a hair of that poor child's head   let alone the rest.
Anybody who knew him, they'd know
      EMILY: Oh those trophies!   he was so proud
one of them is from the, I guess the Lakepointe YMCA
there's some from the New Jersey competition   at Atlantic City
two years ago?

FRANK: no, he was in high school
the first was, Carl was only fifteen years old
    EMILY: Our little muscleman!
    VOICE: Considering the evidence of thousands of years   of human culture
of language   art   religion   the judicial system   "The family
unit"   athletics   hobbies   fraternal organizations
charitable impulses   gods of all species
is   it   possible   that   humankind   desires
        not   to   know
            its   place   in
                the
            food cycle?
    EMILY: One day he said
he wasn't going back to school,
my heart was broken.
    FRANK: Only half his senior year ahead
but you can't argue,   not with
    EMILY: oh his temper!   he takes after,
oh I don't know who
    FRANK: we always have gotten along together
in this household   haven't we
    EMILY: yes but the teachers would laugh at him he said
girls laughed at him he said   stared and pointed at him he said
and there was this pack of   oh we're not prejudiced
against Negros,   it's just that
the edge of the Lakepointe school district
well
    FRANK: Carl got in fights sometimes
in the school cafeteria and   I guess the park?
    EMILY: the park isn't safe for law-abiding people these days
they see the color of your skin,   they'll attack
some of them are just like animals   yes they *are*
    FRANK: Actually our son was attacked first   it isn't like he got
into fights by himself
    EMILY: Who his friends are now, I don't   remember
    FRANK: He is a quiet boy, keeps to himself
    EMILY: he wanted to work
he was looking for work
    FRANK: Well: our daughter Judith was misquoted about that
    EMILY: also about Carl having a bad temper   she never said that
the reporter for the paper twisted her words
Mr. Filco says   we might sue
    FRANK: Look: our son never raised a hand against anybody let alone against
    EMILY: He loves his mother and father,   he respects us
    FRANK: He is a religious boy at heart
    EMILY: He looked me in the eyes he said   Momma you believe me don't
you?   and I said Oh yes   Oh yes   he's just my baby

FRANK: nobody knows him
EMILY: nobody knows him the way we do
FRANK: who would it be, if they did?
I ask you.

Scene 8.

House lights come up, TV screen shows video rewind. Sounds of audio rewind.
Screen shows GULICKS *onstage.*

VOICE: Frank and Mary Gulick we're very sorry   something happened to
the tape we're going to have to re-shoot   Let's go back just to,
we're showing an interior   Carl's room   the trophies
    I will say,   I'll be repeating
     Are you ready?
     (House lights out, all tech returns to normal.)
     Well Mr. and Mrs. Gulick your son has
       quite a collection of trophies!
FRANK: . . . I,   I don't remember what I
EMILY: . . . yes he,
FRANK: Carl was proud of   he had other hobbies though
EMILY: Oh he was so funny, didn't want his mother   poking in his room
he said
FRANK: Yes but that's   how boys are
EMILY: That judge refuses to set bail, which I don't   understand
FRANK: Is this the United States or   is this the Soviet Union?
EMILY: we are willing to sell our house to stand up for what is
VOICE: You were speaking of your son Carl   having quit school,
his senior year?   and then?
EMILY: . . . He had a hard time, the teachers   were down on him.
FRANK: I don't know why,
EMILY: we were never told
And now in the newspapers
FRANK: the kinds of lies they are saying
EMILY: that he got into fights, that he was
FRANK: that kind of thing is all a distortion
EMILY: He was always a quiet boy
FRANK: but he had his own friends
EMILY: they came over to the house sometime, I don't remember   who
FRANK: there was that one boy what was his name
EMILY: Oh Frank   Carl hasn't seen him in years
he had friends in grade school
FRANK: Look: in the newspaper there were false statements
EMILY: Mr. Filco says   we might sue
FRANK: Oh no: he says we can't,   we have to prove "malice"
EMILY: Newspapers and TV are filled with lies

FRANK: Look: our son Carl never raised a hand against anybody let alone
against
    EMILY: He loves his mother and father,
    FRANK: he respects us
    VOICE: Frank and,   it's Emily isn't it   Frank and Emily Gulick
       that is very moving.

Lights down.

Scene 9.

Lights up. Screen shows GULICKS *in theater.*

    VOICE: The discovery of radioactive elements   in the late nineteenth
century enabled scientists to set back the estimated age of the Earth
    to several billion years,   and the discovery in more
recent decades   that the Universe is expanding,   thus that
there is a point in Time when the Universe   was tightly
compressed   smaller than your tiniest fingernail!
    thus that the age of the Universe is many billions
       of   years
       uncountable.
Yet   humankind resides in Time,   God bless us.
    Frank and Emily Gulick as we wind down *our* time together
       What are your plans for the future?
    FRANK: . . . Oh that is, that's hard to   that's hard to answer.
    EMILY: It depends I guess on
    FRANK: Mr. Filco has advised
    EMILY: I guess it's,
next is the grand jury
    FRANK: Yes: the grand jury.
Mr. Filco cannot be present for the session   to protect our boy
I don't understand the law, just the prosecutor is there
swaying the jurors' minds
Oh I try to understand but I can't,
    EMILY: he says we should be prepared
we should be prepared for a trial
    VOICE: You are ready for the trial   to clear your son's name?
    FRANK: Oh yes . . .
    EMILY: yes that is a way of,   of putting it
Yes.   To clear Carl's name.
    FRANK: . . . Oh yes you have to be realistic.
    EMILY: Yes but before that   the true murderer of Edith Kaminsky
might come forward.
If the true murderer is watching this   *Please come forward.*
    FRANK: . . . Well we both believe Carl is protecting someone, some
friend   another boy

EMILY: the one who really   committed that terrible crime
FRANK: So all we can do is pray.   Pray Carl will come
to his senses   give police the other boy's name, or
I believe this: if it's a friend of Carl's
he must have some decency   in his heart
     VOICE: Your faith   in your son remains unshaken?
     EMILY: You would have had to see his   toes,
his tiny baby toes in his bath.
His curly hair,   splashing in the bath.
His yellow rompers or no: I guess that was Denny
     FRANK: If your own flesh and blood looks you in the eye,
you believe
     EMILY: Oh yes.
     VOICE: Human personality, it might be theorized, is a phenomenon of
memory
yet memory   built up from cells, and   atoms does not "exist":
     thus memory   like mind   like personality
        is but a fiction?
     EMILY: Oh   remembering backward is so hard!   oh it's,
     FRANK: it pulls your brain in two.
     EMILY: This medication the doctor gave me, my mouth   my mouth is so
dry
In the middle of the night I wake up drenched in
     FRANK: You don't know who you are   until a thing like this happens,
then you don't know.
     EMILY: It tears your brain in two, trying to   remember,
like even looking at the pictures
Oh you are lost.
     FRANK: in Time you are lost
     EMILY: You fall and fall,
. . . ever since the,   the butcher shop
he wasn't always himself   but
who he was then, I don't know.   But
it's so hard, remembering why.
     FRANK: Yes my wife means thinking backward the way   the way the police
make you, so many questions   you start forgetting right away
it comes out crazy.
Like now,   right here   I don't remember anything up to now
I mean, I can't swear to it: the first time, you see, we just
lived. We lived in our house. I am a, I am a post office employee
I guess I said that?   well, we live in our,   our house.
I mean, it was the first time through.   Just living.
Like the TV, the picture's always on if nobody's watching it
you know?   So,   the people we were then,
I guess I'm trying to say

those actual people, me and her   the ones you see *here*
aren't them. *(laughs)*
I guess that sounds crazy,
    VOICE: We have here the heartbeat   of parental love and faith, it's
a beautiful thing   Frank and Molly Gulick. please comment?
    FRANK: We are that boy's father and mother.
We know that our son is not a murderer and a,   a rapist
    EMILY: We know, if that girl came to harm,   there is some reason
for it to be revealed, but
they never found the knife, for one thing
    FRANK: or whatever it was
    EMILY: They never found the knife, the murderer could tell them where
it's buried, or   whatever it was.
Oh he could help us so   if he just would.
    VOICE: And your plans for the future,   Mr. and Mrs. Gulick of Lakepointe,
    New Jersey?
    FRANK: . . . Well.
I guess,   I guess we don't have any.
    (Long silence, to the point of awkwardness.)
    VOICE: . . . Plans for the future, Mr. and Mrs. Gulick of Lakepointe,
New Jersey?
    FRANK: The thing is, you discover   you need to be protected
from your own thoughts sometimes,   but
who is there to do it?
    EMILY: God didn't make any of us strong enough I guess.
    FRANK: Look: one day in a family like this, it's   like the next day
and the day before.
    EMILY: You could say it *is* the next day, I mean the same   the same day.
    FRANK: Until one day it isn't

Lights slowly down, then out.

(THE END)

ACTIVITIES FOR WRITING AND DISCUSSION

1. What functions do the various devices of electronic imagery—visual and aural—seem to serve in the play? What, if anything, would be lost if they were omitted?

2. The action and **setting** of the play suggest a live TV program, and many of the trappings of the TV medium are blatantly visible such as a "Voice"/interviewer, microphones, nervous interviewees, and monitors. What does the play imply about TV's role in the coverage and presentation of such deeds as Carl's?

3. At the beginning of scene one, the "Voice" is likened to a "television emcee," but often his language is strikingly unlike that of any TV emcee, interviewer, or talk-show host. For instance, he refers to Aristotle, "the food chain," and other matters that seem remote from the subject of the murder/rape and that fail to register any reaction from Frank and Emily. Locate several such speeches by the Voice and analyze Oates's possible motives for writing the speeches as she did.

4. Write up a list of Frank and Emily's major beliefs and values, basing it on evidence in the play. Can you make any connections between these beliefs and values and Carl's personality and crime? If not, explain. If so, give examples that illustrate the connections.

5. Citing evidence in the play about his jobs, interests, personal associations, and so on, compose a character portrait of Carl. In what ways might the character of the son be (a) a result of the character of the parents and (b) a mystery that is beyond the parents' control?

6. Recreate the life and conflicts within the Gulick household through either of the following exercises:
   a. Write a mealtime conversation among Frank, Emily, and Carl (and possibly Denny). Create some situation of conflict (borrowed from the play or invented) that will bring out the personality of each family member.
   b. In the play Emily mentions that Carl didn't like her coming into his room. Imagine that Emily enters Carl's room to vacuum it and discovers him there or that she is vacuuming the room and is caught in the act by him. Write the dialogue that occurs.

7. Like many parents, Emily and Frank try to be "good" parents, yet they conflict and clash with their children. Compose a dialogue or scene that dramatizes relationships and conflicts within a family, either your own or some imaginary family of your own creation.

MILCHA SANCHEZ-SCOTT (b. 1953)

The Cuban Swimmer

CHARACTERS

MARGARITA SUÁREZ, the swimmer
EDUARDO SUÁREZ, her father, the coach
SIMÓN SUÁREZ, her brother
AÍDA SUÁREZ, her mother
ABUELA, her grandmother

VOICE OF MEL MUNSON
VOICE OF MARY BETH WHITE
VOICE OF RADIO OPERATOR

Live conga drums can be used to punctuate the action of the play.

TIME: Summer.
PLACE: The Pacific Ocean between San Pedro and Catalina Island.

Scene 1

Pacific Ocean. Midday. On the horizon, in perspective, a small boat enters U.L.*, crosses to* U.R. *and exits. Pause. Lower on the horizon, the same boat, in larger perspective, enters* U.R.*, crosses and exits* U.L. *Blackout.*

Scene 2

Pacific Ocean. Midday. The swimmer, MARGARITA SUÁREZ, *is swimming. On the boat following behind her are her father,* EDUARDO SUÁREZ, *holding a megaphone, and* SIMÓN, *her brother, sitting on top of the cabin with his shirt off, punk sunglasses on, binoculars hanging on his chest.*

EDUARDO: *(Leaning forward, shouting in time to* MARGARITA's *swimming.) Uno, dos, uno, dos. Y uno, dos* . . . keep your shoulders parallel to the water.

SIMÓN: I'm gonna take these glasses off and look straight into the sun.

EDUARDO: *(Through megaphone.) Muy bien, muy bien* . . . but punch those arms in, baby.

SIMÓN: *(Looking directly at the sun through binoculars.)* Come on, come on, zap me. Show me something. *(He looks behind at the shoreline and ahead at the sea.)* Stop! Stop, Papi! Stop! (AÍDA SUÁREZ *and* ABUELA, *the swimmer's mother and grandmother, enter running from the back of the boat.)*

AÍDA and ABUELA: *Qué? Qué es?*

AÍDA: *Es un* shark?

EDUARDO: Eh?

ABUELA: *Que es un shark dicen?* (EDUARDO *blows whistle.* MARGARITA *looks up at the boat.)*

SIMÓN: No, Papi, no shark, no shark. We've reached the halfway mark.

ABUELA: *(Looking into the water.) A dónde está?*

AÍDA: It's not in the water.

ABUELA: Oh no? Oh no?

AÍDA: No! *A poco* do you think they're gonna have signs in the water to say you are halfway to Santa Catalina? No. It's done very scientific. *A ver, hijo,* explain it to your grandma.

SIMÓN: Well, you see Abuela—*(He points behind.)* There's San Pedro. *(He points ahead.)* And there's Santa Catalina. Looks halfway to me. (ABUELA *shakes her head and is looking back and forth, trying to make the decision, when suddenly the sound of a helicopter is heard.)*

ABUELA: *(Looking up.) Virgencita de la Caridad del Cobre. Qué es eso? (Sound of helicopter gets closer.* MARGARITA *looks up.)*

MARGARITA: Papi, Papi! *(A small commotion on the boat, with everybody pointing at the helicopter above. Shadows of the helicopter fall on the boat.* SIMÓN *looks up at it through binoculars.)* Papi—qué es? What is it?

EDUARDO: *(Through megaphone.)* Uh . . . uh . . . uh *un momentico . . . mi hija..* . . . Your papi's got everything under control, understand? Uh . . . you just keep stroking. And stay . . . uh . . . close to the boat.

SIMÓN: Wow, Papi! We're on TV man! Holy Christ, we're all over the fucking U.S.A.! It's Mel Munson and Mary Beth White!

AÍDA: *Por Dios!* SIMÓN, don't swear. And put on your shirt. (AÍDA *fluffs her hair, puts on her sunglasses and waves to the helicopter.* SIMÓN *leans over the side of the boat and yells to* MARGARITA.)

SIMÓN: Yo, Margo! You're on TV, man.

EDUARDO: Leave your sister alone. Turn on the radio.

MARGARITA: Papi! *Qué está pasando?*

ABUELA: *Que es la televisión dicen? (She shakes her head.) Porque como yo no puedo ver nada sin mis espejuelos.* (ABUELA *rummages through the boat, looking for her glasses. Voices of* MEL MUNSON *and* MARY BETH WHITE *are heard over the boat's radio.)*

MEL'S VOICE: As we take a closer look at the gallant crew of La Havana . . . and there . . . yes, there she is . . . the little Cuban swimmer from Long Beach, California, nineteen-year-old Margarita Suárez. The unknown swimmer is our Cinderella entry . . . a bundle of tenacity, battling her way through the choppy, murky waters of the cold Pacific to reach the Island of Romance . . . Santa Catalina . . . where should she be the first to arrive, two thousand dollars and a gold cup will be waiting for her.

AÍDA: Doesn't even cover our expenses.

ABUELA: *Qué dice?*

EDUARDO: Shhhh!

MARY BETH'S VOICE: This is really a family effort, Mel, and—

MEL'S VOICE: Indeed it is. Her trainer, her coach, her mentor is her father, Eduardo Suárez. Not a swimmer himself, it says here, Mr. Suárez is head usher of the Holy Name Society and the owner-operator of Suárez Treasures of the Sea and Salvage Yard. I guess it's one of those places . . .

MARY BETH'S VOICE: If I might interject a fact here, Mel, assisting in this swim is Mrs. Suárez who is a former Miss Cuba.

MEL'S VOICE: And a beautiful woman in her own right. Let's try and get a closer look. *(Helicopter sound gets louder.* MARGARITA, *frightened, looks up again.)*

MARGARITA: Papi!

EDUARDO: *(Through megaphone.) Mi hija,* don't get nervous . . . it's the press. I'm handling it.

AÍDA: I see how you're handling it.

EDUARDO: *(Through megaphone.)* Do you hear? Everything is under control. Get back into your rhythm. Keep your elbows high and kick and kick and kick and kick . . .

ABUELA: *(Finds her glasses and puts them on.)* Ay sí, es la televisión . . . *(She points to helicopter.)* Qué lindo mira . . . *(She fluffs her hair, gives a big wave.)* Alo América! Viva mi Margarita, viva todo los Cubanos en los Estados Unidos!

AÍDA: *Ay por Dios*, Cecilia, the man didn't come all this way in his helicopter to look at you jumping up and down, making a fool of yourself.

ABUELA: I don't care. I'm proud.

AÍDA: He can't understand you anyway.

ABUELA: *Viva . . . (She stops.) Simón, comó se dice viva?*

SIMÓN: Hurray.

ABUELA: Hurray for *mi* Margarita *y* for all the Cubans living *en* the United States, *y un abrazo . . .* Simón, *abrazo . . .*

SIMÓN: A big hug.

ABUELA: *Sí*, a big hug to all my friends in Miami, Long Beach, Union City, except for my son Carlos who lives in New York in sin! He lives . . . *(She crosses herself.)* in Brooklyn with a Puerto Rican woman in sin! *No decente . . .*

SIMÓN: Decent.

ABUELA: Carlos, *no decente*. This family, *decente*.

AÍDA: Cecilia, *por Dios*.

MEL'S VOICE: Look at that enthusiasm. The whole family has turned out to cheer little Margarita on to victory! I hope they won't be too disappointed.

MARY BETH'S VOICE: She seems to be making good time, Mel.

MEL'S VOICE: Yes, it takes all kinds to make a race. And it's a testimonial to the all-encompassing fairness . . . the greatness of this, the Wrigley Invitational Women's Swim to Catalina, where among all the professionals there is still room for the amateurs . . . like these, the simple people we see below us on the ragtag La Havana, taking their long-shot chance to victory. *Vaya con Dios! (Helicopter sound fading as family, including* MARGARITA, *watch silently. Static as* SIMÓN *turns radio off.* EDUARDO *walks to bow of boat, looks out on the horizon.)*

EDUARDO: *(To himself.)* Amateurs.

AÍDA: Eduardo, that person insulted us. Did you hear, Eduardo? That he called us a simple people in a ragtag boat? Did you hear . . .?

ABUELA: *(Clenching her fist at departing helicopter.) Mal-Rayo los parta!*

SIMÓN: *(Same gesture.)* Asshole! (AÍDA *follows* EDUARDO *as he goes to side of boat and stares at* MARGARITA.)

AÍDA: This person comes in his helicopter to insult your wife, your family, your daughter . . .

MARGARITA: *(Pops her head out of the water.)* Papi?

AÍDA: Do you hear me, Eduardo? I am not simple.

ABUELA: *Sí.*

AÍDA: I am complicated.

ABUELA: *Sí, demasiada complicada.*

AÍDA: Me and my family are not so simple.

SIMÓN: Mom, the guy's an asshole.

ABUELA: *(Shaking her fist at helicopter.)* Asshole!

AÍDA: If my daughter was simple she would not be in that water swimming.

MARGARITA: Simple? Papi . . .?

AÍDA: *Ahora*, Eduardo, this is what I want you to do. When we get to Santa Catalina I want you to call the TV station and demand *un* apology.

EDUARDO: *Cállete mujer! Aquí mando yo.* I will decide what is to be done.

MARGARITA: Papi, tell me what's going on.

EDUARDO: Do you understand what I am saying to you, Aída?

SIMÓN: *(Leaning over side of boat, to* MARGARITA.*)* Yo Margo! You know that Mel Munson guy on TV? He called you a simple amateur and said you didn't have a chance.

ABUELA: *(Leaning directly behind* SIMÓN.*) Mi hija, insultó a la familia. Desgraciado!!*

AÍDA: *(Leaning in behind* ABUELA.*)* He called us peasants! And your father is not doing anything about it. He just knows how to yell at me.

EDUARDO: *(Through megaphone.)* Shut up! All of you! Do you want to break her concentration? Is that what you are after? Eh? *(*ABUELA, AÍDA *and* SIMÓN *shrink back.* EDUARDO *paces before them.)* Swimming is rhythm and concentration. You win a race *aquí. (Pointing to his head.)* Now . . . *(To* SIMÓN.*)* you, take care of the boat, Aída y Mama . . . do something. Anything. Something practical. *(*ABUELA *and* AÍDA *get on knees and pray in Spanish.)* Hija, give it everything, eh? . . . *por la familia. Uno . . . dos. . . .* You must win. *(*SIMÓN *goes into cabin. The prayers continue as lights change to indicate bright sunlight, later in the afternoon.)*

Scene 3

Tableau for a couple of beats. EDUARDO *on bow with timer in one hand as he counts strokes per minute.* SIMÓN *is in the cabin steering, wearing his sunglasses, baseball cap on backwards.* ABUELA *and* AÍDA *are at the side of the boat, heads down, hands folded, still muttering prayers in Spanish.*

AÍDA and ABUELA: *(Crossing themselves.) En el nombre del Padre, del Hijo y del Espíritu Santo amén.*

EDUARDO: *(Through megaphone.)* You're stroking seventy-two!

SIMÓN: *(Singing.)* Mama's stroking, Mama's stroking seventy-two . . .

EDUARDO: *(Through megaphone.)* You comfortable with it?

SIMÓN: *(Singing)* Seventy-two, seventy-two, seventy-two for you.

AÍDA: *(Looking at the heavens.)* Ay, Eduardo, *ven acá*, we should be grateful that *Nuestro* Señor gave us such a beautiful day.

ABUELA: *(Crosses herself.) Sí, gracias a Dios.*

EDUARDO: She's stroking seventy-two, with no problem. *(He throws a kiss to the sky.)* It's a beautiful day to win.

AÍDA: *Qué hermoso!* So clear and bright. Not a cloud in the sky. *Mira! Mira!* Even rainbows on the water . . . a sign from God.

SIMÓN: *(Singing.)* Rainbows on the water . . . you in my arms . . .

ABUELA and EDUARDO: *(Looking the wrong way.) Dónde?*

AÍDA: *(Pointing toward* MARGARITA.*)* There, dancing in front of Margarita, leading her on . . .

EDUARDO: Rainbows on. . . . *Ay coño!* It's an oil slick! You . . . you . . . *(To* SIMÓN.*)* Stop the boat. *(Runs to bow, yelling.)* Margarita! Margarita! *(On the next stroke,* MARGARITA *comes up all covered in black oil.)*

MARGARITA: Papi! Papi! *(Everybody goes to the side and stares at* MARGARITA, *who stares back.* EDUARDO *freezes.)*

AÍDA: *Apúrate* Eduardo, move . . . what's wrong with you . . . *no me oíste,* get my daughter out of the water.

EDUARDO: *(Softly.)* We can't touch her. If we touch her, she's disqualified.

AÍDA: But I'm her mother.

EDUARDO: Not even by her own mother. Especially by her own mother. . . . You always want the rules to be different for you, you always want to be the exception. *(To* SIMÓN*)* And you . . . you didn't see it, eh? You were playing again?

SIMÓN: Papi, I was watching . . .

AÍDA: *(Interrupting.) Pues,* do something Eduardo. You are the big coach, the monitor.

SIMÓN: Mentor! Mentor!

EDUARDO: How can a person think around you? *(He walks off to bow, puts head in hands.)*

ABUELA: *(Looking over side.) Mira como todos los* little birds are dead. *(She crosses herself.)*

AÍDA: Their little wings are glued to their sides.

SIMÓN: Christ, this is like the La Brea tar pits.

AÍDA: They can't move their little wings.

ABUELA: *Esa niña tiene que moverse.*

SIMÓN: Yeah Margo, you gotta move, man. *(*ABUELA *and* SIMÓN *gesture for* MARGARITA *to move.* AÍDA *gestures for her to swim.)*

ABUELA: *Anda niña, muévete.*

AÍDA: Swim, *hija,* swim or the *aceite* will stick to your wings.

MARGARITA: Papi?

ABUELA: *(Taking megaphone.)* Your papi say "move it!" *(*MARGARITA *with difficulty starts moving.)*

ABUELA, AÍDA and SIMÓN. *(Laboriously counting.) Uno, dos . . . uno, dos . . . anda . . . uno, dos.*

EDUARDO: *(Running to take megaphone from* ABUELA.*) Uno, dos . . .* *(*SIMÓN *races into cabin and starts the engine.* ABUELA, AÍDA *and* EDUARDO *count together.)*

SIMÓN: *(Looking ahead.)* Papi, it's over there!

EDUARDO: Eh?

SIMÓN: *(Pointing ahead and to* R.*)* It's getting clearer over there.

EDUARDO: *(Through megaphone.)* Now pay attention to me. Go to the right. *(*SIMÓN, ABUELA, AÍDA *and* EDUARDO *all lean over side. They point ahead and to* R., *except* ABUELA, *who points to* L.*)*

FAMILY: *(Shouting together.) Para yá! Para yá! (Lights go down on boat. A special light on* MARGARITA, *swimming through the oil, and on* ABUELA, *watching her.)*

ABUELA: *Sangre de mi sangre,* you will be another to save us. *En Bolondron,* where your great-grandmother Luz Suárez was born, they say one day it rained blood. All the people, they run into their houses. They cry, they pray, *pero* your great-grandmother Luz she had *cojones* like a man. She run outside. She look straight at the sky. She shake her fist. And she say to the evil one, *"Mira . . . (Beating her chest.) coño, Diablo, aquí estoy si me quieres."* And she open her mouth, and she drunk the blood.

(Blackout.)

Scene 4

Lights up on boat. AÍDA *and* EDUARDO *are on deck watching* MARGARITA *swim.*

We hear the gentle, rhythmic lap, lap, lap, of the water, then the sound of inhaling and exhaling as MARGARITA'*s breathing becomes louder. Then* MARGARITA'*s heartbeat is heard, with the lapping of the water and the breathing under it. These sounds continue beneath the dialogue to the end of the scene.*

AÍDA: *Dios mío.* Look how she moves through the water . . .

EDUARDO: You see, it's very simple. It is a matter of concentration.

AÍDA: The first time I put her in water she came to life, she grew before my eyes. She moved, she smiled, she loved it more than me. She didn't want my breast any longer. She wanted the water.

EDUARDO: And of course, the rhythm. The rhythm takes away the pain and helps the concentration. *(Pause.* AÍDA *and* EDUARDO *watch* MARGARITA.*)*

AÍDA: Is that my child, or a seal. . . .

EDUARDO: Ah a seal, the reason for that is that she's keeping her arms very close to her body. She cups her hands and then she reaches and digs, reaches and digs.

AÍDA: To think that a daughter of mine . . .

EDUARDO: It's the training, the hours in the water. I used to tie weights around her little wrists and ankles.

AÍDA: A spirit, an ocean spirit, must have entered my body when I was carrying her.

EDUARDO: *(To* MARGARITA.*)* Your stroke is slowing down. *(Pause. We hear* MARGARITA'*s heartbeat with the breathing under, faster now.)*

AÍDA: Eduardo, that night, the night on the boat . . .

EDUARDO: Ah, the night on the boat again . . . the moon was . . .

AÍDA: The moon was full. We were coming to America. . . . *Qué romantico. (Heartbeat and breathing continue.)*

EDUARDO: We were cold, afraid, with no money, and on top of everything, you were hysterical, yelling at me, tearing at me with your nails. *(Opens his shirt, points to the base of his neck.)* Look, I still bear the scars . . . telling me that I didn't know what I was doing . . . saying that we were going to die. . . .

AÍDA: You took me, you stole me from my home . . . you didn't give me a chance to prepare. You just said we have to go now, now! Now, you said. You didn't let me take anything. I left everything behind . . . I left everything behind.

EDUARDO: Saying that I wasn't good enough, that your father didn't raise you so that I could drown you in the sea.

AÍDA: You didn't let me say even a goodbye. You took me, you stole me, you tore me from my home.

EDUARDO: I took you so we could be married.

AÍDA: That was in Miami. But that night on the boat, Eduardo. . . . We were not married, that night on the boat.

EDUARDO: *No pasó nada!* Once and for all get it out of your head, it was cold, you hated me and we were afraid. . . .

AÍDA: *Mentiroso!*

EDUARDO: A man can't do it when he is afraid.

AÍDA: Liar! You did it very well.

EDUARDO: I did?

AÍDA: *Sí.* Gentle. You were so gentle and then strong . . . my passion for you so deep. Standing next to you . . . I would ache . . . looking at your hands I would forget to breathe, you were irresistible.

EDUARDO: I was?

AÍDA: You took me into your arms, you touched my face with your finger-tips . . . you kissed my eyes . . . *la esquina de la boca y* . . .

EDUARDO: *Sí, sí,* and then . . .

AÍDA: I look at your face on top of mine, and I see the lights of Havana in your eyes. That's when you seduced me.

EDUARDO: Shhh, they're gonna hear you. *(Lights go down. Special on* AÍDA.*)*

AÍDA: That was the night. A woman doesn't forget those things . . . and later that night was the dream . . . the dream of a big country with fields of fertile land and big, giant things growing. And there by a green, slimy pond I found a giant pea pod and when I opened it, it was full of little, tiny baby frogs. *(*AÍDA *crosses herself as she watches* MARGARITA. *We hear louder breathing and heartbeat.)*

MARGARITA: Santa Teresa. Little Flower of God, pray for me. San Martín de Porres, pray for me. Santa Rosa de Lima, *Virgencita de la Caridad del Cobre,* pray for me. . . . Mother pray for me.

Scene 5

Loud howling of wind is heard, as lights change to indicate unstable weather, fog and mist. Family on deck, braced and huddled against the wind. SIMÓN *is at the helm.*

AÍDA: *Ay Dios mío, qué viento.*

EDUARDO: *(Through megaphone.)* Don't drift out . . . that wind is pushing you out. *(To* SIMÓN*)* You! Slow down. Can't you see your sister is drifting out?

SIMÓN: It's the wind, Papi.

AÍDA: Baby, don't go so far. . . .

ABUELA: *(To heaven.) Ay Gran Poder de Dios, quita este maldito viento.*

SIMÓN: Margo! Margo! Stay close to the boat.

EDUARDO: Dig in. Dig in hard. . . . Reach down from your guts and dig in.

ABUELA: *(To heaven.) Ay Virgen de la Caridad del Cobre, por lo más tú quieres a pararla.*

AÍDA: *(Putting her hand out, reaching for* MARGARITA.*)* Baby, don't go far. (ABUELA *crosses herself. Action freezes. Lights get dimmer, special on* MARGARITA. *She keeps swimming, stops, starts again, stops, then, finally exhausted, stops altogether. The boat stops moving.)*

EDUARDO: What's going on here? Why are we stopping?

SIMÓN: Papi, she's not moving! Yo Margo! *(The family all run to the side.)*

EDUARDO: Hija! . . . Hijita! You're tired, eh?

AÍDA: *Por supuesto* she's tired. I like to see you get in the water, waving your arms and legs from San Pedro to Santa Catalina. A person isn't a machine, a person has to rest.

SIMÓN: Yo, Mama! Cool out, it ain't fucking brain surgery.

EDUARDO: *(To* SIMÓN*)* Shut up, you. *(Louder to* MARGARITA.*)* I guess your mother's right for once, huh? . . . I guess you had to stop, eh? . . . Give your brother, the idiot . . . a chance to catch up with you.

SIMÓN: *(Clowning like Mortimer Snerd.)* Dum dee dum dee dum ooops, ah shucks. . . .

EDUARDO: I don't think he's Cuban.

SIMÓN: *(Like Ricky Ricardo.)* Oye Lucy! I'm home! Ba ba lu!

EDUARDO: *(Joins in clowning, grabbing* SIMÓN *in a headlock.)* What am I gonna do with this idiot, eh? I don't understand this idiot. He's not like us Margarita. *(Laughing.)* You think if we put him into your bathing suit with a cap on his head . . . *(He laughs hysterically.)* you think anyone would know . . . huh? Do you think anyone would know? *(Laughs.)*

SIMÓN: *(Vamping.)* Ay, mi amor. Anybody looking for tits would know. (EDUARDO *slaps* SIMÓN *across the face, knocking him down.* AÍDA *runs to* SIMÓN's *aid.* ABUELA *holds* EDUARDO *back.)*

MARGARITA: *Mía culpa! Mía culpa!*

ABUELA: *Qué dices hija?*

MARGARITA: Papi, it's my fault, it's all my fault. . . . I'm so cold, I can't move. . . . I put my face in the water . . . and I hear them whispering . . . laughing at me. . . .

AÍDA: Who is laughing at you?

MARGARITA: The fish are all biting me . . . they hate me . . . they whisper about me. She can't swim, they say. She can't glide. She has no grace. . . . Yellowtails, bonita, tuna, man-o'-war, snub-nose sharks, los baracudas . . . they all hate me . . . only the dolphins care . . . and sometimes I hear the whales crying . . . she is lost, she is dead. I'm so numb, I can't feel. Papi! Papi! Am I dead?

EDUARDO: *Vamos,* baby, punch those arms in. Come on . . . do you hear me?

MARGARITA: Papi . . . Papi . . . forgive me. . . . *(All is silent on the boat.* EDUARDO *drops his megaphone, his head bent down in dejection.* ABUELA, AÍDA, SIMÓN *all leaning over the side of the boat.* SIMÓN *slowly walks away.)*

AÍDA: *Mi hija, qué tienes?*

SIMÓN: Oh Christ, don't make her say it. Please don't make her say it.

ABUELA: Say what? *Qué cosa?*

SIMÓN: She wants to quit, can't you see she's had enough?

ABUELA: *Mira, para eso. Esta niña* is turning blue.

AÍDA: *Oyeme, mi hija.* Do you want to come out of the water?

MARGARITA: Papi?

SIMÓN: *(To* EDUARDO*)* She won't come out until *you* tell her.

AÍDA: Eduardo . . . answer your daughter.

EDUARDO: *Le dije* to concentrate . . . concentrate on your rhythm. Then the rhythm would carry her . . . ay it's a beautiful thing, Aída. It's like yoga, like meditation, the mind over matter . . . the mind controlling the body . . . that's how the great things in the world have been done. I wish you . . . I wish my wife could understand.

MARGARITA: Papi?

SIMÓN: *(To* MARGARITA*)* Forget him.

AÍDA: *(Imploring.)* Eduardo, *por favor.*

EDUARDO: *(Walking in circles.)* Why didn't you let her concentrate? Don't you understand, the concentration, the rhythm is everything. But no, you wouldn't listen. *(Screaming to the ocean.)* Goddam Cubans, why, God, why do you make us go everywhere with our families? *(He goes to back of boat.)*

AÍDA: *(Opening her arms.)* Mi hija, ven, come to Mami. *(Rocking.)* Your mami knows. (ABUELA *has taken the training bottle, puts it in a net. She and* SIMÓN *lower it to* MARGARITA.*)*

SIMÓN: Take this. Drink it. *(As* MARGARITA *drinks,* ABUELA *crosses herself.)*

ABUELA: *Sangre de mi sangre. (Music comes up softly.* MARGARITA *drinks, gives the bottle back, stretches out her arms, as if on a cross. Floats on her back. She begins a graceful backstroke. Lights fade on boat as special lights come up on* MARGARITA. She stops. *Slowly turns over and starts to swim, gradually picking up speed. Suddenly as if in pain she stops, tries again, then stops in pain again. She becomes disoriented and falls to the bottom of the sea. Special on* MARGARITA *at the bottom of the sea.)*

MARGARITA: *Ya no puedo* . . . I can't . . . A person isn't a machine . . . *es mi culpa* . . . Father forgive me . . . Papi! Papi! One, two. *Uno, dos. (Pause.)* Papi! *A dónde estás? (Pause)* One, two, one, two. Papi! Ay Papi! Where are you . . .? Don't leave me. . . . Why don't you answer me? *(Pause. She starts to swim, slowly.) Uno, dos, uno, dos.* Dig in, dig in. *(Stops swimming.) Por favor,* Papi! *(Starts to swim again.)* One, two, one, two. Kick from your hip, kick from your hip. *(Stops swimming. Starts to cry.)* Oh God, please. . . . *(Pause.)* Hail Mary, full of grace . . . dig in, dig in . . . the Lord is with thee. . . . *(She swims to the rhythm of her Hail Mary.)* Hail Mary, full of grace . . . dig in, dig in, . . . the Lord is with thee . . . dig in, dig in. . . . Blessed art thou among women. . . . Mommie it hurts. You let go of my hand. I'm lost. . . . And blessed is the fruit of thy womb, now and at the hour of our death. Amen. I don't want to die, I don't want to die. (MARGARITA *is still swimming. Blackout. She is gone.)*

Scene 6

Lights up on boat, we hear radio static. There is a heavy mist. On deck we see only black outline of ABUELA *with shawl over her head. We hear the voices of* EDUARDO, AÍDA *and* RADIO OPERATOR.

EDUARDO'S VOICE: La Havana! Coming from San Pedro. Over.

RADIO OPERATOR'S VOICE: Right. DT6-6, you say you've lost a swimmer.

AÍDA'S VOICE: Our child, our only daughter . . . listen to me. Her name is Margarita Inez Suárez, she is wearing a black one-piece bathing suit cut high in the legs with a white racing stripe down the sides, a white bathing cap with goggles and her whole body covered with a . . . with a . . .

EDUARDO'S VOICE: With lanolin and paraffin.

AÍDA'S VOICE: *Sí* . . . *con* lanolin and paraffin. *(More radio static. Special on* SIMÓN, *on the edge of the boat.)*

SIMÓN: Margo! Yo Margo! *(Pause)* Man don't do this. *(Pause.)* Come on. . . . Come on. . . . *(Pause.)* God, why does everything have to be so hard? *(Pause.)* Stupid. You know you're not supposed to die for this. Stupid. It's his dream and he can't even swim. *(Pause.)* Punch those arms in. Come home. Come home. I'm your little brother. Don't forget what Mama said. You're not supposed to leave me behind. *Vamos,* Margarita, take your little brother, hold his hand tight when you cross the street. He's so little. *(Pause.)* Oh Christ, give us a sign. . . . I know! I know! Margo, I'll send you a message . . . like mental telepathy. I'll hold my breath, close my eyes and I'll bring you home. *(He takes a deep breath; a few beats.)* This time I'll beep . . . I'll send out sonar signals like a dolphin. *(He imitates dolphin sounds. The sound of real dolphins takes over from* SIMÓN, *then fades into sound of* ABUELA *saying the Hail Mary in Spanish, as full lights come up slowly.)*

Scene 7

EDUARDO *coming out of cabin, sobbing,* AÍDA *holding him.* SIMÓN *anxiously scanning the horizon.* ABUELA *looking calmly ahead.*

EDUARDO: *Es mi culpa, sí, es mi culpa. (He hits his chest.)*

AÍDA: *Ya, ya viejo* . . . it was my sin . . . I left my home.

EDUARDO: Forgive me, forgive me. I've lost our daughter, our sister, our granddaughter, *mi carne, mi sangre, mis ilusiones. (To heaven.) Dios mío* take me . . . take me, I say . . . Goddammit, take me!

SIMÓN: I'm going in.

AÍDA and EDUARDO: No!

EDUARDO: *(Grabbing and holding* SIMÓN, *speaking to heaven.)* God, take me, not my children. They are my dreams, my illusions . . . and not this one, this one is my mystery . . . he has my secret dreams. In him are the parts of me I cannot see. (EDUARDO *embraces* SIMÓN. *Radio static becomes louder.)*

AÍDA: I . . . I think I see her.

SIMÓN: No it's just a seal.

ABUELA: *(Looking out with binoculars.) Mi nietacita, dónde estás? (She feels her heart.)* I don't feel the knife in my heart . . . my little fish is not lost. *(Radio crackles with static. As lights dim on boat, voices of* MEL *and* MARY BETH *are heard over the radio.)*

MEL'S VOICE: Tragedy has marred the face of the Wrigley Invitational Women's Race to Catalina. The Cuban swimmer, little Margarita Suárez, has reportedly been lost at sea. Coast Guard and divers are looking for her as we speak. Yet in spite of this tragedy the race must go on because . . .

MARY BETH'S VOICE: *(Interrupting loudly.)* Mel!

MEL'S VOICE: *(Startled.)* What!

MARY BETH'S VOICE: Ah . . . excuse me, Mel . . . we have a winner. We've just received word from Catalina that one of the swimmers is just fifty yards from the breakers . . . it's oh, it's Margarita Suárez! *(Special on family in cabin listening to radio.)*

MEL'S VOICE: What? I thought she died! *(Special on* MARGARITA, *taking off bathing cap, trophy in hand, walking on the water.)*

MARY BETH'S VOICE: Ahhh . . . unless . . . unless this is a tragic. . . . No . . . there she is, Mel. Margarita Suárez! The only one in the race wearing a black bathing suit cut high in the legs with a racing stripe down the side. *(Family cheering, embracing.)*

SIMÓN: *(Screaming.)* Way to go Margo!

MEL'S VOICE: This is indeed a miracle! It's a resurrection! Margarita Suárez with a flotilla of boats to meet her, is now walking on the waters, through the breakers . . . onto the beach, with crowds of people cheering her on. What a jubilation! This is a miracle! *(Sound of crowds cheering. Pinspot on* ABUELA.)

ABUELA: *Sangre de mi sangre* you will be another to save us,. . . . to say to the evil one, *Coño Diablo, aqui estoy si me quieres. (Lights and cheering fade. Blackout.)*

END OF PLAY

FAMILIES: ADDITIONAL ACTIVITIES FOR WRITING AND DISCUSSION

1. Reread all or a portion of your notebook. Mark any passages, however long or short, that strike you, for whatever reason. Beside each passage, write a note explaining its significance for you. Finally, pick a favorite passage and either:

    a. Expand it into a new piece of writing, or

    b. Make notes on how you *could* expand or use it at some future date, or

    c. Rewrite it in a different form (e.g., poem, dialogue, letter, memoir).

For a list of strategies for expanding or revising, see Chapter 12.

2. To what extent are children fated to be like their parents, and to what extent can they determine their own personalities and futures? Bring together two or more **characters, speakers,** or **personae** from the different texts and have them discuss this question in a dialogue. Some possible participants might include the father or son in "The Olive Grove," the mother or daughter in Olsen's "I Stand Here Ironing," Kiswana Browne in Gloria Naylor's story, the speaker/son in

Bukowski's "my old man." Begin by listing some pertinent questions and considering how the various speakers might respond to them. Then write the dialogue.

3. Several texts in this section ("Eveline," "Kiswana Browne," "Heritage," *Tone Clusters*, and *The Cuban Swimmer*, to name just a few) indicate ways that families are shaped by the larger cultures of which they are a part. Write an essay about your own family in which you discuss:

      a. Ways in which your family might be perceived as representative of some culture (ethnic, racial, religious, socioeconomic), and

      b. Ways in which your family has an identity that *transcends* that culture.

Make your essay vivid by illustrating it with specific examples and stories. If you wish, supplement your work on this essay with outside research.

4. Several texts in this thematic section incorporate—or refer to—family photographs. Emulate the creative method of Rita Dove ("Fifth Grade Autobiography"), and Joy Harjo ("The Place of Origins"), and use a family photograph (or photographs) as a springboard for writing about your family. *Alternative:* Study a photograph (wife/husband, partners, parent/child, or larger family grouping) of a family other than your own—perhaps a family of a different time or culture—and write from *that* photograph. Obviously, you will need to use your imagination and *invent* details and stories about that family. If possible, do some background research to improve your writing about this "stranger" family.

5. Sibling relationships and rivalries are a theme of several selections in this chapter, such as "The Rich Brother," "Kiswana Browne," "Sadie and Maud," and "The Elder Sister." In each case, who is involved? What are the causes and results of the conflict, and from whose point of view is the conflict related? Analyze the theme in any one text or compare and contrast its treatment in any two or more texts.

6. Review your entire notebook; as you do, make a running list of memorable or striking topics, e.g., "fathers and sons," "mothers and daughters," "siblings," "breaking free of the parent." Then choose a favorite topic, make a Topic/Form Grid (see Chapter 5), and use one of the forms on your grid to create a new notebook entry about the topic. If your chosen form does not work, do a Topic/Form Shift to a different form on your grid.

Interchapter on Notebooks and Journals (II)

"The Stories of How We Lived": Joy Harjo

Poet, essayist, editor, and children's writer, Joy Harjo's work has been closely tied to her identity as a Creek Indian. Harjo was born in 1951 in Tulsa, Oklahoma, in the heart of the Creek Nation. She attended school at the Institute of American Indian Arts in Santa Fe, New Mexico, and graduated with a B.A. degree from the University of New Mexico, Albuquerque in 1976. In 1978 she earned an MFA in creative writing from the University of Iowa Writers' Workshop, and since then she has continued both writing and teaching. Among her books are *She Had Some Horses* (1983), *Secrets from the Center of the World* (1989), *In Mad Love and War* (1990), and *The Woman Who Fell from the Sky: Poems* (1996).

The following journal selections and Harjo's prefatory note are reprinted from *The Poet's Notebook*, an anthology edited by Stephen Kuusisto, Deborah Tall, and David Weiss and published by Norton (1995).

My earliest poems were derived directly from journal work. I would write wildly and in-tuitively in my journal to rev up to the higher frequency of a poem. I'd revise and play out possibilities in the journal, then transfer to a typewriter to revise and see the final poem. Now I do most of my journaling and writing on the computer, though I keep a journal and pen by my bed for dreams. I've included a few dreams here, but most I keep to my-self, especially the very powerful, for I don't wish them to lose power by revealing them to possible misuse.

I sometimes read back through a journal to find scraps of meaning I am missing from some larger piece, when I need something personally historical, or to find a quote or some-thing else I've stuck in the pages: newspaper articles, images, or lists. It's like fishing. Sometimes I see something that totally surprises. Often I write in my journal while I am still quite asleep. These entries are the most surprising, and often include information and leaps of logic I don't figure out until something happens a few years later.

I wish I could include songs. Last night I dreamed a rewrite of a song my band and I have written to go with the poem "She Had Some Horses." We added another movement that enlarged the overall meaning. By the time I awoke to deadlines and the need to bake bread for a lunch for visiting relatives, I had forgotten it. Maybe the skill to notate in shorthand what I hear in dream music will come.

My journal is like the sketch book I used to carry around when I painted. I sketched gestures, ideas for larger drawings and paintings. Eventually everything in the sketchbook was used, whether or not I failed in the exercise of imaging. I gained knowledge of my art through each venture.

7/16/94

I can't help it, I love sweet sad ballads with heartache saxophone: Art Pepper, John Coltrane, especially Coltrane. The music breaks away at any crust of unlove to the longing for that home far from the density of years of soap opera on earth.

1/3/94

The explosion at genesis creates stones who tell the stories of how we lived. I consider the radius of intimacy and imagine you showering in the artificial light of the motel room, before dawn when most earthly spirits are returning from memory. . . . it was a tender arc marked by absolute grace and a little rain.

There is no love beyond faithful love. Le Ly Hayslip's mother, from *When Heaven and Earth Change Places*

10/19/93

The heart has four winds. I heard them last night as my son, his daughter Haleigh and I drove from a birthday dinner. It was raining and dark, difficult to differentiate between shadow and pavement. I remembered weather in the womb. . . . And then the four winds as they created the child, talked to her, shaped the elegant and tiny bones. All humans come out of the dark this way, into the dark. Each human knows a woman intimately. The four winds of the mother's heart directs the fate of the child. Perhaps the path forms the physical heart, consequently.

Remembering and imagination enter and leave from the same area of the soul.

It was hot and wet. To feel was another dimension not available to me, another field in the weave of magnetic waves—yet, approaching me were spirits who rose in waves from the brackish sweet smell of the newly dead whose corpses littered the killing ground. I'm sorry, I said, though I no longer had a mouth or a tongue. Though I no longer had words with which to approach the altar of the living.

There's a lullabye. Made to calm the ruler of sharp things.

UNDATED FROM THIS GENERAL TIME

When you grow up you either make uneasy peace with the density of destiny, and entertain the possibility of a reckless, cruel god, or watch television with the rest of the escapees.

See those sensitive hills? They need to be talked to, sung to. . . .

7/8/90 TUCSON

We descend into the damp city. I anticipate the wet flowering of the desert. And it will remind me of the warm pools of moisture under your body after we have made love, when we are at the mercy of a tenderness beyond this world.

6/3/91 HONOLULU

Full of beans, rice, sweets and a crimson tea. A light mist outside, all seven windows 15 open and trees brushing the second story. Talked of massacres, genocide at dinner last night with Haunani-Kay and her companion David—how those words don't translate, nor do body counts. What's missing are names, terms of endearment, and stories. There's always been a problem negotiating from the language of commerce to the spiritual realm. . . . The smells here are so old, sweet and familiar.

6/4/91

Some spirits go willingly (at death). In the tragedy of massacre the shock of rolling thoughtlessness can trap one in the house of disbelief. The body is a house of memory that decay cannot loosen.

11/10/91

"Blazing above Powell Observatory near Louisburg, Kansas, the aurora borealis filled the sky Friday evening. The northern lights, not usually seen this far south, painted the sky with shimmering curtains of reds, greens, blues and whites. Chances for more displays are good tonight and later this week. Get away from city lights and look north any time after dark." The *Kansas City Star,* Front page.

6/20/91

The first thought is of the angel of death, who can take everything but the heart rooted to acts of imagination. What is imagined and what is not?

In the first dream her spirit had knocked on the door of my truck. She was living in the Fifth World, or are we in it?

I don't think worlds are as easily defineable as that . . . they exist simultaneously. 20 The people are always emerging. They are always falling through the hole in the sky.

I think death has been overrated. I heard too many fire and brimstone stories from the stiff pews of Christians. I saw too many cheap Hollywood movies featuring winners and losers, though no one ever won. No Indians survived. In Ecuador the tribes from the southern hemisphere thought we'd all been killed by John Wayne. Now *there's* an angel of death.

And what of my friend who this afternoon weeded her garden, wielding a cigarette in one hand as she coughed with the cancer eating her, a friend on each side holding her up? She wants to leave with a little grace, yet doesn't want to leave at all. What do we know about anything?

We cannot escape memory, but carry it in us like a huge organ with lungs sucking air for survival. It is an organ like the skin, covering everything, but from the inside.

Was there ever mercy? Is Mercy an errant angel so horrified by cruel acts of humans she cannot bear to look on us? Mercy, come find us in the labyrinth of cruelty.

I don't know what to tell you, beloved.   25

2/10/92 BONN
In Beethoven's house . . . there is no evidence of Beethoven's mother in this place. Who was she? There would be no Beethoven without her.

10/20/92
I felt the immensity of my anger for the first time. I felt totally present as yellow sharpened itself against the blue sky.

3/9/93
Each path reeked of afterbirth, rain and mice. . . . Humans only think we can bend time into increments of money.

3/25/93
As soon as I stepped from the automatic glass doors of the hotel a dragonfly alit on my arm. I once knew that language.

8/10/93
(From these notes came the poem "The Naming," for my granddaughter Haleigh 30
Sara, who was born in Green Bay, Wisconsin. The poem with story follows.)

The most honorable wars weren't fought with swords or the yelling of fools. The greatest thinkers (each representing their tribe) sat on opposite hills and had a contest to outimagine the other. You can manipulate an enemy's weakness so the enemy destroys himself/herself with foolishness.

Names are the least idle of sounds. The night after she was born I spent the night in a hotel near the lake left over from the ice age. A conference of tribes gathered in the ballroom a few floors below.

I think of names that have profoundly changed the direction of disaster. Of the raw whirling wind outlining femaleness emerging from the underworld. It blesses the frog taking refuge under the squash flower cloud, the stubborn weeds leaning in the direction of the wind.

Clouds scheme and provoke a glitter of electricity.

The Naming
For Haleigh Sara Bush

I think of names that have profoundly changed the direction of disaster. Of the raw whirling wind outlining femaleness emerging from the underworld. 35

It blesses the frog taking refuge under the squash-flower cloud, the stubborn weeds leaning in the direction of wind bringing rain.

My grandmother is the color of night as she tells me to move away from the window when it is storming. *The lightning will take you.*

I thought it was my long dark hair appearing as lightning. The lightning appears to be relatives.

Truth can appear as disaster in a land of things unspoken. It can be reached with white arrows, each outlining the meaning of delicate struggle.

And can happen on a night like this when the arrow light is bitten by sweet wind.

My grandmother took leave years ago by way of her aggravated heart. I haven't seen her since, but her warnings against drownings, lightning or anything else portending death by sudden means still cling to my ears.

I take those risks against the current of warnings as if she had invented negative space of wind around the curve of earth.

That night after my granddaughter-born-for-my-son climbed from the underworld we could smell ozone over the lake made of a few centuries of rain.

I went hunting for the right name and found the spirit of the ice age making plans in the bottom of the lake. Eventually the spirit will become rain, remake the shoreline with pines and laughter.

In the rain I saw the child who was carried by lightning to the other side of the storm. I saw my grandmother who never had any peace in this life blessed with animals and songs.

Oh daughter-born-of-my-son, of my grandmother, of my mother; I name you all these things:

The bag of white arrows is heavy with rain.

The earth is wet with happiness.

I never liked my mother's mother, Leona May Baker. When we would visit her and my grandfather in their two-room house in northwestern Arkansas where they were sharecroppers, she would awaken me long before dawn. I would be irritable with lack of sleep as she would sit by my bed and catalogue the gruesome details of every death of every relative and friend as well as each event of personal disaster within her known landscape.

My grandmother, who was half Cherokee and Irish, was orphaned at a very young age and raised by full-blood Cherokees in Jay, Oklahoma. She gave birth to six sons and one daughter—my mother. Each birth added to the burden of life. Once she took out a gun and shot at all of them as they ran through the trees to get away from her. My mother recalls the sounds of bullets flying by her head. My grandmother disliked my mother.

With the impending birth of my son's daughter I was prompted to find out more about this grandmother who I had never made peace with. My mother told me of her incredible gift of storytelling, how she would keep the children entranced for weeks by tales she would invent—they had no books, television or radio. And then she told me this story:

My grandfather Desmond Baker left to work on the railroad when they were especially destitute. While he was away my grandmother had an affair. When he returned nine months later she was near full term with a baby who wasn't his. He beat her until she went into labor and gave birth to the murdered child.

Shortly after the killing my grandparents attempted double suicide. They stood on the 40 *tracks while a train bore down on them as all the children watched in horror. At the last possible second my grandfather pushed my grandmother off to safety and leaped behind her.*

I began to have compassion for this woman who was weighted down with seven children and no opportunities. Maybe her affair was the lightness she needed to stay alive.

When my granddaughter Haleigh was born I felt the spirit of this grandmother in the hospital room. Her presence was a blessing.

I welcomed her.

- The spirit who came to take care of my heart
- The eating and sculpting with shit episode
- Relentless toilet training
- Polio scare and hospital:
      separation
      spinal tap
- Father in jail
- Father chopping the Christmas tree top off with an ax in the living room
- My brother's birth
- My mother's scarlet fever. I am sent far away to relatives I dislike. They take my stuffed black cat away from me and try to replace it with a doll. I am bereft.
- The "following sound" revelation, set off by a trumpet jazz solo on the radio as I am just learning language.
- Difficult birth and separation
- Sun mote language
- Sexual play retribution in public
- Stomach aches, throwing up and castor-oil
- I begin hiding from my father
- Carried home from parents' parties wrapped in my father's brown leather jacket, smells of her perfume White Shoulders

- The babysitter scene, a house at night filled with strange and frightened children cared for by an elderly man and woman. I am terrified. They put me to bed in a crib. My friend Ronnie, whose parents beat him for wetting his pants, comforts me.

3/23/94

My father, too, continued to drink. His white co-workers called him "chief." He 45
just drank off the sting. . . . My parents both liked to dance and party and some of my favorite memories the few years just before the birth of my sister was being a child running with other children at these parties. And carried to the car after I'd fallen asleep, wrapped in the leather bomber jacket that had been my father's but taken over by my mother. It smelled of White Shoulders and tobacco. The smell was home to me, and it was comforting to be carried in, tucked into my Army cot to sleep. I could feel the tenderness well up in my parents as they looked at me, as I feigned sleep. . . . His violence became a thick monster whirling through the rooms of the house. I saw this thing once as it pounded on the front door on Saturday afternoon. My mother grabbed up my little brother and me and we hid in the back bedroom.

4/8/94

Certain numbers chase you through life. The house I was raised in until I was eight was number 419. (Later we moved into a house that had so many traumatic experiences I could not find it when I went back a few years ago, though I knew the street and the number. It was there, though I could not see it. My mother now rented it out.) Nearly forty years later I was picked up at the airport in Albuquerque, from Tucson, by an old friend for a reading to be held at the law school the next afternoon. It was a perfect spring night and my blood went excited at the familiar smell of the land to which I returned as a relative. My blood also felt the halo of impact preceding a life changing event. When I read the address to the house to which I'd been invited for a little wine and talk before retiring, I knew something would change. The house number was distinctly 419. . . . I soon lived in that house. It became the home I had been approaching for many years.

W. H. Auden ". . . poetry makes nothing happen; it survives."

3/24/94 (in between Albuquerque and Chicago)

What was certain was a sensitivity that crackled and burned. I could hear words and the roots of words veering from the base of silence. I wonder where my father is now in the stream of all things that once had a place here? Does he think of me or of the tragedy of connection? Did he ever experience beauty from the inside out? There's a dinosaur under the house, and other bones of those who once walked the surface of the planet, like my father. I've considered this planet as a prison, a school for the hard headed. . . . What comes back to me is the result of my actions for instance—fury begets fury. The form may change. Hatred is self-hatred, though it may mask as xenophobia or other forms of fear and aggression.

1/26/94

In this dream Rainy, Sue and I walk under a huge overpass to watch the planes taking off and landing at an airport about the size of LAX. We are so close it is frightening. One plane falters, then goes down. It is absolutely terrifying, particularly to listen as the breaking apart metal monster slides across the grass towards us. We run hard away from it, in anticipation of the explosion. I've dreamed many variations of this scene. It's always just as horrifying.

2/7/94

Sandra Cisneros is holding a turtle. I am aware that turtles can snap, bite hard, but 50 this turtle reaches out his head to nudge me. The turtle then turns into a baby boy in a high chair. Or he appears to be a baby boy in a high chair. He's pissed because he's a fully conscious human in a baby's body. I tell him he can pass as a dwarf once he can walk.

7/26/94

To be born into a family of mixed nations, involving alliances and enmities from time immemorial, in a land of refugees from persecution in Europe, the Americas, Asia and anywhere else there are evil governments and religious fundamentalists who mete out destiny, or of forced slavery over an ocean turned red from the blood of those who didn't survive, or moved from homelands against the will of the tribes—the land on which all are to be settled amicably into a "melting pot"—is to be disturbed and shaped by the spirits of ancestors who fight it out among themselves in the world intersecting the physical, who cannot rest because the direct track to the original heart has been lost, (and it's easy to get distracted by neon, fast food and the appearance of nude bodies on billboards), as well as fiercely loved and guarded by those who see themselves in you, a promise for continuance when continuance is a myth buried in libraries and in stories told under the stars in sacred languages that have been kept burning by sheer will, sheer love.

SOMETIME EARLIER

I was the first born, arrived with great difficulty to this tempestuous love, this shakey sea. I was born during a new moon, a moon that represents new beginnings, the direction East. East is the harbor for those spirits who point us on our journey. East is the direction of our tribal homelands, the place of forced exile not but a few generations ago—in the southeast of this continent, made of nearly tropical foliage, water, and thick with animal power. My birth contradicted the prediction of destruction, the myth of the vanishing Indian that was bought and sold by the American public, for if we disappeared guilt would vanish, and the right to the land by strangers would be sealed. Though we lost over half the tribe during the forced walk from a land that had nurtured our people through millennia, we didn't die. I was the next loop in the spiral of memory.

ACTIVITIES FOR WRITING AND DISCUSSION

1. Harjo writes, "I keep a journal and pen by my bed for dreams. . . . Often I write in my journal while I am still quite asleep." Following Harjo's example, keep a notepad at your bedside for jotting down dreams or thoughts you have in the middle of the night.

2. Harjo compares rereading her journal to "fishing. Sometimes I see something that totally surprises." Ponder this comparison. Does it jibe with any experiences you have had rereading your own notebook or journal? Explain.

3. While the bulk of your writer's notebook naturally consists of your own writing, Harjo's mention of newspaper articles in the pages of her journal suggests the possibility of including other materials as well, such as photographs, clippings, memorabilia, song lyrics, and drawings. Experiment with incorporating these or any other alternative materials into your notebook. What are the benefits?

4. Respond to Harjo's journal selections using any of the "Generic Ideas for Writing" found on pages 192–193.

Experience and Identity

D. H. Lawrence (1885–1930)

The Rocking-Horse Winner

There was a woman who was beautiful, who started with all the advantages, yet 1
she had no luck. She married for love, and the love turned to dust. She had bonny
children, yet she felt they had been thrust upon her, and she could not love them.
They looked at her coldly, as if they were finding fault with her. And hurriedly she
felt she must cover up some fault in herself. Yet what it was that she must cover up
she never knew. Nevertheless, when her children were present, she always felt the
centre of her heart go hard. This troubled her, and in her manner she was all the
more gentle and anxious for her children, as if she loved them very much. Only
she herself knew that at the centre of her heart was a hard little place that could
not feel love, no, not for anybody. Everybody else said of her: "She is such a good
mother. She adores her children." Only she herself, and her children themselves,
knew it was not so. They read it in each other's eyes.

There were a boy and two little girls. They lived in a pleasant house, with a gar- 2
den, and they had discreet servants, and felt themselves superior to anyone in the
neighbourhood.

Although they lived in style, they felt always an anxiety in the house. There 3
was never enough money. The mother had a small income, and the father had a
small income, but not nearly enough for the social position which they had to
keep up. The father went into town to some office. But though he had good prospects, these prospects never materialised. There was always the grinding sense of
the shortage of money, though the style was always kept up.

At last the mother said: "I will see if *I* can't make something." But she did not 4
know where to begin. She racked her brains, and tried this thing and the other,
but could not find anything successful. The failure made deep lines come into her
face. Her children were growing up, they would have to go to school. There must
be more money, there must be more money. The father, who was always very
handsome and expensive in his tastes, seemed as if he never *would* be able to do
anything worth doing. And the mother, who had a great belief in herself, did not
succeed any better, and her tastes were just as expensive.

And so the house came to be haunted by the unspoken phrase: *There must be* 5
more money! There must be more money! The children could hear it all the time,
though nobody said it aloud. They heard it at Christmas, when the expensive and
splendid toys filled the nursery. Behind the shining modern rocking-horse, behind the smart doll's house, a voice would start whispering: "There *must* be more
money! There *must* be more money!" And the children would stop playing, to listen for a moment. They would look into each other's eyes, to see if they had all
heard. And each one saw in the eyes of the other two that they too had heard.
"There *must* be more money! There *must* be more money!"

It came whispering from the springs of the still-swaying rocking-horse, and 6
even the horse, bending his wooden, champing head, heard it. The big doll, sitting so pink and smirking in her new pram, could hear it quite plainly, and
seemed to be smirking all the more self-consciously because of it. The foolish
puppy, too, that took the place of the teddy-bear, he was looking so extraordinarily foolish for no other reason but that he heard the secret whisper all over the
house: "There *must* be more money!"

Yet nobody ever said it aloud. The whisper was everywhere, and therefore no 7
one spoke it. Just as no one ever says: "We are breathing!" in spite of the fact that
breath is coming and going all the time.

"Mother," said the boy Paul one day, "Why don't we keep a car of our own? 8
Why do we always use uncle's, or else a taxi?"

"Because we're the poor members of the family," said the mother. 9

"But why *are* we, mother?" 10

"Well—I suppose," she said slowly and bitterly, "it's because your father has 11
no luck."

The boy was silent for some time. 12

"Is luck money, mother?" he asked, rather timidly. 13

"No, Paul. Not quite. It's what causes you to have money." 14

"Oh!" said Paul vaguely. "I thought when Uncle Oscar said *filthy lucker*, it 15
meant money."

"*Filthy lucre* does mean money," said the mother. "But it's lucre, not luck." 16

"Oh!" said the boy. "Then what is luck, mother?" 17

"It's what causes you to have money. If you're lucky you have money. That's 18
why it's better to be born lucky than rich. If you're rich, you may lose your money.
But if you're lucky, you will always get more money."

"Oh! Will you? And is father not lucky?" 19

"Very unlucky, I should say," she said bitterly. 20

The boy watched her with unsure eyes.   21

"Why?" he asked.   22

"I don't know. Nobody ever knows why one person is lucky and another   23
unlucky."

"Don't they? Nobody at all? Does *nobody* know?"   24

"Perhaps God. But He never tells."   25

"He ought to, then. And aren't you lucky either, mother?"   26

"I can't be, if I married an unlucky husband."   27

"But by yourself, aren't you?"   28

"I used to think I was, before I married. Now I think I am very unlucky   29
indeed."

"Why?"   30

"Well—never mind! Perhaps I'm not really," she said.   31

The child looked at her to see if she meant it. But he saw, by the lines of her   32
mouth, that she was only trying to hide something from him.

"Well, anyhow," he said stoutly, "I'm a lucky person."   33

"Why?" said his mother, with a sudden laugh.   34

He stared at her. He didn't even know why he had said it.   35

"God told me," he asserted, brazening it out.   36

"I hope He did, dear!" she said, again with a laugh, but rather bitter.   37

"He did, mother!"   38

"Excellent!" said the mother, using one of her husband's exclamations.   39

The boy saw she did not believe him; or rather, that she paid no attention to   40
his assertion. This angered him somewhat, and made him want to compel her
attention.

He went off by himself, vaguely, in a childish way, seeking for the clue to   41
"luck." Absorbed, taking no heed of other people, he went about with a sort of
stealth, seeking inwardly for luck. He wanted luck, he wanted it, he wanted it.
When the two girls were playing dolls in the nursery, he would sit on his big rocking-horse, charging madly into space, with a frenzy that made the little girls peer
at him uneasily. Wildly the horse careered, the waving dark hair of the boy tossed,
his eyes had a strange glare in them. The little girls dared not speak to him.

When he had ridden to the end of his mad little journey, he climbed down and   42
stood in front of his rocking-horse, staring fixedly into its lowered face. Its red
mouth was slightly open, its big eye was wide and glassy-bright.

"Now!" he would silently command the snorting steed. "Now, take me to   43
where there is luck! Now take me!"

And he would slash the horse on the neck with the little whip he had asked   44
Uncle Oscar for. He *knew* the horse could take him to where there was luck, if
only he forced it. So he would mount again and start on his furious ride, hoping
at last to get there. He knew he could get there.

"You'll break your horse, Paul!" said the nurse.   45

"He's always riding like that! I wish he'd leave off!" said his elder sister Joan.   46

But he only glared down on them in silence. Nurse gave him up. She could   47
make nothing of him. Anyhow, he was growing beyond her.

One day his mother and his Uncle Oscar came in when he was on one of his 48
furious rides. He did not speak to them.

"Hallo, you young jockey! Riding a winner?" said his uncle. 49

"Aren't you growing too big for a rocking-horse? You're not a very little boy 50
any longer, you know," said his mother.

But Paul only gave a blue glare from his big, rather close-set eyes. He would 51
speak to nobody when he was in full tilt. His mother watched him with an anxious
expression on her face.

At last he suddenly stopped forcing his horse into the mechanical gallop and 52
slid down.

"Well, I got there!" he announced fiercely, his blue eyes still flaring, and his 53
sturdy long legs straddling apart.

"Where did you get to?" asked his mother. 54

"Where I wanted to go," he flared back at her. 55

"That's right, son!" said Uncle Oscar. "Don't you stop till you get there. What's 56
the horse's name?"

"He doesn't have a name," said the boy. 57

"Gets on without all right?" asked the uncle. 58

"Well, he has different names. He was called Sansovino last week." 59

"Sansovino, eh? Won the Ascot. How did you know this name?" 60

"He always talks about horse-races with Bassett," said Joan. 61

The uncle was delighted to find that his small nephew was posted with all the 62
racing news. Bassett, the young gardener, who had been wounded in the left foot
in the war and had got his present job through Oscar Cresswell, whose batman he
had been, was a perfect blade of the "turf." He lived in the racing events, and the
small boy lived with him.

Oscar Cresswell got it all from Bassett. 63

"Master Paul comes and asks me, so I can't do more than tell him, sir," said 64
Bassett, his face terribly serious, as if he were speaking of religious matters.

"And does he ever put anything on a horse he fancies?" 65

"Well—I don't want to give him away—he's a young sport, a fine sport, sir. 66
Would you mind asking him yourself? He sort of takes a pleasure in it, and perhaps he'd feel I was giving him away, sir, if you don't mind."

Bassett was serious as a church. 67

The uncle went back to his nephew and took him off for a ride in the car. 68

"Say, Paul, old man, do you ever put anything on a horse?" the uncle asked. 69

The boy watched the handsome man closely. 70

"Why, do you think I oughtn't to?" he parried. 71

"Not a bit of it! I thought perhaps you might give me a tip for the Lincoln." 72

The car sped on into the country, going down to Uncle Oscar's place in 73
Hampshire.

"Honour bright?" said the nephew. 74

"Honour bright, son!" said the uncle. 75

"Well, then, Daffodil." 76

"Daffodil! I doubt it, sonny. What about Mirza?" 77

"I only know the winner," said the boy. "That's Daffodil."   78

"Daffodil, eh?"   79

There was a pause. Daffodil was an obscure horse comparatively.   80

"Uncle!"   81

"Yes, son?"   82

"You won't let it go any further, will you? I promised Bassett."   83

"Bassett be damned, old man! What's he got to do with it?"   84

"We're partners. We've been partners from the first. Uncle, he lent me my first   85
five shillings, which I lost. I promised him, honour bright, it was only between me
and him; only you gave me that ten-shilling note I started winning with, so I
thought you were lucky. You won't let it go any further, will you?"

The boy gazed at his uncle from those big, hot, blue eyes, set rather close   86
together. The uncle stirred and laughed uneasily.

"Right you are, son! I'll keep your tip private. Daffodil, eh? How much are you   87
putting on him?"

"All except twenty pounds," said the boy. "I keep that in reserve."   88

The uncle thought it a good joke.   89

"You keep twenty pounds in reserve, do you, you young romancer? What are   90
you betting, then?"

"I'm betting three hundred," said the boy gravely. "But it's between you and   91
me, Uncle Oscar! Honour bright?"

The uncle burst into a roar of laughter.   92

"It's between you and me all right, you young Nat Gould," he said, laughing.   93
"But where's your three hundred?"

"Bassett keeps it for me. We're partners."   94

"You are, are you! And what is Bassett putting on Daffodil?"   95

"He won't go quite as high as I do, I expect. Perhaps he'll go a hundred and   96
fifty."

"What, pennies?" laughed the uncle.   97

"Pounds," said the child, with a surprised look at his uncle. "Bassett keeps a   98
bigger reserve than I do."

Between wonder and amusement Uncle Oscar was silent. He pursued the   99
matter no further, but he determined to take his nephew with him to the Lincoln
races.

"Now, son," he said, "I'm putting twenty on Mirza, and I'll put five on for you   100
on any horse you fancy. What's your pick?"

"Daffodil, uncle."   101

"No, not the fiver on Daffodil!"   102

"I should if it was my own fiver," said the child.   103

"Good! Good! Right you are! A fiver for me and a fiver for you on Daffodil."   104

The child had never been to a race-meeting before, and his eyes were blue fire.   105
He pursed his mouth tight and watched. A Frenchman just in front had put his
money on Lancelot. Wild with excitement, he flayed his arms up and down,
yelling "*Lancelot! Lancelot!*" in his French accent.

Daffodil came in first, Lancelot second, Mirza third. The child, flushed and 106
with eyes blazing, was curiously serene. His uncle brought him four five-pound
notes, four to one.

"What am I to do with these?" he cried, waving them before the boy's eyes. 107

"I suppose we'll talk to Bassett," said the boy. "I expect I have fifteen hundred 108
now; and twenty in reserve; and this twenty."

His uncle studied him for some moments. 109

"Look here, son!" he said. "You're not serious about Bassett and that fifteen 110
hundred, are you?"

"Yes, I am. But it's between you and me, uncle. Honour bright?" 111

"Honour bright all right, son! But I must talk to Bassett." 112

"If you'd like to be a partner, uncle, with Bassett and me, we could all be part- 113
ners. Only, you'd have to promise, honour bright, uncle, not to let it go beyond
us three. Bassett and I are lucky, and you must be lucky, because it was your ten
shillings I started winning with. . . ."

Uncle Oscar took both Bassett and Paul into Richmond Park for an afternoon, 114
and there they talked.

"It's like this, you see, sir," Bassett said. "Master Paul would get me talking 115
about racing events, spinning yarns, you know, sir. And he was always keen on
knowing if I'd made or if I'd lost. It's about a year since, now, that I put five
shillings on Blush of Dawn for him; and we lost. Then the luck turned, with that
ten shillings he had from you: that we put on Singhalese. And since that time, it's
been pretty steady, all things considering. What do you say, Master Paul?"

"We're all right when we're sure," said Paul. "It's when we're not quite sure that 116
we go down."

"Oh, but we're careful then," said Bassett. 117

"But when are you *sure?*" smiled Uncle Oscar. 118

"It's Master Paul, sir," said Bassett in a secret, religious voice. "It's as if he had 119
it from heaven. Like Daffodil, now, for the Lincoln. That was as sure as eggs."

"Did you put anything on Daffodil?" asked Oscar Cresswell. 120

"Yes, sir. I made my bet." 121

"And my nephew?" 122

Bassett was obstinately silent, looking at Paul. 123

"I made twelve hundred, didn't I, Bassett? I told uncle I was putting three hun- 124
dred on Daffodil."

"That's right," said Bassett, nodding. 125

"But where's the money?" asked the uncle. 126

"I keep it safe locked up, sir. Master Paul he can have it any minute he likes to 127
ask for it."

"What, fifteen hundred pounds?" 128

"And twenty! And *forty*, that is, with the twenty he made on the course." 129

"It's amazing!" said the uncle. 130

"If Master Paul offers you to be partners, sir, I would, if I were you: if you'll ex- 131
cuse me," said Bassett.

Oscar Cresswell thought about it. 132

"I'll see the money," he said.   133

They drove home again, and, sure enough, Bassett came round to the garden- 134
house with fifteen hundred pounds in notes. The twenty pounds reserve was left
with Joe Glee, in the Turf Commission deposit.

"You see, it's all right, uncle, when I'm *sure!* Then we go strong, for all we're 135
worth. Don't we, Bassett?"

"We do that, Master Paul."   136

"And when are you sure?" said the uncle, laughing.   137

"Oh, well, sometimes I'm *absolutely* sure, like about Daffodil," said the boy; 138
"and sometimes I have an idea; and sometimes I haven't even an idea, have I,
Bassett? Then we're careful, because we mostly go down."

"You do, do you! And when you're sure, like about Daffodil, what makes you 139
sure, sonny?"

"Oh, well, I don't know," said the boy uneasily. "I'm sure, you know, uncle; 140
that's all."

"It's as if he had it from heaven, sir," Bassett reiterated.   141

"I should say so!" said the uncle.   142

But he became a partner. And when the Leger was coming on Paul was "sure" 143
about Lively Spark, which was a quite inconsiderable horse. The boy insisted on
putting a thousand on the horse, Bassett went for five hundred, and Oscar
Cresswell two hundred. Lively Spark came in first, and the betting had been ten
to one against him. Paul had made ten thousand.

"You see," he said, "I was absolutely sure of him."   144

Even Oscar Cresswell had cleared two thousand.   145

"Look here, son," he said, "this sort of thing makes me nervous."   146

"It needn't, uncle! Perhaps I shan't be sure again for a long time."   147

"But what are you going to do with your money?" asked the uncle.   148

"Of course," said the boy, "I started it for mother. She said she had no luck, 149
because father is unlucky, so I thought if *I* was lucky, it might stop whispering."

"What might stop whispering?"   150

"Our house. I *hate* our house for whispering."   151

"What does it whisper?"   152

"Why—why"—the boy fidgeted—"why, I don't know. But it's always short 153
of money, you know, uncle."

"I know it, son, I know it."   154

"You know people send mother writs, don't you, uncle?"   155

"I'm afraid I do," said the uncle.   156

"And then the house whispers, like people laughing at you behind your back. 157
It's awful, that is! I thought if I was lucky _____"

You might stop it," added the uncle.   158

The boy watched him with big blue eyes, that had an uncanny cold fire in 159
them, and he said never a word.

"Well, then!" said the uncle. "What are we doing?"   160

"I shouldn't like mother to know I was lucky," said the boy.   161

"Why not, son?"   162

"She'd stop me."   163

"I don't think she would."   164

"Oh!"—and the boy writhed in an odd way—"I *don't* want her to know, 165
uncle."

"All right son! We'll manage it without her knowing."   166

They managed it very easily. Paul, at the other's suggestion, handed over five 167
thousand pounds to his uncle, who deposited it with the family lawyer, who was
then to inform Paul's mother that a relative had put five thousand pounds into his
hands, which sum was to be paid out a thousand pounds at a time, on the
mother's birthday, for the next five years.

"So she'll have a birthday present of a thousand pounds for five successive 168
years," said Uncle Oscar. "I hope it won't make it all the harder for her later."

Paul's mother had her birthday in November. The house had been "whisper- 169
ing" worse than ever lately, and, even in spite of his luck, Paul could not bear up
against it. He was very anxious to see the effect of the birthday letter, telling his
mother about the thousand pounds.

When there were no visitors, Paul now took his meals with his parents, as he 170
was beyond the nursery control. His mother went into town nearly every day. She
had discovered that she had an odd knack of sketching furs and dress materials,
so she worked secretly in the studio of a friend who was the chief "artist" for the
leading drapers. She drew the figures of ladies in furs and ladies in silk and sequins
for the newspaper advertisements. This young woman artist earned several thousand pounds a year, but Paul's mother only made several hundred, and she was
again dissatisfied. She so wanted to be first in something, and she did not succeed,
even in making sketches for drapery advertisements.

She was down to breakfast on the morning of her birthday. Paul watched her 171
face as she read her letters. He knew the lawyer's letter. As his mother read it, her
face hardened and became more expressionless. Then a cold, determined look
came on her mouth. She hid the letter under the pile of others, and said not a
word about it.

"Didn't you have anything nice in the post for your birthday, mother?" said 172
Paul.

"Quite moderately nice," she said, her voice cold and absent.   173

She went away to town without saying more.   174

But in the afternoon Uncle Oscar appeared. He said Paul's mother had had a 175
long interview with the lawyer, asking if the whole five thousand could not be advanced at once, as she was in debt.

"What do you think, uncle?" said the boy.   176

"I leave it to you, son."   177

"Oh, let her have it, then! We can get some more with the other," said the boy. 178

"A bird in the hand is worth two in the bush, laddie!" said Uncle Oscar.   179

"But I'm sure to *know* for the Grand National; or the Lincolnshire; or else the 180
Derby. I'm sure to know for *one* of them," said Paul.

So Uncle Oscar signed the agreement, and Paul's mother touched the whole 181
five thousand. Then something very curious happened. The voices in the house

suddenly went mad, like a chorus of frogs on a spring evening. There were certain new furnishings, and Paul had a tutor. He was *really* going to Eton, his father's school, in the following autumn. There were flowers in the winter, and a blossoming of the luxury Paul's mother had been used to. And yet the voices in the house, behind the sprays of mimosa and almond blossom, and from under the piles of iridescent cushions, simply trilled and screamed in a sort of ecstacy: "There *must* be more money! Oh-h-h; there *must* be more money. Oh, now, now-w! Now-w-w—there *must* be more money!—more than ever! More than ever!"

It frightened Paul terribly. He studied away at his Latin and Greek with his tu- 182 tor. But his intense hours were spent with Bassett. The Grand National had gone by: he had not "known," and had lost a hundred pounds. Summer was at hand. He was in agony for the Lincoln. But even for the Lincoln he didn't "know," and he lost fifty pounds. He became wild-eyed and strange, as if something were going to explode in him.

"Let it alone, son! Don't you bother about it!" urged Uncle Oscar. But it was 183 as if the boy couldn't really hear what his uncle was saying.

"I've got to know for the Derby! I've got to know for the Derby!" the child re- 184 iterated, his big blue eyes blazing with a sort of madness.

His mother noticed how overwrought he was. 185

"You'd better go to the seaside. Wouldn't you like to go now to the seaside, in- 186 stead of waiting? I think you'd better," she said, looking down at him anxiously, her heart curiously heavy because of him.

But the child lifted his uncanny blue eyes. 187

"I couldn't possibly go before the Derby, mother!" he said. "I couldn't 188 possibly!"

"Why not?" she said, her voice becoming heavy when she was opposed. "Why 189 not? You can still go from the seaside to see the Derby with your Uncle Oscar, if that's what you wish. No need for you to wait here. Besides, I think you care too much about these races. It's a bad sign. My family has been a gambling family, and you won't know till you grow up how much damage it has done. But it has done damage. I shall have to send Bassett away, and ask Uncle Oscar not to talk racing to you, unless you promise to be reasonable about it: go away to the seaside and forget it. You're all nerves!"

"I'll do what you like, mother, so long as you don't send me away till after the 190 Derby," the boy said.

"Send you away from where? Just from this house?" 191

"Yes," he said, gazing at her. 192

"Why, you curious child, what makes you care about this house so much, sud- 193 denly? I never knew you loved it."

He gazed at her without speaking. He had a secret within a secret, something 194 he had not divulged, even to Bassett or to his Uncle Oscar.

But his mother, after standing undecided and a little bit sullen for some 195 moments, said:

"Very well, then! Don't go to the seaside till after the Derby, if you don't wish 196 it. But promise me you won't let your nerves go to pieces. Promise you won't think so much about horse-racing and *events,* as you call them!"

"Oh no," sad the boy casually. "I won't think much about them, mother. You 197
needn't worry. I wouldn't worry, mother, if I were you."

"If you were me and I were you," said his mother, "I wonder what we *should* 198
do!"

"But you know you needn't worry, mother, don't you?" the boy repeated. 199

"I should be awfully glad to know it," she said wearily. 200

"Oh, well, you *can,* you know. I mean, you *ought* to know you needn't worry," 201
he insisted.

"Ought I? Then I'll see about it," she said. 202

Paul's secret of secrets was his wooden horse, that which had no name. Since 203
he was emancipated from a nurse and a nursery-governess, he had had his rocking-
horse removed to his own bedroom at the top of the house.

"Surely you're too big for a rocking-horse!" his mother had remonstrated. 204

"Well, you see, mother, till I can have a *real* horse, I like to have *some* sort of 205
animal about," had been his quaint answer.

"Do you feel he keeps you company?" she laughed. 206

"Oh yes! He's very good, he always keeps me company, when I'm there," said 207
Paul.

So the horse, rather shabby, stood in an arrested prance in the boy's bedroom. 208

The Derby was drawing near, and the boy grew more and more tense. He 209
hardly heard what was spoken to him, he was very frail, and his eyes were really
uncanny. His mother had sudden strange seizures of uneasiness about him.
Sometimes, for half an hour, she would feel a sudden anxiety about him that was
almost anguish. She wanted to rush to him at once, and know he was safe.

Two nights before the Derby, she was at a big party in town, when one of her 210
rushes of anxiety about her boy, her first-born, gripped her heart till she could
hardly speak. She fought with the feeling, might and main, for she believed in
common sense. But it was too strong. She had to leave the dance and go downstairs to telephone to the country. The children's nursery-governess was terribly
surprised and startled at being rung up in the night.

"Are the children all right, Miss Wilmot?" 211

"Oh yes, they are quite all right." 212

"Master Paul? Is he all right?" 213

"He went to bed as right as a trivet. Shall I run up and look at him?" 214

"No," said Paul's mother reluctantly. "No! Don't trouble. It's all right. Don't sit 215
up. We shall be home fairly soon." She did not want her son's privacy intruded
upon.

"Very good," said the governess. 216

It was about one o'clock when Paul's mother and father drove up to their 217
house. All was still. Paul's mother went to her room and slipped off her white fur
cloak. She had told her maid not to wait up for her. She heard her husband downstairs, mixing a whisky and soda.

And then, because of the strange anxiety at her heart, she stole upstairs to her 218
son's room. Noiselessly she went along the upper corridor. Was there a faint
noise? What was it?

She stood, with arrested muscles, outside his door, listening. There was a 219
strange, heavy, and yet not loud noise. Her heart stood still. It was a soundless
noise, yet rushing and powerful. Something huge, in violent, hushed motion.
What was it? What in God's name was it? She ought to know. She felt that she
knew the noise. She knew what it was.

Yet she could not place it. She couldn't say what it was. And on and on it went, 220
like a madness.

Softly, frozen with anxiety and fear, she turned the doorhandle. 221

The room was dark. Yet in the space near the window, she heard and saw 222
something plunging to and fro. She gazed in fear and amazement.

Then suddenly she switched on the light, and saw her son, in his green pyja- 223
mas, madly surging on the rocking-horse. The blaze of light suddenly lit him up,
as he urged the wooden horse, and lit her up, as she stood, blonde, in her dress of
pale green and crystal, in the doorway.

"Paul!" she cried. "Whatever are you doing?" 224

"It's Malabar!" he screamed in a powerful, strange voice. "It's Malabar!" 225

His eyes blazed at her for one strange and senseless second, as he ceased urg- 226
ing his wooden horse. Then he fell with a crash to the ground, and she, all her tormented motherhood flooding upon her, rushed to gather him up.

But he was unconscious, and unconscious he remained, with some brain- 227
fever. He talked and tossed, and his mother sat stonily by his side.

"Malabar! It's Malabar! Bassett, Bassett, I *know!* It's Malabar!" 228

So the child cried, trying to get up and urge the rocking-horse that gave him 229
his inspiration.

"What does he mean by Malabar?" asked the heart-frozen mother. 230

"I don't know," said the father stonily. 231

"What does he mean by Malabar?" she asked her brother Oscar. 232

"It's one of the horses running for the Derby," was the answer. 233

And, in spite of himself, Oscar Cresswell spoke to Bassett, and himself put a 234
thousand on Malabar: at fourteen to one.

The third day of the illness was critical: they were waiting for a change. The 235
boy, with his rather long, curly hair, was tossing ceaselessly on the pillow. He neither slept nor regained consciousness, and his eyes were like blue stones. His
mother sat, feeling her heart had gone, turned actually into a stone.

In the evening, Oscar Cresswell did not come, but Bassett sent a message, say- 236
ing could he come up for one moment, just one moment? Paul's mother was very
angry at the intrusion, but on second thought she agreed. The boy was the same.
Perhaps Bassett might bring him to consciousness.

The gardener, a shortish fellow with a little brown moustache and sharp little 237
brown eyes, tiptoed into the room, touched his imaginary cap to Paul's mother,
and stole to the bedside, staring with glittering, smallish eyes at the tossing, dying
child.

"Master Paul!" he whispered. "Master Paul! Malabar came in first all right, a 238
clean win. I did as you told me. You've made over seventy thousand pounds, you
have; you've got over eighty thousand. Malabar came in all right, Master Paul."

"Malabar! Malabar! Did I say Malabar, mother? Did I say Malabar? Do you 239 think I'm lucky, mother? I knew Malabar, didn't I? Over eighty thousand pounds! I call that lucky, don't you, mother? Over eighty thousand pounds? I knew, didn't I know I knew? Malabar came in all right. If I ride my horse till I'm sure, then I tell you, Bassett, you can go as high as you like. Did you go for all you were worth, Bassett?"

"I went a thousand on it, Master Paul."   240

"I never told you, mother, that if I can ride my horse, and *get there,* then I'm 241 absolutely sure—oh, absolutely! Mother, did I ever tell you? I *am* lucky!"

"No, you never did," said his mother.   242

But the boy died in the night.   243

And even as he lay dead, his mother heard her brother's voice saying to her: 244 "My God, Hester, you're eighty-odd thousand to the good, and a poor devil of a son to the bad. But, poor devil, poor devil, he's best gone out of a life where he rides his rocking-horse to find a winner."

ACTIVITIES FOR WRITING AND DISCUSSION

1. Annotate the story, and write a notebook response using any of the "Ten Ideas for Writing" summarized on page 35.

2. Reread the opening paragraphs which introduce Paul's family. What problems does the family have? What's missing from their lives? Working alone or collaboratively, take some time to jot down your responses to these questions. Then, working from details and background furnished by the opening paragraphs and your own imagination, write a prequel to the story in which you relate the family's previous history leading up to the events in the story.

3. Why do the voices ("There *must* be more money!") actually *worsen* when more money arrives (paragraph 181)? Imagine you are D. H. Lawrence, and you want to revise the story to *silence* the voices. Imagine the revision required; then make it.

4. Inanimate objects in this story are treated as lifelike—the house (with its voices), the rocking-horse, "the big doll" (paragraph 6). Why does Lawrence do this, and what impact does this have on the characters and on you as a reader? Respond to this question. Then write a **monologue** from the point of view of the voices in the house or the rocking-horse in which you tell your own story (where you came from, what you signify) and comment on the characters and events in the story. *Alternative:* Write from the point of view of the *money* Paul wins.

5. Research Lawrence's opinions on money, greed, and the culture of capitalism. What values did he propose as an alternative to this culture, and how, if at all, are these values implied in "The Rocking-Horse Winner"?

KATHERINE MANSFIELD (1888–1923)

Miss Brill

Although it was so brilliantly fine—the blue sky powdered with gold and great 1
spots of light like white wine splashed over the Jardins Publiques—Miss Brill was
glad that she had decided on her fur. The air was motionless, but when you
opened your mouth there was just a faint chill, like a chill from a glass of iced water before you sip, and now and again a leaf came drifting—from nowhere, from
the sky. Miss Brill put up her hand and touched her fur. Dear little thing! It was
nice to feel it again. She had taken it out of its box that afternoon, shaken out the
moth-powder, given it a good brush, and rubbed the life back into the dim little
eyes. "What has been happening to me?" said the sad little eyes. Oh, how sweet it
was to see them snap at her again from the red eiderdown! . . . But the nose, which
was of some black composition, wasn't at all firm. It must have had a knock,
somehow. Never mind—a little dab of black sealing-wax when the time came—
when it was absolutely necessary. . . . Little rogue! Yes, she really felt like that about
it. Little rogue biting its tail just by her left ear. She could have taken it off and laid
it on her lap and stroked it. She felt a tingling in her hands and arms, but that
came from walking, she supposed. And when she breathed, something light and
sad—no, not sad, exactly—something gentle seemed to move in her bosom.

There were a number of people out this afternoon, far more than last Sunday. 2
And the band sounded louder and gayer. That was because the Season had begun.
For although the band played all the year round on Sundays, out of season it was
never the same. It was like someone playing with only the family to listen; it didn't
care how it played if there weren't any strangers present. Wasn't the conductor
wearing a new coat, too? She was sure it was new. He scraped with his foot and
flapped his arms like a rooster about to crow, and the bandsmen sitting in the
green rotunda blew out their cheeks and glared at the music. Now there came a
little "flutey" bit—very pretty!—a little chain of bright drops. She was sure it
would be repeated. It was; she lifted her head and smiled.

Only two people shared her "special" seat: a fine old man in a velvet coat, his 3
hands clasped over a huge carved walking-stick, and a big old woman, sitting upright, with a roll of knitting on her embroidered apron. They did not speak. This
was disappointing, for Miss Brill always looked forward to the conversation. She
had become really quite expert, she thought, at listening as though she didn't listen, at sitting in other people's lives just for a minute while they talked around her.

She glanced, sideways, at the old couple. Perhaps they would go soon. Last 4
Sunday, too, hadn't been as interesting as usual. An Englishman and his wife, he
wearing a dreadful Panama hat and she button boots. And she'd gone on the
whole time about how she ought to wear spectacles; she knew she needed them;
but that it was no good getting any; they'd be sure to break and they'd never keep
on. And he'd been so patient. He'd suggested everything—gold rims, the kind
that curved round your ears, little pads inside the bridge. No, nothing would

please her. "They'll always be sliding down my nose!" Miss Brill had wanted to shake her.

The old people sat on the bench, still as statues. Never mind, there was always the crowd to watch. To and fro, in front of the flower-beds and the band rotunda, the couples and groups paraded, stopped to talk, to greet, to buy a handful of flowers from the old beggar who had his tray fixed to the railings. Little children ran among them, swooping and laughing; little boys with big white silk bows under their chins, little girls, little French dolls, dressed up in velvet and lace. And sometimes a tiny staggerer came suddenly rocking into the open from under the trees, stopped, stared, as suddenly sat down "flop," until its small high-stepping mother, like a young hen, rushed scolding to its rescue. Other people sat on the benches and green chairs, but they were nearly always the same, Sunday after Sunday, and—Miss Brill had often noticed—there was something funny about nearly all of them. They were odd, silent, nearly all old, and from the way they stared they looked as though they'd just come from dark little rooms or even— even cupboards!

Behind the rotunda the slender trees with yellow leaves down drooping, and through them just a line of sea, and beyond the blue sky with gold-veined clouds.

Tum-tum-tum tiddle-um! tiddle-um! tum tiddley-um tum ta! blew the band.

Two young girls in red came by and two young soldiers in blue met them, and they laughed and paired and went off arm-in-arm. Two peasant women with funny straw hats passed, gravely, leading beautiful smoke-colored donkeys. A cold, pale nun hurried by. A beautiful woman came along and dropped her bunch of violets, and a little boy ran after to hand them to her, and she took them and threw them away as if they'd been poisoned. Dear me! Miss Brill didn't know whether to admire that or not! And now an ermine toque and a gentleman in grey met just in front of her. He was tall, stiff, dignified, and she was wearing the ermine toque she'd bought when her hair was yellow. Now everything, her hair, her face, even her eyes, was the same color as the shabby ermine, and her hand, in its cleaned glove, lifted to dab her lips, was a tiny yellowish paw. Oh, she was so pleased to see him—delighted! She rather thought they were going to meet that afternoon. She described where she'd been—everywhere, here, there, along by the sea. The day was so charming—didn't he agree? And wouldn't he, perhaps? . . . But he shook his head, lighted a cigarette, slowly breathed a great deep puff into her face, and, even while she was still talking and laughing, flicked the match away and walked on. The ermine toque was alone; she smiled more brightly than ever. But even the band seemed to know what she was feeling and played more softly, played tenderly, and the drum beat, "The Brute! The Brute!" over and over. What would she do? What was going to happen now? But as Miss Brill wondered, the ermine toque turned, raised her hand as though she'd seen some one else, much nicer, just over there, and pattered away. And the band changed again and played more quickly, more gaily than ever, and the old couple on Miss Brill's seat got up and marched away, and such a funny old man with long whiskers hobbled along in time to the music and was nearly knocked over by four girls walking abreast.

Oh, how fascinating it was! How she enjoyed it! How she loved sitting here, 9
watching it all! It was like a play. It was exactly like a play. Who could believe the
sky at the back wasn't painted? But it wasn't till a little brown dog trotted on
solemn and then slowly trotted off, like a little "theatre" dog, a little dog that had
been drugged, that Miss Brill discovered what it was that made it so exciting. They
were all on the stage. They weren't only the audience, not only looking on; they
were acting. Even she had a part and came every Sunday. No doubt somebody
would have noticed if she hadn't been there; she was part of the performance after all. How strange she'd never thought of it like that before! And yet it explained
why she made such a point of starting from home at just the same time each
week—so as not to be late for the performance—and it also explained why she
had quite a queer, shy feeling at telling her English pupils how she spent her Sunday afternoons. No wonder! Miss Brill nearly laughed out loud. She was on the
stage. She thought of the old invalid gentleman to whom she read the newspaper
four afternoons a week while he slept in the garden. She had got quite used to
the frail head on the cotton pillow, the hollowed eyes, the open mouth, and the
high pinched nose. If he'd been dead she mightn't have noticed for weeks; she
wouldn't have minded. But suddenly he knew he was having the paper read to
him by an actress! "An actress!" The old head lifted; two points of light quivered
in the old eyes. "An actress—are ye?" And Miss Brill smoothed the newspaper as
though it were the manuscript of her part and said gently: "Yes, I have been an actress for a long time."

The band had been having a rest. Now they started again. And what they 10
played was warm, sunny, yet there was just a faint chill—a something, what was
it?—not sadness—no, not sadness—a something that made you want to sing.
The tune lifted, lifted, the light shone; and it seemed to Miss Brill that in another
moment all of them, all the whole company, would begin singing. The young
ones, the laughing ones who were moving together, they would begin, and the
men's voices, very resolute and brave, would join them. And then she too, she too,
and the others on the benches—they would come in with a kind of accompaniment—something low, that scarcely rose or fell, something so beautiful—
moving. . . . And Miss Brill's eyes filled with tears and she looked smiling at all
the other members of the company. Yes, we understand, we understand, she
thought—though what they understood she didn't know.

Just at that moment a boy and a girl came and sat down where the old couple 11
had been. They were beautifully dressed; they were in love. The hero and heroine,
of course, just arrived from his father's yacht. And still soundlessly singing, still
with that trembling smile, Miss Brill prepared to listen.

"No, not now," said the girl. "Not here, I can't."   12

"But why? Because of that stupid old thing at the end there?" asked the boy. 13
"Why does she come here at all—who wants her? Why doesn't she keep her silly
old mug at home?"

"It's her fu-fur which is so funny," giggled the girl. "It's exactly like a fried 14
whiting."

"Ah, be off with you!" said the boy in an angry whisper. Then: "Tell me, ma   15
petite chère—"

"No, not here," said the girl "Not *yet*."   16

On her way home she usually bought a slice of honey-cake at the baker's. It was   17
her Sunday treat. Sometimes there was an almond in her slice, sometimes not. It
made a great difference. If there was an almond it was like carrying home a tiny
present—a surprise—something that might very well not have been there. She
hurried on the almond Sundays and struck the match for the kettle in quite a
dashing way.

But today she passed the baker's by, climbed the stairs, went into the little dark   18
room—her room like a cupboard—and sat down on the red eiderdown. She sat
there for a long time. The box that the fur came out of was on the bed. She un-
clasped the necklet quickly; quickly, without looking, laid it inside. But when she
put the lid on she thought she heard something crying.

ACTIVITIES FOR WRITING AND DISCUSSION

1. The story reveals nothing about Miss Brill's daily life except that she
teaches English and that she reads the newspaper four times a week to an "old invalid gentleman." Why do you think she looks forward so much to Sunday afternoons and the park? What does she "get" there that she lacks at other times and
places?

2. Reannotate the passages about Miss Brill's fur. What do you think the fur
symbolizes and why? There are many possible answers.

3. Like a writer, Miss Brill enjoys people-watching. Following her example,
go to a public place yourself and observe the people. Record their immediate actions and interactions (briefly or at length) and imagine the stories behind them.

4. Write about Miss Brill from the point of view of some other character in
the story—for instance, the "old invalid gentleman," one of her English pupils,
or someone present in the park.

WILLIAM FAULKNER (1897–1962)

Barn Burning

The store in which the Justice of the Peace's court was sitting smelled of cheese.   1
The boy, crouched on his nail keg at the back of the crowded room, knew he
smelled cheese, and more: from where he sat he could see the ranked shelves

close-packed with the solid, squat, dynamic shapes of tin cans whose labels his stomach read, not from the lettering which meant nothing to his mind but from the scarlet devils and the silver curve of fish—this, the cheese which he knew he smelled and the hermetic meat which his intestines believed he smelled coming in intermittent gusts momentary and brief between the other constant one, the smell and sense just a little of fear because mostly of despair and grief, the old fierce pull of blood. He could not see the table where the Justice sat and before which his father and his father's enemy (*our enemy* he thought in that despair; *ourn! mine and hisn both! He's my father!*) stood, but he could hear them, the two of them that is, because his father had said no word yet:

"But what proof have you, Mr. Harris?"   2

"I told you. The hog got into my corn. I caught it up and sent it back to him.   3 He had no fence that would hold it. I told him so, warned him. The next time I put the hog in my pen. When he came to get it I gave him enough wire to patch up his pen. The next time I put the hog up and kept it. I rode down to his house and saw the wire I gave him still rolled on to the spool in his yard. I told him he could have the hog when he paid me a dollar pound fee. That evening a nigger came with the dollar and got the hog. He was a strange nigger. He said, 'He say to tell you wood and hay kin burn.' I said, 'What?' 'That whut he say to tell you,' the nigger said. 'Wood and hay kin burn.' That night my barn burned. I got the stock out but I lost the barn."

"Where is the nigger? Have you got him?"   4

"He was a strange nigger, I tell you. I don't know what became of him."   5

"But that's not proof. Don't you see that's not proof?"   6

"Get that boy up here. He knows." For a moment the boy thought too that the   7 man meant his older brother until Harris said, "Not him. The little one. The boy," and, crouching, small for his age, small and wiry like his father, in patched and faded jeans even too small for him, with straight, uncombed, brown hair and eyes gray and wild as storm scud, he saw the men between himself and the table part and become a lane of grim faces, at the end of which he saw the Justice, a shabby, collarless, graying man in spectacles, beckoning him. He felt no floor under his bare feet; he seemed to walk beneath the palpable weight of the grim turning faces. His father, stiff in his black Sunday coat donned not for the trial but for the moving, did not even look at him. *He aims for me to lie,* he thought, again with that frantic grief and despair. *And I will have to do hit.*

"What's your name, boy?" the Justice said.   8

"Colonel Sartoris Snopes," the boy whispered.   9

"Hey?" the Justice said. "Talk louder. Colonel Sartoris? I reckon anybody   10 named for Colonel Sartoris in this country can't help but tell the truth, can they?" The boy said nothing. *Enemy! Enemy!* he thought; for a moment he could not even see, could not see that the Justice's face was kindly nor discern that his voice was troubled when he spoke to the man named Harris: "Do you want me to question this boy?" But he could hear, and during those subsequent long seconds while there was absolutely no sound in the crowded little room save that of quiet and intent breathing it was as if he had swung outward at the end of a grape vine, over a ravine, and at the top of the swing had been caught in a prolonged instant of mesmerized gravity, weightless in time.

"No!" Harris said violently, explosively. "Damnation! Send him out of here!"   11 Now time, the fluid world, rushed beneath him again, the voices coming to him again through the smell of cheese and sealed meat, the fear and despair and the old grief of blood:

"This case is closed. I can't find against you, Snopes, but I can give you advice.   12 Leave this country and don't come back to it."

His father spoke for the first time, his voice cold and harsh, level, without em-   13 phasis: "I aim to. I don't figure to stay in a country among people who . . ." he said something unprintable and vile, addressed to no one.

"That'll do," the Justice said. "Take your wagon and get out of this country be-   14 fore dark. Case dismissed."

His father turned, and he followed the stiff black coat, the wiry figure walking   15 a little stiffly from where a Confederate provost's man's musket ball had taken him in the heel on a stolen horse thirty years ago, followed the two backs now, since his older brother had appeared from somewhere in the crowd, no taller than the father but thicker, chewing tobacco steadily, between the two lines of grim-faced men and out of the store and across the worn gallery and down the sagging steps and among the dogs and half-grown boys in the mild May dust, where as he passed a voice hissed:

"Barn burner!"   16

Again he could not see, whirling; there was a face in a red haze, moonlike, big-   17 ger than the full moon, the owner of it half again his size, he leaping in the red haze toward the face, feeling no blow, feeling no shock when his head struck the earth, scrabbling up and leaping again, feeling no blow this time either and tasting no blood, scrabbling up to see the other boy in full flight and himself already leaping into pursuit as his father's hand jerked him back, the harsh, cold voice speaking above him: "Go get in the wagon."

It stood in a grove of locusts and mulberries across the road. His two hulking   18 sisters in their Sunday dresses and his mother and her sister in calico and sun-bonnets were already in it, sitting on and among the sorry residue of the dozen and more movings which even the boy could remember—the battered stove, the broken beds and chairs, the clock inlaid with mother-of-pearl, which would not run, stopped at some fourteen minutes past two o'clock of a dead and forgotten day and time, which had been his mother's dowry. She was crying, though when she saw him she drew her sleeve across her face and began to descend from the wagon. "Get back," the father said.

"He's hurt. I got to get some water and wash his . . ."   19

"Get back in the wagon," his father said. He got in too, over the tail-gate. His   20 father mounted to the seat where the older brother already sat and struck the gaunt mules two savage blows with the peeled willow, but without heat. It was not even sadistic; it was exactly that same quality which in later years would cause his descendants to over-run the engine before putting a motor car into motion, striking and reining back in the same movement. The wagon went on, the store with its quiet crowd of grimly watching men dropped behind; a curve in the road hid it. *Forever* he thought. *Maybe he's done satisfied now, now that he has . . .* stopping himself, not to say it aloud even to himself. His mother's hand touched his shoulder.

"Does hit hurt?" she said.   21

"Naw," he said. "Hit don't hurt. Lemme be."   22

"Can't you wipe some of the blood off before hit dries?"   23

"I'll wash to-night," he said. "Lemme be, I tell you."   24

The wagon went on. He did not know where they were going. None of them   25
ever did or ever asked, because it was always somewhere, always a house of sorts waiting for them a day or two days or even three days away. Likely his father had already arranged to make a crop on another farm before he . . . Again he had to stop himself. He (the father) always did. There was something about his wolflike independence and even courage when the advantage was at least neutral which impressed strangers, as if they got from his latent ravening ferocity not so much a sense of dependability as a feeling that his ferocious conviction in the rightness of his own actions would be of advantage to all whose interest lay with his.

That night they camped, in a grove of oaks and beeches where a spring ran.   26
The nights were still cool and they had a fire against it, of a rail lifted from a nearby fence and cut into lengths—a small fire, neat, niggard almost, a shrewd fire; such fires were his father's habit and custom always, even in freezing weather. Older, the boy might have remarked this and wondered why not a big one; why should not a man who had not only seen the waste and extravagance of war, but who had in his blood an inherent voracious prodigality with material not his own, have burned everything in sight? Then he might have gone a step farther and thought that that was the reason: that niggard blaze was the living fruit of nights passed during those four years in the woods hiding from all men, blue or gray, with his strings of horses (captured horses, he called them). And older still, he might have divined the true reason: that the element of fire spoke to some deep mainspring of his father's being, as the element of steel or of powder spoke to other men, as the one weapon for the preservation of integrity, else breath were not worth the breathing, and hence to be regarded with respect and used with discretion.

But he did not think this now and he had seen those same niggard blazes all   27
his life. He merely ate his supper beside it and was already half asleep over his iron plate when his father called him, and once more he followed the stiff back, the stiff and ruthless limp, up the slope and on to the starlit road where, turning, he could see his father against the stars but without face or depth—a shape black, flat, and bloodless as though cut from tin in the iron folds of the frockcoat which had not been made for him, the voice harsh like tin and without heat like tin:

"You were fixing to tell them. You would have told him." He didn't answer.   28
His father struck him with the flat of his hand on the side of the head, hard but without heat, exactly as he had struck the two mules at the store, exactly as he would strike either of them with any stick in order to kill a horse fly, his voice still without heat or anger: "You're getting to be a man. You got to learn. You got to learn to stick to your own blood or you ain't going to have any blood to stick to you. Do you think either of them, any man there this morning, would? Don't you

know all they wanted was a chance to get at me because they knew I had them beat? Eh?" Later, twenty years later, he was to tell himself, "If I had said they wanted only truth, justice, he would have hit me again." But now he said nothing. He was not crying. He just stood there. "Answer me," his father said.

"Yes," he whispered. His father turned.   29

"Get on to bed. We'll be there tomorrow."   30

Tomorrow they were there. In the early afternoon the wagon stopped before   31 a paintless two-room house identical almost with the dozen others it had stopped before even in the boy's ten years, and again, as on the other dozen occasions, his mother and aunt got down and began to unload the wagon, although his two sisters and his father and brother had not moved.

"Likely hit ain't fitten for hawgs," one of the sisters said.   32

"Nevertheless, fit it will and you'll hog it and like it," his father said. "Get out   33 of them chairs and help your Ma unload."

The two sisters got down, big, bovine, in a flutter of cheap ribbons; one of   34 them drew from the jumbled wagon bed a battered lantern, the other a worn broom. His father handed the reins to the older son and began to climb stiffly over the wheel. "When they get unloaded, take the team to the barn and feed them." Then he said, and at first the boy thought he was still speaking to his brother: "Come with me."

"Me?" he said.   35

"Yes," his father said. "You."   36

"Abner," his mother said. His father paused and looked back—the harsh level   37 stare beneath the shaggy, graying, irascible brows.

"I reckon I'll have a word with the man that aims to begin to-morrow owning   38 me body and soul for the next eight months."

They went back up the road. A week ago—or before last night, that is—he   39 would have asked where they were going, but not now. His father had struck him before last night but never before had he paused afterward to explain why; it was as if the blow and the following calm, outrageous voice still rang, repercussed, divulging nothing to him save the terrible handicap of being young, the light weight of his few years, just heavy enough to prevent his soaring free of the world as it seemed to be ordered but not heavy enough to keep him footed solid in it, to resist it and try to change the course of its events.

Presently he could see the grove of oaks and cedars and the other flowering   40 trees and shrubs where the house would be, though not the house yet. They walked beside a fence massed with honeysuckle and Cherokee roses and came to a gate swinging open between two brick pillars, and now, beyond a sweep of drive, he saw the house for the first time and at that instant he forgot his father and the terror and despair both, and even when he remembered his father again (who had not stopped) the terror and despair did not return. Because, for all the twelve movings, they had sojourned until now in a poor country, a land of small farms and fields and houses, and he had never seen a house like this before. *Hit's big as a courthouse* he thought quietly, with a surge of peace and joy whose reason he could not have thought into words, being too young for that: *They are safe from him. People whose lives are a part of this peace and dignity are beyond his touch, he no more to them than a buzzing wasp: capable of stinging for a little moment but that's all; the spell of this peace and dignity rendering even the barns and stable and cribs which belong to it impervious to the puny flames he might contrive . . .* this, the peace and joy, ebbing for an instant as he looked again at the stiff black back, the stiff and implacable limp of the figure which was not dwarfed by the house, for the reason that it had never looked big anywhere and which now, against the serene columned backdrop, had more than ever that impervious quality of something cut ruthlessly from tin, depthless, as though, sidewise to the sun, it would cast no shadow. Watching him, the boy remarked the absolutely undeviating course which his father held and saw the stiff foot come squarely down in a pile of fresh droppings where a horse had stood in the drive and which his father could have avoided by a simple change of stride. But it ebbed only for a moment, though he could not have thought this into words either, walking on in the spell of the house, which he could even want but without envy, without sorrow, certainly never with that ravening and jealous rage which unknown to him walked in the ironlike black coat before him: *Maybe he will feel it too. Maybe it will even change him now from what maybe he couldn't help but be.*

They crossed the portico. Now he could hear his father's stiff foot as it came 41 down on the boards with clocklike finality, a sound out of all proportion to the displacement of the body it bore and which was not dwarfed either by the white door before it, as though it had attained to a sort of vicious and ravening minimum not to be dwarfed by anything—the flat, wide, black hat, the formal coat of broadcloth which had once been black but which had now that friction-glazed greenish cast of the bodies of old house flies, the lifted sleeve which was too large, the lifted hand like a curled claw. The door opened so promptly that the boy knew the Negro must have been watching them all the time, an old man with neat grizzled hair, in a linen jacket, who stood barring the door with his body, saying, "Wipe yo foots, white man, fo you come in here. Major ain't home nohow."

"Get out of my way, nigger," his father said, without heat too, flinging the 42 door back and the Negro also and entering, his hat still on his head. And now the boy saw the prints of the stiff foot on the doorjamb and saw them appear on the pale rug behind the machinelike deliberation of the foot which seemed to bear (or transmit) twice the weight which the body compassed. The Negro was shouting "Miss Lula! Miss Lula!" somewhere behind them, then the boy, deluged as though by a warm wave by a suave turn of carpeted stair and a pendant glitter of chandeliers and a mute gleam of gold frames, heard the swift feet and saw her too, a lady—perhaps he had never seen her like before either—in a gray, smooth gown with lace at the throat and an apron tied at the waist and the sleeves turned back, wiping cake or biscuit dough from her hands with a towel as she came up the hall, looking not at his father at all but at the tracks on the blond rug with an expression of incredulous amazement.

"I tried," the Negro cried. "I tole him to . . ."   43

"Will you please go away?" she said in a shaking voice. "Major de Spain is not 44 at home. Will you please go away?"

His father had not spoken again. He did not speak again. He did not even look 45
at her. He just stood stiff in the center of the rug, in his hat, the shaggy iron-gray
brows twitching slightly above the pebble-colored eyes as he appeared to examine the house with brief deliberation. Then with the same deliberation he turned;
the boy watched him pivot on the good leg and saw the stiff foot drag round the
arc of the turning, leaving a final long and fading smear. His father never looked
at it, he never once looked down at the rug. The Negro held the door. It closed behind them, upon the hysteric and indistinguishable woman-wail. His father stopped at the top of the steps and scraped his boot clean on the edge of it. At the gate
he stopped again. He stood for a moment, planted stiffly on the stiff foot, looking
back at the house. "Pretty and white, ain't it?" he said. "That's sweat. Nigger sweat.
Maybe it ain't white enough yet to suit him. Maybe he wants to mix some white
sweat with it."

Two hours later the boy was chopping wood behind the house within which 46
his mother and aunt and the two sisters (the mother and aunt, not the two girls,
he knew that; even at this distance and muffled by walls the flat loud voices of the
two girls emanated an incorrigible idle inertia) were setting up the stove to prepare a meal, when he heard the hooves and saw the linen-clad man on a fine sorrel mare, whom he recognized even before he saw the rolled rug in front of the
Negro youth following on a fat bay carriage horse—a suffused, angry face vanishing, still at full gallop, beyond the corner of the house where his father and
brother were sitting in the two tilted chairs; and a moment later, almost before he
could have put the axe down, he heard the hooves again and watched the sorrel
mare go back out of the yard, already galloping again. Then his father began to
shout one of the sisters' names, who presently emerged backward from the
kitchen door dragging the rolled rug along the ground by one end while the other
sister walked behind it.

"If you ain't going to tote, go on and set up the wash pot," the first said.   47

"You, Sarty!" the second shouted. "Set up the wash pot!" His father appeared 48
at the door, framed against that shabbiness, as he had been against that other
bland perfection, impervious to either, the mother's anxious face at his shoulder.

"Go on," the father said. "Pick it up." The two sisters stooped, broad, lethar- 49
gic; stooping, they presented an incredible expanse of pale cloth and a flutter of
tawdry ribbons.

"If I thought enough of a rug to have to git hit all the way from France I 50
wouldn't keep hit where folks coming in would have to tromp on hit," the first
said. They raised the rug.

"Abner," the mother said. "Let me do it."   51

"You go back and git dinner," his father said. "I'll tend to this."   52

From the woodpile through the rest of the afternoon the boy watched them, 53
the rug spread flat in the dust beside the bubbling wash-pot, the two sisters stooping over it with that profound and lethargic reluctance, while the father stood
over them in turn, implacable and grim, driving them though never raising his
voice again. He could smell the harsh homemade lye they were using; he saw
his mother come to the door once and look toward them with an expression not

anxious now but very like despair; he saw his father turn, and he fell to with the axe and saw from the corner of his eye his father raise from the ground a flattish fragment of field stone and examine it and return to the pot, and this time his mother actually spoke: "Abner. Abner. Please don't. Please, Abner."

Then he was done too. It was dusk; the whippoorwills had already begun. He 54 could smell coffee from the room where they would presently eat the cold food remaining from the mid-afternoon meal, though when he entered the house he realized they were having coffee again probably because there was a fire on the hearth, before which the rug now lay spread over the backs of the two chairs. The tracks of his father's foot were gone. Where they had been were now long, water-cloudy scoriations resembling the sporadic course of a lilliputian mowing machine.

It still hung there while they ate the cold food and then went to bed, scattered 55 without order or claim up and down the two rooms, his mother in one bed, where his father would later lie, the older brother in the other, himself, the aunt, and the two sisters on pallets on the floor. But his father was not in bed yet. The last thing the boy remembered was the depthless, harsh silhouette of the hat and coat bending over the rug and it seemed to him that he had not even closed his eyes when the silhouette was standing over him, the fire almost dead behind it, the stiff foot prodding him awake. "Catch up the mule," his father said.

When he returned with the mule his father was standing in the black door, the 56 rolled rug over his shoulder. "Ain't you going to ride?" he said.

"No. Give me your foot." 57

He bent his knee into his father's hand, the wiry, surprising power flowed 58 smoothly, rising, he rising with it, on to the mule's bare back (they had owned a saddle once; the boy could remember it though not when or where) and with the same effortlessness his father swung the rug up in front of him. Now in the starlight they retraced the afternoon's path, up the dusty road rife with honeysuckle, through the gate and up the black tunnel of the drive to the lightless house, where he sat on the mule and felt the rough warp of the rug drag across his thighs and vanish.

"Don't you want me to help?" he whispered. His father did not answer and 59 now he heard again that stiff foot striking the hollow portico with that wooden and clocklike deliberation, that outrageous overstatement of the weight it carried. The rug, hunched, not flung (the boy could tell that even in the darkness) from his father's shoulder, struck the angle of wall and floor with a sound unbelievably loud, thunderous, then the foot again, unhurried and enormous; a light came on in the house and the boy sat, tense, breathing steadily and quietly and just a little fast, though the foot itself did not increase its beat at all, descending the steps now; now the boy could see him.

"Don't you want to ride now?" he whispered. "We kin both ride now," the 60 light within the house altering now, flaring up and sinking. *He's coming down the stairs now,* he thought. He had already ridden the mule up beside the horse block; presently his father was up behind him and he doubled the reins over and slashed the mule across the neck, but before the animal could begin to trot the hard, thin arm came round him, the hard, knotted hand jerking the mule back to a walk.

In the first red rays of the sun they were in the lot, putting plow gear on the   61
mules. This time the sorrel mare was in the lot before he heard it at all, the rider
collarless and even bareheaded, trembling, speaking in a shaking voice as the
woman in the house had done, his father merely looking up once before stooping
again to the hame he was buckling, so that the man on the mare spoke to his
stooping back:

"You must realize you have ruined that rug. Wasn't there anybody here, any of   62
your women . . ." he ceased, shaking, the boy watching him, the older brother
leaning now in the stable door, chewing, blinking slowly and steadily at nothing
apparently. "It cost a hundred dollars. But you never had a hundred dollars. You
never will. So I'm going to charge you twenty bushels of corn against your crop.
I'll add it in your contract and when you come to the commissary you can sign it.
That won't keep Mrs. de Spain quiet but maybe it will teach you to wipe your feet
off before you enter her house again."

Then he was gone. The boy looked at his father, who still had not spoken or   63
even looked up again, who was now adjusting the logger-head in the hame.

"Pap," he said. His father looked at him—the inscrutable face, the shaggy   64
brows beneath which the gray eyes glinted coldly. Suddenly the boy went toward
him, fast, stopping as suddenly. "You done the best you could!" he cried. "If he
wanted hit done different why didn't he wait and tell you how? He won't git no
twenty bushels! He won't git none! We'll gether hit and hide hit! I kin watch . . ."

"Did you put the cutter back in that straight stock like I told you?"   65

"No, sir," he said.   66

"Then go do it."   67

That was Wednesday. During the rest of that week he worked steadily, at what   68
was within his scope and some which was beyond it, with an industry that did not
need to be driven nor even commanded twice; he had this from his mother, with
the difference that some at least of what he did he liked to do, such as splitting
wood with the half-size axe which his mother and aunt had earned, or saved
money somehow, to present him with at Christmas. In company with the two
older women (and on one afternoon, even one of the sisters), he built pens for the
shoat and the cow which were a part of his father's contract with the landlord, and
one afternoon, his father being absent, gone somewhere on one of the mules, he
went to the field.

They were running a middle buster now, his brother holding the plow straight   69
while he handled the reins, and walking beside the straining mule, the rich black
soil shearing cool and damp against his bare ankles, he thought *Maybe this is the
end of it. Maybe even that twenty bushels that seems hard to have to pay for just a
rug will be a cheap price for him to stop forever and always from being what he used
to be;* thinking, dreaming now, so that his brother had to speak sharply to him to
mind the mule: *Maybe he even won't collect the twenty bushels. Maybe it will all add
up and balance and vanish—corn, rug, fire; the terror and grief, the being pulled two
ways like between two teams of horses—gone, done with for ever and ever.*

Then it was Saturday; he looked up from beneath the mule he was harnessing   70
and saw his father in the black coat and hat. "Not that," his father said. "The

wagon gear." And then, two hours later, sitting in the wagon bed behind his father and brother on the seat, the wagon accomplished a final curve, and he saw
the weathered paintless store with its tattered tobacco- and patent-medicine
posters and the tethered wagons and saddle animals below the gallery. He mounted
the gnawed steps behind his father and brother, and there again was the lane of
quiet, watching faces for the three of them to walk through. He saw the man in
spectacles sitting at the plank table and he did not need to be told this was a Justice of the Peace; he sent one glare of fierce, exultant, partisan defiance at the man
in collar and cravat now, whom he had seen but twice before in his life, and that
on a galloping horse, who now wore on his face an expression not of rage but of
amazed unbelief which the boy could not have known was at the incredible circumstance of being sued by one of his own tenants, and came and stood against
his father and cried at the Justice: "He ain't done it! He ain't burnt . . ."

"Go back to the wagon," his father said.   71

"Burnt?" the Justice said. "Do I understand this rug was burned too?"   72

"Does anybody here claim it was?" his father said. "Go back to the wagon."   73
But he did not, he merely retreated to the rear of the room, crowded as that other
had been, but not to sit down this time, instead, to stand pressing among the
motionless bodies, listening to the voices:

"And you claim twenty bushels of corn is too high for the damage you did to   74
the rug?"

"He brought the rug to me and said he wanted the tracks washed out of it.   75
I washed the tracks out and took the rug back to him."

"But you didn't carry the rug back to him in the same condition it was in   76
before you made the tracks on it."

His father did not answer, and now for perhaps half a minute there was no   77
sound at all save that of breathing, the faint, steady suspiration of complete and
intent listening.

"You decline to answer that, Mr. Snopes?" Again his father did not answer.   78
"I'm going to find against you, Mr. Snopes. I'm going to find that you were responsible for the injury to Major de Spain's rug and hold you liable for it. But
twenty bushels of corn seems a little high for a man in your circumstances to have
to pay. Major de Spain claims it cost a hundred dollars. October corn will be
worth about fifty cents. I figure that if Major de Spain can stand a ninety-five-
dollar loss on something he paid cash for, you can stand a five-dollar loss you
haven't earned yet. I hold you in damages to Major de Spain to the amount of ten
bushels of corn over and above your contract with him, to be paid to him out of
your crop at gathering time. Court adjourned."

It had taken no time hardly, the morning was but half begun. He thought they 79
would return home and perhaps back to the field, since they were late, far behind
all other farmers. But instead his father passed on behind the wagon, merely indicating with his hand for the older brother to follow with it, and crossed the road
toward the blacksmith shop opposite, pressing on after his father, overtaking
him, speaking, whispering up at the harsh, calm face beneath the weathered hat:
"He won't git no ten bushels neither. He won't git one. We'll . . ." until his father

glanced for an instant down at him, the face absolutely calm, the grizzled eyebrows tangled above the cold eyes, the voice almost pleasant, almost gentle:

"You think so? Well, we'll wait till October anyway."   80

The matter of the wagon—the setting of a spoke or two and the tightening of   81
the tires—did not take long either, the business of the tires accomplished by driving the wagon into the spring branch behind the shop and letting it stand there,
the mules nuzzling into the water from time to time, and the boy on the seat with
the idle reins, looking up the slope and through the sooty tunnel of the shed
where the slow hammer rang and where his father sat on an upended cypress bolt,
easily, either talking or listening, still sitting there when the boy brought the dripping wagon up out of the branch and halted it before the door.

"Take them on to the shade and hitch," his father said. He did so and returned.   82
His father and the smith and a third man squatting on his heels inside the door
were talking, about crops and animals; the boy, squatting too in the ammoniac
dust and hoof-parings and scales of rust, heard his father tell a long and unhurried story out of the time before the birth of the older brother even when he had
been a professional horsetrader. And then his father came up beside him where he
stood before a tattered last year's circus poster on the other side of the store, gazing rapt and quiet at the scarlet horses, the incredible poisings and convolutions
of tulle and tights and the painted leers of comedians, and said "It's time to eat."

But not at home. Squatting beside his brother against the front wall, he   83
watched his father emerge from the store and produce from a paper sack a segment of cheese and divide it carefully and deliberately into three with his pocket
knife and produce crackers from the same sack. They all three squatted on the
gallery and ate, slowly, without talking; then in the store again, they drank from a
tin dipper tepid water smelling of the cedar bucket and of living beech trees. And
still they did not go home. It was a horse lot this time, a tall rail fence upon and
along which men stood and sat and out of which one by one horses were led, to
be walked and trotted and then cantered back and forth along the road while the
slow swapping and buying went on and the sun began to slant westward, they—
the three of them—watching and listening, the older brother with his muddy
eyes and his steady, inevitable tobacco, the father commenting now and then on
certain of the animals, to no one in particular.

It was after sundown when they reached home. They ate supper by lamplight,   84
then, sitting on the doorstep, the boy watched the night fully accomplish, listening to the whippoorwills and the frogs, when he heard his mother's voice: "Abner!
No! No! Oh, God. Oh, God. Abner!" and he rose, whirled, and saw the altered
light through the door where a candle stub now burned in a bottle neck on the
table and his father, still in the hat and coat, at once formal and burlesque as
though dressed carefully for some shabby and ceremonial violence, emptying the
reservoir of the lamp back into the five-gallon kerosene can from which it had
been filled, while the mother tugged at his arm until he shifted the lamp to the
other hand and flung her back, not savagely or viciously, just hard, into the wall,
her hands flung out against the wall for balance, her mouth open and in her face

the same quality of hopeless despair as had been in her voice. Then his father saw him standing in the door.

"Go to the barn and get that can of oil we were oiling the wagon with," he said. 85 The boy did not move. Then he could speak.

"What . . ." he cried. "What are you . . ." 86

"Go get that oil," his father said. "Go." 87

Then he was moving, running, outside the house, toward the stable: this is the 88 old habit, the old blood which he had not been permitted to choose for himself, which had been bequeathed him willy nilly and which had run for so long (and who knew where, battening on what of outrage and savagery and lust) before it came to him. *I could keep on,* he thought. *I could run on and on and never look back, never need to see his face again. Only I can't. I can't,* the rusted can in his hand now, the liquid sploshing in it as he ran back to the house and into it, into the sound of his mother's weeping in the next room, and handed the can to his father.

"Ain't you going to even send a nigger?" he cried. "At least you sent a nigger 89 before!"

This time his father didn't strike him. The hand came even faster than the 90 blow had, the same hand which had set the can on the table with almost excruciating care flashing from the can toward him too quick for him to follow it, gripping him by the back of his shirt and on to tiptoe before he had seen it quit the can, the face stooping at him in breathless and frozen ferocity, the cold, dead voice speaking over him to the older brother who leaned against the table, chewing with that steady, curious, sidewise motion of cows:

"Empty the can into the big one and go on. I'll catch up with you." 91

"Better tie him up to the bedpost," the brother said. 92

"Do like I told you," the father said. Then the boy was moving, his bunched 93 shirt and the hard, bony hand between his shoulder-blades, his toes just touching the floor, across the room and into the other one, past the sisters sitting with spread heavy thighs in the two chairs over the cold hearth, and to where his mother and aunt sat side by side on the bed, the aunt's arms about his mother's shoulders.

"Hold him," the father said. The aunt made a startled movement. "Not you," 94 the father said. "Lennie. Take hold of him. I want to see you do it." His mother took him by the wrist. "You'll hold him better than that. If he gets loose don't you know what he is going to do? He will go up yonder." He jerked his head toward the road. "Maybe I'd better tie him."

"I'll hold him," his mother whispered. 95

"See you do then." Then his father was gone, the stiff foot heavy and measured 96 upon the boards, ceasing at last.

Then he began to struggle. His mother caught him in both arms, he jerking 97 and wrenching at them. He would be stronger in the end, he knew that. But he had no time to wait for it. "Lemme go!" he cried. "I don't want to have to hit you!"

"Let him go!" the aunt said. "If he don't go, before God, I am going there 98 myself!"

"Don't you see I can't!" his mother cried. "Sarty! Sarty! No! No! Help me, 99 Lizzie!"

Then he was free. His aunt grasped at him but it was too late. He whirled, run- 100 ning, his mother stumbled forward on to her knees behind him, crying to the nearer sister: "Catch him, Net! Catch him!" But that was too late too, the sister (the sisters were twins, born at the same time, yet either of them now gave the impression of being, encompassing as much living meat and volume and weight as any other two of the family) not yet having begun to rise from the chair, her head, face, alone merely turned, presenting to him in the flying instant an astonishing expanse of young female features untroubled by any surprise even, wearing only an expression of bovine interest. Then he was out of the room, out of the house, in the mild dust of the starlit road and the heavy rifeness of honeysuckle, the pale ribbon unspooling with terrific slowness under his running feet, reaching the gate at last and turning in, running, his heart and lungs drumming, on up the drive toward the lighted house, the lighted door. He did not knock, he burst in, sobbing for breath, incapable for the moment of speech; he saw the astonished face of the Negro in the linen jacket without knowing when the Negro had appeared.

"De Spain!" he cried, panted. "Where's . . ." then he saw the white man too 101 emerging from a white door down the hall. "Barn!" he cried. "Barn!"

"What?" the white man said. "Barn?"   102

"Yes!" the boy cried. "Barn!"   103

"Catch him!" the white man shouted.   104

But it was too late this time too. The Negro grasped his shirt, but the entire 105 sleeve, rotten with washing, carried away, and he was out that door too and in the drive again, and had actually never ceased to run even while he was screaming into the white man's face.

Behind him the white man was shouting, "My horse! Fetch my horse!" and he 106 thought for an instant of cutting across the park and climbing the fence into the road, but he did not know the park nor how high the vine-massed fence might be and he dared not risk it. So he ran on down the drive, blood and breath roaring; presently he was in the road again though he could not see it. He could not hear either: the galloping mare was almost upon him before he heard her, and even then he held his course, as if the very urgency of his wild grief and need must in a moment more find him wings, waiting until the ultimate instant to hurl himself aside and into the weed-choked roadside ditch as the horse thundered past and on, for an instant in furious silhouette against the stars, the tranquil early summer night sky which, even before the shape of the horse and rider vanished, stained abruptly and violently upward: a long, swirling roar incredible and soundless, blotting the stars, and he springing up and into the road again, running again, knowing it was too late yet still running even after he heard the shot and, an instant later, two shots, pausing now without knowing he had ceased to run, crying "Pap! Pap!", running again before he knew he had begun to run, stumbling, tripping over something and scrabbling up again without ceasing to run, looking backward over his shoulder at the glare as he got up, running on among the invisible trees, panting, sobbing, "Father! Father!"

At midnight he was sitting on the crest of a hill. He did not know it was mid-   107
night and he did not know how far he had come. But there was no glare behind
him now and he sat now, his back toward what he had called home for four days
anyhow, his face toward the dark woods which he would enter when breath was
strong again, small, shaking steadily in the chill darkness, hugging himself into
the remainder of his thin, rotten shirt, the grief and despair now no longer terror
and fear but just grief and despair. *Father. My father,* he thought. "He was brave!"
he cried suddenly, aloud but not loud, no more than a whisper: "He was! He was
in the war! He was in Colonel Sartoris' cav'ry!" not knowing that his father had
gone to that war a private in the fine old European sense, wearing no uniform,
admitting the authority of and giving fidelity to no man or army or flag, going
to war as Malbrouck himself did: for booty—it meant nothing and less than
nothing to him if it were enemy booty or his own.

The slow constellations wheeled on. It would be dawn and then sun-up after a   108
while and he would be hungry. But that would be to-morrow and now he was only
cold, and walking would cure that. His breathing was easier now and he decided to
get up and go on, and then he found that he had been asleep because he knew it
was almost dawn, the night almost over. He could tell that from the whippoorwills.
They were everywhere now among the dark trees below him, constant and inflec-
tioned and ceaseless, so that, as the instant for giving over to the day birds drew
nearer and nearer, there was no interval at all between them. He got up. He was a
little stiff, but walking would cure that too as it would the cold, and soon there
would be the sun. He went on down the hill, toward the dark woods within which
the liquid silver voices of the birds called unceasing—the rapid and urgent beating of the urgent and quiring heart of the late spring night. He did not look back.

ACTIVITIES FOR WRITING AND DISCUSSION

1. The story is told primarily from the **third-person limited point of view**
of the boy Sarty. How would the story change if it were told by Sarty in the *first
person,* using "I"?

2. Reread the story for details of the Snopes family's life before the story's happenings. What kind of life has the family led? What did Abner (the father) do during the Civil War? What are the personalities and appearances of the sisters,
mother, aunt, and brother? Based on these details, prepare a brief dossier on the
family (perhaps for use by law enforcement officials or social workers).

3. Gather evidence of the range of Sarty's feelings for his father. What attracts
him? repels him? confuses him? How extensive is the father's influence on the
boy's life? In your opinion, will Sarty be able to establish an identity of his own,
separate from his father's? Why or why not?

4. Compose a sequel to the story. Away from his father, what does Sarty do
next? Where does he go? What does he do with his life? Strive to make the facts of
your sequel psychologically consistent with the personality of Sarty as portrayed
in Faulkner's story.

Naguib Mahfouz (b. 1911)

Zaabalawi

Finally I became convinced that I had to find Sheikh Zaabalawi.   1

The first time I had heard of his name had been in a song: 2

"What's wrong with the world, O Zaabalawi?
They've turned it upside down and made it insipid."

It had been a popular song in my childhood and one day it had occurred to   3
me—in the way children have of asking endless questions—to ask my father
about him.

"Who is Zaabalawi, father?"   4

He had looked at me hesitantly as though doubting my ability to understand   5
the answer. However, he had replied:

"May his blessing descend upon you, he's a true saint of God, a remover of   6
worries and troubles. Were it not for him I would have died miserably—"

In the years that followed I heard him many a time sing the praises of this   7
good saint and speak of the miracles he performed. The days passed and brought
with them many illnesses from each one of which I was able, without too much
trouble and at a cost I could afford, to find a cure, until I became afflicted with
that illness for which no one possesses a remedy. When I had tried everything in
vain and was overcome by despair, I remembered by chance what I had heard in
my childhood: Why, I asked myself, should I not seek out Sheikh Zaabalawi? I
recollected that my father had said that he had made his acquaintance in Khan
Gaafar at the house of Sheikh Kamar, one of those sheikhs who practised law in
the religious courts, and I therefore took myself off to his house. Wishing to make
sure that he was still living there, I made enquiries of a vendor of beans whom I
found in the lower part of the house.

"Sheikh Kamar!" he said, looking at me in amazement. "He left the quarter   8
ages ago. They say he's now living in Garden City and has his office in Al-Azhaar
Square."

I looked up the office address in the telephone book and immediately set off   9
to the Chamber of Commerce Building, where it was located. On asking to see
him I was ushered into a room just as a beautiful woman with a most intoxicating perfume was leaving it. The man received me with a smile and motioned me
towards a fine leather-upholstered chair. My feet were conscious of the costly
lushness of the carpet despite the thick soles of my shoes. The man wore a lounge
suit and was smoking a cigar; his manner of sitting was that of someone well
satisfied both with himself and his worldly possessions. The look of warm welcome he gave me left no doubt in my mind that he thought me a prospective
client, and I felt acutely embarrassed at encroaching upon his valuable time.

"Welcome!" he said, prompting me to speak.   10

"I am the son of your old friend Sheikh Ali al-Tatawi," I answered so as to put 11
an end to my equivocal position.

A certain languor was apparent in the glance he cast at me; the languor was 12
not total in that he had not as yet lost all hope in me.

"God rest his soul," he said. "He was a fine man."   13

The very pain that had driven me to go there now prevailed upon me to stay. 14

"He told me," I continued, "of a devout saint named Zaabalawi whom he met 15
at Your Honour's. I am in need of him, sir, if he be still in the land of the living."

The languor became firmly entrenched in his eyes and it would have come as 16
no surprise to me if he had shown the door to both me and my father's memory.

"That," he said in the tone of one who has made up his mind to terminate the 17
conversation, "was a very long time ago and I scarcely recall him now."

Rising to my feet so as to put his mind at rest regarding my intention of going, 18
I asked:

"Was he really a saint?"   19

"We used to regard him as a man of miracles."   20

"And where could I find him today?" I asked, making another move towards 21
the door.

"To the best of my knowledge he was living in the Birgawi Residence in al- 22
Azhar," and he applied himself to some papers on his desk with a resolute movement that indicated he wouldn't open his mouth again. I bowed my head in
thanks, apologized several times for disturbing him and left the office, my head
so buzzing with embarrassment that I was oblivious to all sounds around me.

I went to the Birgawi Residence which was situated in a thickly populated 23
quarter. I found that time had so eaten into the building that nothing was left of
it save an antiquated façade and a courtyard which, despite it being supposedly in
the charge of a caretaker, was being used as a rubbish dump. A small insignificant
fellow, a mere prologue to a man, was using the covered entrance as a place for
the sale of old books on theology and mysticism.

On my asking him about Zaabalawi, he peered at me through narrow, 24
inflamed eyes and said in amazement:

"Zaabalawi! Good heavens, what a time ago that was! Certainly he used to live 25
in this house when it was livable in, and many was the time he would sit with me
talking of bygone days and I would be blessed by his holy presence. Where,
though, is Zaabalawi today?"

He shrugged his shoulders sorrowfully and soon left me to attend to an ap- 26
proaching customer. I proceeded to make enquiries of many shopkeepers in the
district. While I found that a large number of them had never even heard of him,
some, though recalling nostalgically the pleasant times they had spent with
him, were ignorant of his present whereabouts, while others openly made fun of
him, labelled him a charlatan, and advised me to put myself in the hands of a
doctor—as though I had not already done so. I therefore had no alternative but
to return disconsolately home.

With the passing of the days like motes in the air my pains grew so severe that 27
I was sure I would not be able to hold out much lsonger. Once again I fell to

wondering about Zaabalawi and clutching at the hopes his venerable name stirred within me. Then it occurred to me to seek the help of the local Sheikh of the district; in fact, I was surprised I hadn't thought of this to begin with. His office was in the nature of a small shop except that it contained a desk and a telephone, and I found him sitting at his desk wearing a jacket over his striped *galabia*.[1] As he did not interrupt his conversation with a man sitting beside him, I stood waiting till the man had gone. He then looked up at me coldly. I told myself that I should win him over by the usual methods, and it wasn't long before I had him cheerfully inviting me to sit down.

"I'm in need of Sheikh Zaabalawi," I answered his enquiry as to the purpose   28
of my visit.

He gazed at me with the same astonishment as that shown by those I had   29
previously encountered.

"At least," he said, giving me a smile that revealed his gold teeth, "he is still   30
alive. The devil of it is, though, he has no fixed abode. You might well bump into him as you go out of here, on the other hand you might spend days and months in fruitless search of him."

"Even you can't find him!"   31

"Even I! He's a baffling man, but I thank the Lord that he's still alive!"   32

He gazed at me intently, and murmured: 33

"It seems your condition is serious."   34

"Very!"   35

"May God come to your aid! But why don't you go about it rationally?"   36

He spread out a sheet of paper on the desk and drew on it with unexpected   37
speed and skill until he had made a full plan of the district showing all the various quarters, lanes, alleyways, and squares. He looked at it admiringly and said, "These are dwelling-houses, here is the Quarter of the Perfumers, here the Quarter of the Coppersmiths, the Mouski, the Police and Fire Stations. The drawing is your best guide. Look carefully in the cafés, the places where the dervishes perform their rites, the mosques and prayer-rooms, and the Green Gate, for he may well be concealed among the beggars and be indistinguishable from them. Actually, I myself haven't seen him for years, having been somewhat preoccupied with the cares of the world and was only brought back to those most exquisite times of my youth by your enquiry."

I gazed at the map in bewilderment. The telephone rang and he took up the   38
receiver.

"Take it," he told me, generously. "We're at your service."   39

Folding up the map, I left and wandered off through the quarter, from square   40
to street to alleyway, making enquiries of everyone I felt was familiar with the place. At last the owner of a small establishment for ironing clothes told me:

"Go to the calligrapher Hassanein in Umm al-Ghulam—they were friends."   41

I went to Umm al-Ghulam where I found old Hassenein working in a deep,   42
narrow shop full of signboards and jars of colour. A strange smell, a mixture of

---

1. An outer robe.

glue and perfume, permeated its every corner. Old Hassanein was squatting on a sheepskin rug in front of a board propped against the wall; in the middle of it he had inscribed the word "Allah" in silver lettering. He was engrossed in embellishing the letters with prodigious care. I stood behind him, fearful to disturb him or break the inspiration that flowed to his masterly hand. When my concern at not interrupting him had lasted some time, he suddenly enquired with unaffected gentleness:

"Yes?"   43

Realizing that he was aware of my presence, I introduced myself.   44

"I've been told that Sheikh Zaabalawi is your friend and I'm looking for him,"   45
I said.

His hand came to a stop. He scrutinized me in astonishment.   46

"Zaabalawi! God be praised!" he said with a sigh.   47

"He is a friend of yours, isn't he?" I asked eagerly.   48

"He was, once upon a time. A real man of mystery: he'd visit you so often that 49
people would imagine he was your nearest and dearest, then would disappear as though he'd never existed. Yet saints are not to be blamed."

The spark of hope went out with the suddenness of a lamp by a power-cut.   50

"He was so constantly with me," said the man, "that I felt him to be a part of   51
everything I drew. But where is he today?"

"Perhaps he is still alive?"   52

"He's alive, without a doubt. He had impeccable taste and it was due to him   53
that I made my most beautiful drawings."

"God knows," I said, in a voice almost stifled by the dead ashes of hope, "that 54
I am in the direst need of him and no one knows better than you of the ailments in respect of which he is sought."

"Yes—yes. May God restore you to health. He is, in truth, as is said of him, a   55
man, and more—"

Smiling broadly, he added: "And his face is possessed of an unforgettable   56
beauty. But where is he?"

Reluctantly I rose to my feet, shook hands and left. I continued on my way   57
eastwards and westwards through the quarter, enquiring about him from everyone who, by reason of age or experience, I felt was likely to help me. Eventually I was informed by a vendor of lupine that he had met him a short while ago at the house of Sheikh Gad, the well-known composer. I went to the musician's house in Tabakshiyya where I found him in a room tastefully furnished in the old style, its walls redolent with history. He was seated on a divan, his famous lute lying beside him, concealing within itself the most beautiful melodies of our age, while from within the house came the sound of pestle and mortar and the clamour of children. I immediately greeted him and introduced myself, and was put at my ease by the unaffected way in which he received me. He did not ask, either in words or gesture, what had brought me, and I did not feel that he even harboured any such curiosity. Amazed at his understanding and kindness, which boded well, I said:

"O Sheikh Gad, I am an admirer of yours and have long been enchanted by   58
the renderings of your songs."

"Thank you," he said with a smile.   59

"Please excuse my disturbing you," I continued timidly, "but I was told that 60
Zaabalawi was your friend and I am in urgent need of him."

"Zaabalawi!" he said, frowning in concentration. "You need him? God be with 61
you, for who knows, O Zaabalawi, where you are?"

"Doesn't he visit you?" I asked eagerly.   62

"He visited me some time ago. He might well come now; on the other hand I 63
mightn't see him till death!"

I gave an audible sigh and asked: 64

"What made him like that?"   65

He took up his lute. "Such are saints or they would not be saints," he said 66
laughing.

"Do those who need him suffer as I do?"   67

"Such suffering is part of the cure!"   68

He took up the plectrum and began plucking soft strains from the strings. 69
Lost in thought, I followed his movements. Then, as though addressing myself,
I said:

"So my visit has been in vain!"   70

He smiled, laying his cheek against the side of the lute.   71

"God forgive you," he said, "for saying such a thing of a visit that has caused 72
me to know you and you me!"

I was much embarrassed and said apologetically: 73

"Please forgive me; my feelings of defeat made me forget my manners!"   74

"Do not give in to defeat. This extraordinary man brings fatigue to all who 75
seek him. It was easy enough with him in the old days when his place of abode was
known. Today, though, the world has changed and after having enjoyed a position
attained only by potentates, he is now pursued by the police on a charge of false
pretences. It is therefore no longer an easy matter to reach him, but have patience
and be sure that you will do so."

He raised his head from the lute and skillfully led into the opening bars of a 76
melody. Then he sang:

"I make lavish mention, even though I blame myself,
of those I have loved,
For the words of lovers are my wine."

With a heart that was weary and listless I followed the beauty of the melody 77
and the singing.

"I composed the music to this poem in a single night," he told me when he 78
had finished. "I remember that it was the night of the Lesser Bairam. He was my
guest for the whole of that night and the poem was of his choosing. He would sit
for a while just where you are, then would get up and play with my children as
though he were one of them. Whenever I was overcome by weariness or my inspiration failed me he would punch me playfully in the chest and joke with me,
and I would bubble over with melodies and thus I continued working till I
finished the most beautiful piece I have ever composed."

"Does he know anything about music?"   79

"He was the epitome of things musical. He had an extremely beautiful speak-   80
ing voice and you had only to hear him to want to burst into song. His loftiness
of spirit stirred within you—"

"How was it that he cured those diseases before which men are powerless?"   81

"That is his secret. Maybe you will learn it when you meet him."   82

But when would that meeting occur? We relapsed into silence and the hubbub   83
of children once more filled the room.

Again, the Sheikh began to sing. He went on repeating the words "and I have   84
a memory of her" in different and beautiful variations until the very walls danced
in ecstasy. I expressed my wholehearted admiration and he gave me a smile of
thanks. I then got up and asked permission to leave and he accompanied me to
the outer door. As I shook him by the hand he said, "I hear that nowadays he fre-
quents the house of Haag Wanas al-Damanhouri. Do you know him?"

I shook my head, a modicum of renewed hope creeping into my heart.   85

"He is a man of private means," he told me, "who from time to time visits   86
Cairo, putting up at some hotel or other. Every evening, though, he spends at the
Negma Bar in Alfi Street."

I waited for nightfall and went to the Negma Bar. I asked a waiter about Haag   87
Wanas and he pointed to a corner which was semi-secluded because of its position
behind a large pillar with mirrors on its four sides. There I saw a man seated alone
at a table with a bottle three-quarters empty and another empty one in front of
him; there were no snacks or food to be seen and I was sure that I was in the presence of a hardened drinker. He was wearing a loosely flowing silk *galabia* and a
carefully wound turban; his legs were stretched out towards the base of the pillar,
and as he gazed into the mirror in rapt contentment the sides of his face, rounded
and handsome despite the fact that he was approaching old age, were flushed with
wine. I approached quietly till I stood but a few feet away from him. He did not
turn towards me or give any indication that he was aware of my presence.

"Good evening, Mr. Wanas," I said with amiable friendliness.   88

He turned towards me abruptly as though my voice had roused him from   89
slumber and glared at me in disapproval. I was about to explain what had brought
me to him when he interrupted me in an almost imperative tone of voice which
was none the less not devoid of an extraordinary gentleness:

"First, please sit down, and, second, please get drunk!"   90

I opened my mouth to make my excuses but, stopping up his ears with his   91
fingers, he said:

"Not a word till you do what I say."   92

I realized that I was in the presence of a capricious drunkard and told myself 93
that I should go along with him at least halfway.

"Would you permit me to ask one question?" I said with a smile, sitting down. 94

Without removing his hands from his ears he indicated the bottle.   95

"When engaged in a drinking bout like this I do not allow any conversation   96
between myself and another unless, like me, he is drunk, otherwise the session
loses all propriety and mutual comprehension is rendered impossible."

I made a sign indicating that I didn't drink.   97

"That's your look-out," he said offhandedly. "And that's my condition!"   98

He filled me a glass which I meekly took and drank. No sooner had it settled   99 in my stomach than it seemed to ignite. I waited patiently till I had grown used to its ferocity, and said:

"It's very strong, and I think the time has come for me to ask you about—"   100

Once again, however, he put his fingers in his ears.   101

"I shan't listen to you until you're drunk!"   102

He filled up my glass for the second time. I glanced at it in trepidation; then,   103 overcoming my innate objection, I drank it down at a gulp. No sooner had it come to rest inside me than I lost all will-power. With the third glass I lost my memory and with the fourth the future vanished. The world turned round about me and I forgot why I had gone there. The man leaned towards me attentively but I saw him—saw everything—as a mere meaningless series of coloured planes. I don't know how long it was before my head sank down on to the arm of the chair and I plunged into deep sleep. During it I had a beautiful dream the like of which I had never experienced. I dreamed that I was in an immense garden surrounded on all sides by luxuriant trees and the sky was nothing but stars seen between the en-twined branches, all enfolded in an atmosphere like that of sunset or a sky over-cast with cloud. I was lying on a small hummock of jasmine petals which fell upon me like rain, while the lucent spray of a fountain unceasingly sprinkled my head and temples. I was in a state of deep contentedness, of ecstatic serenity. An or-chestra of warbling and cooing played in my ear. There was an extraordinary sense of harmony between me and my inner self, and between the two of us and the world, everything being in its rightful place without discord or distortion. In the whole world there was no single reason for speech or movement, for the universe moved in a rapture of ecstasy. This lasted but a short while. When I opened my eyes consciousness struck at me like a policeman's fist and I saw Wanas al-Damanhouri regarding me with concern. In the bar only a few drowsy people were left.

"You have slept deeply," said my companion; "you were obviously hungry for   104 sleep."

I rested my heavy head in the palms of my hands. When I took them away in   105 astonishment and looked down at them I found that they glistened with drops of water.

"My head's wet," I protested.   106

"Yes, my friend tried to rouse you," he answered quietly.   107

"Somebody saw me in this state?"   108

"Don't worry, he is a good man. Have you not heard of Sheikh Zaabalawi?"   109

"Zaabalawi!" I exclaimed, jumping to my feet.   110

"Yes," he answered in surprise. "What's wrong?"   111

"Where is he?"   112

"I don't know where he is now. He was here and then he left."   113

I was about to run off in pursuit but found I was more exhausted than I had   114 imagined. Collapsed over the table, I cried out in despair:

"My sole reason for coming to you was to meet him. Help me to catch up with   115 him or send someone after him."

The man called a vendor of prawns and asked him to seek out the Sheikh and   116
bring him back. Then he turned to me.

"I didn't realize you were afflicted. I'm very sorry—"   117

"You wouldn't let me speak," I said irritably.   118

"What a pity! He was sitting on this chair beside you the whole time. He was   119
playing with a string of jasmine petals he had round his neck, a gift from one of
his admirers, then, taking pity on you, he began to sprinkle some water on your
head to bring you round."

"Does he meet you here every night?" I asked, my eyes not leaving the door-   120
way through which the vendor of prawns had left.

"He was with me tonight, last night and the night before that, but before that   121
I hadn't seen him for a month."

"Perhaps he will come tomorrow," I answered with a sigh.   122

"Perhaps."   123

"I am willing to give him any money he wants."   124

Wanas answered sympathetically: 125

"The strange thing is that he is not open to such temptations, yet he will cure   126
you if you meet him."

"Without charge?"   127

"Merely on sensing that you love him."   128

The vendor of prawns returned, having failed in his mission.   129

I recovered some of my energy and left the bar, albeit unsteadily. At every   130
street corner I called out, "Zaabalawi!" in the vague hope that I would be rewarded
with an answering shout. The street boys turned contemptuous eyes on me till I
sought refuge in the first available taxi.

The following evening I stayed up with Wanas al-Damanhouri till dawn, but   131
the Sheikh did not put in an appearance. Wanas informed me that he would be
going away to the country and wouldn't be returning to Cairo until he'd sold the
cotton crop.

I must wait, I told myself; I must train myself to be patient. Let me content   132
myself with having made certain of the existence of Zaabalawi, and even of his affection for me, which encourages me to think that he will be prepared to cure me
if a meeting between us takes place.

Sometimes, however, the long delay wearied me. I would become beset by de-   133
spair and would try to persuade myself to dismiss him from my mind completely.
How many weary people in this life know him not or regard him as a mere myth!
Why, then, should I torture myself about him in this way?

No sooner, however, did my pains force themselves upon me than I would   134
again begin to think about him, asking myself as to when I would be fortunate
enough to meet him. The fact that I ceased to have any news of Wanas and was
told he had gone to live abroad did not deflect me from my purpose; the truth of
the matter was that I had become fully convinced that I had to find Zaabalawi.

Yes, I have to find Zaabalawi.   135

— *Translated by Denys Johnson-Davies*

ACTIVITIES FOR WRITING AND DISCUSSION

1. Reread and annotate the reactions of the several people to whom the narrator mentions the name, "Zaabalawi." Do they all react in the same way? in different ways? Working with a partner or small group, try to provide some plausible explanations for the type(s) of reactions you find. Finally, write a description of the Zaabalawi who emerges for you through the impressions of the various characters.

2. After reviewing the context in which it appears, interpret the following dialogue (paragraphs 67 and 68):

Narrator: "Do those who need him suffer as I do?"
Sheikh Gad: "Such suffering is part of the cure!"

Alternative: Identify any other dialogue in the story that intrigues you, annotate it, and give your reading of its literal and/or **symbolic** meanings.

3. At story's end the narrator has yet to "find" Zaabalawi. Does it matter? Have his efforts been wasted? rewarded in any ways? Explain, supporting your response with evidence or quotations from the story.

4. Is the narrator's quest for Zaabalawi symbolic in any ways? If so, *how* or *of what?*

ANNETTE SANFORD (b. 1929)

Nobody Listens When I Talk

Locate me in a swing. Metal, porch type, upholstered in orange-striped canvas by 1
my mother. I am spending the summer. My sixteenth, but the first I have spent in a swing. I could say I'm here because I have a broken leg (it's true I do have pain) or ear trouble or a very strict father. I could say I like to be alone, that I'm cultivating my mind, that I'm meditating on the state of the universe. I could say a lot of things, but nobody listens when I talk, so I don't. Talk. Not often, anyway. And it worries people.

My mother, for instance. She hovers. She lights in a wicker chair by the ban- 2
ister and stares at me periodically. She wears a blue-checked housedress or a green one under the apron I gave her for Christmas with purple rickrack on the hem. She clutches a dustcloth or a broom handle or the woman's section of the *Windsor Chronicle.*

"Marilyn," she says, "a girl your age should be up and doing things." 3

Doing things to her is sweeping out the garage or mending all my underwear. 4
Doing things to me is swimming, hanging on the back of a motorcycle, waterskiing. To her, a girl my age is an apprentice woman in training for three meals a

day served on time and shiny kitchen linoleum, but she would be happy to see me dancing the funky chicken if it would get me on my feet.

I stay prone. I don't want to do her kind of thing, and I can't do mine. The fact 5 is, I don't fit anywhere right now. Except in a swing. So here I am, reading.

My father arrives in the evening. He has worked all day in an office where the 6 air conditioner is broken, or with a client who decides at five minutes to five to invest with another company. He flops in the wicker chair and communes with my mother's ghost.

"Marilyn," he says, "a pretty girl like you ought to realize how lucky she is." 7

Lucky to him is being sixteen with nothing to worry about. My father grew up 8 in Utopia, where everyone between two and twenty dwelt in perpetual joy. If he were sixteen now he would have a motorcycle and a beautiful girl riding behind him. But it wouldn't be me. If he were sixteen and not my father, he wouldn't look at me twice.

From time to time my friend comes. I give her half the swing and she sits like 9 a guru and pops her gum. She can do that and still look great. When she blinks, boys fall dead.

"Marilyn," she says, "a girl like you needs a lot of experience with differ- 10 ent men."

She will get me a date with her cousin. With her sister-in-law's brother. With 11 the preacher's nephew from Syracuse. She will fix me up in the back seat of a car with someone like myself, and we will eat popcorn and watch the drive-in movie and wish it were time to go home.

I could say, *I'm not that kind of girl at all.* I could say, *Someone should be kiss- 12 ing me madly, buying me violets, throwing himself in front of Amtrak for want of my careless glance.*

Who would listen?   13

So I say, "No." I say, "Maybe next week." Then I lie in the swing and watch the 14 stars come out and wonder why I didn't go.

When you lie in a swing all day, you remember a lot. You close your eyes and 15 listen to the locusts humming in the elm trees and you think of who you are.

You think of you at six, crying into a blue corduroy bedspread because your 16 uncle has laughed at your elephant, which has no tusks. You have drawn it as a gift for him. You have never heard of tusks before.

You think of lying in the big iron bed at Grandpa's house, listening to the cis- 17 tern water tapping on the stones outside the window, knowing you are safe be- cause you are the baby and everybody loves you. You think of the dancing class grand ball when you are twelve in a pink dress with ribbons in your hair and a head taller than the boy who brought you. His mother has made a corsage for you, and when you dance it rubs against his nose. You pretend he pulls away because of this, but when you are sixteen lying in a swing, you know it was the scent of your own self-doubt mingling with the rose and lavender that sent you to the chairs waiting by the wall.

When you lie in a swing all day, you live in the world you read about. You drag 18
a bare foot back and forth across the floor and hear the song the chains sing, but
you aren't really you.

You are a woman standing by a table, reading a letter from a box of other let- 19
ters. A dead man wrote them. His face, as young as yours, he has given to the baby
sleeping by the window where the boats pass. He has dreamed his own death and
written a passage from the Psalms: *His days are as grass, in the morning they flour-
ish, in the evening they wither and are cut down.*

You are a father counting cracks in the sidewalk passing under your feet. You 20
have waited a long time in a railroad station for a train carrying the child who
walks beside you, who says, *My mother made me come even though I hate you.*

You are a girl, pregnant, alone in a car you have parked on a country lane. You 21
are kin to the brown cow chewing across the fence. *You are wet and sticky and
blind, curled in the cow's stomach waiting for your birth.* You are sick in the ditch.

You are a boy in a room with bars on the window, an old woman on white 22
sheets looking at the Good Shepherd trapped in a frame, a child with a scar on
his face.

When you aren't really you, then the who that you are is different somehow: 23
strong, and part of everything . . . sure of a harvest for every season . . . glad to be
sad. You are a riddle with hundreds of answers, a song with a thousand tunes.

When you lie in a swing all summer, fall comes before you notice. Suddenly 24
elm leaves pave the street, and you have been seventeen for three days.

It is time to get up. 25

In the kitchen my mother is still in her apron, frying the supper steaks. I sit at 26
the table and eat a grape. I could say, *Don't worry about the underwear. When the
time comes, I can mend it. I can cook and clean a house and love a lonely daughter.
I was watching all summer.*

Instead, I yawn, and she looks at me. "A whole summer," she says, and shakes 27
her head.

In the den the weatherman is promising rain. I kiss the top of my father's head 28
where the hair doesn't grow anymore and lay my cheek on his whiskers. I could
say, *I really am, like you said, beautiful.*

"Try something light for a change," he says, and hands me the funnies. I curl 29
on the couch and call my girlfriend. She tells me she has kissed a trumpet player.
He has an incredible lip. She tells me bikinis are on sale, blond men get bald first,
mud is good for the skin.

I could tell her, *Summer's over.* I could say, *Men are born and die and are born* 30
again. The rest is only details. I could say,

Roses are red,
violets are blue.
I grew up,
but nothing happened to you.

I don't, though. It hurts too much. And besides, nobody listens when I talk. 31
Sometimes not even me. 32

ACTIVITIES FOR WRITING AND DISCUSSION

1. *Do* people "listen" when the **narrator** talks? Write up some conversations that you imagine between the narrator and other people mentioned in the story; or write up conversations between yourself (at age 16 or thereabouts) and significant people who either listened or didn't when *you* talked.

2. Respond to the story using Ideas #1, 2, or 6 of the "Ten Ideas for Writing" on page 35.

TONI CADE BAMBARA (1939–1995)

The Lesson

Back in the days when everyone was old and stupid or young and foolish and me   1
and Sugar were the only ones just right, this lady moved on our block with nappy hair and proper speech and no makeup. And quite naturally we laughed at her, laughed the way we did at the junk man who went about his business like he was some big-time president and his sorry-ass horse his secretary. And we kinda hated her too, hated the way we did the winos who cluttered up our parks and pissed on our handball walls and stank up our hallways and stairs so you couldn't halfway play hide-and-seek without a goddamn gas mask. Miss Moore was her name. The only woman on the block with no first name. And she was black as hell, cept for her feet, which were fish-white and spooky. And she was always planning these boring-ass things for us to do, us being my cousins, mostly, who lived on the block cause we all moved North the same time and to the same apartment then spread out gradual to breathe. And our parents would yank our heads into some kinda shape and crisp up our clothes so we'd be presentable for travel with Miss Moore, who always looked like she was going to church, though she never did. Which is just one of the things the grownups talked about when they talked be-hind her back like a dog. But when she came calling with some sachet she'd sewed up or some gingerbread she'd made or some book, why then they'd all be too em-barrassed to turn her down and we'd get handed over all spruced up. She'd been to college and said it was only right that she should take responsibility for the young ones' education, and she not even related by marriage or blood. So they'd go for it. Specially Aunt Gretchen. She was the main gofer in the family. You got some ole dumb shit foolishness you want somebody to go for, you send for Aunt Gretchen. She been screwed into the go-along for so long, it's a blood-deep nat-ural thing with her. Which is how she got saddled with me and Sugar and Junior in the first place while our mothers were in a la-de-da apartment up the block having a good ole time.

So this one day, Miss Moore rounds us all up at the mailbox and it's purdee   2
hot and she's knockin herself out about arithmetic. And school suppose to let up

in summer I heard, but she don't never let up. And the starch in my pinafore scratching the shit outta me and I'm really hating this nappy-head bitch and her goddamn college degree. I'd much rather go to the pool or to the show where it's cool. So me and Sugar leaning on the mailbox being surly, which is a Miss Moore word. And Flyboy checking out what everybody brought for lunch. And Fat Butt already wasting his peanut-butter-and-jelly sandwich like the pig he is. And Junebug punchin on Q.T.'s arm for potato chips. And Rosie Giraffe shifting from one hip to the other waiting for somebody to step on her foot or ask her if she from Georgia so she can kick ass, preferably Mercedes'. And Miss Moore asking us do we know what money is, like we a bunch of retards. I mean real money, she say, like it's only poker chips or monopoly papers we lay on the grocer. So right away I'm tired of this and say so. And would much rather snatch Sugar and go to the Sunset and terrorize the West Indian kids and take their hair ribbons and their money too. And Miss Moore files that remark away for next week's lesson on brotherhood, I can tell. And finally I say we oughta get to the subway cause it's cooler and besides we might meet some cute boys. Sugar done swiped her mama's lipstick, so we ready.

So we heading down the street and she's boring us silly about what things cost 3 and what our parents make and how much goes for rent and how money ain't divided up right in this country. And then she gets to the part about we all poor and live in the slums, which I don't feature. And I'm ready to speak on that, but she steps out in the street and hails two cabs just like that. Then she hustles half the crew in with her and hands me a five-dollar bill and tells me to calculate 10 percent tip for the driver. And we're off. Me and Sugar and Junebug and Flyboy hangin out the window and hollering to everybody, putting lipstick on each other cause Flyboy a faggot anyway, and making farts with our sweaty armpits. But I'm mostly trying to figure how to spend this money. But they all fascinated with the meter ticking and Junebug starts laying bets as to how much it'll read when Flyboy can't hold his breath no more. Then Sugar lays bets as to how much it'll be when we get there. So I'm stuck. Don't nobody want to go for my plan, which is to jump out at the next light and run off to the first bar-b-que we can find. Then the driver tells us to get the hell out cause we there already. And the meter reads eighty-five cents. And I'm stalling to figure out the tip and Sugar say give him a dime. And I decide he don't need it bad as I do, so later for him. But then he tries to take off with Junebug foot still in the door so we talk about his mamma something ferocious. Then we check out that we on Fifth Avenue and everybody dressed up in stockings. One lady in a fur coat, hot as it is. White folks crazy.

"This is the place," Miss Moore say, presenting it to us in the voice she uses at 4 the museum. "Let's look in the windows before we go in."

"Can we steal?" Sugar asks very serious like she's getting the ground rules 5 squared away before she plays. "I beg your pardon," say Miss Moore, and we fall out. So she leads us around the windows of the toy store and me and Sugar screamin, "This is mine, that's mine, I gotta have that, that was made for me, I was born for that," till Big Butt drowns us out.

"Hey, I'm goin to buy that there." 6

"That there? You don't even know what it is, stupid."   7

"I do so," he say punchin on Rosie Giraffe. "It's a microscope."   8

"Whatcha gonna do with a microscope, fool?"   9

"Look at things."   10

"Like what, Ronald?" ask Miss Moore. And Big Butt ain't got the first notion. 11
So here go Miss Moore gabbing about the thousands of bacteria in a drop of water and the somethinorother in a speck of blood and the million and one living
things in the air around us is invisible to the naked eye. And what she say that for?
Junebug go to town on that "naked" and we rolling. Then Miss Moore ask what
it cost. So we all jam into the window smudgin it up and the price tag say $300.
So then she ask how long'd take for Big Butt and Junebug to save up their allowances. "Too long," I say. "Yeh," adds Sugar, "outgrown it by that time." And
Miss Moore say no, you never outgrow learning instruments. "Why, even medical students and interns and," blah, blah, blah. And we ready to choke Big Butt
for bringing it up in the first damn place.

"This here costs four hundred eighty dollars," say Rosie Giraffe. So we pile up 12
all over her to see what she pointin out. My eyes tell me it's a chunk of glass
cracked with something heavy, and different-color inks dripped into the splits,
then the whole thing put into a oven or something. But for $480 it don't make
sense.

"That's a paperweight made of semi-precious stones fused together under 13
tremendous pressure," she explains slowly, with her hands doing the mining and
all the factory work.

"So what's a paperweight?" ask Rosie Giraffe.   14

"To weigh paper with, dumbbell," say Flyboy, the wise man from the East. 15

"Not exactly," say Miss Moore, which is what she say when you warm or way 16
off too. "It's to weigh paper down so it won't scatter and make your desk untidy."
So right away me and Sugar curtsy to each other and then to Mercedes who is
more the tidy type.

"We don't keep paper on top of the desk in my class," say Junebug, figuring 17
Miss Moore crazy or lyin one.

"At home, then," she say. "Don't you have a calendar and a pencil case and 18
blotter and a letter-opener on your desk at home where you do your homework?"
And she know damn well what our homes look like cause she nosys around in
them every chance she gets.

"I don't even have a desk," say Junebug. "Do we?"   19

"No. And I don't get no homework neither," says Big Butt.   20

"And I don't even have a home," says Flyboy like he do at school to keep the 21
white folks off his back and sorry for him. Send this poor kid to camp posters, is
his specialty.

"I do," says Mercedes. "I have a box of stationery on my desk and a picture of 22
my cat. My godmother bought the stationery and the desk. There's a big rose on
each sheet and the envelopes smell like roses."

"Who wants to know about your smelly-ass stationery," say Rosie Giraffe fore 23
I can get my two cents in.

"It's important to have a work area all your own so that . . ."   24

"Will you look at this sailboat, please," say Flyboy, cutting her off and pointin 25
to the thing like it was his. So once again we tumble all over each other to gaze at
this magnificent thing in the toy store which is just big enough to maybe sail two
kittens across the pond if you strap them to the posts tight. We all start reciting
the price tag like we in assembly. "Handcrafted sailboat of fiberglass at one thousand one hundred ninety-five dollars."

"Unbelievable," I hear myself say and am really stunned. I read it again for 26
myself just in case the group recitation put me in a trance. Same thing. For some
reason this pisses me off. We look at Miss Moore and she lookin at us, waiting for
I dunno what.

"Who'd pay all that when you can buy a sailboat set for a quarter at Pop's, a 27
tube of glue for a dime, and a ball of string for eight cents? It must have a motor
and a whole lot else besides," I say. "My sailboat cost me about fifty cents."

"But will it take water?" say Mercedes with her smart ass.   28

"Took mine to Alley Pond Park once," say Flyboy. "String broke. Lost it. Pity." 29

"Sailed mine in Central Park and it keeled over and sank. Had to ask my fa- 30
ther for another dollar."

"And you got the strap," laugh Big Butt. "The jerk didn't even have a string on 31
it. My old man wailed on his behind."

Little Q.T. was staring hard at the sailboat and you could see he wanted it bad. 32
But he too little and somebody'd just take it from him. So what the hell. "This
boat for kids, Miss Moore?"

"Parents silly to buy something like that just to get all broke up," say Rosie 33
Giraffe.

"That much money it should last forever," I figure.   34

"My father'd buy it for me if I wanted it."   35

"Your father, my ass," say Rosie Giraffe getting a chance to finally push 36
Mercedes.

"Must be rich people shop here," say Q.T.   37

"You are a very bright boy," say Flyboy. "What was your first clue?" And he rap 38
him on the head with back of his knuckles, since Q.T. the only one he could get
away with. Though Q.T. liable to come up behind you years later and get his licks
in when you half expect it.

"What I want to know is," I says to Miss Moore though I never talk to her, I 39
wouldn't give the bitch that satisfaction, "is how much a real boat costs? I figure a
thousand'd get you a yacht any day."

"Why don't you check that out," she says, "and report back to the group?" 40
Which really pains my ass. If you gonna mess up a perfectly good swim day least
you could do is have some answers. "Let's go in," she say like she got something
up her sleeve. Only she don't lead the way. So me and Sugar turn the corner to
where the entrance is, but when we get there I kinda hang back. Not that I'm
scared, what's there to be afraid of, just a toy store. But I feel funny, shame. But
what I got to be shamed about? Got as much right to go in as anybody. But somehow I can't seem to get hold of the door, so I step away from Sugar to lead. But

she hangs back too. And I look at her and she looks at me and this is ridiculous. I mean, damn, I have never ever been shy about doing nothing or going nowhere. But then Mercedes steps up and then Rosie Giraffe and Big Butt crowd in behind and shove, and next thing we all stuffed into the doorway with only Mercedes squeezing past us, smoothing out her jumper and walking right down the aisle. Then the rest of us tumble in like a glued-together jigsaw done all wrong. And people lookin at us. And it's like the time me and Sugar crashed into the Catholic church on a dare. But once we got in there and everything so hushed and holy and the candles and the bowin and the handkerchiefs on all the drooping heads, I just couldn't go through with the plan. Which was for me to run up to the altar and do a tap dance while Sugar played the nose flute and messed around in the holy water. And Sugar kept given me the elbow. Then later teased me so bad I tied her up in the shower and turned it on and locked her in. And she'd be there till this day if Aunt Gretchen hadn't finally figured I was lyin about the boarder takin a shower.

Same thing in the store. We all walkin on tiptoe and hardly touchin the games 41 and puzzles and things. And I watched Miss Moore who is steady watchin us like she waitin for a sign. Like Mama Drewery watches the sky and sniffs the air and takes note of just how much slant is in the bird formation. Then me and Sugar bump smack into each other, so busy gazing at the toys, 'specially the sailboat. But we don't laugh and go into our fat-lady bump-stomach routine. We just stare at that price tag. Then Sugar run a finger over the whole boat. And I'm jealous and want to hit her. Maybe not her, but I sure want to punch somebody in the mouth.

"Watcha bring us here for, Miss Moore?"   42

"You sound angry, Sylvia. Are you mad about something?" Givin me one of 43 them grins like she tellin a grown-up joke that never turns out to be funny. And she's lookin very closely at me like maybe she plannin to do my portrait from memory. I'm mad, but I won't give her that satisfaction. So I slouch around the store bein very bored and say, "Let's go."

Me and Sugar at the back of the train watchin the tracks whizzin by large then 44 small then getting gobbled up in the dark. I'm thinkin about this tricky toy I saw in the store. A clown that somersaults on a bar then does chin-ups just cause you yank lightly at his leg. Cost $35. I could see me askin my mother for a $35 birthday clown. "You wanna who that costs what?" she'd say, cocking her head to the side to get a better view of the hole in my head. Thirty-five dollars could buy new bunk beds for Junior and Gretchen's boy. Thirty-five dollars and the whole household could go visit Granddaddy Nelson in the country. Thirty-five dollars would pay for the rent and the piano bill too. Who are these people that spend that much for performing clowns and $1000 for toy sailboats? What kinda work they do and how they live and how come we ain't in on it? Where we are is who we are, Miss Moore always pointin out. But it don't necessarily have to be that way, she always adds then waits for somebody to say that poor people have to wake up and demand their share of the pie and don't none of us know what kind of pie she talking about in the first damn place. But she ain't so smart cause I still got her four dollars from the taxi and she sure ain't gettin it. Messin up my day with this shit. Sugar nudges me in my pocket and winks.

Miss Moore lines us up in front of the mailbox where we started from, seem 45 like years ago, and I got a headache for thinkin so hard. And we lean all over each other so we can hold up under the draggy-ass lecture she always finishes us off with at the end before we thank her for borin us to tears. But she just looks at us like she readin tea leaves. Finally she say, "Well, what did you think of F. A. O. Schwarz?"

Rosie Giraffe mumbles, "White folks crazy."   46

"I'd like to go there again when I get my birthday money," says Mercedes, and 47 we shove her out the pack so she has to lean on the mailbox by herself.

"I'd like a shower. Tiring day," say Flyboy.   48

Then Sugar surprises me by sayin, "You know, Miss Moore, I don't think all 49 of us here put together eat in a year what that sailboat costs." And Miss Moore lights up like somebody goosed her. "And?" she say, urging Sugar on. Only I'm standin on her foot so she don't continue.

"Imagine for a minute what kind of society it is in which some people can 50 spend on a toy what it would cost to feed a family of six or seven. What do you think?"

"I think," say Sugar pushing me off her feet like she never done before, cause 51 I whip her ass in a minute, "that this is not much of a democracy if you ask me. Equal chance to pursue happiness means an equal crack at the dough, don't it?" Miss Moore is besides herself and I am disgusted with Sugar's treachery. So I stand on her foot one more time to see if she'll shove me. She shuts up, and Miss Moore looks at me, sorrowfully I'm thinkin. And somethin weird is going on, I can feel it in my chest.

"Anybody else learn anything today?" lookin dead at me. I walk away and 52 Sugar has to run to catch up and don't even seem to notice when I shrug her arm off my shoulder.

"Well, we got four dollars anyway," she says.   53

"Uh, hunh."   54

"We could go to Hascombs and get a half a chocolate layer and then go to the 55 Sunset and still have plenty money for potato chips and ice cream sodas."

"Uh hunh."   56

"Race you to Hascombs," she say.   57

We start down the block and she gets ahead which is O.K. by me cause I'm go- 58 ing to the West End and then over to the Drive to think this day through. She can run if she want to and even run faster. But ain't nobody gonna beat me at nuthin.

ACTIVITIES FOR WRITING AND DISCUSSION

1. Respond to the story using the "Four-Step Process for Writing from Reading" described in Chapter 2. For Step #4 use any of the "Ten Ideas" listed on page 35 of Chapter 3.

2. Summarize "the lesson" that Sylvia learns.

3. Jot down your impressions of the story's **first-person** narrator, Sylvia. Then review the various passages of dialogue with her friends (Flyboy, Rosie Giraffe, and so forth). Are there definite advantages to having Sylvia as narrator, or could any of her friends—or even Miss Moore—have served just as well? Explain your answer.

4. Study the story's vernacular language and style. Then write a story of your own with a first-person narrator who uses a strong vernacular.

5. Sylvia's "lesson" isn't from a textbook but out of life—"the school of hard knocks." Recall some "hard knocks" lesson (early or more recent) of your own and write a story about it.

6. Sylvia ends, "But ain't nobody gonna beat me at nuthin." Interpret this closing sentence. How does it follow from the rest of the story? Then:
   a. Write a sequel, in a point of view of your own choice (Miss Moore's perhaps), that traces Sylvia's subsequent life; or
   b. Imagine you are Sylvia in middle age, and write a letter of appreciation to Miss Moore about "the lesson," telling her about your subsequent life.

ALICE WALKER (b. 1944)

The Flowers

It seemed to Myop as she skipped lightly from hen house to pigpen to smoke-   1
house that the days had never been as beautiful as these. The air held a keenness that made her nose twitch. The harvesting of the corn and cotton, peanuts and squash, made each day a golden surprise that caused excited little tremors to run up her jaws.

Myop carried a short, knobby stick. She struck out at random at chickens she   2
liked, and worked out the beat of a song on the fence around the pigpen. She felt light and good in the warm sun. She was ten, and nothing existed for her but her song, the stick clutched in her dark brown hand, and the tat-de-ta-ta-ta of accompaniment.

Turning her back on the rusty boards of her family's sharecropper cabin,   3
Myop walked along the fence till it ran into the stream made by the spring. Around the spring, where the family got drinking water, silver ferns and wildflowers grew. Along the shallow banks pigs rooted. Myop watched the tiny white bubbles disrupt the thin black scale of soil and the water that silently rose and slid away down the stream.

She had explored the woods behind the house many times. Often, in late au-   4
tumn, her mother took her to gather nuts among the fallen leaves. Today she made her own path, bouncing this way and that way, vaguely keeping an eye out for snakes. She found, in addition to various common but pretty ferns and leaves,

an armful of strange blue flowers with velvety ridges and a sweetsuds bush full of the brown, fragrant buds.

By twelve o'clock, her arms laden with sprigs of her findings, she was a mile 5 or more from home. She had often been as far before, but the strangeness of the land made it not as pleasant as her usual haunts. It seemed gloomy in the little cove in which she found herself. The air was damp, the silence close and deep.

Myop began to circle back to the house, back to the peacefulness of the morn- 6 ing. It was then she stepped smack into his eyes. Her heel became lodged in the broken ridge between brow and nose, and she reached down quickly, unafraid, to free herself. It was only when she saw his naked grin that she gave a little yelp of surprise.

He had been a tall man. From feet to neck covered a long space. His head lay 7 beside him. When she pushed back the leaves and layers of earth and debris Myop saw that he'd had large white teeth, all of them cracked or broken, long fingers, and very big bones. All his clothes had rotted away except some threads of blue denim from his overalls. The buckles of the overalls had turned green.

Myop gazed around the spot with interest. Very near where she'd stepped into 8 the head was a wild pink rose. As she picked it to add to her bundle she noticed a raised mound, a ring, around the rose's root. It was the rotted remains of a noose, a bit of shredding plowline, now blending benignly into the soil. Around an overhanging limb of a great spreading oak clung another piece. Frayed, rotted, bleached, and frazzled—barely there—but spinning restlessly in the breeze. Myop laid down her flowers.

And the summer was over.   9

Poems

WILLIAM BLAKE (1757–1827)

Proverbs of Hell

In seed time learn, in harvest teach, in winter enjoy.
Drive your cart and your plow over the bones of the dead.
The road of excess leads to the palace of wisdom.
Prudence is a rich, ugly old maid courted by Incapacity.
He who desires but acts not, breeds pestilence.   5
The cut worm forgives the plow.
Dip him in the river who loves water.
A fool sees not the same tree that a wise man sees.
He whose face gives no light, shall never become a star.
Eternity is in love with the productions of time.   10
The busy bee has no time for sorrow.
The hours of folly are measur'd by the clock; but of wisdom, no clock can
    measure.

All wholesome food is caught without a net or a trap.
Bring out number, weight & measure in a year of dearth.
No bird soars too high, if he soars with his own wings.   15
A dead body revenges not injuries.
The most sublime act is to set another before you.
If the fool would persist in his folly he would become wise.
Folly is the cloke of knavery.
Shame is Pride's cloke.   20
Prisons are built with stones of Law, Brothels with bricks of Religion.
The pride of the peacock is the glory of God.
The lust of the goat is the bounty of God.
The wrath of the lion is the wisdom of God.
The nakedness of woman is the work of God.   25
Excess of sorrow laughs. Excess of joy weeps.
The roaring of lions, the howling of wolves, the raging of the stormy sea, and
    the destructive sword, are portions of eternity, too great for the eye of man.
The fox condemns the trap, not himself.
Joys impregnate. Sorrows bring forth.
Let man wear the fell of the lion, woman the fleece of the sheep.   30
The bird a nest, the spider a web, man friendship.
The selfish, smiling fool, & the sullen, frowning fool shall be both thought
    wise, that they may be a rod.
What is now proved was once only imagin'd.
The rat, the mouse, the fox, the rabbet watch the roots; the lion, the tyger, the
    horse, the elephant watch the fruits.
The cistern contains: the fountain overflows.   35
One thought fills immensity.
Always be ready to speak your mind, and a base man will avoid you.
Every thing possible to be believ'd is an image of truth.
The eagle never lost so much time as when he submitted to learn of the crow.
The fox provides for himself, but God provides for the lion.   40
Think in the morning. Act in the noon. Eat in the evening. Sleep in the night.
He who has suffer'd you to impose on him, knows you.
As the plow follows words, so God rewards prayers.
The tygers of wrath are wiser than the horses of instruction.
Expect poison from the standing water.   45
You never know what is enough unless you know what is more than enough.
Listen to the fool's reproach! it is a kingly title!
The eyes of fire, the nostrils of air, the mouth of water, the beard of earth.
The weak in courage is strong in cunning.
The apple tree never asks the beech how he shall grow; nor the lion, the horse,   50
    how he shall take his prey.
The thankful receiver bears a plentiful harvest.
If others had not been foolish, we should be so.
The soul of sweet delight can never be defil'd.
When thou seest an Eagle, thou seest a portion of Genius; lift up thy head!

As the catterpiller chooses the fairest leaves to lay her eggs on, so the priest lays   55
    his curse on the fairest joys.
To create a little flower is the labour of ages.
Damn braces. Bless relaxes.
The best wine is the oldest, the best water the newest.
Prayers plow not! Praises reap not!
Joys laugh not! Sorrows weep not!   60
The head Sublime, the heart Pathos, the genitals Beauty, the hands & feet
    Proportion.
As the air to a bird or the sea to a fish, so is contempt to the contemptible.
The crow wish'd every thing was black, the owl that every thing was white.
Exuberance is Beauty.
If the lion was advised by the fox, he would be cunning.   65
Improvement makes strait roads; but the crooked roads without Improvement
    are roads of Genius.
Sooner murder an infant in its cradle than nurse unacted desires.
Where man is not, nature is barren.
Truth can never be told so as to be understood, and not be believ'd.
Enough! or Too much.   70

The Tyger

Tyger! Tyger! burning bright
In the forests of the night,
What immortal hand or eye
Could frame thy fearful symmetry?

In what distant deeps or skies   5
Burnt the fire of thine eyes?
On what wings dare he aspire?
What the hand dare seize the fire?

And what shoulder, & what art,
Could twist the sinews of thy heart?   10
And when thy heart began to beat,
What dread hand? & what dread feet?

What the hammer? what the chain?
In what furnace was thy brain?
What the anvil? what dread grasp   15
Dare its deadly terrors clasp?

When the stars threw down their spears
And water'd heaven with their tears,
Did he smile his work to see?
Did he who made the Lamb make thee?   20

Tyger! Tyger! burning bright
In the forests of the night,
What immortal hand or eye
Dare frame thy fearful symmetry?

ACTIVITIES FOR WRITING AND DISCUSSION

1. The "Proverbs of Hell" are Blake's most famous collection of **aphorisms.** Setting aside for a moment the unusual title, read and annotate the "Proverbs," noting especially: (a) proverbs you like; and (b) proverbs that puzzle you. Share your reactions with a partner or small group.

2. Identify striking examples of any of the following: **metaphor, simile, personification, verbal irony,** and **symbolism.** Choose two or three such examples, and, as an experiment, rewrite them using only *literal* language. In each case, how does the **figure** or **trope** pack more power than the flatly *literal* expression you tried in its place?

3. Reread page 11 in Chapter 2, which describes how Blake used annotations to stimulate his thinking and writing. Over the next several weeks use your annotations of readings and your quick notes (see Chapter 4) to compose and collect aphorisms of your own.

4. Blake wrote that "Without Contraries is no progression." His "Proverbs" are excerpted from his prose satire, *The Marriage of Heaven and Hell.* Using these two facts as clues, speculate on why Blake entitled these aphorisms "Proverbs of Hell."

5. Read "The Tyger" aloud several times and determine its **meter.** Then do a **scansion** using the notation described on page 168. Its possible meanings aside, what features (consider **alliteration, assonance,** word choice, imagery, and so on) make the poem exciting or pleasing to the eye and ear? Illustrate your response with examples.

6. Where and how does "The Tyger" upset or transcend conventional (e.g., dictionary) definitions or descriptions of a tiger? What meaning or purpose might underlie the references to "wings," "hammer," "chain," and "anvil"? How do the poem's first and last stanzas differ, and what do you make of the difference?

WILLIAM WORDSWORTH (1770–1850)

I wandered lonely as a cloud

I wandered lonely as a cloud
That floats on high o'er vales and hills,
When all at once I saw a crowd,
A host, of golden daffodils;

Beside the lake, beneath the trees,   5
Fluttering and dancing in the breeze.

Continuous as the stars that shine
And twinkle on the milky way,
They stretched in never-ending line
Along the margin of a bay: 10
Ten thousand saw I at a glance,
Tossing their heads in sprightly dance.

The waves beside them danced; but they
Out-did the sparkling waves in glee:
A poet could not but be gay,   15
In such a jocund company:
I gazed—and gazed—but little thought
What wealth the show to me had brought:

For oft, when on my couch I lie
In vacant or in pensive mood,   20
They flash upon that inward eye
Which is the bliss of solitude;
And then my heart with pleasure fills,
And dances with the daffodils.

ACTIVITIES FOR WRITING AND DISCUSSION

1. Repeat Activity #5 above (about Blake's "The Tyger") for Wordsworth's "I wandered lonely as a cloud."

2. Do you have a valued memory of some place or moment that continues to sustain or feed you in the present? Describe that place or moment and its enduring impact on you.

3. Research the topic of memory and its positive and/or negative consequences. If you wish, focus on memory in Wordsworth and read his best-known poem about memory, "Lines: Composed a Few Miles Above Tintern Abbey," which you can find in any collection of Wordsworth's poems.

WALT WHITMAN (1819–1892)

To You

Whoever you are, I fear you are walking the walks of dreams,
I fear these supposed realities are to melt from under your feet and hands,
Even now your features, joys, speech, house, trade, manners, troubles, follies,
    costume, crimes, dissipate away from you,

Your true soul and body appear before me,
They stand forth out of affairs, out of commerce, shops, work, farms, clothes,   5
    the house, buying, selling, eating, drinking, suffering, dying.

Whoever you are, now I place my hand upon you, that you be my poem,
I whisper with my lips close to your ear,
I have loved many women and men, but I love none better than you.

O I have been dilatory and dumb,
I should have made my way straight to you long ago,   10
I should have blabb'd nothing but you, I should have chanted nothing but you.

I will leave all and come and make the hymns of you,
None has understood you, but I understand you,
None has done justice to you, you have not done justice to yourself,
None but has found you imperfect, I only find no imperfection in you,   15
None but would subordinate you, I only am he who will never consent to
    subordinate you,
I only am he who places over you no master, owner, better, God, beyond what
    waits intrinsically in yourself.

Painters have painted their swarming groups and the centre-figure of all,
From the head of the centre-figure spreading a nimbus of gold-color'd light,
But I paint myriads of heads, but paint no head without its nimbus of gold-   20
    color'd light,
From my hand from the brain of every man and woman it streams, effulgently
    flowing forever.

O I could sing such grandeurs and glories about you!
You have not known what you are, you have slumber'd upon yourself all your
    life,
Your eyelids have been the same as closed most of the time,
What you have done returns already in mockeries,   25
(Your thrift, knowledge, prayers, if they do not return in mockeries, what is
    their return?)

The mockeries are not you,
Underneath them and within them I see you lurk,
I pursue you where none else has pursued you,
Silence, the desk, the flippant expression, the night, the accustom'd routine, if   30
    these conceal you from others or from yourself, they do not conceal you
    from me,
The shaved face, the unsteady eye, the impure complexion, if these balk others
    they do not balk me,
The pert apparel, the deform'd attitude, drunkenness, greed, premature death,
    all these I part aside.

There is no endowment in man or woman that is not tallied in you,
There is no virtue, no beauty in man or woman, but as good is in you,
No pluck, no endurance in others, but as good is in you,   35
No pleasure waiting for others, but an equal pleasure waits for you.

As for me, I give nothing to any one except I give the like carefully to you,
I sing the songs of the glory of none, not God, sooner than I sing the songs of
    the glory of you.

Whoever you are! claim your own at any hazard!
These shows of the East and West are tame compared to you,   40
These immense meadows, these interminable rivers, you are immense and
    interminable as they,
These furies, elements, storms, motions of Nature, throes of apparent
    dissolution, you are he or she who is master or mistress over them,
Master or mistress in your own right over Nature, elements, pain, passion,
    dissolution.

The hopples fall from your ankles, you find an unfailing sufficiency,
Old or young, male or female, rude, low, rejected by the rest, whatever you are   45
    promulges itself,
Through birth, life, death, burial, the means are provided, nothing is scanted,
Through angers, losses, ambition, ignorance, ennui, what you are picks its way.

A Noiseless Patient Spider

A noiseless patient spider,
I mark'd where on a little promontory it stood isolated,
Mark'd how to explore the vacant vast surrounding,
It launch'd forth filament, filament, filament, out of itself,
Ever unreeling them, ever tirelessly speeding them.   5

And you O my soul where you stand,
Surrounded, detached, in measureless oceans of space,
Ceaselessly musing, venturing, throwing, seeking the spheres to connect them,
Till the bridge you will need be form'd, till the ductile anchor hold,
Till the gossamer thread you fling catch somewhere, O my soul.   10

ACTIVITIES FOR WRITING AND DISCUSSION

1. Read "To You" aloud to yourself or communally, with each person taking
a turn reading a few lines. As you read and listen mark any lines, phrases, or
individual words that strike you. At the end of the reading share the passages that
moved you most with a small group or the class.

2. Few poets talk to "you," the reader, as directly and persistently as Whitman did. How does this direct address make you feel? uncomfortable? embarrassed? violated? understood or encouraged? some combination of the preceding? Explain your answer with references to specific lines or passages in the poem.

3. Characterize the speaker in "To You." Who is he? How does he know so much? What gives him the right to talk to you with such familiarity? *Does* he have the right? Consider addressing all of these questions by drafting a verbal portrait or description of the speaker as you imagine him.

4. Write a poem or personal letter to the speaker in "To You" in which you react to his poem and share some stories from your life that bear on its themes.

Emily Dickinson (1830–1886)

Because I could not stop for Death

Because I could not stop for Death—
He kindly stopped for me—
The Carriage held but just Ourselves—
And Immortality.

We slowly drove—He knew no haste   5
And I had put away
My labor and my leisure too,
For His Civility—

We passed the School, where Children strove
At Recess—in the Ring—   10
We passed the Fields of Gazing Grain—
We passed the Setting Sun—

Or rather—He passed Us—
The Dews drew quivering and chill—
For only Gossamer,[1] my Gown—   15
My Tippet[2]—only Tulle—[3]

We paused before a House that seemed
A Swelling of the Ground—

---

1. A finely woven fabric.   2. A covering for the shoulders, such as a shawl.   3. A very fine net of silk or similar fabric.

The Roof was scarcely visible—
The Cornice [4]—in the Ground—   20

Since then—'tis Centuries—and yet
Feels shorter than the Day
I first surmised the Horses Heads
Were toward Eternity—

One need not be a Chamber—to be Haunted—

One need not be a Chamber—to be Haunted—
One need not be a House—
The Brain has Corridors—surpassing
Material Place—

Far safer, of a Midnight Meeting   5
External Ghost
Than its interior Confronting—
That Cooler Host.

Far safer, through an Abbey gallop,
The Stones a'chase—   10
Than Unarmed, one's a'self encounter—
In lonesome Place—

Ourself behind ourself, concealed—
Should startle most—
Assassin hid in our Apartment   15
Be Horror's least.

The Body—borrows a Revolver—
He bolts the Door—
O'erlooking a superior spectre—
Or More—   20

"Faith" is a fine invention

"Faith" is a fine invention
When Gentlemen can *see*—
But *Microscopes* are prudent
In an Emergency.

---

4. Molding that crowns a roof or a wall.

Thomas Hardy (1840–1928)

The Ruined Maid

"O 'mélia, my dear, this does everything crown!
Who could have supposed I should meet you in Town?
And whence such fair garments, such prosperi-ty?"—
"O didn't you know I'd been ruined?" said she.

—"You left us in tatters, without shoes or socks,   5
Tired of digging potatoes, and spudding up docks;
And now you've gay bracelets and bright feathers three!"—
"Yes: that's how we dress when we're ruined," said she.

—"At home in the barton you said 'thee' and 'thou,'
And 'thik oon,' and 'theäs oon,' and 't'other'; but now   10
Your talking quite fits 'ee for high compa-ny!"—
"Some polish is gained with one's ruin," said she.

—"Your hands were like paws then, your face blue and bleak
But now I'm bewitched by your delicate cheek,
And your little gloves fit as on any la-dy!"—   15
"We never do work when we're ruined," said she.

—"You used to call home-life a hag-ridden dream,
And you'd sigh, and you'd sock; but at present you seem
To know not of megrims or melancho-ly!"—
"True. One's pretty lively when ruined," said she.   20

—"I wish I had feathers, a fine sweeping gown,
And a delicate face, and could strut about Town!"—
"My dear—a raw country girl, such as you be,
Cannot quite expect that. You ain't ruined," said she.

ACTIVITIES FOR WRITING AND DISCUSSION

1. Review the material on **meter** in Chapter 15 and Appendix C. Then read the poem aloud and determine its meter.

2. Consider the two speakers in the poem.
   a. How would you characterize their **diction**—as formal or informal? as **abstract** or **concrete**? as general or specific? as literal or **figurative?** Give examples.

b. Judging by the content and diction of their dialogue, what would you suppose the speakers' backgrounds to be? In what sort of environment did they grow up? What is their social status?

3. How do you interpret the word "ruined" as it is used in the poem?

4. In poetry or prose, compose a prequel to the poem. That is, reconstruct the events in the two speakers' lives that have brought them to this moment of conversation. Embellish your narrative with additional details as needed, but strive to remain faithful to the characters of the two women as set forth in the poem.

GERARD MANLEY HOPKINS (1844–1889)

Spring and Fall

TO A YOUNG CHILD

Márgarét, áre you gríeving
Over Goldengrove unleaving?
Leáves, líke the things of man, you
With your fresh thoughts care for, can you?
Áh! ás the heart grows older   5
It will come to such sights colder
By and by, nor spare a sigh
Though worlds of wanwood leafmeal lie;
And yet you *will* weep and know why.
Now no matter, child, the name: 10
Sórrow's spríngs áre the same.
Nor mouth had, no nor mind, expressed
What heart heard of, ghost[1] guessed:
It ís the blight man was born for,
It is Margaret you mourn for.   15

ACTIVITIES FOR WRITING AND DISCUSSION

1. The sound and **meter** of a poem were extremely important to Hopkins. In this poem he has carefully inserted accent marks (e.g., "Márgarét, are you gríeving") to indicate syllables that are to receive special stress in a pattern of what

---

1. Spirit, soul.

he called "sprung rhythm." Read the poem aloud several times to yourself and with a partner or small group. Though the meanings of certain lines may baffle you, concentrate on experiencing the meter and on identifying and marking any examples of sound effects such as **assonance, alliteration,** or **consonance.** Are there any lines or phrases that you find difficult to perform aloud? Explain and discuss.

2. Hopkins also experimented boldly with **diction.** Mark any words in the poem that surprise, please, or puzzle you, and in each case, speculate on *why* Hopkins may have chosen the particular word he did. For instance, why does he use the word "unleaving" in line two or "*fresh* thoughts" in line four? Could he have chosen better alternatives?

3. Following Hopkins's example, use your own notebook or quick notes (see Chapter 4) to experiment with diction. Invent new words (neologisms) and play with unusual word combinations or sounds, as Hopkins does.

4. In one sentence paraphrase what you see as the main point of the poem.

Denise Levertov (1923–1997)

Contraband

The tree of knowledge was the tree of reason.
That's why the taste of it
drove us from Eden. That fruit
was meant to be dried and milled to a fine powder
for use a pinch at a time, a condiment.   5
God had probably planned to tell us later
about this new pleasure.
                         We stuffed our mouths full of it,
gorged on *but* and *if* and *how* and again
but, knowing no better.   10
It's toxic in large quantities; fumes
swirled in our heads and around us
to form a dense cloud that hardened to steel,
a wall between us and God, Who was Paradise.
Not that God is unreasonable—but reason   15
in such excess was tyranny
and locked us into its own limits, a polished cell
reflecting our own faces. God lives
on the other side of that mirror,
but through the slit where the barrier doesn't   20

quite touch ground, manages still
to squeeze in—as filtered light,
splinters of fire, a strain of music heard
then lost, then heard again.

Maya Angelou (b. 1928)

Seven Women's Blessed Assurance

1
One thing about me,
I'm little and low,
find me a man
wherever I go.

2
They call me string bean   5
'cause I'm so tall.
Men see me,
they ready to fall.

2
I'm young as morning
and fresh as dew.   10
Everybody loves me
and so do you.

4
I'm fat as butter
and sweet as cake.
Men start to tremble   15
each time I shake.

5
I'm little and lean,
sweet to the bone.
They like to pick me up
and carry me home.   20

6
When I passed forty
I dropped pretense,

'cause men like women
who got some sense.

7
Fifty-five is perfect,   25
so is fifty-nine,
'cause every man needs
to rest sometime.

Audre Lorde (1934–1992)

Hanging Fire

I am fourteen
and my skin has betrayed me
the boy I cannot live without
still sucks his thumb
in secret   5
how come my knees are
always so ashy
what if I die
before morning
and momma's in the bedroom   10
with the door closed.

I have to learn how to dance
in time for the next party
my room is too small for me
suppose I die before graduation   15
they will sing sad melodies
but finally
tell the truth about me
There is nothing I want to do
and too much   20
that has to be done
and momma's in the bedroom
with the door closed.

Nobody even stops to think
about my side of it   25
I should have been on Math Team
my marks were better than his

why do I have to be
the one
wearing braces   30
I have nothing to wear tomorrow
will I live long enough
to grow up
and momma's in the bedroom
with the door closed.   35

ACTIVITIES FOR WRITING AND DISCUSSION

1. Other than the periods at the ends of stanzas, the poem has no punctuation. How does this lack of punctuation affect the way you read the poem, and how (if at all) does it "fit" the subject of the poem?

2. How do you explain the repetition of the lines "and momma's in the bedroom/with the door closed" at the end of each stanza?

3. After annotating the poem, identify a particular line or group of lines that resonates with your own experience of adolescence. Use the line(s) as a "springboard" to writing about that experience.

4. Rewrite the poem as a dialogue between the **speaker** and her "momma."

MARY OLIVER (b. 1935)

The Black Snake

When the black snake
flashed onto the morning road,
and the truck could not swerve—
death, that is how it happens.

Now he lies looped and useless   5
as an old bicycle tire.
I stop the car
and carry him into the bushes.

He is as cool and gleaming
as a braided whip, he is as beautiful and quiet   10
as a dead brother.
I leave him under the leaves

and drive on, thinking
about *death:* its suddenness,

its terrible weight,   15
its certain coming. Yet under

reason burns a brighter fire, which the bones
have always preferred.
It is the story of endless good fortune.
It says to oblivion: not me!   20

It is the light at the center of every cell.
It is what sent the snake coiling and flowing forward
happily all spring through the green leaves before
he came to the road.

Some Questions You Might Ask

Is the soul solid, like iron?
Or is it tender and breakable, like
the wings of a moth in the beak of the owl?
Who has it, and who doesn't?
I keep looking around me.   5
The face of the moose is as sad
as the face of Jesus.
The swan opens her white wings slowly.
In the fall, the black bear carries leaves into the darkness.
One question leads to another.   10
Does it have a shape? Like an iceberg?
Like the eye of a hummingbird?
Does it have one lung, like the snake and the scallop?
Why should I have it, and not the anteater
who loves her children?   15
Why should I have it, and not the camel?
Come to think of it, what about the maple trees?
What about the blue iris?
What about all the little stones, sitting alone in the moonlight?
What about roses, and lemons, and their shining leaves?   20
What about the grass?

Mark Rudman (b. 1948)

Chrome

On the late news I watch hundreds of helmeted riders
almost indecipherable in the dust
tearing up the holes of desert turtles in the Mojave [1]—

---

1. A desert in the southwestern United States.

and I remember our bravura cycling:
the trick was to go as fast as you could   5
without being thrown by rock or incline.
Hills leeched of color,
the desert a kind of form,
with rimrock and succulents and gulches
providing borders—boundaries.   10
Dust and desire.
I wanted to go down toward the desert floor,
where the spines of the saguaro cactus
guarded the sticky pulp I loved,
the sweet, incomparable, centerless center.   15
O sweet sixteen, to be sprung again and again against
the rock-studded sand, the danger not
in the desert but around it.
The body's oneness with the mind
on the lean machine seemed just right, the body   20
soaring while hovering close
to the sand as the Honda 125
jounced past yucca and cactus and took
the long dip into the arroyo[2] where the ring
of distant chimney rocks and hills   25
like space stations receded, and I
twisted the handle-bars like the horns
of a steer to side-wind up and over the rim.
I was thrown only by breaks in the terrain,
grit and stones and dips in the sand,   30
or by sudden soft patches; or by swerving to avoid
a brush with tumbleweed or a mesquite bush.
Spills were rehearsals for free falling, a way to slow
time down, cease to feel your own weight,
achieve clarity and edge as if edging down   35
off the concrete onto the sand was the aim. . . .
Circling demoniacally, I didn't notice
the ferocious sun, a fusion of horizon and sky,
or the hawks stunned and motionless as clouds.
Each time, bloody but happy,   40
I eased back onto the highway,
and set off down the canyon road
into the sun, whitening as it hung
level with the cliff. Once I rode toward it

---

2. A gully cut by a stream.

hearing only the hush of the tires,   45
the pure elation of it taking my head off as I took
a horseshoe curve at 50 and approached
an even sharper one—the slender cycle shaking apart—;
and I wondered *what to do,* like Porthos[3]
going back to the bomb he'd planted to make sure   50
he'd lit the fuse . . . when—BOOM!—;
I turned the accelerator handle all the way forward
to slow down—gunning the engine
by accident when the cycle bucked, reared,
and surged ahead—I rose, the cliff's gravel   55
gleamed, radiant, it was all over;
I could feel my soul leave my body and see my body flung out
over the canyon rim—
it looked as if I'd leap the cliff and fly
into the sun, time gone, space erased,   60
not a piñon in sight to break my fall, only the cliff
wall, studded with jagged stones.
And I knew if I braked abruptly on the gravel the bike
would catapult me headlong into the open,
so I let go of the throttle—threw up my hands—   65
and the bike went off the highway, keeled over
and died at the cliff's edge.
I owe my life to letting go.

Gary Soto (b. 1952)

Oranges

The first time I walked
With a girl, I was twelve,
Cold, and weighted down
With two oranges in my jacket.
December. Frost cracking   5
Beneath my steps, my breath
Before me, then gone,
As I walked toward
Her house, the one whose
Porch light burned yellow   10

———

3. One of the musketeers in Alexandre Dumas's *The Three Musketeers* (1846).

Night and day, in any weather.
A dog barked at me, until
She came out pulling
At her gloves, face bright
With rouge. I smiled,   15
Touched her shoulder, and led
Her down the street, across
A used car lot and a line
Of newly planted trees,
Until we were breathing   20
Before a drugstore. We
Entered, the tiny bell
Bringing a saleslady
Down a narrow aisle of goods.
I turned to the candies   25
Tiered like bleachers,
And asked what she wanted—
Light in her eyes, a smile
Starting at the corners
Of her mouth. I fingered   30
A nickel in my pocket,
And when she lifted a chocolate
That cost a dime,
I didn't say anything.
I took the nickel from   35
My pocket, then an orange,
And set them quietly on
The counter. When I looked up,
The lady's eyes met mine,
And held them, knowing   40
Very well what it was all
About.

      Outside,
A few cars hissing past,
Fog hanging like old   45
Coats between the trees.
I took my girl's hand
In mine for two blocks,
Then released it to let
Her unwrap the chocolate.   50
I peeled my orange
That was so bright against
The gray of December
That, from some distance,
Someone might have thought   55
I was making a fire in my hands.

ACTIVITIES FOR WRITING AND DISCUSSION

1. What was the incident of the nickel and the orange "all/About" (lines 41–42)? In your notebook, narrate any similar incidents in your own experience.

2. In poetry or prose, retell the incident of the nickel and the orange from the **point of view** of either the girl or the saleslady.

3. With what mixture of emotions does the poem leave you? Explain.

Nonfiction / Essays

G. K. CHESTERTON (1874–1936)

A Defence of Humility

. . . [H]umility has infinitely deeper roots than any modern men suppose; . . . it is a metaphysical and, one might almost say, a mathematical virtue. Probably this can best be tested by a study of those who frankly disregard humility and assert the supreme duty of perfecting and expressing one's self. These people tend, by a perfectly natural process, to bring their own great human gifts of culture, intellect, or moral power to a great perfection, successively shutting out everything that they feel to be lower than themselves. Now shutting out things is all very well, but it has one simple corollary—that from everything that we shut out we are ourselves shut out. When we shut our door on the wind, it would be equally true to say that the wind shuts its door on us. Whatever virtues a triumphant egoism really leads to, no one can reasonably pretend that it leads to knowledge. Turning a beggar from the door may be right enough, but pretending to know all the stories the beggar might have narrated is pure nonsense; and this is practically the claim of the egoism which thinks that self-assertion can obtain knowledge. A beetle may or may not be inferior to a man—the matter awaits demonstration; but if he were inferior by ten thousand fathoms, the fact remains that there is probably a beetle view of things of which a man is entirely ignorant. If he wishes to conceive that point of view, he will scarcely reach it by persistently revelling in the fact that he is not a beetle. The most brilliant exponent of the egoistic school, Nietzsche[1], with deadly and honourable logic, admitted that the philosophy of self-satisfaction led to looking down upon the weak, the cowardly, and the ignorant. Looking down on things may be a delightful experience, only there is nothing, from a mountain to a cabbage, that is really seen when it is seen from a balloon. The philosopher of the ego sees everything, no doubt, from a high and rarefied heaven; only he sees everything foreshortened or deformed.

---

1. German philosopher (1844–1900)

Now if we imagine that a man wished truly, as far as possible, to see everything as it was, he would certainly proceed on a different principle. He would seek to divest himself for a time of those personal peculiarities which tend to divide him from the thing he studies. It is as difficult, for example, for a man to examine a fish without developing a certain vanity in possessing a pair of legs, as if they were the latest article of personal adornment. But if a fish is to be approximately understood, this physiological dandyism must be overcome. The earnest student of fish morality will, spiritually speaking, chop off his legs. And similarly the student of birds will eliminate his arms; the frog-lover will with one stroke of the imagination remove all his teeth, and the spirit wishing to enter into all the hopes and fears of jelly-fish will simplify his personal appearance to a really alarming extent. It would appear, therefore, that this great body of ours and all its natural instincts, of which we are proud, and justly proud, is rather an encumbrance at the moment when we attempt to appreciate things as they should be appreciated. We do actually go through a process of mental asceticism, a castration of the entire being, when we wish to feel the abounding good in all things. It is good for us at certain times that ourselves should be like a mere window—as clear, as luminous, and as invisible.

In a very entertaining work, over which we have roared in childhood, it is stated that a point has no parts and no magnitude. Humility is the luxurious art of reducing ourselves to a point, not to a small thing or a large one, but to a thing with no size at all, so that to it all the cosmic things are what they really are—of immeasurable stature. That the trees are high and the grasses short is a mere accident of our own foot-rules and our own stature. But to the spirit which has stripped off for a moment its own idle temporal standards the grass is an everlasting forest, with dragons for denizens; the stones of the road are as incredible mountains piled one upon the other; the dandelions are like gigantic bonfires illuminating the lands around; and the heathbells on their stalks are like planets hung in heaven each higher than the other. Between one stake of a paling and another there are new and terrible landscapes; here a desert, with nothing but one misshapen rock; here a miraculous forest, of which all the trees flower above the head with the hues of sunset; here, again, a sea full of monsters that Dante would not have dared to dream. These are the visions of him who, like the child in the fairy tales, is not afraid to become small. Meanwhile, the sage whose faith is in magnitude and ambition is, like a giant, becoming larger and larger, which only means that the stars are becoming smaller and smaller. World after world falls from him into insignificance; the whole passionate and intricate life of common things becomes as lost to him as is the life of the infusoria to a man without a microscope. He rises always through desolate eternities. He may find new systems, and forget them; he may discover fresh universes, and learn to despise them. But the towering and tropical vision of things as they really are—the gigantic daisies, the heaven-consuming dandelions, the great Odyssey of strange-coloured oceans and strange-shaped trees, of dust like the wreck of temples, and thistledown like the ruin of stars—all this colossal vision shall perish with the last of the humble.

ACTIVITIES FOR WRITING AND DISCUSSION

1. Understand Chesterton's argument.
   a. Annotate the second paragraph. Summarize the main argument of the paragraph in a sentence or two and share your summary with a partner or small group. (For advice on how to write a summary, see pages 127–128.)
   b. Summarize the main argument of the whole essay. If the summary you write differs substantively from your partner's or groupmates', reach a consensus on a most accurate summary. Then, using evidence (see page 110 in Chapter 9) from your current knowledge or from research, defend or refute Chesterton's argument.

2. Chesterton writes: "Humility is the luxurious art of reducing ourselves to a point, . . . to a thing with no size at all, so that to it all the cosmic things are what they really are—of immeasurable stature" (p. 519). In what sense is humility "luxurious"? As an experiment, reduce yourself imaginatively to "a point" or something very small (e.g., a bug, a grain of sand, a worm, a leaf of grass, a butterfly) and describe what you see, hear, touch, smell, and taste in the course of an hour or a day. Then answer the question, *What does this experiment have to do with "humility"?*

3. In what ways, if any, does Chesterton's concept of "humility" differ from "imagination"?

MAYA ANGELOU (b. 1928)

Graduation

The children in Stamps[1] trembled visibly with anticipation. Some adults were excited too, but to be certain the whole young population had come down with graduation epidemic. Large classes were graduating from both the grammar school and the high school. Even those who were years removed from their own day of glorious release were anxious to help with preparations as a kind of dry run. The junior students who were moving into the vacating classes' chairs were tradition-bound to show their talents for leadership and management. They strutted through the school and around the campus exerting pressure on the lower grades. Their authority was so new that occasionally if they pressed a little too hard it had to be overlooked. After all, next term was coming, and it never hurt a sixth grader to have a play sister in the eighth grade, or a tenth-year student to be able to call a twelfth grader Bubba. So all was endured in a spirit of shared

---

1. A town in Arkansas.

understanding. But the graduating classes themselves were the nobility. Like travelers with exotic destinations on their minds, the graduates were remarkably forgetful. They came to school without their books, or tablets or even pencils. Volunteers fell over themselves to secure replacements for the missing equipment. When accepted, the willing workers might or might not be thanked, and it was of no importance to the pregraduation rites. Even teachers were respectful of the now quiet and aging seniors, and tended to speak to them, if not as equals, as beings only slightly lower than themselves. After tests were returned and grades given, the student body, which acted like an extended family, knew who did well, who excelled, and what piteous ones had failed.

Unlike the white high school, Lafayette County Training School distinguished itself by having neither lawn, nor hedges, nor tennis court, nor climbing ivy. Its two buildings (main classrooms, the grade school and home economics) were set on a dirt hill with no fence to limit either its boundaries or those of bordering farms. There was a large expanse to the left of the school which was used alternately as a baseball diamond or basketball court. Rusty hoops on swaying poles represented the permanent recreational equipment, although bats and balls could be borrowed from the P.E. teacher if the borrower was qualified and if the diamond wasn't occupied.

Over this rocky area relieved by a few shady tall persimmon trees the graduating class walked. The girls often held hands and no longer bothered to speak to the lower students. There was a sadness about them, as if this old world was not their home and they were bound for higher ground. The boys, on the other hand, had become more friendly, more outgoing. A decided change from the closed attitude they projected while studying for finals. Now they seemed not ready to give up the old school, the familiar paths and classrooms. Only a small percentage would be continuing on to college—one of the South's A & M (agricultural and mechanical) schools, which trained Negro youths to be carpenters, farmers, handymen, masons, maids, cooks and baby nurses. Their future rode heavily on their shoulders, and blinded them to the collective joy that had pervaded the lives of the boys and girls in the grammar school graduating class.

Parents who could afford it had ordered new shoes and readymade clothes for themselves from Sears and Roebuck or Montgomery Ward. They also engaged the best seamstresses to make the floating graduating dresses and to cut down secondhand pants which would be pressed to a military slickness for the important event.

Oh, it was important, all right. Whitefolks would attend the ceremony, and two or three would speak of God and home, and the Southern way of life, and Mrs. Parsons, the principal's wife, would play the graduation march while the lower-grade graduates paraded down the aisles and took their seats below the platform. The high school seniors would wait in empty classrooms to make their dramatic entrance. 5

In the Store I was the person of the moment. The birthday girl. The center. Bailey[2] had graduated the year before, although to do so he had had to forfeit all pleasures to make up for his time lost in Baton Rouge.

My class was wearing butter-yellow piqué dresses, and Momma launched out on mine. She smocked the yoke into tiny crisscrossing puckers, then shirred the rest of the bodice. Her dark fingers ducked in and out of the lemony cloth as she embroidered raised daisies around the hem. Before she considered herself finished she had added a crocheted cuff on the puff sleeves, and a pointy crocheted collar.

I was going to be lovely. A walking model of all the various styles of fine hand sewing and it didn't worry me that I was only twelve years old and merely graduating from the eighth grade. Besides, many teachers in Arkansas Negro schools had only that diploma and were licensed to impart wisdom.

The days had become longer and more noticeable. The faded beige of former times had been replaced with strong and sure colors. I began to see my classmates' clothes, their skin tones, and the dust that waved off pussy willows. Clouds that lazed across the sky were objects of great concern to me. Their shiftier shapes might have held a message that in my new happiness and with a little bit of time I'd soon decipher. During that period I looked at the arch of heaven so religiously my neck kept a steady ache. I had taken to smiling more often, and my jaws hurt from the unaccustomed activity. Between the two physical sore spots, I suppose I could have been uncomfortable, but that was not the case. As a member of the winning team (the graduating class of 1940) I had outdistanced unpleasant sensations by miles. I was headed for the freedom of open fields.

Youth and social approval allied themselves with me and we trammeled memories of slights and insults. The wind of our swift passage remodeled my features. Lost tears were pounded to mud and then to dust. Years of withdrawal were brushed aside and left behind, as hanging ropes of parasitic moss. 10

My work alone had awarded me a top place and I was going to be one of the first called in the graduating ceremonies. On the classroom blackboard, as well as on the bulletin board in the auditorium, there were blue stars and white stars and red stars. No absences, no tardinesses, and my academic work was among the best of the year. I could say the preamble to the Constitution even faster than Bailey. We timed ourselves often: "We the people of the United States in order to form a more perfect union . . ." I had memorized the Presidents of the United States from Washington to Roosevelt in chronological as well as alphabetical order.

My hair pleased me too. Gradually the black mass had lengthened and thickened, so that it kept at last to its braided pattern, and I didn't have to yank my scalp off when I tried to comb it.

Louise and I had rehearsed the exercises until we tired out ourselves. Henry Reed was class valedictorian. He was a small, very black boy with hooded eyes, a long, broad nose and an oddly shaped head. I had admired him for years because

---

2. The author's brother.

each term he and I vied for the best grades in our class. Most often he bested me, but instead of being disappointed I was pleased that we shared top places between us. Like many Southern Black children, he lived with his grandmother, who was as strict as Momma and as kind as she knew how to be. He was courteous, respectful and soft-spoken to elders, but on the playground he chose to play the roughest games. I admired him. Anyone, I reckoned, sufficiently afraid or sufficiently dull could be polite. But to be able to operate at a top level with both adults and children was admirable.

His valedictory speech was entitled "To Be or Not to Be." The rigid tenth-grade teacher had helped him write it. He'd been working on the dramatic stresses for months.

The weeks until graduation were filled with heady activities. A group of small children were to be presented in a play about buttercups and daisies and bunny rabbits. They could be heard throughout the building practicing their hops and their little songs that sounded like silver bells. The older girls (nongraduates, of course) were assigned the task of making refreshments for the night's festivities. A tangy scent of ginger, cinnamon, nutmeg and chocolate wafted around the home economics building as the budding cooks made samples for themselves and their teachers. 15

In every corner of the workshop, axes and saws split fresh timber as the wood-shop boys made sets and stage scenery. Only the graduates were left out of the general bustle. We were free to sit in the library at the back of the building or look on quite detachedly, naturally, on the measures being taken for our event.

Even the minister preached on graduation the Sunday before. His subject was, "Let your light so shine that men will see your good works and praise your Father, Who is in Heaven." Although the sermon was purported to be addressed to us, he used the occasion to speak to backsliders, gamblers and general ne'er-do-wells. But since he had called our names at the beginning of the service we were mollified.

Among Negroes the tradition was to give presents to children going only from one grade to another. How much more important this was when the person was graduating at the top of the class. Uncle Willie and Momma had sent away for a Mickey Mouse watch like Bailey's. Louise gave me four embroidered handkerchiefs. (I gave her crocheted doilies.) Mrs. Sneed, the minister's wife, made me an undershirt to wear for graduation, and nearly every customer gave me a nickel or maybe even a dime with the instruction "Keep on moving to higher ground," or some such encouragement.

Amazingly the great day finally dawned and I was out of bed before I knew it. I threw open the back door to see it more clearly, but Momma said, "Sister, come away from that door and put your robe on."

I hoped the memory of that morning would never leave me. Sunlight was itself young, and the day had none of the insistence maturity would bring it in a few hours. In my robe and barefoot in the backyard, under cover of going to see about my new beans, I gave myself up to the gentle warmth and thanked God that no matter what evil I had done in my life He had allowed me to live to see this day. 20

Somewhere in my fatalism I had expected to die, accidentally, and never have the chance to walk up the stairs in the auditorium and gracefully receive my hard-earned diploma. Out of God's merciful bosom I had won reprieve.

Bailey came out in his robe and gave me a box wrapped in Christmas paper. He said he had saved his money for months to pay for it. It felt like a box of chocolates, but I knew Bailey wouldn't save money to buy candy when we had all we could want under our noses.

He was as proud of the gift as I. It was a soft-leather-bound copy of a collection of poems by Edgar Allan Poe, or, as Bailey and I called him, "Eap." I turned to "Annabel Lee" and we walked up and down the garden rows, the cool dirt between our toes, reciting the beautifully sad lines.

Momma made a Sunday breakfast although it was only Friday. After we finished the blessing, I opened my eyes to find the watch on my plate. It was a dream of a day. Everything went smoothly and to my credit I didn't have to be reminded or scolded for anything. Near evening I was too jittery to attend to chores, so Bailey volunteered to do all before his bath.

Days before, we had made a sign for the Store, and as we turned out the lights Momma hung the cardboard over the doorknob. It read clearly: CLOSED, GRADUATION.

My dress fitted perfectly and everyone said that I looked like a sunbeam in it. 25 On the hill, going toward the school, Bailey walked behind with Uncle Willie, who muttered, "Go on, Ju." He wanted him to walk ahead with us because it embarrassed him to have to walk so slowly. Bailey said he'd let the ladies walk together, and the men would bring up the rear. We all laughed, nicely.

Little children dashed by out of the dark like fireflies. Their crepe-paper dresses and butterfly wings were not made for running and we heard more than one rip, dryly, and the regretful "uh oh" that followed.

The school blazed without gaiety. The windows seemed cold and unfriendly from the lower hill. A sense of ill-fated timing crept over me, and if Momma hadn't reached for my hand I would have drifted back to Bailey and Uncle Willie, and possibly beyond. She made a few slow jokes about my feet getting cold, and tugged me along to the now-strange building.

Around the front steps, assurance came back. There were my fellow "greats," the graduating class. Hair brushed back, legs oiled, new dresses and pressed pleats, fresh pocket handkerchiefs and little handbags, all homesewn. Oh, we were up to snuff, all right. I joined my comrades and didn't even see my family go in to find seats in the crowded auditorium.

The school band struck up a march and all classes filed in as had been rehearsed. We stood in front of our seats, as assigned, and on a signal from the choir director, we sat. No sooner had this been accomplished than the band started to play the national anthem. We rose again and sang the song, after which we recited the pledge of allegiance. We remained standing for a brief minute before the choir director and the principal signaled to us, rather desperately I thought, to take our seats. The command was so unusual that our carefully rehearsed and smooth-running machine was thrown off. For a full minute we fumbled for our chairs and bumped into each other awkwardly. Habits change or solidify under pressure, so in our state of nervous tension we had been ready to follow our usual assembly pattern: the American national anthem, then the pledge of allegiance, then the song every Black person I knew called the Negro National Anthem. All done in the same key, with the same passion and most often standing on the same foot.

Finding my seat at last, I was overcome with a presentiment of worse things to 30 come. Something unrehearsed, unplanned, was going to happen, and we were going to be made to look bad. I distinctly remember being explicit in the choice of pronoun. It was "we," the graduating class, the unit, that concerned me then.

The principal welcomed "parents and friends" and asked the Baptist minister to lead us in prayer. His invocation was brief and punchy, and for a second I thought we were getting on the high road to right action. When the principal came back to the dais, however, his voice had changed. Sounds always affected me profoundly and the principal's voice was one of my favorites. During assembly it melted and lowed weakly into the audience. It had not been in my plan to listen to him, but my curiosity was piqued and I straightened up to give him my attention.

He was talking about Booker T. Washington, our "late great leader," who said we can be as close as the fingers on the hand, etc. . . . Then he said a few vague things about friendship and the friendship of kindly people to those less fortunate than themselves. With that his voice nearly faded, thin, away. Like a river diminishing to a stream and then to a trickle. But he cleared his throat and said, "Our speaker tonight, who is also our friend, came from Texarkana to deliver the commencement address, but due to the irregularity of the train schedule, he's going to, as they say, 'speak and run.'" He said that we understood and wanted the man to know that we were most grateful for the time he was able to give us and then something about how we were willing always to adjust to another's program, and without more ado—"I give you Mr. Edward Donleavy."

Not one but two white men came through the door off-stage. The shorter one walked to the speaker's platform, and the tall one moved to the center seat and sat down. But that was our principal's seat, and already occupied. The dislodged gentleman bounced around for a long breath or two before the Baptist minister gave him his chair, then with more dignity than the situation deserved, the minister walked off the stage.

Donleavy looked at the audience once (on reflection, I'm sure that he wanted only to reassure himself that we were really there), adjusted his glasses and began to read from a sheaf of papers.

He was glad "to be here and to see the work going on just as it was in the other 35 schools."

At the first "Amen" from the audience I willed the offender to immediate death by choking on the word. But Amens and Yes, sir's began to fall around the room like rain through a ragged umbrella.

He told us of the wonderful changes we children in Stamps had in store. The Central School (naturally, the white school was Central) had already been granted improvements that would be in use in the fall. A well-known artist was coming from Little Rock to teach art to them. They were going to have the newest micro-scopes and chemistry equipment for their laboratory. Mr. Donleavy didn't leave us long in the dark over who made these improvements available to Central High. Nor were we to be ignored in the general betterment scheme he had in mind.

He said that he had pointed out to people at a very high level that one of the first-line football tacklers at Arkansas Agricultural and Mechanical College had graduated from good old Lafayette County Training School. Here fewer Amen's were heard. Those few that did break through lay dully in the air with the heaviness of habit.

He went on to praise us. He went on to say how he had bragged that "one of the best basketball players at Fisk sank his first ball right here at Lafayette County Training School."

The white kids were going to have a chance to become Galileos and Madame   40 Curies and Edisons and Gauguins, and our boys (the girls weren't even in on it) would try to be Jesse Owenses and Joe Louises.

Owens and the Brown Bomber were great heroes in our world, but what school official in the white-goddom of Little Rock had the right to decide that those two men must be our only heroes? Who decided that for Henry Reed to become a scientist he had to work like George Washington Carver, as a bootblack, to buy a lousy microscope? Bailey was obviously always going to be too small to be an athlete, so which concrete angel glued to what country seat had decided that if my brother wanted to become a lawyer he had to first pay penance for his skin by picking cotton and hoeing corn and studying correspondence books at night for twenty years?

The man's dead words fell like bricks around the auditorium and too many settled in my belly. Constrained by hard-learned manners I couldn't look behind me, but to my left and right the proud graduating class of 1940 had dropped their heads. Every girl in my row had found something new to do with her handker-chief. Some folded the tiny squares into love knots, some into triangles, but most were wadding them, then pressing them flat on their yellow laps.

On the dais, the ancient tragedy was being replayed. Professor Parsons sat, a sculptor's reject, rigid. His large, heavy body seemed devoid of will or willingness, and his eyes said he was no longer with us. The other teachers examined the flag (which was draped stage right) or their notes, or the windows which opened on our now-famous playing diamond.

Graduation, the hush-hush magic time of frills and gifts and congratulations and diplomas, was finished for me before my name was called. The accomplishment was nothing. The meticulous maps, drawn in three colors of ink, learning and spelling decasyllabic words, memorizing the whole of *The Rape of Lucrece*—it was for nothing. Donleavy had exposed us.

We were maids and farmers, handymen and washerwomen, and anything   45 higher that we aspired to was farcical and presumptuous.

Then I wished that Gabriel Prosser and Nat Turner had killed all whitefolks in their beds and that Abraham Lincoln had been assassinated before the signing of the Emancipation Proclamation, and that Harriet Tubman had been killed by that blow on her head and Christopher Columbus had drowned in the *Santa Maria*.

It was awful to be a Negro and have no control over my life. It was brutal to be young and already trained to sit quietly and listen to charges brought against my color with no chance of defense. We should all be dead. I thought I should like to see us all dead, one on top of the other. A pyramid of flesh with the whitefolks on the bottom, as the broad base, then the Indians with their silly tomahawks and teepees and wigwams and treaties, the Negroes with their mops and recipes and cotton sacks and spirituals sticking out of their mouths. The Dutch children should all stumble in their wooden shoes and break their necks. The French should choke to death on the Louisiana Purchase (1803) while silkworms ate all the Chinese with their stupid pigtails. As a species, we were an abomination. All of us.

Donleavy was running for election, and assured our parents that if he won we could count on having the only colored paved playing field in that part of Arkansas. Also—he never looked up to acknowledge the grunts of acceptance— also, we were bound to get some new equipment for the home economics building and the workshop.

He finished, and since there was no need to give any more than the most perfunctory thank-you's, he nodded to the men on the stage, and the tall white man who was never introduced joined him at the door. They left with the attitude that now they were off to something really important. (The graduation ceremonies at Lafayette County Training School had been a mere preliminary.)

The ugliness they left was palpable. An uninvited guest who wouldn't leave. 50 The choir was summoned and sang a modern arrangement of "Onward, Christian Soldiers," with new words pertaining to graduates seeking their place in the world. But it didn't work. Elouise, the daughter of the Baptist minister, recited "Invictus," and I could have cried at the impertinence of "I am the master of my fate, I am the captain of my soul."

My name had lost its ring of familiarity and I had to be nudged to go and receive my diploma. All my preparations had fled. I neither marched up to the stage like a conquering Amazon, nor did I look in the audience for Bailey's nod of approval. Marguerite Johnson, I heard the name again, my honors were read, there were noises in the audience of appreciation, and I took my place on the stage as rehearsed.

I thought about colors I hated: ecru, puce, lavender, beige and black.

There was shuffling and rustling around me, then Henry Reed was giving his valedictory address, "To Be or Not to Be." Hadn't he heard the whitefolks? We couldn't *be*, so the question was a waste of time. Henry's voice came out clear and strong. I feared to look at him. Hadn't he got the message? There was no "nobler in the mind" for Negroes because the world didn't think we had minds, and they let us know it. "Outrageous fortune"? Now, that was a joke. When the ceremony was over I had to tell Henry Reed some things. That is, if I still cared. Not "rub," Henry, "erase." "Ah, there's the erase." Us.

Henry had been a good student in elocution. His voice rose on tides of promise and fell on waves of warnings. The English teacher had helped him to create a sermon winging through Hamlet's soliloquy. To be a man, a doer, a builder, a leader, or to be a tool, an unfunny joke, a crusher of funky toadstools. I marveled that Henry could go through with the speech as if we had a choice.

I had been listening and silently rebutting each sentence with my eyes closed; 55 then there was a hush, which in an audience warns that something unplanned is happening. I looked up and saw Henry Reed, the conservative, the proper, the A student, turn his back to the audience and turn to us (the proud graduating class of 1940) and sing, nearly speaking,

> "Lift ev'ry voice and sing
> Till earth and heaven ring
> Ring with the harmonies of Liberty . . ."

It was the poem written by James Weldon Johnson. It was the music composed by J. Rosamond Johnson. It was the Negro national anthem. Out of habit we were singing it.

Our mothers and fathers stood in the dark hall and joined the hymn of encouragement. A kindergarten teacher led the small children onto the stage and the buttercups and daisies and bunny rabbits marked time and tried to follow:

> "Stony the road we trod
> Bitter the chastening rod
> Felt in the days when hope, unborn, had died.
> Yet with a steady beat
> Have not our weary feet
> Come to the place for which our fathers sighed?"

Each child I knew had learned that song with his ABC's and along with "Jesus Loves Me This I Know." But I personally had never heard it before. Never heard the words, despite the thousands of times I had sung them. Never thought they had anything to do with me.

On the other hand, the words of Patrick Henry had made such an impression on me that I had been able to stretch myself tall and trembling and say, "I know not what course others may take, but as for me, give me liberty or give me death."

And now I heard, really for the first time:

> "We have come over a way that with tears
> has been watered,
> We have come, treading our path through
> the blood of the slaughtered."

While echoes of the song shivered in the air, Henry Reed bowed his head, said 60 "Thank you," and returned to his place in the line. The tears that slipped down many faces were not wiped away in shame.

We were on top again. As always, again. We survived. The depths had been icy and dark, but now a bright sun spoke to our souls. I was no longer simply a member of the proud graduating class of 1940; I was a proud member of the wonderful, beautiful Negro race.

Oh, Black known and unknown poets, how often have your auctioned pains sustained us? Who will compute the lonely nights made less lonely by your songs, or the empty pots made less tragic by your tales?

If we were a people much given to revealing secrets, we might raise monuments and sacrifice to the memories of our poets, but slavery cured us of that weakness. It may be enough, however, to have it said that we survive in exact relationship to the dedication of our poets (include preachers, musicians and blues singers).

ACTIVITY FOR WRITING AND DISCUSSION

1. "Graduation" is one of the most widely anthologized contemporary American essays. Why? Research the background and public reception of the essay. Then, in an essay of your own, assess the popularity of "Graduation" and to what degree you believe it is merited.

EDWARD HOAGLAND (b. 1932)

Learning to Eat Soup

Learning to eat soup: Like little boats that go out to sea, I push my spoon ahead of me.

At my parents' wedding in Michigan, one of Mother's uncles leaned over before the cake cutting and whispered to her, "Feed the brute and flatter the ass." The uncles threw rice at them as they jumped into their car, and Dad, after going a mile down the road, stopped and silently swept it out. That night, before deflowering each other (both over thirty), they knelt by the bed to consecrate the experience.

To strike a balance is everything. If a person sings quietly to himself on the street, people smile with approval; but if he talks, it's not all right; they think he's crazy. The singer is presumed to be happy and the talker unhappy, which counts heavily against him. . . . To strike a balance: If, for example, walking in the woods, we flake off a bit of hangnail skin and an ant drags this bonanza away, we might say that the ants were feasting on human flesh, but probably wouldn't. On the other hand, if a man suffers a heart attack there and festers undiscovered, then we would.

Baby inside M.'s stomach feels like the popping and simmering of oatmeal cooking, as I lay my hand across. Pain, "a revelation to me like fireworks, those comets that whirl," she says in the labor room. She lies like a boy under stress in the canoe-shaped cot, the nurses gathering gravely, listening to the baby's heart-beat through the stethoscope between contractions—heart like a drumbeat sounded a block away. Baby, with bent monkey feet, is born still in its sac. Doctor is unlocatable. The interns gather. A nurse picks up both phones simultaneously and calls him with urgency. The crowd, the rooting and cheering in the delivery room—as if the whole world were gathered there—after the solitary labor room.

Very old people age somewhat as bananas do.   5

Two Vietcong prisoners: An American drew crosses on their foreheads, one guy's cross red, other guy's green, to distinguish which was the target and which the decoy to be thrown out of the helicopter to make the target talk.

Winter travel: Snowbanks on river ice means thin ice because snow layers shield the ice from the cold. And water is always wearing it away from underneath; therefore keep on the *inside* of curves and away from all cutbanks, where the current is fast. Travel on barest ice and avoid obstacles like rocks and drift piles sticking through, which also result in a thinning of the cover. Gravel bars may dam the river, causing overflows, which "smoke" in cold weather like a fire, giving some warning before you sink through the slush on top and into the overflow itself. Overflows also can occur in slow sections of the river where the ice is thick and grinds against itself. A special danger area is the junction of incoming creeks whose whirlpools have kept the water open under a concealment of snow. If the water level falls abruptly, sometimes you can walk on the dry edges of the riverbed under solid ice which remains on top as though you were in a tunnel, but that can be dangerous because bears enjoy following such a route too.

You butter a cat's paws when moving it to a new home, so it can find its way back after going out exploring the first time.

My friend Danny Chapman, the Ringling Bros. clown, had a sliding, circus sort of face, like the eternal survivor, marked by the sun, wind, pain, bad luck, and bad dealings, the standard lusts and equivocations, like a stone that the water has slid over for sixty years. Face was much squarer when not in august-clown black-face, its seams smudged by reacting to all he'd seen, and holding so many expressions in readiness that none could be recognized as characteristic of him.

Success in writing, versus painting, means that your work becomes *cheaper*, 10 purchasable by anybody.

The *New York Times* is a vast democratic souk in which every essayist can find a place to publish his or her voice. But otherwise, for a native New Yorker with proud and lengthy ties to the city, it's not so easy. The *New York Review of Books* is published by a group of sensibilities that give the impression of having been born in this metropolis but of wishing they were Londoners instead. And *The New Yorker* traditionally has been the home of writers and editors born in Columbus, Ohio—who yearned so much to seem like real New Yorkers that their city personalities in print had an artificial, overeager sophistication and snobbery.

I ride my stutter, posting over its jolts, swerving with it, guiding it, if never "mastering" it.

At the annual sports show at the New York Colosseum: "Stay straight with sports," says a poster, a picture of a girl wearing a T-shirt with that slogan over her breasts. An exhibitor tells me he just saw two men fondling each other in the men's room—"It just turns your stomach." A woman wearing a huge odd-looking hat made of dried pheasants' heads is cooing affectionately at a cageful of pheasants. A skinning contest is held in which three taxidermists go to work on the carcasses of three Russian boars.

"If two people are in love they can sleep on the blade of a knife."

Karl Wheeler used a baby bottle until he was five years old, whereupon his mother said to him, "That's your last bottle, Karl. When you break that one you'll never get another one!" and he began to toss it idly in the air to catch it, but missed.   15

First white men in British Columbia sold some of the Indians their names: Ten dollars for a fine name like O'Shaughnessy, five dollars for the more modest Harris.

At six A.M. I shoot a porcupine in the garage (knew about it from seeing Bimbo vomit from a fear reaction after his many tangles with porcupines). It goes under the building to die but not too far for a rake to reach. I take it to Paul Brooks's house. In his freezer he has woodchucks, beaver, bear, deer, bobcat, and porcupine meat (he is a man living only on Social Security), and he cleans it for me. We see it's a mama with milk in her breasts. His mouth fills with saliva as he works; he's also preparing a venison roast for lunch, with garlic salt, Worcestershire sauce, pepper, onions, etc. Says this time of year, first of June, the woodchucks are light as your hat, the winter has been so long for them; you can feel their thin legs. Porcupine liver is a delicacy, the rest not so much. The porcupine had been chewing at my garage for the salts; I eat the porcupine; therefore I'm eating my garage—dark drumsticks that night by kerosene lamp. Game tastes herby even without herbs—best is bobcat and muskrat, in my experience, not counting big meats like moose. One countryman we know had his ashes scattered on his muskrat pond. The porcupine had chattered its teeth and rattled its poor quiver of quills as I approached with my gun. Was so waddly it could not even limp properly when badly wounded. Lay on its side gurgling, choking, and sighing like a man dying.

At the Freifields' one-room cabin, with snowshoes hung under steep roof, I read Larry's father's hectic journal, written in Austro-English, of desperate orphanhood on the Austrian-Russian front in WWI. He, adopted by the rival armies as they overran the town, living in the trenches with them, living off stolen crusts otherwise, surviving the bombardments, dodging the peasants who hated Jews, but cherished by Austrian soldiers, who then were killed—saw one's legs blown off just after he'd changed places with him. That night peed in his pants in the trench and froze himself to the ground.

"Old Bet," the first circus elephant in America, was bought by Hachaliah Bailey from an English ship captain in 1815 but was shot eventually by religious fanatics in Connecticut as resembling the biblical Behemoth of the Book of Job (as indeed she did).

My first overtly sexual memory is of me on my knees in the hallway outside 20
our fifth-grade classroom cleaning the floor, and Lucy Smith in a white blouse and black skirt standing above me, watching me.

My first memory is of being on a train which derailed in a rainstorm in Dakota one night when I was two—and of hearing, as we rode in a hay wagon toward the distant weak lights of a little station, that a boy my age had just choked to death from breathing mud. But maybe my first real memory emerged when my father was dying. I was thirty-five and I dreamed so incredibly vividly of being dandled and rocked and hugged by him, being only a few months old, giggling helplessly and happily.

Had supper at a local commune where they have a fast turnover and have made life hard. They buy twenty-dollar used cars instead of spending two hundred dollars, use kerosene instead of the electricity they have, and a team of horses to plow. They got 180 gallons of maple syrup out of their trees, but they washed 1,400 sugaring pails in the bathtub in cold water, never having put in a hot-water heater. Much husky embracing, like wrestlers; and before they eat their supper they have Grace, where twenty-some people clasp hands around the table, meditating and squeezing fingers. Bread bakes on a puffy wood stove. Rose hips and chili peppers hang from the ceiling on strings, other herbs everywhere and pomegranates and jars of basic grains. The toilet is a car on blocks up the hill. Supper is a soup bowl full of rice and chard and potato pancakes with two sour sauces and apple butter, yogurt for dessert; and we drink from mason jars of water passed around. And the final "course" is dental floss, which everybody solemnly uses. A dulcimer is played with the quill of a feather, accompanied by bongo drums. The women ended the public festivities by each announcing where she was going to sleep that night, which bedroom or which hayloft, in case anyone wished to join her. Clothing is heaped in a feed bin near the bottom of the stairs, and everybody is supposed to reach in in the morning and remove the first items that fit them and come to hand, without regard for which particular sex the clothes were originally made for. The saddest moment of the evening for me was when a little girl came around to her mother carrying a hairbrush in her hand and asking to be put to bed. The mother lost her temper. "Why run to me?" she said. "Everybody in this room is your parent. Anybody can brush your hair and tell you a story and put you to bed."

Manhattan, now 14,310 acres, was 9,800.

Bernard Malamud speaks of writing as a battle: "go to paper" with a novel. At age sixty-one is trying to "write wise," a new aim, and hard. Being between books, I say I'm in a period of withdrawal and inaction like that of a snake that is shedding its skin.

On the crest of Moose Mountain is an old birch growing low and twisty out 25 of the ruins of a still older, bigger bole, surrounded by ferns, and it's there that the deer that feed in my field bed down during the day.

There is a whole literary genre that consists, first, of foolish writing and then later capitalizing upon the foolishness by beating one's breast and crying *mea culpa*. Why *was* I a white Black Panther, a drug swallower, a jackbooted feminist, a jet-set-climbing novelist, a 1940s Communist? How interesting and archetypal of me to have shared my generation's extremes.

Busybodies are called in Yiddish *kochleffl*, "cooking spoon," because they stir people up.

The hollow in the center of the upper lip is where "the angel touched you and told you to forget what you had seen in heaven."

Wife of F.'s uncle, to prevent him from going to work one morning when she preferred he stay home, set the alarm so that it seemed it was too late for him to make the train when he woke. But he did rush so terribly he got to the station, and there collapsed and died, and she, only twenty-seven, never remarried.

Joyce consulted Jung, who diagnosed his poor daughter as incurably schizo- 30 phrenic partly on the evidence of her brilliant, obsessive punning. Joyce remarked that he, too, was a punner. "You are a deep-sea diver," said Jung. "She is drowning."

The cure for stuttering of holding stones in one's mouth works because of the discomfort of them rattling against one's teeth. Stones from a crocodile's stomach were thought to be best.

Amerigo Vespucci said that Indian women enlarged their lovers' sexual parts by applying venomous insects to them.

After losing her virginity at seventeen, she felt unstoppered on the street, like a hollow tube, as though the wind could blow right through her.

The sea, at the village of Soya on Hokkaido island in 1792, was so fertile that twelve quarts of dry rice could be bartered for 1,200 herring, 100 salmon, 300 trout, or 3 sealskins.

How Davy Crockett kept warm when lost in the woods one night: climbing 35 thirty feet up a smooth tree trunk and sliding down.

Am drunk from a soft-shell-crab lunch with Random House's Joe Fox, but stutter so vigorously with William Shawn as to obscure both from him and myself my drunkenness—stutter through it and give myself time to recall names like Numeiry and Assad, necessary to win Shawn's backing for the trip to Africa. He, as reported, is excessively solicitous of my comfort and state of mind; insulated and jittery; heated by electric heater (in August), yet fanned by electric fan; in his shirtsleeves, and immediately suggests I remove my coat. He has an agonized, bulging baby's head with swallowed-up eyes, like that of the tormented child in Francis Bacon's painting *The Scream*. Questions me effectively, however, on my knowledge of the Sudan and the prospects for a salable article there. Says OK. I go to 42nd St. and watch screwing to relax—crazily enough, less is charged to see live souls (twenty-five cents) than for a porno flick—then walk home. Lunch the next day with Alfred Kazin, my old teacher (and the day after that with Barthelme, who has just broken through a writing block, he says, and is therefore more cheerful and sober than I have seen him in a considerable while; says women's movement will produce changes as profound as the abolition of slavery). Kazin as always is a veritable tumult of impressions, like H. S. Commager and other busy intellectuals I have liked, but in Kazin's case it is enormously in earnest and felt. Expresses hurt at Bellow's recent inexplicable anger. Otherwise an outpouring of talk about his new book on the forties, when he published his first book and met the literary figures of the day. Played violin with drunken Alan Tate. Advances the idea that William James, a hero of his, is a better direct heir of Emerson than Thoreau; also the view that students now resent the fact that a professor knows more than they do, want him to learn along with them in class, as in group therapy, and when caught out on homework facts, get offended instead of trying to fake through, as in the old days. On Ph.D. orals, the candidates seem to have no favorite poem, no poem they can quote from, when he asks them for one at the end.

I like Easterners more than Westerners but Western geography more than Eastern geography; and I like the country more than the city, but I like city people more than country people.

Essays, the most conversational form, have naturally drawn me, who have a hard time speaking with my actual mouth.

Tail end of hurricane rains buckets, flooding Barton River. Then the sky clears with nearly full moon, and I hear the deer whickering and whanging to one another gleefully, the mountain behind them gigantic and white.

Bellow says in Jerusalem journal that "light may be the outer garment of God."   40

Oil spills seem to attract aquatic birds; the sheen may resemble schooling fish. Also, oil slicks calm the surface, look like a landing area.

Roth speaks of his debt to both Jean Genet and the Fugs for *Portnoy*. Roth a man who wears his heart on his sleeve, thus rather vulnerable to insult and injury; part of his exceptional generosity. Tells story of man bleeding in front of God but trying to hide blood from His sight apologetically.

William Gaddis: jockeylike, narrow-boned, fastidious Irishman, clever and civilized, with none of the usual hangdog bitterness of the neglected writer.

Warhol: keen, Pan face with tight manipulated skin that makes it ageless except for his eyes. Bleached hair hanging to his leather collar. Fame based upon being immobile.

Pete Hamill, bursting personality, does columns in half an hour, movie script   45 in three weeks, discipline based upon not drinking till day's stint is through. Fewer bar brawls now, more empathetic, though still lives from a suitcase. "Irish Ben Hecht," he laughs.

Malamud: not at all the "Jewish businessman's face" I'd heard about, but a sensitive, gentle face, often silent or dreamy at Podhoretz's, disagreeing with the host and Midge, but holds his tongue and hugs him at the end with professional gratitude to an editor who once published him. When he speaks, his voice is young, light, and quick, an enthusiast's, idealist's. Hurt by attacks on him in *Jerusalem Post*, for dovishness. Extremely solicitous of me, as kind in his way as Bellow, though style of it is modulated lower. Both of us distressed by Israeli's grinning description of Arab prisoners being beaten up. William Phelps says he thinks the Palestinians probably have a point but that he's not interested in hearing what it is. Podhoretz mentions Israel's "Samson option," pulling everything down, and makes fun of Malamud's "ego" when he's left.

Grace Paley: short, stocky woman who at first sight on the Sarah Lawrence campus I mistook for the cleaning woman; asked her where the men's room was. We rode rubbing knees throughout that semester in the back seat of a car pool. She'd been marching in protests since high school (Ethiopia and Spanish civil war), but her exhilaration at being arrested in Washington peace march in midterm reminded me of my own exuberance at completing the hard spells of army basic training. Yes, we were good enough!

Heard MacLeish at YMHA. Afterward unrecovered yet from defeat of his play *Scratch* on B'way. Sweetness and bounce of his voice, however, is unchanged in twenty years; sounds forty, a matinee tenor, and the old lilt to his rhetoric. Face like a sachem's, too wise, too heroic, with a public man's nose. Talks of friendships with Joyce and Hemingway and imitates Sandburg's *O* very well. Talks of Saturday Club in Boston where monthly Harlow Shapley debated Robert Frost. Reminisces of artillery lieutenant days in World War I, "making the world safe for democracy," where his brother was killed. Five years later he and other nondead *did* die a bit when they realized it had been a "commercial" war and they had been lied to. He is a man of Hector-type heroes. Says Andrew Marvell poem was written while going home from Persia after his father's death.

Berryman given five-thousand-dollar prize at the Guggenheim reading, wearing a graybeard's beard which hides tieless collar. Reads best "Dream Songs," plus two sonnets and Rilke, Ralph Hodgson, and eighteenth-century Japanese poet. Emphatically, spoutingly drunk, reads with frail man's grotesqueries, contortions, and his own memorable concoction of earnestness, coyness, staginess, name dropping, and absolutely forceful, rock-bottom directness. Becomes louder and louder at the end of this floodlighted moment after long years of obscurity and hardship. Here was the current Wild Man, people thought, successor to Pound, there being one to a generation, though many others may have been reminded of Dylan Thomas as he fell into the arms of Robert Lowell, punching him affectionately, when he finished. His whole life was thereupon paraded before him, when old mistresses and chums and students like me came up, expecting recognition, and one of his old wives, presenting him with a son whom obviously he hadn't laid eyes on for a long while. He boomed with love and guilt, with repeated thanks for letters informing him that So-and-so had had a child or remarried, till one was wearied of watching. One felt guilty too, as though competing for his attention with the neglected son. I felt Berryman had not long to live and I ought to be content with my memories of him and lessons learned and not join in the hounding of him. Nevertheless, I did go next afternoon to the Chelsea Hotel, with bronze plaques outside memorializing other tragic figures, like Thomas and Brendan Behan. He'd said the son would be there, so I was afraid that, like my last visit with Bellow, I would be taking time away from a son who needed to see him much more. But the son had left—all that remained was a note in Ann B.'s handwriting. Instead a *Life* photographer and reporter were talking with him, plying him with drinks, though he was holding back dignifiedly, talking of fame, of Frost, and his own dog Rufus. Frost was a shit who tried to hurt him, but he quoted the wonderful couplet about God forgiving our little faux pas if we forgive Him His great big joke on us. Is bombastic in his total commitment to words. Legs look very small, but chest inflates with importance of uttering snatches of poems, till he collapses in coughs. Rubs beard and hair exhaustedly, recklessly spendthrift with his strength, and begins harder drinking; leads me to bar, where waiter, thinking from his red face and thin clothing that he is a bum, won't serve him till he lays a ten-dollar bill on the table. I soon leave, but he was hospitalized within a couple of days. "Twinkle" was his favorite word at this time. He used it for commentary, by itself, and irony, or expostulation, quoting an enemy like Oscar Williams, then merely adding a somber "Twinkle."

Turgenev's brain was the heaviest ever recorded, 4.7 pounds; three is average.   50

Child's tale about a man who suffered from shortness of breath. Afraid he would run out, he blew up a bunch of balloons as an extra supply for emergencies. Blew up so many that he floated away holding on to them.

Updike comes to U. of Iowa for first workshop session in three years (hasn't really taught for sixteen years) but handles himself in a classy manner nevertheless, and very well prepared with students' manuscripts beforehand, and in the exhilaration of reading his own work in front of one thousand people in McBride Hall (which we call Mammal Hall because it's part of Nat'l Hist. Museum), freely sheds his private-person role that had made him a bit stiff before, when he'd refused even a newspaper interview. Signs autograph cards for eleven-year-old boys and physics texts for Japanese students and mimeo forms for students with nothing better to offer him. Wife is ample, attractive woman with large, intense face, obviously both loving and sexy, a relaxed, close companion—he is wearing a wedding ring and ignoring the ambitious students who show up for his morning class wearing cocktail dresses. We talk of Africa—both finishing Africa books— and classmates and lit. hierarchies. He mentions Cheever's drunkenness—once he had to dress him after a party like dressing a father. Our mothers are same age. "Poor Johnny," his said, watching a TV program about senility with him recently.

Updike says he quit teaching years ago because he "felt stupid," seeing only one way to write a given story properly, not the endless alternatives students proposed in discussions.

Indians used to scratch small children with mouse teeth fastened to a stick as a punishment for crying in front of white men. (White man, of course, a "skinned" man.)

Short stories tend to be boat-shaped, with a lift at each end, to float.   55

Richard Yates says art is a result of a quarrel with oneself, not others.

Five toes to a track means it's wild, four toes means cat or dog.

Writers customarily write in the morning and try to make news, make love, or make friends in the afternoon. But alas, I write all day.

Bellow says he spent the first third of his life absorbing material, the second third trying to make himself famous, and the last third trying to evade fame.

"A woman without a man is like a fish without a bicycle": T-shirt.   60

People say they'll take a dip in the sea as if it were like dipping into a book, but I nearly drowned in surf's riptide off Martha's Vineyard's South Beach. Repeatedly changed swimming strokes to rest myself as I struggled in the water, surf too loud to shout over, and I'm too nearsighted to see where to shout to. Reaching beach, I sprawled for an hour before moving further. Spent next day in bed, next week aching.

New England is "pot-bound," says Charlton Ogburn; thus superfertile.

Petrarch, climbing Mount Ventoux in 1336, began the Renaissance by being the first learned man ever to climb a mountain only for the view.

Rahv told Roth, "You can't be both Scott Fitzgerald and Franz Kafka."

People who marry their great loves sometimes wish they'd married their best 65
friends; and vice versa.

Trapeze artists some days complain "there's too much gravity," when a change of the weather or the magnetic field affects their bodies. Elvin Bale bought his heel-hook act from Geraldine Soules, who after a fall started doing a dog act instead. Soules had, in turn, bought it from Vander Barbette, who, walking funny after *his* fall, had become a female impersonator and trainer of circus showgirls.

In old-time Georgia you ate mockingbird eggs for a stutter; boiled an egg for jaundice and went and sat beside a red-ant anthill and ate the white and fed the yolk to the ants. For warts, you bled them, put the blood on grains of corn, and fed that to a chicken. Fiddlers like to put a rattlesnake rattle inside their fiddles.

The fifties are an interim decade of life, like the thirties. In the thirties one still has the energy of one's twenties, combined with the judgment (sometimes) of the forties. In the fifties one still has the energy of one's forties, combined with the composure of the sixties.

The forties are the old age of youth and the fifties are the youth of old age.

Adage: "God sends meat, the Devil sends cooks."   70

Carnival stuntman whom Byron Burford banged the drum for used to swallow live rats and Ping-Pong balls, upchucking whichever ones the crowd asked for first. Stunned the rats with cigar smoke before he swallowed them.

> The intellect of man is forced to choose
> Perfection of the life, or of the work,
> And if it take the second must refuse
> A heavenly mansion, raging in the dark.
> —YEATS, "Choice"

Lying to my lieutenant as a private at Fort Sam Houston as to whether I'd shaved that morning before inspection, or only the night before—he reaching out and rubbing his hand down my face.

Glenn Gould liked to practice with the vacuum cleaner on, to hear "the skeleton of the music."

Nature writers, I sometimes think, are second only to cookbook writers in 75 being screwed up.

Deer follow moose in these woods, says Toad. I say maybe they look like father (mother) figures to them.

At Academy-Institute ceremonial, the big scandal is Ellison's lengthy introduction of Malamud for a prize and Barbara Tuchman's brutal interruption of it. Stegner very youthful, as befits an outdoorsman. Cowley very food-hungry as always, as befits a 1930s survivor. Commager tells my wife that his daughter loved me and so he loved me. Lots of cold-faced ambitious poets cluster around each other and Northrop Frye; Galway seems likably unaffected and truthful next to them. Ditto Raymond Carver. Ellison had tried to speak of blacks and Jews.

Joe Flaherty's line for the Brooklyn Bridge: "the Irish gangplank."

Whale mother's milk would stain the sea after she was harpooned, and the calf would circle the ship forlornly. "I do not say that John or Jonathan will realize all this," said Thoreau, in finishing *Walden;* and that's the central and tragic dilemma as the environmental movement fights its rearguard battles.

In starving midwinter, foxes catch cats by rolling on their backs like a kitten 80 ready to play.

Warblers average eight thousand or ten thousand songs a day in spring; vireo twenty thousand. Woodchucks wag their tails like a dog. Blue jays like to scare other birds by imitating a red-shouldered hawk.

My bifocals are like a horse's halter, binding the lower half of my eyes to the day's work.

At my frog pond a blue heron circles low overhead while a brown-muzzled black bear clasps chokecherry bushes and eats off them thirty yards away from me.

Only six hours old, a red calf stumbles toward the barn, as mother is herded in by Hugh Stevens on ATV vehicle, and is eventually tied to its mother's stanchion with hay twine, while a six-inch red tab of its previous cord hangs from its belly.

It's as shiny as a new pair of shoes, its deerlike hooves perfectly formed, including the dew claws. Mother and calf had had a brief wild idyll under the summer sky before they were discovered by Hugh—the last sky this vealer will ever see.

Crocodiles yawn to cool themselves in hot weather, but coyotes yawn as an 85 agonistic device. Mice yawn from sleepiness, as people do, but we also yawn from boredom, which is to say contempt—agonistic again.

Old people seem wise because they have grown resigned and because they remember the axioms, even if they've forgotten the data.

"When you come to the end of your life, make sure you're used up."

I trust love more than friendship, which is why I trust women more than men.

"All hat and no cows." Or, "Big hat, no cattle": Texas saying.

"Eat with the rich, laugh with the poor."   90

Buying a new car after thirteen years, I discover why country people like to keep the old one about the yard. First, it makes the house look occupied. Second, it's a nesting site for ducks and geese and a shelter for chickens during the day. Third, it reminds you of *you*.

ACTIVITIES FOR WRITING AND DISCUSSION

1. You can write long, or you can write short; and there is a place and value for everything you write, whatever its length or apparent individual significance. Hoagland's essay seems to underscore that every thought and experience matters and contributes to a larger picture. Read and annotate the essay.

2. Is this a collection of random and unrelated notes, or is there some sort of focus to it? If there is a focus, what *is* it? Are there paragraphs that don't seem to *fit*—for instance, paragraph 6 about the Vietcong prisoners, or paragraph 23 ("Manhattan, now 14,310 acres, was 9,800")? What do you think, and why? Good arguments can be made either way.

3. Hoagland's essay reads like a selection of journal or notebook entries. Therefore, read and respond to the piece using any of the "Generic Ideas for Writing in Response to Published Notebooks or Journals" listed on page 192.

4. Brainstorm any ideas for writing that this piece gives you. For instance, could you organize a selection of your own notebook entries around some topic or theme? If so, what topic or theme? What would be the advantage(s) of using Hoagland's "selected notes" format instead of the consecutive prose of a traditional essay?

Judith Ortiz Cofer (b. 1952)

Primary Lessons

My mother walked me to my first day at school at La Escuela Segundo Ruiz Belvis, named after the Puerto Rican patriot born in our town. I remember yellow cement with green trim. All the classrooms had been painted these colors to identify them as government property. This was true all over the Island. Everything was color-coded, including the children, who wore uniforms from first through twelfth grade. We were a midget army in white and brown, led by the hand to our battleground. From practically every house in our barrio emerged a crisply ironed uniform inhabited by the savage creatures we had become over a summer of running wild in the sun.

At my grandmother's house where we were staying until my father returned to Brooklyn Yard in New York and sent for us, it had been complete chaos, with several children to get ready for school. My mother had pulled my hair harder than usual while braiding it, and I had dissolved into a pool of total self-pity. I wanted to stay home with her and Mamá, to continue listening to stories in the late afternoon, to drink *café con leche* with them, and to play rough games with my many cousins. I wanted to continue living the dream of summer afternoons in Puerto Rico, and if I could not have it, then I wanted to go back to Paterson, New Jersey, back to where I imagined our apartment waited, peaceful and cool for the three of us to return to our former lives. Our gypsy lifestyle had convinced me, at age six, that one part of life stops and waits for you while you live another for a while—and if you don't like the present, you can always return to the past. Buttoning me into my stiff blouse while I tried to squirm away from her, my mother attempted to explain to me that I was a big girl now and should try to understand that, like all the other children my age, I had to go to school.

"What about him?" I yelled pointing at my brother who was lounging on the tile floor of our bedroom in his pajamas, playing quietly with a toy car.

"He's too young to go to school, you know that. Now stay still." My mother pinned me between her thighs to button my skirt, as she had learned to do from Mamá, from whose grip it was impossible to escape.

"It's not fair, it's not fair. I can't go to school here. I don't speak Spanish." 5
It was my final argument, and it failed miserably because I was shouting my defiance in the language I claimed not to speak. Only I knew what I meant by saying in Spanish that I did not speak Spanish. I had spent my early childhood in the United States, where I lived in a bubble created by my Puerto Rican parents in a home where two cultures and languages became one. I learned to listen to the English from the television with one ear while I heard my mother and father speaking in Spanish with the other. I thought I was an ordinary American kid—like the children on the shows I watched—and that everyone's parents spoke a secret second language at home. When we came to Puerto Rico right before I started first grade, I switched easily to Spanish. It was the language of fun, of summertime games. But school—that was a different matter.

I made one last desperate attempt to make my mother see reason: "Father will be very angry. You know that he wants us to speak good English." My mother, of course, ignored me as she dressed my little brother in his playclothes. I could not believe her indifference to my father's wishes. She was usually so careful about our safety and the many other areas that he was forever reminding her about in his letters. But I was right, and she knew it. Our father spoke to us in English as much as possible, and he corrected my pronunciation constantly—not "jes" but "y-es." Y-es, sir. How could she send me to school to learn Spanish when we would be returning to Paterson in just a few months?

But, of course, what I feared was not language, but loss of freedom. At school there would be no playing, no stories, only lessons. It would not matter if I did not understand a word, and I would not be allowed to make up my own definitions. I would have to learn silence. I would have to keep my wild imagination in check. Feeling locked into my stiffly starched uniform, I only sensed all this. I guess most children can intuit their loss of childhood's freedom on that first day of school. It is separation anxiety too, but mother is just the guardian of the "playground" of our early childhood.

The sight of my cousins in similar straits comforted me. We were marched down the hill of our barrio where Mamá's robin-egg-blue house stood at the top. I must have glanced back at it with yearning. Mamá's house—a place built for children—where anything that could be broken had already been broken by my grandmother's early batch of offspring (they ranged in age from my mother's oldest sisters to my uncle who was six months older than me). Her house had long since been made childproof. It had been a perfect summer place. And now it was September—the cruelest month for a child.

La Mrs., as all the teachers were called, waited for her class of first-graders at the door of the yellow and green classroom. She too wore a uniform: It was a blue skirt and a white blouse. This teacher wore black high heels with her "standard issue." I remember this detail because when we were all seated in rows she called on one little girl and pointed to the back of the room where there were shelves. She told the girl to bring her a shoebox from the bottom shelf. Then, when the box had been placed in her hands, she did something unusual. She had the little girl kneel at her feet and take the pointy high heels off her feet and replace them with a pair of satin slippers from the shoe box. She told the group that every one of us would have a chance to do this if we behaved in her class. Though confused about the prize, I soon felt caught up in the competition to bring *La Mrs.* her slippers in the morning. Children fought over the privilege.

Our first lesson was English. In Puerto Rico, every child has to take twelve 10 years of English to graduate from school. It is the law. In my parents' school days, all subjects were taught in English. The U.S. Department of Education had specified that as a U.S. territory, the Island had to be "Americanized," and to accomplish this task, it was necessary for the Spanish language to be replaced in one generation through the teaching of English in all schools. My father began his school day by saluting the flag of the United States and singing "America" and "The Star-Spangled Banner" by rote, without understanding a word of what he was saying. The logic behind this system was that, though the children did not understand the English words, they would remember the rhythms. Even the games the teacher's manuals required them to play became absurd adaptations. "Here We Go Round the Mulberry Bush" became "Here We Go Round the Mango Tree." I have heard about the confusion caused by the use of a primer in which the sounds of animals were featured. The children were forced to accept that a rooster says *cockadoodledoo*, when they knew perfectly well from hearing their own roosters each morning that in Puerto Rico a rooster says *cocorocó*. Even the vocabulary of their pets was changed; there are still family stories circulating about the bewilderment of a first-grader coming home to try to teach his dog to speak in English. The policy of assimilation by immersion failed on the Island. Teachers adhered to it on paper, substituting their own materials for the texts, but no one took their English home. In due time, the program was minimized to the one class in English per day that I encountered when I took my seat in *La Mrs.*'s first grade class.

Catching us all by surprise, she stood very straight and tall in front of us and began to sing in English:

Pollito	—	Chicken
Gallina	—	Hen
Lápiz	—	Pencil
Y Pluma	—	Pen.

"Repeat after me, children: Pollito—Chicken," she commanded in her heavily accented English that only I understood, being the only child in the room who had ever been exposed to the language. But I too remained silent. No use making waves or showing off. Patiently *La Mrs.* sang her song and gestured for us to join in. At some point it must have dawned on the class that this silly routine was likely to go on all day if we did not "repeat after her." It was not her fault that she had to follow the rule in her teacher's manual stating that she must teach English *in* English, and that she must not translate, but merely repeat her lesson in English until the children "begin to respond" more or less "unconsciously." This was one of the vestiges of the regimen followed by her predecessors in the last generation. To this day I can recite "Pollito—Chicken" mindlessly, never once pausing to visualize chicks, hens, pencils, or pens.

I soon found myself crowned "teacher's pet" without much effort on my part. I was a privileged child in her eyes simply because I lived in "Nueva York," and because my father was in the navy. His name was an old one in our pueblo, associated with once-upon-a-time landed people and long-gone money. Status is judged by unique standards in a culture where, by definition, everyone is a second-class citizen. Remembrance of past glory is as good as titles and money. Old families living in decrepit old houses rank over factory workers living in modern comfort in cement boxes—all the same. The professions raise a person out of the dreaded "sameness" into a niche of status, so that teachers, nurses, and everyone who went to school for a job were given the honorifics of *El Míster* or *La Mrs.* by the common folks, people who were likely to be making more money in American factories than the poorly paid educators and government workers.

My first impressions of the hierarchy began with my teacher's shoe-changing ceremony and the exaggerated respect she received from our parents. *La Mrs.* was always right, and adults scrambled to meet her requirements. She wanted all our schoolbooks covered in the brown paper now used for paper bags (used at that time by the grocer to wrap meats and other foods). That first week of school the grocer was swamped with requests for paper which he gave away to the women. That week and the next, he wrapped produce in newspapers. All school projects became family projects. It was considered disrespectful at Mamá's house to do homework in privacy. Between the hours when we came home from school and dinner time, the table was shared by all of us working together with the women hovering in the background. The teachers communicated directly with the mothers, and it was a matriarchy of far-reaching power and influence.

There was a black boy in my first-grade classroom who was also the teacher's 15 pet but for a different reason than I: I did not have to do anything to win her favor; he would do anything to win a smile. He was as black as the cauldron that Mamá used for cooking stew and his hair was curled into tight little balls on his head—*pasitas,* like little raisins glued to his skull, my mother had said. There had been some talk at Mamá's house about this boy; Lorenzo was his name. I later gathered that he was the grandson of my father's nanny. Lorenzo lived with Teresa, his grandmother, having been left in her care when his mother took off for "Los Nueva Yores" shortly after his birth. And they were poor. Everyone could see that his pants were too big for him—hand-me-downs—and his shoe soles were as thin as paper. Lorenzo seemed unmindful of the giggles he caused when he jumped up to erase the board for *La Mrs.* and his baggy pants rode down to his thin hips as he strained up to get every stray mark. He seemed to relish playing the little clown when she asked him to come to the front of the room and sing his phonetic version of "o-bootifool, forpashios-keeis," leading the class in our incomprehensible tribute to the American flag. He was a bright, loving child, with a talent for song and mimicry that everyone commented on. He should have been chosen to host the PTA show that year instead of me.

At recess one day, I came back to the empty classroom to get something. My cup? My nickel for a drink from the kiosk man? I don't remember. But I remember the conversation my teacher was having with another teacher. I remember because it concerned me, and because I memorized it so that I could ask my mother to explain what it meant.

"He is a funny *negrito,* and, like a parrot, he can repeat anything you teach him. But his Mamá must not have the money to buy him a suit."

"I kept Rafaelito's First Communion suit; I bet Lorenzo could fit in it. It's white with a bow-tie," the other teacher said.

"But, Marisa," laughed my teacher, "in that suit, Lorenzo would look like a fly drowned in a glass of milk."

Both women laughed. They had not seen me crouched at the back of the 20 room, digging into my schoolbag. My name came up then.

"What about the Ortiz girl? They have money."

"I'll talk to her mother today. The superintendent, *El Americano* from San Juan, is coming down for the show. How about if we have her say her lines in both Spanish and English?"

The conversation ends there for me. My mother took me to Mayagüez and bought me a frilly pink dress and two crinoline petticoats to wear underneath so that I looked like a pink and white parachute with toothpick legs sticking out. I learned my lines, "Padres, maestros, Mr. Leonard, bienvenidos/Parents, teachers, Mr. Leonard, welcome. . . ." My first public appearance. I took no pleasure in it. The words were formal and empty. I had simply memorized them. My dress pinched me at the neck and arms, and made me itch all over.

I had asked my mother what it meant to be a "mosca en un vaso de leche," a fly in a glass of milk. She had laughed at the image, explaining that it meant being "different," but that it wasn't something I needed to worry about.

ACTIVITIES FOR WRITING AND DISCUSSION

1. Consider the various meanings of the title. "Primary" can refer to the elementary grades of school; it can also mean "fundamental," "basic," or "of first importance." Do the lessons learned by the six-year-old Cofer fit these different definitions? If so, in what ways?

2. Working with a group, make a list of the "primary lessons" Cofer learned as a six-year-old. Then identify an item on your list that resembles a lesson that *you* once learned, and write the story of that lesson. Either:
   a. Write the story in the form of a personal essay, or
   b. Write a dialogue, set in the past, between yourself and someone who was a key player in the "lesson," or
   c. Tell the story of your particular experience from a **third-person point of view,** i.e., write about yourself as "he" or "she."

3. The final paragraph shows the young Cofer asking her mother an awkward question, which the mother brushes aside. Invent a dialogue in which you either:
   a. Flesh out and expand the conversation you imagine to have taken place between Cofer and her mother, or
   b. Relate a similar type of conversation you had with your own parent, or
   c. Create a fictional conversation of a small child asking a parent about some controversial or "adult" subject.

REBECCA SOLNIT (b. 1961)

The Disembodiment of Everyday Life

The spaces in which people live have changed dramatically, but so have the ways they imagine and experience that space. I found a strange passage in a 1998 *Life* magazine celebrating momentous events over the past thousand years.

Accompanying a picture of a train was this text: "For most of human history, all land transport depended on a single mode of propulsion—feet. Whether the traveller relied on his own extremities or those of another creature, the drawbacks were the same, low cruising speed, vulnerability to weather, the need to stop for food and rest. But on September 15, 1830, foot power began its long slide toward obsolescence. As brass bands played, a million Britons gathered between Liverpool and Manchester to witness the inauguration of the world's first fully steam-driven railway. . . . Despite the death of a member of Parliament who was run down by the train at the opening ceremony, the Liverpool and Manchester inspired a rash of track-laying round the world." The train was, like the factory and the suburb, part of the apparatus of the industrial revolution; just as factories mechanically sped up production, so trains sped up distribution of goods, and then of travelers.

Life maganize's assumptions are interesting; nature as biological and meteorological factors is a drawback rather than an occasional inconvenience; progress consists of the transcendence of time, space, and nature by the train and later the car, airplane, and electronic communications. Eating, resting, moving, experiencing the weather, are primary experiences of being embodied; to view them as negative is to condemn biology and the life of the senses, and the passage does exactly that in its most lurid statement, that "foot power began its long slide toward obsolescence." Perhaps this is why neither *Life* nor the crowd apparently mourned the squashed Parliamentarian. In a way, the train mangled not just that one man's body, but all bodies in the places it transformed, by severing human perception, expectation, and action from the organic world in which our bodies exist. Alienation from nature is usually depicted as estrangement from natural spaces. But the sensing, breathing, living, moving body can be a primary experience of nature too: new technologies and spaces can bring about alienation from both body and space.

In his brilliant *The Railway Journey: The Industrialization of Time and Space in the Nineteenth Century,* Wolfgang Schivelbusch explores the ways trains changed their passengers' perceptions. Early railroad travelers, he writes, characterized this new technology's effects as the elimination of time and space, and to transcend time and space is to begin to transcend the material world altogether—to become disembodied. Disembodiment, however convenient, has side effects. "The speed and mathematical directness with which the railroad proceeds through the terrain destroy the close relationship between the traveller and the travelled space," Schivelbusch writes. "The train was experienced as a projectile, and travelling on it as being shot through the landscape—thus losing control of one's senses. . . . The traveller who sat inside that projectile ceased to be a traveller and became, as noted in a popular metaphor of the century, a parcel." Our own perceptions have sped up since, but trains were then dizzyingly fast. Earlier forms of land travel had intimately engaged travelers with their surroundings, but the railroad moved too fast for nineteenth-century minds to relate visually to the trees, hills, and buildings whipping by. The spatial and sensual engagement with the terrain between here and there began to evaporate. Instead, the two places were separated only by an ever-shortening amount of time. Speed did not make travel more interesting, Schivelbusch writes, but duller; like the suburb, it put its inhabitants in a kind of spatial limbo. People began to read on the train, to sleep, to knit, to complain of boredom. Cars and airplanes have vastly augmented this transformation, and watching a movie on a jetliner 35,000 feet above the earth may be the ultimate disconnection of space, time, and experience. "From the elimination of the physical effort of walking to the sensorimotor loss induced by the first fast transport, we have finally achieved states bordering on sensory deprivation," writes Paul Virilio. "The loss of the thrills of the old voyage is now compensated for by the showing of a film on a central screen."

The *Life* writers may be right. Bodies are not obsolete by any objective standard, but they increasingly are perceived as too slow, frail, and unreliable for our expectations and desires—as parcels to be transported by mechanical means (though of course many steep, rough, or narrow spaces can only be traversed on foot, and many remote parts of the world can't be reached by any other means; it takes a built environment, with tracks, graded roads, landing strips, and energy sources, to accommodate motor transport). A body regarded as adequate to cross continents, like John Muir's or William Wordsworth's or Peace Pilgrim's, is experienced very differently than a body inadequate to go out for the evening under its own power. In a sense the car has become a prosthetic, and though prosthetics are usually for injured or missing limbs, the auto-prosthetic is for a conceptually impaired body or a body impaired by the creation of a world that is no longer human in scale. In one of the *Alien* movies the actress Sigourney Weaver lurches along in a sort of mechanized body armor that wraps around her limbs and magnifies her movements. It makes her bigger, fiercer, stronger, able to battle with monsters, and it seems strange and futuristic. But this is only because the relationship between the body and the prosthetic machine is so explicit here, the latter so obviously an extension of the former. In fact, from the first clasped stick and improvised carrier, tools have extended the body's strength, skill, and reach to a remarkable degree. We live in a world where our hands and feet can direct a ton of metal to go faster than the fastest land animal, where we can speak across thousands of miles, blow holes in things with no muscular exertion but the squeeze of a forefinger.

It is the unaugmented body that is rare now, and that body has begun to atro- 5 phy as both a muscular and a sensory organism. In the century and a half since the railroad seemed to go too fast to be interesting, perceptions and expectations have sped up, so that many now identify with the speed of the machine and look with frustration or alienation at the speed and ability of the body. The world is no longer on the scale of our bodies, but on that of our machines, and many need—or think they need—the machines to navigate that space quickly enough. Of course, like most "time-saving" technologies, mechanized transit more often produces changed expectations than free time; and modern Americans have significantly less time than they did three decades ago. To put it another way, just as the increased speed of factory production did not decrease working hours, so the increased speed of transportation binds people to more diffuse locales rather than liberating them from travel time (many Californians, for example, now spend three or four hours driving to and from work each day). The decline of walking is about the lack of space in which to walk, but it is also about the lack of time—the disappearance of that musing, unstructured space in which so much thinking, courting, daydreaming, and seeing has transpired. Machines have sped up, and lives have kept pace with them.

———————

The suburbs made walking ineffective transportation within their expanses, but the suburbanization of the American mind has made walking increasingly rare even when it is effective. Walking is no longer, so to speak, how many people think. Even in San Francisco, very much a "walking city" by Jackson's criteria,[1] people have brought this suburbanized consciousness to their local travel, or so my observations seem to indicate. I routinely see people drive and take the bus remarkably short distances, often distances that could be covered more quickly by foot. During one of my city's public transit crises, a commuter declared he could *walk* downtown in the time it took the streetcar, as though walking was some kind of damning comparison—but he had apparently been traveling from a destination so near downtown he could've walked every day in less than half an hour, and walking was one transit option the newspaper coverage never proposed (obvious things could be said about bicycling here, were this not a book about walking). Once I made my friend Maria—a surfer, biker, and world traveler—walk the half mile from her house to the bars on Sixteenth Street, and she was startlingly pleased to realize how close they were, for it had never occurred to her before that they were accessible by foot. Last Christmas season, the parking lot of the hip outdoor equipment store in Berkeley was full of drivers idling their engines and waiting for a parking space, while the streets around were full of such spaces. Shoppers weren't apparently willing to walk two blocks to buy their outdoor gear (and since then I have noticed that nowadays drivers often wait for a close parking spot rather than walk in from the farther reaches of the lot). People have a kind of mental radius of how far they are willing to go on foot that seems to be shrinking; in defining neighborhoods and shopping districts, planners say it is about a quarter mile, the distance that can be walked in five minutes, but sometimes it hardly seems to be fifty yards from car to building.

Of course the people idling their engines at the outdoor equipment store may have been there to buy hiking boots, workout clothes, climbing ropes—equipment for the special circumstances in which people will walk. The body has ceased to be a utilitarian entity for many Americans, but it is still a recreational one, and this means that people have abandoned the everyday spaces—the distance from home to work, stores, friends—but created new recreational sites that are most often reached by car: malls, parks, gyms. Parks, from pleasure gardens

———————

1. Kenneth Jackson, author of *Crabgrass Frontier: The Suburbanization of the United States* (NY: Oxford UP, 1985).

to wilderness preserves, have long accommodated bodily recreation, but the gyms that have proliferated wildly in the past couple of decades represent something radically new. If walking is an indicator species, the gym is a kind of wildlife preserve for bodily exertion. A preserve protects species whose habitat is vanishing elsewhere, and the gym (and home gym) accommodates the survival of bodies after the abandonment of the original sites of bodily exertion.

THE TREADMILL

The suburb rationalized and isolated family life as the factory did manufacturing work, and the gym rationalizes and isolates not merely exercise but nowadays even each muscle group, the heart rate, the "burn zone" of most inefficient calorie use. Somehow all this history comes back to the era of the industrial revolution in England. "The Tread-Mill," writes James Hardie in his little book of 1823 on the subject, "was, in the year 1818, invented by Mr. William Cubitt, of Ipswich, and erected in the House of Correction at Brixton, near London." The original treadmill was a large wheel with sprockets that served as steps that several prisoners trod for set periods. It was meant to rationalize prisoners' psyches, but it was already an exercise machine. Their bodily exertion was sometimes used to power grain mills or other machinery, but it was the exertion, not the production, that was the point of the treadmill. "It is its monotonous steadiness and not its severity, which constitutes its terror, and frequently breaks down the obstinate spirit," Hardie wrote of the treadmill's effect in the American prison he oversaw. He added, however, that "the opinions of the medical officers in attendance at the various prisons, concur in declaring that the general health of the prisoners has, in no degree suffered injury, but that, on the contrary, the labor has, in this respect, been productive of considerable benefit." His own prison of Bellevue on New York's East River included 81 male and 101 female vagrants, as well as 109 male and 37 female convicts, and 14 female "maniacs." Vagrancy—wandering without apparent resources or purpose—was and sometimes still is a crime, and doing time on the treadmill was perfect punishment for it.

Repetitive labor has been punitive since the gods of Greek myth sentenced Sisyphus—who had, Robert Graves tells us, "always lived by robbery and often murdered unsuspecting travellers"—to his famous fate of pushing a boulder uphill. "As soon as he has almost reached the summit, he is forced back by the weight of the shameless stone, which bounces to the very bottom once more, where he wearily retrieves it and must begin all over again, though sweat bathes his limbs." It is hard to say if Sisyphus is the first weight lifter or the first treadmiller, but easy to recognize the ancient attitude to repetitive bodily exertion without practical results. Throughout most of human history and outside the first world nowadays, food has been relatively scarce and physical exertion abundant; only when the status of these two things is reversed does "exercise" make sense. Though physical training was part of ancient Greek citizens' education, it had social and cultural dimensions missing from modern workouts and Sisyphean punishments, and while walking as exercise had long been an aristocratic activity, industrial workers' enthusiasm for hiking, particularly in Britain,

Austria, and Germany, suggests that it was far more than a way to make the blood circulate or calories burn. Under the heading "Alienation," Eduardo Galeano wrote a brief essay about fishermen in a remote village of the Dominican Republic puzzling over an advertisement for a rowing machine not very long ago. "Indoors? They use it indoors? Without water? They row without water? And without fish? And without the sun? And without the sky?" they exclaimed, telling the resident alien who has shown them the picture that they like everything about their work *but* the rowing. When he explained that the machine was for exercise, they said "Ah. And exercise—what's that?" Suntans famously became status symbols when most of the poor had moved indoors from the farm to the factory, so that browned skin indicated leisure time rather than work time. That muscles have become status symbols signifies that most jobs no longer call upon bodily strength: like tans, they are an aesthetic of the obsolete.

The gym is the interior space that compensates for the disappearance of out- 10 side and a stopgap measure in the erosion of bodies. The gym is a factory for the production of muscles or of fitness, and most of them look like factories: the stark industrial space, the gleam of metal machines, the isolated figures each absorbed in his or her own repetitive task (and like muscles, factory aesthetics may evoke nostalgia). The industrial revolution institutionalized and fragmented labor; the gym is now doing the same thing, often in the same place, for leisure. Some gyms actually are born-again industrial sites. The Chelsea Piers in Manhattan were built in the first decade of this century for ocean liners—for the work of long-shoremen, stevedores, and clerks, and for the travel of emigrants and elites. They now house a sports center with indoor track, weight machines, pool, climbing gym, and most peculiarly, a four-story golf driving range, destinations in themselves rather than points of arrival and departure. An elevator takes golfers to their stalls, where all the gestures of golf—walking, carrying, gazing, situating, removing, communicating, retrieving or following the ball—have vanished with the landscape of the golf course. Nothing remains but the single arc of a drive: four tiers of solitary stationary figures making the same gesture, the sharp sound of balls being hit, the dull thud of their landing, and the miniaturized armored-car vehicles that go through the green artificial-grass war zone to scoop up the balls and feed them into the mechanism that automatically pops up another ball as each one is hit. Britain has specialized in the conversion of industrial sites into climbing gyms. Among them are a former electrical substation in London, the Warehouse on Gloucester's Severn River waterfront, the Forge in Sheffield on one side of the Peak District, an early factory in downtown Birmingham, and, according to a surveyor friend, a "six-story former cotton mill near Leeds" I couldn't locate (not to mention a desanctified church in Bristol). It was in some of these buildings that the industrial revolution was born, with the Manchester and Leeds textile mills, Sheffield's iron- and steelworks, the innumerable manufactories of "the workshop of the world" that Birmingham once was. Climbing gyms are likewise established in converted industrial buildings in the United States, or at least in those cities old enough to have once had industrial-revolution architecture. In those buildings abandoned because goods are now made elsewhere and First

World work grows ever more cerebral, people now go for recreation, reversing the inclinations of their factory-worker predecessors to go out—to the outskirts of town or at least out-of-doors—in their free time. (In defense of climbing gyms, it should be said they allow people to polish skills and, during foul weather, to stay fit; for some the gym has only augmented the opportunities, not replaced the mountain, though for others the unpredictabilities and splendors of real rock have become dispensible, annoying—or unknown.)

And whereas the industrial revolution's bodies had to adapt to the machines, with terrible consequences of pain, injury, and deformity, exercise machines are adapted to the body. Marx said history happens the first time as tragedy, the second as farce; bodily labor here happens the first time around as productive labor and the second as leisuretime consumption. The deepest sign of transformation is not merely that this activity is no longer productive, that the straining of the arms no longer moves wood or pumps water. It is that the straining of the muscles can require a gym membership, workout gear, special equipment, trainers and instructors, a whole panoply of accompanying expenditures, in this industry of consumption, and the resulting muscles may not be useful or used for any practical purpose. "Efficiency" in exercise means that consumption of calories takes place at the maximum rate, exactly the opposite of what workers aim for, and while exertion for work is about how the body shapes the world, exertion for exercise is about how the body shapes the body. I do not mean to denigrate the users of gyms—I have sometimes been one myself—only to remark on their strangeness. In a world where manual labor has disappeared, the gym is among the most available and efficient compensations. Yet there is something perplexing about this semipublic performance. I used to try to imagine, as I worked out on one or another weight machine, that this motion was rowing, this one pumping water, this one lifting bales or sacks. The everyday acts of the farm had been reprised as empty gestures, for there was no water to pump, no buckets to lift. I am not nostalgic for peasant or farmworker life, but I cannot avoid being struck by how odd it is that we reprise those gestures for other reasons. What exactly is the nature of the transformation in which machines now pump our water but we go to other machines to engage in the act of pumping, not for the sake of water but for the sake of our bodies, bodies theoretically liberated by machine technology? Has something been lost when the relationship between our muscles and our world vanishes, when the water is managed by one machine and the muscles by another in two unconnected processes?

The body that used to have the status of a work animal now has the status of a pet: it does not provide real transport, as a horse might have; instead, the body is exercised as one might walk a dog. Thus the body, a recreational rather than utilitarian entity, doesn't work, but works out. The barbell is only abstracted and quantified materiality to shift around—what used to be a sack of onions or a barrel of beer is now a metal ingot—and the weight machine makes simpler the act of resisting gravity in various directions for the sake of health, beauty, and relaxation. The most perverse of all the devices in the gym is the treadmill (and its steeper cousin, the Stairmaster). Perverse, because I can understand simulating farm labor, since the activities of rural life are not often available—but simulating walking suggests that space itself has disappeared. That is, the weights simulate the objects of work, but the treadmill and Stairmaster simulate the surfaces on which walking takes place. That bodily labor, real or simulated, should be dull and repetitive is one thing; that the multifaceted experience of moving through the world should be made so is another. I remember evenings strolling by Manhattan's many glass-walled second-floor gyms full of rows of treadmillers looking as though they were trying to leap through the glass to their destruction, saved only by the Sisyphean contraption that keeps them from going anywhere at all— though probably they didn't see the plummet before them, only their own reflection in the glass.

I went out the other day, a gloriously sunny winter afternoon, to visit a home-exercise equipment store and en route walked by the University of San Francisco gym, where treadmillers were likewise at work in the plate-glass windows, most of them reading the newspaper (three blocks from Golden Gate Park, where other people were running and cycling, while tourists and Eastern European emigrés were walking). The muscular young man in the store told me that people buy home treadmills because they allow them to exercise after work when it might be too dark for them to go out safely, to exercise in private where the neighbors will not see them sweating, to keep an eye on the kids, and to use their scarce time most efficiently, and because it is a low-impact activity good for people with running injuries. I have a friend who uses a treadmill when it's painfully cold outside in Chicago, and another who uses a no-impact machine whose footpads rise and fall with her steps because she has an injured hamstring (injured by driving cars designed for larger people, not by running). But a third friend's father lives two miles from a very attractive Florida beach, she tells me, full of low-impact sand, but he will not walk there and uses a home treadmill instead.

The treadmill is a corollary to the suburb and the autotropolis: a device with which to go nowhere in places where there is now nowhere to go. Or no desire to go: the treadmill also accommodates the automobilized and suburbanized mind more comfortable in climate-controlled indoor space than outdoors, more comfortable with quantifiable and clearly defined activity than with the seamless engagement of mind, body, and terrain to be found walking out-of-doors. The treadmill seems to be one of many devices that accommodate a retreat from the world, and I fear that such accommodation disinclines people to participate in making that world habitable or to participate in it at all. It too could be called Calvinist technology, in that it provides accurate numerical assessments of the speed, "distance" covered, and even heart rate, and it eliminates the unpredictable and unforeseeable from the routine—no encounters with acquaintances or strangers, no sudden revelatory sights around a bend. On the treadmill, walking is no longer contemplating, courting, or exploring. Walking is the alternate movement of the lower limbs.

Unlike the prison treadmills, of the 1820s, the modern treadmill does not produce mechanical power but consumes it. The new treadmills have two-horse-power engines. Once, a person might have hitched two horses to a carriage to go out into the world without walking; now she might plug in a two-horsepower motor to walk without going out into the world. Somewhere unseen but wired to the home is a whole electrical infrastructure of power generation and distribution transforming the landscape and ecology of the world—a network of electrical cables, meters, workers, of coal mines or oil wells feeding power plants or of hydropower dams on rivers. Somewhere else is a factory making treadmills, though factory work is a minority experience in the United States nowadays. So the treadmill requires far more economic and ecological interconnection than does taking a walk, but it makes far fewer experiential connections. Most treadmillers read or otherwise distract themselves. *Prevention* magazine recommends watching TV while treadmilling and gives instructions on how treadmill users can adapt their routines to walking about outside when spring comes (with the implication that the treadmill, not the walk, is the primary experience). The *New York Times* reports that people have begun taking treadmill classes, like the stationary bicycling classes that have become so popular, to mitigate the loneliness of the long-distance treadmiller. For like factory labor, treadmill time is dull—it was the monotony that was supposed to reform prisoners. Among the features of the Precor Cardiologic Treadmill, says its glossy brochure, are "5 programmed courses" that "vary in distance, time and incline. . . . The Interactive Weight Loss course maintains your heart rate within your optimum weight loss zone by adjusting workload," while "custom courses allow you to easily create and store personalized programs of up to 8 miles, with variations as small as 1/10th mile increments." It's the custom courses that most amaze me; users can create an itinerary like a walking tour over varied terrain, only the terrain is a revolving rubber belt on a platform about six feet long. Long ago when railroads began to erode the experience of space, journeys began to be spoken of in terms of time rather than distance (and a modern Angeleno will say that Beverly Hills is twenty minutes from Hollywood rather than so many miles). The treadmill completes this transformation by allowing travel to be measured entirely by time, bodily exertion, and mechanical motion. Space—as landscape, terrain, spectacle, experience—has vanished.

ACTIVITIES FOR WRITING AND DISCUSSION

1. According to Solnit, how have the functions and purposes of physical exercise changed over time, and what larger socioeconomic factors (for instance, urbanization) have been driving the changes? Give specific examples.

2. How—implicitly or explicitly—does Solnit define "disembodiment"? What adverse effects does she suggest it has on individuals and communities? What, if any, are its personal and social benefits?

3. Are there steps a person or community of persons can take (if so inclined) to counteract or compensate for the trend toward disembodiment? If so, specify a list of steps. If not, explain why not. Alternatively, can you make a good case for continuing or even accelerating "the disembodiment of everyday life"?

4. Research the topic of "disembodiment." Collect and examine examples from a variety of media—books, magazines, and other print sources; commercial advertisements; TV; the Internet; personal interviews and observations; and so on—that support or undercut Solnit's conclusions. Then write up the results of your study and present your own conclusions.

Plays

Eugene O'Neill (1888–1953)

The Hairy Ape

A Comedy of Ancient and Modern Life in Eight Scenes

Characters

ROBERT SMITH, "YANK"

PADDY

LONG

MILDRED DOUGLAS

HER AUNT

SECOND ENGINEER

A GUARD

A SECRETARY OF AN ORGANIZATION

Stokers, Ladies, Gentlemen, etc.

Scenes

Scene I: The firemen's forecastle of an ocean liner—an hour after sailing from New York.

Scene II: Section of promenade deck, two days out—morning.

Scene III: The stokehole. A few minutes later.

Scene IV: Same as Scene I. Half an hour later.

Scene V: Fifth Avenue, New York. Three weeks later.

Scene VI: An island near the city. The next night.

Scene VII: In the city. About a month later.

Scene VIII: In the city. Twilight of the next day.

SCENE ONE

The firemen's forecastle of a transatlantic liner an hour after sailing from New York for the voyage across. Tiers of narrow, steel bunks, three deep, on all sides. An entrance in rear. Benches on the floor before the bunks. The room is crowded with men, shouting, cursing, laughing, singing—a confused, inchoate uproar swelling into a sort of unity, a meaning—the bewildered, furious, baffled defiance of a beast in a cage. Nearly all the men are drunk. Many bottles are passed from hand to hand. All are dressed in dungaree pants, heavy ugly shoes. Some wear singlets, but the majority are stripped to the waist.

The treatment of this scene, or of any other scene in the play, should by no means be naturalistic. The effect sought after is a cramped space in the bowels of a ship, imprisoned by white steel. The lines of bunks, the uprights supporting them, cross each other like the steel framework of a cage. The ceiling crushes down upon the men's heads. They cannot stand upright. This accentuates the natural stooping posture which shoveling coal and the resultant over-development of back and shoulder muscles have given them. The men themselves should resemble those pictures in which the appearance of Neanderthal Man is guessed at. All are hairy-chested, with long arms of tremendous power, and low, receding brows above their small, fierce, resentful eyes. All the civilized white races are represented, but except for the slight differentiation in color of hair, skin, eyes, all these men are like.

The curtain rises on a tumult of sound. YANK *is seated in the foreground. He seems broader, fiercer, more truculent, more powerful, more sure of himself than the rest. They respect his superior strength—the grudging respect of fear. Then, too, he represents to them a self-expression, the very last word in what they are, their most highly developed individual.*

VOICES: Gif me trink dere, you!
'Ave a wet!
Salute!
Gesundheit!
Skoal!
Drunk as a lord, God stiffen you!
Here's how!
Luck!
Pass back that bottle, damn you!
Pourin' it down his neck!
Ho, Froggy! Where the devil have you been?
La Touraine.
I hit him smash in yaw, py Gott!
Jenkins—the First—he's a rotten swine—
And the coppers nabbed him—and I run—
I like peer better. It don't pig head gif you.
A slut, I'm sayin'! She robbed me aslape—
To hell with 'em all!
You're a bloody lair!

Say dot again! *(Commotion. Two men about to fight are pulled apart).*
No scrappin' now!
Tonight—
See who's the best man!
Bloody Dutchman!
Tonight on the for'ard square.
I'll bet on Dutchy.
He packa da wallop, I tella you!
Shut up, Wop!
No fightin', maties. We're all chums, ain't we?
(A voice starts bawling a song).

"Beer, beer, glorious beer!
Fill yourselves right up to here."

YANK *(for the first time seeming to take notice of the uproar about him, turns around threateningly—in a tone of contemptuous authority)*: Choke off dat noise! Where d'yuh get dat beer stuff? Beer, hell! Beer's for goils—and Dutchmen. Me for somep'n wit a kick to it! Gimme a drink, one of youse guys. *(Several bottles are eagerly offered. He takes a tremendous gulp at one of them; then, keeping the bottle in his hand, glares belligerently at the owner, who hastens to acquiesce in this robbery by saying)* All righto, Yank. Keep it and have another. *(YANK contemptuously turns his back on the crowd again. For a second there is an embarrassed silence. Then—)*
   VOICES: We must be passing the Hook.
   She's beginning to roll to it.
   Six days in hell—and then Southampton.
   Py Yesus, I vish somepody take my first vatch for me!
   Gittin' seasick, Square-head?
   Drink up and forget it!
   What's in your bottle?
   Gin.
   Dot's nigger trink.
   Absinthe? It's doped. You'll go off your chump, Froggy.
   Cochon!
   Whisky, that's the ticket!
   Where's Paddy?
   Going asleep.
   Sing us that whisky song, Paddy. *(They all turn to an old, wizened Irishman who is dozing, very drunk, on the benches forward. His face is extremely monkey-like with all the sad, patient pathos of that animal in his small eyes).*
   Singa da song, Caruso Pat!
   He's gettin' old. The drink is too much for him.
   He's too drunk.
   PADDY *(blinking about him, starts to his feet resentfully, swaying, holding on to the edge of a bunk)*: I'm never too drunk to sing. 'Tis only when I'm dead to the

world I'd be wishful to sing at all. *(With a sort of sad contempt)* "Whisky Johnny,"
ye want? A chanty, ye want? Now that's a queer wish from the ugly like of you, God
help you. But no matther. *(He starts to sing in a thin, nasal, doleful tone)*:

> Oh, whisky is the life of man!
> > Whisky! O Johnny! *(They all join in on this)*.
> Oh, whisky is the life of man!
> > Whisky for my Johnny! *(Again chorus)*.

> Oh, whisky drove my old man mad!
> > Whisky! O Johnny!
> Oh, whisky drove my old man mad!
> > Whisky for my Johnny!

YANK *(again turning around scornfully)*: Aw hell! Nix on dat old sailing ship
stuff! All dat bull's dead, see? And you're dead, too, yuh damned old Harp, on'y
yuh don't know it. Take it easy, see. Give us a rest. Nix on de loud noise. *(With
a cynical grin)* Can't youse see I'm tryin' to t'ink?

ALL *(repeating the word after him as one with the same cynical amused
mockery)*: Think! *(The chorused word has a brazen metallic quality as if their
throats were phonograph horns. It is followed by a general uproar of hard, barking
laughter)*.

VOICES: Don't be cracking your head wit ut, Yank.
You gat headache, py yingo!
One thing about it—it rhymes with drink!
Ha, ha, ha!
Drink, don't think!
Drink, don't think!
Drink, don't think! *(A whole chorus of voices has taken up this refrain, stamping
on the floor, pounding on the benches with fists)*.

YANK *(taking a gulp from his bottle—good-naturedly)*: Aw right. Can de noise.
I got yuh de foist time. *(The uproar subsides. A very drunken sentimental tenor begins to sing)*:

"Far away in Canada,
    Far across the sea,
There's a lass who fondly waits
    Making a home for me—"

YANK *(fiercely contemptuous)*: Shut up, yuh lousy boob! Where d'yuh get dat
tripe? Home? Home, hell! I'll make a home for yuh! I'll knock yuh dead. Home!
T'hell wit home! Where d'yuh get dat tripe? Dis is home, see? What d'yuh want
wit home? *(Proudly)* I runned away from mine when I was a kid. On'y too glad to
beat it, dat was me. Home was lickings for me, dat's all. But yuh can bet your shoit
no one ain't never licked me since! Wanter try it, any of youse? Huh! I guess not.

(In a more placated but still contemptuous tone) Goils waitin' for yuh, huh? Aw, hell! Dat's all tripe. Dey don't wait for no one. Dey'd double-cross yuh for a nickel. Dey're all tarts, get me? Treat 'em rough, dat's me. To hell wit 'em. Tarts, dat's what, de whole bunch of 'em.

LONG *(very drunk, jumps on a bench excitedly, gesticulating with a bottle in his hand)*: Listen 'ere, Comrades! Yank 'ere is right. 'E says this 'ere stinkin' ship is our 'ome. And 'e says as 'ome is 'ell. And 'e's right! This is 'ell. We lives in 'ell, Comrades—and right enough we'll die in it. *(Raging)* And who's ter blame, I arsks yer? We ain't. We wasn't born this rotten way. All men is born free and ekal. That's in the bleedin' Bible, maties. But what d'they care for the Bible—them lazy, bloated swine what travels first cabin? Them's the ones. They dragged us down 'til we're on'y wage slaves in the bowels of a bloody ship, sweatin', burnin' up, eatin' coal dust! Hit's them's ter blame—the damned Capitalist clarss! *(There had been a gradual murmur of contemptuous resentment rising among the men until now he is interrupted by a storm of catcalls, hisses, boos, hard laughter).*

VOICES: Turn it off!
Shut up!
Sit down!
Closa da face!
Tamn fool! *(Etc.).*

YANK *(standing up and glaring at* LONG*)*: Sit down before I knock yuh down! *(*LONG *makes haste to efface himself.* YANK *goes on contemptuously)* De Bible, huh? De Cap'tlist class, huh? Aw nix on dat Salvation Army–Socialist bull. Git a soapbox! Hire a hall! Come and be saved, huh? Jerk us to Jesus, huh? Aw g'wan! I've listened to lots of guys like you, see. Yuh're all wrong. Wanter know what I t'ink? Yuh ain't no good for no one. Yuh're de bunk. Yuh ain't got no noive, get me? Yuh're yellow, dat's what. Yellow, dat's you. Say! What's dem slobs in de foist cabin got to do wit us? We're better men dan dey are, ain't we? Sure! One of us guys could clean up de whole mob wit one mit. Put one of 'em down here for one watch in de stokehole, what'd happen? Dey'd carry him off on a stretcher. Dem boids don't amount to nothin'. Dey're just baggage. Who makes dis old tub run? Ain't it us guys? Well den, we belong, don't we? We belong and dey don't. Dat's all. *(A loud chorus of approval.* YANK *goes on)* As for dis bein' hell—aw, nuts! Yuh lost your noive, dat's what. Dis is a man's job, get me? It belongs. It runs dis tub. No stiffs need apply. But yuh're a stiff, see? Yuh're yellow, dat's you.

VOICES *(with a great hard pride in them)*:
Righto!
A man's job!
Talk is cheap, Long.
He never could hold up his end.
Divil take him!
Yank's right. We make it go.
Py Gott, Yank say right ting!
We don't need no one cryin' over us.
Makin' speeches.

Throw him out!
Yellow!
Chuck him overboard!
I'll break his jaw for him!
(They crowd around Long threateningly).

YANK *(half good-natured again—contemptuously)*: Aw, take it easy. Leave him alone. He ain't woith a punch. Drink up. Here's how, whoever owns dis. *(He takes a long swallow from his bottle. All drink with him. In a flash all is hilarious amiability again, backslapping, loud talk, etc.).*

PADDY *(who has been sitting in a blinking, melancholy daze—suddenly cries out in a voice full of old sorrow)*: We belong to this, you're saying? We make the ship to go, you're saying? Yerra then, that Almighty God have pity on us! *(His voice runs into the wail of a keen, he rocks back and forth on his bench. The men stare at him, startled and impressed in spite of themselves)* Oh, to be back in the fine days of my youth, ochone! Oh, there was fine beautiful ships them days—clippers wid tall masts touching the sky—fine strong men in them—men that was sons of the sea as if 'twas the mother that bore them. Oh, the clean skins of them, and the clear eyes, the straight backs and full chests of them! Brave men they was, and bold men surely! We'd be sailing out, bound down round the Horn maybe. We'd be making sail in the dawn, with a fair breeze, singing a chanty song wid no care to it. And astern the land would be sinking low and dying out, but we'd give it no heed but a laugh, and never a look behind. For the day that was, was enough, for we was free men—and I'm thinking 'tis only slaves do be giving heed to the day that's gone or the day to come—until they're old like me. *(With a sort of religious exaltation)* Oh, to be scudding south again wid the power of the Trade Wind driving her on steady through the nights and the days! Full sail on her! Nights and days! Nights when the foam of the wake would be flaming wid fire, when the sky'd be blazing and winking wid stars. Or the full of the moon maybe. Then you'd see her driving through the gray night, her sails stretching aloft all silver and white, not a sound on the deck, the lot of us dreaming dreams, till you'd believe 'twas no real ship at all you was on but a ghost ship like the *Flying Dutchman* they say does be roaming the seas forevermore widout touching a port. And there was the days, too. A warm sun on the clean decks. Sun warming the blood of you, and wind over the miles of shiny green ocean like strong drink to your lungs. Work—aye, hard work—but who'd mind that at all? Sure, you worked under the sky and 'twas work wid skill and daring to it. And wid the day done, in the dog watch, smoking me pipe at ease, the lookout would be raising land maybe, and we'd see the mountains of South Americy wid the red fire of the setting sun painting the white tops and the clouds floating by them! *(His tone of exaltation ceases. He goes on mournfully)* Yerra, what's the use of talking? 'Tis a dead man's whisper. *(To* YANK *resentfully)* 'Twas them days men belonged to ships, not now. 'Twas them days a ship was part of the sea, and a man was part of a ship, and the sea joined all together and made it one. *(Scornfully)* Is it one wid this you'd be, Yank—black smoke from the funnels smudging the sea, smudging the decks—the bloody engines pounding and throbbing and shaking—wid divil a sight of sun or a breath of clean air—choking our lungs wid coal dust—breaking our backs and hearts in the hell of the stokehole—feeding the bloody furnace—feeding our lives along wid the coal, I'm thinking—caged in by steel from a sight of the sky like bloody apes in the Zoo! *(With a harsh laugh)* Ho-ho, divil mend you! Is it to belong to that you're wishing? Is it a flesh and blood wheel of the engines you'd be?

YANK *(who has been listening with a contemptuous sneer, barks out the answer)*: Sure ting! Dat's me. What about it?

PADDY *(as if to himself—with great sorrow)*: Me time is past due. That a great wave wid sun in the heart of it may sweep me over the side sometime I'd be dreaming of the days that's gone!

YANK: Aw, yuh crazy Mick! *(He springs to his feet and advances on* PADDY *threateningly—then stops, fighting some queer struggle within himself—lets his hands fall to his sides—contemptuously)* Aw, take it easy. Yuh're aw right, at dat. Yuh're bugs, dat's all—nutty as a cuckoo. All dat tripe yuh been pullin'—Aw, dat's all right. On'y it's dead, get me? Yuh don't belong no more, see. Yuh don't get de stuff. Yuh're too old. *(Disgustedly)* But aw say, come up for air onct in a while, can't yuh? See what's happened since yuh croaked. *(He suddenly bursts forth vehemently, growing more and more excited)* Say! Sure! Sure I meant it! What de hell— Say, lemme talk! Hey! Hey, you old Harp! Hey, youse guys! Say, listen to me— wait a moment—I gotter talk, see. I belong and he don't. He's dead but I'm livin'. Listen to me! Sure I'm part of de engines! Why de hell not! Dey move, don't dey? Dey're speed, ain't dey? Dey smash trou, don't dey? Twenty-five knots a hour! Dat's goin' some! Dat's new stuff! Dat belongs! But him, he's too old. He gets dizzy. Say, listen. All dat crazy tripe about nights and days; all dat crazy tripe about stars and moons; all dat crazy tripe about suns and winds, fresh air and de rest of it— Aw hell, dat's all a dope dream! Hittin' de pipe of de past, dat's what he's doin'. He's old and don't belong no more. But me, I'm young! I'm in de pink! I move wit it! It, get me! I mean de ting dat's de guts of all dis. It ploughs trou all de tripe he's been sayin'. It blows dat up! It knocks dat dead! It slams dat offen de face of de oith! It, get me! De engines and de coal and de smoke and all de rest of it! He can't breathe and swallow coal dust, but I kin, see? Dat's fresh air for me! Dat's food for me! I'm new, get me? Hell in de stokehole? Sure! It takes a man to work in hell. Hell, sure, dat's my fav'rite climate. I eat it up! I git fat on it! It's me makes it hot! It's me makes it roar! It's me makes it move! Sure, on'y for me everything stops. It all goes dead, get me? De noise and smoke and all de engines movin' de woild, dey stop. Dere ain't nothin' no more! Dat's what I'm sayin'. Everyting else dat makes de woild move, somep'n makes it move. It can't move witout somep'n else, see? Den yuh get down to me. I'm at de bottom, get me! Dere ain't nothin' foither. I'm de end! I'm de start! I start somep'n and de woild moves! It—dat's me!—de new dat's moiderin' de old! I'm de ting in coal dat makes it boin; I'm steam and oil for de engines; I'm de ting in noise dat makes yuh hear it; I'm smoke and express trains and steamers and factory whistles; I'm de ting in gold dat makes it money! And I'm what makes iron into steel! Steel, dat stands for de whole ting! And I'm steel—steel—steel! I'm de muscles in steel, de punch behind it! *(As he says this he pounds with his fist against the steel bunks. All the men, roused to a pitch of frenzied self-glorification by his speech, do likewise. There is a deafening metallic roar, through which* YANK's *voice can be heard bellowing)* Slaves, hell! We run de whole woiks. All de rich guys dat tink dey're somep'n, dey ain't nothin'! Dey don't belong. But us guys, we're in de move, we're at de bottom, de whole ting is us! (PADDY *from the start of* YANK's *speech has been taking one gulp after another from his bottle, at first frightenedly, as if he were afraid to listen, then desperately, as if to drown his senses, but finally has achieved complete indifferent, even amused, drunkenness.* YANK *sees his lips moving. He quells the uproar with a shout)* Hey, youse guys, take it easy! Wait a moment! De nutty Harp is sayin' somep'n.

PADDY (*is heard now—throws his head back with a mocking burst of laughter*): Ho-ho-ho-ho-ho—

YANK (*drawing back his fist, with a snarl*): Aw! Look out who yuh're givin' the bark!

PADDY (*begins to sing the "Miller of Dee" with enormous good nature*):

"I care for nobody, no, not I,
And nobody cares for me."

YANK (*good-natured himself in a flash, interrupts* PADDY *with a slap on the bare back like a report*): Dat's de stuff! Now yuh're gettin' wise to somep'n. Care for nobody, dat's de dope! To hell wit 'em all! And nix on nobody else carin'. I kin care for myself, get me! (*Eight bells sound, muffled, vibrating through the steel walls as if some enormous brazen gong were imbedded in the heart of the ship. All the men jump up mechanically, file through the door silently close upon each other's heels in what is very like a prisoners' lockstep.* YANK *slaps* PADDY *on the back)* Our watch, yuh old Harp! (*Mockingly*) Come on down in hell. Eat up de coal dust. Drink in de heat. It's it, see! Act like yuh liked it, yuh better—or croak yuhself.

PADDY (*with jovial defiance*): To the divil wid it! I'll not report this watch. Let thim log me and be damned. I'm no slave the like of you. I'll be sittin' here at me ease, and drinking, and thinking, and dreaming dreams.

YANK (*contemptuously*): Tinkin' and dreamin', what'll that get yuh? What's tinkin' got to do wit it? We move, don't we? Speed, ain't it? Fog, dat's all you stand for. But we drive trou dat, don't we? We split dat up and smash trou—twenty-five knots a hour! (*Turns his back on* PADDY *scornfully*) Aw, yuh make me sick! Yuh don't belong! (*He strides out the door in rear.* PADDY *hums to himself, blinking drowsily*)

Curtain

SCENE TWO

Two days out. A section of the promenade deck. MILDRED DOUGLAS *and her aunt are discovered reclining in deck chairs. The former is a girl of twenty, slender, delicate, with a pale, pretty face marred by a self-conscious expression of disdainful superiority. She looks fretful, nervous and discontented, bored by her own anemia. Her aunt is a pompous and proud—and fat—old lady. She is a type even to the point of a double chin and lorgnettes. She is dressed pretentiously, as if afraid her face alone would never indicate her position in life.* MILDRED *is dressed all in white.*

The impression to be conveyed by this scene is one of the beautiful, vivid life of the sea all about—sunshine on the deck in a great flood, the fresh sea wind blowing across it. In the midst of this, these two incongruous, artificial figures, inert and disharmonious, the elder like a gray lump of dough touched up with rouge, the younger looking as if the vitality of her stock had been sapped before she was conceived, so that she is the expression not of its life energy but merely of the artificialities that energy had won for itself in the spending.

MILDRED *(looking up with affected dreaminess)*: How the black smoke swirls back against the sky! Is it not beautiful?

AUNT *(without looking up)*: I dislike smoke of any kind.

MILDRED: My great-grandmother smoked a pipe—a clay pipe.

AUNT *(ruffling)*: Vulgar!

MILDRED: She was too distant a relative to be vulgar. Time mellows pipes.

AUNT *(pretending boredom but irritated)*: Did the sociology you took up at college teach you that—to play the ghoul on every possible occasion, excavating old bones? Why not let your great-grandmother rest in her grave?

MILDRED *(dreamily)*: With her pipe beside her—puffing in Paradise.

AUNT *(with spite)*: Yes, you are a natural born ghoul. You are even getting to look like one, my dear.

MILDRED *(in a passionless tone)*: I detest you, Aunt. *(Looking at her critically)* Do you know what you remind me of? Of a cold pork pudding against a background of linoleum tablecloth in the kitchen of a—but the possibilities are wearisome. *(She closes her eyes)*.

AUNT *(with a bitter laugh)*: Merci for your candor. But since I am and must be your chaperon—in appearance, at least—let us patch up some sort of armed truce. For my part you are quite free to indulge any pose of eccentricity that beguiles you—as long as you observe the amenities—

MILDRED *(drawling)*: The inanities?

AUNT *(going on as if she hadn't heard)*: After exhausting the morbid thrills of social service work on New York's East Side—how they must have hated you, by the way, the poor that you made so much poorer in their own eyes!—you are now bent on making your slumming international. Well, I hope Whitechapel will provide the needed nerve tonic. Do not ask me to chaperon you there, however. I told your father I would not. I loathe deformity. We will hire an army of detectives and you may investigate everything—they allow you to see.

MILDRED *(protesting with a trace of genuine earnestness)*: Please do not mock at my attempts to discover how the other half lives. Give me credit for some sort of groping sincerity in that at least. I would like to help them. I would like to be some use in the world. Is it my fault I don't know how? I would like to be sincere, to touch life somewhere. *(With weary bitterness)* But I'm afraid I have neither the vitality nor integrity. All that was burnt out in our stock before I was born. Grandfather's blast furnaces, flaming to the sky, melting steel, making millions—then father keeping those home fires burning, making more millions—and little me at the tail-end of it all. I'm a waste product in the Bessemer process—like the millions. Or rather, I inherit the acquired trait of the by-product, wealth, but none of the energy, none of the strength of the steel that made it. I am sired by gold and damned by it, as they say at the race track—damned in more ways than one. *(She laughs mirthlessly)*.

AUNT *(unimpressed—superciliously)*: You seem to be going in for sincerity today. It isn't becoming to you, really—except as an obvious pose. Be as artificial as you are, I advise. There's a sort of sincerity in that, you know. And, after all, you must confess you like that better.

MILDRED *(again affected and bored)*: Yes, I suppose I do. Pardon me for my outburst. When a leopard complains of its spots, it must sound rather grotesque. *(In a mocking tone)* Purr, little leopard. Purr, scratch, tear, kill, gorge yourself and be happy—only stay in the jungle where your spots are camouflage. In a cage they make you conspicuous.

AUNT: I don't know what you are talking about.

MILDRED: It would be rude to talk about anything to you. Let's just talk. *(She looks at her wrist watch)* Well, thank goodness, it's about time for them to come for me. That ought to give me a new thrill, Aunt.

AUNT *(affectedly troubled)*: You don't mean to say you're really going? The dirt—the heat must be frightful—

MILDRED: Grandfather started as a puddler. I should have inherited an immunity to heat that would make a salamander shiver. It will be fun to put it to the test.

AUNT: But don't you have to have the captain's—or someone's—permission to visit the stokehole?

MILDRED *(with a triumphant smile)*: I have it—both his and the chief engineer's. Oh, they didn't want to at first, in spite of my social service credentials. They didn't seem a bit anxious that I should investigate how the other half lives and works on a ship. So I had to tell them that my father, the president of Nazareth Steel, chairman of the board of directors of this line, had told me it would be all right.

AUNT: He didn't.

MILDRED: How naïve age makes one! But I said he did, Aunt. I even said he had given me a letter to them—which I had lost. And they were afraid to take the chance that I might be lying. *(Excitedly)* So it's ho! for the stokehole. The second engineer is to escort me. *(Looking at her watch again)* It's time. And here he comes, I think. *(The SECOND ENGINEER enters. He is a husky, fine-looking man of thirty-five or so. He stops before the two and tips his cap, visibly embarrassed and ill-at-ease)*.

SECOND ENGINEER: Miss Douglas?

MILDRED: Yes. *(Throwing off her rugs and getting to her feet)* Are we all ready to start?

SECOND ENGINEER: In just a second, ma'am. I'm waiting for the Fourth. He's coming along.

MILDRED *(with a scornful smile)*: You don't care to shoulder this responsibility alone, is that it?

SECOND ENGINEER (*forcing a smile*): Two are better than one. (*Disturbed by her eyes, glances out to sea—blurts out*) A fine day we're having.

MILDRED: Is it?

SECOND ENGINEER: A nice warm breeze—

MILDRED: It feels cold to me.

SECOND ENGINEER: But it's hot enough in the sun—

MILDRED: Not hot enough for me. I don't like Nature. I was never athletic.

SECOND ENGINEER (*forcing a smile*): Well, you'll find it hot enough where you're going.

MILDRED: Do you mean hell?

SECOND ENGINEER (*flabbergasted, decides to laugh*): Ho-ho! No, I mean the stokehole.

MILDRED: My grandfather was a puddler. He played with boiling steel.

SECOND ENGINEER (*all at sea—uneasily*): Is that so? Hum, you'll excuse me, ma'am, but are you intending to wear that dress?

MILDRED: Why not?

SECOND ENGINEER: You'll likely rub against oil and dirt. It can't be helped.

MILDRED: It doesn't matter. I have lots of white dresses.

SECOND ENGINEER: I have an old coat you might throw over—

MILDRED: I have fifty dresses like this. I will throw this one into the sea when I come back. That ought to wash it clean, don't you think?

SECOND ENGINEER (*doggedly*): There's ladders to climb down that are none to clean—and dark alleyways—

MILDRED: I will wear this very dress and none other.

SECOND ENGINEER: No offense meant. It's none of my business. I was only warning you—

MILDRED: Warning? That sounds thrilling.

SECOND ENGINEER (*looking down the deck—with a sigh of relief*): There's the Fourth now. He's waiting for us. If you'll come—

MILDRED: Go on. I'll follow you. (*He goes.* MILDRED *turns a mocking smile on her aunt*) An oaf—but a handsome, virile oaf.

AUNT (*scornfully*): Poser!

MILDRED: Take care. He said there were dark alleyways—

AUNT (*in the same tone*): Poser!

MILDRED (*biting her lips angrily*): You are right. But would that my millions were not so anemically chaste!

AUNT: Yes, for a fresh pose I have no doubt you would drag the name of Douglas in the gutter!

MILDRED: From which it sprang. Good-by, Aunt. Don't pray too hard that I may fall into the fiery furnace.

AUNT: Poser!

MILDRED (*viciously*): Old hag! (*She slaps her aunt insultingly across the face and walks off, laughing gaily*).

AUNT (*screams after her*): I said poser!

Curtain

SCENE THREE

The stokehole. In the rear, the dimly-outlined bulks of the furnaces and boilers. High overhead one hanging electric bulb sheds just enough light through the murky air laden with coal dust to pile up masses of shadows everywhere. A line of men, stripped to the waist, is before the furnace doors. They bend over, looking neither to right nor left, handling their shovels as if they were part of their bodies, with a strange, awkward, swinging rhythm. They use the shovels to throw open the furnace doors. Then from these fiery round holes in the black a flood of terrific light and heat pours full upon the men who are outlined in silhouette in the crouching, inhuman attitudes of chained gorillas. The men shovel with a rhythmic motion, swinging as on a pivot from the coal which lies in heaps on the floor behind to hurl it into the flaming mouths before them. There is a tumult of noise—the brazen clang of the furnace doors as they are flung open or slammed shut, the grating, teeth-gritting grind of steel against steel, of crunching coal. This clash of sounds stuns one's ears with its rending dissonance. But there is order in it, rhythm, a mechanical regulated recurrence, a tempo. And rising above all, making the air hum with the quiver of liberated energy, the roar of leaping flames in the furnaces, the monotonous throbbing beat of the engines.

As the curtain rises, the furnace doors are shut. The men are taking a breathing spell. One or two are arranging the coal behind them, pulling it into more accessible heaps. The others can be dimly made out leaning on their shovels in relaxed attitudes of exhaustion.

PADDY (*from somewhere in the line—plaintively*): Yerra, will this divil's own watch nivir end? Me back is broke. I'm destroyed entirely.

YANK (*from the center of the line—with exuberant scorn*): Aw, yuh make me sick! Lie down and croak, why don't yuh? Always beefin', dat's you! Say, dis is a cinch! Dis was made for me! It's my meat, get me! (*A whistle is blown—a thin, shrill note from somewhere overhead in the darkness.* YANK *curses without resentment*) Dere's de damn engineer crackin' de whip. He tinks we're loafin'.

PADDY (*vindictively*): God stiffen him!

YANK (*in an exultant tone of command*): Come on, youse guys! Git into de game! She's gittin' hungry! Pile some grub in her. Trow it into her belly! Come on now, all of youse! Open her up! (*At this last all the men, who have followed his movements of getting into position, throw open their furnace doors with a deafening clang. The fiery light floods over their shoulders as they bend round for the coal. Rivulets of sooty sweat have traced maps on their backs. The enlarged muscles form bunches of high light and shadow*).

YANK (*chanting a count as he shovels without seeming effort*): One—two—tree— (*His voice rising exultantly in the joy of battle*) Dat's de stuff! Let her have it! All togedder now! Sling it into her! Let her ride! Shoot de piece now! Call de toin on her! Drive her into it! Feel her move! Watch her smoke! Speed, dat's her middle name! Give her coal, youse guys! Coal, dat's her booze! Drink it up, baby! Let's see yuh sprint! Dig in and gain a lap! Dere she go-o-es. (*This last in the chanting formula of the gallery gods at the six-day bike race. He slams his furnace door shut. The others do likewise with as much unison as their wearied bodies will permit. The effect is of one fiery eye after another being blotted out with a series of accompanying bangs).*

PADDY *(groaning)*: Me back is broke. I'm bate out—bate— *(There is a pause. Then the inexorable whistle sounds again from the dim regions above the electric light. There is a growl of cursing rage from all sides).*

YANK *(shaking his fist upward—contemptuously)*: Take it easy dere, you! Who d'yuh tink's runnin' dis game, me or you? When I git ready, we move. Not before! When I git ready, get me!

VOICES *(approvingly)*: That's the stuff!
Yank tal him, py golly!
Yank ain't affeerd.
Goot poy, Yank!
Give him hell!
Tell 'im 'e's a bloody swine!
Bloody slave-driver!

YANK *(contemptuously)*: He ain't got no noive. He's yellow, get me? All de engineers is yellow. Dey got streaks a mile wide. Aw, to hell wit him! Let's move, youse guys. We had a rest. Come on, she needs it! Give her pep! It ain't for him. Him and his whistle, dey don't belong. But we belong, see! We gotter feed de baby! Come on! *(He turns and flings his furnace door open. They all follow his lead. At this instant the* SECOND *and* FOURTH ENGINEERS *enter from the darkness on the left with* MILDRED *between them. She starts, turns paler, her pose is crumbling, she shivers with fright in spite of the blazing heat, but forces herself to leave the* ENGINEERS *and take a few steps nearer the men. She is right behind* YANK. *All this happens quickly while the men have their backs turned).*

YANK: Come on, youse guys! *(He is turning to get coal when the whistle sounds again in a peremptory, irritating note. This drives* YANK *into a sudden fury. While the other men have turned full around and stopped dumfounded by the spectacle of* MILDRED *standing there in her white dress,* YANK *does not turn far enough to see her. Besides, his head is thrown back, he blinks upward through the murk trying to find the owner of the whistle, he brandishes his shovel murderously over his head in one hand, pounding on his chest, gorilla-like, with the other, shouting)* Toin off dat whistle! Come down outa dere, yuh yellow, brass-buttoned, Belfast bum, yuh! Come down and I'll knock yer brains out! Yuh lousy, stinkin', yellow mut of a Catholic-moiderin' bastard! Come down and I'll moider yuh! Pullin' dat whistle on me, huh? I'll show yuh! I'll crash yer skull in! I'll drive yer teet' down yer troat! I'll slam yer nose trou de back of yer head! I'll cut yer guts out for a nickel, yuh lousy boob, yuh dirty, crummy, muckeatin' son of a— *(Suddenly he becomes conscious of all the other men staring at something directly behind his back. He whirls defensively with a snarling, murderous growl, crouching to spring, his lips drawn back over his teeth, his small eyes gleaming ferociously. He sees* MILDRED, *like a white apparition in the full light from the open furnace doors. He glares into her eyes, turned to stone. As for her, during his speech she has listened, paralyzed with horror, terror, her whole* personality crushed, beaten in, collapsed, by the terrific impact of this unknown, abysmal brutality, naked and shameless. As she looks at his gorilla face, as his eyes bore into hers, she utters a low, choking cry and shrinks away from him, putting both hands up before her eyes to shut out the sight of his face, to protect her own. This startles YANK to a reaction. His mouth falls open, his eyes grow bewildered).

MILDRED (about to faint—to the ENGINEERS, who now have her one by each arm—whimperingly): Take me away! Oh, the filthy beast! (She faints. They carry her quickly back, disappearing in the darkness at the left, rear. An iron door clangs shut. Rage and bewildered fury rush back on YANK. He feels himself insulted in some unknown fashion in the very heart of his pride. He roars) God damn yuh! (And hurls his shovel after them at the door which has just closed. It hits the steel bulkhead with a clang and falls clattering on the steel floor. From overhead the whistle sounds again in a long, angry, insistent command).

Curtain

SCENE FOUR

The firemen's forecastle. YANK's *watch has just come off duty and had dinner. Their faces and bodies shine from a soap and water scrubbing but around their eyes, where a hasty dousing does not touch, the coal dust sticks like black make-up, giving them a queer, sinister expression.* YANK *has not washed either face or body. He stands out in contrast to them, a blackened, brooding figure. He is seated forward on a bench in the exact attitude of Rodin's "The Thinker." The others, most of them smoking pipes, are staring at* YANK *half-apprehensively, as if fearing an outburst; half-amusedly, as if they saw a joke somewhere that tickled them.*

VOICES: He ain't ate nothin'.
Py golly, a fallar gat to gat grub in him.
Divil a lie.
Yank feeda da fire, no feeda da face.
Ha-ha.
He aint even washed hisself.
He's forgot.
Hey, Yank, you forgot to wash.
YANK (sullenly): Forgot nothin'! To hell wit washin'.
VOICES: It'll stick to you.
It'll get under your skin.
Give yer the bleedin' itch, that's wot.
It makes spots on you—like a leopard.
Like a piebald nigger, you mean.
Better wash up, Yank.
You sleep better.
Wash up, Yank.
Wash up! Wash up!

YANK (*resentfully*): Aw say, youse guys. Lemme alone. Can't youse see I'm tryin' to tink?

ALL (*repeating the word after him as one with cynical mockery*): Think! (*The word has a brazen, metallic quality as if their throats were phonograph horns. It is followed by a chorus of hard, barking laughter*).

YANK (*springing to his feet and glaring at them belligerently*): Yes, tink! Tink, dat's what I said! What about it? (*They are silent, puzzled by his sudden resentment at what used to be one of his jokes.* YANK *sits down again in the same attitude of "The Thinker"*).

VOICES: Leave him alone.

He's got a grouch on.

Why wouldn't he?

PADDY (*with a wink at the others*): Sure I know what's the matther. 'Tis aisy to see. He's fallen in love, I'm telling you.

ALL (*repeating the word after him as one with cynical mockery*): Love! (*The word has a brazen, metallic quality as if their throats were phonograph horns. It is followed by a chorus of hard, barking laughter*).

YANK (*with a contemptuous snort*): Love, hell! Hate, dat's what. I've fallen in hate, get me?

PADDY (*philosophically*): 'Twould take a wise man to tell one from the other. (*With a bitter, ironical scorn, increasing as he goes on*) But I'm telling you it's love that's in it. Sure what else but love for us poor bastes in the stokehole would be bringing a fine lady, dressed like a white quane, down a mile of ladders and steps to be havin' a look at us? (*A growl of anger goes up from all sides*).

LONG (*jumping on a bench—hectically*): Hinsultin' us! Hinsultin' us, the bloody cow! And them bloody engineers! What right 'as they got to be exhibitin' us 's if we was bleedin' monkeys in a menagerie? Did we sign for hinsults to our dignity as 'onest workers? Is that in the ship's articles? You kin bloody well bet it ain't! But I know why they done it. I asked a deck steward 'o she was and 'e told me. 'Er old man's a bleedin' millionaire, a bloody Capitalist! 'E's got enuf bloody gold to sink this bleedin' ship! 'E makes arf the bloody steel in the world! 'E owns this bloody boat! And you and me, Comrades, we're 'is slaves! And the skipper and mates and engineers, they're 'is slaves! And she's 'is bloody daughter and we're all 'er slaves, too! And she gives 'er orders as 'ow she wants to see the bloody animals below decks and down they takes 'er! (*There is a roar of rage from all sides*).

YANK (*blinking at him bewilderedly*): Say! Wait a moment! Is all dat straight goods?

LONG: Straight as string! The bleedin' steward as waits on 'em, 'e told me about 'er. And what're we goin' ter do, I arsks yer? 'Ave we got ter swaller 'er hinsults like dogs? It ain't in the ship's articles. I tell yer we got a case. We kin go to law—

YANK (*with abysmal contempt*): Hell! Law!

ALL (*repeating the word after him as one with cynical mockery*): Law! (*The word has a brazen metallic quality as if their throats were phonograph horns. It is followed by a chorus of hard, barking laughter*).

LONG (*feeling the ground slipping from under his feet—desperately*): As voters and citizens we kin force the bloody governments—

YANK (*with abysmal contempt*): Hell! Governments!

ALL (*repeating the word after him as one with cynical mockery*): Governments! (*The word has a brazen metallic quality as if their throats were phonograph horns. It is followed by a chorus of hard, barking laughter*).

LONG (*hysterically*): We're free and equal in the sight of God—

YANK (*with abysmal contempt*): Hell! God!

ALL (*repeating the word after him as one with cynical mockery*): God! (*The word has a brazen metallic quality as if their throats were phonograph horns. It is followed by a chorus of hard, barking laughter*).

YANK (*witheringly*): Aw, join de Salvation Army!

ALL: Sit down! Shut up! Damn fool! Sea-lawyer! (LONG *slinks back out of sight*).

PADDY (*continuing the trend of his thoughts as if he had never been interrupted—bitterly*): And there she was standing behind us, and the Second pointing at us like a man you'd hear in a circus would be saying: In this cage is a queerer kind of baboon than ever you'd find in darkest Africy. We roast them in their own sweat—and be damned if you won't hear some of thim saying they like it! (*He glances scornfully at* YANK).

YANK (*with a bewildered uncertain growl*): Aw!

PADDY: And there was Yank roarin' curses and turning round wid his shovel to brain her—and she looked at him, and him at her—

YANK (*slowly*): She was all white. I tought she was a ghost. Sure.

PADDY (*with heavy, biting sarcasm*): 'Twas love at first sight, divil a doubt of it! If you'd seen the endearin' look on her pale mug when she shriveled away with her hands over her eyes to shut out the sight of him! Sure, 'twas as if she'd seen a great hairy ape escaped from the Zoo!

YANK (*stung—with a growl of rage*): Aw!

PADDY: And the loving way Yank heaved his shovel at the skull of her, only she was out the door! (*A grin breaking over his face*) 'Twas touching, I'm telling you! It put the touch of home, swate home in the stokehole. (*There is a roar of laughter from all*).

YANK (*glaring at* PADDY *menacingly*): Aw, choke dat off, see!

PADDY (*not heeding him—to the others*): And her grabbin' at the Second's arm for protection. (*With a grotesque imitation of a woman's voice*) Kiss me, Engineer dear, for it's dark down here and me old man's in Wall Street making money! Hug me tight, darlin', for I'm afeerd in the dark and me mother's on deck makin' eyes at the skipper! (*Another roar of laughter*).

YANK (*threateningly*): Say! What yuh tryin' to do, kid me, yuh old Harp?

PADDY: Divil a bit! Ain't I wishin' myself you'd brained her?

YANK (*fiercely*): I'll brain her! I'll brain her yet, wait 'n' see! (*Coming over to* PADDY—*slowly*) Say, is dat what she called me—a hairy ape?

PADDY: She looked it at you if she didn't say the word itself.

YANK *(grinning horribly)*: Hairy ape, huh? Sure! Dat's de way she looked at me, aw right. Hairy ape! So dat's me, huh? *(Bursting into rage—as if she were still in front of him)* Yuh skinny tart! Yuh white-faced bum, yuh! I'll show yuh who's a ape! *(Turning to the others, bewilderment seizing him again)* Say, youse guys. I was bawlin' him out for pullin' de whistle on us. You heard me. And den I seen youse lookin' at somep'n and I tought he'd sneaked down to come up in back of me, and I hopped round to knock him dead wit de shovel. And dere she was wit de light on her! Christ, yuh coulda pushed me over with a finger! I was scared, get me? Sure! I tought she was a ghost, see? She was all in white like dey wrap around stiffs. You seen her. Kin yuh blame me? She didn't belong, dat's what. And den when I come to and seen it was a real skoit and seen de way she was lookin' at me—like Paddy said—Christ, I was sore, get me? I don't stand for dat stuff from nobody. And I flung de shovel—on'y she'd beat it. *(Furiously)* I wished it'd banged her! I wished it'd knocked her block off!

LONG: And be 'anged for murder or 'lectrocuted? She ain't bleedin' well worth it.

YANK: I don't give a damn what! I'd be square wit her, wouldn't I? Tink I wanter let her put somep'n over on me? Tink I'm goin' to let her git away wit dat stuff? Yuh don't know me! No one ain't never put nothin' over on me and got away wit it, see!—not dat kind of stuff—no guy and no skoit neither! I'll fix her! Maybe she'll come down again—

VOICE: No chance, Yank. You scared her out of a year's growth.

YANK: I scared her? Why de hell should I scare her? Who de hell is she? Ain't she de same as me? Hairy ape, huh? *(With his old confident bravado)* I'll show her I'm better'n her, if she on'y knew it. I belong and she don't, see! I move and she's dead! Twenty-five knots an hour, dat's me! Dat carries her but I make dat. She's on'y baggage. Sure! *(Again bewilderedly)* But, Christ, she was funny lookin'! Did yuh pipe her hands? White and skinny. Yuh could see de bones through 'em. And her mush, dat was dead white, too. And her eyes, dey was like dey'd seen a ghost. Me, dat was! Sure! Hairy ape! Ghost, huh? Look at dat arm! *(He extends his right arm, swelling out the great muscles)* I coulda took her wit dat, wit just my little finger even, and broke her in two. *(Again bewilderedly)* Say, who is dat skoit, huh? What is she? What's she come from? Who made her? Who give her de noive to look at me like dat? Dis ting's got my goat right. I don't get her. She's new to me. What does a skoit like her mean, huh? She don't belong, get me! I can't see her. *(With growing anger)* But one ting I'm wise to, aw right, aw right! Youse all kin bet your shoits I'll git even wit her. I'll show her if she tinks she—She grinds de organ and I'm on de string, huh? I'll fix her! Let her come down again and I'll fling her in de furnace! She'll move den! She won't shiver at nothin', den! Speed, dat'll be her! She'll belong den! *(He grins horribly)*.

PADDY: She'll never come. She's had her belly-full, I'm telling you. She'll be in bed now, I'm thinking, wid ten doctors and nurses feedin' her salts to clean the fear out of her.

YANK *(enraged)*: Yuh tink I made her sick, too, do yuh? Just lookin' at me, huh? Hairy ape, huh? *(In a frenzy of rage)* I'll fix her! I'll tell her where to git off!

She'll git down on her knees and take it back or I'll bust de face offen her! *(Shaking one fist upward and beating on his chest with the other)* I'll find yuh! I'm comin', d'yuh hear? I'll fix yuh, God damn yuh! *(He makes a rush for the door)*.

VOICES: Stop him!
He'll get shot!
He'll murder her!
Trip him up!
Hold him!
He's gone crazy!
Gott, he's strong!
Hold him down!
Look out for a kick!
Pin his arms!

(They have all piled on him and, after a fierce struggle, by sheer weight of numbers have borne him to the floor just inside the door).

PADDY *(who has remained detached)*: Kape him down till he's cooled off. *(Scornfully)* Yerra, Yank, you're a great fool. Is it payin' attention at all you are to the like of that skinny sow widout one drop of rale blood in her?

YANK *(frenziedly, from the bottom of the heap)*: She done me doit! She done me doit, didn't she? I'll git square wit her! I'll get her some way! Git offen me, youse guys! Lemme up! I'll show her who's a ape!

Curtain

SCENE FIVE

Three weeks later. A corner of Fifth Avenue in the Fifties on a fine Sunday morning. A general atmosphere of clean, well-tidied, wide street; a flood of mellow, tempered sunshine; gentle, genteel breezes. In the rear, the show windows of two shops, a jewelry establishment on the corner, a furrier's next to it. Here the adornments of extreme wealth are tantalizingly displayed. The jeweler's window is gaudy with glittering diamonds, emeralds, rubies, pearls, etc., fashioned in ornate tiaras, crowns, necklaces, collars, etc. From each piece hangs an enormous tag from which a dollar sign and numerals in intermittent electric lights wink out the incredible prices. The same in the furrier's. Rich furs of all varieties hang there bathed in a downpour of artificial light. The general effect is of a background of magnificence cheapened and made grotesque by commercialism, a background in tawdry disharmony with the clear light and sunshine on the street itself.

Up the side street YANK *and* LONG *come swaggering.* LONG *is dressed in shore clothes, wears a black Windsor tie, cloth cap.* YANK *is in his dirty dungarees. A fireman's cap with black peak is cocked defiantly on the side of his head. He has not shaved for days and around his fierce, resentful eyes—as around those of* LONG *to a lesser degree—the black smudge of coal dust still sticks like make-up. They hesitate and stand together at the corner, swaggering, looking about them with a forced, defiant contempt.*

LONG (*indicating it all with an oratorical gesture*): Well, 'ere we are. Fif' Avenoo. This 'ere's their bleedin' private lane, as yer might say. (*Bitterly*) We're trespassers 'ere. Proletarians keep orf the grass!

YANK (*dully*): I don't see no grass, yuh boob. (*Staring at the sidewalk*) Clean, ain't it? Yuh could eat a fried egg offen it. The white wings got some job sweepin' dis up. (*Looking up and down the avenue—surlily*) Where's all de white-collar stiffs yuh said was here—and de skoits—*her* kind?

LONG: In church, blast 'em! Arskin' Jesus to give 'em more money.

YANK: Choich, huh? I useter go to choich onct—sure—when I was a kid. Me old man and woman, dey made me. Dey never went demselves, dough. Always got too big a head on Sunday mornin', dat was dem. (*With a grin*) Dey was scrappers for fair, bot' of dem. On Satiday nights when dey bot' got a skinful dey could put up a bout oughter been staged at de Garden. When dey got trough dere wasn't a chair or table wit a leg under it. Or else dey bot' jumped on me for somep'n. Dat was where I loined to take punishment. (*With a grin and a swagger*) I'm a chip offen de old block, get me?

LONG: Did yer old man follow the sea?

YANK: Naw. Worked along shore. I runned away when me old lady croaked wit de tremens. I helped at truckin' and in de market. Den I shipped in de stokehole. Sure. Dat belongs. De rest was nothin'. (*Looking around him*) I ain't never seen dis before. De Brooklyn waterfront, dat was where I was dragged up. (*Taking a deep breath*) Dis ain't so bad at dat, huh?

LONG: Not bad? Well, we pays for it wiv our bloody sweat, if yer wants to know!

YANK (*with sudden angry disgust*): Aw hell! I don't see no one, see—like her. All dis gives me a pain. It don't belong. Say, ain't dere a back room around dis dump? Let's go shoot a ball. All dis is too clean and quiet and dolled-up, get me! It gives me a pain.

LONG: Wait and yer'll bloody well see—

YANK: I don't wait for no one. I keep on de move. Say, what yuh drag me up here for, anyway? Tryin' to kid me, yuh simp, yuh?

LONG: Yer wants to get back at 'er, don't yer? That's what yer been sayin' every bloomin' hour since she hinsulted yer.

YANK (*vehemently*): Sure ting I do! Didn't I try to get even wit her in Southampton? Didn't I sneak on de dock and wait for her by de gangplank? I was goin' to spit in her pale mug, see! Sure, right in her pop-eyes! Dat woulda made me even, see? But no chanct. Dere was a whole army of plainclothes bulls around. Dey spotted me and gimme de bum's rush. I never seen her. But I'll git square wit her yet, you watch! (*Furiously*) De lousy tart! She tinks she kin get away wit moider—but not wit me! I'll fix her! I'll tink of a way!

LONG (*as disgusted as he dares to be*): Ain't that why I brought yer up 'ere—to show yer? Yer been lookin' at this 'ere 'ole affair wrong. Yer been actin' an' talkin' 's if it was all a bleedin' personal matter between yer and that bloody cow. I wants to convince yer she was on'y a representative of 'er clarss. I wants to awaken yer bloody clarss consciousness. Then yer'll see it's 'er clarss yer've got to fight, not 'er alone. There's a 'ole mob of 'em like 'er, Gawd blind 'em!

YANK *(spitting on his hands—belligerently)*: De more de merrier when I gits started. Bring on de gang!

LONG: Yer'll see 'em in arf a mo', when that church lets out. *(He turns and sees the window display in the two stores for the first time)* Blimey! Look at that, will yer? *(They both walk back and stand looking in the jeweler's.* LONG *flies into a fury)* Just look at this 'ere bloomin' mess! Just look at it! Look at the bleedin' prices on 'em— more'n our 'ole bloody stokehole makes in ten voyages sweatin' in 'ell! And they—'er and 'er bloody clarss—buys 'em for toys to dangle on 'em! One of these 'ere would buy scoff for a starvin' family for a year!

YANK: Aw, cut de sob stuff! T' hell wit de starvin' family! Yuh'll be passin' de hat to me next. *(With naïve admiration)* Say, dem tings is pretty, huh? Bet yuh dey'd hock for a piece of change aw right. *(Then turning away, bored)* But, aw hell, what good are dey? Let me have 'em. Dey don't belong no more'n she does. *(With a gesture of sweeping the jewelers into oblivion)* All dat don't count, get me?

LONG *(who has moved to the furrier's—indignantly)*: And I s'pose this 'ere don't count neither—skins of poor, 'armless animals slaughtered so as 'er and 'ers can keep their bleedin' noses warm!

YANK *(who has been staring at something inside—with queer excitement)*: Take a slant at dat! Give it de once-over! Monkey fur—two t'ousand bucks! *(Bewilderedly)* Is dat straight goods—monkey fur? What de hell—?

LONG *(bitterly)*: It's straight enuf. *(With grim humor)* They wouldn't bloody well pay that for a 'airy ape's skin—no, nor for the 'ole livin' ape with all 'is 'ead, and body, and soul thrown in!

YANK *(clenching his fists, his face growing pale with rage as if the skin in the window were a personal insult)*: Trowin' it up in my face! Christ! I'll fix her!

LONG *(excitedly)*: Church is out. 'Ere they come, the bleedin' swine. *(After a glance at* YANK's *lowering face—uneasily)* Easy goes, Comrade. Keep yer bloomin' temper. Remember force defeats itself. It ain't our weapon. We must impress our demands through peaceful means—the votes of the on-marching proletarians of the bloody world!

YANK *(with abysmal contempt)*: Votes, hell! Votes is a joke, see. Votes for women! Let dem do it!

LONG *(still more uneasily)*: Calm, now. Treat 'em wiv the proper contempt. Observe the bleedin' parasites but 'old yer 'orses.

YANK *(angrily)*: Get away from me! Yuh're yellow, dat's what. Force, dat's me! De punch, dat's me every time, see! *(The crowd from church enter from the right, sauntering slowly and affectedly, their heads held stiffly up, looking neither to right nor left, talking in toneless, simpering voices. The women are rouged, calcimined, dyed, overdressed to the nth degree. The men are in Prince Alberts, high hats, spats, canes, etc. A procession of gaudy marionettes, yet with something of the relentless horror of Frankensteins in their detached, mechanical unawareness)*.

VOICES: Dear Doctor Caiaphas! He is so sincere!

What was the sermon? I dozed off.

About the radicals, my dear—and the false doctrines that are being preached.

We must organize a hundred per cent American bazaar.

And let everyone contribute one one-hundredth per cent of their income tax.

What an original idea!

We can devote the proceeds to rehabilitating the veil of the temple.

But that has been done so many times.

YANK (*glaring from one to the other of them—with an insulting snort of scorn*): Huh! Huh! (*Without seeming to see him, they make wide detours to avoid the spot where he stands in the middle of the sidewalk*).

LONG (*frightenedly*): Keep yer bloomin' mouth shut, I tells yer.

YANK (*viciously*): G'wan! Tell it to Sweeney! (*He swaggers away and deliberately lurches into a top-hatted gentleman, then glares at him pugnaciously*) Say, who d'yuh tink yuh're bumpin'? Tink yuh own de oith?

GENTLEMAN (*coldly and affectedly*): I beg your pardon. (*He has not looked at* YANK *and passes on without a glance, leaving him bewildered*).

LONG (*rushing up and grabbing* YANK's *arm*): 'Ere! Come away! This wasn't what I meant. Yer'll 'ave the bloody coppers down on us.

YANK (*savagely—giving him a push that sends him sprawling*): G'wan!

LONG (*picks himself up—hysterically*): I'll pop orf then. This ain't what I meant. And whatever 'appens, yer can't blame me. (*He slinks off left*).

YANK: T' hell wit youse! (*He approaches a lady—with a vicious grin and a smirking wink*) Hello, Kiddo. How's every little ting? Got anyting on for tonight? I know an old boiler down to de docks we kin crawl into. (*The lady stalks by without a look, without a change of pace.* YANK *turns to others—insultingly*) Holy smokes, what a mug! Go hide yuhself before de horses shy at yuh. Gee, pipe de heine on dat one! Say, youse, yuh look like de stoin of a ferryboat. Paint and powder! All dolled up to kill! Yuh look like stiffs laid out for de boneyard! Aw, g'wan, de lot of youse! Yuh give me de eye-ache. Yuh don't belong, get me! Look at me, why don't youse dare? I belong, dat's me! (*Pointing to a skyscraper across the street which is in process of construction—with bravado*) See dat building goin' up dere? See de steel work? Steel, dat's me! Youse guys live on it and tink yuh're somep'n. But I'm *in* it, see! I'm de hoistin' engine dat makes it go up! I'm it—de inside and bottom of it! Sure! I'm steel and steam and smoke and de rest of it! It moves— speed—twenty-five stories up—and me at de top and bottom—movin'! Youse simps don't move. Yuh're on'y dolls I winds up to see 'm spin. Yuh're de garbage, get me—de leavins—de ashes we dump over de side! Now, what 'a' yuh gotta say? (*But as they seem neither to see nor hear him, he flies into a fury*) Bums! Pigs! Tarts! Bitches! (*He turns in a rage on the men, bumping viciously into them but not jarring them the least bit. Rather it is he who recoils after each collision. He keeps growling*) Git off de oith! G'wan, yuh bum! Look where yuh're goin', can't yuh? Git outa here! Fight, why don't yuh? Put up yer mits! Don't be a dog! Fight or I'll knock yuh dead! (*But, without seeming to see him, they all answer with mechnical affected politeness*) I beg your pardon. (*Then at a cry from one of the women, they all scurry to the furrier's window*).

THE WOMAN (*ecstatically, with a gasp of delight*): Monkey fur! (*The whole crowd of men and women chorus after her in the same tone of affected delight*) Monkey fur!

YANK (*with a jerk of his head back on his shoulders, as if he had received a punch full in the face—raging*): I see yuh, all in white! I see yuh, yuh white-faced tart, yuh! Hairy ape, huh? I'll hairy ape yuh! (*He bends down and grips at the street curbing as if to pick it out and hurl it. Foiled in this, snarling with passion, he leaps to the lamp-post on the corner and tries to pull it up for a club. Just at that moment a bus is heard rumbling up. A fat, high-hatted, spatted gentleman runs out from the side street. He calls out plaintively*): Bus! Bus! Stop there! (*and runs full tilt into the bending, straining* YANK, *who is bowled off his balance*).

YANK (*seeing a fight—with a roar of joy as he springs to his feet*): At last! Bus, huh? I'll bust yuh! (*He lets drive a terrific swing, his fist landing full on the fat gentleman's face. But the gentleman stands unmoved as if nothing had happened*).

GENTLEMAN: I beg your pardon. (*Then irritably*) You have made me lose my bus. (*He claps his hands and begins to scream*): Officer! Officer! (*Many police whistles shrill out on the instant and a whole platoon of policemen rush in on* YANK *from all sides. He tries to fight but is clubbed to the pavement and fallen upon. The crowd at the window have not moved or noticed this disturbance. The clanging gong of the patrol wagon approaches with a clamoring din*).

Curtain

SCENE SIX

Night of the following day. A row of cells in the prison on Blackwells Island. The cells extend back diagonally from right front to left rear. They do not stop, but disappear in the dark background as if they ran on, numberless, into infinity. One electric bulb from the low ceiling of the narrow corridor sheds its light through the heavy steel bars of the cell at the extreme front and reveals part of the interior. YANK *can be seen within, crouched on the edge of his cot in the attitude of Rodin's "The Thinker." His face is spotted with black and blue bruises. A blood-stained bandage is wrapped around his head.*

YANK (*suddenly starting as if awakening from a dream, reaches out and shakes the bars—aloud to himself, wonderingly*): Steel. Dis is de Zoo, huh? (*A burst of hard, barking laughter comes from the unseen occupants of the cells, runs back down the tier, and abruptly ceases*).

VOICES (*mockingly*): The Zoo? That's a new name for this coop—a damn good name!

Steel, eh? You said a mouthful. This is the old iron house.

Who is that boob talkin'?

He's the bloke they brung in out of his head. The bulls had beat him up fierce.

YANK (*dully*): I musta been dreamin'. I tought I was in a cage at de Zoo—but de apes don't talk, do dey?

VOICES (*with mocking laughter*): You're in a cage aw right.

A coop!

A pen!

A sty!

A kennel! *(Hard laughter—a pause).*

Say, guy! Who are you? No, never mind lying. What are you?

Yes, tell us your sad story. What's your game?

What did they jug yuh for?

YANK *(dully)*: I was a fireman—stokin' on de liners. *(Then with sudden rage, rattling his cell bars)* I'm a hairy ape, get me? And I'll bust youse all in de jaw if yuh don't lay off kiddin' me.

VOICES: Huh! You're a hard boiled duck, ain't you!

When you spit, it bounces! *(Laughter).*

Aw, can it. He's a regular guy. Ain't you?

What did he say he was—a ape?

YANK *(defiantly)*: Sure ting! Ain't dat what youse all are—apes? *(A silence. Then a furious rattling of bars from down the corridor).*

A VOICE *(thick with rage)*: I'll show yuh who's a ape, yuh bum!

VOICES: Ssshh! Nix!

Can de noise!

Piano!

You'll have the guard down on us!

YANK *(scornfully)*: De guard? Yuh mean de keeper, don't yuh? *(Angry exclamations from all the cells).*

VOICE *(placatingly)*: Aw, don't pay no attention to him. He's off his nut from the beatin'-up he got. Say, you guy! We're waitin' to hear what they landed you for—or ain't yuh tellin'?

YANK: Sure, I'll tell youse. Sure! Why de hell not? On'y—youse won't get me. Nobody gets me but me, see? I started to tell de Judge and all he says was: "Toity days to tink it over." Tink it over! Christ, dat's all I been doin' for weeks! *(After a pause)* I was tryin' to git even with someone, see?—someone dat done me doit.

VOICES *(cynically)*: De old stuff, I bet. Your goil, huh?

Give yuh the double-cross, huh?

That's them every time!

Did yuh beat up de odder guy?

YANK *(disgustedly)*: Aw, yuh're all wrong! Sure dere was a skoit in it—but not what youse mean, not dat old tripe. Dis was a new kind of skoit. She was dolled up all in white—in de stokehole. I tought she was a ghost. Sure. *(A pause).*

VOICES *(whispering)*: Gee, he's still nutty.

Let him rave. It's fun listenin'.

YANK *(unheeding—groping in his thoughts)*: Her hands—dey was skinny and white like dey wasn't real but painted on somep'n. Dere was a million miles from me to her—twenty-five knots a hour. She was like some dead ting de cat brung in. Sure, dat's what. She didn't belong. She belonged in de window of a toy store, or on de top of a garbage can, see! Sure! *(He breaks out angrily)* But would yuh believe it, she had de noive to do me doit. She lamped me like she was seein' somep'n broke loose from de menagerie. Christ, yuh'd oughter seen her eyes! *(He rattles the bars of his cell furiously)* But I'll get back at her yet, you watch! And if I can't find her I'll take it out on de gang she runs wit. I'm wise to where dey hangs out now. I'll show her who belongs! I'll show her who's in de move and who ain't. You watch my smoke!

VOICES *(serious and joking)*: Dat's de talkin'!

Take her for all she's got!

What was this dame, anyway? Who was she, eh?

YANK: I dunno. First cabin stiff. Her old man's a millionaire, dey says—name of Douglas.

VOICES: Douglas? That's the president of the Steel Trust, I bet.

Sure, I seen his mug in de papers.

He's filthy with dough.

VOICE: Hey, feller, take a tip from me. If you want to get back at that dame, you better join the Wobblies. You'll get some action then.

YANK: Wobblies? What de hell's dat?

VOICE: Ain't you ever heard of the I.W.W.?

YANK: Naw. What is it?

VOICE: A gang of blokes—a tough gang. I been readin' about 'em today in the paper. The guard give me the *Sunday Times*. There's a long spiel about 'em. It's from a speech made in the Senate by a guy named Senator Queen. *(He is in the cell next to* YANK'S. *There is a rustling of paper)* Wait'll I see if I got light enough and I'll read you. Listen. *(He reads)* "There is a menace existing in this country today which threatens the vitals of our fair Republic—as foul a menace against the very life-blood of the American Eagle as was the foul conspiracy of Catiline against the eagles of ancient Rome!"

VOICE *(disgustedly)*: Aw, hell! Tell him to salt de tail of dat eagle!

VOICE *(reading)*: "I refer to that devil's brew of rascals, jailbirds, murderers and cutthroats who libel all honest working men by calling themselves the Industrial Workers of the World; but in the light of their nefarious plots, I call them the Industrious *Wreckers* of the World!"

YANK *(with vengeful satisfaction)*: Wreckers, dat's de right dope! Dat belongs! Me for dem!

VOICE: Ssshh! *(reading)* "This fiendish organization is a foul ulcer on the fair body of our Democracy—"

VOICE: Democracy, hell! Give him the boid, fellers—the raspberry! *(They do)*.

VOICE: Ssshh! *(reading)* "Like Cato I say to this Senate, the I.W.W. must be destroyed! For they represent an ever-present dagger pointed at the heart of the greatest nation the world has ever known, where all men are born free and equal, with equal opportunities to all, where the Founding Fathers have guaranteed to each one happiness, where Truth, Honor, Liberty, Justice, and the Brotherhood of Man are a religion absorbed with one's mother's milk, taught at our father's knee, sealed, signed, and stamped upon in the glorious Constitution of these United States!" *(A perfect storm of hisses, catcalls, boos, and hard laughter)*.

VOICES *(scornfully)*: Hurrah for de Fort' of July!

Pass de hat!

Liberty!

Justice!

Honor!

Opportunity!

Brotherhood!

ALL *(with abysmal scorn)*: Aw, hell!

VOICE: Give that Queen Senator guy the bark! All togedder now—one—two—tree—*(A terrific chorus of barking and yapping)*.

GUARD *(from a distance)*: Quiet there, youse—or I'll git the hose. *(The noise subsides)*.

YANK *(with growling rage)*: I'd like to catch dat senator guy alone for a second. I'd loin him some trute!

VOICE: Ssshh! Here's where he gits down to cases on the Wobblies. *(Reads)* "They plot with fire in one hand and dynamite in the other. They stop not before murder to gain their ends, nor at the outraging of defenseless womanhood. They would tear down society, put the lowest scum in the seats of the mighty, turn Almighty God's revealed plan for the world topsy-turvy, and make of our sweet and lovely civilization a shambles, a desolation where man, God's masterpiece, would soon degenerate back to the ape!"

VOICE *(to YANK)*: Hey, you guy. There's your ape stuff again.

YANK *(with a growl of fury)*: I got him. So dey blow up tings, do dey? Dey turn tings round, do dey? Hey, lend me dat paper, will yuh?

VOICE: Sure. Give it to him. On'y keep it to yourself, see. We don't wanter listen to no more of that slop.

VOICE: Here you are. Hide it under your mattress.

YANK *(reaching out)*: Tanks. I can't read much but I kin manage. *(He sits, the paper in the hand at his side, in the attitude of Rodin's "The Thinker." A pause. Several snores from down the corridor. Suddenly YANK jumps to his feet with a furious groan as if some appalling thought had crashed on him—bewilderedly)* Sure—her old man—president of de Steel Trust—makes half de steel in de world—steel—where I tought I belonged—drivin' trou—movin'—in dat—to make her—and cage me in for her to spit on! Christ! *(He shakes the bars of his cell door till the whole tier trembles. Irritated, protesting exclamations from those awakened or trying to get to sleep)* He made dis—dis cage! Steel! *It* don't belong, dat's what! Cages, cells, locks, bolts, bars—dat's what it means!—holdin' me down wit him at de top! But I'll drive trou! Fire, dat melts it! I'll be fire—under de heap—fire dat never goes out—hot as hell—breakin' out in de night—*(While he has been saying this last he has shaken his cell door to a clanging accompaniment. As he comes to the "breakin' out" he seizes one bar with both hands and, putting his two feet up against the others so that his position is parallel to the floor like a monkey's, he gives a great wrench backwards. The bar bends like a licorice stick under his tremendous strength. Just at this moment the PRISON GUARD rushes in, dragging a hose behind him)*.

GUARD *(angrily)*: I'll loin youse bums to wake me up! *(Sees YANK)* Hello, it's you, huh? Got the D.T.'s, hey? Well, I'll cure 'em. I'll drown your snakes for yuh! *(Noticing the bar)* Hell, look at dat bar bended! On'y a bug is strong enough for dat!

YANK (*glaring at him*): Or a hairy ape, yuh big yellow bum! Look out! Here I come! (*He grabs another bar*).

GUARD (*scared now—yelling off left*): Toin de hose on, Ben!—full pressure! And call de others—and a straitjacket! (*The curtain is falling. As it hides* YANK *from view, there is a splattering smash as the stream of water hits the steel of* YANK's *cell*).

Curtain

SCENE SEVEN
Nearly a month later. An I.W.W. local near the waterfront, showing the interior of a front room on the ground floor, and the street outside. Moonlight on the narrow street, buildings massed in black shadow. The interior of the room, which is general assembly room, office, and reading room, resembles some dingy settlement boys' club. A desk and high stool are in one corner. A table with papers, stacks of pamphlets, chairs about it, is at center. The whole is decidedly cheap, banal, commonplace and unmysterious as a room could well be. The secretary is perched on the stool making entries in a large ledger. An eye shade casts his face into shadows. Eight or ten men, longshoremen, iron workers, and the like, are grouped about the table. Two are playing checkers. One is writing a letter. Most of them are smoking pipes. A big signboard is on the wall at the rear, "Industrial Workers of the World—Local No. 57."

YANK (*comes down the street outside. He is dressed as in Scene Five. He moves cautiously, mysteriously. He comes to a point opposite the door; tiptoes softly up to it, listens, is impressed by the silence within, knocks carefully, as if he were guessing at the password to some secret rite. Listens. No answer. Knocks again a bit louder. No answer. Knocks impatiently, much louder*).

SECRETARY (*turning around on his stool*): What the hell is that—someone knocking? (*Shouts*) Come in, why don't you? (*All the men in the room look up.* YANK *opens the door slowly, gingerly, as if afraid of an ambush. He looks around for secret doors, mystery, is taken aback by the commonplaceness of the room and the men in it, thinks he may have gotten in the wrong place, then sees the signboard on the wall and is reassured*).

YANK (*blurts out*): Hello.

MEN (*reservedly*): Hello.

YANK (*more easily*): I thought I'd bumped into de wrong dump.

SECRETARY (*scrutinizing him carefully*): Maybe you have. Are you a member?

YANK: Naw, not yet. Dat's what I came for—to join.

SECRETARY: That's easy. What's your job—longshore?

YANK: Naw. Fireman—stoker on de liners.

SECRETARY (*with satisfaction*): Welcome to our city. Glad to know you people are waking up at last. We haven't got many members in your line.

YANK: Naw. Dey're all dead to de woild.

SECRETARY: Well, you can help to wake 'em. What's your name? I'll make out your card.

YANK (*confused*): Name? Lemme tink.

SECRETARY (*sharply*): Don't you know your own name?

YANK: Sure; but I been just Yank for so long—Bob, dat's it—Bob Smith.

SECRETARY (*writing*): Robert Smith. (*Fills out the rest of card*) Here you are. Cost you half a dollar.

YANK: Is dat all—four bits? Dat's easy. (*Gives the Secretary the money*).

SECRETARY (*throwing it in drawer*): Thanks. Well, make yourself at home. No introductions needed. There's literature on the table. Take some of those pamphlets with you to distribute aboard ship. They may bring results. Sow the seed, only go about it right. Don't get caught and fired. We got plenty out of work. What we need is men who can hold their jobs—and work for us at the same time.

YANK: Sure. (*But he still stands, embarrassed and uneasy*).

SECRETARY (*looking at him—curiously*): What did you knock for? Think we had a coon in uniform to open doors?

YANK: Naw. I tought it was locked—and dat yuh'd wanter give me the once-over trou a peep-hole or somep'n to see if I was right.

SECRETARY (*alert and suspicious but with an easy laugh*): Think we were running a crap game? That door is never locked. What put that in your nut?

YANK (*with a knowing grin, convinced that this is all camouflage, a part of the secrecy*): Dis burg is full of bulls, ain't it?

SECRETARY (*sharply*): What have the cops got to do with us? We're breaking no laws.

YANK (*with a knowing wink*): Sure. Youse wouldn't for woilds. Sure. I'm wise to dat.

SECRETARY: You seem to be wise to a lot of stuff none of us knows about.

YANK (*with another wink*): Aw, dat's aw right, see. (*Then made a bit resentful by the suspicious glances from all sides*) Aw, can it! Youse needn't put me trou de toid degree. Can't youse see I belong? Sure! I'm reg'lar. I'll stick, get me? I'll shoot de woiks for youse. Dat's why I wanted to join in.

SECRETARY (*breezily, feeling him out*): That's the right spirit. Only are you sure you understand what you've joined? It's all plain and above board; still, some guys get a wrong slant on us. (*Sharply*) What's your notion of the purpose of the I.W.W.?

YANK: Aw, I know all about it.

SECRETARY (*sarcastically*): Well, give us some of your valuable information.

YANK (*cunningly*): I know enough not to speak outa my toin. (*Then resentfully again*) Aw, say! I'm reg'lar. I'm wise to de game. I know yuh got to watch your step wit a stranger. For all youse know, I might be a plain-clothes dick, or somep'n, dat's what yuh're tinkin', huh? Aw, forget it! I belong, see? Ask any guy down to de docks if I don't.

SECRETARY: Who said you didn't?

YANK: After I'm 'nitiated, I'll show yuh.

SECRETARY (*astounded*): Initiated? There's no initiation.

YANK (*disappointed*): Ain't there no password—no grip nor nothin'?

SECRETARY: What'd you think this is—the Elks—or the Black Hand?

YANK: De Elks, hell! De Black Hand, dey're a lot of yellow back-stickin' Gi-nees. Naw. Dis is a man's gang, ain't it?

SECRETARY: You said it! That's why we stand on our two feet in the open. We got no secrets.

YANK (*surprised but admiringly*): Yuh mean to say yuh always run wide open—like dis?

SECRETARY: Exactly.

YANK: Den yuh sure got your noive wit youse!

SECRETARY (*sharply*): Just what was it made you want to join us? Come out with that straight.

YANK: Yuh call me? Well, I got noive, too! Here's my hand. Yuh wanter blow tings up, don't yuh? Well, dat's me! I belong!

SECRETARY (*with pretended carelessness*): You mean change the unequal con-ditions of society by legitimate direct action—or with dynamite?

YANK: Dynamite! Blow it offen de oith—steel—all de cages—all de facto-ries, steamers, buildings, jails—de Steel Trust and all dat makes it go.

SECRETARY: So—that's your idea, eh? And did you have any special job in that line you wanted to propose to us? (*He makes a sign to the men, who get up cau-tiously one by one and group behind* YANK).

YANK (*boldly*): Sure, I'll come out wit it. I'll show youse I'm one of de gang. Dere's dat millionaire guy, Douglas—

SECRETARY: President of the Steel Trust, you mean? Do you want to assassi-nate him?

YANK: Naw, dat don't get yuh nothin'. I mean blow up de factory, de woiks, where he makes de steel. Dat's what I'm after—to blow up de steel, knock all de steel in de woild up to de moon. Dat'll fix tings! (*Eagerly, with a touch of bravado*) I'll do it by me lonesome! I'll show yuh! Tell me where his woiks is, how to git there, all de dope. Gimme de stuff, de old butter—and watch me do de rest! Watch de smoke and see it move! I don't give a damn if dey nab me—long as it's done! I'll soive life for it—and give 'em de laugh! (*Half to himself*) And I'll write her a letter and tell her de hairy ape done it. Dat'll square tings.

SECRETARY (*stepping away from* YANK): Very interesting. (*He gives a signal. The men, huskies all, throw themselves on* YANK *and before he knows it they have his legs and arms pinioned. But he is too flabbergasted to make a struggle, anyway. They feel him over for weapons*).

MAN: No gat, no knife. Shall we give him what's what and put the boots to him?

SECRETARY: No. He isn't worth the trouble we'd get into. He's too stupid. (*He comes closer and laughs mockingly in* YANK's *face*) Ho-ho! By God, this is the biggest joke they've put up on us yet. Hey, you Joke! Who sent you—Burns or Pinkerton? No, by God, you're such a bonehead I'll bet you're in the Secret Ser-vice! Well, you dirty spy, you rotten agent provocateur, you can go back and tell whatever skunk is paying you blood-money for betraying your brothers that he's wasting his coin. You couldn't catch a cold. And tell him that all he'll ever get on us, or ever has got, is just his own sneaking plots that he's framed up to put us in jail. We are what our manifesto says we are, neither more nor less—and we'll give him a copy of that any time he calls. And as for you—*(He glares scornfully at* YANK, *who is sunk in an obvious stupor)* Oh, hell, what's the use of talking? You're a brainless ape.

YANK *(aroused by the word to fierce but futile struggles)*: What's dat, yuh Sheeny bum, yuh!

SECRETARY: Throw him out, boys. *(In spite of his struggles, this is done with gusto and éclat. Propelled by several parting kicks,* YANK *lands sprawling in the middle of the narrow cobbled street. With a growl he starts to get up and storm the closed door, but stops bewildered by the confusion in his brain, pathetically impotent. He sits there, brooding, in as near to the attitude of Rodin's "Thinker" as he can get in his position).*

YANK *(bitterly)*: So dem boids don't tink I belong, neider. Aw, to hell wit 'em! Dey're in de wrong pew—de same old bull—soapboxes and Salvation Army—no guts! Cut out an hour offen de job a day and make me happy! Gimme a dollar more a day and make me happy! Tree square a day, and cauliflowers in de front yard—ekal rights—a woman and kids—a lousy vote—and I'm all fixed for Jesus, huh? Aw, hell! What does dat get yuh? Dis ting's in your inside, but it ain't your belly. Feedin' your face—sinkers and coffee—dat don't touch it. It's way down—at de bottom. Yuh can't grab it, and yuh can't stop it. It moves, and everything moves. It stops and de whole woild stops. Dat's me now—I don't tick, see?—I'm a busted Ingersoll, dat's what. Steel was me, and I owned de woild. Now I ain't steel, and de woild owns me. Aw, hell! I can't see—it's all dark, get me? It's all wrong! *(He turns a bitter mocking face up like an ape gibbering at the moon)* Say, youse up dere, Man in de Moon, yuh look so wise, gimme de answer, huh? Slip me de inside dope, de information right from de stable—where do I get off at, huh?

A POLICEMAN *(who has come up the street in time to hear this last—with grim humor)*: You'll get off at the station, you boob, if you don't get up out of that and keep movin'.

YANK *(looking up at him—with a hard, bitter laugh)*: Sure! Lock me up! Put me in a cage! Dat's de on'y answer yuh know. G'wan, lock me up!

POLICEMAN: What you been doin'?

YANK: Enuf to gimme life for! I was born, see? Sure, dat's de charge. Write it in de blotter. I was born, get me!

POLICEMAN *(jocosely)*: God pity your old woman! *(Then matter-of-fact)* But I've no time for kidding. You're soused. I'd run you in but it's too long a walk to the station. Come on now, get up, or I'll fan your ears with this club. Beat it now! *(He hauls* YANK *to his feet).*

YANK *(in vague mocking tone)*: Say, where do I go from here?

POLICEMAN *(giving him a push—with a grin, indifferently)*: Go to hell.

Curtain

SCENE EIGHT

Twilight of the next day. The monkey house at the Zoo. One spot of clear gray light falls on the front of one cage so that the interior can be seen. The other cages are vague, shrouded in shadow from which chatterings pitched in a conversational tone can be heard. On the one cage a sign from which the word "gorilla" stands out. The gigantic animal himself is seen squatting on his haunches on a bench in much the same attitude as Rodin's "Thinker." YANK *enters from the left. Immediately a chorus of angry chattering and screeching breaks out. The gorilla turns his eyes but makes no sound or move.*

YANK (*with a hard, bitter laugh*): Welcome to your city, huh? Hail, hail, de gang's all here! (*At the sound of his voice the chattering dies away into an attentive silence.* YANK *walks up to the gorilla's cage and, leaning over the railing, stares in at its occupant, who stares back at him, silent and motionless. There is a pause of dead stillness. Then* YANK *begins to talk in a friendly confidential tone, half-mockingly, but with a deep undercurrent of sympathy*) Say, yuh're some hard-lookin' guy, ain't yuh? I seen lots of tough nuts dat de gang called gorillas, but yuh're de foist real one I ever seen. Some chest yuh got, and shoulders, and dem arms and mits! I bet yuh got a punch in eider fist dat'd knock 'em all silly! (*This with genuine admiration. The gorilla, as if he understood, stands upright, swelling out his chest and pounding on it with his fist.* YANK *grins sympathetically*) Sure, I get yuh. Yuh challenge de whole woild, huh? Yuh got what I was sayin' even if yuh muffed de woids. (*Then bitterness creeping in*) And why wouldn't yuh get me? Ain't we both members of de same club—de Hairy Apes? (*They stare at each other—a pause—then* YANK *goes on slowly and bitterly*) So yuh're what she seen when she looked at me, de white-faced tart! I was you to her, get me? On'y outa de cage—broke out—free to moider her, see? Sure! Dat's what she tought. She wasn't wise dat I was in a cage, too—worser'n yours—sure—a damn sight—'cause you got some chanct to bust loose—but me—(*He grows confused*) Aw, hell! It's all wrong, ain't it? (*A pause*) I s'pose yuh wanter know what I'm doin' here, huh? I been warmin' a bench down to de Battery—ever since last night. Sure. I seen de sun come up. Dat was pretty, too—all red and pink and green. I was lookin' at de skyscrapers—steel—and all de ships comin' in, sailin' out, all over de oith—and dey was steel, too. De sun was warm, dey wasn't no clouds, and dere was a breeze blowin'. Sure, it was great stuff, I got it aw right—what Paddy said about dat bein' de right dope—on'y I couldn't get *in* it, see? I couldn't belong in dat. It was over my head. And I kept tinkin'—and den I beat it up here to see what youse was like. And I waited till dey was all gone to git yuh alone. Say, how d'yuh feel sittin' in dat pen all de time, havin' to stand for 'em comin' and starin' at yuh—de white-faced, skinny tarts and de boobs that marry 'em—makin' fun of yuh, laughin' at yuh, gittin' scared of yuh—damn 'em! (*He pounds on the rail with his fist. The gorilla rattles the bars of his cage and snarls. All the other monkeys set up an angry chattering in the darkness.* YANK *goes on excitedly*) Sure! Dat's de way it hits me, too. On'y yuh're lucky, see? Yuh don't belong wit 'em and yuh know it. But me, I belong wit 'em—but I don't, see? Dey don't belong wit me, dat's what. Get me? Tinkin' is hard—*(He passes one hand across his forehead with a painful gesture. The gorilla growls impatiently.* YANK *goes on gropingly)* It's dis way, what I'm drivin' at. Youse can sit and dope dream in de past, green woods, de jungle and de rest of it. Den yuh belong and dey don't. Den yuh kin laugh at 'em, see? Yuh're de champ of de woild. But me—I ain't got no past to tink in, nor nothin' dat's comin', on'y what's now—and dat don't belong. Sure, you're de best off! Yuh can't tink, can yuh? Yuh can't talk neider. But I kin make a bluff at talkin' and tinkin'—a'most git away wit it—a'most!—and dat's where de joker comes in. *(He laughs)* I ain't on oith and I ain't in heaven, get me? I'm in de middle tryin' to separate 'em, takin' all de woist punches from bot' of 'em. Maybe dat's what dey call hell, huh? But you, yuh're at de bottom. You belong! Sure! Yuh're de on'y one in de woild dat does, yuh lucky stiff! *(The gorilla growls proudly)* And dat's why dey gotter put yuh in a cage, see? *(The gorilla roars angrily)* Sure! Yuh get me. It beats it when you try to tink it or talk it—it's way down—deep—behind—you 'n' me we feel it. Sure! Bot' members of dis club! *(He laughs—then in a savage tone)* What de hell! T' hell with it! A little action, dat's our meat! Dat belongs! Knock 'em down and keep bustin' 'em till dey croaks yuh with a gat—wit steel! Sure! Are yuh game? Dey've looked at youse, ain't dey—in a cage? Wanter git even? Wanter wind up like a sport 'stead of croakin' slow in dere? *(The gorilla roars an emphatic affirmative.* YANK *goes on with a sort of furious exaltation)* Sure! Yuh're reg'lar! Yuh'll stick to de finish! Me 'n' you, huh?—bot' members of this club! We'll put up one last star bout dat'll knock 'em offen deir seats! Dey'll have to make de cages stronger after we're trou! *(The gorilla is straining at his bars, growling, hopping from one foot to the other.* YANK *takes a jimmy from under his coat and forces the lock on the cage door. He throws this open)* Pardon from de governor! Step out and shake hands. I'll take yuh for a walk down Fif' Avenoo. We'll knock 'em offen de oith and croak wit de band playin'. Come on, Brother. *(The gorilla scrambles gingerly out of his cage. Goes to* YANK *and stands looking at him.* YANK *keeps his mocking tone—holds out his hand)* Shake—de secret grip of our order. *(Something, the tone of mockery, perhaps, suddenly enrages the animal. With a spring he wraps his huge arms around* YANK *in a murderous hug. There is a crackling snap of crushed ribs—a gasping cry, still mocking, from* YANK*)* Hey, I didn't say kiss me! *(The gorilla lets the crushed body slip to the floor; stands over it uncertainly, considering; then picks it up, throws it in the cage, shuts the door, and shuffles off menacingly into the darkness at left. A great uproar of frightened chattering and whimpering comes from the other cages. Then* YANK *moves, groaning, opening his eyes, and there is silence. He mutters painfully)* Say—dey oughter match him—wit Zybszko. He got me, aw right. I'm trou. Even him didn't tink I belonged. *(Then, with sudden passionate despair)* Christ, where do I get off at? Where do I fit in? *(Checking himself as suddenly)* Aw, what de hell! No squawkin', see! No quittin', get me! Croak wit your boots on! *(He grabs hold of the bars of the cage and hauls himself painfully to his feet—looks around him bewilderedly—forces a mocking laugh)* In de cage, huh? *(In the strident *tones of a circus barker)* Ladies and gents, step forward and take a slant at de one and only—*(His voice weakening)*—one and original—Hairy Ape from de wilds of—*(He slips in a heap on the floor and dies. The monkeys set up a chattering, whimpering wail. And, perhaps, the Hairy Ape at last belongs).*

Curtain

ACTIVITIES FOR WRITING AND DISCUSSION

1. *The Hairy Ape* is an example of dramatic **expressionism.** Rather than trying to present characters and events realistically, O'Neill distorts and exaggerates reality in order to produce certain powerful and expressive effects in readers or viewers. Thus, for instance, the coal stokers in scene one are characterized less as individual human beings than as a single beast in a "cage" or as anonymous versions of "Neanderthal Man"; the rich people who are assaulted by Yank in scene five do not even feel the impact of his blows. Mark these and any other passages in the play that strike you as expressionistic. Then write an essay in which you discuss how the expressionistic devices enhance the themes or impact of the play.

2. Reread the scene one speeches of Yank, Long, and Paddy. In your notebook summarize the outlook of each and how those outlooks conflict or clash.

3. In scene one both Yank and Paddy talk about "belonging." To whom or to what does each see himself as belonging? In what ways do their notions of belonging resemble and/or differ from each other? What reasons can you think of for their obsessive concern with "belonging"?

4. Consider the various meanings that "belonging" has in your own life and in the play.
   a. Write about your own concept of "belonging." To what extent and in what ways does your own identity seem to be shaped by the groups, organizations, socioeconomic class, race, religious and ethnic cultures, and so forth to which you "belong"?
   b. Locate recurrences of the words "belong" and "belonging" in *The Hairy Ape.* In each case, annotate what you think the speaker is using the word to mean in that situation.
   c. To whom or what do the following "belong": Yank, Mildred Douglas, the rich people on Fifth Avenue in scene five, the workers in the office of the I.W.W., the gorilla in the zoo?
   d. Interpret O'Neill's final stage direction in the play: *"And, perhaps, the Hairy Ape at last belongs."* Do you take this sentence literally or ironically? Why? To *what* does he "belong" at play's end?

5. Mildred Douglas appears in only two scenes, but her impact on Yank resonates through the entire play. Reread scene two, paying particular attention to Mildred's character, attitudes, and style of speech. Then imagine you are Mildred

and it is the day after your encounter with Yank. In a letter to a friend of your (i.e., Mildred's) own economic and social class, relate the story of your meeting with the "beast" in the stokehole. In addition to mentioning the encounter, use your imagination to fill the letter with chat about other matters—your aunt, impressions of the ship, things you have done and seen. How much of your letter will you devote to the encounter with Yank? While we know the meeting left a profound impact on Yank, how significant an effect did it have on you / Mildred?

6. In an earlier version of the ending of the play, O'Neill had Yank return to the stokehole to live out his prisonlike existence. Draft a new scene eight with this ending. Then compare the new ending with the one O'Neill actually chose. Which do you find more effective, and why?

7. The play makes **allusions** to the I.W.W. (Industrial Workers of the World), antilabor debates in Congress, and "the Steel Trust," allusions that root it firmly in the **setting** of early twentieth-century America, when the play was written. Research the play's historical context and O'Neill's own views on the political and economic issues of his day. Then present your findings in an essay.

Woody Allen (b. 1935)

Death Knocks

The play takes place in the bedroom of the Nat Ackermans' two-story house, somewhere in Kew Gardens. The carpeting is wall-to-wall. There is a big double bed and a large vanity. The room is elaborately furnished and curtained, and on the walls there are several paintings and a not really attractive barometer. Soft theme music as the curtain rises. Nat Ackerman, a bald, paunchy fifty-seven-year-old dress manufacturer, is lying on the bed finishing off tomorrow's Daily News. *He wears a bathrobe and slippers, and reads by a bed light clipped to the white headboard of the bed. The time is near midnight. Suddenly we hear a noise, and Nat sits up and looks at the window.*

NAT: What the hell is that?

[*Climbing awkwardly through the window is a sombre, caped figure. The intruder wears a black hood and skintight black clothes. The hood covers his head but not his face, which is middle-aged and stark white. He is something like* NAT *in appearance. He huffs audibly and then trips over the windowsill and falls into the room.*]

DEATH [*for it is no one else*]: Jesus Christ. I nearly broke my neck.
NAT [*watching with bewilderment*]: Who are you?
DEATH: Death.

NAT: Who?

DEATH: Death. Listen—can I sit down? I nearly broke my neck. I'm shaking like a leaf.

NAT: Who *are* you?

DEATH: *Death.* You got a glass of water?

NAT: Death? What do you mean, Death?

DEATH: What is wrong with you? You see the black costume and the whitened face?

NAT: Yeah.

DEATH: Is it Halloween?

NAT: No.

DEATH: Then I'm Death. Now can I get a glass of water—or a Fresca?

NAT: If this is some joke—

DEATH: What kind of joke? You're fifty-seven? Nat Ackerman? One eighteen Pacific Street? Unless I blew it—where's that call sheet? [*He fumbles through pocket, finally producing a card with an address on it. It seems to check.*]

NAT: What do you want with me?

DEATH: What do I want? What do you think I want?

NAT: You must be kidding. I'm in perfect health.

DEATH [*unimpressed*]: Uh-huh. [*Looking around.*] This is a nice place. You do it yourself?

NAT: We had a decorator, but we worked with her.

DEATH [*looking at picture on the wall*]: I love those kids with the big eyes.

NAT: I don't want to go yet.

DEATH: *You* don't want to go? Please don't start in. As it is, I'm nauseous from the climb.

NAT: What climb?

DEATH: I climbed up the drainpipe. I was trying to make a dramatic entrance. I see the big windows and you're awake reading. I figure it's worth a shot. I'll climb up and enter with a little—you know . . . [*Snaps fingers.*] Meanwhile, I get my heel caught on some vines, the drainpipe breaks, and I'm hanging by a thread. Then my cape begins to tear. Look, let's just go. It's been a rough night.

NAT: You broke my drainpipe?

DEATH: Broke. It didn't break. It's a little bent. Didn't you hear anything? I slammed into the ground.

NAT: I was reading.

DEATH: You must have really been engrossed. [*Lifting newspaper* NAT *was reading.*] "NAB COEDS IN POT ORGY." Can I borrow this?

NAT: I'm not finished.

DEATH: Er—I don't know how to put this to you, pal . . .

NAT: Why didn't you just ring downstairs?

DEATH: I'm telling you, I could have, but how does it look? This way I get a little drama going. Something. Did you read *Faust*?

NAT: What?

DEATH: And what if you had company? You're sitting there with important people. I'm Death—I should ring the bell and traipse right in the front? Where's your thinking?

NAT: Listen, Mister, it's very late.

DEATH: Yeah. Well, you want to go?

NAT: Go where?

DEATH: Death. It. The Thing. The Happy Hunting Grounds. [*Looking at his own knee.*] Y'know, that's a pretty bad cut. My first job, I'm liable to get gangrene yet.

NAT: Now, wait a minute. I need time. I'm not ready to go.

DEATH: I'm sorry. I can't help you. I'd like to, but it's the moment.

NAT: How can it be the moment? I just merged with Modiste Originals.

DEATH: What's the difference, a couple of bucks more or less.

NAT: Sure, what do you care? You guys probably have all your expenses paid.

DEATH: You want to come along now?

NAT [*studying him*]: I'm sorry, but I cannot believe you're Death.

DEATH: Why? What'd you expect—Rock Hudson?

NAT: No, it's not that.

DEATH: I'm sorry if I disappointed you.

NAT: Don't get upset. I don't know, I always thought you'd be . . . uh . . . taller.

DEATH: I'm five seven. It's average for my weight.

NAT: You look a little like me.

DEATH: Who should I look like? I'm your death.

NAT: Give me some time. Another day.

DEATH: I can't. What do you want me to say?

NAT: One more day. Twenty-four hours.

DEATH: What do you need it for? The radio said rain tomorrow.

NAT: Can't we work out something?

DEATH: Like what?

NAT: You play chess?

DEATH: No, I don't.

NAT: I once saw a picture of you playing chess.

DEATH: Couldn't be me, because I don't play chess. Gin rummy, maybe.

NAT: You play gin rummy?

DEATH: Do I play gin rummy? Is Paris a city?

NAT: You're good, huh?

DEATH: Very good.

NAT: I'll tell you what I'll do—

DEATH: Don't make any deals with me.

NAT: I'll play you gin rummy. If you win, I'll go immediately. If I win, give me some more time. A little bit—one more day.

DEATH: Who's got time to play gin rummy?

NAT: Come on. If you're so good.

DEATH: Although I feel like a game . . .

NAT: Come on. Be a sport. We'll shoot for a half hour.

DEATH: I really shouldn't.

NAT: I got the cards right here. Don't make a production.

DEATH: All right, come on. We'll play a little. It'll relax me.

NAT [*getting cards, pad, and pencil*]: You won't regret this.

DEATH: Don't give me a sales talk. Get the cards and give me a Fresca and put out something. For God's sake, a stranger drops in, you don't have potato chips or pretzels.

NAT: There's M&M's downstairs in a dish.

DEATH: M&M's. What if the President came? He'd get M&M's, too?

NAT: You're not the President.

DEATH: Deal.

[NAT *deals, turns up a five.*]

NAT: You want to play a tenth of a cent a point to make it interesting?

DEATH: It's not interesting enough for you?

NAT: I play better when money's at stake.

DEATH: Whatever you say, Newt.

NAT: Nat. Nat Ackerman. You don't know my name?

DEATH: Newt, Nat—I got such a headache.

NAT: You want that five?

DEATH: No.

NAT: So pick.

DEATH [*surveying his hand as he picks*]: Jesus, I got nothing here.

NAT: What's it like?

DEATH: What's what like?

[*Throughout the following, they pick and discard.*]

NAT: Death.

DEATH: What should it be like? You lay there.

NAT: Is there anything after?

DEATH: Aha, you're saving twos.

NAT: I'm asking. Is there anything after?

DEATH [*absently*]: You'll see.

NAT: Oh, then I will actually see something?

DEATH: Well, maybe I shouldn't have put it that way. Throw.

NAT: To get an answer from you is a big deal.

DEATH: I'm playing cards.

NAT: All right, play, play.

DEATH: Meanwhile, I'm giving you one card after another.

NAT: Don't look through the discards.

DEATH: I'm not looking. I'm straightening them up. What was the knock card?

NAT: Four. You ready to knock already?

DEATH: Who said I'm ready to knock? All I asked was what was the knock card.

NAT: And all I asked was is there anything for me to look forward to.

DEATH: Play.

NAT: Can't you tell me anything? Where do we go?

DEATH: We? To tell you the truth, *you* fall in a crumpled heap on the floor.

NAT: Oh, I can't wait for that! Is it going to hurt?

DEATH: Be over in a second.

NAT: Terrific. [*Sighs.*] I needed this. A man merges with Modiste Originals . . .

DEATH: How's four points?

NAT: You're knocking?

DEATH: Four points is good?

NAT: No, I got two.

DEATH: You're kidding.

NAT: No, you lose.

DEATH: Holy Christ, and I thought you were saving sixes.

NAT: No. Your deal. Twenty points and two boxes. Shoot. [*Death deals.*] I must fall on the floor, eh? I can't be standing over the sofa when it happens?

DEATH: No. Play.

NAT: Why not?

DEATH: Because you fall on the floor! Leave me alone. I'm trying to concentrate.

NAT: Why must it be on the floor? That's all I'm saying! Why can't the whole thing happen and I'll stand next to the sofa?

DEATH: I'll try my best. Now can we play?

NAT: That's all I'm saying. You remind me of Moe Lefkowitz. He's also stubborn.

DEATH: I remind him of Moe Lefkowitz. I'm one of the most terrifying figures you could possibly imagine, and him I remind of Moe Lefkowitz. What is he, a furrier?

NAT: You should be such a furrier. He's good for eighty thousand a year. Passementeries. He's got his own factory. Two points.

DEATH: What?

NAT: Two points. I'm knocking. What have you got?

DEATH: My hand is like a basketball score.

NAT: And it's spades.

DEATH: If you didn't talk so much.

[*They redeal and play on.*]

NAT: What'd you mean before when you said this was your first job?

DEATH: What does it sound like?

NAT: What are you telling me—that nobody ever went before?

DEATH: Sure they went. But I didn't take them.

NAT: So who did?

DEATH: Others.

NAT: There's others?

DEATH: Sure. Each one has his own personal way of going.

NAT: I never knew that.

DEATH: Why should you know? Who are you?

NAT: What do you mean who am I? Why—I'm nothing?

DEATH: Not nothing. You're a dress manufacturer. Where do you come to knowledge of the eternal mysteries?

NAT: What are you talking about? I make a beautiful dollar. I sent two kids through college. One is in advertising, the other's married. I got my own home. I drive a Chrysler. My wife has whatever she wants. Maids, mink coat, vacations. Right now she's at the Eden Roc. Fifty dollars a day because she wants to be near her sister. I'm supposed to join her next week, so what do you think I am—some guy off the street?

DEATH: All right. Don't be so touchy.

NAT: Who's touchy?

DEATH: How would you like it if I got insulted quickly?

NAT: Did I insult you?

DEATH: You didn't say you were disappointed in me?

NAT: What do you expect? You want me to throw you a block party?

DEATH: I'm not talking about that. I mean me personally. I'm too short, I'm this, I'm that.

NAT: I said you looked like me. It's like a reflection.

DEATH: All right, deal, deal.

[*They continue to play as music steals in and the lights dim until all is in total darkness. The lights slowly come up again, and now it is later and their game is over.* NAT *tallies.*]

NAT: Sixty-eight . . . one-fifty . . . Well, you lose.

DEATH [*dejectedly looking through the deck*]: I knew I shouldn't have thrown that nine. Damn it.

NAT: So I'll see you tomorrow.

DEATH: What do you mean you'll see me tomorrow?

NAT: I won the extra day. Leave me alone.

DEATH: You were serious?

NAT: We made a deal.

DEATH: Yeah, but—

NAT: Don't "but" me. I won twenty-four hours. Come back tomorrow.

DEATH: I didn't know we were actually playing for time.

NAT: That's too bad about you. You should pay attention.

DEATH: Where am I going to go for twenty-four hours?

NAT: What's the difference? The main thing is I won an extra day.

DEATH: What do you want me to do—walk the streets?

NAT: Check into a hotel and go to a movie. Take a *schvitz*.[1] Don't make a federal case.

DEATH: Add the score again.

NAT: Plus you owe me twenty-eight dollars.

DEATH: *What?*

NAT: That's right, Buster. Here it is—read it.

DEATH [*going through pockets*]: I have a few singles—not twenty-eight dollars.

NAT: I'll take a check.

DEATH: From what account?

NAT: Look who I'm dealing with.

DEATH: Sue me. Where do I keep my checking account?

NAT: All right, gimme what you got and we'll call it square.

DEATH: Listen, I need that money.

NAT: Why should you need money?

DEATH: What are you talking about? You're going to the Beyond.

NAT: So?

DEATH: So—you know how far that is?

NAT: So?

DEATH: So where's gas? Where's tolls?

NAT: We're going by car?

DEATH: You'll find out. [*Agitatedly.*] Look—I'll be back tomorrow, and you'll give me a chance to win the money back. Otherwise I'm in definite trouble.

NAT: Anything you want. Double or nothing we'll play. I'm liable to win an extra week or a month. The way you play, maybe years.

DEATH: Meantime I'm stranded.

NAT: See you tomorrow.

DEATH [*being edged to the doorway*]: Where's a good hotel? What am I talking about hotel, I got no money. I'll go sit in Bickford's. [*He picks up the News.*]

NAT: Out. Out. That's my paper. [*He takes it back.*]

DEATH [*exiting*]: I couldn't just take him and go. I had to get involved in rummy.

NAT [*calling after him*]: And be careful going downstairs. On one of the steps the rug is loose.

[*And, on cue, we hear a terrific crash.* NAT *sighs, then crosses to the bedside table and makes a phone call.*]

NAT: Hello, Moe? Me. Listen, I don't know if somebody's playing a joke, or what, but Death was just here. We played a little gin . . . No, *Death*. In person. Or somebody who claims to be Death. But, Moe, he's such a *schlep!*[2]

Curtain

---

1. Steam bath.   2. A person who is unkempt, down-at-the-heels, clumsy.

ACTIVITIES FOR WRITING AND DISCUSSION

1. Indicate passages in the play that you find funny, and explain how those passages work as comedy. How does the character Death undercut or conflict with traditional images of death? How do other aspects of the play (such as characterization, **setting, stage directions, plot,** and **dialogue**) conflict with what you might expect in an actual encounter between a human being and Death?

2. In a humorous way, *Death Knocks* dramatizes an imaginary conversation between a person (Nat) and a personified abstraction (Death). Try writing such a conversation yourself. Compose an imaginary dialogue between yourself and some abstraction, e.g., your inner self-critic, your conscience, your ideal self, the "child" in you, the "parent" in you, having the abstraction talk as if it were a person.

Steps:
   a. Brainstorm a list of possible abstractions you could personify.
   b. Choose one that looks most interesting.
   c. Imagine what this abstraction would look like if it were a person. Describe such things as facial appearance, eyes, hair, body build, posture, gestures, expressions, how he/she walks, talks, for instance.
   d. Pose some conflict between yourself and this "person."
   e. Write the dialogue.

Note: Your writing for Activity #2 may be quite personal, and you should feel free *not* to share it with anyone else.

EXPERIENCE AND IDENTITY: ADDITIONAL ACTIVITIES FOR WRITING AND DISCUSSION

1. Reread all or a portion of your notebook. Mark any passages, however long or short, that strike you, for whatever reasons. Beside each such passage, write a note explaining its significance for you. Finally, pick a favorite passage and either:
   a. Expand it into a new piece of writing, or
   b. Make notes on how you *could* expand or use it at some future date, or
   c. Rewrite it in a different form, e.g., poem, dialogue, letter, memoir.

For a list of strategies for expanding or revising, see Chapter 12.

2. Explicitly or implicitly, several texts in this section address how growth can occur through experiences of pain, defeat, or personal diminishment (e.g., as described by G.K. Chesterton in "A Defence of Humility").
   a. Compare how this theme plays out in several texts and/or in the text of your own life, or
   b. Create an imaginary "interview" with one or more of the **characters, speakers,** or **personae** who experience such growth. Ask them to explain their outlook and to share some stories (which you may invent yourself) that justify that outlook.

3. The protagonists of several selections in this chapter are on a quest of some sort: Yank (a quest for "belonging"), the narrator of "Zaabalawi" (a quest for the elusive Zaabalawi and personal healing), Paul in "The Rocking-Horse Winner" (a quest for money and possibly/probably love), the narrator of "Nobody Listens When I Talk" (a quest for identity), to name a few. The enormous contrasts among these characters make it tantalizing to imagine them meeting. Each lonely and driven, what would they discuss? Bring two or more of the characters together in an imaginative setting—Paul's bedroom, the zoo at the end of *The Hairy Ape,* or the front porch of Annette Sanford's protagonist's house, for instance—and have them talk.

4. Maya Angelou's "Seven Women's Blessed Assurance" articulates the feelings and attitudes of seven women at various stages of life. Assume the **persona** of someone who has moved through three or more stages of life, e.g., infancy, childhood, adolescence, midlife. Create a text, in poetry or in prose, in which this person reflects on his/her changing perspectives on life and experience. Alternative: Write a dialogue between *yourself* at one stage of life and yourself at a different stage of life. Emphasize age-related conflicts and differences between your two "selves." Does the older self "like" the younger or resent it? Does the younger respect the older . . . scorn it?

5. One subject common to Faulkner's "Barn Burning," Rudman's "Chrome," Angelou's "Graduation," and other texts within this section is the notion of "overcoming." Compare how this subject is treated in any two or three of these texts. Alternative: Write a story about "overcoming" in your own life, and (if you wish) relate it to one of the assigned readings.

6. Several writings in this section are about "firsts." For example, Gary Soto's poem is about a first date, and Judith Ortiz Cofer's essay is about a first experience of school. Write a story, poem, or essay of your own about some actual or imagined "first" experience.

7. Review your entire notebook; as you do, make a running list of memorable or striking topics, such as "childhood experience," "life transitions," "initiations." Then choose a favorite topic, make a Topic/Form Grid (see Chapter 5), and use one of the forms on your grid to create a new notebook entry about the topic. If your chosen form does not work, do a Topic/Form Shift to a different form on your grid.

Interchapter on Notebooks
and Journals (III)

"Pen and Paper and a Breath of Air": Mary Oliver

Born in 1935 in Cleveland, Ohio, Mary Oliver attended Ohio State University and Vassar College. *No Voyage, and Other Poems* (1963) was her first book, followed by *The Night Traveler* (1978), *Twelve Moons* (1978), *Sleeping in the Forest* (1979), and *American Primitive* (Pulitzer Prize, 1984). *New and Selected Poems* won the National Book Award in 1992. Fellow poet Maxine Kumin has called Oliver an "indefatigable guide to the natural world" who is comfortable with being "on the margins of things, on the line between earth and sky, the thin membrane that separates human from what we loosely call animal." One of Oliver's recent books is *West Wind* (1997), a collection of poems and prose poems.

The following notebook selections and introductory note are reprinted from Oliver's book *Blue Pastures* (New York: Harcourt, 1991). A slightly different version of this piece also appeared in *The Poet's Notebook,* an anthology edited by Stephen Kuusisto, Deborah Tall, and David Weiss and published by Norton (1997).

For at least thirty years, and at almost all times, I have carried a notebook with me, 1
in my back pocket. It has always been the same kind of notebook—small, three inches by five inches, and hand-sewn. By no means do I write poems in these notebooks. And yet over the years the notebooks have been laced with phrases that eventually appear in poems. So, they are the pages upon which I begin. Also I record various facts which are permanently or temporarily important to me—when I first see certain birds in the spring, addresses, quotes from books I'm reading, things people say, shopping lists, recipes, thoughts.

Some of the phrases and ideas written down in the notebooks never make the leap 2
into finished prose or poems. They do not elaborate themselves in my unconscious

thoughts, apparently, nor does my conscious mind pluck at them. This does not necessarily mean that they are of a casual or fleeting order of things; it could be that they are seeds broadcast on a chilly day—their time has not yet come. Often I find the same idea will emerge through several phrases before it gets worked on.

I don't use the pages front to back, but randomly, in a disorderly way. I write 3 *wherever I happen to open the notebook. I don't know why this is. When the notebook is fairly full, I start another. In the spring and fall notebooks especially, there are pages where the writing is blurred and hard to read. Spring and fall are the rainy seasons, and almost all of the entries are made somewhere out-of-doors.*

What I write down is extremely exact in terms of phrasing and of cadence. In an 4 *old notebook I can find, "look the trees / are turning / their own bodies / into pillars of light." In a more recent notebook, "the refined anguish of language / passed over him." Sometimes what is written down is not generally understandable at all, but is a kind of private shorthand. The entry "6/8/92 woof!" records for me that on this day, and with this very doggy sound, I first came upon coyotes in the Provincelands. Both the shorthand and the written phrase are intended to return me to the moment and place of the entry. I mean this very exactly. The words do not take me to the reason I made the entry, but back to the felt experience, whatever it was. This is important. I can, then, think forward again to the idea—that is, the significance of the event— rather than back upon it. It is the instant I try to catch in the notebooks, not the comment, not the thought. And, of course, this is so often what I am aiming to do in the finished poems themselves.*

EXCERPTS

Who would tell the mockingbird his song is frivolous, since it lacks words?   5

Do you think the wren ever dreams of a better house?   6

Though you have not seen them, there are swans, even now   7
tapping from the egg and emerging
into the sunlight.
They know who they are.

When will you have a little pity for   8
every soft thing
that walks through the world,
yourself included?

When the main characters of one's life die, is there any replacement? Or, is there   9
anything *but* replacement?

I hope I don't live to be a hundred   10
in the arms of my family.

———————

When you first saw her—beauty, the dream—the human vortex of your life—or 11
him—did you stop, and stand in the crisp air, breathing like a tree? Did you
change your life?

———————

The small deadly voice   12
of vanity.

———————

It's better for the heart to break   13
than not to break.

———————

Elly Ameling during a masterclass at Tanglewood, talking to a young singer: "No! 14
No! No! Make it like peaches in your mouth!"

———————

All my life, and it has not come to any more than this: beauty and terror.   15

———————

Something totally unexpected,   16
like a barking cat.

———————

Sharpsburg: "One well-read member of the 9th New York wrote long afterward: 17
The mental strain was so great that I saw at that moment the singular effect mentioned, I think, in the life of Goethe on a similar occasion—the whole landscape
for an instant turned slightly red."

                                 —B. Catton, *Mr. Lincoln's Army*

———————

The sword, after all, is not built just to glitter like a ribbon in the air.   18

———————

But I want to say something more uncomfortable even than that.   19

———————

"And then, who knows? Perhaps we will be taken in hand by certain memories, as 20
if by angels."

                                      —M. Yourcenar

———————

Molasses, an orange, fennel seed, anise seed, rye flour, two cakes of yeast.   21

———

Culture: power, money, and security (therefore).   22
Art: hope, vision, the soul's need to speak.

———

All culture developed as some wild, raw creature strived to live better and longer.   23

———

Dreams don't have time/space constriction. Of course, in a way Adam naming the   24
things of this world was narrowing his horizons.
    Perhaps dreaming is meditating, before language existed. Animals certainly   25
dream.

———

Language, the tool of consciousness.   26

———

The line is the device upon which the poem spins itself into being. Verse, versus,   27
vers, turn the plough, turn the line. It is impossible to measure the frustration I
feel when, after making careful decisions about where the lines should turn, an
editor snaps off the long limbs to fit some magazine's column-girth or print-line.

———

Who are you? They called out, at the edge of the village.   28
I am one of you, the poet called back.
Though he was dressed like the wind, though he looked like
a waterfall.

———

F. has been to visit us, and now he is gone. The power of last resort, is the power   29
to disrupt.

———

M. arranging the curtains in the next room. "Hello there, darling moon," I hear   30
her say.

———

If you kill for knowledge, what is the name of what you have lost?   31

———

The danger of people becoming infatuated with knowledge. Thoreau gassing the   32
moth to get a perfect specimen. Audubon pushing the needle into the bittern's
heart.

———————

I took the fox bones back into the dunes and buried them. I don't want to hold on   33
to such things anymore. I mean, I'm certainly full of admiration, and curiosity.
But I think something else—a reverence that disavows keeping things—must
come to us all, sooner or later. Like a gift, an understanding, a more happy excitement than possession. Or, of a sudden—too late!—like a stone between the eyes.

———————

Everybody has to have their little tooth of power.   34
Everybody wants to be able to bite.

———————

About poems that don't work—who wants to see a bird almost fly?   35

———————

With what sugar in your voice would you persuade   36
the beach plum
to hurry?

———————

After a cruel childhood, one must reinvent oneself.   37
Then reimagine the world.

———————

van Gogh—he considered everything, and still went crazy with rapture.   38

———————

A snapping turtle was floating today on Little Sister Pond.   39
Goldeneyes still on Great Pond.

———————

Laughing gulls fly by the house laughing.   40
Maybe a hundred pilot whales off the point.

———————

All July and into August, Luke and I see foxes. An adult fox with a young pup. The   41
adult serious and nervous and quick. The young one trailing behind, not serious.
It reached up, swatted the pine boughs with a black paw before it vanished under
the trees.

———————

To Unity College, in Maine, and back. We stayed in Waterville, saw two bald eagles 42
flying over open rivers, though there was still much ice, and snow. A good trip,
friendly people, an interested audience. Luke and Bear were quiet throughout, except that Bear threw up on me just as we arrived in the parking lot. I hope he
learns to ride better than that.

———————

Hundreds of gannets feeding just offshore, plunging, tufts of water rising with 43
a white up-kick. Scary birds, long wings, very white, fearful-looking beaks. We
opened the car windows and there was no sound but the sound of their wings
rustling. They fed at three or four places, then were gone much farther out. We
were at the right place at the right time.

———————

"I am doing pretty well, gathering energy, working . . . and every now and then 44
timor mortis descends over me like midnight."

                                                        Letter from D. H.

———————

Just at the lacy edge of the sea, a dolphin's skull. Recent, but perfectly clean. And 45
entirely beautiful. I held it in my hands, I was so excited I was breathless. What
will I do?

———————

Three deer near the path to Oak Head—of course now they always make me 46
think of Luke. Happiness by association.

———————

Who knows, maybe the root is the flower   47
of that other life.

———————

Money, in our culture, is equal to power. And money, finally, means very little 48
because power, in the end, means nothing.

———————

Lee, as he was dying, called out, "Strike the tent!" Stonewall Jackson said at the 49
end, softly as I imagine it, "Let us cross over the river and rest under the shade of
the trees."

———————

Today I am altogether without ambition. Where did I get such wisdom?   50

———————

A Gallery of Pictures

Not only the written word, but *anything*— memories, experiences, dreams, music, nature, pictures — can work upon a writer's mind, shaping thought, encouraging imagination, stimulating reflection and analysis. With that idea in view, here is a collection of five paintings and a photograph for you to study as prompts for creative or critical writing. You should supplement this modest collection with pictures or other artifacts of your own choosing: paintings, postcards, photographs, scrapbooks or other personal memorabilia, natural or human-made objects. As you do so, and as you contemplate the images you collect, you will likely realize, as Walt Whitman did, that your own mind is a sort of gallery containing "many pictures hanging suspended. . . ./ . . . hundreds and thousands,— all the varieties. . . ."

You can respond to the pictures included here, or the ones you choose yourself, by adapting the methods you have used throughout this book:

1) Use the Four Step Process for Writing outlined in Chapter 2.
2) For Step Two (annotation), write your first-thought reactions in the margins of the page or in your notebook;
3) For Step Four, try any of the Ten Ideas for Writing summarized on pages 27–35 or one of the Activities that accompanies the picture.

To help you think more carefully about each picture, each image is accompanied by a set of prewriting questions. In addition to annotating the pictures, you can jot down a few notes in answer to these questions before you compose your longer notebook response.

1. Jusepe de Ribera, *Boy with a Clubfoot* (1642)

Despite his "clubfoot," the boy in this painting by the Spanish artist Jusepe de Ribera looks defiantly cheerful. Rather than leaning on his crutch, he carries it slung over his shoulder. Though his clothing is torn and tattered, he grins toothily and stands erect and proud before the viewer or passersby. Behind him lies an unpeopled landscape and the vast sky; he seems equal to the emptiness of both. The paper in his hand bears an inscription in Latin asking that he be given alms "for the love of God." The presence of this note suggests that the boy may be deaf and mute.

Prewriting Questions

- At whom or what is the boy looking?

- Why is he grinning, or possibly even laughing?

- Where and how does he live and sleep?

- What does he think about? How does he think? rationally? irrationally? Jot down a few possible strands of his thought.

- Where is he headed, both *literally*, in the sense of toward what physical location, and figuratively, in the sense of into what future?

ACTIVITIES FOR WRITING

1. Tell the boy's story, from either a third-person or first-person (the boy's own) point of view. Consider events surrounding his parentage, birth, infancy, and early childhood.

2. Imagine any of the following individuals approaches the boy: an elderly woman, a small child, a rich or poor person, a physician, a coachful of affluent travellers, or someone else. Narrate the interaction that occurs.

3. Compare the painting with Peter Sharpe's poem, "Waiting for the Idiot to Go Away," on page 18.

BOY WITH A CLUBFOOT

JUSEPE DE RIBERA

Reunion des Musées Nationaux /Art Resource, NY.

2. Arthur Hughes, *Home from Sea* (1862)

In this work by the Englishman Arthur Hughes, a young sailor has returned from overseas to discover that, during his absence, a loved one (probably his mother) has died. In grief he has thrown himself upon her grave. Though the subject of the painting is distressing, the impact is softened by the painter's highly romantic brushwork. The picture evokes, on the one hand, disturbing emotions concerning family loss, grief, and the personal and public sacrifice of a war veteran, and, on the other hand, Victorian sentimentality; the artist emphasizes the intense feelings between the young man and woman and the filial feeling of the son for his dead mother.

Prewriting Questions

- Where and when is the picture set? How does the setting affect the mood of the painting and your own emotional response to it?

- Who is the young woman? What is her relationship to the sailor?

- Has news of the death come as a complete shock to the young man, or was it anticipated? How and in what circumstances was it revealed to him?

ACTIVITIES FOR WRITING

1. With a maximum of drama, recreate the sailor's return, his encounter with the young woman (his sister? fiancee?), and the moment he learns of his mother's death.

2. React to the scene writing in the persona of a passerby—a stranger or a family friend—who comes upon this scene.

3. Create a Topic/Form Grid (see Chapter 5) around topics raised by this painting and compose a notebook response from your Grid.

4. Novelist Thomas Wolfe wrote that "You can't go home again"; when you return home after an absence, neither you nor your home is the same as when you left. Develop this theme by writing your own story—factual or invented—of a homecoming. Center your story around a significant change that has occurred between departure from home and homecoming.

HOME FROM SEA

ARTHUR HUGHES

Ashmolean Museum, Oxford.

3. Unidentified artist, *Running Before the Storm* (ca. 1870)

This American folk painting depicts a potentially disastrous situation in comical terms.

Prewriting Questions

- How is the oncoming storm experienced differently by the man and the dog? Jot down the probable "thoughts" of each.

- What is each of the figures—horses, man, dog, woman, girl—trying to accomplish, if anything, as the storm breaks?

- What emotions do you imagine the artist had as he or she painted this picture? Was the artist trying to make a *point* of some kind through the picture or just having fun? Did he or she paint quickly or create the work over a long period of time?

ACTIVITIES FOR WRITING

1. Write the story of the scene depicted from the point of view of the dog, or of anyone else (human or animal) in the picture.

2. The unknown creator of the painting was most likely an amateur whose main occupation was something other than painting. Writing, if you wish, in the first-person point of view of the artist, invent the artist's life story (or those aspects of it that seem relevant to painting) and the story behind the making of this particular picture.

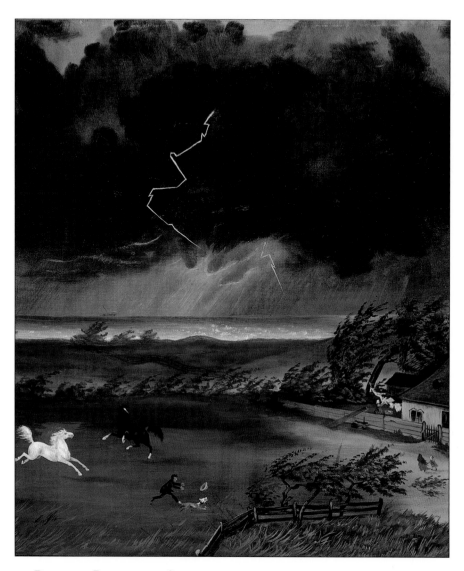

RUNNING BEFORE THE STORM

Photograph © 2004 Museum of Fine Arts, Boston. Unidentified artist, American, 19th century. *Running Before the Storm,* about 1870. Oil on canvas. 60.96 × 92.07 cm (24 × 36¼ in.). Museum of Fine Arts, Boston. Gift of Martha C. Karolik for the M. and M. Karolik Collection of American Paintings, 1815–1865; 46.851.

4. William T. Wiley, *Detail Study from the Bright Side* (1977–88)

This picture was inspired by a Civil War painting entitled *The Bright Side* (1865) by the American artist Winslow Homer. Homer's painting showed several African American soldiers in the Union army waking outside a tent and facing the "bright" sunrise; Wiley concentrates on a single detail in Homer's painting of a head thrust out through a hole in the tent. Wiley's picture is included here because it highlights two focuses of *Reading and Writing from Literature*—intertextuality (described in Chapter 2 as the "conversation" between one text and other texts) and annotation: Wiley has surrounded his own painting with annotations—somewhat cryptic phrases, sayings, images, and quotations, at least some of which seem to represent the thoughts of the man in the painting.

Prewriting Questions

- Read Wiley's annotations. Why do you suppose he included them? In what ways do they relate to or add to the main image in the painting?

- Study Wiley's use of allusions (indirect references to other texts and authors, such as "The Declaration of Independence," "The Samuri Creed," Chief Seattle, Mark Twain, Joseph Conrad, Suzuki Rosh, and the yin/yang symbol). Research as many of these allusions as you can. Then speculate on the artist's reasons for including them. How would the impact of the work suffer if the allusions were eliminated?

ACTIVITY FOR WRITING

1. Following Wiley's example, annotate a painting or photograph. Either use one of the images included in this "Gallery of Pictures" (*Boy with a Clubfoot, Home from the Sea, Before the Storm, Bat Mitzvah Dance, Mother and Child with Dogs Vomiting*) or a picture of your own choosing. Again following Wiley's example, consider selecting a picture that depicts one or more human figures or that alludes to political or historical issues, as "Detail from the Bright Side" alludes to the War for Independence and slavery. Include any of the following among your annotations:

- The thoughts of the person or people in the picture (this might work especially well for Melissa Ann Pinney's *Bat Mitzvah Dance, Chicago, Illinois,* 1991)

- Quotations (culled, perhaps, from your commonplace book—see *Reading and Writing from Literature,* Chapter 4)

- Relevant anecdotes, questions, or pictures, using the examples in *Detail Study from the Bright Side* as models

- Allusions to pertinent political or historical documents

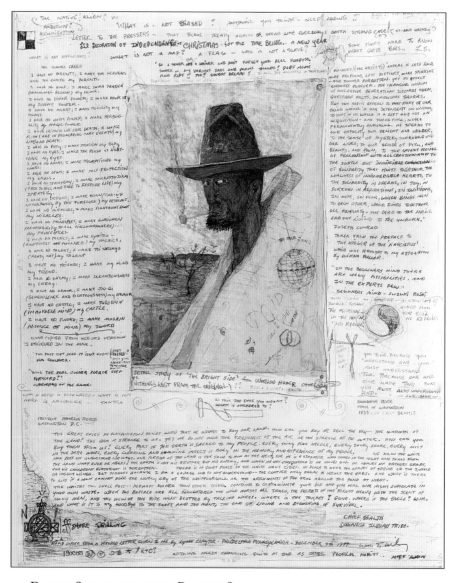

DETAIL STUDY FROM THE BRIGHT SIDE

WILLIAM T. WILEY

William T. Wiley, American, 1937– . *Detail Study from the Bright Side*, 1977–1988. Mixed media on paper, 73.5 × 58.4 cm (image). Fine Arts Museums of San Francisco, Museum Purchase, Achenbach Foundation for Graphic Art Endowment Fund, 1964.4.

5. Melissa Ann Pinney, *Bat Mitzvah Dance, Chicago, Illinois* (1991)

This photograph requires no introduction. Probably most people of high school age or older have had the experience of dancing or decorating a wall at a function like the one pictured.

Prewriting Question

- Take some notes on the young people in the picture—the facial expression of each, their heights and shapes, postures, dress, awareness of or indifference to the camera, who is and isn't dancing and (speculatively) why.

ACTIVITY FOR WRITING

1. Create a Topic/Form Grid (see Chapter 5) around topics raised by this photograph and compose a notebook response from your Grid.

BAT MITZVAH DANCE, CHICAGO, ILLINOIS, 1991

MELISSA ANN PINNEY

6. Brian Kershisnik, *Mother and Child with Dogs Vomiting* (2001)

Contemporary artist Brian Kershisnik depicts human and animal subjects in often whimsical and enigmatic interactions. Like a poet, he invites an unusually high degree of imaginative participation from his audience. Studying his paintings, we become co-creators of the image along with the artist. Thus there are no fixed answers to the prewriting questions; the answers of different viewers may move in radically diverse directions.

Prewriting Questions

- What is the setting for the painting?

- What sort of interaction is occurring between the mother and child? What is the focus of attention of each? What, if anything, is the mother looking at?

- Why are there two dogs, why are they (apparently) identical twins, and why are they vomiting? If this painting were a short story, who would be the **protagonist**? the **antagonist**? What would be the focus of conflict in the **plot**? what would be the **climax** of the plot? How would the story begin and end?

ACTIVITIES FOR WRITING

1. Recreate the painting as a short story or a poem.

2. Writing in **stream of consciousness** mode, capture the mother's thoughts at the moment depicted, or the child's thoughts.

3. Write an essay comparing *Mother and Child with Dogs Vomiting* with Timothy Young's poem "The Thread of Sunlight" or with any other text included in Chapter 21 ("Families").

MOTHER AND CHILD WITH DOGS VOMITING

BRIAN KERSHISNIK

Going Deeper with Pictures

Your work with visual images need not stop here. The following are suggestions for additional writing and reading.

1. Relate any of the six pictures in this insert to one of the short stories, poems, essay/nonfiction works, or plays in Part VI of *Reading and Writing from Literature*. How you "relate" the picture with the verbal text is up to you: perhaps analytically in an essay; or perhaps creatively by bringing one or more characters or personae from the written text into dialogue with a person depicted or included in the picture.

2. After you have done one or more of the Activities for Writing that accompany these pictures, compose a reflective piece in your notebook in which you discuss any special or distinctive ways in which visual images can inspire writing — ways, that is, which strike you as different from writing intertextually from other *writing*.

3. Many well known writers have also been skilled or competent visual artists: William Blake, G. K. Chesterton, Sidonie-Gabrielle Colette, Antoine de Saint-Exupéry, Joy Harjo, Gerard Manley Hopkins, Guy de Maupassant, Flannery O'Connor, Edgar Allan Poe, and James Thurber are a few notable examples among writers included in this book; two other famous examples of authors not included in *Reading and Writing from Literature* are Fyodor Dostoevsky (widely regarded as one of the best novelists of all time) and Victor Hugo (author of *Les Miserables*).

    a. If possible, learn more about the visual artistry of one or more of these authors and its relationship to his or her writing. For example, peruse the multivolume *Notebooks* of Dostoevsky (edited by Edward Wasiolek and published by the University of Chicago Press), and see how this great novelist made sketches of his fictional characters and settings in order, it seems, to facilitate and deepen his writing.

    b. Using what you have learned from activity 3a as inspiration, make sketches and drawings a regular part of your own notebooks. For more ideas on combining writing with visual art in a notebook, see Hannah Hinchman's *A Trail Through Leaves: The Journal As a Path to Place* (New York: Norton, 1997). Hinchman's illustrated journal is punctuated with exercises for writing and drawing that you can try for yourself.

You there, like a red fist under by ribs—   51
be reasonable.

---

little myrtle warblers   52
kissing the air

Let's not pretend we know how the mule feels.   53

Hearing a crow, the first one in a long time. I listened to it, deeply and with plea-   54
sure. And I thought: what if I were dead, lying there dead, and *I heard that!*

Which would you rather be, intellectually deft, or spiritually graceful?   55

The sugar of vanity, the honey of truth.   56

When I was young, I was attracted to sorrow. It seemed interesting. It seemed an   57
energy that would take me somewhere. Now I am older, if not old, and I hate sorrow. I see that it has no energy of its own, but uses mine, furtively. I see that it is
leaden, without breath, and repetitious, and unsolvable.

And now I see that I am sorrowful about only a few things, but over and over.   58

Fairy tales—the great difference is between doing something, and doing nothing.   59
Always, in such tales, the hero or heroine does *something.*

The new baby is all awash with glory.   60
She has a cry that says *I'm here! I'm here!*

Give me that dark moment I will carry it everywhere   61
like a mouthful of rain.

There is a place   62
in the woods
where my swift
and stout-hearted dog

turns and wants to climb
into my arms.

Don't engage in too much fancy footwork before you strike a blow.   63

So much of what Woolf wrote she wrote not because she was a woman, but 64
because she was Woolf.

I would like to do whatever it is that presses the essence from the hour.   65

A fact: one picks it up and reads it, and puts it down, and there is an end to it. But 66
an idea! That one may pick up, and reflect upon, and oppose, and expand, and so
pass a delightful afternoon altogether.

From my way of thinking, Thoreau frequently seems an overly social person.   67

The cry of the killdeer/like a tiny sickle.   68

The translation of experience into contemplation, and the placement of this con- 69
templation within the formality of a certain kind of language, with intent to make
contact—be it across whatever thin or wild a thread—with the spiritual condition
of the reader, is not poetry. Archibald MacLeish: Here is the writer, and over
there—there is "the mystery of the universe." The poem exists—indeed, gets itself written—in the relation *between* the man and the world. The three ingredients
of poetry: the mystery of the universe, spiritual curiosity, the energy of language.

And what is the universe, as far as we are concerned?   70

Leo Frobenius: "It was first the animal world, in its various species, that impressed 71
mankind as a mystery, and that, in its character of admired immediate neighbor,
evoked the impulse to imitative identification. Next, it was the vegetable world
and the miracle of the fruitful earth, wherein death is changed into life. And
finally . . . the focus of attention lifted to the mathematics" of the heavens.

Art cannot separate from these first examples which willed it into existence. Say 72
such forces belong now only to dream or nightmare or to Jung's (our) collective
unconscious—or to the ecologically sensitive—I say it's entirely more primal
than that. Poetry was born in the relationship between men of earth and the earth
itself. Without perceptual experience of life on this earth, how could the following lines be meaningful?

It is the east, and Juliet is the sun. *Or,*

And what rough beast, its hour come round at last,
Slouches toward Bethlehem to be born?

I think as an ecologist. But I feel as a member of a great family—one that includes   73
the elephant and the wheat stalk as well as the schoolteacher and the industrialist.
This is not a mental condition, but a spiritual condition. Poetry is a product of
our history, and our history is inseparable from the natural world. Now, of
course, in the hives and dungeons of the cities, poetry cannot console, it carries
no weight, for the pact between the natural world and the individual has been
broken. There is no more working for harvest—only hunting, for profit. Lives
are no longer exercises in pleasure and valor, but only the means to the amass-
ment of worldly goods. If poetry is ever to become meaningful to such persons, *they* must take the first step—away from their materially bound and self-
interested lives, toward the trees, and the waterfall. It is not poetry's fault that it
has so small an audience, so little effect upon the frightened, money-loving world.
Poetry, after all, is not a miracle. It is an effort to formalize (ritualize) individual
moments and the transcending effects of these moments into a music that all can
use. It is the song of our species.

Hasn't the end of the world been coming absolutely forever?   74

It takes about   75
seventy hours to drag
a poem into
the light.

---

delirious with certainty   76

It's almost six A.M. The mockingbird is still singing. I'm on my way to the ocean,   77
with the sun, just rising, on my left shoulder, and the moon, like a circle of pale
snow, lingering on my right.

ACTIVITIES FOR WRITING AND DISCUSSION

1. In her prefatory note Oliver carefully describes the physical qualities of her
notebook: "It has always been the same kind . . . hand-sewn"; "there are pages
where the writing is blurred and hard to read" from spring and fall rains. Do the
physical properties—size, color, feel or texture, portability, etc.—of your own
notebook make it a place where you *like* to write? If so, why? If not, what alterna-

tive kind of notebook could you buy—or perhaps make—that would be more appealing?

2. In her prefatory note Oliver declares, "Sometimes what is written down is not generally understandable at all, but is a kind of private shorthand. . . . The words do not take me to the reason I made the entry, but back to the felt experience, whatever it was." Shorthand is a device for jotting down a thought or impression quickly and exactly, and in just enough words that you can understand it when rereading. In order to record your own impressions more precisely and economically, strive to develop a "private shorthand" of your own.

3. Respond to Oliver's notebook selections using any of the "Generic Ideas for Writing" found on pages 192–193.

Individual and Society

Short Stories

Nathaniel Hawthorne (1804–1864)

The Birthmark

In the latter part of the last century there lived a man of science, an eminent   1
proficient in every branch of natural philosophy, who not long before our story
opens had made experience of a spiritual affinity more attractive than any chemical one. He had left his laboratory to the care of an assistant, cleared his fine
countenance from the furnace smoke, washed the stain of acids from his fingers,
and persuaded a beautiful woman to become his wife. In those days when the
comparatively recent discovery of electricity and other kindred mysteries of Nature seemed to open paths into the region of miracle, it was not unusual for the
love of science to rival the love of woman in its depth and absorbing energy. The
higher intellect, the imagination, the spirit, and even the heart might all find their
congenial aliment[1] in pursuits which, as some of their ardent votaries believed,
would ascend from one step of powerful intelligence to another, until the philosopher should lay his hand on the secret of creative force and perhaps make new
worlds for himself. We know not whether Aylmer possessed this degree of faith in
man's ultimate control over Nature. He had devoted himself, however, too unre-
servedly to scientific studies ever to be weaned from them by any second passion.

---

1. **aliment:** something that nourishes; food.

His love for his young wife might prove the stronger of the two; but it could only be by intertwining itself with his love of science, and uniting the strength of the latter to his own.

Such a union accordingly took place, and was attended with truly remarkable 2 consequences and a deeply impressive moral. One day, very soon after their marriage, Aylmer sat gazing at his wife with a trouble in his countenance that grew stronger until he spoke.

"Georgiana," said he, "has it never occurred to you that the mark upon your 3 cheek might be removed?"

"No, indeed," said she, smiling; but perceiving the seriousness of his manner, 4 she blushed deeply. "To tell you the truth it has been so often called a charm that I was simple enough to imagine it might be so."

"Ah, upon another face perhaps it might," replied her husband; "but never on 5 yours. No, dearest Georgiana, you came so nearly perfect from the hand of Nature that this slightest possible defect, which we hesitate whether to term a defect or a beauty, shocks me, as being the visible mark of earthly imperfection."

"Shocks you, my husband!" cried Georgiana, deeply hurt; at first reddening 6 with momentary anger, but then bursting into tears. "Then why did you take me from my mother's side? You cannot love what shocks you!"

To explain this conversation it must be mentioned that in the center of 7 Georgiana's left cheek there was a singular mark, deeply interwoven, as it were, with the texture and substance of her face. In the usual state of her complexion—a healthy though delicate bloom—the mark wore a tint of deeper crimson, which imperfectly defined its shape amid the surrounding rosiness. When she blushed it gradually became more indistinct, and finally vanished amid the triumphant rush of blood that bathed the whole cheek with its brilliant glow. But if any shifting motion caused her to turn pale, there was the mark again, a crimson stain upon the snow, in what Aylmer sometimes deemed an almost fearful distinctness. Its shape bore not a little similarity to the human hand, though of the smallest pygmy size. Georgiana's lovers were wont to say that some fairy at her birth hour had laid her tiny hand upon the infant's cheek, and left this impress there in token of the magic endowments that were to give her such sway over all hearts. Many a desperate swain would have risked life for the privilege of pressing his lips to the mysterious hand. It must not be concealed, however, that the impression wrought by this fairy sign-manual varied exceedingly, according to the difference of temperament in the beholders. Some fastidious persons—but they were exclusively of her own sex—affirmed that the bloody hand, as they chose to call it, quite destroyed the effect of Georgiana's beauty, and rendered her countenance even hideous. But it would be as reasonable to say that one of those small blue stains which sometimes occur in the purest statuary marble would convert the Eve of Powers to a monster. Masculine observers, if the birthmark did not heighten their admiration, contented themselves with wishing it away, that the world might possess one living specimen of ideal loveliness without the semblance of a flaw. After his marriage,—for he thought little or nothing of the matter before,—Aylmer discovered that this was the case with himself.

Had she been less beautiful,—if Envy's self could have found aught else to 8
sneer at,—he might have felt his affection heightened by the prettiness of this
mimic hand, now vaguely portrayed, now lost, now stealing forth again and glimmering to and fro with every pulse of emotion that throbbed within her heart; but
seeing her otherwise so perfect, he found this one defect grow more and more
intolerable with every moment of their united lives. It was the fatal flaw of humanity which Nature, in one shape or another, stamps ineffaceably on all her
productions, either to imply that they are temporary and finite, or that their perfection must be wrought by toil and pain. The crimson hand expressed the ineludible gripe[2] in which mortality clutches the highest and purest of earthly mold,
degrading them into kindred with the lowest, and even with the very brutes, like
whom their visible frames return to dust. In this manner, selecting it as the symbol of his wife's liability to sin, sorrow, decay, and death, Aylmer's somber imagination was not long in rendering the birthmark a frightful object, causing him
more trouble and horror than ever Georgiana's beauty, whether of soul or sense,
had given him delight.

At all the seasons which should have been their happiest, he invariably and 9
without intending it, nay, in spite of a purpose to the contrary, reverted to this one
disastrous topic. Trifling as it at first appeared, it so connected itself with innumerable trains of thought and modes of feeling that it became the central point of
all. With the morning twilight Aylmer opened his eyes upon his wife's face and
recognized the symbol of imperfection; and when they sat together at the evening
hearth his eyes wandered stealthily to her cheek, and beheld, flickering with the
blaze of the wood fire, the spectral hand that wrote mortality where he would fain
have worshiped. Georgiana soon learned to shudder at his gaze. It needed but a
glance with the peculiar expression that his face often wore to change the roses of
her cheek into a deathlike paleness, amid which the crimson hand was brought
strongly out, like a bas-relief of ruby on the whitest marble.

Late one night when the lights were growing dim, so as hardly to betray the 10
stain on the poor wife's cheek, she herself, for the first time, voluntarily took up
the subject.

"Do you remember, my dear Aylmer," said she, with a feeble attempt at a 11
smile, "have you any recollection of a dream last night about this odious hand?"

"None! none whatever!" replied Aylmer, starting; but then he added, in a dry, 12
cold tone, affected for the sake of concealing the real depth of his emotion, "I
might well dream of it; for before I fell asleep it had taken a pretty firm hold of my
fancy."

"And you did dream of it?" continued Georgiana hastily, for she dreaded lest 13
a gush of tears should interrupt what she had to say. "A terrible dream! I wonder
that you can forget it. Is it possible to forget this one expression?—'It is in her
heart now; we must have it out!' Reflect, my husband; for by all means I would
have you recall that dream."

---

2. **gripe:** grip.

The mind is in a sad state when Sleep, the all-involving, cannot confine her 14
specters within the dim region of her sway, but suffers them to break forth, af-
frighting this actual life with secrets that perchance belong to a deeper one.
Aylmer now remembered his dream. He had fancied himself with his servant
Aminadab, attempting an operation for the removal of the birthmark; but the
deeper went the knife, the deeper sank the hand, until at length its tiny grasp appeared to have caught hold of Georgiana's heart; whence, however, her husband
was inexorably resolved to cut or wrench it away.

When the dream had shaped itself perfectly in his memory, Aylmer sat in his 15
wife's presence with a guilty feeling. Truth often finds its way to the mind close
muffled in robes of sleep, and then speaks with uncompromising directness of
matters in regard to which we practice an unconscious self-deception during our
waking moments. Until now he had not been aware of the tyrannizing influence
acquired by one idea over his mind, and of the lengths which he might find in his
heart to go for the sake of giving himself peace.

"Aylmer," resumed Georgiana solemnly, "I know not what may be the cost to 16
both of us to rid me of this fatal birthmark. Perhaps its removal may cause cure-
less deformity; or it may be the stain goes as deep as life itself. Again: do we know
that there is a possibility, on any terms, of unclasping the firm grip of this little
hand which was laid upon me before I came into the world?"

"Dearest Georgiana, I have spent much thought upon the subject," hastily in- 17
terrupted Aylmer. "I am convinced of the perfect practicability of its removal."

"If there be the remotest possibility of it," continued Georgiana, "let the at- 18
tempt be made at whatever risk. Danger is nothing to me; for life, while this hateful mark makes me the object of your horror and disgust,—life is a burden which
I would fling down with joy. Either remove this dreadful hand, or take my
wretched life! You have deep science. All the world bears witness of it. You have
achieved great wonders. Cannot you remove this little, little mark, which I cover
with the tips of two small fingers? Is this beyond your power, for the sake of your
own peace, and to save your poor wife from madness?"

"Noblest, dearest, tenderest wife," cried Aylmer rapturously, "doubt not my 19
power. I have already given this matter the deepest thought—thought which
might almost have enlightened me to create a being less perfect than yourself.
Georgiana, you have led me deeper than ever into the heart of science. I feel myself fully competent to render this dear cheek as faultless as its fellow; and then,
most beloved, what will be my triumph when I shall have corrected what Nature
left imperfect in her fairest work! Even Pygmalion,[3] when his sculptured woman
assumed life, felt not greater ecstasy than mine will be."

"It is resolved, then," said Georgiana, faintly smiling. "And, Aylmer, spare me 20
not, though you should find the birthmark take refuge in my heart at last."

Her husband tenderly kissed her cheek—her right cheek—not that which 21
bore the impress of the crimson hand.

---

3. **Pygmalion:** in Greek mythology, a king of Cyprus who carved and then fell in love with a statue of a
woman that the goddess Aphrodite brought to life as Galatea.

The next day Aylmer apprised his wife of a plan that he had formed whereby 22
he might have opportunity for the intense thought and constant watchfulness
which the proposed operation would require; while Georgiana, likewise, would
enjoy the perfect repose essential to its success. They were to seclude themselves
in the extensive apartments occupied by Aylmer as a laboratory, and where, during his toilsome youth, he had made discoveries in the elemental powers of Nature that had roused the admiration of all the learned societies in Europe. Seated
calmly in this laboratory, the pale philosopher had investigated the secrets of the
highest cloud region and of the profoundest mines; he had satisfied himself of
the causes that kindled and kept alive the fires of the volcano; and had explained
the mystery of fountains, and how it is that they gush forth, some so bright and
pure, and others with such rich medicinal virtues, from the dark bosom of the
earth. Here, too, at an earlier period, he had studied the wonders of the human
frame, and attempted to fathom the very process by which Nature assimilates all
her precious influences from earth and air, and from the spiritual world, to create and foster man, her masterpiece. The latter pursuit, however, Aylmer had long
laid aside in unwilling recognition of the truth—against which all seekers sooner
or later stumble—that our great creative Mother, while she amuses us with apparently working in the broadest sunshine, is yet severely careful to keep her own
secrets, and, in spite of her pretended openness, shows us nothing but results. She
permits us, indeed, to mar, but seldom to mend, and, like a jealous patentee, on
no account to make. Now, however, Aylmer resumed these half-forgotten inves-
tigations,—not, of course, with such hopes or wishes as first suggested them,
but because they involved much physiological truth and lay in the path of his
proposed scheme for the treatment of Georgiana.

As he led her over the threshold of the laboratory, Georgiana was cold and 23
tremulous. Aylmer looked cheerfully into her face, with intent to reassure her,
but was so startled with the intense glow of the birthmark upon the whiteness of
her cheek that he could not restrain a strong convulsive shudder. His wife fainted.

"Aminadab! Aminadab!" shouted Aylmer, stamping violently on the floor. 24

Forthwith there issued from an inner apartment a man of low stature, but 25
bulky frame, with shaggy hair hanging about his visage, which was grimed with
the vapors of the furnace. This personage had been Aylmer's under-worker during his whole scientific career, and was admirably fitted for that office by his great
mechanical readiness, and the skill with which, while incapable of comprehend-
ing a single principle, he executed all the details of his master's experiments. With
his vast strength, his shaggy hair, his smoky aspect, and the indescribable earthi-
ness that encrusted him, he seemed to represent man's physical nature; while
Aylmer's slender figure, and pale, intellectual face, were no less apt a type of the
spiritual element.

"Throw open the door of the boudoir, Aminadab," said Aylmer, "and burn a 26
pastille."

"Yes, master," answered Aminadab, looking intently at the lifeless form of 27
Georgiana; and then he muttered to himself, "If she were my wife, I'd never part
with that birthmark."

When Georgiana recovered consciousness she found herself breathing an at-   28
mosphere of penetrating fragrance, the gentle potency of which had recalled her
from her deathlike faintness. The scene around her looked like enchantment.
Aylmer had converted those smoky, dingy, somber rooms, where he had spent his
brightest years in recondite pursuits, into a series of beautiful apartments not
unfit to be the secluded abode of a lovely woman. The walls were hung with gorgeous curtains, which imparted the combination of grandeur and grace that no
other species of adornment can achieve; and as they fell from the ceiling to the
floor, their rich and ponderous folds, concealing all angles and straight lines, appeared to shut in the scene from infinite space. For aught Georgiana knew, it
might be a pavilion among the clouds. And Aylmer, excluding the sunshine,
which would have interfered with his chemical processes, had supplied its place
with perfumed lamps, emitting flames of various hue, but all uniting in a soft,
empurpled radiance. He now knelt by his wife's side, watching her earnestly, but
without alarm; for he was confident in his science, and felt that he could draw a
magic circle round her within which no evil might intrude.

"Where am I? Ah, I remember," said Georgiana faintly; and she placed her   29
hand over her cheek to hide the terrible mark from her husband's eyes.

"Fear not, dearest!" exclaimed he. "Do not shrink from me! Believe me,   30
Georgiana, I even rejoice in this single imperfection, since it will be such a rapture
to remove it."

"Oh, spare me!" sadly replied his wife. "Pray do not look at it again. I never   31
can forget that convulsive shudder."

In order to soothe Georgiana, and, as it were, to release her mind from the   32
burden of actual things, Aylmer now put in practice some of the light and playful
secrets which science had taught him among its profounder lore. Airy figures, absolutely bodiless ideas, and forms of unsubstantial beauty came and danced before her, imprinting their momentary footsteps on beams of light. Though she
had some indistinct idea of the method of these optical phenomena, still the illusion was almost perfect enough to warrant the belief that her husband possessed
sway over the spiritual world. Then again, when she felt a wish to look forth from
her seclusion, immediately, as if her thoughts were answered, the procession of
external existence flitted across a screen. The scenery and the figures of actual life
were perfectly represented, but with that bewitching, yet indescribable difference
which always makes a picture, an image, or a shadow so much more attractive
than the original. When wearied of this, Aylmer bade her cast her eyes upon a vessel containing a quantity of earth. She did so, with little interest at first; but was
soon startled to perceive the germ of a plant shooting upward from the soil. Then
came the slender stalk; the leaves gradually unfolded themselves; and amid them
was a perfect and lovely flower.

"It is magical!" cried Georgiana. "I dare not touch it."   33

"Nay, pluck it," answered Aylmer: "pluck it, and inhale its brief perfume while   34
you may. The flower will wither in a few moments and leave nothing save its
brown seed vessels; but thence may be perpetuated a race as ephemeral as itself."

But Georgiana had no sooner touched the flower than the whole plant 35
suffered a blight, its leaves turning coal-black as if by the agency of fire.

"There was too powerful a stimulus," said Aylmer thoughtfully. 36

To make up for this abortive experiment, he proposed to take her portrait by 37
a scientific process of his own invention. It was to be effected by rays of light striking upon a polished plate of metal. Georgiana assented; but, on looking at the result, was affrighted to find the features of the portrait blurred and indefinable;
while the minute figure of a hand appeared where the cheek should have been.
Aylmer snatched the metallic plate and threw it into a jar of corrosive acid.

Soon, however, he forgot these mortifying failures. In the intervals of study 38
and chemical experiment he came to her flushed and exhausted, but seemed in-
vigorated by her presence, and spoke in glowing language of the resources of his
art. He gave a history of the long dynasty of the alchemists, who spent so many
ages in quest of the universal solvent by which the golden principle might be
elicited from all things vile and base. Aylmer appeared to believe that, by the
plainest scientific logic, it was altogether within the limits of possibility to discover this long-sought medium; "but," he added, "a philosopher who should go
deep enough to acquire the power would attain too lofty a wisdom to stoop to the
exercise of it." Not less singular were his opinions in regard to the elixir vitae. He
more than intimated that it was at his option to concoct a liquid that should pro-
long life for years, perhaps interminably; but that it would produce a discord in
Nature which all the world, and chiefly the quaffer of the immortal nostrum,
would find cause to curse.

"Aylmer, are you in earnest?" asked Georgiana, looking at him with amaze- 39
ment and fear. "It is terrible to possess such power, or even to dream of possessing it."

"Oh, do not tremble, my love," said her husband. "I would not wrong either 40
you or myself by working such inharmonious effects upon our lives; but I would
have you consider how trifling, in comparison, is the skill requisite to remove this
little hand."

At the mention of the birthmark, Georgiana, as usual, shrank as if a red-hot 41
iron had touched her cheek.

Again Aylmer applied himself to his labors. She could hear his voice in the dis- 42
tant furnace-room giving directions to Aminadab, whose harsh, uncouth, misshapen tones were audible in response, more like the grunt or growl of a brute
than human speech. After hours of absence, Aylmer reappeared and proposed
that she should now examine his cabinet of chemical products and natural treasures of the earth. Among the former he showed her a small vial, in which, he remarked, was contained a gentle yet most powerful fragrance, capable of impreg-
nating all the breezes that blow across a kingdom. They were of inestimable value,
the contents of that little vial; and, as he said so, he threw some of the perfume
into the air and filled the room with piercing and invigorating delight.

"And what is this?" asked Georgiana, pointing to a small crystal globe con- 43
taining a gold-colored liquid. "It is so beautiful to the eye that I could imagine it
the elixir of life."

"In one sense it is," replied Aylmer; "or rather, the elixir of immortality. It is 44 the most precious poison that ever was concocted in this world. By its aid I could apportion the lifetime of any mortal at whom you might point your finger. The strength of the dose would determine whether he were to linger out years, or drop dead in the midst of a breath. No king on his guarded throne could keep his life if I, in my private station, should deem that the welfare of millions justified me in depriving him of it."

"Why do you keep such a terrific drug?" inquired Georgiana in horror. 45

"Do not mistrust me, dearest," said her husband, smiling; "its virtuous po- 46 tency is yet greater than its harmful one. But see! here is a powerful cosmetic. With a few drops of this in a vase of water, freckles may be washed away as easily as the hands are cleansed. A stronger infusion would take the blood out of the cheek, and leave the rosiest beauty a pale ghost."

"Is it with this lotion that you intend to bathe my cheek?" asked Georgiana, 47 anxiously.

"Oh, no," hastily replied her husband; "this is merely superficial. Your case 48 demands a remedy that shall go deeper."

In his interviews with Georgiana, Aylmer generally made minute inquiries as 49 to her sensations and whether the confinement of the rooms and the temperature of the atmosphere agreed with her. These questions had such a particular drift that Georgiana began to conjecture that she was already subjected to certain physical influences, either breathed in with the fragrant air or taken with her food. She fancied likewise, but it might be altogether fancy, that there was a stirring up of her system—a strange, indefinite sensation creeping through her veins, and tingling, half painfully, half pleasurably, at her heart. Still, whenever she dared to look into the mirror, there she beheld herself pale as a white rose and with the crimson birthmark stamped upon her cheek. Not even Aylmer now hated it so much as she.

To dispel the tedium of the hours which her husband found it necessary to de- 50 vote to the processes of combination and analysis, Georgiana turned over the volumes of his scientific library. In many dark old tomes she met with chapters full of romance and poetry. They were the works of the philosophers of the middle ages, such as Albertus Magnus, Cornelius Agrippa, Paracelsus, and the famous friar who created the prophetic Brazen Head. All these antique naturalists stood in advance of their centuries, yet were imbued with some of their credulity, and therefore were believed, and perhaps imagined themselves to have acquired from the investigation of Nature a power above Nature, and from physics a sway over the spiritual world. Hardly less curious and imaginative were the early volumes of the Transactions of the Royal Society, in which the members, knowing little of the limits of natural possibility, were continually recording wonders or proposing methods whereby wonders might be wrought.

But to Georgiana the most engrossing volume was a large folio from her 51 husband's own hand, in which he had recorded every experiment of his scientific career, its original aim, the methods adopted for its development, and its final success or failure, with the circumstances to which either event was attributable.

The book, in truth, was both the history and emblem of his ardent, ambitious, imaginative, yet practical and laborious life. He handled physical details as if there were nothing beyond them; yet spiritualized them all, and redeemed himself from materialism by his strong and eager aspiration towards the infinite. In his grasp the veriest clod of earth assumed a soul. Georgiana, as she read, reverenced Aylmer and loved him more profoundly than ever, but with a less entire dependence on his judgment than heretofore. Much as he had accomplished, she could not but observe that his most splendid successes were almost invariably failures, if compared with the ideal at which he aimed. His brightest diamonds were the merest pebbles, and felt to be so by himself, in comparison with the inestimable gems which lay hidden beyond his reach. The volume, rich with achievements that had won renown for its author, was yet as melancholy a record as ever mortal hand had penned. It was the sad confession and continual exemplification of the shortcomings of the composite man, the spirit burdened with clay and working in matter, and of the despair that assails the higher nature at finding itself so miserably thwarted by the earthly part. Perhaps every man of genius in whatever sphere might recognize the image of his own experience in Aylmer's journal.

So deeply did these reflections affect Georgiana that she laid her face upon the 52 open volume and burst into tears. In this situation she was found by her husband.

"It is dangerous to read in a sorcerer's books," said he with a smile, though his 53 countenance was uneasy and displeased. "Georgiana, there are pages in that volume which I can scarcely glance over and keep my senses. Take heed lest it prove as detrimental to you."

"It has made me worship you more than ever," said she. 54

"Ah, wait for this one success," rejoined he, "then worship me if you will. 55 I shall deem myself hardly unworthy of it. But come, I have sought you for the luxury of your voice. Sing to me, dearest."

So she poured out the liquid music of her voice to quench the thirst of his 56 spirit. He then took his leave with a boyish exuberance of gaiety, assuring her that her seclusion would endure but a little longer, and that the result was already certain. Scarcely had he departed when Georgiana felt irresistibly impelled to follow him. She had forgotten to inform Aylmer of a symptom which for two or three hours past had begun to excite her attention. It was a sensation in the fatal birthmark, not painful, but which induced a restlessness throughout her system. Hastening after her husband, she intruded for the first time into the laboratory.

The first thing that struck her eye was the furnace, that hot and feverish 57 worker, with the intense glow of its fire, which by the quantities of soot clustered above it seemed to have been burning for ages. There was a distilling apparatus in full operation. Around the room were retorts, tubes, cylinders, crucibles, and other apparatus of chemical research. An electrical machine stood ready for immediate use. The atmosphere felt oppressively close, and was tainted with gaseous odors which had been tormented forth by the processes of science. The severe and homely simplicity of the apartment, with its naked walls and brick pavement, looked strange, accustomed as Georgiana had become to the fantastic elegance of her boudoir. But what chiefly, indeed almost solely, drew her attention, was the aspect of Aylmer himself.

He was pale as death, anxious and absorbed, and hung over the furnace 58 as if it depended upon his utmost watchfulness whether the liquid which it was distilling should be the draught of immortal happiness or misery. How different from the sanguine and joyous mien that he had assumed for Georgiana's encouragement!

"Carefully now, Aminadab; carefully, thou human machine; carefully, thou 59 man of clay!" muttered Aylmer, more to himself than his assistant. "Now, if there be a thought too much or too little, it is all over."

"Ho! ho!" mumbled Aminadab. "Look, master! look!"   60

Aylmer raised his eyes hastily, and at first reddened, then grew paler than ever, 61 on beholding Georgiana. He rushed towards her and seized her arm with a gripe that left the print of his fingers upon it.

"Why do you come hither? Have you no trust in your husband?" cried he im- 62 petuously. "Would you throw the blight of that fatal birthmark over my labors? It is not well done. Go, prying woman, go!"

"Nay, Aylmer," said Georgiana with the firmness of which she possessed no 63 stinted endowment, "it is not you that have a right to complain. You mistrust your wife; you have concealed the anxiety with which you watch the development of this experiment. Think not so unworthily of me, my husband. Tell me all the risk we run, and fear not that I shall shrink; for my share in it is far less than your own."

"No, no, Georgiana!" said Aylmer impatiently; "it must not be."   64

"I submit," replied she calmly. "And, Aylmer, I shall quaff whatever draught 65 you bring me; but it will be on the same principle that would induce me to take a dose of poison if offered by your hand."

"My noble wife," said Aylmer, deeply moved, "I knew not the height and 66 depth of your nature until now. Nothing shall be concealed. Know, then, that this crimson hand, superficial as it seems, has clutched its grasp into your being with a strength of which I had no previous conception. I have already administered agents powerful enough to do aught except to change your entire physical system. Only one thing remains to be tried. If that fails us we are ruined."

"Why did you hesitate to tell me this?" asked she.   67

"Because, Georgiana," said Aylmer in a low voice, "there is danger."   68

"Danger? There is but one danger—that this horrible stigma shall be left 69 upon my cheek!" cried Georgiana. "Remove it, remove it, whatever be the cost, or we shall both go mad!"

"Heaven knows your words are too true," said Aylmer sadly. "And now, 70 dearest, return to your boudoir. In a little while all will be tested."

He conducted her back and took leave of her with a solemn tenderness which 71 spoke far more than his words how much was now at stake. After his departure Georgiana became rapt in musings. She considered the character of Aylmer, and did it completer justice than at any previous moment. Her heart exulted, while it trembled, at his honorable love—so pure and lofty that it would accept nothing less than perfection nor miserably make itself contented with an earthlier nature than he had dreamed of. She felt how much more precious was such a sentiment than that meaner kind which would have borne with the imperfection for her sake, and have been guilty of treason to holy love by degrading its perfect idea to the level of the actual; and with her whole spirit she prayed that, for a single moment, she might satisfy his highest and deepest conception. Longer than one moment she well knew it could not be; for his spirit was ever on the march, ever ascending, and each instant required something that was beyond the scope of the instant before.

The sound of her husband's footsteps aroused her. He bore a crystal goblet 72 containing a liquor colorless as water, but bright enough to be the draught of immortality. Aylmer was pale; but it seemed rather the consequence of a highly wrought state of mind and tension of spirit than of fear or doubt.

"The concoction of the draught has been perfect," said he, in answer to 73 Georgiana's look. "Unless all my science have deceived me, it cannot fail."

"Save on your account, my dearest Aylmer," observed his wife, "I might wish 74 to put off this birthmark of mortality by relinquishing mortality itself in preference to any other mode. Life is but a sad possession to those who have attained precisely the degree of moral advancement at which I stand. Were I weaker and blinder it might be happiness. Were I stronger, it might be endured hopefully. But, being what I find myself, methinks I am of all mortals the most fit to die."

"You are fit for heaven without tasting death!" replied her husband. "But why 75 do we speak of dying? The draught cannot fail. Behold its effect upon this plant."

On the window seat there stood a geranium diseased with yellow blotches, 76 which had overspread all its leaves. Aylmer poured a small quantity of the liquid upon the soil in which it grew. In a little time, when the roots of the plant had taken up the moisture, the unsightly blotches began to be extinguished in a living verdure.

"There needed no proof," said Georgiana quietly. "Give me the goblet. I 77 joyfully stake all upon your word."

"Drink, then, thou lofty creature!" exclaimed Aylmer, with fervid admiration. 78 "There is no taint of imperfection on thy spirit. Thy sensible frame, too, shall soon be all perfect."

She quaffed the liquid and returned the goblet to his hand. 79

"It is grateful," said she, with a placid smile. "Methinks it is like water from a 80 heavenly fountain; for it contains I know not what of unobtrusive fragrance and deliciousness. It allays a feverish thirst that had parched me for many days. Now, dearest, let me sleep. My earthly senses are closing over my spirit like the leaves around the heart of a rose at sunset."

She spoke the last words with a gentle reluctance, as if it required almost more 81 energy than she could command to pronounce the faint and lingering syllables. Scarcely had they loitered through her lips ere she was lost in slumber. Aylmer sat by her side, watching her aspect with the emotions proper to a man the whole value of whose existence was involved in the process now to be tested. Mingled with this mood, however, was the philosophic investigation characteristic of the man of science. Not the minutest symptom escaped him. A heightened flush of the cheek, a slight irregularity of breath, a quiver of the eyelid, a hardly perceptible tremor through the frame,—such were the details which, as the moments passed, he wrote down in his folio volume. Intense thought had set its stamp upon every previous page of that volume, but the thoughts of years were all concentrated upon the last.

While thus employed, he failed not to gaze often at the fatal hand, and not 82 without a shudder. Yet once, by a strange and unaccountable impulse, he pressed it with his lips. His spirit recoiled, however, in the very act; and Georgiana, out of the midst of her deep sleep, moved uneasily and murmured as if in remonstrance. Again Aylmer resumed his watch. Nor was it without avail. The crimson hand, which at first had been strongly visible upon the marble paleness of Georgiana's cheek, now grew more faintly outlined. She remained not less pale than ever; but the birthmark, with every breath that came and went, lost somewhat of its former distinctness. Its presence had been awful; its departure was more awful still. Watch the stain of the rainbow fading out of the sky, and you will know how that mysterious symbol passed away.

"By Heaven! it is well-nigh gone!" said Aylmer to himself, in almost irrepressi- 83 ble ecstasy. "I can scarcely trace it now. Success! success! And now it is like the faintest rose color. The lightest flush of blood across her cheek would overcome it. But she is so pale!"

He drew aside the window curtain and suffered the light of natural day to fall 84 into the room and rest upon her cheek. At the same time he heard a gross, hoarse chuckle, which he had long known as his servant Aminadab's expression of delight.

"Ah, clod! ah, earthly mass!" cried Aylmer, laughing in a sort of frenzy, "you 85 have served me well! Matter and spirit—earth and heaven—have both done their part in this! Laugh, thing of the senses! You have earned the right to laugh."

These exclamations broke Georgiana's sleep. She slowly unclosed her eyes and 86 gazed into the mirror which her husband had arranged for that purpose. A faint smile flitted over her lips when she recognized how barely perceptible was now that crimson hand which had once blazed forth with such disastrous brilliancy as to scare away all their happiness. But then her eyes sought Aylmer's face with a trouble and anxiety that he could by no means account for.

"My poor Aylmer!" murmured she.   87

"Poor? Nay, richest, happiest, most favored!" exclaimed he. "My peerless 88 bride, it is successful! You are perfect!"

"My poor Aylmer," she repeated, with a more than human tenderness, "you 89 have aimed loftily; you have done nobly. Do not repent that with so high and pure a feeling, you have rejected the best earth could offer. Aylmer, dearest Aylmer, I am dying!"

Alas! it was too true! The fatal hand had grappled with the mystery of life, and 90 was the bond by which an angelic spirit kept itself in union with a mortal frame. As the last crimson tint of the birthmark—that sole token of human imperfection—faded from her cheek, the parting breath of the now perfect woman passed into the atmosphere, and her soul, lingering a moment near her husband, took its heavenward flight. Then a hoarse, chuckling laugh was heard again! Thus ever does the gross fatality of earth exult in its invariable triumph over the immortal essence which, in this dim sphere of half development, demands the completeness of a higher state. Yet, had Aylmer reached a profounder wisdom, he need not thus have flung away the happiness which would have woven his mortal life of the selfsame texture with the celestial. The momentary circumstance was too strong for him; he failed to look beyond the shadowy scope of time, and, living once for all in eternity, to find the perfect future in the present.

ACTIVITIES FOR WRITING AND DISCUSSION

1. Is it plausible that a slight birthmark would have become the all-consuming obsession of Aylmer's and Georgiana's lives? If not, why not? If so, what qualities do you perceive in the characters and personal backgrounds of Aylmer and Georgiana that could account for such an obsession? (If you wish, narrate the characters' backgrounds in fictional form, using either first- or third-person **point of view.**)

2. Aylmer's character is a strange mix of "deep science" and superstition (e.g., he assigns occult and malevolent significance to a slight physical blemish). Is his superstition consistent with his particular kind of science, or not? Explain your answer by discussing specific examples of his scientific and superstitious behaviors.

3. Examine the contrasting characters of Aylmer and Aminadab. The narrator says that each man is "a type"—of whom or of what? What insights into Aylmer's character are provided by the physical appearance, actions, and expressions of his assistant? Look especially at the story's final paragraph.

4. Research Hawthorne's opinions on science. Is "The Birthmark" a critique of science—or is it about other or broader issues?

JAMES THURBER (1894–1961)

The Secret Life of Walter Mitty

"We're going through!" The Commander's voice was like thin ice breaking. He wore his full-dress uniform, with the heavily braided white cap pulled down rakishly over one cold gray eye. "We can't make it, sir. It's spoiling for a hurricane, if you ask me." "I'm not asking you, Lieutenant Berg," said the Commander. "Throw on the power lights! Rev her up to 8,500! We're going through!" The pounding of the cylinders increased: ta-pocketa-pocketa-pocketa-*pocketa-pocketa.* The Commander stared at the ice forming on the pilot window. He walked over and twisted a row of complicated dials. "Switch on No. 8 auxiliary!"

he shouted. "Switch on No. 8 auxiliary!" repeated Lieutenant Berg. "Full strength in No. 3 turret!" shouted the Commander. "Full strength in No. 3 turret!" The crew, bending to their various tasks in the huge, hurtling eight-engined Navy hydroplane, looked at each other and grinned. "The Old Man'll get us through," they said to one another. "The Old Man ain't afraid of Hell!" . . .

"Not so fast! You're driving too fast!" said Mrs. Mitty. "What are you driving 2 so fast for?"

"Hmm?" said Walter Mitty. He looked at his wife, in the seat beside him, with 3 shocked astonishment. She seemed grossly unfamiliar, like a strange woman who had yelled at him in a crowd. "You were up to fifty-five," she said. "You know I don't like to go more than forty. You were up to fifty-five." Walter Mitty drove on toward Waterbury in silence, the roaring of the SN202 through the worst storm in twenty years of Navy flying fading in the remote, intimate airways of his mind. "You're tensed up again," said Mrs. Mitty. "It's one of your days. I wish you'd let Dr. Renshaw look you over."

Walter Mitty stopped the car in front of the building where his wife went to 4 have her hair done. "Remember to get those overshoes while I'm having my hair done," she said. "I don't need overshoes," said Mitty. She put her mirror back into her bag. "We've been all through that," she said, getting out of the car. "You're not a young man any longer." He raced the engine a little. "Why don't you wear your gloves? Have you lost your gloves?" Walter Mitty reached in a pocket and brought out the gloves. He put them on, but after she had turned and gone into the building and he had driven on to a red light, he took them off again. "Pick it up, brother!" snapped a cop as the light changed, and Mitty hastily pulled on his gloves and lurched ahead. He drove around the streets aimlessly for a time, and then he drove past the hospital on his way to the parking lot.

. . . "It's the millionaire banker, Wellington McMillan," said the pretty nurse. 5 "Yes?" said Walter Mitty, removing his gloves slowly. "Who has the case?" "Dr. Renshaw and Dr. Benbow, but there are two specialists here, Dr. Remington from New York and Dr. Pritchard-Mitford from London. He flew over." A door opened down a long, cool corridor and Dr. Renshaw came out. He looked distraught and haggard. "Hello, Mitty," he said. "We're having the devil's own time with McMillan, the millionaire banker and close personal friend of Roosevelt. Obstreosis of the ductal tract. Tertiary. Wish you'd take a look at him." "Glad to," said Mitty.

In the operating room there were whispered introductions: "Dr. Remington, 6 Dr. Mitty, Dr. Pritchard-Mitford, Dr. Mitty." "I've read your book on streptothricosis," said Pritchard-Mitford, shaking hands. "A brilliant performance, sir." "Thank you," said Walter Mitty. "Didn't know you were in the States, Mitty," grumbled Remington. "Coals to Newcastle, bringing Mitford and me up here for a tertiary." "You are very kind," said Mitty. A huge, complicated machine, connected to the operating table, with many tubes and wires, began at this moment to go pocketa-pocketa-pocketa. "The new anesthetizer is giving way!" shouted an intern. "There is no one in the East who knows how to fix it!" "Quiet, man!" said

Mitty, in a low, cool voice. He sprang to the machine, which was now going pocketa-pocketa-queep-pocketa-queep. He began fingering delicately a row of glistening dials. "Give me a fountain pen!" he snapped. Someone handed him a fountain pen. He pulled a faulty piston out of the machine and inserted the pen in its place. "That will hold for ten minutes," he said. "Get on with the operation." A nurse hurried over and whispered to Renshaw, and Mitty saw the man turn pale. "Coreopsis has set in," said Renshaw nervously. "If you would take over, Mitty?" Mitty looked at him and at the craven figure of Benbow, who drank, and at the grave, uncertain faces of the two great specialists. "If you wish," he said. They slipped a white gown on him; he adjusted a mask and drew on thin gloves; nurses handed him shining. . . .

"Back it up, Mac! Look out for that Buick!" Walter Mitty jammed on the   7 brakes. "Wrong lane, Mac," said the parking-lot attendant, looking at Mitty closely. "Gee. Yeh," muttered Mitty. He began cautiously to back out of the lane marked "Exit Only." "Leave her sit there," said the attendant. "I'll put her away." Mitty got out of the car. "Hey, better leave the key." "Oh," said Mitty, handing the man the ignition key. The attendant vaulted into the car, backed it up with insolent skill, and put it where it belonged.

They're so damn cocky, thought Walter Mitty, walking along Main Street; they   8 think they know everything. Once he had tried to take his chains off, outside New Milford, and he had got them wound around the axles. A man had had to come out in a wrecking car and unwind them, a young, grinning garageman. Since then Mrs. Mitty always made him drive to the garage to have the chains taken off. The next time, he thought, I'll wear my right arm in a sling; they won't grin at me then. I'll have my right arm in a sling and they'll see I couldn't possibly take the chains off myself. He kicked at the slush on the sidewalk. "Overshoes," he said to himself, and he began looking for a shoe store.

When he came out into the street again, with the overshoes in a box under his   9 arm, Walter Mitty began to wonder what the other thing was his wife had told him to get. She had told him, twice, before they set out from their house for Waterbury. In a way he hated these weekly trips to town—he was always getting something wrong. Kleenex, he thought, Squibb's, razor blades? No. Toothpaste, toothbrush, bicarbonate, carborundum, initiative and referendum? He gave it up. But she would remember it. "Where's the what's-its-name?" she would ask. "Don't tell me you forgot the what's-its-name." A newsboy went by shouting something about the Waterbury trial.

. . . "Perhaps this will refresh your memory." The District Attorney suddenly   10 thrust a heavy automatic at the quiet figure on the witness stand. "Have you ever seen this before?" Walter Mitty took the gun and examined it expertly. "This is my Webley-Vickers 50.80," he said calmly. An excited buzz ran around the courtroom. The Judge rapped for order. "You are a crack shot with any sort of firearms, I believe?" said the District Attorney, insinuatingly. "Objection!" shouted Mitty's attorney. "We have shown that the defendant could not have fired the shot. We have shown that he wore his right arm in a sling on the night of the fourteenth of July." Walter Mitty raised his hand briefly and the bickering attorneys were stilled.

"With any known make of gun," he said evenly, "I could have killed Gregory Fitzhurst at three hundred feet *with my left hand.*" Pandemonium broke loose in the courtroom. A woman's scream rose above the bedlam and suddenly a lovely, dark-haired girl was in Walter Mitty's arms. The District Attorney struck at her savagely. Without rising from his chair, Mitty let the man have it on the point of the chin. "You miserable cur!" . . .

"Puppy biscuit," said Walter Mitty. He stopped walking and the buildings of 11 Waterbury rose up out of the misty courtroom and surrounded him again. A woman who was passing laughed, "He said 'Puppy biscuit,'" she said to her companion. "That man said 'Puppy biscuit' to himself." Walter Mitty hurried on. He went into an A. & P., not the first one he came to but a smaller one farther up the street. "I want some biscuit for small, young dogs," he said to the clerk. "Any special brand, sir?" The greatest pistol shot in the world thought a moment. "It says 'Puppies Bark for It' on the box," said Walter Mitty.

His wife would be through at the hairdresser's in fifteen minutes, Mitty saw in 12 looking at his watch, unless they had trouble drying it; sometimes they had trouble drying it. She didn't like to get to the hotel first; she would want him to be there waiting for her as usual. He found a big leather chair in the lobby, facing a window, and he put the overshoes and the puppy biscuit on the floor beside it. He picked up an old copy of *Liberty* and sank down into the chair. "Can Germany Conquer the World through the Air?" Walter Mitty looked at the pictures of bombing planes and of ruined streets.

. . . "The cannonading has got the wind up in young Raleigh, sir," said the 13 sergeant. Captain Mitty looked up at him through tousled hair. "Get him to bed," he said wearily. "With the others. I'll fly alone." "But you can't, sir," said the sergeant anxiously. "It takes two men to handle that bomber and the Archies are pounding hell out of the air. Von Richtman's circus is between here and Saulier." "Somebody's got to get that ammunition dump," said Mitty. "I'm going over. Spot of brandy?" He poured a drink for the sergeant and one for himself. War thundered and whined around the dugout and battered at the door. There was a rending of wood and splinters flew through the room. "A bit of a near thing," said Captain Mitty carelessly. "The box barrage is closing in," said the sergeant. "We only live once, Sergeant," said Mitty, with his faint, fleeting smile. "Or do we?" He poured another brandy and tossed it off. "I never see a man could hold his brandy like you, sir," said the sergeant. "Begging your pardon, sir." Captain Mitty stood up and strapped on his huge Webley-Vickers automatic. "It's forty kilometers through hell, sir," said the sergeant. Mitty finished one last brandy. "After all," he said softly, "what isn't?" The pounding of the cannon increased; there was the rat-tat-tatting of machine guns, and from somewhere came the menacing pocket-pocketa-pocketa of the new flame-throwers. Walter Mitty walked to the door of the dugout humming "Auprès de Ma Blonde." He turned and waved to the sergeant. "Cheerio!" he said. . . .

Something struck his shoulder. "I've been looking all over this hotel for you," 14 said Mrs. Mitty. "Why do you have to hide in this old chair? How did you expect me to find you?" "Things close in," said Walter Mitty vaguely. "What?" Mrs. Mitty said. "Did you get the what's-its-name? The puppy biscuit? What's in that box?" "Overshoes," said Mitty. "Couldn't you have put them on in the store?" "I was thinking," said Walter Mitty. "Does it ever occur to you that I am sometimes thinking?" She looked at him. "I'm going to take your temperature when I get you home," she said.

They went out through the revolving doors that made a faintly derisive 15 whistling sound when you pushed them. It was two blocks to the parking lot. At the drugstore on the corner she said, "Wait here for me. I forgot something. I won't be a minute." She was more than a minute. Walter Mitty lighted a cigarette. It began to rain, rain with sleet in it. He stood up against the wall of the drugstore, smoking. . . . He put his shoulders back and his heels together. "To hell with the handkerchief," said Walter Mitty scornfully. He took one last drag on his cigarette and snapped it away. Then, with that faint, fleeting smile playing about his lips, he faced the firing squad; erect and motionless, proud and disdainful, Walter Mitty the Undefeated, inscrutable to the last.

RAY BRADBURY (b. 1920)

The Murderer

Music moved with him in the white halls. He passed an office door: "The Merry 1 Widow Waltz." Another door: "Afternoon of a Faun." A third: "Kiss Me Again." He turned into a cross corridor: "The Sword Dance" buried him in cymbals, drums, pots, pans, knives, forks, thunder and tin lightning. All washed away as he hurried through an anteroom where a secretary sat nicely stunned by Beethoven's Fifth. He moved himself before her eyes like a hand; she didn't see him.

His wrist radio buzzed. 2

"Yes?" 3

"This is Lee, Dad. Don't forget about my allowance." 4

"Yes, son, yes. I'm busy." 5

"Just didn't want you to forget, Dad," said the wrist radio. Tchaikovsky's 6 "Romeo and Juliet" swarmed about the voice and flushed into the long halls.

The psychiatrist moved in the beehive of offices, in the cross-pollination 7 of themes, Stravinsky mating with Bach, Haydn unsuccessfully repulsing Rachmaninoff, Schubert slain by Duke Ellington. He nodded to the humming secretaries and the whistling doctors fresh to their morning work. At his office he checked a few papers with his stenographer, who sang under her breath, then phoned the police captain upstairs. A few minutes later a red light blinked, a voice said from the ceiling:

"Prisoner delivered to Interview Chamber Nine." 8

He unlocked the chamber door, stepped in, heard the door lock behind him. 9

"Go away," said the prisoner, smiling. 10

The psychiatrist was shocked by that smile. A very sunny, pleasant warm 11
thing, a thing that shed bright light upon the room. Dawn among the dark hills.
High noon at midnight, that smile. The blue eyes sparkled serenely above that
display of self-assured dentistry.

"I'm here to help you," said the psychiatrist, frowning. Something was wrong 12
with the room. He had hesitated the moment he entered. He glanced around. The
prisoner laughed. "If you're wondering why it's so quiet in here, I just kicked the
radio to death."

Violent, thought the doctor.   13

The prisoner read this thought, smiled, put out a gentle hand. "No, only to 14
machines that yak-yak-yak."

Bits of the wall radio's tubes and wires lay on the gray carpeting. Ignoring 15
these, feeling that smile upon him like a heat lamp, the psychiatrist sat across from
his patient in the unusual silence which was like the gathering of a storm.

"You're Mr. Albert Brock, who calls himself The Murderer?"   16

Brock nodded pleasantly. "Before we start . . ." He moved quietly and quickly 17
to detach the wrist radio from the doctor's arm. He tucked it in his teeth like a
walnut, gritted and heard it crack, handed it back to the appalled psychiatrist as if
he had done them both a favor. "That's better."

The psychiatrist stared at the ruined machine. "You're running up quite a 18
damage bill."

"I don't care," smiled the patient. "As the old song goes: 'Don't Care What 19
Happens to Me!'" He hummed it.

The psychiatrist said: "Shall we start?"   20

"Fine. The first victim, or one of the first, was my telephone. Murder most 21
foul. I shoved it in the kitchen Insinkerator! Stopped the disposal unit in mid-
swallow. Poor thing strangled to death. After that I shot the television set!"

The psychiatrist said, "Mmm."   22

"Fired six shots right through the cathode. Made a beautiful tinkling crash, 23
like a dropped chandelier."

"Nice imagery."   24

"Thanks, I always dreamt of being a writer."   25

"Suppose you tell me when you first began to hate the telephone."   26

"It frightened me as a child. Uncle of mine called it the Ghost Machine. Voices 27
without bodies. Scared the living hell out of me. Later in life I was never comfortable. Seemed to me a phone was an impersonal instrument. If it *felt* like it, it
let your personality go through its wires. If it didn't *want* to, it just drained your
personality away until what slipped through at the other end was some cold fish
of a voice all steel, copper, plastic, no warmth, no reality. It's easy to say the wrong
thing on telephones; the telephone changes your meaning on you. First thing you
know, you've made an enemy. Then, of course, the telephone's such a *convenient*
thing; it just sits there and *demands* you call someone who doesn't want to be
called. Friends were always calling, calling, calling me. Hell, I hadn't any time of
my own. When it wasn't the telephone it was the television, the radio, the phonograph. When it wasn't the television or radio or the phonograph it was motion

pictures at the corner theater, motion pictures projected, with commercials on low-lying cumulus clouds. It doesn't rain rain any more, it rains soapsuds. When it wasn't High-Fly Cloud advertisements, it was music by Mozzek in every restaurant; music and commercials on the busses I rode to work. When it wasn't music, it was interoffice communications, and my horror chamber of a radio wrist watch on which my friends and my wife phoned every five minutes. What is there about such 'conveniences' that makes them so *temptingly* convenient? The average man thinks, Here I am, time on my hands, and there on my wrist is a wrist telephone, so why not just buzz old Joe up, eh? 'Hello, hello!' I love my friends, my wife, humanity, very much, but when one minute my wife calls to say, 'Where are you *now* dear?' and a friend calls and says, 'Got the best off-color joke to tell you. Seems there was a guy—' and a stranger calls and cries out, 'This is the Find-Fax Poll. What gum are you chewing at this very *instant!*' Well!"

"How did you feel during the week?"   28

"The fuse lit. On the edge of the cliff. That same afternoon I did what I did at   29
the office."

"Which was?"   30

"I poured a paper cup of water into the intercommunications system."   31

The psychiatrist wrote on his pad.   32

"And the system shorted?"   33

"Beautifully! The Fourth of July on wheels! My God, stenographers ran   34
around looking *lost!* What an uproar!"

"Felt better temporarily, eh?"   35

"Fine! Then I got the idea at noon of stomping my wrist radio on the sidewalk. 36
A shrill voice was just yelling out of it at me, 'This is People's Poll Number Nine. What did you eat for lunch?' when I kicked the Jesus out of the wrist radio!"

"Felt even *better,* eh?"   37

"It *grew* on me!" Brock rubbed his hands together. "Why didn't I start a 38
solitary revolution, deliver man from certain 'conveniences'? 'Convenient for whom?' I cried. Convenient for friends: 'Hey, Al, thought I'd call you from the locker room out here at Green Hills. Just made a sockdolager hole in one! A hole in one, Al! A *beautiful* day. Having a shot of whiskey now. Thought you'd want to know, Al!' Convenient for my office, so when I'm in the field with my car radio there's no moment when I'm not in touch. In *touch! There's* a slimy phrase. Touch, hell. *Gripped!* Pawed, rather. Mauled and massaged and pounded by FM voices. You can't leave your car without checking in: 'Have stopped to visit gas-station men's room.' 'Okay, Brock, step on it!' 'Brock, what *took* you so long?' 'Sorry, sir.' 'Watch it next time, Brock.' '*Yes, sir!*' So, do you know what I did, Doctor? I bought a quart of French chocolate ice cream and spooned it into the car radio transmitter."

"Was there any *special* reason for selecting French chocolate ice cream to 39
spoon into the broadcasting unit?"

Brock thought about it and smiled. "It's my favorite flavor."   40

"Oh," said the doctor.   41

"I figured, hell, what's good enough for me is good enough for the radio   42
transmitter."

"What made you think of spooning *ice cream* into the radio?"   43

"It was a hot day."   44

The doctor paused.   45

"And what happened next?"   46

"Silence happened next. God, it was *beautiful.* That car radio cackling all day,   47
Brock go here, Brock go there, Brock check in, Brock check out, okay Brock, hour
lunch, Brock, lunch over, Brock, Brock, Brock. Well, that silence was like putting
ice cream in my ears."

"You seem to like ice cream a lot."   48

"I just rode around feeling of the silence. It's a big bolt of the nicest, softest   49
flannel ever made. Silence. A whole hour of it. I just sat in my car; smiling, feeling
of that flannel with my ears. I felt *drunk* with Freedom!"

"Go on."   50

"Then I got the idea of the portable diathermy machine. I rented one, took it   51
on the bus going home that night. There sat all the tired commuters with their
wrist radios, talking to their wives, saying, 'Now I'm at Forty-third, now I'm at
Forty-fourth, here I am at Forty-ninth, now turning at Sixty-first.' One husband
cursing, 'Well, get *out* of that bar, damn it, and get home and get dinner started,
I'm at Seventieth!' And the transit-system radio playing 'Tales from the Vienna
Woods,' a canary singing words about a first-rate wheat cereal. Then—I switched
on my diathermy! Static! Interference! All wives cut off from husbands grousing
about a hard day at the office. All husbands cut off from wives who had just seen
their children break a window! The 'Vienna Woods' chopped down, the canary
mangled! *Silence!* A terrible, unexpected silence. The bus inhabitants faced with
having to converse with each other. Panic! Sheer, animal panic!"

"The police seized you?"   52

"The bus *had* to stop. After all, the music *was* being scrambled, husbands and   53
wives *were* out of touch with reality. Pandemonium, riot, and chaos. Squirrels
chattering in cages! A trouble unit arrived, triangulated on me instantly, had me
reprimanded, fined, and home, minus my diathermy machine, in jig time."

"Mr. Brock, may I suggest that so far your whole pattern here is not very—   54
practical? If you didn't like transit radios or office radios or car business radios,
why didn't you join a fraternity of radio haters, start petitions, get legal and
constitutional rulings? After all, this is a democracy."

"And I," said Brock, "am that thing called a minority. I *did* join fraternities,   55
picket, pass petitions, take it to court. Year after year I protested. Everyone
laughed. Everyone else *loved* bus radios and commercials. *I* was out of step."

"Then you should have taken it like a good soldier, don't you think? The   56
majority rules."

"But they went too far. If a little music and 'keeping in touch' was charming,   57
they figured a lot would be ten times as charming. I went *wild!* I got home to find
my wife hysterical. *Why?* Because she had been completely out of touch with me

for half a day. Remember, I did a dance on my wrist radio? Well, that night I laid plans to murder my house."

"Are you *sure* that's how you want me to write it down?"   58

"That's semantically accurate. Kill it dead. It's one of those talking, singing, 59 humming, weather-reporting, poetry-reading, novel-reciting, jingle-jangling, rockaby-crooning-when-you-go-to-bed houses. A house that screams opera to you in the shower and teaches you Spanish in your sleep. One of those blathering caves where all kinds of electronic Oracles make you feel a trifle larger than a thimble, with stoves that say, 'I'm apricot pie, and I'm *done*,' or 'I'm prime roast beef, so *baste* me!' and other nursery gibberish like that. With beds that rock you to sleep and *shake* you awake. A house that *barely* tolerates humans, I tell you. A front door that barks: 'You've mud on your feet, sir!' And an electronic vacuum hound that snuffles around after you from room to room, inhaling every finger-nail or ash you drop. Jesus God, *I* say, Jesus God!"

"Quietly," suggested the psychiatrist.   60

"Remember that Gilbert and Sullivan song—'I've Got It on My List, It Never 61 Will Be Missed'? All night I listed grievances. Next morning early I bought a pis-tol. I *purposely* muddied my feet. I stood at our front door. The front door shrilled, 'Dirty feet, muddy feet! Wipe your feet! Please be *neat!*' I shot the damn thing in its keyhole. I ran to the kitchen, where the stove was just whining, 'Turn me *over!*' In the middle of a mechanical omelet I did the stove to death. Oh, how it sizzled and screamed, 'I'm *shorted!*' Then the telephone rang like a spoiled brat. I shoved it down the Insinkerator. I must state here and now I have *nothing* what-ever against the Insinkerator; it was an innocent bystander. I feel sorry for it now, a practical device indeed, which never said a word, purred like a sleepy lion most of the time, and digested our leftovers. I'll have it restored. Then I went in and shot the televisor, that insidious beast, that Medusa, which freezes a billion peo-ple to stone every night, staring fixedly, that Siren which called and sang and promised so much and gave, after all, so little, but myself always going back, going back, hoping and waiting until—bang! Like a headless turkey, gobbling, my wife whooped out the front door. The police came. Here I *am!*"

He sat back happily and lit a cigarette.   62

"And did you realize, in committing these crimes, that the wrist radio, the 63 broadcasting transmitter, the phone, the bus radio, the office intercoms, all were rented or were someone else's property?"

"I would do it all over again, so help me God."   64

The psychiatrist sat there in the sunshine of that beatific smile.   65

"You don't want any further help from the Office of Mental Health? You're 66 ready to take the consequences?"

"This is only the beginning," said Mr. Brock. "I'm the vanguard of the small 67 public which is tired of noise and being taken advantage of and pushed around and yelled at, every moment music, every moment in touch with some voice somewhere, do this, do that, quick, quick, now here, now there. You'll see. The revolt begins. My name will go down in history!"

"Mmm." The psychiatrist seemed to be thinking.   68

"It'll take time, of course. It was all so enchanting at first. The very *idea* of 69 these things, the practical uses, was wonderful. They were almost toys, to be played with, but the people got too involved, went too far, and got wrapped up in a pattern of social behavior and couldn't get out, couldn't admit they were *in,* even. So they rationalized their nerves as something else. 'Our modern age,' they said. 'Conditions,' they said. 'High-strung,' they said. But mark my words, the seed has been sown. I got world-wide coverage on TV, radio, films; *there's* an irony for you. That was five days ago. A billion people know about me. Check your financial columns. Any day now. Maybe today. Watch for a sudden spurt, a rise in sales for French chocolate ice cream!"

"I see," said the psychiatrist.   70

"Can I go back to my nice private cell now, where I can be alone and quiet for 71 six months?"

"Yes," said the psychiatrist quietly.   72

"Don't worry about me," said Mr. Brock, rising. "I'm just going to sit around 73 for a long time stuffing that nice soft bolt of quiet material in both ears."

"Mmm," said the psychiatrist, going to the door.   74

"Cheers," said Mr. Brock.   75

"Yes," said the psychiatrist.   76

He pressed a code signal on a hidden button, the door opened, he stepped out, 77 the door shut and locked. Alone, he moved in the offices and corridors. The first twenty yards of his walk were accompanied by "Tambourine Chinois." Then it was "Tzigane," Bach's "Passacaglia" and Fugue in something Minor, "Tiger Rag," "Love Is Like a Cigarette." He took his broken wrist radio from his pocket like a dead praying mantis. He turned in at his office. A bell sounded; a voice came out of the ceiling, "Doctor?"

"Just finished with Brock," said the psychiatrist.   78

"Diagnosis?"   79

"Seems completely disorientated, but convivial. Refuses to accept the simplest 80 realities of his environment and work *with* them."

"Prognosis?"   81

"Indefinite. Left him enjoying a piece of invisible material."   82

Three phones rang. A duplicate wrist radio in his desk drawer buzzed like a 83 wounded grasshopper. The intercom flashed a pink light and click-clicked. Three phones rang. The drawer buzzed. Music blew in through the open door. The psychiatrist, humming quietly, fitted the new wrist radio to his wrist, flipped the intercom, talked a moment, picked up one telephone, talked, picked up another telephone, talked, picked up the third telephone, talked, touched the wrist-radio button, talked calmly and quietly, his face cool and serene, in the middle of the music and the lights flashing, the two phones ringing again, and his hands moving, and his wrist radio buzzing, and the intercoms talking, and voices speaking from the ceiling. And he went on quietly this way through the remainder of a cool, air-conditioned, and long afternoon; telephone, wrist radio, intercom, telephone, wrist radio, intercom, telephone, wrist radio, intercom, telephone, wrist radio, intercom, telephone, wrist radio, intercom, telephone, wrist radio . . .

ACTIVITIES FOR WRITING AND DISCUSSION

1. Read and annotate the story. Then:
    a. Share and discuss a few of your favorite annotations with a small group, and take notes on your groupmates' annotations to enrich your response to the story.
    b. React to "The Murderer" in your notebook using any of the "Ten Ideas for Writing" described in Chapter 3 and summarized on page 35.

2. Reannotate the psychiatrist's half of the dialogue, his comments and questions. Choose two or three specific comments or questions that seem particularly interesting to you and react to them in your notebook. How do the psychiatrist's concerns and values differ from Brock's?

3. Identify and explain any **ironies** in the story—its title, Brock's attitude toward prison, the various ironies surrounding the words "conveniences" and "convenient," and other ironies you find.

4. Modifying the characters and plot as necessary, recreate the story in a twenty-first-century **setting.**

KURT VONNEGUT, JR. (b. 1922)

Harrison Bergeron

The year was 2081, and everybody was finally equal. They weren't only equal 1
before God and the law. They were equal every which way. Nobody was smarter than anybody else. Nobody was better looking than anybody else. Nobody was stronger or quicker than anybody else. All this equality was due to the 211th, 212th, and 213th Amendments to the Constitution, and to the unceasing vigilance of agents of the United States Handicapper General.

Some things about living still weren't quite right, though. April, for instance, 2
still drove people crazy by not being springtime. And it was in that clammy month that the H-G men took George and Hazel Bergeron's fourteen-year-old son, Harrison, away.

It was tragic, all right, but George and Hazel couldn't think about it very hard. 3
Hazel had a perfectly average intelligence, which meant she couldn't think about anything except in short bursts. And George, while his intelligence was way above normal, had a little mental handicap radio in his ear. He was required by law to wear it at all times. It was tuned to a government transmitter. Every twenty seconds or so, the transmitter would send out some sharp noise to keep people like George from taking unfair advantage of their brains.

George and Hazel were watching television. There were tears on Hazel's 4
cheeks, but she'd forgotten for the moment what they were about.

On the television screen were ballerinas.   5

A buzzer sounded in George's head. His thoughts fled in panic, like bandits 6
from a burglar alarm.

"That was a real pretty dance, that dance they just did," said Hazel.   7

"Huh?" said George.   8

"That dance—it was nice," said Hazel.   9

"Yup," said George. He tried to think a little about the ballerinas. They weren't 10
really very good—no better than anybody else would have been, anyway. They
were burdened with sashweights and bags of birdshot, and their faces were
masked, so that no one, seeing a free and graceful gesture or a pretty face, would
feel like something the cat drug in. George was toying with the vague notion that
maybe dancers shouldn't be handicapped. But he didn't get very far with it before
another noise in his ear radio scattered his thoughts.

George winced. So did two out of the eight ballerinas.   11

Hazel saw him wince. Having no mental handicap herself, she had to ask 12
George what the latest sound had been.

"Sounded like somebody hitting a milk bottle with a ball peen hammer," said 13
George.

"I'd think it would be real interesting, hearing all the different sounds," said 14
Hazel, a little envious. "All the things they think up."

"Um," said George.   15

"Only, if I was Handicapper General, you know what I would do?" said Hazel. 16
Hazel, as a matter of fact, bore a strong resemblance to the Handicapper General,
a woman named Diana Moon Glampers. "If I was Diana Moon Glampers," said
Hazel, "I'd have chimes on Sunday—just chimes. Kind of in honor of religion."

"I could think, if it was just chimes," said George.   17

"Well—maybe make 'em real loud," said Hazel. "I think I'd make a good 18
Handicapper General."

"Good as anybody else," said George.   19

"Who knows better'n I do what normal is?" said Hazel.   20

"Right," said George. He began to think glimmeringly about his abnormal 21
son who was now in jail, about Harrison, but a twenty-one-gun salute in his head
stopped that.

"Boy!" said Hazel, "that was a doozy, wasn't it?"   22

It was such a doozy that George was white and trembling, and tears stood on 23
the rims of his red eyes. Two of the eight ballerinas had collapsed to the studio
floor, were holding their temples.

"All of a sudden you look so tired," said Hazel. "Why don't you stretch out on 24
the sofa, so's you can rest your handicap bag on the pillows, honeybunch." She
was referring to the forty-seven pounds of birdshot in a canvas bag, which was
padlocked around George's neck. "Go on and rest the bag for a little while," she
said. "I don't care if you're not equal to me for a while."

George weighed the bag with his hands. "I don't mind it," he said. "I don't 25
notice it any more. It's just a part of me."

"You been so tired lately—kind of wore out," said Hazel. "If there was just 26 some way we could make a little hole in the bottom of the bag, and just take out a few of them lead balls. Just a few."

"Two years in prison and two thousand dollars fine for every ball I took out," 27 said George. "I don't call that a bargain."

"If you could just take a few out when you came home from work," said Hazel. 28 "I mean—you don't compete with anybody around here. You just set around."

"If I tried to get away with it," said George, "then other people'd get away with 29 it—and pretty soon we'd be right back to the dark ages again, with everybody competing against everybody else. You wouldn't like that, would you?"

"I'd hate it," said Hazel. 30

"There you are," said George. "The minute people start cheating on laws, what 31 do you think happens to society?"

If Hazel hadn't been able to come up with an answer to this question, George 32 couldn't have supplied one. A siren was going off in his head.

"Reckon it'd fall all apart," said Hazel. 33

"What would?" said George blankly. 34

"Society," said Hazel uncertainly. "Wasn't that what you just said?" 35

"Who knows?" said George. 36

The television program was suddenly interrupted for a news bulletin. It was- 37 n't clear at first as to what the bulletin was about, since the announcer, like all announcers, had a serious speech impediment. For about half a minute, and in a state of high excitement, the announcer tried to say, "Ladies and gentlemen—"

He finally gave up, handed the bulletin to a ballerina to read. 38

"That's all right—" Hazel said of the announcer, "he tried. That's the big 39 thing. He tried to do the best he could with what God gave him. He should get a nice raise for trying so hard."

"Ladies and gentlemen—" said the ballerina, reading the bulletin. She must 40 have been extraordinarily beautiful, because the mask she wore was hideous. And it was easy to see that she was the strongest and most graceful of all the dancers, for her handicap bags were as big as those worn by two-hundred-pound men.

And she had to apologize at once for her voice, which was a very unfair voice 41 for a woman to use. Her voice was a warm, luminous, timeless melody. "Excuse me—" she said, and she began again, making her voice absolutely uncompetitive.

"Harrison Bergeron, age fourteen," she said in a grackle squawk, "has just 42 escaped from jail, where he was held on suspicion of plotting to overthrow the government. He is a genius and an athlete, is under-handicapped, and should be regarded as extremely dangerous."

A police photograph of Harrison Bergeron was flashed on the screen—upside 43 down, then sideways, upside down again, then right side up. The picture showed the full length of Harrison against a background calibrated in feet and inches. He was exactly seven feet tall.

The rest of Harrison's appearance was Halloween and hardware. Nobody had 44 ever born heavier handicaps. He had outgrown hindrances faster than the H-G men could think them up. Instead of a little ear radio for a mental handicap, he wore a tremendous pair of earphones, and spectacles with thick wavy lenses. The spectacles were intended to make him not only half blind, but to give him whanging headaches besides.

Scrap metal was hung all over him. Ordinarily, there was a certain symmetry, 45 a military neatness to the handicaps issued to strong people, but Harrison looked like a walking junkyard. In the race of life, Harrison carried three hundred pounds.

And to offset his good looks, the H-G men required that he wear at all times 46 a red rubber ball for a nose, keep his eyebrows shaved off, and cover his even white teeth with black caps at snaggle-tooth random.

"If you see this boy," said the ballerina, "do not—I repeat, do not—try to 47 reason with him."

There was the shriek of a door being torn from its hinges. 48

Screams and barking cries of consternation came from the television set. The 49 photograph of Harrison Bergeron on the screen jumped again and again, as though dancing to the tune of an earthquake.

George Bergeron correctly identified the earthquake, and well he might 50 have—for many was the time his own home had danced to the same crashing tune. "My God—" said George, "that must be Harrison!"

The realization was blasted from his mind instantly by the sound of an auto- 51 mobile collision in his head.

When George could open his eyes again, the photograph of Harrison was 52 gone. A living, breathing Harrison filled the screen.

Clanking, clownish, and huge, Harrison stood in the center of the studio. The 53 knob of the uprooted studio door was still in his hand. Ballerinas, technicians, musicians, and announcers cowered on their knees before him, expecting to die.

"I am the Emperor!" cried Harrison. "Do you hear? I am the Emperor! Every- 54 body must do what I say at once!" He stamped his foot and the studio shook.

"Even as I stand here—" he bellowed, "crippled, hobbled, sickened—I am 55 a greater ruler than any man who ever lived! Now watch me become what I *can* become!"

Harrison tore the straps of his handicap harness like wet tissue paper, tore 56 straps guaranteed to support five thousand pounds.

Harrison's scrap-iron handicaps crashed to the floor. 57

Harrison thrust his thumbs under the bar of the padlock that secured his head 58 harness. The bar snapped like celery. Harrison smashed his headphones and spec- tacles against the wall.

He flung away his rubber-ball nose, revealed a man that would have awed 59 Thor, the god of thunder.

"I shall now select my Empress!" he said, looking down on the cowering 60 people. "Let the first woman who dares rise to her feet claim her mate and her throne!"

A moment passed, and then a ballerina arose, swaying like a willow. 61

Harrison plucked the mental handicap from her ear, snapped off her physical 62 handicaps with marvellous delicacy. Last of all, he removed her mask.

She was blindingly beautiful. 63

"Now—" said Harrison, taking her hand, "shall we show the people the 64 meaning of the word dance? Music!" he commanded.

The musicians scrambled back into their chairs, and Harrison stripped them 65 of their handicaps, too. "Play your best," he told them, "and I'll make you barons and dukes and earls."

The music began. It was normal at first—cheap, silly, false. But Harrison 66 snatched two musicians from their chairs, waved them like batons as he sang the music as he wanted it played. He slammed them back into their chairs.

The music began again and was much improved. 67

Harrison and his Empress merely listened to the music for a while—listened 68 gravely, as though synchronizing their heartbeats with it.

They shifted their weights to their toes. 69

Harrison placed his big hands on the girl's tiny waist, letting her sense the 70 weightlessness that would soon be hers.

And then, in an explosion of joy and grace, into the air they sprang! 71

Not only were the laws of the land abandoned, but the law of gravity and the 72 laws of motion as well.

They reeled, whirled, swiveled, flounced, capered, gamboled, and spun. 73

They leaped like deer on the moon. 74

The studio ceiling was thirty feet high, but each leap brought the dancers 75 nearer to it.

It became their obvious intention to kiss the ceiling. 76

They kissed it. 77

And then, neutralizing gravity with love and pure will, they remained 78 suspended in air inches below the ceiling, and they kissed each other for a long, long time.

It was then that Diana Moon Glampers, the Handicapper General, came into 79 the studio with a double-barreled ten-gauge shotgun. She fired twice, and the Emperor and the Empress were dead before they hit the floor.

Diana Moon Glampers loaded the gun again. She aimed it at the musicians 80 and told them they had ten seconds to get their handicaps back on.

It was then that the Bergerons' television tube burned out. 81

Hazel turned to comment about the blackout to George. But George had gone 82 out into the kitchen for a can of beer.

George came back in with the beer, paused while a handicap signal shook him 83 up. And then he sat down again. "You been crying?" he said to Hazel.

"Yup," she said. 84

"What about?" he said. 85

"I forget," she said. "Something real sad on television." 86

"What was it?" he said. 87

"It's all kind of mixed up in my mind," said Hazel. 88

"Forget sad things," said George. 89

"I always do," said Hazel. 90

"That's my girl," said George. He winced. There was the sound of a rivetting 91
gun in his head.

"Gee—I could tell that one was a doozy," said Hazel.   92

"You can say that again," said George.   93

"Gee—" said Hazel, "I could tell that one was a doozy."   94

ACTIVITIES FOR WRITING AND DISCUSSION

1. Annotate the story and respond to it using any of the "Ten Ideas for Writing" described in Chapter 3 and summarized on page 35.

2. "Harrison Bergeron" is a satire, i.e., "a literary work that attacks human vice or folly through irony, derision, or wit" *(American Heritage College Dictionary)*.

  a. What, specifically, is Vonnegut satirizing? (Several answers are possible.)

  b. What passages in the story strike you as particularly satiric? Focus on one or two such passages, and use them as examples to explain how Vonnegut's satire works. Share your analysis orally or in an essay.

3. The futuristic America Vonnegut depicts is dedicated to the eradication of excellence and the enforcement of mediocrity. How the country got that way is left for us to imagine. Suppose it is the year 2081, and you have been hired as the official national historian. In the **persona** of the historian write the history of the events that culminated in Harrison Bergeron's America. (Bear in mind that your version of events should be acceptable to those who hired you.)

4. Vonnegut's story is set in the distant future, but are there any aspects of the society he imagines—for instance, Hazel and George's inability to think for more than a few seconds at a time, or the need for outstanding people to apologize for their excellence (paragraph 41)—that could be read as **symbolic** of realities today? Explain.

FLANNERY O'CONNOR (1925–1964)

Everything That Rises Must Converge

Her doctor had told Julian's mother that she must lose twenty pounds on account 1
of her blood pressure, so on Wednesday nights Julian had to take her downtown
on the bus for a reducing class at the Y. The reducing class was designed for working girls over fifty, who weighed from 165 to 200 pounds. His mother was one of
the slimmer ones, but she said ladies did not tell their age or weight. She would
not ride the buses by herself at night since they had been integrated, and because

the reducing class was one of her few pleasures, necessary for her health, and *free,* she said Julian could at least put himself out to take her, considering all she did for him. Julian did not like to consider all she did for him, but every Wednesday night he braced himself and took her.

She was almost ready to go, standing before the hall mirror, putting on her 2 hat, while he, his hands behind him, appeared pinned to the door frame, waiting like Saint Sebastian for the arrows to begin piercing him. The hat was new and had cost her seven dollars and a half. She kept saying, "Maybe I shouldn't have paid that for it. No, I shouldn't have. I'll take it off and return it tomorrow. I shouldn't have bought it."

Julian raised his eyes to heaven. "Yes, you should have bought it," he said. "Put 3 it on and let's go." It was a hideous hat. A purple velvet flap came down on one side of it and stood up on the other; the rest of it was green and looked like a cushion with the stuffing out. He decided it was less comical than jaunty and pathetic. Everything that gave her pleasure was small and depressed him.

She lifted the hat one more time and set it down slowly on top of her head. 4 Two wings of gray hair protruded on either side of her florid face, but her eyes, sky-blue, were as innocent and untouched by experience as they must have been when she was ten. Were it not that she was a widow who had struggled fiercely to feed and clothe and put him through school and who was supporting him still, "until he got on his feet," she might have been a little girl that he had to take to town.

"It's all right, it's all right," he said. "Let's go." He opened the door himself and 5 started down the walk to get her going. The sky was a dying violet and the houses stood out darkly against it, bulbous liver-colored monstrosities of a uniform ugliness though no two were alike. Since this had been a fashionable neighborhood forty years ago, his mother persisted in thinking they did well to have an apartment in it. Each house had a narrow collar of dirt around it in which sat, usually, a grubby child. Julian walked with his hands in his pockets, his head down and thrust forward, and his eyes glazed with the determination to make himself completely numb during the time he would be sacrificed to her pleasure.

The door closed and he turned to find the dumpy figure, surmounted by 6 the atrocious hat, coming toward him. "Well," she said, "you only live once and paying a little more for it, I at least won't meet myself coming and going."

"Some day I'll start making money," Julian said gloomily—he knew he never 7 would—"and you can have one of those jokes whenever you take the fit." But first they would move. He visualized a place where the nearest neighbor would be three miles away on either side.

"I think you're doing fine," she said, drawing on her gloves. "You've only been 8 out of school a year. Rome wasn't built in a day."

She was one of the few members of the Y reducing class who arrived in hat and 9 gloves and who had a son who had been to college. "It takes time," she said, "and the world is in such a mess. This hat looked better on me than any of the others, though when she brought it out I said, 'Take that thing back. I wouldn't have it on my head,' and she said, 'Now wait till you see it on,' and when she put it on me,

I said, 'We-ull,' and she said, 'If you ask me, that hat does something for you and you do something for the hat, and besides,' she said, 'with that hat, you won't meet yourself coming and going.'"

Julian thought he could have stood his lot better if she had been selfish, if she 10 had been an old hag who drank and screamed at him. He walked along, saturated in depression, as if in the midst of his martyrdom he had lost his faith. Catching sight of his long, hopeless, irritated face, she stopped suddenly with a grief-stricken look, and pulled back on his arm. "Wait on me," she said. "I'm going back to the house and take this thing off and tomorrow I'm going to return it. I was out of my head. I can pay the gas bill with the seven-fifty."

He caught her arm in a vicious grip. "You are not going to take it back," he 11 said. "I like it."

"Well," she said, "I don't think I ought . . ." 12

"Shut up and enjoy it," he muttered, more depressed than ever. 13

"With the world in the mess it's in," she said, "it's a wonder we can enjoy 14 anything. I tell you, the bottom rail is on the top."

Julian sighed. 15

"Of course," she said, "if you know who you are, you can go anywhere." 16 She said this every time he took her to the reducing class. "Most of them in it are not our kind of people," she said, "but I can be gracious to anybody. I know who I am."

"They don't give a damn for your graciousness," Julian said savagely. "Know- 17 ing who you are is good for one generation only. You haven't the foggiest idea where you stand now or who you are."

She stopped and allowed her eyes to flash at him. "I most certainly do know 18 who I am," she said, "and if you don't know who you are, I'm ashamed of you."

"Oh hell," Julian said. 19

"Your great-grandfather was a former governor of this state," she said. "Your 20 grandfather was a prosperous landowner. Your grandmother was a Godhigh."

"Will you look around you," he said tensely, "and see where you are now?" 21 and he swept his arm jerkily out to indicate the neighborhood, which the growing darkness at least made less dingy.

"You remain what you are," she said. "Your great-grandfather had a plantation 22 and two hundred slaves."

"There are no more slaves," he said irritably. 23

"They were better off when they were," she said. He groaned to see that she 24 was off on that topic. She rolled onto it every few days like a train on an open track. He knew every stop, every junction, every swamp along the way, and knew the exact point at which her conclusion would roll majestically into the station: "It's ridiculous. It's simply not realistic. They should rise, yes, but on their own side of the fence."

"Let's skip it," Julian said. 25

"The ones I feel sorry for," she said, "are the ones that are half white. They're 26 tragic."

"Will you skip it?" 27

"Suppose we were half white. We would certainly have mixed feelings."   28

"I have mixed feelings now," he groaned.   29

"Well let's talk about something pleasant," she said. "I remember going to   30
Grandpa's when I was a little girl. Then the house had double stairways that went
up to what was really the second floor—all the cooking was done on the first. I
used to like to stay down in the kitchen on account of the way the walls smelled.
I would sit with my nose pressed against the plaster and take deep breaths. Actually the place belonged to the Godhighs but your grandfather Chestny paid the
mortgage and saved it for them. They were in reduced circumstances," she said,
"but reduced or not, they never forgot who they were."

"Doubtless that decayed mansion reminded them," Julian muttered. He never   31
spoke of it without contempt or thought of it without longing. He had seen it
once when he was a child before it had been sold. The double stairways had rotted and had been torn down. Negroes were living in it. But it remained in his
mind as his mother had known it. It appeared in his dreams regularly. He would
stand on the wide porch, listening to the rustle of oak leaves, then wander through
the high-ceilinged hall into the parlor that opened onto it and gaze at the worn
rugs and faded draperies. It occurred to him that it was he, not she, who would
have appreciated it. He preferred its threadbare elegance to anything he could
name and it was because of it that all the neighborhoods they had lived in had
been a torment to him—whereas she had hardly known the difference. She called
her insensitivity "being adjustable."

"And I remember the old darky who was my nurse, Caroline. There was no   32
better person in the world. I've always had a great respect for my colored friends,"
she said. "I'd do anything in the world for them and they'd . . ."

"Will you for God's sake get off that subject?" Julian said. When he got on a   33
bus by himself, he made it a point to sit down beside a Negro, in reparation as it
were for his mother's sins.

"You're mighty touchy tonight," she said. "Do you feel all right?"   34

"Yes I feel all right," he said. "Now lay off."   35

She pursed her lips. "Well, you certainly are in a vile humor," she observed. "I   36
just won't speak to you at all."

They had reached the bus stop. There was no bus in sight and Julian, his hands   37
still jammed in his pockets and his head thrust forward, scowled down the empty
street. The frustration of having to wait on the bus as well as ride on it began to
creep up his neck like a hot hand. The presence of his mother was borne in upon
him as she gave a pained sigh. He looked at her bleakly. She was holding herself
very erect under the preposterous hat, wearing it like a banner of her imaginary
dignity. There was in him an evil urge to break her spirit. He suddenly unloosened
his tie and pulled it off and put it in his pocket.

She stiffened. "Why must you look like *that* when you take me to town?" she   38
said. "Why must you deliberately embarrass me?"

"If you'll never learn where you are," he said, "you can at least learn where   39
I am."

"You look like a—thug," she said.   40

"Then I must be one," he murmured.   41

"I'll just go home," she said. "I will not bother you. If you can't do a little thing 42
like that for me . . ."

Rolling his eyes upward, he put his tie back on. "Restored to my class," he 43
muttered. He thrust his face toward her and hissed, "True culture is in the mind,
the *mind*," he said, and tapped his head, "the mind."

"It's in the heart," she said, "and in how you do things and how you do things 44
is because of who you *are*."

"Nobody in the damn bus cares who you are."   45

"I care who I am," she said icily.   46

The lighted bus appeared on top of the next hill and as it approached, they 47
moved out into the street to meet it. He put his hand under her elbow and hoisted
her up on the creaking step. She entered with a little smile, as if she were going
into a drawing room where everyone had been waiting for her. While he put in
the tokens, she sat down on one of the broad front seats for three which faced the
aisle. A thin woman with protruding teeth and long yellow hair was sitting on the
end of it. His mother moved up beside her and left room for Julian beside herself.
He sat down and looked at the floor across the aisle where a pair of thin feet in red
and white canvas sandals were planted.

His mother immediately began a general conversation meant to attract any- 48
one who felt like talking. "Can it get any hotter?" she said and removed from her
purse a folding fan, black with a Japanese scene on it, which she began to flutter
before her.

"I reckon it might could," the woman with the protruding teeth said, "but I 49
know for a fact my apartment couldn't get no hotter."

"It must get the afternoon sun," his mother said. She sat forward and looked 50
up and down the bus. It was half filled. Everybody was white. "I see we have the
bus to ourselves," she said. Julian cringed.

"For a change," said the woman across the aisle, the owner of the red and 51
white canvas sandals. "I come on one the other day and they were thick as fleas—
up front and all through."

"The world is in a mess everywhere," his mother said. "I don't know how 52
we've let it get in this fix."

"What gets my goat is all those boys from good families stealing automobile 53
tires," the woman with the protruding teeth said. "I told my boy, I said you may
not be rich but you been raised right and if I ever catch you in any such mess, they
can send you on to the reformatory. Be exactly where you belong."

"Training tells," his mother said. "Is your boy in high school?"   54

"Ninth grade," the woman said.   55

"My son just finished college last year. He wants to write but he's selling type- 56
writers until he gets started," his mother said.

The woman leaned forward and peered at Julian. He threw her such a malev- 57
olent look that she subsided against the seat. On the floor across the aisle there
was an abandoned newspaper. He got up and got it and opened it out in front of
him. His mother discreetly continued the conversation in a lower tone but the

woman across the aisle said in a loud voice, "Well that's nice. Selling typewriters is close to writing. He can go right from one to the other."

"I tell him," his mother said, "that Rome wasn't built in a day."   58

Behind the newspaper Julian was withdrawing into the inner compartment of   59
his mind where he spent most of his time. This was a kind of mental bubble in which he established himself when he could not bear to be part of what was going on around him. From it he could see out and judge but in it he was safe from any kind of penetration from without. It was the only place where he felt free of the general idiocy of his fellows. His mother had never entered it but from it he could see her with absolute clarity.

The old lady was clever enough and he thought that if she had started from   60
any of the right premises, more might have been expected of her. She lived according to the laws of her own fantasy world, outside of which he had never seen her set foot. The law of it was to sacrifice herself for him after she had first created the necessity to do so by making a mess of things. If he had permitted her sacrifices, it was only because her lack of foresight had made them necessary. All of her life had been a struggle to act like a Chestny without the Chestny goods, and to give him everything she thought a Chestny ought to have; but since, said she, it was fun to struggle, why complain? And when you had won, as she had won, what fun to look back on the hard times! He could not forgive her that she had enjoyed the struggle and that she thought *she* had won.

What she meant when she said she had won was that she had brought him up   61
successfully and had sent him to college and that he had turned out so well— good looking (her teeth had gone unfilled, so that his could be straightened), intelligent (he realized he was too intelligent to be a success), and with a future ahead of him (there was of course no future ahead of him). She excused his gloominess on the grounds that he was still growing up and his radical ideas on his lack of practical experience. She said he didn't yet know a thing about "life," that he hadn't even entered the real world—when already he was as disenchanted with it as a man of fifty.

The further irony of all this was that in spite of her, he had turned out so well.   62
In spite of going to only a third-rate college, he had, on his own initiative, come out with a first-rate education; in spite of growing up dominated by a small mind, he had ended up with a large one; in spite of all her foolish views, he was free of prejudice and unafraid to face facts. Most miraculous of all, instead of being blinded by love for her as she was for him, he had cut himself emotionally free of her and could see her with complete objectivity. He was not dominated by his mother.

The bus stopped with a sudden jerk and shook him from his meditation. A   63
woman from the back lurched forward with little steps and barely escaped falling in his newspaper as she righted herself. She got off and a large Negro got on. Julian kept his paper lowered to watch. It gave him a certain satisfaction to see injustice in daily operation. It confirmed his view that with a few exceptions there was no one worth knowing within a radius of three hundred miles. The Negro was well dressed and carried a briefcase. He looked round and then sat down on

the other end of the seat where the woman with the red and white canvas sandals was sitting. He immediately unfolded a newspaper and obscured himself behind it. Julian's mother's elbow at once prodded insistently into his ribs. "Now you see why I won't ride on these buses by myself," she whispered.

The woman with the red and white canvas sandals had risen at the same time   64
the Negro sat down and had gone further back in the bus and taken the seat of the woman who had got off. His mother leaned forward and cast her an approving look.

Julian rose, crossed the aisle, and sat down in the place of the woman with the   65
canvas sandals. From this position, he looked serenely across at his mother. Her face had turned an angry red. He stared at her, making his eyes the eyes of a stranger. He felt his tension suddenly lift as if he had openly declared war on her.

He would have liked to get in conversation with the Negro and to talk with   66
him about art or politics or any subject that would be above the comprehension of those around them, but the man remained entrenched behind his paper. He was either ignoring the change of seating or had never noticed it. There was no way for Julian to convey his sympathy.

His mother kept her eyes fixed reproachfully on his face. The woman with   67
the protruding teeth was looking at him avidly as if he were a type of monster new to her.

"Do you have a light?" he asked the Negro.   68

Without looking away from his paper, the man reached in his pocket and   69
handed him a packet of matches.

"Thanks," Julian said. For a moment he held the matches foolishly. A NO   70
SMOKING sign looked down upon him from over the door. This alone would not have deterred him; he had no cigarettes. He had quit smoking some months before because he could not afford it. "Sorry," he muttered and handed back the matches. The Negro lowered the paper and gave him an annoyed look. He took the matches and raised the paper again.

His mother continued to gaze at him but she did not take the advantage of his   71
momentary discomfort. Her eyes retained their battered look. Her face seemed to be unnaturally red, as if her blood pressure had risen. Julian allowed no glimmer of sympathy to show on his face. Having got the advantage, he wanted desperately to keep it and carry it through. He would have liked to teach her a lesson that would last her a while, but there seemed no way to continue the point. The Negro refused to come out from behind his paper.

Julian folded his arms and looked stolidly before him, facing her but as if he   72
did not see her, as if he had ceased to recognize her existence. He visualized a scene in which, the bus having reached their stop, he would remain in his seat and when she said, "Aren't you going to get off?" he would look at her as a stranger who had rashly addressed him. The corner they got off on was usually deserted, but it was well lighted and it would not hurt her to walk by herself the four blocks to the Y. He decided to wait until the time came and then decide whether or not he would let her get off by herself. He would have to be at the Y at ten to bring her

back, but he could leave her wondering if he was going to show up. There was no reason for her to think she could always depend on him.

He retired again into the high-ceilinged room sparsely settled with large 73 pieces of antique furniture. His soul expanded momentarily but then he became aware of his mother across from him and the vision shriveled. He studied her coldly. Her feet in little pumps dangled like a child's and did not quite reach the floor. She was training on him an exaggerated look of reproach. He felt completely detached from her. At that moment he could with pleasure have slapped her as he would have slapped a particularly obnoxious child in his charge.

He began to imagine various unlikely ways by which he could teach her a les- 74 son. He might make friends with some distinguished Negro professor or lawyer and bring him home to spend the evening. He would be entirely justified but her blood pressure would rise to 300. He could not push her to the extent of making her have a stroke, and moreover, he had never been successful at making any Negro friends. He had tried to strike up an acquaintance on the bus with some of the better types, with ones that looked like professors or ministers or lawyers. One morning he had sat down next to a distinguished-looking dark brown man who had answered his questions with a sonorous solemnity but who had turned out to be an undertaker. Another day he had sat down beside a cigar-smoking Negro with a diamond ring on his finger, but after a few stilted pleasantries, the Negro had rung the buzzer and risen, slipping two lottery tickets into Julian's hand as he climbed over him to leave.

He imagined his mother lying desperately ill and his being able to secure only 75 a Negro doctor for her. He toyed with that idea for a few minutes and dropped it for a momentary vision of himself participating as a sympathizer in a sit-in demonstration. This was possible but he did not linger with it. Instead, he approached the ultimate horror. He brought home a beautiful suspiciously Negroid woman. Prepare yourself, he said. There is nothing you can do about it. This is the woman I've chosen. She's intelligent, dignified, even good, and she's suffered and she hasn't thought it *fun*. Now persecute us, go ahead and persecute us. Drive her out of here, but remember, you're driving me too. His eyes were narrowed and through the indignation he had generated, he saw his mother across the aisle, purplefaced, shrunken to the dwarf-like proportions of her moral nature, sitting like a mummy beneath the ridiculous banner of her hat.

He was tilted out of his fantasy again as the bus stopped. The door opened 76 with a sucking hiss and out of the dark a large, gaily dressed, sullen-looking colored woman got on with a little boy. The child, who might have been four, had on a short plaid suit and a Tyrolean hat with a blue feather in it. Julian hoped that he would sit down beside him and that the woman would push in beside his mother. He could think of no better arrangement.

As she waited for her tokens, the woman was surveying the seating possibili- 77 ties—he hoped with the idea of sitting where she was least wanted. There was something familiar-looking about her but Julian could not place what it was. She was a giant of a woman. Her face was set not only to meet opposition but to seek it out. The downward tilt of her large lower lip was like a warning sign: DON'T

TAMPER WITH ME. Her bulging figure was encased in a green crepe dress and her feet overflowed in red shoes. She had on a hideous hat. A purple velvet flap came down on one side of it and stood up on the other; the rest of it was green and looked like a cushion with the stuffing out. She carried a mammoth red pocket-book that bulged throughout as if it were stuffed with rocks.

To Julian's disappointment, the little boy climbed up on the empty seat beside his mother. His mother lumped all children, black and white, into the common category, "cute," and she thought little Negroes were on the whole cuter than little white children. She smiled at the little boy as he climbed on the seat.   78

Meanwhile the woman was bearing down upon the empty seat beside Julian. To his annoyance, she squeezed herself into it. He saw his mother's face change as the woman settled herself next to him and he realized with satisfaction that this was more objectionable to her than it was to him. Her face seemed almost gray and there was a look of dull recognition in her eyes, as if suddenly she had sickened at some awful confrontation. Julian saw that it was because she and the woman had, in a sense, swapped sons. Though his mother would not realize the symbolic significance of this, she would feel it. His amusement showed plainly on his face.   79

The woman next to him muttered something unintelligible to herself. He was conscious of a kind of bristling next to him, muted growling like that of an angry cat. He could not see anything but the red pocketbook upright on the bulging green thighs. He visualized the woman as she had stood waiting for her tokens— the ponderous figure, rising from the red shoes upward over the solid hips, the mammoth bosom, the haughty face, to the green and purple hat.   80

His eyes widened.   81

The vision of the two hats, identical, broke upon him with the radiance of a brilliant sunrise. His face was suddenly lit with joy. He could not believe that Fate had thrust upon his mother such a lesson. He gave a loud chuckle so that she would look at him and see that he saw. She turned her eyes on him slowly. The blue in them seemed to have turned a bruised purple. For a moment he had an uncomfortable sense of her innocence, but it lasted only a second before principle rescued him. Justice entitled him to laugh. His grin hardened until it said to her as plainly as if he were saying aloud: Your punishment exactly fits your pettiness. This should teach you a permanent lesson.   82

Her eyes shifted to the woman. She seemed unable to bear looking at him and to find the woman preferable. He became conscious again of the bristling presence at his side. The woman was rumbling like a volcano about to become active. His mother's mouth began to twitch slightly at one corner. With a sinking heart, he saw incipient signs of recovery on her face and realized that this was going to strike her suddenly as funny and was going to be no lesson at all. She kept her eyes on the woman and an amused smile came over her face as if the woman were a monkey that had stolen her hat. The little Negro was looking up at her with large fascinated eyes. He had been trying to attract her attention for some time.   83

"Carver," the woman said suddenly. "Come heah!"   84

When he saw that the spotlight was on him at last, Carver drew his feet up and   85
turned himself toward Julian's mother and giggled.

"Carver!" the woman said. "You heah me? Come Heah!"   86

Carver slid down from the seat but remained squatting with his back against   87
the base of it, his head turned slowly around toward Julian's mother, who was
smiling at him. The woman reached a hand across the aisle and snatched him to
her. He righted himself and hung backwards on her knees, grinning at Julian's
mother. "Isn't he cute?" Julian's mother said to the woman with the protruding
teeth.

"I reckon he is," the woman said without conviction.   88

The Negress yanked him upright but he eased out of her grip and shot across   89
the aisle and scrambled, giggling wildly, onto the seat beside his love.

"I think he likes me," Julian's mother said, and smiled at the woman. It was the   90
smile she used when she was being particularly gracious to an inferior. Julian saw
everything lost. The lesson had rolled off her like rain on a roof.

The woman stood up and yanked the little boy off the seat as if she were   91
snatching him from contagion. Julian could feel the rage in her at having no
weapon like his mother's smile. She gave the child a sharp slap across his leg. He
howled once and then thrust his head into her stomach and kicked his feet against
her shins. "Behave," she said vehemently.

The bus stopped and the Negro who had been reading the newspaper got off.   92
The woman moved over and set the little boy down with a thump between herself and Julian. She held him firmly by the knee. In a moment he put his hands in
front of his face and peeped at Julian's mother through his fingers.

"I see yoooooooo!" she said and put her hand in front of her face and peeped   93
at him.

The woman slapped his hand down. "Quit yo' foolishness," she said, "before   94
I knock the living Jesus out of you!"

Julian was thankful that the next stop was theirs. He reached up and pulled the   95
cord. The woman reached up and pulled it at the same time. Oh my God, he
thought. He had the terrible intuition that when they got off the bus together, his
mother would open her purse and give the little boy a nickel. The gesture would
be as natural to her as breathing. The bus stopped and the woman got up and
lunged to the front, dragging the child, who wished to stay on, after her. Julian
and his mother got up and followed. As they neared the door, Julian tried to relieve her of her pocketbook.

"No," she murmured, "I want to give the little boy a nickel."   96

"No!" Julian hissed. "No!"   97

She smiled down at the child and opened her bag. The bus door opened and   98
the woman picked him up by the arm and descended with him, hanging at her
hip. Once in the street she set him down and shook him.

Julian's mother had to close her purse while she got down the bus step but as   99
soon as her feet were on the ground, she opened it again and began to rummage
inside. "I can't find but a penny," she whispered, "but it looks like a new one."

"Don't do it!" Julian said fiercely between his teeth. There was a streetlight on   100
the corner and she hurried to get under it so that she could better see into her
pocketbook. The woman was heading off rapidly down the street with the child
still hanging backward on her hand.

"Oh little boy!" Julian's mother called and took a few quick steps and caught   101
up with them just beyond the lamppost. "Here's a bright new penny for you," and
she held out the coin, which shone bronze in the dim light.

The huge woman turned and for a moment stood, her shoulders lifted and her   102
face frozen with frustrated rage, and stared at Julian's mother. Then all at once she
seemed to explode like a piece of machinery that had been given one ounce of
pressure too much. Julian saw the black fist swing out with the red pocketbook.
He shut his eyes and cringed as he heard the woman shout, "He don't take nobody's pennies!" When he opened his eyes, the woman was disappearing down
the street with the little boy staring wide-eyed over her shoulder. Julian's mother
was sitting on the sidewalk.

"I told you not to do that," Julian said angrily. "I told you not to do that!"   103

He stood over her for a minute, gritting his teeth. Her legs were stretched out   104
in front of her and her hat was on her lap. He squatted down and looked her in
the face. It was totally expressionless. "You got exactly what you deserved," he
said. "Now get up."

He picked up her pocketbook and put what had fallen out back in it. He   105
picked the hat up off her lap. The penny caught his eye on the sidewalk and he
picked that up and let it drop before her eyes into the purse. Then he stood up and
leaned over and held his hands out to pull her up. She remained immobile. He
sighed. Rising above them on either side were black apartment buildings, marked
with irregular rectangles of light. At the end of the block a man came out of a door
and walked off in the opposite direction. "All right," he said, "suppose somebody
happens by and wants to know why you're sitting on the sidewalk?"

She took the hand and, breathing hard, pulled heavily up on it and then stood   106
for a moment, swaying slightly as if the spots of light in the darkness were circling
around her. Her eyes, shadowed and confused, finally settled on his face. He did
not try to conceal his irritation. "I hope this teaches you a lesson," he said. She
leaned forward and her eyes raked his face. She seemed trying to determine his
identity. Then, as if she found nothing familiar about him, she started off with a
headlong movement in the wrong direction.

"Aren't you going to the Y?" he asked.   107

"Home," she muttered.   108

"Well, are we walking?"   109

For answer she kept going. Julian followed along, his hands behind him. He   110
saw no reason to let the lesson she had had go without backing it up with an explanation of its meaning. She might as well be made to understand what had happened to her. "Don't think that was just an uppity Negro woman," he said. "That
was the whole colored race which will no longer take your condescending pennies. That was your black double. She can wear the same hat as you, and to be
sure," he added gratuitously (because he thought it was funny), "it looked better
on her than it did on you. What all this means," he said, "is that the old world is
gone. The old manners are obsolete and your graciousness is not worth a damn."

He thought bitterly of the house that had been lost for him. "You aren't who you think you are," he said.

She continued to plow ahead, paying no attention to him. Her hair had come 111 undone on one side. She dropped her pocketbook and took no notice. He stopped and picked it up and handed it to her but she did not take it.

"You needn't act as if the world had come to an end," he said, "because it has- 112 n't. From now on you've got to live in a new world and face a few realities for a change. Buck up," he said, "it won't kill you."

She was breathing fast.   113

"Let's wait on the bus," he said.   114

"Home," she said thickly.   115

"I hate to see you behave like this," he said. "Just like a child. I should be able to 116 expect more of you." He decided to stop where he was and make her stop and wait for a bus. "I'm not going any farther," he said, stopping. "We're going on the bus."

She continued to go on as if she had not heard him. He took a few steps and 117 caught her arm and stopped her. He looked into her face and caught his breath. He was looking into a face he had never seen before. "Tell Grandpa to come get me," she said.

He stared, stricken.   118

"Tell Caroline to come get me," she said.   119

Stunned, he let her go and she lurched forward again, walking as if one leg 120 were shorter than the other. A tide of darkness seemed to be sweeping her from him. "Mother!" he cried. "Darling, sweetheart, wait!" Crumpling, she fell to the pavement. He dashed forward and fell at her side, crying, "Mamma, Mamma!" He turned her over. Her face was fiercely distorted. One eye, large and staring, moved slightly to the left as if it had become unmoored. The other remained fixed on him, raked his face again, found nothing, and closed.

"Wait here, wait here!" he cried and jumped up and began to run for help to- 121 ward a cluster of lights he saw in the distance ahead of him. "Help, help!" he shouted, but his voice was thin, scarcely a thread of sound. The lights drifted farther away the faster he ran and his feet moved numbly as if they carried him nowhere. The tide of darkness seemed to sweep him back to her, postponing from moment to moment his entry into the world of guilt and sorrow.

ACTIVITIES FOR WRITING AND DISCUSSION

1. Working alone or with a group, make a list of conflicts—personal, social, moral—that make this story suspenseful. Identify places where your interest was greatest and why.

2. Pick one specific *moment* or *scene* in the story that is particularly intense or powerful for you. Annotate or reannotate that passage, emphasizing aspects of the moment or scene that make it tense. Then:
   a. Share your scene and annotations with a small group.
   b. Write an analysis of the moment or scene you have chosen and explain how it reinforces the impact of the story as a whole.

3. Describe the **point of view** of the story. Then return to the moment or scene you examined in Activity #2 and rewrite it from the **first-person** point of view of either Julian, Julian's mother, or some other character in the story. What is lost, gained, or changed by using the alternative point of view?

4. Julian believes that his mother "lived according to the laws of her own fantasy world. . . ." Could the same be said of Julian himself? Assuming the point of view of some detached observer (e.g., one of Julian's college counselors or professors, his boss at the typewriter business) compose an informal letter of evaluation that describes what Julian's "fantasy world" is.

5. Imagine you are Julian.
   a. What thoughts and feelings go through your mind the moment after your mother collapses on the pavement at the end of the story? Write out the rapid flow of thoughts exactly as they occur to you.
   b. Writing from Julian's point of view or some other, draft a sequel to the story. What becomes of Julian? Is he changed by the events in the story? If not, why not? If so, how—and for better or for worse?

6. O'Connor once described her stories as "parables." A parable is "a simple story illustrating a moral or religious lesson" *(American Heritage College Dictionary)*. Is the term applicable to "Everything That Rises Must Converge," and if so, what "moral or religious lesson" does the story illustrate?

7. O'Connor's stories often end with an act of violence. Is the violence gratuitous? Consulting O'Connor's letters, interviews, and other nonfiction prose (a good place to start is with her collection *Mystery and Manners*), ascertain her views on the role of violence in her fiction and assess its impact and significance in "Everything That Rises Must Converge."

Alice Walker (b. 1944)

Nineteen Fifty-five

1955

The car is a brandnew red Thunderbird convertible, and it's passed the house 1
more than once. It slows down real slow now, and stops at the curb. An older gentleman dressed like a Baptist deacon gets out on the side near the house, and a young fellow who looks about sixteen gets out on the driver's side. They are white, and I wonder what in the world they doing in this neighborhood.

Well, I say to J. T., put your shirt on, anyway, and let me clean these glasses 2
offa the table.

We had been watching the ballgame on TV. I wasn't actually watching, I was 3
sort of daydreaming, with my foots up in J.T.'s lap.

I seen 'em coming on up the walk, brisk, like they coming to sell something, 4
and then they rung the bell, and J. T. declined to put on a shirt but instead disappeared into the bedroom where the other television is. I turned down the one in
the living room; I figured I'd be rid of these two double quick and J. T. could come
back out again.

Are you Gracie Mae Still? asked the old guy, when I opened the door and put 5
my hand on the lock inside the screen

And I don't need to buy a thing, said I.   6

What makes you think we're sellin'? he asks, in that hearty Southern way that 7
makes my eyeballs ache.

Well, one way or another and they're inside the house and the first thing the 8
young fellow does is raise the TV a couple of decibels. He's about five feet nine,
sort of womanish looking, with real dark white skin and a red pouting mouth. His
hair is black and curly and he looks like a Loosianna creole.

About one of your songs, says the deacon. He is maybe sixty, with white hair and 9
beard, white silk shirt, black linen suit, black tie and black shoes. His cold grey
eyes look like they're sweating.

One of my songs?   10

Traynor here just *loves* your songs. Don't you, Traynor? He nudges Traynor 11
with his elbow. Traynor blinks, says something I can't catch in a pitch I don't
register.

The boy learned to sing and dance livin' round you people out in the country. 12
Practically cut his teeth on you.

Traynor looks up at me and bites his thumbnail.   13

I laugh.   14

Well, one way or another they leave with my agreement that they can record 15
one of my songs. The deacon writes me a check for five hundred dollars, the boy
grunts his awareness of the transaction, and I am laughing all over myself by the
time I rejoin J. T.

Just as I am snuggling down beside him though I hear the front door bell go- 16
ing off again.

Forgit his hat? asks J. T.   17

I hope not, I say.   18

The deacon stands there leaning on the door frame and once again I'm think- 19
ing of those sweaty-looking eyeballs of his. I wonder if sweat makes your eyeballs
pink because his are sure pink. Pink and gray and it strikes me that nobody I'd
care to know is behind them.

I forgot one little thing, he says pleasantly. I forgot to tell you Traynor and I 20
would like to buy up all of those records you made of the song. I tell you we sure
do love it.

Well, love it or not, I'm not so stupid as to let them do that without making 21
'em pay. So I says, Well, that's gonna cost you. Because, really, that song never did
sell all that good, so I was glad they was going to buy it up. But on the other hand,
them two listening to my song by themselves, and nobody else getting to hear me
sing it, give me a pause.

Well, one way or another the deacon showed me where I would come out ahead 22
on any deal he had proposed so far. Didn't I give you five hundred dollars? he asked.
What white man—and don't even need to mention colored—would give you
more? We buy up all your records of that particular song: first, you git royalties. Let
me ask you, how much you sell that song for in the first place? Fifty dollars? A hundred, I say. And no royalties from it yet, right? Right. Well, when we buy up all of
them records you gonna git royalties. And that's gonna make all them race record
shops sit up and take notice of Gracie Mae Still. And they gonna push all them other
records of yourn they got. And you no doubt will become one of the big name colored recording artists. And then we can offer you another five hundred dollars for
letting us do all this for you. And by God you'll be sittin' pretty! You can go out and
buy you the kind of outfit a star should have. Plenty sequins and yards of red satin.

I had done unlocked the screen when I saw I could get some more money out 23
of him. Now I held it wide open while he squeezed through the opening between
me and the door. He whipped out another piece of paper and I signed it.

He sort of trotted out to the car and slid in beside Traynor, whose head was 24
back against the seat. They swung around in a u-turn in front of the house and
then they was gone.

J. T. was putting his shirt on when I got back to the bedroom. Yankees beat the 25
Orioles 10–6, he said. I believe I'll drive out to Paschal's pond and go fishing.
Wanta go?

While I was putting on my pants J. T. was holding the two checks.   26

I'm real proud of a woman that can make cash money without leavin' home, 27
he said. And I said *Umph*. Because we met on the road with me singing in first one
little low-life jook after another, making ten dollars a night for myself if I was
lucky, and sometimes bringin' home nothing but my life. And J. T. just loved
them times. The way I was fast and flashy and always on the go from one town to
another. He loved the way my singin' made the dirt farmers cry like babies and
the womens shout Honey, hush! But that's mens. They loves any style to which
you can get 'em accustomed.

1956

My little grandbaby called me one night on the phone: Little Mama, Little Mama, 28
there's a white man on the television singing one of your songs! Turn on channel 5.

Lord, if it wasn't Traynor. Still looking half asleep from the neck up, but kind 29
of awake in a nasty way from the waist down. He wasn't doing too bad with my
song either, but it wasn't just the song the people in the audience was screeching
and screaming over, it was that nasty little jerk he was doing from the waist down.

Well, Lord have mercy, I said, listening to him. If I'da closed my eyes, it could 30
have been me. He had followed every turning of my voice, side streets, avenues,
red lights, train crossings and all. It give me a chill.

Everywhere I went I heard Traynor singing my song, and all the little white 31
girls just eating it up. I never had so many ponytails switched across my line of vision in my life. They was so *proud.* He was a *genius.*

Well, all that year I was trying to lose weight anyway and that and high blood 32
pressure and sugar kept me pretty well occupied. Traynor had made a smash from
a song of mine, I still had seven hundred dollars of the original one thousand dollars in the bank, and I felt if I could just bring my weight down, life would be sweet.

1957

I lost ten pounds in 1956. That's what I give myself for Christmas. And J. T. and 33
me and the children and their friends and grandkids of all description had just
finished dinner—over which I had put on nine and a half of my lost ten—when
who should appear at the front door but Traynor. Little Mama, Little Mama! It's
that white man who sings —— —— ——. The children didn't call it my song
anymore. Nobody did. It was funny how that happened. Traynor and the deacon had bought up all my records, true, but on his record he had put "written by
Gracie Mae Still." But that was just another name on the label, like "produced
by Apex Records."

On the TV he was inclined to dress like the deacon told him. But now he 34
looked presentable.

Merry Christmas, said he.   35

And same to you, Son.   36

I don't know why I called him Son. Well, one way or another they're all our 37
sons. The only requirement is that they be younger than us. But then again,
Traynor seemed to be aging by the minute.

You looks tired, I said. Come on in and have a glass of Christmas cheer.   38

J. T. ain't never in his life been able to act decent to a white man he wasn't 39
working for, but he poured Traynor a glass of bourbon and water, then he took
all the children and grandkids and friends and whatnot out to the den. After while
I heard Traynor's voice singing the song, coming from the stereo console. It was
just the kind of Christmas present my kids would consider cute.

I looked at Traynor, complicit. But he looked like it was the last thing in the 40
world he wanted to hear. His head was pitched forward over his lap, his hands
holding his glass and his elbows on his knees.

I done sung that song seem like a million times this year, he said. I sung it on 41
the Grand Ole Opry, I sung it on the Ed Sullivan show. I sung it on Mike Douglas,
I sung it at the Cotton Bowl, the Orange Bowl. I sung it at Festivals. I sung it
at Fairs. I sung it overseas in Rome, Italy, and once in a submarine *underseas.*
I've sung it and sung it, and I'm making forty thousand dollars a day offa it, and
you know what, I don't have the faintest notion what that song means.

Whatchumean, what do it mean? It mean what it says. All I could think was: 42
These suckers is making forty thousand a *day* offa my song and now they gonna
come back and try to swindle me out of the original thousand.

It's just a song, I said. Cagey. When you fool around with a lot of no count   43
mens you sing a bunch of 'em. I shrugged.

Oh, he said. Well. He started brightening up. I just come by to tell you I think   44
you are a great singer.

He didn't blush, saying that. Just said it straight out.   45

And I brought you a little Christmas present too. Now you take this little box   46
and you hold it until I drive off. Then you take it outside under that first streetlight back up the street aways in front of that green house. Then you open the box
and see . . . Well, just *see*.

What had come over this boy, I wondered, holding the box. I looked out the   47
window in time to see another white man come up and get in the car with him
and then two more cars full of white mens start out behind him. They was all in
long black cars that looked like a funeral procession.

Little Mama, Little Mama, what is it? One of my grandkids come running up   48
and started pulling at the box. It was wrapped in gay Christmas paper — the thick,
rich kind that it's hard to picture folks making just to throw away.

J. T. and the rest of the crowd followed me out the house, up the street to the   49
streetlight and in front of the green house. Nothing was there but somebody's
gold-grilled white Cadillac. Brandnew and most distracting. We got to looking at
it so till I almost forgot the little box in my hand. While the others were busy making 'miration I carefully took off the paper and ribbon and folded them up and
put them in my pants pocket. What should I see but a pair of genuine solid gold
caddy keys.

Dangling the keys in front of everybody's nose, I unlocked the caddy, motioned   50
for J. T. to git in on the other side, and us didn't come back home for two days.

1960

Well, the boy was sure nuff famous by now. He was still a mite shy of twenty but   51
already they was calling him the Emperor of Rock and Roll.

Then what should happen but the draft.   52

Well, says J. T. There goes all this Emperor of Rock and Roll business.   53

But even in the army the womens was on him like white on rice. We watched   54
it on the News.

Dear Gracie Mae [he wrote from Germany],   55

How you? Fine I hope as this leaves me doing real well. Before I come in the army   56
I was gaining a lot of weight and gitting jittery from making all them dumb movies.
But now I exercise and eat right and get plenty of rest. I'm more awake than I been
in ten years.

I wonder if you are writing any more songs? 57

Sincerely,
Traynor

I wrote him back:

Dear Son, 58
    We is all fine in the Lord's good grace and hope this finds you the same. J. T. and 59 *me be out all times of the day and night in that car you give me—which you know you didn't have to do. Oh, and I do appreciate the mink and the new self-cleaning oven. But if you send anymore stuff to eat from Germany I'm going to have to open up a store in the neighborhood just to get rid of it. Really, we have more than enough of everything. The Lord is good to us and we don't know Want.*
    Glad to hear you is well and gitting your right rest. There ain't nothing like exer- 60 *cising to help that along. J. T. and me work some part of every day that we don't go fishing in the garden.*
    Well, so long Soldier. 61

Sincerely, 62
Gracie Mae

He wrote: 63

Dear Gracie Mae, 64
    I hope you and J. T. like that automatic power tiller I had one of the stores back 65 *home send you. I went through a mountain of catalogs looking for it—I wanted something that even a woman could use.*
    I've been thinking about writing some songs of my own but every time I finish one 66 *it don't seem to be about nothing I've actually lived myself. My agent keeps sending me other people's songs but they just sound mooney. I can hardly git through 'em without gagging.*
    Everybody still loves that song of yours. They ask me all the time what do I think 67 *it means, really. I mean, they want to know just what I want to know. Where out of your life did it come from?*

Sincerely,
Traynor

1968

I didn't see the boy for seven years. No. Eight. Because just about everybody was 68 dead when I saw him again. Malcolm X, King, the president and his brother, and even J. T. J. T. died of a head cold. It just settled in his head like a block of ice, he said, and nothing we did moved it until one day he just leaned out the bed and died.

His good friend Horace helped me put him away, and then about a year later   69
Horace and me started going together. We was sitting out on the front porch
swing one summer night, dusk-dark, and I saw this great procession of lights
winding to a stop.

Holy Toledo! said Horace. (He's got a real sexy voice like Ray Charles.) Look   70
at it. He meant the long line of flashy cars and the white men in white summer
suits jumping out on the drivers' sides and standing at attention. With wings they
could pass for angels, with hoods they could be the Klan.

Traynor comes waddling up the walk.   71

And suddenly I know what it is he could pass for. An Arab like the ones you   72
see in storybooks. Plump and soft and with never a care about weight. Because
with so much money, who cares? Traynor is almost dressed like someone from a
storybook too. He has on, I swear, about ten necklaces. Two sets of bracelets on
his arms, at least one ring on every finger, and some kind of shining buckles on
his shoes, so that when he walks you get quite a few twinkling lights.

Gracie Mae, he says, coming up to give me a hug. J. T.   73

I explain that J. T. passed. That this is Horace.   74

Horace, he says, puzzled but polite, sort of rocking back on his heels, Horace.   75

That's it for Horace. He goes in the house and don't come back.   76

Looks like you and me is gained a few, I say.   77

He laughs. The first time I ever heard him laugh. It don't sound much like a   78
laugh and I can't swear that it's better than no laugh a'tall.

He's gitting fat for sure, but he's still slim compared to me. I'll never see three   79
hundred pounds again and I've just about said (excuse me) fuck it. I got to thinking about it one day an' I thought: aside from the fact that they say it's unhealthy,
my fat ain't never been no trouble. Mens always have loved me. My kids ain't
never complained. Plus they's fat. And fat like I is I looks distinguished. You see
me coming and know somebody's *there.*

Gracie Mae, he says, I've come with a personal invitation to you to my house   80
tomorrow for dinner. He laughed. What did it sound like? I couldn't place it. See
them men out there? he asked me. I'm sick and tired of eating with them. They
don't never have nothing to talk about. That's why I eat so much. But if you come
to dinner tomorrow we can talk about the old days. You can tell me about that
farm I bought you.

I sold it, I said.   81

You did?   82

Yeah, I said, I did. Just cause I said I liked to exercise by working in a garden   83
didn't mean I wanted five hundred acres! Anyhow, I'm a city girl now. Raised in
the country it's true. Dirt poor—the whole bit—but that's all behind me now.

Oh well, he said, I didn't mean to offend you.   84

We sat a few minutes listening to the crickets.   85

Then he said: You wrote that song while you was still on the farm, didn't you,   86
or was it right after you left?

You had somebody spying on me? I asked.   87

You and Bessie Smith got into a fight over it once, he said.   88

You *is* been spying on me!   89

But I don't know what the fight was about, he said. Just like I don't know what   90
happened to your second husband. Your first one died in the Texas electric chair.
Did you know that? Your third one beat you up, stole your touring costumes and
your car and retired with a chorine to Tuskegee. He laughed. He's still there.

I had been mad, but suddenly I calmed down. Traynor was talking very   91
dreamily. It was dark but seems like I could tell his eyes weren't right. It was like
some*thing* was sitting there talking to me but not necessarily with a person behind it.

You gave up on marrying and seem happier for it. He laughed again. I married   92
but it never went like it was supposed to. I never could squeeze any of my own life
either into it or out of it. It was like singing somebody else's record. I copied the
way it was sposed to be *exactly* but I never had a clue what marriage meant.

I bought her a diamond ring big as your fist. I bought her clothes. I built her   93
a mansion. But right away she didn't want the boys to stay there. Said they smoked
up the bottom floor. Hell, there were *five* floors.

No need to grieve, I said. No need to. Plenty more where she come from.   94

He perked up. That's part of what that song means, ain't it? No need to grieve.   95
Whatever it is, there's plenty more down the line.

I never really believed that way back when I wrote that song, I said. It was all   96
bluffing then. The trick is to live long enough to put your young bluffs to use.
Now if I was to sing that song today I'd tear it up. 'Cause I done lived long enough
to know it's *true.* Them words could hold me up.

I ain't lived that long, he said.   97

Look like you on your way, I said. I don't know why, but the boy seemed to   98
need some encouraging. And I don't know, seem like one way or another you talk
to rich white folks and you end up reassuring *them.* But what the hell, by now I
feel something for the boy. I wouldn't be in his bed all alone in the middle of the
night for nothing. Couldn't be nothing worse than being famous the world over
for something you don't even understand. That's what I tried to tell Bessie. She
wanted that same song. Overheard me practicing it one day, said, with her hands
on her hips: Gracie Mae, I'ma sing your song tonight. I *likes* it.

Your lips be too swole to sing, I said. She was mean and she was strong, but I   99
trounced her.

Ain't you famous enough with your own stuff? I said. Leave mine alone. Later   100
on, she thanked me. By then she was Miss Bessie Smith to the World, and I was
still Miss Gracie Mae Nobody from Notasulga.

———————

The next day all these limousines arrived to pick me up. Five cars and twelve   101
bodyguards. Horace picked that morning to start painting the kitchen.

Don't paint the kitchen, fool, I said. The only reason that dumb boy of ours is   102
going to show me his mansion is because he intends to present us with a new house.

What you gonna do with it? he asked me, standing there in his shirtsleeves   103
stirring the paint.

Sell it. Give it to the children. Live in it on weekends. It don't matter what I do.   104
He sure don't care.

Horace just stood there shaking his head. Mama you sure looks *good,* he says.   105
Wake me up when you git back.

Fool, I say, and pat my wig in front of the mirror.   106

The boy's house is something else. First you come to this mountain, and then you   107
commence to drive and drive up this road that's lined with magnolias. Do magnolias grow on mountains? I was wondering. And you come to lakes and you
come to ponds and you come to deer and you come up on some sheep. And I
figure these two is sposed to represent England and Wales. Or something out of
Europe. And you just keep on coming to stuff. And it's all pretty. Only the man
driving my car don't look at nothing but the road. Fool. And then *finally,* after all
this time, you begin to go up the driveway. And there's more magnolias—only
they're not in such good shape. It's sort of cool up this high and I don't think
they're gonna make it. And then I see this building that looks like if it had a name
it would be The Tara Hotel. Columns and steps and outdoor chandeliers and
rocking chairs. Rocking chairs? Well, and there's the boy on the steps dressed in a
dark green satin jacket like you see folks wearing on TV late at night, and he looks
sort of like a fat dracula with all that house rising behind him, and standing beside him there's this little white vision of loveliness that he introduces as his wife.

He's nervous when he introduces us and he says to her: This is Gracie Mae   108
Still, I want you to know me. I mean . . . and she gives him a look that would fry
meat.

Won't you come in, Gracie Mae, she says, and that's the last I see of her.   109

He fishes around for something to say or do and decides to escort me to the   110
kitchen. We go through the entry and the parlor and the breakfast room and the
dining room and the servants' passage and finally get there. The first thing I notice is that, altogether, there are five stoves. He looks about to introduce me to
one.

Wait a minute, I say. Kitchens don't do nothing for me. Let's go sit on the front   111
porch.

Well, we hike back and we sit in the rocking chairs rocking until dinner.   112

Gracie Mae, he says down the table, taking a piece of fried chicken from the   113
woman standing over him, I got a little surprise for you.

It's a house, ain't it? I ask, spearing a chitlin.   114

You're getting *spoiled,* he says. And the way he says *spoiled* sounds funny. He   115
slurs it. It sounds like his tongue is too thick for his mouth. Just that quick he's
finished the chicken and is now eating chitlins *and* a pork chop. *Me* spoiled, I'm
thinking.

I already got a house. Horace is right this minute painting the kitchen. I   116
bought that house. My kids feel comfortable in that house.

But this one I bought you is just like mine. Only a little smaller. 117

I still don't need no house. And anyway who would clean it? 118

He looks surprised. 119

Really, I think, some peoples advance *so* slowly. 120

I hadn't thought of that. But what the hell, I'll get you somebody to live in. 121

I don't want other folks living 'round me. Makes me nervous. 122

You *don't?* It *do?* 123

What I want to wake up and see folks I don't even know for? 124

He just sits there downtable staring at me. Some of that feeling is in the song, 125 ain't it? Not the words, the *feeling*. What I want to wake up and see folks I don't even know for? But I see twenty folks a day I don't even know, including my wife.

This food wouldn't be bad to wake up to though, I said. The boy had found 126 the genius of corn bread.

He looked at me real hard. He laughed. Short. They want what you got but they 127 don't want you. They want what I got only it ain't mine. That's what makes 'em so hungry for me when I sing. They getting the flavor of something but they ain't getting the thing itself. They like a pack of hound dogs trying to gobble up a scent.

Your talking 'bout your fans? 128

Right. Right. He says. 129

Don't worry 'bout your fans, I say. They don't know their asses from a hole in 130 the ground. I doubt there's a honest one in the bunch.

That's the point. Dammit, that's the point! He hits the table with his fist. It's so 131 solid it don't even quiver. You need a honest audience! You can't have folks that's just gonna lie right back to you.

Yeah, I say, it was small compared to yours, but I had one. It would have been 132 worth my life to try to sing 'em somebody else's stuff that I didn't know nothing about.

He must have pressed a buzzer under the table. One of his flunkies zombies up. 133

Git Johnny Carson, he says. 134

On the phone? asks the zombie. 135

On the phone, says Traynor, what you think I mean, git him offa the front 136 porch? Move your ass.

So two weeks later we's on the Johnny Carson show. 137

Traynor is all corseted down nice and looks a little bit fat but mostly good. And 138 all the women that grew up on him and my song squeal and squeal. Traynor says: The lady who wrote my first hit record is here with us tonight, and she's agreed to sing it for all of us, just like she sung it forty-five years ago. Ladies and Gentlemen, the great Gracie Mae Still!

Well, I had tried to lose a couple of pounds my own self, but failing that I had 139 me a very big dress made. So I sort of rolls over next to Traynor, who is dwarfted by me, so that when he puts his arm around back of me to try to hug me it looks funny to the audience and they laugh.

I can see this pisses him off. But I smile out there at 'em. Imagine squealing 140
for twenty years and not knowing why you're squealing? No more sense of endings and beginnings than hogs.

It don't matter, Son, I say. Don't fret none over me.   141

I commence to sing. And I sound——wonderful. Being able to sing good 142
ain't all about having a good singing voice a'tall. A good singing voice helps. But when you come up in the Hard Shell Baptist church like I did you understand early that the fellow that sings is the singer. Them that waits for programs and arrangements and letters from home is just good voices occupying body space.

So there I am singing my own song, my own way. And I give it all I got and en- 143
joy every minute of it. When I finish Traynor is standing up clapping and clapping and beaming at first me and then the audience like I'm his mama for true. The audience claps politely for about two seconds.

Traynor looks disgusted.   144

He comes over and tries to hug me again. The audience laughs.   145

Johnny Carson looks at us like we both weird.   146

Traynor is mad as hell. He's supposed to sing something called a love ballad. 147
But instead he takes the mike, turns to me and says: Now see if my imitation still holds up. He goes into the same song, *our* song, I think, looking out at his flaky audience. And he sings it just the way he always did. My voice, my tone, my inflection, everything. But he forgets a couple of lines. Even before he's finished the matronly squeals begin.

He sits down next to me looking whipped.   148

It don't matter, Son, I say, patting his hand. You don't even know those people. 149
Try to make the people you know happy.

Is that in the song? he asks.   150

Maybe, I say.   151

1977

For a few years I hear from him, then nothing. But trying to lose weight takes all 152
the attention I got to spare. I finally faced up to the fact that my fat is the hurt I don't admit, not even to myself, and that I been trying to bury it from the day I was born. But also when you git real old, to tell the truth, it ain't as pleasant. It gits lumpy and slack. Yuck. So one day I said to Horace, I'ma git this shit offa me.

And he fell in with the program like he always try to do and Lord such a pro- 153
cession of salads and cottage cheese and fruit juice!

One night I dreamed Traynor had split up with his fifteenth wife. He said: *You* 154
meet 'em for no reason. You date 'em for no reason. You marry 'em for no reason. I do it all but I swear it's just like somebody else doing it. I feel like I can't remember Life.

The boy's in trouble, I said to Horace.   155

You've always said that, he said.   156

I have?   157

Yeah. You always said he looked asleep. You can't sleep through life if you 158 wants to live it.

You not such a fool after all, I said, pushing myself up with my cane and hob- 159 bling over to where he was. Let me sit down on your lap, I said, while this salad I ate takes effect.

In the morning we heard Traynor was dead. Some said fat, some said heart, 160 some said alcohol, some said drugs. One of the children called from Detroit. Them dumb fans of his is on a crying rampage, she said. You just ought to turn on the t.v.

But I didn't want to see 'em. They was crying and crying and didn't even know 161 what they was crying for. One day this is going to be a pitiful country, I thought.

ACTIVITIES FOR WRITING AND DISCUSSION

1. Respond to the story using the "Four-Step Process for Writing from Reading" described in Chapter 2.

2. What effects does Walker achieve by narrating the story from the **first-person point of view** of Gracie Mae? What advantages, if any, does her choice of first-person have over a **third-person** narration?

3. The story's events take place over a span of twenty-two years. What purposes are served by dividing the story up according to years? If you wish, compose a first-person narrative of your own that is similarly structured, i.e., by years.

4. Events in the story are a weave of the personal and the cultural. For instance, in 1956 Gracie Mae is trying to lose weight (personal) and Traynor makes a smash hit out of her song (cultural). Write a story of your own that portrays a person embedded in some culture, time, or movement of your own choosing.

Poems

SHAMS-UD-DIN MUHAMMAD (HAFIZ) (c. 1320–1389)

Elephant Wondering

A seed
Has sprouted beneath a golden leaf
In a dark forest.

This seed is seriously contemplating,
Seriously wondering about   5

The moseying habits
Of the Elephant.

Why?

Because
In this lucid, wine-drenched tale   10
The Elephant is really—
God,

Who has His big foot upon us,
Upon the golden leaf under which lies
This sprouting   15
Universe

Wherein
We are all a little concerned
And

Nervous.   20

For Three Days

Not many teachers in this world
Can give you as much enlightenment
In one year

As sitting all alone, for three days,
In your closet   5
Would
Do.

That means not leaving.
Better get a friend to help with
A few sandwiches   10
And
The chamber
Pot.

And no reading in there or writing poems,
That would be cheating;   15
Aim high—for a 360 degree
Detox.

This sitting alone, though, is
Not recommended

If you are normally   20
Sedated

Or have ever been under a doctor's
Surveillance because of your
Brain.

Dear one,   25
Don't let Hafiz fool you—

A ruby is buried
Here.

What Should We Do About That Moon?

A wine bottle fell from a wagon
And broke open in a field.

That night one hundred beetles and all their cousins
Gathered

And did some serious binge drinking.   5

They even found some seed husks nearby
And began to play them like drums and whirl.
This made God very happy.

Then the "night candle" rose into the sky
And one drunk creature, laying down his instrument,   10
Said to his friend—for no apparent
Reason,

"What should we do about that moon?"

Seems to Hafiz
Most everyone has laid aside the music   15

Tackling such profoundly useless
Questions.

Walt Whitman (1819–1892)

Excerpts from "Song of Myself" (1855 version)

[1]
I celebrate myself,
And what I assume you shall assume,
For every atom belonging to me as good belongs to you.

I loafe and invite my soul,
I lean and loafe at my ease . . . . observing a spear of summer grass.   5

[2]
Houses and rooms are full of perfumes . . . . the shelves are crowded
    with perfumes,
I breathe the fragrance myself, and know it and like it,
The distillation would intoxicate me also, but I shall not let it.

The atmosphere is not a perfume . . . . it has no taste of the
    distillation . . . . it is odorless,
It is for my mouth forever . . . . I am in love with it,   10
I will go to the bank by the wood and become undisguised and naked,
I am mad for it to be in contact with me.

The smoke of my own breath,
Echoes, ripples, and buzzed whispers . . . . loveroot, silkthread,
    crotch and vine,
My respiration and inspiration . . . . the beating of my heart . . . .
    the passing of blood and air through my lungs,   15
The sniff of green leaves and dry leaves, and of the shore and
    darkcolored sea-rocks, and of hay in the barn,
The sound of the belched words of my voice . . . . words loosed to
    the eddies of the wind,
A few light kisses . . . . a few embraces . . . . a reaching around of arms,
The play of shine and shade on the trees as the supple boughs wag,
The delight alone or in the rush of the streets, or along the fields
    and hillsides,   20
The feeling of health . . . . the full-noon trill . . . . the song of me
    rising from bed and meeting the sun.

Have you reckoned a thousand acres much? Have you reckoned the
    earth much?

Have you practiced so long to learn to read?
Have you felt so proud to get at the meaning of poems?

Stop this day and night with me and you shall possess the origin of
    all poems,   25
You shall possess the good of the earth and sun . . . . there are millions
    of suns left,
You shall no longer take things at second or third hand . . . . nor look through
    the eyes of the dead . . . . nor feed on the specters in
    books,
You shall not look through my eyes either, nor take things from me,
You shall listen to all sides and filter them from yourself.

[3]
I have heard what the talkers were talking . . . . the talk of the
    beginning and the end,   30
But I do not talk of the beginning or the end.

There was never any more inception than there is now,
Nor any more youth or age than there is now;
And will never be any more perfection than there is now,
Nor any more heaven or hell than there is now.   35

Urge and urge and urge,
Always the procreant urge of the world.

Out of the dimness opposite equals advance . . . . Always substance
    and increase,
Always a knit of identity . . . . always distinction . . . . always a breed
    of life.

To elaborate is no avail . . . . Learned and unlearned feel that it
    is so.   40

Sure as the most certain sure . . . . plumb in the uprights, well
    entretied, braced in the beams,
Stout as a horse, affectionate, haughty, electrical,
I and this mystery here we stand. . . .

[6]
A child said, What is the grass? fetching it to me with full hands;   90
How could I answer the child? . . . . I do not know what it is any
    more than he.

I guess it must be the flag of my disposition, out of hopeful green stuff woven.

Or I guess it is the handkerchief of the Lord,
A scented gift and remembrancer designedly dropped,
Bearing the owner's name someway in the corners, that we may see
    and remark, and say Whose?   95

Or I guess the grass is itself a child . . . . the produced babe of the
    vegetation.

Or I guess it is a uniform hieroglyphic,
And it means, Sprouting alike in broad zones and narrow zones,
Growing among black folks as among white,
Kanuck, Tuckahoe, Congressman, Cuff, I give them the same, I
    receive them the same.   100

And now it seems to me the beautiful uncut hair of graves.

Tenderly will I use you curling grass,
It may be you transpire from the breasts of young men,
It may be if I had known them I would have loved them;
It may be you are from old people and from women, and from
    offspring taken soon out of their mothers' laps,   105
And here you are the mothers' laps. . . .

[24]
Walt Whitman, an American, one of the roughs, a kosmos,
Disorderly fleshy and sensual . . . . eating drinking and breeding,   500
No sentimentalist . . . . no stander above men and women or apart
    from them . . . . no more modest than immodest.

Unscrew the locks from the doors!
Unscrew the doors themselves from their jambs!

Whoever degrades another degrades me . . . . and whatever is done or
    said returns at last to me,
And whatever I do or say I also return. . . .   505

Through me many long dumb voices,
Voices of the interminable generations of slaves,   510
Voices of prostitutes and of deformed persons,
Voices of the diseased and despairing, and of thieves and dwarfs,
Voices of cycles of preparation and accretion,
And of the threads that connect the stars—and of wombs, and of the
    fatherstuff,
And of the rights of them the others are down upon,   515

Of the trivial and flat and foolish and despised,
Of fog in the air and beetles rolling balls of dung.

Through me forbidden voices,
Voices of sexes and lusts . . . . voices veiled, and I remove the veil,
Voices indecent by me clarified and transfigured.   520

I do not press my finger across my mouth,
I keep as delicate around the bowels as around the head and heart,
Copulation is no more rank to me than death is.

I believe in the flesh and the appetites,
Seeing hearing and feeling are miracles, and each part and tag of
    me is a miracle.   525

Divine am I inside and out, and I make holy whatever I touch or
    am touched from;
The scent of these arm-pits is aroma finer than prayer,
This head is more than churches or bibles or creeds . . . .

[31]
I believe a leaf of grass is no less than the journeywork of the stars,
And the pismire is equally perfect, and a grain of sand, and the egg
    of the wren,
And the tree-toad is a chef-d' œuvre for the highest,
And the running blackberry would adorn the parlors of heaven,   665
And the narrowest hinge in my hand puts to scorn all machinery,
And the cow crunching with depressed head surpasses any statue,
And a mouse is miracle enough to stagger sextillions of infidels . . .

[52]
The spotted hawk swoops by and accuses me . . . . he complains of
    my gab and my loitering.

I too am not a bit tamed . . . . I too am untranslatable,
I sound my barbaric yawp over the roofs of the world.

The last scud of day holds back for me,
It flings my likeness after the rest and true as any on the shadowed
    wilds,   1325
It coaxes me to the vapor and the dusk.

I depart as air . . . . I shake my white locks at the runaway sun,
I effuse my flesh in eddies and drift it in lacy jags.

I bequeath myself to the dirt to grow from the grass I love,
If you want me again look for me under your bootsoles.   1330

You will hardly know who I am or what I mean,
But I shall be good health to you nevertheless,
And filter and fibre your blood.

Failing to fetch me at first keep encouraged,
Missing me one place search another,   1335
I stop some where waiting for you

I Sing the Body Electric

1

I sing the body electric,
The armies of those I love engirth me and I engirth them,
They will not let me off till I go with them, respond to them,
And discorrupt them, and charge them full with the charge of the
    soul.

Was it doubted that those who corrupt their own bodies conceal
    themselves?   5
And if those who defile the living are as bad as they who defile
    the dead?
And if the body does not do fully as much as the soul?
And if the body were not the soul, what is the soul?

2

The love of the body of man or woman balks account, the body
    itself balks account,
That of the male is perfect, and that of the female is perfect.   10

The expression of the face balks account,
But the expression of a well-made man appears not only in his
    face,
It is in his limbs and joints also, it is curiously in the joints of
    his hips and wrists,
It is in his walk, the carriage of his neck, the flex of his waist and
    knees, dress does not hide him,
The strong sweet quality he has strikes through the cotton and
    broadcloth,   15
To see him pass conveys as much as the best poem, perhaps more,
You linger to see his back, and the back of his neck and shoulder-
    side.

The sprawl and fullness of babes, the bosoms and heads of women,
    the folds of their dress, their style as we pass in the street,
    the contour of their shape downwards,

The swimmer naked in the swimming-bath, seen as he swims
    through the transparent green-shine, or lies with his face
    up and rolls silently to and fro in the heave of the water,
The bending forward and backward of rowers in row-boats,
    the horseman in his saddle.   20
Girls, mothers, house-keepers, in all their performances,
The group of laborers seated at noon-time with their open dinner-
    kettles, and their wives waiting,
The female soothing a child, the farmer's daughter in the garden
    or cow-yard,
The young fellow hoeing corn, the sleigh-driver driving his six
    horses through the crowd,
The wrestle of wrestlers, two apprentice-boys, quite grown, lusty,
    good-natured, native-born, out on the vacant lot at sun down
    after work,   25
The coats and caps thrown down, the embrace of love and resistance,
The upper-hold and under-hold, the hair rumpled over and blind-
    ing the eyes;
The march of firemen in their own costumes, the play of mascu-
    line muscle through clean-setting trowsers and waist-straps,
The slow return from the fire, the pause when the bell strikes
    suddenly again, and the listening on the alert,
The natural, perfect, varied attitudes, the bent head, the curv'd
    neck and the counting;   30
Such-like I love—I loosen myself, pass freely, am at the mother's
    breast with the little child,
Swim with the swimmers, wrestle with wrestlers, march in line with
    the firemen, and pause, listen, count.

3
I knew a man, a common farmer, the father of five sons,
And in them the fathers of sons, and in them the fathers of sons.

This man was of wonderful vigor, calmness, beauty of person,   35
The shape of his head, the pale yellow and white of his hair and
    beard, the immeasurable meaning of his black eyes, the
    richness and breadth of his manners,
These I used to go and visit him to see, he was wise also,
He was six feet tall, he was over eighty years old, his sons were
    massive, clean, bearded, tan-faced, handsome,
They and his daughters loved him, all who saw him loved him,
They did not love him by allowance, they loved him with personal
    love,   40
He drank water only, the blood show'd like scarlet through the
    clear-brown skin of his face,

He was a frequent gunner and fisher, he sail'd his boat himself,
    he had a fine one presented to him by a ship-joiner,
    he had fowling-pieces presented to him by men that loved him,
When he went with his five sons and many grand-sons to hunt or
    fish, you would pick him out as the most beautiful and
    vigorous of the gang,
You would wish long and long to be with him, you would wish to
    sit by him in the boat that you and he might touch each
    other.

4
I have perceiv'd that to be with those I like is enough,   45
To stop in company with the rest at evening is enough,
To be surrounded by beautiful, curious, breathing, laughing flesh
    is enough,
To pass among them or touch any one, or rest my arm ever so
    lightly round his or her neck for a moment, what is this
    then?
I do not ask any more delight, I swim in it as in a sea.

There is something in staying close to men and women and look-
    ing on them, and in the contact and odor of them, that
    pleases the soul well,   50
All things please the soul, but these please the soul well.

5
This is the female form,
A divine nimbus exhales from it from head to foot,
It attracts with fierce undeniable attraction,
I am drawn by its breath as if I were no more than a helpless
    vapor, all falls aside but myself and it,   55
Books, art, religion, time, the visible and solid earth, and what was
    expected of heaven or fear'd of hell, are now consumed,
Mad filaments, ungovernable shoots play out of it, the response
    likewise ungovernable,
Hair, bosom, hips, bend of legs, negligent falling hands all dif-
    fused, mine too diffused,
Ebb stung by the flow and flow stung by the ebb, love-flesh swel-
    ling and deliciously aching,
Limitless limpid jets of love hot and enormous, quivering jelly of
    love, white-blow and delirious juice,   60
Bridegroom night of love working surely and softly into the pros-
    trate dawn,

Undulating into the willing and yielding day,
Lost in the cleave of the clasping and sweet-flesh'd day.
This the nucleus—after the child is born of woman, man is born
    of woman,
This the bath of birth, this the merge of small and large, and the
    outlet again.   65

Be not ashamed women, your privilege encloses the rest, and is the
    exit of the rest,
You are the gates of the body, and you are the gates of the soul.

The female contains all qualities and tempers them,
She is in her place and moves with perfect balance,
She is all things duly veil'd, she is both passive and active,   70
She is to conceive daughters as well as sons, and sons as well as
    daughters.

As I see my soul reflected in Nature,
As I see through a mist, One with inexpressible completeness,
    sanity, beauty,
See the bent head and arms folded over the breast, the Female
    I see.

6
The male is not less the soul nor more, he too is in his place,   75
He too is all qualities, he is action and power,
The flush of the known universe is in him,
Scorn becomes him well, and appetite and defiance become him
    well,
The wildest largest passions, bliss that is utmost, sorrow that is
    utmost become him well, pride is for him,
The full-spread pride of man is calming and excellent to the soul,   80
Knowledge becomes him, he likes it always, he brings every thing
    to the test of himself,
Whatever the survey, whatever the sea and the sail he strikes
    soundings at last only here,
(Where else does he strike soundings except here?)

The man's body is sacred and the woman's body is sacred,
No matter who it is, it is sacred—is it the meanest one in the
    laborers' gang?   85
Is it one of the dull-faced immigrants just landed on the wharf?
Each belongs here or anywhere just as much as the well-off, just
    as much as you,

Each has his or her place in the procession.

(All is a procession,
The universe is a procession with measured and perfect motion.)   90

Do you know so much yourself that you call the meanest ignorant?
Do you suppose you have a right to a good sight, and he or she
    has no right to a sight?
Do you think matter has cohered together from its diffuse float,
    and the soil is on the surface, and water runs and vegeta-
    tion sprouts,
For you only, and not for him and her?

7
A man's body at auction,   95
(For before the war I often go to the slave-mart and watch the
    sale,)
I help the auctioneer, the sloven does not half know his business.

Gentlemen look on this wonder,
Whatever the bids of the bidders they cannot be high enough for it,
For it the globe lay preparing quintillions of years without one
    animal or plant,   100
For it the revolving cycles truly and steadily roll'd.

In this head the all-baffling brain,
In it and below it the makings of heroes.

Examine these limbs, red, black, or white, they are cunning in
    tendon and nerve,
They shall be stript that you may see them.   105

Exquisite senses, life-lit eyes, pluck, volition,
Flakes of breast-muscle, pliant backbone and neck, flesh not
    flabby, good-sized arms and legs,
And wonders within there yet.

Within there runs blood,
The same old blood! the same red-running blood!   110
There swells and jets a heart, there all passions, desires, reachings,
    aspirations,
(Do you think they are not there because they are not express'd in
    parlors and lecture-rooms?)

This is not only one man, this the father of those who shall be
    fathers in their turns,
In him the start of populous states and rich republics,
Of him countless immortal lives with countless embodiments and
    enjoyments.   115

How do you know who shall come from the offspring of his off-
    spring through the centuries?
(Who might you find you have come from yourself, if you could
    trace back through the centuries?)

8

A woman's body at auction,
She too is not only herself, she is the teeming mother of mothers,
She is the bearer of them that shall grow and be mates to the
    mothers.   120

Have you ever loved the body of a woman?
Have you ever loved the body of a man?
Do you not see that these are exactly the same to all in all nations
    and times all over the earth?

If any thing is sacred the human body is sacred,
And the glory and sweet of a man is the token of manhood
    untainted,   125
And in man or woman a clean, strong, firm-fibred body, is more
    beautiful than the most beautiful face.

Have you seen the fool that corrupted his own live body? or the
    fool that corrupted her own live body?
For they do not conceal themselves, and cannot conceal themselves.

9

O my body! I dare not desert the likes of you in other men and
    women, nor the likes of the parts of you,
I believe the likes of you are to stand or fall with the likes of the
    soul, (and that they are the soul,)   130
I believe the likes of you shall stand or fall with my poems, and
    that they are my poems,
Man's, woman's, child's, youth's, wife's, husband's, mother's, father's,
    young man's, young woman's poems,
Head, neck, hair, ears, drop and tympan of the ears,
Eyes, eye-fringes, iris of the eye, eyebrows, and the waking or
    sleeping of the lids,

Mouth, tongue, lips, teeth, roof of the mouth, jaws, and the jaw-
hinges,   135
Nose, nostrils of the nose, and the partition,
Cheeks, temples, forehead, chin, throat, back of the neck, neck-
slue,
Strong shoulders, manly beard, scapula, hind-shoulders, and the
ample side-round of the chest,
Upper-arm, armpit, elbow-socket, lower-arm, arm-sinews, arm-
bones,
Wrist and wrist-joints, hand, palm, knuckles, thumb, forefinger,
finger-joints, finger-nails,   140
Broad breast-front, curling hair of the breast, breast-bone, breast-side,
Ribs, belly, backbone, joints of the backbone,
Hips, hip-sockets, hip-strength, inward and outward round, man-
balls, man-root,
Strong set of thighs, well carrying the trunk above,
Leg-fibres, knee, knee-pan, upper-leg, under-leg,   145
Ankles, instep, foot-ball, toes, toe-joints, the heel;
All attitudes, all the shapeliness, all the belongings of my or your
body or of any one's body, male or female,
The lung-sponges, the stomach-sac, the bowels sweet and clean,
The brain in its folds inside the skull-frame,
Sympathies, heart-valves, palate-valves, sexuality, maternity,   150
Womanhood, and all that is a woman, and the man that comes
from woman,
The womb, the teats, nipples, breast-milk, tears, laughter, weeping,
love-looks, love-perturbations and risings,
The voice, articulation, language, whispering, shouting aloud,
Food, drink, pulse, digestion, sweat, sleep, walking, swimming,
Poise on the hips, leaping, reclining, embracing, arm-curving and
tightening,   155
The continual changes of the flex of the mouth, and around the
eyes,
The skin, the sunburnt shade, freckles, hair,
The curious sympathy one feels when feeling with the hand the
naked meat of the body,
The circling rivers the breath, and breathing it in and out,
The beauty of the waist, and thence of the hips, and thence down-
ward toward the knees,   160
The thin red jellies within you or within me, the bones and the
marrow in the bones,
The exquisite realization of health;
O I say these are not the parts and poems of the body only, but
of the soul,
O I say now these are the soul!

ACTIVITIES FOR WRITING AND DISCUSSION

1. Whitman urged people to read his poems "in the open air every season of every year of your life." Taking this advice literally, read "Song of Myself" and "I Sing the Body Electric" aloud outdoors and live with them over a period of days. Feel free to read and reread the poems in several sittings, focusing on sections that strike you and skimming over others that don't. In your notebook, keep a record of your impressions of the poems and any thoughts or feelings they prompt in you.

2. Whitman saw poetry as a force for bringing people together. Follow your private reading of the poems with a communal reading in class or with a small group. Have each person take a turn at reading a verse paragraph or numbered section, and pause after each section to share and discuss your annotations of particular lines or passages.

3. How does it make you feel when the speaker addresses "you" directly in "Song of Myself"? How would the poem change if this element of direct address to the reader were eliminated?

4. Whitman's poetry is disarmingly personal: "Have you ever loved the body of a woman?/Have you ever loved the body of a man?" ("I Sing the Body Electric," lines 121–122). Identify other passages in the Whitman poems that strike you as personal or that move you personally, and respond to them using Ideas #1 or 2 of the "Ten Ideas for Writing" on page 35.

5. How would you characterize Whitman's concept of the human body: as hedonistic? sensuous? religious? some combination? As you answer, consider his graphic descriptions of bodies alongside such passages as "The scent of these armpits is aroma finer than prayer" ("Song of Myself," line 527) and "Have you seen the fool that corrupted his own live body? or the fool that corrupted her own live body?" ("I Sing the Body Electric," line 127). From your reading of these poems, write a paragraph or essay summarizing what it is about human bodies (and material life) that prompts Whitman to celebrate.

6. Research Whitman's views on the human body, love, friendship, or some other topic and summarize your findings in an essay.

EMILY DICKINSON (1830–1886)

Much Madness is divinest Sense

Much Madness is divinest Sense—
To a discerning Eye—
Much Sense—the starkest Madness—

'Tis the Majority
In this, as All, prevail—
Assent—and you are sane—   5
Demur [1]—you're straightway dangerous—
And handled with a Chain—

The Soul selects her own Society

The Soul selects her own Society—
Then—shuts the Door—
To her divine Majority—
Present no more—

Unmoved—she notes the Chariots—pausing—   5
At her low Gate—
Unmoved—an Emperor be kneeling
Upon her Mat—

I've known her—from an ample nation—
Choose One—   10
Then—close the Valves of her attention—
Like Stone—

Tell all the Truth but tell it slant

Tell all the Truth but tell it slant—
Success in Circuit lies
Too bright for our infirm Delight
The Truth's superb surprise
As Lightning to the Children eased   5
With explanation kind
The Truth must dazzle gradually
Or every man be blind—

What Soft—Cherubic Creatures

What Soft—Cherubic Creatures—
These Gentlewomen are—
One would as soon assault a Plush—
Or violate a Star—

---

1. Disagree.

Such Dimity Convictions— 5
A Horror so refined
Of freckled Human Nature—
Of Deity—ashamed—

It's such a common—Glory—
A Fisherman's—Degree— 10
Redemption—Brittle Lady—
Be so—ashamed of Thee—

ACTIVITIES FOR WRITING AND DISCUSSION

1. Read the four Dickinson poems aloud, identifying the **meter, rhymes,** and other sound effects such as **assonance** and **alliteration.** Attempting, for the moment, to set aside issues of "meaning," what passages—words, phrases, or lines— please you because of their sound or rhythm?

2. In a small group or as a class, progress towards strong readings of the poems by assuming, initially, the role of "dumb" readers. Simply go through a poem, line by line, and brainstorm any images, associations, or feelings that occur to you. Rather than suppressing "dumb," "irrelevant," or "eccentric" responses, *honor* them and write them down. Then discuss how people's diverse responses illuminate the poem and/or evoke thoughts about life experiences that may not be explicitly addressed in the poem itself.

3. Dickinson's astonishing **metaphors, similes,** and **paradoxes** challenge and subvert logical or rational ways of thinking and our desire for neatly packaged meanings. Working with a group:
   a. Identify and mark as many metaphors, similes, and paradoxes—or other **figures**—as you can.
   b. Select two or three favorites.
   c. Orally or in an essay, explain how these favorites work, i.e., what makes them striking or powerful.

4. Respond to one or more of the poems using one of the "Ten Ideas for Writing from Reading" described in Chapter 3 and summarized on page 35.

EDWIN ARLINGTON ROBINSON (1869–1935)

Richard Cory

Whenever Richard Cory went down town,
We people on the pavement looked at him:

He was a gentleman from sole to crown,
Clean favored, and imperially slim.

And he was always quietly arrayed,   5
And he was always human when he talked;
But still he fluttered pulses when he said,
"Good-morning," and he glittered when he walked.

And he was rich—yes, richer than a king—
And admirably schooled in every grace: 10
In fine, we thought that he was everything
To make us wish that we were in his place.

So on we worked, and waited for the light,
And went without the meat, and cursed the bread;
And Richard Cory, one calm summer night,   15
Went home and put a bullet through his head.

ACTIVITIES FOR WRITING AND DISCUSSION

1. Is it significant that the **speaker** uses the first-person *plural* pronoun ("we") instead of the singular ("I")? Why or why not?

2. Why does Richard Cory kill himself? To enrich what might be a rather pat answer to this question, invent a series of entries from "The Diary of Richard Cory" in which you (Richard) narrate experiences and describe feelings that are weighing on you. *Alternative:* Write Richard's suicide note, or compose a character biography of Richard.

3. Write a conversation between two townsfolk (gossips, perhaps) discussing Richard Cory, before and/or just after his death.

ANTONIO MACHADO (1875–1939)

Excerpts from *Proverbs and Song-verse*

To José Ortega y Gasset.

I

The eye you see is an eye
not because you see it;
it's an eye because it sees you.

II
    For dialogue,
first ask,   5
then . . . listen.

III
    Any narcissism
is an ugly vice—
and an old one by now.

IV
    But seek out the other in your mirror,   10
the other who keeps you company.

VIII
    Today always is still.

XI
    Once again my attention
is bound by water—
but water in the live   15
rock of my heart.

XII
    From the sound of water, can you tell
if it's water of peak or valley,
town fountain, garden or grove?

XIV
    Never set down your limits   20
or fuss with your profile;
they're only externals.

XV
    Look for your counterpart
who's always alongside you
and is usually your opposite.   25

XVI
    Now that spring's here,
fly off to the flowers;
don't chew on the wax.

XXIV
Slowly now, nice neat letters:
the point is to do things well,   30
not just to do them.

XXVIII
Singers, the clapping
and cheers should be left
to the others.

XXIX
Singers, wake up.   35
Time for echoes to end
and voices to start.

XXX
But don't hunt for dissonance:
There is no such thing;
people dance to all tunes.   40

XXXVI
It's not the basic I
that the poet is after
but the essential you.

XXXIX
Find a mirror in your fellow man,
but not one for shaving   45
or dyeing your hair.

XL
Those eyes you long for;
make no mistake,
eyes you see yourself in—
are eyes because they see you.   50

XLIV
Don't look down on words.
The world is noisy and mute,
poets; God alone speaks.

XLVIII
Doubtless the worst of the wicked
is the rogue who forgets   55
his devil's vocation.

XLIX
   Did you speak a half-truth?
They'll call you liar twice over
if you speak the other half.

LIII
   After living and dreaming   60
comes what matters most:
waking up.

LVI
   Gypsy conversation:
"Pal, how're we doing?"
"Taking a stroll on the shortcut."   65

LVII
   Some who give up
end it all with a rope;
others with four little words:
faith's back in style.

— *Translated by Alan S. Trueblood*

ACTIVITIES FOR WRITING AND DISCUSSION

1. These short poems shouldn't be hurried and probably do not need to be read in sequence. Skip around, hovering over the poems that strike you. What do you like? What thoughts and feelings do the "Proverbs" evoke from you? Are there particular images, **metaphors** or other **figures** that stand out for you? Describe your thoughts and feelings in your notebook or orally.

2. In your notebook react to Machado's **persona** in the "Proverbs." Do you find the persona preachy? appealing? a combination of both? Explain with reference to specific lines and passages.

3. Think about the format of the "Proverbs."
   a. Based on these excerpts, does there seem to be an underlying pattern of organization, or do the proverbs seem to be set down in a random order? If you detect a pattern of organization, what is it?
   b. Reformat some of the verse sections into prose. What is lost, gained, or changed by doing so?
   c. Skim through your own notebook. Identify any passages of intellectually or emotionally heightened prose that tend toward poetry and reformat them into verse.

4. As a long-term project, compose a collection of "proverbs in verse" of your own. Carrying a small notepad (see Chapter 4) will enable you to jot down and collect the sorts of passing thoughts, images, and intuitions that are found in Machado's proverbs.

Bertolt Brecht (1898–1956)

Questions from a Worker Who Reads

Who built Thebes of the seven gates?
In the books you will find the names of kings.
Did the kings haul up the lumps of rock?
And Babylon, many times demolished
Who raised it up so many times? In what houses   5
Of gold-glittering Lima did the builders live?
Where, the evening that the Wall of China was finished
Did the masons go? Great Rome
Is full of triumphal arches. Who erected them? Over whom
Did the Caesars triumph? Had Byzantium, much praised in song   10
Only palaces for its inhabitants? Even in fabled Atlantis
The night the ocean engulfed it
The drowning still bawled for their slaves.

The young Alexander conquered India.
Was he alone?   15
Caesar beat the Gauls.
Did he not have even a cook with him?
Philip of Spain wept when his armada
Went down. Was he the only one to weep?
Frederick the Second won the Seven Years War. Who   20
Else won it?

Every page a victory.
Who cooked the feast for the victors?
Every ten years a great man.
Who paid the bill?   25

So many reports.
So many questions.

—Translated by Michael Hamburger

ACTIVITIES FOR WRITING AND DISCUSSION

1. What seems to be the point of Brecht's poem? Why are the last two words of the title important?

2. Countless unnamed people, some of them probably heroic, stand behind each story and historical event the speaker mentions. Research one of the stories or events and retell it from the first-person **point of view** of one individual (e.g., Caesar's cook) among the anonymous multitude who made the history happen.

3. Write your own poem of difficult or imponderable questions. For additional inspiration, see Mary Oliver's "Some Questions You Might Ask" (p. 514).

STANISLAW J. LEC (1909–1966)

Excerpts from *Unkempt Thoughts*

You will always find some Eskimos ready to instruct the Congolese on how to cope with heat waves. 1

———

On the neck of a giraffe a flea begins to believe in immortality. 2

———

I prefer the sign NO ENTRY to the one that says NO EXIT. 3

———

Only the dead can be resurrected. It's more difficult with the living. 4

———

Truth will always be naked, even when turned out in the latest fashion. 5

———

All is in the hands of man. Therefore wash them often. 6

———

Thoughts, like fleas, jump from man to man. But they don't bite everybody. 7

———

If only we could also *milk* the scapegoat! 8

If the art of conversation stood a little higher, we would have a lower birthrate. 9

——————

Men, enough of this modesty. Don't pretend to be lions. 10

——————

In prison cells the sun draws shadows of the bars on the floor. In the squares the 11
prisoners can play crossword puzzles. The possibilities depend on the size of the
bars.

——————

The aspen trembles under every regime, but it grows green under every regime 12
anyway.

——————

I give you bitter pills in sugar coating. The pills are harmless; the poison is in the 13
sugar.

——————

When I eat sardines I sometimes tremble that I may be biting a Jonah from the 14
bible of the little people.

——————

The fact that he died does not prove that he lived. 15

——————

If you want to hide your face, walk naked. 16

——————

Do not walk on the well-trodden path—you may slip. 17

——————

On every summit you are on the brink of an abyss. 18

——————

You can spit on yourself without opening your mouth. 19

— Translated by Jacek Galazka

ACTIVITIES FOR WRITING AND DISCUSSION

1. Read Lec's **aphorisms** aloud to yourself or in a group. Mark or annotate
any aphorisms that particularly strike you, and identify the particular features

(e.g., ideas, themes, word choice, **metaphors, ironies,** or other kinds of **figurative language**) that make those selections memorable or appealing. Put your reactions in writing, and be prepared to share them with classmates.

2. Lec's tiny but explosive thoughts seem to have been drafted on the run, perhaps in odd places or at odd times on scrap paper or in a small notepad. Over the next several weeks compose a collection of aphorisms of your own—when and as they occur to you—in which you imitate the ironic style of Lec, or, if you prefer, compose in a style of your own. For other aphorisms, see Blake's "Proverbs of Hell" on page 499, Machado's aphoristic verse on page 672, and Joubert's notebooks on page 319.

Julio Cortázar (1914–1984)

Preamble to the Instructions on How to Wind a Watch

Think of this: When they present you with a watch they are gifting you with a tiny flowering hell, a wreath of roses, a dungeon of air. They aren't simply wishing the watch on you, and many more, and we hope it will last you, it's a good brand, Swiss, seventeen rubies; they aren't just giving you this minute stonecutter which will bind you by the wrist and walk along with you. They are giving you—they don't know it, it's terrible that they don't know it—they are gifting you with a new, fragile, and precarious piece of yourself, something that's yours but not a part of your body, that you have to strap to your body like your belt, like a tiny, furious bit of something hanging onto your wrist. They gift you with the job of having to wind it every day, an obligation to wind it, so that it goes on being a watch; they gift you with the obsession of looking into jewelry-shop windows to check the exact time, check the radio announcer, check the telephone service. They give you the gift of fear, someone will steal it from you, it'll fall on the street and get broken. They give you the gift of your trademark and the assurance that it's a trademark better than the others, they gift you with the impulse to compare your watch with other watches. They aren't giving you a watch, you are the gift, they're giving you yourself for the watch's birthday.

—Translated by Paul Blackburn

Activities for Writing and Discussion

1. Though few people "wind" watches anymore, is this **prose poem** still timely? Explain. Are there any actions or "obligations" in the digital age that are analogous to the old obligation of winding a watch? If so, what are they?

2. Read the poem aloud with a partner or small group, with your pen or pencil out to mark arresting words or phrases as you read and listen. Then reread the poem, pausing after each sentence to share your moment by moment reactions to striking or puzzling words, phrases, and/or ideas.

3. The poem is packed with **metaphors** and other comparisons. Practice carrying a small notepad (see Chapter 4) for jotting down metaphors of your own, on whatever topics, as they occur to you. (Note: This will probably work best if you don't *try* to write metaphors but rather, *detect* them as they occur.) If possible, expand one of your jottings into a prose poem.

4. React to the poem using the "Four-Step Process" (see Chapter 2).

5. Read Cortázar's book *Cronopios and Famas,* from which "Preamble to the Instructions on How to Wind a Watch" is taken, or read some other collection or anthology of prose poems. Some prose poets you might consider are Robert Bly, Russell Edson, Ana Hatherly, Franz Kafka, Mary Oliver, Francis Ponge, and Wislawa Szymborska. In an essay, discuss the work you read and the distinctive qualities that make prose poetry compelling.

Margaret Atwood (b. 1939)

The City Planners

Cruising these residential Sunday
streets in dry August sunlight:
what offends us is
the sanities:
the houses in pedantic rows, the planted   5
sanitary trees, assert
levelness of surface like a rebuke
to the dent in our car door.

No shouting here, or
shatter of glass; nothing more abrupt   10
than the rational whine of a power mower
cutting a straight swath in the discouraged grass.

But though the driveways neatly
sidestep hysteria
by being even, the roofs all display   15
the same slant of avoidance to the hot sky,
certain things:
the smell of spilled oil a faint

sickness lingering in the garages,
a splash of paint on brick surprising as a bruise,   20
a plastic hose poised in a vicious
coil; even the too-fixed stare of the wide windows

give momentary access to
the landscape behind or under
the future cracks in the plaster   25

when the houses, capsized, will slide
obliquely into the clay seas, gradual as glaciers
that right now nobody notices.

That is where the City Planners
with the insane faces of political conspirators   30
are scattered over unsurveyed
territories, concealed from each other,
each in his own private blizzard;

guessing directions, they sketch
transitory lines rigid as wooden borders   35
on a wall in the white vanishing air

tracing the panic of suburb
order in a bland madness of snows.

Laure-Anne Bosselaar (b. 1943)

The Bumper-Sticker

   "Yield" says the road-sign, so you do.
The bearded man nods thank-you, and passes,
It's never too late to have a happy childhood!
reads his bumper-sticker. You want to stop him,
ask if he knows how. No one waits for you at home,   5
so you follow: it could be God in that Dodge,
leading you to where you can change the past
like worn tires, or get a quick lube: the old stuff
dripping out murky and dark.

   You'd get a new mother first: the pick   10
of the lot, a bright color—green maybe—
with safety features and a lifelong warranty.

A good reliable car, never running on empty,
with all kinds of options and lots of room
for both of you. You'd test-drive head high,   15
motor humming, gears changing noiselessly,
and never look back at the old jalopy that always
stalled and left you standing by the side of the road.

    A new father next. He'd slide
into the passenger's seat and teach you how   20
to drive like a pro: check the rearview often,
and stop holding your foot on the brake fearing
you'll get in a wreck. He'd pull out
Technicolor maps, highlight the best itinerary:
no dead-ends, no potholes, it'll be a smooth ride   25
my baby, tell me where you're heading
and I'll show you the way.

    The Dodge signals left. You follow, but
lose him in a tunnel when a sixteen-wheeler
reading *Safeway* passes so close it nearly   30
sends you to the wall.

ACTIVITIES FOR WRITING AND DISCUSSION

    1. How would you describe the speaker's response to the bumper sticker? Is it believing? critical? ironic? something else? Explain.

    2. As a primary research assignment, keep a running list of bumper stickers you see. Assemble them into a poem, interpret them individually (especially the strangest or most provocative), react to a specific bumper sticker imaginatively (as Bosselaar did), or write an essay on "what our bumper stickers say about us" or on some related topic.

CATHY APPEL (b. 1948)

Letters

Don't put your disembodied voice in an envelope —
send objects,
tangibles from Vermont, like the broken thread
from the last shirt button you've lost,
photographs of the house;   5

I should see you as you are.
What kind of soap is in your bathroom;
where do you keep your car keys? Send me
your favorite recipe, something from your pocket
like a ticket stub or tattered list.   10
I'll answer promptly
enclosing dust from my closet,
mud from the soles of my shoes.
Can you imagine me exhausted,
tissues tucked in a sleeve,   15
lying beside my husband, who, regardless,
caresses my hip? I could send you
a toenail clipping
or the umpteen odd barrettes, rubber bands,
unanswered letters scattered in my drawer.   20
Don't write in sentences.
No matter how we feel, send specifics—a branch
of your family's Christmas tree,
your daughter's loose tooth, crumbs
from the toast you ate this morning.   25
Send me what defies
language, something of which
there isn't any doubt.

LEO ROMERO (b. 1950)

What the Gossips Saw

Everyone pitied Escolastica, her leg
had swollen like a watermelon in the summer
It had practically happened over night
She was seventeen, beautiful and soon
to be married to Guillermo who was working   5
in the mines at Terreros, eighty miles away
far up in the mountains, in the wilderness
Poor Escolastica, the old women would say
on seeing her hobble to the well with a bucket
carrying her leg as if it were the weight   10
of the devil, surely it was a curse from heaven
for some misdeed, the young women who were
jealous would murmur, yet they were grieved too
having heard that the doctor might cut
her leg, one of a pair of the most perfect legs   15

in the valley, and it was a topic of great
interest and conjecture among the villagers
whether Guillermo would still marry her
if she were crippled, a one-legged woman—
as if life weren't hard enough for a woman   20
with two legs—how could she manage

Guillermo returned and married Escolastica
even though she had but one leg, the sound
of her wooden leg pounding down the wooden aisle
stayed in everyone's memory for as long   25
as they lived, women cried at the sight
of her beauty, black hair so dark
that the night could get lost in it, a face
more alluring than a full moon

Escolastica went to the dances with her husband   30
and watched and laughed but never danced
though once she had been the best dancer
and could wear holes in a pair of shoes
in a matter of a night, and her waist had been
as light to the touch as a hummingbird's flight   35
And Escolastica bore five children, only half
what most women bore, yet they were healthy
In Escolastica's presence, no one would mention
the absence of her leg, though she walked heavily
And it was not long before the gossips   40
spread their poison, that she must be in cohorts
with the devil, had given him her leg
for the power to bewitch Guillermo's heart
and cloud his eyes so that he could not see
what was so clear to them all   45

ACTIVITIES FOR WRITING AND DISCUSSION

1. Why do you suppose Romero is vague about the precise medical causes of Escolastica's loss of a leg?

2. Jot down your impressions of the village in which Escolastica lives. What are the people like? What sorts of beliefs and attitudes do they have? What are their families like? their entertainments? Then, using details provided in the poem (and fabricating others where necessary), invent the conversation about Escolastica that occurs among any of the following: "the old women," "the young women," "the villagers," or "the gossips."

3. Recall a situation out of your own experience or knowledge in which one person was an object of gossip. Make a few notes about the person, the source of the gossip, and the gossipers. Then write the text of the gossip. *Alternative:* Invent such a situation.

Nonfiction/Essays

Sei Shōnagon (b. ca. 967)

Excerpts from *The Pillow Book of Sei Shōnagon*

92. Things Without Merit

An ugly person with a bad character.

Rice starch that has become mixed with water. . . . I know that this is a very vulgar item and everyone will dislike my mentioning it. But that should not stop me. In fact I must feel free to include anything, even tongs used for the parting-fires. After all, these objects do exist in our world and people all know about them. I admit they do not belong to a list that others will see. But I never thought that these notes would be read by anyone else, and so I included everything that came into my head, however strange or unpleasant.

134. Letters Are Commonplace

Letters are commonplace enough, yet what splendid things they are! When someone is in a distant province and one is worried about him, and then a letter suddenly arrives, one feels as though one were seeing him face to face. Again, it is a great comfort to have expressed one's feelings in a letter even though one knows it cannot yet have arrived. If letters did not exist, what dark depressions would come over one! When one has been worrying about something and wants to tell a certain person about it, what a relief it is to put it all down in a letter! Still greater is one's joy when a reply arrives. At that moment a letter really seems like an elixir of life.

149. One Day, When Her Majesty Was Surrounded by Several Ladies

One day, when Her Majesty was surrounded by several ladies, I remarked in connexion with something that she had said, "There are times when the world so exasperates me that I feel I cannot go on living in it for another moment and I want to disappear for good. But then, if I happen to obtain some nice white paper, Michinoku paper, or white decorated paper, I decide that I can put up with things as they are a little longer. Or, if I can spread out a finely woven, green straw mat and examine the white bordering with its vivid black patterns, I somehow feel that I cannot turn my back on this world, and life actually seems precious to me."

"It really doesn't take much to console you," said the Empress laughing. "I wonder what sort of a person it was who gazed at the moon on Mount Obasute."

The ladies who were in attendance also teased me. "You've certainly found a cheap prayer for warding off evil," they said.

Some time later, when I was staying at home and absorbed in various petty worries, a messenger brought me twenty rolls of magnificent paper from Her Majesty. "Come back quickly," she wrote, adding, "I am sending you this because of what you told me the other day. It seems to be of poor quality, however, and I am afraid you will not be able to use it for copying the Sutra of Longevity." It delighted me that Her Majesty should have remembered something that I myself had completely forgotten. Even if an ordinary person had sent me the present, I should have been overjoyed. How much more pleasing when it came from the Empress herself! I was so excited that I could not frame a proper reply, but simply sent Her Majesty this poem:

> Thanks to the paper that the Goddess gave,
> My years will now be plenteous as the crane's.

"Make sure that the Empress is asked the following," I told the messenger. "Am I expecting too many years?" My reward for the messenger, a general maid from the Table Room, was an unlined green costume.

Then I immediately used the paper I had received to write my collection of notes. I felt a glow of delight and all my worries began to disappear. . . .

184. WHEN THE MIDDLE CAPTAIN

When the Middle Captain of the Left Guards Division was still Governor of Ise, he visited me one day at my home. There was a straw mat at the edge of the veranda, and I pulled it out for him. This notebook of mine happened to be lying on the mat, but I did not notice it in time. I snatched at the book and made a desperate effort to get it back; but the Captain instantly took it off with him and did not return it until much later. I suppose it was from this time that my book began to be passed about at Court.

185. IT IS GETTING SO DARK

It is getting so dark that I can scarcely go on writing; and my brush is all worn out. Yet I should like to add a few things before I end.

I wrote these notes at home, when I had a good deal of time to myself and thought no one would notice what I was doing. Everything that I have seen and felt is included. Since much of it might appear malicious and even harmful to other people, I was careful to keep my book hidden. But now it has become public, which is the last thing I expected.

One day Lord Korechika, the Minister of the Centre, brought the Empress a bundle of notebooks. "What shall we do with them?" Her Majesty asked me. "The Emperor has already made arrangements for copying the 'Records of the Historian.'"

"Let me make them into a pillow," I said.[1]

"Very well," said Her Majesty. "You may have them."

I now had a vast quantity of paper at my disposal, and I set about filling the notebooks with odd facts, stories from the past, and all sorts of other things, often including the most trivial material. On the whole I concentrated on things and people that I found charming and splendid; my notes are also full of poems and observations on trees and plants, birds and insects. I was sure that when people saw my book they would say, "It's even worse than I expected. Now one can really tell what she is like." After all, it is written entirely for my own amusement and I put things down exactly as they came to me. How could my casual jottings possibly bear comparison with the many impressive books that exist in our time? Readers have declared, however, that I can be proud of my work. This has surprised me greatly; yet I suppose it is not so strange that people should like it, for, as will be gathered from these notes of mine, I am the sort of person who approves of what others abhor and detests the things they like.

Whatever people may think of my book, I still regret that it ever came to light.

ACTIVITIES FOR WRITING AND DISCUSSION

1. Sei Shōnagon writes, "Letters are commonplace" and goes on to describe their benefits, specifically to the writer. In the twenty-first century letters are less commonplace than in the past; what kinds of writing, if any, have replaced them, and do these provide the same benefits to the contemporary writer as letters have in the past? Illustrate your answer with examples. Alternatively, if you are a letter writer, compare your experiences with Sei Shōnagon's.

2. In excerpt #149 Sei Shōnagon expresses her passion for a particular art—writing notes—and articulates its effect on her (it restores her enthusiasm for life). Identify an art or craft (fine or everyday) that inspires you with a similar passion, and write about it in a brief essay like one of Sei Shōnagon's.

3. Starting with Ivan Morris's translation of *The Pillow Book of Sei Shōnagon* and his accompanying notes, research the tradition and purposes of pillow books in Japan. If you wish, consider how this Japanese form compares with diaries and notebooks in the West.

---

1. *Majura no sōshi* ("pillow book") referred to a notebook or a collection of notebooks kept in some accessible but relatively private place, and in which the author would from time to time record impressions, daily events, poems, letters, stories, ideas, descriptions of people, etc. [Translator's note].

Samuel Johnson (1709–1784)

The Rambler, No. 146 [On Celebrity]

None of the projects or designs which exercise the mind of man, are equally subject to obstructions and disappointments with the pursuit of fame. Riches cannot easily be denied to them who have something of greater value to offer in exchange; he whose fortune is endangered by litigation, will not refuse to augment the wealth of the lawyer; he whose days are darkened by languor, or whose nerves are excruciated by pain, is compelled to pay tribute to the science of healing. But praise may be always omitted without inconvenience. When once a man has made celebrity necessary to his happiness, he has put it in the power of the weakest and most timorous malignity, if not to take away his satisfaction, at least to withhold it. His enemies may indulge their pride by airy negligence, and gratify their malice by quiet neutrality. They that could never have injured a character by invectives may combine to annihilate it by silence; as the women of Rome threatened to put an end to conquest and dominion, by supplying no children to the commonwealth.

When a writer has with long toil produced a work intended to burst upon mankind with unexpected lustre, and withdraw the attention of the learned world from every other controversy or enquiry, he is seldom contented to wait long without the enjoyment of his new praises. With an imagination full of his own importance, he walks out like a monarch in disguise, to learn the various opinions of his readers. Prepared to feast upon admiration; composed to encounter censures without emotion; and determined not to suffer his quiet to be injured by a sensibility too exquisite of praise or blame, but to laugh with equal contempt at vain objections and injudicious commendations, he enters the places of mingled conversation, sits down to his tea in an obscure corner, and while he appears to examine a file of antiquated journals, catches the conversation of the whole room. He listens, but hears no mention of his book, and therefore supposes that he has disappointed his curiosity by delay, and that as men of learning would naturally begin their conversation with such a wonderful novelty, they had digressed to other subjects before his arrival. The company disperses, and their places are supplied by others equally ignorant, or equally careless. The same expectation hurries him to another place, from which the same disappointment drives him soon away. His impatience then grows violent and tumultuous; he ranges over the town with restless curiosity, and hears in one quarter of a cricket-match, in another of a pick-pocket; is told by some of an unexpected bankrupcy, by others of a turtle feast; is sometimes provoked by importunate enquiries after the white bear, and sometimes with praises of the dancing dog; he is afterwards entreated to give his judgment upon a wager about the height of the monument; invited to see a foot race in the adjacent villages; desired to read a ludicrous advertisement; or consulted about the most effectual method of making enquiry after a favourite cat. The whole world is busied in affairs, which he thinks below the notice of reasonable creatures, and which are nevertheless sufficient to withdraw all regard from his labours and his merits.

He resolves at last to violate his own modesty, and to recal the talkers from their folly by an enquiry after himself. He finds every one provided with an answer; one has seen the work advertised, but never met with any that had read it; another has been so often imposed upon by specious titles, that he never buys a book till its character is established; a third wonders what any man can hope to produce after so many writers of greater eminence; the next has enquired after the author, but can hear no account of him, and therefore suspects the name to be fictitious; and another knows him to be a man condemned by indigence to write too frequently what he does not understand.

Many are the consolations with which the unhappy author endeavours to allay his vexation, and fortify his patience. He has written with too little indulgence to the understanding of common readers; he has fallen upon an age in which solid knowledge, and delicate refinement, have given way to low merriment and idle buffoonry, and therefore no writer can hope for distinction, who has any higher purpose than to raise laughter. He finds that his enemies, such as superiority will always raise, have been industrious, while his performance was in the press, to vilify and blast it; and that the bookseller, whom he had resolved to enrich, has rivals that obstruct the circulation of his copies. He at last reposes upon the consideration, that the noblest works of learning and genius have always made their way slowly against ignorance and prejudice; and that reputation which is never to be lost, must be gradually obtained, as animals of longest life are observed not soon to attain their full stature and strength.

By such arts of voluntary delusion does every man endeavour to conceal his 5 own unimportance from himself. It is long before we are convinced of the small proportion which every individual bears to the collective body of mankind; or learn how few can be interested in the fortune of any single man; how little vacancy is left in the world for any new object of attention; to how small extent the brightest blaze of merit can be spread amidst the mists of business and of folly; and how soon it is clouded by the intervention of other novelties. Not only the writer of books, but the commander of armies, and the deliverer of nations, will easily outlive all noisy and popular reputation: he may be celebrated for a time by the public voice, but his actions and his name will soon be considered as remote and unaffecting, and be rarely mentioned but by those whose alliance gives them some vanity to gratify by frequent commemoration.

It seems not to be sufficiently considered how little renown can be admitted in the world. Mankind are kept perpetually busy by their fears or desires, and have not more leisure from their own affairs, than to acquaint themselves with the accidents of the current day. Engaged in contriving some refuge from calamity, or in shortening the way to some new possession, they seldom suffer their thoughts to wander to the past or future; none but a few solitary students have leisure to enquire into the claims of ancient heroes or sages, and names which hoped to range over kingdoms and continents shrink at last into cloisters or colleges.

Nor is it certain, that even of these dark and narrow habitations, these last retreats of fame, the possession will be long kept. Of men devoted to literature very few extend their views beyond some particular science, and the greater part seldom enquire, even in their own profession, for any authors but those whom the present mode of study happens to force upon their notice; they desire not to fill their minds with unfashionable knowledge, but contentedly resign to oblivion those books which they now find censured or neglected.

The hope of fame is necessarily connected with such considerations as must abate the ardour of confidence, and repress the vigour of pursuit. Whoever claims renown from any kind of excellence, expects to fill the place which is now possessed by another, for there are already names of every class sufficient to employ all that will desire to remember them; and surely he that is pushing his predecessors into the gulph of obscurity, cannot but sometimes suspect, that he must himself sink in like manner, and as he stands upon the same precipice, be swept away with the same violence.

It sometimes happens, that fame begins when life is at an end; but far the greater number of candidates for applause have owed their reception in the world to some favourable casualties, and have therefore immediately sunk into neglect, when death stripped them of their casual influence, and neither fortune nor patronage operated in their favour. Among those who have better claims to regard, the honour paid to their memory is commonly proportionate to the reputation which they enjoyed in their lives, though still growing fainter, as it is at a greater distance from the first emission; and since it is so difficult to obtain the notice of contemporaries, how little is to be hoped from future times? What can merit effect by its own force, when the help of art or friendship can scarcely support it?

The Rambler, No. 159 [On Bashfulness]

No cause more frequently produces bashfulness than too high an opinion of our own importance. He that imagines an assembly filled with his merit, panting with expectation, and hushed with attention, easily terrifies himself with the dread of disappointing them, and strains his imagination in pursuit of something that may vindicate the veracity of fame, and shew that his reputation was not gained by chance. He considers, that what he shall say or do will never be forgotten; that renown or infamy are suspended upon every syllable, and that nothing ought to fall from him which will not bear the test of time. Under such solicitude, who can wonder that the mind is overwhelmed, and by struggling with attempts above her strength, quickly sinks into languishment and despondency.

The most useful medicines are often unpleasing to the taste. Those who are oppressed by their own reputation, will perhaps not be comforted by hearing that their cares are unnecessary. But the truth is, that no man is much regarded by the rest of the world. He that considers how little he dwells upon the condition of others, will learn how little the attention of others is attracted by himself. While we see multitudes passing before us, of whom perhaps not one appears to deserve our notice, or excites our sympathy, we should remember, that we likewise are lost in the same throng, that the eye which happens to glance upon us is turned in a moment on him that follows us, and that the utmost which we can reasonably hope or fear is to fill a vacant hour with prattle, and be forgotten.

ACTIVITIES FOR WRITING AND DISCUSSION

1. Analyze the **irony** in either of Johnson's essays, and discuss the present-day relevance of these 250-year-old writings.

2. Annotate **one** of Johnson's paragraphs intensively, summarize it, and express your thoughts about it in an essay.

3. Johnson writes about the illusory character of fame or celebrity. Create a Topic/Form Grid (see Chapter 5) that includes "fame" and "celebrity" as two of your topics. Then write on either topic (or some related topic) using one of the forms on your grid.

4. Most of us objectify other people rather routinely. For instance, we reduce them to stereotypes, notice them only in terms of their immediate importance to ourselves, or do not notice them at all. Johnson challenges you to reverse the situation and objectify yourself; that is, to appreciate how *you* are observed or summarized (when you are observed at all) by other people. As an exercise, respond descriptively to the following question: *What would it be like to be someone else (e.g., my mother, father, sibling, roommate, friend, enemy, etc.) and live with me?* or pick out a stranger at random and write about yourself from his or her point of view.

ARTHUR SCHOPENHAUER (1788–1860)

On Thinking for Oneself

257

Just as the largest library, badly arranged, is not so useful as a very moderate one that is well arranged, so the greatest amount of knowledge, if not elaborated by our own thoughts, is worth much less than a far smaller volume that has been abundantly and repeatedly thought over. For only by universally combining what we know, by comparing every truth with every other, do we fully assimilate our own knowledge and get it into our power. We can think over only what we know, and so we should learn something; but we know only what we have thought out....

258

... Therefore the mind is deprived of all its elasticity by *much* reading as is a spring when a weight is continually applied to it; and the surest way not to have thoughts of our own is for us at once to take up a book when we have a moment to spare. This practice is the reason why erudition makes most men more stupid and simple than they are by nature and also deprives their literary careers of every success. As Pope says, they remain:

For ever reading, never to be read.

The Dunciad, 3:193–94.

Scholars are those who have read in books, but thinkers, men of genius, world enlighteners, and reformers of the human race are those who have read directly in the book of the world.

259

At bottom, only our own fundamental ideas have truth and life; for it is they alone that we really and thoroughly understand. The ideas of someone else that we have read are the scraps and leavings of someone else's meal, the cast-off clothes of a stranger.

The idea of another that we have read is related to our own that occurs to us as the impression in stone of a plant from the primeval world to the blossoming plant of spring.

260

Reading is a mere makeshift for original thinking. When we read, we allow another to guide our thoughts in leading strings. Moreover, many books merely serve to show how many false paths there are and how seriously we could go astray if we allowed ourselves to be guided by them. But whoever is guided by genius, in other words thinks for himself, thinks freely and of his own accord and thinks correctly; he has the compass for finding the right way. We should, therefore, read only when the source of our own ideas dries up, which will be the case often enough even with the best minds. On the other hand, to scare away our own original and powerful ideas in order to take up a book, is a sin against the Holy Ghost. We then resemble the man who runs away from free nature in order to look at a herbarium, or to contemplate a beautiful landscape in a copper engraving.

Even if occasionally we had been able very easily and conveniently to find in a book a truth or view that we very laboriously and slowly discovered through our own thinking and combining, it is nevertheless a hundred times more valuable if we have arrived at it through our own original thinking. Only then does it enter into the whole system of our ideas as an integral part and living member; only then is it completely and firmly connected therewith, is understood in all its grounds and consequents, bears the color, tone, and stamp of our whole mode of thought, has come at the very time when the need for it was keen, is therefore firmly established and cannot again pass away. Accordingly, Goethe's verse here finds its most perfect application and even explanation:

> What from your fathers' heritage is lent,
> Earn it anew, really to possess it!

Thus the man who thinks for himself only subsequently becomes acquainted with the authorities for his opinions when they serve merely to confirm him therein and to encourage him. The book-philosopher, on the other hand, starts from those authorities in that he constructs for himself an entire system from the opinions of others that he has collected in the course of his reading. Such a system is then like an automaton composed of foreign material, whereas that of the original thinker resembles a living human being. For it originated like this, since the external world fertilized the thinking mind that afterwards carried it and gave birth to it.

The truth that has been merely learned sticks to us like an artificial limb, a false tooth, a nose of wax, or at best like a rhinoplastic nose formed from someone else's flesh. On the other hand, the truth acquired through our own thinking is like the natural limb; it alone really belongs to us. On this rests the distinction between the thinker and the mere scholar. The intellectual gain of the man who thinks for himself is, therefore, like a beautiful painting that vividly stands out with correct light and shade, sustained tone, and perfect harmony of colors. The intellectual acquisition of the mere scholar, on the other hand, is like a large palette full of bright colors, systematically arranged perhaps, but without harmony, sequence, and significance.

261

Reading is equivalent to thinking with someone else's head instead of with one's own. Now for our own thinking, whence a coherent and connected whole, a system though not strictly rounded off, endeavors to evolve, nothing is more detrimental than too strong an influx of other people's ideas through constant reading. For each of them has sprung from the mind of another, belongs to another system, bears another tint; and never do they flow of themselves into a totality of thought, knowledge, insight, and conviction. On the contrary, they set up in the head a slight Babylonian confusion of tongues, and a mind so crammed is now robbed of all clear insight and thus is well-nigh disorganized. This state can be observed in many scholars and results in their being inferior to many illiterate men as regards common sense, correct judgment, and practical tact. The latter have always subordinated to, and incorporated in, their own thinking the little knowledge that has come to them from without through experience, conversation, and a little reading. Now it is just this that the scientific *thinker* also does to a greater degree. Although he needs much knowledge and must, therefore, read a great deal, his mind is nevertheless strong enough to master all this, to assimilate it, to incorporate it into his system of ideas, and thus to subordinate it to the organically consistent totality of his vast and ever-growing insight. Here his own thinking, like the ground-bass of an organ, always dominates everything and is never drowned by the notes and tones of others, as is the case with the minds of mere pundits and polyhistors, where fragments of music in all keys run into one another, so to speak, and the fundamental note can no longer be detected at all.

262

Those who have spent their lives in reading, and have drawn their wisdom from   10
books, resemble men who have acquired precise information about a country from many descriptions of travel. They are able to give much information about things, but at bottom they have really no coherent, clear, and thorough knowledge

of the nature of the country. On the other hand, those who have spent their lives in thinking are like men who have themselves been in that country. They alone really know what they are talking about; they have a consistent and coherent knowledge of things there and are truly at home in them. . . .

265

. . . The characteristic sign of all first-rate minds is the directness of all their judgments and opinions. All that they express and assert is the result of their own original thinking and everywhere proclaims itself as such even by the style of delivery. Accordingly, like princes, they have an imperial immediacy in the realm of the mind; the rest are all mediatized, as is already seen from their style that has no stamp of originality.

Therefore every genuine and original thinker is to this extent like a monarch; he is immediate and perceives no one who is his superior. Like the decrees of a monarch, his judgments spring from his own supreme power and come directly from himself. For he no more accepts authorities than does the monarch take orders; on the contrary, he admits nothing but what he himself has confirmed. On the other hand, minds of the common ruck who labor under all kinds of current opinions, authorities, and prejudices, are like the crowd that silently obeys laws and orders. . . .

268

The presence of an idea is like that of a loved one. We imagine that we shall never forget it and that the beloved can never become indifferent to us; but out of sight, out of mind! The finest thought runs the risk of being irretrievably forgotten if it is not written down, and the beloved of being taken from us unless she has been wedded.

— Translated by E.F.J. Payne

ACTIVITIES FOR WRITING AND DISCUSSION

1. Review your annotations of Schopenhauer's text. Choose one or more that speak(s) most powerfully to your own experiences of reading or thinking. Then use the annotated passage(s) as a springboard to writing and reflecting on your experiences. Write in essay form, or, if you wish, compose a letter to Schopenhauer or a dialogue with him in which you share your experiences of reading and thinking.

2. Schopenhauer's text is rich in **metaphors, similes,** and analogies. Working alone or in a group, underline and annotate as many examples of these figures as you can. Then choose two or three and show how they help explain or clarify Schopenhauer's ideas.

3. Working from your annotations of "On Thinking for Oneself," summarize the distinctions Schopenhauer makes between "reading" and "thinking." Then agree or disagree with the distinctions.

Adrienne Rich (b. 1929)

A Leak in History

I'm staying in a house in the Vermont countryside, shaded in front by three big sugar maples. Behind it lies a grove of the same trees, and on a hillside far away I can see another grove, glowing green in rich late-afternoon light. In autumn the leaves turn scarlet; in late winter thaw the pale aqueous sap starts rising and is gathered and laboriously evaporated, in little steamy shacks and cabins, down to its essence, a syrup fine as honey. The Abnaki Indians knew this process before the Yankees came to clear scattered pools of land for grazing, leaving old forest lands in between. Taught by the Abnaki, the first white men made maple sugar in Vermont in 1752.

Under snow, the sap shrinks back. In early thaw, farmers trudge and horse-sledge through the woods to drill little taps into the rough-barked trunks. The sap used to be collected in wooden firkins, then in tin pails hung over the taps; more recently, where terrain and weather allow, plastic tubing is used. A culture formed around this labor-intensive harvesting, first ritual of the northern spring, the culture of the sugarhouse with its ancient sprung castoff chairs, steaming evaporation trays, wet snow and mud trodden inside on heavy boots, doughnuts and coffee, pickles, frankfurters, and beer brought down by women from farm kitchens, eaten and drunk by men lugging and pouring sap and stoking the wood fires. Hard manual labor—about forty gallons of sap being collected and boiled down to obtain one gallon of syrup—and adept, sensitive calculation of the cycles of thaw and freeze that make for the best sugaring-off; testing for the moment when the thin, faintly sweet sap has reached the density of amber syrup. The sour crispness of pickle on the tongue amid all that sweaty sweetness. There is a summer culture too, at church suppers and county fairs, where "sugar on snow" still competes with cotton-candy machines and barbecue—pans of last winter's snow from icehouse, cemetery vault, or freezer, sticky arabesques of hot syrup poured on, served on paper plates with the necessary pickle and doughnut on the side.

Maple trees reproduce with energy: Under any big tree you will find dozens of seedlings crowding each other; in spring the seeds, or keys, blow far afield on little brown wings soon after the new leaves uncurl. The root system of a full-grown maple is many times the circumference of the great crown. In their early-summer-evening green, in the hectic flare of their October changing, in the strong, stripped upreaching of their winter bareness, they are presences of enormous vitality and generosity, trees that yield much to the eye, to the tongue, to the modest cash assets of farm families.

It's said that acid rain and road salt are slowly dooming the sugar maples. Studying and testing the rings of mature trees, scientists have found that up until 1955 they show no evidence of chemical stress; since 1955 acidity has been wearing into the trees and will eventually destroy them. I look out at the grove on the hill, the old trees just outside the window; all seems as it has always been, without smirch or taint.

I remember other trees that stood in this landscape when I first knew it: the   5
wineglass elms. Every village common, every roadside, had them. *Ulmus ameri-*
canus, outspreading limbs sweeping up from a straight and slender trunk in the
form of a true wineglass, green in summer, golden in autumn, architecturally
elegant in nakedness. An old pamphlet from the State Agricultural Service, found
in a drawer, implores cooperation in destroying infested bark and wood and
protecting still-healthy trees. But the fungus-carrying elm bark beetle won out.
Throughout New England, elms fell barren in summer, sick to death, easily splintered by winds. Soon a living elm in leaf was something rare and precious. Now
it's hard to remember where they stood.

The poorer we become, the less we remember what we had. Whenever I walk
into this house after an absence, I drink, slowly and deliberately, a glass of pure
cold water from the spring-fed tap. I don't drink from most taps because I don't
like their ill flavor. And the taste of bottled water from the supermarket has no savor; it reminds me of nothing. The spring water flowing into this house does — in
its transparency, its lucidity, its original cold. Of course it tastes of this place,
sharp with memories, but also of water I drank as a child in the 1930s, from an
iron pipe set in the side of a ravine where I used to play. It seemed like the saving,
merciful drink of water in legends or poetry; through it I sensuously understood
the beautiful, lip-smacking words "to quench a thirst." This was not in the country, but in a wooded park in Baltimore. There was a stream there too, where we
waded, and plunged our hands in to the wrists, and never got sick.

Three thousand miles to the west, where I live now, on a much-traveled hill
road winding eastward from the coast, there is a standing pipe called the Lom-
bardi Spring. A few cars and trucks are almost always parked on the shoulder,
people lined up with jugs and bottles, because that water is held to be particularly
delicious and good. And it is free.

Sensual vitality is essential to the struggle for life. It's as simple — and as
threatened — as that. To have no love for the taste of the water you drink is a loss
of vitality. If your appetite is embalmed in prescriptives, you are weakened for the
struggle. Under the most crushing conditions of deprivation, people have to fill
their stomachs, eat earth, eat plain starch, force down watery and rancid soup,
drink urine for survival. Yet there's another story. In the newsletter produced by
inmates in a women's facility, among columns on law, religion, politics, current
prison issues, there is the "Konvict Kitchen," with recipes for special microwaved
dishes to be created by combining items from the prison store:

> 1 can Mixin' Chicken
> 1 Shrimp Noodle Cup
> jalapeño peppers (optional)
> onions (optional)
> bell peppers (optional)
> 2 packages margarine

> Crush noodles and put in large microwave bowl with enough water to cover
> them. Let sit for three minutes. Take bell peppers, onions, and hot peppers
> and saute in microwave for two minutes. Take mixture out, add noodles, stir
> thoroughly and cook in microwave for approximately 20–25 minutes, until

noodles are crisp. Stir every five minutes. Keep lid lightly on mixture but not tightly closed. Serves 2.

—Gloria Bolden

Poetry being a major form of prison literature, it goes without saying that there are poems in the newsletter. Like the recipe above, they work within the prison context but refuse to be subdued:

This is prison not the Hilton
Heard we got it made in here?
This is livin' at its finest?
Country clubs with kegs of beer?
Say—listen up my friend
let me tell you what it's like
to be livin' in the sewer
flushed further down the pipe . . .

This is prison not the Hilton
Election time is on its way
you'll hear it on the TV
we should suffer every day
days of torture
nights of terror—
feel your heart's been torn in shreds?
Say you're showered with asbestos,
drinking nitrate in your bed? . . .

This is prison not the Hilton
care to change your place for mine?
Think that 20 out of 60
isn't doing enough time?
Care to try this life of leisure?
Care to leave your folks behind?
This is prison not the Hilton
and its hell here all the time.[1]

Sensual vitality is essential to the struggle for life. Many people drink as if filling themselves with dirt or starch: the filling of an emptiness. But what comes after is a greater emptiness. In the reputations of poets like Hart Crane, Dylan Thomas, Kenneth Rexroth, James Wright, Richard Hugo, Delmore Schwartz, Robert Lowell, Elizabeth Bishop, John Berryman, Anne Sexton, drinking has been romanticized as part of the "poetic fate," the "despondency and madness"

10

---

1. Composed by Jacqueline Dixon-Bey and Mary Glover, inside Florence Crane Women's Prison, Coldwater, Michigan, Spring 1990; recipe and poem from *Insight: Serving the Women of Florence Crane Women's Facility*, 2d quarter ed. (1990). [Rich's note.]

of the poet—as if bricklayers, surgeons, housewives, miners, generals, salesmen haven't also poured down liquids to fire up or numb interior spaces of dread. A politician's wife confesses to having drunk aftershave, nail-polish remover, in desperate substitute for confiscated bottles. Whether done with nail-polish remover or antique liqueur of pear, this is self-poisoning.

But there's a sensual vitality in drinking wine and "spirits" as in drinking pure water. Both belong to ancient human rites and memories. People have fermented the apple, the grape, the palm, hops and barley, rice, berries, the potato, the dandelion, the plum. Along with the rising of the yeast in bread was the fermentation of the grain, the fruit. Blessed be the Spirit of the Universe, who created the fruit of the vine. For us to use it as we may.

That so many of us use, or have used, the fruit of the vine in an attempt to fill our terrifying voids may point to the failure of a general communal vitality more than to some inherent poisoning in the fermentation process. I don't minimize the ultimate transaction between the individual and the bottle. But the individual's sense of emptiness reflects—and helps perpetuate—a public emptiness.

When a vast, stifling denial in the public realm is felt by every individual yet there is no language, no depiction, of what is being denied, it becomes for each his or her own anxious predicament, a daily struggle to act "as if" everything were normal. Alcohol, drugs offer a reprieve—not ceremony or celebration, but a substitute for vital bonds of community and friendship, for collective memory and responsibility. Where there is no public face of interdependence, of justice and mercy, where there is no social language for "picking up the pieces when we don't know what/where they are," anomie and amnesia, alcohol and drug abuse can work as social controls and, because they appear "normal," can be more effective—in a very large country—than terrorization by a secret police.

The danger lies in forgetting what we had. The flow between generations becomes a trickle, grandchildren tape-recording grandparents' memories on special occasions perhaps—no casual storytelling jogged by daily life, there being no shared daily life what with migrations, exiles, diasporas, rendings, the search for work. Or there is a shared daily life riddled with holes of silence. In 1979 Helen Epstein published her book of interviews, *Children of the Holocaust*. In 1985 Judy Kaplan and Linn Shapiro edited *Red Diaper Babies: Children of the Left*, a compilation of transcripts of taped sessions at two conferences held in 1982 and 1983 by children of leftist and Communist families, then in their thirties and forties. There are haunting resonances between the two groups of testimony: the children's experience of knowing that there was something of major weight at the center of their parents' lives, something secret, unspoken, unspeakable. (Epstein refers to "that quiet, invisible community, that peer group without a sign.") Both groups of children knowing about things that could not be discussed on the playground or with "strangers," that were to a greater or lesser degree unmentionable even at home. A tattoo on an aunt's wrist. A neighbor's withdrawal. A mother's nightmares; a parent's terror when a child left the house or came home late. A father in jail or underground. Close friends who suddenly could not be mentioned. Certain newspapers having to be hidden; jobs inexplicably lost; children trained that "the walls have ears"; a car parked across the street for hours, one day every week, two men sitting inside. There can be no question of equalizing the events that catalyzed these two silences. Yet the passing on of living history is an essential ingredient of individual and communal self-knowledge, and in both cases that continuity was breached. Forty years is a wilderness of silence.

The loss can be a leak in history or a shrinking in the vitality of everyday life. 15 Fewer and fewer people in this country entertain each other with verbal games, recitations, charades, singing, playing on instruments, doing anything as amateurs—people who are good at something because they enjoy it. To be good at talk, not pompously eloquent or didactic, but having a vivid tongue, savoring turns of phrase—to sing on key and know many songs by heart—to play fiddle, banjo, mandolin, flute, accordion, harmonica—to write long letters—to draw pictures or whittle wood with some amount of skill—to do moderately and pleasingly well, in short, a variety of things without solemn investment or disenabling awe—these were common talents till recently, crossing class and racial lines. People used their human equipment—memory, image making, narrative, voice, hand, eye—unselfconsciously, to engage with other people, and not as specialists or "artistes." My father and his mother both loved to recite poetry learned long ago in school. He had Poe's "The Raven" and "Annabel Lee" from memory, and he had won a school medal for his recitation of a long narrative poem called "Lasca," which began:

> I want free life and I want fresh air,
> And I sigh for the canter after the cattle,
> The crack of whips like shots in a battle,
> The green below, and the blue above,
> And dash, and danger, and life, and love—
>   And Lasca.

And my grandmother still remembered a poem she'd learned in Vicksburg, Mississippi—Jewish girl sent to a convent school where there were no secular schools. In her seventies she could recite, black eyes glowing, "Asleep at the Switch":

> It was down in the Lehigh Valley,
> At the bottom of the bottomless ditch,
> I lived alone in a cabin,
> And attended the railway switch.

The reciters of these two poems could not have been in person more unlike the "speaker" of each poem, and that was part of the excitement: to see a known person become someone new and different, change his or her identity but within a framework that allowed each to change back at the end—from Texan desperado to my sedentary, scholarly father; from negligent, solitary switchman to my sheltered, precise grandmother. And such recitations let a child feel that poetry (verse, really, with its structured rhymes, meters, and ringingly fulfilled aural expectations) was not just words on the page, but could live in people's minds for decades, to be summoned up with relish and verve, and that poetry was not just literature, but embodied in voices.

For ordinary people to sing or whistle used to be as common as breathing. I remember men whistling, briskly or hauntingly, women humming with deep-enclosed chest tones. Where did it go? A technology of "canned" music available through car radios, portable "boom boxes," and cassette players, programmed music piped into the workplace, has left people born in the 1950s and later largely alien to the experience of hearing or joining in casual music making. Knowing how to pitch your voice isn't the privilege of the conservatory; people used to learn it from hearing others casually, unself-consciously sing, as they learned language, accent, inflection in speech. Now singing belongs to professionals, is preserved in churches; rap, a spontaneous and sophisticated expression of black street youth at first, quickly became a commodity on videotape, adapted as a new style for television commercials. (Yet rap goes on around the world, picking up on local griefs, local insurgencies.)

Part of the experience of casual singing was the undeliberate soaking up of many songs, many verses. Ballads, hymns, work songs, opera arias, folk songs, popular songs, labor songs, schoolchildren's playground songs. And, of course, with the older songs words changed over time, new generations of singers misremembering or modifying. Tunes changed, too, as songs traveled: from England or Wales to Appalachia, from Africa to the Sea Islands, France to Québec, and across the continent.

To ears accustomed to high-technology amplification and recording processes, the unamplified human voice, the voice not professionally trained, may sound acoustically lacking, even perhaps embarrassing. And so we're severed from a physical release and pleasure, whether in solitude or community—the use of breath to produce song. But breath is also *Ruach*, spirit, the human connection to the universe.

ACTIVITIES FOR WRITING AND DISCUSSION

1. Twice in the essay Rich writes, "Sensual vitality is essential to the struggle for life," and the phrase "sensual vitality" occurs several times elsewhere. On the basis of the stories in the first dozen paragraphs of the essay, explain what you think Rich means by the phrases "sensual vitality" and "struggle for life." Jot down and share some stories or examples of your own that reinforce her point that such vitality is "essential."

2. Reread and annotate paragraphs 12 and 13. Then:
   a. Use the process described on pages 127–128 to write a summary of Rich's argument in these paragraphs.
   b. Share your summary—and any of your annotations (including questions or confusions over difficult concepts)—with a partner or small group.
   c. Write a notebook entry agreeing or disagreeing with Rich's argument.

3. In paragraph 14, Rich says that we have "no shared daily life" today, or that it is "a shared daily life riddled with holes of silence." On the basis of your own

experiences, do you tend to agree or disagree? Share—orally or in writing—your own stories of "shared" or alienated life.

4. Reread and reannotate paragraphs 15 to 19. Then react (in writing) to the picture of contemporary life and lifestyle that Rich presents in these paragraphs. If you believe her picture is accurate, are there ways of reversing the trends she describes, and, if so, what are they?

Carol Bly (b. 1930)

Growing Up Expressive

Love, death, the cruelty of power, and time's curve past the stars are what children want to look at. For convenience's sake, let's say these are the four most vitally touching things in life. Little children ask questions about them with relish. Children, provided they are still little enough, have no eye to doing any problem solving about love or death or injustice or the universe; they are simply interested. I've noticed that as we read aloud literature to them, about Baba Yaga, and Dr. Doolittle, and Ivan and the Firebird, and Rat and Mole, children are not only interested, they are prepared to be vitally touched by the great things of life. If you like the phrase, they are what some people call "being as a little child." Another way of looking at it is to say that in our minds we have two kinds of receptivity to life going on all the time: first, being vitally touched and enthusiastic (grateful, enraged, puzzled—but, at all events, *moved*) and, second, having a will to solve problems.

Our gritty society wants and therefore deliberately trains problem solvers, however, not mystics. We teach human beings to keep themselves conscious only of problems that *can* conceivably be solved. There must be no hopeless causes. Now this means that some subjects, of which death and sexual love come to mind straight off, should be kept at as low a level of consciousness as possible. Both resist problem solving. A single-minded problem solver focuses his consciousness, of course, on problems to be solved, but even he realizes there is a concentric, peripheral band of other material around the problems. This band appears to him as "issues." He is not interested in these issues for themselves; he sees them simply as impacting on the problems. He will allow us to talk of love, death, injustice, and eternity—he may even encourage us to do so because his group-dynamics training advises him to let us have our say, thus dissipating our willfulness—but his heart is circling, circling, looking for an opening to *wrap up* these "issues" so he can return attention to discrete, solvable problems. For example, a physician who has that mentality does not wish to be near dying patients very much. They are definitely not a solvable problem. If he is wicked, he will regard them as a present issue with impact on a future problem: then he will order experimentation done on them during their last weeks with us. It means his ethic is toward the healing process only, but not toward the dying person. His ethic is toward problem solving, not toward wonder. He will feel quite conscientious while doing the experiments on the dying patient, because he feels he is saving lives of future patients.

To return to little children for a second: they simply like to contemplate life and death. So our difficulty, in trying to educate adults so they will be balanced but enthusiastic, is to keep both streams going—the problem solving, which seems to be the mental genius of our species, and the fearless contemplation of gigantic things, the spiritual genius of our species.

The problem-solving mentality is inculcated no less in art and English classes than in mathematics and science. Its snake oil is hope of success: by setting very small topics in front of people, for which it is easy for them to see the goals, the problems, the solutions, their egos are not threatened. They feel hopeful of being effective. Therefore, to raise a generation of problem solvers, you encourage them to visit the county offices (as our sixth-grade teachers do) and you lead them to understand that this is citizenship. You carefully do not suggest that citizenship also means comparatively complex and hopeless activities like Amnesty International's pressure to get prisoners in far places released or at least no longer tortured. Small egos are threatened by huge, perhaps insoluble problems. Therefore, one feeds the small ego confidence by setting before it dozens and dozens of very simple situations. The ego is nourished by feeling it understands the relationship between the county recorder's office and the county treasurer's office; in later life, when young people find a couple of sticky places in county government, they will confidently work at smoothing them. How very different an experience such problem solving is from having put before one the spectacle of the United States' various stances and activities with respect to germ warfare. Educators regularly steer off all interest in national and international government to one side, constantly feeding our rural young people on questions to which one can hope for answers on a short timeline. We do not ask them to exercise that muscle which bears the weight of vast considerations—such as cruelty in large governments. By the time the average rural Minnesotan is eighteen, he or she expects to stay in cheerful places, devote some time to local government and civic work, and "win the little ones." Rural young people have a repertoire of pejorative language for hard causes: "opening that keg of worms," "no end to that once you get into it," "don't worry—you can't do anything about that from where you are," "we could go on about that forever!" They are right, of course: we could, and our species, at its most cultivated, does go on forever about love, death, power, time, the universe. But some of us, alas, have been conditioned by eighteen fashionably to despise those subjects because there are no immediate answers to all the questions they ask us.

The other way we negatively reinforce any philosophical bent in children is to 5 pretend we don't see the content in their artwork. We comment only on the technique, in somewhat the same way you can scarcely get a comment on rural preachers' sermon content: the response is always, He does a good (or bad) job of speaking. "Well, but what did he say?" "Oh, he talked really well. The man can preach!"

The way to devalue the content of a child's painting is to say, "Wow, you sure can paint!" The average art teacher in Minnesota is at pains to find something to say to the third grader's painting of a space machine with complicated, presumably electronic equipment in it. Here is the drawing in words: A man is sitting at some controls. Outside his capsule, fire is flying from emission points on his ship toward another spaceship at right, hitting it. Explosions are coming out of its side and tail. What is an art teacher to do with this? Goodness knows. So he or she says, "My goodness, I can see there's a lot of action there!" It is said in a deliberately encouraging way but anyone can hear under the carefully supportive comment: "A lot of work going into nothing but more TV-inspired violence." One might as well have told the child, "Thank you for sharing."

I once attended a regional writers' group at which a young poet wrote about his feelings of being a single parent and trying to keep his sanity as he cared for his children. In his poem, he raced up the staircase, grabbed a gun, and shot the clock. When he finished reading it aloud to us, someone told him, "I certainly am glad you shared with us. I'd like to really thank you for sharing."

If we are truly serious about life we are going to have to stop thanking people for sharing. It isn't enough response to whatever has been offered. It is half ingenuous, and sometimes it is insincere, and often it is patronizing. It is the *dictum excrementi* of our decade.

I would like to keep in mind for a moment the art works described above: the child's painting of a spaceship assaulting another spaceship, and the harrowed father's racing up the staircase and shooting the clock. Here is a third. It is a twelve-year-old's theme for English class.

> They were their four days and nights before anyone found them. It was wet and cold down there. As little kids at the orphanage, they had been beaten every night until they could scarcely make it to bed. Now they were older. Duane and Ellen leaned together. "I love you forever," she told him. He asked her, "Even though my face is marked from getting scarlet fever and polio and small pox and newmonya and they wouldn't take decent care of me, not call the doctor or anything, so the marks will always be on me?" "You know I love you," Ellen told him. "You know that time they tortured me for information and I was there but I didn't talk and later I found out it was your uncle who did it. I didn't talk because I remembered the American flag." Just then they heard someone shout, "Anyone alive down there in this mess?" You see a bomb had gone off destroying a entire U.S.A. city where they lived. Duane had lived with his cruel uncle who took him out of the orphanage to get cheap labor and Ellen lived at a boardinghouse where there were rats that ate pages of her diary all the time. Now they both looked up and shouted "We're here!" A head appeared at the top of the well into which they had fallen or they would of been in 6,500 pieces like all the other men and ladies even pregnant ones and little kids in that town. Now this head called down, "Oh—a boy and a girl!" then the head explained it was going for a ladder and ropes and it ducked away and where it had been they saw the beginnings of stars for that

night, the stars still milky in front of the bright blue because the sky wasn't dark enough yet to show them up good.

The English teacher will typically comment on this story by observing that the 10 spelling is uneven, and adjectives get used as adverbs. In rural Minnesota (if not elsewhere) an English teacher can spend every class hour on adjectives used as adverbs: it is meat and potatoes to a nag. But when we discuss spelling, syntax, and adverbs, we are talking method, not content. The child notices that nothing is said of the story's *plot*. No one remarks on the *feelings* in it. Now if this happens every time a child hands in fiction or a poem, the child will realize by the time he reaches twelfth grade that meaning or feelings are not worth anything, that "mechanics" (note the term) are all that matter.

It is rare for a public school English teacher to comment on a child's content unless the material is *factual*. Minnesota teachers encourage writing booklets about the state, themes on ecology and county government, on how Dad strikes the field each autumn, on how Mom avoids open-kettle canning because the USDA advises against it. In this way, our children are conditioned to regard writing as problem solving instead of contemplation, as routine thinking instead of imaginative inquiry.

How can we manage it otherwise?

I would like to suggest some questions we can ask children about their artwork which will encourage them to grow up into lovers, lobby supporters, and Amnesty International members, instead of only township officers and annual protestors against daylight saving time. Let us gather all the elements of the three artworks presented in this Letter: the little boy's spaceship-war painting, the young divorced father's narrative poem, and the twelve-year-old girl's story of love in a well. We have a set of images before us, then:

Man directing spaceship fire
Another aircraft being obliterated
Staircase, man shooting a clock; children
Cruel orphanage
Torture
Last survivors of a decimated city

Let us, instead of lending the great sneer to these images, be respectful of them. It may help to pretend the painting is by Picasso, that Flaubert wrote the father/clock scene, and that Tolstoy wrote the well story. It helps to remember that Picasso felt the assault of historical events on us—like Guernica; Flaubert, as skillfully as Dostoyevsky and with less self-pity, was an observer of violent detail; and the Tolstoy who wrote *Resurrection* or the scene of Pierre's imprisonment in *War and Peace* would turn to the well/love story without qualm.

We know we would never say to Picasso, Flaubert, or Tolstoy, "Why don't you draw something you know about from everyday life? Why don't you write about something you know about? You say Anna was smashed beneath a train? Thank you for sharing!"

The fact is that a child's feelings about orphanages and torture and love are   15
things that he does know about. They are psychic realities inside him, and when he draws them, he is drawing something from everyday life. Sometimes they are from his night life of dreaming, but in any event they are images of passion and he is drawing from his genuine if garbled experience. A few years ago there was a stupid movement to discourage children's reading of Grimms' fairy tales. Later, with a more sophisticated psychology, we learned that the stepmother who is hostile and overweening is a reality to all children; the cutting-off of the hero's right hand and replacing of it with a hand of silver is a reality to all children. Spaceships, witches' gingerbread houses, orphanages, being the last two people to survive on earth—all these are part of the inner landscape, something children know about. Therefore, in examining their artwork, we need better sets of questions to ask them. Young people who are not repressed are going to lay their wild stuff in front of adults (hoping for comment of some kind, praise if possible) until the sands of life are run, so we had better try to be good at responding to them. And unless we want to raise drones suitable only for conveyor-belt shifts, we had better be at least half as enthusiastic as when they tell us, Mama, I got the mowing finished.

Here are some questions to ask our young artist. How much of that electronic equipment is used for firepower and how much just to run the ship? After the other spaceship is blown up and the people in it are dead, what will this man do? Will he go home somewhere? Were the stars out that night? You said he'll go home to his parents. Did the other man have parents? How soon will that man's parents find out that his spaceship was destroyed? Could you draw in the stars? You said they were out—could you draw them into the picture some way? but don't ruin anything you've got in there now. Also, that wire you said ran to the solar plates, will you darken it so it shows better? Don't change it—just make it clearer. Yes— terrific! Can you see the planet where the other man would have returned to if he had lived till morning?

The young father's story: There is an obvious psychic complication to this story: the violence in his shooting out the clock face is gratuitous, and the plea for attention on the part of the author directed at the reader is glaring: clock faces as psychological symbols are in the public domain. Anyone who tells a friend (or a group of strangers) I am going to shoot up a clock face at 11 P.M. is asking for psychological attention. In a civil world, to ask is to receive, so if we are civilized we have to pay attention and ask the young author: Why does the father in the story blast the clock? And, when he replies, we have to ask some more. If there was ever an instance in which it was O.K. to say, "Thanks for sharing," this is not it.

I should like to add that this will be especially difficult for rural teachers because the traditional country way to treat any kind of mental problem is to stare it down. It didn't happen. I didn't hear that insane thing you just said, and you know you don't really hate your mother. What nice parent would shoot a clock?

We uniformly do what Dr. Vaillant in *Adaptations to Life* would call a denial adaptation. It takes a brave questioner when the young person brings in a crazy story.

The well/love story: Did you know there really are such orphanages? There are orphanages where the children have to get up at four-thirty to work in the dairy, and the girls work hours and hours in the kitchens, and the children's growth is stunted. Did you make the girl so brave on purpose? Were they a lucky couple or an unlucky couple, or is that the sort of a question you can't ask? You made a point of telling us they'd been through a lot of hardship. What would it have been like for them if they hadn't? Do you want to talk about what blew up the city? Did you imagine yourself in the well?

Those are not brilliant questions; they are simply respectful, because the art 20 works described are concerned with death by violence; cruelty by institutions; treachery by relations; bravery (or cowardice—either one is important); sexual love, either despite or encouraged by dreadful circumstances.

They are some of the subjects in *War and Peace,* in Dürer's etchings, paintings, and woodcuts, and in *Madame Bovary.*

It is a moot question in my mind which of two disciplines will be the more useful in helping people stay vitally touched by the Great Things: psychology might do it—and English literature in high school might do it (instruction on the college level is generally so dutiful to methodology that it seems a lost cause to me. "How did D. H. Lawrence foreshadow this event?" and "What metaphors does Harold Rosenberg use in his discussion of Action Painting?" are the questions of technocrats, not preservers of spirit. It is as if we got home from church and the others said, "How was church?" "We had Eucharist," we tell them. "Well, how was it?" they ask. "Pretty good," we reply. "Bishop Anderson was there. He held the chalice eight inches above the rail so no one spilled, then he turned and wiped the chalice after each use so no germs were passed along. People who had already communed returned to their benches using the north aisle so there was no bottlenecking at the chancel.")

I don't think churches will be helpful in preserving the mystical outlook as long as they see life and death as a *problem*—a problem of salvation—with a solution to be worked at. Churches have an axe to grind. They might take the father running up the staircase to be an impact subject: they would wish to use their program to solve his problem. Churchmen often appear to be companionable counselors, but the appearance is largely manner and habit. Under the manner, the clergyman's mindset is nearly always to see a disturbed or grieving person's imagery as the *issues.* From there, he swings into psychological problem solving.

I would like to commend this responsibility to our English teachers: that they help our children preserve pity, happiness, and grief inside themselves. They can enhance those feelings by having young children both write and draw pictures. They can be very enthusiastic about the children's first drawings of death in the sky. Adults, particularly mature ones who have *not* got children in school at the moment, should make it clear that we expect this of English teachers and that we don't give a damn if LeRoy and Merv never in their lives get the sentence balance of past conditional and perfect subjunctive clauses right. We need to protect some of the Things Invisible inside LeRoy and Merv and the rest of us.

This is my last Letter from the Country. That is why it is so shrill. Gadflies are 25 always looking out a chance to be shrill anyway, so I jumped to this one and have shouted my favorite hope: that we can educate children not to be problem solvers but to be madly expressive all their lives.

ACTIVITIES FOR WRITING AND DISCUSSION

1. Working in a group, jot down what you think Bly means by the terms "problem solvers" (or "the problem-solving mentality") and "expressive." Then draw upon Bly's essay and your own experience to give some examples of each. Do you find the terms meaningful for thinking about learning and education? Why or why not?

2. Throughout her essay, Bly reviles the expression "Thank you for sharing." Identify some situations in which people use this expression, and explain the reasons Bly dislikes it. Do you share her dislike? Why or why not? *Additional activity:* Compose a text (story, dialogue, public speech, poem) in which this expression either recurs or serves as the focal subject.

3. In paragraph 18 Bly says that "the traditional country way to treat any kind of mental problem is to stare it down. It didn't happen." Bly is a rural Minnesotan. Is the phenomenon of "staring it down" confined to rural America? Write a dialogue between two people or characters in which one tries to "stare down" the other's "mental problem."

4. Bly criticizes the ways that some teachers teach. For instance, in paragraph 10 she says that English teachers focus their comments on students' "spelling, syntax, and adverbs" in order to avoid responding to the content and ideas in students' papers. "Now if this happens every time a child hands in fiction or a poem, the child will realize by the time he reaches twelfth grade that meaning or feelings are not worth anything, that 'mechanics' . . . are all that matter."
    a. Does this jibe—or conflict—with your own experience in English classes? Explain, and illustrate with some specific stories of your experiences.
    b. Imagine a situation in which a student is "madly expressive" in his or her writing, drawing, or other creative work. Create the student's madly expressive work and invent the comments that a "problem-solving" teacher might put on it.

5. In the last paragraph Bly states that her "favorite hope" is "that we can educate children not to be problem solvers but to be madly expressive all their

lives." Take a point of view that is opposed to Bly's and argue for the importance and value of teaching children to be problem solvers. *Alternative:* Write a dialogue between someone who shares Bly's view (expressed in the above quotation) and someone who opposes it. Emphasize the conflict between the two speakers and avoid an easy resolution of the conflict.

Play

William Shakespeare

The Tragedy of Othello, the Moor of Venice

The Names of the Actors
DUKE OF VENICE
BRABANTIO, [*a senator,*] *father to Desdemona*
[*Other*] SENATORS
GRATIANO, [*brother to Brabantio*]
two noble Venetians
LODOVICO, [*kinsman to Brabantio*]
OTHELLO, *The Moor,* [*in the military service of Venice*]
CASSIO, *an honorable lieutenant*
IAGO, [*an ensign,*] *a villain*
RODERIGO, *a gull'd gentleman*
MONTANO, *governor of Cyprus* [*before Othello*]
CLOWN, [*servant to Othello*]
DESDEMONA, [*daughter to Brabantio and*] *wife to Othello*
EMILIA, *wife to Iago*
BIANCA, *a courtezan*
GENTLEMEN *of Cyprus,* SAILORS, [OFFICERS, MESSENGER, HERALD, MUSICIANS, *and* ATTENDANTS]

[Scene: *Venice; a sea-port in Cyprus*]

Words and passages enclosed in square brackets in the text above are either emendations of the copy-text or additions to it.
I. i. Location: Venice. A street.

Act I, Scene I

Enter RODERIGO *and* IAGO.

> RODERIGO: [Tush,] never tell me! I take it much unkindly
> That thou, Iago, who hast had my purse
> As if the strings were thine, shouldst know of this.
> IAGO: ['Sblood,] but you'll not hear me.
> If ever I did dream of such a matter,   5
> Abhor me.
> RODERIGO: Thou toldst me thou didst hold him in thy hate.
> IAGO: Despise me if I do not. Three great ones of the city,
> In personal suit to make me his lieutenant,
> Off-capp'd to him; and, by the faith of man,   10
> I know my price, I am worth no worse a place.
> But he (as loving his own pride and purposes)
> Evades them with a bumbast circumstance
> Horribly stuff'd with epithites of war,
> [And in conclusion]   15
> Nonsuits my mediators; for, "Certes," says he,
> "I have already chose my officer."
> And what was he?
> Forsooth, a great arithmetician,
> One Michael Cassio, a Florentine   20
> (A fellow almost damn'd in a fair wife),
> That never set a squadron in the field,
> Nor the division of a battle knows
> More than a spinster—unless the bookish theoric,
> Wherein the [toged] consuls can propose   25
> As masterly as he. Mere prattle, without practice,
> Is all his soldiership. But he, sir, had th' election;
> And I, of whom his eyes had seen the proof
> At Rhodes, at Cyprus, and on [other] grounds
> Christen'd and heathen, must be belee'd and calm'd   30
> by debitor and creditor—this counter-caster,
> He (in good time!) must his lieutenant be,
> And I ([God] bless the mark!) his Moorship's ancient.

---

3. **this:** i.e. Othello's marriage to Desdemona.   4. **'Sblood:** by God's (Christ's) blood.   13. **bumbast:** bombast, a cotton material used for padding; here, inflated. The figure is continued in *stuff'd* (line 14). **circumstance:** circumlocution, rigmarole.   14. **epithites of war:** military jargon (*epithites,* a variant spelling of *epithets,* = expressions, terms).   16. **Nonsuits:** refuses. **Certes:** certainly.   19. **arithmetician:** i.e. one adept at figures, not at fighting; cf. line 31.   21. **almost . . . wife.** Unexplained. Perhaps Shakespeare originally intended to follow his source Cinthio in giving Cassio a wife. There is no evidence that Cassio has yet met Bianca.   23. **division:** arrangement. **battle:** battalion.   24. **spinster:** i.e. housewife (one of whose duties was spinning).   25. **toged:** wearing togas (dressed for the council-chamber, not the battlefield). **consuls:** senators. **propose:** talk.   28. **his:** i.e. Othello's.   30. **be . . . calm'd:** have the wind taken out of my sails and be left becalmed.   31. **debitor and creditor:** i.e. bookkeeper. **counter-caster:** accountant; literally, one who calculates with the aid of metal counters.   32. **in good time.** Ironic. 33. **ancient:** ensign, standard-bearer.

RODERIGO: By heaven, I rather would have been his hangman.

IAGO: Why, there's no remedy. 'Tis the curse of service;   35
Preferment goes by letter and affection,
And not by old gradation, where each second
Stood heir to th' first. Now, sir, be judge yourself
Whether I in any just term am affin'd
To love the Moor.

RODERIGO: I would not follow him then.   40

IAGO: O, sir, content you;
I follow him to serve my turn upon him.
We cannot all be masters, nor all masters
Cannot be truly follow'd. You shall mark
Many a duteous and knee-crooking knave   45
That (doting on his own obsequious bondage)
Wears out his time, much like his master's ass,
For nought but provender, and when he's old, cashier'd.
Whip me such honest knaves. Others there are
Who, trimm'd in forms and visages of duty,   50
Keep yet their hearts attending on themselves,
And throwing but shows of service on their lords,
Do well thrive by them; and when they have lin'd their coats,
Do themselves homage. These fellows have some soul,
And such a one do I profess myself. For, sir,   55
It is as sure as you are Roderigo,
Were I the Moor, I would not be Iago.
In following him, I follow but myself;
Heaven is my judge, not I for love and duty,
But seeming so, for my peculiar end;   60
For when my outward action doth demonstrate
The native act and figure of my heart
In complement extern, 'tis not long after
But I will wear my heart upon my sleeve
For daws to peck at: I am not what I am.   65

RODERIGO: What a [full] fortune does the thick-lips owe
If he can carry't thus!

IAGO: Call up her father.
Rouse him, make after him, poison his delight,
Proclaim him in the streets; incense her kinsmen,
And though he in a fertile climate dwell,   70

---

34. **his hangman:** the one to hang him.   36. **Preferment:** advancement. **letter and affection:** private recommendation and favoritism.   37. **old gradation:** seniority, as in the good old days.   39. **term:** respect. **affin'd:** bound.   41. **content you:** calm yourself.   48. **cashier'd:** dismissed.   50. **trimm'd ... duty:** wearing the manners and countenance of humble service.   60. **peculiar:** private.   62. **figure:** shape. 63. **complement extern:** external show corresponding to these hidden motives.   66. **thick-lips:** i.e. Othello. **owe:** own.   67. **carry't thus:** carry this off.   70. **though ... dwell:** i.e. though his general situation is a fortunate one. *Climate* = region, country.

Plague him with flies. Though that his joy be joy,
Yet throw such [changes] of vexation on't,
As it may lose some color.
    RODERIGO: Here is her father's house, I'll call aloud.
    IAGO: Do, with like timorous accent and dire yell
As when, by night and negligence, the fire   76
Is spied in populous cities.
    RODERIGO: What ho! Brabantio, Signior Brabantio, ho!
    IAGO: Awake! what ho, Brabantio! thieves, thieves!
Look to your house, your daughter, and your bags!
Thieves, thieves!   81
[*Enter* BRABANTIO] *above* [*at a window*].
    BRABANTIO: What is the reason of this terrible summons?
What is the matter there?
    RODERIGO: Signior, is all your family within?
    IAGO: Are your doors lock'd?
    BRABANTIO: Why? Wherefore ask you this?
    IAGO: ['Zounds,] sir, y' are robb'd! For shame, put on your gown;   86
Your heart is burst, you have lost half your soul;
Even now, now, very now, an old black ram
Is tupping your white ewe. Arise, arise!
Awake the snorting citizens with the bell,   90
Or else the devil will make a grandsire of you.
Arise, I say!
    BRABANTIO: What, have you lost your wits?
    RODERIGO: Most reverend signior, do you know my voice?
    BRABANTIO: Not I; what are you?
    RODERIGO: My name is Roderigo.
    BRABANTIO: The worser welcome;
I have charg'd thee not to haunt about my doors.   96
In honest plainness thou hast heard me say
My daughter is not for thee; and now, in madness
(being full of supper and distemp'ring draughts),
Upon malicious [bravery] dost thou come   100
To start my quiet.
    RODERIGO: Sir, sir, sir—
    BRABANTIO: But thou must needs be sure
My spirits and my place have in their power
To make this bitter to thee.
    RODERIGO: Patience, good sir.

---

71. **flies:** i.e. petty annoyances.   72. **changes of vexation:** vexatious changes.   73. **some color:** i.e. some of its fresh gloss.   75. **timorous:** terrifying.   76. **by . . . negligence:** at night and as the result of negligence.   86. **'Zounds:** by God's (Christ's) wounds.   90. **snorting:** snoring.   99. **distemp'ring:** disordering, intoxicating.   100. **Upon malicious bravery:** with hostile intent to defy me.   101. **start:** startle.

BRABANTIO: What tell'st thou me of robbing? This is Venice;   105
My house is not a grange.
    RODERIGO: Most grave Brabantio,
In simple and pure soul I come to you.
    IAGO: ['Zounds,] sir, you are one of those that will
not serve God, if the devil bid you. Because we come
to do you service, and you think we are ruffians,   110
you'll have your daughter cover'd with a Barbary
horse, you'll have your nephews neigh to you; you'll
have coursers for cousins, and gennets for germans.
    BRABANTIO: What profane wretch art thou?   114
    IAGO: I am one, sir, that comes to tell you your
daughter and the Moor are [now] making the beast
with two backs.
    BRABANTIO: Thou art a villain.
    IAGO: You are a senator.
    BRABANTIO: This thou shalt answer; I know thee, Roderigo.
    RODERIGO: Sir, I will answer any thing. But I beseech you,   120
If't be your pleasure and most wise consent
(As partly I find it is) that your fair daughter,
At this odd-even and dull watch o' th' night,
Transported with no worse nor better guard
But with a knave of common hire, a gundolier,   125
To the gross clasps of a lascivious Moor—
If this be known to you, and your allowance,
We then have done you bold and saucy wrongs;
But if you know not this, my manners tell me
We have your wrong rebuke. Do not believe   130
That, from the sense of all civility,
I thus would play and trifle with your reverence.
Your daughter (if you have not given her leave),
I say again, hath made a gross revolt,
Tying her duty, beauty, wit, and fortunes   135
In an extravagant and wheeling stranger
Of here and every where. Straight satisfy yourself.
If she be in her chamber or your house,
Let loose on me the justice of the state
For thus deluding you.

---

106. **grange:** isolated farmhouse.   107. **simple:** sincere.   112. **nephews:** i.e. grandsons.   113. **coursers:** horses. **cousins:** kinsmen. **gennets:** Spanish horses. **germans:** close relatives.   118. **villain:** base fellow. 119. **answer:** be held answerable for.   123. **odd-even:** i.e. about midnight, when there is scarcely any distinction between the end of one day and the beginning of the next.   124. **with:** by.   125. **But:** than. **gundolier:** gondolier.   127. **allowance:** approval.   128. **saucy:** insolent.   131. **from ... civility:** contrary to all sense of decency.   136. **extravagant:** expatriate; literally, wandering beyond his due limits. **wheeling:** roving. **stranger:** foreigner.   137. **Straight:** straightway.

BRABANTIO: Strike on the tinder, ho!   140
Give me a taper! Call up all my people!
This accident is not unlike my dream,
Belief of it oppresses me already.
Light, I say, light! *Exit [above].*
     IAGO: Farewell; for I must leave you.
It seems not meet, nor wholesome to my place,   145
To be producted (as, if I stay, I shall)
Against the Moor; for I do know the state
(How ever this may gall him with some check)
Cannot with safety cast him, for he's embark'd
With such loud reason to the Cyprus wars   150
(Which even now stands in act) that, for their souls,
Another of his fadom they have none
To lead their business; in which regard,
Though I do hate him as I do hell-pains,
Yet, for necessity of present life,   155
I must show out a flag and sign of love,
Which is indeed but sign. That you shall surely find him,
Lead to the Sagittary the raised search;
And there will I be with him. So farewell. *Exit.*
Enter [below] BRABANTIO *[in his night-gown] with* SERVANTS *and torches.*
     BRABANTIO: It is too true an evil; gone she is;   160
And what's to come of my despised time
Is nought but bitterness. Now, Roderigo,
Where didst thou see her?— O unhappy girl!—
With the Moor, say'st thou?—Who would be a father!—
How didst thou know 'twas she?— O, she deceives me   165
Past thought—What said she to you?— Get moe tapers;
Raise all my kindred.—Are they married, think you?
     RODERIGO: Truly, I think they are.
     BRABANTIO: O heaven! how got she out? O treason of the blood!   169
Fathers, from hence trust not your daughters' minds
By what you see them act. Is there not charms
By which the property of youth and maidenhood
May be abus'd? Have you not read, Roderigo,
Of some such thing?

---

142. **accident:** occurrence.   146. **producted:** produced, brought forward (to give evidence).   148. **gall
. . . check:** bring on him some irritating rebuke (*gall* = rub sore).   149. **cast:** dismiss.   150. **loud reason:**
i.e. evident rightness of choice.   151. **stands in act:** are under way.   152. **fadom:** fathom, i.e. capability.
153. **in which regard:** because of which consideration.   158. **Sagittary:** an inn (so called because its sign
bore the conventional figure of Sagittarius, the Archer—a Centaur shooting an arrow). **raised search:**
party of searchers who have been roused from their beds.   159. s.d. **night-gown:** dressing gown.
161. **what's . . . time:** the hateful remainder of my life.   166. **moe:** more.   169. **of the blood:** within the
family.   171. **charms:** magic spells.   172. **property:** nature.   173. **abus'd:** deceived.

RODERIGO: Yes, sir, I have indeed.
BRABANTIO: Call up my brother.— O would you had had her!—   175
Some one way, some another.— Do you know
Where we may apprehend her and the Moor?
   RODERIGO: I think I can discover him, if you please
To get good guard and go along with me.   179
   BRABANTIO: Pray you lead on. At every house I'll call
(I may command at most).— Get weapons, ho!
And raise some special officers of [night].—
On, good Roderigo, I will deserve your pains.
Exeunt.

SCENE II
Enter OTHELLO, IAGO, ATTENDANTS *with torches.*
   IAGO: Though in the trade of war I have slain men,
Yet do I hold it very stuff o' th' conscience
To do no contriv'd murder. I lack iniquity
Sometime to do me service. Nine or ten times
I had thought t' have yerk'd him here under the ribs.   5
   OTHELLO: 'Tis better as it is.
   IAGO: Nay, but he prated,
And spoke such scurvy and provoking terms
Against your honor,
That with the little godliness I have
I did full hard forbear him. But I pray you, sir,   10
Are you fast married? Be assur'd of this,
That the magnifico is much belov'd,
And hath in his effect a voice potential
As double as the Duke's. He will divorce you,
Or put upon you what restraint or grievance   15
The law (with all his might to enforce it on)
Will give him cable.
   OTHELLO: Let him do his spite;
My services which I have done the signiory
Shall out-tongue his complaints. 'Tis yet to know—
which, when I know that boasting is an honor,   20
I shall [provulgate]—I fetch my life and being
From men of royal siege, and my demerits

---

178. **discover:** uncover, bring to light.   181. **I . . . most:** i.e. I can be sure of help from most of them.
183. **deserve:** i.e. reward.   I.ii. Location: Venice. Another street.   1. **trade:** i.e. actual business.   2. **stuff:**
material, substance.   3. **contriv'd:** premeditated.   5. **yerk'd:** stabbed.   10. **did . . . him:** had a hard time
keeping my hands off him.   13. **potential:** powerful.   14. **double:** of double strength (like the Duke's
voting power in the Senate).   17. **cable:** scope (cf. "give one rope enough").   18. **signiory:** Venetian
government.   19. **yet to know:** not yet public knowledge.   21. **provulgate:** make publicly known.
22. **siege:** seat, i.e. rank. **demerits:** deserts, merits.

May speak, unbonneted, to as proud a fortune
As this that I have reach'd; for know, Iago,
But that I love the gentle Desdemona,   25
I would not my unhoused free condition
Put into circumscription and confine
For the sea's worth. But look, what lights come yond?
Enter CASSIO *with* [OFFICERS *and*] *torches.*
    IAGO: Those are the raised father and his friends.
You were best go in.
    OTHELLO: Not I; I must be found.   30
My parts, my title, and my perfect soul
Shall manifest me rightly. Is it they?
    IAGO: By Janus, I think no.
    OTHELLO: The servants of the [Duke]? And my lieutenant?
The goodness of the night upon you, friends!   35
What is the news?
    CASSIO: The Duke does greet you, general,
And he requires your haste-post-haste appearance,
Even on the instant.
    OTHELLO: What is the matter, think you?
    CASSIO: Something from Cyprus, as I may divine;
It is a business of some heat. The galleys   40
Have sent a dozen sequent messengers
This very night at one another's heels;
And many of the consuls, rais'd and met,
Are at the Duke's already. You have been hotly call'd for;
When, being not at your lodging to be found,   45
The Senate hath sent about three several quests
To search you out.
    OTHELLO: 'Tis well I am found by you.
I will but spend a word here in the house,
And go with you. [*Exit.*]
    CASSIO: Ancient, what makes he here?
    IAGO: Faith, he to-night hath boarded a land carract.
If it prove lawful prize, he's made for ever.   51
    CASSIO: I do not understand.
    IAGO: He's married.
    CASSIO: To who?

---

23. **unbonneted.** Explained either as "without taking my hat off, i.e. on equal terms" (the opposite of the word's expected meaning, but in *Coriolanus*, II.ii.27, *bonneted* = took off their caps) or as a parenthetical "I say it in all due modesty." 26. **unhoused:** unconfined. 28. **the sea's worth:** all the treasure in the sea. 31. **parts:** qualities, personal merits. **title:** position. **perfect soul:** clear conscience, conviction that I have done no wrong. 33. **Janus:** the two-faced god (dear to Iago). 38. **matter:** business. 41. **sequent:** one after another. 49. **makes he:** is he doing. 50. **carract:** carrack, large trading ship. 51. **prize:** booty.

[*Enter* OTHELLO.]
    IAGO: Marry, to—Come, captain, will you go?
    OTHELLO: Have with you.
    CASSIO: Here comes another troop to seek for you.
Enter BRABANTIO, RODERIGO, *with* OFFICERS [*with*] *torches* [*and weapons*].
    IAGO: It is Brabantio. General, be advis'd,   55
He comes to bad intent.
    OTHELLO: Holla, stand there!
    RODERIGO: Signior, it is the Moor.
    BRABANTIO: Down with him, thief!
[*They draw on both sides.*]
    IAGO: You, Roderigo! come, sir, I am for you.
    OTHELLO: Keep up your bright swords, for the dew will rust them.
Good signior, you shall more command with years   60
Than with your weapons.
    BRABANTIO: O thou foul thief, where hast thou stow'd my daughter?
Damn'd as thou art, thou hast enchanted her,
For I'll refer me to all things of sense,
If she in chains of magic were not bound,   65
Whether a maid so tender, fair, and happy,
So opposite to marriage that she shunn'd
The wealthy curled [darlings] of our nation,
Would ever have, t' incur a general mock,
Run from her guardage to the sooty bosom   70
Of such a thing as thou—to fear, not to delight!
Judge me the world, if 'tis not gross in sense,
That thou hast practic'd on her with foul charms,
Abus'd her delicate youth with drugs or minerals
That weakens motion. I'll have't disputed on,   75
'Tis probable, and palpable to thinking.
I therefore apprehended and do attach thee
For an abuser of the world, a practicer
Of arts inhibited and out of warrant.
Lay hold upon him, if he do resist   80
Subdue him at his peril.
    OTHELLO: Hold your hands,
Both you of my inclining, and the rest.
Were it my cue to fight, I should have known it

---

53. **Marry:** indeed (originally, the name of the Virgin Mary used as an oath). **Have with you:** a formula equivalent to "yes, let's go."   55. **advis'd:** on your guard.   59. **Keep up:** sheathe.   63. **enchanted:** bewitched, cast a spell upon.   64. **refer . . . sense:** i.e. submit my case to the court of ordinary common sense.   71. **fear:** frighten.   72. **gross in sense:** obvious to perception (synonymous with *palpable to thinking* in line 76).   73. **practic'd on:** plotted against.   75. **motion:** the mental powers. **I'll . . . on:** I'll submit it to experts for judgment.   77. **attach:** arrest.   79. **inhibited:** prohibited. **out of warrant:** unwarrantable, illegal.   82. **inclining:** party.

Without a prompter. Whither will you that I go
To answer this your charge?
 BRABANTIO: To prison, till fit time
Of law and course of direct session   86
Call thee to answer.
 OTHELLO: What if [I] do obey?
How may the Duke be therewith satisfied,
Whose messengers are here about my side,
Upon some present business of the state,   90
To bring me to him?
 OFFICER: 'Tis true, most worthy signior;
The Duke's in council, and your noble self
I am sure is sent for.
 BRABANTIO: How? the Duke in council?
In this time of the night? Bring him away;
Mine's not an idle cause. The Duke himself,   95
Or any of my brothers of the state,
Cannot but feel this wrong as 'twere their own;
For if such actions may have passage free,
Bond-slaves and pagans shall our statesmen be.
Exeunt.

SCENE III

Enter DUKE [*and*] SENATORS [*set at a table, with lights*] *and* OFFICERS.
 DUKE: There's no composition in [these] news
That gives them credit.
 1. SENATOR: Indeed, they are disproportioned;
My letters say a hundred and seven galleys.
 DUKE: And mine, a hundred forty.
 2. SENATOR: And mine, two hundred!
But though they jump not on a just accompt   5
(As in these cases where the aim reports,
'Tis oft with difference), yet do they all confirm
A Turkish fleet, and bearing up to Cyprus.
 DUKE: Nay, it is possible enough to judgment.
I do not so secure me in the error   10
But the main article I do approve
In fearful sense.
 SAILOR: (*Within.*)   What ho, what ho, what ho!
Enter SAILOR.

---

86. **direct:** regular. 94. **away:** right along. 95. **idle:** trivial. I.iii. Location: Venice. A council-chamber.
1. **composition:** consistency. 5. **jump:** agree. **just:** exact. **accompt:** accounting, number. 6. **the aim:** i.e. conjecture. 10–11. **so . . . approve:** take such assurance from the discrepancy that I don't accept the central item. 12. **fearful:** alarming.

OFFICER: A messenger from the galleys.
DUKE: Now? what's the business?
SAILOR: The Turkish preparation makes for Rhodes,
So was I bid report here to the state   15
By Signior Angelo. [*Exit* SAILOR.]
    DUKE: How say you by this change?
    FIRST SENATOR: This cannot be
By no assay of reason; 'tis a pageant
To keep us in false gaze. When we consider
Th' importancy of Cyprus to the Turk,   20
And let ourselves again but understand
That, as it more concerns the Turk than Rhodes,
So may he with more facile question bear it,
For that it stands not in such warlike brace,
But altogether lacks th' abilities   25
That Rhodes is dress'd in—if we make thought of this,
We must not think the Turk is so unskillful
To leave that latest which concerns him first,
Neglecting an attempt of ease and gain
To wake and wage a danger profitless.   30
    DUKE: Nay, in all confidence, he's not for Rhodes.
    OFFICER: Here is more news.
Enter a MESSENGER.
    MESSENGER: The Ottomites, reverend and gracious,
Steering with due course toward the isle of Rhodes,
Have there injointed them with an after fleet.   35
    FIRST SENATOR: Ay, so I thought. How many, as you guess?
    MESSENGER: Of thirty sail; and now they do restem
Their backward course, bearing with frank appearance
Their purposes toward Cyprus. Signior Montano,
Your trusty and most valiant servitor,   40
With his free duty recommends you thus,
And prays you to believe him. [*Exit* MESSENGER.]
    DUKE: 'Tis certain then for Cyprus.
Marcus Luccicos, is not he in town?
    FIRST SENATOR: He's now in Florence.   45
    DUKE: Write from us to him, post-post-haste. Dispatch!
    FIRST SENATOR: Here comes Brabantio and the valiant Moor.

---

14. **preparation:** force prepared for war; here, fleet (so also at line 221 below).   17. **by:** about.
18. **assay of reason:** test of common sense. **pageant:** mere show.   19. **in false gaze:** looking in the wrong
direction.   23. **with . . . it:** capture it more easily.   24. **brace:** readiness.   27. **unskillful:** unable to weigh
the situation, undiscriminating.   28. **latest:** last.   29. **of . . . gain:** i.e. that will yield easy success.
30. **wage:** risk.   38. **with frank appearance:** openly, without disguising their intention.   41. **his free
duty:** i.e. expressions of unwavering loyalty. **recommends:** informs.

Enter BRABANTIO, OTHELLO, CASSIO, IAGO, RODERIGO, *and* OFFICERS.

DUKE: Valiant Othello, we must straight employ you
Against the general enemy Ottoman.
[*To* BRABANTIO.] I did not see you; welcome, gentle signior,   50
We lack'd your counsel and your help to-night.
    BRABANTIO: So did I yours. Good your Grace, pardon me:
Neither my place, nor aught I heard of business,
Hath rais'd me from my bed, nor doth the general care
Take hold on me; for my particular grief   55
Is of so flood-gate and o'erbearing nature
That it engluts and swallows other sorrows,
And it is still itself.
    DUKE: Why? what's the matter?
    BRABANTIO: My daughter! O, my daughter!
    [ALL:]   Dead?
    BRABANTIO: Ay, to me:
She is abus'd, stol'n from me, and corrupted   60
By spells and medicines bought of mountebanks;
For nature so prepost'rously to err
(Being not deficient, blind, or lame of sense)
Sans witchcraft could not.
    DUKE: Who e'er he be that in this foul proceeding
Hath thus beguil'd your daughter of herself,   66
And you of her, the bloody book of law
You shall yourself read in the bitter letter
After your own sense; yea, though our proper son
Stood in your action.
    BRABANTIO: Humbly I thank your Grace.   70
Here is the man—this Moor, whom now, it seems,
Your special mandate for the state affairs
Hath hither brought.
    ALL: We are very sorry for't.
    DUKE: [*To* OTHELLO.] What, in your own part, can you say to this?
    BRABANTIO: Nothing, but this is so.   75
    OTHELLO: Most potent, grave, and reverend signiors,
My very noble and approv'd good masters:
That I have ta'en away this old man's daughter,
It is most true; true I have married her;
The very head and front of my offending   80

---

49. **general:** universal, i.e. of all Christendom.   50. **gentle:** noble.   55. **particular:** private.   56. **flood-gate:** i.e. overwhelming (like the onrushing water when flood-gates are opened).   57. **engluts:** engulfs. 60. **abus'd:** deceived, deluded.   62. **err:** suffer aberration.   63. **deficient:** defective. **sense:** reason. 64. **Sans:** without.   69. **After ... sense:** giving it your own interpretation. **proper:** own.   70. **Stood ... action:** were the one who faced your charges.   77. **approv'd:** proved.   80. **The very ... offending:** i.e. my offense at the utmost.

Hath this extent, no more. Rude am I in my speech,
And little bless'd with the soft phrase of peace;
For since these arms of mine had seven years' pith,
Till now some nine moons wasted, they have us'd
Their dearest action in the tented field;   85
And little of this great world can I speak
More than pertains to feats of broils and battle,
And therefore little shall I grace my cause
In speaking for myself. Yet (by your gracious patience)
I will a round unvarnish'd tale deliver   90
Of my whole course of love—what drugs, what charms,
What conjuration, and what mighty magic
(For such proceeding I am charg'd withal)
I won his daughter.
        BRABANTIO: A maiden, never bold;
Of spirit so still and quiet that her motion   95
Blush'd at herself; and she, in spite of nature,
Of years, of country, credit, every thing,
To fall in love with what she fear'd to look on!
It is a judgment main'd, and most imperfect,
That will confess perfection so could err   100
Against all rules of nature, and must be driven
To find our practices of cunning hell
Why this should be. I therefore vouch again
That with some mixtures pow'rful o'er the blood,
Or with some dram (conjur'd to this effect)   105
He wrought upon her.
        [DUKE:]   To vouch this is no proof,
Without more wider and more [overt] test
Than these thin habits and poor likelihoods
Of modern seeming do prefer against him.
        FIRST SENATOR: But, Othello, speak.   110
Did you by indirect and forced courses
Subdue and poison this young maid's affections?
Or came it by request, and such fair question
As soul to soul affordeth?
        OTHELLO: I do beseech you,
Send for the lady to the Sagittary,   115

---

81. **Rude:** unpolished.   83. **pith:** i.e. strength.   90. **round:** plain.   93. **withal:** with.   95–96. **her . . . herself:** any stirring of her feelings made her blush (as if it were improper).   97. **credit:** reputation. 99. **main'd:** maimed.   100. **confess:** aver, declare.   101. **must:** i.e. the unmaimed judgment must. 102. **practices:** plots.   103. **vouch:** affirm.   104. **blood:** passions.   105. **conjur'd . . . effect:** made thus efficacious by spells.   107. **more wider:** i.e. fuller.   108. **thin habits:** thin clothing, i.e. slight appearances.   109. **modern:** commonplace, insignificant. **seeming:** supposition. **prefer:** present.   113. **question:** conversation.

And let her speak of me before her father.
If you do find me foul in her report,
The trust, the office I do hold of you,
Not only take away, but let your sentence
Even fall upon my life.
    DUKE: Fetch Desdemona hither.   120
[*Exeunt two or three.*]
    OTHELLO: Ancient, conduct them; you best know the place. [*Exit* IAGO.]
And, [till] she come, as truly as to heaven
I do confess the vices of my blood,
So justly to your grave ears I'll present
How I did thrive in this fair lady's love,   125
And she in mine.
    DUKE: Say it, Othello.
    OTHELLO: Her father lov'd me, oft invited me;
Still question'd me the story of my life
From year to year—the [battles], sieges, [fortunes],
That I have pass'd.   131
I ran it through, even from my boyish days
To th' very moment that he bade me tell it;
Wherein I spoke of most disastrous chances:
Of moving accidents by flood and field,   135
Of hair-breadth scapes i' th' imminent deadly breach,
Of being taken by the insolent foe
And sold to slavery, of my redemption thence
And portance in my [travel's] history;
Wherein of antres vast and deserts idle,   140
Rough quarries, rocks, [and] hills whose [heads] touch heaven,
It was my hint to speak—such was my process—
And of the Cannibals that each [other] eat,
The Anthropophagi, and men whose heads
[Do grow] beneath their shoulders. These things to hear   145
Would Desdemona seriously incline;
But still the house affairs would draw her [thence],
Which ever as she could with haste dispatch,
She'ld come again, and with a greedy ear
Devour up my discourse. Which I observing,   150
Took once a pliant hour, and found good means
To draw from her a prayer of earnest heart

---

123. **vices ... blood:** my human failings.   124. **justly:** exactly, truthfully.   129. **Still:** continually.
135. **accidents:** events.   136. **imminent deadly:** threatening death. **breach:** gap made in fortifications.
139. **portance:** behavior.   140. **antres:** caves. **idle:** barren, empty.   141. **Rough quarries:** rugged stone-
masses.   142. **hint:** occasion. **process:** proceeding (?) or story (?).   144. **Anthropophagi:** man-eaters.
151. **pliant:** convenient, favorable.

That I would all my pilgrimage dilate,
Whereof by parcels she had something heard,
But not [intentively]. I did consent,   155
And often did beguile her of her tears,
When I did speak of some distressful stroke
That my youth suffer'd. My story being done,
She gave me for my pains a world of [sighs];
She swore, in faith 'twas strange, 'twas passing strange;
'Twas pitiful, 'twas wondrous pitiful.   161
She wish'd she had not heard it, yet she wish'd
That heaven had made her such a man. She thank'd me,
And bade me, if I had a friend that lov'd her,
I should but teach him how to tell my story,   165
And that would woo her. Upon this hint I spake:
She lov'd me for the dangers I had pass'd,
And I lov'd her that she did pity them.
This only is the witchcraft I have us'd.
Here comes the lady; let her witness it.   170
Enter DESDEMONA, IAGO, ATTENDANTS.
    DUKE: I think this tale would win my daughter too.
Good Brabantio,
Take up this mangled matter at the best;
Men do their broken weapons rather use
Than their bare hands.
    BRABANTIO: I pray you hear her speak.
If she confess that she was half the wooer,   176
Destruction on my head if my bad blame
Light on the man! Come hither, gentle mistress.
Do you perceive in all this noble company
Where most you owe obedience?
    DESDEMONA: My noble father,
I do perceive here a divided duty: 181
To you I am bound for life and education;
My life and education both do learn me
How to respect you; you are the lord of duty;
I am hitherto your daughter. But here's my husband;
And so much duty as my mother show'd   186
To you, preferring you before her father,
So much I challenge that I may profess
Due to the Moor, my lord.

---

153. **dilate:** relate in detail.   154. **by parcels:** by snatches, in bits and pieces.   155. **intentively:** with continuous attention.   166. **hint:** opportunity.   173. **Take . . . best:** make the best of this badly damaged situation.   182. **education:** rearing.   183. **learn:** teach.   184. **respect:** regard.   185. **I . . . daughter:** i.e. until now I have owed all my obedience to you as my father.   188. **challenge:** claim.

BRABANTIO: God be with you! I have done.
Please it your Grace, on to the state affairs.   190
I had rather to adopt a child than get it.
Come hither, Moor:
I here do give thee that with all my heart
Which but thou hast already, with all my heart
I would keep from thee. For your sake, jewel,   195
I am glad at soul I have no other child,
For thy escape would teach me tyranny,
To hang clogs on them. I have done, my lord.
    DUKE: Let me speak like yourself, and lay a sentence,
Which as a grise or step, may help these lovers   200
[Into your favor].
When remedies are past, the griefs are ended
By seeing the worst, which late on hopes depended.
To mourn a mischief that is past and gone
Is the next way to draw new mischief on.   205
What cannot be preserv'd when Fortune takes,
Patience her injury a mock'ry makes.
The robb'd that smiles steals something from the thief;
He robs himself that spends a bootless grief.
    BRABANTIO: So let the Turk of Cyprus us beguile,   210
We lose it not, so long as we can smile.
He bears the sentence well that nothing bears
But the free comfort which from thence he hears;
But he bears both the sentence and the sorrow
That, to pay grief, must of poor patience borrow.   215
These sentences, to sugar or to gall,
Being strong on both sides, are equivocal.
But words are words; I never yet did hear
That the bruis'd heart was pierced through the [ear].
I humbly beseech you proceed to th' affairs of state.   220
    DUKE: The Turk with a most mighty preparation
makes for Cyprus. Othello, the fortitude of the place is
best known to you; and though we have there a sub-
stitute of most allow'd sufficiency, yet opinion, a

---

189. **God . . . you:** good-bye.   191. **get:** beget.   195. **For your sake:** because of what you have done.
197. **escape:** transgression.   198. **clogs:** blocks of wood hung on criminals or animals to prevent their
running away.   199. **like yourself:** as you should. **sentence:** maxim, moral saying.   200. **grise:** degree,
step.   202. **remedies:** i.e. hopes of remedy.   203. **which:** i.e. the griefs. **hopes:** anticipations.   204. **mischief:** injury.   205. **next:** nearest.   207. **Patience . . . makes:** patient endurance of the loss makes a
mockery of Fortune's intended injury.   209. **bootless:** unavailing.   213. **free:** i.e. unmixed with sorrow.
215. **poor patience:** i.e., endurance, which hasn't much to lend.   219. **pierced:** i.e. relieved as by a surgeon's lancet. Some editors adopt Warburton's emendation *pieced* = mended.   221. **preparation:** fleet.
222. **fortitude:** military strength.   223–24. **substitute:** representative.   224. **allow'd:** acknowledged.
224–25. **opinion . . . effects:** public opinion, the ultimate arbiter of what is to be done.

sovereign mistress of effects, throws a more   225
safer voice on you. You must therefore be content to
slubber the gloss of your new fortunes with this more
stubborn and boist'rous expedition.
    OTHELLO: The tyrant custom, most grave senators,
Hath made the flinty and steel [couch] of war   230
My thrice-driven bed of down. I do agnize
A natural and prompt alacrity
I find in hardness; and do undertake
This present wars against the Ottomites.
Most humbly therefore bending to your state,   235
I crave fit disposition for my wife,
Due reference of place and exhibition,
With such accommodation and besort
As levels with her breeding.
    DUKE: [If you please,
Be't] at her father's.
    BRABANTIO: I will not have it so.   240
    OTHELLO: Nor I.
    DESDEMONA: Nor [I; I would not] there reside,
To put my father in impatient thoughts
By being in his eye. Most gracious Duke,
To my unfolding lend your prosperous ear,
And let me find a charter in your voice   245
T' assist my simpleness.
    DUKE: What would you, Desdemona?
    DESDEMONA: That I [did] love the Moor to live with him,
My downright violence, and storm of fortunes,
May trumpet to the world. My heart's subdu'd   250
Even to the very quality of my lord.
I saw Othello's visage in his mind,
And to his honors and his valiant parts
Did I my soul and fortunes consecrate.
So that, dear lords, if I be left behind,   255
A moth of peace, and he go to the war,

225–26. **throws . . . you:** gives you the reputation of being safer.   227. **slubber:** sully.   228. **stubborn:** rough.   231. **thrice-driven:** thrice-winnowed (to obtain the smallest and softest feathers). **agnize:** recognize.   232. **alacrity:** readiness.   233. **hardness:** hardship.   235. **state:** i.e. authority.   236. **fit disposition:** suitable provision.   237. **reference of place:** assignment of residence. **exhibition:** allowance of money.   238. **besort:** suitable company.   244. **prosperous:** favorable.   245. **charter:** authorization, privilege.   249. **downright:** plain, open. **violence:** i.e. boldly aggressive action, breach of customary behavior. **storm of fortunes:** taking my fortune by storm.   250–51. **subdu'd Even to:** brought completely into accord with.   251. **quality:** (1) nature, character; (2) profession, mode of life.   253. **parts:** qualities.   256. **moth:** mere idle consumer, parasite.

The rites for why I love him are bereft me,
And I a heavy interim shall support
By his dear absence. Let me go with him.
    OTHELLO: Let her have your voice.   260
Vouch with me, heaven, I therefore beg it not
To please the palate of my appetite,
Nor to comply with heat (the young affects
In [me] defunct) and proper satisfaction;
But to be free and bounteous to her mind.   265
And heaven defend your good souls, that you think
I will your serious and great business scant
[For] she is with me. No, when light-wing'd toys
Of feather'd Cupid seel with wanton dullness
My speculative and offic'd [instruments],   270
That my disports corrupt and taint my business,
Let housewives make a skillet of my helm,
And all indign and base adversities
Make head against my estimation!
    DUKE: Be it as you shall privately determine,   275
Either for her stay or going; th' affair cries haste,
And speed must answer it.
    [FIRST] SENATOR: You must away to-night.
    [DESDEMONA: To-night, my lord?
    DUKE: This night.]
    OTHELLO: With all my heart.
    DUKE: At nine i' th' morning here we'll meet again.
Othello, leave some officer behind,   280
And he shall our commission bring to you;
And such things else of quality and respect
As doth import you.
    OTHELLO: So please your Grace, my ancient;
A man he is of honesty and trust.
To his conveyance I assign my wife,   285
With what else needful your good Grace shall think
To be sent after me.

---

257. **rites.** Perhaps to be taken as a variant spelling of *rights,* i.e. all the rights (including love-rites) in- volved in sharing his life to the full.   259. **dear:** heartfelt.   263–64. **Nor ... defunct:** nor to serve sexual appetite—since the excesses of youthful passion are in me over and done with.   264. **proper:** personal, private.   266. **defend:** forbid.   268. **For:** because.   269. **seel:** blind (literally, sew shut the eyelids of a hawk to tame it). **wanton dullness:** dullness produced by sexual indulgence.   270. **My ... instruments:** my faculties of perception when they have duties to perform. *Speculative* means literally "having power to see," and the line has been explained by some annotators as referring to the eyes, but it probably refers to the powers of mental perception, the "mind's eye."   271. **That:** so that.   273. **indign:** unworthy, shame- ful.   274. **Make head:** raise an armed force. **estimation:** reputation.   282. **of ... respect:** pertaining to your rank and privilege.   283. **import:** concern.   284. **honesty:** honor.

DUKE: Let it be so.
Good night to every one. [*To* BRABANTIO.] And, noble signior,
If virtue no delighted beauty lack,
Your son-in-law is far more fair than black.   290
    FIRST SENATOR: Adieu, brave Moor, use Desdemona well.
    BRABANTIO: Look to her, Moor, if thou hast eyes to see;
She has deceiv'd her father, and may thee.
Exeunt [DUKE, SENATORS, OFFICERS, *etc.*].
    OTHELLO: My life upon her faith! Honest Iago,
My Desdemona must I leave to thee.   295
I prithee let thy wife attend on her,
And bring them after in the best advantage.
Come, Desdemona, I have but an hour
Of love, of worldly matter and direction,
To spend with thee. We must obey the time.   300
Exit [*with* DESDEMONA].
    RODERIGO: Iago—
    IAGO: What say'st thou, noble heart?
    RODERIGO: What will I do, think'st thou?
    IAGO: Why, go to bed and sleep.
    RODERIGO: I will incontinently drown myself.   305
    IAGO: If thou dost, I shall never love thee after.
Why, thou silly gentleman?
    RODERIGO: It is silliness to live, when to live is torment;
and then have we a prescription to die, when death is
our physician.   310
    IAGO: O villainous! I have look'd upon the world
for four times seven years, and since I could distinguish betwixt a benefit and an injury, I never found
man that knew how to love himself. Ere I would say I
would drown myself for the love of a guinea hen,
I would change my humanity with a baboon.   316
    RODERIGO: What should I do? I confess it is my shame to
be so fond, but it is not in my virtue to amend it.
    IAGO: Virtue? a fig! 'tis in ourselves that we are
thus or thus. Our bodies are our gardens, to the   320
which our wills are gardeners; so that if we will plant
nettles or sow lettuce, set hyssop and weed up [tine],
supply it with one gender of herbs or distract it with

---

289. **delighted:** delightful.   297. **in . . . advantage:** at . . . opportunity.   299. **worldly:** worldly (a variant
spelling).   305. **incontinently:** at once.   309. **prescription:** (1) perfect right; (2) doctor's order.
311. **villainous:** wretched nonsense.   318. **virtue:** nature.   319–20. **'tis . . . thus:** it is in our own power
to make ourselves what we will.   322. **hyssop:** a fragrant herb. **tine:** tares, wild grasses.   323. **gender:**
kind.

many, either to have it sterile with idleness or manur'd
with industry—why, the power and corrigible
authority of this lies in our wills. If the [beam] of our
lives had not one scale of reason to poise another of
sensuality, the blood and baseness of our natures would
conduct us to most prepost'rous conclusions. But we
have reason to cool our raging motions, our carnal   330
stings, [our] unbitted lusts; whereof I take this that
you call love to be a sect or scion.

    RODERIGO: It cannot be.

    IAGO: It is merely a lust of the blood and a per-
mission of the will. Come, be a man! Drown   335
thyself? drown cats and blind puppies! I have pro-
fess'd me thy friend, and I confess me knit to thy
deserving with cables of perdurable toughness. I could
never better stead thee than now. Put money in thy
purse; follow thou the wars; defeat thy favor with   340
an usurp'd beard. I say put money in thy purse. It
cannot be long that Desdemona should continue her
love to the Moor—put money in thy purse—nor he his
to her. It was a violent commencement in her, and
thou shalt see an answerable sequestration—put   345
but money in thy purse. These Moors are changeable
in their wills—fill thy purse with money. The food
that to him now is as luscious as locusts, shall be to him
shortly as [acerb] as [the] coloquintida. She must change
for youth; when she is sated with his body, she   350
will find the [error] of her choice. [She must have
change, she must;] therefore put money in thy purse.
If thou wilt needs damn thyself, do it a more delicate
way than drowning. Make all the money thou canst.
If sanctimony and a frail vow betwixt an erring   355
barbarian and [a] super-subtle Venetian be not too hard
for my wits and all the tribe of hell, thou shalt enjoy
her; therefore make money. A pox of drowning thyself, it is clean out of the way. Seek thou rather to be

---

325. **corrigible:** corrective.   326. **beam:** balance.   327. **poise:** counterbalance.   328. **blood and
baseness:** base passions.   330. **motions:** desires, appetites.   332. **sect or scion:** cutting or offshoot.
338. **perdurable:** lasting.   339. **stead:** serve, help.   340. **defeat thy favor:** alter your appearance.
341. **usurp'd:** to which you have no right (because you are scarcely old enough to grow it).
345. **answerable sequestration:** correspondingly abrupt ending (or separation).   347. **wills:** lusts.
348. **locusts:** the sweet fruit of the carob tree.   349. **acerb:** bitter. **coloquintida:** colocynth or "bitter
apple," used as a purgative.   354. **Make:** raise, get together.   355. **sanctimony:** religious bond or ceremony. **erring:** vagabond.   356. **super-subtle:** highly refined and sensitive.

hang'd in compassing thy joy than to be drown'd and
go without her.   361

    RODERIGO: Wilt thou be fast to my hopes, if I depend on
the issue?

    IAGO: Thou art sure of me—go make money. I
have told thee often, and I retell thee again and   365
again, I hate the Moor. My cause is hearted; thine
hath no less reason. Let us be conjunctive in our
revenge against him. If thou canst cuckold him, thou
dost thyself a pleasure, me a sport. There are many
events in the womb of time which will be deliver'd.
Traverse, go, provide thy money. We will have more
of this to-morrow. Adieu.   372

    RODERIGO: Where shall we meet i' th' morning?

    IAGO: At my lodging.

    RODERIGO: I'll be with thee betimes.   375

    IAGO: Go to, farewell. Do you hear, Roderigo?

    [RODERIGO: What say you?

    IAGO: No more of drowning, do you hear?

    RODERIGO: I am chang'd.

    IAGO: Go to, farewell. Put money enough in your
purse.]   381

    RODERIGO: I'll sell all my land. *Exit.*

    IAGO: Thus do I ever make my fool my purse;
For I mine own gain'd knowledge should profane
If I would time expend with such [a] snipe   385
But for my sport and profit. I hate the Moor,
And it is thought abroad that 'twixt my sheets
[H'as] done my office. I know not if't be true,
But I, for mere suspicion in that kind,
Will do as if for surety. He holds me well,   390
The better shall my purpose work on him.
Cassio's a proper man. Let me see now:
To get his place and to plume up my will
In double knavery—How? how?—Let's see—
After some time, to abuse Othello's [ear]   395
That he is too familiar with his wife.
He hath a person and a smooth dispose
To be suspected—fram'd to make women false.

---

362. **fast:** true.   366. **hearted:** rooted in my heart, i.e. deeply and passionately felt.   367. **conjunctive:** united.   371. **Traverse:** forward.   376. **Do you hear:** just a minute, one more thing.   385. **snipe:** woodcock; used contemptuously of an insignificant or silly person.   387. **it . . . abroad:** there is gossip.   390. **do . . . surety:** act as if on the basis of proved fact.   392. **proper:** handsome.   393. **plume . . . will:** pamper my ego.   397. **dispose:** bearing.

The Moor is of a free and open nature,
That thinks men honest that but seem to be so,   400
And will as tenderly be led by th' nose
As asses are.
I have't. It is engend'red. Hell and night
Must bring this monstrous birth to the world's light.
[*Exit.*]

ACT II, SCENE I
Enter MONTANO *and two* GENTLEMEN.
   MONTANO: What from the cape can you discern at sea?
   FIRST GENTLEMEN: Nothing at all, it is a high-wrought flood.
I cannot, 'twixt the heaven and the main,
Descry a sail.
   MONTANO: Methinks the wind hath spoke aloud at land,
A fuller blast ne'er shook our battlements.   6
If it hath ruffian'd so upon the sea,
What ribs of oak, when mountains melt on them,
Can hold the mortise? What shall we hear of this?
   SECOND GENTLEMEN: A segregation of the Turkish fleet: 10
For do but stand upon the foaming shore,
The chidden billow seems to pelt the clouds,
The wind-shak'd surge, with high and monstrous mane,
Seems to cast water on the burning Bear,
And quench the guards of th' ever-fixed Pole;   15
I never did like molestation view
On the enchafed flood.
   MONTANO: If that the Turkish fleet
Be not enshelter'd and embay'd, they are drown'd;
It is impossible to bear it out.
Enter a [*third*] GENTLEMAN.
   THIRD GENTLEMEN: News, lads! our wars are done.   20
The desperate tempest hath so bang'd the Turks,
That their designment halts. A noble ship of Venice
Hath seen a grievous wrack and sufferance
On most part of their fleet.
   MONTANO: How? is this true?
   THIRD GENTLEMEN: The ship is here put in,
A Veronesa; Michael Cassio,   26

---

401. **tenderly:** readily.   II.i. Location: A seaport in Cyprus. An open place near the quay.   9. **hold the mortise:** hold their joints together.   10. **segregation:** dispersion.   13. **mane.** Many editors prefer *main* = power. F1 *Maine* and Q1 *mayne* are ambiguous.   15. **guards:** two stars in the Little Bear, in line with the pole star.   22. **designment:** plan. **halts:** is lame.   23. **sufferance:** damage.   26. **Veronesa.** If this word means "Veronese," there is difficulty about applying it either to the ship, which has just been described as "of Venice," or to Cassio, who is called a Florentine at I.i.20. Modern editors usually explain it as designating a ship furnished by Verona for the Venetian service. But the word may not mean "Veronese" at all; some suspect a connection with an Italian word for a particular type of ship.

Lieutenant to the warlike Moor Othello,
Is come on shore; the Moor himself at sea,
And is in full commission here for Cyprus.
  MONTANO: I am glad on't; 'tis a worthy governor.   30
  THIRD GENTLEMEN: But this same Cassio, though he speak of comfort
Touching the Turkish loss, yet he looks sadly,
And [prays] the Moor be safe; for they were parted
With foul and violent tempest.
  MONTANO: Pray [heaven] he be;
For I have serv'd him, and the man commands   35
Like a full soldier. Let's to the sea-side, ho!
As well to see the vessel that's come in
As to throw out our eyes for brave Othello,
Even till we make the main and th' aerial blue
An indistinct regard.
  [THIRD] GENTLEMEN: Come, let's do so;   40
For every minute is expectancy
Of more [arrivance].
Enter CASSIO.
  CASSIO: Thanks you, the valiant of [this] warlike isle,
That so approve the Moor! O, let the heavens
Give him defense against the elements,   45
For I have lost him on a dangerous sea.
  MONTANO: Is he well shipp'd?
  CASSIO: His bark is stoutly timber'd, and his pilot
Of very expert and approv'd allowance;
Therefore my hopes (not surfeited to death)   50
Stand in bold cure. *Within,* "A sail, a sail, a sail!"
[*Enter a* MESSENGER.]
  CASSIO: What noise?
  [MESSENGER:] The town is empty; on the brow o' th' sea
Stand ranks of people, and they cry, "A sail!"
  CASSIO: My hopes do shape him for the governor.   55
[*A shot.*]
  [SECOND] GENTLEMEN: They do discharge their shot of courtesy;
Our friends at least.
  CASSIO: I pray you, sir, go forth,
And give us truth who 'tis that is arriv'd.
  [SECOND] GENTLEMEN: I shall. *Exit.*
  MONTANO: But, good lieutenant, is your general wiv'd?
  CASSIO: Most fortunately: he hath achiev'd a maid

---

39. **An indistinct regard:** indistinguishable to the sight. 43. **Thanks you:** thanks to you. 44. **approve:** commend, admire. 49. **expert . . . allowance:** i.e. of acknowledged and proved skill. 50–51. **my . . . cure:** since I have not had to indulge my hopes so long that they are near death, I am confident that they will be fulfilled.

That paragons description and wild fame;   62
One that excels the quirks of blazoning pens,
And in th' essential vesture of creation
Does tire the [ingener].
Enter [SECOND] GENTLEMAN.
         How now? who has put in?
     [SECOND] GENTLEMEN: 'Tis one Iago, ancient to the general.   66
     CASSIO: H'as had most favorable and happy speed:
Tempests themselves, high seas, and howling winds,
The gutter'd rocks and congregated sands,
Traitors ensteep'd to enclog the guiltless keel,   70
As having sense of beauty, do omit
Their mortal natures, letting go safely by
The divine Desdemona.
     MONTANO: What is she?
     CASSIO: She that I spake of, our great captain's captain,
Left in the conduct of the bold Iago,   75
Whose footing here anticipates our thoughts
A se'nnight's speed. Great Jove, Othello guard,
And swell his sail with thine own pow'rful breath,
That he may bless this bay with his tall ship,
Make love's quick pants in Desdemona's arms,   80
Give renew'd fire to our extincted spirits,
[And bring all Cyprus comfort!]
Enter DESDEMONA, IAGO, RODERIGO, *and* EMILIA, [*with* ATTENDANTS].
         O, behold,
The riches of the ship is come on shore!
You men of Cyprus, let her have your knees.
Hail to thee, lady! and the grace of heaven,   85
Before, behind thee, and on every hand,
Enwheel thee round!
     DESDEMONA: I thank you, valiant Cassio.
What tidings can you tell [me] of my lord?
     CASSIO: He is not yet arriv'd, nor know I aught
But that he's well and will be shortly here.   90
     DESDEMONA: O, but I fear—How lost you company?
     CASSIO: The great contention of [the] sea and skies
Parted our fellowship.

---

62. **paragons description:** surpasses whatever praise is uttered of her.   63. **quirks:** conceits, flourishes. **blazoning:** listing her beauties.   64–65. **in . . . ingener:** in her native beauty defeats all attempts of the inventive poet to praise her adequately.   69. **gutter'd:** jagged.   70. **ensteep'd:** submerged.   71. **omit:** give up, do not act in accordance with.   72. **mortal:** deadly.   76. **footing:** landing, arrival.   83. **riches.** Singular (from French *richesse*).

Within, "A sail, a sail!" [*A shot.*]
                    But hark! a sail.
     [SECOND] GENTLEMEN: They give [their] greeting to the citadel.
This likewise is a friend.
          CASSIO: See for the news.   95
[*Exit* SECOND GENTLEMEN.]
Good ancient, you are welcome. [*To* EMILIA] Welcome, mistress.
Let it not gall your patience, good Iago,
That I extend my manners; 'tis my breeding
That gives me this bold show of courtesy.   99
[*Kissing her.*]
          IAGO: Sir, would she give you so much of her lips
As of her tongue she oft bestows on me,
You would have enough.
          DESDEMONA: Alas! she has no speech.
          IAGO: In faith, too much;
I find it still, when I have [list] to sleep.
Marry, before your ladyship, I grant,   105
She puts her tongue a little in her heart,
And chides with thinking.
          EMILIA: You have little cause to say so.
          IAGO: Come on, come on; you are pictures out [a' doors],
Bells in your parlors, wild-cats in your kitchens,   110
Saints in your injuries, devils being offended,
Players in your huswifery, and huswives in your beds.
          DESDEMONA: O, fie upon thee, slanderer!
          IAGO: Nay, it is true, or else I am a Turk:
You rise to play, and go to bed to work.   115
          EMILIA: You shall not write my praise.
          IAGO: No, let me not.
          DESDEMONA: What wouldst write of me, if thou shouldst praise me?
          IAGO: O gentle lady, do not put me to't,
For I am nothing if not critical.
          DESDEMONA: Come on, assay.—There's one gone to the harbor?   120
          IAGO: Ay, madam.
          DESDEMONA: I am not merry; but I do beguile
The thing I am by seeming otherwise.—
Come, how wouldst thou praise me?
          IAGO: I am about it, but indeed my invention   125

---

98. **extend:** show.   104. **list:** inclination.   107. **with thinking:** i.e. without speaking her thoughts.
109. **pictures:** i.e. painted.   110. **Bells:** i.e. with tongues going like bell-clappers.   111. **Saints ...**
injuries: when you offend, you do it with an air of sanctity.   112. **Players:** actors, i.e. people making a
pretense (?) or perfunctory triflers (?). **huswifery:** household management. **huswives:** hussies, wantons.
119. **critical:** censorious.   120. **assay:** try.   123. **The thing I am:** my anxious self.

Comes from my pate as birdlime does from frieze,
It plucks out brains and all. But my Muse labors,
And thus she is deliver'd:
If she be fair and wise, fairness and wit,
The one's for use, the other useth it.   130
    DESDEMONA: Well prais'd! How if she be black and witty?
    IAGO: If she be black, and thereto have a wit,
She'll find a white that shall her blackness [hit].
    DESDEMONA: Worse and worse.
    EMILIA: How if fair and foolish?   135
    IAGO: She never yet was foolish that was fair,
For even her folly help'd her to an heir.
    DESDEMONA: These are old fond paradoxes to make fools
laugh i' th' alehouse. What miserable praise hast thou
for her that's foul and foolish?   140
    IAGO: There's none so foul and foolish thereunto,
But does foul pranks which fair and wise ones do.
    DESDEMONA: O heavy ignorance! thou praisest the worst
best. But what praise couldst thou bestow on a   144
deserving woman indeed—one that in the authority of
her merit, did justly put on the vouch of very malice
itself?
    IAGO: She that was ever fair, and never proud,
Had tongue at will, and yet was never loud,
Never lack'd gold, and yet went never gay,   150
Fled from her wish, and yet said, "Now I may";
She that being ang'red, her revenge being nigh,
Bade her wrong stay, and her displeasure fly;
She that in wisdom never was so frail
To change the cod's head for the salmon's tail;   155
She that could think, and nev'r disclose her mind,
See suitors following, and not look behind:
She was a wight (if ever such [wight] were)—
    DESDEMONA: To do what?   159
    IAGO: To suckle fools and chronicle small beer.

---

126. **birdlime:** sticky substance used to catch birds. **frieze:** coarse wool.   131. **black:** brunette.
133. **white.** With a pun on *wight,* "person." **hit:** suit, fit (with sexual quibble).   137. **folly.** With second
sense "wantonness."   138. **fond:** foolish.   140. **foul:** ugly.   145. **in the authority:** by virtue.   146. **put
. . . vouch:** compel the favorable testimony.   150. **gay:** extravagantly dressed.   151. **Fled . . . may:** i.e.
did not indulge herself even though she was free to do so.   153. **wrong stay:** sense of injury cease.
155. **change . . . tail.** Obscure. Perhaps "give up something common but valuable in exchange for something showy but worthless," but more probably a sexual innuendo.   160. **suckle . . . beer:** tend babies
and keep petty household accounts.

DESDEMONA: O most lame and impotent conclusion! Do
not learn of him, Emilia, though he be thy husband.
How say you, Cassio? is he not a most profane and
liberal counsellor?

CASSIO: He speaks home, madam. You may relish him
more in the soldier than in the scholar.   166

IAGO [*Aside.*]: He takes her by the palm; ay, well
said, whisper. With as little a web as this will I en-
snare as great a fly as Cassio. Ay, smile upon her, do;
I will gyve thee in thine own courtship. You   170
say true, 'tis so indeed. If such tricks as these strip
you out of your lieutenantry, it had been better you
had not kiss'd your three fingers so oft, which now
again you are most apt to play the sir in. Very good;
well kiss'd! [an] excellent [courtesy]! 'Tis so   175
indeed. Yet again, your fingers to your lips? Would
they were clyster-pipes for your sake! [*Trumpets
within.*]—The Moor! I know his trumpet.

CASSIO: 'Tis truly so.

DESDEMONA: Let's meet him and receive him.   180

CASSIO: Lo, where he comes!

Enter OTHELLO *and* ATTENDANTS.

OTHELLO: O my fair warrior!

DESDEMONA: My dear Othello!

OTHELLO: It gives me wonder great as my content
To see you here before me. O my soul's joy!
If after every tempest come such calms,   185
May the winds blow till they have waken'd death!
And let the laboring bark climb hills of seas
Olympus-high, and duck again as low
As hell's from heaven! If it were now to die,
'Twere now to be most happy; for I fear   190
My soul hath her content so absolute
That not another comfort like to this
Succeeds in unknown fate.

DESDEMONA: The heavens forbid
But that our loves and comforts should increase
Even as our days do grow!

OTHELLO: Amen to that, sweet powers!   195
I cannot speak enough of this content,

---

164. **liberal:** free-spoken.   165. **home:** bluntly.   166. **in:** in the character of.   167–68. **well said:** well
done.   170. **gyve:** fetter, entangle.   **courtship:** display of courtly manners.   174. **sir:** gentleman, gallant.
175. **courtesy:** bow.   177. **clyster-pipes:** enema tubes.

It stops me here; it is too much of joy.
And this, and this, the greatest discords be
[*They kiss.*]
That e'er our hearts shall make!
  IAGO: [*Aside.*]   O, you are well tun'd now!
But I'll set down the pegs that make this music,   200
As honest as I am.
  OTHELLO: Come; let us to the castle.
News, friends: our wars are done; the Turks are drown'd.
How does my old acquaintance of this isle?
Honey, you shall be well desir'd in Cyprus,
I have found great love amongst them. O my sweet,
I prattle out of fashion, and I dote   206
In mine own comforts. I prithee, good Iago,
Go to the bay and disembark my coffers.
Bring thou the master to the citadel;
He is a good one, and his worthiness   210
Does challenge much respect. Come, Desdemona,
Once more, well met at Cyprus.
Exeunt OTHELLO *and* DESDEMONA [*with all but* IAGO *and* RODERIGO].
  IAGO: [*To an* ATTENDANT, *as he is going out.*] Do thou
meet me presently at the harbor.—Come [hither]. If
thou be'st valiant (as they say base men being in   215
love have then a nobility in their natures more than is
native to them), list me. The lieutenant to-night
watches on the court of guard. First, I must tell thee
this: Desdemona is directly in love with him.
  RODERIGO: With him? why, 'tis not possible.   220
  IAGO: Lay thy finger thus; and let thy soul be instructed. Mark me with what violence she first lov'd
the Moor, but for bragging and telling her fantastical
lies. To love him still for prating—let not thy discreet
heart think it. Her eye must be fed; and what de-   225
light shall she have to look on the devil? When the
blood is made dull with the act of sport, there should
be, [again] to inflame it and to give satiety a fresh
appetite, loveliness in favor, sympathy in years,
manners, and beauties—all which the Moor is de-   230

---

200. **set ... pegs:** i.e. untune the instrument (and so produce discords). 204. **desir'd:** welcomed, loved.
206. **out of fashion:** irrelevantly (?) or unconventionally (?) 208. **coffers:** baggage. 209. **master:** ship's
captain. 211. **challenge:** claim, deserve. 215. **base men:** even men of low birth. 218. **watches ...
guard:** has charge of the watch. 221. **thus:** i.e. on your lips. 224. **still:** always. 226. **the devil.** Traditionally black. 229. **favor:** face, appearance. **sympathy:** similarity, correspondence.

fective in. Now for want of these requir'd conveniences, her delicate tenderness will find itself abus'd, begin to heave the gorge, disrelish and abhor the Moor; very nature will instruct her in it and compel her to some second choice. Now, sir, this granted (as it is a most pregnant and unforc'd position), who stands so eminent in the degree of this fortune as Cassio does? a knave very voluble; no further conscionable than in putting on the mere form of civil and humane seeming, for the better compass of his salt and most hidden loose affection? Why, none, why, none—a slipper and subtle knave, a finger[-out] of occasion; that [has] an eye can stamp and counterfeit advantages, though true advantage never present itself; a devilish knave. Besides, the knave is handsome, young, and hath all those requisites in him that folly and green minds look after; a pestilent complete knave, and the woman hath found him already.

RODERIGO: I cannot believe that in her, she's full of most bless'd condition.

IAGO: Bless'd fig's-end! The wine she drinks is made of grapes. If she had been bless'd, she would never have lov'd the Moor. Bless'd pudding! Didst thou not see her paddle with the palm of his hand? Didst not mark that?

RODERIGO: Yes, that I did; but that was but courtesy.

IAGO: Lechery, by this hand; an index and obscure prologue to the history of lust and foul thoughts. They met so near with their lips that their breaths embrac'd together. Villainous thoughts, Roderigo! When these [mutualities] so marshal the way, hard at hand comes the master and main exercise, th' incorporate conclusion. Pish! But, sir, be you rul'd by me. I have brought you from Venice. Watch you to-night; for the command, I'll lay't upon you. Cassio knows you not. I'll not be far from you. Do you find some occasion to anger Cassio, either by speak-

235

242

245

250

255

258

262

267

231–32. **conveniences:** compatibilities.   233. **heave the gorge:** feel nauseated.   236. **pregnant:** obvious. 238. **conscionable:** bound by considerations of conscience.   239. **civil and humane:** polite and courteous.   240. **salt:** lewd.   241. **affection:** passion.   242. **slipper:** slippery.   243. **stamp:** coin, manufacture. **advantages:** opportunities.   246. **folly:** wantonness.   247. **green:** youthful, lusty.   248. **found him:** sized him up.   250. **condition:** disposition, character.   253. **pudding:** sausage.   257. **index:** table of contents at the beginning of a book.   261. **mutualities:** exchanges.   261–62. **hard at hand:** very soon after.   263. **incorporate:** carnal.   264. **Watch:** serve as a member of the watch.   265. **lay't upon you:** arrange for your orders.

ing too loud, or tainting his discipline, or from what
other course you please, which the time shall more
favorably minister.   270

RODERIGO: Well.

IAGO: Sir, he's rash and very sudden in choler, and
happily may strike at you—provoke him that he may;
for even out of that will I cause these of Cyprus to
mutiny, whose qualification shall come into no true
taste again but by the displanting of Cassio. So shall
you have a shorter journey to your desires by the   277
means I shall then have to prefer them; and the impediment most profitably remov'd, without the which
there were no expectation of our prosperity.   280

RODERIGO: I will do this, if you can bring it to any
opportunity.

IAGO: I warrant thee. Meet me by and by at the
citadel. I must fetch his necessaries ashore. Farewell.

RODERIGO: Adieu. *Exit.*   285

IAGO: That Cassio loves her, I do well believe't;
That she loves him, 'tis apt and of great credit.
The Moor (howbeit that I endure him not)
Is of a constant, loving, noble nature,
And I dare think he'll prove to Desdemona   290
A most dear husband. Now I do love her too,
Not out of absolute lust (though peradventure
I stand accomptant for as great a sin),
But partly led to diet my revenge,
For that I do suspect the lusty Moor   295
Hath leap'd into my seat; the thought whereof
Doth (like a poisonous mineral) gnaw my inwards;
And nothing can or shall content my soul
Till I am even'd with him, wife for wife;
Or failing so, yet that I put the Moor   300
At least into a jealousy so strong
That judgment cannot cure. Which thing to do,
If this poor trash of Venice, whom I trace
For his quick hunting, stand the putting on,
I'll have our Michael Cassio on the hip,   305

---

268. **tainting:** discrediting.   272. **rash:** impetuous.   273. **happily:** haply, perhaps.   275. **mutiny:** riot.
275–76. **whose . . . taste:** whose anger will not be acceptably diluted.   283. **I warrant thee:** I guarantee
you'll have opportunity.   287. **apt . . . credit:** likely and credible.   293. **accomptant:** accountable.
303. **trace.** Obscure. The meaning must be something like "train," or "check to make more eager"; the
latter is the sense of Steevens' widely accepted emendation *trash,* meaning to hang weights on a hound to
prevent his hunting too fast.   304. **stand . . . on:** perform properly when the moment comes for me to
set him on.   305. **on the hip:** in a position where I can throw him (wrestling term).

Abuse him to the Moor in the [rank] garb
(For I fear Cassio with my night-cap too),
Make the Moor thank me, love me, and reward me,
For making him egregiously an ass,
And practicing upon his peace and quiet   310
Even to madness. 'Tis here; but yet confus'd,
Knavery's plain face is never seen till us'd. *Exit.*

SCENE II
Enter Othello's HERALD *with a proclamation;* [*people
following*].

    HERALD: It is Othello's pleasure, our noble and valiant
general, that upon certain tidings now arriv'd, import-
ing the mere perdition of the Turkish fleet, every man
put himself into triumph; some to dance, some to make
bonfires, each man to what sport and revels his   5
[addiction] leads him; for besides these beneficial
news, it is the celebration of his nuptial. So much was
his pleasure should be proclaim'd. All offices are open,
and there is full liberty of feasting from this present
hour of five till the bell have told eleven. [Heaven]
bless the isle of Cyprus and our noble general   11
Othello! *Exeunt.*

[SCENE III]
    Enter OTHELLO, DESDEMONA, CASSIO, *and* ATTENDANTS.
    OTHELLO: Good Michael, look you to the guard to-night.
Let's teach ourselves that honorable stop,
Not to outsport discretion.
    CASSIO: Iago hath direction what to do;
But notwithstanding with my personal eye   5
Will I look to't.
    OTHELLO: Iago is most honest.
Michael, good night. To-morrow with your earliest
Let me have speech with you. [*To* DESDEMONA.] Come, my dear love,
The purchase made, the fruits are to ensue;
That profit's yet to come 'tween me and you.—   10
Good night. *Exit* [*with* DESDEMONA *and* ATTENDANTS].
Enter IAGO.
    CASSIO: Welcome, Iago; we must to the watch.

---

306. **rank garb:** coarse fashion.   310. **practicing upon:** plotting against.   II.ii. Location: Cyprus.
A street.   3. **mere perdition:** utter destruction.   8. **offices:** kitchens, food storerooms, etc.
II.iii. Location: Cyprus. The citadel.   3. **outsport:** carry our sports beyond.

IAGO: Not this hour, lieutenant; 'tis not yet ten o' th' clock. Our general cast us thus early for the love of his Desdemona; who let us not therefore blame. He hath not yet made wanton the night with her; and she is sport for Jove.   15

CASSIO: She's a most exquisite lady.

IAGO: And I'll warrant her, full of game.   19

CASSIO: Indeed she's a most fresh and delicate creature.

IAGO: What an eye she has! Methinks it sounds a parley to provocation.

CASSIO: An inviting eye; and yet methinks right modest.   25

IAGO: And when she speaks, is it not an alarum to love?

CASSIO: She is indeed perfection.

IAGO: Well—happiness to their sheets! Come, lieutenant, I have a stope of wine, and here without   30
are a brace of Cyprus gallants that would fain have a measure to the health of black Othello.

CASSIO: Not to-night, good Iago, I have very poor and unhappy brains for drinking. I could well wish courtesy would invent some other custom of entertainment.   36

IAGO: O, they are our friends—but one cup, I'll drink for you.

CASSIO: I have drunk but one cup to-night—and that was craftily qualified too—and behold what innovation it makes here. I am infortunate in the infirmity, and dare not task my weakness with any more.   42

IAGO: What, man? 'Tis a night of revels, the gallants desire it.

CASSIO: Where are they?   45

IAGO: Here, at the door; I pray you call them in.

CASSIO: I'll do't, but it dislikes me. *Exit.*

IAGO: If I can fasten but one cup upon him,
With that which he hath drunk to-night already,
He'll be as full of quarrel and offense   50
As my young mistress' dog. Now, my sick fool Roderigo,
Whom love hath turn'd almost the wrong side out,

---

13. **Not this hour:** not for an hour yet.   14. **cast:** dismissed.   23. **parley:** trumpet signal for a conference.   26. **alarum:** trumpet signal to arms.   30. **stope:** stoup, large drinking vessel.   40. **craftily qualified:** cannily diluted.   40–41. **innovation:** insurrection.   41. **here:** i.e. in his head.   47. **it dislikes me:** I don't care for it.   51. **my . . . dog:** a young lady's pet dog (likely to be spoiled).

To Desdemona hath to-night carous'd
Potations pottle-deep; and he's to watch.
Three else of Cyprus, noble swelling spirits   55
That hold their honors in a wary distance,
The very elements of this warlike isle,
Have I to-night fluster'd with flowing cups,
And they watch too. Now 'mongst this flock of drunkards
Am I [to put] our Cassio in some action   60
That may offend the isle. But here they come.
Enter CASSIO, MONTANO, *and* GENTLEMEN; [SERVANTS *follow with wine*].
If consequence do but approve my dream,
My boat sails freely, both with wind and stream.

CASSIO: 'Fore [God], they have given me a rouse
already.   65

MONTANO: Good faith, a little one; not past a pint, as I
am a soldier.

IAGO: Some wine ho!
[*Sings.*] "And let me the canakin clink, clink;
         And let me the canakin clink.   70
             A soldier's a man;
             O, man's life's but a span;
         Why then let a soldier drink."
Some wine, boys!

CASSIO: 'Fore [God], an excellent song.   75

IAGO: I learn'd it in England, where indeed they
are most potent in potting; your Dane, your German,
and your swag-bellied Hollander—Drink ho!—are
nothing to your English.

CASSIO: Is your [Englishman] so exquisite in his
drinking?   81

IAGO: Why, he drinks you, with facility, your Dane
dead drunk; he sweats not to overthrow your Almain;
he gives your Hollander a vomit ere the next pottle
can be fill'd.   85

CASSIO: To the health of our general!

MONTANO: I am for it, lieutenant; and I'll do you
justice.

IAGO: O sweet England!

---

53. **carous'd:** drunk off.   54. **pottle-deep:** to the bottom of the tankard. A pottle was a two-quart vessel.
55. **else:** others. **swelling:** proud.   56. **hold . . . distance:** i.e. are very touchy about their honor.
57. **very elements:** typical products.   62. **If . . . dream:** if the sequel corresponds to my fond hope.
63. **stream:** current.   64. **rouse:** drink.   69–73. **And . . . drink.** Probably an old drinking song.
72. **span:** i.e. brief stretch of time.   83. **Almain:** German.   87. **do you justice:** i.e. match you in drinking
that toast.

[*Sings.*]
> "King Stephen was and-a worthy peer,
>> His breeches cost him but a crown;   90
> He held them sixpence all too dear,
>> With that he call'd the tailor lown;
> He was a wight of high renown,
>> And thou art but of low degree.
> 'Tis pride that pulls the country down,   95
>> [Then] take thy auld cloak about thee."

Some wine ho!

CASSIO: ['Fore God,] this is a more exquisite song than the other.

IAGO: Will you hear't again?   100

CASSIO: No; for I hold him to be unworthy of his place that does those things. Well, [God's] above all; and there be souls must be sav'd, and there be souls must not be sav'd.

IAGO: It's true, good lieutenant.   105

CASSIO: For mine own part—no offense to the general, nor any man of quality—I hope to be sav'd.

IAGO: And so do I too, lieutenant.

CASSIO: Ay; but by your leave, not before me; the lieutenant is to be sav'd before the ancient. Let's   110
have no more of this; let's to our affairs.—[God] forgive us our sins!—Gentlemen, let's look to our business. Do not think, gentlemen, I am drunk: this is my ancient, this is my right hand, and this is my left [hand]. I am not drunk now; I can stand well enough, and I speak well enough.   116

[ALL.] Excellent well.

CASSIO: Why, very well then; you must not think then that I am drunk. *Exit.*

MONTANO: To th' platform, masters, come, let's set the watch. [*The* GENTLEMEN *follow* CASSIO *off.*]

IAGO: You see this fellow that is gone before: 121
He's a soldier fit to stand by Caesar
And give direction; and do but see his vice,
'Tis to his virtue a just equinox,
The one as long as th' other. 'Tis pity of him.   125
I fear the trust Othello puts him in,

89–96. **King . . . thee.** From an old ballad which is also alluded to in *The Tempest,* IV.i.222. 92. **lown:** rascal. 95. **pride:** ostentation, extravagance. 124. **just equinox:** exact counterpart (of dark against light).

On some odd time of his infirmity,
Will shake this island.
    MONTANO: But is he often thus?
    IAGO: 'Tis evermore [the] prologue to his sleep.
He'll watch the horologe a double set   130
If drink rock not his cradle.
    MONTANO: It were well
The general were put in mind of it.
Perhaps he sees it not, or his good nature
Prizes the virtue that appears in Cassio,
And looks not on his evils. Is not this true?   135
Enter RODERIGO.
    IAGO: [*Aside to him.*] How now, Roderigo?
I pray you, after the lieutenant, go. [*Exit* RODERIGO.]
    MONTANO: And 'tis great pity that the noble Moor
Should hazard such a place as his own second
With one of an ingraft infirmity;   140
It were an honest action to say
So to the Moor.
    IAGO: Not I, for this fair island.
I do love Cassio well; and would do much
To cure him of this evil. [*Cry within:* "Help! help!"]
          But hark, what noise?
Enter CASSIO *pursuing* RODERIGO.
    CASSIO: ['Zounds,] you rogue! you rascal!   145
    MONTANO: What's the matter, lieutenant?
    CASSIO: A knave teach me my duty? I'll beat the knave
into a twiggen bottle.
    RODERIGO: Beat me?   149
    CASSIO: Dost thou prate, rogue? [*Striking* RODERIGO.]
    MONTANO: Nay, good lieutenant; I pray you, sir, hold
your hand. [*Staying him.*]
    CASSIO: Let me go, sir, or I'll knock you o'er the
mazzard.
    MONTANO: Come, come—you're drunk.   155
    CASSIO: Drunk? [*They fight.*]
    IAGO: [*Aside to* RODERIGO.] Away, I say; go out and cry a mutiny. [*Exit*
RODERIGO.]
Nay, good lieutenant—[God's will], gentlemen—
Help ho!—lieutenant—sir—Montano—[sir]—

---

130. **watch . . . set:** stay awake twice round the clock.   139–40. **hazard . . . With:** take risks with a position as important as that of his own deputy by appointing.   140. **ingraft:** ingrained, inveterate.
148. **twiggen:** wicker-covered.   154. **mazzard:** head.

Help, masters!—Here's a goodly watch indeed!   160
[*A Bell rung.*]
Who's that which rings the bell? *Diablo,* ho!
The town will rise. [God's will], lieutenant, [hold]!
You'll be asham'd for ever.
Enter OTHELLO *and* [GENTLEMEN *with weapons*].
    OTHELLO: What is the matter here?
    MONTANO: ['Zounds,] I bleed still,
I am hurt to th' death. He dies.
    [*Assailing* CASSIO *again.*]
    OTHELLO: Hold, for your lives!   165
    IAGO: Hold ho! Lieutenant—sir—Montano—gentlemen—
Have you forgot all place of sense and duty?
Hold! the general speaks to you; hold, for shame!
    OTHELLO: Why, how now ho? from whence ariseth this?
Are we turn'd Turks, and to ourselves do that   170
Which heaven hath forbid the Ottomites?
For Christian shame, put by this barbarous brawl.
He that stirs next to carve for his own rage
Holds his soul light; he dies upon his motion.
Silence that dreadful bell, it frights the isle   175
From her propriety. What is the matter, masters?
Honest Iago, that looks dead with grieving,
Speak: who began this? On thy love, I charge thee!
    IAGO: I do not know. Friends all, but now, even now;
In quarter, and in terms like bride and groom   180
Devesting them for bed; and then, but now
(As if some planet had unwitted men),
Swords out, and tilting one at other's [breast],
In opposition bloody. I cannot speak
Any beginning to this peevish odds;   185
And would in action glorious I had lost
Those legs that brought me to a part of it.
    OTHELLO: How comes it, Michael, you are thus forgot?
    CASSIO: I pray you pardon me, I cannot speak.
    OTHELLO: Worthy Montano, you were wont to be civil;
The gravity and stillness of your youth   191
The world hath noted, and your name is great
In mouths of wisest censure. What's the matter

---

167. **place of sense:** i.e. the ordinary decencies. Some editors adopt Hanmer's emendation *sense of place.*
171. **Which . . . Ottomites:** i.e. by wrecking their fleet.   173. **carve . . . rage:** indulge his own impulse.
174. **light:** of small value.   176. **propriety:** natural temper (of calmness and order).   180. **quarter:**
bounds.   185. **peevish odds:** childish quarrel.   188. **are thus forgot:** have forgotten yourself in this way.
193. **censure:** judgment.

That you unlace your reputation thus,
And spend your rich opinion for the name   195
Of a night-brawler? Give me answer to it.
    MONTANO: Worthy Othello, I am hurt to danger.
Your officer, Iago, can inform you—
While I spare speech, which something now offends me—
Of all that I do know, nor know I aught   200
By me that's said or done amiss this night,
Unless self-charity be sometimes a vice,
And to defend ourselves it be a sin
When violence assails us.
    OTHELLO: Now by heaven,
My blood begins my safer guides to rule,   205
And passion, having my best judgment collied,
Assays to lead the way. ['Zounds,] if I stir,
Or do but lift this arm, the best of you
Shall sink in my rebuke. Give me to know
How this foul rout began; who set it on;   210
And he that is approv'd in this offense,
Though he had twinn'd with me, both at a birth,
Shall lose me. What, in a town of war,
Yet wild, the people's hearts brimful of fear,
To manage private and domestic quarrel?   215
In night, and on the court and guard of safety?
'Tis monstrous. Iago, who began't?
    MONTANO: If partially affin'd, or [leagu'd] in office,
Thou dost deliver more or less than truth,
Thou art no soldier.
    IAGO: Touch me not so near;   220
I had rather have this tongue cut from my mouth
Than it should do offense to Michael Cassio;
Yet I persuade myself, to speak the truth
Shall nothing wrong him. [Thus] it is, general:
Montano and myself being in speech,   225
There comes a fellow crying out for help,
And Cassio following him with determin'd sword
To execute upon him. Sir, this gentleman
Steps in to Cassio and entreats his pause;
Myself the crying fellow did pursue,   230
Lest by his clamor (as it so fell out)

---

194. **unlace:** lay open.   195. **opinion:** reputation.   199. **offends:** pains.   205. **blood:** anger. **safer guides:** i.e. rational controls.   206. **collied:** darkened.   211. **approv'd . . . offense:** found guilty. 215. **manage:** carry on.   216. **on . . . safety:** i.e. at the very headquarters on which the security of the town depends.   218. **partially affin'd:** biased (in Cassio's favor) because of your connection with him.

The town might fall in fright. He, swift of foot,
Outran my purpose; and I return'd [the] rather
For that I heard the clink and fall of swords,
And Cassio high in oath; which till to-night   235
I ne'er might say before. When I came back
(For this was brief), I found them close together
At blow and thrust, even as again they were
When you yourself did part them.
More of this matter cannot I report.   240
But men are men; the best sometimes forget.
Though Cassio did some little wrong to him,
As men in rage strike those that wish them best,
Yet surely Cassio, I believe, receiv'd
From him that fled some strange indignity   245
Which patience could not pass.
    OTHELLO: I know, Iago,
Thy honesty and love doth mince this matter,
Making it light to Cassio. Cassio, I love thee,
But never more be officer of mine.
Enter DESDEMONA *attended.*
Look if my gentle love be not rais'd up!   250
I'll make thee an example.
    DESDEMONA: What is the matter, dear?
    OTHELLO: All's well [now], sweeting;
Come away to bed. [*To* MONTANO.] Sir, for your hurts,
Myself will be your surgeon.—Lead him off.
[*Some lead* MONTANO *off.*]
Iago, look with care about the town,   255
And silence those whom this vild brawl distracted.
Come, Desdemona, 'tis the soldiers' life
To have their balmy slumbers wak'd with strife.
Exit [*with* DESDEMONA, GENTLEMEN, *and* ATTENDANTS].
    IAGO: What, are you hurt, lieutenant?
    CASSIO: Ay, past all surgery.   260
    IAGO: Marry, [God] forbid!
    CASSIO: Reputation, reputation, reputation! O, I have
lost my reputation! I have lost the immortal part of
myself, and what remains is bestial. My reputation,
Iago, my reputation!   265
    IAGO: As I am an honest man, I had thought you had
receiv'd some bodily wound; there is more sense in that

---

233. **rather:** sooner, i.e. more speedily.   246. **pass:** pass over.   247. **mince:** cut fine, i.e. try to make light of.   267. **sense:** physical sensation.

than in reputation. Reputation is an idle and most false imposition; oft got without merit, and lost without deserving. You have lost no reputation at all, unless you repute yourself such a loser. What, man, there are more ways to recover the general again. You are but now cast in his mood, a punishment more in policy than in malice, even so as one would beat his offenseless dog to affright an imperious lion. Sue to him again, and he's yours.

CASSIO: I will rather sue to be despis'd than to deceive so good a commander with so slight, so drunken, and so indiscreet an officer. Drunk? and speak parrot? and squabble? swagger? swear? and discourse fustian with one's own shadow? O thou invisible spirit of wine, if thou hast no name to be known by, let us call thee devil!

IAGO: What was he that you follow'd with your sword? What had he done to you?

CASSIO: I know not.

IAGO: Is't possible?

CASSIO: I remember a mass of things, but nothing distinctly; a quarrel, but nothing wherefore. O [God], that men should put an enemy in their mouths to steal away their brains! that we should, with joy, pleasance, revel, and applause, transform ourselves into beasts!

IAGO: Why, but you are now well enough. How came you thus recover'd?

CASSIO: It hath pleas'd the devil drunkenness to give place to the devil wrath: one unperfectness shows me another, to make me frankly despise myself.

IAGO: Come, you are too severe a moraler. As the time, the place, and the condition of this country stands, I could heartily wish this had not befall'n; but since it is as it is, mend it for your own good.

CASSIO: I will ask him for my place again, he shall tell me I am a drunkard! Had I as many mouths as Hydra, such an answer would stop them all. To be now a sensible man, by and by a fool, and presently a beast!

270

276

280

285

290

295

300

305

---

269. **imposition:** i.e. something laid on from outside; what others say of him, and not the man himself. 272. **recover:** regain the favor of.   273. **cast:** dismissed. **mood:** anger.   274. **policy:** expediency. **malice:** ill will.   274–75. **as . . . lion.** Proverbial.   278. **slight:** worthless.   279. **speak parrot:** talk nonsense. 280. **fustian:** gibberish.   304. **Hydra:** many-headed snake killed by Hercules as one of his twelve labors. 306. **sensible:** in possession of one's faculties.

O strange! Every inordinate cup is unbless'd, and the
ingredient is a devil.

    IAGO: Come, come; good wine is a good familiar
creature, if it be well us'd; exclaim no more against it.
And, good lieutenant, I think you think I love you.   311

    CASSIO: I have well approv'd it, sir. I drunk!

    IAGO: You, or any man living, may be drunk at a
time, man. [I'll] tell you what you shall do. Our
general's wife is now the general—I may say so in this
respect, for that he hath devoted and given up   316
himself to the contemplation, mark, and [denotement]
of her parts and graces. Confess yourself freely to her;
importune her help to put you in your place again. She
is of so free, so kind, so apt, so bless'd a disposition,
she holds it a vice in her goodness not to do more   321
than she is requested. This broken joint between you
and her husband entreat her to splinter; and my fortunes against any lay worth naming, this crack of your
love shall grow stronger than it was before.   325

    CASSIO: You advise me well.

    IAGO: I protest, in the sincerity of love and honest
kindness.

    CASSIO: I think it freely; and betimes in the morning
I will beseech the virtuous Desdemona to undertake
for me. I am desperate of my fortunes if they check
me [here].   332

    IAGO: You are in the right. Good night, lieutenant,
I must to the watch.

    CASSIO: Good night, honest Iago. *Exit* CASSIO.

    IAGO: And what's he then that says I play the villain,   336
When this advice is free I give, and honest,
Probal to thinking, and indeed the course
To win the Moor again? For 'tis most easy
Th' inclining Desdemona to subdue   340
In any honest suit; she's fram'd as fruitful
As the free elements. And then for her
To win the Moor, were['t] to renounce his baptism,
All seals and symbols of redeemed sin,
His soul is so enfetter'd to her love,   345

---

309. **familiar:** domestic, serviceable.   312. **approv'd:** tested and found true.   313–14. **at a time:** at
some time, on some occasion.   317. **mark:** marking, observing. **denotement:** noting.   318. **parts:** good
qualities.   320. **free:** generous. **apt:** willing.   321. **vice:** defect.   323. **splinter:** bind up with splints.
324. **lay:** wager.   327. **protest:** declare.   337. **free:** free from guile.   338. **Probal to thinking:** something
that thought would show to be true.   341. **fruitful:** generous.

That she may make, unmake, do what she list,
Even as her appetite shall play the god
With his weak function. How am I then a villain,
To counsel Cassio to this parallel course,
Directly to his good? Divinity of hell!   350
When devils will the blackest sins put on,
They do suggest at first with heavenly shows,
As I do now; for whiles this honest fool
Plies Desdemona to repair his fortune,
And she for him pleads strongly to the Moor,   355
I'll pour this pestilence into his ear—
That she repeals him for her body's lust,
And by how much she strives to do him good,
She shall undo her credit with the Moor.
So will I turn her virtue into pitch,   360
And out of her own goodness make the net
That shall enmesh them all.
Enter RODERIGO.
          How now, Roderigo?
    RODERIGO: I do follow here in the chase, not like a hound
that hunts, but one that fills up the cry. My money is
almost spent; I have been to-night exceedingly well
cudgell'd; and I think the issue will be, I shall have   366
so much experience for my pains; and so, with no
money at all and a little more wit, return again to
Venice.
    IAGO: How poor are they that have not patience!
What wound did ever heal but by degrees?   371
Thou know'st we work by wit, and not by witchcraft,
And wit depends on dilatory time.
Does't not go well? Cassio hath beaten thee,
And thou by that small hurt [hast] cashier'd Cassio.
Though other things grow fair against the sun,   376
Yet fruits that blossom first will first be ripe.
Content thyself a while. [By the mass], 'tis morning;
Pleasure and action make the hours seem short.
Retire thee, go where thou art billeted.   380
Away, I say, thou shalt know more hereafter.
Nay, get thee gone. (*Exit* RODERIGO.) Two things are to be done:
My wife must move for Cassio to her mistress—
I'll set her on—

---

348. **function:** mental faculties.   349. **parallel:** i.e. conforming with these facts.   350. **Divinity:** theology.   352. **suggest:** tempt.   357. **repeals:** recalls, i.e. seeks to reinstate.   364. **cry:** pack.

Myself a while to draw the Moor apart,   385
And bring him jump when he may Cassio find
Soliciting his wife. Ay, that's the way;
Dull not device by coldness and delay. *Exit.*

ACT III, SCENE I
Enter CASSIO [*with*] MUSICIANS.
  CASSIO: Masters, play here, I will content your pains;
Something that's brief; and bid "Good morrow, general."
[*They play, and enter the*] CLOWN.
  CLOWN: Why, masters, have your instruments been in
Naples, that they speak i' th' nose thus?
  [FIRST] MUSICIAN: How, sir? how?   5
  CLOWN: Are these, I pray you, wind instruments?
  [FIRST] MUSICIAN: Ay, marry, are they, sir.
  CLOWN: O, thereby hangs a tail.
  [FIRST] MUSICIAN: Whereby hangs a tale, sir?   9
  CLOWN: Marry, sir, by many a wind instrument that I
know. But, masters, here's money for you; and the
general so likes your music, that he desires you for
love's sake to make no more noise with it.
  [FIRST] MUSICIAN: Well, sir, we will not.   14
  CLOWN: If you have any music that may not be heard,
to't again; but (as they say) to hear music the general
does not greatly care.
  [FIRST] MUSICIAN: We have none such, sir.
  CLOWN: Then put up your pipes in your bag, for I'll
away. Go, vanish into air, away! *Exeunt* Musicians.
  CASSIO: Dost thou hear, mine honest friend?   21
  CLOWN: No, I hear not your honest friend; I hear you.
  CASSIO: Prithee keep up thy quillets. There's a poor
piece of gold for thee. If the gentlewoman that attends
the [general's wife] be stirring, tell her there's one   25
Cassio entreats her a little favor of speech. Wilt thou
do this?
  CLOWN: She is stirring, sir. If she will stir hither, I
shall seem to notify unto her.
  CASSIO: [Do, good my friend.] *Exit* CLOWN.
  Enter IAGO.
          In happy time, Iago.   30

---

386. **jump:** at the precise moment.   388. **device:** plotting.   III.i. Location: The citadel.   1. **content:**
requite.   4. **speak . . . thus:** i.e. sound like a man whose nose has been affected by syphilis (a disease
supposed to have originated in Naples).   15. **may not:** cannot.   23. **keep up:** do not bring out. **quillets:**
quibbles, puns.   26. **a little . . . speech:** the favor of a brief conference.   30. **In happy time:** oppor-
tunely met.

IAGO: You have not been a-bed then?

CASSIO: Why, no; the day had broke
Before we parted. I have made bold, Iago,
To send in to your wife. My suit to her
Is that she will to virtuous Desdemona   35
Procure me some access.

IAGO: I'll send her to you presently;
And I'll devise a mean to draw the Moor
Out of the way, that your converse and business
May be more free.

CASSIO: I humbly thank you for't. *Exit* [IAGO].
I never knew a Florentine more kind and honest.   40
Enter EMILIA.

EMILIA: Good morrow, good lieutenant. I am sorry
For your displeasure; but all will sure be well.
The general and his wife are talking of it,
And she speaks for you stoutly. The Moor replies
That he you hurt is of great fame in Cyprus,   45
And great affinity; and that in wholesome wisdom
He might not but refuse you. But he protests he loves you,
And needs no other suitor but his likings
[To take the safest occasion by the front]
To bring you in again.

CASSIO: Yet I beseech you,   50
If you think fit, or that it may be done,
Give me advantage of some brief discourse
With Desdemon alone.

EMILIA: Pray you come in.
I will bestow you where you shall have time   54
To speak your bosom freely.

CASSIO: I am much bound to you. [*Exeunt.*]

SCENE II
Enter OTHELLO, IAGO, *and* GENTLEMEN.

OTHELLO: These letters give, Iago, to the pilot,
And by him do my duties to the Senate.
That done, I will be walking on the works;
Repair there to me.

IAGO: Well, my good lord, I'll do't.   4

OTHELLO: This fortification, gentlemen, shall we see't?

GENTLEMEN: We'll wait upon your lordship. *Exeunt.*

---

40. **a Florentine:** i.e. even a Florentine, one of my own townsmen.   42. **displeasure:** loss of favor.   46.
affinity: family connections.   49. **occasion:** opportunity. **front:** forelock.   55. **bosom:** most private concerns.   III.ii. Location: The citadel.   2. **do my duties:** send my dutiful respects.   3. **works:**
fortifications.

Scene III

Enter DESDEMONA, CASSIO, *and* EMILIA.

DESDEMONA: Be thou assur'd, good Cassio, I will do
All my abilities in thy behalf.

EMILIA: Good madam, do. I warrant it grieves my husband
As if the cause were his.

DESDEMONA: O, that's an honest fellow. Do not doubt, Cassio, 5
But I will have my lord and you again
As friendly as you were.

CASSIO: Bounteous madam,
What ever shall become of Michael Cassio,
He's never any thing but your true servant.

DESDEMONA: I know't; I thank you. You do love my lord;
You have known him long, and be you well assur'd
He shall in strangeness stand no farther off 12
Than in a politic distance.

CASSIO: Ay, but, lady,
That policy may either last so long,
Or feed upon such nice and waterish diet, 15
Or breed itself so out of circumstances,
That I being absent and my place supplied,
My general will forget my love and service.

DESDEMONA: Do not doubt that; before Emilia here,
I give thee warrant of thy place. Assure thee, 20
If I do vow a friendship, I'll perform it
To the last article. My lord shall never rest,
I'll watch him tame, and talk him out of patience;
His bed shall seem a school, his board a shrift,
I'll intermingle every thing he does 25
With Cassio's suit. Therefore be merry, Cassio,
For thy solicitor shall rather die
Than give thy cause away.

Enter OTHELLO *and* IAGO.

EMILIA: Madam, here comes my lord.

CASSIO: Madam, I'll take my leave. 30

DESDEMONA: Why, stay, and hear me speak.

CASSIO: Madam, not now; I am very ill at ease,
Unfit for mine own purposes.

DESDEMONA: Well, do your discretion. *Exit* CASSIO.

III.iii. Location: The garden of the citadel.   12. **strangeness:** aloofness.   13. **politic:** dictated by policy.
15. **feed . . . diet:** i.e. require so little to keep it alive (*nice* = trivial).   16. **breed . . . circumstances:** be re-
vived by some accident or other.   17. **supplied:** filled.   19. **doubt:** fear.   21. **friendship:** friendly act.
23. **watch him tame:** keep him awake till he capitulates (as in training a hawk). **talk . . . patience:** keep
talking until he can't endure it any longer.   24. **shrift:** confessional.   28. **away:** up.

IAGO: Hah? I like not that.

OTHELLO: What dost thou say?

IAGO: Nothing, my lord; or if—I know not what.   36

OTHELLO: Was not that Cassio parted from my wife?

IAGO: Cassio, my lord? No, sure, I cannot think it,

That he would steal away so guilty-like,

Seeing your coming.

OTHELLO: I do believe 'twas he.   40

DESDEMONA: How now, my lord?

I have been talking with a suitor here,

A man that languishes in your displeasure.

OTHELLO: Who is't you mean?   44

DESDEMONA: Why, your lieutenant, Cassio. Good my lord,

If I have any grace or power to move you,

His present reconciliation take;

For if he be not one that truly loves you,

That errs in ignorance and not in cunning,

I have no judgment in an honest face.   50

I prithee call him back.

OTHELLO: Went he hence now?

DESDEMONA: [Yes, faith]; so humbled

That he hath left part of his grief with me

To suffer with him. Good love, call him back.   54

OTHELLO: Not now, sweet Desdemon, some other time.

DESDEMONA: But shall't be shortly?

OTHELLO: The sooner, sweet, for you.

DESDEMONA: Shall't be to-night at supper?

OTHELLO: No, not to-night.

DESDEMONA: To-morrow dinner then?

OTHELLO: I shall not dine at home;

I meet the captains at the citadel.

DESDEMONA: Why then to-morrow night, [or] Tuesday morn;   60

On Tuesday noon, or night; on We'n'sday morn.

I prithee name the time, but let it not

Exceed three days. In faith, he's penitent;

And yet his trespass, in our common reason

(Save that they say the wars must make example   65

(Out of her best), is not almost a fault

T' incur a private check. When shall he come?

Tell me, Othello. I wonder in my soul

What you would ask me that I should deny,

---

47. **reconciliation:** repentance.   49. **in cunning:** wittingly.   66. **her.** *Wars* was frequently construed as a singular. See I.i.150–51, I.iii.234, III.iii.349–50. **not almost:** scarcely.   67. **a private check:** even a private rebuke.

Or stand so mamm'ring on. What? Michael Cassio,   70
That came a-wooing with you, and so many a time,
When I have spoke of you dispraisingly,
Hath ta'en your part—to have so much to do
To bring him in! [By'r lady], I could do much—   74
    OTHELLO: Prithee no more; let him come when he will;
I will deny thee nothing.
    DESDEMONA: Why, this is not a boon;
'Tis as I should entreat you wear your gloves,
Or feed on nourishing dishes, or keep you warm,
Or sue to you to do a peculiar profit
To your own person. Nay, when I have a suit   80
Wherein I mean to touch your love indeed,
It shall be full of poise and difficult weight,
And fearful to be granted.
    OTHELLO: I will deny thee nothing;
Whereon, I do beseech thee, grant me this,
To leave me but a little to myself.   85
    DESDEMONA: Shall I deny you? No. Farewell, my lord.
    OTHELLO: Farewell, my Desdemona, I'll come to thee straight.
    DESDEMONA: Emilia, come.—Be as your fancies teach you;
What e'er you be, I am obedient. *Exit* [*with* EMILIA].
    OTHELLO: Excellent wretch! Perdition catch my soul   90
But I do love thee! and when I love thee not,
Chaos is come again.
    IAGO: My noble lord—
    OTHELLO: What dost thou say, Iago?
    IAGO: Did Michael Cassio, when [you] woo'd my lady,
Know of your love?   95
    OTHELLO: He did, from first to last. Why dost thou ask?
    IAGO: But for a satisfaction of my thought,
No further harm.
    OTHELLO: Why of thy thought, Iago?
    IAGO: I did not think he had been acquainted with her.
    OTHELLO: O yes, and went between us very oft.   100
    IAGO: Indeed!
    OTHELLO: Indeed? ay, indeed. Discern'st thou aught in that?
Is he not honest?
    IAGO: Honest, my lord?
    OTHELLO: Honest? ay, honest.
    IAGO: My lord, for aught I know.
    OTHELLO: What dost thou think?

---

70. **mamm'ring:** hesitating.   73. **to do:** ado, fuss.   74. **bring him in:** i.e. restore him to your favor.
79. **peculiar profit:** personal benefit.   82. **poise:** weight.   84. **Whereon:** in return for which.   91. **But I do:** if I do not.

IAGO: Think, my lord?   105
    OTHELLO: Think, my lord? [By heaven], thou echo'st me,
As if there were some monster in thy thought
Too hideous to be shown. Thou dost mean something.
I heard thee say even now, thou lik'st not that,
When Cassio left my wife. What didst not like?   110
And when I told thee he was of my counsel
[In] my whole course of wooing, thou criedst, "Indeed!"
And didst contract and purse thy brow together,
As if thou then hadst shut up in thy brain
Some horrible conceit. If thou dost love me,   115
Show me thy thought.
    IAGO: My lord, you know I love you.
    OTHELLO: I think thou dost;
And for I know thou'rt full of love and honesty,
And weigh'st thy words before thou giv'st them breath,
Therefore these stops of thine fright me the more;
For such things in a false disloyal knave   121
Are tricks of custom; but in a man that's just
They're close dilations, working from the heart,
That passion cannot rule.
    IAGO: For Michael Cassio,
I dare be sworn I think that he is honest.   125
    OTHELLO: I think so too.
    IAGO: Men should be what they seem,
Or those that be not, would they might seem none!
    OTHELLO: Certain, men should be what they seem.
    IAGO: Why then I think Cassio's an honest man.
    OTHELLO: Nay, yet there's more in this.   130
I prithee speak to me as to thy thinkings,
As thou dost ruminate, and give thy worst of thoughts
The worst of words.
    IAGO: Good my lord, pardon me:
Though I am bound to every act of duty,
I am not bound to that all slaves are free [to].   135
Utter my thoughts? Why, say they are vild and false,
As where's that palace whereinto foul things
Sometimes intrude not? Who has that breast so pure
[But some] uncleanly apprehensions
Keep leets and law-days and in sessions sit   140

---

111. **of my counsel:** in my confidence.   123. **close dilations:** expressions of secret thought.
124. **passion cannot rule:** i.e. the man because of his impassioned state cannot control.   131. **as to:** with
respect to.   135. **that . . . to:** that which even a slave is not bound to.   139. **apprehensions:** thoughts.
140. **leets:** sessions of local courts.

With meditations lawful?
    OTHELLO: Thou dost conspire against thy friend, Iago,
If thou but think'st him wrong'd, and mak'st his ear
A stranger to thy thoughts.
    IAGO: I do beseech you,
Though I perchance am vicious in my guess   145
(As I confess it is my nature's plague
To spy into abuses, and [oft] my jealousy
Shapes faults that are not), that your wisdom [then],
From one that so imperfectly [conjects],
Would take no notice, nor build yourself a trouble   150
Out of his scattering and unsure observance.
It were not for your quiet nor your good,
Nor for my manhood, honesty, and wisdom,
To let you know my thoughts.
    OTHELLO: ['Zounds,] what dost thou mean?
    IAGO: Good name in man and woman, dear my lord,
Is the immediate jewel of their souls.   156
Who steals my purse steals trash; 'tis something, nothing;
'Twas mine, 'tis his, and has been slave to thousands;
But he that filches from me my good name
Robs me of that which not enriches him,   160
And makes me poor indeed.
    OTHELLO: [By heaven,] I'll know thy thoughts.
    IAGO: You cannot, if my heart were in your hand,
Nor shall not, whilst 'tis in my custody.
    OTHELLO: Ha?
    IAGO: O, beware, my lord, of jealousy!   165
It is the green-ey'd monster which doth mock
The meat it feeds on. That cuckold lives in bliss
Who, certain of his fate, loves not his wronger;
But O, what damned minutes tells he o'er
Who dotes, yet doubts; suspects, yet [strongly] loves!
    OTHELLO: O misery!   171
    IAGO: Poor and content is rich, and rich enough,
But riches fineless is as poor as winter
To him that ever fears he shall be poor.
Good [God], the souls of all my tribe defend   175
From jealousy!
    OTHELLO: Why? why is this?
Think'st thou I'ld make a life of jealousy?
To follow still the changes of the moon

---

141. **With meditations lawful:** along with innocent thoughts.   147. **jealousy:** suspicion.   148. **then:** on that account.   163. **if:** even if.   167. **meat . . . on:** i.e. the heart of the man who suffers it.   173. **fineless:** boundless.

With fresh suspicions? No! to be once in doubt
Is [once] to be resolv'd. Exchange me for a goat,   180
When I shall turn the business of my soul
To such [exsufflicate] and [blown] surmises,
Matching thy inference. 'Tis not to make me jealous
To say my wife is fair, feeds well, loves company,
Is free of speech, sings, plays, and dances [well];   185
Where virtue is, these are more virtuous.
Nor from mine own weak merits will I draw
The smallest fear or doubt of her revolt,
For she had eyes, and chose me. No, Iago,
I'll see before I doubt; when I doubt, prove;   190
And on the poof, there is no more but this—
Away at once with love or jealousy!
    IAGO: I am glad of this, for now I shall have reason
To show the love and duty that I bear you
With franker spirit; therefore (as I am bound)   195
Receive it from me. I speak not yet of proof.
Look to your wife, observe her well with Cassio,
Wear your eyes thus, not jealous nor secure.
I would not have your free and noble nature,
Out of self-bounty, be abus'd; look to't.   200
I know our country disposition well:
In Venice they do let [God] see the pranks
They dare not show their husbands; their best conscience
Is not to leave't undone, but keep't unknown.
    OTHELLO: Dost thou say so?   205
    IAGO: She did deceive her father, marrying you,
And when she seem'd to shake and fear your looks,
She lov'd them most.
    OTHELLO: And so she did.
    IAGO: Why, go to then.
She that so young could give out such a seeming
To seel her father's eyes up, close as oak,   210
He thought 'twas witchcraft—but I am much to blame;
I humbly do beseech you of your pardon
For too much loving you.
    OTHELLO: I am bound to thee for ever.
    IAGO: I see this hath a little dash'd your spirits.

---

180. **once:** once for all.   182. **exsufflicate and blown.** Both adjectives may mean "blown-up, inflated," or the phrase may mean "spat-out and fly-blown."   183. **jealous:** jealous, suspicious.   188. **doubt:** suspicion. **revolt:** unfaithfulness.   190. **prove:** test.   198. **secure:** culpably free of anxiety, overconfident.   200. **self-bounty:** inherent goodness.   210. **oak.** A close-grained wood.   213. **bound:** indebted.

OTHELLO: Not a jot, not a jot.

IAGO: [I' faith], I fear it has.

I hope you will consider what is spoke   216

Comes from [my] love. But I do see y' are mov'd.

I am to pray you not to strain my speech

To grosser issues nor to larger reach

Than to suspicion.   220

OTHELLO: I will not.

IAGO: Should you do so, my lord,

My speech should fall into such vild success

Which my thoughts aim'd not. Cassio's my worthy friend—

My lord, I see y' are mov'd.

OTHELLO: No, not much mov'd:

I do not think but Desdemona's honest.   225

    IAGO: Long live she so! and long live you to think so!

    OTHELLO: And yet how nature erring from itself—

    IAGO: Ay, there's the point; as (to be bold with you)

Not to affect many proposed matches

Of her own clime, complexion, and degree,   230

Whereto we see in all things nature tends—

Foh, one may smell in such, a will most rank,

Foul disproportions, thoughts unnatural.

But (pardon me) I do not in position

Distinctly speak of her, though I may fear   235

Her will, recoiling to her better judgment,

May fall to match you with her country forms,

And happily repent.

    OTHELLO: Farewell, farewell!

If more thou dost perceive, let me know more;

Set on thy wife to observe. Leave me, Iago.   240

    IAGO: [*Going.*] My lord, I take my leave.

    OTHELLO: Why did I marry? This honest creature, doubtless,

Sees and knows more, much more, than he unfolds.

    IAGO: [*Returning.*] My lord, I would I might entreat your honor

To scan this thing no farther; leave it to time.   245

Although 'tis fit that Cassio have his place—

For sure he fills it up with great ability—

Yet if you please to [hold] him off awhile,

You shall by that perceive him and his means.

Note if your lady strain his entertainment   250

---

219. **issues:** conclusions. **reach:** scope.   222. **success:** effect.   225. **honest:** chaste.   229. **affect:** desire,
look with favor on.   230. **clime:** region, country.   232. **will:** desire, appetite.   233. **disproportions:**
abnormality.   234. **in position:** i.e. in arguing thus.   235. **Distinctly speak of:** refer specifically to.
236. **recoiling ... judgment:** reverting to a more natural preference.   237. **match:** compare. **her country
forms:** the appearance of her countrymen.   238. **happily:** haply, perchance.   250. **strain his entertainment:** repeatedly urge his reappointment.

With any strong or vehement importunity;
Much will be seen in that. In the mean time,
Let me be thought too busy in my fears
(As worthy cause I have to fear I am)
And hold her free, I do beseech your honor.   255
    OTHELLO: Fear not my government.
    IAGO: I once more take my leave. *Exit.*
    OTHELLO: This fellow's of exceeding honesty,
And knows all [qualities], with a learned spirit,
Of human dealings. If I do prove her haggard,   260
Though that her jesses were my dear heart-strings,
I'ld whistle her off, and let her down the wind
To prey at fortune. Haply, for I am black,
And have not those soft parts of conversation
That chamberers have, or for I am declin'd   265
Into the vale of years (yet that's not much),
She's gone. I am abus'd, and my relief
Must be to loathe her. O curse of marriage!
That we can call these delicate creatures ours,
And not their appetites! I had rather be a toad   270
And live upon the vapor of a dungeon
Than keep a corner in the thing I love
For others' uses. Yet 'tis the plague [of] great ones,
Prerogativ'd are they less than the base;
'Tis destiny unshunnable, like death.   275
Even then this forked plague is fated to us
When we do quicken. Look where she comes:
    Enter DESDEMONA *and* EMILIA.
If she be false, [O then] heaven [mocks] itself!
I'll not believe't.
    DESDEMONA: How now, my dear Othello?
Your dinner, and the generous islanders   280
By you invited, do attend your presence.
    OTHELLO: I am to blame.
    DESDEMONA: Why do you speak so faintly?
Are you not well?
    OTHELLO: I have a pain upon my forehead, here.
    DESDEMONA: [Faith], that's with watching, 'twill away again.   285

---

255. **free:** guiltless.   256. **government:** conduct, self-control.   259. **qualities:** types, conditions.
260. **haggard:** wild (a term from falconry).   261. **jesses:** leather straps on the hawk's legs, by which it
was fastened to the leash held by the falconer.   262. **down the wind.** To release the hawk downwind was
to court its loss.   263. **at fortune:** at random. **for:** because.   264. **soft . . . conversation:** pleasing qualities of social behavior.   265. **chamberers:** gallants.   274. **Prerogativ'd:** privileged.   276. **forked plague:**
curse of cuckold's horns.   277. **quicken:** begin to live.   280. **generous:** noble.   285. **with watching:**
from lack of sleep.

Let me but bind it hard, within this hour
It will be well.
  OTHELLO: Your napkin is too little;
[*He puts the handkerchief from him, and it drops.*]
Let it alone. Come, I'll go in with you.
  DESDEMONA: I am very sorry that you are not well.
Exit [*with* OTHELLO].
  EMILIA: I am glad I have found this napkin;   290
This was her first remembrance from the Moor.
My wayward husband hath a hundred times
Woo'd me to steal it; but she so loves the token
(For he conjur'd her she should ever keep it)
That she reserves it evermore about her   295
To kiss and talk to. I'll have the work ta'en out,
And give't Iago. What he will do with it
Heaven knows, not I;
I nothing but to please his fantasy.
Enter IAGO.
  IAGO: How now? what do you here alone?   300
  EMILIA: Do not you chide; I have a thing for you.
  IAGO: You have a thing for me? It is a common thing—
  EMILIA: Hah?
  IAGO: To have a foolish wife.
  EMILIA: O, is that all? What will you give me now
For that same handkerchief?
  IAGO: What handkerchief?   306
  EMILIA: What handkerchief?
Why, that the Moor first gave to Desdemona,
That which so often you did bid me steal.
  IAGO: Hast stol'n it from her?   310
  EMILIA: No, [faith]; she let it drop by negligence,
And to th' advantage, I, being here, took't up.
Look, here 'tis.
  IAGO: A good wench, give it me.
  EMILIA: What will you do with't, that you have been so earnest
To have me filch it?
  IAGO: [*Snatching it*].   Why, what is that to you?
  EMILIA: If it be not for some purpose of import,   316
Give't me again. Poor lady, she'll run mad
When she shall lack it.
  IAGO: Be not acknown on't; I have use for it.

287. **napkin:** handkerchief. 288. **Let it alone:** don't trouble yourself about it. 292. **wayward:** capricious. 296. **work ta'en out:** pattern copied. 299. **I nothing but:** my only thought is. **fantasy:** fancy, whim. 312. **to th' advantage:** upon the opportunity. 319. **Be . . . on't:** pretend not to know of it.

Go, leave me. *Exit* EMILIA.   320
I will in Cassio's lodging lose this napkin,
And let him find it. Trifles light as air
Are to the jealous confirmations strong
As proofs of holy writ; this may do something.
The Moor already changes with my poison: 325
Dangerous conceits are in their natures poisons,
Which at the first are scarce found to distaste,
But with a little act upon the blood
Burn like the mines of sulphur.
Enter OTHELLO.
              I did say so.
Look where he comes! Not poppy, nor mandragora,
Nor all the drowsy syrups of the world   331
Shall ever medicine thee to that sweet sleep
Which thou ow'dst yesterday.
    OTHELLO: Ha, ha, false to me?
    IAGO: Why, how now, general? No more of that.
    OTHELLO: Avaunt, be gone! thou hast set me on the rack.
I swear 'tis better to be much abus'd   336
Than but to know't a little.
    IAGO: How now, my lord?
    OTHELLO: What sense had I in her stol'n hours of lust?
I saw't not, thought it not; it harm'd not me.
I slept the next night well, fed well, was free and merry;   340
I found not Cassio's kisses on her lips.
He that is robb'd, not wanting what is stol'n,
Let him not know't, and he's not robb'd at all.
    IAGO: I am sorry to hear this.
    OTHELLO: I had been happy, if the general camp,   345
Pioners and all, had tasted her sweet body,
So I had nothing known. O now, for ever
Farewell the tranquil mind! farewell content!
Farewell the plumed troops and the big wars
That makes ambition virtue! O, farewell!   350
Farewell the neighing steed and the shrill trump,
The spirit-stirring drum, th' ear-piercing fife,
The royal banner, and all quality,
Pride, pomp, and circumstance of glorious war!
And O you mortal engines, whose rude throats   355

---

328. **with . . . act:** after they have acted for a little while.   330. **mandragora:** an opiate, made of the mandrake.   333. **ow'dst:** didst own.   338. **in:** of.   340. **free:** carefree.   342. **wanting:** missing.   346. **Pioneers:** the lowest rank of soldier, primarily used for manual labor, not fighting.   349. **big:** stately.   353. **quality:** character, attributes.   354. **Pride:** proud display. **pomp:** dignity. **circumstance:** ceremonial splendor.   355. **mortal:** deadly. **engines:** instruments of war; here, cannon.

Th' immortal Jove's dread clamors counterfeit,
Farewell! Othello's occupation's gone.
    IAGO: Is't possible, my lord?
    OTHELLO: Villain, be sure thou prove my love a whore;
[*Taking him by the throat.*]
Be sure of it. Give me the ocular proof,   360
Or by the worth of mine eternal soul,
Thou hadst been better have been born a dog
Than answer my wak'd wrath!
    IAGO: Is't come to this?
    OTHELLO: Make me to see't; or (at the least) so prove it
That the probation bear no hinge nor loop   365
To hang a doubt on; or woe upon thy life!
    IAGO: My noble lord—
    OTHELLO: If thou dost slander her and torture me,
Never pray more; abandon all remorse;
On horror's head horrors accumulate;   370
Do deeds to make heaven weep, all earth amaz'd;
For nothing canst thou to damnation add
Greater than that.
    IAGO: O grace! O heaven forgive me!
Are you a man? Have you a soul? or sense?   374
God buy you; take mine office. O wretched fool,
That lov'st to make thine honesty a vice!
O monstrous world! Take note, take note, O world,
To be direct and honest is not safe.
I thank you for this profit, and from hence
I'll love no friend, sith love breeds such offense.   380
    OTHELLO: Nay, stay. Thou shouldst be honest.
    IAGO: I should be wise—for honesty's a fool
And loses that it works for.
    OTHELLO: By the world,
I think my wife be honest, and think she is not;
I think that thou art just, and think thou art not.   385
I'll have some proof. [Her] name, that was as fresh
As Dian's visage, is now begrim'd and black
As mine own face. If there be cords, or knives,
Poison, or fire, or suffocating streams,
I'll not endure it. Would I were satisfied!   390

---

365. **probation:** proof.   369. **remorse:** pity.   371. **amaz'd:** utterly confounded.   375. **God buy you:** God be with you, i.e. goodbye.   376. **vice:** flaw, failing.   379. **profit:** valuable lesson.   380. **sith:** since. **offense:** injury (to the one who loves).   381. **Thou shouldst be:** i.e. all indications point to the fact that you are.   382. **should be:** ought to be.

IAGO: I see, [sir], you are eaten up with passion;
I do repent me that I put it to you.
You would be satisfied?
    OTHELLO: Would? nay, and I will.
    IAGO: And may; but how? How satisfied, my lord?
Would you, the [supervisor], grossly gape on?   395
Behold her topp'd?
    OTHELLO: Death and damnation! O!
    IAGO: It were a tedious difficulty, I think,
To bring them to that prospect; damn them then,
If ever mortal eyes do see them bolster
More than their own. What then? How then?   400
What shall I say? Where's satisfaction?
It is impossible you should see this,
Were they as prime as goats, as hot as monkeys,
As salt a wolves in pride, and fools as gross
As ignorance made drunk. But yet, I say,   405
If imputation and strong circumstances
Which lead directly to the door of truth
Will give you satisfaction, you might have't.
    OTHELLO: Give me a living reason she's disloyal.
    IAGO: I do not like the office;   410
But sith I am ent'red in this cause so far
(Prick'd to't by foolish honesty and love),
I will go on. I lay with Cassio lately,
And being troubled with a raging tooth,
I could not sleep.   415
There are a kind of men, so loose of soul,
That in their sleeps will mutter their affairs;
One of this kind is Cassio.
In sleep I heard him say, "Sweet Desdemona,
Let us be wary, let us hide our loves";   420
And then, sir, would he gripe and wring my hand;
Cry, "O sweet creature!" then kiss me hard,
As if he pluck'd up kisses by the roots
That grew upon my lips; [then] laid his leg   424
[Over] my thigh, and [sigh'd], and [kiss'd], and then
[Cried], "Cursed fate that gave thee to the Moor!"
    OTHELLO: O monstrous! monstrous!
    IAGO: Nay, this was but his dream.

---

395. **supervisor:** onlooker, spectator.   398–99. **damn . . . ever:** i.e. to condemn them only if.   399. **bolster:** go to bed together.   400. **More:** other (eyes).   402. **see:** i.e. contrive to be an actual witness of.
403. **prime:** lustful.   404. **salt:** lecherous. **pride:** heat.   421. **gripe:** grip, clasp.

OTHELLO: But this denoted a foregone conclusion.
[IAGO:] 'Tis a shrewd doubt, though it be but a dream,
And this may help to thicken other proofs   430
That do demonstrate thinly.
    OTHELLO: I'll tear her all to pieces.
    IAGO: Nay, yet be wise; yet we see nothing done;
She may be honest yet. Tell me but this,
Have you not sometimes seen a handkerchief
Spotted with strawberries in your wive's hand?   435
    OTHELLO: I gave her such a one; 'twas my first gift.
    IAGO: I know not that; but such a handkerchief
(I am sure it was your wive's) did I to-day
See Cassio wipe his beard with.
    OTHELLO: If it be that—
    IAGO: If it be that, or any [that] was hers,   440
It speaks against her with the other proofs.
    OTHELLO: O that the slave had forty thousand lives!
One is too poor, too weak for my revenge.
Now do I see 'tis true. Look here, Iago,
All my fond love thus do I blow to heaven.   445
'Tis gone.
Arise, black vengeance, from the hollow hell!
Yield up, O love, thy crown and hearted throne
To tyrannous hate! Swell, bosom, with thy fraught,
For 'tis of aspics' tongues!
    IAGO: Yet be content.   450
    OTHELLO: O blood, blood, blood!
    IAGO: Patience, I say; your mind [perhaps] may change.
    OTHELLO: Never, Iago. Like to the Pontic Sea,
Whose icy current and compulsive course
Nev'r [feels] retiring ebb, but keeps due on   455
To the Propontic and the Hellespont,
Even so my bloody thoughts, with violent pace,
Shall nev'r look back, nev'r ebb to humble love,
Till that a capable and wide revenge   459
Swallow them up. [*He kneels.*] Now by yond marble heaven,
In the due reverence of a sacred vow
I here engage my words.
    IAGO: Do not rise yet. [IAGO *kneels.*]

---

428. **foregone conclusion:** act already performed.   429. **shrewd doubt:** strong reason for suspicion.
430. **thicken:** substantiate.   435. **wive's:** wife's.   442. **the slave:** i.e. Cassio.   448. **hearted:** established
in my heart.   449. **fraught:** burden.   450. **aspics':** asps'.   453. **Pontic Sea:** Black Sea.   459. **capable:**
capacious, comprehensive.   460. **marble:** shining (?) or enduring, changeless (cf. *marble-constant,* in
Antony and Cleopatra, V.ii.240) (?).

Witness, you ever-burning lights above,
You elements that clip us round about,
Witness that here Iago doth give up   465
The execution of his wit, hands, heart,
To wrong'd Othello's service! Let him command,
And to obey shall be in me remorse,
What bloody business ever. [*They rise.*]
    OTHELLO: I greet thy love,
Not with vain thanks, but with acceptance bounteous,
And will upon the instant put thee to't: 471
Within these three days let me hear thee say
That Cassio's not alive.
    IAGO: My friend is dead; 'tis done at your request.
But let her live.
    OTHELLO: Damn her, lewd minx! O, damn her, damn her!   476
Come go with me apart, I will withdraw
To furnish me with some swift means of death
For the fair devil. Now art thou my lieutenant.
    IAGO: I am your own for ever. *Exeunt.*

SCENE IV
Enter DESDEMONA, EMILIA, *and* CLOWN.
    DESDEMONA: Do you know, sirrah, where Lieutenant
Cassio lies?
    CLOWN: I dare not say he lies any where.
    DESDEMONA: Why, man?
    CLOWN: He's a soldier, and for me to say a soldier lies,
'tis stabbing.   6
    DESDEMONA: Go to! where lodges he?
    CLOWN: To tell you where he lodges, is to tell you
where I lie.
    DESDEMONA: Can any thing be made of this?   10
    CLOWN: I know not where he lodges, and for me to de-
vise a lodging and say he lies here, or he lies there,
were to lie in mine own throat.
    DESDEMONA: Can you inquire him out, and be edified by
report?   15
    CLOWN: I will catechize the world for him, that is,
make questions, and by them answer.

---

464. **clip:** embrace.   466. **execution:** action.   468–69. **to . . . ever:** i.e. in Othello's service even the cruellest acts will be as allowable as if they were gentle and prompted by pity (*remorse*).   476. **minx:** wanton.   III.iv. Location: Before the citadel.   1. **sirrah:** term of address to inferiors.   2. **lies:** lodges. 13. **lie . . . throat:** tell a gross and deliberate lie.

DESDEMONA: Seek him, bid him come hither. Tell him I
have mov'd my lord on his behalf, and hope all will be
well.   20
    CLOWN: To do this is within the compass of man's wit,
and therefore I will attempt the doing it. *Exit* CLOWN.
    DESDEMONA: Where should I lose the handkerchief, Emilia?
    EMILIA: I know not, madam.
    DESDEMONA: Believe me, I had rather have lost my purse   25
Full of crusadoes; and but my noble Moor
Is true of mind, and made of no such baseness
As jealous creatures are, it were enough
To put him to ill thinking.
    EMILIA: Is he not jealous?
    DESDEMONA: Who, he? I think the sun where he was born
Drew all such humors from him.
    EMILIA: Look where he comes.   31
Enter OTHELLO.
    DESDEMONA: I will not leave him now till Cassio
Be call'd to him.—How is't with you, my lord?
    OTHELLO: Well, my good lady. [*Aside.*] O, hardness to dissemble!—   .
How do you, Desdemona?
    DESDEMONA: Well, my good lord.   35
    OTHELLO: Give me your hand. This hand is moist, my lady.
    DESDEMONA: It [yet] hath felt no age nor known no sorrow.
    OTHELLO: This argues fruitfulness and liberal heart;
Hot, hot, and moist. This hand of yours requires
A sequester from liberty: fasting and prayer,   40
Much castigation, exercise devout,
For here's a young and sweating devil here
That commonly rebels. 'Tis a good hand,
A frank one.
    DESDEMONA: You may, indeed, say so;
For 'twas that hand that gave away my heart.   45
    OTHELLO: A liberal hand. The hearts of old gave hands;
But our new heraldry is hands, not hearts.
    DESDEMONA: I cannot speak of this. Come now, your promise.
    OTHELLO: What promise, chuck?
    DESDEMONA: I have sent to bid Cassio come speak with you.

---

19. **mov'd:** urged, made suit to.   23. **should I lose:** could I have lost.   26. **crusadoes:** Portuguese
coins stamped with a cross.   31. **humors:** bodily fluids (which were thought to determine temperament).   40. **sequester:** sequestration, separation.   41. **castigation:** corrective discipline, penance.
44. **frank:** Desdemona takes this as meaning "generous," but Othello may have in mind also the meanings "lusty, vigorous" and "open, unable to conceal secrets." So *liberal* in line 46 means both "generous"
and "licentious."   47. **our . . . hearts:** under our newfangled heraldry, hands (given in marriage) no
longer signify that hearts are given also.   49. **chuck:** a term of endearment, related to *chick.*

OTHELLO: I have a salt and sorry rheum offends me;   51
Lend me thy handkerchief.
    DESDEMONA: Here, my lord.
    OTHELLO: That which I gave you.
    DESDEMONA: I have it not about me.
    OTHELLO: Not?
    DESDEMONA: No, [faith], my lord.
    OTHELLO: That's a fault. That handkerchief   55
Did an Egyptian to my mother give;
She was a charmer, and could almost read
The thoughts of people. She told her, while she kept it,
'Twould make her amiable, and subdue my father
Entirely to her love; but if she lost it,   60
Or made a gift of it, my father's eye
Should hold her loathed, and his spirits should hunt
After new fancies. She, dying, gave it me,
And bid me, when my fate would have me wiv'd,
To give it her. I did so; and take heed on't,   65
Make it a darling like your precious eye.
To lose't or give't away were such perdition
As nothing else could match.
    DESDEMONA: Is't possible?
    OTHELLO: 'Tis true; there's a magic in the web of it.
A sibyl, that had numb'red in the world   70
The sun to course two hundred compasses,
In her prophetic fury sew'd the work;
The worms were hallowed that did breed the silk,
And it was dy'd in mummy which the skillful
Conserv'd of maidens' hearts.
    DESDEMONA: [I' faith]! is't true?   75
    OTHELLO: Most veritable, therefore look to't well.
    DESDEMONA: Then would to [God] that I had never seen't!
    OTHELLO: Ha? wherefore?
    DESDEMONA: Why do you speak so startingly and rash?
    OTHELLO: Is't lost? Is't gone? Speak, is't out o' th' way?   80
    DESDEMONA: [Heaven] bless us!
    OTHELLO: Say you?
    DESDEMONA: It is not lost; but what and if it were?
    OTHELLO: How?
    DESDEMONA: I say, it is not lost.

---

51. **salt . . . rheum:** distressing watering of the eyes.   57. **charmer:** magician.   59. **amiable:** desirable.
65. **her:** i.e. to my wife.   67. **perdition:** loss.   69. **web:** fabric.   70. **sibyl:** prophetess.   72. **prophetic fury:** the divine frenzy which enabled her to prophesy.   74. **mummy:** fluid drawn from embalmed bodies.   75. **Conserv'd:** prepared.   79. **startingly and rash:** disjointedly and impetuously.   83. **and if:** if.

OTHELLO: Fetch't, let me see't.   85
DESDEMONA: Why, so I can, [sir,] but I will not now.
This is a trick to put me from my suit.
Pray you let Cassio be receiv'd again.
    OTHELLO: Fetch me the handkerchief, my mind misgives.
    DESDEMONA: Come, come;   90
You'll never meet a more sufficient man.
    OTHELLO: The handkerchief!
    [DESDEMONA: I pray talk me of Cassio.
    OTHELLO: The handkerchief!]
DESDEMONA: A man that all his time
Hath founded his good fortunes on your love,
Shar'd dangers with you—   95
    OTHELLO: The handkerchief!
    DESDEMONA: [I' faith], you are to blame.
    OTHELLO: ['Zounds!] *Exit* OTHELLO.
    EMILIA: Is not this man jealous?
    DESDEMONA: I nev'r saw this before.   100
Sure, there's some wonder in this handkerchief;
I am most unhappy in the loss of it.
    EMILIA: 'Tis not a year or two shows us a man:
They are all but stomachs, and we all but food;
They eat us hungerly, and when they are full   105
They belch us.
    Enter IAGO *and* CASSIO.
                Look you, Cassio, and my husband!
    IAGO: There is no other way: 'tis she must do't;
And lo the happiness! Go, and importune her.
    DESDEMONA: How now, good Cassio, what's the news with you?
    CASSIO: Madam, my former suit. I do beseech you   110
That by your virtuous means I may again
Exist, and be a member of his love
Whom I, with all the office of my heart,
Entirely honor. I would not be delay'd.
If my offense be of such mortal kind   115
That nor my service past, nor present sorrows,
Nor purpos'd merit in futurity,
Can ransom me into his love again,
But to know so must be my benefit;
So shall I clothe me in a forc'd content,   120

---

91. **sufficient:** able, complete.   104. **but:** nothing but.   108. **happiness:** good luck.   111. **virtuous:** efficacious.   113. **office:** devoted service.   115. **mortal:** fatal.   117. **purpos'd ... futurity:** intention to serve well in the future.   119. **But:** merely.

And shut myself up in some other course,
To fortune's alms.
  DESDEMONA: Alas, thrice-gentle Cassio,
My advocation is not now in tune.
My lord is not my lord; nor should I know him
Were he in favor as in humor alter'd.   125
So help me every spirit sanctified,
As I have spoken for you all my best,
And stood within the blank of his displeasure
For my free speech! You must awhile be patient.
What I can do, I will; and more I will   130
Than for myself I dare. Let that suffice you.
  IAGO: Is my lord angry?
  EMILIA: He went hence but now;
And certainly in strange unquietness.
  IAGO: Can he be angry? I have seen the cannon
When it hath blown his ranks into the air,   135
And like the devil from his very arm
Puff'd his own brother—and is he angry?
Something of moment then. I will go meet him.
There's matter in't indeed, if he be angry.
  DESDEMONA: I prithee do so. *Exit* [IAGO].
     Something sure of state,
Either from Venice, or some unhatch'd practice   141
Made demonstrable here in Cyprus to him,
Hath puddled his clear spirit; and in such cases
Men's natures wrangle with inferior things,
Though great ones are their object. 'Tis even so;   145
For let our finger ache, and it endues
Our other healthful members even to a sense
Of pain. Nay, we must think men are not gods,
Nor of them look for such observancy
As fits the bridal. Beshrew me much, Emilia,   150
I was (unhandsome warrior as I am)
Arraigning his unkindness with my soul;
But now I find I had suborn'd the witness,
And he's indicted falsely.
  EMILIA: Pray heaven it be state matters, as you think,

---

122. **fortune's alms:** pittances handed out by Fortune to beggars. 125. **favor:** appearance. 128. **blank:** centre of a target, i.e. direct line of aim. 141. **unhatch'd practice:** plot not yet ready for execution. 143. **puddled:** muddied. 146. **endues:** makes conformable. 149. **observancy:** devoted attention. 150. **Beshrew me.** A very mild imprecation. 151. **unhandsome:** unskillful. 152. **with:** before the bar of. 153. **suborn'd the witness:** caused the witness to lie, i.e. misinterpreted Othello's behavior.

And no conception nor no jealous toy   156
Concerning you.
    DESDEMONA: Alas the day, I never gave him cause.
    EMILIA: But jealous souls will not be answer'd so;
They are not ever jealous for the cause,   160
But jealous for they're jealous. It is a monster
Begot upon itself, born on itself.
    DESDEMONA: Heaven keep the monster from Othello's mind!
    EMILIA: Lady, amen.
    DESDEMONA: I will go seek him. Cassio, walk hereabout;
If I do find him fit, I'll move your suit   166
And seek to effect it to my uttermost.
    CASSIO: I humbly thank your ladyship.
Exeunt [DESDEMONA *and* EMILIA].
Enter BIANCA.
    BIANCA: 'Save you, friend Cassio!
    CASSIO: What make you from home?
How is't with you, my most fair Bianca?   170
[I'faith], sweet love, I was coming to your house.
    BIANCA: And I was going to your lodging, Cassio.
What? keep a week away? seven days and nights?
Eightscore eight hours? and lovers' absent hours,
More tedious than the dial eightscore times?   175
O weary reck'ning!
    CASSIO: Pardon me, Bianca.
I have this while with leaden thoughts been press'd,
But I shall in a more continuate time
Strike off this score of absence. Sweet Bianca,
[*Giving her* DESDEMONA*'s handkerchief.*]
Take me this work out.
    BIANCA: O Cassio, whence came this?
This is some token from a newer friend;   181
To the felt absence now I feel a cause.
Is't come to this? Well, well.
    CASSIO: Go to, woman!
Throw your vild guesses in the devil's teeth,   184
From whence you have them. You are jealous now
That this is from some mistress, some remembrance;
No, [by my faith], Bianca.
    BIANCA: Why, whose is it?
    CASSIO: I know not, neither; I found it in my chamber.

---

156. **toy:** fancy.   162. **Begot . . . itself:** i.e. spontaneously generated, without cause.   169. **'Save you:** God save you.   178. **continuate:** uninterrupted.   179. **Strike . . . score:** settle this account.

I like the work well; ere it be demanded
(As like enough it will) I would have it copied.   190
Take it, and do't, and leave me for this time.
    BIANCA: Leave you? Wherefore?
    CASSIO: I do attend here on the general,
And think it no addition, nor my wish,   194
To have him see me woman'd.
    BIANCA: Why, I pray you?
    CASSIO: Not that I love you not.
    BIANCA: But that you do not love me.
I pray you bring me on the way a little,
And say if I shall see you soon at night.
    CASSIO: 'Tis but a little way that I can bring you,
For I attend here; but I'll see you soon.   200
    BIANCA: 'Tis very good; I must be circumstanc'd.
Exeunt omnes.

ACT IV, SCENE I
Enter OTHELLO *and* IAGO.
    IAGO: Will you think so?
    OTHELLO: Think so, Iago?
    IAGO: What,
To kiss in private?
    OTHELLO: An unauthoriz'd kiss!
    IAGO: Or to be naked with her friend in bed
An hour, or more, not meaning any harm?
    OTHELLO: Naked in bed, Iago, and not mean harm?   5
It is hypocrisy against the devil.
They that mean virtuously, and yet do so,
The devil their virtue tempts, and they tempt heaven.
    IAGO: If they do nothing, 'tis a venial slip;
But if I give my wife a handkerchief—   10
    OTHELLO: What then?
    IAGO: Why then 'tis hers, my lord, and being hers,
She may, I think, bestow't on any man.
    OTHELLO: She is protectress of her honor too;
May she give that?   15
    IAGO: Her honor is an essence that's not seen;
They have it very oft that have it not.
But for the handkerchief—

---

189. **demanded:** inquired for.   194. **addition:** credit.   201. **be circumstanc'd:** yield to circumstances, accept your conditions.   IV.i. Location: Before the citadel.   17. **They . . . oft:** i.e. often individuals are credited with it.

OTHELLO: By heaven, I would most gladly have forgot it.
Thou saidst (O, it comes o'er my memory,   20
As doth the raven o'er the infectious house,
Boding to all) he had my handkerchief.
     IAGO: Ay; what of that?
     OTHELLO: That's not so good now.
     IAGO: What
If I had said I had seen him do you wrong?
Or heard him say—as knaves be such abroad,   25
Who having by their own importunate suit,
Or voluntary dotage of some mistress,
Convinced or supplied them, cannot choose
But they must blab—
     OTHELLO: Hath he said any thing?   29
     IAGO: He hath, my lord, but be you well assur'd,
No more than he'll unswear.
     OTHELLO: What hath he said?
     IAGO: [Faith], that he did—I know not what he did.
     OTHELLO: What? what?   33
     IAGO: Lie—
     OTHELLO: With her?
     IAGO: With her? On her; what you will.
     OTHELLO: Lie with her? lie on her? We say lie on her,
when they belie her. Lie with her! ['Zounds,] that's
fulsome!   Handkerchief — confessions — handkerchief!
To confess, and be hang'd for his labor—first to be
hang'd, and then to confess. I tremble at it. Nature
would not invest herself in such shadowing passion   40
without some instruction. It is not words that shakes
me thus. Pish! Noses, ears, and lips. Is't possible?
Confess? Handkerchief? O devil! *Falls in a trance.*
     IAGO: Work on,
My medicine, [work]! Thus credulous fools are caught,   45
And many worthy and chaste dames even thus
(All guiltless) meet reproach.—What ho! my lord!
My lord, I say! Othello!
Enter CASSIO.
        How now, Cassio?
     CASSIO: What's the matter?
     IAGO: My lord is fall'n into an epilepsy.   50

---

28. **Convinced or supplied:** conquered or satisfied.   40. **shadowing:** coming over one like a shadow, i.e. overwhelming suddenly (?) or filling the imagination with shapes and figures (?). **passion:** paroxysm of emotion.   41. **instruction:** prompting, cause.

This is his second fit; he had one yesterday.
    CASSIO: Rub him about the temples.
    IAGO: [No, forbear,]
The lethargy must have his quiet course;
If not, he foams at mouth, and by and by
Breaks out to savage madness. Look, he stirs.   55
Do you withdraw yourself a little while,
He will recover straight. When he is gone,
I would on great occasions speak with you.
[*Exit* CASSIO.]
How is it, general? Have you not hurt your head?
    OTHELLO: Dost thou mock me?
    IAGO: I mock you not, by heaven.   60
Would you would bear your fortune like a man!
    OTHELLO: A horned man's a monster and a beast.
    IAGO: There's many a beast then in a populous city,
And many a civil monster.
    OTHELLO: Did he confess it?
    IAGO: Good sir, be a man;   65
Think every bearded fellow that's but yok'd
May draw with you. There's millions now alive
That nightly lie in those unproper beds
Which they dare swear peculiar; your case is better.
O, 'tis the spite of hell, the fiend's arch-mock,   70
To lip a wanton in a secure couch,
And to suppose her chaste! No, let me know,
And knowing what I am, I know what she shall be.
    OTHELLO: O, thou art wise; 'tis certain.
    IAGO: Stand you a while apart,
Confine yourself but in a patient list.   75
Whilst you were here o'erwhelmed with your grief
(A passion most [unsuiting] such a man),
Cassio came hither. I shifted him away,
And laid good 'scuses upon your ecstasy;
Bade him anon return and here speak with me,   80
The which he promis'd. Do but encave yourself,
And mark the fleers, the gibes, and notable scorns
That dwell in every region of his face,
For I will make him tell the tale anew:
Where, how, how oft, how long ago, and when   85

---

53. **lethargy:** coma. **his:** its.   59. **hurt your head.** Othello takes this as alluding to the cuckold's horns.
64. **civil:** i.e. among the citizenry, city-dwelling.   66. **yok'd:** married.   67. **draw:** pull (like oxen under the yoke).   68. **unproper:** not their own.   69. **peculiar:** their own.   71. **secure:** free from suspicion.
75. **in . . . list:** within the bounds of patience.   79. **ecstasy:** trance.   82. **fleers:** sneers. **notable:** obvious.

He hath, and is again to cope your wife.
I say, but mark his gesture. Marry, patience,
Or I shall say y' are all in all in spleen,
And nothing of a man.
    OTHELLO: Dost thou hear, Iago,
I will be found most cunning in my patience;   90
But (dost thou hear) most bloody.
    IAGO: That's not amiss,
But yet keep time in all. Will you withdraw?
[OTHELLO *withdraws.*]
Now will I question Cassio of Bianca,
A huswife that by selling her desires
Buys herself bread and [clothes]. It is a creature   95
That dotes on Cassio (as 'tis the strumpet's plague
To beguile many and be beguil'd by one);
He, when he hears of her, cannot restrain
From the excess of laughter. Here he comes.
Enter CASSIO.
As he shall smile, Othello shall go mad;   100
And his unbookish jealousy must [conster]
Poor Cassio's smiles, gestures, and light behaviors
Quite in the wrong. How do you [now], lieutenant?
    CASSIO: The worser that you give me the addition
Whose want even kills me.   105
    IAGO: Ply Desdemona well, and you are sure on't.
[*Speaking lower.*] Now, if this suit lay in Bianca's [pow'r],
How quickly should you speed!
    CASSIO: Alas, poor caitiff!
    OTHELLO: Look how he laughs already!
    IAGO: I never knew woman love man so.   110
    CASSIO: Alas, poor rogue, I think [i' faith], she loves me.
    OTHELLO: Now he denies it faintly, and laughs it out.
    IAGO: Do you hear, Cassio?
    OTHELLO: Now he importunes him
To tell it o'er. Go to, well said, well said.
    IAGO: She gives it out that you shall marry her.
Do you intend it?   116
    CASSIO: Ha, ha, ha!
    OTHELLO: Do [you] triumph, Roman? do you triumph?

---

86. **cope:** encounter with.   88. **spleen.** Considered the seat of sudden and capricious impulses.   94. **huswife:** hussy.   101. **unbookish:** uninstructed, unpracticed. **conster:** construe, interpret. The figure is of a person trying to translate a language he is ignorant of.   104. **addition:** title.   108. **caitiff:** wretch. 112. **faintly:** not very earnestly.   118. **Roman:** exultant fellow (suggested by *triumph*).

CASSIO: I marry [her]! What? a customer! Prithee bear some charity to my wit, do not think it so un- wholesome. Ha, ha, ha!   121

OTHELLO: So, so, so, so; they laugh that wins.

IAGO: [Faith], the cry goes that you marry her.

CASSIO: Prithee say true.

IAGO: I am a very villain else.   125

OTHELLO: Have you scor'd me? Well.

CASSIO: This is the monkey's own giving out. She is persuaded I will marry her, out of her own love and flattery, not out of my promise.

OTHELLO: Iago [beckons] me; now he begins the story.   131

CASSIO: She was here even now; she haunts me in every place. I was the other day talking on the sea- bank with certain Venetians, and thither comes the bauble, and [by this hand,] falls me thus about my neck—   136

OTHELLO: Crying, "O dear Cassio!" as it were; his gesture imports it.

CASSIO: So hangs, and lolls, and weeps upon me; so [hales] and pulls me. Ha, ha, ha!   140

OTHELLO: Now he tells how she pluck'd him to my chamber. O, I see that nose of yours, but not that dog I shall throw it to.

CASSIO: Well, I must leave her company.

IAGO: Before me! look where she comes.   145

Enter BIANCA.

CASSIO: 'Tis such another fitchew! marry, a perfum'd one!—What do you mean by this haunting of me?

BIANCA: Let the devil and his dam haunt you! What did you mean by that same handkerchief you gave me even now? I was a fine fool to take it. I must take   150 out the work? A likely piece of work, that you should find it in your chamber, and know not who left it there! This is some minx's token, and I must take out the work? There, give it your hobby-horse. Where- soever you had it, I'll take out no work on't.   155

CASSIO: How now, my sweet Bianca? how now? how now?

---

119. **customer:** prostitute.   120–21. **unwholesome:** unsound.   126. **scor'd:** scored off, beaten.   128– 29. **own . . . flattery:** self-love and self-satisfaction.   130. **beckons:** signals.   135. **bauble:** plaything. 146. **fitchew:** polecat (thought to be very lecherous as well as strong-smelling).   154. **hobby-horse:** woman of easy virtue.

OTHELLO: By heaven, that should be my handkerchief!

BIANCA: [An'] you'll come to supper to-night, you may; [an'] you will not, come when you are next pre-par'd for. *Exit.*   161

IAGO: After her, after her.

CASSIO: [Faith,] I must, she'll rail in the streets else.

IAGO: Will you sup there?

CASSIO: [Faith], I intend so.   165

IAGO: Well, I may chance to see you; for I would very fain speak with you.

CASSIO: Prithee come; will you?

IAGO: Go to; say no more. [*Exit* CASSIO.]

OTHELLO: [*Advancing.*] How shall I murther him, Iago?

IAGO: Did you perceive how he laugh'd at his vice?

OTHELLO: O Iago!   172

IAGO: And did you see the handkerchief?

OTHELLO: Was that mine?

IAGO: Yours, by this hand. And to see how he prizes the foolish woman your wife! She gave it him, and he hath giv'n it his whore.   177

OTHELLO: I would have him nine years a-killing. A fine woman! a fair woman! a sweet woman!

IAGO: Nay, you must forget that.   180

OTHELLO: Ay, let her rot, and perish, and be damn'd to-night, for she shall not live. No, my heart is turn'd to stone; I strike it, and it hurts my hand. O, the world hath not a sweeter creature! she might lie by an emperor's side and command him tasks.   185

IAGO: Nay, that's not your way.

OTHELLO: Hang her, I do but say what she is. So deli-cate with her needle! an admirable musician! O, she will sing the savageness out of a bear. Of so high and plenteous wit and invention!   190

IAGO: She's the worse for all this.

OTHELLO: O, a thousand, a thousand times. And then of so gentle a condition!

IAGO: Ay, too gentle.   194

OTHELLO: Nay, that's certain. But yet the pity of it, Iago! O Iago, the pity of it, Iago!

IAGO: If you are so fond over her iniquity, give her patent to offend, for if it touch not you, it comes near nobody.

---

159. **An':** and, i.e. if.   186. **your way:** your proper course, the direction your mind should take.   193. **of ... condition:** so nobly born and bred.   194. **gentle:** i.e. generous with her favors.   197. **fond:** dotingly foolish.   198. **patent:** license.

OTHELLO: I will chop her into messes. Cuckold me!

IAGO: O, 'tis foul in her.   201

OTHELLO: With mine officer!

IAGO: That's fouler.

OTHELLO: Get me some poison, Iago, this night. I'll not
expostulate with her, lest her body and beauty   205
unprovide my mind again. This night, Iago.

IAGO: Do it not with poison; strangle her in her bed,
even the bed she hath contaminated.

OTHELLO: Good, good; the justice of it pleases; very
good.   210

IAGO: And for Cassio, let me be his undertaker.
You shall hear more by midnight.

OTHELLO: Excellent good. [*A trumpet.*] What trumpet is that same?

IAGO: I warrant, something from Venice.

Enter LODOVICO, DESDEMONA, *and* ATTENDANTS.

       'Tis Lodovico—   214
This comes from the Duke. See, your wife's with him.

LODOVICO: [God] save you, worthy general!

OTHELLO: With all my heart, sir.

LODOVICO: The Duke and the senators of Venice greet you. [*Gives him a letter.*]

OTHELLO: I kiss the instrument of their pleasures.

[*Opens the letter and reads.*]

DESDEMONA: And what's the news, good cousin Lodovico?

IAGO: I am very glad to see you, signior;   220
Welcome to Cyprus.

LODOVICO: I thank you. How does Lieutenant Cassio?

IAGO: Lives, sir.

DESDEMONA: Cousin, there's fall'n between him and my lord
An unkind breach; but you shall make all well.   225

OTHELLO: Are you sure of that?

DESDEMONA: My lord?

OTHELLO: [*Reads.*] "This fail you not to do, as you will—"

LODOVICO: He did not call; he's busy in the paper.   230
Is there division 'twixt my lord and Cassio?

DESDEMONA: A most unhappy one. I would do much
T' atone them, for the love I bear to Cassio.

OTHELLO: Fire and brimstone!

DESDEMONA: My lord?

OTHELLO: Are you wise?   234

DESDEMONA: What, is he angry?

LODOVICO: May be th' letter mov'd him;

---

200. **messes:** portions of food, i.e. little pieces.   205. **body and beauty:** physical beauty.   211. **be his undertaker:** undertake to dispatch him.   216. **With . . . heart:** i.e. I heartily thank you.   233. **atone:** reconcile.

For as I think, they do command him home,
Deputing Cassio in his government.
    DESDEMONA: [By my troth], I am glad on't.
    OTHELLO: Indeed?
    DESDEMONA: My lord?
    OTHELLO: I am glad to see you mad.
    DESDEMONA: Why, sweet Othello?
    OTHELLO: [*Striking her.*] Devil!   240
    DESDEMONA: I have not deserv'd this.
    LODOVICO: My lord, this would not be believ'd in Venice,
Though I should swear I saw't. 'Tis very much,
Make her amends; she weeps.
    OTHELLO: O devil, devil!
If that the earth could teem with woman's tears,   245
Each drop she falls would provide a crocodile.
Out of my sight!
    DESDEMONA: I will not stay to offend you. [*Going.*]
    LODOVICO: Truly, [an] obedient lady:
I do beseech your lordship call her back.   249
    OTHELLO: Mistress!
    DESDEMONA: My lord?
    OTHELLO: What would you with her, sir?
    LODOVICO: Who, I, my lord?
    OTHELLO: Ay, you did wish that I would make her turn.
Sir, she can turn, and turn; and yet go on
And turn again; and she can weep, sir, weep;
And she's obedient, as you say, obedient;   255
Very obedient.—Proceed you in your tears.—
Concerning this, sir—O well-painted passion!—
I am commanded home.—Get you away;
I'll send for you anon.—Sir, I obey the mandate,
And will return to Venice.—Hence, avaunt!   260
    [*Exit* DESDEMONA.]
Cassio shall have my place. And, sir, to-night
I do entreat that we may sup together.
You are welcome, sir, to Cyprus.—Goats and monkeys! *Exit.*
    LODOVICO: Is this the noble Moor whom our full Senate
Call all in all sufficient? Is this the nature   265
Whom passion could not shake? whose solid virtue
The shot of accident nor dart of chance
    Could neither graze nor pierce?
    IAGO: He is much chang'd.
    LODOVICO: Are his wits safe? Is he not light of brain?

---

245. **teem with:** be made pregnant by. 246. **falls:** lets fall. 260. **avaunt:** begone. 263. **Goats and monkeys.** Cf. III.iii.403. 269. **safe:** sound.

IAGO: He's that he is; I may not breathe my censure
What he might be. If what he might he is not,   271
I would to heaven he were!
    LODOVICO: What? strike his wife?
    IAGO: Faith, that was not so well; yet would I knew
That stroke would prove the worst!
    LODOVICO: Is it his use?
Or did the letters work upon his blood,   275
And new-create [this] fault?
    IAGO: Alas, alas!
It is not honesty in me to speak
What I have seen and known. You shall observe him,
And his own courses will denote him so
That I may save my speech. Do but go after,   280
And mark how he continues.
    LODOVICO: I am sorry that I am deceiv'd in him.
Exeunt.

SCENE *II*
Enter OTHELLO *and* EMILIA.
    OTHELLO: You have seen nothing then?
    EMILIA: Nor ever heard—nor ever did suspect.
    OTHELLO: Yes, you have seen Cassio and she together.
    EMILIA: But then I saw no harm, and then I heard
Each syllable that breath made up between them.   5
    OTHELLO: What? did they never whisper?
    EMILIA: Never, my lord.
    OTHELLO: Nor send you out o' th' way?
    EMILIA: Never.
    OTHELLO: To fetch her fan, her gloves, her mask, nor nothing?
    EMILIA: Never, my lord.   10
    OTHELLO: That's strange.
    EMILIA: I durst, my lord, to wager she is honest;
Lay down my soul at stake. If you think other,
Remove your thought; it doth abuse your bosom.
If any wretch have put this in your head,   15
Let heaven requite it with the serpent's curse!
For if she be not honest, chaste, and true,
There's no man happy; the purest of their wives
Is foul as slander.

270–71. **censure . . . be:** i.e. opinion as to whether he is insane.   272. **I . . . were:** i.e. because otherwise his behavior is unpardonable.   274. **use:** habit.   275. **blood:** passions.   IV.ii. Location: The citadel. 16. **the serpent's curse:** the curse laid by God on the serpent that tempted Eve. Emilia implies that the crime of a slanderer of Desdemona, who is as innocent as Eve was before the fall, would be of the same magnitude.

OTHELLO: Bid her come hither; go. *Exit* Emilia.
She says enough; yet she's a simple bawd   20
That cannot say as much. This is a subtile whore,
A closet lock and key of villainous secrets;
And yet she'll kneel and pray; I have seen her do't.
Enter DESDEMONA *and* EMILIA.
    DESDEMONA: My lord, what is your will?
    OTHELLO: Pray you, chuck, come hither.
    DESDEMONA: What is your pleasure?
    OTHELLO: Let me see your eyes;
Look in my face.
    DESDEMONA: What horrible fancy's this?   26
    OTHELLO: [*To* EMILIA.] Some of your function, mistress;
Leave procreants alone, and shut the door;
Cough, or cry "hem," if anybody come.
Your mystery, your mystery; [nay], dispatch.   30
Exit EMILIA.
    DESDEMONA: Upon my knee, what doth your speech import?
I understand a fury in your words,
[But not the words].
    OTHELLO: Why? what art thou?
    DESDEMONA: Your wife, my lord; your true
And loyal wife.
    OTHELLO: Come swear it, damn thyself,   35
Lest being like one of heaven, the devils themselves
Should fear to seize thee; therefore be double damn'd:
Swear thou art honest.
    DESDEMONA: Heaven doth truly know it.
    OTHELLO: Heaven truly knows that thou art false as hell
    DESDEMONA: To whom, my lord? With whom? How am I false?   40
    OTHELLO: Ah, Desdemon! Away, away, away!
    DESDEMONA: Alas the heavy day! Why do you weep?
Am I the motive of these tears, my lord?
If happily you my father do suspect
An instrument of this your calling back,   45
Lay not your blame on me. If you have lost him,
[Why,] I have lost him too.
    OTHELLO: Had it pleas'd heaven
To try me with affliction, had they rain'd
All kind of sores and shames on my bare head,
Steep'd me in poverty to the very lips,   50

20–21. **she's ... much:** the bawd who cannot say as much is a stupid one.   22. **closet:** place where private papers could be locked up.   27. **Some ... function:** go about your bawd's business (of standing watch outside the door).   30. **mystery:** trade.   43. **motive:** moving force, cause.   48. **they:** i.e. the gods.

Given to captivity me and my utmost hopes,
I should have found in some place of my soul
A drop of patience; but, alas, to make me
The fixed figure for the time of scorn
To point his slow [unmoving] finger at!   55
Yet could I bear that too, well, very well;
But there, where I have garner'd up my heart,
Where either I must live or bear no life;
The fountain from the which my current runs
Or else dries up: to be discarded thence!   60
Or keep it as a cestern for foul toads
To knot and gender in! Turn thy complexion there,
Patience, thou young and rose-lipp'd cherubin—
Ay, here look grim as hell!
    DESDEMONA: I hope my noble lord esteems me honest.   65
    OTHELLO: O ay, as summer flies are in the shambles,
That quicken even with blowing. O thou weed!
Who art so lovely fair and smell'st so sweet
That the sense aches at thee, would thou hadst never been born!   69
    DESDEMONA: Alas, what ignorant sin have I committed?
    OTHELLO: Was this fair paper, this most goodly book,
Made to write "whore" upon? What committed?
Committed? O thou public commoner,
I should make very forges of my cheeks,
That would to cinders burn up modesty,   75
Did I but speak thy deeds. What committed?
Heaven stops the nose at it, and the moon winks;
The bawdy wind, that kisses all it meets,
Is hush'd within the hollow mine of earth
And will not hear't. What committed?   80
[Impudent strumpet!]
    DESDEMONA: By heaven, you do me wrong.
    OTHELLO: Are not you a strumpet?
    DESDEMONA: No, as I am a Christian.
If to preserve this vessel for my lord
From any other foul unlawful touch
Be not to be a strumpet, I am none.   85
    OTHELLO: What, not a whore?
    DESDEMONA: No, as I shall be sav'd.

---

54. **time of scorn:** scornful world.   55. **slow unmoving finger.** A troublesome phrase; perhaps the meaning is that the finger points steadily and is slow to alter its aim, or that it rises slowly to its aim and then remains fixed.   59. **fountain:** source, spring.   61. **cestern:** cistern.   62. **turn:** change. **there:** at that point, when that happens.   67. **quicken … blowing:** come to life as soon as the eggs are deposited.
73. **commoner:** prostitute.   77. **winks:** shuts her eyes.   81. **Impudent:** shameless.

OTHELLO: Is't possible?

DESDEMONA: O, heaven forgive us!

OTHELLO: I cry you mercy then.

I took you for that cunning whore of Venice

That married with Othello.—[*Raising his voice.*] You, mistress,   90

Enter EMILIA.

That have the office opposite to Saint Peter,

And keeps the gate of hell! You, you! ay, you!

We have done our course; there's money for your pains.

I pray you turn the key and keep our counsel. *Exit.*

EMILIA: Alas, what does this gentleman conceive?

How do you, madam? how do you, my good lady?   96

DESDEMONA: Faith, half asleep.

EMILIA: Good madam, what's the matter with my lord?

DESDEMONA: With who?

EMILIA: Why, with my lord, madam.   100

DESDEMONA: Who is thy lord?

EMILIA: He that is yours, sweet lady.

DESDEMONA: I have none. Do not talk to me, Emilia;

I cannot weep, nor answers have I none

But what should go by water. Prithee to-night

Lay on my bed my wedding-sheets—remember;   105

And call thy husband hither.

EMILIA: Here's a change indeed! *Exit.*

DESDEMONA: 'Tis meet I should be us'd so, very meet.

How have I been behav'd, that he might stick

The small'st opinion on my least misuse?

Enter IAGO *and* EMILIA.

IAGO: What is your pleasure, madam? How is't with you?   110

DESDEMONA: I cannot tell. Those that do teach young babes

Do it with gentle means and easy tasks.

He might have chid me so; for in good faith

I am a child to chiding.

IAGO: What is the matter, lady?

EMILIA: Alas, Iago, my lord hath so bewhor'd her,

Thrown such despite and heavy terms upon her,   116

That true hearts cannot bear it.

DESDEMONA: Am I that name, Iago?

IAGO: What name, fair lady?

DESDEMONA: Such as she said my lord did say I was.

EMILIA: He call'd her whore. A beggar in his drink

---

88. **cry you mercy:** beg your pardon.   104. **go by water:** be rendered by tears.   109. **opinion:** censure.
my least misuse: the slightest misconduct on my part.

Could not have laid such terms upon his callet.   121
    IAGO: Why did he so?
    DESDEMONA: I do not know; I am sure I am none such.
    IAGO: Do not weep, do not weep. Alas the day!
    EMILIA: Hath she forsook so many noble matches?
Her father? and her country? and her friends?   126
To be call'd whore? Would it not make one weep?
    DESDEMONA: It is my wretched fortune.
    IAGO: Beshrew him for't!
How comes this trick upon him?
    DESDEMONA: Nay, heaven doth know.
    EMILIA: I will be hang'd if some eternal villain,   130
Some busy and insinuating rogue,
Some cogging, cozening slave, to get some office,
Have not devis'd this slander. I will be hang'd else.
    IAGO: Fie, there is no such man; it is impossible.
    DESDEMONA: If any such there be, heaven pardon him!   135
    EMILIA: A halter pardon him! and hell gnaw his bones!
Why should he call her whore? Who keeps her company?
What place? what time? what form? what likelihood?
The Moor's abus'd by some most villainous knave,
Some base notorious knave, some scurvy fellow.   140
O [heaven], that such companions thou'dst unfold,
And put in every honest hand a whip
To lash the rascals naked through the world
Even from the east to th' west!
    IAGO: Speak within door.
    EMILIA: O fie upon them! Some such squire he was
That turn'd your wit the seamy side without,   146
And made you to suspect me with the Moor.
    IAGO: You are a fool; go to.
    DESDEMONA: Alas, Iago,
What shall I do to win my lord again?
Good friend, go to him; for by this light of heaven,
I know not how I lost him. Here I kneel: 151
If e'er my will did trespass 'gainst his love,
Either in discourse of thought or actual deed,
Or that mine eyes, mine ears, or any sense
Delighted them [in] any other form;   155
Or that I do not yet, and ever did,

---

121. **callet:** whore.   129. **trick:** odd behavior.   130. **eternal:** inveterate.   131. **insinuating:** worming his way into favor.   132. **cogging:** cheating. **cozening:** deceiving.   138. **form:** shape, i.e. specific circumstances.   141. **companions:** fellows. **unfold:** expose.   144. **within door:** i.e. less loudly.   146. **seamy side without:** wrong side out.   153. **discourse of thought:** process of thinking.

And ever will (though he do shake me off
To beggarly divorcement) love him dearly,
Comfort forswear me! Unkindness may do much,
And his unkindness may defeat my life,   160
But never taint my love. I cannot say "whore."
It does abhor me now I speak the word;
To do the act that might the addition earn,
Not the world's mass of vanity could make me.
    IAGO: I pray you be content; 'tis but his humor.
The business of the state does him offense,   166
[And he does chide with you].
    DESDEMONA: If 'twere no other—
    IAGO: It is but so, I warrant.
[*Trumpets within.*]
Hark how these instruments summon to supper!
The messengers of Venice stays the meat.   170
Go in, and weep not; all things shall be well.
Exeunt DESDEMONA *and* EMILIA.
Enter RODERIGO.
    How now, Roderigo?
    RODERIGO: I do not find that thou deal'st justly with me.
    IAGO: What in the contrary?   174
    RODERIGO: Every day thou daff'st me with some device,
Iago, and rather, as it seems to me now, keep'st from
me all conveniency than suppliest me with the least
advantage of hope. I will indeed no longer endure it;
nor am I yet persuaded to put up in peace what already
I have foolishly suff'red.   180
    IAGO: Will you hear me, Roderigo?
    RODERIGO: [Faith,] I have heard too much; [for] your
words and performances are no kin together.
    IAGO: You charge me most unjustly.   184
    RODERIGO: With nought but truth. I have wasted myself
out of my means. The jewels you have had from me to
deliver Desdemona would half have corrupted a votarist. You have told me she hath receiv'd them and
return'd me expectations and comforts of sudden
respect and acquaintance, but I find none.   190
    IAGO: Well, go to; very well.

---

160. **defeat:** destroy.   162. **abhor me:** fill me with abhorrence.   163. **addition:** designation.
165. **humor:** mood.   170. **stays the meat:** wait to dine.   175. **daff'st me:** puttest me off.   177. **conveniency:** i.e. opportunity to meet Desdemona.   179. **put up:** tolerate, stomach.   187–88. **votarist:**
nun.   189–90. **sudden respect:** immediate consideration.

RODERIGO: Very well! go to! I cannot go to, man, nor
'tis not very well. [By this hand,] I think it is scurvy,
and begin to find myself fopp'd in it.

IAGO: Very well.   195

RODERIGO: I tell you 'tis not very well. I will make myself known to Desdemona. If she will return me my
jewels, I will give over my suit and repent my unlawful
solicitation; if not, assure yourself I will seek satisfaction of you.   200

IAGO: You have said now.

RODERIGO: Ay; and said nothing but what I protest
intendment of doing.

IAGO: Why, now I see there's mettle in thee, and
even from this instant do build on thee a better   205
opinion than ever before. Give me thy hand, Roderigo.
Thou hast taken against me a most just exception; but
yet I protest I have dealt most directly in thy affair.

RODERIGO: It hath not appear'd.   209

IAGO: I grant indeed it hath not appear'd; and your
suspicion is not without wit and judgment. But,
Roderigo, if thou hast that in thee indeed, which I have
greater reason to believe now than ever (I mean purpose, courage, and valor), this night show it. If thou
the next night following enjoy not Desdemona, take
me from this world with treachery and devise engines
for my life.   217

RODERIGO: Well; what is it? Is it within reason and
compass?

IAGO: Sir, there is especial commission come from
Venice to depute Cassio in Othello's place.   221

RODERIGO: Is that true? Why then Othello and
Desdemona return again to Venice.

IAGO: O no; he goes into Mauritania and taketh
away with him the fair Desdemona, unless his   225
abode be ling'red here by some accident; wherein none
can be so determinate as the removing of Cassio.

RODERIGO: How do you mean, removing him?

IAGO: Why, by making him uncapable of Othello's
place: knocking out his brains.   230

RODERIGO: And that you would have me to do?

IAGO: Ay; if you dare do yourself a profit and a
right. He sups to-night with a harlotry, and thither

---

194. **fopp'd:** made a fool of, duped.   216–17. **engines for:** plots against.   227. **determinate:** effectual.
233. **harlotry:** slut.

will I go to him—he knows not yet of his honorable
fortune. If you will watch his going thence   235
(which I will fashion to fall out between twelve and
one), you may take him at your pleasure. I will be
near to second your attempt, and he shall fall between
us. Come, stand not amaz'd at it, but go along with
me; I will show you such a necessity in his death   240
that you shall think yourself bound to put it on him.
It is now high supper-time, and the night grows to
waste. About it.
    RODERIGO: I will hear further reason for this.
    IAGO: And you shall be satisfied. *Exeunt.*   245

SCENE III
Enter OTHELLO, LODOVICO, DESDEMONA, EMILIA, *and* ATTENDANTS.
    LODOVICO: I do beseech you, sir, trouble yourself no further.
    OTHELLO: O, pardon me; 'twill do me good to walk.
    LODOVICO: Madam, good night; I humbly thank your ladyship.
    DESDEMONA: Your honor is most welcome.
    OTHELLO: Will you walk, sir?
O, Desdemona!   5
    DESDEMONA: My lord?
    OTHELLO: Get you to bed on th' instant, I will be re-
turn'd forthwith. Dismiss your attendant there.
Look't be done.
    DESDEMONA: I will, my lord.   10
Exeunt [OTHELLO, LODOVICO, *and* ATTENDANTS].
    EMILIA: How goes it now? He looks gentler than he did.
    DESDEMONA: He says he will return incontinent,
And hath commanded me to go to bed,
And bid me to dismiss you.
    EMILIA: Dismiss me?   14
    DESDEMONA: It was his bidding; therefore, good Emilia,
Give me my nightly wearing, and adieu.
We must not now displease him.
    EMILIA: I would you had never seen him!   18
    DESDEMONA: So would not I. My love doth so approve him,
That even his stubbornness, his checks, his frowns—
Prithee unpin me—have grace and favor [in them].
    EMILIA: I have laid those sheets you bade me on the bed.
    DESDEMONA: All's one. Good [faith], how foolish are our minds!

242–43. **grows to waste:** is being wasted.   IV.iii. Location: The citadel.   12. **incontinent:** at once.
20. **stubbornness:** roughness.   21. **favor:** attractiveness.

If I do die before [thee], prithee shroud me   24
In one of these same sheets.
    EMILIA: Come, come; you talk.
    DESDEMONA: My mother had a maid call'd Barbary;
She was in love, and he she lov'd prov'd mad,
And did forsake her. She had a song of "Willow,"
An old thing 'twas, but it express'd her fortune,
And she died singing it. That song to-night   30
Will not go from my mind; I have much to do
But to go hang my head all at one side
And sing it like poor Barbary. Prithee dispatch.
    EMILIA: Shall I go fetch your night-gown?
    DESDEMONA: No, unpin me here.
This Lodovico is a proper man.   35
    EMILIA: A very handsome man.
    DESDEMONA: He speaks well.
    EMILIA: I know a lady in Venice would have walk'd
barefoot to Palestine for a touch of his nether lip.
    DESDEMONA: [*Singing.*]
"The poor soul sat [sighing] by a sycamore tree,   40
    Sing all a green willow;
Her hand on her bosom, her head on her knee,
    Sing willow, willow, willow.
The fresh streams ran by her, and murmur'd her moans,
    Sing willow, willow, willow;   45
Her salt tears fell from her, and soft'ned the stones,
    Sing willow"—
Lay by these—
[*Singing.*] "—willow, willow"—
Prithee hie thee; he'll come anon—   50
[*Singing.*]
"Sing all a green willow must be my garland.
Let nobody blame him, his scorn I approve"—
Nay, that's not next. Hark, who is't that knocks?
    EMILIA: It's the wind.
    DESDEMONA: [*Singing.*]
"I call'd my love false love; but what said he then?   55
Sing willow, willow, willow;
If I court moe women, you'll couch with moe men."—
So get thee gone, good night. Mine eyes do itch;
Doth that bode weeping?

---

25. **talk:** i.e. prattle idly.　27. **mad:** wild, i.e. untrue.　28. **Willow.** Symbolic of disappointed love.　31–
32. **I . . . to:** it's all I can do not to.　50. **hie thee:** make haste.

EMILIA: 'Tis neither here nor there.

DESDEMONA: I have heard it said so. O, these men, these men!   60
Dost thou in conscience think—tell me, Emilia—
That there be women do abuse their husbands
In such gross kind?

EMILIA: There be some such, no question.

DESDEMONA: Wouldst thou do such a deed for all the world?   64

EMILIA: Why, would not you?

DESDEMONA: No, by this heavenly light!

EMILIA: Nor I neither by this heavenly light;
I might do't as well i' th' dark.

DESDEMONA: Wouldst thou do such a deed for all the world?

EMILIA: The world's a huge thing; it is a great price
For a small vice.

DESDEMONA: [Good] troth, I think thou wouldst not.   70

EMILIA: [By my] troth, I think I should, and undo't
when I had done['t]. Marry, I would not do such a
thing for a joint-ring, nor for measures of lawn, nor for
gowns, petticoats, nor caps, nor any petty exhibition;
but, for all the whole world—['ud's pity], who   75
would not make her husband a cuckold to make him a
monarch? I should venture purgatory for't.

DESDEMONA: Beshrew me, if I would do such a wrong
For the whole world.   79

EMILIA: Why, the wrong is but a wrong i' th' world;
and having the world for your labor, 'tis a wrong in
your own world, and you might quickly make it right.

DESDEMONA I do not think there is any such woman.

EMILIA: Yes, a dozen; and as many to th' vantage as
would store the world they play'd for.   85
But I do think it is their husbands' faults
If wives do fall. Say that they slack their duties,
And pour our treasures into foreign laps;
Or else break out in peevish jealousies,
Throwing restraint upon us; or say they strike us,   90
Or scant our former having in despite:
Why, we have galls; and though we have some grace,
Yet have we some revenge. Let husbands know
Their wives have sense like them; they see, and smell,

---

61. **in conscience:** sincerely, truly.   69. **price:** prize.   73. **joint-ring:** cheap ring made in separable
halves. **lawn:** fine linen.   74. **exhibition:** gift.   75. **'ud's:** a corruption of *God's.*   84. **to th' vantage:** in
addition.   87. **duties:** marital duties.   88. **foreign laps:** i.e. the laps of other women.   89. **peevish:** silly,
childish.   91. **scant:** reduce. **having:** allowance. **despite:** spite.   92. **galls:** tempers, the capacity to resent
such treatment.   94. **sense:** bodily senses.

And have their palates both for sweet and sour,   95
As husbands have. What is it that they do
When they change us for others? Is it sport?
I think it is. And doth affection breed it?
I think it doth. Is't frailty that thus errs?
It is so too. And have not we affections,   100
Desires for sport, and frailty, as men have?
Then let them use us well; else let them know,
The ills we do, their ills instruct us so.
    DESDEMONA: Good night, good night. [God] me such uses send,   104
Not to pick bad from bad, but by bad mend. *Exeunt.*

ACT V, SCENE I
Enter IAGO *and* RODERIGO.
    IAGO: Here, stand behind this [bulk], straight will he come.
Wear thy good rapier bare, and put it home.
Quick, quick, fear nothing; I'll be at thy elbow.
It makes us, or it mars us, think on that,
And fix most firm thy resolution.   5
    RODERIGO: Be near at hand, I may miscarry in't.
    IAGO: Here, at thy hand; be bold, and take thy stand. [*Retires.*]
    RODERIGO: I have no great devotion to the deed,
And yet he hath given me satisfying reasons.
'Tis but a man gone. Forth my sword; he dies.   10
    IAGO: I have rubb'd this young quat almost to the sense,
And he grows angry. Now, whether he kill Cassio,
Or Cassio him, or each do kill the other,
Every way makes my gain. Live Roderigo,
He calls me to a restitution large   15
Of gold and jewels that I bobb'd from him
As gifts to Desdemona;
It must not be. If Cassio do remain,
He hath a daily beauty in his life
That makes me ugly; and besides, the Moor   20
May unfold me to him; there stand I in much peril.
No, he must die. [Be't] so. I [hear] him coming.
Enter CASSIO.
    RODERIGO: I know his gait, 'tis he.—Villain, thou diest!
[*Makes a pass at* CASSIO.]
    CASSIO: That thrust had been mine enemy indeed,

---

104. **me . . . send:** i.e. enable me to make it my practice.   105. **Not . . . mend:** not to use others' ill conduct as an excuse for behaving likewise, but rather to learn from it how to behave otherwise.   V.i. Location: A street near the citadel.   1. **bulk:** shop-stall protruding into the street.   11. **quat:** pimple, small
boil. **sense:** quick.   16. **obb'd:** swindled.

But that my coat is better than thou know'st.   25
I will make proof of thine.
[*Draws, and wounds* RODERIGO.]
   RODERIGO: O, I am slain.
[IAGO *from behind wounds* CASSIO *in the leg, and exit.*]
   CASSIO: I am maim'd for ever. Help ho! murther, murther! [*Falls.*]
Enter OTHELLO.
   OTHELLO: The voice of Cassio! Iago keeps his word
   RODERIGO: O, villain that I am!
   OTHELLO: It is even so.
   CASSIO: O, help ho! light! a surgeon!   30
   OTHELLO: 'Tis he!— O brave Iago, honest and just,
That hast such noble sense of thy friend's wrong!
Thou teachest me. Minion, your dear lies dead,
And your unblest fate hies. Strumpet, I come.
[Forth] of my heart those charms, thine eyes, are blotted;   35
Thy bed, lust-stain'd, shall with lust's blood be spotted.
Exit OTHELLO.
Enter LODOVICO *and* GRATIANO.
   CASSIO: What ho! no watch? no passage? Murther, murther!
   GRATIANO: 'Tis some mischance, the voice is very direful.
   CASSIO: O, help!
   LODOVICO: Hark!   40
   RODERIGO: O wretched villain!
   LODOVICO: Two or three groan. 'Tis heavy night;
These may be counterfeits; let's think't unsafe
To come in to the cry without more help.
   RODERIGO: Nobody come? Then shall I bleed to death.
Enter IAGO [*with a light*].
   LODOVICO: Hark!   46
   GRATIANO: Here's one comes in his shirt, with light and weapons.
   IAGO: Who's there? Whose noise is this that cries on murther?
   LODOVICO: We do not know.
   IAGO: [Did] not you hear a cry?
   CASSIO: Here, here! for heaven sake help me!
   IAGO: What's the matter?   50
   GRATIANO: This is Othello's ancient, as I take it.
   LODOVICO: The same indeed, a very valiant fellow.
   IAGO: What are you here that cry so grievously?
   CASSIO: Iago? O, I am spoil'd, undone by villains!
Give me some help.   55

---

25. **coat.** Possibly he wears a rapier-proof vest under his outer clothing.   31. **brave:** excellent, noble.
33. **Minion:** hussy.   34. **hies:** approaches rapidly.   37. **passage:** passers-by.   42. **heavy:** dark.   48. **cries
on:** cries out.   50. **heaven:** heaven's.   54. **spoil'd:** destroyed.

IAGO: O me, lieutenant! what villains have done this?

CASSIO: I think that one of them is hereabout,
And cannot make away.

IAGO: O treacherous villains!
[*To* LODOVICO *and* GRATIANO.]   What are you there?
Come in, and give some help.

RODERIGO: O, help me there!   60

CASSIO: That's one of them.

IAGO: O murd'rous slave! O villain!
[*Stabs* RODERIGO.]

RODERIGO: O damn'd Iago! O inhuman dog!

IAGO: Kill men i' th' dark?—Where be these bloody thieves?—
How silent is this town!—Ho, murther, murther!—
What may you be? Are you of good or evil?   65

LODOVICO: As you shall prove us, praise us.

IAGO: Signior Lodovico?

LODOVICO: He, sir.

IAGO: I cry you mercy. Here's Cassio hurt by villains.

GRATIANO: Cassio?   70

IAGO: How is't, brother?

CASSIO: My leg is cut in two.

IAGO: Marry, heaven forbid!
Light, gentlemen! I'll bind it with my shirt.
Enter BIANCA.

BIANCA: What is the matter ho? Who is't that cried?

IAGO: Who is't that cried?   75

BIANCA: O my dear Cassio, my sweet Cassio!
O Cassio, Cassio, Cassio!

IAGO: O notable strumpet! Cassio, may you suspect
Who they should be that have thus mangled you?

CASSIO: No.   80

GRATIANO: I am sorry to find you thus; I have been to seek you.

IAGO: Lend me a garter. So.—O for a chair
To bear him easily hence!

BIANCA: Alas, he faints! O Cassio, Cassio, Cassio!

IAGO: Gentlemen all, I do suspect this trash   85
To be a party in this injury.—
Patience awhile, good Cassio.—Come, come;
Lend me a light. Know we this face or no?
Alas, my friend and my dear countryman
Roderigo! No—yes, sure—[O heaven,] Roderigo!

GRATIANO: What, of Venice?   91

IAGO: Even he, sir; did you know him?

GRATIANO: Know him? ay.

IAGO: Signior Gratiano? I cry your gentle pardon;

These bloody accidents must excuse my manners
That so neglected you.
    GRATIANO: I am glad to see you.   95
    IAGO: How do you, Cassio? O, a chair, a chair!
    GRATIANO: Roderigo!
    IAGO: He, he, 'tis he. [*A chair brought in.*] O, that's well said: the chair.
Some good man bear him carefully from hence,
I'll fetch the general's surgeon. [*To* BIANCA.] For you, mistress.   100
Save you your labor.—He that lies slain here, Cassio,
Was my dear friend. What malice was between you?
    CASSIO: None in the world; nor do I know the man.
    IAGO: [*To* BIANCA.] What? look you pale?— O, bear im [out] o' th' air.
[CASSIO *and* RODERIGO *are borne off.*]
Stay you, good gentlemen.—Look you pale, mistress?—   105
Do you perceive the gastness of her eye?—
Nay, [an'] you stare, we shall hear more anon.—
Behold her well; I pray you look upon her.
Do you see, gentlemen? Nay, guiltiness will speak,
Though tongues were out of use.   110
[*Enter* EMILIA.]
    EMILIA: Alas, what is the matter? What is the matter, husband?
    IAGO: Cassio hath here been set on in the dark
By Roderigo and fellows that are scap'd.
He's almost slain, and Roderigo quite dead.
    EMILIA: Alas, good gentleman! alas, good Cassio!
    IAGO: This is the fruits of whoring. Prithee, Emilia,   116
Go know of Cassio where he supp'd to-night.
[*To* BIANCA.] What, do you shake at that?
    BIANCA: He supp'd at my house, but I therefore shake not.
    IAGO: O, did he so? I charge you go with me.   120
    EMILIA: O fie upon thee, strumpet!
    BIANCA: I am no strumpet, but of life as honest
As you that thus abuse me.
    EMILIA: As I? [Fough,] fie upon thee!
    IAGO: Kind gentlemen, let's go see poor Cassio dress'd.
Come, mistress, you must tell 's another tale.   125
Emilia, run you to the citadel,
And tell my lord and lady what hath happ'd.—
Will you go on afore? [*Aside.*] This is the night
That either makes me, or foredoes me quite. *Exeunt.*

----

98. **well said:** well done.   102. **malice:** enmity.   104. **out . . . air.** Fresh air was considered bad for wounds.   106. **gastness:** terror.   129. **foredoes:** destroys.

Scene II

Enter OTHELLO [*with a light*] *and* DESDEMONA *in her
bed* [*asleep*].

OTHELLO: It is the cause, it is the cause, my soul;
Let me not name it to you, you chaste stars,
It is the cause. Yet I'll not shed her blood,
Nor scar that whiter skin of hers than snow,
And smooth as monumental alablaster.   5
Yet she must die, else she'll betray more men.
Put out the light, and then put out the light:
If I quench thee, thou flaming minister,
I can again thy former light restore,
Should I repent me; but once put out thy light,   10
Thou cunning'st pattern of excelling nature,
I know not where is that Promethean heat
That can thy light relume. When I have pluck'd thy rose,
I cannot give it vital growth again,
It needs must wither. I'll smell thee on the tree.   15
[*Kisses her.*]
O balmy breath, that dost almost persuade
Justice to break her sword! One more, one more.
Be thus when thou art dead, and I will kill thee
And love thee after. One more, and that's the last.
So sweet was ne'er so fatal. I must weep,   20
But they are cruel tears. This sorrow's heavenly,
It strikes where it doth love. She wakes.
    DESDEMONA: Who's there? Othello?
    OTHELLO: Ay, Desdemona.
    DESDEMONA: Will you come to bed, my lord?
    OTHELLO: Have you pray'd to-night, Desdemon?
    DESDEMONA: Ay, my lord.
    OTHELLO: If you bethink yourself of any crime   26
Unreconcil'd as yet to heaven and grace,
    Solicit for it straight.
    DESDEMONA: Alack, my lord, what may you mean by that?
    OTHELLO: Well, do it, and be brief, I will walk by.   30
I would not kill thy unprepared spirit,
No, [heaven] forefend! I would not kill thy soul.
    DESDEMONA: Talk you of killing?

V.ii. Location: The citadel.   1. **the cause:** the crime (not the criminal). Othello sees himself as an agent of
justice, not an avenger of his own honor.   5. **alablaster:** alabaster.   10. **repent me:** change my mind.
12. **Promethean:** i.e. divine (since Prometheus brought down fire from heaven).   13. **relume:** rekindle.
21. **cruel:** unrelenting.   21–22. **This . . . love.** Cf. Hebrews 12:6: "For whom the Lord loveth he chas-
teneth. . . ."   26. **crime:** sin.   32. **forefend:** forfend, forbid.

OTHELLO: Ay, I do.

DESDEMONA: Then heaven
Have mercy on me!

OTHELLO: Amen, with all my heart!

DESDEMONA: If you say [so], I hope you will not kill me.   35

OTHELLO: Humh!

DESDEMONA: And yet I fear you; for you're fatal then
When your eyes roll so. Why I should fear I know not,
    Since guiltiness I know not; but yet I feel I fear.

OTHELLO: Think on thy sins.

DESDEMONA: They are loves I bear to you.   40

OTHELLO: Ay, and for that thou di'st.

DESDEMONA: That death's unnatural that kills for loving.
Alas, why gnaw you so your nether lip?
Some bloody passion shakes your very frame.
These are portents; but yet I hope, I hope,   45
They do not point on me.

OTHELLO: Peace, and be still!

DESDEMONA: I will so. What's the matter?

OTHELLO: That handkerchief which I so lov'd, and gave thee,
Thou gav'st to Cassio.

DESDEMONA: No, by my life and soul!
Send for the man, and ask him.

OTHELLO: Sweet soul, take heed,   50
Take heed of perjury, thou art on thy death-bed.

DESDEMONA: Ay, but not yet to die.

OTHELLO: [Yes,] presently:
Therefore confess thee freely of thy sin;
For to deny each article with oath
Cannot remove nor choke the strong conception   55
That I do groan withall. Thou art to die.

DESDEMONA: [Then Lord] have mercy on me!

OTHELLO: I say, amen.

DESDEMONA: And have you mercy too! I never did
Offend you in my life; never lov'd Cassio
But with such general warranty of heaven   60
As I might love. I never gave him token.

OTHELLO: By heaven, I saw my handkerchief in 's hand.
O perjur'd woman, thou dost stone my heart,
And [mak'st] me call what I intend to do
A murther, which I thought a sacrifice.   65
I saw the handkerchief.

---

46. **point on:** point to, aim at.   52. **presently:** at once.   55. **conception:** i.e. conviction of your guilt.
59. **Offend:** wrong.   60. **warranty:** approval, allowance.   63. **stone:** turn to stone.   65. **sacrifice:** i.e. offering to justice.

DESDEMONA: He found it then;
I never gave it him. Send for him hither;
Let him confess a truth.
    OTHELLO: He hath confess'd.
    DESDEMONA: What, my lord?   69
    OTHELLO: That he hath us'd thee.
    DESDEMONA: How? unlawfully?
    OTHELLO: Ay.
    DESDEMONA: He will not say so.
    OTHELLO: No—his mouth is stopp'd;
Honest Iago hath ta'en order for't.
    DESDEMONA: O, my fear interprets. What, is he dead?
    OTHELLO: Had all his hairs been lives, my great revenge
Had stomach for them all.   75
    DESDEMONA: Alas, he is betray'd and I undone!
    OTHELLO: Out, strumpet! weep'st thou for him to my face?
    DESDEMONA: O, banish me, my lord, but kill me not!
    OTHELLO: Down, strumpet!
    DESDEMONA: Kill me to-morrow, let me live to-night!   80
    OTHELLO: Nay, [an'] you strive—
    DESDEMONA: But half an hour!
    OTHELLO: Being done, there is no pause.
    DESDEMONA: But while I say one prayer!
    OTHELLO: It is too late. *Smothers her.*
    [DESDEMONA: O Lord, Lord, Lord!]
    EMILIA: (*At the door, [within].*)   My lord, my lord!
What ho! my lord, my lord!   85
    OTHELLO: What noise is this? Not dead? not yet quite dead?
I that am cruel am yet merciful,
I would not have thee linger in thy pain.
So, so.
    EMILIA: (*Within.*)   What ho! my lord, my lord!
    OTHELLO: Who's there?
    EMILIA: [*Within.*] O, good my lord, I would speak a word with you!   90
    OTHELLO: Yes.—'Tis Emilia.—By and by.—She's dead.
'Tis like she comes to speak of Cassio's death;
The noise was high. Hah, no more moving?
Still as the grave. Shall she come in? Were't good?
I think she stirs again. No. What's best to do?   95
If she come in, she'll sure speak to my wife.
My wife, my wife! what wife? I have no wife.
O insupportable! O heavy hour!

---

72. **ta'en order for't:** taken steps to effect it.   81. **strive:** struggle.   82. **Being done:** since all is over.
93. **The noise was high:** i.e. it caused a great commotion. Many editors, following Q1, read *The noise was here,* referring to the noise in the bed (line 86).

Methinks it should be now a huge eclipse
Of sun and moon, and that th' affrighted globe   100
Did yawn at alteration.
    EMILIA: [*Within.*]   I do beseech you
That I may speak with you. O, good my lord!
    OTHELLO: I had forgot thee. O, come in, Emilia.—
Soft, by and by, let me the curtains draw.—   104
Where art thou? [*Unlocks the door.*]
Enter EMILIA.
           What's the matter with thee now?
    EMILIA: O, my good lord, yonder's foul murthers done!
    OTHELLO: What? now?
    EMILIA: But now, my lord.
    OTHELLO: It is the very error of the moon,
She comes more nearer earth than she was wont,   110
And makes men mad.
    EMILIA: Cassio, my lord, hath kill'd a young Venetian
Call'd Roderigo.
    OTHELLO: Roderigo kill'd?
And Cassio kill'd?
    EMILIA: No, Cassio is not kill'd.
    OTHELLO: Not Cassio kill'd? Then murther's out of tune,   115
And sweet revenge grows harsh.
    DESDEMONA: O, falsely, falsely murder'd!
    EMILIA: [O Lord], what cry is that?
    OTHELLO: That? what?
    EMILIA: Out, and alas, that was my lady's voice.
Help, help, ho, help! O lady, speak again!   120
Sweet Desdemona, O sweet mistress, speak!
    DESDEMONA: A guiltless death I die.
    EMILIA: O, who hath done this deed?
    DESDEMONA: Nobody; I myself. Farewell!   124
Commend me to my kind lord. O, farewell! [*Dies.*]
    OTHELLO: Why, how should she be murd'red?
    EMILIA: Alas! who knows?
    OTHELLO: You [heard] her say herself, it was not I.
    EMILIA: She said so; I must needs report the truth.
    OTHELLO: She's like a liar gone to burning hell:
'Twas I that kill'd her.
    EMILIA: O, the more angel she,   130
And you the blacker devil!
    OTHELLO: She turn'd to folly, and she was a whore.
    EMILIA: Thou dost belie her, and thou art a devil.

---

101. **yawn.** It was commonly believed that eclipses were accompanied by earthquakes. **alteration:** the great change on earth.   104. **Soft:** wait a moment.   109. **error:** aberration, deviation from the normal course.   119. **Out:** exclamation of grief.

OTHELLO: She was false as water.

EMILIA: Thou art rash as fire to say

That she was false. O, she was heavenly true!   135

OTHELLO: Cassio did top her; ask thy husband else.

O, I were damn'd beneath all depth in hell

But that I did proceed upon just grounds

To this extremity. Thy husband knew it all.

EMILIA: My husband?   140

OTHELLO: Thy husband.

EMILIA: That she was false to wedlock?

OTHELLO: Ay, with Cassio. [Nay,] had she been true,

If heaven would make me such another world

Of one entire and perfect chrysolite,   145

I'ld not have sold her for it.

EMILIA: My husband?

OTHELLO: Ay, 'twas he that told me on her first.

An honest man he is, and hates the slime

That sticks on filthy deeds.

EMILIA: My husband?

OTHELLO: What needs this iterance, woman? I say thy husband.   150

EMILIA: O mistress, villainy hath made mocks with love!

My husband say she was false?

OTHELLO: He, woman:

I say thy husband; dost understand the word?

My friend, thy husband, honest, honest Iago.

EMILIA: If he say so, may his pernicious soul   155

Rot half a grain a day! He lies to th' heart.

She was too fond of her most filthy bargain.

OTHELLO: Hah?

EMILIA: Do thy worst!

This deed of thine is no more worthy heaven   160

Than thou wast worthy her.

OTHELLO: Peace, you were best.

EMILIA: Thou hast not half that pow'r to do me harm

As I have to be hurt. O gull, O dolt,

As ignorant as dirt! Thou hast done a deed—

I care not for thy sword, I'll make thee known,   165

Though I lost twenty lives. Help, help, ho, help!

The Moor hath kill'd my mistress! Murther, murther!

Enter MONTANO, GRATIANO, *and* IAGO, [*with others*].

MONTANO: What is the matter? How now, general?

EMILIA: O, are you come, Iago? You have done well,

That men must lay their murthers on your neck.   170

GRATIANO: What is the matter?

---

134. **rash:** impetuous.   145. **chrysolite:** topaz.   150. **iterance:** repetition.   151. **with:** at.   163. **be hurt:** i.e. endure hurt. **gull:** dupe.

EMILIA: Disprove this villain, if thou be'st a man.
He says thou toldst him that his wife was false.
I know thou didst not; thou'rt not such a villain.
Speak, for my heart is full.   175
    IAGO: I told him what I thought, and told no more
Than what he found himself was apt and true.
    EMILIA: But did you ever tell him she was false?
    IAGO: I did.
    EMILIA: You told a lie, an odious, damned lie;   180
Upon my soul, a lie, a wicked lie.
She false with Cassio? did you say with Cassio?
    IAGO: With Cassio, mistress. Go to, charm your tongue.
    EMILIA: I will not charm my tongue; I am bound to speak.
My mistress here lies murthered in her bed—   185
    ALL: O heavens forefend!
    EMILIA: And your reports have set the murder on.
    OTHELLO: Nay, stare not, masters, it is true indeed.
    GRATIANO: 'Tis a strange truth.   189
    MONTANO: O monstrous act!
    EMILIA: Villainy, villainy, villainy!
I think upon't, I think—I smell't—O villainy!
I thought so then—I'll kill myself for grief—
O villainy! villainy!
    IAGO: What, are you mad? I charge you get you home.   194
    EMILIA: Good gentlemen, let me have leave to speak.
'Tis proper I obey him; but not now.
Perchance, Iago, I will ne'er go home.
    OTHELLO: O, O, O! [OTHELLO *falls on the bed.*]
    EMILIA: Nay, lay thee down and roar;
For thou hast kill'd the sweetest innocent   199
That e'er did lift up eye.
    OTHELLO: [*Rising.*]   O, she was foul!
I scarce did know you, uncle; there lies your niece,
Whose breath, indeed, these hands have newly stopp'd.
I know this act shows horrible and grim.
    GRATIANO: Poor Desdemon! I am glad thy father's dead.
Thy match was mortal to him, and pure grief   205
Shore his old thread in twain. Did he live now,
This sight would make him do a desperate turn,
Yea, curse his better angel from his side,
And fall to reprobance.
    OTHELLO: 'Tis pitiful; but yet Iago knows   210
That she with Cassio hath the act of shame

---

177. **apt:** credible.   183. **charm:** i.e. silence, as if with a magic spell.   192. **I...then.** See IV.ii.130–33.
206. **Shore:** sheared, cut. **thread:** i.e. thread of life.   207. **turn:** act.   209. **to reprobance:** into
damnation.

A thousand times committed. Cassio confess'd it,
And she did gratify his amorous works
With that recognizance and pledge of love
Which I first gave her. I saw it in his hand;   215
It was a handkerchief, an antique token
My father gave my mother.
    EMILIA: O [God]! O heavenly [God]!
    IAGO: ['Zounds], hold your peace.
    EMILIA: 'Twill out, 'twill out! I peace?
No, I will speak as liberal as the north: 220
Let heaven and men and devils, let them all,
All, all, cry shame against me, yet I'll speak.
    IAGO: Be wise, and get you home.
    EMILIA: I will not. [IAGO *offers to stab* EMILIA.]
    GRATIANO: Fie,
Your sword upon a woman?
    EMILIA: O thou dull Moor, that handkerchief thou speak'st of   225
I found by fortune, and did give my husband;
For often, with a solemn earnestness
(More than indeed belong'd to such a trifle),
He begg'd of me to steal't.
    IAGO: Villainous whore!   229
    EMILIA: She give it Cassio? No, alas, I found it,
And I did give't my husband.
    IAGO: Filth, thou liest!
    EMILIA: By heaven, I do not, I do not, gentlemen.
O murd'rous coxcomb, what should such a fool
Do with so good a wife?
    OTHELLO: Are there no stones in heaven   234
But what serves for the thunder?—Precious villain!
[*The Moor runs at* IAGO; MONTANO *disarms* OTHELLO; IAGO *kills his wife.*]
    GRATIANO: The woman falls; sure he hath kill'd his wife.
    EMILIA: Ay, ay! O, lay me by my mistress' side.
[*Exit* IAGO.]
    GRATIANO: He's gone, but his wife's kill'd.
    MONTANO: 'Tis a notorious villain. Take you this weapon
Which I have [here] recover'd from the Moor.   240
Come guard the door without; let him not pass,
But kill him rather. I'll after that same villain,
For 'tis a damned slave.
Exit [*with all but* OTHELLO *and* EMILIA].
    OTHELLO: I am not valiant neither,

---

214. **recognizance:** token.   220. **liberal:** unrestrainedly. **as the north:** as the north wind blows.
228. **belong'd:** was appropriate.   233. **coxcomb:** fool.   235. **for the thunder:** i.e. as thunderbolts.
239. **notorious:** exceptional, egregious.   240. **recover'd:** taken away.

But every puny whipster gets my sword.
But why should honor outlive honesty?   245
Let it go all.
    EMILIA: What did thy song bode, lady?
Hark, canst thou hear me? I will play the swan,
And die in music. [*Sings.*] "Willow, willow, willow."
Moor, she was chaste; she lov'd thee, cruel Moor;
So come my soul to bliss, as I speak true;   250
So speaking as I think, alas, I die. [*Dies.*]
    OTHELLO: I have another weapon in this chamber;
It was a sword of Spain, the ice-brook's temper—
O, here it is. Uncle, I must come forth.
    GRATIANO: [*Within.*] If thou attempt it, it will cost thee dear: 255
Thou hast no weapon, and perforce must suffer.
    OTHELLO: Look in upon me then and speak with me,
Or naked as I am I will assault thee.
[*Enter* GRATIANO.]
    GRATIANO: What is the matter?
    OTHELLO: Behold, I have a weapon;
    A better never did itself sustain   260
Upon a soldier's thigh. I have seen the day
That with this little arm, and this good sword,
I have made my way through more impediments
Than twenty times your stop. But (O vain boast!)
Who can control his fate? 'tis not so now.   265
Be not afraid though you do see me weapon'd;
Here is my journey's end, here is my butt
And very sea-mark of my utmost sail.
Do you go back dismay'd? 'Tis a lost fear;
Man but a rush against Othello's breast,   270
And he retires. Where should Othello go?
Now—how dost thou look now? O ill-starr'd wench,
Pale as thy smock! when we shall meet at compt,
This look of thine will hurl my soul from heaven,
And fiends will snatch at it. Cold, cold, my girl?   275
Even like thy chastity. O cursed, cursed slave!
Whip me, ye devils,
From the possession of this heavenly sight!
Blow me about in winds! roast me in sulphur!
Wash me in steep-down gulfs of liquid fire!   280

---

244. **whipster:** insignificant or contemptible person.   245. **honor:** i.e. personal prowess and courage, and one's reputation for them. **honesty:** inward integrity.   253. **the ice-brook's temper:** i.e. its steel tempered in icy water.   258. **naked:** unarmed.   264. **stop:** power to stop.   267. **butt:** goal.   268. **sea-mark:** beacon or other object marking the entrance to a harbor; hence, destination, end.   269. **lost:** idle, unnecessary.   270. **Man . . . rush:** hold a mere reed.   273. **compt:** accounting, i.e. Judgment Day.

O Desdemon! dead, Desdemon! dead!
O, O!
Enter LODOVICO, CASSIO [*in a chair*], MONTANO, *and* IAGO [*guarded*], *with* OFFICERS.

> LODOVICO: Where is this rash and most unfortunate man?
> OTHELLO: That's he that was Othello; here I am.   284
> LODOVICO: Where is that viper? Bring the villain forth.
> OTHELLO: I look down towards his feet; but that's a fable.

If that thou be'st a devil, I cannot kill thee.
[*Wounds* IAGO.]

> LODOVICO: Wrench his sword from him.
> IAGO: I bleed, sir, but not kill'd.
> OTHELLO: I am not sorry neither, I'ld have thee live;

For in my sense, 'tis happiness to die.   290

> LODOVICO: O thou Othello, that was once so good,

Fall'n in the practice of a [damned] slave,
What shall be said to thee?

> OTHELLO: Why, any thing:

An honorable murderer, if you will;
For nought I did in hate, but all in honor.   295

> LODOVICO: This wretch hath part confess'd his villainy.

Did you and he consent in Cassio's death?

> OTHELLO: Ay.
> CASSIO: Dear general, I never gave you cause.
> OTHELLO: I do believe it, and I ask your pardon.   300

Will you, I pray, demand that demi-devil
Why he hath thus ensnar'd my soul and body?

> IAGO: Demand me nothing; what you know, you know:

From this time forth I never will speak word.   304

> LODOVICO: What? not to pray?
> GRATIANO: Torments will ope your lips.
> OTHELLO: Well, thou dost best.
> LODOVICO: Sir, you shall understand what hath befall'n,

Which, as I think, you know not. Here is a letter
Found in the pocket of the slain Roderigo,
And here another. The one of them imports   310
The death of Cassio to be undertook
By Roderigo.

> OTHELLO: O villain!
> CASSIO: Most heathenish and most gross!
> LODOVICO: Now here's another discontented paper,

---

283. **rash:** overhasty.   286. **I . . . feet:** i.e. to see if they are cloven, as the devil's were thought to be. **that's a fable:** i.e. the fact that your feet aren't cloven doesn't prove that you aren't a devil.   290. **in my sense:** i.e. to one who feels as I do.   292. **practice:** plotting.   313. **gross:** monstrous.

Found in his pocket too; and this it seems   315
Roderigo meant t' have sent this damned villain;
But that, belike, Iago in the [nick]
Came in and satisfied him.

    OTHELLO: O thou pernicious caitiff!—
How came you, Cassio, by that handkerchief
That was my wive's?

    CASSIO: I found it in my chamber: 320
And he himself confess'd it but even now,
That there he dropp'd it for a special purpose
Which wrought to his desire.

    OTHELLO: O fool, fool, fool!

    CASSIO: There is besides, in Roderigo's letter,
How he upbraids Iago, that he made him   325
Brave me upon the watch, whereon it came
That I was cast; and even but now he spake
(After long seeming dead) Iago hurt him,
Iago set him on.   329

    LODOVICO: You must forsake this room and go with us.
Your power and your command is taken off,
And Cassio rules in Cyprus. For this slave,
If there be any cunning cruelty
That can torment him much, and hold him long,
It shall be his. You shall close prisoner rest,   335
Till that the nature of your fault be known
To the Venetian state. Come, bring away.

    OTHELLO: Soft you; a word or two before you go.
I have done the state some service, and they know't—
No more of that. I pray you, in your letters,   340
When you shall these unlucky deeds relate,
Speak of me as I am; nothing extenuate,
Nor set down aught in malice. Then must you speak
Of one that lov'd not wisely but too well;
Of one not easily jealous, but being wrought,   345
Perplexed in the extreme; of one whose hand
(Like the base [Indian]) threw a pearl away
Richer than all his tribe; of one whose subdu'd eyes,
Albeit unused to the melting mood,

---

323. **wrought to:** worked toward, fitted in with.   326. **Brave:** defy, behave insolently toward.   342. **extenuate:** tone down (literally, make thin).   345. **wrought:** worked upon.   346. **Perplexed:** bewildered, distraught.   347. **Indian.** This, the Q1 reading, relates to the not unfamiliar notion of an Indian ignorant of the value of some precious object he finds. (*Base* = low in the scale of civilization.) A few editors prefer to read *Judean,* after F1; this is taken as an allusion to Judas, or to Herod the Great, who in a fit of jealousy had his beloved wife Mariamne killed.

Drops tears as fast as the Arabian trees   350
Their medicinable gum. Set you down this;
And say besides, that in Aleppo once,
Where a malignant and a turban'd Turk
Beat a Venetian and traduc'd the state,
I took by th' throat the circumcised dog,   355
And smote him—thus. [*He stabs himself.*]
    LODOVICO: O bloody period!
    GRATIANO: All that is spoke is marr'd.
    OTHELLO: I kiss'd thee ere I kill'd thee. No way but this,
Killing myself, to die upon a kiss.   359
    [*Falls on the bed and*] *dies.*
    CASSIO: This did I fear, but thought he had no weapon;
For he was great of heart.
    LODOVICO: [*To* IAGO.] O Spartan dog,
More fell than anguish, hunger, or the sea!
Look on the tragic loading of this bed;
This is thy work. The object poisons sight,
Let it be hid. Gratiano, keep the house,   365
And seize upon the fortunes of the Moor,
For they succeed on you. To you, Lord Governor,
Remains the censure of this hellish villain,
The time, the place, the torture, O, enforce it!
Myself will straight aboard, and to the state   370
This heavy act with heavy heart relate. *Exeunt.*

ACTIVITIES FOR WRITING AND DISCUSSION

    1. An irony is a type of incongruity. For example, throughout this play, Othello ironically places his full trust in the completely untrustworthy Iago. Read the section on "Irony" on pp. 208–210 of Chapter 19. Then:
        a. Brainstorm a list of ironies in *Othello.*
        b. Choose what are for you the two or three most significant ironies and discuss them in a short essay.

    2. Reread and annotate pages 751–764 in which Iago begins fomenting jealousy in Othello's mind.
        a. Does Iago create or *plant* the jealousy, or does he *nurture* a jealousy that was already present? Find support for both views and back up your ar-

---

351. **medicinable:** medicinal.   357. **period:** conclusion.   361. **Spartan dog:** a kind of bloodhound, noted for its silence as well as its skill.   362. **fell:** cruel.   364. **object:** sight, spectacle.   365. **keep:** remain in.   366. **seize upon:** take legal possession of.   368. **censure:** judgment, sentence.

guments with analysis and illustrative examples. What concrete evidence, if any, does Othello have for believing Desdemona unfaithful? To what extent is his jealousy the product of mere imagination, stirred up by Iago?

b. What reasons, other than concrete evidence, could Othello have for suspecting infidelity in Desdemona, who is elsewhere and consistently presented as the paragon of faithfulness?

3. One critic has hypothesized that the tragedy of *Othello* would never have occurred if the invading Turkish fleet had made it to Cyprus. A battle, the argument goes, would have kept Othello occupied and prevented him from indulging the jealous speculations that begin to obsess him when he sits relaxed and idle in the citadel. Agree or disagree with this hypothesis. If accepted, what particular strengths and/or weaknesses does it suggest in Othello's character?

4. The play reveals ironic contrasts between Othello the public persona (the brave and steady general) and Othello the private human being (the frightened and jealous husband). A similarly ironic disparity between public and private personae is sometimes exposed in the lives of modern public figures (political, popular).

a. Cite some present-day examples and examine any parallels between their stories or circumstances and Othello's; or

b. Invent a story about an imaginary celebrated person whose public and private lives display such a disparity.

5. The public and private Othellos converge in Act IV, scene i, when, acting on his private jealousies, the celebrated general strikes his wife in plain view of Lodovico, a nobleman, and various "attendants." (A modern parallel might be a famous world leader, renowned for sober judgment, arriving drunk at a well-publicized speaking engagement.) Explain Lodovico's astonished reaction in lines 264–268 on page 777. Then imagine a newspaper reporter is present at the scene. Write the story as he or she assembles it from first-hand observation, background research, and interviews.

6. Othello, a great general who has conquered enemy armies, is himself defeated by his own passions, particularly the passion of jealousy. Imagine Othello steals a reflective moment between his discovery of Iago's treachery and his own suicide (Act V, scene ii; p. 802) and reads Emily Dickinson's poem "One need not be a Chamber to be Haunted" (p. 507). How might he see the poem as written for or about *himself*?

7. Research the historical background of *Othello*—its first performances, public reception, and publication, and the source material upon which Shakespeare drew for his plot and characters.

INDIVIDUAL AND SOCIETY: ADDITIONAL ACTIVITIES FOR WRITING AND DISCUSSION

1. Reread all or a portion of your notebook. Mark any passages, however long or short, that strike you, for whatever reason. Beside each such passage, write a note explaining its significance for you. Finally, pick a favorite passage and either:

    a. Expand it into a new piece of writing, or

    b. Make notes on how you could expand or use it at some future date, or

    c. Rewrite it in a different form, e.g., a poem, dialogue, letter, memoir.

For a list of strategies for expanding or revising, see Chapter 12.

2. Write down your own definitions of "individual" and "society." Then think about this question: Is society essentially the *enemy* of the individual or the *friend?* Finally, bring together two or more **characters, speakers,** or **personae** from the texts in this section and write a dialogue in which they debate the question. Some participants in this dialogue might include James Thurber's Walter Mitty, Ray Bradbury's Brock, one of Margaret Atwood's "City Planners," the Cathy Appel of "Letters," Carol Bly. If you wish, include yourself in the dialogue as a participant or moderator.

3. Is "individuality" mainly a matter of being independent, or does it include dependence of various kinds? Are there kinds of dependence that can enhance individuality, or is dependence generally at odds with individuality? Compare the ways in which "independence" and "dependence" interweave as themes in any of the texts within this section, such as Whitman's "Song of Myself," O'Connor's "Everything That Rises Must Converge," or Rich's "A Leak in History."

4. As a variation on Activity #3, write about the same issues in some alternative literary form, e.g., in a dialogue between or among characters or speakers, a personal essay, or a short story.

5. Several writings in this chapter explore ironic contradictions between the public personae of celebrities and their private lives. Examples include Alice Walker's Traynor, Edward Arlington Robinson's Richard Cory, and William Shakespeare's Othello. Samuel Johnson addresses the irony of celebrity directly in *Rambler,* no. 146. Write a dialogue among two or more characters in which, momentarily risen from their graves, they reflect back candidly on their public lives, private dreams, and what went wrong. Alternatively, bring these characters together in a panel discussion with either yourself or Samuel Johnson as the moderator.

6. Imagine you are Arthur Schopenhauer. Apply the ideas in your work "On Thinking for Oneself" to write an interpretation of the character of Shakespeare's Othello.

7. Write about any common themes you see in Schopenhauer's "On Thinking for Oneself" and Bly's "Growing Up Expressive." Do the two essays articulate a common message? Are there any important differences?

8. Review your entire notebook; as you do, make a running list of memorable or striking topics, e.g., "individuality," "nonconformists," "communities," "friendship." Then choose a favorite topic, make a Topic/Form Grid (see Chapter 5), and use one of the forms on your grid to create a new notebook entry about the topic. If your chosen form does not work, do a Topic/Form Shift to a different form on your grid.

9. Walker's "Nineteen Fifty-five" is a *mix* of literary forms, combining **first-person** narrative by Gracie Mae with imaginary letters between Traynor and Gracie Mae. Use the topic you chose for Activity #8 and compose a notebook piece that mixes two or more forms from your Topic/Form Grid.

Interchapter on Notebooks and Journals (IV)

"These Notes Are My Daily Prayer": Jules Renard

> I am a man continually astonished, each instant just fallen from the moon.
> —JULES RENARD, *JOURNAL*

Jules Renard was born in Chalons-sur-Mayenne (in France) in 1864 and grew up in Chitry, a village some 140 miles south of Paris. His mother was, in the words of one editor, "a bigot . . . a compulsive talker and fibber." His father stopped talking to his wife after Jules's birth and remained largely indifferent to his son and his son's career. Renard later mined his tormented childhood and family relationships for some of his best work, particularly *Poil de Carotte* ("Carrot-top"—Jules was redheaded), a collection of stories which he later revised into a play. Both parents also figure prominently in his *Journal,* which he began keeping in 1887.

Renard moved to Paris when he was seventeen and soon resolved to become a writer. Living on clerking and tutoring jobs and a small allowance from his father, he began producing poetry and short stories but had to publish his first collections in both genres at his own expense. By the late 1880s he had started attracting widespread critical notice. His marriage in 1888 to a woman of property enabled him to concentrate more exclusively on his writing, and with *Poil de*

Carotte (1894) he became famous. After 1895 he and his family divided their time between Paris and the countryside near Chitry, with homes in both places.

In addition to short stories, Renard wrote and published novels, numerous commercially successful plays, and a book of brief descriptions of animals and plants entitled *Natural Histories* written in a poetic prose similar to that found in his *Journal*. Widely honored as an author, Renard was also elected mayor of his hometown of Chitry in 1904. He died in 1910, in Paris, of artereosclerosis.

Though Renard's writings can be wonderfully witty, whimsical, and light:

> The chattering of the chairs, lined up before the guests arrive on a reception day

> If I were a bird, I would sleep only in the clouds

he regarded the practice of writing with profound seriousness. He hated hypocrisy and sham, which he believed degrade language: when people are false, words are cheapened and lose their original meaning and power. For instance, of the word "love" he wrote:

> We no longer know what love is. The thing itself is lost, drowned in a verbal deluge. It is impossible to come through to reality, which should be simple and clear.

Renard's answer to the "verbal deluge" was to strive relentlessly to make his own writing plainer and more economical, "to reproduce in compressed and resistant [prose] life completely pure and completely simple."

> When he drinks with a couple, he always pays, so that people may believe he is the lover.

> The life of a cat asleep. From time to time, a leap, a slash of claws, a stretch that resembles action, then everything returns into its fur and goes back to sleep.

> A boy from the orphan asylum, hired out near Cervon, at thirteen. He is a little deaf. He receives 120 francs for fifteen months. I am thoughtless enough to say it is not much. Whereupon, lifting his eyes, which he had kept lowered, he says, with pride:
>   "There's something else too. You get your washing done, and a pair of shoes."

Never falsely modest, Renard pursued fame and honors and relished his successes, which he viewed with self-amused irony. "It's many a day since I've felt ashamed of my vanity," he wrote when his career was in full stride, "or even tried to correct it. Of all my faults, it is the one that amuses me most." At the same time, he denied that writers are special or extraordinary people to be put on pedestals:

> No novel exists which an ordinary intelligence could not conceive; there is no sentence, no matter how lovely, that a beginner could not construct. What remains is to pick up the pen, to rule the paper, patiently to fill it up. The strong do not hesitate. They settle down, they sweat, they go on to the end. They exhaust the ink, they use up the paper. . . . In literature, there are only oxen.

A "great" writer was simply an ordinary person with a farm animal's capacity for work.

Renard's comparison of writers to oxen reflects his rural upbringing among peasants whose "animal" virtues he both satirized and admired. It also suggests a certain envy of brute energy and instinct. "I don't give a fig for intelligence," he once wrote; "I should be satisfied with a lot of instinct." Most people probably assume the *more* "intelligence" they have the better; in Renard's view intelligence can actually impede the senses and cloud understanding with excessive analysis, equivocations, and theorizing. Writers need to *un*learn some of what intelligence has taught them—become more like the "dumb" oxen that go to work each day with muscle, energy, and humility.

Renard strove to experience life at first hand, through his own senses, as if he were the first person alive. "To think," he wrote, "is to search for clearings in a wood." If he did not always succeed ("Every time I want to settle down to work, literature gets between"), in his *Journal* at least his writing never seems to get tired. In the midst of his busy life Renard extracted the poetry from every moment and renewed himself by enjoying and recording the ordinary:

> In my church, there is no vaulting between me and the sky.

> I like rain that lasts all day, and don't feel that I am really in the country until I am well caked with mud.

For further reading:
Renard, Jules. *The Journal of Jules Renard.* Ed. and trans. Louise Bogan and Elizabeth Roget. New York: George Braziller, 1964.

Excerpts from *The Journal of Jules Renard*

The true artist will write in, as it were, small leaps, on a hundred subjects that 1
surge unawares into his mind. In this way, nothing is forced. Everything has an unwilled, natural charm. One does not provoke: one waits.

I have an almost incessant need of speaking evil of others; but no interest at all 2
in doing evil to them.

To lie watching one's mind, pen raised, ready to spear the smallest thought 3 that may come out.

The chatting of the chairs, lined up before the guests arrive on a reception day. 4

Work thinks; laziness muses.   5

Sometimes conversation dies out like a lamp. You turn up the wick. A few 6 ideas bring out another gleam, but, decidedly, there is no oil left.

The ideal of calm exists in a sitting cat.   7

All I have read, all I have thought, all my forced paradoxes, my hatred of the 8 conventional, my contempt for the commonplace, do not prevent me from turning soft on the first day of spring, from looking for violets under the hedges, among the turds and the scraps of decayed paper; from playing with the village youngsters, giving close attention to lizards and yellow-robed butterflies, bringing home a little blue flower to my wife. Everlasting contradiction. Continual effort to get beyond stupidity, and inevitable backsliding. Happily!

Today, Marie Pierry's cow calved. Marie, in tears, said: "I can't watch that. I'm 9 getting out of here."
Then she'd come back. "Oh, the poor dear! The poor dear! There! She is dead! 10 I can see she is dead. She'll never pull out of it!"
The cow lowed and heaved sighs. Lexandre, pulling at the calf's legs, pouted 11 his lips at her: "There, my beauty!" Father Castel presided: "Pull, children, pull!"
Everyone felt himself to be a mother, and when the cow, having produced her 12 calf and drunk a bottle of sweetened wine, began licking the salt that had been sprinkled over the calf, everyone had tears in his eyes.

When I make a joke, I watch the maid out of the corner of my eye to see if she 13 is laughing.

The geese had retired, but they could still be heard stirring.   14
They jabbered, deep in their throats. They raised their wings a little in order 15 to close them more comfortably. They settled down like ladies rustling and drawing together around someone who is about to tell them a piece of gossip.

I like rain that lasts all day, and don't feel that I am really in the country until 16 I am well caked with mud.

Visit to the zoo: 17
Tiny parakeets, like tie-pins that sing.   18

How monotonous snow would be if God had not created crows!   19

With its purring, the cat accompanies the tick-tock of the clock; it is the only   20
music in the room.

I want my ear to be a shell that keeps in itself all the sounds of nature.   21

Be modest! It is the kind of pride least likely to offend.   22

My brother Maurice tells me: "Papa and I sit together on the wall. He waits for   23
me to talk, and I wait for him. And that goes on until we go to bed." He can no
longer shoot. He has a pain in the left arm. When a partridge starts out from
somewhere, or a hare goes barreling off, he can't lift his arm. It is as though someone were to put a hand on his shoulder to prevent him from killing, saying:
"That's enough!"
     In the old bedroom, the paper is coming off the walls and the plaster is crum-   24
bling. Holes are forming. There is one big enough for me to put my watch into,
as in a niche.
     Papa walked with me as far as the Bargeot fields, and he wearies me. When we   25
got back, he said: "I am no more tired than when we started, because at my age
you are always tired."

     Papa. The swollen veins of his temples. Moles are digging around and rav-   26
aging him under the skin.

     The little light existing in the mystery that surrounds us comes from our-   27
selves: it is a false light. The mystery has never shown us its own.

     When he drinks with a couple, he always pays, so that people may believe he   28
is the lover.

     By six o'clock in the morning, she has finished cleaning her house. Someone   29
may go by her door, who stops and talks. This talk may go on till noon, and the
rest of the day is spent in the same way.
     No one ever sees her working. You knock. She opens the door, in wooden   30
shoes, neat and clean, her hands over her belly. Everything is in order. How does
she keep busy? Sometimes, she knits. She is so happy over having lost her husband
who drank, and beat her, that even the death of one of her two boys did not sad-
den her. She could go on living like this for ever.

     When the little peasant girls see us from a distance, they turn aside to smile.   31

     The bird alights on the rosebush not because of the rose, but because of the   32
plant lice.

     Men like my father respect only those that get rich, and admire only those that   33
die poor.

The magpie fluttered about, dressed up as a sister of charity.   34

Return to Paris. My father and I did not love each other outwardly. We did not 35
hang together by our branches: we loved each other by our roots.

When laziness makes us miserable, it has the same value as work.   36

I read what I write as though I were my mortal enemy.   37

Old woman, your eyes are like the reflection of a star in the water of a wagon 38
rut.

The duck tries to jump over a wall and go through a hedge. Halfway up the 39
wall, she falls back heavily. She does not insist: she goes to fetch the drake. Together, their heads held straight up, they examine the wall, look for an opening in
the hedge. From time to time, they desist, go around by the field, cut a little grass,
and come back.
    The duck gets half-way into the hedge; but it is too thick: she gives up the idea. 40
    They make the turn of the meadow, wasting their day and mine.   41
    And their jerky bows.   42
    It is a confused act. It would take a comic playwright to straighten it out. 43

Like the soil, my courage needs rain.   44

Our egoism is so excessive that, in a storm, we believe the thunder to be di- 45
rected only at us.

All day, the woods hold in their branches a little of the night.   46

I don't give a fig for intelligence: I should be satisfied with a lot of instinct. 47

I turn home, my heart filled with anguish because I have watched the sun set 48
and heard the birds sing, and because I shall have had so few days on this earth I
love, and there are so many dead before me.

When I used to see my father walking from one window to the other, bent, 49
silent, his hands behind his back, his look deep, I used to ask myself: "What is he
thinking about?" Today I know, because I walk about in exactly the same manner,
with the same air, and I can answer in all certainty: "Nothing."

I cannot look at the leaf of a tree without being crushed by the universe.   50

We no longer know what love is. The thing itself is lost, drowned in a verbal 51
deluge. It is impossible to come through to reality, which should be simple and
clear.

Love kills intelligence. The brain and the heart act upon each other in the 52
manner of an hour-glass. One fills itself only to empty the other.

If I were a bird, I would sleep only in the clouds.   53

It is hailing. A disaster! But, once the hail has melted, the peasant does not 54
spend time being sorry for himself: he goes back to work.

The wind that makes the chimney look as though it were smoking while on 55
the run.

Toward morning, when you can't sleep, you are possessed with genius. You see 56
luminous things on that black canvas. In the dark, you scribble on a piece of paper.
The next day, all you find is meaningless scratches.   57

Too fast, the auto. So many pretty landscapes where one does not stop.   58

If I were to begin life again, I should want it as it was. I would only open my 59
eyes a little more. I did not see properly, and I did not see everything in that little
universe in which I was feeling my way.

A boy from the orphan asylum, hired out near Cervon, at thirteen. He is a 60
little deaf. He receives 120 francs for fifteen months. I am thoughtless enough to
say it is not much. Whereupon, lifting his eyes, which he had kept lowered, he says
with pride:
"There's something else too. You get your washing done, and a pair of shoes." 61

The life of a cat asleep. From time to time, a leap, a slash of claws, a stretch that 62
resembles action, then everything returns into its fur and goes back to sleep.

Laziness: the habit of resting before fatigue sets in.   63

These notes are my daily prayer.   64

On the horizon, the moon, like a balloon unencumbered by a basket, says: 65
"Let go!" It rises. All the cables are cut.
Not a man, not a tree, not a dry branch was able to hang on to its net and un- 66
awares rise too.
The red woods burn under it and inflate it.   67
It reaches a cloud, seems caught, stops moving.   68
It disappeared behind a mass of clouds. It was never seen again. Not that 69
moon, at least.

I have an idea the way I look at a bird: I am always afraid it will fly away, and I   70
don't dare touch it.

To the young. I shall tell you a truth that you may not like, because you look   71
forward to novelty. This truth is that one does not grow old. Where the heart is
concerned, the fact is accepted, at least in matters of love. Well, it is the same with
the mind. It always remains young. You do not understand life any more at forty
than you did at twenty, but you are aware of this fact, and you admit it. To admit
it is to remain young.

We are in the world to laugh.   72
In purgatory or in hell we shall no longer be able to do so.   73
And in heaven it would not be proper.   74

After seeing what the bourgeois crave, I feel myself capable of doing without   75
everything.

Evening. A soul is wandering; you can hear its little bell.   76

Walks. The body advances, while the mind flutters around it like a bird.   77

A new maid. Marie. Believes in the number thirteen and doesn't work on Sun-   78
days. At thirty-eight, she is no more advanced than she was at thirteen. She was
married once, and feels that it's enough.
She remembers only one good situation, at the Spanish embassy.   79
She has been in homes where the coffee was weighed out, and where her   80
dinner consisted of a hard-boiled egg when the masters, who were rich, dined out.
She eats the crusts of the day before. She hasn't tasted fresh bread for a year.   81
Shy, with an Alsatian accent and a lisp, she begs pardon when she crosses in front
of an armchair.

Rain mixed with piano drops.   82

The Luxembourg gardens are nothing but a dome of leaves under which   83
people dream.

Snow on water: silence upon silence.   84

— Translated by Louise Bogan and Elizabeth Roget

ACTIVITIES FOR WRITING AND DISCUSSION

1. Consider Renard's notion of a "verbal deluge" (page 807). Do you experience this "verbal deluge" anywhere today? If so, what forms does it take, and

what are its effects, positive and/or negative, on yourself and society? (For an interesting comparison, see paragraphs 32 and 33 of Whitecloud's "Blue Winds Dancing" on page 879.) Illustrate your responses with stories and examples from your own experience and knowledge.

2. Respond to Renard's journal selections using any of the "Generic Ideas for Writing" found on pages 192–193.

24

People and Cultures in Conflict and Change

EDGAR ALLAN POE (1809–1849)

The Black Cat

For the most wild yet most homely narrative which I am about to pen, I neither 1
expect nor solicit belief. Mad indeed would I be to expect it, in a case where my
very senses reject their own evidence. Yet, mad am I not—and very surely do I
not dream. But tomorrow I die, and today I would unburden my soul. My immediate purpose is to place before the world, plainly, succinctly, and without
comment, a series of mere household events. In their consequences, these events
have terrified—have tortured—have destroyed me. Yet I will not attempt to ex-
pound them. To me, they have presented little but horror—to many they will
seem less terrible than *baroques*. Hereafter, perhaps, some intellect may be found
which will reduce my phantasm to the commonplace—some intellect more
calm, more logical, and far less excitable than my own, which will perceive, in the
circumstances I detail with awe, nothing more than an ordinary succession of
very natural causes and effects.

From my infancy I was noted for the docility and humanity of my disposition. 2
My tenderness of heart was even so conspicuous as to make me the jest of my
companions. I was especially fond of animals, and was indulged by my parents
with a great variety of pets. With these I spent most of my time, and never was so
happy as when feeding and caressing them. This peculiarity of character grew
with my growth, and, in my manhood, I derived from it one of my principal
sources of pleasure. To those who have cherished an affection for a faithful and

sagacious dog, I need hardly be at the trouble of explaining the nature or the intensity of the gratification thus derivable. There is something in the unselfish and self-sacrificing love of a brute, which goes directly to the heart of him who has had frequent occasion to test the paltry friendship and gossamer fidelity of mere *Man*.

I married early, and was happy to find in my wife a disposition not uncongenial with my own. Observing my partiality for domestic pets, she lost no opportunity of procuring those of the most agreeable kind. We had birds, goldfish, a fine dog, rabbits, a small monkey, and a *cat*. 3

This latter was a remarkably large and beautiful animal, entirely black, and sagacious to an astonishing degree. In speaking of his intelligence, my wife, who at heart was not a little tinctured with superstition, made frequent allusion to the ancient popular notion, which regarded all black cats as witches in disguise. Not that she was ever *serious* upon this point—and I mention the matter at all for no better reason than that it happens, just now, to be remembered. 4

Pluto—this was the cat's name—was my favorite pet and playmate. I alone fed him, and he attended me wherever I went about the house. It was even with difficulty that I could prevent him from following me through the streets. 5

Our friendship lasted, in this manner, for several years, during which my general temperament and character—through the instrumentality of the Fiend Intemperance—had (I blush to confess it) experienced a radical alteration for the worse. I grew, day by day, more moody, more irritable, more regardless of the feelings of others. I suffered myself to use intemperate language to my wife. At length, I even offered her personal violence. My pets, of course, were made to feel the change in my disposition. I not only neglected, but ill-used them. For Pluto, however, I still retained sufficient regard to restrain me from maltreating him, as I made no scruple of maltreating the rabbits, the monkey, or even the dog, when, by accident, or through affection, they came in my way. But my disease grew upon me—for what disease is like Alcohol!—and at length even Pluto, who was now becoming old, and consequently somewhat peevish—even Pluto began to experience the effects of my ill temper. 6

One night, returning home, much intoxicated, from one of my haunts about town, I fancied that the cat avoided my presence. I seized him; when, in his fright at my violence, he inflicted a slight wound upon my hand with his teeth. The fury of a demon instantly possessed me. I knew myself no longer. My original soul seemed, at once, to take its flight from my body; and a more than fiendish malevolence, gin-nurtured, thrilled every fibre of my frame. I took from my waistcoat-pocket a penknife, opened it, grasped the poor beast by the throat, and deliberately cut one of its eyes from the socket! I blush, I burn, I shudder, while I pen the damnable atrocity. 7

When reason returned with the morning—when I had slept off the fumes of the night's debauch—I experienced a sentiment half of horror, half of remorse, for the crime of which I had been guilty; but it was, at best, a feeble and equivocal feeling, and the soul remained untouched. I again plunged into excess, and soon drowned in wine all memory of the deed. 8

In the meantime the cat slowly recovered. The socket of the lost eye presented, 9 it is true, a frightful appearance, but he no longer appeared to suffer any pain. He went about the house as usual, but, as might be expected, fled in extreme terror at my approach. I had so much of my old heart left, as to be at first grieved by this evident dislike on the part of a creature which had once so loved me. But this feeling soon gave place to irritation. And then came, as if to my final and irrevocable overthrow, the spirit of PERVERSENESS. Of this spirit philosophy takes no account. Yet I am not more sure that my soul lives, than I am that perverseness is one of the primitive impulses of the human heart—one of the indivisible primary faculties, or sentiments, which give direction to the character of Man. Who has not, a hundred times, found himself committing a vile or a stupid action, for no other reason than because he knows he should *not*? Have we not a perpetual inclination, in the teeth of our best judgment, to violate that which is *Law,* merely because we understand it to be such? This spirit of perverseness, I say, came to my final overthrow. It was this unfathomable longing of the soul *to vex itself*—to offer violence to its own nature—to do wrong for the wrong's sake only—that urged me to continue and finally to consummate the injury I had inflicted upon the unoffending brute. One morning, in cold blood, I slipped a noose about its neck and hung it to the limb of a tree;—hung it with the tears streaming from my eyes, and with the bitterest remorse at my heart;—hung it *because* I knew that it had loved me, and *because* I felt it had given me no reason of offence;—hung it *because* I knew that in so doing I was committing a sin—a deadly sin that would so jeopardize my immortal soul as to place it—if such a thing were possible—even beyond the reach of the infinite mercy of the Most Merciful and Most Terrible God.

On the night of the day on which this most cruel deed was done, I was aroused 10 from sleep by the cry of fire. The curtains of my bed were in flames. The whole house was blazing. It was with great difficulty that my wife, a servant, and myself, made our escape from the conflagration. The destruction was complete. My entire worldly wealth was swallowed up, and I resigned myself thenceforward to despair.

I am above the weakness of seeking to establish a sequence of cause and effect, 11 between the disaster and the atrocity. But I am detailing a chain of facts—and wish not to leave even a possible link imperfect. On the day succeeding the fire, I visited the ruins. The walls, with one exception, had fallen in. This exception was found in a compartment wall, not very thick, which stood about the middle of the house, and against which had rested the head of my bed. The plastering had here, in great measure, resisted the action of the fire—a fact which I attributed to its having been recently spread. About this wall a dense crowd were collected, and many persons seemed to be examining a particular portion of it with very minute and eager attention. The words "strange!" "singular!" and other similar expressions, excited my curiosity. I approached and saw, as if graven in *bas-relief* upon the white surface, the figure of a gigantic *cat*. The impression was given with an accuracy truly marvellous. There was a rope about the animal's neck.

When I first beheld this apparition—for I could scarcely regard it as less— 12 my wonder and my terror were extreme. But at length reflection came to my aid. The cat, I remembered, had been hung in a garden adjacent to the house. Upon the alarm of fire, this garden had been immediately filled by the crowd—by some one of whom the animal must have been cut from the tree and thrown, through an open window, into my chamber. This had probably been done with the view of arousing me from sleep. The falling of other walls had compressed the victim of my cruelty into the substance of the freshly spread plaster; the lime of which, with the flames, and the *ammonia* from the carcass, had then accomplished the portraiture as I saw it.

Although I thus readily accounted to my reason, if not altogether to my con-   13
science, for the startling fact just detailed, it did not the less fail to make a deep impression upon my fancy. For months I could not rid myself of the phantasm of the cat; and, during this period, there came back into my spirit a half-sentiment that seemed, but was not, remorse. I went so far as to regret the loss of the animal, and to look about me, among the vile haunts which I now habitually frequented, for another pet of the same species, and of somewhat similar appearance, with which to supply its place.

One night as I sat, half stupefied, in a den of more than infamy, my attention   14
was suddenly drawn to some black object, reposing upon the head of one of the immense hogsheads of gin, or of rum, which constituted the chief furniture of the apartment. I had been looking steadily at the top of this hogshead for some min-utes, and what now caused me surprise was the fact that I had not sooner per-ceived the object thereupon. I approached it, and touched it with my hand. It was a black cat—a very large one—fully as large as Pluto, and closely resembling him in every respect but one. Pluto had not a white hair upon any portion of his body; but this cat had a large, although indefinite splotch of white, covering nearly the whole region of the breast.

Upon my touching him, he immediately arose, purred loudly, rubbed against   15
my hand, and appeared delighted with my notice. This, then, was the very crea-ture of which I was in search. I at once offered to purchase it of the landlord; but this person made no claim to it—knew nothing of it—had never seen it before.

I continued my caresses, and when I prepared to go home, the animal evinced   16
a disposition to accompany me. I permitted it to do so; occasionally stooping and patting it as I proceeded. When it reached the house it domesticated itself at once, and became immediately a great favorite with my wife.

For my own part, I soon found a dislike to it arising within me. This was just   17
the reverse of what I had anticipated; but—I know not how or why it was—its evident fondness for myself rather disgusted and annoyed me. By slow degrees these feelings of disgust and annoyance rose into the bitterness of hatred. I avoided the creature; a certain sense of shame, and the remembrance of my for-mer deed of cruelty, preventing me from physically abusing it. I did not, for some weeks, strike, or otherwise violently ill use it; but gradually—very gradually—I came to look upon it with unutterable loathing, and to flee silently from its odious presence, as from the breath of a pestilence.

What added, no doubt, to my hatred of the beast, was the discovery, on the   18
morning after I brought it home, that, like Pluto, it also had been deprived of one of its eyes. This circumstance, however, only endeared it to my wife, who, as I

have already said, possessed, in a high degree, that humanity of feeling which had once been my distinguishing trait, and the source of many of my simplest and purest pleasures.

With my aversion to this cat, however, its partiality for myself seemed to in-   19
crease. It followed my footsteps with a pertinacity which it would be difficult to make the reader comprehend. Whenever I sat, it would crouch beneath my chair, or spring upon my knees, covering me with its loathsome caresses. If I arose to walk it would get between my feet and thus nearly throw me down, or, fastening its long and sharp claws in my dress, clamber, in this manner, to my breast. At such times, although I longed to destroy it with a blow, I was yet withheld from so doing, partly by a memory of my former crime, but chiefly—let me confess it at once—by absolute *dread* of the beast.

This dread was not exactly a dread of physical evil—and yet I should be at a loss   20
how otherwise to define it. I am almost ashamed to own—yes, even in this felon's cell, I am almost ashamed to own—that the terror and horror with which the an-imal inspired me, had been heightened by one of the merest chimeras it would be possible to conceive. My wife had called my attention, more than once, to the char-acter of the mark of white hair, of which I have spoken, and which constituted the sole visible difference between the strange beast and the one I had destroyed. The reader will remember that this mark, although large, had been originally very indefinite; but, by slow degrees—degrees nearly imperceptible, and which for a long time my reason struggled to reject as fanciful—it had, at length, assumed a rigorous distinctness of outline. It was now the representation of an object that I shudder to name—and for this, above all, I loathed, and dreaded, and would have rid myself of the monster *had I dared*—it was now, I say, the image of a hideous—of a ghastly thing—of the GALLOWS!—oh, mournful and terrible engine of Hor-ror and of Crime—of Agony and of Death!

And now was I indeed wretched beyond the wretchedness of mere Humanity.   21
And *a brute beast*—whose fellow I had contemptuously destroyed—*a brute beast* to work out for *me*—for me, a man fashioned in the image of the High God—so much of insufferable woe! Alas! neither by day nor by night knew I the blessing of rest any more! During the former the creature left me no moment alone, and in the latter I started hourly from dreams of unutterable fear to find the hot breath of *the thing* upon my face, and its vast weight—an incarnate nightmare that I had no power to shake off—incumbent eternally upon my *heart!*

Beneath the pressure of torments such as these the feeble remnant of the good   22
within me succumbed. Evil thoughts became my sole intimates—the darkest and most evil of thoughts. The moodiness of my usual temper increased to hatred of all things and of all mankind; while from the sudden, frequent, and ungovernable outbursts of a fury to which I now blindly abandoned myself, my uncomplaining wife, alas, was the most usual and the most patient of sufferers.

One day she accompanied me, upon some household errand, into the cellar   23
of the old building which our poverty compelled us to inhabit. The cat followed me down the steep stairs, and, nearly throwing me headlong, exasperated me to madness. Uplifting an axe, and forgetting in my wrath the childish dread which

had hitherto stayed my hand, I aimed a blow at the animal, which, of course, would have proved instantly fatal had it descended as I wished. But this blow was arrested by the hand of my wife. Goaded by the interference into a rage more than demoniacal, I withdrew my arm from her grasp and buried the axe in her brain. She fell dead upon the spot without a groan.

This hideous murder accomplished, I set myself forthwith, and with entire 24 deliberation, to the task of concealing the body. I knew that I could not remove it from the house, either by day or by night, without the risk of being observed by the neighbors. Many projects entered my mind. At one period I thought of cutting the corpse into minute fragments, and destroying them by fire. At another, I resolved to dig a grave for it in the floor of the cellar. Again, I deliberated about casting it in the well in the yard—about packing it in a box, as if merchandise, with the usual arrangements, and so getting a porter to take it from the house. Finally I hit upon what I considered a far better expedient than either of these. I determined to wall it up in the cellar, as the monks of the Middle Ages are recorded to have walled up their victims.

For a purpose such as this the cellar was well adapted. Its walls were loosely 25 constructed, and had lately been plastered throughout with a rough plaster, which the dampness of the atmosphere had prevented from hardening. Moreover, in one of the walls was a projection, caused by a false chimney, or fireplace, that had been filled up and made to resemble the rest of the cellar. I made no doubt that I could readily displace the bricks at this point, insert the corpse, and wall the whole up as before, so that no eye could detect any thing suspicious.

And in this calculation I was not deceived. By means of a crowbar I easily dis- 26 lodged the bricks, and, having carefully deposited the body against the inner wall, I propped it in that position, while with little trouble I relaid the whole structure as it originally stood. Having procured mortar, sand, and hair, with every possible precaution, I prepared a plaster which could not be distinguished from the old, and with this I very carefully went over the new brick-work. When I had finished, I felt satisfied that all was right. The wall did not present the slightest appearance of having been disturbed. The rubbish on the floor was picked up with the minutest care. I looked around triumphantly, and said to myself: "Here at least, then, my labor has not been in vain."

My next step was to look for the beast which had been the cause of so much 27 wretchedness; for I had, at length, firmly resolved to put it to death. Had I been able to meet with it at the moment, there could have been no doubt of its fate; but it appeared that the crafty animal had been alarmed at the violence of my previous anger, and forbore to present itself in my present mood. It is impossible to describe or to imagine the deep, the blissful sense of relief which the absence of the detested creature occasioned in my bosom. It did not make its appearance during the night; and thus for one night, at least, since its introduction into the house, I soundly and tranquilly slept; aye, *slept* even with the burthen of murder upon my soul.

The second and the third day passed, and still my tormentor came not. Once 28 again I breathed as a freeman. The monster, in terror, had fled the premises for ever! I should behold it no more! My happiness was supreme! The guilt of my dark deed disturbed me but little. Some few inquiries had been made, but these had been readily answered. Even a search had been instituted—but of course nothing was to be discovered. I looked upon my future felicity as secured.

Upon the fourth day of the assassination, a party of the police came, very un- 29 expectedly, into the house, and proceeded again to make rigorous investigation of the premises. Secure, however, in the inscrutability of my place of concealment, I felt no embarrassment whatever. The officers bade me accompany them in their search. They left no nook or corner unexplored. At length, for the third or fourth time, they descended into the cellar. I quivered not in a muscle. My heart beat calmly as that of one who slumbers in innocence. I walked the cellar from end to end. I folded my arms upon my bosom, and roamed easily to and fro. The police were thoroughly satisfied and prepared to depart. The glee at my heart was too strong to be restrained. I burned to say if but one word, by way of triumph, and to render doubly sure their assurance of my guiltlessness.

"Gentlemen," I said at last, as the party ascended the steps, "I delight to have al- 30 layed your suspicions. I wish you all health and a little more courtesy. By the bye, gentlemen, this—this is a very well-constructed house" (in the rabid desire to say something easily, I scarcely knew what I uttered at all),—"I may say an *excellently* well-constructed house. These walls—are you going, gentlemen?—these walls are solidly put together"; and here, through the mere frenzy of bravado, I rapped heavily with a cane which I held in my hand, upon that very portion of the brick-work behind which stood the corpse of the wife of my bosom.

But may God shield and deliver me from the fangs of the Arch-Fiend! No 31 sooner had the reverberation of my blows sunk into silence, than I was answered by a voice from within the tomb!—by a cry, at first muffled and broken, like the sobbing of a child, and then quickly swelling into one long, loud, and continuous scream, utterly anomalous and inhuman—a howl—a wailing shriek, half of horror and half of triumph, such as might have arisen only out of hell, conjointly from the throats of the damned in their agony and of the demons that exult in the damnation.

Of my own thoughts it is folly to speak. Swooning, I staggered to the opposite 32 wall. For one instant the party on the stairs remained motionless, through extremity of terror and awe. In the next a dozen stout arms were toiling at the wall. It fell bodily. The corpse, already greatly decayed and clotted with gore, stood erect before the eyes of the spectators. Upon its head, with red extended mouth and solitary eye of fire, sat the hideous beast whose craft had seduced me into murder, and whose informing voice had consigned me to the hangman. I had walled the monster up within the tomb.

ACTIVITIES FOR WRITING AND DISCUSSION

1. Would you describe the narrator as reliable or **unreliable?** Explain. What factors or influences impel his bizarre and brutal actions?

2. The narrator professes to have killed two cats because they loved him, and his third murder victim—his wife—appears to have been a model of patient forbearance and endurance.

    a. Get inside the narrator's household and invent some scenes that dramatize, and perhaps even explain, these "perverse" domestic relationships.

    b. With a partner or small group, speculate on what the cats might symbolize (there are several possibilities).

3. Write a "Poe" story of your own using a first-person narrator.

4. In addition to being a writer of tales and poems, Poe was a respected literary critic. Read the 1842 review of Nathaniel Hawthorne's *Twice-Told Tales* in which Poe articulates his own theory of the short story. Then write an essay discussing how "The Black Cat" embodies—or fails to embody—Poe's theory.

CLARICE LISPECTOR (1924–1977)

The Smallest Woman in the World

In the depths of Equatorial Africa the French explorer, Marcel Pretre, hunter and 1 man of the world, came across a tribe of surprisingly small pygmies. Therefore he was even more surprised when he was informed that a still smaller people existed, beyond forests and distances. So he plunged farther on.

In the Eastern Congo, near Lake Kivu, he really did discover the smallest pyg- 2 mies in the world. And—like a box within a box within a box—obedient, perhaps, to the necessity nature sometimes feels of outdoing herself—among the smallest pygmies in the world there was the smallest of the smallest pygmies in the world.

Among mosquitoes and lukewarm trees, among leaves of the most rich and 3 lazy green, Marcel Pretre found himself facing a woman seventeen and three-quarter inches high, full-grown, black, silent—"Black as a monkey," he informed the press—who lived in a treetop with her little spouse. In the tepid miasma of the jungle, that swells the fruits so early and gives them an almost intolerable sweetness, she was pregnant.

So there she stood, the smallest woman in the world. For an instant, in the 4 buzzing heat, it seemed as if the Frenchman had unexpectedly reached his final destination. Probably only because he was not insane, his soul neither wavered nor broke its bounds. Feeling an immediate necessity for order and for giving names to what exists, he called her Little Flower. And in order to be able to classify her among the recognizable realities, he immediately began to collect facts about her.

Her race will soon be exterminated. Few examples are left of this species, which, 5 if it were not for the sly dangers of Africa, might have multiplied. Besides disease, the deadly effluvium of the water, insufficient food, and ranging beasts, the great threat to the Likoualas are the savage Bahundes, a threat that surrounds them in the silent air, like the dawn of battle. The Bahundes hunt them with nets, like monkeys. And eat them. Like that: they catch them in nets and *eat* them. The tiny race, retreating, always retreating, has finished hiding away in the heart of Africa, where the lucky explorer discovered it. For strategic defense, they live in the highest trees. The women descend to grind and cook corn and to gather vegetables, the men to hunt. When a child is born, it is left free almost immediately. It is true that, what with the beasts, the child frequently cannot enjoy this freedom for very long. But then it is true that it cannot be lamented that for such a short life there had been any long, hard work. And even the language that the child learns is short and simple, merely the essentials. The Likoualas use few names; they name things by gestures and animal noises. As for things of the spirit, they have a drum. While they dance to the sound of the drum, a little male stands guard against the Bahundes, who come from no one knows where.

That was the way, then, that the explorer discovered, standing at his very feet, 6 the smallest existing human thing. His heart beat, because no emerald in the world is so rare. The teachings of the wise men of India are not so rare. The richest man in the world has never set eyes on such strange grace. Right there was a woman that the greed of the most exquisite dream could never have imagined. It was then that the explorer said timidly, and with a delicacy of feeling of which his wife would never have thought him capable: "You are Little Flower."

At that moment, Little Flower scratched herself where no one scratches. The 7 explorer—as if he were receiving the highest prize for chastity to which an idealistic man dares aspire—the explorer, experienced as he was, looked the other way.

A photograph of Little Flower was published in the colored supplement of the 8 Sunday Papers, life-size. She was wrapped in a cloth, her belly already very big. The flat nose, the black face, the splay feet. She looked like a dog.

On that Sunday, in an apartment, a woman seeing the picture of Little Flower 9 in the paper didn't want to look a second time because "It gives me the creeps."

In another apartment, a lady felt such perverse tenderness for the smallest of 10 the African women that—an ounce of prevention being worth a pound of cure— Little Flower could never be left alone to the tenderness of that lady. Who knows to what murkiness of love tenderness can lead? The woman was upset all day, almost as if she were missing something. Besides, it was spring and there was a dangerous leniency in the air.

In another house, a little girl of five, seeing the picture and hearing the com- 11 ments, was extremely surprised. In a houseful of adults, this little girl had been the smallest human being up until now. And, if this was the source of all caresses, it was also the source of the first fear of the tyranny of love. The existence of Little Flower made the little girl feel—with a deep uneasiness that only years and years later, and for very different reasons, would turn into thought—made her feel, in her first wisdom, that "sorrow is endless."

In another house, in the consecration of spring, a girl about to be married felt 12 an ecstacy of pity: "Mama, look at her little picture, poor little thing! Just look how sad she is!"

"But," said the mother, hard and defeated and proud, "it's the sadness of an 13
animal. It isn't human sadness."

"Oh, Mama!" said the girl, discouraged.   14

In another house, a clever little boy had a clever idea: "Mummy, if I could put 15
this little woman from Africa in little Paul's bed when he's asleep? When he woke
up wouldn't he be frightened? Wouldn't he howl? When he saw her sitting on his
bed? And then we'd play with her! She would be our toy!"

His mother was setting her hair in front of the bathroom mirror at the moment, 16
and she remembered what a cook had told her about life in an orphanage. The or-
phans had no dolls, and, with terrible maternity already throbbing in their hearts,
the little girls had hidden the death of one of the children from the nun. They kept
the body in a cupboard and when the nun went out they played with the dead child,
giving her baths and things to eat, punishing her only to be able to kiss and console
her. In the bathroom, the mother remembered this, and let fall her thoughtful
hands, full of curlers. She considered the cruel necessity of loving. And she considered the malignity of our desire for happiness. She considered how ferociously we
need to play. How many times we will kill for love. Then she looked at her clever
child as if she were looking at a dangerous stranger. And she had a horror of her
own soul that, more than her body, had engendered that being, adept at life and
happiness. She looked at him attentively and with uncomfortable pride, that child
who had already lost two front teeth, evolution evolving itself, teeth falling out to
give place to those that could bite better. "I'm going to buy him a new suit," she decided, looking at him, absorbed. Obstinately, she adorned her gap-toothed son
with fine clothes; obstinately, she wanted him very clean, as if his cleanliness could
emphasize a soothing superficiality, obstinately perfecting the polite side of beauty.
Obstinately drawing away from, and drawing him away from, something that
ought to be "black as a monkey." Then, looking in the bathroom mirror, the
mother gave a deliberately refined and social smile, placing a distance of insuper-
able millenniums between the abstract lines of her features and the crude face
of Little Flower. But, with years of practice, she knew that this was going to be a
Sunday on which she would have to hide from herself anxiety, dreams, and lost
millenniums.

In another house, they gave themselves up to the enthralling task of measur- 17
ing the seventeen and three-quarter inches of Little Flower against the wall. And,
really, it was a delightful surprise: she was even smaller than the sharpest imagination could have pictured. In the heart of each member of the family was born,
nostalgic, the desire to have that tiny and indomitable thing for itself, that thing
spared having been eaten, that permanent source of charity. The avid family soul
wanted to devote itself. To tell the truth, who hasn't wanted to own a human being just for himself? Which, it is true, wouldn't always be convenient; there are
times when one doesn't want to have feelings.

"I bet if she lived here it would end in a fight," said the father, sitting in the 18
armchair and definitely turning the page of the newspaper. "In this house everything ends in a fight."

"Oh, you, José—always a pessimist," said the mother.   19

"But, Mama, have you thought of the size her baby's going to be?" said the old- 20
est little girl, aged thirteen, eagerly.

The father stirred uneasily behind his paper.   21

"It should be the smallest black baby in the world," the mother answered, 22
melting with pleasure. "Imagine her serving our table, with her big little belly!"

"That's enough!" growled father.   23

"But you have to admit," said the mother, unexpectedly offended, "that it is 24
something very rare. You're the insensitive one."

And the rare thing itself?   25

In the meanwhile, in Africa, the rare thing herself, in her heart—and who 26
knows if the heart wasn't black, too, since once nature has erred she can no longer
be trusted—the rare thing herself had something even rarer in her heart, like the
secret of her own secret: a minimal child. Methodically, the explorer studied that
little belly of the smallest mature human being. It was at this moment that the explorer, for the first time since he had known her, instead of feeling curiosity, or
exaltation, or victory, or the scientific spirit, felt sick.

The smallest woman in the world was laughing.   27

She was laughing, warm, warm—Little Flower was enjoying life. The rare thing 28
herself was experiencing the ineffable sensation of not having been eaten yet. Not
having been eaten yet was something that at any other time would have given her
the agile impulse to jump from branch to branch. But, in this moment of tranquility, amid the thick leaves of the Eastern Congo, she was not putting this impulse into action—it was entirely concentrated in the smallness of the rare thing
itself. So she was laughing. It was a laugh such as only one who does not speak
laughs. It was a laugh that the explorer, constrained, couldn't classify. And she kept
on enjoying her own soft laugh, she who wasn't being devoured. Not to be devoured is the most perfect feeling. Not to be devoured is the secret goal of a whole
life. While she was not being eaten, her bestial laughter was as delicate as joy is
delicate. The explorer was baffled.

In the second place, if the rare thing herself was laughing, it was because, 29
within her smallness, a great darkness had begun to move.

The rare thing herself felt in her breast a warmth that might be called love. She 30
loved that sallow explorer. If she could have talked and had told him that she loved
him, he would have been puffed up with vanity. Vanity that would have collapsed
when she added that she also loved the explorer's ring very much, and the explorer's boots. And when that collapse had taken place, Little Flower would not
have understood why. Because her love for the explorer—one might even say
"profound love," since, having no other resources, she was reduced to profun-
dity—her profound love for the explorer would not have been at all diminished by
the fact that she also loved his boots. There is an old misunderstanding about the
word love, and, if many children are born from this misunderstanding, many others have lost the unique chance of being born, only because of the susceptibility

that demands that it be me! me! that is loved, and not my money. But in the humidity of the forest these cruel refinements do not exist, and love is not to be eaten, love is to find a boot pretty, love is to like the strange color of a man who isn't black, is to laugh for love of a shiny ring. Little Flower blinked with love, and laughed warmly, small, gravid, warm.

The explorer tried to smile back, without knowing exactly to what abyss his 31 smile responded, and then he was embarrassed as only a very big man can be embarrassed. He pretended to adjust his explorer's hat better; he colored, prudishly. He turned a lovely color, a greenish-pink, like a lime at sunrise. He was undoubtedly sour.

Perhaps adjusting the symbolic helmet helped the explorer to get control 32 of himself, severely recapture the discipline of his work, and go on with his note-taking. He had learned how to understand some of the tribe's few articulate words, and to interpret their signs. By now, he could ask questions.

Little Flower answered "Yes." That it was very nice to have a tree of her own to 33 live in. Because—she didn't say this but her eyes became so dark that they said it—because it is good to own, good to own, good to own. The explorer winked several times.

Marcel Pretre had some difficult moments with himself. But at least he kept 34 busy taking notes. Those who didn't take notes had to manage as best they could:

"Well," suddenly declared one old lady, folding up the newspaper decisively, 35 "well, as I always say: God knows what He's doing."

— Translated by Elizabeth Bishop

ACTIVITIES FOR WRITING AND DISCUSSION

1. Describe the narrative **point of view** in the story. Could the story "work" as well or have the same effect if told from a different point of view than the one Lispector chose? Explain.

2. Annotate the different reactions people have to the photograph of "Little Flower" in the newspaper. How do you account for the wide diversity of reactions? Do the various viewers of the picture identify with "Little Flower"? objectify her? What does each person see? Explain your answer and its implications for the meaning of the story.

3. Identify and interpret any examples of **irony** or **verbal irony** in the story.

4. Respond to the story using any of the "Ten Ideas for Writing" on page 35.

5. Research the cultural context of Lispector's writings and of "The Smallest Woman in the World" specifically. Can the story be read as a critique of European colonialism? What other interpretations are possible?

MARGARET ATWOOD (b. 1939)

The Man from Mars

A long time ago Christine was walking through the park. She was still wearing her 1
tennis dress; she hadn't had time to shower and change, and her hair was held
back with an elastic band. Her chunky reddish face, exposed with no softening
fringe, looked like a Russian peasant's, but without the elastic band the hair got in
her eyes. The afternoon was too hot for April; the indoor courts had been steaming, her skin felt poached.

The sun had brought the old men out from wherever they spent the winter: 2
she had read a story recently about one who lived for three years in a manhole.
They sat weedishly on the benches or lay on the grass with their heads on squares
of used newspaper. As she passed, their wrinkled toadstool faces drifted towards
her, drawn by the movement of her body, then floated away again, uninterested.

The squirrels were out, too, foraging; two or three of them moved towards her 3
in darts and pauses, eyes fixed on her expectantly, mouths with the ratlike receding chins open to show the yellowed front teeth. Christine walked faster, she had
nothing to give them. People shouldn't feed them, she thought; it makes them
anxious and they get mangy.

Halfway across the park she stopped to take off her cardigan. As she bent over 4
to pick up her tennis racquet again someone touched her on her freshly bared
arm. Christine seldom screamed; she straightened up suddenly, gripping the
handle of her racquet. It was not one of the old men, however; it was a dark-
haired boy of twelve or so.

"Excuse me," he said, "I search for Economics Building. Is it there?" He mo- 5
tioned towards the west.

Christine looked at him more closely. She had been mistaken: he was not 6
young, just short. He came a little above her shoulder, but then, she was above the
average height; "statuesque," her mother called it when she was straining. He was
also what was referred to in their family as "a person from another culture": oriental without a doubt, though perhaps not Chinese. Christine judged he must be
a foreign student and gave him her official welcoming smile. In high school she
had been president of the United Nations Club; that year her school had been
picked to represent the Egyptian delegation at the Mock Assembly. It had been an
unpopular assignment—nobody wanted to be the Arabs—but she had seen it
through. She had made rather a good speech about the Palestinian refugees.

"Yes," she said, "that's it over there. The one with the flat roof. See it?" 7

The man had been smiling nervously at her the whole time. He was wearing 8
glasses with transparent plastic rims, through which his eyes bulged up at her as
though through a goldfish bowl. He had not followed where she was pointing. Instead he thrust towards her a small green paper and a ball-point pen.

"You make map," he said. 9

Christine set down her tennis racquet and drew a careful map. "We are here," 10
she said, pronouncing distinctly. "You go this way. The building is here." She indicated the route with a dotted line and an X. The man leaned close to her, watching the progress of the map attentively; he smelled of cooked cauliflower and an
unfamiliar brand of hair grease. When she had finished Christine handed the paper and pen back to him with a terminal smile.

"Wait," the man said. He tore the piece of paper with the map off the pad, 11
folded it carefully and put it in his jacket pocket; the jacket sleeves came down
over his wrists and had threads at the edges. He began to write something; she noticed with a slight feeling of revulsion that his nails and the ends of his fingers were
so badly bitten they seemed almost deformed. Several of his fingers were blue
from the leaky ball-point.

"Here is my name," he said, holding the pad out to her.   12

Christine read an odd assemblage of Gs, Ys and Ns, neatly printed in block let- 13
ters. "Thank you," she said.

"You now write *your* name," he said, extending the pen.   14

Christine hesitated. If this had been a person from her own culture she would 15
have thought he was trying to pick her up. But then, people from her own culture
never tried to pick her up; she was too big. The only one who had made the attempt was the Moroccan waiter at the beer parlour where they sometimes went
after meetings, and he had been direct. He had just intercepted her on the way to
the Ladies' Room and asked and she said no; that had been that. This man was not
a waiter though, but a student; she didn't want to offend him. In his culture, whatever it was, this exchange of names on pieces of paper was probably a formal politeness, like saying thank you. She took the pen from him.

"That is a very pleasant name," he said. He folded the paper and placed it in 16
his jacket with the map.

Christine felt she had done her duty. "Well, goodbye," she said. "It was nice 17
to have met you." She bent for her tennis racquet but he had already stooped and
retrieved it and was holding it with both hands in front of him, like a captured
banner.

"I carry this for you."   18

"Oh no, please. Don't bother, I am in a hurry," she said, articulating clearly. 19
Deprived of her tennis racquet she felt weaponless. He started to saunter along the
path; he was not nervous at all now, he seemed completely at ease.

"*Vous parlez français?*" he asked conversationally.   20

"*Oui, un petit peu,*" she said. "Not very well." How am I going to get my rac- 21
quet away from him without being rude? she was wondering.

"*Mais vous avez un bel accent.*" His eyes goggled at her through the glasses: was 22
he being flirtatious? She was well aware that her accent was wretched.

"Look," she said, for the first time letting her impatience show, "I really have 23
to go. Give me my racquet, please."

He quickened his pace but gave no sign of returning the racquet. "Where you 24
are going?"

"Home," she said. "My house."   25

"I go with you now," he said hopefully.   26

"*No*," she said: she would have to be firm with him. She made a lunge and got   27
a grip on her racquet; after a brief tug of war it came free.

"Goodbye," she said, turning away from his puzzled face and setting off at   28
what she hoped was a discouraging jog-trot. It was like walking away from a
growling dog: you shouldn't let on you were frightened. Why should she be frightened anyway? He was only half her size and she had the tennis racquet, there was
nothing he could do to her.

Although she did not look back she could tell he was still following. Let there   29
be a streetcar, she thought, and there was one, but it was far down the line, stuck
behind a red light. He appeared at her side, breathing audibly, a moment after she
reached the stop. She gazed ahead, rigid.

"You are my friend," he said tentatively.   30

Christine relented: he hadn't been trying to pick her up after all, he was a   31
stranger, he just wanted to meet some of the local people; in his place she would
have wanted the same thing.

"Yes," she said, doling him out a smile.   32

"That is good," he said. "My country is very far."   33

Christine couldn't think of an apt reply. "That's interesting," she said. "*Très in-*   34
teressant." The streetcar was coming at last; she opened her purse and got out a
ticket.

"I go with you now," he said. His hand clamped on her arm above the elbow.   35

"You . . . stay . . . *here*," Christine said, resisting the impulse to shout but paus-   36
ing between each word as though for a deaf person. She detached his hand—his
hold was quite feeble and could not compete with her tennis biceps—and leapt
off the curb and up the streetcar steps, hearing with relief the doors grind shut behind her. Inside the car and a block away she permitted herself a glance out a side
window. He was standing where she had left him; he seemed to be writing something on his little pad of paper.

When she reached home she had only time for a snack, and even then she was   37
almost late for the Debating Society. The topic was, "Resolved: That War Is Obsolete." Her team took the affirmative and won.

Christine came out of her last examination feeling depressed. It was not the   38
exam that depressed her but the fact that it was the last one: it meant the end of
the school year. She dropped into the coffee shop as usual, then went home early
because there didn't seem to be anything else to do.

"Is that you, dear?" her mother called from the living room. She must have   39
heard the front door close. Christine went in and flopped on the sofa, disturbing
the neat pattern of cushions.

"How was your exam, dear?" her mother asked.   40

"Fine," said Christine flatly. It had been fine; she had passed. She was not a   41
brilliant student, she knew that, but she was conscientious. Her professors always
wrote things like "A serious attempt" and "Well thought out but perhaps lacking
in élan" on her term papers; they gave her Bs, the occasional B+. She was taking

Political Science and Economics, and hoped for a job with the Government after she graduated; with her father's connections she had a good chance.

"That's nice."   42

Christine felt, resentfully, that her mother had only a hazy idea of what an   43 exam was. She was arranging gladioli in a vase; she had rubber gloves on to protect her hands as she always did when engaged in what she called "housework." As far as Christine could tell her housework consisted of arranging flowers in vases: daffodils and tulips and hyacinths through gladioli, irises and roses, all the way to asters and mums. Sometimes she cooked, elegantly and with chafing-dishes, but she thought of it as a hobby. The girl did everything else. Christine thought it faintly sinful to have a girl. The only ones available now were either foreign or pregnant; their expressions usually suggested they were being taken advantage of somehow. But her mother asked what they would do otherwise; they'd either have to go into a Home or stay in their own countries, and Christine had to agree this was probably true. It was hard, anyway, to argue with her mother. She was so delicate, so preserved-looking, a harsh breath would scratch the finish.

"An interesting young man phoned today," her mother said. She had finished   44 the gladioli and was taking off her rubber gloves. "He asked to speak with you and when I said you weren't in we had quite a little chat. You didn't tell me about him, dear." She put on the glasses which she wore on a decorative chain around her neck, a signal that she was in her modern, intelligent mood rather than her old-fashioned whimsical one.

"Did he leave his name?" Christine asked. She knew a lot of young men but   45 they didn't often call her; they conducted their business with her in the coffee shop or after meetings.

"He's a person from another culture. He said he would call back later."   46

Christine had to think a moment. She was vaguely acquainted with several   47 people from other cultures, Britain mostly; they belonged to the Debating Society.

"He's studying Philosophy in Montreal," her mother prompted. "He sounded   48 French."

Christine began to remember the man in the park. "I don't think he's French,   49 exactly," she said.

Her mother had taken off her glasses again and was poking absentmindedly at   50 a bent gladiolus. "Well, he sounded French." She meditated, flowery sceptre in hand. "I think it would be nice if you had him to tea."

Christine's mother did her best. She had two other daughters, both of whom   51 took after her. They were beautiful; one was well married already and the other would clearly have no trouble. Her friends consoled her about Christine by saying, "She's not fat, she's just big-boned, it's the father's side," and "Christine is so healthy." Her other daughters had never gotten involved in activities when they were at school, but since Christine could not possibly ever be beautiful even if she took off weight, it was just as well she was so athletic and political, it was a good thing she had interests. Christine's mother tried to encourage her interests whenever possible. Christine could tell when she was making an extra effort, there was a reproaching edge to her voice.

She knew her mother expected enthusiasm but she could not supply it. "I 52
don't know, I'll have to see," she said dubiously.

"You look tired, darling," said her mother. "Perhaps you'd like a glass of milk." 53

Christine was in the bathtub when the phone rang. She was not prone to fan- 54
tasy but when she was in the bathtub she often pretended she was a dolphin, a
game left over from one of the girls who used to bathe her when she was small.
Her mother was being bell-voiced and gracious in the hall; then there was a tap at
the door.

"It's that nice young French student, Christine," her mother said. 55

"Tell him I'm in the bathtub," Christine said, louder than necessary. "He isn't 56
French."

She could hear her mother frowning. "That wouldn't be very polite, Christine. 57
I don't think he'd understand."

"Oh, all right," Christine said. She heaved herself out of the bathtub, swathed 58
her pink bulk in a towel and splattered to the phone.

"Hello," she said gruffly. At a distance he was not pathetic, he was a nuisance. 59
She could not imagine how he had tracked her down: most likely he went through
the phone book, calling all the numbers with her last name until he hit on the
right one.

"It is your friend." 60

"I know," she said. "How are you?" 61

"I am very fine." There was a long pause, during which Christine had a vicious 62
urge to say, "Well goodbye then," and hang up; but she was aware of her mother
poised figurine-like in her bedroom doorway. Then he said, "I hope you also are
very fine."

"Yes," said Christine. She wasn't going to participate. 63

"I come to tea," he said. 64

This took Christine by surprise. "You do?" 65

"Your pleasant mother ask me. I come Thursday, four o'clock." 66

"Oh," Christine said, ungraciously. 67

"See you then," he said, with the conscious pride of one who has mastered a 68
difficult idiom.

Christine set down the phone and went along the hall. Her mother was in her 69
study, sitting innocently at her writing desk.

"Did you ask him to tea on Thursday?" 70

"Not exactly, dear," her mother said. "I did mention he might come round to 71
tea *some*time, though."

"Well, he's coming Thursday. Four o'clock." 72

"What's wrong with that?" her mother said serenely. "I think it's a very nice 73
gesture for us to make. I do think you might try to be a little more co-operative."
She was pleased with herself.

"Since you invited him," said Christine, "you can bloody well stick around and 74
help me entertain him. I don't want to be left making nice gestures all by myself."

"Christine, *dear*," her mother said, above being shocked. "You ought to put 75
on your dressing gown, you'll catch a chill."

After sulking for an hour Christine tried to think of the tea as a cross between 76
an examination and an executive meeting: not enjoyable, certainly, but to be got
through as tactfully as possible. And it *was* a nice gesture. When the cakes her
mother had ordered arrived from The Patisserie on Thursday morning she began
to feel slightly festive; she even resolved to put on a dress, a good one, instead of
a skirt and blouse. After all, she had nothing against him, except the memory of
the way he had grabbed her tennis racquet and then her arm. She suppressed a
quick impossible vision of herself pursued around the living room, fending him
off with thrown sofa cushions and vases of gladioli; nevertheless she told the girl
they would have tea in the garden. It would be a treat for him, and there was more
space outdoors.

She had suspected her mother would dodge the tea, would contrive to be go- 77
ing out just as he was arriving: that way she could size him up and then leave them
alone together. She had done things like that to Christine before; the excuse this
time was the Symphony Committee. Sure enough, her mother carefully mislaid
her gloves and located them with a faked murmur of joy when the doorbell rang.
Christine relished for weeks afterwards the image of her mother's dropped jaw
and flawless recovery when he was introduced: he wasn't quite the foreign poten-
tate her optimistic, veil-fragile mind had concocted.

He was prepared for celebration. He had slicked on so much hair cream that 78
his head seemed to be covered with a tight black patent-leather cap, and he had
cut the threads off his jacket sleeves. His orange tie was overpoweringly splendid.
Christine noticed, however, as he shook her mother's suddenly braced white
glove that the ball-point ink on his fingers was indelible. His face had broken out,
possibly in anticipation of the delights in store for him; he had a tiny camera slung
over his shoulder and was smoking an exotic-smelling cigarette.

Christine led him through the cool flowery softly padded living room and out 79
by the French doors into the garden. "You sit here," she said. "I will have the girl
bring tea."

This girl was from the West Indies: Christine's parents had been enraptured 80
with her when they were down at Christmas and had brought her back with them.
Since that time she had become pregnant, but Christine's mother had not dismissed her. She said she was slightly disappointed but what could you expect, and
she didn't see any real difference between a girl who was pregnant before you
hired her and one who got that way afterwards. She prided herself on her toler-
ance; also there was a scarcity of girls. Strangely enough, the girl became progressively less easy to get along with. Either she did not share Christine's mother's view
of her own generosity, or she felt she had gotten away with something and was
therefore free to indulge in contempt. At first Christine had tried to treat her as
an equal. "Don't call me 'Miss Christine,'" she had said with an imitation of light,
comradely laughter. "What you want me to call you then?" the girl had said,
scowling. They had begun to have brief, surly arguments in the kitchen, which
Christine decided were like the arguments between one servant and another: her
mother's attitude towards each of them was similar, they were not altogether satisfactory but they would have to do.

The cakes, glossy with icing, were set out on a plate and the teapot was stand- 81
ing ready; on the counter the electric kettle boiled. Christine headed for it, but the
girl, till then sitting with her elbows on the kitchen table and watching her ex-
pressionlessly, made a dash and intercepted her. Christine waited until she had
poured the water into the pot. Then, "I'll carry it out, Elvira," she said. She had
just decided she didn't want the girl to see her visitor's orange tie; already, she
knew, her position in the girl's eyes had suffered because no one had yet attempted
to get *her* pregnant.

"What you think they pay me for, Miss Christine?" the girl said insolently. She 82
swung towards the garden with the tray; Christine trailed her, feeling lumpish and
awkward. The girl was at least as big as she was but in a different way.

"Thank you, Elvira," Christine said when the tray was in place. The girl de- 83
parted without a word, casting a disdainful backward glance at the frayed jacket
sleeves, the stained fingers. Christine was now determined to be especially kind
to him.

"You are very rich," he said. 84

"No," Christine protested, shaking her head, "we're not." She had never 85
thought of her family as rich; it was one of her father's sayings that nobody made
any money with the Government.

"Yes," he repeated, "you are very rich." He sat back in his lawn chair, gazing 86
about him as though dazed.

Christine set his cup of tea in front of him. She wasn't in the habit of paying 87
much attention to the house or the garden; they were nothing special, far from
being the largest on the street; other people took care of them. But now she
looked where he was looking, seeing it all as though from a different height: the
long expanses, the border flowers blazing in the early-summer sunlight, the
flagged patio and walks, the high walls and the silence.

He came back to her face, sighing a little. "My English is not good," he said, 88
"but I improve."

"You do," Christine said, nodding encouragement. 89

He took sips of his tea, quickly and tenderly, as though afraid of injuring the 90
cup. "I like to stay here."

Christine passed him the cakes. He took only one, making a slight face as he 91
ate it; but he had several more cups of tea while she finished the cakes. She managed to find out from him that he had come over on a church fellowship—she
could not decode the denomination—and was studying Philosophy or Theology,
or possibly both. She was feeling well-disposed towards him: he had behaved
himself, he had caused her no inconvenience.

The teapot was at last empty. He sat up straight in his chair, as though alerted 92
by a soundless gong. "You look this way, please," he said. Christine saw that he
had placed his miniature camera on the stone sundial her mother had shipped
back from England two years before. He wanted to take her picture. She was flattered, and settled herself to pose, smiling evenly.

He took off his glasses and laid them beside his plate. For a moment she saw 93
his myopic, unprotected eyes turned towards her, with something tremulous and

confiding in them she wanted to close herself off from knowing about. Then he went over and did something to the camera, his back to her. The next instant he was crouched beside her, his arm around her waist as far as it could reach, his other hand covering her own hands which she had folded in her lap, his cheek jammed up against hers. She was too startled to move. The camera clicked.

He stood up at once and replaced his glasses, which glittered now with a sad   94 triumph. "Thank you, miss," he said to her. "I go now." He slung the camera back over his shoulder, keeping his hand on it as though to hold the lid on and prevent escape. "I send to my family; they will like."

He was out the gate and gone before Christine had recovered; then she   95 laughed. She had been afraid he would attack her, she could admit it now, and he had; but not in the usual way. He had raped, *rapeo, rapere, rapui, to seize and carry off*, not herself but her celluloid image, and incidently that of the silver tea service, which glinted mockingly at her as the girl bore it away, carrying it regally, the insignia, the official jewels.

Christine spent the summer as she had for the past three years: she was the   96 sailing instructress at an expensive all-girls camp near Algonquin Park. She had been a camper there, everything was familiar to her; she sailed almost better than she played tennis.

The second week she got a letter from him, postmarked Montreal and for-   97 warded from her home address. It was printed in block letters on a piece of the green paper, two or three sentences. It began, "I hope you are well," then described the weather in monosyllables and ended, "I am fine." It was signed, "Your friend." Each week she got another of these letters, more or less identical. In one of them a colour print was enclosed: himself, slightly cross-eyed and grinning hilariously, even more spindly than she remembered him against her billowing draperies, flowers exploding around them like firecrackers, one of his hands an equivocal blur in her lap, the other out of sight; on her own face, astonishment and outrage, as though he was sticking her in the behind with his hidden thumb.

She answered the first letter, but after that the seniors were in training for the   98 races. At the end of the summer, packing to go home, she threw all the letters away.

When she had been back for several weeks she received another of the green   99 letters. This time there was a return address printed at the top which Christine noted with foreboding was in her own city. Every day she waited for the phone to ring; she was so certain his first attempt at contact would be a disembodied voice that when he came upon her abruptly in midcampus she was unprepared.

"How are you?"   100

His smile was the same, but everything else about him had deteriorated. He   101 was, if possible, thinner; his jacket sleeves had sprouted a lush new crop of threads, as though to conceal hands now so badly bitten they appeared to have been gnawed by rodents. His hair fell over his eyes, uncut, ungreased; his eyes in the hollowed face, a delicate triangle of skin stretched on bone, jumped behind his glasses like hooded fish. He had the end of a cigarette in the corner of his mouth, and as they walked he lit a new one from it.

"I'm fine," Christine said. She was thinking, I'm not going to get involved 102
again, enough is enough, I've done my bit for internationalism. "How are you?"

"I live here now," he said. "Maybe I study Economics." 103

"That's nice." He didn't sound as though he was enrolled anywhere. 104

"I come to see you." 105

Christine didn't know whether he meant he had left Montreal in order to be 106
near her or just wanted to visit her at her house as he had done in the spring; either way she refused to be implicated. They were outside the Political Science
Building. "I have a class here," she said. "Goodbye." She was being callous, she realized that, but a quick chop was more merciful in the long run, that was what her
beautiful sisters used to say.

Afterwards she decided it had been stupid of her to let him find out where her 107
class was. Though a timetable was posted in each of the colleges: all he had to do
was look her up and record her every probable movement in block letters on his
green notepad. After that day he never left her alone.

Initially he waited outside the lecture rooms for her to come out. She said 108
hello to him curtly at first and kept on going, but this didn't work; he followed her
at a distance, smiling his changeless smile. Then she stopped speaking altogether
and pretended to ignore him, but it made no difference, he followed her anyway.
The fact that she was in some way afraid of him—or was it just embarrassment?—seemed only to encourage him. Her friends started to notice, asking her
who he was and why he was tagging along behind her; she could hardly answer,
because she hardly knew.

As the weekdays passed and he showed no signs of letting up, she began to jog- 109
trot between classes, finally to run. He was tireless, and had an amazing wind for
one who smoked so heavily: he would speed along behind her, keeping the distance between them the same, as though he were a pull-toy attached to her by a
string. She was aware of the ridiculous spectacle they must make, galloping across
campus, something out of a cartoon short, a lumbering elephant stampeded by a
smiling, emaciated mouse, both of them locked in the classic pattern of comic
pursuit and flight; but she found that to race made her less nervous than to walk
sedately, the skin on the back of her neck crawling with the feel of his eyes on it.
At least she could use her muscles. She worked out routines, escapes: she would
dash in the front door of the Ladies' Room in the coffee shop and out the back
door, and he would lose the trail, until he discovered the other entrance. She
would try to shake him by detours through baffling archways and corridors, but
he seemed as familiar with the architectural mazes as she was herself. As a last refuge she could head for the women's dormitory and watch from safety as he was
skidded to a halt by the receptionist's austere voice: men were not allowed past the
entrance.

Lunch became difficult. She would be sitting, usually with other members 110
of the Debating Society, just digging nicely into a sandwich, when he would appear suddenly as though he'd come up through an unseen manhole. She then
had the choice of barging out through the crowded cafeteria, sandwich half-eaten,
or finishing her lunch with him standing behind her chair, everyone at the

table acutely aware of him, the conversation stilting and dwindling. Her friends learned to spot him from a distance; they posted lookouts. "Here he comes," they would whisper, helping her collect her belongings for the sprint they knew would follow.

Several times she got tired of running and turned to confront him. "What do   111 you want?" she would ask, glowering belligerently down at him, almost clenching her fists; she felt like shaking him, hitting him.

"I wish to talk with you."   112

"Well, here I am," she would say. "What do you want to talk about?"   113

But he would say nothing; he would stand in front of her, shifting his feet,   114 smiling perhaps apologetically (though she could never pinpoint the exact tone of that smile, chewed lips stretched apart over the nicotine-yellowed teeth, rising at the corners, flesh held stiffly in place for an invisible photographer), his eyes jerking from one part of her face to another as though he saw her in fragments.

Annoying and tedious though it was, his pursuit of her had an odd result: 115 mysterious in itself, it rendered her equally mysterious. No one had ever found Christine mysterious before. To her parents she was a beefy heavyweight, a plodder, lacking in flair, ordinary as bread. To her sisters she was the plain one, treated with an indulgence they did not give to each other: they did not fear her as a rival. To her male friends she was the one who could be relied on. She was helpful and a hard worker, always good for a game of tennis with the athletes among them. They invited her along to drink beer with them so they could get into the cleaner, more desirable Ladies and Escorts side of the beer parlour, taking it for granted she would buy her share of the rounds. In moments of stress they confided to her their problems with women. There was nothing devious about her and nothing interesting.

Christine had always agreed with these estimates of herself. In childhood she   116 had identified with the false bride or the ugly sister; whenever a story had begun, "Once there was a maiden as beautiful as she was good," she had known it wasn't her. That was just how it was, but it wasn't so bad. Her parents never expected her to be a brilliant social success and weren't overly disappointed when she wasn't. She was spared the manoeuvring and anxiety she witnessed among others her age, and she even had a kind of special position among men: she was an exception, she fitted none of the categories they commonly used when talking about girls; she wasn't a cock-teaser, a cold fish, an easy lay or a snarky bitch; she was an honorary person. She had grown to share their contempt for most women.

Now, however, there was something about her that could not be explained. A   117 man was chasing her, a peculiar sort of man, granted, but still a man, and he was without doubt attracted to her, he couldn't leave her alone. Other men examined her more closely than they ever had, appraising her, trying to find out what it was those twitching bespectacled eyes saw in her. They started to ask her out, though they returned from these excursions with their curiosity unsatisfied, the secret of her charm still intact. Her opaque dumpling face, her solid bearshaped body became for them parts of a riddle no one could solve. Christine sensed this. In the bathtub she no longer imagined she was a dolphin; instead she imagined she was an elusive water-nixie, or sometimes, in moments of audacity, Marilyn Monroe. The daily chase was becoming a habit; she even looked forward to it. In addition to its other benefits she was losing weight.

All these weeks he had never phoned her or turned up at the house. He must 118 have decided however that his tactics were not having the desired result, or perhaps he sensed she was becoming bored. The phone began to ring in the early morning or late at night when he could be sure she would be there. Sometimes he would simply breathe (she could recognize, or thought she could, the quality of his breathing), in which case she would hang up. Occasionally he would say again that he wanted to talk to her, but even when she gave him lots of time nothing else would follow. Then he extended his range: she would see him on her streetcar, smiling at her silently from a seat never closer than three away; she could feel him tracking her down her own street, though when she would break her resolve to pay no attention and would glance back he would be invisible or in the act of hiding behind a tree or hedge.

Among crowds of people and in daylight she had not really been afraid of him; 119 she was stronger than he was and he had made no recent attempt to touch her. But the days were growing shorter and colder, it was almost November. Often she was arriving home in twilight or a darkness broken only by the feeble orange streetlamps. She brooded over the possibility of razors, knives, guns; by acquiring a weapon he could quickly turn the odds against her. She avoided wearing scarves, remembering the newspaper stories about girls who had been strangled by them. Putting on her nylons in the morning gave her a funny feeling. Her body seemed to have diminished, to have become smaller than his.

Was he deranged, was he a sex maniac? He seemed so harmless, yet it was that 120 kind who often went berserk in the end. She pictured those ragged fingers at her throat, tearing at her clothes, though she could not think of herself as screaming. Parked cars, the shrubberies near her house, the driveways on either side of it, changed as she passed them from unnoticed background to sinister shadowed foreground, every detail distinct and harsh: they were places a man might crouch, leap out from. Yet every time she saw him in the clear light of morning or afternoon (for he still continued his old methods of pursuit), his aging jacket and jittery eyes convinced her that it was she herself who was the tormentor, the persecutor. She was in some sense responsible; from the folds and crevices of the body she had treated for so long as a reliable machine was emanating, against her will, some potent invisible odour, like a dog's in heat or a female moth's, that made him unable to stop following her.

Her mother, who had been too preoccupied with the unavoidable fall enter- 121 taining to pay much attention to the number of phone calls Christine was getting or to the hired girl's complaints of a man who hung up without speaking, announced that she was flying down to New York for the weekend; her father decided to go too. Christine panicked: she saw herself in the bathtub with her throat slit, the blood drooling out of her neck and running in a little spiral down the drain (for by this time she believed he could walk through walls, could be everywhere at once). The girl would do nothing to help; she might even stand in the bathroom door with her arms folded, watching. Christine arranged to spend the weekend at her married sister's.

When she arrived back Sunday evening she found the girl close to hysterics. 122 She said that on Saturday she had gone to pull the curtains across the French doors at dusk and had found a strangely contorted face, a man's face, pressed against the glass, staring in at her from the garden. She claimed she had fainted and had almost had her baby a month too early right there on the living-room carpet. Then she had called the police. He was gone by the time they got there but she had recognized him from the afternoon of the tea; she had informed them he was a friend of Christine's.

They called Monday evening to investigate, two of them. They were very po- 123 lite, they knew who Christine's father was. Her father greeted them heartily; her mother hovered in the background, fidgeting with her porcelain hands, letting them see how frail and worried she was. She didn't like having them in the living room but they were necessary.

Christine had to admit he'd been following her around. She was relieved he'd 124 been discovered, relieved also that she hadn't been the one to tell, though if he'd been a citizen of the country she would have called the police a long time ago. She insisted he was not dangerous, he had never hurt her.

"That kind don't hurt you," one of the policemen said. "They just kill you. 125 You're lucky you aren't dead."

"Nut cases," the other one said. 126

Her mother volunteered that the thing about people from another culture was 127 that you could never tell whether they were insane or not because their ways were so different. The policemen agreed with her, deferential but also condescending, as though she was a royal halfwit who had to be humoured.

"You know where he lives?" the first policeman asked. Christine had long ago 128 torn up the letter with his address on it; she shook her head.

"We'll have to pick him up tomorrow then," he said. "Think you can keep him 129 talking outside your class if he's waiting for you?"

After questioning her they held a murmured conversation with her father in 130 the front hall. The girl, clearing away the coffee cups, said if they didn't lock him up she was leaving, she wasn't going to be scared half out of her skin like that again.

Next day when Christine came out of her Modern History lecture he was 131 there, right on schedule. He seemed puzzled when she did not begin to run. She approached him, her heart thumping with treachery and the prospect of freedom. Her body was back to its usual size; she felt herself a giantess, self-controlled, in-vulnerable.

"How are you?" she asked, smiling brightly. 132

He looked at her with distrust. 133

"How have you been?" she ventured again. His own perennial smile faded; he 134 took a step back from her.

"This the one?" said the policeman, popping out from behind a notice board 135 like a Keystone Cop and laying a competent hand on the worn jacket shoulder. The other policeman lounged in the background; force would not be required.

"Don't *do* anything to him," she pleaded as they took him away. They nodded 136 and grinned, respectful, scornful. He seemed to know perfectly well who they were and what they wanted.

The first policeman phoned that evening to make his report. Her father talked 137 with him, jovial and managing. She herself was now out of the picture; she had been protected, her function was over.

"What did they *do* to him?" she asked anxiously as he came back into the liv- 138 ing room. She was not sure what went on in police stations.

"They didn't do anything to him," he said, amused by her concern. "They 139 could have booked him for Watching and Besetting, they wanted to know if I'd like to press charges. But it's not worth a court case: he's got a visa that says he's only allowed in the country as long as he studies in Montreal, so I told them to just ship him down there. If he turns up here again they'll deport him. They went around to his rooming house, his rent's two weeks overdue; the landlady said she was on the point of kicking him out. He seems happy enough to be getting his back rent paid and a free train ticket to Montreal." He paused. "They couldn't get anything out of him though."

"*Out* of him?" Christine asked. 140

"They tried to find out why he was doing it; following you, I mean." Her fa- 141 ther's eyes swept her as though it was a riddle to him also. "They said when they asked him about that he just clammed up. Pretended he didn't understand English. He understood well enough, but he wasn't answering."

Christine thought this would be the end, but somehow between his arrest and 142 the departure of the train he managed to elude his escort long enough for one more phone call.

"I see you again," he said. He didn't wait for her to hang up. 143

Now that he was no longer an embarrassing present reality, he could be talked 144 about, he could become an amusing story. In fact, he was the only amusing story Christine had to tell, and telling it preserved both for herself and for others the aura of her strange allure. Her friends and the men who continued to ask her out speculated about his motives. One suggested he had wanted to marry her so he could remain in the country; another said that oriental men were fond of well-built women: "It's your Rubens quality."

Christine thought about him a lot. She had not been attracted to him, rather 145 the reverse, but as an idea only he was a romantic figure, the one man who had found her irresistible; though she often wondered, inspecting her unchanged pink face and hefty body in her full-length mirror, just what it was about her that had done it. She avoided whenever it was proposed the theory of his insanity: it was only that there was more than one way of being sane.

But a new acquaintance, hearing the story for the first time, had a different ex- 146 planation. "So he got you, too," he said, laughing. "That has to be the same guy who was hanging around our day camp a year ago this summer. He followed all the girls like that, a short guy, Japanese or something, glasses, smiling all the time."

"Maybe it was another one," Christine said. 147

"There couldn't be two of them, everything fits. This was a pretty weird guy." 148

"What . . . *kind* of girls did he follow?" Christine asked.   149

"Oh, just anyone who happened to be around. But if they paid any attention   150
to him at first, if they were nice to him or anything, he was unshakeable. He was
a bit of a pest, but harmless."

Christine ceased to tell her amusing story. She had been one among many,   151
then. She went back to playing tennis, she had been neglecting her game.

A few months later the policeman who had been in charge of the case tele-   152
phoned her again.

"Like you to know, miss, that fellow you were having the trouble with was sent   153
back to his own country. Deported."

"What for?" Christine asked. "Did he try to come back here?" Maybe she had   154
been special after all, maybe he had dared everything for her.

"Nothing like it," the policeman said. "He was up to the same tricks in Mon-   155
treal but he really picked the wrong woman this time—a Mother Superior of a
convent. They don't stand for things like that in Quebec—had him out of here
before he knew what happened. I guess he'll be better off in his own place."

"How old was she?" Christine asked, after a silence.   156

"Oh, around sixty, I guess."   157

"Thank you very much for letting me know," Christine said in her best official   158
manner. "It's such a relief." She wondered if the policeman had called to make fun
of her.

She was almost crying when she put down the phone. What *had* he wanted   159
from her then? A Mother Superior. Did she really look sixty, did she look like a
mother? What did convents mean? Comfort, charity? Refuge? Was it that something had happened to him, some intolerable strain just from being in this country; her tennis dress and exposed legs too much for him, flesh and money seemingly
available everywhere but withheld from him wherever he turned, the nun the symbol of some final distortion, the robe and veil reminiscent to his nearsighted eyes
of the women of his homeland, the ones he was able to understand? But he was back
in his own country, remote from her as another planet; she would never know.

He hadn't forgotten her though. In the spring she got a postcard with a for-   160
eign stamp and the familiar block-letter writing. On the front was a picture of a
temple. He was fine, he hoped she was fine also, he was her friend. A month later
another print of the picture he had taken in the garden arrived, in a sealed manila
envelope otherwise empty.

Christine's aura of mystery soon faded; anyway, she herself no longer believed   161
in it. Life became again what she had always expected. She graduated with
mediocre grades and went into the Department of Health and Welfare; she did a
good job, and was seldom discriminated against for being a woman because nobody thought of her as one. She could afford a pleasant-sized apartment, though
she did not put much energy into decorating it. She played less and less tennis;
what had been muscle with a light coating of fat turned gradually into fat with a
thin substratum of muscle. She began to get headaches.

As the years were used up and the war began to fill the newspapers and mag-   162
azines, she realized which Eastern country he had actually been from. She had

known the name but it hadn't registered at the time, it was such a minor place; she could never keep them separate in her mind.

But though she tried, she couldn't remember the name of the city, and the 163 postcard was long gone—had he been from the North or the South, was he near the battle zone or safely far from it? Obsessively she bought magazines and pored over the available photographs, dead villagers, soldiers on the march, colour blowups of frightened or angry faces, spies being executed; she studied maps, she watched the late-night newscasts, the distant country and terrain becoming almost more familiar to her than her own. Once or twice she thought she could recognize him but it was no use, they all looked like him.

Finally she had to stop looking at the pictures. It bothered her too much, it 164 was bad for her; she was beginning to have nightmares in which he was coming through the French doors of her mother's house in his shabby jacket, carrying a packsack and a rifle and a huge bouquet of richly coloured flowers. He was smiling in the same way but the blood streaked over his face, partly blotting out the features. She gave her television set away and took to reading nineteenth-century novels instead; Trollope and Galsworthy were her favourites. When, despite herself, she would think about him, she would tell herself that he had been crafty and agile-minded enough to survive, more or less, in her country, so surely he would be able to do it in his own, where he knew the language. She could not see him in the army, on either side; he wasn't the type, and to her knowledge he had not believed in any particular ideology. He would be something nondescript, something in the background, like herself; perhaps he had become an interpreter.

ACTIVITIES FOR WRITING AND DISCUSSION

1. Working alone or in a group, identify any moments or junctures in the story that made you wonder, "What's going to happen next?" Then compare what you *expected* would happen with what *actually* happened. What conclusions can you draw from the contrast, if any, between your expectations and what happened?

2. Reread any passages pertaining to Christine's self-image. How did she get her self-image, and what was it like before she met "the man from Mars"? How does it evolve in the course of her relationship with the alien man? Why?

3. What motivations do various **characters** ascribe to "the man from Mars"? What reasons do they believe he has for pursuing Christine? What motivations, if any, are implied by the man himself? Investigate these questions. Then:
   a. Invent some diary entries or letters home in which you ("the man from Mars") talk about Christine, or
   b. Write an imaginary interview with the man in which you get the man to explain himself, or
   c. Invent an exchange of letters between yourself and the **author** in which she discusses her intentions in the story.

4. What is the native land of "the man from Mars"? A sentence in the second-to-last paragraph begins, "Obsessively [Christine] bought magazines and pored over the available photographs." How can you account for this obsession? In the **persona** of Christine, write about your "obsession" and your inability to forget the man.

JAMES ALAN MCPHERSON (b. 1943)

A Loaf of Bread

It was one of those obscene situations, pedestrian to most people, but invested with   1
meaning for a few poor folk whose lives are usually spent outside the imaginations of their fellow citizens. A grocer named Harold Green was caught red-handed selling to one group of people the very same goods he sold at lower prices at similar outlets in better neighborhoods. He had been doing this for many years, and at first he could not understand the outrage heaped upon him. He acted only from habit, he insisted, and had nothing personal against the people whom he served. They were his neighbors. Many of them he had carried on the cuff during hard times. Yet, through some mysterious access to a television station, the poor folk were now empowered to make grand denunciations of the grocer. Green's children now saw their father's business being picketed on the Monday evening news.

No one could question the fact that the grocer had been overcharging the   2
people. On the news even the reporter grimaced distastefully while reading the statistics. His expression said, "It is my job to report the news, but sometimes even I must disassociate myself from it to protect my honor." This, at least, was the impression the grocer's children seemed to bring away from the television. Their father's name had not been mentioned, but there was a close-up of his store with angry black people, and a few outraged whites, marching in groups of three in front of it. There was also a close-up of his name. After seeing this, they were in no mood to watch cartoons. At the dinner table, disturbed by his children's silence, Harold Green felt compelled to say, "I am not a dishonest man." Then he felt ashamed. The children, a boy and his older sister, immediately left the table, leaving Green alone with his wife. "Ruth, I am not dishonest," he repeated to her.

Ruth Green did not say anything. She knew, and her husband did not, that the   3
outraged people had also picketed the school attended by their children. They had threatened to return each day until Green lowered his prices. When they called her at home to report this, she had promised she would talk with him. Since she could not tell him this, she waited for an opening. She looked at her husband across the table.

"I did not make the world," Green began, recognizing at once the seriousness   4
in her stare. "My father came to this country with nothing but his shirt. He was

exploited for as long as he couldn't help himself. He did not protest or picket. He put himself in a position to play by the rules he had learned." He waited for his wife to answer, and when she did not, he tried again. "I did not make this world," he repeated. "I only make my way in it. Such people as these, they do not know enough to not be exploited. If not me, there would be a Greek, a Chinaman, maybe an Arab or a smart one of their own kind. Believe me, I deal with them. There is something in their style that lacks the patience to run a concern such as mine. If I closed down, take my word on it, someone else would do what has to be done."

But Ruth Green was not thinking of his leaving. Her mind was on other mat- 5 ters. Her children had cried when they came home early from school. She had no special feeling for the people who picketed, but she did not like to see her children cry. She had kissed them generously, then sworn them to silence. "One day this week," she told her husband, "you will give free, for eight hours, anything your customers come in to buy. There will be no publicity, except what they spread by word of mouth. No matter what they say to you, no matter what they take, you will remain silent." She stared deeply into him for what she knew was there. "If you refuse, you have seen the last of your children and myself."

Her husband grunted. Then he leaned toward her. "I will not knuckle under," 6 he said. "I will *not* give!"

"We shall see," his wife told him.   7

The black pickets, for the most part, had at first been frightened by the au- 8 dacity of their undertaking. They were peasants whose minds had long before become resigned to their fate as victims. None of them, before now, had thought to challenge this. But now, when they watched themselves on television, they hardly recognized the faces they saw beneath the hoisted banners and placards. Instead of reflecting the meekness they all felt, the faces looked angry. The close-ups looked especially intimidating. Several of the first pickets, maids who worked in the suburbs, reported that their employers, seeing the activity on the afternoon news, had begun treating them with new respect. One woman, midway through the weather report, called around the neighborhood to disclose that her employer had that very day given her a new china plate for her meals. The paper plates, on which all previous meals had been served, had been thrown into the wastebasket. One recipient of this call, a middle-aged woman known for her bashfulness and humility, rejoined that her husband, a sheet-metal worker, had only a few hours before been called "Mister" by his supervisor, a white man with a passionate hatred of color. She added the tale of a neighbor down the street, a widow-woman named Murphy, who had at first been reluctant to join the picket; this woman now was insisting it should be made a daily event. Such talk as this circulated among the people who had been instrumental in raising the issue. As news of their victory leaked into the ears of others who had not participated, they received all through the night calls from strangers requesting verification, offering advice, and vowing support. Such strangers listened, and then volunteered stories about indignities inflicted on them by city officials, policemen, other grocers. In this way, over a period of hours, the community became even more incensed and restless than it had been at the time of the initial picket.

Soon, the man who had set events in motion found himself a hero. His name ⁹ was Nelson Reed, and all his adult life he had been employed as an assembly-line worker. He was a steady husband, the father of three children, and a deacon in the Baptist church. All his life he had trusted in God and gotten along. But now something in him capitulated to the reality that came suddenly into focus. "I was wrong," he told people who called him. "The onliest thing that matters in this world is *money.* And when was the last time you seen a picture of Jesus on a dollar bill?" This line, which he repeated over and over, caused a few callers to laugh nervously, but not without some affirmation that this was indeed the way things were. Many said they had known it all along. Others argued that although it was certainly true, it was one thing to live without money and quite another to live without faith. But still most callers laughed and said, "You right. You *know* I know you right. Ain't it the truth, though?" Only a few people, among them Nelson Reed's wife, said nothing and looked very sad.

Why they looked sad, however, they would not communicate. And anyone ¹⁰ observing their troubled faces would have to trust his own intuition. It is known that Reed's wife, Betty, measured all events against the fullness of her own experience. She was skeptical of everything. Brought to the church after a number of years of living openly with a jazz musician, she had embraced religion when she married Nelson Reed. But though she no longer believed completely in the world, she nonetheless had not fully embraced God. There was something in the nature of Christ's swift rise that had always bothered her, and something in the blood and vengeance of the Old Testament that was mellowing and refreshing. But she had never communicated these thoughts to anyone, especially her husband. Instead, she smiled vacantly while others professed leaps of faith, remained silent when friends spoke fiercely of their convictions. The presence of this vacuum in her contributed to her personal mystery; people said she was beautiful, although she was not outwardly so. Perhaps it was because she wished to protect this inner beauty that she did not smile now, and looked extremely sad, listening to her husband on the telephone.

Nelson Reed had no reason to be sad. He seemed to grow more energized and ¹¹ talkative as the days passed. He was invited by an alderman, on the Tuesday after the initial picket, to tell his story on a local television talk show. He sweated heavily under the hot white lights and attempted to be philosophical. "I notice," the host said to him, "that you are not angry at this exploitative treatment. What, Mr. Reed, is the source of your calm?" The assembly-line worker looked unabashedly into the camera and said, "I have always believed in *Justice* with a capital *J.* I was raised up from a baby believin' that God ain't gonna let nobody go *too* far. See, in *my* mind God is in charge of *all* the capital letters in the alphabet of this world. It say in the Scripture He is Alpha and Omega, the first and the last. He is just about the *onliest* capitalizer they is." Both Reed and the alderman laughed. "Now, when *men* start to capitalize, they gets *greedy*. They put a little *j* in *joy* and a littler one in *justice*. They raise up a big *G* in *Greed* and a big *E* in *Evil*. Well, soon as they commence to put a little *g* in *god,* you can expect some kind of reaction. The Savior will just raise up the *H* in *Hell* and go on from there. And that's just what I'm doin', giving these sharpies *HELL* with a big *H*." The talk show host laughed along with Nelson Reed and the alderman. After the taping they drank coffee in the back room of the studio and talked about the sad shape of the world.

Three days before he was to comply with his wife's request, Green, the grocer, 12 saw this talk show on television while at home. The words of Nelson Reed sent a chill through him. Though Reed had attempted to be philosophical, Green did not perceive the statement in this light. Instead, he saw a vindictive-looking black man seated between an ambitious alderman and a smug talk-show host. He saw them chatting comfortably about the nature of evil. The cameraman had shot mostly close-ups, and Green could see the set in Nelson Reed's jaw. The color of Reed's face was maddening. When his children came into the den, the grocer was in a sweat. Before he could think, he had shouted at them and struck the button turning off the set. The two children rushed from the room screaming. Ruth Green ran in from the kitchen. She knew why he was upset because she had received a call about the show; but she said nothing and pretended ignorance. Her children's school had been picketed that day, as it had the day before. But both children were still forbidden to speak of this to their father.

"Where do they get so much power?" Green said to his wife. "Two days ago, 13 nobody would have cared. Now, everywhere, even in my home, I am condemned as a rascal. And what do I own? An airline? A multinational? Half of South America? *No!* I own three stores, one of which happens to be in a certain neighborhood inhabited by people who cost me money to run it." He sighed and sat upright on the sofa, his chubby legs spread wide. "A cab driver has a meter that clicks as he goes along. I pay extra for insurance, iron bars, pilfering by customers and employees. Nothing clicks. But when I add a little overhead to my prices, suddenly everything clicks. But for someone else. When was there last such a world?" He pressed the palms of both hands to his temples, suggesting a bombardment of brain-stinging sounds.

This gesture evoked no response from Ruth Green. She remained standing by 14 the door, looking steadily at him. She said, "To protect yourself, I would not stock any more fresh cuts of meat in the store until after the giveaway on Saturday. Also, I would not tell it to the employees until after the first customer of the day has begun to check out. But I would urge you to hire several security guards to close the door promptly at seven-thirty, as is usual." She wanted to say much more than this, but did not. Instead she watched him. He was looking at the blank gray television screen, his palms still pressed against his ears. "In case you need to hear again," she continued in a weighty tone of voice, "I said two days ago, and I say again now, that if you fail to do this you will not see your children again for many years."

He twisted his head and looked up at her. "What is the color of these people?"   15
he asked.

"Black," his wife said.   16

"And what is the name of my children?"   17

"Green."   18

The grocer smiled. "There is your answer," he told his wife. "Green is the only   19
color I am interested in."

His wife did not smile. "Insufficient," she said.   20

"The world is mad!" he moaned. "But it is a point of sanity with me to not   21
bend. I will not bend." He crossed his legs and pressed one hand firmly atop his
knee. "*I will not bend*," he said.

"We will see," his wife said.   22

———

Nelson Reed, after the television interview, became the acknowledged leader   23
of the disgruntled neighbors. At first a number of them met in the kitchen at his
house; then, as space was lacking for curious newcomers, a mass meeting was held
on Thursday in an abandoned theater. His wife and three children sat in the front
row. Behind them sat the widow Murphy, Lloyd Dukes, Tyrone Brown, Les
Jones—those who had joined him on the first picket line. Behind these sat people
who bought occasionally at the store, people who lived on the fringes of the
neighborhood, people from other neighborhoods come to investigate the problem, and the merely curious. The middle rows were occupied by a few people
from the suburbs, those who had seen the talk show and whose outrage at the grocer proved much more powerful than their fear of black people. In the rear of the
theater crowded aging, old-style leftists, somber students, cynical young black
men with angry grudges to explain with inarticulate gestures. Leaning against the
walls, and huddled near the doors at the rear, tape-recorder-bearing social scientists looked as detached and serene as bookies at the track. Here and there, in this
diverse crowd, a politician stationed himself, pumping hands vigorously and
pressing his palms gently against the shoulders of elderly people. Other visitors
passed out leaflets, buttons, glossy color prints of men who promoted causes, the
familiar and obscure. There was a hubbub of voices, a blend of the strident and
the playful, the outraged and the reverent, lending an undercurrent of ominous
energy to the assembly.

Nelson Reed spoke from a platform on the stage, standing before a yellowed,   24
shredded screen that had once reflected the images of matinee idols. "I don't mind
sayin' that I have always been a sucker," he told the crowd. "All my life I have been
a sucker for the words of Jesus. Being a natural-born fool, I just ain't never had the
sense to learn no better. Even right today, while the whole world is sayin' wrong is
right and up is down, I'm so dumb I'm *still* steady believin' what is wrote in the
Good Book . . ."

From the audience, especially the front rows, came a chorus singing,   25
"Preach!"

"I have no doubt," he continued in a low baritone, "that it's true what is writ   26
in the Good Book: 'The last shall be first and the first shall be last.' I don't know
about y'all, but I have *always* been the last. I never wanted to be the first, but
sometimes it look like the world get so bad that them that's holdin' onto the tree
of life is the onliest ones left when God commence to blowin' dead leafs off the
branches."

"Now you preaching," someone called.   27

In the rear of the theater a white student shouted an awkward "Amen."   28

Nelson Reed began walking across the stage to occupy the major part of his   29
nervous energy. But to those in the audience, who now hung on his every word, it
looked as though he strutted. "All my life," he said, "I have claimed to be a man
without earnin' the right to call myself that. You know, the *average* man ain't really a man. The average man is a *bootlicker*. In fact, the *average* man would *run
away* if he found hisself standing alone facin' down a adversary. I have done that
too many a time in my life! But *not no more*. Better to be *once* was than *never* was
a man. I will tell you tonight, there is somethin' *wrong* in being average. *I intend
to stand up!* Now, if your average man that ain't really a man stand up, two things
gonna happen: *One*, he g'on bust through all the weights that been place on his
head, and, *two*, he g'on feel a lot of pain. But that same hurt is what make things
fall in place. That, and gettin' your hands on one of these slick four-flushers tight
enough so's you can squeeze him and say, '*No more!*' You do that, you g'on hurt
some, but *you won't be average no more . . .*"

"*No more!*" a few people in the front rows repeated.   30

"I say *no more!*" Nelson Reed shouted.   31

"*No more! No more! No more!*" The chant rustled through the crowd like the   32
rhythm of an autumn wind against a shedding tree.

Then people laughed and chattered in celebration.   33

As for the grocer, from the evening of the television interview he had begun   34
to make plans. Unknown to his wife, he cloistered himself several times with his
brother-in-law, an insurance salesman, and plotted a course. He had no intention
of tossing steaks to the crowd. "And why should I, Tommy?" he asked his wife's
brother, a lean, bald-headed man named Thomas. "I don't cheat anyone. I have
never cheated anyone. The businesses I run are always on the up-and-up. So why
should I pay?"

"Quite so," the brother-in-law said, chewing an unlit cigarillo. "The world has   35
gone crazy. Next they will say that people in my business are responsible for pro-
longing life. I have found that people who refuse to believe in death refuse also to
believe in the harshness of life. I sell well by saying that death is a long happiness.
I show people the realities of life and compare this to a funeral with dignity, *and*
the promise of a bundle for every loved one salted away. When they look around
hard at life, they usually buy."

"So?" asked Green. Thomas was a college graduate with a penchant for   36
philosophy.

"So," Thomas answered. "You must fight to show these people the reality of   37
both your situation and theirs. How would it be if you visited one of their meetings and chalked out, on a blackboard, the dollars and cents of your operation?
Explain your overhead, your security fees, all the additional expenses. If you treat
them with respect, they might understand."

Green frowned. "That I would never do," he said. "It would be admission of a   38
certain guilt."

The brother-in-law smiled, but only with one corner of his mouth. "Then you   39
have something to feel guilty about?" he asked.

The grocer frowned at him. "*Nothing!*" he said with great emphasis.   40

"So?" Thomas said.   41

This first meeting between the grocer and his brother-in-law took place on   42
Thursday, in a crowded barroom.

At the second meeting, in a luncheonette, it was agreed that the grocer should   43
speak privately with the leader of the group, Nelson Reed. The meeting at which
this was agreed took place on Friday afternoon. After accepting this advice from
Thomas, the grocer resigned himself to explain to Reed, in as finite detail as possible, the economic structure of his operation. He vowed to suppress no information. He would explain everything: inventories, markups, sale items, inflation,
balance sheets, specialty items, overhead, and that mysterious item called profit.
This last item, promising to be the most difficult to explain, Green and his
brother-in-law debated over for several hours. They agreed first of all that a man
should not work for free, then they agreed that it was unethical to ruthlessly exploit. From these parameters, they staked out an area between fifteen and forty
percent, and agreed that someplace between these two borders lay an amount of
return that could be called fair. This was easy, but then Thomas introduced the
factor of circumstance. He questioned whether the fact that one serviced a risky
area justified the earning of profits closer to the forty-percent edge of the scale.
Green was unsure. Thomas smiled. "Here is a case that will point out an analogy,"
he said, licking a cigarillo. "I read in the papers that a family wants to sell an electric stove. I call the home and the man says fifty dollars. I ask to come out and inspect the merchandise. When I arrive I see they are poor, have already bought a
new stove that is connected and are selling the old one for fifty dollars because
they want it out of the place. The electric stove is in good condition, worth much
more than fifty. But because I see what I see I offer forty-five."

Green, for some reason, wrote down this figure on the back of the sales slip   44
for the coffee they were drinking.

The brother-in-law smiled. He chewed his cigarillo. "The man agrees to take   45
forty-five dollars, saying he has had no other calls. I look at the stove again and
see a spot of rust. I say I will give him forty dollars. He agrees to this, on condition that I myself haul it away. I say I will haul it away if he comes down to thirty.
You, of course, see where I am going."

The grocer nodded. "The circumstances of his situation, his need to get rid of   46
the stove quickly, placed him in a position where he has little room to bargain?"

"Yes," Thomas answered. "So? Is it ethical, Harry?"   47

Harold Green frowned. He had never liked his brother-in-law, and now he 48 thought the insurance agent was being crafty. "But," he answered, "this man does not *have* to sell! It is his choice whether to wait for other calls. It is not the fault of the buyer that the seller is in a hurry. It is the right of the buyer to get what he wants at the lowest price possible. That is the rule. That has *always* been the rule. And the reverse of it applies to the seller as well."

"Yes," Thomas said, sipping coffee from the Styrofoam cup. "But suppose that 49 in addition to his hurry to sell, the owner was also of a weak soul. There are, after all, many such people." He smiled. "Suppose he placed no value on the money?"

"Then," Green answered, "your example is academic. Here we are not talking 50 about real life. One man lives by the code, one man does not. Who is there free enough to make a judgment?" He laughed. "Now you see," he told his brother-in-law. "Much more than a few dollars are at stake. If this one buyer is to be condemned, then so are most people in the history of the world. An examination of history provides the only answer to your question. This code will be here tomorrow, long after the ones who do not honor it are not."

They argued fiercely late into the afternoon, the brother-in-law leaning heavi- 51 ly on his readings. When they parted, a little before 5:00 P.M., nothing had been resolved.

Neither was much resolved during the meeting between Green and Nelson 52 Reed. Reached at home by the grocer in the early evening, the leader of the group spoke coldly at first, but consented finally to meet his adversary at a nearby drugstore for coffee and a talk. They met at the lunch counter, shook hands awkwardly, and sat for a few minutes discussing the weather. Then the grocer pulled two gray ledgers from his briefcase. "You have for years come into my place," he told the man. "In my memory I have always treated you well. Now our relationship has come to this." He slid the books along the counter until they touched Nelson Reed's arm.

Reed opened the top book and flipped the thick green pages with his thumb. 53 He did not examine the figures. "All I know," he said, "is over at your place a can of soup cost me fifty-five cents, and two miles away at your other store for white folks you chargin' thirty-nine cents." He said this with the calm authority of an outraged soul. A quality of condescension tinged with pity crept into his gaze.

The grocer drummed his fingers on the counter top. He twisted his head and 54 looked away, toward shelves containing cosmetics, laxatives, toothpaste. His eyes lingered on a poster of a woman's apple red lips and milk white teeth. The rest of the face was missing.

"Ain't no use to hide," Nelson Reed said, as to a child. "*I* know you wrong, *you* 55 know you wrong, and before I finish, *everybody in this city* g'on know you wrong. God don't *like* ugly." He closed his eyes and gripped the cup of coffee. Then he swung his head suddenly and faced the grocer again. "Man, why you want to *do* people that way?" he asked. "We human, same as you."

"Before *God!*" Green exclaimed, looking squarely into the face of Nelson Reed. 56 "Before God!" he said again. "*I am not an evil man!*" These last words sounded more like a moan as he tightened the muscles in his throat to lower the sound of his voice. He tossed his left shoulder as if adjusting the sleeve of his coat, or as if throwing off some unwanted weight. Then he peered along the countertop. No one was watching. At the end of the counter the waitress was scrubbing the coffee urn. "Look at these figures, please," he said to Reed.

The man did not drop his gaze. His eyes remained fixed on the grocer's face. 57

"All right," Green said. "Don't look. I'll tell you what is in these books, believe 58 me if you want. I work twelve hours a day, one day off per week, running my business in three stores. I am not a wealthy person. In one place, in the area you call white, I get by barely by smiling lustily at old ladies, stocking gourmet stuff on the chance I will build a reputation as a quality store. The two clerks there cheat me; there is nothing I can do. In this business you must be friendly with everybody. The second place is on the other side of town, in a neighborhood as poor as this one. I get out there seldom. The profits are not worth the gas. I use the loss there as a write-off against some other properties." He paused. "Do you understand write-off?" he asked Nelson Reed.

"Naw," the man said. 59

Harold Green laughed. "What does it matter?" he said in a tone of voice in- 60 tended for himself alone. "In this area I will admit I make a profit, but it is not so much as you think. But I do not make a profit here because the people are black. I make a profit because a profit is here to be made. I invest more here in window bars, theft losses, insurance, spoilage; I deserve to make more here than at the other places." He looked, almost imploringly, at the man seated next to him. "You don't accept this as the right of a man in business?"

Reed grunted. "Did the bear shit in the woods?" he said. 61

Again Green laughed. He gulped his coffee awkwardly, as if eager to go. Yet his 62 motions slowed once he had set the coffee cup down on the blue plastic saucer. "Place yourself in *my* situation," he said, his voice high and tentative. "If *you* were running my store in this neighborhood, what would be *your* position? Say on a profit scale of fifteen to forty percent, at what point in between would you draw the line?"

Nelson Reed thought. He sipped his coffee and seemed to chew the liquid. 63 "Fifteen to forty?" he repeated.

"Yes." 64

"I'm a churchgoin' man," he said. "Closer to fifteen than to forty." 65

"How close?" 66

Nelson Reed thought. "In church you tithe ten percent." 67

"In restaurants you tip fifteen," the grocer said quickly. 68

"All right," Reed said. "Over fifteen." 69

"How much over?" 70

Nelson Reed thought. 71

"Twenty, thirty, thirty-five?" Green chanted, leaning closer to Reed. 72

Still the man thought. 73

"Forty? Maybe even forty-five or fifty?" the grocer breathed in Reed's ear. "In 74 the supermarkets, you know, they have more subtle ways of accomplishing such feats."

Reed slapped his coffee cup with the back of his right hand. The brown liquid 75
swirled across the counter top, wetting the books. "*Damn this!*" he shouted.

Startled, Green rose from his stool. 76

Nelson Reed was trembling. "I ain't *you*," he said in a deep baritone. "I ain't 77
the *supermarket* neither. All I is is a poor man that works *too* hard to see his pay
slip through his fingers like rainwater. All I know is you done *cheat* me, you done
cheat everybody in the neighborhood, and we organized now to get some of it
back!" Then he stood and faced the grocer. "My daddy sharecropped down in
Mississippi and bought in the company store. He owed them twenty-three years
when he died. I paid off five of them years and then run away to up here. Now,
I'm a deacon in the Baptist church. I raised my kids the way my daddy raise me
and don't bother nobody. Now come to find out, after all my runnin', they done
lift that *same company store* up out of Mississippi and slip it down on us here!
Well, my daddy was a *fighter,* and if he hadn't owed all them years he would of
raise him some hell. Me, I'm steady my daddy's child, plus I got seniority in my
union. I'm a free man. Buddy, don't you know *I'm gonna raise me some hell!*"

Harold Green reached for a paper napkin to sop the coffee soaking into his 78
books.

Nelson Reed threw a dollar on top of the books and walked away. 79

"I *will not* do it!" Harold Green said to his wife that same evening. They were 80
in the bathroom of their home. Bending over the face bowl, she was washing her
hair with a towel draped around her neck. The grocer stood by the door, looking
in at her. "I will not bankrupt myself tomorrow," he said.

"I've been thinking about it, too," Ruth Green said, shaking her wet hair. 81
"You'll do it, Harry."

"Why should I?" he asked. "You won't leave. You know it was a bluff. I've 82
waited this long for you to calm down. Tomorrow is Saturday. This week has been
a hard one. Tonight let's be realistic."

"Of course you'll do it," Ruth Green said. She said it the way she would say 83
"Have some toast." She said, "You'll do it because you want to see your children
grow up."

"And for what other reason?" he asked. 84

She pulled the towel tighter around her neck. "Because you are at heart a 85
moral man."

He grinned painfully. "If I am, why should I have to prove it to *them?*" 86

"Not them," Ruth Green said, freezing her movements and looking in the 87
mirror. "Certainly not them. By no means them. They have absolutely nothing to
do with this."

"Who, then?" he asked, moving from the door into the room. "Who else 88
should I prove something to?"

His wife was crying. But her entire face was wet. The tears moved secretly 89
down her face.

"Who else?" Harold Green asked. 90

It was almost 11:00 P.M. and the children were in bed. They had also cried   91
when they came home from school. Ruth Green said, "For yourself, Harry. For
the love that lives inside your heart."

All night the grocer thought about this.   92

———————

Nelson Reed also slept little that Friday night. When he returned home from   93
the drugstore, he reported to his wife as much of the conversation as he could remember. At first he had joked about the exchange between himself and the grocer, but as more details returned to his conscious mind he grew solemn and then
bitter. "He ask me to put myself in *his* place," Reed told his wife. "Can you imagine that kind of gumption? I never cheated nobody in my life. All my life I have
lived on Bible principles. I am a deacon in the church. I have work all my life for
other folks and I don't even own the house I live in." He paced up and down the
kitchen, his big arms flapping loosely at his sides. Betty Reed sat at the table,
watching. "This here's a low-down, ass-kicking world," he said. "I swear to God it
is! All my life I have lived on principle and I ain't got a dime in the bank. Betty,"
he turned suddenly toward her, "don't you think I'm a fool?"

"Mr. Reed," she said. "Let's go on to bed."   94

But he would not go to bed. Instead, he took the fifth of bourbon from the   95
cabinet under the sink and poured himself a shot. His wife refused to join him.
Reed drained the glass of whiskey, and then another, while he resumed pacing the
kitchen floor. He slapped his hands against his sides. "*I* think I'm a fool," he said.
"Ain't got a dime in the bank, ain't got a pot to *pee* in or a wall to pitch it over, and
that there *cheat* ask me to put myself inside *his* shoes. Hell, I can't even *afford* the
kind of shoes he wears." He stopped pacing and looked at his wife.

"Mr. Reed," she whispered, "tomorrow ain't a work day. Let's go to bed."   96

Nelson Reed laughed, the bitterness in his voice rattling his wife. "The *hell* I   97
will!" he said.

He strode to the yellow telephone on the wall beside the sink and began to   98
dial. The first call was to Lloyd Dukes, a neighbor two blocks away and a lieutenant in the organization. Dukes was not at home. The second call was to McEl-
roy's Bar on the corner of 65th and Carroll, where Stanley Harper, another of the
lieutenants, worked as a bartender. It was Harper who spread the word, among
those men at the bar, that the organization would picket the grocer's store the following morning. And all through the night, in the bedroom of their house, Betty
Reed was awakened by telephone calls coming from Lester Jones, Nat Lucas, Mrs.
Tyrone Brown, the widow-woman named Murphy, all coordinating the time
when they would march in a group against the store owned by Harold Green.
Betty Reed's heart beat loudly beneath the covers as she listened to the bitterness
and rage in her husband's voice. On several occasions, hearing him declare himself a fool, she pressed the pillow against her eyes and cried.

———————

The grocer opened later than usual this Saturday morning, but still it was early 99
enough to make him one of the first walkers in the neighborhood. He parked his
car one block from the store and strolled to work. There were no birds singing.
The sky in this area was not blue. It was smog-smutted and gray, seeming on the
verge of a light rain. The street, as always, was littered with cans, papers, bits of
broken glass. As always the garbage cans overflowed. The morning breeze plastered a sheet of newspaper playfully around the sides of a rusted garbage can. For
some reason, using his right foot, he loosened the paper and stood watching it
slide into the street and down the block. The movement made him feel good. He
whistled while unlocking the bars shielding the windows and door of his store.
When he had unlocked the main door he stepped in quickly and threw a switch
to the right of the jamb, before the shrill sound of the alarm could shatter his
mood. Then he switched on the lights. Everything was as it had been the night before. He had already telephoned his two employees and given them the day off.
He busied himself doing the usual things—hauling milk and vegetables from the
cooler, putting cash in the till—not thinking about the silence of his wife, or the
look in her eyes, only an hour before when he left home. He had determined, at
some point while driving through the city, that today it would be business as
usual. But he expected very few customers.

The first customer of the day was Mrs. Nelson Reed. She came in around 9:30 100
A.M. and wandered about the store. He watched her from the checkout counter.
She seemed uncertain of what she wanted to buy. She kept glancing at him down
the center aisle. His suspicions aroused, he said finally, "Yes, may I help you, Mrs.
Reed?" His words caused her to jerk, as if some devious thought had been perceived going through her mind. She reached over quickly and lifted a loaf of
whole wheat bread from the rack and walked with it to the counter. She looked at
him and smiled. The smile was a broad, shy one, that rare kind of smile one sees
on virgin girls when they first confess love to themselves. Betty Reed was a woman
of about forty-five. For some reason he could not comprehend, this gesture
touched him. When she pulled a dollar from her purse and laid it on the counter,
an impulse, from no place he could locate with his mind, seized control of his
tongue. "Free," he told Betty Reed. She paused, then pushed the dollar toward
him with a firm and determined thrust of her arm. "Free," he heard himself saying strongly, his right palm spread and meeting her thrust with absolute force.
She clutched the loaf of bread and walked out of his store.

The next customer, a little girl, arriving well after 10:30 A.M., selected a candy 101
bar from the rack beside the counter. "Free," Green said cheerfully. The little girl
left the candy on the counter and ran out of the store.

At 11:15 A.M. a wino came in looking desperate enough to sell his soul. The 102
grocer watched him only for an instant. Then he went to the wine counter and selected a half-gallon of medium-grade red wine. He shoved the jug into the belly
of the wino, the man's sour breath bathing his face. "Free," the grocer said. "But
you must not drink it in here."

He felt good about the entire world, watching the wino through the window 103
gulping the wine and looking guiltily around.

At 11:25 A.M. the pickets arrived.   104

Two dozen people, men and women, young and old, crowded the pavement   105
in front of his store. Their signs, placards, and voices denounced him as a parasite. The grocer laughed inside himself. He felt lighthearted and wild, like a man
drugged. He rushed to the meat counter and pulled a long roll of brown wrapping
paper from the rack, tearing it neatly with a quick shift of his body resembling a
dance step practiced fervently in his youth. He laid the paper on the chopping
block and with the black-inked, felt-tipped marker scrawled, in giant letters, the
word FREE. This he took to the window and pasted in place with many strands of
Scotch tape. He was laughing wildly. "Free!" he shouted from behind the brown
paper. "Free! Free! Free! Free! Free! Free!" He rushed to the door, pushed his head
out, and screamed to the confused crowd, "*Free!*" Then he ran back to the counter
and stood behind it, like a soldier at attention.

They came in slowly.   106

Nelson Reed entered first, working his right foot across the dirty tile as if   107
tracking a squiggling worm. The others followed: Lloyd Dukes dragging a placard, Mr. and Mrs. Tyrone Brown, Stanley Harper walking with his fists clenched,
Lester Jones with three of his children, Nat Lucas looking sheepish and detached,
a clutch of winos, several bashful nuns, ironic-smiling teenagers and a few students. Bringing up the rear was a bearded social scientist holding a tape recorder
to his chest. "Free!" the grocer screamed. He threw up his arms in a gesture that
embraced, or dismissed, the entire store. "*All free!*" he shouted. He was grinning
with the grace of a madman.

The winos began grabbing first. They stripped the shelf of wine in a matter of   108
seconds. Then they fled, dropping bottles on the tile in their wake. The others,
stepping quickly through this liquid, soon congealed it into a sticky, blood-like
consistency. The young men went for the cigarettes and luncheon meats and beer.
One of them had the prescience to grab a sack from the counter, while the others
loaded their arms swiftly, hugging cartons and packages of cold cuts like long-lost
friends. The students joined them, less for greed than for the thrill of the experience. The two nuns backed toward the door. As for the older people, men and
women, they stood at first as if stuck to the wine-smeared floor. Then Stanley
Harper, the bartender, shouted, "The man said *free,* y'all heard him." He paused.
"Didn't you say *free* now?" he called to the grocer.

"I said free," Harold Green answered, his temples pounding.   109

A cheer went up. The older people began grabbing, as if the secret lusts of a life-   110
time had suddenly seized command of their arms and eyes. They grabbed toilet
tissue, cold cuts, pickles, sardines, boxes of raisins, boxes of starch, cans of soup,
tins of tuna fish and salmon, bottles of spices, cans of boned chicken, slippery cans
of olive oil. Here a man, Lester Jones, burdened himself with several heads of lettuce, while his wife, in another aisle, shouted for him to drop those small items
and concentrate on the gourmet section. She herself took imported sardines,
wheat crackers, bottles of candied pickles, herring, anchovies, imported olives,

French wafers, an ancient, half-rusted can of paté, stocked, by mistake, from the inventory of another store. Others packed their arms with detergents, hams, chocolate-coated cereal, whole chickens with hanging asses, wedges of bologna and salami like squashed footballs, chunks of cheeses, yellow and white, shriveled onions, and green peppers. Mrs. Tyrone Brown hung a curve of pepperoni around her neck and seemed to take on instant dignity, much like a person of noble birth in possession now of a long sought-after gem. Another woman, the widow Murphy, stuffed tomatoes into her bosom, holding a half-chewed lemon in her mouth. The more enterprising fought desperately over the three rusted shopping carts, and the victors wheeled these along the narrow aisles, sweeping into them bulk items—beer in sixpacks, sacks of sugar, flour, glass bottles of syrup, toilet cleanser, sugar cookies, prune, apple and tomato juices—while others endeavored to snatch the carts from them. There were several fistfights and much cursing. The grocer, standing behind the counter, hummed and rang his cash register like a madman.

Nelson Reed, the first into the store, followed the nuns out, empty-handed.   111

In less than half an hour the others had stripped the store and vanished in   112
many directions up and down the block. But still more people came, those late in hearing the news. And when they saw the shelves were bare, they cursed soberly and chased those few stragglers still bearing away goods. Soon only the grocer and the social scientist remained, the latter stationed at the door with his tape recorder sucking in leftover sounds. Then he too slipped away up the block.

By 12:10 P.M. the grocer was leaning against the counter, trying to make his   113
mind slow down. Not a man given to drink during work hours he nonetheless took a swallow from a bottle of wine, a dusty bottle from beneath the wine shelf, somehow overlooked by the winos. Somewhat recovered, he was preparing to remember what he should do next when he glanced toward a figure at the door. Nelson Reed was standing there, watching him.

"All gone," Harold Green said. "My friend, Mr. Reed, there is no more." Still   114
the man stood in the doorway, peering into the store.

The grocer waved his arms about the empty room. Not a display case had a   115
single item standing. "All gone," he said again, as if addressing a stupid child. "There is nothing left to get. You, my friend, have come back too late for a second load. I am cleaned out."

Nelson Reed stepped into the store and strode toward the counter. He moved   116
through wine-stained flour, lettuce leaves, red, green, and blue labels, bits and pieces of broken glass. He walked toward the counter.

"All day," the grocer laughed not quite hysterically now, "all day long I have   117
not made a single cent of profit. The entire day was a loss. This store, like the others, is *bleeding* me." He waved his arms about the room in a magnificent gesture of uncaring loss. "Now do you understand?" he said. "Now will you put yourself

in my shoes? I have nothing here. Come, now, Mr. Reed, would it not be so bad a thing to walk in my shoes?"

"Mr. Green," Nelson Reed said coldly. "My wife bought a loaf of bread in here 118 this mornin'. She forgot to pay you. I, myself, have come here to pay you your money."

"Oh," the grocer said. 119

"I think it was brown bread. Don't that cost more than white?" 120

The two men looked away from each other, but not at anything in the store. 121

"In my store, yes," Harold Green said. He rang the register with the most ca- 122 sual movement of his finger. The register read fifty-five cents.

Nelson Reed held out a dollar. 123

"And two cents tax," the grocer said. 124

The man held out the dollar. 125

"After all," Harold Green said. "We are all, after all, Mr. Reed, in debt to the 126 government."

He rang the register again. It read fifty-seven cents. 127

Nelson Reed held out a dollar. 128

ACTIVITIES FOR WRITING AND DISCUSSION

1. At the beginning of the fourth paragraph, Green says, "I did not make the world." He contends that he is only doing what he *must* and that anyone else in his position would do the same.

   a. Identify a situation that placed someone in a dilemma similar to Green's. Who was involved? What was the focus of conflict? How was (or wasn't) the conflict resolved? Provide the facts and write the story of that situation.

   b. Agree with Green's statement that he "did not make the world," summarizing arguments in the text (or your own) that support his claim. Then disagree with him, summarizing arguments in the text (or your own) that take an opposing point of view.

2. Reread Thomas's story (paragraphs 43–51) about the sale of the electric stove. Then offer your own answer to Thomas's follow-up question, "Is it ethical?" Provide reasons for your answer.

3. Why do you suppose Betty Reed comes to buy something in Green's store on Saturday morning, even though she knows the store is to be picketed that day? To answer this question, first reread and annotate any passages in the story that talk about Betty, her character, or her motivations. Then assume Betty's **persona** and express the thoughts and motives leading up to your action.

4. Using one of the "Ten Ideas for Writing from Reading" in Chapter 3 (page 35)—or some other approach of your own choosing—respond to any of the events that occur in Green's store on that fateful Saturday.

LANGSTON HUGHES (1902–1967)

Theme for English B

The instructor said,

> Go home and write
> a page tonight.
> And let that page come out of you—
> Then, it will be true.   5

I wonder if it's that simple?
I am twenty-two, colored, born in Winston-Salem.
I went to school there, then Durham, then here
to this college on the hill above Harlem.
I am the only colored student in my class.   10
The steps from the hill lead down to Harlem,
through a park, then I cross St. Nicholas,
Eighth Avenue, Seventh, and I come to the Y,
the Harlem Branch Y, where I take the elevator
up to my room, sit down, and write this page: 15

It's not easy to know what is true for you or me
at twenty-two, my age. But I guess I'm what
I feel and see and hear. Harlem, I hear you:
hear you, hear me—we two—you, me talk on this page.
(I hear New York, too.) Me—who?   20
Well, I like to eat, sleep, drink, and be in love.
I like to work, read, learn, and understand life.
I like a pipe for a Christmas present,
or records—Bessie,[1] bop,[2] or Bach.[3]
I guess being colored doesn't make me not like   25
the same things other folks like who are other races.
So will my page be colored that I write?
Being me, it will not be white.
But it will be
a part of you, instructor.   30

---

1. Bessie Smith (1894–1937), legendary blues singer.   2. A kind of jazz popular in the 1940s and 1950s.
3. Johann Sebastian Bach (1685–1750), German composer.

You are white—
yet a part of me, as I am a part of you.
That's American.
Sometimes perhaps you don't want to be a part of me.
Nor do I often want to be a part of you.   35
But we are, that's true!
As I learn from you,
I guess you learn from me—
although you're older—and white—
and somewhat more free.   40

This is my page for English B.

ACTIVITIES FOR WRITING AND DISCUSSION

1. How does the structure of the speaker's "theme" (or English paper) compare or contrast with your sense of the standard structure for an English paper? Is there an introduction? a conclusion? Why or why not? What are the main ideas, and what connects one idea with another? How do you react when the student addresses the instructor directly (as "you") in his paper? Finally, how are any of these structural or tonal features significant to the poem's meaning?

2. Imagine you are the instructor. It is late at night; you are nodding off over the twenty or thirty student themes you have collected in response to this assignment when you come across this theme. Does the speaker's "page" of writing satisfy your expectations? fail to meet them? surpass them? How does it compare with the other students' themes? Take some notes in response to these questions. Then, as instructor, write a letter of reply or evaluation to the student.

3. Hughes wrote poems, plays, novels, short stories, and autobiography. He was also a key figure in the 1920s movement of African American arts and letters known as the Harlem Renaissance. Research either Hughes's career as a writer or his role in the Harlem Renaissance.

Ballad of the Landlord

Landlord, landlord,
My roof has sprung a leak.
Don't you 'member I told you about it
Way last week?

Landlord, landlord,   5
These steps is broken down.
When you come up yourself
It's a wonder you don't fall down.

Ten Bucks you say I owe you?
Ten Bucks you say is due?   10
Well, that's Ten Bucks more'n I'll pay you
Till you fix this house up new.

What? You gonna get eviction orders?
You gonna cut off my heat?
You gonna take my furniture and   15
Throw it in the street?

Um-huh! You talking high and mighty.
Talk on—till you get through.
You ain't gonna be able to say a word
If I land my fist on you.   20

Police! Police!
Come and get this man!
He's trying to ruin the government
And overturn the land!

Copper's whistle!   25
Patrol bell!
Arrest.

Precinct Station.
Iron cell.
Headlines in press: 30

MAN THREATENS LANDLORD
TENANT HELD NO BAIL
JUDGE GIVES NEGRO 90 DAYS IN COUNTY JAIL

Anna Swir (1909–1984)

The Same Inside

Walking to your place for a love feast
I saw at a street corner
an old beggar woman.

I took her hand,
kissed her delicate cheek,   5

we talked, she was
the same inside as I am,
from the same kind,
I sensed this instantly
as a dog knows by scent   10
another dog.

I gave her money,
I could not part from her.
After all, one needs
someone who is close.   15

And then I no longer knew
why I was walking to your place.

—*Translated by Czeslaw Milosz and Leonard Nathan*

GWENDOLYN BROOKS (b. 1917)

The Boy Died in My Alley

The Boy died in my alley
without my Having Known.
Policeman said, next morning,
"Apparently died Alone."

"You heard a shot?" Policeman said.   5
Shots I hear and Shots I hear.
I never see the Dead.

The Shot that killed him yes I heard
as I heard the Thousand shots before;
careening tinnily down the nights   10
across my years and arteries.

Policeman pounded on my door.
 "Who is it?" "POLICE!" Policeman yelled.
"A Boy was dying in your alley.
A Boy is dead, and in your alley.   15
And have you known this Boy before?"

I have known this Boy before.
I have known this Boy before, who

ornaments my alley.
I never saw his face at all.
I never saw his futurefall.
But I have known this Boy.

I have always heard him deal with death.
I have always heard the shout, the volley.
I have closed my heart-ears late and early.
And I have killed him ever.

I joined the Wild and killed him
with knowledgeable unknowing.
I saw where he was going.
I saw him Crossed. And seeing,
I did not take him down.

He cried not only "Father!"
but "Mother!
Sister!
Brother."
The cry climbed up the alley.
It went up to the wind.
It hung upon the heaven
for a long
stretch-strain of Moment.

The red floor of my alley
is a special speech to me.

ACTIVITIES FOR WRITING AND DISCUSSION

1. Annotate and discuss any words, phrases, or lines that strike or puzzle you. (An example of a puzzling passage might be lines 27–28 with the closing **oxymoron:** "I joined the Wild and killed him / with knowledgeable unknowing.") What strikes you and why? What puzzles you and why?

2. What are the effects of certain phrases being repeated, e.g., "I have known," "I never saw," "I have always heard"?

3. Using details from the poem and inventing others as necessary, tell the story of the Boy. Who (or what) is he? Try narrating from any of a variety of **points of view**—the Boy's mother's or father's, a sibling's, a friend's.

4. Tell the story of the **speaker.** Where does the speaker live? What is his/her life like? What sorts of things does he/she do, see, hear, experience in a typical

day? If you wish, compose your narrative in the form of a series of diary entries by the speaker.

Wislawa Szymborska (b. 1923)

Hatred

See how efficient it still is,
how it keeps itself in shape —
our century's hatred.
How easily it vaults the tallest obstacles.
How rapidly it pounces, tracks us down.   5

It's not like other feelings.
At once both older and younger.
It gives birth itself to the reasons
that give it life.
When it sleeps, it's never eternal rest.   10
And sleeplessness won't sap its strength; it feeds it.

One religion or another —
whatever gets it ready, in position.
One fatherland or another —
whatever helps it get a running start.   15
Justice also works well at the outset
until hate gets its own momentum going.
Hatred. Hatred.
Its face twisted in a grimace
of erotic ecstasy.   20

Oh these other feelings,
listless weaklings.
Since when does brotherhood
draw crowds?
Has compassion   25
ever finished first?
Does doubt ever really rouse the rabble?
Only hatred has just what it takes.

Gifted, diligent, hard-working.
Need we mention all the songs it has composed?   30
All the pages it has added to our history books?

All the human carpets it has spread
over countless city squares and football fields?

Let's face it:
it knows how to make beauty.   35
The splendid fire-glow in midnight skies.
Magnificent bursting bombs in rosy dawns.
You can't deny the inspiring pathos of ruins
and a certain bawdy humor to be found
in the sturdy column jutting from their midst.   40

Hatred is a master of contrast—
between explosions and dead quiet,
red blood and white snow.
Above all, it never tires
of its leitmotif—the impeccable executioner   45
towering over its soiled victim.

It's always ready for new challenges.
If it has to wait awhile, it will.
They say it's blind. Blind?
It has a sniper's keen sight   50
and gazes unflinchingly at the future
as only it can.

—Translated by Stanislaw Barańczak and Clare Cavanagh

ACTIVITIES FOR WRITING AND DISCUSSION

1. Where—and with what effect(s)—does Szymborska use **personification** in this poem? What other figures are present, and how do they intensify the poem's impact? Illustrate your answer with specific phrases or lines.

2. Individually or collaboratively, jot down some adjectives to describe the poem's tone. Grim? Angry? Playful? Impassioned? Support your choice of adjectives with evidence from specific lines. Then discuss *why* Szymborska might have chosen the particular tone she did.

3. Rather than condemning hatred, the speaker seems to praise it. How can you tell that the praise is meant to be taken **ironically?** What are some particular words and passages that underscore the irony? Finally, how does this ironic stance do a better job of portraying hatred than would literal condemnation?

4. Do Activity #2 on page 593.

CARTER REVARD (b. 1931)

Discovery of the New World

The creatures that we met this morning
    marveled at our green skins
            and scarlet eyes.
They lack antennae
    and can't be made to grasp   5
      your proclamation that they are
our lawful food and prey and slaves,
    nor can they seem to learn
      their body-space is needed to materialize
        our oxygen-absorbers—   10
which they conceive are breathing
    and thinking creatures whom they implore
at first as angels, then as devils,
      when they are being snuffed out
        by an absorber swelling   15
          into their space.
Their history bled from one this morning,
    while we were tasting his brain,
      in holographic rainbows,
which we assembled into quite an interesting   20
    set of legends—
      that's all it came to, though
the colors were quite lovely before we
    poured them into our time;
      the blue shift bleached away   25
meaningless circumstances, and they would not fit
    any of our truth-matrices—
      there was, however,
      a curious visual echo in their history
        of our own coming to their earth;   30
a certain General Sherman said
    about one group of them precisely what
      we have been telling you about these creatures:
it is our destiny to asterize this planet,
    and they WILL not be asterized,   35
      so they must be wiped out.
    WE NEED their space and nitrogen
    which they do not know how to *use,*

nor will they breathe ammonia, as we do;
    yet they will not give up their "air" unforced,   40
      so it is clear,
        whatever our "agreements" made this
                    morning,
    we'll have to kill them all:
      the more we cook this orbit,   45
    the fewer next time round.
We've finished lazing all their crops and stores,
    we've killed their meat-slaves, now
      they'll have to come into our pens
    and we can use them for our final studies   50
      of how our heart attacks and cancers spread
                  among them,
    since they seem not immune to these.
—If we didn't have this mission it might be sad
      to see such helpless creatures die   55
chanting their sacred psalms and bills of rights; but
                  never fear
    the riches of this globe are ours
    and worth whatever pains others may have to
                feel.   60
    We'll soon have it cleared
completely, as it now is, at the poles, and then
    we will be safe, and rich, and happy here, forever.

ACTIVITIES FOR WRITING AND DISCUSSION

1. Where do the "discoverers" seem to be from? What "New World" are they discovering, and how do you know? To whom might the "your" in line 6 refer? What type of writing is this poem meant to represent—a diary entry? report? letter? oral communication of some sort? Explain.

2. Working alone or in a group, underline or circle any odd, puzzling, or striking terms or expressions you find in the poem. Then look for definitions in a dictionary, or attempt to translate the terms into more familiar language. Finally, discuss how these terms or expressions function meaningfully in the poem.

3. Does the poem parody (i.e., provide a satirical imitation of) any actual events in human history? If so, give examples of some such events. Then, in your notebook, analyze how the parody works.

4. React to the final line. Do you take it literally or **ironically?** Why? Write a sequel (in poetry or prose) in which you trace the subsequent fortunes of the "discoverers."

WOLE SOYINKA (b. 1934)

Telephone Conversation

The price seemed reasonable, location
Indifferent. The landlady swore she lived
Off premises. Nothing remained
But self-confession. 'Madam,' I warned,
'I hate a wasted journey—I am—African.'   5
Silence. Silenced transmission of
Pressurized good-breeding. Voice, when it came,
Lipstick coated, long gold-rolled
Cigarette-holder pipped. Caught I was, foully.
'HOW DARK?' . . . I had not misheard. . . . 'ARE YOU LIGHT   10
OR VERY DARK?' Button B. Button A. Stench
Of rancid breath of public-hide-and-speak.
Red booth.[1] Red pillar-box.[2] Red double-tiered
Omnibus squelching tar. It *was* real! Shamed
By ill-mannered silence, surrender   15
Pushed dumbfoundment to beg simplification.
Considerate she was, varying the emphasis—
'ARE YOU DARK? OR VERY LIGHT?' Revelation came.
'You mean—like plain or milk chocolate?'
Her assent was clinical, crushing in its light   20
Impersonality. Rapidly, wave-length adjusted,
I chose, 'West African sepia'—and as afterthought,
'Down in my passport.' Silence for spectroscopic
Flight of fancy, till truthfulness clanged her accent
Hard on the mouthpiece. 'WHAT'S THAT?' conceding   25
'DON'T KNOW WHAT THAT IS.' 'Like brunette.'
'THAT'S DARK, ISN'T IT?' 'Not altogether.
Facially, I am brunette, but madam, you should see
The rest of me. Palm of my hand, soles of my feet
Are a peroxid blonde. Friction, caused—   30
Foolishly madam—by sitting down, has turned
My bottom raven black—One moment madam!'—sensing
Her receiver rearing on the thunder clap
About my ears—'Madam,' I pleaded, 'wouldn't you rather
See for yourself?'   35

---

1. Phone booth.   2. Mailbox.

ACTIVITIES FOR WRITING AND DISCUSSION

1. How, if at all, would the poem change if this "conversation" took place via e-mail rather than over the phone? Invent the alternative conversation.

2. Analyze the poem's language, e.g., the varied sentence lengths, the choice and use of quoted dialogue, the use of ellipsis points and capitalization in lines 10 and 11 and elsewhere, and other punctuation devices used to depict the rhythms and tensions of the conversation. How do these features enhance the poem's effect? Illustrate your analysis with examples.

3. Soyinka uses a phone conversation to dramatize an example of racial prejudice. In a dialogue within a poem or a prose dialogue, do a takeoff on Soyinka's text. Include one or more of the following elements:
   a. A conflict that goes beyond opinion or thought to the essential selves, e.g., racial, ethnic, linguistic, religious, of the two speakers,
   b. A conflict that threatens to explode but is controlled by a conscious effort at politeness,
   c. A conflict in which one speaker clearly enjoys an implicit position of power over the other.

PAULA GUNN ALLEN (b. 1939)

Pocahontas to Her English Husband, John Rolfe

Had I not cradled you in my arms,
oh beloved perfidious one,
you would have died.
And how many times did I pluck you
from certain death in the wilderness—   5
my world through which you stumbled
as though blind?
Had I not set you tasks
your masters far across the sea
would have abandoned you—   10
did abandon you, as many times they
left you to reap the harvest of their lies;
still you survived, oh my fair husband,
and brought them gold
wrung from a harvest I taught you   15
to plant: Tobacco.   It
is not without irony that by this crop
your descendants die, for other powers
than those you know take part in this.

And indeed I did rescue you   20
not once but a thousand thousand times
and in my arms you slept, a foolish child,
and beside me you played,
chattering nonsense about a God
you had not wit to name;   25
and wondered you at my silence—
simple foolish wanton maid you saw,
dusky daughter of heathen sires
who knew not the ways of grace—
no doubt, no doubt.   30
I spoke little, you said.
And you listened less.
But played with your gaudy dreams
and sent ponderous missives to the throne
striving thereby to curry favor   35
with your king.   I saw you well.   I
understood the ploy and still protected you,
going so far as to die in your keeping—
a wasting, putrifying death, and you,
deceiver, my husband, father of my son,   40
survived, your spirit bearing crop
slowly from my teaching, taking
certain life from the wasting of my bones.

Sharon Olds (b. 1942)

On the Subway

The boy and I face each other.
His feet are huge, in black sneakers
laced with white in a complex pattern like a
set of intentional scars. We are stuck on
opposite sides of the car, a couple of   5
molecules stuck in a rod of light
rapidly moving through darkness. He has the
casual cold look of a mugger,
alert under hooded lids. He is wearing
red, like the inside of the body   10
exposed. I am wearing dark fur, the
whole skin of an animal taken and

used. I look at his raw face,
he looks at my fur coat, and I don't
know if I am in his power—   15
he could take my coat so easily, my
briefcase, my life—
or if he is in my power, the way I am
living off his life, eating the steak
he does not eat, as if I am taking   20
the food from his mouth. And he is black
and I am white, and without meaning or
trying to I must profit from his darkness,
the way he absorbs the murderous beams of the
nation's heart, as black cotton   25
absorbs the heat of the sun and holds it. There is
no way to know how easy this
white skin makes my life, this
life he could take so easily and
break across his knee like a stick the way his   30
own back is being broken, the
rod of his soul that at birth was dark and
fluid and rich as the heart of a seedling
ready to thrust up into any available light.

ACTIVITIES FOR WRITING AND DISCUSSION

1. Describe the emotions you have as you read the first several lines. What words or images contribute to these emotions?

2. Is the **speaker** male or female? Does it matter? Why or why not? What evidence, if any, do you have of the speaker's race and socioeconomic background? of his/her political leanings? Quote and discuss such evidence. Does it matter that the speaker describes the large person across the car as a "boy" rather than a "man"?

3. Working alone or with a group, underline and annotate any **metaphors** and **similes.** Choose two or three that particularly strike you and brainstorm a list of any thoughts, reactions, or images they stir in you. Finally, in your notebook explain how those two or three metaphors or similes work in the poem.

4. The poem captures a momentary encounter, all from the speaker's **point of view.** In poetry or prose, narrate the same encounter from the boy's point of view. Consider the possibility that the boy has no interest in assaulting Olds's speaker. *Alternative:* Narrate the encounter between the speaker and the boy from the point of view of someone else aboard the subway car.

Jim Sagel (b. 1947)

Baca Grande

Una vaca se topó con un ratón y le dice:
"Tú—¿tan chiquito y con bigote?" Y le responde el ratón:
"Y tú tan grandota—¿y sin brassiere?"

It was nearly a miracle
James Baca remembered anyone at all
from the old hometown gang
having been two years at Yale
  no less   5
and halfway through law school
at the University of California at Irvine

They hardly recognized him either
in his three-piece grey business suit
and surfer-swirl haircut   10
with just the menacing hint
of a tightly trimmed Zapata moustache
  for cultural balance
and relevance

He had come to deliver the keynote address   15
to the graduating class of 80
at his old alma mater
and show off his well-trained lips
which laboriously parted
  each Kennedyish "R"   20
and drilled the first person pronoun
through the microphone
like an oil bit
with the slick, elegantly honed phrases
that slid so smoothly   25
off his meticulously bleached
  tongue
He talked Big Bucks
with astronautish fervor and if he
  the former bootstrapless James A. Baca   30
could dazzle the ass
off the universe
then even you
  yes you

Joey Martinez toying with your yellow   35
        tassle
and staring dumbly into space
could emulate Mr. Baca someday
        possibly
well   40
there was of course
such a thing
as being an outrageously successful
gas station attendant too
        let us never forget   45
it doesn't really matter what you do
so long as you excel
        James said
never believing a word
of it   50
for he had already risen
        as high as they go

Wasn't nobody else
from this deprived environment
who'd ever jumped   55
        straight out of college
into the Governor's office
and maybe one day
he'd sit in that big chair
        himself   60
and when he did
he'd forget this damned town
and all the petty little people
in it
once and for all   65

That much he promised himself

ACTIVITIES FOR WRITING AND DISCUSSION

1. Describe the occasion depicted and the **speaker.** Do you imagine the speaker is a member of the student audience being addressed by Baca or an outside observer? someone older or younger than Baca? Cite evidence to support your answers.

2. In lines 34–35 the speaker suddenly shifts attention to "you / Joey Martinez," and by the last line he seems to be inside the mind of James Baca. How do

you account for these shifts in focus and perspective? Are they clumsy, or are they purposeful in some way? Explain.

3. From clues in the poem (and other material from your own imagination), create an outline—or the complete text—of Baca's speech.

Gary Soto (b. 1952)

Black Hair

At eight I was brilliant with my body.
In July, that ring of heat
We all jumped through, I sat in the bleachers
Of Romain Playground, in the lengthening
Shade that rose from our dirty feet.   5
The game before us was more than baseball.
It was a figure—Hector Moreno
Quick and hard with turned muscles,
His crouch the one I assumed before an altar
Of worn baseball cards, in my room.   10

I came here because I was Mexican, a stick
Of brown light in love with those
Who could do it—the triple and hard slide,
The gloves eating balls into double plays.
What could I do with 50 pounds, my shyness,   15
My black torch of hair, about to go out?
Father was dead, his face no longer
Hanging over the table or our sleep,
And mother was the terror of mouths
Twisting hurt by butter knives.   20

In the bleachers I was brilliant with my body,
Waving players in and stomping my feet,
I chewed sunflower seeds. I drank water
And bit my arm through the late innings.
When Hector lined balls into deep   25
Center, in my mind I rounded the bases
With him, my face flared, my hair lifting
Beautifully, because we were coming home
To the arms of brown people.

Sook Lyol Ryu (b. 1954)

Poem by a Yellow Woman

When I first saw America,
it was like a huge giant,
and I was like a pygmy woman.
I made a desperate struggle with this giant
not to fall. He whistled merrily, waving his hands.   5
He was a huge man, but a man like a snake.

Now, here I am in America, where
people drink Coca-Cola, where
people are crazy about Spielberg's silly films, where
people chase endless desires, where   10
people choose an old anachronistic
movie star as their president, where
people enjoy powerful wealth,
but keep homeless people in the street, where
people shout, "ladies first,"   15
and don't allow a woman to be president.
Now here I am from the country, where
the people are burning American flags,
singing, "Yankee, go home!"
Now here I am in America, where   20
most of my yellow people are hungry
for McDonald's and greedy for "Made in U.S.A."
My brother, who has a master's degree in English literature
thinks about Norman Mailer's American Dream
while selling fishes and vegetables   25
to his white neighbors 24 hours a day.
My sister, who liked paintings of
Picasso's Blue Period
is working on a sewing machine, with dyed blond hair.

When colored friends are making a rainbow coalition,   30
my yellow people wonder whether yellow is on the rainbow.
They think the lighter the skin, the closer to heaven,
the darker the skin, the closer to hell.
They decide yellow is in between.
So they smile at white and frown at black.   35
They make money in the hope of becoming a majority
and forget about the minority.

Martín Espada (b. 1957)

Coca-Cola and Coco Frío

On his first visit to Puerto Rico,
island of family folklore,
the fat boy wandered
from table to table
with his mouth open.   5
At every table, some great-aunt
would steer him with cool spotted hands
to a glass of Coca-Cola.
One even sang to him, in all the English
she could remember, a Coca-Cola jingle   10
from the forties. He drank obediently, though
he was bored with this potion, familiar
from soda fountains in Brooklyn.

Then, at a roadside stand off the beach, the fat boy
opened his mouth to coco frío, a coconut   15
chilled, then scalped by a machete
so that a straw could inhale the clear milk.
The boy tilted the green shell overhead
and drooled coconut milk down his chin;
suddenly, Puerto Rico was not Coca-Cola   20
or Brooklyn, and neither was he.

For years afterward, the boy marveled at an island
where the people drank Coca-Cola
and sang jingles from World War II
in a language they did not speak,   25
while so many coconuts in the trees
sagged heavy with milk, swollen
and unsuckled.

ACTIVITIES FOR WRITING AND DISCUSSION

1. What is the ethnic and personal background of "the fat boy"? Why do his great-aunts "steer him" to Coca-Cola? What political and economic issues does the poem raise?

2. Interpret the **irony** in lines 22–28 and the **metaphor** in lines 26–28.

3. Based on the poem's descriptive details and the boy's reaction to the two beverages, compare and contrast Coca-Cola and Coco-Frío.

4. Research the topic of globalization. What are its benefits and/or disadvantages to local cultures and economies?

Thomas S. Whitecloud (1914–1972)

Blue Winds Dancing

There is a moon out tonight. Moon and stars and clouds tipped with moonlight. And there is a fall wind blowing in my heart. Ever since this evening, when against a fading sky I saw geese wedge southward. They were going home. . . . Now I try to study, but against the pages I see them again, driving southward. Going home.

Across the valley there are heavy mountains holding up the night sky, and beyond the mountains there is home. Home, and peace, and the beat of drums, and blue winds dancing over snow fields. The Indian lodge will fill with my people, and our gods will come and sit among them. I should be there then. I should be at home.

But home is beyond the mountains, and I am here. Here where fall hides in the valleys, and winter never comes down from the mountains. Here where all the trees grow in rows; the palms stand stiffly by the roadsides, and in the groves the orange trees line in military rows, and endlessly bear fruit. Beautiful, yes; there is always beauty in order, in rows of growing things! But it is the beauty of captivity. A pine fighting for existence on a windy knoll is much more beautiful.

In my Wisconsin, the leaves change before the snows come. In the air there is the smell of wild rice and venison cooking; and when the winds come whispering through the forests, they carry the smell of rotting leaves. In the evenings, the loon calls, lonely; and birds sing their last songs before leaving. Bears dig roots and eat late fall berries, fattening for their long winter sleep. Later, when the first snows fall, one awakens in the morning to find the world white and beautiful and clean. Then one can look back over his trail and see the tracks following. In the woods there are tracks of deer and snowshoe rabbits, and long streaks where partridges slide to alight. Chipmunks make tiny footprints on the limbs; and one can hear squirrels busy in hollow trees, sorting acorns. Soft lake waves wash the shores, and sunsets burst each evening over the lakes, and make them look as if they were afire.

That land which is my home! Beautiful, calm—where there is no hurry to get 5 anywhere, no driving to keep up in a race that knows no ending and no goal. No classes where men talk and talk, and then stop now and then to hear their own words come back to them from the students. No constant peering into the maelstrom of one's mind; no worries about grades and honors; no hysterical preparing for life until that life is half over; no anxiety about one's place in the thing they call Society.

I hear again the ring of axes in deep woods, the crunch of snow beneath my feet. I feel again the smooth velvet of ghost-birch bark. I hear the rhythm of the drums. . . . I am tired. I am weary of trying to keep up this bluff of being civilized. Being civilized means trying to do everything you don't want to, never doing anything you want to. It means dancing to the strings of custom and tradition; it means living in houses and never knowing or caring who is next door. These civilized white men want us to be like them—always dissatisfied, getting a hill and wanting a mountain.

Then again, maybe I am not tired. Maybe I'm licked. Maybe I am just not smart enough to grasp these things that go to make up civilization. Maybe I am just too lazy to think hard enough to keep up.

Still, I know my people have many things that civilization has taken from the whites. They know how to give; how to tear one's piece of meat in two and share it with one's brother. They know how to sing—how to make each man his own songs and sing them; for their music they do not have to listen to other men singing over a radio. They know how to make things with their hands, how to shape beads into design and make a thing of beauty from a piece of birch bark.

But we are inferior. It is terrible to have to feel inferior; to have to read reports of intelligence tests, and learn that one's race is behind. It is terrible to sit in classes and hear men tell you that your people worship sticks of wood—that your gods are all false, that the Manitou forgot your people and did not write them a book.

I am tired. I want to walk again among the ghost-birches. I want to see the leaves 10 turn in autumn, the smoke rise from the lodgehouses, and to feel the blue winds. I want to hear the drums; I want to hear the drums and feel the blue whispering winds.

There is a train wailing into the night. The trains go across the mountains. It would be easy to catch a freight. They will say he has gone back to the blanket; I don't care. The dance at Christmas. . . .

———

A bunch of bums warming at a tiny fire talk politics and women and joke about the Relief and the WPA and smoke cigarettes. These men in caps and overcoats and dirty overalls living on the outskirts of civilization are free, but they pay the price of being free in civilization. They are outcasts. I remember a sociology professor lecturing on adjustment to society; hobos and prostitutes and criminals are individuals who never adjusted, he said. He could learn a lot if he came and listened to a bunch of bums talk. He would learn that work and a woman and a place to hang his hat are all the ordinary man wants. These are all he wants, but other men are not content to let him want only these. He must be taught to want radios and automobiles and a new suit every spring. Progress would stop if he did not want these things. I listen to hear if there is any talk of communism or socialism in the hobo jungles. There is none. At best there is a sort of disgusted philosophy about life. They seem to think there should be a better distribution of wealth, or more work, or something. But they are not rabid about it. The radicals live in the cities.

I find a fellow headed for Albuquerque, and talk road-talk with him. "It is hard to ride fruit cars. Bums break in. Better to wait for a cattle car going back to the Middle West, and ride that." We catch the next east-bound and walk the tops until we find a cattle car. Inside, we crouch near the forward wall, huddle, and try to sleep. I feel peaceful and content at last. I am going home. The cattle car rocks. I sleep.

Morning and the desert. Noon and the Salton Sea, lying more lifeless than a mirage under a somber sun in a pale sky. Skeleton mountains rearing on the sky-line, thrusting out of the desert floor, all rock and shadow and edges. Desert. Good country for an Indian reservation. . . .

Yuma and the muddy Colorado. Night again, and I wait shivering for the 15 dawn.

Phoenix. Pima country. Mountains that look like cardboard sets on a forgot-ten stage. Tucson. Papago country. Giant cacti that look like petrified hitchhikers along the highways. Apache country. At El Paso my road-buddy decides to go on to Houston. I leave him, and head north to the mesa country. Las Cruces and the terrible Organ Mountains, jagged peaks that instill fear and wondering. Albu-querque. Pueblos along the Rio Grande. On the boardwalk there are some Indian women in colored sashes selling bits of pottery. The stone age offering its art to the twentieth century. They hold up a piece and fix the tourist with black eyes un-til, embarrassed, he buys or turns away. I feel suddenly angry that my people should have to do such things for a living. . . .

Santa Fe trains are fast, and they keep them pretty clean of bums. I decide to hurry and ride passenger coaltenders. Hide in the dark, judge the speed of the train as it leaves, and then dash out, and catch it. I hug the cold steel wall of the tender and think of the roaring fire in the engine ahead, and of the passengers back in the dining car reading their papers over hot coffee. Beneath me there is blur of rails. Death would come quick if my hands should freeze and I fall. Up over the Sangre De Cristo range, around cliffs and through canyons to Denver. Bitter cold here, and I must watch out for Denver Bob. He is a railroad bull who has thrown bums from fast freights. I miss him. It is too cold, I suppose. On north to the Sioux country.

Small towns lit for the coming Christmas. On the streets of one I see a beam-shouldered young farmer gazing into a window filled with shining silver toasters. He is tall and wears a blue shirt buttoned, with no tie. His young wife by his side looks at him hopefully. He wants decorations for his place to hang his hat to please his woman. . . .

Northward again. Minnesota, and great white fields of snow; frozen lakes, and dawn running in dusk without noon. Long forests wearing white. Bitter cold, and one night the northern lights. I am nearing home.

I reach Woodruff at midnight. Suddenly I am afraid, now that I am but twenty 20 miles from home. Afraid of what my father will say, afraid of being looked on as a stranger by my own people. I sit by a fire and think about myself and all the other young Indians. We just don't seem to fit in anywhere—certainly not among the whites, and not among the older people. I think again about the learned soci-ology professor and his professing. So many things seem to be clear now that I am away from school and do not have to worry about some man's opinion of my ideas. It is easy to think while looking at dancing flames.

Morning. I spend the day cleaning up, and buying some presents for my family with what is left of my money. Nothing much, but a gift is a gift, if a man buys it with his last quarter. I wait until evening, then start up the track toward home.

Christmas Eve comes in on a north wind. Snow clouds hang over the pines, and the night comes early. Walking along the railroad bed, I feel the calm peace of snow-bound forests on either side of me. I take my time; I am back in a world where time does not mean so much now. I am alone; alone but not nearly so lonely as I was back on the campus at school. Those are never lonely who love the snow and the pines; never lonely when the pines are wearing white shawls and snow crunches coldly underfoot. In the woods I know there are the tracks of deer and rabbit; I know that if I leave the rails and go into the woods I shall find them. I walk along feeling glad because my legs are light and my feet seem to know that they are home. A deer comes out of the woods just ahead of me, and stands silhouetted on the rails. The North, I feel, has welcomed me home. I watch him and am glad that I do not wish for a gun. He goes into the woods quietly, leaving only the design of his tracks in the snow. I walk on. Now and then I pass a field, white under the night sky, with houses at the far end. Snow comes from the chimneys of the houses, and I try to tell what sort of wood each is burning by the smoke; some burn pine, others aspen, others tamarack. There is one from which comes black coal smoke that rises lazily and drifts out over the tops of the trees. I like to watch houses and try to imagine what might be happening in them.

Just as a light snow begins to fall, I cross the reservation boundary; somehow it seems as though I have stepped into another world. Deep woods in a white-and-black winter night. A faint trail leading to the village.

The railroad on which I stand comes from a city sprawled by a lake—a city with a million people who walk around without seeing one another; a city sucking the life from all the country around; a city with stores and police and intellectuals and criminals and movies and apartment houses; a city with its politics and libraries and zoos.

Laughing, I go into the woods. As I cross a frozen lake I begin to hear the   25 drums. Soft in the night the drums beat. It is like the pulse beat of the world. The white line of the lake ends at a black forest, and above the trees the blue winds are dancing.

I come to the outlying houses of the village. Simple box houses, etched black in the night. From one or two windows soft lamp light falls on the snow. Christmas here, too, but it does not mean much; not much in the way of parties and presents. Joe Sky will get drunk. Alex Bodidash will buy his children red mittens and a new sled. Alex is a Carlisle man, and tries to keep his home up to white standards. White standards. Funny that my people should be ever falling farther behind. The more they try to imitate whites the more tragic the result. Yet they want us to be imitation white men. About all we imitate well are their vices.

The village is not a sight to instill pride, yet I am not ashamed; one can never be ashamed of his own people when he knows they have dreams as beautiful as white snow on a tall pine.

Father and my brother and sister are seated around the table as I walk in. Father stares at me for a moment, then I am in his arms, crying on his shoulder. I give them the presents I have brought, and my throat tightens as I watch my sister save carefully bits of red string from the packages. I hide my feelings by wrestling with my brother when he strikes my shoulder in token of affection. Father looks at me, and I know he has many questions, but he seems to know why I have come. He tells me to go on alone to the lodge, and he will follow.

I walk along the trail to the lodge, watching the northern lights forming in the heavens. White waving ribbons that seem to pulsate with the rhythm of the drums. Clean snow creaks beneath my feet, and a soft wind sighs through the trees, singing to me. Everything seems to say "Be happy! You are home now—you are free. You are among friends—we are your friends; we, the trees, and the snow, and the lights." I follow the trail to the lodge. My feet are light, my heart seems to sing to the music, and I hold my head high. Across white snow fields blue winds are dancing.

Before the lodge door I stop, afraid. I wonder if my people will remember me. 30 I wonder—"Am I Indian, or am I white?" I stand before the door a long time. I hear the ice groan on the lake, and remember the story of the old woman who is under the ice, trying to get out, so she can punish some runaway lovers. I think to myself, "If I am white I will not believe that story; if I am Indian, I will know that there is an old woman under the ice." I listen for a while, and I know that there is an old woman under the ice. I look again at the lights, and go in.

Inside the lodge there are many Indians. Some sit on benches around the walls, others dance in the center of the floor around a drum. Nobody seems to notice me. It seems as though I were among a people I have never seen before. Heavy women with long black hair. Women with children on their knees—small children that watch with intent black eyes the movements of the dancers, whose small faces are solemn and serene. The faces of the old people are serene, too, and their eyes are merry and bright. I look at the old men. Straight, dressed in dark trousers and beaded velvet vests, wearing soft moccasins. Dark, lined faces intent on the music. I wonder if I am at all like them. They dance on, lifting their feet to the rhythm of the drums, swaying lightly, looking upward. I look at their eyes, and am startled at the rapt attention to the rhythm of the music.

The dance stops. The men walk back to the walls, and talk in low tones or with their hands. There is little conversation, yet everyone seems to be sharing some secret. A woman looks at a small boy wandering away, and he comes back to her.

Strange, I think, and then remember. These people are not sharing words—they are sharing a mood. Everyone is happy. I am so used to white people that it seems strange so many people could be together without someone talking. These Indians are happy because they are together, and because the night is beautiful outside, and the music is beautiful. I try hard to forget school and white people, and be one of these—my people. I try to forget everything but the night, and it is a part of me; that I am one with my people and we are all a part of something universal. I watch eyes, and see now that the old people are speaking to me. They nod slightly, imperceptibly, and their eyes laugh into mine. I look around the room. All the eyes are friendly; they all laugh. No one questions my being here. The drums begin to beat again, and I catch the invitation in the eyes of the old men. My feet begin to lift to the rhythm, and I look out beyond the walls into the night and see the lights. I am happy. It is beautiful. I am home.

ACTIVITIES FOR WRITING AND DISCUSSION

1. Read and annotate the essay. Then:
    a. Share and discuss a few of your favorite annotations with a small group, and take notes on your groupmates' annotations to enrich your response to the essay.
    b. Respond to "Blue Winds Dancing" in your notebook using any of the "Ten Ideas for Writing" described in Chapter 3 and summarized on page 35.

2. React to Whitecloud's **persona.** What qualities of the persona attract or repel you, and how and where—specifically—are those qualities conveyed in the language and content of the text? Consider word choice, vocabulary, sentence length and style, tone, and ideas. If you wish, focus your analysis on the opening paragraphs.

3. Working alone or collaboratively, make as long a list as you can of Whitecloud's criticisms of white society. Then, drawing upon the text and your own experience or knowledge, pick one or two criticisms and debate their justness or accuracy—first orally and then in writing in your notebook.

4. List any topics that are suggested to you by the essay, e.g., "silence," "civilization," "home," etc. Then make a Topic/Form Grid (see Chapter 5), choose a favorite topic, and use one of the forms on your grid to create a notebook entry about the topic. If your chosen form or topic does not work, do a Topic/Form Shift to a different form or topic on your grid.

WENDELL BERRY (b. 1934)

Think Little

First there was Civil Rights, and then there was the War, and now it is the Environment. The first two of this sequence of causes have already risen to the top of the nation's consciousness and declined somewhat in a remarkably short time. I mention this in order to begin with what I believe to be a justifiable skepticism.

For it seems to me that the Civil Rights Movement and the Peace Movement, as popular causes in the electronic age, have partaken far too much of the nature of fads. Not for all, certainly, but for too many they have been the fashionable politics of the moment. As causes they have been undertaken too much in ignorance; they have been too much simplified; they have been powered too much by impatience and guilt of conscience and short-term enthusiasm, and too little by an authentic social vision and long-term conviction and deliberation. For most people those causes have remained almost entirely abstract; there has been too little personal involvement, and too much involvemnet in organizations that were insisting that *other* organizations should do what was right.

There is considerable danger that the Environment Movement will have the same nature: that it will be a public cause, served by organizations that will self-righteously criticize and condemn other organizations, inflated for a while by a lot of public talk in the media, only to be replaced in its turn by another fashionable crisis. I hope that will not happen, and I believe that there are ways to keep it from happening, but I know that if this effort is carried on solely as a public cause, if millions of people cannot or will not undertake it as a *private* cause as well, then it is *sure* to happen. In five years the energy of our present concern will have petered out in a series of public gestures—and no doubt in a series of empty laws— and a great, and perhaps the last, human opportunity will have been lost.

It need not be that way. A better possibility is that the movement to preserve the environment will be seen to be, as I think it has to be, not a digression from the civil rights and peace movements, but the logical culmination of those movements. For I believe that the separation of these three problems is artificial. They have the same cause, and that is the mentality of greed and exploitation. The mentality that exploits and destroys the natural environment is the same that abuses racial and economic minorities, that imposes on young men the tyranny of the military draft, that makes war against peasants and women and children with the indifference of technology. The mentality that destroys a watershed and then panics at the threat of flood is the same mentality that gives institutionalized insult to black people and then panics at the prospect of race riots. It is the same mentality that can mount deliberate warfare against a civilian population and then express moral shock at the logical consequence of such warfare at My Lai. We would be fools to believe that we could solve any one of these problems without solving the others.

To me, one of the most important aspects of the environmental movement is that it brings us not just to another public crisis, but to a crisis of the protest movement itself. For the environmental crisis should make it dramatically clear, as perhaps it has not always been before, that there is no public crisis that is not also private. To most advocates of civil rights, racism has seemed mostly the fault of someone else. For most advocates of peace the war has been a remote reality, and the burden of the blame has seemed to rest mostly on the government. I am certain that these crises have been more private, and that we have each suffered more from them and been more responsible for them than has been readily apparent, but the connections have been difficult to see. Racism and militarism have been institutionalized among us for too long for our personal involvement in those evils to be easily apparent to us. Think, for example, of all the Northerners who assumed—until black people attempted to move into *their* neighborhoods—that racism was a Southern phenomenon. And think how quickly—one might almost say how naturally—among some of its members the peace movement has spawned policies of deliberate provocation and violence.

———

But the environmental crisis rises closer to home. Every time we draw a breath,   5
every time we drink a glass of water, every time we eat a bite of food we are suffering from it. And more important, every time we indulge in, or depend on, the wastefulness of our economy—and our economy's first principle is waste—we are *causing* the crisis. Nearly every one of us, nearly every day of his life, is contributing *directly* to the ruin of this planet. A protest meeting on the issue of environmental abuse is not a convocation of accusers, it is a convocation of the guilty. That realization ought to clear the smog of self-righteousness that has almost conventionally hovered over these occasions, and let us see the work that is to be done.

In this crisis it is certain that every one of us has a public responsibility. We must not cease to bother the government and the other institutions to see that they never become comfortable with easy promises. For myself, I want to say that I hope never again to go to Frankfort to present a petition to the governor on an issue so vital as that of strip mining, only to be dealt with by some ignorant functionary—as several of us were not so long ago, the governor himself being "too busy" to receive us. Next time I will go prepared to wait as long as necessary to see that the petitioners' complaints and their arguments are heard *fully*—and by the governor. And then I will hope to find ways to keep those complaints and arguments from being forgotten until something is done to relieve them. The time is past when it was enough merely to elect our officials. We will have to elect them and then go and *watch* them and keep our hands on them, the way the coal companies do. We have made a tradition in Kentucky of putting self-servers, and worse, in charge of our vital interests. I am sick of it. And I think that one way to change it is to make Frankfort a less comfortable place. I believe in American political principles, and I will not sit idly by and see those principles destroyed by sorry practice. I am ashamed and deeply distressed that American government should have become the chief cause of disillusionment with American principles.

And so when the government in Frankfort again proves too stupid or too blind or too corrupt to see the plain truth and to act with simple decency, I intend to be there, and I trust that I won't be alone. I hope, moreover, to be there, not with a sign or a slogan or a button, but with the facts and the arguments. A crowd whose discontent has risen no higher than the level of slogans is *only* a crowd. But a crowd that understands the reasons for its discontent and knows the remedies is a vital community, and it will have to be reckoned with. I would rather go before the government with two people who have a competent understanding of an issue, and who therefore deserve a hearing, than with two thousand who are vaguely dissatisfied.

But even the most articulate public protest is not enough. We don't live in the government or in institutions or in our public utterances and acts, and the environmental crisis has its roots in our *lives.* By the same token, environmental health will also be rooted in our lives. That is, I take it, simply a fact, and in the light of it we can see how superficial and foolish we would be to think that we could correct what is wrong merely by tinkering with the institutional machinery. The changes that are required are fundamental changes in the way we are living.

———

What we are up against in this country, in any attempt to invoke private responsibility, is that we have nearly destroyed private life. Our people have given up their independence in return for the cheap seductions and the shoddy merchandise of so-called "affluence." We have delegated all our vital functions and responsibilities to salesmen and agents and bureaus and experts of all sorts. We cannot feed or clothe ourselves, or entertain ourselves, or communicate with each other, or be charitable or neighborly or loving, or even respect ourselves, without recourse to a merchant or a corporation or a public-service organization or an agency of the government or a style-setter or an expert. Most of us cannot think of dissenting from the opinions or the actions of one organization without first forming a new organization. Individualism is going around these days in uniform, handing out the party line on individualism. Dissenters want to publish their personal opinions over a thousand signatures.

The Confucian *Great Digest* says that the "chief way for the production of 10 wealth" (and he is talking about real goods, not money) is "that the producers be many and that the mere consumers be few. . . ." But even in the much-publicized rebellion of the young against the materialism of the affluent society, the consumer mentality is too often still intact: the standards of behavior are still those of kind and quantity, the security sought is still the security of numbers, and the chief motive is still the consumer's anxiety that he is missing out on what is "in." In this state of total consumerism—which is to say a state of helpless dependence on things and services and ideas and motives that we have forgotten how to provide ourselves—all meaningful contact between ourselves and the earth is broken. We do not understand the earth in terms either of what it offers us or of what it requires of us, and I think it is the rule that people inevitably destroy what they do not understand. Most of us are not directly responsible for strip mining and extractive agriculture and other forms of environmental abuse. But we are guilty nevertheless, for we connive in them by our ignorance. We are ignorantly dependent on them. We do not know enough about them; we do not have a particular enough sense of their danger. Most of us, for example, not only do not know how to produce the best food in the best way—we don't know how to produce any kind in any way. Our model citizen is a sophisticate who before puberty understands how to produce a baby, but who at the age of thirty will not know how to produce a potato. And for this condition we have elaborate rationalizations, instructing us that dependence for everything on somebody else is efficient and economical and a scientific miracle. I say, instead, that it is madness, mass produced.

A man who understands the weather only in terms of golf is participating in a chronic public insanity that either he or his descendants will be bound to realize as suffering. I believe that the death of the world is breeding in such minds much more certainly and much faster than in any political capital or atomic arsenal.

For an index of our loss of contact with the earth we need only look at the condition of the American farmer—who must in our society, as in every society, enact man's dependence on the land, and his responsibility to it. In an age of unparalleled affluence and leisure, the American farmer is harder pressed and harder worked than ever before; his margin of profit is small, his hours are long; his outlays for land and equipment and the expenses of maintenance and operation are growing rapidly greater; he cannot compete with industry for labor; he is being forced more and more to depend on the use of destructive chemicals and on the wasteful methods of haste and anxiety. As a class, farmers are one of the despised minorities. So far as I can see, farming is considered marginal or incidental to the economy of the country, and farmers, when they are thought of at all, are thought of as hicks and yokels whose lives do not fit into the modern scene. The average American farmer is now an old man whose sons have moved away to the cities. His knowledge, and his intimate connection with the land, are about to be lost. The small independent farmer is going the way of the small independent craftsmen and storekeepers. He is being forced off the land into the cities, his place taken by absentee owners, corporations, and machines. Some would justify all this in the name of efficiency. As I see it, it is an enormous social and economic and cultural blunder. For the small farmers who lived on their farms *cared* about their land. And given their established connection to their land—which was often hereditary and traditional as well as economic—they could have been encouraged to care for it more competently than they have so far. The corporations and machines that replace them will never be bound to the land by the sense of birthright and continuity, or by the love that enforces care. They will be bound by the rule of efficiency, which takes thought only of the volume of the year's produce, and takes no thought of the slow increment of the life of the land, not measurable in pounds or dollars, which will assure the livelihood and the health of the coming generations.

If we are to hope to correct our abuses of each other and of other races and of our land, and if our effort to correct these abuses is to be more than a political fad that will in the long run be only another form of abuse, then we are going to have to go far beyond public protest and political action. We are going to have to rebuild the substance and the integrity of private life in this country. We are going to have to gather up the fragments of knowledge and responsibility that we have parceled out to the bureaus and the corporations and the specialists, and we are going to have to put those fragments back together again in our own minds and in our families and households and neighborhoods. We need better government, no doubt about it. But we also need better minds, better friendships, better marriages, better communities. We need persons and households that do not have to wait upon organizations, but can make necessary changes in themselves, on their own.

For most of the history of this country our motto, implied or spoken, has been Think Big. I have come to believe that a better motto, and an essential one now, is Think Little. That implies the necessary change of thinking and feeling, and suggests the necessary work. Thinking Big has led us to the two biggest and cheapest political dodges of our time: plan-making and law-making. The lotus-eaters of this era are in Washington, D.C., Thinking Big. Somebody comes up with a problem, and somebody in the government comes up with a plan or a law. The result, mostly, has been the persistence of the problem, and the enlargement and enrichment of the government.

But the discipline of thought is not generalization; it is detail, and it is personal behavior. While the government is "studying" and funding and organizing its Big Thought, nothing is being done. But the citizen who is willing to Think Little, and, accepting the discipline of that, to go ahead on his own, is already solving the problem. A man who is trying to live as a neighbor to his neighbors will have a lively and practical understanding of the work of peace and brotherhood, and let there be no mistake about it—he is *doing* that work. A couple who make a good marriage, and raise healthy, morally competent children, are serving the world's future more directly and surely than any political leader, though they never utter a public word. A good farmer who is dealing with the problem of soil erosion on an acre of ground has a sounder grasp of that problem and *cares* more about it and is probably doing more to solve it than any bureaucrat who is talking about it in general. A man who is willing to undertake the discipline and the difficulty of mending his own ways is worth more to the conservation movement than a hundred who are insisting merely that the government and the industries mend *their* ways.

If you are concerned about the proliferation of trash, then by all means start an organization in your community to do something about it. But before—*and while*—you organize, pick up some cans and bottles yourself. That way, at least, you will assure yourself and others that you mean what you say. If you are concerned about air pollution, help push for government controls, but drive your car less, use less fuel in your home. If you are worried about the damming of wilderness rivers, join the Sierra Club, write to the government, but turn off the lights you're not using, don't install an air conditioner, don't be a sucker for electrical gadgets, don't waste water. In other words, if you are fearful of the destruction of the environment, then learn to quit being an environmental parasite. We all are, in one way or another, and the remedies are not always obvious, though they certainly will always be difficult. They require a new kind of life—harder, more laborious, poorer in luxuries and gadgets, but also, I am certain, richer in meaning and more abundant in real pleasure. To have a healthy environment we will all have to give up things we like; we may even have to give up things we have come to think of as necessities. But to be fearful of the disease and yet unwilling to pay for the cure is not just to be hypocritical; it is to be doomed. If you talk a good line without being changed by what you say, then you are not just hypocritical and doomed; you have become an agent of the disease. Consider, for an example, President Nixon, who advertises his grave concern about the destruction of the environment, and who turns up the air conditioner to make it cool enough to build a fire.

Odd as I am sure it will appear to some, I can think of no better form of personal involvement in the cure of the environment than that of gardening. A person who is growing a garden, if he is growing it organically, is improving a piece of the world. He is producing something to eat, which makes him somewhat independent of the grocery business, but he is also enlarging, for himself, the meaning of food and the pleasure of eating. The food he grows will be fresher, more nutritious, less contaminated by poisons and preservatives and dyes than what he can buy at a store. He is reducing the trash problem; a garden is not a disposable container, and it will digest and reuse its own wastes. If he enjoys working in his garden, then he is less dependent on an automobile or a merchant for his pleasure. He is involving himself directly in the work of feeding people.

If you think I'm wandering off the subject, let me remind you that most of the vegetables necessary for a family of four can be grown on a plot of forty by sixty feet. I think we might see in this an economic potential of considerable importance, since we now appear to be facing the possibility of widespread famine. How much food could be grown in the dooryards of cities and suburbs? How much could be grown along the extravagant rights-of-way of the interstate system? Or how much could be grown, by the intensive practices and economics of the small farm, on so-called marginal lands? Louis Bromfield liked to point out that the people of France survived crisis after crisis because they were a nation of gardeners, who in times of want turned with great skill to their own small plots of ground. And F. H. King, an agriculture professor who traveled extensively in the Orient in 1907, talked to a Chinese farmer who supported a family of twelve, "one donkey, one cow . . . and two pigs on 2.5 acres of cultivated land"—and who did this, moreover, by agricultural methods that were sound enough organically to have maintained his land in prime fertility through several thousand years of such use. These are possibilities that are readily apparent and attractive to minds that are prepared to Think Little. To Big Thinkers—the bureaucrats and businessmen of agriculture—they are quite simply invisible. But intensive, organic agriculture kept the farms of the Orient thriving for thousands of years, whereas extensive—which is to say, exploitive or extractive—agriculture has critically reduced the fertility of American farmlands in a few centuries or even a few decades.

A person who undertakes to grow a garden at home, by practices that will preserve rather than exploit the economy of the soil, has set his mind decisively against what is wrong with us. He is helping himself in a way that dignifies him and that is rich in meaning and pleasure. But he is doing something else that is more important: he is making vital contact with the soil and the weather on which his life depends. He will no longer look upon rain as an impediment of traffic, or upon the sun as a holiday decoration. And his sense of man's dependence on the world will have grown precise enough, one would hope, to be politically clarifying and useful.

What I am saying is that if we apply our minds directly and competently to the needs of the earth then we will have begun to make fundamental and necessary changes in our minds. We will begin to understand and to mistrust *and to change* our wasteful economy, which markets not just the produce of the earth, but also the earth's ability to produce. We will see that beauty and utility are alike dependent upon the health of the world. But we will also see through the fads and the fashions of protest. We will see that war and oppression and pollution are not separate issues, but are aspects of the same issue. Amid the outcries for the liberation of this group or that, we will know that no person is free except in the freedom of other persons, and that man's only real freedom is to know and faithfully occupy his place—a much humbler place than we have been taught to think—in the order of creation.

But the change of mind I am talking about involves not just a change of knowl- 20
edge, but also a change of attitude toward our essential ignorance, a change in our bearing in the face of mystery. The principle of ecology, if we will take it to heart, should keep us aware that our lives depend upon other lives and upon processes and energies in an interlocking system that, though we can destroy it, we can neither fully understand nor fully control. And our great dangerousness is that, locked in our selfish and myopic economics, we have been willing to change or destroy far beyond our power to understand. We are not humble enough or reverent enough.

Some time ago, I heard a representative of a paper company refer to conservation as a "no-return investment." This man's thinking was exclusively oriented to the annual profit of his industry. Circumscribed by the demand that the profit be great, he simply could not be answerable to any other demand—not even to the obvious needs of his own children.

Consider, in contrast, the profound ecological intelligence of Black Elk, "a holy man of the Oglala Sioux," who in telling his story said that it was not his own life that was important to him, but what he had shared with all life: "It is the story of all life that is holy and it is good to tell, and of us two-leggeds sharing in it with the four-leggeds and the wings of the air and all green things. . . ." And of the great vision that came to him when he was a child he said: "I saw that the sacred hoop of my people was one of many hoops that made one circle, wide as daylight and as starlight, and in the center grew one mighty flowering tree to shelter all the children of one mother and father. And I saw that it was holy."

ACTIVITIES FOR WRITING AND DISCUSSION

1. In paragraph 4 Berry states that "there is no public crisis that is not also private." After a careful rereading of the opening paragraphs, explain what he means. Then relate the quotation to the essay's title, "Think Little," and to paragraphs 13 and 14, which articulate the thesis of the essay.

2. Berry asserts that we (Americans) live in a "state of total consumerism," which he defines as a "state of helpless dependence on things and services and ideas and motives that we have forgotten how to provide ourselves" (paragraph 10). Annotate his examples of "dependence" in paragraph 10; then defend or challenge his assertion with evidence and examples of your own.

3. In addition to criticizing "total consumerism" Berry proposes actions that private citizens and communities can take to counteract its effects. Identify these proposed actions. Then evaluate them or (if you see a problem) suggest alternative actions of your own devising.

4. Read other of Berry's writings on the topics of "consumerism," "dependence," and economy—for instance, the classic title essay in his collection *Sex, Economy, Freedom & Community* (New York: Pantheon, 1993). In an essay of your own, defend or challenge his arguments and conclusions.

LESLIE MARMON SILKO (b. 1948)

Language and Literature from a Pueblo Indian Perspective

Where I come from, the words most highly valued are those spoken from the heart, unpremeditated and unrehearsed. Among the Pueblo people, a written speech or statement is highly suspect because the true feelings of the speaker remain hidden as she reads words that are detached from the occasion and the audience. I have intentionally not written a formal paper because I want you to *hear* and to experience English in a structure that follows patterns from the oral tradition. For those of you accustomed to being taken from point A to point B to point C, this presentation may be somewhat difficult to follow. Pueblo expression resembles something like a spider's web—with many little threads radiating from the center, crisscrossing each other. As with the web, the structure emerges as it is made and you must simply listen and trust, as the Pueblo people do, that meaning will be made.

My task is a formidable one: I ask you to set aside a number of basic approaches that you have been using, and probably will continue to use, and instead, to approach language from the Pueblo perspective, one that embraces the whole of creation and the whole of history and time.

What changes would Pueblo writers make to English as a language for literature? I have some examples of stories in English that I will use to address this question. At the same time, I would like to explain the importance of storytelling and how it relates to a Pueblo theory of language.

So, I will begin, appropriately enough, with the Pueblo Creation story, an all-inclusive story of how life began. In this story, Tséitsínako, Thought Woman, by thinking of her sisters, and together with her sisters, thought of everything that is.

In this way, the world was created. Everything in this world was a part of the original creation; the people at home understood that far away there were other human beings, also a part of this world. The Creation story even includes a prophecy, which describes the origin of European and African peoples and also refers to Asians.

This story, I think, suggests something about why the Pueblo people are more 5
concerned with story and communication and less concerned with a particular language. There are at least six, possibly seven, distinct languages among the twenty pueblos of the southwestern United States, for example, Zuñi and Hopi. And from mesa to mesa there are subtle differences in language. But the particular language being spoken isn't as important as what a speaker is trying to say, and this emphasis on the story itself stems, I believe, from a view of narrative particular to the Pueblo and other Native American peoples—that is, that language *is* story.

I will try to clarify this statement. At Laguna Pueblo, for example, many individual words have their own stories. So when one is telling a story, and one is using words to tell the story, each word that one is speaking has a story of its own, too. Often the speakers or tellers will go into these word-stories, creating an elaborate structure of stories-within-stories. This structure, which becomes very apparent in the actual telling of a story, informs contemporary Pueblo writing and storytelling as well as the traditional narratives. This perspective on narrative—of story within story, the idea that one story is only the beginning of many stories, and the sense that stories never truly end—represents an important contribution of Native American cultures to the English language.

Many people think of storytelling as something that is done at bedtime, that it is something done for small children. But when I use the term *storytelling*, I'm talking about something much bigger than that. I'm talking about something that comes out of an experience and an understanding of that original view of creation—that we are all part of a whole; we do not differentiate or fragment stories and experiences. In the beginning, Tséitsínako, Thought Woman, thought of all things, and all of these things are held together as one holds many things together in a single thought.

So in the telling (and you will hear a few of the dimensions of this telling) first of all, as mentioned earlier, the storytelling always includes the audience, the listeners. In fact, a great deal of the story is believed to be inside the listener: the storyteller's role is to draw the story out of the listeners. The storytelling continues from generation to generation.

Basically, the origin story constructs our identity—within this story, we know who we are. We are the Lagunas. This is where we come from. We came this way. We came by this place. And so from the time we are very young, we hear these stories, so that when we go out into the world, when one asks who we are, or where we are from, we immediately know: we are the people who came from the north. We are the people of these stories.

In the Creation story, Antelope says that he will help knock a hole in the earth 10
so that the people can come up, out into the next world. Antelope tries and tries; he uses his hooves, but is unable to break through. It is then that Badger says, "Let me help you." And Badger very patiently uses his claws and digs a way through,

bringing the people into the world. When the Badger clan people think of themselves, or when the Antelope people think of themselves, it is as people who are of *this* story, and this is *our* place, and we fit into the very beginning when the people first came, before we began our journey south.

Within the clans there are stories that identify the clan. One moves, then, from the idea of one's identity as a tribal person into clan identity, then to one's identity as a member of an extended family. And it is the notion of "extended family" that has produced a kind of story that some distinguish from other Pueblo stories, though Pueblo people do not. Anthropologists and ethnologists have, for a long time, differentiated the types of stories the Pueblos tell. They tended to elevate the old, sacred, and traditional stories and to brush aside family stories, the family's account of itself. But in Pueblo culture, these family stories are given equal recognition. There is no definite, preset pattern for the way one will hear the stories of one's own family, but it is a very critical part of one's childhood, and the storytelling continues throughout one's life. One will hear stories of importance to the family—sometimes wonderful stories—stories about the time a maternal uncle got the biggest deer that was ever seen and brought it back from the mountains. And so an individual's identity will extend from the identity constructed around the family—"I am from the family of my uncle who brought in this wonderful deer and it was a wonderful hunt."

Family accounts include negative stories, too; perhaps an uncle did something unacceptable. It is very important that one keep track of all these stories—both positive and not so positive—about one's own family and other families. Because even when there is no way around it—old Uncle Pete *did* do a terrible thing—by knowing the stories that originate in other families, one is able to deal with terrible sorts of things that might happen within one's own family. If a member of the family does something that cannot be excused, one always knows stories about similarly inexcusable things done by a member of another family. But this knowledge is not communicated for malicious reasons. It is very important to understand this. Keeping track of all the stories within the community gives us all a certain distance, a useful perspective, that brings incidents down to a level we can deal with. If others have done it before, it cannot be so terrible. If others have endured, so can we.

The stories are always bringing us together, keeping this whole together, keeping this family together, keeping this clan together. "Don't go away, don't isolate yourself, but come here, because we have all had these kinds of experiences." And so there is this constant pulling together to resist the tendency to run or hide or separate oneself during a traumatic emotional experience. This separation not only endangers the group but the individual as well—one does not recover by oneself.

Because storytelling lies at the heart of Pueblo culture, it is absurd to attempt to fix the stories in time. "When did they tell the stories?" or "What time of day does the storytelling take place?"—these questions are nonsensical from a Pueblo perspective, because our storytelling goes on constantly: as some old grandmother puts on the shoes of a child and tells her the story of a little girl who didn't wear her shoes, for instance, or someone comes into the house for coffee to talk with a teenage boy who has just been in a lot of trouble, to reassure him that someone else's son has been in that kind of trouble, too. Storytelling is an ongoing process, working on many different levels.

Here's one story that is often told at a time of individual crisis (and I want to remind you that we make no distinctions between types of story—historical, sacred, plain gossip—because these distinctions are not useful when discussing the Pueblo *experience* of language). There was a young man who, when he came back from the war in Vietnam, had saved up his army pay and bought a beautiful red Volkswagen. He was very proud of it. One night he drove up to a place called the King's Bar right across the reservation line. The bar is notorious for many reasons, particularly for the deep *arroyo* located behind it. The young man ran in to pick up a cold six-pack, but he forgot to put on his emergency brake. And his little red Volkswagen rolled back into the *arroyo* and was all smashed up. He felt very bad about it, but within a few days everybody had come to him with stories about other people who had lost cars and family members to that *arroyo*, for instance, George Day's station wagon, with his mother-in-law and kids inside. So everybody was saying, "Well, at least your mother-in-law and kids weren't in the car when it rolled in," and one can't argue with that kind of story. The story of the young man and his smashed-up Volkswagen was now joined with all the other stories of cars that fell into that *arroyo*.

Now I want to tell you a very beautiful little story. It is a very old story that is sometimes told to people who suffer great family or personal loss. This story was told by my Aunt Susie. She is one of the first generation of people at Laguna who began experimenting with English—who began working to make English speak for us—that is, to speak from the heart. (I come from a family intent on getting the stories told.) As you read the story, I think you will hear that. And here and there, I think, you will also hear the influence of the Indian school at Carlisle, Pennsylvania, where my Aunt Susie was sent (like being sent to prison) for six years.

This scene is set partly in Acoma, partly in Laguna. Waithea was a little girl living in Acoma and one day she said, "Mother, I would like to have some *yashtoah* to eat." *Yashtoah* is the hardened crust of corn mush that curls up. *Yashtoah* literally means "curled up." She said, "I would like to have some *yashtoah*," and her mother said, "My dear little girl, I can't make you any *yashtoah* because we haven't any wood, but if you will go down off the mesa, down below, and pick up some pieces of wood and bring them home, I will make you some *yashtoah*." So Waithea was glad and ran down the precipitous cliff of Acoma mesa. Down below, just as her mother had told her, there were pieces of wood, some curled, some crooked in shape, that she was to pick up and take home. She found just such wood as these.

She brought them home in a little wicker basket. First she called to her mother as she got home, "*Nayah, deeni!* Mother, upstairs!" The Pueblo people always called "upstairs" because long ago their homes were two, three stories, and they entered from the top. She said, "*Deeni!* UPSTAIRS!" and her mother came. The little girl said, "I have brought the wood you wanted me to bring." And she opened her little wicker basket to lay out the pieces of wood but here they were snakes. They were snakes instead of the crooked sticks of wood. And her mother said, "Oh my dear child, you have brought snakes instead!" She said, "Go take them back and put them back just where you got them." And the little girl ran down the mesa again, down below to the flats. And she put those snakes back just where she got them. They were snakes instead and she was very hurt about this and so she said, "I'm not going home. I'm going to *Kawaik,* the beautiful lake place, *Kawaik,* and drown myself in that lake, *byn'yah'nah* [the "west lake"]. I will go there and drown myself."

So she started off, and as she passed by the Enchanted Mesa near Acoma she met an old man, very aged, and he saw her running, and he said, "My dear child, where are you going?" "I'm going to *Kawaik* and jump into the lake there." "Why?" "Well, because," she said, "my mother didn't want to make any *yashtoah* for me." The old man said, "Oh, no! You must not go my child. Come with me and I will take you home." He tried to catch her, but she was very light and skipped along. And every time he would try to grab her she would skip faster away from him.

The old man was coming home with some wood strapped to his back and tied   20 with yucca. He just let that strap go and let the wood drop. He went as fast as he could up the cliff to the little girl's home. When he got to the place where she lived, he called to her mother. "*Deeni!*" "Come on up!" And he said, "I can't. I just came to bring you a message. Your little daughter is running away. She is going to *Kawaik* to drown herself in the lake there." "Oh my dear little girl!" the mother said. So she busied herself with making the *yashtoah* her little girl liked so much. Corn mush curled at the top. (She must have found enough wood to boil the corn meal and make the *yashtoah.*)

While the mush was cooling off, she got the little girl's clothing, her *manta* dress and buckskin moccasins and all her other garments, and put them in a bundle—probably a yucca bag. And she started down as fast as she could on the east side of Acoma. (There used to be a trail there, you know. It's gone now, but it was accessible in those days.) She saw her daughter way at a distance and she kept calling: "Stsamaku! My daughter! Come back! I've got your *yashtoah* for you." But the little girl would not turn. She kept on ahead and she cried: "My mother, my mother, she didn't want me to have any *yashtoah.* So now I'm going to *Kawaik* and drown myself." Her mother heard her cry and said, "My little daughter, come back here!" "No," and she kept a distance away from her. And they came nearer and nearer to the lake. And she could see her daughter now, very plain. "Come back, my daughter! I have your *yashtoah.*" But no, she kept on, and finally she reached the lake and she stood on the edge.

She had tied a little feather in her hair, which is traditional (in death they tie this feather on the head). She carried a feather, the little girl did, and she tied it in her hair with a piece of string, right on top of her head she put the feather. Just as her mother was about to reach her, she jumped into the lake. The little feather was whirling around and around in the depths below. Of course the mother was very sad. She went, grieved, back to Acoma and climbed her mesa home. She stood on the edge of the mesa and scattered her daughter's clothing, the little moccasins, the *yashtoah*. She scattered them to the east, to the west, to the north, to the south. And the pieces of clothing and the moccasins and *yashtoah*, all turned into butterflies. And today they say that Acoma has more beautiful butterflies, red ones, white ones, blue ones, yellow ones. They came from this little girl's clothing.

Now this is a story anthropologists would consider very old. The version I have given you is just as Aunt Susie tells it. You can occasionally hear some English she picked up at Carlisle—words like "precipitous." You will also notice that there is a great deal of repetition, and a little reminder about *yashtoah*, and how it is made. There is a remark about the cliff trail at Acoma—that it was once there, but is there no longer. The story may be told at a time of sadness or loss, but within this story many other elements are brought together. Things are not separated out and categorized; all things are brought together, so that the reminder about the *yashtaoh* is valuable information that is repeated—a recipe, if you will. The information about the old trail at Acoma reveals that stories are, in a sense, maps, since even to this day there is little information or material about trails that is passed around with writing. In the structure of this story the repetitions are, of course, designed to help you remember. It is repeated again and again, and then it moves on.

The next story I would like to tell is by Simon Ortiz, from Acoma Pueblo. He is a wonderful poet who also works in narrative. One of the things I find very interesting in this short story is that if you listen very closely, you begin to hear what I was talking about in terms of a story never beginning at the beginning, and certainly never ending. As the Hopis sometimes say, "Well, it has gone this far for a while." There is always that implication of a continuing. The other thing I want you to listen for is the many stories within one story. Listen to the kinds of stories contained within the main story—stories that give one a family identity and an individual identity, for example. This story is called "Home Country":

"Well, it's been a while. I think in 1947 was when I left. My husband had   25
been killed in Okinawa some years before. And so I had no more husband.
And I had to make a living. O I guess I could have looked for another man but
I didn't want to. It looked like the war had made some of them into a bad way
anyway. I saw some of them come home like that. They either got drunk or
just stayed around a while or couldn't seem to be satisfied anymore with what
was there. I guess now that I think about it, that happened to me too although
I wasn't in the war not in the Army or even much off the reservation just that
several years at the Indian School. Well there was that feeling things were
changing not only the men the boys, but things were changing.
   "One day the home nurse the nurse that came from the Indian health service
was at my mother's home my mother was getting near the end real sick and she
said that she had been meaning to ask me a question. I said what is the question.
And the home nurse said well your mother is getting real sick and after she is no
longer around for you to take care of, what will you be doing you and her are the
only ones here. And I said I don't know. But I was thinking about it what she

said made me think about it. And then the next time she came she said to me Eloise the government is hiring Indians now in the Indian schools to take care of the boys and girls I heard one of the supervisors saying that Indians are hard workers but you have to supervise them a lot and I thought of you well because you've been taking care of your mother real good and you follow all my instructions. She said I thought of you because you're a good Indian girl and you would be the kind of person for that job. I didn't say anything I had not ever really thought about a job but I kept thinking about it.

"Well my mother she died and we buried her up at the old place the cemetery there it's real nice on the east side of the hill where the sun shines warm and the wind doesn't blow too much sand around right there. Well I was sad we were all sad for a while but you know how things are. One of my aunties came over and she advised me and warned me about being too sorry about it and all that she wished me that I would not worry too much about it because old folks they go along pretty soon life is that way and then she said that maybe I ought to take in one of my aunties kids or two because there was a lot of them kids and I was all by myself now. But I was so young and I thought that I might do that you know take care of someone but I had been thinking too of what the home nurse said to me about working. Hardly anybody at our home was working at something like that no woman anyway. And I would have to move away.

"Well I did just that. I remember that day very well. I told my aunties and they were all crying and we all went up to the old highway where the bus to town passed by everyday. I was wearing an old kind of bluish sweater that was kind of big that one of my cousins who was older had got from a white person a tourist one summer in trade for something she had made a real pretty basket. She gave me that and I used to have a picture of me with it on it's kind of real ugly. Yeah that was the day I left wearing a baggy sweater and carrying a suitcase that someone gave me too I think or maybe it was the home nurse there wasn't much in it anyway either. I was scared and everybody seemed to be sad I was so young and skinny then. My aunties said one of them who was real fat you make sure you eat now make your own tortillas drink the milk and stuff like candies is no good she learned that from the nurse. Make sure you got your letter my auntie said. I had it folded into my purse. Yes I had one too a brown one that my husband when he was still alive one time on furlough he brought it on my birthday it was a nice purse and still looked new because I never used it.

"The letter said that I had a job at Keams Canyon the boarding school there but I would have to go to the Agency first for some papers to be filled and that's where I was going first. The Agency. And then they would send me out to Keams Canyon. I didn't even know where it was except that someone of our relatives said that it was near Hopi. My uncles teased me about watching out for the Hopi men and boys don't let them get too close they said well you know how they are and they were pretty strict too about those things and then they were joking and then they were not too and so I said aw they won't get near to me I'm too ugly and I promised I would be careful anyway.

"So we all gathered for a while at my last auntie's house and then the old man   30
my grandfather brought his wagon and horses to the door and we all got in and
sat there for a while until my auntie told her father okay father let's go and
shook his elbow because the poor old man was old by then and kind of going
to sleep all the time you had to talk to him real loud. I had about ten dollars I
think that was a lot of money more than it is now you know and when we got
to the highway where the Indian road which is just a dirt road goes off the pave
road my grandfather reached into his blue jeans and pulled out a silver dollar
and put it into my hand. I was so shocked. We were all so shocked. We all
looked around at each other we didn't know where the old man had gotten it
because we were real poor two of my uncles had to borrow on their accounts
at the trading store for the money I had in my purse but there it was a silver
dollar so big and shining in my grandfather's hand and then in my hand.

"Well I was so shocked and everybody was so shocked that we all started crying right there at the junction of that Indian road and the pave highway I wanted
to be a little girl again running after the old man when he hurried with his long
legs to the cornfields or went for water down to the river. He was old then and
his eye was turned gray and he didn't do much anymore except drive the wagon
and chop a little bit of wood but I just held him and I just held him so tightly.

"Later on I don't know what happened to the silver dollar it had a date of
1907 on it but I kept it for a long time because I guess I wanted to have it to
remember when I left my home country. What I did in between then and now
is another story but that's the time I moved away," is what she said.*

There are a great many parallels between Pueblo experiences and those of African and Caribbean peoples—one is that we have all had the conqueror's language imposed on us. But our experience with English has been somewhat different in that the Bureau of Indian Affairs schools were not interested in teaching us
the canon of Western classics. For instance, we never heard of Shakespeare. We
were given Dick and Jane, and I can remember reading that the robins were heading south for the winter. It took me a long time to figure out what was going on. I
worried for quite a while about our robins in Laguna because they didn't leave in
the winter, until I finally realized that all the big textbook companies are up in Boston and *their* robins do go south in the winter. But in a way, this dreadful formal
education freed us by encouraging us to maintain our narratives. Whatever literature we were exposed to at school (which was damn little), at home the storytelling,
the special regard for telling and bringing together through the telling, was going
on constantly.

And as the old people say, "If you can remember the stories, you will be all right.
Just remember the stories." When I returned to Laguna Pueblo after attending college, I wondered how the storytelling was continuing (anthropologists say that Laguna Pueblo is one of the more acculturated pueblos), so I visited an English class
at Laguna-Acoma High School. I knew the students had cassette tape recorders in
their lockers and stereos at home, and that they listened to Kiss and Led Zeppelin

---

*Simon J. Oritz, *Howbah Indians* (Tucson: Blue Moon Press, 1978). [Author's note] and were well informed about popular culture in general. I had with me an anthology of short stories by Native American writers, *The Man to Send Rain Clouds*. One story in the book is about the killing of a state policeman in New Mexico by three Acoma Pueblo men in the early 1950s. I asked the students how many had heard this story and steeled myself for the possibility that the anthropologists were right, that the old traditions were indeed dying out and the students would be ignorant of the story. But instead, all but one or two raised their hands—they had heard the story, just as I had heard it when I was young, some in English, some in Laguna.

One of the other advantages that we Pueblos have enjoyed is that we have always been able to stay with the land. Our stories cannot be separated from their geographical locations, from actual physical places on the land. We were not relocated like so many Native American groups who were torn away from their ancestral land. And our stories are so much a part of these places that it is almost impossible for future generations to lose them—there is a story connected with every place, every object in the landscape.   35

Dennis Brutus has talked about the "yet unborn" as well as "those from the past," and how we are still *all* in *this* place, and language—the storytelling—is our way of passing through or being with them, or being together again. When Aunt Susie told her stories, she would tell a younger child to go open the door so that our esteemed predecessors might bring in their gifts to us. "They are out there," Aunt Susie would say. "Let them come in. They're here, they're here with us *within* the stories."

A few years ago, when Aunt Susie was 106, I paid her a visit, and while I was there she said, "Well, I'll be leaving here soon. I think I'll be leaving here next week, and I will be going over to the Cliff House." She said, "It's going to be real good to get back over there." I was listening, and I was thinking that she must be talking about her house at Paguate Village, just north of Laguna. And she went on, "Well, my mother's sister (and she gave her Indian name) will be there. She has been living there. She will be there and we will be over there, and I will get a chance to write down these stories I've been telling you." Now you understand, of course, that Aunt Susie's mother's sister, a great storyteller herself, has long since passed over into the land of the dead. But then I realized, too, that Aunt Susie wasn't talking about death the way most of us do. She was talking about "going over" as a journey, a journey that perhaps we can only begin to understand through an appreciation for the boundless capacity of language that, through storytelling, brings us together, despite great distances between cultures, despite great distances in time.

ACTIVITIES FOR WRITING AND DISCUSSION

1. In the first paragraph Silko comments on the structure her essay will take:

> For those of you accustomed to being taken from point A to point B to point C, this presentation may be somewhat difficult to follow. Pueblo expression resembles something like a spider's web—with many little threads radiating

from the center, crisscrossing each other. As with the web, the structure emerges as it is made and you must simply listen and trust, as the Pueblo people do, that meaning will be made.

Do a postdraft outline (see Chapter 8) of all—or some sizable part of—Silko's essay. Then use your outline to show where and how her essay bears out her comments about "structure." Finally, what sorts of things does a "web"-like structure (as opposed to one that goes "from point A to point B to point C") imply about the outlook and values of the culture to which she belongs?

2. Based on your annotations of Silko's text, list and comment on the functions storytelling plays in Pueblo culture. Then, in your notebook, tell one or two particular stories that are important in your own family. What roles do the stories—and storytelling—play in your own family or larger culture? Do they serve any of the functions described by Silko?

3. Look again at the title of Silko's piece. Where in her essay does she discuss "literature"? Jot down your own definition of "literature"; then, as best you can, write down what you think Silko means by the term. How does her Pueblo concept of "literature" resemble and/or differ from your own? Finally, what do the differences suggest about differences between your culture and Silko's?

4. Reread the long story Silko quotes from Simon Ortiz.
   a. Identify and annotate "the many stories within one story" to which she refers.
   b. List and discuss any ways that Ortiz's narrative differs from ones common in your own culture.
   c. If you wish, write a story of your own in which you attempt to imitate the structure and oral style of Ortiz's text.

Judith Ortiz Cofer (b. 1952)

The Myth of the Latin Woman: I Just Met a Girl Named Maria

On a bus trip to London from Oxford University where I was earning some graduate credits one summer, a young man, obviously fresh from a pub, spotted me and as if struck by inspiration went down on his knees in the aisle. With both hands over his heart he broke into an Irish tenor's rendition of "Maria" from *West Side Story*. My politely amused fellow passengers gave his lovely voice the round of gentle applause it deserved. Though I was not quite as amused, I managed my version of an English smile: no show of teeth, no extreme contortions of the facial muscles—I was at this time of my life practicing reserve and cool. Oh, that

British control, how I coveted it. But "Maria" had followed me to London, re-minding me of a prime fact of my life: you can leave the island, master the English language, and travel as far as you can, but if you are a Latina, especially one like me who so obviously belongs to Rita Moreno's gene pool, the island travels with you.

This is sometimes a very good thing—it may win you that extra minute of someone's attention. But with some people, the same things can make *you* an is-land—not a tropical paradise but an Alcatraz, a place nobody wants to visit. As a Puerto Rican girl living in the United States and wanting like most children to "belong," I resented the stereotype that my Hispanic appearance called forth from many people I met.

Growing up in a large urban center in New Jersey during the 1960s, I suffered from what I think of as "cultural schizophrenia." Our life was designed by my parents as a microcosm of their *casas* on the island. We spoke in Spanish, ate Puerto Rican food bought at the *bodega,* and practiced strict Catholicism at a church that allotted us a one-hour slot each week for mass, performed in Spanish by a Chinese priest trained as a missionary for Latin America.

As a girl I was kept under strict surveillance by my parents, since my virtue and modesty were, by their cultural equation, the same as their honor. As a teen-ager I was lectured constantly on how to behave as a *proper señorita.* But it was a conflicting message I received, since the Puerto Rican mothers also encouraged their daughters to look and act like women and to dress in clothes our Anglo friends and their mothers found too "mature" and flashy. The difference was, and is, cultural; yet I often felt humiliated when I appeared at an American friend's party wearing a dress more suitable to a semi-formal than to a playroom birthday celebration. At Puerto Rican festivities, neither the music nor the colors we wore could be too loud.

I remember Career Day in our high school, when teachers told us to come 5 dressed as if for a job interview. It quickly became obvious that to the Puerto Ri-can girls "dressing up" meant wearing their mother's ornate jewelry and clothing, more appropriate (by mainstream standards) for the company Christmas party than as daily office attire. That morning I had agonized in front of my closet, try-ing to figure out what a "career girl" would wear. I knew how to dress for school (at the Catholic school I attended, we all wore uniforms), I knew how to dress for Sunday mass, and I knew what dresses to wear for parties at my relatives' homes. Though I do not recall the precise details of my Career Day outfit, it must have been a composite of these choices. But I remember a comment my friend (an Ital-ian American) made in later years that coalesced my impressions of that day. She said that at the business school she was attending, the Puerto Rican girls al-ways stood out for wearing "everything at once." She meant, of course, too much jewelry, too many accessories. On that day at school we were simply made the negative models by the nuns, who were themselves not credible fashion experts to any of us. But it was painfully obvious to me that to the others, in their tailored skirts and silk blouses, we must have seemed "hopeless" and "vulgar." Though I now know that most adolescents feel out of step much of the time, I also know that for the Puerto Rican girls of my generation that sense was intensified. The way our teachers and classmates looked at us that day in school was just a taste of the cultural clash that awaited us in the real world, where prospective employers and men on the street would often misinterpret our tight skirts and jingling bracelets as a "come-on."

Mixed cultural signals have perpetuated certain stereotypes—for example, that of the Hispanic woman as the "hot tamale" or sexual firebrand. It is a one-dimensional view that the media have found easy to promote. In their special vocabulary, advertisers have designated "sizzling" and "smoldering" as the adjectives of choice for describing not only the foods but also the women of Latin America. From conversations in my house I recall hearing about the harassment that Puerto Rican women endured in factories where the "boss-men" talked to them as if sexual innuendo was all they understood, and worse, often gave them the choice of submitting to their advances or being fired.

It is custom, however, not chromosomes, that leads us to choose scarlet over pale pink. As young girls, it was our mothers who influenced our decisions about clothes and colors—mothers who had grown up on a tropical island where the natural environment was a riot of primary colors, where showing your skin was one way to keep cool as well as to look sexy. Most important of all, on the island, women perhaps felt freer to dress and move more provocatively since, in most cases, they were protected by the traditions, mores, and laws of a Spanish/Catholic system of morality and machismo whose main rule was: *You may look at my sister, but if you touch her I will kill you.* The extended family and church structure could provide a young woman with a circle of safety in her small pueblo on the island; if a man "wronged" a girl, everyone would close in to save her family honor.

My mother has told me about dressing in her best party clothes on Saturday nights and going to the town's plaza to promenade with her girlfriends in front of the boys they liked. The males were thus given an opportunity to admire the women and to express their admiration in the form of *piropos:* erotically charged street poems they composed on the spot. (I have myself been subjected to a few *piropos* while visiting the island, and they can be outrageous, although custom dictates that they must never cross into obscenity.) This ritual, as I understand it, also entails a show of studied indifference on the woman's part; if she is "decent," she must not acknowledge the man's impassioned words. So I do understand how things can be lost in translation. When a Puerto Rican girl dressed in her idea of what is attractive meets a man from the mainstream culture who has been trained to react to certain types of clothing as a sexual signal, a clash is likely to take place. I remember the boy who took me to my first formal dance leaning over to plant a sloppy, over-eager kiss painfully on my mouth; when I didn't respond with sufficient passion, he remarked resentfully: "I thought you Latin girls were supposed to mature early," as if I were expected to *ripen* like a fruit or vegetable, not just grow into womanhood like other girls.

It is surprising to my professional friends that even today some people, including those who should know better, still put others "in their place." It happened to me most recently during a stay at a classy metropolitan hotel favored by young professional couples for weddings. Late one evening after the theater, as I walked toward my room with a colleague (a woman with whom I was coordinating an arts program), a middle-aged man in a tuxedo, with a young girl in satin and lace on his arm, stepped directly into our path. With his champagne glass extended toward me, he exclaimed "Evita!"

Our way blocked, my companion and I listened as the man half-recited, half-bellowed "Don't Cry for Me, Argentina." When he finished, the young girl said: "How about a round of applause for my daddy?" We complied, hoping this would bring the silly spectacle to a close. I was becoming aware that our little group was attracting the attention of the other guests. "Daddy" must have perceived this too, and he once more barred the way as we tried to walk past him. He began to shout-sing a ditty to the tune of "La Bamba"—except the lyrics were about a girl named Maria whose exploits rhymed with her name and gonorrhea. The girl kept saying "Oh, Daddy" and looking at me with pleading eyes. She wanted me to laugh along with the others. My companion and I stood silently waiting for the man to end his offensive song. When he finished, I looked not at him but at his daughter. I advised her calmly never to ask her father what he had done in the army. Then I walked between them and to my room. My friend complimented me on my cool handling of the situation, but I confessed that I had really wanted to push the jerk into the swimming pool. This same man—probably a corporate executive, well-educated, even worldly by most standards—would not have been likely to regale an Anglo woman with a dirty song in public. He might have checked his impulse by assuming that she could be somebody's wife or mother, or at least *somebody* who might take offense. But, to him, I was just an Evita or a Maria: merely a character in his cartoon-populated universe.

Another facet of the myth of the Latin woman in the United States is the menial, the domestic—Maria the housemaid or countergirl. It's true that work as domestics, as waitresses, and in factories is all that's available to women with little English and few skills. But the myth of the Hispanic menial—the funny maid, mispronouncing words and cooking up a spicy storm in a shiny California kitchen—has been perpetuated by the media in the same way that "Mammy" from *Gone with the Wind* became America's idea of the black woman for generations. Since I do not wear my diplomas around my neck for all to see, I have on occasion been sent to that "kitchen" where some think I obviously belong.

One incident has stayed with me, though I recognize it as a minor offense. My first public poetry reading took place in Miami, at a restaurant where a luncheon was being held before the event. I was nervous and excited as I walked in with notebook in hand. An older woman motioned me to her table, and thinking (foolish me) that she wanted me to autograph a copy of my newly published slender volume of verse, I went over. She ordered a cup of coffee from me, assuming I was the waitress. (Easy enough to mistake my poems for menus, I suppose.) I know it wasn't an intentional act of cruelty. Yet of all the good things that happened later, I remember that scene most clearly, because it reminded me of what I had to overcome before anyone would take me seriously. In retrospect I understand that my anger gave my reading fire. In fact, I have almost always taken any doubt in my abilities as a challenge, the result most often being the satisfaction of winning a convert, of seeing the cold, appraising eyes warm to my words, the body language change, the smile that indicates I have opened some avenue for communication. So that day as I read, I looked directly at that woman. Her lowered eyes told me she was embarrassed at her faux pas, and when I willed her to look up at me, she graciously allowed me to punish her with my full attention. We shook hands at the end of the reading and I never saw her again. She has probably forgotten the entire incident, but maybe not.

Yet I am one of the lucky ones. There are thousands of Latinas without the privilege of an education or the entrees into society that I have. For them life is a constant struggle against the misconceptions perpetuated by the myth of the Latina. My goal is to try to replace the old stereotypes with a much more interesting set of realities. Every time I give a reading, I hope the stories I tell, the dreams and fears I examine in my work, can achieve some universal truth that will get my audience past the particulars of my skin color, my accent, or my clothes.

I once wrote a poem in which I called all Latinas "God's brown daughters." This poem is really a prayer of sorts, offered upward, but also, through the human-to-human channel of art, outward. It is a prayer for communication and for respect. In it, Latin women pray "in Spanish to an Anglo God / with a Jewish heritage," and they are "fervently hoping / that if not omnipotent, / at least He be bilingual."

Activities for Writing and Discussion

1. In paragraph #13 Cofer writes that "My goal is to try to replace the old stereotypes with a much more interesting set of realities." What, specifically, are "the old stereotypes" she wants to remove (list and describe them) and what is the "more interesting set of realities" she wants to substitute? Does she achieve her goal in this essay? Explain.

2. Explain what Cofer means by the phrase "mixed cultural signals" (see paragraph #6). Then share any stories of times when *you* have experienced "mixed cultural signals" (or, alternatively, when someone you know has experienced them). What was the context? Who was involved, and what was the source of the confusion? How did you react? What was the final outcome? What, if anything, did you learn about yourself and/or "cultures" through the experience? For this activity, "culture" can be understood variously to refer to race, ethnicity, religion, belief, social group, social class, and so forth.

3. After you have drafted a response to Activity #2, expand it by adding, where appropriate, illustrative dialogue or description as Cofer does in *her* stories.

4. Some debates over "cultures" seem only to inflame passions and prejudices on all sides. Does Cofer's essay, her submission to the debate, do so? Why or why not? To answer this question, examine Cofer's **persona** and how, paragraph by paragraph, it goes about dismantling "the myth of the Latin woman." What

strategies does Cofer use to appeal to her readers, and how do those strategies persuade—or repel—*you*?

5. Augment your work on Activity #2 or 3 with outside research on the topic of "mixed cultural signals," how and why they occur and how they can be avoided.

BELL HOOKS (b. 1952)

Keeping Close to Home: Class and Education

We are both awake in the almost dark of 5 A.M. Everyone else is sound asleep. Mama asks the usual questions. Telling me to look around, make sure I have everything, scolding me because I am uncertain about the actual time the bus arrives. By 5:30 we are waiting outside the closed station. Alone together, we have a chance to really talk. Mama begins. Angry with her children, especially the ones who whisper behind her back, she says bitterly, "Your childhood could not have been that bad. You were fed and clothed. You did not have to do without—that's more than a lot of folks have and I just can't stand the way y'all go on." The hurt in her voice saddens me. I have always wanted to protect mama from hurt, to ease her burdens. Now I am part of what troubles. Confronting me, she says accusingly, "It's not just the other children. You talk too much about the past. You don't just listen." And I do talk. Worse, I write about it.

Mama has always come to each of her children seeking different responses. With me she expresses the disappointment, hurt, and anger of betrayal: anger that her children are so critical, that we can't even have the sense to like the presents she sends. She says, "From now on there will be no presents. I'll just stick some money in a little envelope the way the rest of you do. Nobody wants criticism. Everybody can criticize me but I am supposed to say nothing." When I try to talk, my voice sounds like a twelve year old. When I try to talk, she speaks louder, interrupting me, even though she has said repeatedly, "Explain it to me, this talk about the past." I struggle to return to my thirty-five year old self so that she will know by the sound of my voice that we are two women talking together. It is only when I state firmly in my very adult voice, "Mama, you are not listening," that she becomes quiet. She waits. Now that I have her attention, I fear that my explanations will be lame, inadequate. "Mama," I begin, "people usually go to therapy because they feel hurt inside, because they have pain that will not stop, like a wound that continually breaks open, that does not heal. And often these hurts, that pain has to do with things that have happened in the past, sometimes in childhood, often in childhood, or things that we believe happened." She wants to know, "What hurts, what hurts are you talking about?" "Mom, I can't answer that. I can't speak for all of us, the hurts are different for everybody. But the point is you try to make the hurt better, to heal it, by understanding how it came to be. And I know you feel mad when we say something happened or hurt that you don't remember being that way, but the past isn't like that, we don't have the same memory of it. We remember things differently. You know that. And sometimes folk feel hurt about stuff and you just don't know or didn't realize it, and they need to talk about it. Surely you understand the need to talk about it."

Our conversation is interrupted by the sight of my uncle walking across the park toward us. We stop to watch him. He is on his way to work dressed in a familiar blue suit. They look alike, these two who rarely discuss the past. This interruption makes me think about life in a small town. You always see someone you know. Interruptions, intrusions are part of daily life. Privacy is difficult to maintain. We leave our private space in the car to greet him. After the hug and kiss he has given me every year since I was born, they talk about the day's funerals. In the distance the bus approaches. He walks away knowing that they will see each other later. Just before I board the bus I turn, staring into my mother's face. I am momentarily back in time, seeing myself eighteen years ago, at this same bus stop, staring into my mother's face, continually turning back, waving farewell as I returned to college—that experience which first took me away from our town, from family. Departing was as painful then as it is now. Each movement away makes return harder. Each separation intensifies distance, both physical and emotional.

To a southern black girl from a working-class background who had never been on a city bus, who had never stepped on an escalator, who had never travelled by plane, leaving the comfortable confines of a small town Kentucky life to attend Stanford University was not just frightening; it was utterly painful. My parents had not been delighted that I had been accepted and adamantly opposed my going so far from home. At the time, I did not see their opposition as an expression of their fear that they would lose me forever. Like many working-class folks, they feared what college education might do to their children's minds even as they unenthusiastically acknowledged its importance. They did not understand why I could not attend a college nearby, an all-black college. To them, any college would do. I would graduate, become a school teacher, make a decent living and a good marriage. And even though they reluctantly and skeptically supported my educational endeavors, they also subjected them to constant harsh and bitter critique. It is difficult for me to talk about my parents and their impact on me because they have always felt wary, ambivalent, mistrusting of my intellectual aspirations even as they have been caring and supportive. I want to speak about these contradictions because sorting through them, seeking resolution and reconciliation has been important to me both as it affects my development as a writer, my effort to be fully self-realized, and my longing to remain close to the family and community that provided the groundwork for much of my thinking, writing, and being.

Studying at Stanford, I began to think seriously about class differences. To be   5 materially underprivileged at a university where most folks (with the exception of workers) are materially privileged provokes such thought. Class differences were boundaries no one wanted to face or talk about. It was easier to downplay them, to act as though we were all from privileged backgrounds, to work around them, to confront them privately in the solitude of one's room, or to pretend that just being chosen to study at such an institution meant that those of us who did not come from privilege were already in transition toward privilege. To not long for such transition marked one as rebellious, as unlikely to succeed. It was a kind of treason not to believe that it was better to be identified with the world of material privilege than with the world of the working class, the poor. No wonder our working-class parents from poor backgrounds feared our entry into such a world, intuiting perhaps that we might learn to be ashamed of where we had come from, that we might never return home, or come back only to lord it over them.

Though I hung with students who were supposedly radical and chic, we did not discuss class. I talked to no one about the sources of my shame, how it hurt me to witness the contempt shown the brown-skinned Filipina maids who cleaned our rooms, or later my concern about the $100 a month I paid for a room off-campus which was more than half of what my parents paid for rent. I talked to no one about my efforts to save money, to send a little something home. Yet these class realities separated me from fellow students. We were moving in different directions. I did not intend to forget my class background or alter my class allegiance. And even though I received an education designed to provide me with a bourgeois sensibility, passive acquiescence was not my only option. I knew that I could resist. I could rebel. I could shape the direction and focus of the various forms of knowledge available to me. Even though I sometimes envied and longed for greater material advantages (particularly at vacation times when I would be one of few if any students remaining in the dormitory because there was no money for travel), I did not share the sensibility and values of my peers. That was important—class was not just about money; it was about values which showed and determined behavior. While I often needed more money, I never needed a new set of beliefs and values. For example, I was profoundly shocked and disturbed when peers would talk abut their parents without respect, or would even say that they hated their parents. This was especially troubling to me when it seemed that these parents were caring and concerned. It was often explained to me that such hatred was "healthy and normal." To my white, middle-class California roommate, I explained the way we were taught to value our parents and their care, to understand that they were not obligated to give us care. She would always shake her head, laughing all the while, and say, "Missy, you will learn that it's different here, that we think differently." She was right. Soon, I lived alone, like the one Mormon student who kept to himself as he made a concentrated effort to remain true to his religious beliefs and values. Later in graduate school I found that classmates believed "lower class" people had no beliefs and values. I was silent in such discussions, disgusted by their ignorance.

Carol Stack's anthropological study, *All Our Kin,* was one of the first books I read which confirmed my experiential understanding that within black culture (especially among the working class and poor, particularly in southern states), a value system emerged that was counter-hegemonic, that challenged notions of individualism and private property so important to the maintenance of white-supremacist, capitalist patriarchy. Black folk created in marginal spaces a world of community and collectivity where resources were shared. In the preface to

Feminist Theory: from margin to center, I talked about how the point of difference, this marginality can be the space for the formation of an oppositional world view. That world view must be articulated, named if it is to provide a sustained blue-print for change. Unfortunately, there has existed no consistent framework for such naming. Consequently both the experience of this difference and documentation of it (when it occurs) gradually loses presence and meaning.

Much of what Stack documented about the "culture of poverty," for example, would not describe interactions among most black poor today irrespective of geographical setting. Since the black people she described did not acknowledge (if they recognized it in theoretical terms) the oppositional value of their world view, apparently seeing it more as a survival strategy determined less by conscious efforts to oppose oppressive race and class biases than by circumstance, they did not attempt to establish a framework to transmit their beliefs and values from generation to generation. When circumstances changed, values altered. Efforts to assimilate the values and beliefs of privileged white people, presented through media like television, undermine and destroy potential structures of opposition.

Increasingly, young black people are encouraged by the dominant culture (and by those black people who internalize the values of this hegemony) to believe that assimilation is the only possible way to survive, to succeed. Without the framework of an organized civil rights or black resistance struggle, individual and collective efforts at black liberation that focus on the primacy of self-definition and self-determination often go unrecognized. It is crucial that those among us who resist and rebel, who survive and succeed, speak openly and honestly about our lives and the nature of our personal struggles, the means by which we resolve and reconcile contradictions. This is no easy task. Within the educational institutions where we learn to develop and strengthen our writing and analytical skills, we also learn to think, write, and talk in a manner that shifts attention away from personal experience. Yet if we are to reach our people and all people, if we are to remain connected (especially those of us whose familial backgrounds are poor and working-class), we must understand that the telling of one's personal story provides a meaningful example, a way for folks to identify and connect.

Combining personal with critical analysis and theoretical perspectives can engage listeners who might otherwise feel estranged, alienated. To speak simply with language that is accessible to as many folks as possible is also important. Speaking about one's personal experience or speaking with simple language is often considered by academics and/or intellectuals (irrespective of their political inclinations) to be a sign of intellectual weakness or even anti-intellectualism. Lately, when I speak, I do not stand in place—reading my paper, making little or no eye contact with audiences—but instead make eye contact, talk extemporaneously, digress, and address the audience directly. I have been told that people assume I am not prepared, that I am anti-intellectual, unprofessional (a concept that has everything to do with class as it determines actions and behavior), or that I am reinforcing the stereotype of black people as non-theoretical and gutsy. 10

Such criticism was raised recently by fellow feminist scholars after a talk I gave at Northwestern University at a conference on "Gender, Culture, Politics" to an audience that was mainly students and academics. I deliberately chose to speak in a very basic way, thinking especially about the few community folks who had come to hear me. Weeks later, KumKum Sangari, a fellow participant who shared with me what was said when I was no longer present, and I engaged in quite rigorous critical dialogue about the way my presentation had been perceived primarily by privileged white female academics. She was concerned that I not mask my knowledge of theory, that I not appear anti-intellectual. Her critique compelled me to articulate concerns that I am often silent about with colleagues. I spoke about class allegiance and revolutionary commitments, explaining that it was disturbing to me that intellectual radicals who speak about transforming society, ending the domination of race, sex, class, cannot break with behavior patterns that reinforce and perpetuate domination, or continue to use as their sole reference point how we might be or are perceived by those who dominate whether or not we gain their acceptance and approval.

This is a primary contradiction which raises the issue of whether or not the academic setting is a place where one can be truly radical or subversive. Concurrently, the use of a language and style of presentation that alienates most folks who are not also academically trained reinforces the notion that the academic world is separate from real life, that everyday world where we constantly adjust our language and behavior to meet diverse needs. The academic setting is separate only when we work to make it so. It is a false dichotomy which suggests that academics and/or intellectuals can only speak to one another, that we cannot hope to speak with the masses. What is true is that we make choices, that we choose our audiences, that we choose voices to hear and voices to silence. If I do not speak in a language that can be understood, then there is little chance for dialogue. This issue of language and behavior is a central contradiction all radical intellectuals, particularly those who are members of oppressed groups, must continually confront and work to resolve. One of the clear and present dangers that exists when we move outside our class of origin, our collective ethnic experience, and enter hierarchical institutions which daily reinforce domination by race, sex, and class, is that we gradually assume a mindset similar to those who dominate and oppress, that we lose critical consciousness because it is not reinforced or affirmed by the environment. We must be ever vigilant. It is important that we know who we are speaking to, who we most want to hear us, who we most long to move, motivate, and touch with our words.

When I first came to New Haven to teach at Yale, I was truly surprised by the marked class divisions between black folks—students and professors—who identify with Yale and those black folks who work at Yale or in surrounding communities. Style of dress and self-presentation are most often the central markers of one's position. I soon learned that the black folks who spoke on the street were likely to be part of the black community and those who carefully shifted their glance were likely to be associated with Yale. Walking with a black female colleague one day, I spoke to practically every black person in sight (a gesture which reflects my upbringing), an action which disturbed my companion. Since I addressed black folk who were clearly not associated with Yale, she wanted to know whether or not I knew them. That was funny to me. "Of course not," I answered. Yet when I thought about it seriously, I realized that in a deep way, I knew them for they, and not my companion or most of my colleagues at Yale, resemble my family. Later that year, in a black women's support group I started for undergraduates, students from poor backgrounds spoke about the shame they sometimes feel when faced with the reality of their connection to working-class and poor black people. One student confessed that her father is a street person, addicted to drugs, someone who begs from passersby. She, like other Yale students, turns away from street people often, sometimes showing anger or contempt; she hasn't wanted anyone to know that she was related to this kind of person. She struggles with this, wanting to find a way to acknowledge and affirm this reality, to claim this connection. The group asked me and one another what we [should] do to remain connected, to honor the bonds we have with working-class and poor people even as our class experience alters.

Maintaining connections with family and community across class boundaries demands more than just summary recall of where one's roots are, where one comes from. It requires knowing, naming, and being ever-mindful of those aspects of one's past that have enabled and do enable one's self-development in the present, that sustain and support, that enrich. One must also honestly confront barriers that do exist, aspects of that past that do diminish. My parents' ambivalence about my love for reading led to intense conflict. They (especially my mother) would work to ensure that I had access to books, but would threaten to burn the books or throw them away if I did not conform to other expectations. Or they would insist that reading too much would drive me insane. Their ambivalence nurtured in me a like uncertainty about the value and significance of intellectual endeavor which took years for me to unlearn. While this aspect of our class reality was one that wounded and diminished, their vigilant insistence that being smart did not make me a "better" or "superior" person (which often got on my nerves because I think I wanted to have that sense that it did indeed set me apart, make me better) made a profound impression. From them I learned to value and respect various skills and talents folk might have, not just to value people who read books and talk about ideas. They and my grandparents might say about somebody, "Now he don't read nor write a lick, but he can tell a story," or as my grandmother would say, "call out the hell in words."

Empty romanticization of poor or working-class backgrounds undermines the   15 possibility of true connection. Such connection is based on understanding difference in experience and perspective and working to mediate and negotiate these terrains. Language is a crucial issue for folk whose movement outside the boundaries of poor and working-class backgrounds changes the nature and direction of their speech. Coming to Stanford with my own version of a Kentucky accent, which I think of always as a strong sound quite different from Tennessee or Georgia speech, I learned to speak differently while maintaining the speech of my region, the sound of my family and community. This was of course much easier to keep up when I returned home to stay often. In recent years, I have endeavored to use various speaking styles in the classroom as a teacher and find it disconcerts those who feel that the use of a particular patois excludes them as listeners, even if there is translation into the usual, acceptable mode of speech. Learning to listen to different voices, having different speech challenges the notion that we must all assimilate—share a single, similar talk—in educational institutions. Language reflects the culture from which we emerge. To deny ourselves daily use of speech patterns that are common and familiar, that embody the unique and distinctive aspect of our self is one of the ways we become estranged and alienated from our past. It is important for us to have as many languages on hand as we can know or learn. It is important for those of us who are black, who speak in particular patois as well as standard English, to express ourselves in both ways.

Often I tell students from poor and working-class backgrounds that if you believe what you have learned and are learning in schools and universities separates you from your past, this is precisely what will happen. It is important to stand firm in the conviction that nothing can truly separate us from our pasts when we nurture and cherish that connection. An important strategy for maintaining contact is ongoing acknowledgement of the primacy of one's past, of one's background, affirming the reality that such bonds are not severed automatically solely because one enters a new environment or moves toward a different class experience.

Again, I do not wish to romanticize this effort, to dismiss the reality of conflict and contradiction. During my time at Stanford, I did go through a period of more than a year when I did not return home. That period was one where I felt that it was simply too difficult to mesh my profoundly disparate realities. Critical reflection about the choice I was making, particularly about why I felt a choice had to be made, pulled me through this difficult time. Luckily I recognized that the insistence on choosing between the world of family and community and the new world of privileged white people and privileged ways of knowing was imposed upon me by the outside. It is as though a mythical contract had been signed somewhere which demanded of us black folks that once we entered these spheres we would immediately give up all vestiges of our underprivileged past. It was my responsibility to formulate a way of being that would allow me to participate fully in my new environment while integrating and maintaining aspects of the old.

One of the most tragic manifestations of the pressure black people feel to assimilate is expressed in the internalization of racist perspectives. I was shocked and saddened when I first heard black professors at Stanford downgrade and express contempt for black students, expecting us to do poorly, refusing to establish nurturing bonds. At every university I have attended as a student or worked at as a teacher, I have heard similar attitudes expressed with little or no understanding of factors that might prevent brilliant black students from performing to their full capability. Within universities, there are few educational and social spaces where students who wish to affirm positive ties to ethnicity—to blackness, to working-class backgrounds—can receive affirmation and support. Ideologically, the message is clear—assimilation is the way to gain acceptance and approval from those in power.

Many white people enthusiastically supported Richard Rodriguez's vehement contention in his autobiography, *Hunger of Memory,* that attempts to maintain ties with his Chicano background impeded his progress, that he had to sever ties with community and kin to succeed at Stanford and in the larger world, that family language, in his case Spanish, had to be made secondary or discarded. If the terms of success as defined by the standards of ruling groups within white-supremacist, capitalist patriarchy are the only standards that exist, then assimilation is indeed necessary. But they are not. Even in the face of powerful structures of domination, it remains possible for each of us, especially those of us who are members of oppressed and/or exploited groups as well as those radical visionaries who may have race, class, and sex privilege, to define and determine alternative standards, to decide on the nature and extent of compromise. Standards by which one's success is measured, whether student or professor, are quite different from those of us who wish to resist reinforcing the domination of race, sex, and class, who work to maintain and strengthen our ties with the oppressed, with those who lack material privilege, with our families who are poor and working-class.

When I wrote my first, book, *Ain't I a Woman: black women and feminism,* the   20 issue of class and its relationship to who one's reading audience might be came up for me around my decision not to use footnotes, for which I have been sharply criticized. I told people that my concern was that footnotes set class boundaries for readers, determining who a book is for. I was shocked that many academic folks scoffed at this idea. I shared that I went into working-class black communities as well as talked with family and friends to survey whether or not they ever read books with footnotes and found that they did not. A few did not know what they were, but most folks saw them as indicating that a book was for college-educated people. These responses influenced my decision. When some of my more radical college-educated friends freaked out about the absence of footnotes, I seriously questioned how we could ever imagine revolutionary transformation of society if such a small shift in direction could be viewed as threatening. Of course, many folks warned that the absence of footnotes would make the work less credible in academic circles. This information also highlighted the way in which class informs our choices. Certainly I did feel that choosing to use simple language, absence of footnotes, etc. would mean I was jeopardizing the possibility of being taken seriously in academic circles but then this was a political matter and a political decision. It utterly delights me that this has proven not to be the case and that the book is read by many academics as well as by people who are not college-educated.

Always our first response when we are motivated to conform or compromise within structures that reinforce domination must be to engage in critical reflection. Only by challenging ourselves to push against oppressive boundaries do we make the radical alternative possible, expanding the realm and scope of critical inquiry. Unless we share radical strategies, ways of rethinking and revisioning with students, with kin and community, with a larger audience, we risk perpetuating the stereotype that we succeed because we are the exception, different from the rest of our people. Since I left home and entered college, I am often asked, usually by white people, if my sisters and brothers are also high achievers. At the root of this question is the longing for reinforcement of the belief in "the exception" which enables race, sex, and class biases to remain intact. I am careful to separate what it means to be exceptional from a notion of "the exception."

Frequently I hear smart black folks, from poor and working-class backgrounds, stressing their frustration that at times family and community do not recognize that they are exceptional. Absence of positive affirmation clearly diminishes the longing to excel in academic endeavors. Yet it is important to distinguish between the absence of basic positive affirmation and the longing for continued reinforcement that we are special. Usually liberal white folks will willingly offer continual reinforcement of us as exceptions—as special. This can be both patronizing and very seductive. Since we often work in situations where we are isolated from other black folks, we can easily begin to feel that encouragement from white people is the primary or only source of support and recognition. Given the internalization of racism, it is easy to view this support as more validating and legitimizing than similar support from black people. Still, nothing takes the place of being valued and appreciated by one's own, by one's family and community. We share a mutual and reciprocal responsibility for affirming one another's successes. Sometimes we have to talk to our folks about the fact that we need their ongoing support and affirmation, that it is unique and special to us. In some cases we may never receive desired recognition and acknowledgement of specific achievements from kin. Rather than seeing this as a basis for estrangement, for severing connection, it is useful to explore other sources of nourishment and support.

I do not know that my mother's mother ever acknowledged my college education except to ask me once, "How can you live so far away from your people?" Yet she gave me sources of affirmation and nourishment, sharing the legacy of her quilt-making, of family history, of her incredible way with words. Recently, when our father retired after more than thirty years of work as a janitor, I wanted to pay tribute to this experience, to identify links between his work and my own as writer and teacher. Reflecting on our family past, I recalled ways he had been an impressive example of diligence and hard work, approaching tasks with a seriousness of concentration I work to mirror and develop, with a discipline I struggle to maintain. Sharing these thoughts with him keeps us connected, nurtures our respect for each other, maintaining a space, however large or small, where we can talk.

Open, honest communication is the most important way we maintain relationships with kin and community as our class experience and backgrounds change. It is as vital as the sharing of resources. Often financial assistance is given in circumstances where there is no meaningful contact. However helpful, this can also be an expression of estrangement and alienation. Communication between black folks from various experiences of material privilege was much easier when we were all in segregated communities sharing common experiences in relation to social institutions. Without this grounding, we must work to maintain ties, connection. We must assume greater responsibility for making and maintaining contact, connections that can shape our intellectual visions and inform our radical commitments.

The most powerful resource any of us can have as we study and teach in 25 university settings is full understanding and appreciation of the richness, beauty, and primacy of our familial and community backgrounds. Maintaining awareness of class differences, nurturing ties with the poor and working-class people who are our most intimate kin, our comrades in struggle, transforms and enriches our intellectual experience. Education as the practice of freedom becomes not a force which fragments or separates, but one that brings us closer, expanding our definitions of home and community.

Play

August Wilson (b. 1945)

Fences

Characters

TROY MAXSON
JIM BONO, *Troy's friend*
ROSE, *Troy's wife*
LYONS, *Troy's oldest son by previous marriage*
GABRIEL, *Troy's brother*
CORY, *Troy and Rose's son*
RAYNELL, *Troy's daughter*

Setting: *The setting is the yard which fronts the only entrance to the Maxson household, an ancient two-story brick house set back off a small alley in a big-city neighborhood. The entrance to the house is gained by two or three steps leading to a wooden porch badly in need of paint.*

A relatively recent addition to the house and running its full width, the porch lacks congruence. It is a sturdy porch with a flat roof. One or two chairs of dubious value sit at one end where the kitchen window opens onto the porch. An old-fashioned icebox stands silent guard at the opposite end.

The yard is a small dirt yard, partially fenced, except for the last scene, with a wooden sawhorse, a pile of lumber, and other fence-building equipment set off to the side. Opposite is a tree from which hangs a ball made of rags. A baseball bat leans against the tree. Two oil drums serve as garbage receptacles and sit near the house at right to complete the setting.

The Play: *Near the turn of the century, the destitute of Europe sprang on the city with tenacious claws and an honest and solid dream. The city devoured them. They swelled its belly until it burst into a thousand furnaces and sewing machines, a thousand butcher shops and bakers' ovens, a thousand churches and hospitals and funeral parlors and money-lenders. The city grew. It nourished itself and offered each man a partnership limited only by his talent, his guile, and his willingness and capacity for hard work. For the immigrants of Europe, a dream dared and won true.*

The descendants of African slaves were offered no such welcome or participation. They came from places called the Carolinas and the Virginias, Georgia, Alabama, Mississippi, and Tennessee. They came strong, eager, searching. The city rejected them and they fled and settled along the riverbanks and under bridges in shallow, ramshackle houses made of sticks and tarpaper. They collected rags and wood. They sold the use of their muscles and their bodies. They cleaned houses and washed clothes, they shined shoes, and in quiet desperation and vengeful pride, they stole, and lived in pursuit of their own dream. That they could breathe free, finally, and stand to meet life with the force of dignity and whatever eloquence the heart could call upon.

By 1957, the hard-won victories of the European immigrants had solidified the industrial might of America. War had been confronted and won with new energies that used loyalty and patriotism as its fuel. Life was rich, full, and flourishing. The Milwaukee Braves won the World Series, and the hot winds of change that would make the sixties a turbulent, racing, dangerous, and provocative decade had not yet begun to blow full.

ACT I • SCENE I

It is 1957. TROY *and* BONO *enter the yard, engaged in conversation.* TROY *is fifty-three years old, a large man with thick, heavy hands; it is this largeness that he strives to fill out and make an accommodation with. Together with his blackness, his largeness informs his sensibilities and the choices he has made in his life.*

Of the two men, BONO *is obviously the follower. His commitment to their friendship of thirty-odd years is rooted in his admiration of* TROY's *honesty, capacity for hard work, and his strength, which* BONO *seeks to emulate.*

It is Friday night, payday, and the one night of the week the two men engage in a ritual of talk and drink. TROY *is usually the most talkative and at times he can be crude and almost vulgar, though he is capable of rising to profound heights of expression. The men carry lunch buckets and wear or carry burlap aprons and are dressed in clothes suitable to their jobs as garbage collectors.*

BONO: Troy, you ought to stop that lying!

TROY: I ain't lying! The nigger had a watermelon this big.

(He indicates with his hands.)

Talking about . . . "What watermelon, Mr. Rand?" I liked to fell out! "What watermelon, Mr. Rand?" . . . And it sitting there big as life.

BONO: What did Mr. Rand say?

TROY: Ain't said nothing. Figure if the nigger too dumb to know he carrying a watermelon, he wasn't gonna get much sense out of him. Trying to hide that great big old watermelon under his coat. Afraid to let the white man see him carry it home.

BONO: I'm like you . . . I ain't got no time for them kind of people.

TROY: Now what he look like getting mad cause he see the man from the union talking to Mr. Rand?

BONO: He come to me talking about . . . "Maxson gonna get us fired." I told him to get away from me with that. He walked away from me calling you a troublemaker. What Mr. Rand say?

TROY: Ain't said nothing. He told me to go down the Commissioner's office next Friday. They called me down there to see them.

BONO: Well, as long as you got your complaint filed, they can't fire you. That's what one of them white fellows tell me.

TROY: I ain't worried about them firing me. They gonna fire me cause I asked a question? That's all I did. I went to Mr. Rand and asked him, "Why? Why you got the white mens driving and the colored lifting?" Told him, "what's the matter, don't I count? You think only white fellows got sense enough to drive a truck. That ain't no paper job! Hell, anybody can drive a truck. How come you got all whites driving and the colored lifting?" He told me "take it to the union." Well, hell, that's what I done! Now they wanna come up with this pack of lies.

BONO: I told Brownie if the man come and ask him any questions . . . just tell the truth! It ain't nothing but something they done trumped up on you cause you filed a complaint on them.

TROY: Brownie don't understand nothing. All I want them to do is change the job description. Give everybody a chance to drive the truck. Brownie can't see that. He ain't got that much sense.

BONO: How you figure he be making out with that gal be up at Taylors' all the time . . . that Alberta gal?

TROY: Same as you and me. Getting just as much as we is. Which is to say nothing.

BONO: It is, huh? I figure you doing a little better than me . . . and I ain't saying what I'm doing.

TROY: Aw, nigger, look here . . . I know you. If you had got anywhere near that gal, twenty minutes later you be looking to tell somebody. And the first one you gonna tell . . . that you gonna want to brag to . . . is gonna be me.

BONO: I ain't saying that. I see where you be eyeing her.

TROY: I eye all the women. I don't miss nothing. Don't never let nobody tell you Troy Maxson don't eye the women.

BONO: You been doing more than eyeing her. You done bought her a drink or two.

TROY: Hell yeah, I bought her a drink! What that mean? I bought you one, too. What that mean cause I buy her a drink? I'm just being polite.

BONO: It's all right to buy her one drink. That's what you call being polite. But when you wanna be buying two or three . . . that's what you call eyeing her.

TROY: Look here, as long as you known me . . . you ever known me to chase after women?

BONO: Hell yeah! Long as I done known you. You forgetting I knew you when.

TROY: Naw, I'm talking about since I been married to Rose?

BONO: Oh, not since you been married to Rose. Now, that's the truth, there. I can say that.

TROY: All right then! Case closed.

BONO: I see you be walking up around Alberta's house. You supposed to be at Taylors' and you be walking up around there.

TROY: What you watching where I'm walking for? I ain't watching after you.

BONO: I seen you walking around there more than once.

TROY: Hell, you liable to see me walking anywhere! That don't mean nothing cause you see me walking around there.

BONO: Where she come from anyway? She just kinda showed up one day.

TROY: Tallahassee. You can look at her and tell she one of them Florida gals. They got some big healthy women down there. Grow them right up out of the ground. Got a little bit of Indian in her. Most of them niggers down in Florida got some Indian in them.

BONO: I don't know about that Indian part. But she damn sure big and healthy. Woman wear some big stockings. Got them great big old legs and hips as wide as the Mississippi River.

TROY: Legs don't mean nothing. You don't do nothing but push them out of the way. But them hips cushion the ride!

BONO: Troy, you ain't got no sense.

TROY: It's the truth! Like you riding on Goodyears!

(ROSE *enters from the house. She is ten years younger than* TROY, *her devotion to him stems from her recognition of the possibilities of her life without him: a succession of abusive men and their babies, a life of partying and running the streets, the Church, or aloneness with its attendant pain and frustration. She recognizes* TROY's *spirit as a fine and illuminating one and she either ignores or forgives his faults, only some of which she recognizes. Though she doesn't drink, her presence is an integral part of the Friday night rituals. She alternates between the porch and the kitchen, where supper preparations are under way.*)

ROSE: What you all out here getting into?

TROY: What you worried about what we getting into for? This is men talk, woman.

ROSE: What I care what you all talking about? Bono, you gonna stay for supper?

BONO: No, I thank you, Rose. But Lucille say she cooking up a pot of pigfeet.

TROY: Pigfeet! Hell, I'm going home with you! Might even stay the night if you got some pigfeet. You got something in there to top them pigfeet, Rose?

ROSE: I'm cooking up some chicken. I got some chicken and collard greens.

TROY: Well, go on back in the house and let me and Bono finish what we was talking about. This is men talk. I got some talk for you later. You know what kind of talk I mean. You go on and powder it up.

ROSE: Troy Maxson, don't you start that now!

TROY (*puts his arm around her*): Aw, woman . . . come here. Look here, Bono . . . when I met this woman . . . I got out that place, say, "Hitch up my pony, saddle up my mare . . . there's a woman out there for me somewhere. I looked here. Looked there. Saw Rose and latched on to her." I latched on to her and told her— I'm gonna tell you the truth—I told her, "Baby, I don't wanna marry, I just wanna be your man." Rose told me . . . tell him what you told me, Rose.

ROSE: I told him if he wasn't the marrying kind, then move out the way so the marrying kind could find me.

TROY: That's what she told me. "Nigger, you in my way. You blocking the view! Move out the way so I can find me a husband." I thought it over two or three days. Come back—

ROSE: Ain't no two or three days nothing. You was back the same night.

TROY: Come back, told her . . . "Okay, baby . . . but I'm gonna buy me a banty rooster and put him out there in the backyard . . . and when he see a stranger come, he'll flap his wings and crow . . ." Look here, Bono, I could watch the front door by myself . . . it was that back door I was worried about.

ROSE: Troy, you ought not talk like that. Troy ain't doing nothing but telling a lie.

TROY: Only thing is . . . when we first got married . . . forget the rooster . . . we ain't had no yard!

BONO: I hear you tell it. Me and Lucille was staying down there on Logan Street. Had two rooms with the outhouse in the back. I ain't mind the outhouse none. But when that goddamn wind blow through there in the winter . . . that's what I'm talking about! To this day I wonder why in the hell I ever stayed down there for six long years. But see, I didn't know I could do no better. I thought only white folks had inside toilets and things.

ROSE: There's a lot of people don't know they can do no better than they doing now. That's just something you got to learn. A lot of folks still shop at Bella's.

TROY: Ain't nothing wrong with shopping at Bella's. She got fresh food.

ROSE: I ain't said nothing about if she got fresh food. I'm talking about what she charge. She charge ten cents more than the A&P.

TROY: The A&P ain't never done nothing for me. I spends my money where I'm treated right. I go down to Bella, say, "I need a loaf of bread, I'll pay you Friday." She give it to me. What sense that make when I got money to go and spend it somewhere else and ignore the person who done right by me? That ain't in the Bible.

ROSE: We ain't talking about what's in the Bible. What sense it make to shop there when she overcharge?

TROY: You shop where you want to. I'll do my shopping where the people been good to me.

ROSE: Well, I don't think it's right for her to overcharge. That's all I was saying.

BONO: Look here . . . I got to get on. Lucille going be raising all kind of hell.

TROY: Where you going, nigger? We ain't finished this pint. Come here, finish this pint.

BONO: Well, hell, I am . . . if you ever turn the bottle loose.

TROY (*hands him the bottle*): The only thing I say about the A&P is I'm glad Cory got that job down there. Help him take care of his school clothes and things. Gabe done moved out and things getting tight around here. He got that job. . . . He can start to look out for himself.

ROSE: Cory done went and got recruited by a college football team.

TROY: I told that boy about that football stuff. The white man ain't gonna let him get nowhere with that football. I told him when he first come to me with it.

Now you come telling me he done went and got more tied up in it. He ought to go and get recruited in how to fix cars or something where he can make a living.

ROSE: He ain't talking about making no living playing football. It's just something the boys in school do. They gonna send a recruiter by to talk to you. He'll tell you he ain't talking about making no living playing football. It's a honor to be recruited.

TROY: It ain't gonna get him nowhere. Bono'll tell you that.

BONO: If he be like you in the sports . . . he's gonna be all right. Ain't but two men ever played baseball as good as you. That's Babe Ruth and Josh Gibson. Them's the only two men ever hit more home runs than you.

TROY: What it ever get me? Ain't got a pot to piss in or a window to throw it out of.

ROSE: Times have changed since you was playing baseball, Troy. That was before the war. Times have changed a lot since then.

TROY: How in hell they done changed?

ROSE: They got lots of colored boys playing ball now. Baseball and football.

BONO: You right about that, Rose. Times have changed, Troy. You just come along too early.

TROY: There ought not never have been no time called too early! Now you take that fellow . . . what's that fellow they had playing right field for the Yankees back then? You know who I'm talking about, Bono. Used to play right field for the Yankees.

ROSE: Selkirk?

TROY: Selkirk! That's it! Man batting .269, understand? .269. What kind of sense that make? I was hitting .432 with thirty-seven home runs! Man batting .269 and playing right field for the Yankees! I saw Josh Gibson's daughter yesterday. She walking around with raggedy shoes on her feet. Now I bet you Selkirk's daughter ain't walking around with raggedy shoes on her feet! I bet you that!

ROSE: They got a lot of colored baseball players now. Jackie Robinson was the first. Folks had to wait for Jackie Robinson.

TROY: I done seen a hundred niggers play baseball better than Jackie Robinson. Hell, I know some teams Jackie Robinson couldn't even make! What you talking about Jackie Robinson. Jackie Robinson wasn't nobody. I'm talking about if you could play ball then they ought to have let you play. Don't care what color you were. Come telling me I come along too early. If you could play . . . then they ought to have let you play.

(TROY *takes a long drink from the bottle.*)

ROSE: You gonna drink yourself to death. You don't need to be drinking like that.

TROY: Death ain't nothing. I done seen him. Done wrassled with him. You can't tell me nothing about death. Death ain't nothing but a fastball on the outside corner. And you know what I'll do to that! Lookee here, Bono . . . am I lying? You get one of them fastballs, about waist high, over the outside corner of the plate where you can get the meat of the bat on it . . . and good god! You can kiss it goodbye. Now, am I lying?

BONO: Naw, you telling the truth there. I seen you do it.

TROY: If I'm lying . . . that 450 feet worth of lying!

(Pause.)

That's all death is to me. A fastball on the outside corner.

ROSE: I don't know why you want to get on talking about death.

TROY: Ain't nothing wrong with talking about death. That's part of life. Everybody gonna die. You gonna die, I'm gonna die. Bono's gonna die. Hell, we all gonna die.

ROSE: But you ain't got to talk about it. I don't like to talk about it.

TROY: You the one brought it up. Me and Bono was talking about baseball . . . you tell me I'm gonna drink myself to death. Ain't that right, Bono? You know I don't drink this but one night out of the week. That's Friday night. I'm gonna drink just enough to where I can handle it. Then I cuts it loose. I leave it alone. So don't you worry about me drinking myself to death. 'Cause I ain't worried about Death. I done seen him. I done wrestled with him.

Look here, Bono . . . I looked up one day and Death was marching straight at me. Like Soldiers on Parade! The Army of Death was marching straight at me. The middle of July, 1941. It got real cold just like it be winter. It seem like Death himself reached out and touched me on the shoulder. He touch me just like I touch you. I got cold as ice and Death standing there grinning at me.

ROSE: Troy, why don't you hush that talk.

TROY: I say . . . What you want, Mr. Death? You be wanting me? You done brought your army to be getting me? I looked him dead in the eye. I wasn't fearing nothing. I was ready to tangle. Just like I'm ready to tangle now. The Bible say be ever vigilant. That's why I don't get but so drunk. I got to keep watch.

ROSE: Troy was right down there in Mercy Hospital. You remember he had pneumonia? Laying there with a fever talking plumb out of his head.

TROY: Death standing there staring at me . . . carrying that sickle in his hand. Finally he say, "You want bound over for another year?" See, just like that . . . "You want bound over for another year?" I told him, "Bound over hell! Let's settle this now!"

It seem like he kinda fell back when I said that, and all the cold went out of me. I reached down and grabbed that sickle and threw it just as far as I could throw it . . . and me and him commenced to wrestling.

We wrestled for three days and three nights. I can't say where I found the strength from. Every time it seemed like he was gonna get the best of me, I'd reach way down deep inside myself and find the strength to do him one better.

ROSE: Every time Troy tell that story he find different ways to tell it. Different things to make up about it.

TROY: I ain't making up nothing. I'm telling you the facts of what happened. I wrestled with Death for three days and three nights and I'm standing here to tell you about it.

(Pause.)

All right. At the end of the third night we done weakened each other to where we can't hardly move. Death stood up, throwed on his robe . . . had him a white robe with a hood on it. He threw on that robe and went off to look for his sickle. Say, "I'll be back." Just like that. "I'll be back." I told him, say, "Yeah, but . . . you gonna have to find me!" I wasn't no fool. I wan't going looking for him. Death ain't nothing to play with. And I know he's gonna get me. I know I got to join his army . . . his camp followers. But as long as I keep my strength and see him coming . . . as long as I keep up my vigilance . . . he's gonna have to fight to get me. I ain't going easy.

BONO: Well, look here, since you got to keep up your vigilance . . . let me have the bottle.

TROY: Aw hell, I shouldn't have told you that part. I should have left out that part.

ROSE: Troy be talking that stuff and half the time don't even know what he be talking about.

TROY: Bono know me better than that.

BONO: That's right. I know you. I know you got some Uncle Remus in your blood. You got more stories than the devil got sinners.

TROY: Aw hell, I done seen him too! Done talked with the devil.

ROSE: Troy, don't nobody wanna be hearing all that stuff.

(LYONS *enters the yard from the street. Thirty-four years old,* TROY's *son by a previous marriage, he sports a neatly trimmed goatee, sport coat, white shirt, tieless and buttoned at the collar. Though he fancies himself a musician, he is more caught up in the rituals and "idea" of being a musician than in the actual practice of the music. He has come to borrow money from* TROY, *and while he knows he will be successful, he is uncertain as to what extent his lifestyle will be held up to scrutiny and ridicule.*)

LYONS: Hey, Pop.

TROY: What you come "Hey, Popping" me for?

LYONS: How you doing, Rose?

(*He kisses her.*)

Mr. Bono. How you doing?

BONO: Hey, Lyons . . . how you been?

TROY: He must have been doing all right. I ain't seen him around here last week.

ROSE: Troy, leave your boy alone. He come by to see you and you wanna start all that nonsense.

TROY: I ain't bothering Lyons.

(*Offers him the bottle.*)

Here . . . get you a drink. We got an understanding. I know why he come by to see me and he know I know.

LYONS: Come on, Pop . . . I just stopped by to say hi . . . see how you was doing.

TROY: You ain't stopped by yesterday.

ROSE: You gonna stay for supper, Lyons? I got some chicken cooking in the oven.

LYONS: No, Rose . . . thanks. I was just in the neighborhood and thought I'd stop by for a minute.

TROY: You was in the neighborhood all right, nigger. You telling the truth there. You was in the neighborhood cause it's my payday.

LYONS: Well, hell, since you mentioned it . . . let me have ten dollars.

TROY: I'll be damned! I'll die and go to hell and play blackjack with the devil before I give you ten dollars.

BONO: That's what I wanna know about . . . that devil you done seen.

LYONS: What . . . Pop done seen the devil? You too much, Pops.

TROY: Yeah, I done seen him. Talked to him too!

ROSE: You ain't seen no devil. I done told you that man ain't had nothing to do with the devil. Anything you can't understand, you want to call it the devil.

TROY: Look here, Bono . . . I went down to see Hertzberger about some furniture. Got three rooms for two-ninety-eight. That what it say on the radio. "Three rooms . . . two-ninety-eight." Even made up a little song about it. Go down there . . . man tell me I can't get no credit. I'm working every day and can't get no credit. What to do? I got an empty house with some raggedy furniture in it. Cory ain't got no bed. He's sleeping on a pile of rags on the floor. Working every day and can't get no credit. Come back here—Rose'll tell you—madder than hell. Sit down . . . try to figure what I'm gonna do. Come a knock on the door. Ain't been living here but three days. Who know I'm here? Open the door . . . devil standing there bigger than life. White fellow . . . got on good clothes and everything. Standing there with a clipboard in his hand. I ain't had to say nothing. First words come out of his mouth was . . . "I understand you need some furniture and can't get no credit." I liked to fell over. He say, "I'll give you all the credit you want, but you got to pay the interest on it." I told him, "Give me three rooms worth and charge whatever you want." Next day a truck pulled up here and two men unloaded them three rooms. Man what drove the truck gave me a book. Say send ten dollars, first of every month to the address in the book and everything will be all right. Say if I miss a payment the devil was coming back and it'll be hell to pay. That was fifteen years ago. To this day . . . the first of the month I send my ten dollars, Rose'll tell you.

ROSE: Troy lying.

TROY: I ain't never seen that man since. Now you tell me who else that could have been but the devil? I ain't sold my soul or nothing like that, you understand. Naw, I wouldn't have truck with the devil about nothing like that. I got my furniture and pays my ten dollars the first of the month just like clockwork.

BONO: How long you say you been paying this ten dollars a month?

TROY: Fifteen years!

BONO: Hell, ain't you finished paying for it yet? How much the man done charged you?

TROY: Ah hell, I done paid for it. I done paid for it ten times over! The fact is I'm scared to stop paying it.

ROSE: Troy lying. We got that furniture from Mr. Glickman. He ain't paying no ten dollars a month to nobody.

TROY: Aw hell, woman. Bono know I ain't that big a fool.

LYONS: I was just getting ready to say . . . I know where there's a bridge for sale.

TROY: Look here, I'll tell you this . . . it don't matter to me if he was the devil. It don't matter if the devil give credit. Somebody has got to give it.

ROSE: It ought to matter. You going around talking about having truck with the devil . . . God's the one you gonna have to answer to. He's the one gonna be at the Judgment.

LYONS: Yeah, well, look here, Pop . . . let me have that ten dollars. I'll give it back to you. Bonnie got a job working at the hospital.

TROY: What I tell you, Bono? The only time I see this nigger is when he wants something. That's the only time I see him.

LYONS: Come on, Pop, Mr. Bono don't want to hear all that. Let me have the ten dollars. I told you Bonnie working.

TROY: What that mean to me? "Bonnie working." I don't care if she working. Go ask her for the ten dollars if she working. Talking about "Bonnie working." Why ain't you working?

LYONS: Aw, Pop, you know I can't find no decent job. Where am I gonna get a job at? You know I can't get no job.

TROY: I told you I know some people down there. I can get you on the rubbish if you want to work. I told you that the last time you came by here asking me for something.

LYONS: Naw, Pop . . . thanks. That ain't for me. I don't wanna be carrying nobody's rubbish. I don't wanna be punching nobody's time clock.

TROY: What's the matter, you too good to carry people's rubbish? Where you think that ten dollars you talking about come from? I'm just supposed to haul people's rubbish and give my money to you cause you too lazy to work. You too lazy to work and wanna know why you ain't got what I got.

ROSE: What hospital Bonnie working at? Mercy?

LYONS: She's down at Passavant working in the laundry.

TROY: I ain't got nothing as it is. I give you that ten dollars and I got to eat beans the rest of the week. Naw . . . you ain't getting no ten dollars here.

LYONS: You ain't got to be eating no beans. I don't know why you wanna say that.

TROY: I ain't got no extra money. Gabe done moved over to Miss Pearl's paying her the rent and things done got tight around here. I can't afford to be giving you every payday.

LYONS: I ain't asked you to give me nothing. I asked you to loan me ten dollars. I know you got ten dollars.

TROY: Yeah, I got it. You know why I got it? Cause I don't throw my money away out there in the streets. You living the fast life . . . wanna be a musician . . . running around in them clubs and things . . . then, you learn to take care of yourself. You ain't gonna find me going and asking nobody for nothing. I done spent too many years without.

LYONS: You and me is two different people, Pop.

TROY: I done learned my mistake and learned to do what's right by it. You still trying to get something for nothing. Life don't owe you nothing. You owe it to yourself. Ask Bono. He'll tell you I'm right.

LYONS: You got your way of dealing with the world . . . I got mine. The only thing that matters to me is the music.

TROY: Yeah, I can see that! It don't matter how you gonna eat . . . where your next dollar is coming from. You telling the truth there.

LYONS: I know I got to eat. But I got to live too. I need something that gonna help me to get out of the bed in the morning. Make me feel like I belong in the world. I don't bother nobody. I just stay with my music cause that's the only way I can find to live in the world. Otherwise there ain't no telling what I might do. Now I don't come criticizing you and how you live. I just come by to ask you for ten dollars. I don't wanna hear all that about how I live.

TROY: Boy, your mamma did a hell of a job raising you.

LYONS: You can't change me, Pop. I'm thirty-four years old. If you wanted to change me, you should have been there when I was growing up. I come by to see you . . . ask for ten dollars and you want to talk about how I was raised. You don't know nothing about how I was raised.

ROSE: Let the boy have ten dollars, Troy.

TROY (*to* LYONS): What the hell you looking at me for? I ain't got no ten dollars. You know what I do with my money.
(*To* ROSE.)
Give him ten dollars if you want him to have it.

ROSE: I will. Just as soon as you turn it loose.

TROY (*handing* ROSE *the money*): There it is. Seventy-six dollars and forty-two cents. You see this, Bono? Now, I ain't gonna get but six of that back.

ROSE: You ought to stop telling that lie. Here, Lyons. (*She hands him the money.*)

LYONS: Thanks, Rose. Look . . . I got to run . . . I'll see you later.

TROY: Wait a minute. You gonna say, "thanks, Rose" and ain't gonna look to see where she got that ten dollars from? See how they do me, Bono?

LYONS: I knew she got it from you, Pop. Thanks. I'll give it back to you.

TROY: There he go telling another lie. Time I see that ten dollars . . . he'll be owing me thirty more.

LYONS: See you, Mr. Bono.

BONO: Take care, Lyons!

LYONS: Thanks, Pop. I'll see you again.
(LYONS *exits the yard.*)

TROY: I don't know why he don't go out and get him a decent job and take care of that woman he got.

BONO: He'll be all right, Troy. The boy is still young.

TROY: The *boy* is thirty-four years old.

ROSE: Let's not get off into all that.

BONO: Look here . . . I got to be going. I got to be getting on. Lucille gonna be waiting.

TROY (*puts his arm around* ROSE): See this woman, Bono? I love this woman. I love this woman so much it hurts. I love her so much . . . I done run out of ways of loving her. So I got to go back to basics. Don't you come by my house Monday morning talking about time to go to work . . . 'cause I'm still gonna be stroking!

ROSE: Troy! Stop it now!

BONO: I ain't paying him no mind, Rose. That ain't nothing but gin-talk. Go on, Troy. I'll see you Monday.

TROY: Don't you come by my house, nigger! I done told you what I'm gonna be doing.

(The lights go down to black.)

SCENE II

(The lights come up on ROSE *hanging up clothes. She hums and sings softly to herself. It is the following morning.)*

ROSE *(sings):* Jesus, be a fence all around me every day

Jesus, I want you to protect me as I travel on my way.

Jesus, be a fence all around me every day.

*(*TROY *enters from the house.)*

Jesus, I want you to protect me

As I travel on my way.

(To TROY*.)* 'Morning. You ready for breakfast? I can fix it soon as I finish hanging up these clothes?

TROY: I got the coffee on. That'll be all right. I'll just drink some of that this morning.

ROSE: That 651 hit yesterday. That's the second time this month. Miss Pearl hit for a dollar . . . seem like those that need the least always get lucky. Poor folks can't get nothing.

TROY: Them numbers don't know nobody. I don't know why you fool with them. You and Lyons both.

ROSE: It's something to do.

TROY: You ain't doing nothing but throwing your money away.

ROSE: Troy, you know I don't play foolishly. I just play a nickel here and a nickel there.

TROY: That's two nickels you done thrown away.

ROSE: Now I hit sometimes . . . that makes up for it. It always comes in handy when I do hit. I don't hear you complaining then.

TROY: I ain't complaining now. I just say it's foolish. Trying to guess out of six hundred ways which way the number gonna come. If I had all the money niggers, these Negroes, throw away on numbers for one week—just one week—I'd be a rich man.

ROSE: Well, you wishing and calling it foolish ain't gonna stop folks from playing numbers. That's one thing for sure. Besides . . . some good things come from playing numbers. Look where Pope done bought him that restaurant off of numbers.

TROY: I can't stand niggers like that. Man ain't had two dimes to rub together. He walking around with his shoes all run over bumming money for cigarettes. All right. Got lucky there and hit the numbers . . .

ROSE: Troy, I know all about it.

TROY: Had good sense, I'll say that for him. He ain't throwed his money away. I seen niggers hit the numbers and go through two thousand dollars in four days.

Man bought him that restaurant down there . . . fixed it up real nice . . . and then didn't want nobody to come in it! A Negro go in there and can't get no kind of service. I seen a white fellow come in there and order a bowl of stew. Pope picked all the meat out the pot for him. Man ain't had nothing but a bowl of meat! Negro come behind him and ain't got nothing but the potatoes and carrots. Talking about what numbers do for people, you picked a wrong example. Ain't done nothing but make a worser fool out of him than he was before.

ROSE: Troy, you ought to stop worrying about what happened at work yesterday.

TROY: I ain't worried. Just told me to be down there at the Commissioner's office on Friday. Everybody think they gonna fire me. I ain't worried about them firing me. You ain't got to worry about that.

(Pause.)

Where's Cory? Cory in the house? *(Calls.)* Cory?

ROSE: He gone out.

TROY: Out, huh? He gone out 'cause he know I want him to help me with this fence. I know how he is. That boy scared of work.

(GABRIEL enters. He comes halfway down the alley and, hearing TROY's voice, stops.)

TROY *(continues)*: He ain't done a lick of work in his life.

ROSE: He had to go to football practice. Coach wanted them to get in a little extra practice before the season start.

TROY: I got his practice . . . running out of here before he get his chores done.

ROSE: Troy, what is wrong with you this morning? Don't nothing set right with you. Go on back in there and go to bed . . . get up on the other side.

TROY: Why something got to be wrong with me? I ain't said nothing wrong with me.

ROSE: You got something to say about everything. First it's the numbers . . . then it's the way the man runs his restaurant . . . then you done got on Cory. What's it gonna be next? Take a look up there and see if the weather suits you . . . or is it gonna be how you gonna put up the fence with the clothes hanging in the yard.

TROY: You hit the nail on the head then.

ROSE: I know you like I know the back of my hand. Go in there and get you some coffee . . . see if that straighten you up. 'Cause you ain't right this morning.

(TROY starts into the house and sees GABRIEL. GABRIEL starts singing. TROY's brother, he is seven years younger than TROY. Injured in World War II, he has a metal plate in his head. He carries an old trumpet tied around his waist and believes with every fiber of his being that he is the Archangel Gabriel. He carries a chipped basket with an assortment of discarded fruits and vegetables he has picked up in the strip district and which he attempts to sell.)

GABRIEL *(singing)*: Yes, ma'am, I got plums
You ask me how I sell them
Oh ten cents apiece
Three for a quarter
Come and buy now

'Cause I'm here today
And tomorrow I'll be gone
(GABRIEL *enters.*)
Hey, Rose!

>   ROSE: How you doing, Gabe?

>   GABRIEL: There's Troy . . . Hey, Troy!

>   TROY: Hey, Gabe.

(*Exits into kitchen.*)

>   ROSE (*to* GABRIEL): What you got there?

>   GABRIEL: You know what I got, Rose. I got fruits and vegetables.

>   ROSE (*looking in basket*): Where's all these plums you talking about?

>   GABRIEL: I ain't got no plums today, Rose. I was just singing that. Have some
tomorrow. Put me in a big order for plums. Have enough plums tomorrow for St.
Peter and everybody.

(TROY *reenters from kitchen, crosses to steps.*)
(*To* ROSE.)
Troy's mad at me.

>   TROY: I ain't mad at you. What I got to be mad at you about? You ain't done
nothing to me.

>   GABRIEL: I just moved over to Miss Pearl's to keep out from in your way. I ain't
mean no harm by it.

>   TROY: Who said anything about that? I ain't said anything about that.

>   GABRIEL: You ain't mad at me, is you?

>   TROY: Naw . . . I ain't mad at you, Gabe. If I was mad at you I'd tell you about it.

>   GABRIEL: Got me two rooms. In the basement. Got my own door too. Wanna
see my key?

(*He holds up a key.*)
That's my own key! Ain't nobody else got a key like that. That's my key! My two
rooms!

>   TROY: Well, that's good, Gabe. You got your own key . . . that's good.

>   ROSE: You hungry, Gabe? I was just fixing to cook Troy his breakfast.

>   GABRIEL: I'll take some biscuits. You got some biscuits? Did you know when
I was in heaven . . . every morning me and St. Peter would sit down by the gate and
eat some big fat biscuits? Oh, yeah! We had us a good time. We'd sit there and eat
us them biscuits and then St. Peter would go off to sleep and tell me to wake him
up when it's time to open the gates for the judgment.

>   ROSE: Well, come on . . . I'll make up a batch of biscuits.

(ROSE *exits into the house.*)

>   GABRIEL: Troy . . . St. Peter got your name in the book. I seen it. It say . . . Troy
Maxson. I say . . . I know him! He got the same name like what I got. That's my
brother!

>   TROY: How many times you gonna tell me that, Gabe?

>   GABRIEL: Ain't got my name in the book. Don't have to have my name. I done
died and went to heaven. He got your name though. One morning St. Peter was
looking at his book . . . marking it up for the judgment . . . and he let me see your

name. Got it in there under M. Got Rose's name . . . I ain't seen it like I seen yours . . . but I know it's in there. He got a great big book. Got everybody's name what was ever been born. That's what he told me. But I seen your name. Seen it with my own eyes.

TROY: Go on in the house there. Rose going to fix you something to eat.

GABRIEL: Oh, I ain't hungry. I done had breakfast with Aunt Jemimah. She come by and cooked me up a whole mess of flapjacks. Remember how we used to eat them flapjacks?

TROY: Go on in the house and get you something to eat now.

GABRIEL: I got to go sell my plums. I done sold some tomatoes. Got me two quarters. Wanna see?

(He shows TROY *his quarters.)*

I'm gonna save them and buy me a new horn so St. Peter can hear me when it's time to open the gates.

*(*GABRIEL *stops suddenly. Listens.)*

Hear that? That's the hellhounds. I got to chase them out of here! Go on get out of here! Get out!

*(*GABRIEL *exits singing.)*

Better get ready for the judgment

Better get ready for the judgment

My Lord is coming down

*(*ROSE *enters from the house.)*

TROY: He gone off somewhere.

GABRIEL *(offstage):* Better get ready for the judgment

Better get ready for the judgment morning

Better get ready for the judgment

My God is coming down

ROSE: He ain't eating right. Miss Pearl say she can't get him to eat nothing.

TROY: What you want me to do about it, Rose? I done did everything I can for the man. I can't make him get well. Man got half his head blown away . . . what you expect?

ROSE: Seem like something ought to be done to help him.

TROY: Man don't bother nobody. He just mixed up from that metal plate he got in his head. Ain't no sense for him to go back into the hospital.

ROSE: Least he be eating right. They can help him take care of himself.

TROY: Don't nobody wanna be locked up, Rose. What you wanna lock him up for? Man go over there and fight the war . . . messin' around with them Japs, get half his head blown off . . . and they give him a lousy three thousand dollars. And I had to swoop down on that.

ROSE: Is you fixing to go into that again?

TROY: That's the only way I got a roof over my head . . . cause of that metal plate.

ROSE: Ain't no sense you blaming yourself for nothing. Gabe wasn't in no condition to manage that money. You done what was right by him. Can't nobody say you ain't done what was right by him. Look how long you took care of him . . . till he wanted to have his own place and moved over there with Miss Pearl.

TROY: That ain't what I'm saying, woman! I'm just stating the facts. If my brother didn't have that metal plate in his head . . . I wouldn't have a pot to piss in or a window to throw it out of. And I'm fifty-three years old. Now see if you can understand that!

(TROY gets up from the porch and starts to exit the yard.)

ROSE: Where you going off to? You been running out of here every Saturday for weeks. I thought you was gonna work on this fence?

TROY: I'm gonna walk down to Taylors'. Listen to the ball game. I'll be back in a bit. I'll work on it when I get back.

(He exits the yard. The lights go to black.)

SCENE III

(The lights come up on the yard. It is four hours later. ROSE is taking down the clothes from the line. CORY enters carrying his football equipment.)

ROSE: Your daddy like to had a fit with you running out of here this morning without doing your chores.

CORY: I told you I had to go to practice.

ROSE: He say you were supposed to help him with this fence.

CORY: He been saying that the last four or five Saturdays, and then he don't never do nothing but go down to Taylors'. Did you tell him about the recruiter?

ROSE: Yeah, I told him.

CORY: What he say?

ROSE: He ain't said nothing too much. You get in there and get started on your chores before he gets back. Go on and scrub down them steps before he gets back here hollering and carrying on.

CORY: I'm hungry. What you got to eat, Mama?

ROSE: Go on and get started on your chores. I got some meat loaf in there. Go on and make you a sandwich . . . and don't leave no mess in there.

(CORY exits into the house. ROSE continues to take down the clothes. TROY enters the yard and sneaks up and grabs her from behind.)

Troy! Go on, now. You liked to scared me to death. What was the score of the game? Lucille had me on the phone and I couldn't keep up with it.

TROY: What I care about the game? Come here, woman. *(He tries to kiss her.)*

ROSE: I thought you went down Taylors' to listen to the game. Go on, Troy! You supposed to be putting up this fence.

TROY *(attempting to kiss her again)*: I'll put it up when I finish with what is at hand.

ROSE: Go on, Troy. I ain't studying you.

TROY *(chasing after her)*: I'm studying you . . . fixing to do my homework!

ROSE: Troy, you better leave me alone.

TROY: Where's Cory? That boy brought his butt home yet?

ROSE: He's in the house doing his chores.

TROY (*calling*): Cory! Get your butt out here, boy!

(ROSE *exits into the house with the laundry.* TROY *goes over to the pile of wood, picks up a board, and starts sawing.* CORY *enters from the house.*)

TROY: You just now coming in here from leaving this morning?

CORY: Yeah, I had to go to football practice.

TROY: Yeah, what?

CORY: Yessir.

TROY: I ain't but two seconds off you noway. The garbage sitting in there overflowing . . . you ain't done none of your chores . . . and you come in here talking about "Yeah."

CORY: I was just getting ready to do my chores now, Pop . . .

TROY: Your first chore is to help me with this fence on Saturday. Everything else come after that. Now get that saw and cut them boards.

(CORY *takes the saw and begins cutting the boards.* TROY *continues working. There is a long pause.*)

CORY: Hey, Pop . . . why don't you buy a TV?

TROY: What I want with a TV? What I want one of them for?

CORY: Everybody got one. Earl, Ba Bra . . . Jesse!

TROY: I ain't asked you who had one. I say what I want with one?

CORY: So you can watch it. They got lots of things on TV. Baseball games and everything. We could watch the World Series.

TROY: Yeah . . . and how much this TV cost?

CORY: I don't know. They got them on sale for around two hundred dollars.

TROY: Two hundred dollars, huh?

CORY: That ain't that much, Pop.

TROY: Naw, it's just two hundred dollars. See that roof you got over your head at night? Let me tell you something about that roof. It's been over ten years since that roof was last tarred. See now . . . the snow come this winter and sit up there on that roof like it is . . . and it's gonna seep inside. It's just gonna be a little bit . . . ain't gonna hardly notice it. Then the next thing you know, it's gonna be leaking all over the house. Then the wood rot from all that water and you gonna need a whole new roof. Now, how much you think it cost to get that roof tarred?

CORY: I don't know.

TROY: Two hundred and sixty-four dollars . . . cash money. While you thinking about a TV, I got to be thinking about the roof . . . and whatever else go wrong around here. Now if you had two hundred dollars, what would you do . . . fix the roof or buy a TV?

CORY: I'd buy a TV. Then when the roof started to leak . . . when it needed fixing . . . I'd fix it.

TROY: Where you gonna get the money from? You done spent it for a TV. You gonna sit up and watch the water run all over your brand new TV.

CORY: Aw, Pop. You got money. I know you do.

TROY: Where I got it at, huh?

CORY: You got it in the bank.

TROY: You wanna see my bankbook? You wanna see that seventy-three dollars and twenty-two cents I got sitting up in there?

CORY: You ain't got to pay for it all at one time. You can put a down payment on it and carry it on home with you.

TROY: Not me. I ain't gonna owe nobody nothing if I can help it. Miss a payment and they come and snatch it right out your house. Then what you got? Now, soon as I get two hundred dollars clear, then I'll buy a TV. Right now, as soon as I get two hundred and sixty-four dollars, I'm gonna have this roof tarred.

CORY: Aw . . . Pop!

TROY: You go on and get you two hundred dollars and buy one if ya want it. I got better things to do with my money.

CORY: I can't get no two hundred dollars. I ain't never seen two hundred dollars.

TROY: I'll tell you what . . . you get you a hundred dollars and I'll put the other hundred with it.

CORY: All right, I'm gonna show you.

TROY: You gonna show me how you can cut them boards right now.

(CORY *begins to cut the boards. There is a long pause.*)

CORY: The Pirates won today. That makes five in a row.

TROY: I ain't thinking about the Pirates. Got an all-white team. Got that boy . . . that Puerto Rican boy . . . Clemente. Don't even half-play him. That boy could be something if they give him a chance. Play him one day and sit him on the bench the next.

CORY: He gets a lot of chances to play.

TROY: I'm talking about playing regular. Playing every day so you can get your timing. That's what I'm talking about.

CORY: They got some white guys on the team that don't play every day. You can't play everybody at the same time.

TROY: If they got a white fellow sitting on the bench . . . you can bet your last dollar he can't play! The colored guy got to be twice as good before he get on the team. That's why I don't want you go get all tied up in them sports. Man on the team and what it get him? They got colored on the team and don't use them. Same as not having them. All them teams the same.

CORY: The Braves got Hank Aaron and Wes Covington. Hank Aaron hit two home runs today. That makes forty-three.

TROY: Hank Aaron ain't nobody. That's what you supposed to do. That's how you supposed to play the game. Ain't nothing to it. It's just a matter of timing . . . getting the right follow-through. Hell, I can hit forty-three home runs right now!

CORY: Not off no major-league pitching, you couldn't.

TROY: We had better pitching in the Negro leagues. I hit seven home runs off of Satchel Paige.[1] You can't get no better than that!

CORY: Sandy Koufax. He's leading the league in strikeouts.

TROY: I ain't thinking of no Sandy Koufax.

---

1. Legendary black pitcher (1906?–1982) in the Negro leagues.

CORY: You got Warren Spahn and Lew Burdette. I bet you couldn't hit no home runs off of Warren Spahn.

TROY: I'm through with it now. You go on and cut them boards.

(Pause.)

Your mama tell me you done got recruited by a college football team? Is that right?

CORY: Yeah. Coach Zellman say the recruiter gonna be coming by to talk to you. Get you to sign the permission papers.

TROY: I thought you supposed to be working down there at the A&P. Ain't you suppose to be working down there after school?

CORY: Mr. Stawicki say he gonna hold my job for me until after the football season. Say starting next week I can work weekends.

TROY: I thought we had an understanding about this football stuff? You suppose to keep up with your chores and hold that job down at the A&P. Ain't been around here all day on a Saturday. Ain't none of your chores done . . . and now you telling me you done quit your job.

CORY: I'm gonna be working weekends.

TROY: You damn right you are! And ain't no need for nobody coming around here to talk to me about signing nothing.

CORY: Hey, Pop . . . you can't do that. He's coming all the way from North Carolina.

TROY: I don't care where he coming from. The white man ain't gonna let you get nowhere with that football noway. You go on and get your book-learning so you can work yourself up in that A&P or learn how to fix cars or build houses or something, get you a trade. That way you have something can't nobody take away from you. You go on and learn how to put your hands to some good use. Besides hauling people's garbage.

CORY: I get good grades, Pop. That's why the recruiter wants to talk with you. You got to keep up your grades to get recruited. This way I'll be going to college. I'll get a chance . . .

TROY: First you gonna get your butt down there to the A&P and get your job back.

CORY: Mr. Stawicki done already hired somebody else 'cause I told him I was playing football.

TROY: You a bigger fool than I thought . . . to let somebody take away your job so you can play some football. Where you gonna get your money to take out your girlfriend and whatnot? What kind of foolishness is that to let somebody take away your job?

CORY: I'm still gonna be working weekends.

TROY: Naw . . . naw. You getting your butt out of here and finding you another job.

CORY: Come on, Pop! I got to practice. I can't work after school and play football too. The team needs me. That's what Coach Zellman say . . .

TROY: I don't care what nobody else say. I'm the boss . . . you understand? I'm the boss around here. I do the only saying what counts.

CORY: Come on, Pop!

TROY: I asked you . . . did you understand?

CORY: Yeah . . .

TROY: What?!

CORY: Yessir.

TROY: You go on down there to that A&P and see if you can get your job back. If you can't do both . . . then you quit the football team. You've got to take the crookeds with the straights.

CORY: Yessir.

(Pause.)

Can I ask you a question?

TROY: What the hell you wanna ask me? Mr. Stawicki the one you got the questions for.

CORY: How come you ain't never liked me?

TROY: Liked you? Who the hell say I got to like you? What law is there say I got to like you? Wanna stand up in my face and ask a damn fool-ass question like that. Talking about liking somebody. Come here, boy, when I talk to you.

(CORY *comes over to where* TROY *is working. He stands slouched over and* TROY *shoves him on his shoulder.)*

Straighten up, goddammit! I asked you a question . . . what law is there say I got to like you?

CORY: None.

TROY: Well, all right then! Don't you eat every day?

(Pause.)

Answer me when I talk to you! Don't you eat every day?

CORY: Yeah.

TROY: Nigger, as long as you in my house, you put that sir on the end of it when you talk to me!

CORY: Yes . . . sir.

TROY: You eat every day.

CORY: Yessir!

TROY: Got a roof over your head.

CORY: Yessir!

TROY: Got clothes on your back.

CORY: Yessir.

TROY: Why you think that is?

CORY: Cause of you.

TROY: Ah, hell I know it's 'cause of me . . . but why do you think that is?

CORY *(hesitant):* Cause you like me.

TROY: Like you? I go out of here every morning . . . bust my butt . . . putting up with them crackers every day . . . cause I like you? You about the biggest fool I ever saw.

(Pause.)

It's my job. It's my responsibility! You understand that? A man got to take care of his family. You live in my house . . . sleep you behind on my bedclothes . . . fill you belly up with my food . . . cause you my son. You my flesh and blood. Not 'cause I like you! Cause it's my duty to take care of you. I owe a responsibility to you! Let's get this straight right here . . . before it go along any further . . . I ain't got to like you. Mr. Rand don't give me my money come payday cause he likes me. He gives me cause he owe me. I done give you everything I had to give you. I gave you your life! Me and your mama worked that out between us. And liking your black ass wasn't part of the bargain. Don't you try and go through life worrying about if somebody like you or not. You best be making sure they doing right by you. You understand what I'm saying, boy?

CORY: Yessir.

TROY: Then get the hell out of my face, and get on down to that A&P.

(ROSE *has been standing behind the screen door for much of the scene. She enters as* CORY *exits.*)

ROSE: Why don't you let the boy go ahead and play football, Troy? Ain't no harm in that. He's just trying to be like you with the sports.

TROY: I don't want him to be like me! I want him to move as far away from my life as he can get. You the only decent thing that ever happened to me. I wish him that. But I don't wish him a thing else from my life. I decided seventeen years ago that boy wasn't getting involved in no sports. Not after what they did to me in the sports.

ROSE: Troy, why don't you admit you was too old to play in the major leagues? For once . . . why don't you admit that?

TROY: What do you mean too old? Don't come telling me I was too old. I just wasn't the right color. Hell, I'm fifty-three years old and can do better than Selkirk's .269 right now!

ROSE: How's was you gonna play ball when you were over forty? Sometimes I can't get no sense out of you.

TROY: I got good sense, woman. I got sense enough not to let my boy get hurt over playing no sports. You been mothering that boy too much. Worried about if people like him.

ROSE: Everything that boy do . . . he do for you. He wants you to say "Good job, son." That's all.

TROY: Rose, I ain't got time for that. He's alive. He's healthy. He's got to make his own way. I made mine. Ain't nobody gonna hold his hand when he get out there in that world.

ROSE: Times have changed from when you was young, Troy. People change. The world's changing around you and you can't even see it.

TROY (*slow, methodical*): Woman . . . I do the best I can do. I come in here every Friday. I carry a sack of potatoes and a bucket of lard. You all line up at the door with your hands out. I give you the lint from my pockets. I give you my sweat and my blood. I ain't got no tears. I done spent them. We go upstairs in that room at night . . . and I fall down on you and try to blast a hole into forever. I get up Monday morning . . . find my lunch on the table. I go. Make my way. Find my strength to carry me through to the next Friday.

(*Pause.*)

That's all I got, Rose. That's all I got to give. I can't give nothing else.
(TROY *exits into the house. The lights go down to black.*)

Scene IV
(*It is Friday. Two weeks later.* CORY *starts out of the house with his football equipment. The phone rings.*)

 CORY (*calling*): I got it!
(*He answers the phone and stands in the screen door talking.*)
Hello? Hey, Jesse. Naw . . . I was just getting ready to leave now.

 ROSE (*calling*): Cory!

 CORY: I told you, man, them spikes is all tore up. You can use them if you want, but they ain't no good. Earl got some spikes.

 ROSE (*calling*): Cory!

 CORY (*calling to* ROSE): Mam? I'm talking to Jesse.
(*Into phone.*)
When she say that? (*Pause.*) Aw, you lying, man. I'm gonna tell her you said that.

 ROSE (*calling*): Cory, don't you go nowhere!

 CORY: I got to go to the game, Ma!
(*Into the phone.*)
Yeah, hey, look, I'll talk to you later. Yeah, I'll meet you over Earl's house. Later. Bye, Ma.
(CORY *exits the house and starts out the yard.*)

 ROSE: Cory, where you going off to? You got that stuff all pulled out and thrown all over your room.

 CORY (*in the yard*): I was looking for my spikes. Jesse wanted to borrow my spikes.

 ROSE: Get up there and get that cleaned up before your daddy get back in here.

 CORY: I got to go to the game! I'll clean it up *when I get back.*
(CORY *exits.*)

 ROSE: That's all he need to do is see that room all messed up.
(ROSE *exits into the house.* TROY *and* BONO *enter the yard.* TROY *is dressed in clothes other than his work clothes.*)

 BONO: He told him the same thing he told you. Take it to the union.

 TROY: Brownie ain't got that much sense. Man wasn't thinking about nothing. He wait until I confront them on it . . . then he wanna come crying seniority.
(*Calls.*)
Hey, Rose!

 BONO: I wish I could have seen Mr. Rand's face when he told you.

 TROY: He couldn't get it out of his mouth! Liked to bit his tongue! When they called me down there to the Commissioner's office . . . he thought they was gonna fire me. Like everybody else.

 BONO: I didn't think they was gonna fire you. I thought they was gonna put you on the warning paper.

 TROY: Hey, Rose!
(*To* BONO.)

Yeah, Mr. Rand like to bit his tongue.

(TROY *breaks the seal on the bottle, takes a drink, and hands it to* BONO.)

BONO: I see you run right down to Taylors' and told that Alberta gal.

TROY *(calling):* Hey, Rose! *(To* BONO.) I told everybody. Hey, Rose! I went down there to cash my check.

ROSE *(entering from the house):* Hush all that hollering, man! I know you out here. What they say down there at the Commissioner's office?

TROY: You supposed to come when I call you, woman. Bono'll tell you that. *(To* BONO.)

Don't Lucille come when you call her?

ROSE: Man, hush your mouth. I ain't no dog . . . talk about "come when you call me."

TROY *(puts his arm around* ROSE): You hear this, Bono? I had me an old dog used to get uppity like that. You say, "C'mere, Blue!" . . . and he just lay there and look at you. End up getting a stick and chasing him away trying to make him come.

ROSE: I ain't studying you and your dog. I remember you used to sing that old song.

TROY *(he sings):* Hear it ring! Hear it ring! I had a dog his name was Blue.

ROSE: Don't nobody wanna hear you sing that old song.

TROY *(sings):* You know Blue was mighty true.

ROSE: Used to have Cory running around here singing that song.

BONO: Hell, I remember that song myself.

TROY *(sings):* You know Blue was a good old dog.

Blue treed a possum in a hollow log.

That was my daddy's song. My daddy made up that song.

ROSE: I don't care who made it up. Don't nobody wanna hear you sing it.

TROY *(makes a song like calling a dog):* Come here, woman.

ROSE: You come in here carrying on, I reckon they ain't fired you. What they say down there at the Commissioner's office?

TROY: Look here, Rose . . . Mr. Rand called me into his office today when I got back from talking to them people down there . . . it come from up top . . . he called me in and told me they was making me a driver.

ROSE: Troy, you kidding!

TROY: No I ain't. Ask Bono.

ROSE: Well, that's great, Troy. Now you don't have to hassle them people no more.

(LYONS *enters from the street.*)

TROY: Aw hell, I wasn't looking to see you today. I thought you was in jail. Got it all over the front page of the *Courier* about them raiding Sefus' place . . . where you be hanging out with all them thugs.

LYONS: Hey, Pop . . . that ain't got nothing to do with me. I don't go down there gambling. I go down there to sit in with the band. I ain't got nothing to do with the gambling part. They got some good music down there.

TROY: They got some rogues . . . is what they got.

LYONS: How you been, Mr. Bono? Hi, Rose.

BONO: I see where you playing down at the Crawford Grill tonight.

ROSE: How come you ain't brought Bonnie like I told you. You should have brought Bonnie with you, she ain't been over in a month of Sundays.

LYONS: I was just in the neighborhood . . . thought I'd stop by.

TROY: Here he come . . .

BONO: Your daddy got a promotion on the rubbish. He's gonna be the first colored driver. Ain't got to do nothing but sit up there and read the paper like them white fellows.

LYONS: Hey, Pop . . . if you knew how to read you'd be all right.

BONO: Naw . . . naw . . . you mean if the nigger knew how to *drive* he'd be all right. Been fighting with them people about driving and ain't even got a license. Mr. Rand know you ain't got no driver's license?

TROY: Driving ain't nothing. All you do is point the truck where you want it to go. Driving ain't nothing.

BONO: Do Mr. Rand know you ain't got no driver's license? That's what I'm talking about. I ain't asked if driving was easy. I asked if Mr. Rand know you ain't got no driver's license.

TROY: He ain't got to know. The man ain't got to know my business. Time he find out, I have two or three driver's licenses.

LYONS *(going into his pocket):* Say, look here, Pop . . .

TROY: I knew it was coming. Didn't I tell you, Bono? I know what kind of "Look here, Pop" that was. The nigger fixing to ask me for some money. It's Friday night. It's my payday. All them rogues down there on the avenue . . . the ones that ain't in jail . . . and Lyons is hopping in his shoes to get down there with them.

LYONS: See, Pop . . . if you give somebody else a chance to talk sometime, you'd see that I was fixing to pay you back your ten dollars like I told you. Here . . . I told you I'd pay you when Bonnie got paid.

TROY: Naw . . . you go ahead and keep that ten dollars. Put it in the bank. The next time you feel like you wanna come by here and ask me for something . . . you go on down there and get that.

LYONS: Here's your ten dollars, Pop. I told you I don't want you to give me nothing. I just wanted to borrow ten dollars.

TROY: Naw . . . you go on and keep that for the next time you want to ask me.

LYONS: Come on, Pop . . . here go your ten dollars.

ROSE: Why don't you go on and let the boy pay you back, Troy?

LYONS: Here you go, Rose. If you don't take it I'm gonna have to hear about it for the next six months.

(He hands her the money.)

ROSE: You can hand yours over here too, Troy.

TROY: You see this, Bono. You see how they do me.

BONO: Yeah, Lucille do me the same way.

(GABRIEL *is heard singing offstage. He enters.*)

GABRIEL: Better get ready for the Judgment! Better get ready for . . . Hey! . . . Hey! . . . There's Troy's boy!

LYONS: How are you doing, Uncle Gabe?

GABRIEL: Lyons . . . The King of the Jungle! Rose . . . hey, Rose. Got a flower for you.

(He takes a rose from his pocket.)

Picked it myself. That's the same rose like you is!

ROSE: That's right nice of you, Gabe.

LYONS: What you been doing, Uncle Gabe?

GABRIEL: Oh, I been chasing hellhounds and waiting on the time to tell St. Peter to open the gates.

LYONS: You been chasing hellhounds, huh? Well . . . you doing the right thing, Uncle Gabe. Somebody got to chase them.

GABRIEL: Oh, yeah . . . I know it. The devil's strong. The devil ain't no pushover. Hellhounds snipping at everybody's heels. But I got my trumpet waiting on the judgment time.

LYONS: Waiting on the Battle of Armageddon, huh?

GABRIEL: Ain't gonna be too much of a battle when God get to waving that Judgment sword. But the people's gonna have a hell of a time trying to get into heaven if them gates ain't open.

LYONS *(putting his arm around* GABRIEL*):* You hear this, Pop. Uncle Gabe, you all right!

GABRIEL *(laughing with* LYONS*):* Lyons! King of the Jungle.

ROSE: You gonna stay for supper, Gabe. Want me to fix you a plate?

GABRIEL: I'll take a sandwich, Rose. Don't want no plate. Just wanna eat with my hands. I'll take a sandwich.

ROSE: How about you, Lyons? You staying? Got some short ribs cooking.

LYONS: Naw, I won't eat nothing till after we finished playing.

(Pause.)

You ought to come down and listen to me play, Pop.

TROY: I don't like that Chinese music. All that noise.

ROSE: Go on in the house and wash up, Gabe . . . I'll fix you a sandwich.

GABRIEL *(to* LYONS, *as he exits):* Troy's mad at me.

LYONS: What you mad at Uncle Gabe for, Pop?

ROSE: He think Troy's mad at him cause he moved over to Miss Pearl's.

TROY: I ain't mad at the man. He can live where he want to live at.

LYONS: What he move over there for? Miss Pearl don't like nobody.

ROSE: She don't mind him none. She treats him real nice. She just don't allow all that singing.

TROY: She don't mind that rent he be paying . . . that's what she don't mind.

ROSE: Troy, I ain't going through that with you no more. He's over there cause he want to have his own place. He can come and go as he please.

TROY: Hell, he could come and go as he please here. I wasn't stopping him. I ain't put no rules on him.

ROSE: It ain't the same thing, Troy. And you know it.

*(*GABRIEL *comes to the door.)*

Now, that's the last I wanna hear about that. I don't wanna hear nothing else about Gabe and Miss Pearl. And next week . . .

GABRIEL: I'm ready for my sandwich, Rose.

ROSE: And next week . . . when that recruiter come from that school . . . I want you to sign that paper and go on and let Cory play football. Then that'll be the last I have to hear about that.

TROY (*to* ROSE *as she exits into the house*): I ain't thinking about Cory nothing.

LYONS: What . . . Cory got recruited? What school he going to?

TROY: That boy walking around here smelling his piss . . . thinking he's grown. Thinking he's gonna do what he want, irrespective of what I say. Look here, Bono . . . I left the Commissioner's office and went down to the A&P . . . that boy ain't working down there. He lying to me. Telling me he got his job back . . . telling me he working weekends . . . telling me he working after school . . . Mr. Stawicki tell me he ain't working down there at all!

LYONS: Cory just growing up. He's just busting at the seams trying to fill out your shoes.

TROY: I don't care what he's doing. When he get to the point where he wanna disobey me . . . then it's time for him to move on. Bono'll tell you that. I bet he ain't never disobeyed his daddy without paying the consequences.

BONO: I ain't never had a chance. My daddy came on through . . . but I ain't never knew him to see him . . . or what he had on his mind or where he went. Just moving on through. Searching out the New Land. That's what the old folks used to call it. See a fellow moving around from place to place . . . woman to woman . . . called it searching out the New Land. I can't say if he ever found it. I come along, didn't want no kids. Didn't know if I was gonna be in one place long enough to fix on them right as their daddy. I figured I was going searching too. As it turned out I been hooked up with Lucille near about as long as your daddy been with Rose. Going on sixteen years.

TROY: Sometimes I wish I hadn't known my daddy. He ain't cared nothing about no kids. A kid to him wasn't nothing. All he wanted was for you to learn how to walk so he could start you to working. When it come time for eating . . . he ate first. If there was anything left over, that's what you got. Man would sit down and eat two chickens and give you the wing.

LYONS: You ought to stop that, Pop. Everybody feed their kids. No matter how hard times is . . . everybody care about their kids. Make sure they have something to eat.

TROY: The only thing my daddy cared about was getting them bales of cotton in to Mr. Lubin. That's the only thing that mattered to him. Sometimes I used to wonder why he was living. Wonder why the devil hadn't come and got him. "Get them bales of cotton in to Mr. Lubin" and find out he owe him money . . .

LYONS: He should have just went on and left when he saw he couldn't get no-where. That's what I would have done.

TROY: How he gonna leave with eleven kids? And where he gonna go? He ain't knew how to do nothing but farm. No, he was trapped and I think he knew it. But I'll say this for him . . . he felt a responsibility toward us. Maybe he ain't treated us the way I felt he should have . . . but without that responsibility he could have walked off and left us . . . made his own way.

BONO: A lot of them did. Back in those days what you talking about . . . they walk out their front door and just take on down one road or another and keep on walking.

LYONS: There you go! That's what I'm talking about.

BONO: Just keep on walking till you come to something else. Ain't you never heard of nobody having the walking blues? Well, that's what you call it when you just take off like that.

TROY: My daddy ain't had them walking blues! What you talking about? He stayed right there with his family. But he was just as evil as he could be. My mama couldn't stand him. Couldn't stand that evilness. She run off when I was about eight. She sneaked off one night after he had gone to sleep. Told me she was coming back for me. I ain't never seen her no more. All his women run off and left him. He wasn't good for nobody.

When my turn come to head out, I was fourteen and got to sniffing around Joe Canewell's daughter. Had us an old mule we called Greyboy. My daddy sent me out to do some plowing and I tied up Greyboy and went to fooling around with Joe Canewell's daughter. We done found us a nice little spot, got real cozy with each other. She about thirteen and we done figured we was grown anyway . . . so we down there enjoying ourselves . . . ain't thinking about nothing. We didn't know Greyboy had got loose and wandered back to the house and my daddy was looking for me. We down there by the creek enjoying ourselves when my daddy come up on us. Surprised us. He had them leather straps off the mule and commenced to whupping me like there was no tomorrow. I jumped up, mad and embarrassed. I was scared of my daddy. When he commenced to whupping on me . . . quite naturally I run to get out of the way.

(Pause.)

Now I thought he was mad cause I ain't done my work. But I see where he was chasing me off so he could have the gal for himself. When I see what the matter of it was, I lost all fear of my daddy. Right there is where I become a man . . . at fourteen years of age.

(Pause.)

Now it was my turn to run him off. I picked up them same reins that he had used on me. I picked up them reins and commenced to whupping on him. The gal jumped up and run off . . . and when my daddy turned to face me, I could see why the devil had never come to get him . . . cause he was the devil himself. I don't know what happened. When I woke up, I was laying right there by the creek, and Blue . . . this old dog we had . . . was licking my face. I thought I was blind. I couldn't see nothing. Both my eyes were swollen shut. I layed there and cried. I didn't know what I was gonna do. The only thing I knew was the time had come for me to leave my daddy's house. And right there the world suddenly got big. And it was a long time before I could cut it down to where I could handle it.

Part of that cutting down was when I got to the place where I could feel him kicking in my blood and knew that the only thing that separated us was the matter of a few years.

(GABRIEL *enters from the house with a sandwich.*)

LYONS: What you got there, Uncle Gabe?

GABRIEL: Got me a ham sandwich. Rose gave me a ham sandwich.

TROY: I don't know what happened to him. I done lost touch with everybody except Gabriel. But I hope he's dead. I hope he found some peace.

LYONS: That's a heavy story, Pop. I didn't know you left home when you was fourteen.

TROY: And didn't know nothing. The only part of the world I knew was the forty-two acres of Mr. Lubin's land. That's all I knew about life.

LYONS: Fourteen's kinda young to be out on your own. *(Phone rings.)* I don't even think I was ready to be out on my own at fourteen. I don't know what I would have done.

TROY: I got up from the creek and walked on down to Mobile. I was through with farming. Figured I could do better in the city. So I walked the two hundred miles to Mobile.

LYONS: Wait a minute . . . you ain't walked no two hundred miles, Pop. Ain't nobody gonna walk no two hundred miles. You talking about some walking there.

BONO: That's the only way you got anywhere back in them days.

LYONS: Shhh. Damn if I wouldn't have hitched a ride with somebody!

TROY: Who you gonna hitch it with? They ain't had no cars and things like they got now. We talking about 1918.

ROSE *(entering):* What you all out here getting into?

TROY *(to ROSE):* I'm telling Lyons how good he got it. He don't know nothing about this I'm talking.

ROSE: Lyons, that was Bonnie on the phone. She say you supposed to pick her up.

LYONS: Yeah, okay, Rose.

TROY: I walked on down to Mobile and hitched up with some of them fellows that was heading this way. Got up here and found out . . . not only couldn't you get a job . . . you couldn't find no place to live. I thought I was in freedom. Shhh. Colored folks living down there on the riverbanks in whatever kind of shelter they could find for themselves. Right down there under the Brady Street Bridge. Living in shacks made of sticks and tarpaper. Messed around there and went from bad to worse. Started stealing. First it was food. Then I figured, hell, if I steal money I can buy me some food. Buy me some shoes too! One thing led to another. Met your mama. I was young and anxious to be a man. Met your mama and had you. What I do that for? Now I got to worry about feeding you and her. Got to steal three times as much. Went out one day looking for somebody to rob . . . that's what I was, a robber. I'll tell you truth. I'm ashamed of it today. But it's the truth. Went to rob this fellow . . . pulled out my knife . . . and he pulled out a gun. Shot me in the chest. It felt just like somebody had taken a hot branding iron and laid it on me. When he shot me I jumped at him with my knife. They told me I killed him and they put me in the penitentiary and locked me up for fifteen years. That's where I met Bono. That's where I learned how to play baseball. Got out that place and your mama had taken you and went on to make life without me. Fifteen years was a long time for her to wait. But that fifteen years cured me of that robbing stuff. Rose'll tell you. She asked me when I met her if I had gotten all that foolishness out of my system. And I told her, "Baby, it's you and baseball all what count with me." You hear me, Bono? I meant it too. She say, "Which one comes first?" I told her, "Baby, ain't no doubt it's baseball . . . but you stick and get old with me and we'll both outlive this baseball." Am I right, Rose? And it's true.

ROSE: Man, hush your mouth. You ain't said no such thing. Talking about, "Baby, you know you'll always be number one with me." That's what you was talking.

TROY: You hear that, Bono. That's why I love her.

BONO: Rose'll keep you straight. You get off the track, she'll straighten you up.

ROSE: Lyons, you better get on up and get Bonnie. She waiting on you.

LYONS (gets up to go): Hey, Pop, why don't you come on down to the Grill and hear me play?

TROY: I ain't going down there. I'm too old to be sitting around in them clubs.

BONO: You got to be good to play down at the Grill.

LYONS: Come on, Pop . . .

TROY: I got to get up in the morning.

LYONS: You ain't got to stay long.

TROY: Naw, I'm gonna get my supper and go on to bed.

LYONS: Well, I got to go. I'll see you again.

TROY: Don't you come around my house on my payday.

ROSE: Pick up the phone and let somebody know you coming. And bring Bonnie with you. You know I'm always glad to see her.

LYONS: Yeah, I'll do that, Rose. You take care now. See you, Pop. See you, Mr. Bono. See you, Uncle Gabe.

GABRIEL: Lyons! King of the Jungle!

(LYONS exits.)

TROY: Is supper ready, woman? Me and you got some business to take care of. I'm gonna tear it up too.

ROSE: Troy, I done told you now!

TROY (puts his arm around BONO): Aw hell, woman . . . this is Bono. Bono like family. I done known this nigger since . . . how long I done know you?

BONO: It's been a long time.

TROY: I done known this nigger since Skippy was a pup. Me and him done been through some times.

BONO: You sure right about that.

TROY: Hell, I done know him longer than I known you. And we still standing shoulder to shoulder. Hey, look here, Bono . . . a man can't ask for no more than that.

(Drinks to him.)

I love you, nigger.

BONO: Hell, I love you too . . . but I got to get home see my woman. You got yours in hand. I got to go get mine.

(BONO *starts to exit as* CORY *enters the yard, dressed in his football uniform. He gives* TROY *a hard, uncompromising look.*)

CORY: What you do that for, Pop?

(He throws his helmet down in the direction of TROY.*)*

ROSE: What's the matter? Cory . . . what's the matter?

CORY: Papa done went up to the school and told Coach Zellman I can't play football no more. Wouldn't even let me play the game. Told him to tell the recruiter not to come.

ROSE: Troy . . .

TROY: What you Troying me for. Yeah, I did it. And the boy know why I did it.

CORY: Why you wanna do that to me? That was the one chance I had.

ROSE: Ain't nothing wrong with Cory playing football, Troy.

TROY: The boy lied to me. I told the nigger if he wanna play football . . . to keep up his chores and hold down that job at the A&P. That was the conditions. Stopped down there to see Mr. Stawicki . . .

CORY: I can't work after school during the football season, Pop! I tried to tell you that Mr. Stawicki's holding my job for me. You don't never want to listen to nobody. And then you wanna go and do this to me!

TROY: I ain't done nothing to you. You done it to yourself.

CORY: Just cause you didn't have a chance! You just scared I'm gonna be better than you, that's all.

TROY: Come here.

ROSE: Troy . . .

(CORY *reluctantly crosses over to* TROY.*)*

TROY: All right! See. You done made a mistake.

CORY: I didn't even do nothing!

TROY: I'm gonna tell you what your mistake was. See . . . you swung at the ball and didn't hit it. That's strike one. See, you in the batter's box now. You swung and you missed. That's strike one. Don't you strike out!

(Lights fade to black.)

ACT II • SCENE I

(The following morning. CORY *is at the tree hitting the ball with the bat. He tries to mimic* TROY, *but his swing is awkward, less sure.* ROSE *enters from the house.*)

ROSE: Cory, I want you to help me with this cupboard.

CORY: I ain't quitting the team. I don't care what Poppa say.

ROSE: I'll talk to him when he gets back. He had to go see about your Uncle Gabe. The police done arrested him. Say he was disturbing the peace. He'll be back directly. Come on in here and help me clean out the top of this cupboard.

*(CORY *exits into the house.* ROSE *sees* TROY *and* BONO *coming down the alley.*)

Troy . . . what they say down there?

TROY: Ain't said nothing. I give them fifty dollars and they let him go. I'll talk to you about it. Where's Cory?

ROSE: He's in there helping me clean out these cupboards.

TROY: Tell him to get his butt out here.

(TROY *and* BONO *go over to the pile of wood.* BONO *picks up the saw and begins sawing.*)

TROY *(to* BONO*):* All they want is the money. That makes six or seven times I done went down there and got him. See me coming they stick out their *hands.*

BONO: Yeah, I know what you mean. That's all they care about . . . that money. They don't care about what's right.

(*Pause.*)

Nigger, why you got to go and get some hard wood? You ain't doing nothing but building a little old fence. Get you some soft pine wood. That's all you need.

TROY: I know what I'm doing. This is outside wood. You put pine wood inside the house. Pine wood is inside wood. This here is outside wood. Now you tell me where the fence is gonna be?

BONO: You don't need this wood. You can put it up with pine wood and it'll stand as long as you gonna be here looking at it.

TROY: How you know how long I'm gonna be here, nigger? Hell, I might just live forever. Live longer than old man Horsely.

BONO: That's what Magee used to say.

TROY: Magee's a damn fool. Now you tell me who you ever heard of gonna pull their own teeth with a pair of rusty pliers.

BONO: The old folks . . . my granddaddy used to pull his teeth with pliers. They ain't had no dentists for the colored folks back then.

TROY: Get clean pliers! You understand? Clean pliers! Sterilize them! Besides we ain't living back then. All Magee had to do was walk over to Doc Goldblum's.

BONO: I see where you and that Tallahassee gal . . . that Alberta . . . I see where you all done got tight.

TROY: What you mean "got tight"?

BONO: I see where you be laughing and joking with her all the time.

TROY: I laughs and jokes with all of them, Bono. You know me.

BONO: That ain't the kind of laughing and joking I'm talking about.

(CORY *enters from the house.*)

CORY: How you doing, Mr. Bono?

TROY: Cory? Get that saw from Bono and cut some wood. He talking about the wood's too hard to cut. Stand back there, Jim, and let that young boy show you how it's done.

BONO: He's sure welcome to it.

(CORY *takes the saw and begins to cut the wood.*)

Whew-e-e! Look at that. Big old strong boy. Look like Joe Louis. Hell, must be getting old the way I'm watching that boy whip through that wood.

CORY: I don't see why Mama want a fence around the yard noways.

TROY: Damn if I know either. What the hell she keeping out with it? She ain't got nothing nobody want.

BONO: Some people build fences to keep people out . . . and other people build fences to keep people in. Rose wants to hold on to you all. She loves you.

TROY: Hell, nigger, I don't need nobody to tell me my wife loves me, Cory . . . go on in the house and see if you can find that other saw.

CORY: Where's it at?

TROY: I said find it! Look for it till you find it!

(CORY *exits into the house.*)

What's that supposed to mean? Wanna keep us in?

BONO: Troy . . . I done known you seem like damn near my whole life. You and Rose both. I done know both of you all for a long time. I remember when you met Rose. When you was hitting them baseball out the park. A lot of them old gals was after you then. You had the pick of the litter. When you picked Rose, I was happy for you. That was the first time I knew you had any sense. I said . . . My man Troy knows what he's doing . . . I'm gonna follow this nigger . . . he might take me somewhere. I been following you too. I done learned a whole heap of things about life watching you. I done learned how to tell where the shit lies. How to tell it from the alfalfa. You done learned me a lot of things. You showed me how to not make the same mistakes . . . to take life as it comes along and keep putting one foot in front of the other.

(*Pause.*)

Rose a good woman, Troy.

TROY: Hell, nigger, I know she a good woman. I been married to her for eighteen years. What you got on your mind, Bono?

BONO: I just say she a good woman. Just like I say anything. I ain't got to have nothing on my mind.

TROY: You just gonna say she a good woman and leave it hanging out there like that? Why you telling me she a good woman?

BONO: She loves you, Troy. Rose loves you.

TROY: You saying I don't measure up. That's what you trying to say. I don't measure up cause I'm seeing this other gal. I know what you trying to say.

BONO: I know what Rose means to you, Troy. I'm just trying to say I don't want to see you mess up.

TROY: Yeah, I appreciate that, Bono. If you was messing around on Lucille I'd be telling you the same thing.

BONO: Well, that's all I got to say. I just say that because I love you both.

TROY: Hell, you know me . . . I wasn't out there looking for nothing. You can't find a better woman than Rose. I know that. But seems like this woman just stuck onto me where I can't shake her loose. I done wrestled with it, tried to throw her off me . . . but she just stuck on tighter. Now she's stuck on for good.

BONO: You's in control . . . that's what you tell me all the time. You responsible for what you do.

TROY: I ain't ducking the responsibility of it. As long as it sets right in my heart . . . then I'm okay. Cause that's all I listen to. It'll tell me right from wrong every time. And I ain't talking about doing Rose no bad turn. I love Rose. She done carried me a long ways and I love and respect her for that.

BONO: I know you do. That's why I don't want to see you hurt her. But what you gonna do when she find out? What you got then? If you try and juggle both of them . . . sooner or later you gonna drop one of them. That's common sense.

TROY: Yeah, I hear what you saying, Bono. I been trying to figure a way to work it out.

BONO: Work it out right, Troy. I don't want to be getting all up between you and Rose's business . . . but work it so it come out right.

TROY: Ah hell, I get all up between you and Lucille's business. When you gonna get that woman that refrigerator she been wanting? Don't tell me you ain't got no money now. I know who your banker is. Mellon don't need that money bad as Lucille want that refrigerator. I'll tell you that.

BONO: Tell you what I'll do . . . when you finish building this fence for Rose . . . I'll buy Lucille that refrigerator.

TROY: You done stuck your foot in your mouth now!

(TROY *grabs up a board and begins to saw.* BONO *starts to walk out the yard.*)

Hey, nigger . . . where you going?

BONO: I'm going home. I know you don't expect me to help you now. I'm protecting my money. I wanna see you put that fence up by yourself. That's what I want to see. You'll be here another six months without me.

TROY: Nigger, you ain't right.

BONO: When it comes to my money . . . I'm right as fireworks on the Fourth of July.

TROY: All right, we gonna see now. You better get your bankbook.

(BONO *exits, and* TROY *continues to work.* ROSE *enters from the house.*)

ROSE: What they say down there? What's happening with Gabe?

TROY: I went down there and got him out. Cost me fifty dollars. Say he was disturbing the peace. Judge set up a hearing for him in three weeks. Say to show cause why he shouldn't be recommitted.

ROSE: What was he doing that cause them to arrest him?

TROY: Some kids was teasing him and he run them off home. Say he was howling and carrying on. Some folks seen him and called the police. That's all it was.

ROSE: Well, what's you say? What'd you tell the judge?

TROY: Told him I'd look after him. It didn't make no sense to recommit the man. He stuck out his big greasy palm and told me to give him fifty dollars and take him on home.

ROSE: Where's he at now? Where'd he go off to?

TROY: He's gone on about his business. He don't need nobody to hold his hand.

ROSE: Well, I don't know. Seem like that would be the best place for him if they did put him into the hospital. I know what you're gonna say. But that's what I think would be best.

TROY: The man done had his life ruined fighting for what? And they wanna take and lock him up. Let him be free. He don't bother nobody.

ROSE: Well, everybody got their own way of looking at it I guess. Come on and get your lunch. I got a bowl of lima beans and some cornbread in the oven. Come on get something to eat. Ain't no sense you fretting over Gabe.

(ROSE *turns to go into the house.*)

TROY: Rose . . . got something to tell you.

ROSE: Well, come on . . . wait till I get this food on the table.

TROY: Rose!

(*She stops and turns around.*)

I don't know how to say this.

(*Pause.*)

I can't explain it none. It just sort of grows on you till it gets out of hand. It starts out like a little bush . . . and the next thing you know it's a whole forest.

ROSE: Troy . . . what is you talking about?

TROY: I'm talking, woman, let me talk. I'm trying to find a way to tell you . . . I'm gonna be a daddy. I'm gonna be somebody's daddy.

ROSE: Troy . . . you're not telling me this? You're gonna be . . . what?

TROY: Rose . . . now . . . see . . .

ROSE: You telling me you gonna by somebody's daddy? You telling your *wife* this?

(GABRIEL *enters from the street. He carries a rose in his hand.*)

GABRIEL: Hey, Troy! Hey, Rose!

ROSE: I have to wait eighteen years to hear something like this.

GABRIEL: Hey, Rose . . . I got a flower for you.

(*He hands it to her.*)

That's a rose. Same rose like you is.

ROSE: Thanks, Gabe.

GABRIEL: Troy, you ain't mad at me is you? Them bad mens come and put me away. You ain't mad at me is you?

TROY: Naw, Gabe, I ain't mad at you.

ROSE: Eighteen years and you wanna come with this.

GABRIEL (*takes a quarter out of his pocket*): See what I got? Got a brand new quarter.

TROY: Rose . . . it's just . . .

ROSE: Ain't nothing you can say, Troy. Ain't no way of explaining that.

GABRIEL: Fellow that gave me this quarter had a whole mess of them. I'm gonna keep this quarter till it stop shining.

ROSE: Gabe, go on in the house there. I got some watermelon in the frigidaire. Go on and get you a piece.

GABRIEL: Say, Rose . . . you know I was chasing hellhounds and them bad mens come and get me and take me away. Troy helped me. He come down there and told them they better let me go before he beat them up. Yeah, he did!

ROSE: You go on and get you a piece of watermelon, Gabe. Them bad mens is gone now.

GABRIEL: Okay, Rose . . . gonna get me some watermelon. The kind with the stripes on it.

(GABRIEL *exits into the house.*)

ROSE: Why, Troy? Why? After all these years to come dragging this in to me now. It don't make no sense at your age. I could have expected this ten or fifteen years ago, but not now.

TROY: Age ain't got nothing to do with it, Rose.

ROSE: I done tried to be everything a wife should be. Everything a wife could be. Been married eighteen years and I got to live to see the day you tell me you been seeing another woman and done fathered a child by her. And you know I ain't never wanted no half nothing in my family. My whole family is half. Everybody got different fathers and mothers . . . my two sisters and my brother. Can't hardly tell who's who. Can't never sit down and talk about Papa and Mama. It's your papa and your mama and my papa and my mama . . .

TROY: Rose . . . stop it now.

ROSE: I ain't never wanted that for none of my children. And now you wanna drag your behind in here and tell me something like this.

TROY: You ought to know. It's time for you to know.

ROSE: Well, I don't want to know, goddamn it!

TROY: I can't just make it go away. It's done now. I can't wish the circumstance of the thing away.

ROSE: And you don't want to either. Maybe you want to wish me and my boy away. Maybe that's what you want? Well, you can't wish us away. I've got eighteen years of my life invested in you. You ought to have stayed upstairs in my bed where you belong.

TROY: Rose . . . now listen to me . . . we can get a handle on this thing. We can talk this out . . . come to an understanding.

ROSE: All of a sudden it's "we." Where was "we" at when you was down there rolling around with some godforsaken woman? "We" should have come to an understanding before you started making a damn fool of yourself. You're a day late and a dollar short when it comes to an understanding with me.

TROY: It's just . . . She gives me a different idea . . . a different understanding about myself. I can step out of this house and get away from the pressures and problems . . . be a different man. I ain't got to wonder how I'm gonna pay the bills or get the roof fixed. I can just be a part of myself that I ain't never been.

ROSE: What I want to know . . . is do you plan to continue seeing her. That's all you can say to me.

TROY: I can sit up in her house and laugh. Do you understand what I'm saying. I can laugh out loud . . . and it feels good. It reaches all the way down to the bottom of my shoes.

(*Pause.*)

Rose, I can't give that up.

ROSE: Maybe you ought to go on and stay down there with her . . . if she's a better woman than me.

TROY: It ain't about nobody being a better woman or nothing. Rose, you ain't the blame. A man couldn't ask for no woman to be a better wife than you've been.

I'm responsible for it. I done locked myself into a pattern trying to take care of you all that I forgot about myself.

ROSE: What the hell was I there for? That was my job, not somebody else's.

TROY: Rose, I done tried all my life to live decent . . . to live a clean . . . hard . . . useful life. I tried to be a good husband to you. In every way I knew how. Maybe I come into the world backwards, I don't know. But . . . you born with two strikes on you before you come to the plate. You got to guard it closely . . . always looking for the curve ball on the inside corner. You can't afford to let none get past you. You can't afford a call strike. If you going down . . . you going down swinging. Everything lined up against you. What you gonna do. I fooled them, Rose. I bunted. When I found you and Cory and a halfway decent job . . . I was safe. Couldn't nothing touch me. I wasn't gonna strike out no more. I wasn't going back to the penitentiary. I wasn't gonna lay in the streets with a bottle of wine. I was safe. I had me a family. A job. I wasn't gonna get that last strike. I was on first looking for one of them boys to knock me in. To get me home.

ROSE: You should have stayed in my bed, Troy.

TROY: Then when I saw that gal . . . she firmed up my backbone. And I got to thinking that if I tried . . . I just might be able to steal second. Do you understand after eighteen years I wanted to steal second.

ROSE: You should have held me tight. You should have grabbed me and held on.

TROY: I stood on first base for eighteen years and I thought . . . well, goddamn it . . . go on for it!

ROSE: We're not talking about baseball! We're talking about you going off to lay in bed with another woman . . . and then bring it home to me. That's what we're talking about. We ain't talking about no baseball.

TROY: Rose, you're not listening to me. I'm trying the best I can to explain it to you. It's not easy for me to admit that I been standing in the same place for eighteen years.

ROSE: I been standing with you! I been right here with you, Troy. I got a life too. I gave eighteen years of my life to stand in the same spot with you. Don't you think I ever wanted other things? Don't you think I had dreams and hopes? What about my life? What about me? Don't you think it ever crossed my mind to want to know other men? That I wanted to lay up somewhere and forget about my responsibilities? That I wanted someone to make me laugh so I could feel good? You not the only one who's got wants and needs. But I held on to you, Troy. I took all my feelings, my wants and needs, my dreams . . . and I buried them inside you. I planted a seed and watched and prayed over it. I planted myself inside you and waited to bloom. And it didn't take me no eighteen years to find out the soil was hard and rocky and it wasn't never gonna bloom.

But I held on to you, Troy. I held you tighter. You was my husband. I owed you everything I had. Every part of me I could find to give you. And upstairs in that room . . . with the darkness falling in on me . . . I gave everything I had to try and erase the doubt that you wasn't the finest man in the world. And wherever you was going . . . I wanted to be there with you. Cause you was my husband. Cause that's the only way I was gonna survive as your wife. You always talking about what you give . . . and what you don't have to give. But you take too. You take . . . and don't even know nobody's giving!

(ROSE *turns to exit into the house;* TROY *grabs her arm.*)

TROY: You say I take and don't give!

ROSE: Troy! You're hurting me!

TROY: You say I take and don't give.

ROSE: Troy . . . you're hurting my arm! Let go!

TROY: I done give you everything I got. Don't you tell that lie on me.

ROSE: Troy!

TROY: Don't you tell that lie on me!

(CORY *enters from the house.*)

CORY: Mama!

ROSE: Troy. You're hurting me.

TROY: Don't you tell me about no taking and giving.

(CORY *comes up behind* TROY *and grabs him.* TROY, *surprised, is thrown off balance just as* CORY *throws a glancing blow that catches him on the chest and knocks him down.* TROY *is stunned, as is* CORY.)

ROSE: Troy. Troy. No!

(TROY *gets to his feet and starts at* CORY.)

Troy . . . no. Please! Troy!

(ROSE *pulls on* TROY *to hold him back.* TROY *stops himself.*)

TROY (*to* CORY): All right. That's strike two. You stay away from around me, boy. Don't you strike out. You living with a full count. Don't you strike out.

(TROY *exits out the yard as the lights go down.*)

Scene II

(*It is six months later, early afternoon.* TROY *enters from the house and starts to exit the yard.* ROSE *enters from the house.*)

ROSE: Troy, I want to talk to you.

TROY: All of a sudden, after all this time, you want to talk to me, huh? You ain't wanted to talk to me for months. You ain't wanted to talk to me last night. You ain't wanted no part of me then. What you wanna talk to me about now?

ROSE: Tomorrow's Friday.

TROY: I know what day tomorrow is. You think I don't know tomorrow's Friday? My whole life I ain't done nothing but look to see Friday coming and you got to tell me it's Friday.

ROSE: I want to know if you're coming home.

TROY: I always come home, Rose. You know that. There ain't never been a night I ain't come home.

ROSE: That ain't what I mean . . . and you know it. I want to know if you're coming straight home after work.

TROY: I figure I'd cash my check . . . hang out at Taylors' with the boys . . . maybe play a game of checkers . . .

ROSE: Troy, I can't live like this. I won't live like this. You livin' on borrowed time with me. It's been going on six months now you ain't been coming home.

TROY: I be here every night. Every night of the year. That's 365 days.

ROSE: I want you to come home tomorrow after work.

TROY: Rose . . . I don't mess up my pay. You know that now. I take my pay and I give it to you. I don't have no money but what you give me back. I just want to have a little time to myself . . . a little time to enjoy life.

ROSE: What about me? When's my time to enjoy life?

TROY: I don't know what to tell you, Rose. I'm doing the best I can.

ROSE: You ain't been home from work but time enough to change your clothes and run out . . . and you wanna call that the best you can do?

TROY: I'm going over to the hospital to see Alberta. She went into the hospital this afternoon. Look like she might have the baby early. I won't be gone long.

ROSE: Well, you ought to know. They went over to Miss Pearl's and got Gabe today. She said you told them to go ahead and lock him up.

TROY: I ain't said no such thing. Whoever told you that is telling a lie. Pearl ain't doing nothing but telling a big fat lie.

ROSE: She ain't had to tell me. I read it on the papers.

TROY: I ain't told them nothing of the kind.

ROSE: I saw it right there on the papers.

TROY: What it say, huh?

ROSE: It said you told them to take him.

TROY: Then they screwed that up, just the way they screw up everything. I ain't worried about what they got on the paper.

ROSE: Say the government send part of his check to the hospital and the other part to you.

TROY: I ain't got nothing to do with that if that's the way it works. I ain't made up the rules about how it work.

ROSE: You did Gabe just like you did Cory. You wouldn't sign the paper for Cory . . . but you signed for Gabe. You signed that paper.

(*The telephone is heard ringing inside the house.*)

TROY: I told you I ain't signed nothing, woman! The only thing I signed was the release form. Hell, I can't read, I don't know what they had on that paper! I ain't signed nothing about sending Gabe away.

ROSE: I said send him to the hospital . . . you said let him be free . . . now you done went down there and signed him to the hospital for half his money. You went back on yourself, Troy. You gonna have to answer for that.

TROY: See now . . . you been over there talking to Miss Pearl. She done got mad cause she ain't getting Gabe's rent money. That's all it is. She's liable to say anything.

ROSE: Troy, I seen where you signed the paper.

TROY: You ain't seen nothing I signed. What she doing got papers on my brother anyway? Miss Pearl telling a big fat lie. And I'm gonna tell her about it too! You ain't seen nothing I signed. Say . . . you ain't seen nothing I signed.

(ROSE *exits into the house to answer the telephone. Presently she returns.*)

ROSE: Troy . . . that was the hospital. Alberta had the baby.

TROY: What she have? What is it?

ROSE: It's a girl.

TROY: I better get on down to the hospital to see her.

ROSE: Troy . . .

TROY: Rose . . . I got to go see her now. That's only right . . . what's the matter . . . the baby's all right, ain't it?

ROSE: Alberta died having the baby.

TROY: Died . . . you say she's dead? Alberta's dead?

ROSE: They said they done all they could. They couldn't do nothing for her.

TROY: The baby? How's the baby?

ROSE: They say it's healthy. I wonder who's gonna bury her.

TROY: She had family, Rose. She wasn't living in the world by herself.

ROSE: I know she wasn't living in the world by herself.

TROY: Next thing you gonna want to know if she had any insurance.

ROSE: Troy, you ain't got to talk like that.

TROY: That's the first thing that jumped out your mouth. "Who's gonna bury her?" Like I'm fixing to take on that task for myself.

ROSE: I am your wife. Don't push me away.

TROY: I ain't pushing nobody away. Just give me some space. That's all. Just give me some room to breathe.

(ROSE *exits into the house.* TROY *walks about the yard.*)

TROY (*with a quiet rage that threatens to consume him*): All right . . . Mr. Death. See now . . . I'm gonna tell you what I'm gonna do. I'm gonna take and build me a fence around this yard. See? I'm gonna build me a fence around what belongs to me. And then I want you to stay on the other side. See? You stay over there until you're ready for me. Then you come on. Bring your army. Bring your sickle. Bring your wrestling clothes. I ain't gonna fall down on my vigilance this time. You ain't gonna sneak up on me no more. When you ready for me . . . when the top of your list say Troy Maxson . . . that's when you come around here. You come up and knock on the front door. Ain't nobody else got nothing to do with this. This is between you and me. Man to man. You stay on the other side of that fence until you ready for me. Then you come up and knock on the front door. Anytime you want. I'll be ready for you.

(*The lights go down to black.*)

Scene III

(*The lights come up on the porch. It is late evening three days later.* ROSE *sits listening to the ball game waiting for* TROY. *The final out of the game is made and* ROSE *switches off the radio.* TROY *enters the yard carrying an infant wrapped in blankets. He stands back from the house and calls.*)

(ROSE *enters and stands on the porch. There is a long, awkward silence, the weight of which grows heavier with each passing second.*)

TROY: Rose . . . I'm standing here with my daughter in my arms. She ain't but a wee bittie little old thing. She don't know nothing about grownups' business. She innocent . . . and she ain't got no mama.

ROSE: What you telling me for, Troy?

(She turns and exits into the house.)

    TROY: Well . . . I guess we'll sit out here on the porch.

(He sits down on the porch. There is an awkward indelicateness about the way he handles the baby. His largeness engulfs and seems to swallow it. He speaks loud enough for ROSE *to hear.)*

A man's got to do what's right for him. I ain't sorry for nothing I done. It felt right in my heart.

(To the baby.)

What you smiling at? Your daddy's a big man. Got these great big old hands. But sometimes he's scared. And right now your daddy's scared cause we sitting out here and ain't got no home. Oh, I been homeless before. I ain't had no little baby with me. But I been homeless. You just be out on the road by your lonesome and you see one of them trains coming and you just kinda go like this . . .

(He sings as a lullaby.)

Please, Mr. Engineer let a man ride the line

Please, Mr. Engineer let a man ride the line

I ain't got no ticket please let me ride the blinds

*(*ROSE *enters from the house.* TROY *hearing her steps behind him, stands and faces her.)*

She's my daughter, Rose. My own flesh and blood. I can't deny her no more than I can deny them boys.

(Pause.)

You and them boys is my family. You and them and this child is all I got in the world. So I guess what I'm saying is . . . I'd appreciate it if you'd help me take care of her.

    ROSE: Okay, Troy . . . you're right. I'll take care of your baby for you . . . cause . . . like you say . . . she's innocent . . . and you can't visit the sins of the father upon the child. A motherless child has got a hard time.

(She takes the baby from him.)

From right now . . . this child got a mother. But you a womanless man.

*(*ROSE *turns and exits into the house with the baby. Lights go down to black.)*

SCENE IV

(It is two months later. LYONS *enters from the street. He knocks on the door and calls.)*

    LYONS: Hey, Rose! *(Pause.)* Rose!

    ROSE *(from inside the house):* Stop that yelling. You gonna wake up Raynell. I just got her to sleep.

    LYONS: I just stopped by to pay Papa this twenty dollars I owe him. Where's Papa at?

    ROSE: He should be here in a minute. I'm getting ready to go down to the church. Sit down and wait on him.

    LYONS: I got to go pick up Bonnie over her mother's house.

    ROSE: Well, sit it down there on the table. He'll get it.

    LYONS *(enters the house and sets the money on the table):* Tell Papa I said thanks. I'll see you again.

ROSE: All right, Lyons. We'll see you.

(LYONS *starts to exit as* CORY *enters.*)

CORY: Hey, Lyons.

LYONS: What's happening, Cory. Say man, I'm sorry I missed your graduation. You know I had a gig and couldn't get away. Otherwise, I would have been there, man. So what you doing?

CORY: I'm trying to find a job.

LYONS: Yeah I know how that go, man. It's rough out here. Jobs are scarce.

CORY: Yeah, I know.

LYONS: Look here, I got to run. Talk to Papa . . . he know some people. He'll be able to help get you a job. Talk to him . . . see what he say.

CORY: Yeah . . . all right, Lyons.

LYONS: You take care. I'll talk to you soon. We'll find some time to talk.

(LYONS *exits the yard.* CORY *wanders over to the tree, picks up the bat, and assumes a batting stance. He studies an imaginary pitcher and swings. Dissatisfied with the result, he tries again.* TROY *enters. They eye each other for a beat.* CORY *puts the bat down and exits the yard.* TROY *starts into the house as* ROSE *exits with* RAYNELL. *She is carrying a cake.*)

TROY: I'm coming in and everybody's going out.

ROSE: I'm taking this cake down to the church for the bake sale. Lyons was by to see you. He stopped by to pay you your twenty dollars. It's laying in there on the table.

TROY (*going into his pocket*): Well . . . here go this money.

ROSE: Put it in there on the table, Troy. I'll get it.

TROY: What time you coming back?

ROSE: Ain't no use in you studying me. It don't matter what time I come back.

TROY: I just asked you a question, woman. What's the matter . . . can't I ask you a question?

ROSE: Troy, I don't want to go into it. Your dinner's in there on the stove. All you got to do is heat it up. And don't you be eating the rest of them cakes in there. I'm coming back for them. We having a bake sale at the church tomorrow.

(ROSE *exits the yard.* TROY *sits down on the steps, takes a pint bottle from his pocket, opens it, and drinks. He begins to sing.*)

TROY: Hear it ring! Hear it ring!
Had an old dog his name was Blue
You know Blue was mighty true
You know Blue was a good old dog
Blue treed a possum in a hollow log
You know from that he was a good old dog

(BONO *enters the yard.*)

BONO: Hey, Troy.

TROY: Hey, what's happening, Bono?

BONO: I just thought I'd stop by to see you.

TROY: What you stop by and see me for? You ain't stopped by in a month of Sundays. Hell, I must owe you money or something.

BONO: Since you got your promotion I can't keep up with you. Used to see you every day. Now I don't even know what route you working.

TROY: They keep switching me around. Got me out in Greentree now . . . hauling white folks' garbage.

BONO: Greentree, huh? You lucky, at least you ain't got to be lifting them barrels. Damn if they ain't getting heavier. I'm gonna put in my two years and call it quits.

TROY: I'm thinking about retiring myself.

BONO: You got it easy. You can drive for another five years.

TROY: It ain't the same, Bono. It ain't like working the back of the truck. Ain't got nobody to talk to . . . feel like you working by yourself. Naw, I'm thinking about retiring. How's Lucille?

BONO: She all right. Her arthritis get to acting up on her sometime. Saw Rose on my way in. She going down to the church, huh?

TROY: Yeah, she took up going down there. All them preachers looking for somebody to fatten their pockets.

(Pause.)

Got some gin here.

BONO: Naw, thanks. I just stopped by to say hello.

TROY: Hell, nigger . . . you can take a drink. I ain't never known you to say no to a drink. You ain't got to work tomorrow.

BONO: I just stopped by. I'm fixing to go over to Skinner's. We got us a domino game going over his house every Friday.

TROY: Nigger, you can't play no dominoes. I used to whup you four games out of five.

BONO: Well, that learned me. I'm getting better.

TROY: Yeah? Well, that's all right.

BONO: Look here . . . I got to be getting on. Stop by sometime, huh?

TROY: Yeah, I'll do that, Bono. Lucille told Rose you bought her a new refrigerator.

BONO: Yeah, Rose told Lucille you had finally built your fence . . . so I figured we'd call it even.

TROY: I knew you would.

BONO: Yeah . . . okay. I'll be talking to you.

TROY: Yeah, take care, Bono. Good to see you. I'm gonna stop over.

BONO: Yeah. Okay, Troy.

*(*BONO *exits.* TROY *drinks from the bottle.)*

TROY: Old Blue died and I dig his grave

Let him down with a golden chain

Every night when I hear old Blue bark

I know Blue treed a possum in Noah's Ark.

Hear it ring! Hear it ring!

*(*CORY *enters the yard. They eye each other for a beat.* TROY *is sitting in the middle of the steps.* CORY *walks over.)*

CORY: I got to get by.

TROY: Say what? What's you say?

CORY: You in my way. I got to get by.

TROY: You got to get by where? This is my house. Bought and paid for. In full. Took me fifteen years. And if you wanna go in my house and I'm sitting on the steps . . . you say excuse me. Like your mama taught you.

CORY: Come on, Pop . . . I got to get by.

(CORY *starts to maneuver his way past* TROY. TROY *grabs his leg and shoves him back.*)

TROY: You just gonna walk over top of me?

CORY: I live here too!

TROY *(advancing toward him):* You just gonna walk over top of me in my own house?

CORY: I ain't scared of you.

TROY: I ain't asked if you was scared of me. I asked you if you was fixing to walk over top of me in my own house? That's the question. You ain't gonna say excuse me? You just gonna walk over top of me?

CORY: If you wanna put it like that.

TROY: How else am I gonna put it?

CORY: I was walking by you to go into the house cause you sitting on the steps drunk, singing to yourself. You can put it like that.

TROY: Without saying excuse me???

(CORY *doesn't respond.*)

I asked you a question. Without saying excuse me???

CORY: I ain't got to say excuse me to you. You don't count around here no more.

TROY: Oh, I see . . . I don't count around here no more. You ain't got to say excuse me to your daddy. All of a sudden you done got so grown that your daddy don't count around here no more . . . Around here in his own house and yard that he done paid for with the sweat of his brow. You done got so grown to where you gonna take over. You gonna take over my house. Is that right? You gonna wear my pants. You gonna go in there and stretch out on my bed. You ain't got to say excuse me cause I don't count around here no more. Is that right?

CORY: That's right. You always talking this dumb stuff. Now, why don't you just get out my way.

TROY: I guess you got someplace to sleep and something to put in your belly. You got that, huh? You got that? That's what you need. You got that, huh?

CORY: You don't know what I got. You ain't got to worry about what I got.

TROY: You right! You one hundred percent right! I done spent the last seventeen years worrying about what you got. Now it's your turn, see? I'll tell you what to do. You grown . . . we done established that. You a man. Now, let's see you act like one. Turn you behind around and walk out this yard. And when you get out there in the alley . . . you can forget about this house. See? 'Cause this is my house. You go on and be a man and get your own house. You can forget about this. 'Cause this is mine. You go on and get yours 'cause I'm through with doing for you.

CORY: You talking about what you did for me . . . what'd you ever give me?

TROY: Them feet and bones! That pumping heart, nigger! I give you more than anybody else is ever gonna give you.

CORY: You ain't never gave me nothing! You ain't never done nothing but hold me back. Afraid I was gonna be better than you. All you ever did was try and make me scared of you. I used to tremble every time you called my name. Every time I heard your footsteps in the house. Wondering all the time . . . what's Papa gonna say if I do this? . . . What's he gonna say if I do that? . . . What's Papa gonna say if I turn on the radio? And Mama, too . . . she tries . . . but she's scared of you.

TROY: You leave your mama out of this. She ain't got nothing to do with this.

CORY: I don't know how she stand you . . . after what you did to her.

TROY: I told you to leave your mama out of this!

(He advances toward CORY.*)*

CORY: What you gonna do . . . give me a whupping? You can't whup me no more. You're too old. You just an old man.

TROY *(shoves him on his shoulder):* Nigger! That's what you are. You just another nigger on the street to me!

CORY: You crazy! You know that?

TROY: Go on now! You got the devil in you. Get on away from me!

CORY: You just a crazy old man . . . talking about I got the devil in me.

TROY: Yeah, I'm crazy! If you don't get on the other side of that yard . . . I'm gonna show you how crazy I am! Go on . . . get the hell out of my yard.

CORY: It ain't your yard. You took Uncle Gabe's money he got from the army to buy this house and then you put him out.

TROY *(*TROY *advances on* CORY*):* Get your black ass out of my yard!

*(*TROY'S *advance backs* CORY *up against the tree.* CORY *grabs up the bat.)*

CORY: I ain't going nowhere! Come on . . . put me out! I ain't scared of you.

TROY: That's my bat!

CORY: Come on!

TROY: Put my bat down!

CORY: Come on, put me out.

*(*CORY *swings at* TROY, *who backs across the yard.)*

What's the matter? You so bad . . . put me out!

*(*TROY *advances toward* CORY.*)*

CORY *(backing up):* Come on! Come on!

TROY: You're gonna have to use it! You wanna draw that bat back on me . . . you're gonna have to use it.

CORY: Come on! . . . Come on!

*(*CORY *swings the bat at* TROY *a second time. He misses.* TROY *continues to advance toward him.)*

TROY: You're gonna have to kill me! You wanna draw that bat back on me. You're gonna have to kill me.

*(*CORY, *backed up against the tree, can go no farther.* TROY *taunts him. He sticks out his head and offers him a target.)*

Come on! Come on!

*(*CORY *is unable to swing the bat.* TROY *grabs it.)*

TROY: Then I'll show you.

(CORY *and* TROY *struggle over the bat. The struggle is fierce and fully engaged.* TROY *ultimately is the stronger and takes the bat from* CORY *and stands over him ready to swing. He stops himself.*)

Go on and get away from around my house.

(CORY, *stung by his defeat, picks himself up, walks slowly out of the yard and up the alley.*)

CORY: Tell Mama I'll be back for my things.

TROY: They'll be on the other side of that fence.

(CORY *exits.*)

TROY: I can't taste nothing. Helluljah! I can't taste nothing no more. (TROY *assumes a batting posture and begins to taunt Death, the fastball on the outside corner.*) Come on! It's between you and me now! Come on! Anytime you want! Come on! I be ready for you . . . but I ain't gonna be easy.

(*The lights go down on the scene.*)

SCENE V

(*The time is 1965. The lights come up in the yard. It is the morning of* TROY'S *funeral. A funeral plaque with a light hangs beside the door. There is a small garden plot off to the side. There is noise and activity in the house as* ROSE, LYONS, *and* BONO *have gathered. The door opens and* RAYNELL, *seven years old, enters dressed in a flannel nightgown. She crosses to the garden and pokes around with a stick.* ROSE *calls from the house.*)

ROSE: Raynell!

RAYNELL: Mam?

ROSE: What you doing out there?

RAYNELL: Nothing.

(ROSE *comes to the door.*)

ROSE: Girl, get in here and get dressed. What you doing?

RAYNELL: Seeing if my garden growed.

ROSE: I told you it ain't gonna grow overnight. You got to wait.

RAYNELL: It don't look like it never gonna grow. Dang!

ROSE: I told you a watched pot never boils. Get in here and get dressed.

RAYNELL: This ain't even no pot, Mama.

ROSE: You just have to give it a chance. It'll grow. Now you come on and do what I told you. We got to be getting ready. This ain't no morning to be playing around. You hear me?

RAYNELL: Yes, mam.

(ROSE *exits into the house.* RAYNELL *continues to poke at her garden with a stick.* CORY *enters. He is dressed in a Marine corporal's uniform, and carries a duffel bag. His posture is that of a military man, and his speech has a clipped sternness.*)

CORY (*to* RAYNELL): Hi.

(*Pause.*)

I bet your name is Raynell.

RAYNELL: Uh huh.

CORY: Is your mama home?

(RAYNELL *runs up on the porch and calls through the screen door.*)

RAYNELL: Mama . . . there's some man out here. Mama?

(ROSE *comes to the door.*)

ROSE: Cory? Lord have mercy! Look here, you all!

(ROSE *and* CORY *embrace in a tearful reunion as* BONO *and* LYONS *enter from the house dressed in funeral clothes.*)

BONO: Aw, looka here . . .

ROSE: Done got all grown up!

CORY: Don't cry, Mama. What you crying about?

ROSE: I'm just so glad you made it.

CORY: Hey Lyons. How you doing, Mr. Bono.

(LYONS *goes to embrace* CORY.)

LYONS: Look at you, man. Look at you. Don't he look good, Rose? Got them Corporal stripes.

ROSE: What took you so long?

CORY: You know how the Marines are, Mama. They got to get all their paperwork straight before they let you do anything.

ROSE: Well, I'm sure glad you made it. They let Lyons come. Your Uncle Gabe's still in the hospital. They don't know if they gonna let him out or not. I just talked to them a little while ago.

LYONS: A Corporal in the United States Marines.

BONO: Your daddy knew you had it in you. He used to tell me all the time.

LYONS: Don't he look good, Mr. Bono?

BONO: Yeah, he remind me of Troy when I first met him.

(*Pause.*)

Say, Rose, Lucille's down at the church with the choir. I'm gonna go down and get the pallbearers lined up. I'll be back to get you all.

ROSE: Thanks, Jim.

CORY: See you, Mr. Bono.

LYONS (*with his arm around* RAYNELL): Cory . . . look at Raynell. Ain't she precious? She gonna break a whole lot of hearts.

ROSE: Raynell, come and say hello to your brother. This is your brother, Cory. You remember Cory.

RAYNELL: No, Mam.

CORY: She don't remember me, Mama.

ROSE: Well, we talk about you. She heard us talk about you. (*To* RAYNELL.) This is your brother, Cory. Come on and say hello.

RAYNELL: Hi.

CORY: Hi. So you're Raynell. Mama told me a lot about you.

ROSE: You all come on into the house and let me fix you some breakfast. Keep up your strength.

CORY: I ain't hungry, Mama.

LYONS: You can fix me something, Rose. I'll be in there in a minute.

ROSE: Cory, you sure you don't want nothing? I know they ain't feeding you right.

CORY: No, Mama . . . thanks. I don't feel like eating. I'll get something later.

ROSE: Raynell . . . get on upstairs and get that dress on like I told you.

(ROSE *and* RAYNELL *exit into the house.*)

LYONS: So . . . I hear you thinking about getting married.

CORY: Yeah, I done found the right one, Lyons. It's about time.

LYONS: Me and Bonnie been split up about four years now. About the time Papa retired. I guess she just got tired of all them changes I was putting her through.

(*Pause.*)

I always knew you was gonna make something out yourself. Your head was always in the right direction. So . . . you gonna stay in . . . make it a career . . . put in your twenty years?

CORY: I don't know. I got six already, I think that's enough.

LYONS: Stick with Uncle Sam and retire early. Ain't nothing out here. I guess Rose told you what happened with me. They got me down the workhouse. I thought I was being slick cashing other people's checks.

CORY: How much time you doing?

LYONS: They give me three years. I got that beat now. I ain't got but nine more months. It ain't so bad. You learn to deal with it like anything else. You got to take the crookeds with the straights. That's what Papa used to say. He used to say that when he struck out. I seen him strike out three times in a row . . . and the next time up he hit the ball over the grandstand. Right out there in Homestead Field. He wasn't satisfied hitting in the seats . . . he want to hit it over everything! After the game he had two hundred people standing around waiting to shake his hand. You got to take the crookeds with the straights. Yeah, Papa was something else.

CORY: You still playing?

LYONS: Cory . . . you know I'm gonna do that. There's some fellows down there we got us a band . . . we gonna try and stay together when we get out . . . but yeah, I'm still playing. It still helps me to get out of bed in the morning. As long as it do that I'm gonna be right there playing and trying to make some sense out of it.

ROSE (*calling*): Lyons, I got these eggs in the pan.

LYONS: Let me go on and get these eggs, man. Get ready to go bury Papa.

(*Pause.*)

How you doing? You doing all right?

(CORY *nods.* LYONS *touches him on the shoulder and they share a moment of silent grief.* LYONS *exits into the house.* CORY *wanders about the yard.* RAYNELL *enters.*)

RAYNELL: Hi.

CORY: Hi.

RAYNELL: Did you used to sleep in my room?

CORY: Yeah . . . that used to be my room.

RAYNELL: That's what Papa call it. "Cory's room." It got your football in the closet.

(ROSE *comes to the door.*)

ROSE: Raynell, get in there and get them good shoes on.

RAYNELL: Mama, can't I wear these? Them other one hurt my feet.

ROSE: Well, they just gonna have to hurt your feet for a while. You ain't said they hurt your feet when you went down to the store and got them.

RAYNELL: They didn't hurt then. My feet done got bigger.

ROSE: Don't you give me no backtalk now. You get in there and get them shoes on.

(RAYNELL *exits into the house.*)

Ain't too much changed. He still got that piece of rag tied to that tree. He was out here swinging that bat. I was just ready to go back in the house. He swung that bat and then he just fell over. Seem like he swung it and stood there with this grin on his face . . . and then he just fell over. They carried him on down to the hospital, but I knew there wasn't no need . . . why don't you come on in the house?

CORY: Mama . . . I got something to tell you. I don't know how to tell you this . . . but I've got to tell you . . . I'm not going to Papa's funeral.

ROSE: Boy, hush your mouth. That's your daddy you talking about. I don't want hear that kind of talk this morning. I done raised you to come to this? You standing there all healthy and grown talking about you ain't going to your daddy's funeral?

CORY: Mama . . . listen . . .

ROSE: I don't want to hear it, Cory. You just get that thought out of your head.

CORY: I can't drag Papa with me everywhere I go. I've got to say no to him. One time in my life I've got to say no.

ROSE: Don't nobody have to listen to nothing like that. I know you and your daddy ain't seen eye to eye, but I ain't got to listen to that kind of talk this morning. Whatever was between you and your daddy . . . the time has come to put it aside. Just take it and set it over there on the shelf and forget about it. Disrespecting your daddy ain't gonna make you a man, Cory. You got to find a way to come to that on your own. Not going to your daddy's funeral ain't gonna make you a man.

CORY: The whole time I was growing up . . . living in his house . . . Papa was like a shadow that followed you everywhere. It weighed on you and sunk into your flesh. It would wrap around you and lay there until you couldn't tell which one was you anymore. That shadow digging in your flesh. Trying to crawl in. Trying to live through you. Everywhere I looked, Troy Maxson was staring back at me . . . hiding under the bed . . . in the closet. I'm just saying I've got to find a way to get rid of that shadow, Mama.

ROSE: You just like him. You got him in you good.

CORY: Don't tell me that, Mama.

ROSE: You Troy Maxson all over again.

CORY: I don't want to be Troy Maxson. I want to be me.

ROSE: You can't be nobody but who you are, Cory. That shadow wasn't nothing but you growing into yourself. You either got to grow into it or cut it down to fit you. But that's all you got to make life with. That's all you got to measure yourself against that world out there. Your daddy wanted you to be everything he wasn't . . . and at the same time he tried to make you into everything he was. I don't know if he was right or wrong . . . but I do know he meant to do more good than he meant to do harm. He wasn't always right. Sometimes when he touched he bruised. And sometimes when he took me in his arms he cut.

When I first met your daddy I thought . . . Here is a man I can lay down with and make a baby. That's the first thing I thought when I seen him. I was thirty years old and had done seen my share of men. But when he walked up to me and said, "I can dance a waltz that'll make you dizzy," I thought, Rose Lee, here is a man that you can open yourself up to and be filled to bursting. Here is a man that can fill all them empty spaces you been tipping around the edges of. One of them empty spaces was being somebody's mother.

I married your daddy and settled down to cooking his supper and keeping clean sheets on the bed. When your daddy walked through the house he was so big he filled it up. That was my first mistake. Not to make him leave some room for me. For my part in the matter. But at that time I wanted that. I wanted a house that I could sing in. And that's what your daddy gave me. I didn't know to keep up his strength I had to give up little pieces of mine. I did that. I took on his life as mine and mixed up the pieces so that you couldn't hardly tell which was which anymore. It was my choice. It was my life and I didn't have to live it like that. But that's what life offered me in the way of being a woman and I took it. I grabbed hold of it with both hands.

By the time Raynell came into the house, me and your daddy had done lost touch with one another. I didn't want to make my blessing off of nobody's misfortune . . . but I took on to Raynell like she was all them babies I had wanted and never had.
(The phone rings.)
Like I'd been blessed to relive a part of my life. And if the Lord see fit to keep up my strength . . . I'm gonna do her just like your daddy did you . . . I'm gonna give her the best of what's in me.

RAYNELL *(entering, still with her old shoes):* Mama . . . Reverend Tollivier on the phone.
(ROSE exits into the house.)

RAYNELL: Hi.

CORY: Hi.

RAYNELL: You in the Army or the Marines?

CORY: Marines.

RAYNELL: Papa said it was the Army. Did you know Blue?

CORY: Blue? Who's Blue?

RAYNELL: Papa's dog what he sing about all the time.

CORY *(singing):* Hear it ring! Hear it ring!
I had a dog his name was Blue
You know Blue was mighty true
You know Blue was a good old dog
Blue treed a possum in a hollow log

You know from that he was a good old dog.
Hear it ring! Hear it ring!
(RAYNELL *joins in singing.*)
    CORY AND RAYNELL: Blue treed a possum out on a limb
Blue looked at me and I looked at him
Grabbed that possum and put him in a sack
Blue stayed there till I came back
Old Blue's feets was big and round
Never allowed a possum to touch the ground.

Old Blue died and I dug his grave
I dug his grave with a silver spade
Let him down with a golden chain
And every night I call his name
Go on Blue, you good dog you
Go on Blue, you good dog you

    RAYNELL: Blue laid down and died like a man
Blue laid down and died . . .
    BOTH: Blue laid down and died like a man
Now he's treeing possums in the Promised Land
I'm gonna tell you this to let you know
Blue's gone where the good dogs go
When I hear old Blue bark
When I hear old Blue bark
Blue treed a possum in Noah's Ark
Blue treed a possum in Noah's Ark.
(ROSE *comes to the screen door.*)
    ROSE: Cory, we gonna be ready to go in a minute.
    CORY *(to* RAYNELL*):* You go on in the house and change them shoes like Mama
told you so we can go to Papa's funeral.
    RAYNELL: Okay, I'll be back.
(RAYNELL *exits into the house.* CORY *gets up and crosses over to the tree.* ROSE *stands
in the screen door watching him.* GABRIEL *enters from the alley.*)
    GABRIEL *(calling)*: Hey, Rose!
    ROSE: Gabe?
    GABRIEL: I'm here, Rose. Hey Rose, I'm here!
(ROSE *enters from the house.*)
    ROSE: Lord . . . Look here, Lyons!
    LYONS: See, I told you, Rose . . . I told you they'd let him come.
    CORY: How you doing, Uncle Gabe?
    LYONS: How you doing, Uncle Gabe?
    GABRIEL: Hey, Rose. It's time. It's time to tell St. Peter to open the gates. Troy,
you ready? You ready, Troy. I'm gonna tell St. Peter to open the gates. You get
ready now.

(GABRIEL, *with great fanfare, braces himself to blow. The trumpet is without a mouthpiece. He puts the end of it into his mouth and blows with great force, like a man who has been waiting some twenty-odd years for this single moment. No sound comes out of the trumpet. He braces himself and blows again with the same result. A third time he blows. There is a weight of impossible description that falls away and leaves him bare and exposed to a frightful realization. It is a trauma that a sane and normal mind would be unable to withstand. He begins to dance. A slow, strange dance, eerie and life-giving. A dance of atavistic signature and ritual.* LYONS *attempts to embrace him.* GABRIEL *pushes* LYONS *away. He begins to howl in what is an attempt at song, or perhaps a song turning back into itself in an attempt at speech. He finishes his dance and the gates of heaven stand open as wide as God's closet.*)
That's the way that go!

ACTIVITIES FOR WRITING AND DISCUSSION

1. How do you account for the rather long history of migration at the beginning of the play?

2. Working with a group, identify the different conflicts you see between Troy and Cory, and illustrate the conflicts with specific passages from the play. Which of these conflicts strike you as fairly typical of any father/son relationship? Give examples. Which, if any, seem more unique to an African American father and son? Again, give examples.

3. Examine Troy's motives for not wanting Cory to play football. Citing evidence from the play, argue that he is motivated by:
   a. A desire to protect Cory, to prevent him from getting hurt
   b. Jealousy that Cory has better opportunities than he did
   c. Considerations other than a or b.

4. Find and annotate all the references you find in the play to "fences." What are Rose's thoughts and feelings about the fence around the yard? What are Troy's? What finally prompts Troy to complete the fence? What literal purposes does the fence serve? How, if at all, is it **symbolic**? Finally, give some reasons why Wilson might have chosen "Fences" as the title for his play.

5. Wilson has said that "Troy's flaw is that he does not recognize that the world was changing. That's because he spent fifteen years in a penitentiary." Explain what you think Wilson means. Then consider how this "flaw" affects Troy's family. Does Troy himself suffer as a result of it? Does Rose? Do Lyons and Cory? Explain with references to specific passages in the play.

6. In the play's final scene Rose tells Cory, "You Troy Maxson all over again." In what respects does she seem to be correct? incorrect? Could the same be said of Troy, i.e., that he is *his* father "all over again"? How might such a comparison be accurate, and where (if at all) would it break down?

7. The play ends on the day of Troy's funeral. Cory doesn't plan to attend but then changes his mind.
   a. Write down the thoughts you believe are going through his mind at the end of the play as he "gets up and crosses over to the tree," or
   b. Write a dialogue, set on the day of the funeral, between Cory and the dead Troy, or
   c. Imagine thirty years have passed and you are Cory and now have a teenage son of your own. Tell your son the story of your relationship with Troy, just as Troy told the family about his relationship with *his* father. Invent some pretext or reason for telling this story, e.g., your son is about to make some important life decision or he wants to do something you resist.

PEOPLE AND CULTURES IN CONFLICT AND CHANGE: ADDITIONAL ACTIVITIES FOR WRITING AND DISCUSSION

1. Reread all or a portion of your notebook. Mark any passages, however long or short, that strike you, for whatever reason. Beside each such passage, write a note explaining its significance for you. Finally, pick a favorite passage and either:
   a. Expand it into a new piece of writing, or
   b. Make notes on how you could expand or use it at some future date, or
   c. Rewrite it in a different form, e.g., poem, dialogue, letter, or memoir.

For a list of strategies for expanding or revising, see Chapter 12.

2. Explore the concept of "cultures in conflict and change." Is it meaningful to the **characters, speakers,** and **personae** represented in this thematic section? If so, in what ways? Is it meaningful for you? Create a dialogue, with two or more participants, around these questions. Draw your participants from the reading selections and/or the world of your own experience.

3. Harold Green in "A Loaf of Bread" says he is only doing what he must when he charges higher prices to the patrons of his store in the poor black neighborhood. In a sense, he—the ostensible "oppressor" in the story—sees himself as a victim. Are "oppressors" "victims"? Write a dialogue in which you have different characters or speakers from the works in this section take opposing perspectives on this issue.

4. Think of any situations in which you find (or have found) yourself to be a minority because of your race, religion, ethnicity, sexual preference, values, or a disability. In an essay:
   a. Relate some stories or examples that illustrate your minority status.
   b. Characterize the role in which your status places you. Do you perceive yourself as a victim? a hero? a crusader? in some other way, or as some combination of the above? Explain.

5. Scott Russell Sanders, in "Looking at Women" in Chapter 20 (pages 291–300), describes "objectification" as a process by which people treat those who are "different" from themselves as objects, dehumanizing them so that they can be ignored, set apart, persecuted, or destroyed. Review what Sanders says about objectification. Then discuss objectification as a theme in any two or more of the texts in this section.

6. The topic of "fear" is important in many readings within this chapter— Poe's "The Black Cat," Atwood's "The Man from Mars," Olds's "On the Subway," and others. Identify one or two readings that address this topic and analyze it. If you wish, relate the topic and text(s) to experiences of your own.

7. Review your entire notebook. As you do, make a running list of memorable or striking topics, e.g., "racism," "crossing boundaries," "diversity," "multiculturalism," "fear." Then choose a favorite topic, make a Topic/Form Grid (see Chapter 5), and use one of the forms on your grid to create a new notebook entry about the topic. If your chosen form does not work, do a Topic/Form Shift to a different form on your grid.

Interchapter on Notebooks and Journals (V)

Your Passing Thoughts: Ralph Waldo Emerson

> Emerson has special talents unequalled. . . . His personal influence upon young persons greater than any man's. In his world every man would be a poet. . . .
>
> —HENRY DAVID THOREAU

> [A] moment is a concentrated eternity.
>
> —EMERSON

The words of Ralph Waldo Emerson (1803–1882) have punctuated much of this book. They provide the epigraph to the book as a whole: "Books are the best of things, well used; abused, among the worst. . . . They are for nothing but to inspire." Essayist and poet, Emerson was among the most influential American writers of the nineteenth century and was also an avid notetaker and journal writer. He began his first journal at age sixteen and eventually filled over 250 volumes (each 300 to 400 pages long) with thoughts, quotations, observations, facts, aphorisms, and germinal essays. These notes supplied most of the material for his published writings, which include *Nature* (1836), *Essays* (*First* and *Second Series,* 1841 and 1844), *Poems* (1846), *Representative Men* (1850), *English Traits* (1856), and *The Conduct of Life* (1860). Emerson's views on reading and writing helped inspire this textbook and thus form a fitting close to these interchapters on notebooks and journals.

For me, Emerson's story begins with someone an ocean away and two generations removed from him who was an Emersonian not in name but in heart: Jules Renard (1864–1910; see page 806). Renard was a busy man. A writer, husband, parent, and public official, he could easily have lost himself in a cyclone of activity but for a life-changing event that occurred in his twenty-third year: he started keeping a journal. Renard developed the habit of carrying notepaper wherever he went and of pausing in the middle of his busy hours to record his passing thoughts. At the zoo he took notes on birds:

Tiny parakeets, like tie-pins that sing. (Renard 67)

In the park he noted his emotional reactions to nature:

I cannot look at the leaf of a tree without being crushed by the universe. (127)

Elsewhere he had a thought about composing and wrote:

I have an idea the way I look at a bird: I am always afraid it will fly away, and I don't dare touch it. (209)

Renard commented, "These notes are my daily prayer" (204). Notetaking was his way of slowing the moments of life so they could be savored and valued, a way of being simultaneously in time and in the transcendent.

Renard's notes provide a natural segue into the life and thought of Emerson and one of Emerson's important messages for us today:

Listen to and record your passing thoughts.

This message is vital, because to pay attention to your thoughts is to be "awake" in the Emersonian sense of the word: alive, aware, conscious.

To understand this consider two scenarios. In Scenario #1 you race down the road to an appointment and arrive in record time but exhausted and stressed out. Are you happy about the trip? Not especially; all you have thought about is the slow drivers in front of you and the clock. At best, you may experience a brief spasm of relief at not being punished for tardiness. In Scenario #2, you are enjoying the scenery as you drive to the appointment; you have a thought and pull off the road to write it down:

Slate mountains, gaslight clouds.

For a moment time stops: your blood pressure dips, your mind deserts the hustling traffic and wings its way into the mountains and clouds. You know then what William Blake meant when he wrote, "One thought fills immensity," because your own experience confirms it. You reach your destination a few minutes later than in Scenario #1, but no one notices or cares; and you arrive feeling a little less like a robot and a bit more like a human being. Moreover, in the note you jotted down you have *made* something. During your trip you have indulged two of the human soul's basic needs: to contemplate and to create.

Emerson heeded and wrote down his thoughts in just this way and tirelessly advised others to do the same: "Make your own Bible," he wrote. "Select & Collect all those words & sentences that . . . have been to you like the blast of trumpet out of Shakspear [sic], Seneca, Moses, John, & Paul" (*Emerson in His Journals* 148). Inspired by Emerson's stirring words, several years ago I began carrying a small notepad—I still carry one—so that when a thought grabs me I can write it down. At times people look askance at me as I stop on the sidewalk to scribble something, or prop my notepad on the steering wheel to take a note as I brake for a red light. Maybe I am a little crazy, certainly eccentric, but I don't mind. I take notes because I can't stop myself. I have been lit by the Emersonian fire.

What explains Emerson's incendiary effect on people in his own time and ours? Why does he make ordinary people like me believe that what we think is important—important enough to write down? The answer, I think, is in the story of Emerson's life. That life, particularly the early part of it, is a validation of *listening to yourself think,* a validation of self-trust.

Emerson, the "sage of Concord," began life unremarkably, cutting a rather mediocre figure in the eyes of the world. His siblings all looked more promising as children than he did (Richardson 19). As a student at Harvard he was chosen class poet, but only after six of his classmates had declined the honor (Richardson 6). He graduated in the bottom half of his college class (number 30 out of 59; Allen 58). After that he taught briefly in an all-girls' school—a bad choice, since young Waldo, growing up in a houseful of brothers—was awkward around girls and knew it. In his twenties he became a Unitarian minister, largely because it seemed the thing to do (both his father and paternal grandfather had been ministers), but he had to resign in 1832, at age twenty-nine, over doctrinal and philosophic differences with the church. Another failure. Making matters worse, his first wife, whom he loved passionately, died of tuberculosis less than two years into their marriage. As he was stumbling from job to job, Emerson was reading and writing voraciously on the side, educating himself. He knew that he *really* wanted to be a writer but was afraid to commit himself to so uncertain a vocation.

In short, Emerson at twenty-nine felt like many of us do from time to time: a bit like a cipher, a nonentity. He had read the great literature and knew, perhaps too well, the famous names: Plato, Shakespeare, Goethe, and other figures in the pantheon. Like many of *us,* who are deterred from doing something creative or adventurous by thoughts of our own insignificance, he seems to have doubted his ability to do what he truly *wanted* to do. Who was *he* to write? The crisis of vocation was a crisis of thought: he didn't trust his own thought and instinct enough; he didn't trust himself.

By the end of 1832 Emerson's spirits were at low ebb. In the words of a concerned brother, he was "sick" and "disheartened," his life "flying to pieces" (Richardson 5). He gave up his house, sold his furniture, and on Christmas Day, boarded a boat for Europe in quest of a new beginning.

And a new beginning it was. Nine months abroad gave Emerson badly needed distance from his past. More importantly, it helped awaken his slumbering sense of individual power. In England and Scotland he met the literary giants of the day, including Samuel Taylor Coleridge, Thomas Carlyle, and William Wordsworth. Instead of feeling eclipsed by these luminaries, as he half-expected, he was struck by their ordinariness. They were good writers, but they were only human. They were all "deficient" in important areas—notably, "insight into religious truth" (*Emerson in His Journals* 115). While he liked Carlyle, he found Wordsworth somewhat pompous and Coleridge disappointingly narrow-minded. In his journal Emerson wrote:

> Many things I owe to the sight of these men. I shall judge more justly, less timidly, of wise men forevermore. . . . it is an *idealized* portrait which always we draw of them. (115)

"An *idealized* portrait. . . ." Till then Emerson had put the great writers on pedestals and imagined they *owned* poetry and thought. Now, encountering them face-to-face, he acquired a new perspective on fame and celebrity. Writing in his journal he affirmed that "fame is a conventional thing" (115). At the same time he felt new confidence in his own powers. What was exemplary in Wordsworth and the others was not their public renown but their frankness and self-trust—qualities independent of fame that he also found in himself. Emerson began to discard conventional ideas of "genius" for a more democratic one that would become the cornerstone of all this thought: Genius isn't the property of an elite few; it is innate in every human being.

What is genius? Nothing other than self-trust. "To believe your own thought . . . —that is genius" ("Self-Reliance" 138). Our passing thoughts—the thousands that dart evanescently through our minds each day—are sparks from what Emerson called the "universal soul" or "oversoul." Who you are is inscribed in your passing thoughts: they are the stuff of poetic inspiration and can point you toward your individual destiny. Moreover, the individual soul and the universal soul are coterminous; to honor your individual, private thought is to arrive, simultaneously, at the universal. "Speak your latent conviction, and it shall be the universal sense; for the inmost in due time becomes the outmost, and our first thought is rendered back to us by the trumpets of the Last Judgment" ("Self-Reliance" 138). Our intuitive thoughts are visitations of the divine.

The problem is, caught up in our routinized and conventional lives we reject most of these thoughts as "silly," "strange," or "inappropriate" or don't even notice them. Genius is the faculty of heeding the thought and recording it. Thus "In every work of genius we recognize our own rejected thoughts . . ." ("Self-Reliance" 139). The great literature of the world is full of things that you and I have thought and that we instantly recognize when reading. The authors of the great literature honored the thoughts and wrote them down, while we had those same ideas but dismissed or ignored them.

In his own work and practice Emerson's cardinal rule was *trust your first thought,* however plain, awkward, or strange it might seem. If it occurs to you, any thought is important—not fixed or final but worth writing down as it may, at the least, be the prelude to better thoughts. Not to miss the divine visitations, Emerson carried paper with him everywhere and took notes on all that he read, thought, and experienced, always striving to capture the passing thought in its fresh and original form. "For the best part . . . of every mind," he wrote, "is not that which a [person] knows, but that which hovers in gleams, suggestions, tantalizing un-possessed before him" (qtd. in Richardson 201).

Emerson had gone to Europe feeling unsure of himself and his abilities; by the time he returned home, in October 1833, he had found himself and his mission: to write; and to spread, as a public lecturer and essayist, the message of self-trust. Of his listeners and readers he asked: Why bask in the reflected genius of others—the great men and women of past and present—when you have your own ge-nius—the universal soul—within you and speaking to you at all times of the day?

Emerson's younger contemporaries devoured this message. With Emerson's encouragement the young Thoreau started keeping a journal and adopted the habit of taking pencil and notepaper on his long daily walks for recording on-the-spot reflections and observations. Thoreau admonished himself to "Obey the spur of the moment. These accumulated it is that make the impulse and impetus of the life of genius. . . . Let the spurs of countless moments goad us incessantly into life" (*H. D. Thoreau: A Writer's Journal* 82–83).

In Brooklyn, New York, a brawny son of a carpenter-father and a semiliterate mother was also touched by Emerson and began disciplining himself to become the quintessential American poet. Walt Whitman read and reread Emerson's *Essays* during the 1840s and early 1850s when he was gestating what would become his great book and life's work, *Leaves of Grass*. "I was simmering, simmering, simmering," he later recalled; "Emerson brought me to a boil" (qtd. in Townsend 367). Like Emerson, Whitman learned to pause and jot down everything he saw, heard, felt, touched, and thought. He gathered notes everywhere, filing them away to form nascent poems and copying his poems and fragments of poems into notebooks. Whitman later summarized Emerson's unique effect on him:

> The best part of Emersonianism is, it breeds the giant that destroys itself. Who wants to be any man's mere follower? lurks behind every page. No teacher ever taught, that has so provided for his pupil's setting up independently. . . . (qtd. in Harding 118)

In other words, for Emerson the job of the poet/writer was not to overwhelm and eclipse readers with his own brilliance but to inspire readers—all readers—to think and be poets themselves.

Emerson helped empower people like Whitman to work in their own individual ways, in calm defiance of social and literary conventions. Whitman largely invented free verse and wrote exuberantly of sex and the human body when such subjects were considered off-limits to poets, and he stuck firmly to his task through decades of public criticism and censure.

In Amherst, Massachusetts, Emily Dickinson also drew inspiration from Emerson. Emily Dickinson was largely unknown during her lifetime. She never made money from writing or gained any public reputation by it. In that respect she was much like you or me as *we* might reflect and write in the quiet obscurity of our own homes. She was a private person with no paid occupation, but she could as well have been a teacher, a carpenter, or a nurse stealing moments on the side to write. In Emersonian fashion she heeded all her passing thoughts as visitations of the divine and recorded them in nearly eighteen hundred poems. Rather than pushing to place her work in periodicals or publish them in books, she wove many of her poems into hand-sewn booklets (which remained unpublished till after her death) and shared individual poems with family and friends in her personal letters.

But for a lucky sequence of events that led to posthumous publication of her poems, Emily Dickinson might be as unknown today as she was during her lifetime. Would she have cared? I doubt it. For Emily Dickinson the life of the mind was the great thing. She was as drunk on it as Whitman was. Near the end of her life she wrote the following lines, which she incorporated into three different letters (Sewall 589):

> Take all away from me, but leave me Ecstasy,
> And I am richer then than all my Fellow Men. (Dickinson Poem #1640)

So to repeat: *Listen to and record your passing thoughts.* The stories of Emerson, Whitman, and Dickinson show that the ability to do so depends on self-trust, on learning from great examples without being intimidated by them, and on heeding the still small voice of "Yes" that comes from within over and against the societal "No" that comes from without. This message is tonic in a time like our own that places such emphasis on celebrity. You need only watch five minutes of a TV talk show or open a magazine to see that celebrity worship is about the *negation* of self-trust. Today more than ever we need to open our ears to our own thoughts.

At this point a question is appropriate: Suppose you listen to and write down your passing thoughts. What do you *do* with them? What did Emerson do? Emerson collected his notes (into some 250 notebooks, no less!) and habitually reread them—for amusement and pleasure, and to stimulate additional thought and writing. He compared his journal to a "Savings Bank." He deposited ideas there and earned interest on them by saving and rereading them:

> I grow richer because I have somewhere to deposit my earnings; and fractions are worth more to me because corresponding fractions are waiting here that shall be made integers by their addition. (*Emerson in His Journals* 119)

Hard-working professional writer though he was, I don't believe Emerson would have done any of this if it hadn't been *fun*—if he hadn't thrilled to the spectacle of seeing ideas grow. An idea written down is like a seed planted in the subconscious: it stays there and germinates and can blossom at surprising times and in unusual places—while you're housecleaning, taking a walk, mowing the lawn, doing dishes, enjoying a bath, or waiting for an appointment. That's part of the fun: the process can go on anywhere.

A short personal example will illustrate. I have long been fascinated by the contrast between the sheer volume of thought that passes through our heads and the little of it that we ever write down. Sophisticated as our technology becomes, the speed of thought still massively outpaces our ability to articulate the tiniest fraction of what we think. Some time ago I was thinking about this during a walk and paused to write the following in my notepad:

Note-taking is good practice for those who can't write as fast as they think.

A month later I reread this note and a metaphor came to mind:

Writing plods. A rickshaw.

The new version seemed better than the first, more striking and compact. A few weeks later I was in the yard raking leaves and the thought came back yet again, this time in the form of a comparison:

Writing is to thought as rickshaw to rocket.

This version stuck. It said what I meant, and I liked the sound of it.

The point? I had fun shaping and honing my sentence to say exactly what I meant. Nor did I torture the idea; I just thought about it for a few minutes now and then (over a span of two months!) in my rereading and daily reflection. Finally, as an added benefit, it made activities like walking and raking leaves even more pleasant than they already are.

I'll end on a personal note. Like many people, I feel as if I am always on the run—between family, work, meetings, appointments, social obligations of all kinds, distractions. Emerson's message is about *time.* After years of complaining about time (there never seems to be enough of it) I've concluded that no one really gives us time or takes it away from us; we have to create it ourselves. Is there *time* to scribble down thoughts as Jules Renard did, or Emerson? Yes. It takes effort, but I think the rewards are worth it.

I teach writing professionally; but if I were an accountant, a plumber, an attorney, an engineer, a homemaker, a grocery clerk, a mechanic, retired, or unemployed I would still be carrying my notepad around, writing at stoplights and in grocery lines, whenever a thought comes. To be Emersonian is to be eccentric.

I once read where a certain poet—whose name I've forgotten—said that he never let himself walk faster than two miles per hour. (Try doing that for even five minutes and you'll see how hard it is!) He explained that the slow pace helped clear his head for thinking. At the time his statement baffled me. Was he serious? Slow down—when what we need is to go *faster?*

Now I understand what he meant. I've learned that if you like to think you actually *want* to move more slowly; you find yourself instinctively slowing down. (Perhaps the most subversive consequence of Emersonian habits is that they make you slow down while everyone else is speeding up.) I don't mind *waiting* anymore. If I'm stuck in highway construction or in a line somewhere, I just take out my notepad. In fact, strangely enough, I *like* having to wait, because it gives me more time to reflect.

The demand for speed will remain a constant in American life; we will always need to do more things more quickly and *will* do them more quickly. Electronic technology is taking care of that need, a material need. But over and against this is another need—call it a spiritual one—the need to slow down so we can hear ourselves think.

The best teachers teach us to wait, and Emerson was among the best of teachers.

Give yourself time.

Works Cited

Allen, Gay Wilson. *Waldo Emerson.* New York: Penguin, 1981.

Dickinson, Emily. *The Complete Poems of Emily Dickinson.* Ed. Thomas H. Johnson. Boston: Little, Brown, 1960.

Emerson, Ralph Waldo. *Emerson in His Journals.* Selected and edited by Joel Porte. Cambridge: The Belknap Press of Harvard UP, 1982.

———. "Self-Reliance." *The Portable Emerson.* Ed. Carl Bode in collaboration with Malcolm Cowley. New York: Viking Penguin, 1981. 138–164.

Harding, Walter. *A Thoreau Handbook.* New York: New York UP, 1961.

Renard, Jules. *The Journal of Jules Renard.* Ed. and trans. Louise Bogan and Elizabeth Roget. New York: George Braziller, 1964.

Richardson, Robert D., Jr. *Emerson: The Mind on Fire.* Berkeley: U of California P, 1995.

Sewall, Richard B. *The Life of Emily Dickinson.* Cambridge: Harvard UP, 1994.

Thoreau, Henry David. *H. D. Thoreau: A Writer's Journal.* Selected and edited by Laurence Stapleton. New York: Dover, 1960.

Trowbridge, John Townsend. *My Own Story: With Recollections of Noted Persons.* Boston: Houghton Mifflin, 1903.

Excerpts from Emerson's *Journals*

UNDATED   1

It is excellent advice both in writing and in action to avoid a too great elevation at first. Let one's beginnings be temperate and unpretending, and the more elevated parts will rise from these with a just and full effect. We were not made to breathe oxygen, or to talk poetry, or to be always wise.

FEBRUARY 1827   2

Much of what we learn, and to the highest purposes, of life is caught in moments, and rather by a sublime instinct than by modes which can be explained in
detail.

BOSTON, AUGUST 24, 1828 [TO MISS EMERSON]   3

When I attended church, and the man in the pulpit was all clay and not of
tuneable metal, I thought that if men would avoid that general language and general manner in which they strive to hide all that is peculiar, and would say only
what was uppermost in their own minds, after their own individual manner,
every man would be interesting.

AUGUST 18, 1830   4

The sun shines and warms and lights us and we have no curiosity to know why
this is so; but we ask the reason of all evil, of pain, and hunger, and musquitoes
and silly people.

JULY 15, 1831   5

The things taught in colleges and schools are not an education, but the means
of education.

MAY 21, 1833   6

I like the sayers of No better than the sayers of Yes.

JANUARY 1, 1834   7

This Book is my Savings Bank. I grow richer because I have somewhere to deposit my earnings; and fractions are worth more to me because corresponding
fractions are waiting here that shall be made integers by their addition.

APRIL 11, 1834   8

Went yesterday to Cambridge and spent most of the day at Mount Auburn[1];
got my luncheon at Fresh Pond, and went back again to the woods. After much
wandering and seeing many things, four snakes gliding up and down a hollow for
no purpose that I could see—not to eat, not for love, but only gliding; then a
whole bed of *Hepatica triloba*, cousins of the Anemone, all blue and beautiful, but
constrained by niggard nature to wear their last year's faded jacket of leaves; then
a black-capped titmouse, who came upon a tree, and when I would know his
name, sang *chick-a-dee-dee*; then a far-off tree full of clamorous birds, I know not
what, but you might hear them half a mile. I forsook the tombs, and found a
sunny hollow where the east wind would not blow, and lay down against the side
of a tree to most happy beholdings. At least I opened my eyes and let what would
pass through them into the soul. I saw no more my relation, how near and petty,
to Cambridge or Boston; I heeded no more what minute or hour our Massachu-

---

1. A rural cemetery

setts clocks might indicate—I saw only the noble earth on which I was born, with the great Star which warms and enlightens it. I saw the clouds that hang their significant drapery over us. It was Day—that was all Heaven said. The pines glittered with their innumerable green needles in the light, and seemed to challenge me to read their riddle. The drab oak-leaves of the last year turned their little somersets and lay still again. And the wind bustled high overhead in the forest top. This gay and grand architecture, from the vault to the moss and lichen on which I lay,—who shall explain to me the laws of its proportions and adornments?

APRIL 12, 1834 9

All the mistakes I make arise from forsaking my own station and trying to see the object from another person's point of view.

APRIL 13, 1834 10

We are always getting ready to live, but never living. We have many years of technical education; then many years of earning a livelihood, and we get sick, and take journeys for our health, and compass land and sea for improvement by travelling, but the work of self-improvement,—always under our nose,—nearer than the nearest, is seldom seldom engaged in. A few, few hours in the longest life.

MAY 21, 1834 11

I will trust my instincts. For always a reason halts after an instinct, and when I have deviated from the instinct, comes somebody with a profound theory teaching that I ought to have followed it. . . . "Our first and third thought coincide."

JULY 18, 1834 12

What is there of the divine in a load of bricks? What is there of the divine in a barber's shop? . . . Much. All.

OCTOBER 14, 1834 13

Every involuntary repulsion that arises in your mind, give heed unto. It is the surface of a central truth.

DECEMBER 22, 1834 14

It is very easy in the world to live by the opinion of the world. It is very easy in solitude to be self-centred. But the finished man is he who in the midst of the crowd keeps with perfect sweetness the independence of solitude.

JULY 21, 1836 15

Make your own Bible. Select and collect all the words and sentences that in all your reading have been to you like the blast of triumph out of Shakspear, Seneca, Moses, John and Paul.

OCTOBER 29, 1836 16

There is one advantage which every man finds in setting himself a literary task,—as these my lectures,—that it gives him the high pleasure of reading, which does not in other circumstances attain all its zest. . . . When the mind is braced by the weighty expectation of a prepared work, the page of whatever book we read becomes luminous with manifold allusion. Every sentence is doubly significant, and the sense of our author is as broad as the world. There is creative reading as well as creative writing.

November 12, 1836   17

How many attractions for us have our passing fellows in the streets, both male and female, which our ethics forbid us to express, which yet infuse so much pleasure into life. A lovely child, a handsome youth, a beautiful girl, a heroic man, a maternal woman, a venerable old man, charm us, though strangers, and we cannot say so, or look at them but for a moment.

August 2, 1837   18

An enchanting night of south wind and clouds; mercury at 73°; all the trees are wind-harps; blessed be light and darkness; ebb and flow, cold and heat; these restless pulsations of nature which by and by will throb no more.

February 17, 1838   19

How much self-reliance it implies to write a true description of anything, for example, Wordsworth's picture of skating; that leaning back on your heels and stopping in mid-career. So simple a fact no common man would have trusted himself to detach as a thought.

April 1, 1838   20

Preaching, especially false preaching, is for able men a sickly employment. Study of books is also sickly; and the garden and the family, wife, mother, son, and brother are a balsam. There is health in table-talk and nursery play. We must wear old shoes and have aunts and cousins.

April 26, 1838   21

Yesterday afternoon I went to the Cliff with Henry Thoreau. Warm, pleasant, misty weather, which the great mountain amphitheatre seemed to drink in with gladness. A crow's voice filled all the miles of air with sound. A bird's voice, even a piping frog, enlivens a solitude and makes world enough for us. At night I went out into the dark and saw a glimmering star and heard a frog, and Nature seemed to say, Well do not these suffice? Here is a new scene, a new experience. Ponder it, Emerson, and not like the foolish world, hanker after thunders and multitudes and vast landscapes, the sea or Niagara.

June 8, 1838   22

A man must have aunts and cousins, must buy carrots and turnips, must have barn and woodshed, must go to market and to the blacksmith's shop, must saunter and sleep and be inferior and silly.

SEPTEMBER 29, 1838   23

Censure and Praise.—I hate to be defended in a newspaper. As long as all that is said is said *against* me, I feel a certain sublime assurance of success, but as soon as honied words of praise are spoken for me, I feel as one that lies unprotected before his enemies.

OCTOBER 5, 1838   24

Books.—It seems meritorious to read: but from everything but history or the works of the old commanding writers I come back with a conviction that the slightest *wood-thought,* the least significant native emotion of my own, is more to me.

NOVEMBER 14, 1838   25

What is the hardest task in the world? To think. . . .

JUNE 12, 1839   26

I know no means of calming the fret and perturbation into which too much sitting, too much talking, brings me, so perfect as labor. I have no animal spirits; therefore, when surprised by company and kept in a chair for many hours, my heart sinks, my brow is clouded and I think I will run for Acton woods, and live with the squirrels henceforward. But my garden is nearer, and my good hoe, as it bites the ground, revenges my wrongs, and I have less lust to bite my enemies. I confess I work at first with a little venom, lay to a little unnecessary strength. But by smoothing the rough hillocks, I smooth my temper; by extracting the long roots of the piper-grass, I draw out my own splinters; and in a short time I can hear the bobolink's song and see the blessed deluge of light and colour that rolls around me.

JUNE 22, 1839   27

It is one of the signs of our time, the ill health of all people. All the young people are nearsighted in the towns.

SEPTEMBER 14, 1839   28

How sad a spectacle, so frequent nowadays, to see a young man after ten years of college education come out, ready for his voyage of life,—and to see that the entire ship is made of rotten timber, of rotten, honeycombed, traditional timber without so much as an inch of new plank in the hull.

NOVEMBER 14, 1839   29

Systems.—I need hardly say to anyone acquainted with my thoughts that I have no System. When I was quite young, I fancied that by keeping a manuscript Journal by me, over whose pages I wrote a list of the great topics of human study, as, *Religion, Poetry, Politics, Love,* etc., in the course of a few years I should be able to complete a sort of encyclopædia containing the net value of all the definitions at which the world had yet arrived. But at the end of a couple of years, my Cabinet Cyclopædia, though much enlarged, was no nearer to a completeness than on its first day. Nay, somehow the whole plan of it needed alteration, nor did the following months promise any speedier term to it than the foregoing. At last I discovered that my curve was a parabola whose arcs would never meet, and came to acquiesce in the perception that, although no diligence can rebuild the universe in a model by the best accumulation of disposition of details, yet does the world reproduce itself in miniature in every event that transpires, so that all the laws of nature may be read in the smallest fact. So that the truth-speaker may dismiss all solicitude as to the proportion and congruency of the aggregate of his thoughts, so long as he is a faithful reporter of particular impressions.

JUNE 4, 1840   30

Waldo says, "The flowers talk when the wind blows over them." My little boy grows thin in the hot summer, and runs all to eyes and eyelashes.

SEPTEMBER 16, 1840   31

A sleeping child gives me the impression of a traveller in a very far country.

JULY, UNDATED (1841)   32

Let us answer a book of ink with a book of flesh and blood.

AUGUST, UNDATED (1841)   33

The trumpet-like lowing of a cow—what does that speak to in me? Not to my understanding. No. Yet somewhat in me hears and loves it well.

OCTOBER 9, 1841   34

The sum of life ought to be valuable when the fractions and particles are so sweet.

NOVEMBER 11, 1842   35

Do not be too timid and squeamish about your actions. All life is an experiment. The more experiments you make the better. What if they are a little coarse, and you may get your coat soiled or torn? What if you do fail, and get fairly rolled in the dirt once or twice? Up again you shall never be so afraid of a tumble.

MAY 20, 1843   36

It is greatest to believe and to hope well of the world, because he who does so, quits the world of experience, and makes the world he lives in.

JANUARY, (1844) UNDATED   37

Finish each day before you begin the next, and interpose a solid wall of sleep between two. This you cannot do without temperance.

MARCH, (1845) UNDATED   38

Good manners require a great deal of time, as does a wise treatment of children. Orientals have time, the desert, and stars; the Occidentals have not.

MARCH, (1846) UNDATED   39

What a discovery I made one day, that the more I spent the more I grew, that it was as easy to occupy a large place and do much work as an obscure place to do little; and that in the winter in which I communicated all my results to classes, I was full of new thoughts.

AUGUST, (1847) UNDATED   40

Life consists in what a man is thinking of all day.

MAY (?) 1856 UNDATED   41

Education. Don't let them eat their seed-corn; don't let them anticipate, antedate, and be young men, before they have finished their boyhood. Let them have the fields and woods, and learn their secret and the base- and football, and wrestling, and brickbats, and suck all the strength and courage that lies for them in these games; let them ride bare-back, and catch their horse in his pasture, let them hook and spear their fish, and shin a post and a tall tree, and shoot their partridge and trap the woodchuck, before they begin to dress like collegians and sing in serenades, and make polite calls.

APRIL (?) 1859   42

I am a natural reader, and only a writer in the absence of natural writers. In a true time, I should never have written.

MAY 25, 1862   43

Resources or feats. I like people who can do things. When Edward and I struggled in vain to drag our big calf into the barn, the Irish girl put her finger into the calf's mouth, and led her in directly.

OCTOBER 1872   44

Look sharply after your thoughts. They come unlooked for, like a new bird seen on your trees, and, if you turn to your usual task, disappear; and you shall never find that perception again; never, I say,—but perhaps years, ages, and I know not what events and worlds may lie between you and its return!

For Further Reading:
Emerson, Ralph Waldo. *The Heart of Emerson's Journals.* Ed. Bliss Perry. New York: Dover, 1995.

ACTIVITIES FOR WRITING AND DISCUSSION

1. In your notebook relate some of your own experiences of encountering literary greatness in your readings. Think of a favorite author whose work you greatly admire. How has that author's presence affected your writing, for better and/or for worse? Has it intimidated or overwhelmed you? inspired you? some combination of both? Explain with a story.

2. In your notebook react to the following Emerson comment (on page 973):

I will trust my instincts. For always a reason halts after an instinct, and when I have deviated from the instinct, comes somebody with a profound theory teaching that I ought to have followed it. . . . "Our first and third thought coincide."

First, what do you think Emerson means? Second, how does or doesn't his observation jibe with your own experience of "thoughts"?

3. In his notebook, *The Burning Brand,* the Italian writer Cesar Pavese writes:

[G]enius is not a matter of discovering some external theme and treating it skillfully, but of finally achieving complete possession of one's own experience, own body, own memories—one's own rhythm, and expressing this rhythm, above and beyond the limitations of plot or subject matter, with the perennial fruitfulness of inexhaustible thought. (141)

How do you interpret this comment? How might one achieve "complete possession of one's own experience, own body, own memories"? Can a journal or notebook help? How?

4. Respond to Emerson's journal selections using any of the "Generic Ideas for Writing" found on pages 192–193.

Work and the Quality of Life

KATE CHOPIN (1850–1904)

A Pair of Silk Stockings

Little Mrs. Sommers one day found herself the unexpected possessor of fifteen 1
dollars. It seemed to her a very large amount of money, and the way in which it
stuffed and bulged her worn old *porte-monnaie*[1] gave her a feeling of importance
such as she had not enjoyed for years.

The question of investment was one that occupied her greatly. For a day or two 2
she walked about apparently in a dreamy state, but really absorbed in speculation
and calculation. She did not wish to act hastily, to do anything she might afterward regret. But it was during the still hours of the night when she lay awake revolving plans in her mind that she seemed to see her way clearly toward a proper
and judicious use of the money.

A dollar or two should be added to the price usually paid for Janie's shoes, 3
which would insure their lasting an appreciable time longer than they usually did.
She would buy so and so many yards of percale for new shirt waists for the boys
and Janie and Mag. She had intended to make the old ones do by skilful patching.
Mag should have another gown. She had seen some beautiful patterns, veritable
bargains in the shop windows. And still there would be left enough for new stockings—two pairs apiece—and what darning that would save for a while! She
would get caps for the boys and sailor-hats for the girls. The vision of her little
brood looking fresh and dainty and new for once in their lives excited her and
made her restless and wakeful with anticipation.

---

1. Purse.

The neighbors sometimes talked of certain "better days" that little 4
Mrs. Sommers had known before she had ever thought of being Mrs. Sommers.
She herself indulged in no such morbid retrospection. She had no time—no second of time to devote to the past. The needs of the present absorbed her every
faculty. A vision of the future like some dim, gaunt monster sometimes appalled
her, but luckily tomorrow never comes.

Mrs. Sommers was one who knew the value of bargains; who could stand for 5
hours making her way inch by inch toward the desired object that was selling below cost. She could elbow her way if need be; she had learned to clutch a piece of
goods and hold it and stick to it with persistence and determination till her turn
came to be served, no matter when it came.

But that day she was a little faint and tired. She had swallowed a light lun- 6
cheon—no! when she came to think of it, between getting the children fed and
the place righted, and preparing herself for the shopping bout, she had actually
forgotten to eat any luncheon at all!

She sat herself upon a revolving stool before a counter that was comparatively 7
deserted, trying to gather strength and courage to charge through an eager multitude that was besieging breast-works of shirting and figured lawn. An all-gone
limp feeling had come over her and she rested her hand aimlessly upon the
counter. She wore no gloves. By degrees she grew aware that her hand had encountered something very soothing, very pleasant to touch. She looked down to
see that her hand lay upon a pile of silk stockings. A placard near by announced
that they had been reduced in price from two dollars and fifty cents to one dollar
and ninety-eight cents; and a young girl who stood behind the counter asked her
if she wished to examine their line of silk hosiery. She smiled, just as if she had
been asked to inspect a tiara of diamonds with the ultimate view of purchasing it.
But she went on feeling the soft, sheeny luxurious things—with both hands now,
holding them up to see them glisten, and to feel them glide serpent-like through
her fingers.

Two hectic blotches came suddenly into her pale cheeks. She looked up at 8
the girl.

"Do you think there are any eights-and-a-half among these?"   9

There were any number of eights-and-a-half. In fact, there were more of that 10
size than any other. Here was a light-blue pair; there were some lavender, some
all black and various shades of tan and gray. Mrs. Sommers selected a black pair
and looked at them very long and closely. She pretended to be examining their
texture, which the clerk assured her was excellent.

"A dollar and ninety-eight cents," she mused aloud. "Well, I'll take this pair." 11
She handed the girl a five-dollar bill and waited for her change and for her parcel.
What a very small parcel it was! It seemed lost in the depths of her shabby old
shopping-bag.

Mrs. Sommers after that did not move in the direction of the bargain counter. 12
She took the elevator, which carried her to an upper floor into the region of the
ladies' waiting-rooms. Here, in a retired corner, she exchanged her cotton stockings for the new silk ones which she had just bought. She was not going through

any acute mental process or reasoning with herself, nor was she striving to explain to her satisfaction the motive of her action. She was not thinking at all. She seemed for the time to be taking a rest from that laborious and fatiguing function and to have abandoned herself to some mechanical impulse that directed her actions and freed her of responsibility.

How good was the touch of the raw silk to her flesh! She felt like lying back in 13 the cushioned chair and reveling for a while in the luxury of it. She did for a little while. Then she replaced her shoes, rolled the cotton stockings together and thrust them into her bag. After doing this she crossed straight over to the shoe department and took her seat to be fitted.

She was fastidious. The clerk could not make her out; he could not reconcile 14 her shoes with her stockings, and she was not too easily pleased. She held back her skirts and turned her feet one way and her head another way as she glanced down at the polished, pointed-tipped boots. Her foot and ankle looked very pretty. She could not realize that they belonged to her and were a part of herself. She wanted an excellent and stylish fit, she told the young fellow who served her, and she did not mind the difference of a dollar or two more in the price so long as she got what she desired.

It was a long time since Mrs. Sommers had been fitted with gloves. On rare 15 occasions when she had bought a pair they were always "bargains," so cheap that it would have been preposterous and unreasonable to have expected them to be fitted to the hand.

Now she rested her elbow on the cushion of the glove counter, and a pretty, 16 pleasant young creature, delicate and deft of touch, drew a long-wristed "kid" over Mrs. Sommers's hand. She smoothed it down over the wrist and buttoned it neatly, and both lost themselves for a second or two in admiring contemplation of the little symmetrical gloved hand. But there were other places where money might be spent.

There were books and magazines piled up in the window of a stall a few paces 17 down the street. Mrs. Sommers bought two high-priced magazines such as she had been accustomed to read in the days when she had been accustomed to other pleasant things. She carried them without wrapping. As well as she could she lifted her skirts at the crossings. Her stockings and boots and well fitting gloves had worked marvels in her bearing—had given her a feeling of assurance, a sense of belonging to the well-dressed multitude.

She was very hungry. Another time she would have stilled the cravings for food 18 until reaching her own home, where she would have brewed herself a cup of tea and taken a snack of anything that was available. But the impulse that was guiding her would not suffer her to entertain any such thought.

There was a restaurant at the corner. She had never entered its doors; from the 19 outside she had sometimes caught glimpses of spotless damask and shining crystal, and soft-stepping waiters serving people of fashion.

When she entered her appearance created no surprise, no consternation, as 20 she had half feared it might. She seated herself at a small table alone, and an attentive waiter at once approached to take her order. She did not want a profusion;

she craved a nice and tasty bite—a half dozen blue-points, a plump chop with cress, a something sweet—a crème-frappée, for instance; a glass of Rhine wine, and after all a small cup of black coffee.

While waiting to be served she removed her gloves very leisurely and laid 21 them beside her. Then she picked up a magazine and glanced through it, cutting the pages with a blunt edge of her knife. It was all very agreeable. The damask was even more spotless than it had seemed through the window, and the crystal more sparkling. There were quiet ladies and gentlemen, who did not notice her, lunching at the small tables like her own. A soft, pleasing strain of music could be heard, and a gentle breeze was blowing through the window. She tasted a bite, and she read a word or two, and she sipped the amber wine and wiggled her toes in the silk stockings. The price of it made no difference. She counted the money out to the waiter and left an extra coin on his tray, whereupon he bowed before her as before a princess of royal blood.

There was still money in her purse, and her next temptation presented itself 22 in the shape of a matinée poster.

It was a little later when she entered the theatre, the play had begun and the 23 house seemed to her to be packed. But there were vacant seats here and there, and into one of them she was ushered, between brilliantly dressed women who had gone there to kill time and eat candy and display their gaudy attire. There were many others who were there solely for the play and acting. It is safe to say there was no one present who bore quite the attitude which Mrs. Sommers did to her surroundings. She gathered in the whole—stage and players and people in one wide impression, and absorbed it and enjoyed it. She laughed at the comedy and wept— she and the gaudy woman next to her wept over the tragedy. And they talked a little together over it. And the gaudy woman wiped her eyes and sniffled on a tiny square of filmy, perfumed lace and passed little Mrs. Sommers her box of candy.

The play was over, the music ceased, the crowd filed out. It was like a dream 24 ended. People scattered in all directions. Mrs. Sommers went to the corner and waited for the cable car.

A man with keen eyes, who sat opposite to her, seemed to like the study of her 25 small, pale face. It puzzled him to decipher what he saw there. In truth, he saw nothing unless he were wizard enough to detect a poignant wish, a powerful longing that the cable car would never stop anywhere, but go on and on with her forever.

ACTIVITIES FOR WRITING AND DISCUSSION

1. Compare Mrs. Sommers with Louise Mallard, the protagonist of Chopin's "The Story of an Hour" (see p. 221). How are the characters or life situations of the two women alike? different? Then:

    a. Draft an essay comparing and contrasting the two women; or

    b. Imagine a scene in which Mrs. Mallard joins Mrs. Sommers at the corner restaurant described in paragraph 19, and write a dialogue between the two women.

2. Mrs. Sommers meant to spend the fifteen dollars on her children but ends up spending it on herself. Why? Looking carefully at the motivations mentioned for each of her purchases, find any evidence in the text that you think justifies her behavior. Then find evidence that suggests her behavior was "wrong" or inappropriately selfish. Finally, form your own judgment of Mrs. Sommers and argue it in class.

3. From the evidence in the story do you think Mrs. Sommers is married, widowed, or divorced? Does her marital status affect how you feel about her actions? Is it significant that there is no explicit mention in the story of a *Mr.* Sommers? What possible interpretations can you give of the first sentence in paragraph 4 ("The neighbors sometimes talked of certain 'better days' that little Mrs. Sommers had known before she had ever thought of being Mrs. Sommers") and of paragraph 17?

4. Write a sequel in which Mrs. Sommers returns home with her purchases and encounters her husband and/or children. Do they react? If so, how do they react? What does she reveal—or conceal—about her day's activities?

ANTON CHEKHOV (1860–1904)

Gooseberries

The sky had been overcast since early morning; it was a still day, not hot, but tedious, as it usually is when the weather is gray and dull, when clouds have been hanging over the fields for a long time, and you wait for the rain that does not come. Ivan Ivanych, a veterinary, and Burkin, a high school teacher, were already tired with walking, and the plain seemed endless to them. Far ahead were the scarcely visible windmills of the village of Mironositzkoe; to the right lay a range of hills that disappeared in the distance beyond the village, and both of them knew that over there were the river, and fields, green willows, homesteads, and if you stood on one of the hills, you could see from there another vast plain, telegraph poles, and a train that from afar looked like a caterpillar crawling, and in clear weather you could even see the town. Now, when it was still and when nature seemed mild and pensive, Ivan Ivanych and Burkin were filled with love for this plain, and both of them thought what a beautiful land it was. 1

"Last time when we were in Elder Prokofy's barn," said Burkin, "you were going to tell me a story." 2

"Yes; I wanted to tell you about my brother." 3

Ivan Ivanych heaved a slow sigh and lit his pipe before beginning his story, but just then it began to rain. And five minutes later there was a downpour, and it was hard to tell when it would be over. The two men halted, at a loss; the dogs, already wet, stood with their tails between their legs and looked at them feelingly. 4

"We must find shelter somewhere," said Burkin. "Let's go to Alyohin's; it's 5 quite near."

"Let's." 6

They turned aside and walked across a mown meadow, now going straight 7 ahead, now bearing to the right, until they reached the road. Soon poplars came into view, a garden, then the red roofs of barns; the river gleamed, and the view opened on a broad expanse of water with a mill and a white bathing-cabin. That was Sofyino, Alyohin's place.

The mill was going, drowning out the sound of the rain; the dam was shaking. 8 Wet horses stood near the carts, their heads drooping, and men were walking about, their heads covered with sacks. It was damp, muddy, dreary; and the water looked cold and unkind. Ivan Ivanych and Burkin felt cold and messy and uncomfortable through and through; their feet were heavy with mud and when, having crossed the dam, they climbed up to the barns, they were silent as though they were cross with each other.

The noise of a winnowing-machine came from one of the barns, the door was 9 open, and clouds of dust were pouring from within. On the threshold stood Alyohin himself, a man of forty, tall and rotund, with long hair, looking more like a professor or an artist than a gentleman farmer. He was wearing a white blouse, badly in need of washing, that was belted with a rope, and drawers, and his high boots were plastered with mud and straw. His eyes and nose were black with dust. He recognized Ivan Ivanych and Burkin and was apparently very glad to see them.

"Please go up to the house, gentlemen," he said, smiling; "I'll be there directly, 10 in a moment."

It was a large structure of two stories. Alyohin lived downstairs in what was 11 formerly the stewards' quarters: two rooms that had arched ceilings and small windows; the furniture was plain, and the place smelled of rye bread, cheap vodka, and harness. He went into the showy rooms upstairs only rarely, when he had guests. Once in the house, the two visitors were met by a chambermaid, a young woman so beautiful that both of them stood still at the same moment and glanced at each other.

"You can't imagine how glad I am to see you, gentlemen," said Alyohin, join- 12 ing them in the hall. "What a surprise! Pelageya," he said, turning to the chambermaid, "give the guests a change of clothes. And, come to think of it, I will change, too. But I must go and bathe first, I don't think I've had a wash since spring. Don't you want to go into the bathing-cabin? In the meanwhile things will be got ready here."

The beautiful Pelageya, with her soft, delicate air, brought them bath towels 13 and soap, and Alyohin went to the bathing-cabin with his guests.

"Yes, it's a long time since I've bathed," he said, as he undressed. "I've an ex- 14 cellent bathing-cabin, as you see—it was put up by my father—but somehow I never find time to use it." He sat down on the steps and lathered his long hair and neck, and the water around him turned brown.

"I say—" observed Ivan Ivanych significantly, looking at his head. 15

"I haven't had a good wash for a long time," repeated Alyohin, embarrassed, 16 and soaped himself once more; the water about him turned dark-blue, the color of ink.

Ivan Ivanych came out of the cabin, plunged into the water with a splash and 17 swam in the rain, thrusting his arms out wide; he raised waves on which white lilies swayed. He swam out to the middle of the river and dived and a minute later came up in another spot and swam on and kept diving, trying to touch bottom. "By God!" he kept repeating delightedly, "by God!" He swam to the mill, spoke to the peasants there, and turned back and in the middle of the river lay floating, exposing his face to the rain. Burkin and Alyohin were already dressed and ready to leave, but he kept on swimming and diving. "By God!" he kept exclaiming. "Lord, have mercy on me."

"You've had enough!" Burkin shouted to him. 18

They returned to the house. And only when the lamp was lit in the big draw- 19 ing room upstairs, and the two guests, in silk dressing-gowns and warm slippers, were lounging in armchairs, and Alyohin himself, washed and combed, wearing a new jacket, was walking about the room, evidently savoring the warmth, the cleanliness, the dry clothes and light footwear, and when pretty Pelageya, stepping noiselessly across the carpet and smiling softly, brought in a tray with tea and jam, only then did Ivan Ivanych begin his story, and it was as though not only Burkin and Alyohin were listening, but also the ladies, old and young, and the military men who looked down upon them, calmly and severely, from their gold frames.

"We are two brothers," he began, "I, Ivan Ivanych, and my brother, Nikolay 20 Ivanych, who is two years my junior. I went in for a learned profession and became a veterinary; Nikolay at nineteen began to clerk in a provincial branch of the Treasury. Our father was a *kantonist*,[1] but he rose to be an officer and so a nobleman, a rank that he bequeathed to us together with a small estate. After his death there was a lawsuit and we lost the estate to creditors, but be that as it may, we spent our childhood in the country. Just like peasant children we passed days and nights in the fields and the woods, herded horses, stripped bast from the trees, fished, and so on. And, you know, whoever even once in his life has caught a perch or seen thrushes migrate in the autumn, when on clear, cool days they sweep in flocks over the village, will never really be a townsman and to the day of his death will have a longing for the open. My brother was unhappy in the government office. Years passed, but he went on warming the same seat, scratching away at the same papers, and thinking of one and the same thing: how to get away to the country. And little by little this vague longing turned into a definite desire, into a dream of buying a little property somewhere on the banks of a river or a lake.

"He was a kind and gentle soul and I loved him, but I never sympathized with 21 his desire to shut himself up for the rest of his life on a little property of his own. It is a common saying that a man needs only six feet of earth. But six feet is what a corpse needs, not a man. It is also asserted that if our educated class is drawn to

---

1. The son of a private, registered at birth in the army and trained in a military school.

the land and seeks to settle on farms, that's a good thing. But these farms amount to the same six feet of earth. To retire from the city, from the struggle, from the hubbub, to go off and hide on one's own farm—that's not life, it is selfishness, sloth, it is a kind of monasticism, but monasticism without works. Man needs not six feet of earth, not a farm, but the whole globe, all of Nature, where unhindered he can display all the capacities and peculiarities of his free spirit.

"My brother Nikolay, sitting in his office, dreamed of eating his own *shchi*, 22 which would fill the whole farmyard with a delicious aroma, of picnicking on the green grass, of sleeping in the sun, of sitting for hours on the seat by the gate gazing at field and forest. Books on agriculture and the farming items in almanacs were his joy, the delight of his soul. He liked newspapers too, but the only things he read in them were advertisements of land for sale, so many acres of tillable land and pasture, with house, garden, river, mill, and millpond. And he pictured to himself garden paths, flowers, fruit, birdhouses with starlings in them, crucians in the pond, and all that sort of thing, you know. These imaginary pictures varied with the advertisements he came upon, but somehow gooseberry bushes figured in every one of them. He could not picture to himself a single country-house, a single rustic nook, without gooseberries.

" 'Country life has its advantages,' he used to say. 'You sit on the veranda hav- 23 ing tea, and your ducks swim in the pond, and everything smells delicious and— the gooseberries are ripening.'

"He would draw a plan of his estate and invariably it would contain the fol- 24 lowing features: a) the master's house; b) servants' quarters; c) kitchen-garden; d) a gooseberry patch. He lived meagerly: he deprived himself of food and drink; he dressed God knows how, like a beggar, but he kept on saving and salting money away in the bank. He was terribly stingy. It was painful for me to see it, and I used to give him small sums and send him something on holidays, but he would put that away too. Once a man is possessed by an idea, there is no doing anything with him.

"Years passed. He was transferred to another province, he was already past 25 forty, yet he was still reading newspaper advertisements and saving up money. Then I heard that he was married. Still for the sake of buying a property with a gooseberry patch he married an elderly, homely widow, without a trace of affection for her, but simply because she had money. After marrying her, he went on living parsimoniously, keeping her half-starved, and he put her money in the bank in his own name. She had previously been the wife of a postmaster, who had got her used to pies and cordials. This second husband did not even give her enough black bread. She began to sicken, and some three years later gave up the ghost. And, of course, it never for a moment occurred to my brother that he was to blame for her death. Money, like vodka, can do queer things to a man. Once in our town a merchant lay on his deathbed; before he died, he ordered a plateful of honey and he ate up all his money and lottery tickets with the honey, so that no one should get it. One day when I was inspecting a drove of cattle at a railway station, a cattle dealer fell under a locomotive and it sliced off his leg. We carried him in to the infirmary, the blood was gushing from the wound—a terrible business, but he kept begging us to find his leg and was very anxious about it: he had twenty rubles in the boot that was on that leg, and he was afraid they would be lost."

"That's a tune from another opera," said Burkin.   26

Ivan Ivanych paused a moment and then continued: 27

"After his wife's death, my brother began to look around for a property. Of   28 course, you may scout about for five years and in the end make a mistake, and buy something quite different from what you have been dreaming of. Through an agent my brother bought a mortgaged estate of three hundred acres with a house, servants' quarters, a park, but with no orchard, no gooseberry patch, no duck-pond. There was a stream, but the water in it was the color of coffee, for on one of its banks there was a brickyard and on the other a glue factory. But my brother was not at all disconcerted: he ordered a score of gooseberry bushes, planted them, and settled down to the life of a country gentleman.

"Last year I paid him a visit. I thought I would go and see how things were   29 with him. In his letter to me my brother called his estate 'Chumbaroklov Waste, or Himalaiskoe' (our surname was Chimsha-Himalaisky). I reached the place in the afternoon. It was hot. Everywhere there were ditches, fences, hedges, rows of fir trees, and I was at a loss as to how to get to the yard and where to leave my horse. I made my way to the house and was met by a fat dog with reddish hair that looked like a pig. It wanted to bark, but was too lazy. The cook, a fat, barelegged woman, who also looked like a pig, came out of the kitchen and said that the master was resting after dinner. I went in to see my brother, and found him sitting up in bed, with a quilt over his knees. He had grown older, stouter, flabby; his cheeks, his nose, his lips jutted out: It looked as though he might grunt into the quilt at any moment.

"We embraced and dropped tears of joy and also of sadness at the thought that   30 the two of us had once been young, but were now gray and nearing death. He got dressed and took me out to show me his estate.

"'Well, how are you getting on here?' I asked.   31

"'Oh, all right, thank God. I am doing very well.'   32

"He was no longer the poor, timid clerk he used to be but a real landowner, a   33 gentleman. He had already grown used to his new manner of living and developed a taste for it. He ate a great deal, steamed himself in the bathhouse, was growing stout, was already having a lawsuit with the village commune and the two factories and was very much offended when the peasants failed to address him as 'Your Honor.' And he concerned himself with his soul's welfare too in a substantial, upper-class manner, and performed good deeds not simply, but pompously. And what good works! He dosed the peasants with bicarbonate and castor oil for all their ailments and on his name day he had a thanksgiving service celebrated in the center of the village, and then treated the villagers to a gallon of vodka, which he thought was the thing to do. Oh, those horrible gallons of vodka! One day a fat landowner hauls the peasants up before the rural police officer for trespassing, and the next, to mark a feast day, treats them to a gallon of vodka, and they drink and shout 'Hurrah' and when they are drunk bow down at his feet. A higher standard of living, overeating and idleness develop the most insolent self-conceit in a

Russian. Nikolay Ivanych, who when he was a petty official was afraid to have opinions of his own even if he kept them to himself, now uttered nothing but incontrovertible truths and did so in the tone of a minister of state: 'Education is necessary, but the masses are not ready for it; corporal punishment is generally harmful, but in some cases it is useful and nothing else will serve.'

   "'I know the common people, and I know how to deal with them,' he would 34 say. 'They love me. I only have to raise my little finger, and they will do anything I want.'

   "And all this, mark you, would be said with a smile that bespoke kindness and 35 intelligence. Twenty times over he repeated: 'We, of the gentry,' 'I, as a member of the gentry.' Apparently he no longer remembered that our grandfather had been a peasant and our father just a private. Even our surname, 'Chimsha-Himalaisky,' which in reality is grotesque, seemed to him sonorous, distinguished, and delightful.

   "But I am concerned now not with him, but with me. I want to tell you about 36 the change that took place in me during the few hours that I spent on his estate. In the evening when we were having tea, the cook served a plateful of gooseberries. They were not bought, they were his own gooseberries, the first ones picked since the bushes were planted. My brother gave a laugh and for a minute looked at the gooseberries in silence, with tears in his eyes—he could not speak for excitement. Then he put one berry in his mouth, glanced at me with the triumph of a child who has at last been given a toy he was longing for and said: 'How tasty!' And he ate the gooseberries greedily, and kept repeating: 'Ah, how delicious! Do taste them!'

   "They were hard and sour, but as Pushkin[2] has it,   37

> The falsehood that exalts we cherish more
> Than meaner truths that are a thousand strong.

I saw a happy man, one whose cherished dream had so obviously come true, who had attained his goal in life, who had got what he wanted, who was satisfied with his lot and with himself. For some reason an element of sadness had always mingled with my thoughts of human happiness, and now at the sight of a happy man I was assailed by an oppressive feeling bordering on despair. It weighed on me particularly at night. A bed was made up for me in a room next to my brother's bedroom, and I could hear that he was wakeful, and that he would get up again and again, go to the plate of gooseberries and eat one after another. I said to myself: how many contented, happy people there really are! What an overwhelming force they are! Look at life: the insolence and idleness of the strong, the ignorance and brutishness of the weak, horrible poverty everywhere, overcrowding, degeneration, drunkenness, hypocrisy, lying——Yet in all the houses and on all the streets there is peace and quiet; of the fifty thousand people who live in our town

---

2. Russian poet (1799–1837).

there is not one who would cry out, who would vent his indignation aloud. We see the people who go to market, eat by day, sleep by night, who babble nonsense, marry, grow old, good-naturedly drag their dead to the cemetery, but we do not see or hear those who suffer, and what is terrible in life goes on somewhere behind the scenes. Everything is peaceful and quiet and only mute statistics protest: so many people gone out of their minds, so many gallons of vodka drunk, so many children dead from malnutrition——And such a state of things is evidently necessary; obviously the happy man is at ease only because the unhappy ones bear their burdens in silence, and if there were not this silence, happiness would be impossible. It is a general hypnosis. Behind the door of every contented, happy man there ought to be someone standing with a little hammer and continually reminding him with a knock that there are unhappy people, that however happy he may be, life will sooner or later show him its claws, and trouble will come to him—illness, poverty, losses, and then no one will see or hear him, just as now he neither sees nor hears others. But there is no man with a hammer. The happy man lives at his ease, faintly fluttered by small daily cares, like an aspen in the wind—and all is well.

"That night I came to understand that I too had been contented and happy," 38 Ivan Ivanych continued, getting up. "I too over the dinner table or out hunting would hold forth on how to live, what to believe, the right way to govern the people. I too would say that learning was the enemy of darkness, that education was necessary but that for the common people the three R's were sufficient for the time being. Freedom is a boon, I used to say, it is as essential as air, but we must wait awhile. Yes, that's what I used to say, and now I ask: Why must we wait?" said Ivan Ivanych, looking wrathfully at Burkin. "Why must we wait, I ask you? For what reason? I am told that nothing can be done all at once, that every idea is realized gradually, in its own time. But who is it that says so? Where is the proof that it is just? You cite the natural order of things, the law governing all phenomena, but is there law, is there order in the fact that I, a living, thinking man, stand beside a ditch and wait for it to close up of itself or fill up with silt, when I could jump over it or throw a bridge across it? And again, why must we wait? Wait, until we have no strength to live, and yet we have to live and are eager to live!

"I left my brother's place early in the morning, and ever since then it has be- 39 come intolerable for me to stay in town. I am oppressed by the peace and the quiet, I am afraid to look at the windows, for there is nothing that pains me more than the spectacle of a happy family sitting at table having tea. I am an old man now and unfit for combat, I am not even capable of hating. I can only grieve inwardly, get irritated, worked up, and at night my head is ablaze with the rush of ideas and I cannot sleep. Oh, if I were young!"

Ivan Ivanych paced up and down the room excitedly and repeated, "If I were 40 young!"

He suddenly walked up to Alyohin and began to press now one of his hands, 41 now the other.

"Pavel Konstantinych," he said imploringly, "don't quiet down, don't let your- 42 self be lulled to sleep! As long as you are young, strong, alert, do not cease to do good! There is no happiness and there should be none, and if life has a meaning and a purpose, that meaning and purpose is not our happiness but something greater and more rational. Do good!"

All this Ivan Ivanych said with a pitiful, imploring smile, as though he were 43
asking a personal favor.

Afterwards all three of them sat in armchairs in different corners of the draw- 44
ing room and were silent. Ivan Ivanych's story satisfied neither Burkin nor Alyohin. With the ladies and generals looking down from the golden frames, seeming alive in the dim light, it was tedious to listen to the story of the poor devil of
a clerk who ate gooseberries. One felt like talking about elegant people, about
women. And the fact that they were sitting in a drawing room where everything—
the chandelier under its cover, the armchairs, the carpets underfoot—testified
that the very people who were now looking down from the frames had once
moved about here, sat and had tea, and the fact that lovely Pelageya was noiselessly moving about—that was better than any story.

Alyohin was very sleepy; he had gotten up early, before three o'clock in the 45
morning, to get some work done, and now he could hardly keep his eyes open,
but he was afraid his visitors might tell an interesting story in his absence, and he
would not leave. He did not trouble to ask himself if what Ivan Ivanych had just
said was intelligent or right. The guests were not talking about groats, or hay, or
tar, but about something that had no direct bearing on his life, and he was glad of
it and wanted them to go on.

"However, it's bedtime," said Burkin, rising. "Allow me to wish you good 46
night."

Alyohin took leave of his guests and went downstairs to his own quarters, 47
while they remained upstairs. They were installed for the night in a big room in
which stood two old wooden beds decorated with carvings and in the corner was
an ivory crucifix. The wide cool beds which had been made by the lovely Pelageya
gave off a pleasant smell of clean linen.

Ivan Ivanych undressed silently and got into bed. 48

"Lord forgive us sinners!" he murmured, and drew the bedclothes over his 49
head.

His pipe, which lay on the table, smelled strongly of burnt tobacco, and 50
Burkin, who could not sleep for a long time, kept wondering where the unpleasant
odor came from.

The rain beat against the window panes all night. 51

—Translated by Avrahm Yarmolinsky

ACTIVITIES FOR WRITING AND DISCUSSION

1. In paragraph 37, Ivan Ivanych criticizes his brother for being "a happy man." Why? In your notebook write a summary of his reasoning. Do you think his criticism is fair? Why or why not?

2. In paragraph 44 we are told that "Ivan Ivanych's story satisfied neither Burkin nor Alyohin." Describe the two friends' reactions to the story. Can their reactions be said to relate in any ways to the **themes** of Ivan's story about his brother Nikolay?

3. How do you assess Ivan Ivanych's outlook and attitudes? Is he mentally sick? too intense and serious? wiser than his friends or the world he criticizes? Of what people (if any) in your own experience does he remind you?

4. Like the **characters** in many Chekhov stories, Ivan Ivanych doesn't just tell a story: he philosophizes; he wrestles with the meaning of life. Who are we? Why are we alive? What are our lives for? Create a character of your own and a subject about which he or she can philosophize. For a context, consider two or three friends conversing around a campfire or college students talking late at night in the dorm or over beers.

Sloan Wilson (b. 1920)

Excerpt from *The Man in the Gray Flannel Suit*

Walker's outer office was impressive. As soon as Tom saw it, he knew he was be- 1
ing seriously considered for a job, and maybe a pretty good one. Walker had two secretaries, one chosen for looks, apparently, and one for utility. A pale-yellow carpet lay on the floor, and there was a yellow leather armchair for callers. Walker himself was closeted in an inner office which was separated from the rest of the room by a partition of opaque glass brick.

The utilitarian secretary told Tom to wait. It was extremely quiet. Neither of the 2
two girls was typing, and although each had two telephones on her desk and an interoffice communication box, there was no ringing or buzzing. Both the secretaries sat reading typewritten sheets in black notebooks. After Tom had waited about half an hour, the pretty secretary, with no audible or visible cue, suddenly looked up brightly and said, "Mr Walker will see you now. Just open the door and go in."

Tom opened the door and saw a fat pale man sitting in a high-backed uphol- 3
stered chair behind a kidney-shaped desk with nothing on it but a blotter and pen. He was in his shirt sleeves, and he weighed about two hundred and fifty pounds. His face was as white as a marshmallow. He didn't stand up when Tom came in, but he smiled. It was a surprisingly warm, spontaneous smile, as though he had unexpectedly recognized an old friend. "Thomas Rath?" he said. "Sit down! Make yourself comfortable! Take off your coat!"

Tom thanked him and, although it wasn't particularly warm, took off his coat. 4
There wasn't any place to put it, so, sitting down in the comfortable chair in front of Walker's desk, he laid the coat awkwardly across his lap.

"I've read the application forms you filled out, and it seems to me you might 5
be qualified for a new position we may have opening up here," Walker said.

"There are just a few questions I want to ask you." He was still smiling. Suddenly he touched a button on the arm of his chair and the back of the chair dropped, allowing him to recline, as though he were in an airplane seat. Tom could see only his face across the top of the desk.

"You will excuse me," Walker said, still smiling. "The doctor says I must get 6 plenty of rest, and this is the way I do it."

Tom couldn't think of anything more appropriate to say than "It looks com- 7 fortable . . ."

"Why do you want to work for the United Broadcasting Corporation?" 8 Walker asked abruptly.

"It's a good company . . ." Tom began hesitantly, and was suddenly impatient 9 at the need for hypocrisy. The sole reason he wanted to work for United Broadcasting was that he thought he might be able to make a lot of money there fast, but he felt he couldn't say that. It was sometimes considered fashionable for the employees of foundations to say that they were in it for the money, but people were supposed to work at advertising agencies and broadcasting companies for spiritual reasons.

"I believe," Tom said, "that television is developing into the greatest medium 10 for mass education and entertainment. It has always fascinated me, and I would like to work with it . . ."

"What kind of salary do you have in mind?" Walker asked. Tom hadn't ex- 11 pected the question that soon. Walker was still smiling.

"The salary isn't the primary consideration with me," Tom said, trying des- 12 perately to come up with stock answers to stock questions. "I'm mainly interested in finding something useful and worth while to do. I have personal responsibilities, however, and I would hope that something could be worked out to enable me to meet them . . ."

"Of course," Walker said, beaming more cheerily than ever. "I understand you 13 applied for a position in the public-relations department. Why did you choose that?"

Because I heard there was an opening, Tom wanted to say, but quickly thought 14 better of it and substituted a halting avowal of lifelong interest in public relations. "I think my experience in working with *people* at the Schanenhauser Foundation would be helpful," he concluded lamely.

"I see," Walker said kindly. There was a short silence before he added," Can 15 you write?"

"I do most of the writing at the Schanenhauser Foundation," Tom said. "The 16 annual report to the trustees is my job, and so are most of the reports on individual projects. I used to be editor of my college paper."

"That sounds fine," Walker said casually. "I have a little favour I want to ask of 17 you. I want you to write me your autobiography."

"What?" Tom asked in astonishment.   18

"Nothing very long," Walker said. "Just as much as you can manage to type 19 out in an hour. One of my girls will give you a room with a typewriter."

"Is there anything in particular you want me to tell you about?"   20

"Yourself," Walker said, looking hugely pleased. "Explain yourself to me. Tell 21 me what kind of person you are. Explain why we should hire you."

"I'll try," Tom said weakly. 22

"You'll have precisely an hour," Walker said. "You see, this is a device I use in 23 employing people—I find it most helpful. For this particular job, I have twenty or thirty applicants. It's hard to tell from a brief interview whom to choose, so I ask them all to write about themselves for an hour. You'd be surprised how revealing the results are . . ."

He paused, still smiling. Tom said nothing. 24

"Just a few hints," Walker continued. "Write anything you want, but at the 25 end of your last page, I'd like you to finish this sentence: 'The most significant fact about me is . . .'"

"The most significant fact about me is . . ." Tom repeated idiotically. 26

"The results, of course, will be entirely confidential." Walker lifted a bulky 27 arm and inspected his wrist watch. "It's now five minutes to twelve," he concluded. "I'll expect your paper on my desk at precisely one o'clock."

ACTIVITIES FOR WRITING AND DISCUSSION

1. Tom seems to have rehearsed for the interview. In what specific ways does the interview upset or destroy his expectations?

2. Write a prequel or a sequel to the story.

3. Rewrite the interview with the interviewer and the applicant as women, or the interviewer as a woman and the applicant as a man, or with Tom as a middle-aged person between jobs and the interviewer a young professional superstar; or rewrite the story along other imaginative lines of your own.

4. Do Walker's assignment yourself. First decide on your audience (for instance, a prospective employer, a scholarship committee, your family or descendants). Give yourself exactly one hour to write your autobiography. If appropriate, conclude your autobiography by finishing the sentence, "The most significant fact about me is. . . ."

RAYMOND CARVER (1938–1988)

Kindling

It was the middle of August and Myers was between lives. The only thing differ- 1 ent about this time from the other times was that this time he was sober. He'd just spent twenty-eight days at a drying-out facility. But during this period his wife took it into her head to go down the road with another drunk, a friend of theirs.

The man had recently come into some money and had been talking about buying into a bar and restaurant in the eastern part of the state.

Myers called his wife, but she hung up on him. She wouldn't even talk to him, 2 let alone have him anywhere near the house. She had a lawyer and a restraining order. So he took a few things, boarded a bus, and went to live near the ocean in a room in a house owned by a man named Sol who had run an ad in the paper.

Sol was wearing jeans and a red T-shirt when he opened the door. It was about 3 ten o'clock at night and Myers had just gotten out of a cab. Under the porch light Myers could see that Sol's right arm was shorter than his other arm, and the hand and fingers of the right arm were withered. He didn't offer either his good left hand or his withered hand for Myers to shake, and this was fine with Myers. Myers felt plenty rattled as it was.

You just called, right? Sol said. You're here to see the room. Come on in.   4

Myers gripped his suitcase and stepped inside.   5

This is my wife. This is Bonnie, Sol said.   6

Bonnie was watching TV, but she moved her eyes to see who it was coming in- 7 side. She muted the TV with the remote, then turned it off altogether. Then she got up off the sofa onto her feet. She was a fat girl. She was fat all over and she huffed when she breathed.

I'm sorry it's so late, Myers said. Nice to meet you.   8

It's all right, Bonnie said. Did my husband tell you on the phone what we're 9 asking?

Myers nodded. He was still holding the suitcase.   10

Well, this is the living room, Sol said, as you can see for yourself. He shook his 11 head and brought the fingers of his good hand up to his chin. I may as well tell you that we're new at this. We never rented a room to anybody before. But it's just back there not being used, and we thought what the hell. A person can always use a little extra.

I don't blame you a bit, Myers said.   12

Where are you from? Bonnie said. You're not from anywhere around town.   13

My wife wants to be a writer, Sol said. Who, what, where, why, and how 14 much?

I just got here, Myers said. He moved the suitcase to his other hand. I got off 15 the bus about an hour ago, read your ad in the paper, and called up.

What sort of work do you do? Bonnie wanted to know.   16

I've done everything, Myers said. He set the suitcase down and opened and 17 closed his fingers. Then he picked up the suitcase again.

Bonnie didn't pursue it. Sol didn't either, though Myers could see he was 18 curious.

Myers took in a photograph of Elvis Presley on top of the TV. Elvis's signature 19 ran across the breast of his white sequined jacket. He moved a step closer.

The King, Bonnie said.   20

Myers nodded but didn't say anything. Alongside the picture of Elvis was a 21 wedding picture of Sol and Bonnie. In the picture Sol was dressed up in a suit and tie. Sol's good strong left arm reached around Bonnie's waist as far as it would go.

Sol's right hand and Bonnie's right hand were joined over Sol's belt buckle. Bonnie wasn't going anywhere if Sol had anything to say about it. Bonnie didn't mind. In the picture Bonnie wore a hat and was all smiles.

I love her, Sol said, as if Myers had said something to the contrary.   22

How about that room you were going to show me? Myers said.   23

I knew there was something we were forgetting, Sol said.   24

They moved out of the living room into the kitchen, Sol first, then Myers, carrying his suitcase, then Bonnie. They passed through the kitchen and turned left just before the back door. There were some open cupboards along the wall, and a washer and dryer. Sol opened a door at the end of the little corridor and turned on the light in the bathroom.   25

Bonnie moved up and huffed and said, This is your private bathroom. That door in the kitchen is your own entrance. Sol opened the door to the other side of the bathroom and turned on another light.   26

This is the room, Sol said.   27

I made up the bed with clean sheets, Bonnie said. But if you take the room you'll have to be responsible from here on out.   28

Like my wife says, this is not a hotel, Sol said. But you're welcome, if you want to stay.   29

There was a double bed against one wall, along with a nightstand and lamp, a chest of drawers, and a pinochle table with a metal chair. A big window gave out onto the backyard. Myers put his suitcase on the bed and moved to the window. He raised the shade and looked out. A moon rode high in the sky. In the distance he could see a forested valley and mountain peaks. Was it his imagination, or did he hear a stream or a river?   30

I hear water, Myers said.   31

That's the Little Quilcene River you hear, Sol said. That river has the fastest per-foot drop to it of any river in the country.   32

Well, what do you think? Bonnie said. She went over and turned down the covers on the bed, and this simple gesture almost caused Myers to weep.   33

I'll take it, Myers said.   34

I'm glad, Sol said. My wife's glad, too, I can tell. I'll have them pull that ad out of the paper tomorrow. You want to move in right now, don't you?   35

That's what I hoped, Myers said.   36

We'll let you get settled, Bonnie said. I gave you two pillows, and there's an extra quilt in that closet.   37

Myers could only nod.   38

Well, good night, Sol said.   39

Good night, Bonnie said.   40

Good night, Myers said. And thank you.   41

Sol and Bonnie went through his bathroom and into the kitchen. They closed the door, but not before Myers heard Bonnie say, He seems okay.   42

Pretty quiet, Sol said.   43

I think I'll fix buttered popcorn.   44

I'll eat some with you, Sol said.   45

Pretty soon Myers heard the TV come on again in the living room, but it was 46
a very faint sound and he didn't think it would bother him. He opened the window all the way and heard the sound of the river as it raced through the valley on
its way to the ocean.

He took his things out of the suitcase and put them away in the drawers. Then 47
he used the bathroom and brushed his teeth. He moved the table so that it sat directly in front of the window. Then he looked at where she'd turned the covers
down. He drew out the metal chair and sat down and took a ballpoint out of his
pocket. He thought for a minute, then opened the notebook, and at the top of a
blank white page he wrote the words *Emptiness is the beginning of all things.* He
stared at this, and then he laughed. Jesus, what rubbish! He shook his head. He
closed the notebook, undressed, and turned off the light. He stood for a moment
looking out the window and listening to the river. Then he moved to get into bed.

———

Bonnie fixed the popcorn, salted it and poured butter over it, and took it in a big 48
bowl to where Sol was watching TV. She let him help himself to some first. He
used his left hand to good effect and then he reached his little hand over for the
paper towel she offered. She took a little popcorn for herself.

What do you make of him? she wanted to know. Our new roomer. 49

Sol shook his head and went on watching TV and eating popcorn. Then, as if 50
he'd been thinking about her question, he said, I like him all right. He's okay. But
I think he's on the run from something.

What? 51

I don't know that. I'm just guessing. He isn't dangerous and he isn't going to 52
make any trouble.

His eyes, Bonnie said. 53

What about his eyes? 54

They're sad eyes. Saddest eyes I ever saw on a man. 55

Sol didn't say anything for a minute. He finished his popcorn. He wiped his 56
fingers and dabbed his chin with the paper towel. He's okay. He's just had some
trouble along the way, that's all. No disgrace attached to that. Give me a sip of that,
will you? He reached over for the glass of orange drink that she was holding and
took some. You know, I forgot to collect the rent from him tonight. I'll have to get
it in the morning, if he's up. And I should have asked him how long he intends to
stay. Damn, what's wrong with me? I don't want to turn this place into a hotel.

You couldn't think of everything. Besides, we're new at this. We never rented 57
a room out before.

Bonnie decided she was going to write about the man in the notebook she was 58
filling up. She closed her eyes and thought about what she was going to write. *This
tall, stooped—but handsome!—curly headed stranger with sad eyes walked into our
house one fateful night in August.* She leaned into Sol's left arm and tried to write
some more. Sol squeezed her shoulder, which brought her back to the present
moment. She opened her eyes and closed them, but she couldn't think of anything
else to write about him. Time will tell, she thought. She was glad he was here.

This show's for the birds, Sol said. Let's go to bed. We have to get up in the 59
morning.

In bed, Sol loved her up and she took him and held him and loved him back, 60
but all the time she was doing it she was thinking about the big, curly headed man
in the back room. What if he suddenly opened the bedroom door and looked in
on them?

Sol, she said, is this bedroom door locked? 61

What? Be still, Sol said. Then he finished and rolled off, but he kept his little 62
arm on her breast. She lay on her back and thought for a minute, then she patted
his fingers, let air out through her mouth, and went off to sleep thinking about
blasting caps, which is what had gone off in Sol's hand when he was a teenager,
severing nerves and causing his arm and fingers to wither.

Bonnie began to snore. Sol took her arm and shook it until she turned over 63
on her side, away from him.

In a minute, he got up and put on his underwear. He went into the living 64
room. He didn't turn on the light. He didn't need a light—the moon was out, and
he didn't want a light. He went from the living room into the kitchen. He checked
to make sure the back door was locked, and then he stood for a while outside the
bathroom door listening, but he couldn't hear anything out of the ordinary. The
faucet dripped—it needed a washer, but then, it always dripped. He went back
through the house and closed and locked their bedroom door. He checked the
clock and made sure the stem was pulled. He got into bed and moved right up
against Bonnie. He put his leg over her leg, and in that way he finally went to sleep.

These three people slept and dreamed, while outside the house the moon grew 65
large and seemed to move across the sky until it was out over the ocean and growing smaller and paler. In his dream, someone is offering Myers a glass of Scotch, but
just as he is about to take it, reluctantly, he wakes up in a sweat, his heart racing.

Sol dreams that he is changing a tire on a truck and that he has the use of both 66
of his arms.

Bonnie dreams that she is taking two—no, three—children to the park. She 67
even has names for the children. She's named them just before the trip to the park.
Millicent, Dionne, and Randy. Randy keeps wanting to pull away from her and go
his own way.

Soon, the sun breaks over the horizon and birds begin calling to each other. 68
The Little Quilcene River rushes down through the valley, shoots under the highway bridge, rushes another hundred yards over sand and sharp rocks, and pours
into the ocean. An eagle flies down from the valley and over the bridge and begins to pass up and down the beach. A dog barks.

At this minute, Sol's alarm goes off. 69

Myers stayed in his room that morning until he heard them leave. Then he went 70
out and made instant coffee. He looked in the fridge and saw that one of the

shelves had been cleared for him. A little sign was scotch-taped to the shelf: MR. MYERS SHELF.

Later, he walked a mile toward town to a little service station he remembered 71 from the night before that sold a few groceries. He bought milk, cheese, bread, and tomatoes. That afternoon, before it was time for them to come home, he left the rent money in cash on the table and went back into his own room. Late that night, before going to bed, he opened his notebook and on a clean page he wrote, *Nothing.*

He adjusted his schedule to theirs. Mornings he'd stay in the room until he 72 heard Sol in the kitchen making coffee and getting his breakfast. Then he would hear Sol calling Bonnie to get up and then they'd have breakfast, but they wouldn't talk much. Then Sol would go out to the garage and start the pickup, back out, and drive away. In a little while, Bonnie's ride would pull up in front of the house, a horn would toot, and Bonnie would say, every time, I'm coming.

It was then that Myers would go out to the kitchen, put on water for coffee, 73 and eat a bowl of cereal. But he didn't have much of an appetite. The cereal and coffee would keep him for most of the day until the afternoon, when he knew they would arrive home. He'd eat something else, a sandwich, then stay out of the kitchen for the rest of the time when they might be in there or in the living room watching TV. He didn't want any conversation.

She'd go into the kitchen for a snack the first thing after she got in from work. 74 Then she'd turn on the TV and wait until Sol came in, and then she'd get up and fix something for the two of them to eat. They might talk on the telephone to friends, or else go sit outside in the backyard between the garage and Myers's bedroom window and talk about their day and drink iced tea until it was time to go inside and turn on the TV. Once he heard Bonnie say to someone on the telephone, How'd she expect me to pay any attention to Elvis Presley's weight when my own weight was out of control at the time?

They'd said he was welcome anytime to sit in the living room with them and 75 watch TV. He'd thanked them but said, No, television hurt his eyes.

They were curious about him. Especially Bonnie, who'd asked him one day, 76 when she came home early and surprised him in the kitchen, if he'd been married and if he had any kids. Myers had nodded. Bonnie had looked at him and waited for him to go on, but he hadn't.

Sol was curious, too. What kind of work do you do? he wanted to know. I'm 77 just curious. This is a small town and I know people. I grade lumber at the mill myself. Only need one good arm to do that. But sometimes there are openings. I could put in a word, maybe. What's your regular line of work?

Do you play any instruments? Bonnie asked. Sol has a guitar, she said. 78

But I don't know how to play a guitar, Sol said. I wish I did. 79

Myers kept to his room, where he was writing a letter to his wife. It was a long 80 letter and, he felt, an important letter. Perhaps the most important letter he'd ever written in his life. In the letter he was attempting to tell his wife that he was *sorry* for everything that had happened and that he hoped someday she would forgive him. *I would get down on my knees and ask forgiveness if that would help.*

After Sol and Bonnie had both left for the day, he sat in the living room with 81
his feet on the coffee table and drank instant coffee while he read the newspaper
from the evening before. Once in a while his hands trembled and the newspaper
began rattling in the empty house. Now and then the telephone rang, but he never
made a move to answer it. It wasn't for him, because nobody knew he was here.

Through his window at the rear of the house he could see up the valley to a se- 82
ries of steep mountain peaks whose tops were covered with snow, even though it
was August. Lower down on the mountains, timber covered the slopes and the
sides of the valley. The river coursed down the valley, frothing and boiling over
rocks and under granite embankments until it burst out of its confines at the
mouth of the valley, slowed a little, as if it had spent itself, then picked up strength
again and plunged into the ocean. Days when Sol and Bonnie were gone, Myers
sat in the sun in a lawn chair out back and looked up the valley toward the peaks.
Once he saw an eagle soaring down the valley, and on another occasion he saw a
deer picking its way along the riverbank.

He was sitting out there like that one afternoon when a big flatbed truck 83
pulled up in the drive with a load of wood.

You must be Sol's roomer, the driver of the truck said. He was talking out the 84
truck window.

Myers nodded. 85

Sol said to just dump this wood in the backyard and he'd take care of it from 86
there, the driver said.

I'll move out of your way, Myers said. He took the chair and moved to the 87
back step, where he stood and watched the driver of the truck back it up onto the
lawn, then push something inside the cab until the truck bed began to elevate. In
a minute, the six-foot logs began to slide off the truck bed and pile up on the
ground. The bed rose even higher, and all of the logs rolled with a loud bang
down onto the lawn.

The driver touched the lever again and the truck bed went back to its normal 88
place. Then the driver revved his engine, honked, and drove away.

What are you going to do with that wood out there? Myers asked Sol that night. 89
Sol was standing at the stove frying smelt when Myers surprised him by coming into the kitchen. Bonnie was in the shower—Myers could hear the water
running.

Why, I'm going to saw it up and stack it, if I can find the time between now 90
and September. I'd like to do it before the rain starts.

Maybe I could do it for you, Myers said. 91

You ever cut wood before? Sol said. He'd taken the frying pan off the stove and 92
was wiping the fingers of his left hand with a paper towel.

I couldn't pay you anything for doing it, Sol said. It's something I was going to 93
do anyway. Just as soon as I get a weekend to my name.

I'll do it, Myers said. I can use the exercise. 94

You know how to use a power saw? And an ax and an awl? 95

You can show me, Myers said. I learn fast. It was important to him that he cut 96
the wood.

Sol put the pan of smelt back on the burner. Then he said, Okay, I'll show you 97
after supper. You had anything to eat yet? Why don't you have a bite to eat with us?

I ate something already, Myers said. 98

Sol nodded. Let me get this grub on the table for Bonnie and me then, and af- 99
ter we eat I'll show you.

I'll be out back, Myers said. 100

Sol didn't say anything more. He nodded to himself, as if he was thinking 101
about something else.

Myers took one of the folding chairs that was out back and sat down on it. He 102
looked at the pile of wood and then up the valley at the mountain peaks that had
the sun shining off the snow. It was nearly evening. The tops of the mountains
thrust up into some clouds. Mist seemed to be falling from the clouds. He could
hear the river crashing through the undergrowth down in the valley.

I heard talking, Myers overheard Bonnie say to Sol in the kitchen. 103

It's the roomer, Sol said. He asked me if he could cut up that load of wood 104
out back.

How much does he want to do it? Bonnie wanted to know. Did you tell him 105
we can't pay much?

I told him we can't pay anything. He wants to do it for nothing. That's what he 106
said, anyway.

Nothing? She didn't say anything for a time. Then Myers heard her say, I guess 107
he doesn't have anything else to do.

Later, Sol came outside and said, I guess we can get started now, if you're 108
still game.

Myers got up out of the lawn chair and followed Sol over to the garage. Sol 109
brought out two sawhorses and set them up on the lawn. Then he brought out a
power saw. The sun had dropped behind the town. In another thirty minutes it
would be dark. Myers rolled down the sleeves of his shirt and buttoned the cuffs.
Sol worked without saying anything. He grunted as he lifted one of the six-foot
logs and positioned it on the sawhorses. Then he began to use the saw, working
steadily for a while. Sawdust flew. Finally he stopped sawing and stepped back.

You get the idea, he said. 110

Myers took the saw and nosed the blade into a length where Sol had left off. 111
He found a rhythm and stayed with it. He kept pressing, leaning into the saw. In
a few minutes, he had sawed through several logs, which dropped in sections onto
the ground.

That's the idea, Sol said. You'll do, he said. He picked up two blocks of wood, 112
carried them over, and put them alongside the garage.

Every so often—not every piece of wood, but maybe every fifth or sixth 113
piece—you'll want to split it with the ax down the middle, Sol said. Don't worry
about making kindling—I'll take care of that later. Just split about every fifth or
sixth chunk. I'll show you. He propped the chunk up and, with a blow of the ax,
split the wood into two pieces. You try it now, he said.

Myers stood the block on its end, just as Sol had done, and he brought the ax 114 down and split the wood.

That's good, Sol said. He placed the chunks of wood alongside the garage. 115 Stack them up about so high, and then come out this way with your stack. I'll lay some plastic sheeting over it once it's all finished. But you don't have to do this, you know.

It's all right, Myers said. I want to, or I wouldn't have asked. 116

Sol shrugged. Then he turned and went back to the house. Bonnie was stand- 117 ing in the doorway, watching, and Sol stopped in the doorway, too, reached his arm around Bonnie, and they both looked at Myers.

Myers picked up the saw and looked at them. He felt good suddenly, and he 118 grinned. Sol and Bonnie were taken by surprise at first. Sol grinned back, and then Bonnie. Then she and Sol went back inside.

Myers put another piece of wood on the sawhorses and worked awhile, saw- 119 ing, until the sweat on his forehead began to feel chill and the sun had gone down. The porch light came on. Myers kept on working until he'd finished the piece he was on. He carried the two pieces over to the garage and then he went in, used his bathroom to wash up, then sat at the table in his room and wrote in his notebook. *I have sawdust in my shirt sleeves tonight,* he wrote. *It's a sweet smell.*

That night he lay awake for a long time. Once he got out of bed and looked 120 out the window at the mound of wood which lay in the backyard, and then his eyes were drawn up the valley to the mountains. The moon was partially obscured by clouds, but he could see the peaks and the white snow, and when he raised his window, the sweet, cool air poured in, and farther off he could hear the river coursing down the valley.

The next morning it was all he could do to wait until they'd left the house be- 121 fore he went out back to begin work. He found a pair of gloves on the back step that Sol must have left for him. He started up the saw and went back and forth sawing and splitting wood until the sun was directly over his head. Then he went inside and ate a sandwich and drank some milk.

When he went back outside and began again, he noticed that his shoulders 122 hurt and his fingers were sore. In spite of the gloves, he'd picked up a few splin-ters and could feel blisters rising, but he kept on. He decided that he would cut this wood and split it and stack it before sunset, and that it was a matter of life and death that he do so. I must finish this job, he thought, or else . . . He stopped to wipe his sleeve over his face.

By the time Sol and Bonnie came in from work that night—first Bonnie, as 123 usual, and then Sol—Myers was nearly through. A thick pile of sawdust lay be-tween the sawhorses, and, except for two or three blocks of wood still in the yard, all of the wood lay stacked in tiers against the garage. Sol and Bonnie stood in the doorway without saying anything. Myers looked up from his work for a minute and nodded, and Sol nodded back. Bonnie just stood there looking, breathing through her mouth. Myers kept on.

Sol and Bonnie went back inside and began their supper. Afterwards, Sol 124 turned on the porch light, as he'd done the evening before. Just as the sun went down and the moon appeared over the mountains, Myers split the last chunk and gathered up the two pieces and carried the wood over to the garage. He put away the sawhorses, the power saw, the ax, a steel splitting wedge, and the awl. Then he went inside.

Sol and Bonnie sat still at their table, but they hadn't begun on their food.   125

You better sit down and eat with us, Sol said.   126

Sit down, Bonnie said.   127

I'm not hungry just yet, Myers said.   128

Sol didn't say anything. He nodded. Bonnie waited a minute and then reached   129
for a platter.

You got it all, I'll bet, Sol said.   130

Myers said, I'll clean up that sawdust tomorrow.   131

Sol moved his knife back and forth over his plate as if to say, Forget it.   132

I'll be leaving in a day or two, Myers said.   133

Somehow I figured you would be, Sol said. I don't know why I felt that, but I   134
didn't think somehow when you moved in you'd be here all that long.

No refunds on the rent, Bonnie said.   135

Hey, Bonnie, Sol said.   136

It's okay, Myers said.   137

No, it isn't, Sol said.   138

It's all right, Myers said. He opened the door to the bathroom, stepped inside,   139
then shut the door. As he ran water into the sink he could hear them talking out there, but he couldn't hear what they were saying.

He showered, washed his hair, and put on clean clothes. He looked at the   140
things of his in the room that had come out of his suitcase just a few days ago, a week ago, and figured it would take him about ten minutes to pack up and be gone. He could hear the TV start up on the other side of the house. He went to the window and raised it and looked again at the mountains, with the moon lying over them—no clouds now, just the moon, and the snowcapped mountains. He looked at the pile of sawdust out in back and at the wood stacked against the shadowy recesses of the garage. He listened to the river for a while. Then he went over to the table and sat down and opened the notebook and began to write.

The country I'm in is very exotic. It reminds me of someplace I've read about but   141
never traveled to before now. Outside my window I can hear a river of fast-moving water, and in the valley behind the house there is a forest and precipices and mountain peaks covered with snow. Today I saw a wild eagle, and a deer, and I cut and chopped two cords of wood.

Then he put the pen down and held his head in his hands for a moment. Pretty   142
soon he got up and undressed and turned off the light. After he'd gotten into bed he realized he'd left the window open. But he didn't get up. It was okay like that.

ACTIVITIES FOR WRITING AND DISCUSSION

1. Interpret the phrase "between lives" in the opening sentence. What is the "old" life Myers has left? the "new" life he is attempting to find? If you have ever been "between lives" yourself, describe the experience.

2. As specifically as you can, describe your first impressions of Myers, Sol, and Bonnie. As you continue and finish reading the story, how or in what ways are these first impressions confirmed or rejected?

3. Character is revealed in even the smallest details. For example, what does Myers's handling of his suitcase during his first conversation with Sol and Bonnie suggest to you about Myers or about his emerging relationship with his new landlords? Identify and comment on any other similarly small but telling details you find in the story.

4. Paragraph #96 states, "It was important to [Myers] that he cut the wood." Why was it important? Describe the effect the work has on Myers. Then compose an imaginary interview between yourself and Raymond Carver in which Carver explains the thematic significance of work in his story.

ALLAN GURGANUS (b. 1947)

He's at the Office

Till the Japanese bombed Pearl Harbor, most American men wore hats to work. 1 What happened? Did our guys—suddenly scouting overhead for worse Sunday raids—come to fear their hat brims' interference? My unsuspecting father wore his till yesterday. He owned three. A gray, a brown, and a summer straw one, whose maroon-striped rayon band could only have been woven in America in the 1940s.

Last month, I lured him from his self-imposed office hours for a walk around 2 our block. My father insisted on bringing his briefcase. "You never know," he said. We soon passed a huge young hipster, creaking in black leather. The kid's pierced face flashed more silver than most bait shops sell. His jeans, half down, exposed hat racks of white hipbone; the haircut arched high over jug ears. He was scouting Father's shoes. Long before fashion joined him, Dad favored an under-evolved antique form of orthopedic Doc Martens. These impressed a punk now scanning the Sherman tank of a cowhide briefcase with chromium corner braces. The camel-hair overcoat was cut to resemble some boxy-backed 1947 Packard. And, of course, up top sat "the gray."

Pointing to it, the boy smiled. "Way bad look on you, guy." 3

My father, seeking interpretation, stared at me. I simply shook my head no. 4 I could not explain Dad to himself in terms of tidal fashion trends. All I said was "I think he likes you."

Dad's face folded. "Uh-oh." 5

By the end, my father, the fifty-two-year veteran of Integrity Office Supplier, 6 Unlimited, had become quite cool again, way.

We couldn't vacation for more than three full days. He'd veer our Plymouth to-   7
ward some way-station pay phone. We soon laughed as Dad, in the glass booth,
commenced to wave his arms, shake his head, shift his weight from foot to foot.
We knew Miss Green must be telling him of botched orders, delivery mistakes.
We were nearly to Gettysburg. I'd been studying battle maps. Now I knew we'd
never make it.

My father bounded back to the car and smiled in. "Terrible mixup with the   8
Wilmington school system's carbon paper for next year. Major goof, but typical.
Guy's got to do it all himself. Young Green didn't insist I come back, but she sure
hinted."

We U-turned southward, and my father briefly became the most charming   9
man on earth. He now seemed to be selling something we needed, whatever we
needed. Traveling north into a holiday—the very curse of leisure—he had kept
as silent as some fellow with toothaches. Now he was our tour guide, interviewing us, telling and retelling his joke. Passing a cemetery, he said (over his family's
dry carbon-paper unison), "I hear they're dying to get in there!" "Look on the
bright side," I told myself: "we'll arrive home and escape him as he runs—literally runs—to the office."

Dad was, like me, an early riser. Six days a week, Mom sealed his single-   10
sandwich lunch into its Tupperware jacket; this fit accidentally yet exactly within
the lid compartment of his durable briefcase. He would then pull on his overcoat—
bulky, war-efficient, strong-seamed, four buttons as big as silver dollars and
carved from actual shell. He'd place the cake-sized hat in place, nod in our general direction, and set off hurrying. Dad faced each day as one more worthy enemy. If he had been Dwight Eisenhower saving the Western world, or Jonas Salk
freeing kids our age from crutches, okay. But yellow Eagle pencils? Utility paper-
weights in park-bench green?

Once a year, Mom told my brother and me how much the war had darkened   11
her young husband; he'd enlisted with three other guys from Falls; he alone came
back alive with all his limbs. "Before that," she smiled, "your father was funnier,
funny. And smarter. Great dancer. You can't blame mustard gas, not this time. It's
more what Dick saw. He came home and he was all business. Before that, he'd
been mischievous and talkative and strange. He was always playing around with
words. Very entertaining. Eyelashes out to here. For years, I figured that in time
he'd come back to being whole. But since June of forty-five it's been All Work and
No Play Makes Jack."

Mom remembered their fourth anniversary. "I hired an overnight sitter for   12
you two. We drove to an inn near Asheville. It had the state's best restaurant, candlelight, a real string quartet. I'd made myself a green velvet dress. I was twenty-
eight and never in my whole life have I ever looked better. You just know it. Dick
recognized some man who'd bought two adding machines. Dick invited him to
join us. Then I saw how much his work was going to have to mean to him. Don't
be too hard on him, please. He feeds us, he puts aside real savings for you boys'
college. Dick pays our taxes. Dick has no secrets. He's not hurting anyone."

Brother and I gave each other a look Mom recognized and understood but refused to return.

The office seemed to tap some part of him that was either off limits to us or simply did not otherwise exist. My brother and I griped that he'd never attended our Little League games (not that we ever made the starting lineup). He missed our father-son Cub Scout banquet; it conflicted with a major envelope convention in Newport News. Mother neutrally said he loved us as much as he could. She was a funny, energetic person—all that wasted good will. And even as kids, we knew not to blame her.

Ignored, Mom created a small sewing room. Economizing needlessly, she stayed busy stitching all our school clothes, cowboy motifs galore. For a while, each shirt pocket bristled with Mom-designed embroidered cacti. But Simplicity patterns were never going to engage a mind as complex as hers. Soon Mom was spending most mornings playing vicious duplicate bridge. Our toothbrush glasses briefly broke out in rashes of red hearts, black clubs. Mom's new pals were society ladies respectful of her brainy speed, her impenitent wit; she never bothered introducing them to her husband. She laughed more now. She started wearing rouge.

We lived a short walk from both our school and his wholesale office. Dad sometimes left the Plymouth parked all night outside the workplace, his desk lamp the last one burning on the whole third floor. Integrity's president, passing headquarters late, always fell for it. "Dick, what do you do up there all night, son?" My father's shrug became his finest boast. The raises kept pace; Integrity Office Supplier was still considered quite a comer. And R. Richard Markham, Sr.—as handsome as a collar ad, a hat ad, forever at the office—was the heir apparent.

Dad's was Integrity's flagship office: "Maker of World's Highest Quality Clerical Supplies." No other schoolboys had sturdier pastel subject dividers, more clip-in see-through three-ring pen caddies. The night before school started, Dad would be up late at our kitchen table, swilling coffee, "getting you boys set." Zippered leather cases, English slide rules, folders more suitable for treaties than for book reports ("*Skipper, A Dog of the Pyrenees,* by Marjorie Hopgood Purling"). Our notebooks soon proved too heavy to carry far; we secretly stripped them, swapping gear for lunchbox treats more exotic than Mom's hard-boiled eggs and Sun-Maid raisin packs.

Twenty years ago, Dad's Integrity got bought out by a German firm. The business's vitality proved somewhat hobbled by computers' onslaught. "A fad," my father called computers in 1976. "Let others retool. We'll stand firm with our yellow legals, erasers, Parker ink, fountain pens. Don't worry, our regulars'll come back. True vision always lets you act kind in the end, boys. Remember."

Yeah, right.

My father postponed his retirement. Mom encouraged that and felt relieved; she could not imagine him at home all day. As Integrity's market share dwindled,

Dad spent more time at the office, as if to compensate with his own body for the course of modern life.

His secretary, the admired Miss Green, had once been what Pop still called "some-   20
thing of a bombshell." (He stuck with a Second World War terminology that had, like the hat, served him too well ever to leave behind.)

Still favoring shoulder pads, dressed in unyielding woolen Joan Crawford   21
solids, Green wore an auburn pageboy that looked burned by decades of ungrateful dyes. She kicked off her shoes beneath her desk, revealing feet that told the tale
of high heels' worthless weekday brutality. She'd quit college to tend an ailing
mother, who proved demanding, then immortal. Brother and I teased Mom:
poor Green appeared to worship her longtime boss, a guy whose face was as
smooth and wedged and classic as his hat. Into Dick Markham's blunted constancy she read actual "moods."

He still viewed Green, now past sixty, as a promising virginal girl. In their   22
small adjoining offices, these two thrived within a fond impersonality that permeated the ads of the period.

Integrity's flagship headquarters remained enameled a flavorless mint green,   23
unaltered for five decades. The dark Mission coatrack was made by Limbert—
quite a good piece. One ashtray—upright, floor model, brushed chromium—
proved the size and shape of some landlocked torpedo. Moored to walls, dented
metal desks were as gray as battleships. A series of forest green filing cabinets
seemed banished, as patient as a family of trolls, to one shaming little closet all
their own. Dad's office might've been decorated by a firm called Edward Hopper &
Sam Spade, Unlimited.

For more than half a century, he walked in each day at seven-oh-nine sharp,   24
as Miss Green forever said, "Morning, Mr. Markham. I left your appointments
written on your desk pad, can I get you your coffee? Is now good, sir?" And Dad
said, "Yes, why, thanks, Miss Green, how's your mother, don't mind if I do."

Four years ago, I received a panicked phone call: "You the junior to a guy about   25
eighty, guy in a hat?"

"Probably." I was working at home. I pressed my computer's "Save" function.   26
This, I sensed, might take a while. "Save."

"Exit? No? Yes?"   27

"Yes."   28

"Mister, your dad thinks we're camped out in his office and he's been banging   29
against our door. He's convinced we've evicted his files and what he calls his
Green. 'What have you done with young Green?' Get down here A.S.A.P. Get him
out of our hair or it's nine-one-one in three minutes, swear to God."

From my car, I phoned home. Mom must have been off somewhere playing   30
bridge with the mayor's blond wife and his blond ex-wife; they'd sensibly become
excellent friends. The best women are the best people on earth; and the worst men

the very worst. Mother, overlooked by Dad for years, had continued finding what she called "certain outlets."

When I arrived, Dad was still heaving himself against an office door, deadbolt- 31 locked from within. Since its upper panel was frosted glass, I could make out the colors of the clothes of three or four people pressing from their side. They'd used masking tape to crosshatch the glass, as if bracing for a hurricane. The old man held his briefcase, wore his gray hat, the tan boxy coat.

"Dad?" He stopped with a mechanical cartoon verve, jumped my way, and 32 smiled so hard it warmed my heart and scared me witless. My father had never acted so glad to see me—not when I graduated summa cum laude, not at my wedding, not after the birth of my son—and I felt joy in the presence of such joy from him.

"Reinforcements. Good man. We've got quite a hostage situation here. Let's 33 put our shoulders to it, shall we?"

"Dad?" I grabbed the padded shoulders of his overcoat. These crumpled to 34 reveal a man far sketchier hiding in there somewhere—a guy only twenty years from a hundred, after all.

"Dad? Dad. We have a good-news, bad-news setup here today. It's this. You 35 found the right building, Dad. Wrong floor."

I led him back to the clattering, oil-smelling elevator. I thought to return, tap 36 on the barricaded door, explain. But, in time, hey, they'd peek, they'd figure out the coast was clear. That they hadn't recognized him, after his fifty-two years of long days in this very building, said something. New people, everywhere.

I saw at once that Miss Green had been crying. Her face was caked with so 37 much powder it looked like calamine. "Little mixup," I said.

"Mr. Markham? We got three calls about those gum erasers," she said, faking 38 a frontal normality. "I think they're putting sawdust in them these days, sir. They leave skid marks, apparently. I put the information on your desk. With your day's appointments. Like your coffee? Like it now? Sir?"

I hung his hat on the hat tree; I slid his coat onto its one wooden Deco hanger 39 that could, at any flea market today, bring thirty-five dollars easy, two tones of wood, inlaid.

I wanted to have a heart-to-heart. I was so disoriented as to feel half-sane my- 40 self. But I overheard Father already returning his calls. He ignored me, and that seemed, within this radically altered gravitational field, a good sign. I sneaked back to Miss Green's desk, and admitted, "I'll need to call his doctor. I want him seen today, Miss Green. He was up on four, trying to get into that new headhunting service. He told them his name. Mom was out. So they, clever, looked him up in the book and found his junior and phoned me to come help."

She sat forward, strenuously feigning surprise. She looked rigid, chained to 41 this metal desk by both gnarled feet. "How long?" I somehow knew to ask.

Green appeared ecstatic, then relieved, then, suddenly, happily weeping, tears 42 pouring down—small tears, lopsided, mascaraed grit. She blinked up at me with a spaniel's gratitude. Suddenly, if slowly, I began to understand. In mere seconds, she had caved about Dad's years-long caving-in. It was my turn now.

Miss Green now whispered certain of his mistakes. There were forgotten   43
parking tickets by the dozen. There was his attempt to purchase a lake house on
land already flooded for a dam. Quietly, she admitted years of covering.

From her purse, she lifted a page covered in Dad's stern Germanic cursive,   44
blue ink fighting to stay isometrically between red lines.

"I found this one last week." Green's voice seemed steadied by the joy of hav-   45
ing told. "I fear this is about the worst, to date, we've been."

If they say "Hot enough for you?," it means recent weather. "Yes indeed" still   46
a good comeback. Order forms pink. Requisition yellow. Miss green's birthday June 12. She work with you fifty-one years. Is still unmarried. Mother now
dead, since '76, so stop asking about Mother, health of. Home address, 712
Marigold Street: Left at Oak, can always walk there. After last week, never go
near car again. Unfair to others. Take second left at biggest tree. Your new
Butcher's name is: Al. Wife: Betty. Sons: Matthew and Dick Junior. Grandson
Richie (your name with a III added on it). List of credit cards, licnse etc. below in case you lose walet agn, you big dope. Put copies somewhere safe, 3
places, write down, hide many. You are 80, yes, eighty.

And yet, as we now eavesdropped, Dick Markham dealt with a complaining   47
customer. He sounded practiced, jokey, conversant, exact.

"Dad, you have an unexpected doctor's appointment." I handed Dad his hat.   48
I'd phoned our family physician from Miss Green's extension.

For once, they were ready for us. The nurses kept calling him by name, smil-   49
ing, overinsistent, as if hinting at answers for a kid about to take his make-or-
break college exam. I could see they'd always liked him. In a town this small,
they'd maybe heard about his trouble earlier today.

As Dad got ushered in for tests, he glowered accusations back at me as if I had   50
just dragged him to a Nazi medical experiment. He finally reemerged, scarily pale,
pressing a bit of gauze into the crook of his bare arm, its long veins the exact blue
of Parker's washable ink. They directed him toward the lobby bathroom. They
gave him a cup for his urine specimen. He held it before him with two hands like
some Magus's treasure.

His hat, briefcase, and overcoat remained behind, resting on an orange plas-   51
tic chair all their own. Toward these I could display a permissible tenderness. I
lightly set my hand on each item. Call it superstition. I now lifted the hat and
sniffed it. It smelled like Dad. It smelled like rope. Physical intimacy has never
been a possibility. My brother and I, half-drunk, once tried to picture the im-
probable, the sexual conjunction of our parents. Brother said, "Well, he probably
pretends he's at the office, unsealing her like a good manila envelope that requires
a rubber stamp—legible, yes, keep it legible, *legible,* now speed-mail!"

I had flipped through four stale magazines before I saw the nurses peeking   52
from their crudely cut window. "He has been quite a while, Mr. Markham. Going on thirty minutes."

"Shall I?" I rose and knocked. No answer. "Would you come stand behind 53 me?" Cowardly, I signaled to an older nurse.

The door proved unlocked. I opened it. I saw one old man aimed the other 54 way and trembling with hesitation. Before him, a white toilet, a white sink, and a white enamel trash can, the three aligned—each its own insistent invitation. In one hand, the old man held an empty specimen cup. In the other hand, his dick.

Turning my way, grateful, unashamed to be caught sobbing, he cried, "Which 55 one, son? Fill which one?"

Forcibly retired, my father lived at home in his pajamas. Mom made him wear 56 the slippers and robe to help with his morale. "Think *Thin Man*. Think William Powell." But the poor guy literally hung his head with shame. That phrase took on new meaning now that his routine and dignity proved so reduced. Dad's mopey presence clogged every outlet she'd perfected to avoid him. The two of them were driving each other crazy.

Lacking the cash for live-in help, she was forced to cut way back on her bridge 57 game and female company. She lost ten pounds—it showed in her neck and face—and then she gave up rouge. You could see Mom missed her fancy friends. I soon pitied her nearly as much as I pitied him—no, more. At least he allowed himself to be distracted. She couldn't forget.

Mom kept urging him to get dressed. She said they needed to go to the zoo. 58 She had to get out and "do" something. One morning, she was trying to force Dad into his dress pants when he struck her. She fell right over the back of an armchair. The whole left side of her head stayed a rubber-stamp pad's blue-black for one whole week. Odd, this made it easier for both of them to stay home. Now two people hung their heads in shame.

At a window overlooking the busy street, Dad would stand staring out, one 59 way. On the window glass, his forehead left a persistent oval of human oil. His pajama knees pressed against the radiator. He silently second-guessed parallel parkers. He studied westerly-moving traffic. Sometimes he'd stand guard there for six uninterrupted hours. Did he await some detained patriotic parade? I pictured poor Green on a passing float—hoisting his coffee mug and the black phone receiver, waving him back down to street level, reality, use.

One December morning, Mom—library book in lap, trying to reinterest her- 60 self in Daphne du Maurier, in anything—smelled scorching. Like Campbell's mushroom soup left far too long on simmer. Twice she checked their stove and toaster oven. Finally, around his nap time, she pulled Dad away from the radiator: his shins had cooked. "Didn't it hurt you, Dick? Darling, didn't you ever feel anything?"

Next morning at six-thirty, I got her call. Mom's husky tone sounded too jolly 61 for the hour. She described bandaging both legs. "As you kids say, I don't think this is working for us. This might be beyond me. Integrity's fleabag insurance won't provide him with that good a home. We have just enough to go on living here as usual. Now, I'll maybe shock you and you might find me weak or, worse, disloyal. But would you consider someday checking out some nice retreats or facilities in driving distance? Even if it uses up the savings. Your father is the love of my life—one per customer. I just hate to get any more afraid of him!"

I said I'd phone all good local places, adding, giddy, "I hear they're dying to 62 get in there."

This drew a silence as cold as his. "Your dad's been home from the office— 63 what, seven months? Most men lean toward their leisure years, but who ever hated leisure more than Dick? When I think of everything he gave Integrity and how little he's getting back . . . I'm not strong enough to *keep* him, but I can't bear to *put* him anywhere. Still, at this rate, all I'll want for Christmas is a nice white padded cell for two."

I wished my mother belonged to our generation, where the women work. She 64 could've done anything. And now to be saddled with a man who'd known nothing but enslavement to one so-so office. The workaholic, tabled. He still refused to dress; she focused on the sight of his pajamas. My folks now argued with the energy of newlyweds; then she felt ashamed of herself and he forgot to do whatever he'd just promised.

On Christmas Eve, she was determined to put up a tree for him. But Dad, 65 somehow frightened by the ladder and all the unfamiliar boxes everywhere, got her into such a lethal headlock she had to scream for help. Now the neighbors were involved. People I barely knew interrupted my work hours, saying, "Something's got to be done. It took three of us to pull him off of her. He's still strong as a horse. It's getting dangerous over there. He could escape."

Sometimes, at two in the morning, she'd find him standing in their closet, 66 wearing his p.j.s and the season's correct hat. He'd be looking at his business suits. The right hand would be filing, "walking," back and forth across creased pant legs, as if seeking the . . . exact . . . right . . . pair . . . for . . . the office . . . today.

I tried to keep Miss Green informed. She'd sold her duplex and moved into our 67 town's most stylish old-age home. When she swept downstairs to greet me, I didn't recognize her. "God, you look fifteen years younger." I checked her smile for hints of a possible lift.

She just laughed, giving her torso one mild shimmy. "Look, Ma. No shoulder 68 pads."

Her forties hairdo, with its banked, rolled edges, had softened into pretty little 69 curls around her face. She'd let its color go her natural silvery blond. Green gave me a slow look. If I didn't know her better, I'd have sworn she was flirting.

She appeared shorter in flats. I now understood: her toes had been so mangled 70 by wearing those forties Quonset-huts of high heels, ones she'd probably owned since age eighteen. Her feet had grown, but she'd stayed true to the old shoes, part of some illusion she felt my dad required.

Others in the lobby perked up at her fond greeting; I saw she'd already become 71 the belle of this place. She let me admire her updated charms.

"No." She smiled simply. "It's that I tried to keep it all somewhat familiar for 72 him. How I looked and all. We got to where Mr. Markham found any change a kind of danger, so . . . I mean, it wasn't as if a dozen other suitors were beating down my door. What with Mother being moody and sick that long. And so, day to day, well . . ." She shrugged.

Now, in my life I've had very few inspired ideas. Much of me, like Pop, is help- 73 lessly a company man. So forgive my boasting of this.

Leaving Miss Green's, I stopped by a huge Salvation Army store. It was a good 74 one. Over the years, I've found a few fine Federal side chairs here and many a great tweed jacket. Browsing through the used-furniture room, I wandered beneath a cardboard placard hand-lettered "The World of Early American." Ladder-back deacon's chairs and plaid upholstered things rested knee to knee, like sad and separate families.

I chanced to notice a homeless man, asleep, a toothless white fellow. His over- 75 coat looked filthy. His belongings were bunched around him in six rubber-banded shoeboxes. His feet, in paint-stained shoes, rested on an ordinary school administrator's putty-colored desk. "The Wonderful World of Work" hung over hand-me-down waiting rooms still waiting. Business furniture sat parlored— forlorn as any gray-green Irish wake. There was something about the sight of this old guy's midday snoring in so safe a fluorescent make-work cubicle.

Mom now used her sewing room only for those few overnight third cousins 76 willing to endure its lumpy foldout couch. The room had become a catchall, cold storage, since about 1970. We waited for Dad's longest nap of the day. Then, in a crazed burst of energy, we cleared her lair, purging it of boxes, photo albums, four unused exercise machines. I paint-rolled its walls in record time, the ugliest latex junior-high-school green that Sherwin-Williams sells (there's still quite a range). The Salvation Army delivers: within two days, I had arranged this new-used-junk to resemble Integrity's workspace, familiarly anonymous. A gray desk nuzzled one wall—the window wasted behind. Three green file cabinets made a glum herd. One swivel wooden chair rode squeaky casters. The hat rack antlered upright over a dented tin wastebasket. The ashtray looked big enough to serve an entire cancer ward. Wire shelves predicted a neutral "in," a far more optimistic "out." I stuffed desk drawers with Parker ink, cheap fountain pens, yellow legal pads, four dozen paper clips. I'd bought a big black rotary phone, and Mom got him his own line.

Against her wishes, I'd saved most of Dad's old account ledgers. Yellowed al- 77 ready, they could've come from a barrister's desk in a Dickens novel. I scattered "1959–62." In one corner I piled all Dad's boxed records, back taxes, old Christmas cards from customers. The man saved everything.

The evening before we planned introducing him to his new quarters, I dis- 78 arranged the place a bit. I tossed a dozen pages on the floor near his chair. I left the desk lamp lit all night. It gave this small room a strange hot smell, overworked. The lamp was made of nubbly brown cast metal (recast war surplus?), its red button indicating "on." Black meant "off."

That morning I was there to help him dress. Mom made us a hearty oatmeal 79 breakfast, packed his lunch, and snapped the Tupperware insert into his briefcase.

"And where am *I* going?" he asked us in a dead voice.   80

"To the office," I said. "Where else do you go this time of day?"   81

He appeared sour, puffy, skeptical. Soon as I could, I glanced at Mom. This   82
was not going to be as easy as we'd hoped.

I got Dad's coat and hat. He looked gray and dubious. He would never believe   83
in this new space if I simply squired him down the hall to it. So, after handing him
his briefcase, I led Dad back along our corridor and out onto the street.

Some of the old-timers, recognizing him, called, "Looking good, Mr.   84
Markham," or "Cold enough for you?" Arm in arm, we nodded past them.

My grammar school had been one block from his office. Forty years back,   85
we'd set out on foot like this together. The nearer Dad drew to Integrity, the live-
lier he became; the closer I got to school, the more withdrawn I acted. But today
I kept up a mindless overplentiful patter. My tone neither cheered nor deflected
him. One block before his office building, I swerved back down an alley toward
the house. As we approached, I saw that Mom had been imaginative enough to
leave our front door wide open. She'd removed a bird print that had hung in our
foyer hall unloved forever. A mere shape, it still always marked this as our hall,
our home.

"*Here* we are!" I threw open his office door. I took his hat and placed it on its   86
hook. I helped him free of his coat. Just as his face had grown bored, then irked,
and finally enraged at our deception, the phone rang. From where I stood—half
in the office, half in the hall—I could see Mom holding the white phone in the
kitchen.

My father paused—since when did he answer the phone?—and, finally,   87
flushed, reached for it himself. "Dick?" Mom said. "You'll hate me, I'm getting so
absentminded. But you did take your lunch along today, right? I mean, go check.
Be patient with me, okay?" Phone cradled between his head and shoulder, he
lifted his briefcase and snapped it open—his efficiency still water-clear, and scary.
Dad then said to the receiver, "Lunch is definitely here, per usual. But, honey,
haven't I told you about these personal calls at the office?"

Then I saw him bend to pick up scattered pages. I saw him touch one yellow   88
legal pad and start to square all desktop pens at sharp right angles. As he pulled
the chair two inches forward I slowly shut his door behind me. Then Mother and
I, hidden in the kitchen, held each other and, not expecting it, cried, if very, very
silently.

When we peeked in two hours later, he was filing.

Every morning, Sundays included, Dad walked to the office. Even our ruse of   89
walking him around the block was relaxed. Mom simply set a straw hat atop him
(after Labor Day, she knew to switch to his gray). With his packed lunch, he would
stride nine paces from the kitchen table, step in, and pull the door shut, muttering complaints of overwork, no rest ever.

Dad spent a lot of time on the phone. Long-distance directory-assistance   90
charges constituted a large part of his monthly bill. But he "came home" for supper
with the weary sense of blurred accomplishment we recalled from olden times.

Once, having dinner with them, I asked Dad how he was. He sighed. "Well, 91
July is peak for getting their school supplies ordered. So the pressure is on. My
heart's not what it was, heart's not completely in it lately, I admit. They downsized
Green. Terrible loss to me. With its being crunch season, I get a certain shortness
of breath. Suppliers aren't where they were, the gear is often second-rate, little of
it any longer American-made. But you keep going, because it's what you know
and because your clients count on you. I may be beat, but, hey—it's still a job."

"Aha," I said. 92

Mom received a call on her own line. It was from some kindergarten owner. 93
Dad—plundering his old red address book—had somehow made himself a go-
between, arranging sales, but working freelance now. He appeared to be doing it
unsalaried, not for whole school systems but for small local outfits like day care
centers. This teacher had to let Mom know that he'd sent too much of the paste.
No invoice with it, a pallet of free jarred white school paste waiting out under the
swing sets. Whom to thank?

Once, I tiptoed in and saw a long list of figures he kept meaning to add up. I 94
noticed that, in his desperate daily fight to keep his desktop clear, he'd placed
seven separate five-inch piles of papers at evened intervals along the far wall. I
found such ankle-level filing sad till slowly I recognized a pattern—oh, yeah,
"The Pile System." It was my own technique for maintaining provisional emergency order, and one which I now rejudged to be quite sane.

Inked directly into the wooden bottom of his top desk drawer was this: 95

Check Green's sick leave ridic. long. Nazis still soundly defeated. Double enter 96
all new receipts, nincompoop. Yes, you . . . eighty-one. Old Woman roommate
is: "Betty."

Mom felt safe holding bridge parties at the house again, telling friends 97
that Dad was in there writing letters and doing paperwork, and who could say he
wasn't? Days, Mom could now shop or attend master-point tournaments at
good-driving-distance hotels. In her own little kitchen-corner office, she entered
bridge chat rooms, E-mailing game-theory arcana to well-known French and
Russian players. She'd regained some weight and her face was fuller, and prettier
for that. She bought herself a bottle-green velvet suit. "It's just a cheap Chanel
knockoff, but these ol' legs still ain't that bad, hmm?" She looked more rested
than I'd seen her in a year or two.

I cut a mail slot in Dad's office door, and around eleven Mom would slip in 98
his today's *Wall Street Journal.* You'd hear him fall upon it like a zoo animal, fed.

Since Dad had tried to break down the headhunters' door I hadn't dared go on 99
vacation myself. But Mother encouraged me to take my family to Hawaii. She
laughed. "Go ahead, enjoy yourself, for Pete's sake. Everything under control. I'm
playing what friends swear is my best bridge ever, and Dick's sure working good
long hours again. By now I should know the drill, huh?"

I was just getting into my bathing suit when the hotel phone rang. I could see 100
my wife and son down there on the white beach.

"Honey? Me. There's news about your father." 101

Mom's voice sounded vexed but contained. Her businesslike tone seemed as- 102
signed. It let me understand.

"When?" 103

"This afternoon around six-thirty our time. Maybe it happened earlier, I don't 104
know. I found him. First I convinced myself he was just asleep. But I guess, even
earlier, I knew."

I stood here against glass, on holiday. I pictured my father facedown at his 105
desk. The tie still perfectly knotted, his hat yet safe on its hook. I imagined Dad's
head at rest atop those forty pages of figures he kept meaning to add up.

I told Mom I was sorry; I said we'd fly right back. 106

"No, please," she said. "I've put everything off till next week. It's just us now. 107
Why hurry? And, son? Along with the bad news, I think there's something good.
He died at the office."

ACTIVITIES FOR WRITING AND DISCUSSION

1. The topics of "*work*" and "*family*" loom large in this story. Mr. Markham
is a workaholic whose needs and habits significantly affect his wife and sons.
Write about the interrelationship of work and family as depicted in the story or
as you have experienced it in your own life (as a son, daughter, parent, spouse ...).

2. Trace the evolution of Miss Green, who served as Markham's reliable office
assistant for over half a century. What sort of relationship (professional and emotional) did she have with her boss? How do her own last years (as revealed to us)
and Markham's differ? Then, writing in the character of Miss Green, narrate your
own life story.

3. Create a Topic/Form Grid (see Chapter 5) for the story. On the "topics"
axis list all the topics the story suggests to you (e.g., "work," "aging,"
"Alzheimer's"); on the "forms" axis list all the forms of writing you could use to
address those topics. Then, using your grid, compose a response of at least three
hundred words.

LORRIE MOORE (b. 1957)

How to Become a Writer

First, try to be something, anything, else. A movie star/astronaut. A movie 1
star/missionary. A movie star/kindergarten teacher. President of the World.
Fail miserably. It is best if you fail at an early age—say, fourteen. Early, critical

disillusionment is necessary so that at fifteen you can write long haiku sequences about thwarted desire. It is a pond, a cherry blossom, a wind brushing against sparrow wing leaving for mountain. Count the syllables. Show it to your mom. She is tough and practical. She has a son in Vietnam and a husband who may be having an affair. She believes in wearing brown because it hides spots. She'll look briefly at your writing, then back up at you with a face blank as a donut. She'll say: "How about emptying the dishwasher?" Look away. Shove the forks in the fork drawer. Accidentally break one of the freebie gas station glasses. This is the required pain and suffering. This is only for starters.

In your high school English class look only at Mr. Killian's face. Decide faces 2 are important. Write a villanelle about pores. Struggle. Write a sonnet. Count the syllables: nine, ten, eleven, thirteen. Decide to experiment with fiction. Here you don't have to count syllables. Write a short story about an elderly man and woman who accidentally shoot each other in the head, the result of an inexplicable malfunction of a shotgun which appears mysteriously in their living room one night. Give it to Mr. Killian as your final project. When you get it back, he has written on it: "Some of your images are quite nice, but you have no sense of plot." When you are home, in the privacy of your own room, faintly scrawl in pencil beneath his black-inked comments: "Plots are for dead people, pore-face."

Take all the babysitting jobs you can get. You are great with kids. They love 3 you. You tell them stories about old people who die idiot deaths. You sing them songs like "Blue Bells of Scotland," which is their favorite. And when they are in their pajamas and have finally stopped pinching each other, when they are fast asleep, you read every sex manual in the house, and wonder how on earth anyone could ever do those things with someone they truly loved. Fall asleep in a chair reading Mr. McMurphy's *Playboy*. When the McMurphys come home, they will tap you on the shoulder, look at the magazine in your lap, and grin. You will want to die. They will ask you if Tracey took her medicine all right. Explain, yes, she did, that you promised her a story if she would take it like a big girl and that seemed to work out just fine. "Oh, marvelous," they will exclaim.

Try to smile proudly.   4

Apply to college as a child psychology major.   5

As a child psychology major, you have some electives. You've always liked 6 birds. Sign up for something called "The Ornithological Field Trip." It meets Tuesdays and Thursdays at two. When you arrive at Room 134 on the first day of class, everyone is sitting around a seminar table talking about metaphors. You've heard of these. After a short, excruciating while, raise your hand and say diffidently, "Excuse me, isn't this Bird-watching One-oh-one?" The class stops and turns to look at you. They seem to all have one face—giant and blank as a vandalized clock. Someone with a beard booms out, "No, this is Creative Writing," Say: "Oh—right," as if perhaps you knew all along. Look down at your schedule. Wonder how the hell you ended up here. The computer, apparently, has made an error. You start to get up to leave and then don't. The lines at the registrar this week are huge. Perhaps you should stick with this mistake. Perhaps your creative writing isn't all that bad. Perhaps it is fate. Perhaps this is what your dad meant when he said, "It's the age of computers, Francie, it's the age of computers."

Decide that you like college life. In your dorm you meet many nice people. 7 Some are smarter than you. And some, you notice, are dumber than you. You will continue, unfortunately, to view the world in exactly these terms for the rest of your life.

The assignment this week in creative writing is to narrate a violent happening. 8 Turn in a story about driving with your Uncle Gordon and another one about two old people who are accidentally electrocuted when they go to turn on a badly wired desk lamp. The teacher will hand them back to you with comments: "Much of your writing is smooth and energetic. You have, however, a ludicrous notion of plot." Write another story about a man and a woman who, in the very first paragraph, have their lower torsos accidentally blitzed away by dynamite. In the second paragraph, with the insurance money, they buy a frozen yogurt stand together. There are six more paragraphs. You read the whole thing out loud in class. No one likes it. They say your sense of plot is outrageous and incompetent. After class someone asks you if you are crazy.

Decide that perhaps you should stick to comedies. Start dating someone who 9 is funny, someone who has what in high school you called a "really great sense of humor" and what now your creative writing class calls "self-contempt giving rise to comic form." Write down all of his jokes, but don't tell him you are doing this. Make up anagrams of his old girlfriend's name and name all of your socially handicapped characters with them. Tell him his old girlfriend is in all of your stories and then watch how funny he can be, see what a really great sense of humor he can have.

Your child psychology advisor tells you you are neglecting courses in your 10 major. What you spend the most time on should be what you're majoring in. Say yes, you understand.

In creative writing seminars over the next two years, everyone continues to 11 smoke cigarettes and ask the same things: "But does it work?" "Why should we care about this character?" "Have you earned this cliché?" These seem like important questions.

On days when it is your turn, you look at the class hopefully as they scour your 12 mimeographs for a plot. They look back up at you, drag deeply, and then smile in a sweet sort of way.

You spend too much time slouched and demoralized. Your boyfriend sug- 13 gests bicycling. Your roommate suggests a new boyfriend. You are said to be self-mutilating and losing weight, but you continue writing. The only happiness you have is writing something new, in the middle of the night, armpits damp, heart pounding, something no one has yet seen. You have only those brief, fragile, untested moments of exhilaration when you know: you are a genius. Understand what you must do. Switch majors. The kids in your nursery project will be disappointed, but you have a calling, an urge, a delusion, an unfortunate habit. You have, as your mother would say, fallen in with a bad crowd.

Why write? Where does writing come from? These are questions to ask your- 14 self. They are like: Where does dust come from? Or: Why is there war? Or: If there's a God, then why is my brother now a cripple?

These are questions that you keep in your wallet, like calling cards. These are 15 questions, your creative writing teacher says, that are good to address in your journals but rarely in your fiction.

The writing professor this fall is stressing the Power of the Imagination. 16 Which means he doesn't want long descriptive stories about your camping trip last July. He wants you to start in a realistic context but then to alter it. Like recombinant DNA. He wants you to let your imagination sail, to let it grow big-bellied in the wind. This is a quote from Shakespeare.

Tell your roommate your great idea, your great exercise of imaginative power: 17 a transformation of Melville to contemporary life. It will be about monomania and the fish-eat-fish world of life insurance in Rochester, New York. The first line will be "Call me Fishmeal," and it will feature a menopausal suburban husband named Richard, who because he is so depressed all the time is called "Mopey Dick" by his witty wife Elaine. Say to your roommate: "Mopey Dick, get it?" Your roommate looks at you, her face blank as a large Kleenex. She comes up to you, like a buddy, and puts an arm around your burdened shoulders. "Listen, Francie," she says, slow as speech therapy. "Let's go out and get a big beer."

The seminar doesn't like this one either. You suspect they are beginning to feel 18 sorry for you. They say: "You have to think about what is happening. Where is the story here?"

The next semester the writing professor is obsessed with writing from per- 19 sonal experience. You must write from what you know, from what has happened to you. He wants deaths, he wants camping trips. Think about what has happened to you. In three years there have been three things: you lost your virginity; your parents got divorced; and your brother came home from a forest ten miles from the Cambodian border with only half a thigh, a permanent smirk nestled into one corner of his mouth.

About the first you write: "It created a new space, which hurt and cried in a 20 voice that wasn't mine, 'I'm not the same anymore, but I'll be okay.'"

About the second you write an elaborate story of an old married couple who 21 stumble upon an unknown land mine in their kitchen and accidentally blow themselves up. You call it: "For Better or for Liverwurst."

About the last you write nothing. There are no words for this. Your typewriter 22
hums. You can find no words.

At undergraduate cocktail parties, people say, "Oh, you write? What do you 23
write about?" Your roommate, who has consumed too much wine, too little
cheese, and no crackers at all, blurts: "Oh, my god, she always writes about her
dumb boyfriend."

Later on in life you will learn that writers are merely open, helpless texts with 24
no real understanding of what they have written and therefore must half-believe
anything and everything that is said of them. You, however, have not yet reached
this stage of literary criticism. You stiffen and say, "I do not," the same way you
said it when someone in the fourth grade accused you of really liking oboe lessons
and your parents really weren't just making you take them.

Insist you are not very interested in any one subject at all, that you are inter- 25
ested in the music of language, that you are interested in—in—syllables, because
they are the atoms of poetry, the cells of the mind, the breath of the soul. Begin to
feel woozy. Stare into your plastic wine cup.

"Syllables?" you will hear someone ask, voice trailing off, as they glide slowly 26
toward the reassuring white of the dip.

Begin to wonder what you do write about. Or if you have anything to say. Or 27
if there even is such a thing as a thing to say. Limit these thoughts to no more than
ten minutes a day; like sit-ups, they can make you thin.

You will read somewhere that all writing has to do with one's genitals. Don't 28
dwell on this. It will make you nervous.

Your mother will come visit you. She will look at the circles under your eyes 29
and hand you a brown book with a brown briefcase on the cover. It is entitled:
How to Become a Business Executive. She has also brought the *Names for Baby* encyclopedia you asked for; one of your characters, the aging clown-school teacher,
needs a new name. Your mother will shake her head and say: "Francie, Francie,
remember when you were going to be a child psychology major?"

Say: "Mom, I like to write."   30
She'll say: "Sure you like to write. Of course. Sure you like to write."   31

Write a story about a confused music student and title it: "Schubert Was the 32
One with the Glasses, Right?" It's not a big hit, although your roommate likes the
part where the two violinists accidentally blow themselves up in a recital room. "I
went out with a violinist once," she says, snapping her gum.

Thank god you are taking other courses. You can find sanctuary in nineteenth- 33
century ontological snags and invertebrate courting rituals. Certain globular
mollusks have what is called "Sex by the Arm." The male octopus, for instance,
loses the end of one arm when placing it inside the female body during intercourse.
Marine biologists call it "Seven Heaven." Be glad you know these things. Be glad
you are not just a writer. Apply to law school.

From here on in, many things can happen. But the main one will be this: you 34
decide not to go to law school after all, and, instead, you spend a good, big chunk
of your adult life telling people how you decided not to go to law school after all.
Somehow you end up writing again. Perhaps you go to graduate school. Perhaps
you work odd jobs and take writing courses at night. Perhaps you are working on
a novel and writing down all the clever remarks and intimate personal confessions
you hear during the day. Perhaps you are losing your pals, your acquaintances,
your balance.

You have broken up with your boyfriend. You now go out with men who, in- 35
stead of whispering "I love you," shout: "Do it to me, baby." This is good for your
writing.

Sooner or later you have a finished manuscript more or less. People look at it 36
in a vaguely troubled sort of way and say, "I'll bet becoming a writer was always a
fantasy of yours, wasn't it?" Your lips dry to salt. Say that of all the fantasies possible in the world, you can't imagine being a writer even making the top twenty.
Tell them you were going to be a child psychology major. "I bet," they always sigh,
"you'd be great with kids." Scowl fiercely. Tell them you're a walking blade.

Quit classes. Quit jobs. Cash in old savings bonds. Now you have time like 37
warts on your hands. Slowly copy all of your friends' addresses into a new address book.

Vacuum. Chew cough drops. Keep a folder full of fragments. 38

An eyelid darkening sideways.
World as conspiracy.
Possible plot? A woman gets on a bus.
Suppose you threw a love affair and nobody came.

At home drink a lot of coffee. At Howard Johnson's order the cole slaw. Con- 39
sider how it looks like the soggy confetti of a map: where you've been, where
you're going—"You Are Here," says the red star on the back of the menu.

Occasionally a date with a face blank as a sheet of paper asks you whether writ- 40
ers often become discouraged. Say that sometimes they do and sometimes they
do. Say it's a lot like having polio.

"Interesting," smiles your date, and then he looks down at his arm hairs and 41
starts to smooth them, all, always, in the same direction.

ACTIVITIES FOR WRITING AND DISCUSSION

1. Why isn't the story formatted as one piece of *continuous* prose? What are
the advantages, if any, to the piece being organized as a series of short segments
separated by white spaces?

2. Moore writes in an unusual **point of view,** *second*-person. How is, or isn't, it appropriate to the story she tells? How would the effect of the story change if the persistent use of "you" were suppressed? Try recasting a part of the story in either the first or third person, and assess the result.

3. Compose a story or essay of your own, on a topic of your choice, with the second-person point of view.

4. Following Moore's example, write a "How to Become a ——————" piece on a topic of your own choice. Before you draft, brainstorm ideas to determine:
    a. Who your audience for the piece will be (e.g., a specific person or group of persons, some more general audience), and
    b. Whether your treatment will be comic (like Moore's) or serious.

———————————————————————————————————————

Poems

WILLIAM WORDSWORTH (1770–1850)

The World Is Too Much with Us

The world is too much with us; late and soon,
Getting and spending, we lay waste our powers:
Little we see in Nature that is ours;
We have given our hearts away, a sordid boon!
This Sea that bares her bosom to the moon;   5
The winds that will be howling at all hours,
And are up-gathered now like sleeping flowers;
For this, for every thing, we are out of tune;
It moves us not.—Great God! I'd rather be
A Pagan suckled in a creed outworn;   10
So might I, standing on this pleasant lea,
Have glimpses that would make me less forlorn;
Have sight of Proteus[1] rising from the sea;
Or hear old Triton[2] blow his wreathèd horn.

———————

1. In Greek mythology, an old man of the sea who was able to assume a variety of shapes.   2. A god of the sea, often depicted as blowing on a seashell.

John Keats (1795–1821)

When I have fears that I may cease to be

When I have fears that I may cease to be
   Before my pen has glean'd my teeming brain,
Before high piled books, in charactry,
   Hold like rich garners the full ripen'd grain;
When I behold, upon the night's starr'd face,   5
   Huge cloudy symbols of a high romance,
And think that I may never live to trace
   Their shadows, with the magic hand of chance;
And when I feel, fair creature of an hour,
   That I shall never look upon thee more,   10
Never have relish in the fairy power
   Of unreflecting love;—then on the shore
Of the wide world I stand alone, and think
Till love and fame to nothingness do sink.

Activities for Writing and Discussion

1. Read "When I have fears that I may cease to be" aloud with a partner or small group. Together, do a scansion of the poem, and map out its rhyme pattern (see pp. 167–169).

2. Postponing (for now) questions about meaning, reread the poem aloud once more, and concentrate on its sound effects. Mark or underline examples of **alliteration, assonance,** or **consonance.** Also note any images or phrases you find compelling or beautiful.

3. The aphorist Logan Pearsall Smith once wrote, "Sound is more than sense." What do you suppose he meant by this statement, and is Keats's poem a proof of it? Can a poem be pleasurable or beautiful even if you don't fully understand it? Why or why not, and if "yes," in what ways?

4. Keats was a poet who burned for love and fame and died young, at the age of twenty-five. Explain the logic of the poem. What sorts of thoughts would reduce "love and fame to nothingness" in the mind of a profoundly passionate and ambitious poet?

5. As this poem attests, Keats did not shy away from the Big Themes. Following his example, take the concerns and anxieties addressed in the poem and recast them in a prose format using present-day or modern language. For instance, write a meditation, a personal letter, or a series of journal entries ranging over issues of ambition, mortality, love, and fame or success.

WILLIAM BUTLER YEATS (1865–1939)

Adam's Curse

We sat together at one summer's end,
That beautiful mild woman, your close friend,
And you and I, and talked of poetry.
I said: "A line will take us hours maybe;
Yet if it does not seem a moment's thought,   5
Our stitching and unstitching has been naught.
Better go down upon your marrow-bones
And scrub a kitchen pavement, or break stones
Like an old pauper, in all kinds of weather;
For to articulate sweet sounds together   10
Is to work harder than all these, and yet
Be thought an idler by the noisy set
Of bankers, schoolmasters, and clergymen
The martyrs call the world."

                And thereupon   15
That beautiful mild woman for whose sake
There's many a one shall find out all heartache
On finding that her voice is sweet and low
Replied: "To be born woman is to know—
Although they do not talk of it at school—   20
That we must labour to be beautiful."

I said: "It's certain there is no fine thing
Since Adam's fall but needs much labouring.
There have been lovers who thought love should be
So much compounded of high courtesy   25
That they would sigh and quote with learned looks
Precedents out of beautiful old books;
Yet now it seems an idle trade enough."

We sat grown quiet at the name of love;
We saw the last embers of daylight die,   30
And in the trembling blue-green of the sky
A moon, worn as if it had been a shell
Washed by time's waters as they rose and fell
About the stars and broke in days and years.

I had a thought for no one's but your ears: 35
That you were beautiful, and that I strove

To love you in the old high way of love;
That it had all seemed happy, and yet we'd grown
As weary-hearted as that hollow moon.

Robert Frost (1874–1963)

Stopping by Woods on a Snowy Evening

Whose woods these are I think I know.
His house is in the village though;
He will not see me stopping here
To watch his woods fill up with snow.

My little horse must think it queer   5
To stop without a farmhouse near
Between the woods and frozen lake
The darkest evening of the year.

He gives his harness bells a shake
To ask if there is some mistake.   10
The only other sound's the sweep
Of easy wind and downy flake.

The woods are lovely, dark and deep,
But I have promises to keep,
And miles to go before I sleep,   15
And miles to go before I sleep.

"Out, Out—"

The buzz-saw snarled and rattled in the yard
And made dust and dropped stove-length sticks of wood,
Sweet-scented stuff when the breeze drew across it.
And from there those that lifted eyes could count
Five mountain ranges one behind the other   5
Under the sunset far into Vermont.
And the saw snarled and rattled, snarled and rattled,
As it ran light, or had to bear a load.
And nothing happened: day was all but done.
Call it a day, I wish they might have said   10

To please the boy by giving him the half hour
That a boy counts so much when saved from work.
His sister stood beside them in her apron
To tell them "Supper." At the word, the saw,
As if to prove saws knew what supper meant,   15
Leaped out at the boy's hand, or seemed to leap—
He must have given the hand. However it was,
Neither refused the meeting. But the hand!
The boy's first outcry was a rueful laugh,
As he swung toward them holding up the hand   20
Half in appeal, but half as if to keep
The life from spilling. Then the boy saw all—
Since he was old enough to know, big boy
Doing a man's work, though a child at heart—
He saw all spoiled. "Don't let him cut my hand off—   25
The doctor, when he comes. Don't let him, sister!"
So. But the hand was gone already.
The doctor put him in the dark of ether.
He lay and puffed his lips out with his breath.
And then—the watcher at his pulse took fright.   30
No one believed. They listened at his heart.
Little—less—nothing!—and that ended it.
No more to build on there. And they, since they
Were not the one dead, turned to their affairs.

ACTIVITIES FOR WRITING AND DISCUSSION

1. Respond to either of Frost's poems using the "Four-Step Process for Writing from Reading" discussed in Chapter 2.

2. Working with a group or as a class, read "Out, Out—" aloud. Have each person take a turn reading several lines, and pause periodically to do either or both of the following:

   a. Share and discuss your annotations of specific lines and passages. What parts puzzle you or leave you with questions? What parts strike or "grab" you? Why?

   b. Analyze Frost's **metaphors** and **similes** and how they enhance the poem.

Based on this process and on your annotations, write a response to the poem using one of the "Ten Ideas for Writing" from Chapter 3 (page 35) or a different idea of your own devising.

ISHIGAKI RIN (b. 1920)

The Pan, the Pot, the Fire I Have Before Me

For a long time
these things have always been placed
before us women:

the pan of a reasonable size
suited to the user's strength,   5
the pot in which it's convenient for rice
to begin to swell and shine, grain by grain,
the glow of the fire inherited from time immemorial—
before these there have always been
mothers, grandmothers, and their mothers   10

What measures of love and sincerity
these persons must have poured
into these utensils—
now red carrots,
now black seaweed,   15
now crushed fish

in the kitchen, always accurately
for morning, noon, and evening, preparations have been made
and before the preparations, in a row, there have always been
some pairs of warm knees and hands.   20

Ah without those persons waiting
how could women have gone on
cooking so happily?
their unflagging care,
so daily a service they became unconscious of it.   25

Cooking was mysteriously assigned
to women, as a role,
but I don't think that was unfortunate;
because of that, their knowledge and positions in society
may have lagged behind the times   30
but it isn't too late:
the things we have before us,
the pan and the pot, and the burning fire,

before these familiar things,
let us study government, economy, literature   35

as sincerely
as we cook potatoes and meat.

not for vanity and promotion
but so everyone
may serve all   40
so everyone may work for love.

— *Translated by Hiroaki Sato*

ACTIVITIES FOR WRITING AND DISCUSSION

1. Make a list of stories you have heard or read about cooking, women, or politics. Jot down notes on the **characters** in these stories (from books, film, television) and be prepared to share them in your small group.

2. Reread the fourth and fifth **stanzas.** To whom might "pairs of warm knees and hands" refer, and why might the speaker allude to them as "knees" and "hands" instead of as people?

3. Commenting on specific lines or phrases in the poem, attack and/or defend the following statement: "Experiences with 'the pan, the pot, [and] the fire' have nothing to do with preparing women for a role in 'government, economy, [and] literature.'"

DENISE LEVERTOV (1923–1997)

O Taste and See

The world is
not with us enough.
O taste and see

the subway Bible poster said,
meaning *The Lord,* meaning   5
if anything all that lives
to the imagination's tongue,

grief, mercy, language,
tangerine, weather, to
breathe them, bite,   10
savor, chew, swallow, transform

into our flesh our
deaths, crossing the street, plum, quince,
living in the orchard and being

hungry, and plucking   15
the fruit.

ACTIVITIES FOR WRITING AND DISCUSSION

1. This poem is a reply to Wordsworth's sonnet "The World Is Too Much with
Us" (p. 1020). Reread both poems carefully, inferring as much information as you
can about the two poets' worldviews and values. Then:

> a. Working alone or with a group, identify and list points of probable
> agreement and disagreement between the two poets.
> b. Imagine a setting—such as a home, park, or café—in which the two
> poets meet. Have them discuss—and possibly debate—their different
> views of "the world," along with any other topics that happen to arise.
> Try to infer the speaking style of each poet from the poetic style you de-
> tect in their poems. How does the meeting end? In agreement? cordial
> disagreement? with one or the other poet leaving angrily?

2. Write an essay in which you compare and contrast the two poems. In addition to considering ideas or outlooks, you might also examine differences and
similarities in **diction,** imagery, tone, and poetic type (Wordsworth's poem is traditional verse, while Levertov's is free verse).

WISLAWA SZYMBORSKA (b. 1923)

Advertisement

I'm a tranquilizer.
I'm effective at home.
I work in the office.
I can take exams
or the witness stand.   5
I mend broken cups with care.
All you have to do is take me,
let me melt beneath your tongue,
just gulp me   10
with a glass of water.

I know how to handle misfortune,
how to take bad news.
I can minimize injustice,
lighten up God's absence,
or pick the widow's veil that suits your face.   15
What are you waiting for—
have faith in my chemical compassion.

You're still a young man / woman.
It's not too late to learn how to unwind.
Who said   20
you have to take it on the chin?

Let me have your abyss.
I'll cushion it with sleep.
You'll thank me for giving you
four paws to fall on.   25

Sell me your soul.
There are no other takers.

There is no other devil anymore.

> —*Translated by Stanislaw Barańczak
> and Clare Cavanagh*

ACTIVITIES FOR WRITING AND DISCUSSION

1. Why do you suppose Szymborska titled the poem "Advertisement" instead of "Tranquilizer"?

2. What strategies of advertising in general does the "Advertisement" mimic? What fears and desires does it exploit? Annotate and discuss specific lines and the strategies they illustrate.

3. A more conventional version of this poem might have featured a salesperson extolling the virtues of the tranquilizer in the **third person.** What effects does Szymborska achieve by **personifying** the tranquilizer and having it speak for itself? If you wish, write a poem of your own from the point of view of some personified commercial product (e.g., a car, item of clothing, television, cell phone) in which you have the product "sell" itself.

4. Judging from hints in the poem, what are the personal characteristics and needs of the "you" who will likely buy the tranquilizer? Use your experience and imagination to write his or her life story.

5. The poem is rich in **figures** (e.g., "Let me have your abyss"; "Sell me your soul"). Identify several that are most notable to you, and analyze their power and impact orally or in an essay.

JAMES WRIGHT (1927–1980)

Lying in a Hammock at William Duffy's Farm in Pine Island, Minnesota

Over my head, I see the bronze butterfly,
Asleep on the black trunk,
Blowing like a leaf in green shadow.
Down the ravine behind the empty house,
The cowbells follow one another   5
Into the distances of the afternoon.
To my right,
In a field of sunlight between two pines,
The droppings of last year's horses
Blaze up into golden stones.   10
I lean back, as the evening darkens and comes on.
A chicken hawk floats over, looking for home.
I have wasted my life.

URSULA FANTHORPE (b. 1929)

You Will Be Hearing from Us Shortly

You feel adequate to the demands of this position?
What qualities do you feel you
Personally have to offer?

                                                       Ah

Let us consider your application form.   5
Your qualifications, though impressive, are
Not, we must admit, precisely what
We had in mind. Would you care
To defend their relevance?

                                              Indeed   10

Now your age. Perhaps you feel able
To make your own comment about that,
Too? We are conscious ourselves
Of the need for a candidate with precisely
The right degree of immaturity.   15

                                                        So glad we agree

And now a delicate matter: your looks.
You do appreciate this work involves
Contact with the actual public? Might they,
Perhaps, find your appearance   20
Disturbing?

                                                        Quite so

And your accent. That is the way
You have always spoken, is it? What
Of your education? Were   25
You educated? We mean, of course,
Where were you educated?
                           And how
Much of a handicap is that to you,
Would you say?   30

                      Married, children,
We see. The usual dubious
Desire to perpetuate what had better
Not have happened at all. We do not
Ask what domestic disasters shimmer   35
Behind that vaguely unsuitable address.

And you were born—?

                                                        Yes. Pity.

So glad we agree.

ACTIVITIES FOR WRITING AND DISCUSSION

   1. The poem implies a dialogue but includes only one side of that conversation. In fact, more is left unsaid in this poem than is actually said. Why? What do the silences mean or convey?

   2. Mark and annotate any lines that seem odd, surprising, or out of place in an interview. Share your "take" on those lines with a partner or small group.

3. Write from the poem creatively.
    a. Respond using Idea #1 or #2 of the "Ten Ideas for Writing" on page 35; or
    b. Rewrite the poem as a short story told from either the third- or first-person **point of view;** or
    c. Rewrite the poem as a brief play with **scene description, stage directions,** and **character descriptions;** or
    d. Rewrite the poem to include *only* the *interviewee's* side of the conversation as you imagine it.

GARY SNYDER (b. 1930)

Axe Handles

One afternoon the last week in April
Showing Kai how to throw a hatchet
One-half turn and it sticks in a stump.
He recalls the hatchet-head
Without a handle, in the shop   5
And go gets it, and wants it for his own.
A broken-off axe handle behind the door
Is long enough for a hatchet,
We cut it to length and take it
With the hatchet head   10
And working hatchet, to the wood block.
There I begin to shape the old handle
With the hatchet, and the phrase
First learned from Ezra Pound[1]
Rings in my ears!   15
"When making an axe handle
        the pattern is not far off."
And I say this to Kai
"Look: We'll shape the handle
By checking the handle   20
Of the axe we cut with—"
And he sees. And I hear it again:
It's in Lu Ji's *Wên Fu*, fourth century
A.D. "Essay on Literature"—in the

---

1. American poet (1885–1972).

Preface: "In making the handle   25
Of an axe
By cutting wood with an axe
The model is indeed near at hand."
My teacher Shih-hsiang Chen
Translated that and taught it years ago   30
And I see: Pound was an axe,
Chen was an axe, I am an axe
And my son a handle, soon
To be shaping again, model
And tool, craft of culture,   35
How we go on.

ACTIVITIES FOR WRITING AND DISCUSSION

1. Study the quotation from Ezra Pound in lines 16–17. Think of other objects or works (pictures, handcrafts, songs, gardens, and so on) you can make or create with your hands. Is there a "pattern" for each of these? What does the word "pattern" signify?

2. The poem contains several literary **allusions.** The speaker *quotes* Pound and Lu Ji exactly. Why doesn't he just *paraphrase* their ideas instead?

3. Make a Topic/Form Grid (see Chapter 5) for the poem, including such items as "modeling," "patterns," "role models," "mentors," and "tradition" among your topics. Then address one of your topics using one of the forms on your grid.

4. Would you describe the vision of this poem as forward-looking? backward-looking? neither? both? Explain.

HERBERT SCOTT (b. 1931)

Boss in the Back Room

1

I love to work the checkstands Saturdays.
The carts lined up, bulging with goods.
You weigh the produce heavy, ring the prices

high. That's where you make your wages.
Keep the customers talking. They don't know   5
which way their money went.

2

There's too much money in groceries.
I seen it happen in my life.
The bankers in their high hats,

they own this place.   10
They don't care nothing about groceries.
It's paper and ink to them.

3

I know the clerks steal.
You got to keep them happy.
Jack the prices a little,   15

let the customers pay.
They got their own racket,
somewheres. They take you,

you take them. Live and let live,
I always say. It ain't the worst   20
business in the world.

4

Marriage, that's the travesty of your life.
You spend the rest of your days
picking the fleas out of your ears.

My wife got married so young   25
she don't remember her maiden name.
And the women you see come in,

day after day, they ain't stupid.
Their old man's sleeping on the couch
or out playing pig's knuckle   30

with the boys. I'm telling you,
this world is full of lonely women.
It's a great place to be.

ACTIVITIES FOR WRITING AND DISCUSSION

1. Describe the poem's **diction,** and illustrate your description with examples. Herbert Scott is a poet. Is his **speaker** in this poem a "poet"? Explain your answer.

2. React to the speaker. Do you trust him? like him? admire him? Why or why not?

3. Describe the speaker's philosophy of life.

4. Describe the speaker's implied audience, the person or people to whom he seems to be speaking. How does his implied audience affect the content and style of his speech? Rewrite all or a part of the poem with a different implied audience—say, of the boss's *boss*, his wife, his peers, or a customer. *Alternative:* Imagine the boss stepping from the back room into the front room, and write what he says in the latter space.

5. The poem is a **monologue.** Following Scott's example and writing in either verse or prose, create a monologue of your own in which a speaker—real or imagined—talks candidly about his or her work to an implied listener or listeners. Choose both your speaker and listener(s) carefully.

TED KOOSER (b. 1939)

A Death at the Office

The news goes desk to desk
like a memo: *Initial*
and pass on. Each of us marks
Surprised or *Sorry.*

The management came early   5
and buried her nameplate
deep in her desk. They have boxed up
the Midol and Lip-Ice,

the snapshots from home,
wherever it was—nephews   10
and nieces, a strange, blurred cat
with fiery, flashbulb eyes

as if it grieved. But who grieves here?
We have her ballpoints back,
her bud vase. One of us tears   15
the scribbles from her calendar.

ACTIVITIES FOR WRITING AND DISCUSSION

1. Identify as many **figures—metaphors, similes, verbal ironies,** and others—as you can. From these choose several that stand out for you, and explain how each enhances the poem's overall effect on you.

2. Based on this poem about a *death* at the office, tell the story of typical day-to-day *life* in this office as you imagine it. If you wish, focus your story on one particular imagined worker.

3. Assess the personality and emotions of the poem's **speaker.** Make a list of adjectives that describe the speaker. If you wish, imagine the habits, personal values, and home life of the speaker. Then invent a dialogue between yourself and the speaker in which you talk about life (and death) at the office—the office in the poem and/or offices you have known yourself.

4. In the **persona** of the dead woman (imagine the dead can speak):
    a. Tell the story of your life, with emphasis on the subject of your work; or
    b. Share your thoughts and feelings about the way your coworkers and office management have reacted to your death.

5. Do you interpret the last stanza literally or ironically? Explain.

Jack Ridl (b. 1944)

Last Ditch

for Billy Mayer

Thirty-one seconds on the clock. Coach is down on one knee, screaming at Tommy to get the ball across mid-court and call time out. We're down by one. Time out. In the huddle, Coach slaps Frank behind the head, "Look at this. Look. Now, you Frank, you get the ball to Jimmy. Frank, you hear me? Ok. Now, get the ball to Jimmy. Then, Frank, you break down the lane like you're gonna get it back. Got it? Ok. Then, Jimmy, you look for Carl who'll be breaking out to the line after Frank goes by. Frank, you're gonna screen Carl's man. Ok? Now, it's just the same as in practice. No different. No different. Just the same. Just the ..." And all I can hear is this roar, this sense that the roof is opening and a train is tumbling slowly across the sky. I look over at Jeannie. She's shoving her fist toward the scoreboard and yelling, "Come on Blue. Come on Blue." The horn sounds. We all reach in, grab Coach's hand. "OK. OK. OK. OK. OK. OK." Frank tosses it in to Jimmy. 28, 27, 26, 25. Jimmy dribbles, left, back right; his man presses close; Jimmy keeps the ball tight to his right side, keeps his left arm out. He holds his head high, at one angle. 18, 17, 16, 15. He passes to Tommy. Tommy looks inside, fakes a pass, head fakes, tosses back to Jimmy. The train is rolling, the crowd, the clock, Jeannie is shrieking "C'mon, C'mon, C'mon." 12, 11, 10, Jimmy's still dribbling. Coach is back down on his knee, clapping, "OK. OK. OK." Frank cuts down the lane. Carl fakes left, then starts for the line; Jimmy looks to his right, catches Carl open; Carl turns, fires . . . The last dance, "Goodnight sweetheart, well, it's time to go. Goodnight sweetheart, goodnight." And Jeannie cups her hand around my neck.

ACTIVITIES FOR WRITING AND DISCUSSION

1. Write a **prose poem** that captures a suspenseful moment — or sequence of moments — in a sporting event or other competition.

TARA PATEL (b. 1949)

In Bombay

Time passes even when unemployed.

After summer the incessant monologue of rain.
There is a professional touch to it all.
I have been employed as many times
as unemployed.   5
And now I am unemployed.
Repetition does not make it easier.

In the beginning one leaves the house
in the morning as usual.
Pretences increase, imaginary interviews   10
outnumber unimaginary ones.
Waiting to be interviewed is a
test by itself.

Unemployed, one makes friends who
are unemployed.   15
Picked up at the employment bureau
where silence is articulate.
The unemployed dare not lose their temper.

The afternoons are reserved for exhibitions,
libraries, bookstalls.   20
Movies. Today it was *Wait until Dark*
for the second time.
I am an outsider in an auditorium of
college students.

The boys are quick with gilded wit, the   25
girls gay dolls
with "Choosy Cherry" lips and expensive eyes.
My white-washed presence marred the
illustration.

Of course, when unemployed, the need to spend,   30
to do everything in excess, increases.

Cursing comes easily, when a hundred-rupee
note is lost or stolen
it is God who is a so and so.

Unemployed people try to sleep at any   35
time of the day.

JAN BEATTY (b. 1952)

A Waitress's Instructions on Tipping
or
Get the Cash Up and Don't Waste My Time

20% minimum as long as the waitress doesn't inflict bodily harm.
If you're two people at a four top, tip extra.
If you sit a long time, pay rent.
Double tips for special orders.
Always tip extra when using coupons.   5
Better yet, don't use coupons.
Never leave change instead of bills.
Never leave pennies at all.
Never hide a tip for fun.
Overtip, overtip, overtip.   10
Remember, I am somebody's mother or daughter.
Large parties *must* overtip, no separate piles of change.
If people in your party don't show up, tip *for* them.
Don't wait around for gratitude if you overtip.
Take a risk. Don't adjust your tip so your credit card total is even.   15
Don't ever, ever pull out a tipping guide in public.
If you leave 10% or less, eat at home.
If I call a taxi for you, tip me.
If I hang up your coat for you, tip me.
If I get cigarettes for you, tip me.   20
Better yet, do it yourself.
If you buy a $50 bottle of wine, pull out a $10.
If I serve you one cocktail, don't hand me $.35.
If you're just having coffee, leave a $5.
Don't fold a bill and hand it to me like you're a big shot.   25
Don't say, *There's a big tip in it for you if . . .*
Don't say, *I want to make sure you get this,* like a busboy would steal it.
Don't say, *Here, honey, this is for you*—ever.
Don't say, *I'll make it worth your while.*
If you're miserable, there's not enough money in the world.   30

JANICE M. LYNCH (b. 1962)

Excerpts from "Sixty-Four Caprices for a Long-Distance Swimmer: Notes on Swimming 100 Miles"

1. A friend asks why I swim. Why not a movie? A drink? Dinner? I answer that I swim for strength, for a rippling tricep and a dimple in my thigh. I hide the lie with a stroke: I swim for the silence of water.

2. An older woman stopped swimming and watched me. What a graceful stroke! What she loved, of course, was the mirrored beauty of her youth—the forgotten pleasure of her toughened skin.

3. The water undulates like a womb I do not remember. My fingers poke through for life. The air is unfamiliar.

4. I tell a friend that life is water. With a pretended fluidity his heart mimics the ocean—but he cannot swim. He answers that a cell full of water explodes.

5. Seventy-year old women stand naked in the locker room. Some use walkers, others have artificial hips, scarred legs and missing breasts, still, they love this morning swim with the distant sun rising.

6. In these women, I witness how I too will age. I avert my eyes, move to far lanes and other shadows.

7. I swim past men to prove my strength—after years of "throwing like a girl"—I lap them twice.

10. I tap slower swimmers' feet to pass them. Their skin startles me, as though I've come upon schools of spot running south for winter.

15. I dream of fire. I dream of fire and combustion. The things water does not heal.

17. How do we breathe underwater? A moment without air is magic. Through goggles, I watch the bubbles insist on my life.

18. Fifty others swim in the pool. Water molecules vibrate with our personalities. I swallow each person's breath, yet remain alone.

21. This—is—the—point—where I always—want to stop. Turn—legs—ache—lungs heave—arms weary—the distance—is forever—force the push—break water.

22. Every morning, two crows perch near the pool's glass doors and peck madly at their reflections. When no one watches, I jump out of the pool and run, arms raised and mouth squawking, to chase them away.

23. Then all three of us jump—the crows with fright to the sky—and me, chilled, to the diving well.

24. Every other breath my face sculpts a water mask.

26. Blood throbs, echoing the physics of water and sound. It sets up a rhythm between myself and other swimmers.

29. At a certain angle, the hand slices sheets of water. This requires a force the body is unaware of, even as pounds of water move away like the curtain rising over the first act.

30. What does it mean to drown in a dream? Is there the hope of bellying-up like a fish? Are we forced to forget breathing?

31. Some days there is no difference between sleep and dreams, between swimming and drowning, water and air.

36. After a winter of depression, inches of sadness float across the pool.

37. Sometimes, breathing, the heaviness of my own life amazes me. Sucking on air, I consume the world.

40. Breaststroke beads the surface like mercury on skin. I'm a skeet barely touching water, needing it only to serve my own motion.

41. I try to describe my father, but he eludes me, fast as a rock skipping the ocean. I try to describe my mother, but she is too much myself—familiar as oxygen gurgling about my waist.

42. I learned to walk because my sister was born and I knew that I would never be carried again.

43. I learned to swim because my father threw me in the deep end and shouted "Swim!"

44. I sweat in the water and my face is cooled, ice cooled on ice.

45. As children, my sisters and I linked arms with my father and ran into the Atlantic, afraid only of letting go and coming up in some other ocean.

46. A man paralyzed from the waist down swims slowly, his legs quivering with the dream of motion. In a dream that my strength reaches him through the water, I swim faster, give up another length.

47. At dawn the moon fits the socket of the sky like a great white bulb.

61. When I swim I am the totality of water. I am hydrogen and oxygen. I am pure strength and energy.

64. I shed the water's silk cocoon for the certain embrace of air; my body emerges from the pool, form from cut crystal.

ACTIVITIES FOR WRITING AND DISCUSSION

1. Lynch calls the numbered sections of her poem "caprices" or "notes," and they resemble the kinds of notes you might jot down in a notebook. Therefore, react to the piece using any of the "Generic Ideas for Writing in Response to Published Notebooks and Journals" that are listed on pages 192–193.

2. React to the *form* of the piece. Do the numbered sections need to be read in sequence? Do they suggest any underlying pattern of organization? Do they constitute *a* poem or 64 *separate* poems? Support your opinions with references to specific passages.

3. Compare "Sixty-Four Caprices" with Edward Hoagland's essay, "Learning to Eat Soup" (p. 529), which is somewhat similar in format. In what specific ways do the two pieces differ and/or resemble each other? What ideas, if any, does either suggest to you for a writing project of your own?

4. Following Lynch's example, compose and collect a number of "notes" or "caprices" based on experiencing some favorite activity of your own.

Nonfiction/Essays

HENRY DAVID THOREAU (1817–1862)

Where I Lived, and What I Lived For

At a certain season of our life we are accustomed to consider every spot as the possible site of a house. I have thus surveyed the country on every side within a dozen miles of where I live. In imagination I have bought all the farms in succession, for all were to be bought, and I knew their price. I walked over each farmer's premises, tasted his wild apples, discoursed on husbandry with him, took his farm at his price, at any price, mortgaging it to him in my mind; even put a higher price on it,—took everything but a deed of it,—took his word for his deed, for I dearly love to talk,—cultivated it, and him too to some extent, I trust, and withdrew when I had enjoyed it long enough, leaving him to carry it on. This experience entitled me to be regarded as a sort of real-estate broker by my friends. Wherever I sat, there I might live, and the landscape radiated from me accordingly. What is a house but a *sedes*, a seat?—better if a country seat. I discovered many a site for a house not likely to be soon improved, which some might have thought too far from the village, but to my eyes the village was too far from it. Well, there I might live, I said; and there I did live, for an hour, a summer and a winter life; saw how I could let the years run off, buffet the winter through, and see the spring come in. The future inhabitants of this region, wherever they may place their houses, may be sure that they have been anticipated. An afternoon sufficed to lay out the land into orchard, woodlot, and pasture, and to decide what fine oaks or pines should be left to stand before the door, and whence each blasted tree could be seen to the best advantage; and then I let it lie, fallow perchance, for a man is rich in proportion to the number of things which he can afford to let alone. . . .

The present was my next experiment of this kind, which I purpose to describe more at length, for convenience, putting the experience of two years into one. As I have said, I do not propose to write an ode to dejection, but to brag as lustily as chanticleer in the morning, standing on his roost, if only to wake my neighbors up.

When first I took up my abode in the woods, that is, began to spend my nights as well as days there, which, by accident, was on Independence day, or the fourth of July, 1845, my house was not finished for winter, but was merely a defence against the rain, without plastering or chimney, the walls being of rough weather-stained boards, with wide chinks, which made it cool at night. The upright white hewn studs and freshly planed door and window casings gave it a clean and airy look, especially in the morning, when its timbers were saturated with dew, so that I fancied that by noon some sweet gum would exude from them. To my imagination it retained throughout the day more or less of this auroral character, reminding me of a certain house on a mountain which I had visited a year before. This was an airy and unplastered cabin, fit to entertain a travelling god, and where a goddess might trail her garments. The winds which passed over my dwelling were such as sweep over the ridges of mountains, bearing the broken strains, or celestial parts only, of terrestrial music. The morning wind forever blows, the poem of creation is uninterrupted; but few are the ears that hear it. Olympus is but the outside of the earth everywhere.

The only house I had been the owner of before, if I except a boat, was a tent, which I used occasionally when making excursions in the summer, and this is still rolled up in my garret; but the boat, after passing from hand to hand, has gone down the stream of time. With this more substantial shelter about me, I had made some progress toward settling in the world. This frame, so slightly clad, was a sort of crystallization around me, and reacted on the builder. It was suggestive somewhat as a picture in outlines. I did not need to go out doors to take the air, for the atmosphere within had lost none of its freshness. It was not so much within doors as behind a door where I sat, even in the rainiest weather. The Harivansa says, "An abode without birds is like a meat without seasoning." Such was not my abode, for I found myself suddenly neighbor to the birds; not by having imprisoned one, but having caged myself near them. I was not only nearer to some of those which commonly frequent the garden and the orchard, but to those wilder and more thrilling songsters of the forest which never, or rarely, serenade a villager,—the wood-thrush, the veery, the scarlet tanager, the field-sparrow, the whippoorwill, and many others. . . .

Every morning was a cheerful invitation to make my life of equal simplicity, 5 and I may say innocence, with Nature herself. I have been as sincere a worshipper of Aurora as the Greeks. I got up early and bathed in the pond; that was a religious exercise, and one of the best things which I did. They say that characters were engraven on the bathing tub of king Tching-thang to this effect: "Renew thyself completely each day; do it again, and again, and forever again." I can understand that. Morning brings back the heroic ages. I was as much affected by the faint hum of a mosquito making its invisible and unimaginable tour through my apartment at earliest dawn, when I was sitting with door and windows open, as I could be by any trumpet that ever sang of fame. It was Homer's requiem; itself an Iliad and Odyssey in the air, singing its own wrath and wanderings. There was something cosmical about it; a standing advertisement, till forbidden, of the everlasting vigor and fertility of the world. The morning, which is the most memorable season of the day, is the awakening hour. Then there is least somnolence in us; and for an hour, at least, some part of us awakes which slumbers all the rest of the day and night. Little is to be expected of that day, if it can be called a day, to which we are not awakened by our Genius, but by the mechanical nudgings of some servitor, are not awakened by our own newly-acquired force and aspirations from within, accompanied by the undulations of celestial music, instead of factory bells, and a fragrance filling the air—to a higher life than we fell asleep from; and thus the darkness bear its fruit, and prove itself to be good, no less than the light. That man who does not believe that each day contains an earlier, more sacred, and auroral hour than he has yet profaned, has despaired of life, and is pursuing a descending and darkening way. After a partial cessation of his sensuous life, the soul of man, or its organs rather, are reinvigorated each day, and his Genius tries again what noble life it can make. All memorable events, I should say, transpire in morning time and in a morning atmosphere. The Vedas say, "All intelligences awake with the morning." Poetry and art, and the fairest and most memorable of the actions of men, date from such an hour. All poets and heroes, like Memnon, are the children of Aurora, and emit their music at sunrise. To him whose elastic and vigorous thought keeps pace with the sun, the day is a perpetual morning. It matters not what the clocks say or the attitudes and labors of men. Morning is when I am awake and there is a dawn in me. Moral reform is the effort to throw off sleep. Why is it that men give so poor an account of their day if they have not been slumbering? They are not such poor calculators. If they had not been overcome with drowsiness they would have performed something. The millions are awake enough for physical labor; but only one in a million is awake enough for effective intellectual exertion, only one in a hundred millions to a poetic or divine life. To be awake is to be alive. I have never yet met a man who was quite awake. How could I have looked him in the face?

We must learn to reawaken and keep ourselves awake, not by mechanical aids, but by an infinite expectation of the dawn, which does not forsake us in our soundest sleep. I know of no more encouraging fact than the unquestionable ability of man to elevate his life by a conscious endeavor. It is something to be able to paint a particular picture, or to carve a statue, and so to make a few objects beautiful; but it is far more glorious to carve and paint the very atmosphere and medium through which we look, which morally we can do. To affect the quality of the day, that is the highest of arts. Every man is tasked to make his life, even in its details, worthy of the contemplation of his most elevated and critical hour. If we refused, or rather used up, such paltry information as we get, the oracles would distinctly inform us how this might be done.

I went to the woods because I wished to live deliberately, to front only the essential facts of life, and see if I could not learn what it had to teach, and not, when I came to die, discover that I had not lived. I did not wish to live what was not life, living is so dear; nor did I wish to practise resignation, unless it was quite necessary. I wanted to live deep and suck out all the marrow of life, to live so sturdily and Spartan-like as to put to rout all that was not life, to cut a broad swath and shave close, to drive life into a corner, and reduce it to its lowest terms, and, if it proved to be mean, why then to get the whole and genuine meanness of it, and publish its meanness to the world; or if it were sublime, to know it by experience, and be able to give a true account of it in my next excursion. For most men, it appears to me, are in a strange uncertainty about it, whether it is of the devil or of God, and have *somewhat hastily* concluded that it is the chief end of man here to "glorify God and enjoy him forever." . . .

Why should we live with such hurry and waste of life? We are determined to be starved before we are hungry. Men say that a stitch in time saves nine, and so they take a thousand stitches to-day to save nine to-morrow. As for *work,* we haven't any of any consequence. We have the Saint Vitus' dance, and cannot possibly keep our heads still. If I should only give a few pulls at the parish bell-rope, as for a fire, that is, without setting the bell, there is hardly a man on his farm in the outskirts of Concord, notwithstanding that press of engagements which was his excuse so many times this morning, nor a boy, nor a woman, I might almost say, but would forsake all and follow that sound, not mainly to save property from the flames, but, if we will confess the truth, much more to see it burn, since burn it must, and we, be it known, did not set it on fire,—or to see it put out, and have a hand in it, if that is done as handsomely; yes, even if it were the parish church itself. Hardly a man takes a half hour's nap after dinner, but when he wakes he holds up his head and asks, "What's the news?" as if the rest of mankind had stood his sentinels. Some give directions to be waked every half hour, doubtless for no other purpose; and then, to pay for it, they tell what they have dreamed. After a night's sleep the news is as indispensable as the breakfast. "Pray tell me anything new that has happened to a man anywhere on this globe,"—and he reads it over his coffee and rolls, that a man has had his eyes gouged out this morning on the Wachito River; never dreaming the while that he lives in the dark unfathomed mammoth cave of this world, and has but the rudiment of an eye himself.

For my part, I could easily do without the post-office. I think that there are very few important communications made through it. To speak critically, I never received more than one or two letters in my life—I wrote this some years ago— that were worth the postage. The penny-post is, commonly, an institution through which you seriously offer a man that penny for his thoughts which is so often safely offered in jest. And I am sure that I never read any memorable news in a newspaper. If we read of one man robbed, or murdered, or killed by accident, or one house burned, or one vessel wrecked, or one steamboat blown up, or one cow run over on the Western Railroad, or one mad dog killed, or one lot of grasshoppers in the winter,—we never need read of another. One is enough. If you are acquainted with the principle, what do you care for a myriad instances and applications? To a philosopher all *news,* as it is called, is gossip, and they who edit and read it are old women over their tea. . . .

What news! how much more important to know what that is which was never   10 old! "Kieou-he-yu (great dignitary of the state of Wei) sent a man to Khoung-tseu to know his news. Khoung-tseu caused the messenger to be seated near him, and questioned him in these terms: What is your master doing? The messenger answered with respect: My master desires to diminish the number of his faults, but he cannot come to the end of them. The messenger being gone, the philosopher remarked: What a worthy messenger! What a worthy messenger!" The preacher, instead of vexing the ears of drowsy farmers on their day of rest at the end of the week,—for Sunday is the fit conclusion of an ill-spent week, and not the fresh and brave beginning of a new one,—with this one other draggle-tail of a sermon, should shout with thundering voice,—"Pause! Avast! Why so seeming fast, but deadly slow?"

Shams and delusions are esteemed for soundest truths, while reality is fabulous. If men would steadily observe realities only, and not allow themselves to be deluded, life, to compare it with such things as we know, would be like a fairy tale and the Arabian Nights' Entertainments. If we respected only what is inevitable and has a right to be, music and poetry would resound along the streets. When we are unhurried and wise, we perceive that only great and worthy things have any permanent and absolute existence,—that petty fears and petty pleasures are but the shadow of the reality. This is always exhilarating and sublime. By closing the eyes and slumbering, and consenting to be deceived by shows, men establish and confirm their daily life of routine and habit everywhere, which still is built on purely illusory foundations. Children, who play life, discern its true law and relations more clearly than men, who fail to live it worthily, but who think that they are wiser by experience, that is, by failure. I have read in a Hindoo book, that "there was a king's son, who, being expelled in infancy from his native city, was brought up by a forester, and, growing up to maturity in that state, imagined himself to belong to the barbarous race with which he lived. One of his father's ministers having discovered him, revealed to him what he was, and the misconception of his character was removed, and he knew himself to be a prince. So soul," continues the Hindoo philosopher, "from the circumstances in which it is placed, mistakes its own character, until the truth is revealed to it by some holy teacher, and then it knows itself to be *Brahme.*" I perceive that we inhabitants of New England live this mean life that we do because our vision does not penetrate the surface of things. We think that that *is* which *appears* to be. If a man should walk through this town and see only the reality, where, think you, would the "Milldam" go to? If he should give us an account of the realities he beheld there, we should not recognize the place in his description. Look at a meeting-house, or a courthouse, or a jail, or a shop, or a dwelling-house, and say what that thing really is before a true gaze, and they would all go to pieces in your account of them.

Men esteem truth remote, in the outskirts of the system, behind the farthest star, before Adam and after the last man. In eternity there is indeed something true and sublime. But all these times and places and occasions are now and here. God himself culminates in the present moment, and will never be more divine in the lapse of all the ages. And we are enabled to apprehend at all what is sublime and noble only by the perpetual instilling and drenching of the reality that surrounds us. The universe constantly and obediently answers to our conceptions; whether we travel fast or slow, the track is laid for us. Let us spend our lives in conceiving then. The poet or the artist never yet had so fair and noble a design but some of his posterity at least could accomplish it.

Let us spend one day as deliberately as Nature, and not be thrown off the track by every nutshell and mosquito's wing that falls on the rails. Let us rise early and fast, or break fast, gently and without perturbation; let company come and let company go, let the bells ring and the children cry,— determined to make a day of it. Why should we knock under and go with the stream? Let us not be upset and overwhelmed in that terrible rapid and whirlpool called a dinner, situated in the meridian shallows. Weather this danger and you are safe, for the rest of the way is down hill. With unrelaxed nerves, with morning vigor, sail by it, looking another way, tied to the mast like Ulysses. If the engine whistles, let it whistle till it is hoarse for its pains. If the bell rings, why should we run? We will consider what kind of music they are like. Let us settle ourselves, and work and wedge our feet downward through the mud and slush of opinion, and prejudice, and tradition, and delusion, and appearance, that alluvion which covers the globe, through Paris and London, through New York and Boston and Concord, through church and state, through poetry and philosophy and religion, till we come to a hard bottom and rocks in place, which we can call *reality*, and say, This is, and no mistake; and then begin, having a *point d' appui*, below freshet and frost and fire, a place where you might found a wall or a state, or set a lamppost safely, or perhaps a gauge, not a Nilometer, but a Realometer, that future ages might know how deep a freshet of shams and appearances had gathered from time to time. If you stand right fronting and face to face to a fact, you will see the sun glimmer on both its surfaces, as if it were a cimeter, and feel its sweet edge dividing you through the heart and marrow, and so you will happily conclude your mortal career. Be it life or death, we crave only reality. If we are really dying, let us hear the rattle in our throats and feel cold in the extremities; if we are alive, let us go about our business.

Time is but the stream I go a-fishing in. I drink at it; but while I drink I see the sandy bottom and detect how shallow it is. Its thin current slides away, but eternity remains. I would drink deeper; fish in the sky, whose bottom is pebbly with stars. I cannot count one. I know not the first letter of the alphabet. I have always been regretting that I was not as wise as the day I was born. The intellect is a cleaver; it discerns and rifts its way into the secret of things. I do not wish to be any more busy with my hands than is necessary. My head is hands and feet. I feel all my best faculties concentrated in it. My instinct tells me that my head is an organ for burrowing, as some creatures use their snout, and fore-paws, and with it

I would mine and burrow my way through these hills. I think that the richest vein is somewhere hereabouts; so by the divining rod and thin rising vapors I judge; and here I will begin to mine.

ACTIVITIES FOR WRITING AND DISCUSSION

1. Thoreau's prose abounds with memorable sentences. Underline and annotate any that strike you, and be prepared to share and discuss them in class. If you wish, copy some or all of these sentences into a notepad or a commonplace book (see Chapter 4).

2. One distinctive aspect of Thoreau's style is his use of **allusions,** i.e., references to other literary works or characters or to historical persons, places, or events. Identify two or three allusions in the essay, look up the references, and analyze how the allusions work. Then generalize about how you think allusions strengthen or weaken the effectiveness of Thoreau's prose.

3. Thoreau takes a dim view of newspapers, the postal service, and other cultural resources and institutions that many of us regard as essential. Reread the relevant passages and summarize—as objectively as possible—the rationale behind Thoreau's criticisms. Then agree or disagree with Thoreau's critique.

4. Imagine you are Thoreau and you are living somewhere in America in the 2000s. In a personal essay, reveal how and where you (Thoreau) presently choose to live and why. Then review some contemporary American institutions, values, technologies, and/or behaviors as you believe Thoreau would.

5. Research the history of the two-year sojourn at Walden Pond that inspired Thoreau to write *Walden,* from which "Where I Lived, and What I Lived For" is excerpted.

THOMAS MOORE (b. 1940)

The Sacred Arts of Life

We can return now to one of Plato's expressions for care of the soul, *techne tou biou,* the craft of life. Care of the soul requires craft (*techne*)—skill, attention, and art. To live with a high degree of artfulness means to attend to the small things that keep the soul engaged in whatever we are doing, and it is the very heart of soul-making. From some grand overview of life, it may seem that only the big events are ultimately important. But to the soul, the most minute details and the most ordinary activities, carried out with mindfulness and art, have an effect far beyond their apparent insignificance.

Art is not found only in the painter's studio or in the halls of a museum, it also has its place in the store, the shop, the factory, and the home. In fact, when art is reserved as the province of professional artists, a dangerous gulf develops between the fine arts and the everyday arts. The fine arts are elevated and set apart from life, becoming too precious and therefore irrelevant. Having banished art to the museum, we fail to give it a place in ordinary life. One of the most effective forms of repression is to give a thing excessive honor.

Even in our art schools, a technical viewpoint is often dominant. The young painter learns about materials and schools of thought, but not about the soul of his vocation or the deeper significance of the content of his artwork. A voice major in a university music department expects to become an artist, but in her first lesson she is hooked up to an oscilloscope that will measure the parameters of her voice and indicate areas to be improved. The soul makes a quick exit before these purely technical approaches to learning.

The arts are important for all of us, whether or not we ourselves practice a particular discipline. Art, broadly speaking, is that which invites us into contemplation—a rare commodity in modern life. In that moment of contemplation, art intensifies the presence of the world. We see it more vividly and more deeply. The emptiness that many people complain dominates their lives comes in part from a failure to let the world in, to perceive it and engage it fully. Naturally, we'll feel empty if everything we do slides past without sticking. As we have seen, art *arrests* attention, an important service to the soul. Soul cannot thrive in a fast-paced life because being affected, taking things in and chewing on them, requires time.

Living artfully, therefore, might require something as simple as *pausing*. Some 5 people are incapable of being arrested by things because they are always on the move. A common symptom of modern life is that there is no time for thought, or even for letting impressions of a day sink in. Yet it is only when the world enters the heart that it can be made into soul. The vessel in which soulmaking takes place is an inner container scooped out by reflection and wonder. There is no doubt that some people could spare themselves the expense and trouble of psychotherapy simply by giving themselves a few minutes each day for quiet reflection. This simple act would provide what is missing in their lives: a period of nondoing that is essential nourishment to the soul.

Akin to pausing, and just as important in care of the soul, is *taking time*. I realize these are extremely simple suggestions, but taken to heart they could transform a life, by allowing soul to enter. Taking time with things, we get to know them more intimately and to feel more genuinely connected to them. One of the symptoms of modern soullessness, an alienation from nature and things as well as from our fellow human beings, might be overcome if we took time with whatever we are dealing with.

Living artfully might require taking the time to buy things with soul for the home. Good linens, a special rug, or a simple teapot can be a source of enrichment not only in our own life, but also in the lives of our children and grandchildren. The soul basks in this extended sense of time. But we can't discover the soul in a thing without first taking time to observe it and be with it for a while. This kind of observation has a quality of intimacy about it; it's not just studying a consumer guide for factual and technical analysis. Surfaces, textures, and feel count as much as efficiency.

Certain things stimulate the imagination more than others, and that very blossoming of fantasy might be a sign of soul. An airline executive once talked to me about the struggle he was having in deciding between two jobs that had opened up for him. One was full of prestige and power, while the other was comfortable but quite ordinary. The first he felt he should consider because it was highly prized among his peers, but his thoughts about it were dry. The second one he imagined all day long. In his mind he had already begun to design his office and set his schedule. From the richness of his imagination of it, it was quite clear that the more lowly job appealed to his soul.

The ordinary arts we practice every day at home are of more importance to the soul than their simplicity might suggest. For example, I can't explain it, but I enjoy doing dishes. I've had an automatic dishwasher in my home for over a year, and I have never used it. What appeals to me, as I think about it, is the reverie induced by going through the ritual of washing, rinsing, and drying. Marie-Louise von Franz, the Swiss Jungian author, observes that weaving and knitting, too, are particularly good for the soul because they encourage reflection and reverie.

I also cherish the opportunity to hang clothes on a line outdoors. The fresh 10
smell, the wet fabrics, the blowing wind, and the drying sun go together to make an experience of nature and culture that is unique and particularly pleasurable for its simplicity. Deborah Hunter, a photographer, made a study several years ago of clothes on a line tossed by the wind. There was an element in these photographs, difficult to name, that touched upon vitality, the deep pleasures of ordinary life, and unseen forces of nature, all of which can be found around the house.

In a book not yet published, Jean Lall, the astrologer, observes that daily life at home is full of epiphanies. "Within our daily experience," she writes, "as keepers of home and gardens the spirits still move and speak if we but attend. They slip in through the cracks, making themselves felt in little breakdowns in appliances, unplanned sproutings in the flowerbeds, and sudden moments of blinding beauty, as where sunlight glances across a newly-waxed table or the wind stirs clean laundry into fresh choreography."

Many of the arts practiced at home are especially nourishing to the soul because they foster contemplation and demand a degree of artfulness, such as arranging flowers, cooking, and making repairs. I have a friend who is taking time over several months to paint a garden scene on a low panel of her dining room wall. Sometimes these ordinary arts bring out the individual, so that when you go into a home you can see the special character of your hosts in a particular aspect of their home.

Attending to the soul in these ordinary things usually leads to a more individual life, if not to an eccentric style. One of the things I love to do on a free afternoon is to visit Sleepy Hollow cemetery in Concord, Massachusetts. On a small, knobby hill deep in the cemetery is Emerson's grave, marked by a large, red-streaked boulder that contrasts with the typical gray rectangular gravestones all around him. Thoreau and Hawthorne lie a short distance away. For any who love Emerson's writing, this place is filled with soul. To me, his remarkable gravestone reflects his love of nature and mirrors both his greatness of soul and the irrepressible eccentricity of his imagination. The particular thrust of nature and the presence of a community of writers buried together make the place truly sacred.

When imagination is allowed to move to deep places, the sacred is revealed. The more different kinds of thoughts we experience around a thing and the deeper our reflections go as we are arrested by its artfulness, the more fully its sacredness can emerge. It follows, then, that living artfully can be a tonic for the secularization of life that characterizes our time. We can, of course, bring religion more closely in tune with ordinary life by immersing ourselves in formal rituals and traditional teachings; but we can also serve religion's soul by discovering the "natural religion" in all things. The route to this discovery is art, both the fine arts and those of everyday life. If we could loosen our grip on the functionality of life and let ourselves be arrested by the imaginal richness that surrounds all objects, natural and human-made, we might ground our secular attitudes in a religious sensibility and give ordinary life soul.

I'm suggesting that we consider sacredness from the point of view of soul 15 rather than spirit. From that angle, the sacred appears when imagination achieves unusual depth and fullness. The Bible, the Koran, Buddhist writings, and ritual books of all religions move us to imagine with exceptional range and depth. They bring us into wonder about the cosmos, about the far reaches of time past and present, and about ultimate values. But in a less formal way, any source of imagination that approaches this richness and depth helps create a religious sensibility. When they expose the deep images and themes that course through human life, so-called secular literature and art serve the religious impulse.

The medieval idea about learning, that theology is the ultimate science and all the others are "ancillary"—in humble service—is, to me, absolutely correct. Every issue, no matter how secular it appears to be, has a sacred dimension. If you press anything far enough, you will come up against either the holy or the demonic. Our secular sciences of physics, sociology, psychology, and the rest stop short of theological categories, thus preserving their scientific "objectivity," but also losing soul. Religious sensibility and soul are inseparable. I'm not saying that any particular religious affiliation or belief is essential to soul, but that a solid, palpable, and intellectually satisfying appreciation of the sacred is a sine qua non of living soulfully.

The theme requires a book of its own, but suffice it to say that theology is of concern for everyone, because our most ordinary experiences touch upon issues of such immense depth that they can only be considered religious. Recall Nicholas of Cusa's observation that God is the minimum as well as the maximum. The small things in everyday life are no less sacred than the great issues of human existence.

Becoming the artists and theologians of our own lives, we can approach the depth that is the domain of soul. When we leave art only to the accomplished painter and the museum, instead of fostering our own artful sensibilities through them, then our lives lose opportunities for soul. The same is true when we leave religion to church on the weekend. Then religion remains on the periphery of life, even if it is an exalted periphery, and life loses opportunities for soul. Fine art, like formal religion, is at times quite lofty, while soul in any context is lower case, ordinary, daily, familial and communal, felt, intimate, attached, engaged, involved, affected, ruminating, stirred, and poetic. The soul of a piece of art is known intimately, not remotely. It is felt, not just understood. So, too, the soul of religion lies in an immediate acquaintance with the angelic and the demonic. It is a daily involvement in mysteries and a personal quest for a corresponding ethic. Without soul, religion's truths and moral principles might be believed in, perhaps, and discussed, but they are not taken truly to heart and lived from the core of one's being.

Dreams: A Royal Road to Soul

Care of the soul involves "work," in the alchemical sense. It is impossible to care for the soul and live at the same time in unconsciousness. Sometimes soul work is exciting and inspiring, but often it is also challenging, requiring genuine courage. Rarely easy, work with the soul is usually placed squarely in that place we would rather not visit, in that emotion we don't want to feel, and in that understanding we would prefer to do without. The most honest route may be the most difficult to take. It is not easy to visit the place in ourselves that is most challenging and to look straight into the image that gives us the most fright; yet, there, where the work is most intense, is the source of soul.

Since we never want to take up the piece of our emotion that is most in need 20 of attention, I usually recommend to my patients that they give increased awareness to their dreams; for there they will find images that in waking life are very difficult to face. Dreams truly are the mythology of the soul and working with them forms a major piece in the project of making life more artful.

As a visit to any bookstore will demonstrate, there are many approaches to working with dreams. I would like to make a few concrete suggestions about what I consider key attitudes and strategies in dealing with dreams in a manner that preserves their integrity, allows meaning to emerge, and generally serves care of the soul.

Therapeutic work with dreams could be a model for less formal habits of giving dreams a serious place in our ordinary lives. When a person comes to me for an hour of therapy, I like to hear a dream or two early in the session. I don't like to listen to a dream and then immediately reach for an interpretation. It is better to let the dream lead us into new territory than to try to master the dream and figure it out at once. After the dream has been told, we might go on to talk about the person's life, since the therapy is almost always concerned with life situations. I may notice ways in which the dream offers us images and a language for talking about life with depth and imagination. Instead of trying to figure out the dream, we are letting the dream figure us out, allowing the dream to influence and shape our way of imagining. Usually, the main problem with life conundrums is that we don't bring to them enough imagination. We understand our difficulties literally and look for literal solutions, which rarely work precisely because they are part of the problem—lack of imagination. Dreams offer a fresh point of view.

In therapy it's tempting for both therapist and patient to translate a dream into theories and rationalizations that merely support the ideas of the therapist or the problematical attitudes of the patient. It is much better to let the dream interpret us rather than for us to become clever in interpreting the dream in ways most compatible with our existing ideas.

It is my experience that a dream reveals itself to the patient and the therapist slowly, gradually. I hear the dream and usually have a few impressions and ideas come to the surface immediately. But there might also be a great deal of confusion about the imagery. I try to hold back my need to overcome a dream with meaning. I tolerate its mood and let its puzzling imagery confound me, turn me away from my convictions in order to consider *its* mystery. Having patience with dreams is extremely important, and is more effective in the long run than any exercise of knowledge, techniques, and tricks. The dream reveals itself on its own timetable, but it does reveal itself.

It's important to trust your intuitions, which are not the same as your intel- 25 lectual interpretations. For example, sometimes a person will tell me a dream and immediately recommend a way of understanding it or offer a bias toward one of the characters. A woman, for instance, relates a dream in which she has absentmindedly left her front door open, allowing a man to sneak into her house. "It was a nightmare," she says, "I think the dream is telling me that I'm not careful enough about keeping myself protected. I'm too open."

You see, I'm given a dream and an interpretation. Even though I have considerable experience working with dreams and have been trained not to buy into whatever idea a patient gives me, I'm sometimes unconsciously affected by the interpretation. It's so reasonable. Of course, she is too vulnerable and is threatened by an intruder. But then I remember my first rule: trust your intuitions. I wonder if the "accidental" opening in the door might not be a good thing for this person. The opening may allow new personalities to enter her living space. I'm also aware that the unintentional may not be unintended at all: someone else besides the "I" may wish to leave the door open. The crack in the door may be an accident only to the ego.

There is often an apparent collusion between the dream-ego and the waking dreamer. As the dreamer tells the dream, she may slant her story in the direction of the "I" in the dream, thus convincing the listener to take a certain position in relation to the figures in the dream. Therefore, perhaps sometimes too much in compensation, I like to assume a rather perverse attitude when I hear the dream. I make a point of considering an angle different from the dreamer's. To put it more technically, I assume that in the telling of the dream the dreamer may be locked in the same complex as is the dream-ego. If I simply accept what the dreamer tells me, I may get caught in the dreamer's complex, and then I'm of no use. So I say to this dreamer: "Maybe it's not so bad that your usual thought about closing doors failed in this case. Maybe it allowed an entry that will prove to be beneficial. At least we can keep an open mind."

Speaking for other figures in the dream, sometimes against the bias of the dreamer, can open up a perspective on the dream that is extraordinarily revealing. Care of the soul, remember, does not necessarily mean care of the ego. Other characters may need acceptance and understanding. We may need to consider objectionable actions and characters as somehow necessary and even valuable.

A woman who is a writer tells a dream in which she catches a friend of hers smearing crayons all over the dreamer's typewriter. "It was an awful dream," she said, "and I know what it means. My inner child is always interfering with my adult work. If only I could grow up!"

Notice that this person, too, is quick to move toward interpretation. More than that, she wants me to take a certain position in relation to her dream. In a very subtle way, this desire is a defense against the otherness of the dream, its challenge. Soul and ego are often in a struggle which is sometimes mild and sometimes savage. So, I am careful not to assume that she is right about the content of the dream.

"Was your friend in the dream a child?" I ask.

"No, she was an adult. She was the age she is in life."

"Then why do you think she is being childish?"

"Crayons are a childish thing," she says as if stating the obvious.

"Can you tell me something about this friend of yours?" I am trying to break free of her strong views about her dream.

"She's very seductive, always wearing outlandish clothes—you know, bright colors and always low-cut."

"Is it possible," I say, taking a leap on the basis of her association, "that this colorful, sensual woman could be adding color, body, and some positive qualities of the child to your writing?"

"I suppose it's possible," she says, still unconvinced by this affront to her more satisfying interpretation.

One of the things that turned me away from her reading of the dream, apart from the general principle that we should avoid getting caught in the dream ego's complexes, was the negative narcissism in her judgment about the child: she didn't want to accept her own childlike ways. Once we moved away from her attachment to her usual way of thinking about herself, an attitude that strongly colored her own thoughts about the dream, we could go on to consider some truly fresh ideas about her life situation and her personal habits.

I am going into some detail about dreams not only because they give us a great deal of insight into our habits and our nature, but also because the way we relate to our dreams can be indicative of our way of dealing with all kinds of things, including our interpretations of the past, our current situation and problems, and the culture in the larger sense.

For example, another rule of thumb about dreams is that there is never a single, definitive reading. At another time, the same dream might reveal something altogether new. I like to treat dreams as if they were paintings, and paintings as if they were dreams. A Monet landscape might "mean" something different to various people who contemplate it. It might evoke entirely different reactions in the same person at different viewings. Over many years, a good painting will retain its power to mesmerize, satisfy, and evoke new reverie and wonder.

The same is true with dreams. A dream may survive a lifetime of neglect or an onslaught of interpretations and remain an icon and a fertile enigma for years of reflection. The point in working with a dream is never to translate it into a final meaning, but always to give it honor and respect, drawing from it as much meaningfulness and imaginative meditation as possible. Entering a dream should revitalize the imagination, not keep it in fixed and tired habits.

A simple but effective approach in working with images—whether they are from dreams, art, or personal stories—is never to stop listening to them and exploring them. Why do we listen to Bach's St. Matthew Passion more than once? Because it is the nature of a work of art, of any image, to reveal itself endlessly, one of the methods I use in therapy and in teaching is to listen to a reading of a dream or a story and say, when it is finished, "All right, let's try that again, differently."

Once a young man came to me with a letter he had written to his sweetheart. It was important to him because it expressed his deep feelings. He said he'd like to read it to me aloud. He read it slowly and expressively. When he was finished, I asked him if he'd read it again, with different emphasis. He did, and in this reading we heard different nuances of meaning. We tried it a third and a fourth time, and each time we learned something new. This little exercise points out the rich, multilayered nature of images of all kinds, and the advantage of never stopping in our exploration of them. The images, dreams, and experiences that are important to us will always have a multitude of possible readings and interpretations, because they are rich with imagination and soul.

I understand that this approach to imagination goes against the part of us that   45 longs for a conclusion and a destination in our search for meaning. This is another reason why *care* of the soul, in contrast to *understanding* the soul, amounts to a new paradigm for our modern way of life. It asks us to make a complete turnaround in our usual efforts to figure things out, suggesting a different set of values and new techniques in which we actually appreciate and enjoy the endless unraveling of meaning, the infinitely rich and deep layering of poetics within the shifting, fluid fabric of experience.

The desire to squeeze a single meaning out of a dream or a work of art or a tale from life is inherently and profoundly Promethean. We want to steal fire from the gods for the sake of humanity. We want to replace divine mystery with human rationality. But this loss of complexity and mystery in our everyday response to life stories entails a loss of soul as well, because soul always manifests itself in mystery and multiplicity.

Dreams themselves often show us the way to understand them: they pull the dreamer deep into a body of water, or down into a pit, or down an elevator to a basement, or down a dark stairway, or deep into an alley. Typically, the dreamer, preferring height and light, is afraid to make the downward move into darkness. When I taught in the university, students frequently told me dreams of going into the library, getting on an elevator, then finding themselves in an ancient basement. The dream is not surprising, given the fact that the life of academia is so much an Apollonic, upper-world, ivory tower affair, and stands as a metaphor for all our attempts at understanding.

A woman who worked for a large appliance corporation once told me a dream in which she and her husband got off an elevator on a lower floor of the building, only to find the entire area under water. Together they floated in the water through hallways and streets until they arrived at a wonderful restaurant where they sat and ate a delicious dinner. This, too, is an image of dreamwork: allowing oneself to move around in the liquid atmosphere of fantasy and finding nourishment there. In dreams, which need never be taken literally or according to the laws of nature, we can breathe in a watery atmosphere. Dreams *are* watery: they resist all efforts to make them fixed and solid. We think we can only survive in the airy realms of thought and reason, but this dreamer found that she could be fed in gourmet style in that thicker atmosphere where imagination and life are fluid.

The Guiding Daimon

An approach often taken to images is to find a meaning outside the image itself. A cigar in a dream is considered a phallic symbol instead of a cigar. A woman is an anima figure instead of a particular woman. A child is the "child part of myself" instead of simply the child of the dream. We think of imagination as a kind of symbolic thinking, with, as Freud put it, a latent and a manifest meaning. If we could "decipher" the given symbols, to use a popular rationalistic word, we could learn the meaning that is hidden in the image.

But there is another possible way to understand the creations of the dream 50 world. What if there were no hidden meaning, no underlying message? What if we chose to confront images in all their mystery, deciding whether to follow their lead or to struggle with them?

The Greeks referred to the multitude of unnamed spirits that motivate and guide life as daimons. Socrates claimed to have lived his life according to the dictates of his daimon. In more recent times, W.B. Yeats warned that the daimon both inspires and threatens. In the chapter of *Memories, Dreams, Reflections* entitled "Late Thoughts," Jung, too, discusses the daimon. "We know that something unknown, alien, does come our way, just as we know that we do not ourselves *make* a dream or an inspiration, but that it somehow arises of its own accord. What does happen to us in this manner can be said to emanate from mana, from a daimon, a god, or the unconscious." He goes on to say that he prefers the term *the unconscious,* but he might just as well say *daimon.* Daimonic living is a response to the movements of imagination. When Jung was building his tower, workmen delivered a large piece of stone that was the wrong size. He took this "mistake" as the work of his Mercurial daimon and used the stone for one of his most important sculptures, the Bollingen Stone.

In the fifteenth century, Ficino, in *his* book on care of the soul, recommended finding the guardian daimon that is with us from the beginning: "Whoever examines himself thoroughly will find his own daimon." Rilke also regarded the daimon with respect. In his *Letters to a Young Poet* he suggests diving deeply into oneself in order to find one's own nature: "Go into yourself and see how deep the place is from which your life flows." Rilke is giving advice to a young man who wants to know whether he is called to be an artist, but his recommendation applies to anyone who wants to live everyday life with art. The soul wants to be in touch with that deep place from which life flows, without translating its offerings into familiar concepts. The best way to fulfill this desire is to give attention to the images that arise as independent beings from the springs of day-to-day imagination.

One implication of offering respect to the dream world is that we have to re-imagine imagination itself. Instead of seeing it as a particularly creative form of mind work, we could understand it more along Greek mythological lines, as a spring from which autonomous beings arise. Our relationship to it would change as well, from attempting to translate florid fantasy into reasonable terms to observing and entering a veritable world of personalities, geographies, animals, and events—all irreducible to completely understandable or controllable terms.

We would realize that the images of dreams and art are not puzzles to be solved, and that imagination hides its meaningfulness as much as it reveals it. In order to be affected by a dream, it isn't necessary to understand it or even to mine it for meanings. Merely giving our attention to such imagery, granting its autonomy and mystery, goes a long way toward shifting the center of consciousness from understanding to response. To live in the presence of the daimonic is to obey inner laws and urgencies. Cicero said that it is the *animus*—the Latin translation of *daimon*—that accounts for who you are. Ficino warned against living in conflict with the daimon lest you succumb to the worst kind of soul sickness. As an example, he says you should never decide where to live without taking into full consideration the demands of the daimon, which may appear as an intuitive attraction or inhibition.

The source from which life flows is so deep that it is experienced as "other." 55 Speaking in the ancient language of the daimonic helps bring imagination into our very sense of self. Our relationship to the deep source of life becomes interpersonal, a dramatic tension between self and angel. In this dialogue, life also becomes more artful, in some cases even dramatic. We see this in people we label psychotic. Most of their actions are explicitly dramatic. Their deep "others," the personalities who play significant roles in their lives, appear in full dress. Writers talk about the characters of their fiction as people with will and intention. The novelist Margaret Atwood said once in an interview, "If the author gets too bossy, the characters may remind her that, though she is their creator, they are to some extent her creator as well."

Art teaches us to respect imagination as something far beyond human creation and intention. To live our ordinary life artfully is to have this sensibility about the things of daily life, to live more intuitively and to be willing to surrender a measure of our rationality and control in return for the gifts of soul.

The Soul Arts

Care of the soul may take the form of living in a fully embodied imagination, being an artist at home and at work. You don't have to be a professional in order to bring art into the care of your soul; anyone can have an art studio at home, for instance. Like Jung, Black Elk, and Ficino, we could decorate our homes with images from our dreams and waking fantasy.

One of my own forms of expression is to play the piano in times of strong emotion. I remember well the day Martin Luther King, Jr., was killed. I was so overwhelmed that I went to the piano and played Bach for three hours. The music gave form and voice to my scrambled emotions, without explanations and rational interpretations.

The stuff of the world is there to be made into images that become for us tabernacles of spirituality and containers of mystery. If we don't allow soul its place in our lives, we are forced to encounter these mysteries in fetishes and symptoms, which in a sense are pathological art forms, the gods in our diseases. The example of artists teaches us that every day we can transform ordinary experience into the material of soul—in diaries, poems, drawings, music, letters, watercolors.

In a letter on soul-making to his brother George, Keats describes the process of 60 transforming world into soul with the image of a school: "I will call the world a School instituted for the purpose of teaching little children to read—I will call the human heart the hornbook used in that School—and I will call the child able to read, the Soul made from that school and its hornbook. Do you not see how necessary a World of Pains and troubles is to school an Intelligence and make it a soul?"

As we read our experiences and learn to express them artfully, we are making life more soulful. Our homely arts arrest the flow of life momentarily so that events can be submitted to the alchemy of reflection. In a letter to a friend, we can deepen the impressions of experience and settle them in the heart where they can become the foundation for soul. Our great museums of art are simply a grand model for the more modest museum that is our home. There is no reason not to imagine our own homes as a place where the Muses can do their work of inspiration daily.

Another advantage to the soul of practicing the ordinary arts is the gift they leave for future generations. Tradition says that the soul thrives in a sense of time much greater than that of consciousness. To the soul the past is alive and valuable, and so is the future. As we perform the alchemy of sketching or writing upon our daily experience, we are preserving our thoughts for those who follow us. The community made by art transcends the limits of a personal lifetime, so that we can be instructed in our own soul work by the letters of John Keats to his brother.

In the modern world, in which we live mainly for the moment, it is easy to overlook the taste of the soul for a greater sense of time and a profound notion of community. We tend to give superficial explanations for our actions, to speak in literal terms instead of focusing on the reasons of the heart. A man explaining to me why he was getting a divorce went on and on with minor complaints about his wife. What he didn't say was what was obvious from our other conversations, that his heart was going through a major change. He wanted a new life, but tried to justify all the accompanying pain with superficial reasons. Because he didn't speak deeply about what was going on with him, he was cutting himself off from the soul of his divorce.

But when you read the letters of Keats, Rilke, or other poets you find a passionate search for expression and language adequate to the pleasures and pains of life. We can learn from them the importance to everyone, not just poets, of the effort to translate experience into words and pictures. The point of art is not simply to express ourselves, but to create an external, concrete form in which the soul of our lives can be evoked and contained.

Children paint every day and love to show their works on walls and refrigerator doors. But as we become adults, we abandon this important soul task of childhood. We assume, I suppose, that children are just learning motor coordination and alphabets. But maybe they are doing something more fundamental: finding forms that reflect what is going on in their souls. When we grow up and begin to think of the art gallery as much more advanced than the refrigerator door, we lose an important ritual of childhood, giving it away to the professional artist. We are then left with mere rational reasons for our lives, feelings of emptiness and confusion, expensive visits to a psychotherapist, and a compulsive attachment to pseudoimages, such as shallow television programs. When our own images no longer have a home, a personal museum, we drown our sense of loss in pale substitutes, trashy novels or formulaic movies.

As the poets and painters of centuries have tried to tell us, art is not about the expression of talent or the making of pretty things. It is about the preservation and containment of soul. It is about arresting life and making it available for contemplation. Art captures the eternal in the everyday, and it is the eternal that feeds soul—the whole world in a grain of sand.

Leonardo da Vinci asks an interesting question in one of his notebooks: "Why does the eye see a thing more clearly in dreams than the imagination when awake?" One answer is that the eye of the soul perceives the eternal realities so important to the heart. In waking life, most of us see only with our physical eyes, even though we could, with some effort of imagination, glimpse fragments of eternity in the most ordinary passing events. Dream teaches us to look with that other eye, the eye that in waking life belongs to the artist, to each of us as artist.

When we see pain on a tortured person's face, we might glimpse for a second the image of Jesus crucified, a reality that artists for centuries have shown in infinite variation and detail and one that enters the lives of all of us at one time or another. We might look at a woman in a jewelry shop with the eyes of D.H. Lawrence, who saw Aphrodite in the body of the woman washing her clothes in a river. We might see a Cézanne still life in a momentary glance at our own kitchen table. When a summer breeze blows through an open window as we sit reading in a rare half-hour of quiet, we might recall one of the hundreds of annunciations painters have given us, reminding us that it is the habit of angels to visit in moments of silent reading.

A soul-centered understanding of art sees the interpenetration of poetic image and ordinary life. Art shows us what is already there in the ordinary, but without art we live under the illusion that there is only time, and not eternity. As we practice our daily arts, if only in the composing of a heart-felt letter, we are unearthing the eternal from within ordinary time, engaging in the special qualities, themes, and circumstances of the soul. Soul thrives as we jot down a thought in our diary or note a dream, and give body to a slight influx of eternity. Our notebooks then truly become our own private gospels and sutras, our holy books, and our simple paintings truly serve as icons, every bit as significant in the work of our own soul as the wonderful icons of the Eastern churches are for their congregations.

Care of the soul is not a project of self-improvement nor a way of being released   70
from the troubles and pains of human existence. It is not at all concerned with living properly or with emotional health. These are the concerns of temporal, heroic, Promethean life. Care of the soul touches another dimension, in no way separate from life, but not identical either with the problem solving that occupies so much of our consciousness. We care for the soul solely by honoring its expressions, by giving it time and opportunity to reveal itself, and by living life in a way that fosters the depth, interiority, and quality in which it flourishes. Soul is its own purpose and end.

To the soul, memory is more important than planning, art more compelling than reason, and love more fulfilling than understanding. We know we are well on the way toward soul when we feel attachment to the world and the people around us and when we live as much from the heart as from the head. We know soul is being cared for when our pleasures feel deeper than usual, when we can let go of the need to be free of complexity and confusion, and when compassion takes the place of distrust and fear. Soul is interested in the differences among cultures and individuals, and within ourselves it wants to be expressed in uniqueness if not in outright eccentricity.

Therefore, when in the midst of my confusion and my stumbling attempts to live a transparent life, *I* am the fool, and not everyone around me, then I know I am discovering the power of the soul to make a life interesting. Ultimately, care of the soul results in an individual "I" I never would have planned for or maybe even wanted. By caring for the soul faithfully, every day, we step out of the way and let our full genius emerge. Soul coalesces into the mysterious philosophers' stone, that rich, solid core of personality the alchemists sought, or it opens into the peacock's tail—a revelation of the soul's colors and a display of its dappled brilliance.

ACTIVITIES FOR WRITING AND DISCUSSION

1. Since Moore's essay is quite long, try to read it in two or more sittings, focusing on sections that strike you and skimming over those that don't. In your notebook, respond using either:

   a. The "Four-Step Process for Writing from Reading" described in Chapter 2; or

   b. Idea #1 from the "Ten Ideas" described in Chapter 3.

2. In paragraph 45 Moore writes: "*[C]are* of the soul, in contrast to *understanding* the soul, amounts to a new paradigm for our modern way of life." Read the context in which this sentence appears. Then consider:

    a. Some differences between "caring" and "understanding" as Moore seems to use those terms. Can caring and understanding be at odds with each other? If so how and in what situations?

    b. In what ways do you think Moore's statement, quoted above, is accurate or inaccurate?

3. In his discussion of "The Guiding Daimon," Moore writes:

The source from which life flows is so deep that it is experienced as "other." . . . Our relationship to the deep source of life [i.e., the daimon] becomes interpersonal, a dramatic tension between self and angel.

Explain what you think Moore means by "the daimon." Then do one of the following:

    a. Over a period of days, think about the nature of your own "angel" or "daimon"; describe its power, mystery, promises, and dangers. Then write a dialogue—or a series of short dialogues—between your own "self" and this angel or daimon.

    b. List the names of some outstanding people, living or dead, whom you admire. Choose one such person and write about the nature of the "daimon" that you imagine guides (or guided) that person in his or her life.

MICHAEL DORRIS (1945–1997)

Life Stories

In most cultures, adulthood is equated with self-reliance and responsibility, yet often Americans do not achieve this status until we are in our late twenties or early thirties—virtually the entire average lifespan of a person in a traditional non-Western society. We tend to treat prolonged adolescence as a warm-up for real life, as a wobbly ladder between childhood and legal maturity. Whereas a nineteenth-century Cheyenne or Lakota teenager was expected to alter self-conception in a split-second vision, we often meander through an analogous rite of passage for more than a decade—through high school, college, graduate school.

Though he had never before traveled alone outside his village, the Plains Indian male was expected at puberty to venture solo into the wilderness. There he had to fend for and sustain himself while avoiding the menace of unknown dangers, and there he had absolutely to remain until something happened that would transform him. Every human being, these tribes believed, was entitled to at least one moment of personal, enabling insight.

Anthropology proposes feasible psychological explanations for why this flash was eventually triggered: fear, fatigue, reliance on strange foods, the anguish of loneliness, stress, and the expectation of ultimate success all contributed to a state of receptivity. Every sense was quickened, alerted to perceive deep meaning, until at last the interpretation of an unusual event—a dream, a chance encounter, or an unexpected vista—reverberated with significance. Through this unique prism, abstractly preserved in a vivid memory or song, a boy caught foresight of both his adult persona and his vocation, the two inextricably entwined.

The best approximations that many of us get to such a heady sense of eventuality come in the performance of the jobs we hold during summer vacation. Summers are intermissions, and once we hit our teens it is during these breaks in our structured regimen that we initially taste the satisfaction of remuneration that is earned, not merely doled. Tasks defined as work are not graded, they are compensated; they have a worth that is inarguable because it translates into hard currency. Wage labor—and in the beginning, this generally means a confining, repetitive chore for which we are quickly overqualified—paradoxically brings a sense of blooming freedom. At the outset, the complaint to a peer that business supersedes fun is oddly liberating—no matter what drudgery requires your attention, it is by its very required nature serious and adult.

At least that's how it seemed to me. I come from a line of people hard hit by 5 the Great Depression. My mother and her sisters went to work early in their teens—my mother operated a kind of calculator known as a comptometer while her sisters spent their days, respectively, at a peanut factory and at Western Union. My grandmother did piecework sewing. Their efforts, and the Democratic Party, saw them through, and to this day they never look back without appreciation for their later solvency. They take nothing for granted. Accomplishments are celebrated, possessions are valuable, in direct proportion to the labor entailed to acquire them; anything easily won or bought on credit is suspect. When I was growing up we were far from wealthy, but what money we had was correlated to the hours one of us had logged. My eagerness to contribute to, or at least not diminish, the coffer was countered by the arguments of those whose salaries kept me in school: my higher education was a sound group investment. The whole family was adamant that I have the opportunities they had missed and, no matter how much I objected, they stinted themselves to provide for me.

Summer jobs were therefore a relief, an opportunity to pull a share of the load. As soon as the days turned warm I began to peruse the classifieds, and when the spring semester was done, I was ready to punch a clock. It even felt right. Work in June, July, and August had an almost biblical aspect: in the hot, canicular weather your brow sweats, just as God had ordained. Moreover, summer jobs had the luxury of being temporary. No matter how onerous, how off my supposed track, employment terminated with the falling leaves and I was back to real life. So, during each annual three-month leave from secondary school and later from the university, I compiled an eclectic resumé: lawn cutter, hair sweeper in a barber shop, lifeguard, delivery boy, mail carrier, file clerk, youth program coordinator on my Montana reservation, ballroom dance instructor, theater party promoter, night-shift hospital records keeper, human adding machine in a Paris bank, encyclopedia salesman, newspaper stringer, recreation bus manager, salmon fisherman.

The summer I was eighteen a possibility arose for a rotation at the post office, and I grabbed it. There was something casually sophisticated about work that required a uniform, about having a federal ranking, even if it was GS-1 (Temp/Sub), and it was flattering to be entrusted with a leather bag containing who knew what important correspondence. Every day I was assigned a new beat, usually in a rough neighborhood avoided whenever possible by regular carriers, and I proved quite capable of complicating what would normally be fairly routine missions. The low point came on the first of August when I diligently delivered four blocks' worth of welfare checks to the right numbers on the wrong streets. It is no fun to snatch unexpected wealth from the hands of those who had but moments previously opened their mailboxes and received a bonus.

After my first year of college, I lived with relatives on an Indian reservation in eastern Montana and filled the only post available: Coordinator of Youth Programs. I was seduced by the language of the announcement into assuming that there existed Youth Programs to be coordinated. In fact, the Youth consisted of a dozen bored, disgruntled kids—most of them my cousins—who had nothing better to do each day than to show up at what was euphemistically called "the gym" and hate whatever Program I had planned for them. The Youth ranged in age from fifteen to five and seemed to have as their sole common ambition the determination to smoke cigarettes. This put them at immediate and ongoing odds with the Coordinator, who on his first day naively encouraged them to sing the "Doe, a deer, a female deer" song from *The Sound of Music*. They looked at me, that bleak morning, and I looked at them, each boy and girl equipped with a Pall Mall behind an ear, and we all knew we faced a long, struggle-charged battle. It was to be a contest of wills, the hearty and wholesome versus prohibited vice. I stood for dodge ball, for collecting bugs in glass jars, for arts and crafts; they had pledged a preternatural allegiance to sloth. The odds were not in my favor and each waking dawn I experienced the lightheadedness of anticipated exhaustion, that thrill of giddy dissociation in which nothing seems real or of great significance. Finally, I went with the flow and learned to inhale.

The next summer, I decided to find work in an urban setting for a change, and was hired as a general office assistant in the Elsa Hoppenfeld Theatre Party Agency, located above Sardi's restaurant in New York City. The agency consisted of Elsa Hoppenfeld herself, Rita Frank, her regular deputy, and me. Elsa was a gregarious Viennese woman who established contacts through honesty, hard work, and personal charm, and she spent much of the time away from the building courting trade. Rita was therefore both my immediate supervisor and constant companion; she had the most incredible fingernails I had ever seen—long, carefully shaped pegs lacquered in cruel primary colors and hard as stone—and an attitude about her that could only be described as zeal.

The goal of a theater party agent is to sell blocks of tickets to imminent Broad- 10 way productions, and the likely buyers are charities, B'nai B'riths, Hadassahs, and assorted other fund-raising organizations. We received commissions on volume, and so it was necessary to convince a prospect that a play—preferably an expensive musical—for which we had reserved the rights to seats would be a boffo smash hit.

The object of our greatest expectation that season was an extravaganza called *Chu Chem*, a saga that aspired to ride the coattails of *Fiddler on the Roof* into entertainment history. It starred the estimable Molly Picon and told the story of a family who had centuries ago gone from Israel to China during the Diaspora, yet had, despite isolation in an alien environment, retained orthodox culture and habits. The crux of the plot revolved around a man with several marriageable daughters and nary a kosher suitor within five thousand miles. For three months Rita and I waxed eloquent in singing the show's praises. We sat in our little office, behind facing desks, and every noon while she redid her nails I ordered out from a deli that offered such exotic (to me) delicacies as fried egg sandwiches, lox and cream cheese, pastrami, tongue. I developed of necessity and habit a telephone voice laced with a distinctly Yiddish accent. It could have been a great career. However, come November, *Chu Chem* bombed. Its closing was such a financial catastrophe for all concerned that when the following January one Monsieur Dupont advertised on the placement board at my college, I decided to put an ocean between me and my former trusting clientele.

M. Dupont came to campus with the stated purpose of interviewing candidates for teller positions in a French bank. Successful applicants, required to be fluent *en français,* would be rewarded with three well-paid months and a rent-free apartment in Paris. On my way to the language lab, I registered for an appointment.

The only French in the interview was *Bonjour, ça va?*, after which M. Dupont switched into English and described the wonderful deal on charter air flights that would be available to those who got the nod. Round-trip to Amsterdam, via Reykjavík, leaving the day after exams and returning in mid-September, no changes or substitutions. I signed up on the spot. I was to be a *banquier,* with a *pied-à-terre* in Montparnasse!

Unfortunately, when I arrived with only $50 in traveler's checks in my pocket—the flight had cleaned me out, but who needed money since my paycheck started right away—no one in Paris had ever heard of M. Dupont. *Alors.*

I stood in the Gare du Nord and considered my options. There weren't any. 15 I scanned a listing of Paris hotels and headed for the cheapest one: the Hotel Villedo, $10 a night. The place had an ambiance that I persuaded myself was antique, despite the red light above the sign. The only accommodation available was "the bridal suite," a steal at $20. The glass door to my room didn't lock and in the adjacent room there was a rather continual floor show, but at some point I must have dozed off. When I awoke the church bells were ringing, the sky was pink, and I felt renewed. No little setback was going to spoil my adventure. I stretched, then walked to a mirror that hung above the sink next to the bed. I leaned forward to punctuate my resolve with a confident look in the eye.

The sink disengaged and fell to the floor. Water gushed. In panic I rummaged through my open suitcase, stuffed two pairs of underpants into the pipe to quell the flow, and before the dam broke, I was out the door. I barreled through the lobby of the first bank I passed, asked to see the director, and told the startled man my sad story. For some reason, whether from shock or pity, he hired me at $1.27 an hour to be a cross-checker of foreign currency transactions, and with two phone calls found me lodgings at a commercial school's dormitory.

From 8 to 5 each weekday my duty was to sit in a windowless room with six impeccably dressed people, all of whom were totaling identical additions and subtractions. We were highly dignified with each other, very professional, no *tu-toyer*ing. Monsieur Saint presided, but the formidable Mademoiselle was the true power; she oversaw each of our columns and shook her head sadly at my American-shaped numbers.

My legacy from that summer, however, was more than an enduring penchant for crossed 7s. After I had worked for six weeks, M. Saint asked me during a coffee break why I didn't follow the example of other foreign students he had known and depart the office at noon in order to spend the afternoon touring the sights of Paris with the Alliance Française.

"Because," I replied in my halting French, "that costs money. I depend upon my full salary the same as any of you." M. Saint nodded gravely and said no more, but then on the next Friday he presented me with a white envelope along with my check.

"Do not open this until you have left the Société Général," he said ominously. 20 I thought I was fired for the time I had mixed up kroner and guilders, and, once on the sidewalk, I steeled myself to read the worst. I felt the quiet panic of blankness.

"Dear Sir," I translated the perfectly formed script. "You are a person of value. It is not correct that you should be in our beautiful city and not see it. Therefore we have amassed a modest sum to pay the tuition for a two-week afternoon program for you at the Alliance Française. Your wages will not suffer, for it is your assignment to appear each morning in this bureau and reacquaint us with the places you have visited. We shall see them afresh through your eyes." The letter had thirty signatures, from the director to the janitor, and stuffed inside the envelope was a sheaf of franc notes in various denominations.

I rushed back to the tiny office. M. Saint and Mademoiselle had waited, and accepted my gratitude with their usual controlled smiles and precise handshakes. But they had blown their Gallic cover, and for the next ten days and then through all the weeks until I went home in September, our branch was awash with sightseeing paraphernalia. Everyone had advice, favorite haunts, criticisms of the Alliance's choices or explanations. Paris passed through the bank's granite walls as sweetly as a June breeze through a window screen, and ever afterward the lilt of overheard French, a photograph of Sacre-Coeur or the Louvre, even a monthly bank statement, recalls to me that best of all summers.

I didn't wind up in an occupation with any obvious connection to the careers I sampled during my school breaks, but I never altogether abandoned those brief professions either. They were jobs not so much to be held as to be weighed, absorbed, and incorporated, and, collectively, they carried me forward into adult life like an escalator, unfolding a particular pattern at once amazing and inevitable.

ACTIVITIES FOR WRITING AND DISCUSSION

1. Reread the last sentence in the essay.
   a. Interpret this concluding statement. What do you think Dorris means by it?
   b. In an essay, discuss one or two jobs in your own past that had a particular impact on you. Tell some specific stories about those jobs (as Dorris does) to make them vivid for a reader. Think of a crucial moment in any of the stories when there was dialogue, and write the dialogue. To what extent have you "weighed, absorbed, and incorporated" those jobs, and what "particular pattern" (if any) do you perceive in them?

2. Think of an early job that particularly influenced you. Write a letter (sent or unsent) to your employer, in which you recount your experiences on that job and how they affected you, for better or worse, in the short and/or long term.

LINDA HOGAN (b. 1947)

Waking Up the Rake

In the still dark mornings, my grandmother would rise up from her bed and put wood in the stove. When the fire began to burn, she would sit in front of its warmth and let down her hair. It had never been cut and it knotted down in two long braids. When I was fortunate enough to be there, in those red Oklahoma mornings, I would wake up with her, stand behind her chair, and pull the brush through the long strands of her hair. It cascaded down her back, down over the chair, and touched the floor.

We were the old and the new, bound together in front of the snapping fire, woven like a lifetime's tangled growth of hair. I saw my future in her body and face, and her past was alive in me. We were morning people, and in all of earth's mornings the new intertwines with the old. Even new, a day itself is ancient, old with earth's habit of turning over and over again.

Years later, I was sick, and I went to a traditional healer. The healer was dark and thin and radiant. The first night I was there, she also lit a fire. We sat before it, smelling the juniper smoke. She asked me to tell her everything, my life spoken in words, a case history of living, with its dreams and losses, the scars and wounds we all bear from being in the world. She smoked me with cedar smoke, wrapped a sheet around me, and put me to bed, gently, like a mother caring for her child.

The next morning she nudged me awake and took me outside to pray. We faced east where the sun was beginning its journey on our side of earth.

The following morning in red dawn, we went outside and prayed. The sun was 5 a full orange eye rising up the air. The morning after that we did the same, and on Sunday we did likewise.

The next time I visited her it was a year later, and again we went through the same prayers, standing outside facing the early sun. On the last morning I was there, she left for her job in town. Before leaving, she said, "Our work is our altar."

Those words have remained with me.

Now I am a disciple of birds. The birds that I mean are eagles, owls, and hawks. I clean cages at the Birds of Prey Rehabilitation Foundation. It is the work I wanted to do, in order to spend time inside the gentle presence of the birds.

There is a Sufi saying that goes something like this: "Yes, worship God, go to church, sing praises, but first tie your camel to the post." This cleaning is the work of tying the camel to a post.

I pick up the carcasses and skin of rats, mice, and of rabbits. Some of them have 10 been turned inside out by the sharp-beaked eaters, so that the leathery flesh becomes a delicately veined coat for the inner fur. It is a boneyard. I rake the smooth fragments of bones. Sometimes there is a leg or shank of deer to be picked up.

In this boneyard, the still-red vertebrae lie on the ground beside an open rib cage. The remains of a rabbit, a small intestinal casing, holds excrement like beads in a necklace. And there are the clean, oval pellets the birds spit out, filled with fur, bone fragments and now and then, a delicate sharp claw that looks as if it were woven inside. A feather, light and soft, floats down a current of air, and it is also picked up.

Over time, the narrow human perspective from which we view things expands. A deer carcass begins to look beautiful and rich in its torn redness, the muscle and bone exposed in the shape life took on for a while as it walked through meadows and drank at creeks.

And the bone fragments have their own stark beauty, the clean white jaw bones with ivory teeth small as the head of a pin still in them. I think of medieval physicians trying to learn about our private, hidden bodies by cutting open the stolen dead and finding the splendor inside, the grace of every red organ, and the smooth, gleaming bone.

This work is an apprenticeship, and the birds are the teachers. Sweet-eyed barn owls, such taskmasters, asking us to be still and slow and to move in time with their rhythms, not our own. The short-eared owls with their startling yellow eyes require the full presence of a human. The marsh hawks, behind their branches, watch our every move.

There is a silence needed here before a person enters the bordered world the 15 birds inhabit, so we stop and compose ourselves before entering their doors, and we listen to the musical calls of the eagles, the sound of wings in air, the way their feet with sharp claws, many larger than our own hands, grab hold of a perch. Then we know we are ready to enter, and they are ready for us.

The most difficult task the birds demand is that we learn to be equal to them, to feel our way into an intelligence that is different from our own. A friend, awed at the thought of working with eagles, said, "Imagine knowing an eagle." I answered her honestly, "It isn't so much that we know the eagles. It's that they know us."

And they know that we are apart from them, that as humans we have some-how fallen from our animal grace, and because of that we maintain a distance from them, though it is not always a distance of heart. The places we inhabit, even sharing a common earth, must remain distinct and separate. It was our presence that brought most of them here in the first place, nearly all of them injured in a clash with the human world. They have been shot, or hit by cars, trapped in leg hold traps, poisoned, ensnared in wire fences. To ensure their survival, they must remember us as the enemies that we are. We are the embodiment of a paradox; we are the wounders and we are the healers.

There are human lessons to be learned here, in the work. Fritjof Capra wrote: "Doing work that has to be done over and over again helps us to recognize the natural cycles of growth and decay, of birth and death, and thus become aware of the dynamic order of the universe." And it is true, in whatever we do, the brush-ing of hair, the cleaning of cages, we begin to see the larger order of things. In this place, there is a constant coming to terms with both the sacred place life occupies, and with death. Like one of those early physicians who discovered the strange, in-ner secrets of our human bodies, I'm filled with awe at the very presence of life, not just the birds, but a horse contained in its living fur, a dog alive and running. What a marvel it is, the fine shape life takes in all of us. It is equally marvelous that life is quickly turned back to earth-colored ants and the soft white maggots that are time's best and closest companions. To sit with the eagles and their flute-like songs, listening to the longer flute of wind sweep through the lush grasslands, is to begin to know the natural laws that exist apart from our own written ones.

One of those laws, that we carry deep inside us, is intuition. It is lodged in a place even the grave-robbing doctors could not discover. It's a blood-written code that directs us through life. The founder of this healing center, Sigrid Ueblacker, depends on this inner knowing. She watches, listens, and feels her way to an un-derstanding of each eagle and owl. This vision, as I call it, directs her own daily work at healing the injured birds and returning them to the wild.

"Sweep the snow away," she tells me. "The Swainson's hawks should be in   20 Argentina this time of year and should not have to stand in the snow."

I sweep.

And that is in the winter when the hands ache from the cold, and the water freezes solid and has to be broken out for the birds, fresh buckets carried over icy earth from the well. In summer, it's another story. After only a few hours the food begins to move again, as if resurrected to life. A rabbit shifts a bit. A mouse turns. You could say that they have been resurrected, only with a life other than the one that left them. The moving skin swarms with flies and their offspring, ants, and a few wasps, busy at their own daily labor.

Even aside from the expected rewards for this work, such as seeing an eagle healed and winging across the sky it fell from, there are others. An occasional snake, beautiful and sleek, finds its way into the cage one day, eats a mouse and is too fat to leave, so we watch its long muscular life stretched out in the tall grasses. Or, another summer day, taking branches to be burned with a pile of wood near the little creek, a large turtle with a dark and shining shell slips soundlessly into the water, its presence a reminder of all the lives beyond these that occupy us.

One green morning, an orphaned owl perches nervously above me while I clean. Its downy feathers are roughed out. It appears to be twice its size as it clacks its beak at me, warning me: Stay back. Then, fearing me the way we want it to, it bolts off the perch and flies, landing by accident onto the wooden end of my rake, before it sees that a human is an extension of the tool, and it flies again to a safer place, while I return to raking.

The word *rake* means to gather or heap up, to smooth the broken ground. 25 And that's what this work is, all of it, the smoothing over of broken ground, the healing of the severed trust we humans hold with earth. We gather it back together again with great care, take the broken pieces and fragments and return them to the sky. It is work at the borderland between species, at the boundary between injury and healing.

There is an art to raking, a very fine art, one with rhythm in it, and life. On the days I do it well, the rake wakes up. Wood that came from dark dense forests seems to return to life. The water that rose up through the rings of that wood, the minerals of earth mined upward by the burrowing tree roots, all come alive. My own fragile hand touches the wood, a hand full of my own life, including that which rose each morning early to watch the sun return from the other side of the planet. Over time, these hands will smooth the rake's wooden handle down to a sheen.

Raking. It is a labor round and complete, smooth and new as an egg, and the rounding seasons of the world revolving in time and space. All things, even our own heartbeats and sweat, are in it, part of it. And that work, that watching the turning over of life, becomes a road into what is essential. Work is the country of hands, and they want to live there in the dailiness of it, the repetition that is time's language of prayer, a common tongue. Everything is there, in that language, in the humblest of labor. The rake wakes up and the healing is in it. The shadows of leaves that once fell beneath the tree the handle came from are in that labor, and the rabbits that passed this way, on the altar of our work. And when the rake wakes up, all earth's gods are reborn and they dance and sing in the dusty air around us.

ACTIVITIES FOR WRITING AND DISCUSSION

1. The traditional healer whom Hogan visits says, "Our work is our altar." Judging from the narrative that precedes this statement, explain what you think the healer means by this **metaphor.** Then write about ways in which your own "work" (paid or unpaid, vocation or avocation) is—or isn't—an "altar."

2. Hogan says that her work for the Birds of Prey Rehabilitation Foundation is monotonous, yet she seems to value this very monotony. She performs a task (raking) that would seem to be easy and "mindless," yet she insists "there is an art to [it]." How can monotony be valuable, and how can a menial job—raking or any other—involve "art"? In your notebook try to explain either of these observations. *Alternative:* Write about any other ideas in the essay that you find surprising or striking, and relate them to your own experience.

3. Hogan says that birds require us "to feel our way into an intelligence that is different from our own." She also regards birds and other animals as soulful creatures from which we humans can learn. Reread and annotate passages about this "teacher"/"apprentice" relationship between animals and humans. Then assume the **point of view** of one such animal—from Hogan's essay or your own experience—and compose a text about your past, your life and its beauty, and your perspective on humans.

Barbara Kingsolver (b. 1955)

The One-Eyed Monster, and Why I Don't Let Him In

"Nobody ever gets killed at our house," begins a song by Charlie King, and it continues with a litany of other horrors—"no one gets shot at, run over, or stabbed, / nobody goes up in flames"—that you'd surely agree you wouldn't want to see in *your* house, either, until you realize he's discussing what routinely happens on the screen that most people happily host in their living rooms. Maybe you have one in yours, and maybe you don't, but I'm with Charlie. People very rarely get killed at our house, and I'm trying to keep it that way.

The subject isn't entirely closed, of course, because we are not Amish. We are what you'd call a regular American family, surrounded by regular America, and I believe in raising children who express themselves freely. This they do. The other night they raised the question once again of whether it might not be time for us to join the twenty-first century and every other upright-walking family we know of, at least in this neighborhood, and get cable TV.

"Why are you asking me?" I said, pretending to be dismayed. "Do I look like the dictator of this house?"

My efforts to stall weren't fooling anybody. I am not the dictator of this house, but I am the designated philosopher-king of its television-watching habits. That is to say, when my subjects become restless on the topic of TV, as they do from time to time, I sit down once again and explain to them in the kindest of tones why it is in their best interest to drop it.

But this time I'd been blindsided. Teenager and kindergartner were in league, with perhaps even the sympathies of my husband, though he was precluded from

offering an opinion by his diplomatic ties. But the indentured serfs were foment-
ing a small rebellion.

"OK, look," I said to my serfs. "Watching TV takes *time*. When are you going   6
to do it?"

They answered this without blinking: Evening. Morning. Prime time. Only   7
when something good is on.

Which was just what I was afraid of. I explained that while I could understand   8
there were probably some good things on TV that they were missing, they would
have to miss out on *other* things in order to watch them, and when I looked around
at what everybody was doing in our house, I couldn't really see what would give.
I asked them, particularly my teenager (who likes to watch *Daria* and MTV at
other people's houses, and whom I immediately sniffed out as our Robespierre
here), to spend a few days paying careful attention to the hours of her life and exactly how she spent them. Kind of like keeping a calorie record, only with minutes. If she could come up with two expendable hours per day, I'd consider letting
her spend them with the one-eyed monster.

She agreed to this, and at that moment I knew I'd already won. Here is what   9
she does with her time: goes to school, does homework, practices the upright bass,
talks with friends on the phone, eats dinner with the family, does more homework, reads for fun, hangs out with friends at their houses or ours, works out, listens to music, jams on the electric bass, tries to form an all-girl band, maintains
various pets, participates in family outings, and gets exactly enough sleep. (In
summertime the routine is different but the subject is moot, because then we live
beyond the reach of cables, in a tiny house with no room for a TV and antique
electricity that likely wouldn't support one anyway.) Her time card, in short, is
full. Friends, exercise, music—not one minute of these would she give up, nor
would I want her to. Even hanging out with friends—*especially* that—should not
be sacrificed for solitary confinement with a talking box. If she wants to watch
MTV at a friend's house, fine, that's *their* way of socializing—at our house her pals
like to beat on my conga drums. And while she might have offered to trade in
some hours of math homework, she knew better. Everything else she simply likes
too much to cut out of her day.

So the discussion was shelved for the time being. I intend to keep a firm hand   10
on at least this one aspect of my kingdom. To me, that ubiquitous cable looks an
awful lot like the snake that batted its eyes at Eve.

Probably I shouldn't use such a morally loaded metaphor. I don't mean to   11
equate my freedom from TV with freedom from sin, or to suggest that it confers
on me any special virtue, though others generally interpret the discussion that
way. If ever it comes up in conversation that my life is largely a TV void, people
instantly get defensive about their own television-viewing habits and extol the
value of the *few* things they like to watch (invariably citing something called the
History Channel). But no defense is necessary, I promise; this is not about high-
culture snobbery. If you knew me, you'd know there's almost nothing that is cat-
egorically beneath my dignity: I can get teary-eyed over a song about family re-
unions on the country radio station; I love to borrow my teenager's impractical

shoes; on a dance floor I'm more at home with salsa and hip-hop than the tango; I have been known to do the Macarena. At a party more recent than I care to admit (I was definitely past forty), my friends voted me Most Likely to Dance on the Table. Before I dig this hole any deeper, why don't you just take my word for it? I'm not too high-minded for television, I really just don't like it. It's a taste I never got to acquire, having been raised by parents who made it painfully clear that life offered no bigger waste of time than watching the "boob tube" (one of the rare slang terms that've become more apt with the years). From there I proceeded to live an adult life with lots to do and very little cash, so that purposefully setting out to pay money for a time-wasting device just never crossed my mind. I made it to the childbearing phase without TV dependence, then looked around and thought, Well gee, why start *now*? Why get a pet python on the *day* you decide to raise fuzzy little gerbils?

The advantages of raising kids without commercial TV seem obvious, and yet   12 I know plenty of parents who express dismay as their children demand sugar-frosted sugar for breakfast, then expensive name-brand clothing, then the right to dress up as hookers not for Halloween but for school. *Hello?* Anyone who feels powerless against the screaming voice of materialistic youth culture should remember that power comes out of those two little holes in the wall. The plug is detachable. Human young are not born with the knowledge that wearing somebody's name in huge letters on a T-shirt is a thrilling privilege for which they should pay eighty dollars. It takes years of careful instruction to arrive at that piece of logic.

I ask my kids, on principle, to live without wasteful and preposterous things   13 (e.g., clothing that extorts from customers the right to wear labels on the outside), and it's a happier proposition to follow through if we don't have an extra blabber-mouth in the room telling them every fourteen minutes about six brand-*new* wasteful, preposterous things they'll die without. It's fairly well documented that TV creates a net loss in contentment. The average household consumption of goods and services has doubled since 1957, when TV began to enter private homes, but according to a University of Chicago study, over all those years the fraction of Americans who describe themselves as "very happy" has remained steady, at about one third. The amount of money people believed they *needed* to buy happiness actually doubled between the mid-1980s and the mid-1990s, and the figure is still reaching for the sky. Think the kids would be unhappy without TV? I say pull the plug, quick, before they get more miserable. My daughters are by no means immune to peer pressure, but the kindergartner couldn't pick Tommy Hilfiger out of a lineup, and the ninth grader dresses way cool on an impressively frugal clothing budget, and they both find a hundred things to do each day that are more fun than sitting in front of a box. They agree with me about TV, once they're forced to accept the theory that there are only twenty-four hours in a day.

I can't think how anyone, child or adult, could sit still for the daily three hours   14 and forty-six minutes that is our national TV-watching average. For my own purposes, sitting still is probably the most difficult part of the proposition. I have struggled all my life with a constitutional impatience with anything that threatens to waste what's left of my minutes here on earth. I start fidgeting at any community meeting where the first item on the agenda is to discuss and vote on the order of the other items on the agenda; I have to do discreet yoga relaxation postures in my chair to keep myself from hollering, "Yo, people, life is short!" I was born like this; I need to get a move on. I'm the kind of person who races around the kitchen so fast while cooking (with my mind on two other things), that I sometimes snag the fabric of my pants pocket on a drawer knob, and may either rip my trousers or fling the forks and spoons across the room. But reading can hold me spellbound, provided I'm the one turning the pages. And so I'm the kind of person who would rather *read* history (skipping over the parts I don't need) than have to sit and *watch* the eight-hour docudrama (baloney included). As a habitual reader I find the pace of information delivery on television noticeably sluggish. There's a perfectly good reason for this: The script for a one-hour TV documentary is only about fifteen or twenty double-spaced pages in length, whereas most any competent reader can cover three to five times that much material in an hour. Devoted as our culture is to efficiency, convenience, and DSL Internet access, I'm surprised so many Americans are content to get their up-to-the-minute news delivered in such a slow, vacuum-packed format.

I did get a chance, recently, to watch CNN for a few minutes, and I was bedazzled by what I presume to be its post–September 11 format, in which the main story is at the top of the screen, "Coming Up Next" occupies the middle, and completely unrelated headlines run constantly across the bottom. Yikes. It looked to me like a TV trying very hard to be a newspaper, about as successfully as my five-year-old imitates her big sister's smooth teenage dance steps. Ten minutes of that visual three-ring circus gave me a headache; when I want *newspaper,* I'll read one. 15

It's true that being a reader rather than a viewer gives me a type of naïveté that amuses my friends. I'm in the dark, for instance, about what many public figures look like, at least in color rather than newsprint (for the longest time I thought Phil Donahue was *blond*), and in some cases I may not know quite how to pronounce their names. When people began talking about the dreadful anthrax attack on the congressional offices, I kept scratching my head and asking, "*Dashell?* There's a Senator *Dashell?*" It took me nearly a day to identify the man whose name my brain had been registering as something like "Dask-lee." 16

But I don't mind being somebody's fool. I don't think I'm missing too much. Of course, every two weeks or so someone will tell me about the latest should-be-required-viewing-for-the-human-race documentary that I've missed. No problem: I know how to send off for it, usually from Annenburg CPB. Then some winter evening I'll put the tape in the machine, and if I agree it's wonderful I will see it out. Often it turns out I've long since read an article that told me exactly the same things about Muslim women or Mongolian mummies unearthed or whatever-have-you, or a book that told me more. For bringing events quickly to the world, the imaginative reporter's pad and the still photographer's snap are far more streamlined instruments than bulky video cameras and production committees. But sometimes, I won't deny it, there is a video image that stops me cold and rearranges the furniture of my heart. An African mother's gesture of resignation, the 17 throat-singing of a Tuva shepherd, a silent pan of the untouched horizon of a Central Asian steppe—these things can carry an economy of feeling in so many unspoken words that they're pure instruction for a wordy novelist. For exactly this reason I love to watch movies, domestic and especially foreign ones, and we see lots of them at home. We do own a VCR. My kids would point out to you that it's old and somewhat antiquated; I would point out that so am I, by some standards, but we both still work just fine.

I'm happy to use the machine; I just don't want a cable or a dish or an antenna.   18 Having a sieve up there on the roof collecting wild beams from everywhere does seem poetic, but the image that strikes me as more realistic is that of a faucet into the house that runs about 5 percent clear water and 95 percent raw sewage. I know some people who stay on guard all the time and carefully manage this flow so their household gets a healthy intake; I know a lot more who don't. Call me a control freak, but I have this thing about my household appliances—blender, lawn mower, TV monitor—which is that I like to feel I am in charge of the machine, and not vice versa. I have gotten so accustomed to this balance of power with my VCR that I behave embarrassingly in front of real television. When I watch those stony-faced men (I swear one of them is named Stone) deliver the official news with their pursed mouths and woeful countenances, I feel compelled to mutter back at them, insolently, while my teenager puts her forearms over her face. (Now you know what I really am—more insolent than my own teenager.) "You're completely ignoring what *caused* this," I mumble at Ted-Peter-Dan, "and anyway who did your *hair?*"

Well, honestly, who do those guys think I am? Thirteen seconds of whatever   19 incident produced the most alarming visuals today, and I'm supposed to believe that's all I really need to know? One overturned fuel tanker in Nebraska is more important to me than, say, global warming? Television news is driven by compelling visuals, not by the intrinsic importance of the story being cast. Complicated, nonphotogenic issues requiring any considerable background information (global warming, for example) get left out of the running every time.

Meanwhile, viewers are lured into assuming, at least subconsciously, that this   20 "news" is a random sampling of everything that happened on planet earth that day, and so represents reality. One friend of mine argued (even though, as I say, I'm not trying to start a fight) that he felt a moral obligation to watch CNN so he could see all there was and sort out what was actually true—as if CNN were some huge window thrown wide on the whole world at once. Not true, not *remotely* true. The world, a much wider place than seventeen inches, includes songbird migration, emphysema, pollinating insects, the Krebs cycle, my neighbor who recycles knitting-factory scraps to make quilts, natural selection, the Loess Hills of Iowa, and a trillion other things outside the notice of CNN. Are they important? Everything on that list I just tossed off is life or death to somebody somewhere, half of them are life and death to you and me, and you may well agree that they're all more interesting than Monica Lewinski. It's just a nasty, tiny subset of reality they're subsisting on there in TV land—the subset invested with some visual component likely to cause an adrenal reaction, ideally horror.

Print news has its multitude of agendas, to be sure, but they are not all so po- 21
tently biased *against* the deeper assessment that interests me most. The overwhelming drive toward visuals in newscasting acts as a powerful influence on
which bits of information will reach us. It also influences what we will retain. We
are a predominantly visual species, and that's a biological fact that will never
change; our brains are carefully wired to put the most stock in what they see,
rather than what they hear. If we listen to a presidential candidates' debate over
the radio, for instance, we'll be apt to recall, afterward, the visual components of
the room in which we were sitting while we listened; if it was a fairly boring room,
we'll also remember much of what the candidates said. If we watch that same debate on television, however, we will remember everything about the candidates'
appearance—who was smug, who was tense, who made a funny face—but relatively few of their words. No matter what we may think of this prioritizing, it's the
biological destiny of sighted people. It makes me wonder, frankly, why certain
things are televised at all. If our aim is to elect candidates on the basis of their stature, clothing, and facial expressiveness, then fine, we should look at them. But if
our intention is to evaluate their ideas, we should probably just listen and not
look. Give us one good gander and we'll end up electing cheerleaders instead of
careful thinkers. In a modern election, Franklin D. Roosevelt in his wheelchair
wouldn't have a prayer—not to mention the homely but honest Abe Lincoln.

Still, there is this thing in us that wants to have a look, a curiosity that was 22
quite useful to our ancestors on the savannah but is not so helpful now when it
makes us rubberneck as we drive past the awful car crash. So the gods that gave us
TV now bring us the awfulest car crash of the day and name it *The World Tonight*.
This running real-time horror show provides a peculiarly unbalanced diet for the
human psyche, tending to make us feel that we're living in the most dangerous
time and place imaginable. When the eyes see a building explode, and then an airplane burning, and the ears hear, "Car bomb in Oklahoma City . . . far away from
here . . . equipment failure . . . odds of this one in a million," the message stashed
away by the brain goes something like, "Uh-oh, cars explode, buildings collapse,
planes plunge to the ground—oh, *man*, better hunker down." As a person who
either reads the news or hears it on the radio, I am a bit more of a stranger to this
scary-world phenomenon, so I notice its impact on other people.

The day after all the world became a ghastly stage for the terrified high school 23
students fleeing from murder by their classmates in Littleton, Colorado, it happened that I was to give an afternoon staff writing workshop at my sixth grader's
school. When we assembled, I could see that the teachers were jumpy and wanted
to talk rather than write. Several confessed that they had experienced physical
panic that morning at the prospect of coming to school. I sympathized with their
anxiety, but since nobody ever gets shot in my house, I didn't share the visceral
sense of doom that surely came from seeing a live-camera feed of bloody children
just like ours racing from a school so very much like this one. I remarked that
while the TV coverage might make us *feel* endangered, the real probability of our
own kids' getting shot at school today had been lower than the odds of their being
bitten by a rattlesnake while waiting for the bus. And more to the point, the chance

of such horror's happening here was hardly greater than it had been two days before, when we weren't remotely worried about it. (The TV coverage apparently did
increase the likelihood of other school shootings, but only faintly.) It was such a
small thing to offer—merely another angle on the truth—but I was amazed to see
that it helped, as these thoughtful teachers breathed deeply, looked around at the
quiet campus, and reclaimed the relative kindness of their lives. Anyone inclined
toward chemical sedatives might first consider, seriously, turning off the TV. I
know the vulnerability of my own psyche well enough to avoid certain films that
are no doubt instructive and artful but will nevertheless insert violent images into
my brain that I'll regret for many years. Obviously, I read verbal accounts of violence and construct from them my own mental pictures, but for whatever reason,
these self-created images rarely have the same power as external ones to invade my
mind and randomly, recurrently, savage my sense of wellbeing.

So I glean my news from many written sources and the radio, but even that 24
isn't constant. I purposefully spend a few weeks each year avoiding national and
international news altogether, and attending only to the news of my own community, since that is the only place I can actually do very much about the falling-
apart-things of the moment. Some of my friends can't believe I do this, or can't
understand it. One summer I was talking on the phone with a friend when she derived from our conversation that I had not yet heard about the tragic crash of the
small airplane piloted by John Kennedy Jr.

"You're *kidding!*" she cried, again and again. "It happened three days ago, and 25
you haven't heard about it yet?"

I hadn't. 26

My friend was amazed and amused. "People in Turkestan already know about 27
this," she said.

I could have observed that everybody in the world, Turkestanis included, 28
already knows global warming is the most important news on every possible
agenda—except here in the United States, where that info has been successfully
suppressed. We know so very much about the trees, and miss the forest. I was
talking with a friend, though, so I told her only that I was deeply sorry for the
Kennedy family, to whom this tragedy belonged, but that it would make no real
difference in my life.

It's not that I'm callous about the calamities suffered by famous people; they 29
are heartaches, to be sure, but heartaches genuinely experienced only by their
own friends and families. It seems somewhat voyeuristic, and also absurd, to expect that JFK Jr.'s death should change my life any more than a recent death in *my*
family affected the Kennedys. The same is true of a great deal—maybe most—of
the other bad news that pounds at our doors day and night. On the matter of individual tragic deaths, I believe that those in my own neighborhood are the ones
I need to attend to first, by means of casseroles and whatever else I can offer. I also
believe it's possible to be so overtaken and stupefied by the tragedies of the world
that we don't have any time or energy left for those closer to home, the hurts we
should take as our own.

Many view this opinion as quaint. Truly, I'm in awe of the news junkies who 30 can watch three screens at once and maintain their up-to-the-minute data without plunging into despair or cynicism. But I have a different sort of brain. For me, knowing does not replace doing. I find I sometimes need time off from the world of things I can't do anything about so I may be granted (as the famous prayer says) the serenity to accept the things I cannot change, the courage to change the things I can, and the wisdom to know the difference.

So for the duration of every summer, when our family migrates to a farm in 31 rural Virginia (the place whose antique wiring would short out at the very idea of TV), I gather books and read up, seeking background information on the likes of genetic engineering, biodiversity, the history of U.S. relations in the Middle East—drifts of event too large and slow to be called news. I still listen almost daily to radio news (the Kennedy crash must not have been among All the Things to be Considered), but I limit myself to one national newspaper per week, usually the Sunday edition of the *Washington Post,* which I can buy on Monday or Tuesday at our little town's bookstore. Here's a big secret I've discovered that I will share with you now: This strategy saves me the time of reading about the sports hero/politician/movie star whose shocking assault charge/affair/heart attack was huge breaking news in the middle of last week, because by Sunday he has already confessed/apologized/died. You'd be amazed how little time it takes to catch up, not on "all the news that's fit to print," as one news organ boasts, but on all I really needed to be a responsible citizen.

The rest of the week I try to remember to stop by the hardware store and pick 32 up our folkloric *County News,* which is comprised largely of farm forecasts and obituaries. I read them and make casseroles; it's a healthy exercise. It helps me remember what death really is, and helps me feel less useless in the face of it. And I decide with fresh conviction that we just don't need anybody getting killed at our house.

ACTIVITIES FOR WRITING AND DISCUSSION

1. In your notebook, describe your own TV viewing habits—what you watch, how often and how long, and at what times of day or night. Also describe your feelings about TV. What aspects of the medium attract or repel you? Do you regard watching TV as an addiction? a simple pleasure? an innocent mode of entertainment? a manipulative influence? Illustrate your opinions with examples.

2. Review the discussion of Kingsolver's **persona** on page 108 of Chapter 9. Is her idea of a "philosopher-king" exercising sovereignty over what comes into her home (or head) unrealistic in the twenty-first century, or is it viable? Argue that it is unrealistic. Then argue that it is viable. Support each argument with carefully chosen evidence.

3. Kingsolver contends that there is no *time* to watch TV and challenges her daughter "to spend a few days paying careful attention to the hours of her life and

exactly how she spent them" (p. 1069). Reannotate paragraphs 8 and 9 and take the same test Kingsolver's daughter did. What are your results, and do they impel you to change your habits or to keep them the same? Explain.

4. An old proverb suggests that it is hard to understand someone else without "walking a mile" in that person's shoes. As an experiment, walk in Kingsolver's shoes and watch no TV for two or three days. Describe the results. When you didn't watch TV, what did you do instead?

5. Research the topic of TV watching, and in an essay, compose your own conclusions concerning its positive and/or adverse effects on individuals and society.

Play

Henrik Ibsen (1828–1906)

The Master Builder

Persons

HALVARD SOLNESS, *the Master Builder*
ALINE SOLNESS, *his wife*
DOCTOR HERDAL, *physician*
KNUT BROVIK, *formerly an architect, now in* SOLNESS'S *employment*
RAGNAR BROVIK, *his son, draughtsman*
KAIA FOSLI, *his niece, book-keeper*
MISS HILDA WANGEL
Some Ladies.
A Crowd in the street.

The action passes in and about the house of SOLNESS.

ACT FIRST

A plainly-furnished work-room in the house of HALVARD SOLNESS. *Folding doors on the left lead out to the hall. On the right is the door leading to the inner rooms of the house. At the back is an open door into the draughtsmen's office. In front, on the left, a desk with books, papers, and writing materials. Further back than the folding door, a stove. In the right-hand corner, a sofa, a table, and one or two chairs. On the table a water-bottle and glass. A smaller table, with a rocking-chair and arm-chair, in front on the right. Lighted lamps with shades on the table in the draughtsmen's office, on the table in the corner, and on the desk.*

In the draughtsmen's office sit KNUT BROVIK *and his son* RAGNAR, *occupied with plans and calculations. At the desk in the outer office stands* KAIA FOSLI, *writing in the ledger.* KNUT BROVIK *is a spare old man with white hair and beard. He wears a rather threadbare but well-brushed black coat, spectacles, and a somewhat discolored white neckcloth.* RAGNAR BROVIK *is a well-dressed, light-haired man of about thirty, who stoops a little.* KAIA FOSLI *is a slightly-built girl, a little over twenty, carefully dressed, and delicate-looking. She has a green shade over her eyes.—All three go on working for some time in silence.*

KNUT BROVIK: *(Rises suddenly, as if in distress, from the table; breathes heavily and laboriously as he comes forward into the doorway.)* No, I can't bear it much longer!

KAIA: *(Going up to him.)* You're feeling very ill this evening, aren't you, Uncle?

BROVIK: Oh, I seem to get worse every day.

RAGNAR: *(Has risen and advances.)* You ought to go home, father. Try to get a little sleep——

BROVIK: *(Impatiently.)* Go to bed, I suppose? Would you have me stifled outright?

KAIA: Then take a little walk.

RAGNAR: Yes, do. I will come with you.

BROVIK: *(With warmth.)* I'll not go till he comes! I'm determined to have it out this evening with—*(in a tone of suppressed bitterness)*—with him—with the chief.

KAIA: *(Anxiously.)* Oh no, uncle,—do wait awhile before doing *that!*

RAGNAR: Yes, better wait, father!

BROVIK: *(Draws his breath laboriously.)* Ha—ha—! *I* haven't much time for waiting.

KAIA: *(Listening.)* Hush! I hear him on the stairs. *(All three go back to their work. A short silence.)*

(HALVARD SOLNESS comes in through the hall-door. He is a man of mature age, healthy and vigorous, with close-cut curly hair, dark mustache and dark thick eyebrows. He wears a grayish-green buttoned jacket with an upstanding collar and broad lapels. On his head he wears a soft gray felt hat, and he has one or two light portfolios under his arm.)

SOLNESS: *(Near the door, points towards the draughtsmen's office, and asks in a whisper:)* Are they gone?

KAIA: *(Softly, shaking her head.)* No.

(She takes the shade off her eyes. SOLNESS crosses the room, throws his hat on a chair, places the portfolios on the table by the sofa, and approaches the desk again. KAIA goes on writing without intermission, but seems nervous and uneasy.)

SOLNESS: *(Aloud.)* What is that you're entering, Miss Fosli?

KAIA: *(Starts.)* Oh, it's only something that—

SOLNESS: Let me look at it, Miss Fosli. *(Bends over her, pretends to be looking into the ledger, and whispers:)* Kaia?

KAIA: *(Softly, still writing.)* Well?

SOLNESS: Why do you always take that shade off when I come?

KAIA: *(As before.)* I look so ugly with it on.

SOLNESS: *(Smiling.)* Then you don't like to look ugly, Kaia?

KAIA: *(Half glancing up at him.)* Not for all the world. Not in *your* eyes.

SOLNESS: *(Strokes her hair gently.)* Poor, poor little Kaia——

KAIA: *(Bending her head.)* Hush, they can hear you!

(SOLNESS *strolls across the room to the right, turns and pauses at the door of the draughtsmen's office.*)

SOLNESS: Has any one been here for me?

RAGNAR: *(Rising.)* Yes, the young couple who want a villa built out at Lövstrand.

SOLNESS: *(Growling.)* Oh, those two! They must wait. I'm not quite clear about the plans yet.

RAGNAR: *(Advancing, with some hesitation.)* They were very anxious to have the drawings at once.

SOLNESS: *(As before.)* Yes, of course—so they all are.

BROVIK: *(Looks up.)* They say they're longing so to get into a house of their own.

SOLNESS: Yes, yes—we know all that! And so they're content to take what-ever's offered them. They get a—a roof over their heads—an address—but nothing to call a home. No thank you! In that case, let them apply to somebody else. Tell them *that*, the next time they call.

BROVIK: *(Pushes his glasses up on to his forehead and looks in astonishment at him.)* To somebody else? Are you prepared to give up the commission?

SOLNESS: *(Impatiently.)* Yes, yes, yes, devil take it! If that's to be the way of it. —Rather that, than build away at random. *(Vehemently.)* Besides, I know very little about these people as yet.

BROVIK: The people are safe enough. Ragnar knows them. He's a friend of the family. Perfectly safe people.

SOLNESS: Oh, safe—safe enough! That's not at all what I mean. Good lord—don't *you* understand me either? *(Angrily.)* I won't have anything to do with these strangers. They may apply to whom they please, so far as I'm concerned.

BROVIK: *(Rising.)* Do you really mean it?

SOLNESS: *(Sulkily.)* Yes I do.—For once in a way. *(He comes forward.)*

(BROVIK *exchanges a glance with* RAGNAR, *who makes a warning gesture. Then* BROVIK *comes into the front room.*)

BROVIK: May I have a few words with you?

SOLNESS: Certainly.

BROVIK: *(To* KAIA.*)* Just go in there for a moment, Kaia.

KAIA: *(Uneasily.)* Oh, but Uncle—

BROVIK: Do as I say, child. And shut the door after you.

(KAIA *goes reluctantly into the draughtsmen's office, glances anxiously and entreatingly at* SOLNESS, *and shuts the door.*)

BROVIK: *(Lowering his voice a little.)* I don't want the poor children to know how ill I am.

SOLNESS: Yes, you've been looking very poorly of late.

BROVIK: It will soon be all over with me. My strength is ebbing from day to day.

SOLNESS: Won't you sit down?

BROVIK: Thanks—may I?

SOLNESS: *(Placing the arm-chair more conveniently.)* Here—take this chair.— And now?

BROVIK: *(Has seated himself with difficulty.)* Well, you see, it's about Ragnar. That's what weighs most upon me. What is to become of him?

SOLNESS: Of course your son will stay with me as long as ever he likes.

BROVIK: But that's just what he doesn't like. He feels that he can't stay any longer.

SOLNESS: Why, I should say he was very well off here. But if he wants a raise, I shouldn't object to——

BROVIK: No, no! It's not *that*. *(Impatiently.)* But sooner or later he, too, must have a chance of doing something on his own account.

SOLNESS: *(Without looking at him.)* Do you think that Ragnar has quite talent enough to stand alone?

BROVIK: No, that's just the heart-breaking part of it—I've begun to have my doubts about the boy. For you've never said so much as—as one encouraging word about him. And yet I can't help thinking there must be something in him— he can't possibly be without talent.

SOLNESS: Well, but he has learnt nothing—nothing thoroughly, I mean. Except, of course, to draw.

BROVIK: *(Looks at him with covert hatred, and says hoarsely,)* You had learned little enough of the business when you were in my employment. But that didn't prevent you from setting to work—*(breathing with difficulty)*—and pushing your way up, and taking the wind out of my sails—mine, and other people's.

SOLNESS: Yes, you see—circumstances favored me.

BROVIK: You're right there. Everything favored you. But then how can you have the heart to let me go to my grave—without having seen what Ragnar is fit for? And of course I'm anxious to see them married, too—before I go.

SOLNESS: *(Sharply.)* Is it she who wishes it?

BROVIK: Not Kaia so much as Ragnar—he talks about it every day. *(Appealingly.)* You must—you *must* help him to get some independent work now! I *must* see something that the lad has done. Do you hear?

SOLNESS: *(Peevishly.)* You can't expect me to drag commissions down from the moon for him!

BROVIK: He has the chance of a capital commission at this very moment. A big bit of work.

SOLNESS: *(Uneasily, startled.)* Has he?

BROVIK: If *you* would give your consent.

SOLNESS: What sort of work do you mean?

BROVIK: *(With some hesitation.)* He can have the building of that villa out at Lövstrand.

SOLNESS: That! Why, I'm going to build that myself!

BROVIK: Oh, you don't much care about doing it.

SOLNESS: *(Flaring up.)* Don't care! I! Who dares to say that?

BROVIK: You said so yourself just now.

SOLNESS: Oh, never mind what I *say*.—Would they give Ragnar the building of that villa?

BROVIK: Yes. You see, he knows the family. And then—just for the fun of the thing—he's made drawings and estimates and so forth——

SOLNESS: Are they pleased with the drawings? The people who've got to live in the house?

BROVIK: Yes. If you would only look through them and approve of them——

SOLNESS: Then they would let Ragnar build their home for them?

BROVIK: They were immensely pleased with his idea. They thought it exceedingly original, they said.

SOLNESS: Oho! Original! Not the old-fashioned stuff that *I'm* in the habit of turning out.

BROVIK: It seemed to them *different*.

SOLNESS: *(With suppressed irritation.)* So it was to see Ragnar that they came here—whilst I was out!

BROVIK: They came to call upon you—and at the same time to ask whether you would mind retiring——

SOLNESS: *(Angrily.)* Retire? I?

BROVIK: In case you thought that Ragnar's drawings——

SOLNESS: I? Retire in favor of your son?

BROVIK: Retire from the agreement, they meant.

SOLNESS: Oh, it comes to the same thing. *(Laughs angrily.)* So that's it, is it? Halvard Solness is to see about retiring now! To make room for younger men! For the very youngest, perhaps! He's got to make room! Room! Room!

BROVIK: Why, good heavens! there's surely room for more than one single man——

SOLNESS: Oh, there's not so very much room to spare either. But be that as it may—I will never retire! I will never give way to anybody! Never of my own free will. Never in this world will I do *that*!

BROVIK: *(Rises with difficulty.)* Then I am to pass out of life without any certainty? Without a gleam of happiness? Without any faith or trust in Ragnar? Without having seen a single piece of work of his doing? Is that to be the way of it?

SOLNESS: *(Turns half aside, and mutters.)* H'm—don't ask more just now.

BROVIK: But answer me this one thing. Am I to pass out of life in such utter poverty?

SOLNESS: *(Seems to struggle with himself; finally he says in a low but firm voice:)* You must pass out of life as best you can.

BROVIK: Then be it so.

(He goes up the room.)

SOLNESS: *(Following him, half in desperation.)* Don't you understand that I *cannot* help it? I am what I am, and I can't change my nature!

BROVIK: No, no; you evidently can't. *(Reels and supports himself against the sofa-table.)* May I have a glass of water?

SOLNESS: By all means. *(Fills a glass and hands it to him.)*

BROVIK: Thanks. *(Drinks and puts the glass down again.)*
(SOLNESS *goes up and opens the door of the draughtsmen's office.*)

SOLNESS: Ragnar—you must come and take your father home.
(RAGNAR *rises quickly. He and* KAIA *come into the work-room.*)

RAGNAR: What's the matter, father?

BROVIK: Give me your arm. Now let us go.

RAGNAR: All right. You'd better put your things on, too, Kaia.

SOLNESS: Miss Fosli must stay—just a moment. There's a letter I want written.

BROVIK: *(Looks at* SOLNESS.*)* Good-night. Sleep well—if you can.

SOLNESS: Good-night.
(BROVIK *and* RAGNAR *go out through the hall-door.* KAIA *goes to the desk.* SOLNESS *stands with bent head, to the right, by the arm-chair.*)

KAIA: *(Dubiously.) Is* there any letter——?

SOLNESS: *(Curtly.)* No, of course not. *(Looks sternly at her.)* Kaia!

KAIA: *(Anxiously, in a low voice.)* Yes?

SOLNESS: *(Points imperatively to a spot on the floor.)* Come here! At once!

KAIA: *(Hesitatingly.)* Yes.

SOLNESS: *(As before.)* Nearer!

KAIA: *(Obeying.)* What do you want with me?

SOLNESS: *(Looks at her for a while.)* Is it you I have to thank for all this?

KAIA: No, no, don't think that!

SOLNESS: But confess now—you want to get married!

KAIA: *(Softly.)* Ragnar and I have been engaged for four or five years, and so——

SOLNESS: And so you think it's time there were an end of it. Isn't that so?

KAIA: Ragnar and Uncle say I *must.* So I suppose I'll have to give in.

SOLNESS: *(More gently.)* Kaia, don't you really care a little bit for Ragnar, too?

KAIA: I cared very much for Ragnar once—before I came here to you.

SOLNESS: But you don't now? Not in the least?

KAIA: *(Passionately, clasping her hands and holding them out towards him.)* Oh, you know very well that there's only *one* person I care for now! One, and one only, in all the world. I shall never care for any one else again!

SOLNESS: Yes, you say that. And yet you go away from me—leave me alone here with everything on my hands.

KAIA: But couldn't I stay with you, even if Ragnar——?

SOLNESS: *(Repudiating the idea.)* No, no, that's quite impossible. If Ragnar leaves me and starts work on his own account, then of course he'll need you himself.

KAIA: *(Wringing her hands.)* Oh, I feel as if I *couldn't* be separated from you! It's quite, quite impossible!

SOLNESS: Then be sure you get those foolish notions out of Ragnar's mind. Marry him as much as you please—*(Alters his tone.)* I mean—don't let him throw up his good situation with me. For then I can keep *you* too, my dear Kaia.

KAIA: Oh yes, how lovely that would be, if it could only be managed.

SOLNESS: *(Clasps her head with his two hands and whispers.)* For I *can't* get on without you, you see. I must have you with me every single day.

KAIA: *(In nervous exaltation.)* My God! My God!

SOLNESS: *(Kisses her hair.)* Kaia—Kaia!

KAIA: *(Sinks down before him.)* Oh, how good you are to me! How unspeakably good you are!

SOLNESS: *(Vehemently.)* Get up! For goodness' sake get up! I think I hear some one!

(He helps her to rise. She staggers over to the desk. MRS. SOLNESS *enters by the door on the right. She looks thin and wasted with grief, but shows traces of bygone beauty. Blonde ringlets. Dressed with good taste, wholly in black. Speaks somewhat slowly and in a plaintive voice.)*

MRS. SOLNESS: *(In the doorway.)* Halvard!

SOLNESS: *(Turns.)* Oh, are you there, dear——?

MRS. SOLNESS: *(With a glance at* KAIA.*)* I'm afraid I'm disturbing you.

SOLNESS: Not in the least. Miss Fosli has only a short letter to write.

MRS. SOLNESS: Yes, so I see.

SOLNESS: What do you want with me, Aline?

MRS. SOLNESS: I merely wanted to tell you that Dr. Herdal is in the drawing-room. Won't you come and see him, Halvard?

SOLNESS: *(Looks suspiciously at her.)* H'm—is the doctor so very anxious to talk to me?

MRS. SOLNESS: Well, not exactly anxious. He really came to see me; but he would like to say how-do-you-do to you at the same time.

SOLNESS: *(Laughs to himself.)* Yes, I dare say. Well, you must ask him to wait a little.

MRS. SOLNESS: Then you'll come in later on?

SOLNESS: Perhaps I will. Later on, later on, dear. Presently.

MRS. SOLNESS: *(Glancing again at* KAIA.*)* Well now, don't forget, Halvard. *(Withdraws and closes the door behind her.)*

KAIA: *(Softly.)* Oh dear, oh dear—I'm sure Mrs. Solness thinks ill of me in some way!

SOLNESS: Oh, not in the least. Not more than usual at any rate. But you'd better go now, all the same, Kaia.

KAIA: Yes, yes, now I must go.

SOLNESS: *(Severely.)* And mind you get that matter settled for me. Do you hear?

KAIA: Oh, if it only depended on *me*——

SOLNESS: I *will* have it settled, I say! And to-morrow too—not a day later!

KAIA: *(Terrified.)* If there's nothing else for it, I'm quite willing to break off the engagement.

SOLNESS: *(Angrily.)* Break it off! Are you mad? Would you think of breaking it off?

KAIA: *(Distracted.)* Yes, if necessary. For I *must*—I *must* stay here with you! I can't leave you! That's utterly—utterly impossible!

SOLNESS: *(With a sudden outburst.)* But deuce take it—how about Ragnar then! It's Ragnar that I——

KAIA: *(Looks at him with terrified eyes.)* It is chiefly on Ragnar's account, that—that you——?

SOLNESS: *(Collecting himself.)* No, no, of course not! You don't understand me either. *(Gently and softly.)* Of course it's *you* I want to keep—you above everything, Kaia. But for that very reason you must prevent Ragnar too from throwing up his situation. There, there,—now go home.

KAIA: Yes, yes—good-night, then.

SOLNESS: Good-night. *(As she is going.)* Oh! stop a moment! Are Ragnar's drawings in there?

KAIA: I didn't see him take them with him.

SOLNESS: Then just go in and find them for me. I might perhaps glance over them.

KAIA: *(Happy.)* Oh yes, please do!

SOLNESS: For your sake, Kaia dear. Now, let me have them at once, please. (KAIA *hurries into the draughtsmen's office, searches anxiously in the table-drawer, finds a portfolio and brings it with her.*)

KAIA: Here are all the drawings.

SOLNESS: Good. Put them down there on the table.

KAIA: *(Putting down the portfolio.)* Good-night, then. *(Beseechingly.)* And think kindly of me.

SOLNESS: Oh, that I always do. Good-night, my dear little Kaia. *(Glances to the right.)* Go, go now!

(MRS. SOLNESS *and* DR. HERDAL *enter by the door on the right. He is a stoutish, elderly man, with a round, good-humored face, clean shaven, with thin, light hair, and gold spectacles.*)

MRS. SOLNESS: *(Still in the doorway.)* Halvard, I cannot keep the doctor any longer.

SOLNESS: Well then, come in here.

MRS. SOLNESS: *(To* KAIA, *who is turning down the desk-lamp.)* Have you finished the letter already, Miss Fosli?

KAIA: *(In confusion.)* The letter——?

SOLNESS: Yes, it was quite a short one.

MRS. SOLNESS: It must have been very short.

SOLNESS: You may go now, Miss Fosli. And please come in good time tomorrow morning.

KAIA: I will be sure to. Good-night, Mrs. Solness. *(She goes out by the hall-door.)*

MRS. SOLNESS: She must be quite an acquisition to you, Halvard, this Miss Fosli.

SOLNESS: Yes, indeed. She's useful in all sorts of ways.

MRS. SOLNESS: So it seems.

DR. HERDAL: Is she good at book-keeping, too?

SOLNESS: Well—of course she's had a good deal of practice during these two years. And then she's so nice and obliging in every possible way.

MRS. SOLNESS: Yes, that must be very delightful.

SOLNESS: It *is*. Especially when one doesn't get too much of that sort of thing.

MRS. SOLNESS: *(In a tone of general remonstrance.)* Can *you* say that, Halvard?

SOLNESS: Oh, no, no, my dear Aline; I beg your pardon.

MRS. SOLNESS: There's no occasion. Well, then, doctor, you'll come back later on and have a cup of tea with us?

DR. HERDAL: I've only a professional visit to pay, and then I'll come back.

MRS. SOLNESS: Thank you. *(She goes out by the door on the right.)*

SOLNESS: Are you in a hurry, doctor?

DR. HERDAL: No, not at all.

SOLNESS: May I have a little chat with you?

DR. HERDAL: With the greatest of pleasure.

SOLNESS: Then let us sit down.

(He motions the doctor to take the rocking-chair and sits down himself in the arm-chair.)

SOLNESS: *(Looks searchingly at him.)* Tell me, did you notice anything odd about Aline?

DR. HERDAL: Do you mean just now when she was here?

SOLNESS: Yes, in her manner to me. Did you notice anything?

DR. HERDAL: *(Smiling.)* Well, I admit—one couldn't well avoid noticing that your wife—h'm——

SOLNESS: Well?

DR. HERDAL: —that your wife isn't particularly fond of this Miss Fosli.

SOLNESS: Is that all? I've noticed that myself.

DR. HERDAL: And I must say it doesn't surprise me.

SOLNESS: What doesn't?

DR. HERDAL: That she shouldn't exactly approve of you seeing so much of another woman, all day and every day.

SOLNESS: No, no, I suppose you're right there—and Aline too. But it's impossible to make any change.

DR. HERDAL: Could you not engage a clerk?

SOLNESS: The first man that came to hand? No, thanks—that would never do for me.

DR. HERDAL: But now, if your wife——? Suppose, with her delicate health, all this tries her too much?

SOLNESS: Well then there's no help for it—I could almost say. I *must* keep Kaia Fosli. No one else could fill her place.

DR. HERDAL: No one else?

SOLNESS: *(Curtly.)* No, no one.

DR. HERDAL: *(Drawing his chair closer.)* Now listen to me, my dear Mr. Solness. May I ask you a question, quite between ourselves?

SOLNESS: By all means.

DR. HERDAL: Women, you see—in certain matters, they have a deucedly keen intuition——

SOLNESS: They have indeed. There's not the least doubt of that. But——?

DR. HERDAL: Well, tell me now—if your wife can't endure this Kaia Fosli——?

SOLNESS: Well, what then?

DR. HERDAL: —hasn't she got just—just the least little bit of reason for this involuntary dislike?

SOLNESS: *(Looks at him and rises.)* Oho!

DR. HERDAL: Now don't be offended—but *hasn't* she?

SOLNESS: *(With curt decision.)* No.

DR. HERDAL: No reason of any sort?

SOLNESS: No other reason than her own suspicious nature.

DR. HERDAL: I know you've known a good many women in your time.

SOLNESS: Yes, I have.

DR. HERDAL: And have been a good deal taken with some of them, too?

SOLNESS: Oh yes, I don't deny it.

DR. HERDAL: But as regards Miss Fosli, then—there's nothing of that sort in the case?

SOLNESS: No; nothing at all—on *my* side.

DR. HERDAL: But on her side?

SOLNESS: I don't think you have any right to ask that question, doctor.

DR. HERDAL: Well, you know, we were discussing your wife's intuition.

SOLNESS: So we were. And for that matter—*(lowers his voice)*—Aline's intuition, as you call it—in a certain sense, it's not been so far out.

DR. HERDAL: Ah! there we have it!

SOLNESS: *(Sits down.)* Doctor Herdal—I'm going to tell you a strange story— if you care to listen to it.

DR. HERDAL: I like listening to strange stories.

SOLNESS: Very well then. I daresay you recollect that I took Knut Brovik and his son into my service—after the old man's business had gone to the dogs.

DR. HERDAL: Yes, so I've understood.

SOLNESS: You see, they really are clever fellows, these two. Each of them has talent in his way. But then the son took it into his head to get engaged; and the next thing, of course, was that he wanted to get married—and begin to build on his own account. That's the way with all these young people.

DR. HERDAL: *(Laughing.)* Yes, they've a bad habit of wanting to marry.

SOLNESS: Just so. But of course that didn't suit *my* plans; for I needed Ragnar myself—and the old man, too. He's exceedingly good at calculating bearing-strains and cubic contents—and all that sort of devilry, you know.

DR. HERDAL: Oh yes, no doubt that's very important.

SOLNESS: Yes, it is. But Ragnar was absolutely bent on setting to work for himself. He wouldn't hear of anything else.

DR. HERDAL: But he has stayed with you all the same.

SOLNESS: Yes, I'll tell you how that came about. One day this girl, Kaia Fosli, came to see them on some errand or other. She had never been here before. And when I saw how utterly infatuated they were with each other, the thought occurred to me: If only I could get her into the office here, then perhaps Ragnar too would stay where she is.

DR. HERDAL: That was not at all a bad idea.

SOLNESS: Yes, but at the time I didn't breathe a word of what was in my mind. I merely stood and looked at her, and kept wishing intently that I could have her here. Then I talked to her a little, in a friendly way—about one thing and another. And then she went away.

DR. HERDAL: Well?

SOLNESS: Well then, next day, pretty late in the evening, when old Brovik and Ragnar had gone home, she came here again, and behaved as if I had made an arrangement with her.

DR. HERDAL: An arrangement? What about?

SOLNESS: About the very thing my mind had been fixed on. But I hadn't said one single word about it.

DR. HERDAL: That was most extraordinary.

SOLNESS: Yes, wasn't it? And now she wanted to know what she was to do here, whether she could begin the very next morning, and so forth.

DR. HERDAL: Don't you think she did it in order to be with her sweetheart?

SOLNESS: That was what occurred to me at first. But no, that wasn't it. She seemed to drift quite away from *him*—when once she had come here to me.

DR. HERDAL: She drifted over to you, then?

SOLNESS: Yes, entirely. If I happen to look at her when her back is turned, I can tell that she feels it. She quivers and trembles the moment I come near her. What do you think of that?

DR. HERDAL: H'm—that's not very hard to explain.

SOLNESS: Well, but what about the other thing? That she believed I had said to her what I had only wished and willed—silently—inwardly—to myself? What do you say to that? Can you explain that, Dr. Herdal?

DR. HERDAL: No, I won't undertake to do that.

SOLNESS: I felt sure you wouldn't; and so I've never cared to talk about it till now. But it's a cursed nuisance to me in the long run, you understand. Here have I got to go on day after day pretending—. And it's a shame to treat her so, too, poor girl. *(Vehemently.)* But I *can't* do anything else. For if *she* runs away from me—then Ragnar will be off too.

DR. HERDAL: And you haven't told your wife the rights of the story?

SOLNESS: No.

DR. HERDAL: Then why on earth don't you?

SOLNESS: *(Looks fixedly at him and says in a low voice:)* Because I seem to find a sort of—of salutary self-torture in allowing Aline to do me an injustice.

DR. HERDAL: *(Shakes his head.)* I don't in the least understand what you mean.

SOLNESS: Well, you see, it's like paying off a little bit of a huge, immeasurable debt——

DR. HERDAL: To your wife?

SOLNESS: Yes; and that always helps to relieve one's mind a little. One can breathe more freely for a while, you see.

DR. HERDAL: No, goodness knows, I don't see at all——

SOLNESS: *(Breaking off, rises again.)* Well, well, well—then we won't talk any more about it. *(He saunters across the room, returns, and stops beside the table. Looks at the doctor with a sly smile.)* I suppose you think you've drawn me out nicely now, doctor?

DR. HERDAL: *(With some irritation.)* Drawn you out? Again I haven't the faintest notion what you mean, Mr. Solness.

SOLNESS: Oh come, out with it; for I've seen it quite clearly, you know.

DR. HERDAL: *What* have you seen?

SOLNESS: *(In a low voice, slowly.)* That you've been quietly keeping an eye upon me.

DR. HERDAL: That *I* have! And why in all the world should I do *that?*

SOLNESS: Because you think that I——*(Passionately.)* Well, devil take it—you think the same of me as Aline does.

DR. HERDAL: And what does *she* think about you?

SOLNESS: *(Having recovered his self-control.)* She has begun to think that I'm—that I'm—ill.

DR. HERDAL: Ill! *You!* She has never hinted such a thing to me. Why, what can she think is the matter with you?

SOLNESS: *(Leans over the back of the chair and whispers.)* Aline has made up her mind that I am mad. *That's* what she thinks.

DR. HERDAL: *(Rising.)* Why, my dear, good fellow——!

SOLNESS: Yes, on my soul she does! I tell you it's so! And she has got you to think the same. Oh, I can assure you, doctor, I see it in your face as clearly as possible. You don't take me in so easily, I can tell you.

DR. HERDAL: *(Looks at him in amazement.)* Never, Mr. Solness—never has such a thought entered my mind.

SOLNESS: *(With an incredulous smile.)* Really? Has it not?

DR. HERDAL: No, never! Nor your wife's mind either, I'm convinced. I could almost swear to that.

SOLNESS: Well, I wouldn't advise you to. For, in a certain sense, you see, per-haps—perhaps she's not so far wrong in thinking something of the kind.

DR. HERDAL: Come now, I really must say——

SOLNESS: *(Interrupting with a sweep of his hand.)* Well, well, my dear doctor—don't let us discuss this any further. We had better agree to differ. *(Changes to a tone of quiet merriment.)* But look here now, doctor—hm—

DR. HERDAL: Well?

SOLNESS: Since you don't believe that I am—ill—and crazy—and mad, and so forth——

DR. HERDAL: What then?

SOLNESS: Then I daresay you fancy that I'm an extremely happy man?

DR. HERDAL: Is *that* mere fancy?

SOLNESS: *(Laughs.)* No, no—of course not! Heaven forbid! Only think—to be Solness the master builder! Halvard Solness! What could be more delightful?

DR. HERDAL: Yes, I must say it seems to me you've had the luck on your side to an astounding degree.

SOLNESS: *(Suppresses a gloomy smile.)* So I have. I can't complain on *that* score.

DR. HERDAL: First of all that grim old robber's-castle was burnt down for you. And that was certainly a great piece of luck.

SOLNESS: *(Seriously.)* It was the home of Aline's family. Remember that.

DR. HERDAL: Yes, it must have been a great grief to *her*.

SOLNESS: She hasn't got over it to this day—not in all these twelve or thirteen years.

DR. HERDAL: Ah, but what followed must have been the worst blow for her.

SOLNESS: The one thing with the other.

DR. HERDAL: But you—yourself—*you* rose upon the ruins. You began as a poor boy from a country village—and now you're at the head of your profession. Ah, yes, Mr. Solness, you've undoubtedly had the luck on your side.

SOLNESS: *(Looks doubtfully across at him.)* Yes, but that's just what makes me so horribly afraid.

DR. HERDAL: Afraid? Because you have the luck on your side!

SOLNESS: It terrifies me—terrifies me every hour of the day. For sooner or later the luck must turn, you see.

DR. HERDAL: Oh, nonsense! What should make the luck turn?

SOLNESS: *(With firm assurance.)* The younger generation.

DR. HERDAL: Pooh! The younger generation! You're not laid on the shelf yet, I should hope. Oh no—your position here is probably firmer now than it has ever been.

SOLNESS: The luck *will* turn. I know it—I feel the day approaching. Some one or other will take it into his head to say: Give *me* a chance! And then all the rest will come clamoring after him, and shake their fists at me and shout: Make room—make room—make room! Yes, just you see, doctor—presently the younger generation will come knocking at my door——

DR. HERDAL: *(Laughing.)* Well, and what if they do?

SOLNESS: What if they do? Then there's an end of Halvard Solness. *(There is a knock at the door on the left.)*

SOLNESS: *(Starts.)* What's that? Didn't you hear something?

DR. HERDAL: Some one is knocking at the door.

SOLNESS: *(Loudly.)* Come in.

(HILDA WANGEL *enters through the hall door. She is of middle height, supple, and delicately built. Somewhat sunburnt. Dressed in a tourist costume, with skirt caught up for walking, a sailor's collar open at the throat, and a small sailor hat on her head. Knapsack on back, plaid shawl in strap, and alpenstock.)*

HILDA: *(Goes straight up to* SOLNESS, *her eyes sparkling with happiness.)* Good-evening!

SOLNESS: *(Looks doubtfully at her.)* Good-evening——

HILDA: *(Laughs.)* I almost believe you don't recognize me!

SOLNESS: No—I must admit that—just for the moment——

DR. HERDAL: *(Approaching.)* But *I* recognize you, my dear young lady——

HILDA: *(Pleased.)* Oh, is it you that——

DR. HERDAL: Of course it is. *(To* SOLNESS.*)* We met at one of the mountain stations this summer. *(To* HILDA.*)* What became of the other ladies?

HILDA: Oh, they went westward.

DR. HERDAL: They didn't much like all the fun we used to have in the evenings.

HILDA: No, I believe they didn't.

DR. HERDAL: *(Holds up his finger at her.)* And I'm afraid it can't be denied that you flirted a little with us.

HILDA: Well, that was better fun than to sit there knitting stockings with all those old women.

DR. HERDAL: *(Laughs.)* There I entirely agree with you!

SOLNESS: Have you come to town this evening?

HILDA: Yes, I've just arrived.

DR. HERDAL: Quite alone, Miss Wangel?

HILDA: Oh yes!

SOLNESS: Wangel? Is your name Wangel?

HILDA: *(Looks in amused surprise at him.)* Yes, of course it is.

SOLNESS: Then you must be the daughter of the district doctor up at Lysanger?

HILDA: *(As before.)* Yes, who else's daughter should I be?

SOLNESS: Oh, then I suppose we met up there, that summer when I was building a tower on the old church.

HILDA: *(More seriously.)* Yes, of course it was then we met.

SOLNESS: Well, that's a long time ago.

HILDA: *(Looks hard at him.)* It's just the ten years.

SOLNESS: You must have been a mere child then, I should think.

HILDA: *(Carelessly.)* Well, I was twelve or thirteen.

DR. HERDAL: Is this the first time you've ever been up to town, Miss Wangel?

HILDA: Yes, it is indeed.

SOLNESS: And don't you know any one here?

HILDA: Nobody but you. And of course, your wife.

SOLNESS: So you know *her* too?

HILDA: Only a little. We spent a few days together at the sanatorium.

SOLNESS: Ah, up there?

HILDA: She said I might come and pay her a visit if ever I came up to town. *(Smiles.)* Not that that was necessary.

SOLNESS: Odd that she should never have mentioned it.

(HILDA *puts her stick down by the stove, takes off the knapsack and lays it and the plaid on the sofa.* DR. HERDAL *offers to help her.* SOLNESS *stands and gazes at her.*)

HILDA: *(Going towards him.)* Well, now I must ask you to let me spend the night here.

SOLNESS: I'm sure we can manage that.

HILDA: For I've no other clothes than those I stand in, except a change of linen in my knapsack. And that has to go to the wash, for it's very dirty.

SOLNESS: Oh yes, we'll see to that. Now I'll just let my wife know——

DR. HERDAL: Meanwhile, I'll visit my patient.

SOLNESS: Yes, do; and come again later on.

DR. HERDAL: *(Playfully, with a glance at* HILDA.*)* Oh that I will, you may be very certain! *(Laughs)* So your prediction has come true, Mr. Solness!

SOLNESS: How so?

DR. HERDAL: The younger generation *did* come knocking at your door.

SOLNESS: *(Cheerfully.)* Yes, but in a very different way from what I meant.

DR. HERDAL: Very different, yes. That's undeniable.

(He goes out by the hall-door. SOLNESS *opens the door on the right and speaks into the side room.)*

SOLNESS: Aline! Will you come in here, please. Here's a friend of yours—Miss Wangel.

MRS. SOLNESS: *(Appears in the door-way.)* Who do you say it is? *(Sees* HILDA.*)* Oh, is it you, Miss Wangel? *(Goes up to her and offers her hand.)* So you've come to town after all.

SOLNESS: Miss Wangel has this moment arrived; and she would like to stay the night here.

MRS. SOLNESS: Here with us? Oh yes, with pleasure.

SOLNESS: So as to get her things a little in order, you see.

MRS. SOLNESS: I will do the best I can for you. It's no more than my duty. I suppose your trunk is coming on later?

HILDA: I *have* no trunk.

MRS. SOLNESS: Well, it will be all right, I daresay. In the meantime, you must excuse my leaving you here with my husband until I can get a room made a little comfortable for you.

SOLNESS: Can't we give her one of the nurseries? *They* are all ready as it is.

MRS. SOLNESS: Oh yes. There we have room and to spare. *(To* HILDA.*)* Sit down now and rest a little.

(She goes out to the right. HILDA, *with her hands behind her back, strolls about the room and looks at various objects.* SOLNESS *stands in front, beside the table, also with his hands behind his back, and follows her with his eyes.)*

HILDA: *(Stops and looks at him.)* Have you several nurseries?

SOLNESS: There are three nurseries in the house.

HILDA: That's a lot. Then I suppose you have a great many children?

SOLNESS: No. We have no child. But now *you* can be the child here, for the time being.

HILDA: For to-night, yes. I sha'n't cry. I mean to sleep as sound as a stone.

SOLNESS: Yes, you must be very tired, I should think.

HILDA: Oh no! But all the same——It's so delicious to lie and dream.

SOLNESS: Do you dream much of nights?

HILDA: Oh yes! Almost always.

SOLNESS: What do you dream about most?

HILDA: I sha'n't tell you to-night. Another time, perhaps.

(She again strolls about the room, stops at the desk and turns over the books and papers a little.)

SOLNESS: *(Approaching.)* Are you searching for anything?

HILDA: No, I'm merely looking at all these things. *(Turns.)* Perhaps I mustn't?

SOLNESS: Oh, by all means.

HILDA: Is it you that writes in this great ledger?

SOLNESS: No, it's my book-keeper.

HILDA: Is it a woman?

SOLNESS: *(Smiles).* Yes.

HILDA: One you employ here, in your office?

SOLNESS: Yes.

HILDA: Is she married?

SOLNESS: No, she's single.

HILDA: Ah!

SOLNESS: But I believe she's soon going to be married.

HILDA: That's a good thing for *her.*

SOLNESS: But not such a good thing for *me.* For then I shall have nobody to help me.

HILDA: Can't you get hold of some one else who'll do just as well?

SOLNESS: Perhaps *you* would stop here and—and write in the ledger?

HILDA: *(Measures him with a glance.)* Yes, I daresay! No, thanks—nothing of that sort for *me*—(*She again strolls across the room, and sits down in the rocking-chair.* SOLNESS *too goes to the table.* HILDA *continues:*)—for there must surely be other things than *that* to be done here. *(Looks smilingly at him.)* Don't you think so too?

SOLNESS: Of course. First and foremost, I suppose you want to make a round of the shops, and get yourself up in the height of fashion.

HILDA: *(Amused.)* No, I think I shall let that alone.

SOLNESS: Indeed!

HILDA: For you must know I've run through all my money.

SOLNESS: *(Laughs.)* Neither trunk nor money, then!

HILDA: Neither one nor the other. But never mind—it doesn't matter now.

SOLNESS: Come now, I like you for *that.*

HILDA: Only for *that?*

SOLNESS: For that among other things. *(Sits in the arm-chair.)* Is your father alive still?

HILDA: Yes, father's alive.

SOLNESS: Perhaps you're thinking of studying here?

HILDA: No, that hadn't occurred to me.

SOLNESS: But I suppose you'll be stopping for some time.

HILDA: That must depend upon circumstances.

(She sits awhile rocking herself and looking at him, half seriously, half with a suppressed smile. Then she takes off her hat and puts it on the table in front of her.)

HILDA: Mr. Solness!

SOLNESS: Well?

HILDA: Have you a very bad memory?

SOLNESS: A bad memory? No, not that I'm aware of.

HILDA: Then haven't you anything to say to me about what happened up there?

SOLNESS: *(In momentary surprise.)* Up at Lysanger? *(Indifferently.)* Why, it was nothing much to talk about, it seems to me.

HILDA: *(Looks reproachfully at him.)* How can you sit there and say such things?

SOLNESS: Well, then, *you* talk to *me* about it.

HILDA: When the tower was finished, we had grand doings in the town.

SOLNESS: Yes, I sha'n't easily forget that day.

HILDA: *(Smiles.)* Won't you? That's good of you!

SOLNESS: Good?

HILDA: There was music in the churchyard—and many, many hundreds of people. We school-girls were dressed in white; and we all carried flags.

SOLNESS: Ah yes, those flags—I can tell you I remember them!

HILDA: Then you climbed up over the scaffolding, straight to the very top; and you had a great wreath with you; and you hung that wreath right away up on the weathercock.

SOLNESS: *(Curtly interrupting.)* I always did that in those days. It's an old custom.

HILDA: It was so wonderfully thrilling to stand below and look up at you. Fancy, if he should fall over! He—the master builder himself!

SOLNESS: *(As if to lead her away from the subject.)* Yes, yes, yes, that might very well have happened, too. For one of those white-frocked little devils—she went on in such a way, and screamed up at me so——

HILDA: *(Sparkling with pleasure.)* "Hurra for Mr. Solness!" Yes!

SOLNESS: —and waved and flourished with her flag so that I—so that it almost made me giddy to look at it.

HILDA: *(In a lower voice, seriously.)* That little devil—that was *I.*

SOLNESS: *(Fixes his eyes steadily upon her.)* I'm sure of that now. It *must* have been you.

HILDA: *(Lively again.)* Oh, it was so gloriously thrilling! I couldn't have believed there was a builder in the whole world that could have built such a tremendously high tower. And then, that you yourself should stand at the very top of it, as large as life! And that you shouldn't be the least bit dizzy! It was that above everything that made one—made one dizzy to think of.

SOLNESS: How could you be so certain that I wasn't——?

HILDA: *(Scouting the idea.)* No indeed! Oh no! I knew that instinctively. For if you had been you could never have stood up there and sung.

SOLNESS: *(Looks at her in astonishment.)* Sung? Did I sing?

HILDA: Yes, I should think you did.

SOLNESS: *(Shakes his head.)* I've never sung a note in my life.

HILDA: Yes, you sang then. It sounded like harps in the air.

SOLNESS: *(Thoughtfully.)* This is very strange—all this.

HILDA: *(Is silent awhile, looks at him and says in a low voice:)* But then,—it was after that—that the *real* thing happened.

SOLNESS: The real thing?

HILDA: *(Sparkling with vivacity.)* Yes, I surely don't need to remind you of *that?*

SOLNESS: Oh yes, do remind me a little of *that,* too.

HILDA: Don't you remember that a great dinner was given in your honor at the Club?

SOLNESS: Yes, to be sure. It must have been the same afternoon, for I left the place next morning.

HILDA: And from the Club you were invited to come round to our house to supper.

SOLNESS: Quite right, Miss Wangel. It's wonderful how all these trifles have impressed themselves on your mind.

HILDA: Trifles! I like that! Perhaps it was a trifle, too, that I was *alone* in the room when you came in?

SOLNESS: *Were* you alone?

HILDA: *(Without answering him.)* You didn't call me a little devil *then.*

SOLNESS: No, I probably didn't.

HILDA: You said I was lovely in my white dress, and that I looked like a little princess.

SOLNESS: I've no doubt you did, Miss Wangel.—And besides—I was feeling so buoyant and free that day——

HILDA: And then you said that when I grew up I should be *your* princess.

SOLNESS: *(Laughing a little.)* Dear, dear—did I say *that* too?

HILDA: Yes, you did. And when I asked how long I should have to wait, you said that you would come again in ten years—like a troll—and carry me off—to Spain or some such place. And you promised you would buy me a kingdom there.

SOLNESS: *(As before.)* Yes, after a good dinner one doesn't haggle about the halfpence. But did I really *say* all that?

HILDA: *(Laughs to herself.)* Yes. And you told me, too, what the kingdom was to be called.

SOLNESS: Well, what was it?

HILDA: It was to be called the kingdom of Orangia,[1] you said.

SOLNESS: Well, that was an appetizing name.

HILDA: No, I didn't like it a bit; for it seemed as though you wanted to make game of me.

SOLNESS: I'm sure *that* can't have been my intention.

HILDA: No, I should hope not—considering what you did next——

SOLNESS: What in the world did I do next?

HILDA: Well, that's the finishing touch, if you've forgotten *that* too. I should have thought one couldn't help remembering such a thing as that.

SOLNESS: Yes, yes, just give me a hint, and then perhaps—. Well?

HILDA: *(Looks fixedly at him.)* You came and kissed me, Mr. Solness.

SOLNESS: *(Open-mouthed, rising from his chair.)* I did!

---

1. In the original "Appelsinia," "appelsin" meaning "orange."

HILDA: Yes, indeed you did. You took me in both your arms, and bent my head back, and kissed me—many times.

SOLNESS: Now, really, my dear Miss Wangel——!

HILDA: *(Rises.)* You surely don't mean to deny it?

SOLNESS: Yes, I do. I deny it altogether!

HILDA: *(Looks scornfully at him.)* Oh, indeed!

(She turns and goes slowly close up to the stove, where she remains standing motionless, her face averted from him, her hands behind her back. Short pause.)

SOLNESS: *(Goes cautiously up behind her.)* Miss Wangel!——

HILDA: *(Is silent and does not move.)*

SOLNESS: Don't stand there like a statue. You must have dreamt all this. *(Lays his hand on her arm.)* Now just listen——

HILDA: *(Makes an impatient movement with her arm.)*

SOLNESS: *(As a thought flashes upon him.)* Or——! Wait a moment! There is something under all this, you may depend!

HILDA: *(Does not move.)*

SOLNESS: *(In a low voice, but with emphasis.)* I must have *thought* all that. I must have *wished* it—have *willed* it—have *longed* to do it. And then——. May not that be the explanation?

HILDA: *(Is still silent.)*

SOLNESS: *(Impatiently.)* Oh very well, deuce take it all—then I *did* do it, I suppose!

HILDA: *(Turns her head a little, but without looking at him.)* Then you admit it now?

SOLNESS: Yes—whatever you like.

HILDA: You came and put your arms round me?

SOLNESS: Oh yes.

HILDA: And bent my head back?

SOLNESS: Very far back.

HILDA: And kissed me?

SOLNESS: Yes, I did.

HILDA: Many times?

SOLNESS: As many as ever you like.

HILDA: *(Turns quickly towards him and has once more the sparkling expression of gladness in her eyes.)* Well, you see, I got it out of you at last!

SOLNESS: *(With a slight smile.)* Yes—just think of my forgetting such a thing as that.

HILDA: *(Again a little sulky, retreats from him.)* Oh, you've kissed so many people in your time, I suppose.

SOLNESS: No, you mustn't think *that* of me.

(HILDA seats herself in the arm-chair. SOLNESS stands and leans against the rocking-chair.)

SOLNESS: *(Looks observantly at her.)* Miss Wangel?

HILDA: Yes?

SOLNESS: How *was* it now? What came of all this—between us two?

HILDA: Why, nothing more came of it. You know that quite well. For then the other guests came in, and then—bah!

SOLNESS: Quite so! The others came in. To think of my forgetting *that* too!

HILDA: Oh, you haven't really forgotten anything: you're only a little ashamed of it all. I'm sure one doesn't forget things of that kind.

SOLNESS: No, one would suppose not.

HILDA: *(Lively again looks at him.)* Perhaps you've even forgotten what day it was?

SOLNESS: What day?

HILDA: Yes, on what day did you hang the wreath on the tower? Well? Tell me at once!

SOLNESS: H'm—I confess I've forgotten the particular day. I only know it was ten years ago. Some time in the autumn.

HILDA: *(Nods her head slowly several times.)* It was ten years ago—on the 19th of September.

SOLNESS: Yes, it must have been about that time. Fancy your remembering that too! *(Stops.)* But wait a moment—! Yes—it's the 19th of September to-day.

HILDA: Yes, it is; and the ten years are gone. And you didn't come—as you had promised me.

SOLNESS: Promised you? Threatened, I suppose you mean?

HILDA: I don't think there was any sort of threat in *that.*

SOLNESS: Well then, a little bit of a hoax.

HILDA: Was that all you wanted to do? To hoax me?

SOLNESS: Well, or to have a little joke with you! Upon my soul I don't recollect. But it must have been something of that kind; for you were a mere child then.

HILDA: Oh, perhaps I wasn't quite such a child either. Not such a mere chit as you imagine.

SOLNESS: *(Looks searchingly at her.)* Did you really and seriously expect me to come again?

HILDA: *(Conceals a half-teasing smile.)* Yes, indeed! I did expect *that* of you.

SOLNESS: That I should come back to your home, and take you away with me?

HILDA: Just like a troll—yes.

SOLNESS: And make a princess of you?

HILDA: That's what you promised.

SOLNESS: And give you a kingdom as well?

HILDA: *(Looks up at the ceiling.)* Why not? Of course it needn't have been an actual, every-day sort of a kingdom.

SOLNESS: But something else just as good?

HILDA: Yes, at least as good. *(Looks at him a moment.)* I thought if you could build the highest church-towers in the world, you could surely manage to raise a kingdom of one sort or another as well.

SOLNESS: *(Shakes his head.)* I can't quite make you out, Miss Wangel.

HILDA: Can't you? To me it seems all so simple.

SOLNESS: No, I can't make up my mind whether you mean all you say, or are simply having a joke with me.

HILDA: *(Smiles.)* Hoaxing you, perhaps? I, too?

SOLNESS: Yes, exactly. Hoaxing—both of us. *(Looks at her.)* Is it long since you found out that I was married?

HILDA: I've known it all along. Why do you ask me *that?*

SOLNESS: *(Lightly.)* Oh, well, it just occurred to me. *(Looks earnestly at her, and says in a low voice:)* What have you come for?

HILDA: I want my kingdom. The time is up.

SOLNESS: *(Laughs involuntarily.)* What a girl you are!

HILDA: *(Gayly.)* Out with my kingdom, Mr. Solness! *(Raps with her fingers.)* The kingdom on the table!

SOLNESS: *(Pushing the rocking-chair nearer and sitting down.)* Now, seriously speaking—what have you come for? What do you really want to do here?

HILDA: Oh, first of all, I want to go round and look at all the things that you've built.

SOLNESS: That will give you plenty of exercise.

HILDA: Yes, I know you've built a tremendous lot.

SOLNESS: I have indeed—especially of late years.

HILDA: Many church-towers among the rest? Immensely high ones?

SOLNESS: No. I build no more church-towers now. Nor churches either.

HILDA: What *do* you build then?

SOLNESS: Homes for human beings.

HILDA: *(Reflectively.)* Couldn't you build a little—a little bit of a church-tower over these homes as well?

SOLNESS: *(Starting.)* What do you mean by *that?*

HILDA: I mean—something that points—points up into the free air. With the vane at a dizzy height.

SOLNESS: *(Pondering a little.)* Strange that you should say *that*—for that's just what I'm most anxious to do.

HILDA: *(Impatiently.)* Then why don't you do it?

SOLNESS: *(Shakes his head.)* No, the people won't have it.

HILDA: Fancy their not wanting it!

SOLNESS: *(More lightly.)* But now I'm building a new home for myself—just opposite here.

HILDA: For yourself?

SOLNESS: Yes. It's almost finished. And on that there's a tower.

HILDA: A high tower?

SOLNESS: Yes.

HILDA: Very high?

SOLNESS: No doubt people will say that it's too high—too high for a dwelling-house.

HILDA: I'll go out and look at that tower the first thing to-morrow morning.

SOLNESS: *(Sits with his hand under his cheek and gazes at her.)* Tell me, Miss Wangel—what is your name? Your Christian name, I mean?

HILDA: Why, Hilda, of course.

SOLNESS: *(As before.)* Hilda? Ah?

HILDA: Don't you remember *that?* You called me Hilda yourself—that day when you misbehaved.

SOLNESS: Did I really?

HILDA: But then you said "*little* Hilda"; and I didn't like that.

SOLNESS: Oh, you didn't like that, Miss Hilda?

HILDA: No, not at such a time as that. But—"Princess Hilda"—that will sound very well, I think.

SOLNESS: Very well indeed. Princess Hilda of—of—what was to be the name of the kingdom?

HILDA: Pooh! I won't have anything to do with *that* stupid kingdom. I've set my heart upon quite a different one!

SOLNESS: *(Has leaned back in the chair, still gazing at her.)* Isn't it strange——? The more I think of it now, the more it seems to me as though I had gone about all these years torturing myself with—h'm——

HILDA: With what?

SOLNESS: With the effort to recover something—some experience, which I seemed to have forgotten. But I never had the least inkling of what it would be.

HILDA: You should have tied a knot in your pocket-handkerchief, Mr. Solness.

SOLNESS: In that case, I should simply have had to go racking my brains to discover what the knot could mean.

HILDA: Oh, yes, I suppose there are trolls of *that* kind in the world, too.

SOLNESS: *(Rises slowly.)* What a good thing it is that *you* have come to me now.

HILDA: *(Looks deeply into his eyes.)* *Is* it a good thing?

SOLNESS: For I've been so lonely here. I've been gazing so helplessly at it all. *(In a lower voice.)* I must tell you—I've begun to be so afraid—so terribly afraid of the younger generation.

HILDA: *(With a little snort of contempt.)* Pooh—is the younger generation a thing to be afraid of?

SOLNESS: It is indeed. And that's why I've locked and barred myself in. *(Mysteriously.)* I tell you the younger generation will one day come and thunder at my door! They'll break in upon me!

HILDA: Then I should say you ought to go out and open the door to the younger generation.

SOLNESS: Open the door?

HILDA: Yes. Let them come in to you on friendly terms, as it were.

SOLNESS: No, no, no! The younger generation—it means retribution, you see. It comes, as if under a new banner, heralding the turn of fortune.

HILDA: *(Rises, looks at him, and says with a quivering twitch of her lips.)* Can *I* be of any use to you, Mr. Solness?

SOLNESS: Yes, you can indeed! For you, too, come—under a new banner, it seems to me. Youth marshalled against youth——!

(DR. HERDAL comes in by the hall-door.)

DR. HERDAL: What—you and Miss Wangel here still?

SOLNESS: Yes. We've had no end of things to talk about.

HILDA: Both old and new.

DR. HERDAL: Have you really?

HILDA: Oh, it has been the greatest fun. For Mr. Solness—he has such a miraculous memory. All the least little details he remembers instantly.

(MRS. SOLNESS *enters by the door on the right.*)

MRS. SOLNESS: Well, Miss Wangel, your room is quite ready for you now.

HILDA: Oh, how kind you are to me!

SOLNESS: *(To* MRS. SOLNESS.*)* The nursery?

MRS. SOLNESS: Yes, the middle one. But first let us go in to supper.

SOLNESS: *(Nods to* HILDA.*)* Hilda shall sleep in the nursery.

MRS. SOLNESS: *(Looks at him.)* Hilda?

SOLNESS: Yes, Miss Wangel's name is Hilda. I knew her when she was a child.

MRS. SOLNESS: Did you really, Halvard? Well, shall we go? Supper is on the table.

(*She takes* DR. HERDAL'S *arm and goes out with him to the right.* HILDA *has meanwhile been collecting her travelling things.*)

HILDA: *(Softly and rapidly to* SOLNESS.*)* Is it true, what you said? *Can* I be of use to you?

SOLNESS: *(Takes the things from her.) You* are the very one I have most needed.

HILDA: *(Looks at him with happy, wondering eyes and clasps her hands.)* Oh heavens, how lovely——!

SOLNESS: *(Eagerly.)* What——?

HILDA: Then I *have* my kingdom!

SOLNESS: *(Involuntarily.)* Hilda——!

HILDA: *(Again with the quivering twitch of her lips.) Almost*—I was going to say. (*She goes out to the right.* SOLNESS *follows her.*)

SECOND ACT

A prettily furnished small drawing-room in the house of SOLNESS. *In the back, a glass-door leading out to the veranda and garden. The right-hand corner is cut off transversely by a large bay-window, in which are flower-stands. The left-hand corner is similarly cut off by a transverse wall, in which is a small door papered like the wall. On each side, an ordinary door. In front, on the right, a console table with a large mirror over it. Well-filled stands of plants and flowers. In front, on the left, a sofa with a table and chairs. Further back, a bookcase. Well forward in the room, before the bay-window, a small table and some chairs. It is early in the day.*

SOLNESS *sits by the little table with* RAGNAR BROVIK'S *portfolio open in front of him. He is turning the drawings over and closely examining some of them.* MRS. SOLNESS *walks about noiselessly with a small watering-pot, attending to her flowers. She is dressed in black as before. Her hat, cloak and parasol lie on a chair near the mirror. Unobserved by her,* SOLNESS *now and again follows her with his eyes. Neither of them speaks.*

KAIA FOSLI *enters quietly by the door on the left.*

SOLNESS: *(Turns his head and says in an off-hand tone of indifference.)* Well, is that you?

KAIA: I merely wished to let you know I've come.

SOLNESS: Yes, yes, that's all right. Hasn't Ragnar come too?

KAIA: No, not yet. He had to wait a little while to see the doctor. But he's coming presently to hear——

SOLNESS: How is the old man to-day?

KAIA: Not well. He begs you to excuse him, for he must keep his bed to-day.

SOLNESS: Quite so; by all means let him rest. But now, get to your work.

KAIA: Yes. *(Pauses at the door.)* Do you wish to speak to Ragnar when he comes?

SOLNESS: No—I don't know that I've anything special to say to him.

(KAIA goes out again to the left. SOLNESS remains seated, turning over the drawings.)

MRS. SOLNESS: *(Over beside the plants.)* I wonder if *he* isn't going to die now, as well?

SOLNESS: *(Looks up at her.)* As well as who?

MRS. SOLNESS: *(Without answering.)* Yes, yes—depend upon it, Halvard, old Brovik's going to die too. You'll see that he will.

SOLNESS: My dear Aline, oughtn't you to go out for a little walk?

MRS. SOLNESS: Yes, I suppose I ought to. *(She continues to attend to the flowers.)*

SOLNESS: *(Bending over the drawings.)* Is she still asleep?

MRS. SOLNESS: *(Looking at him.)* Is it Miss Wangel you're sitting there thinking about?

SOLNESS: *(Indifferently.)* I just happened to recollect her.

MRS. SOLNESS: Miss Wangel was up long ago.

SOLNESS: Oh, was she?

MRS. SOLNESS: When I went in to see her, she was busy putting her things in order.

(She goes in front of the mirror and slowly begins to put on her hat.)

SOLNESS: *(After a short pause.)* So we've found a use for one of our nurseries after all, Aline.

MRS. SOLNESS: Yes, we have.

SOLNESS: That seems to me better than to have them all standing empty.

MRS. SOLNESS: That emptiness is dreadful; you're right there.

SOLNESS: *(Closes the portfolio, rises and approaches her.)* You'll find that we shall get on far better after this, Aline. Things will be more comfortable. Life will be easier—especially for *you.*

MRS. SOLNESS: *(Looks at him.)* After this?

SOLNESS: Yes, believe me, Aline——

MRS. SOLNESS: Do you mean—because *she* has come here?

SOLNESS: *(Checking himself.)* I mean, of course—when once we've moved into the new house.

MRS. SOLNESS: *(Takes her cloak.)* Ah, do you think so, Halvard? Will it be better then?

SOLNESS: I can't think otherwise. And surely you think so too?

MRS. SOLNESS: I think nothing at all about the new house.

SOLNESS: *(Cast down.)* It's hard for me to hear you say that; for you know it's mainly for your sake that I've built it.

(He offers to help her on with her cloak.)

MRS. SOLNESS: *(Evades him.)* The fact is, you do far too much for my sake.

SOLNESS: *(With a certain vehemence.)* No, no, you really mustn't say that, Aline. I can't bear to hear you say such things.

MRS. SOLNESS: Very well, then I won't say it, Halvard.

SOLNESS: But I stick to what *I* said. You'll see that things'll be easier for you in the new place.

MRS. SOLNESS: Oh heavens—easier for me—!

SOLNESS: *(Eagerly.)* Yes, indeed they will! You may be quite sure of that! For you see—there'll be so very, very much there that'll remind you of your own home——

MRS. SOLNESS: The home that used to be father's and mother's—and that was burnt to the ground——

SOLNESS: *(In a low voice.)* Yes, yes, my poor Aline. That was a terrible blow for you.

MRS. SOLNESS: *(Breaking out in lamentation.)* You may build as much as ever you like, Halvard—you can never build up again a real home for *me!*

SOLNESS: *(Crosses the room.)* Well, in Heaven's name, let us talk no more about it then.

MRS. SOLNESS: We're not in the habit of talking about it. For you always put the thought away from you——

SOLNESS: *(Stops suddenly and looks at her.)* Do I? And why should I do *that?* Put the thought away from me?

MRS. SOLNESS: Oh yes, Halvard, I understand very well. You're so anxious to spare me—and to find excuses for me too—as much as ever you can.

SOLNESS: *(With astonishment in his eyes.)* You! Is it *you*—yourself, that you're talking about, Aline?

MRS. SOLNESS: Yes, who else should it be but myself?

SOLNESS: *(Involuntarily, to himself.)* That too!

MRS. SOLNESS: As for the old house, I wouldn't mind so much about that. When once misfortune was in the air—why——

SOLNESS: Ah, you're right there. Misfortune will have its way—as the saying goes.

MRS. SOLNESS: But it's what came of the fire—the dreadful thing that followed—! *That* is the thing! That, that, that!

SOLNESS: *(Vehemently.)* Don't think about *that,* Aline.

MRS. SOLNESS: Ah, that's exactly what I can't help thinking about. And now, at last, I must speak about it, too; for I don't seem able to bear it any longer. And then never to be able to forgive myself——

SOLNESS: *(Vehemently.)* Yourself?

MRS. SOLNESS: Yes, for I had duties on both sides—both towards you and towards the little ones. I ought to have hardened myself—not to have let the horror take such hold upon me, nor the grief for the burning of my home.

(Wrings her hands.) Oh, Halvard, if I'd only had the strength!

SOLNESS: *(Softly, much moved, comes closer.)* Aline—you must promise me never to think these thoughts any more. Promise me that, dear!

MRS. SOLNESS: Oh, promise, promise! One can promise anything.

SOLNESS: *(Clenches his hands and crosses the room.)* Oh, but this is hopeless, hopeless! Never a ray of sunlight! Not so much as a gleam of brightness to light up our home!

MRS. SOLNESS: This *is* no home, Halvard.

SOLNESS: Oh no, you may well say that. *(Gloomily.)* And God knows whether you're not right in saying that it will be no better for us in the new house, either.

MRS. SOLNESS: It will never be any better. Just as empty—just as desolate—there as here.

SOLNESS: *(Vehemently.)* Why in all the world have we built it then? Can you tell me that?

MRS. SOLNESS: No; you must answer that question for yourself.

SOLNESS: *(Glances suspiciously at her.)* What do you mean by *that*, Aline?

MRS. SOLNESS: What do I mean?

SOLNESS: Yes, in the devil's name! You said it so strangely—as if you had some hidden meaning in it.

MRS. SOLNESS: No, indeed, I assure you——

SOLNESS: *(Comes closer.)* Oh, come now—I know what I know. I've both my eyes and my ears about me, Aline—you may depend upon that!

MRS. SOLNESS: Why, what are you talking about? What is it?

SOLNESS: *(Places himself in front of her.)* Do you mean to say you don't find a kind of lurking, hidden meaning in the most innocent word I happen to say?

MRS. SOLNESS: *I*, do you say? I do that?

SOLNESS: *(Laughs.)* Ho-ho-ho! It's natural enough, Aline! When you've a sick man on your hands——

MRS. SOLNESS: *(Anxiously.)* Sick? Are you ill, Halvard?

SOLNESS: *(Violently.)* A half-mad man, then! A crazy man! Call me what you will.

MRS. SOLNESS: *(Feels gropingly for a chair and sits down.)* Halvard—for God's sake——

SOLNESS: But you're wrong, both you and the doctor. That's not what's the matter with me.

(He walks up and down the room. MRS. SOLNESS follows him anxiously with her eyes. Finally he goes up to her.)

SOLNESS: *(Calmly.)* In reality there's nothing whatever wrong with me.

MRS. SOLNESS: No, there isn't, is there? But then what is it that troubles you so?

SOLNESS: Why this, that I often feel ready to sink under this terrible burden of debt——

MRS. SOLNESS: Debt, do you say? But you owe no one anything, Halvard!

SOLNESS: *(Softly, with emotion.)* I owe a boundless debt to you—to you—to you, Aline.

MRS. SOLNESS: *(Rises slowly.)* What is behind all this? You may just as well tell me at once.

SOLNESS: But there *is* nothing behind it. I've never done you any wrong—not wittingly and wilfully, at any rate. And yet—and yet it seems as though a crushing debt rested upon me and weighed me down.

MRS. SOLNESS: A debt to me?

SOLNESS: Chiefly to you.

MRS. SOLNESS: Then you are—ill after all, Halvard.

SOLNESS: *(Gloomily.)* I suppose I must be—or not far from it. *(Looks towards the door to the right, which is opened at this moment.)* Ah! now it grows lighter. (HILDA WANGEL *comes in. She has made some alterations in her dress, and let down her skirt.)*

HILDA: Good-morning, Mr. Solness!

SOLNESS: *(Nods.)* Slept well?

HILDA: Quite deliciously! As if in a cradle. Oh—I lay and stretched myself like—like a princess!

SOLNESS: *(Smiles a little.)* You were thoroughly comfortable then?

HILDA: I should think so.

SOLNESS: And no doubt you dreamed, too.

HILDA: Yes, I did. But *that* was horrid.

SOLNESS: Indeed?

HILDA: Yes, for I dreamed I was falling over a frightfully high, sheer precipice. Do you never have that kind of dream?

SOLNESS: Oh yes—now and then——

HILDA: It's tremendously thrilling—when you fall and fall——

SOLNESS: It seems to make one's blood run cold.

HILDA: Do you draw your legs up under you while you're falling?

SOLNESS: Yes, as high as ever I can.

HILDA: So do I.

MRS. SOLNESS: *(Takes her parasol.)* I must go into town now, Halvard. *(To* HILDA.*)* And I'll try to get one or two things that may be of use to you.

HILDA: *(Making a motion to throw her arms round her neck.)* Oh, you dear, sweet Mrs. Solness! You're really much too kind to me! Frightfully kind——

MRS. SOLNESS: *(Deprecatingly, freeing herself.)* Oh, far from it. It's only my duty, so I'm very glad to do it.

HILDA: *(Offended, pouts.)* But really, I think I'm quite fit to be seen in the streets—now that I've put my dress to rights. Or do you think I'm not?

MRS. SOLNESS: To tell you the truth, I think people would stare at you a little.

HILDA: *(Contemptuously.)* Pooh! Is that all? That only amuses me.

SOLNESS: *(With suppressed ill-humor.)* Yes, but people might take it into their heads that *you* were mad too, you see.

HILDA: Mad? Are there so many mad people here in town, then?

SOLNESS: *(Points to his own forehead.)* Here you see *one* at all events.

HILDA: You—Mr. Solness!

MRS. SOLNESS: Oh, don't talk like that, my dear Halvard!

SOLNESS: Haven't you noticed *that* yet?

HILDA: No, I certainly haven't. (*Reflects and laughs a little.*) And yet—perhaps in one single thing.

SOLNESS: Ah, do you hear *that,* Aline?

MRS. SOLNESS: What is that one single thing, Miss Wangel?

HILDA: No, I won't say.

SOLNESS: Oh yes, do!

HILDA: No thanks—I'm not so mad as all that.

MRS. SOLNESS: When you and Miss Wangel are alone, I daresay she'll tell you, Halvard.

SOLNESS: Ah—you think she will?

MRS. SOLNESS: Oh yes, certainly. For you've known her so well in the past. Ever since she was a child—you tell me.

(*She goes out by the door on the left.*)

HILDA: (*After a little while.*) Does your wife dislike me very much?

SOLNESS: Did you think you noticed anything of the kind?

HILDA: Didn't you notice it yourself?

SOLNESS: (*Evasively.*) Aline has become exceedingly shy with strangers of late years.

HILDA: Has she really?

SOLNESS: But if only you could get to know her thoroughly—Ah, she's so nice—and so kind—and so good at heart.

HILDA: (*Impatiently.*) But if she's all that—what made her say that about her duty?

SOLNESS: Her duty?

HILDA: She said that she would go out and buy something for me, because it was her *duty.* Oh I can't bear that ugly, horrid word!

SOLNESS: Why not?

HILDA: It sounds so cold, and sharp, and stinging. Duty—duty—duty. Don't *you* think so, too? Doesn't it seem to sting you?

SOLNESS: H'm—haven't thought much about it.

HILDA: Yes, it does. And if she's so nice—as you say she is—why should she talk in that way?

SOLNESS: But, good Lord, what would you have had her say, then?

HILDA: She might have said she would do it because she had taken a tremendous fancy to me. She might have said something like that—something really warm and cordial, you understand.

SOLNESS: (*Looks at her.*) Is that how you'd like to have it?

HILDA: Yes, precisely.

(*She wanders about the room, stops at the bookcase and looks at the books.*)

HILDA: What a lot of books you have!

SOLNESS: Yes, I've got together a good many.

HILDA: Do you read them all, too?

SOLNESS: I used to try to. Do you read much?

HILDA: No, never! I've given it up. For it all seems so irrelevant.

SOLNESS: That's just my feeling.

(HILDA *wanders about a little, stops at the small table, opens the portfolio and turns over the contents.*)

HILDA: Are all these drawings yours?

SOLNESS: No, they're drawn by a young man whom I employ to help me.

HILDA: Some one you've taught?

SOLNESS: Oh yes, no doubt he's learnt something from me, too.

HILDA: (*Sits down.*) Then I suppose he's very clever. (*Looks at a drawing.*) Isn't he?

SOLNESS: Oh, he's not bad. For *my* purpose——

HILDA: Oh yes—I'm sure he's frightfully clever.

SOLNESS: Do you think you can see that in the drawings?

HILDA: Pooh—these scrawlings! But if he's been learning from *you*——

SOLNESS: Oh, as far as that goes——there are plenty of people here that have learnt from *me,* and have come to little enough for all that.

HILDA: (*Looks at him and shakes her head.*) No, I can't for the life of me understand how you can be so stupid.

SOLNESS: Stupid? Do you think I'm so very stupid?

HILDA: Yes, I do indeed. If you're content to go about here teaching all these people——

SOLNESS: (*With a slight start.*) Well, and why not?

HILDA: (*Rises, half-serious, half-laughing.*) No indeed, Mr. Solness! What can be the good of that? No one but yourself should be allowed to build. You should stand quite alone—do it all yourself. Now you know it.

SOLNESS: (*Involuntarily.*) Hilda——!

HILDA: Well!

SOLNESS: How in the world did that come into your head?

HILDA: Do you think I'm so very far wrong then?

SOLNESS: No, that's not what I mean. But now I'll tell you something.

HILDA: Well?

SOLNESS: I keep on—incessantly—in silence and alone—brooding on that very thought.

HILDA: Yes, that seems to me perfectly natural.

SOLNESS: (*Looks somewhat searchingly at her.*) Perhaps you've already noticed it?

HILDA: No, indeed I haven't.

SOLNESS: But just now—when you said you thought I was—off my balance? In one thing you said——

HILDA: Oh, I was thinking of something quite different.

SOLNESS: What was it?

HILDA: I'm not going to tell you.

SOLNESS: (*Crosses the room.*) Well, well—as you please. (*Stops at the bay-window.*) Come here and I'll show you something.

HILDA: (*Approaching.*) What is it?

SOLNESS: Do you see—over there in the garden——?

HILDA: Yes?

SOLNESS: *(Points.)* Right above the great quarry——?

HILDA: That new house, you mean?

SOLNESS: The one that's being built, yes. Almost finished.

HILDA: It seems to have a very high tower.

SOLNESS: The scaffolding is still up.

HILDA: Is that your new house?

SOLNESS: Yes.

HILDA: The house you're soon going to move into?

SOLNESS: Yes.

HILDA: *(Looks at him.)* Are there nurseries in *that* house, too?

SOLNESS: Three, as there are here.

HILDA: And no child.

SOLNESS: And there never will be one.

HILDA: *(With a half-smile.)* Well, isn't it just as I said——

SOLNESS: That——?

HILDA: That you *are* a little—a little mad after all.

SOLNESS: Was that what you were thinking of?

HILDA: Yes, of all the empty nurseries I slept in.

SOLNESS: *(Lowers his voice.)* We *have* had children—Aline and I.

HILDA: *(Looks eagerly at him.)* Have you——?

SOLNESS: Two little boys. They were of the same age.

HILDA: Twins, then.

SOLNESS: Yes, twins. It's eleven or twelve years ago now.

HILDA: *(Cautiously.)* And so both of them——? You have lost both the twins, then?

SOLNESS: *(With quiet emotion.)* We only kept them about three weeks. Or scarcely so much. *(Bursts forth.)* Oh, Hilda, I can't tell you what a good thing it is for me that you have come! For now at last I have some one I can talk to!

HILDA: Can't you talk to—to *her,* too?

SOLNESS: Not about this. Not as I want to talk and must talk. *(Gloomily.)* And not about so many other things, too.

HILDA: *(In a subdued voice.)* Was that all you meant when you said you needed me?

SOLNESS: That was mainly what I meant—at all events, yesterday. For to-day I'm not so sure. *(Breaking off.)* Come here and let us sit down, Hilda. Sit there on the sofa—so that you can look into the garden. (HILDA *seats herself in the corner of the sofa.* SOLNESS *brings a chair closer.)* Would you like to hear about it?

HILDA: Yes, I shall love to sit and listen to you.

SOLNESS: *(Sits down.)* Then I'll tell you all about it.

HILDA: Now I can see both the garden and you, Mr. Solness. So now, tell away! Go on!

SOLNESS: *(Points towards the bay-window.)* Out there on the rising ground—where you see the new house——

HILDA: Yes?

SOLNESS: Aline and I lived there in the first years of our married life. There was an old house up there that had belonged to her mother; and we inherited it, and the whole of the great garden with it.

HILDA: Was there a tower on *that* house, too?

SOLNESS: No, nothing of the kind. From the outside it looked like a great, dark, ugly wooden box; but, all the same, it was snug and comfortable enough inside.

HILDA: Then did you pull down the ramshackle old place?

SOLNESS: No, it was burnt down.

HILDA: The whole of it?

SOLNESS: Yes.

HILDA: Was that a great misfortune for you?

SOLNESS: That depends on how you look at it. As a builder, the fire was the making of me——

HILDA: Well, but——?

SOLNESS: It was just after the birth of the two little boys.

HILDA: The poor little twins, yes.

SOLNESS: They came healthy and bonny into the world. And they were growing too—you could see the difference from day to day.

HILDA: Little children do grow quickly at first.

SOLNESS: It was the prettiest sight in the world to see Aline lying with the two of them in her arms. But then came the night of the fire——

HILDA: *(Excitedly.)* What happened? Do tell me! Was any one burnt?

SOLNESS: No, not that. Every one got safe and sound out of the house——

HILDA: Well, and what then?

SOLNESS: The fright had shaken Aline terribly. The alarm—the escape—the break-neck hurry—and then the ice-cold night air—for they had to be carried out just as they lay—both she and the little ones——

HILDA: Was it too much for them?

SOLNESS: Oh no, *they* stood it well enough. But Aline fell into a fever, and it affected her milk. She would insist on nursing them herself; because it was her duty, she said. And both our little boys, they—*(clenching his hands)*—they—oh!

HILDA: They didn't get over *that*?

SOLNESS: No, *that* they didn't get over. That was how we lost them.

HILDA: It must have been terribly hard for you.

SOLNESS: Hard enough for me; but ten times harder for Aline. *(Clenching his hands in suppressed fury.)* Oh, that such things should be allowed to happen here on earth! *(Shortly and firmly.)* From the day I lost them, I had no heart for building churches.

HILDA: Didn't you like building the church-tower in our town?

SOLNESS: I didn't like it. I know how free and happy I felt when that tower was finished.

HILDA: *I* know that, too.

SOLNESS: And now I shall never—never build anything of that sort again! Neither churches nor church-towers.

HILDA: *(Nods slowly.)* Nothing but houses for people to live in.

SOLNESS: Homes for human beings, Hilda.

HILDA: But homes with high towers and pinnacles upon them.

SOLNESS: If possible. *(Adopts a lighter tone.)* Well, you see, as I said, that fire was the making of me—as a builder, I mean.

HILDA: Why don't you call yourself an architect, like the others?

SOLNESS: I haven't been systematically enough taught for that. Most of what I know, I've found out for myself.

HILDA: But you succeeded all the same.

SOLNESS: Yes, thanks to the fire. I laid out almost the whole of the garden in villa-lots; and *there* I was able to build entirely after my own heart. So I came to the front with a rush.

HILDA: *(Looks keenly at him.)* You must surely be a very happy man—situated as you are.

SOLNESS: *(Gloomily.)* Happy? Do *you* say that, too—like all the rest of them?

HILDA: Yes, I should say you must be. If you could only get the two little children out of your head——

SOLNESS: *(Slowly.)* The two little children—they're not so easy to forget, Hilda.

HILDA: *(Somewhat uncertainly.)* Do you still feel their loss so much—after all these years?

SOLNESS: *(Looks fixedly at her, without replying.)* A happy man, you said——

HILDA: Well now, *are* you not happy—in other respects?

SOLNESS: *(Continues to look at her.)* When I told you all this about the fire—h'm——

HILDA: Well?

SOLNESS: Was there not one special thought that you—that you seized upon?

HILDA: *(Reflects in vain.)* No. What thought should that be?

SOLNESS: *(With subdued emphasis.)* It was simply and solely by that fire that I was enabled to build homes for human beings. Cosy, comfortable, bright homes, where father and mother and the whole troop of children can live in safety and gladness, feeling what a happy thing it is to be alive in the world—and most of all to belong to each other—in great things and in small.

HILDA: *(Ardently.)* Well, and isn't it a great happiness for you to be able to build such beautiful homes?

SOLNESS: The price, Hilda! The terrible price I had to pay for it!

HILDA: But can you *never* get over that?

SOLNESS: No. That I might build homes for others, I had to forego—to forego for all time—the home that might have been my own. I mean a home for a troop of children—and for father and mother, too.

HILDA: *(Cautiously.)* But need you have done that? For all time, you say?

SOLNESS: *(Nods slowly.)* That was the price of this happiness that people talk about. *(Breathes heavily.)* This happiness—h'm—this happiness was not to be bought any cheaper, Hilda.

HILDA: *(As before.)* But may it not come right even yet?

SOLNESS: Never in this world—never. That is another consequence of the fire—and of Aline's illness afterwards.

HILDA: *(Looks at him with an indefinable expression.)* And yet you build all these nurseries?

SOLNESS: *(Seriously.)* Have you never noticed, Hilda, how the impossible— how it seems to beckon and cry aloud to one?

HILDA: *(Reflecting.)* The impossible? *(With animation.)* Yes, indeed! Is that how *you* feel too?

SOLNESS: Yes, I do.

HILDA: Then there must be—a little of the troll in you too?

SOLNESS: Why of the troll?

HILDA: What would *you* call it, then?

SOLNESS: *(Rises.)* Well, well, perhaps you're right. *(Vehemently.)* But how can I help turning into a troll, when this is how it always goes with me in everything— in everything!

HILDA: How do you mean?

SOLNESS: *(Speaking low, with inward emotion.)* Mark what I say to you, Hilda. All that I have succeeded in doing, building, creating—all the beauty, security, cheerful comfort—ay, and magnificence too—*(clenches his hands)*—oh, isn't it terrible even to think of——!

HILDA: *What* is so terrible?

SOLNESS: That all this I have to make up for, to pay for—not in money, but in human happiness. And not with my own happiness only, but with other people's too. Yes, yes, do you see that, Hilda? That is the price which my position as an art- ist has cost me—and others. And every single day I have to look on while the price is paid for me anew. Over again, and over again—and over again forever.

HILDA: *(Rises and looks steadily at him.)* Now I can see you're thinking of— of *her.*

SOLNESS: Yes, mainly of Aline. For Aline—she, too, had her vocation in life, just as much as I had mine. *(His voice quivers.)* But her vocation has had to be stunted, and crushed, and shattered—in order that mine might force its way to— to a sort of great victory. For you must know that Aline—she, too, had a turn for building.

HILDA: She? For building?

SOLNESS: *(Shakes his head.)* Not houses, and towers, and spires—not such things as I work away at——

HILDA: Well, but *what,* then?

SOLNESS: *(Softly, with emotion.)* For building up the souls of little children, Hilda. For building up children's souls in perfect balance, and in noble and beau- tiful forms. For enabling them to soar up into erect and full-grown human souls. That was Aline's talent. And there it all lies now—unused and unusable forever— of no earthly service to any one—just like the ruins left by a fire.

HILDA: Yes, but even if this were so——

SOLNESS: It *is* so! It *is* so! I know it.

HILDA: Well, but in any case it's not *your* fault.

SOLNESS: *(Fixes his eyes on her, and nods slowly.)* Ah, *that* is the great, the ter- rible question. *That* is the doubt that's gnawing me—night and day.

HILDA: That?

SOLNESS: Yes. Suppose the fault *was* mine—in a certain sense.

HILDA: Your fault! The fire!

SOLNESS: All of it; the whole thing. And yet, perhaps—I mayn't have had anything to do with it.

HILDA: *(Looks at him with a troubled expression.)* Oh, Mr. Solness, if you can talk like that, I'm afraid you must be—ill, after all.

SOLNESS: H'm—I don't think I shall ever be of quite sound mind on that point.

*(*RAGNAR BROVIK *cautiously opens the little door in the left-hand corner.* HILDA *comes forward.)*

RAGNAR: *(When he sees* HILDA.*)* Oh—I beg pardon, Mr. Solness—— *(He makes a movement to withdraw.)*

SOLNESS: No, no, don't go. Let's get it over.

RAGNAR: Oh, yes—if only we could.

SOLNESS: I hear your father is no better?

RAGNAR: Father is fast growing weaker—and therefore I beg and implore you to write a few kind words for me on one of the plans! Something for father to read before he——

SOLNESS: *(Vehemently.)* I won't hear anything more about those drawings of yours!

RAGNAR: Have you looked at them?

SOLNESS: Yes, I have.

RAGNAR: And they're good for nothing? And *I* am good for nothing, too?

SOLNESS: *(Evasively.)* Stay here with me, Ragnar. You shall have everything your own way. And then you can marry Kaia, and live at your ease—and—and happily too, who knows? Only don't think of building on your own account.

RAGNAR: Well, well, then I must go home and tell father what you say—I promised I would. *Is* this what I am to tell father—before he dies?

SOLNESS: *(With a groan.)* Oh tell him—tell him what you will for me. Best to say nothing at all to him! *(With a sudden outburst.)* I *cannot* do anything else, Ragnar!

RAGNAR: May I have the drawings to take with me?

SOLNESS: Yes, take them—take them by all means! They're lying there on the table.

RAGNAR: *(Goes to the table.)* Thanks.

HILDA: *(Puts her hand on the portfolio.)* No, no; leave them here.

SOLNESS: Why?

HILDA: Because I want to look at them too.

SOLNESS: But you *have* been—— *(To* RAGNAR.*)* Well, leave them here, then.

RAGNAR: Very well.

SOLNESS: And go home at once to your father.

RAGNAR: Yes, I suppose I must.

SOLNESS: *(As if in desperation.)* Ragnar—you *must* not ask me to do what's beyond my power! Do you hear, Ragnar? You *must* not!

RAGNAR: No, no. I beg your pardon——
(He bows, and goes out by the corner door. HILDA *goes over and sits down on a chair near the mirror.)*

HILDA: *(Looks angrily at* SOLNESS.*)* That was a very ugly thing to do.

SOLNESS: Do *you* think so, too?

HILDA: Yes, it was horribly ugly—and hard and bad and cruel as well.

SOLNESS: Oh, you don't understand my position.

HILDA: All the same——. No, you oughtn't to be like that.

SOLNESS: You said yourself, only just now, that no one but *I* ought to be allowed to build.

HILDA: *I* may say such things—but *you* mayn't.

SOLNESS: I most of all, surely, who have paid so dear for my position.

HILDA: Oh, yes—with what you call domestic comfort—and that sort of thing.

SOLNESS: And with my peace of soul into the bargain.

HILDA: *(Rising.)* Peace of soul! *(With feeling.)* Yes, yes, you're right in that! Poor Mr. Solness—you fancy that——

SOLNESS: *(With a quiet, chuckling laugh.)* Just sit down again, Hilda, and I'll tell you something funny.

HILDA: *(Sits down; with intent interest.)* Well?

SOLNESS: It sounds such a ludicrous little thing; for, you see, the whole story turns upon nothing but a crack in a chimney.

HILDA: No more than that?

SOLNESS: No, not to begin with.
(He moves a chair nearer to HILDA *and sits down.)*

HILDA: *(Impatiently, taps on her knee.)* Well, now for the crack in the chimney!

SOLNESS: I had noticed the split in the flue long, long before the fire. Every time I went up into the attic, I looked to see if it was still there.

HILDA: And it was?

SOLNESS: Yes; for no one else knew about it.

HILDA: And you said nothing?

SOLNESS: Nothing.

HILDA: And didn't think of repairing the flue either.

SOLNESS: Oh yes, I thought about it—but never got any further. Every time I intended to set to work, it seemed just as if a hand held me back. Not to-day, I thought—to-morrow; and nothing ever came of it.

HILDA: But why did you keep putting it off like that?

SOLNESS: Because I was revolving something in my mind. *(Slowly, and in a low voice.)* Through that little black crack in the chimney I might, perhaps, force my way upwards—as a builder.

HILDA: *(Looking straight in front of her.)* That must have been thrilling.

SOLNESS: Almost irresistible—quite irresistible. For at that time it appeared to me a perfectly simple and straightforward matter. I would have had it happen in the winter time—a little before midday. I was to be out driving Aline in the sleigh. The servants at home would have made a huge fire in the stove.

HILDA: For, of course, it was to be bitterly cold that day?

SOLNESS: Rather biting, yes—and they would want Aline to find it thoroughly snug and warm when she came home.

HILDA: I suppose she's very chilly by nature?

SOLNESS: She *is*. And as we drove home, we were to see the smoke.

HILDA: Only the smoke?

SOLNESS: The smoke first. But when we came up to the garden gate, the whole of the old timber-box was to be a rolling mass of flames.— That's how I wanted it to be, you see.

HILDA: Oh, why, *why* couldn't it have happened so!

SOLNESS: You may well say that, Hilda.

HILDA: Well, but now listen, Mr. Solness. Are you perfectly certain that the fire was caused by that little crack in the chimney?

SOLNESS: No, on the contrary—I'm perfectly certain that the crack in the chimney had nothing whatever to do with the fire.

HILDA: What!

SOLNESS: It has been clearly ascertained that the fire broke out in a clothes-cupboard—in a totally different part of the house.

HILDA: Then what's all this nonsense you're talking about the crack in the chimney?

SOLNESS: May I go on talking to you a little, Hilda?

HILDA: Yes, if you'll only talk sensibly,——

SOLNESS: I'll try to. (*He moves his chair nearer.*)

HILDA: Out with it, then, Mr. Solness.

SOLNESS: (*Confidentially.*) Don't you agree with me, Hilda, that there exist special, chosen people who have been endowed with the power and faculty of *desiring* a thing, *craving* for a thing, willing a thing—so persistently and so—so inexorably—that at last it *has* to happen? Don't you believe that?

HILDA: (*With an indefinable expression in her eyes.*) If that is so, we shall see one of these days—whether *I* am one of the chosen.

SOLNESS: It's not one's self alone that can do such great things. Oh, no—the helpers and the servers—they must do their part too, if it's to be of any good. But they never come of themselves. One has to call upon them very persistently—inwardly, you understand.

HILDA: What are these helpers and servers?

SOLNESS: Oh, we can talk about that some other time. For the present, let us keep to this business of the fire.

HILDA: Don't you think the fire would have happened all the same—even if you hadn't wished for it?

SOLNESS: If my house had been old Knut Brovik's, it would never have burnt down so conveniently for *him*. I'm sure of that; for he doesn't know how to call for the helpers—no, nor for the servers, either. (*Rises in agitation.*) So you see, Hilda—it's my fault, after all, the lives of the two little boys had to be sacrificed. And do you think it isn't my fault, too, that Aline has never been the woman she should and might have been—and that she most longed to be?

HILDA: Yes, but if it's all the work of those helpers and servers——?

SOLNESS: *Who* called for the helpers and servers? It was *I*! And they came and obeyed my will. *(In increasing excitement.) That's* what good people call having the luck on your side; but I must tell you what this sort of luck feels like! It feels like a great raw place here on my breast. And the helpers and servers keep on flaying pieces of skin off other people in order to close my sore. But still the sore is not healed—never, never! Oh, if you knew how it can sometimes gnaw and burn.

HILDA: *(Looks attentively at him.)* You *are* ill, Mr. Solness. Very ill, I almost think.

SOLNESS: Say *mad;* for that's what you mean.

HILDA: No, I don't think there's much amiss with your intellect.

SOLNESS: With *what,* then? Out with it!

HILDA: I wonder whether you weren't sent into the world with a sickly conscience.

SOLNESS: A sickly conscience? What devilry is that?

HILDA: I mean that your conscience is feeble—too delicately built, as it were—hasn't strength to take a grip of things—to lift and bear what's heavy.

SOLNESS: *(Growls.)* H'm! May I ask, then, what sort of a conscience one ought to have?

HILDA: I should like *your* conscience to be thoroughly robust.

SOLNESS: Indeed? Robust, eh? Is your own conscience robust.

HILDA: Yes, I think it is. I've never noticed that it wasn't.

SOLNESS: It hasn't been put very severely to the test, I should think.

HILDA: *(With a quivering of the lips.)* Oh, it wasn't such a simple matter to leave father—I'm so awfully fond of him.

SOLNESS: Dear me! for a month or two——

HILDA: I don't think I shall ever go home again.

SOLNESS: Never? Then why did you leave him?

HILDA: *(Half-seriously, half-banteringly.)* Have you forgotten again that the ten years are up?

SOLNESS: Oh, nonsense. Was anything wrong at home? Eh?

HILDA: *(Quite seriously.)* It *was* this something within me that drove and spurred me here—and allured and attracted me, too.

SOLNESS: *(Eagerly.)* There we have it! There we have it, Hilda! There's a troll in you too, as in me. For it's the troll in one, you see—it's *that* that calls to the powers outside us. And then you *must* give in—whether you will or no.

HILDA: I almost think you're right, Mr. Solness.

SOLNESS: *(Walks about the room.)* Oh, there are devils innumerable abroad in the world, Hilda, that one never *sees!*

HILDA: Devils, too?

SOLNESS: *(Stops.)* Good devils and bad devils; light-haired devils and black-haired devils. If only you could always tell whether it's the light or the dark ones that have got hold of you! *(Paces about.)* Ho, ho! Then it would be simple enough!

HILDA: *(Follows him with her eyes.)* Or if one had a really vigorous, radiantly healthy conscience—so that one *dared* to do what one *would.*

SOLNESS: *(Stops beside the console table.)* I believe, now, that most people are just as puny creatures as I am in this respect.

HILDA: I shouldn't wonder.

SOLNESS: *(Leaning against the table.)* In the sagas——Have you read any of the old sagas?

HILDA: Oh yes! When I used to read books, I——

SOLNESS: In the sagas you read about vikings, who sailed to foreign lands, and plundered and burned and killed men——

HILDA: And carried off women——

SOLNESS: ——and kept them in captivity——

HILDA: ——took them home in their ships——

SOLNESS: ——and behaved to them like——like the very worst of trolls.

HILDA: *(Looks straight before her with a half-veiled look.)* I think *that* must have been thrilling.

SOLNESS: *(With a short, deep laugh.)* To carry off women, eh!

HILDA: To *be* carried off.

SOLNESS: *(Looks at her a moment.)* Oh, indeed.

HILDA: *(As if breaking the thread of conversation.)* But what made you speak of these vikings, Mr. Solness?

SOLNESS: Because *those* fellows must have had robust consciences, if you like! When they got home again they could eat and drink, and be as happy as children. And the women, too! They often wouldn't leave them on any account. Can you understand that, Hilda?

HILDA: Those women I can understand exceedingly well.

SOLNESS: Oho! Perhaps you could do the same yourself?

HILDA: Why not?

SOLNESS: Live—of your own free will—with a ruffian like that?

HILDA: If it was a ruffian I had come to love——

SOLNESS: *Could* you come to love a man like that?

HILDA: Good heavens, you know very well one can't choose whom one's going to love.

SOLNESS: *(Looks meditatively at her.)* Oh no, I suppose it's the troll within one that's responsible for that.

HILDA: *(Half laughing.)* And all those blessed devils, that *you* know so well—both the light-haired and the dark-haired ones.

SOLNESS: *(Quietly and warmly.)* Then I hope with all my heart that the devils will choose carefully for you, Hilda.

HILDA: For me they *have* chosen already—once and for all.

SOLNESS: *(Looks earnestly at her.)* Hilda, you are like a wild bird of the woods.

HILDA: Far from it. I don't hide myself away under the bushes.

SOLNESS: No, no. There's rather something of the bird of prey in you.

HILDA: That's nearer it—perhaps. *(Very vehemently.)* And why not a bird of prey? Why shouldn't *I* go a-hunting—I, as well as the rest? Carry off the prey I want—if I can only get my claws into it, and have my own way with it.

SOLNESS: Hilda,—do you know what you are?

HILDA: Yes, I suppose I'm a strange sort of bird.

SOLNESS: No. You are like a dawning day. When I look at you, I seem to be looking towards the sunrise.

HILDA: Tell me, Mr. Solness—are you certain that you've never called me to you?—Inwardly, you know?

SOLNESS: *(Softly and slowly.)* I almost think I must have.

HILDA: What did you want with me?

SOLNESS: You are the younger generation, Hilda.

HILDA: *(Smiles.)* That younger generation that you're so afraid of.

SOLNESS: *(Nods slowly.)* And which, in my heart, I yearn towards so deeply. (HILDA *rises, goes to the little table, and fetches* RAGNAR BROVIK'S *portfolio.*)

HILDA: *(Holds out the portfolio to him.)* We were talking of these drawings——

SOLNESS: *(Shortly, waving them away.)* Put those things away! I've seen enough of them.

HILDA: Yes, but you have to write your approval on them.

SOLNESS: Write my approval on them? Never!

HILDA: But the poor old man is lying at death's door! Can't you give him and his son this pleasure before they're parted? And perhaps he might get the commission to carry them out, too.

SOLNESS: Yes, that's just what he would get. He's made sure of that—has my fine gentleman!

HILDA: Then good heavens—if that's so—can't you tell the least little bit of a lie for once?

SOLNESS: A lie? *(Raging.)* Hilda—take those devil's drawings out of my sight!

HILDA: *(Draws the portfolio a little nearer to herself.)* Well, well, well—don't bite me.—You talk of trolls—but I think you go on like a troll yourself. *(Looks round.)* Where do you keep your pen and ink?

SOLNESS: There's nothing of the sort in here.

HILDA: *(Goes towards the door.)* But in the office where that young lady is——

SOLNESS: Stay where you are, Hilda!—I ought to tell a lie, you say. Oh yes, for the sake of his old father I might well do that—for in my time I've crushed him, trodden him under foot——

HILDA: Him, too?

SOLNESS: I needed room for myself. But this Ragnar—he must on no account be allowed to come to the front.

HILDA: Poor fellow, there's surely no fear of that. If he has nothing in him——

SOLNESS: *(Comes closer, looks at her, and whispers.)* If Ragnar Brovik comes to the front he will strike *me* to the earth. Crush me—as I crushed his father.

HILDA: Crush you? Has he the ability for that?

SOLNESS: Yes, you may depend upon it *he* has the ability! He is the younger generation that stands ready to knock at my door—to make an end of Halvard Solness.

HILDA: *(Looks at him with quiet reproach.)* And yet you would bar him out. Fie, Mr. Solness!

SOLNESS: The fight I have been fighting has cost heart's blood enough.—And I'm afraid, too, that the helpers and servers won't obey me any longer.

HILDA: Then you must go ahead without them. There's nothing else for it.

SOLNESS: It's hopeless, Hilda. The luck is bound to turn. A little sooner or a little later. Retribution is inexorable.

HILDA: *(In distress putting her hands over her ears.)* Don't talk like that! Do you want to kill me? To take from me what is more than my life?

SOLNESS: And what is that?

HILDA: The longing to see you great. To see you, with a wreath in your hand, high, high up upon a church-tower. *(Calm again.)* Come, out with your pencil now. You must have a pencil about you!

SOLNESS: *(Takes out his pocket-book.)* I have one here.

HILDA: *(Puts the portfolio on the sofa-table.)* Very well. Now let us two sit down here, Mr. Solness.

(SOLNESS *seats himself at the table.*)

HILDA: *(Behind him leaning over the back of the chair.)* And now we'll write on the drawings. We must write very, very nicely and cordially—for this horrid Ruar—or whatever his name is.

SOLNESS: *(Writes a few words, turns his head and looks at her.)* Tell me one thing, Hilda.

HILDA: Yes?

SOLNESS: If you've been waiting for me all these ten years——

HILDA: What then?

SOLNESS: Why have you never written to me? Then I could have answered you.

HILDA: *(Hastily.)* No, no, no! That was just what I didn't want.

SOLNESS: Why not?

HILDA: I was afraid the whole thing might fall to pieces.—But we were going to write on the drawings, Mr. Solness.

SOLNESS: So we were.

HILDA: *(Bends forward and looks over his shoulder while he writes.)* Mind now! kindly and cordially! Oh how I hate—how I hate this Ruald——

SOLNESS: *(Writing.)* Have you never really cared for anyone, Hilda?

HILDA: *(Harshly.)* What do you say?

SOLNESS: Have you never cared for any one?

HILDA: For any one else, I suppose you mean?

SOLNESS: *(Looks up at her.)* For any one else, yes. Have you never? In all these ten years? Never?

HILDA: Oh yes, now and then. When I was perfectly furious with you for not coming.

SOLNESS: Then you did take an interest in other people, too?

HILDA: A little bit—for a week or so. Good heavens, Mr. Solness, you surely know how such things come about.

SOLNESS: Hilda—what is it you've come for?

HILDA: Don't waste time in talking. The poor old man might go and die in the mean time.

SOLNESS: Answer me, Hilda. What do you want of me?

HILDA: I want my kingdom.

SOLNESS: H'm——

(He gives a rapid glance towards the door on the left, and then goes on writing on the drawings. At the same moment MRS. SOLNESS *enters; she has some packages in her hand.)*

MRS. SOLNESS: Here are a few things I've got for you, Miss Wangel. The large parcels will be sent later on.

HILDA: Oh, how very, very kind of you!

MRS. SOLNESS: Only my simple duty. Nothing more than that.

SOLNESS: *(Reading over what he has written.)* Aline!

MRS. SOLNESS: Yes?

SOLNESS: Did you notice whether the—the book-keeper was out there?

MRS. SOLNESS: Yes, of course, *she* was there.

SOLNESS: *(Puts the drawings in the portfolio.)* H'm——

MRS. SOLNESS: She was standing at the desk, as she always is—when *I* go through the room.

SOLNESS: *(Rises.)* Then I'll give this to her, and tell her that——

HILDA: *(Takes the portfolio from him.)* Oh, no, let me have the pleasure of doing that! *(Goes to the door, but turns.)* What's her name?

SOLNESS: Her name is Miss Fosli.

HILDA: Pooh, that sounds so cold. Her Christian name, I mean?

SOLNESS: Kaia—I believe.

HILDA: *(Opens the door and calls out.)* Kaia, come in here! Make haste! Mr. Solness wants to speak to you.

(KAIA FOSLI *appears at the door.)*

KAIA: *(Looking at him in alarm.)* Here I am.

HILDA: *(Handing her the portfolio.)* See here, Kaia? You can take these home; Mr. Solness has written on them now.

KAIA: Oh, at last!

SOLNESS: Give them to the old man as soon as you can.

KAIA: I will go straight home with them.

SOLNESS: Yes, do. Now Ragnar will have a chance of building for himself.

KAIA: Oh, may he come and thank you for all——

SOLNESS: *(Harshly.)* I won't have any thanks. Tell him *that* from me.

KAIA: Yes, I will——

SOLNESS: And tell him at the same time that henceforward I don't require his services—nor yours either.

KAIA: *(Softly and quiveringly.)* Not mine either?

SOLNESS: You will have other things to think of now, and to attend to; and that's a very good thing for you. Well, go home with the drawings now, Miss Fosli. Quickly! Do you hear?

KAIA: *(As before.)* Yes, Mr. Solness.

(She goes out.)

MRS. SOLNESS: Heavens! what deceitful eyes she has.

SOLNESS: She? That poor little creature?

MRS. SOLNESS: Oh—I can see what I can see, Halvard.——Are you really dismissing them?

SOLNESS: Yes.

MRS. SOLNESS: Her as well?

SOLNESS: Wasn't that what you wished?

MRS. SOLNESS: But how can you get on without *her*——? Oh well, no doubt you have some one else in reserve, Halvard.

HILDA: *(Playfully.)* Well, *I* for one am not the person to stand at that desk.

SOLNESS: Never mind, never mind—it'll be all right, Aline. Now all you have to do is to think about moving into our new home—as quickly as you can. This evening we'll hang up the wreath—*(Turns to* HILDA*)*—right on the very pinnacle of the tower. What do you say to that, Miss Hilda?

HILDA: *(Looks at him with sparkling eyes.)* It'll be splendid to see you so high up once more.

SOLNESS: Me!

MRS. SOLNESS: For Heaven's sake, Miss Wangel, don't imagine such a thing! My husband!—when he always gets so dizzy!

HILDA: *He* get dizzy! No, I know quite well he doesn't.

MRS. SOLNESS: Oh, yes, indeed he does.

HILDA: But I've seen him with my own eyes right up at the top of a high church-tower.

MRS. SOLNESS: Yes, I hear people talk of that; but its utterly impossible——

SOLNESS: *(Vehemently.)* Impossible—impossible, yes! But there I stood all the same!

MRS. SOLNESS: Oh, how can you say so, Halvard? Why, you can't even bear to go out on the second-story balcony here. You've always been like that.

SOLNESS: You may perhaps see something different this evening.

MRS. SOLNESS: *(In alarm.)* No, no, no! Please God, I shall never see that! I'll write at once to the doctor—and I'm sure he won't let you do it.

SOLNESS: Why, Aline——!

MRS. SOLNESS: Oh, you know you're ill, Halvard. This *proves* it! Oh God—Oh God!

(She goes hastily out to the right.)

HILDA: *(Looks intently at him.)* Is it so, or is it not?

SOLNESS: That I turn dizzy?

HILDA: That *my* master builder *dares* not—*cannot*—climb as high as he builds?

SOLNESS: Is that the way you look at it?

HILDA: Yes.

SOLNESS: I believe there's scarcely a corner in me safe from you.

HILDA: *(Looks towards the bay-window.)* Up there, then. Right up there——

SOLNESS: *(Approaches her.)* You might have the topmost chamber in the tower, Hilda—there you might live like a princess.

HILDA: *(Indefinably, between earnest and jest.)* Yes, that's what you promised me.

SOLNESS: *Did* I really?

HILDA: Fie, Mr. Solness! You said, I should be a princess, and that you would give me a kingdom. And then you went and————Well!

SOLNESS: *(Cautiously.)* Are you quite certain that this is not a dream—a fancy, that has fixed itself in your mind?

HILDA: *(Sharply.)* Do you mean that you didn't do it?

SOLNESS: I scarcely know myself. *(More softly.)* But now I know *so much* for certain, that I————

HILDA: That you————? Say it at once!

SOLNESS: ————that I *ought* to have done it.

HILDA: *(In a bold outburst.)* Don't tell me *you* can ever be dizzy!

SOLNESS: This evening, then, we'll hang up the wreath—Princess Hilda.

HILDA: *(With a bitter curve of the lips.)* Over your new home, yes.

SOLNESS: Over the new house, which will never be a *home* for *me*. *(He goes out through the garden door.)*

HILDA: *(Looks straight in front of her with a far-away expression, and whispers to herself. The only words audible are:)*————frightfully thrilling————

THIRD ACT

A large, broad veranda attached to SOLNESS'S *dwelling-house. Part of the house, with outer door leading to the veranda, is seen to the left. A railing along the veranda to the right. At the back, from the end of the veranda, a flight of steps leads down to the garden below. Tall old trees in the garden spread their branches over the veranda and towards the house. Far to the right, in among the trees, a glimpse is caught of the lower part of the new villa, with scaffolding round so much as is seen of the tower. In the background the garden is bounded by an old wooden fence. Outside the fence, a street with low, tumble-down cottages.*

Evening sky with sun-lit clouds.

On the veranda a garden bench stands along the wall of the house, and in front of the bench a long table. On the other side of the table, an arm-chair and some stools. All the furniture is of wicker-work.

MRS. SOLNESS, *wrapped in a large white crape shawl, sits resting in the arm-chair and gazes over to the right. Shortly after,* HILDA WANGEL *comes up the flight of steps from the garden. She is dressed as in the last act and wears her hat. She has in her bodice a little nosegay of small common flowers.*

MRS. SOLNESS: *(Turning her head a little.)* Have you been round the garden, Miss Wangel?

HILDA: Yes, I've been taking a look at it.

MRS. SOLNESS: And found some flowers too, I see.

HILDA: Yes, indeed. There are such heaps of them in among the bushes.

MRS. SOLNESS: Are there really? Still? You see I scarcely ever go there.

HILDA: *(Closer.)* What! Don't you take a run down into the garden every day, then?

MRS. SOLNESS: *(With a faint smile.)* I don't "run" anywhere, nowadays.

HILDA: Well, but don't you go down now and then, to look at all the lovely things there?

MRS. SOLNESS: It has all become so strange to me. I'm almost afraid to see it again.

HILDA: Your own garden!

MRS. SOLNESS: I don't feel that it is *mine* any longer.

HILDA: What do you mean——?

MRS. SOLNESS: No, no, it *is* not—not as it was in my mother's and father's time. They have taken away so much—so much of the garden, Miss Wangel. Fancy—they've parcelled it out—and built houses for strangers—people that I don't know. And *they* can sit and look in upon me from their windows.

HILDA: *(With a bright expression.)* Mrs. Solness?

MRS. SOLNESS: Yes?

HILDA: May I stay here with you a little?

MRS. SOLNESS: Yes, by all means, if you care to.

(HILDA *moves a stool close to the arm-chair and sits down.*)

HILDA: Ah—one can sit here and sun oneself like a cat.

MRS. SOLNESS: *(Lays her hand softly on* HILDA'S *neck.)* It's nice of you to be willing to sit with *me.* I thought you wanted to go in to my husband.

HILDA: What should I want with him?

MRS. SOLNESS: To help him, I thought.

HILDA: No, thanks. And besides, he's not in. He's over there with his workmen. But he looked so fierce that I didn't dare to talk to him.

MRS. SOLNESS: He's so kind and gentle in reality.

HILDA: *He!*

MRS. SOLNESS: You don't really know him yet, Miss Wangel.

HILDA: *(Looks affectionately at her.)* Are you pleased at the thought of moving over to the new house?

MRS. SOLNESS: I *ought* to be pleased; for it's what Halvard wants——

HILDA: Oh, not just on that account, surely.

MRS. SOLNESS: Yes, yes, Miss Wangel; for it's simply my duty to submit myself to *him.* But very often it's dreadfully difficult to force one's mind to obedience.

HILDA: Yes, *that* must be difficult indeed.

MRS. SOLNESS: I can tell you it is—when one has so many faults as I have——

HILDA: When one has gone through so much as *you* have——

MRS. SOLNESS: How do you know about that?

HILDA: Your husband told me.

MRS. SOLNESS: To me he very seldom mentions these things.—Yes, I can tell you I've gone through more than enough trouble in my life, Miss Wangel.

HILDA: *(Looks sympathetically at her and nods slowly.)* Poor Mrs. Solness. First of all there was the fire——

MRS. SOLNESS: *(With a sigh.)* Yes, everything that was *mine* was burnt.

HILDA: And then came what was worse.

MRS. SOLNESS: *(Looking inquiringly at her.)* Worse?

HILDA: The worst of all.

MRS. SOLNESS: What do you mean?

HILDA: *(Softly.)* You lost the two little boys.

MRS. SOLNESS: Oh yes, the boys. But you see, *that* was a thing apart. That was a dispensation of Providence; and in such things one can only bow in submission—yes, and be thankful, too.

HILDA: Then are you so?

MRS. SOLNESS: Not always, I'm sorry to say. I know well enough that it's my duty—but all the same I *cannot.*

HILDA: No, no, I think that's only natural.

MRS. SOLNESS: And often and often I have to remind myself that it was a righteous punishment for me—

HILDA: Why?

MRS. SOLNESS: Because I hadn't fortitude enough in misfortune.

HILDA: But I don't see that——

MRS. SOLNESS: Oh, no, no, Miss Wangel—don't talk to me any more about the two little boys. We ought to feel nothing but joy in thinking of *them;* for they are so happy—so happy now. No, it's the *small* losses in life that cut one to the heart—the loss of all that other people look upon as almost nothing.

HILDA: *(Lays her arms on* MRS. SOLNESS' *knees and looks at her affectionately.)* Dear Mrs. Solness—tell me what things you mean!

MRS. SOLNESS: As I say, only little things. All the old portraits were burnt on the walls. And all the old silk dresses were burnt, that had belonged to the family for generations and generations. And all mother's and grandmother's lace—that was burnt too. And only think—the jewels too! *(Sadly.)* And then all the dolls.

HILDA: The dolls?

MRS. SOLNESS: *(Choking with tears.)* I had nine lovely dolls.

HILDA: And *they* were burnt too?

MRS. SOLNESS: All of them. Oh, it was hard—so hard for me.

HILDA: Had you put by all these dolls, then? Ever since you were little?

MRS. SOLNESS: I hadn't put them by. The dolls and I had gone on living together.

HILDA: After you were grown up?

MRS. SOLNESS: Yes, long after that.

HILDA: After you were married too?

MRS. SOLNESS: Oh yes, indeed. So long as he didn't see it.—But they were all burnt up, poor things. No one thought of saving them. Oh, it's so miserable to think of. You mustn't laugh at me, Miss Wangel.

HILDA: I'm not laughing in the least.

MRS. SOLNESS: For you see, in a certain sense there was life in them, too. I carried them under my heart—like little unborn children.

*(*DR. HERDAL, *with his hat in his hand, comes out through the door and observes* MRS. SOLNESS *and* HILDA.*)*

DR. HERDAL: Well, Mrs. Solness, so you're sitting out here catching cold?

MRS. SOLNESS: I find it so pleasant and warm here to-day.

DR. HERDAL: Yes, yes. But is there anything going on here? I got a note from you.

MRS. SOLNESS: *(Rises.)* Yes, there's something I must talk to you about.

DR. HERDAL: Very well; then perhaps we'd better go in. (*To* HILDA.) Still in your mountaineering dress, Miss Wangel?

HILDA: *(Gayly, rising.)* Yes—in full uniform! But to-day I'm not going climbing and breaking my neck. We two will stop quietly below and look on, doctor.

DR. HERDAL: What are we to look on at?

MRS. SOLNESS: *(Softly, in alarm, to* HILDA.) Hush, hush—for God's sake! He's coming! Try to get that idea out of his head. And let us be friends, Miss Wangel. Don't you think we can?

HILDA: *(Throws her arms impetuously round* MRS. SOLNESS' *neck.)* O, if we only could!

MRS. SOLNESS: *(Gently disengages herself.)* There, there, there! There he comes, doctor. Let me have a word with you.

DR. HERDAL: Is it about *him?*

MRS. SOLNESS: Yes, to be sure it's about him. Do come in.

(She and the doctor enter the house. Next moment SOLNESS *comes up from the garden by the flight of steps. A serious look comes over* HILDA'S *face.)*

SOLNESS: *(Glances at the house-door, which is closed cautiously from within.)* Have you noticed, Hilda, that as soon as I come, she goes?

HILDA: I've noticed that as soon as you come, you make her go.

SOLNESS: Perhaps so. But I cannot help it. *(Looks observantly at her.)* Are you cold, Hilda? I think you look so.

HILDA: I've just come up out of a tomb.

SOLNESS: What do you mean by *that?*

HILDA: That I've got chilled through and through, Mr. Solness.

SOLNESS: *(Slowly.)* I believe I understand——

HILDA: What brings you up here just now?

SOLNESS: I caught sight of you from over there.

HILDA: But then you must have seen her too?

SOLNESS: I knew she would go at once if I came.

HILDA: Is it very painful for you that she should avoid you in this way?

SOLNESS: In one sense, it's a relief as well.

HILDA: Not to have her before your eyes?

SOLNESS: Yes.

HILDA: Not to be always seeing how heavily the loss of the little boys weighs upon her?

SOLNESS: Yes. Chiefly that.

(HILDA drifts across the veranda with her hands behind her back, stops at the railing and looks out over the garden.)

SOLNESS: *(After a short pause.)* Did you have a long talk with her?

(HILDA stands motionless and does not answer.)

SOLNESS: Had you a long talk, I asked?

(HILDA *is silent as before.*)

    SOLNESS: What was she talking about, Hilda?

(HILDA *continues silent.*)

    SOLNESS: Poor Aline! I suppose it was about the little boys.

    HILDA: *(A nervous shudder runs through her; then she nods hurriedly once or twice.)*

    SOLNESS: She will never get over it—never in this world. *(Approaches her.)* Now you're standing there again like a statue; just as you stood last night.

    HILDA: *(Turns and looks at him with great serious eyes.)* I am going away.

    SOLNESS: *(Sharply.)* Going away!

    HILDA: Yes.

    SOLNESS: But I won't allow you to.

    HILDA: What am I to do *here* now?

    SOLNESS: Simply to *be* here, Hilda!

    HILDA: *(Measures him with a look.)* Oh, thank you. You know it wouldn't end there.

    SOLNESS: *(Without consideration.)* So much the better.

    HILDA: *(Vehemently.)* I *can't* do any harm to one I *know!* I can't take away anything that belongs to her.

    SOLNESS: Who wants you to do that?

    HILDA: *(Continuing.)* A stranger, yes! for that's quite a different thing. A person I've never set eyes on. But one that I've come into close contact with——! No! Oh no! Ugh!

    SOLNESS: Yes, but I never proposed you should.

    HILDA: Oh, Mr. Solness, you know quite well what the end of it would be. And that's why I'm going away.

    SOLNESS: And what's to become of me when you're gone? What shall I have to live for *then?*—After that?

    HILDA: *(With the indefinable look in her eyes.)* It's surely not so hard for *you.* You have your duties to her. Live for those duties.

    SOLNESS: Too late. These powers—these—these——

    HILDA: ——devils——

    SOLNESS: Yes, these devils! And the troll within me as well—they have drawn all the life-blood out of her. *(Laughs in desperation.)* They did it for my *happiness.* Yes, yes! *(Sadly.)* And now she's dead—for my sake. And I am chained alive to a dead woman. *(In wild anguish.)* I——I who *cannot* live without joy in life!

(HILDA *walks round the table and seats herself on the bench with her elbows on the table, and her head supported by her hands.*)

    HILDA: *(Sits and looks at him awhile.)* What will you build next?

    SOLNESS: *(Shakes his head.)* I don't believe I shall build much more.

    HILDA: Not those cosy, happy homes for mother and father, and for the troop of children?

    SOLNESS: I wonder whether there will be any use for such homes in the times that are coming.

HILDA: Poor Mr. Solness! And you have gone all these ten years—and staked your whole life—on that alone.

SOLNESS: Yes, you may well say so, Hilda.

HILDA: *(With an outburst.)* Oh, it all seems to me so foolish—so foolish!

SOLNESS: All what?

HILDA: Not to be able to grasp at your own happiness—at your own life! Merely because some one you know happens to stand in the way!

SOLNESS: One whom you have no right to set aside.

HILDA: I wonder whether one really *hasn't* the right? And yet, and yet——. Oh! If one could only sleep the whole thing away!
(She lays her arms flat down on the table, rests the left side of her head on her hand and shuts her eyes.)

SOLNESS: *(Turns the arm-chair and sits down at the table.)* Had *you* a cosy, happy home—up with your father, Hilda?

HILDA: *(Without stirring, answers as if half asleep.)* I had only a cage.

SOLNESS: And you're determined not to return to it?

HILDA: *(As before.)* The wild bird never wants to go into the cage.

SOLNESS: Rather range through the free air——

HILDA: *(Still as before.)* The bird of prey loves to range—

SOLNESS: *(Lets his eyes rest on her.)* If only one had the viking-spirit in life—

HILDA: *(In her usual voice; opens her eyes but does not move.)* And the other thing? Say what *that* was!

SOLNESS: A robust conscience.
*(*HILDA *sits upon the bench with animation. Her eyes have once more the sparkling expression of gladness.)*

HILDA: *(Nods to him.)* I know what you're going to build next!

SOLNESS: Then you know more than I do, Hilda.

HILDA: Yes, builders are such stupid people.

SOLNESS: What is it to be then?

HILDA: *(Nods again.)* The castle.

SOLNESS: What castle?

HILDA: *My* castle, of course.

SOLNESS: Do you want a castle now?

HILDA: Don't you owe me a kingdom, I'd like to know?

SOLNESS: You say I do.

HILDA: Well—you admit you owe me this kingdom. And you can't have a kingdom without a royal castle, I should think!

SOLNESS: *(More and more animated.)* Yes, they usually go together.

HILDA: Good! Then build it for me this moment!

SOLNESS: *(Laughing.)* Must you have that on the instant, too?

HILDA: Yes, to be sure! For the ten years are up now, and I'm not going to wait any longer. So—out with the castle, Mr. Solness!

SOLNESS: It's no light matter to owe you anything, Hilda.

HILDA: You should have thought of that before. It's too late now. So— *(tapping the table)*—the castle on the table! It's *my* castle. I will have it *at once!*

SOLNESS: *(More seriously, leans over towards her, with his arms on the table.)* What sort of castle have you imagined, Hilda?

(Her expression becomes more and more veiled. She seems gazing inwards at herself.)

HILDA: *(Slowly.)* My castle shall stand on a height—on a very great height— with a clear outlook on all sides, so that I can see far—far around.

SOLNESS: And no doubt it's to have a high tower?

HILDA: A tremendously high tower. And at the very top of the tower there shall be a balcony. And I will stand out upon it—

SOLNESS: *(Involuntarily clutches at his forehead.)* How can you like to stand at such a dizzy height——?

HILDA: Yes, I will! Right up there will I stand and look down on the other people—on those that are building churches, and homes for mother and father and the troop of children. And *you* may come up and look on at it, too.

SOLNESS: *(In a low tone.)* Is the builder to be allowed to come up beside the princess?

HILDA: If the builder *will.*

SOLNESS: *(More softly.)* Then I think the builder will come.

HILDA: *(Nods.)* The builder—he'll come.

SOLNESS: But he'll never be able to build any more. Poor builder!

HILDA: *(Animated.)* Oh yes, he will! We two will set to work together. And then we'll build the loveliest—the very loveliest—thing in all the world.

SOLNESS: *(Intently.)* Hilda, tell me what that is!

HILDA: *(Looks smilingly at him, shakes her head a little, pouts, and speaks as if to a child.)* Builders—they are such very—very stupid people.

SOLNESS: Yes, no doubt they're stupid. But now tell me what it is—the loveliest thing in the world—that we two are to build together?

HILDA: *(Is silent a little while, then says with an indefinable expression in her eyes.)* Castles in the air.

SOLNESS: Castles in the air?

HILDA: *(Nods.)* Castles in the air, yes! Do you know what sort of thing a castle in the air is?

SOLNESS: It's the loveliest thing in the world, you say.

HILDA: *(Rises with vehemence, and makes a gesture of repulsion with her hand.)* Yes, to be sure it is! Castles in the air—they're so easy to take refuge in. And so easy to build, too—*(looks scornfully at him)*—especially for the builders who have a—a dizzy conscience.

SOLNESS: *(Rises.)* After this day we two will build together, Hilda.

HILDA: *(With a half-dubious smile.)* A *real* castle in the air?

SOLNESS: Yes. One with a firm foundation under it.

(RAGNAR BOVIK comes out from the house. He is carrying a large, green wreath with flowers and silken ribbons.)

HILDA: *(With an outburst of pleasure.)* The wreath! Oh, that'll be glorious!

SOLNESS: *(In surprise.)* Have *you* brought the wreath, Ragnar?

RAGNAR: I promised the foreman I would.

SOLNESS: *(Relieved.)* Ah, then I suppose your father's better?

RAGNAR: No.

SOLNESS: Wasn't he cheered by what I wrote?

RAGNAR: It came too late.

SOLNESS: Too late!

RAGNAR: When she came with it he was unconscious. He has had a stroke.

SOLNESS: Why, then, you must go home to him! You must attend to your father!

RAGNAR: He doesn't need me any more.

SOLNESS: But surely you ought to be with him.

RAGNAR: *She* is sitting by his bed.

SOLNESS: *(Rather uncertainly.)* Kaia?

RAGNAR: *(Looking darkly at him.)* Yes—Kaia.

SOLNESS: Go home, Ragnar—both to him and to her. Give *me* the wreath.

RAGNAR: *(Suppresses a mocking smile.)* You don't mean that you yourself—

SOLNESS: I will take it down to them myself. *(Takes the wreath from him.)* And now, you go home; we don't require you to-day.

RAGNAR: I know you don't require me any more; but to-day I shall stop.

SOLNESS: Well, stop then, since you're bent upon it.

HILDA: *(At the railing.)* Mr. Solness, I will stand here and look on at you.

SOLNESS: At me!

HILDA: It will be fearfully thrilling.

SOLNESS: *(In a low tone.)* We'll talk about that another time, Hilda.

(He goes down the flight of steps with the wreath, and away through the garden.)

HILDA: *(Looks after him, then turns to* RAGNAR.*)* You might at least have thanked him, I think.

RAGNAR: Thanked him? Ought I to have thanked *him?*

HILDA: Yes, of course you ought!

RAGNAR: I think it's rather you I ought to thank.

HILDA: How can you say such a thing?

RAGNAR: *(Without answering her.)* But I advise you to take care, Miss Wangel! For you don't know *him* rightly yet.

HILDA: *(Ardently.)* Oh, I know him better than any one!

RAGNAR: *(Laughs in exasperation.)* Thank him, when he's held me down year after year! When he made father disbelieve in me—made me disbelieve in myself. And all merely that he might——!

HILDA: *(As if divining something.)* That he might——? Tell me at once!

RAGNAR: That he might keep her with him.

HILDA: *(With a start towards him.)* The girl at the desk!

RAGNAR: Yes.

HILDA: *(Threateningly, clenching her hands.)* That is not true! You're telling falsehoods about him!

RAGNAR: I wouldn't believe it either until to-day—when she said so herself.

HILDA: *(As if beside herself.)* What did she say? I *will* know! At once! at once!

RAGNAR: She said that he had taken possession of her mind—her whole mind—centred all her thoughts upon himself alone. She says that she can never leave him—that she will remain here, where *he* is——

HILDA: *(With flashing eyes.)* She won't be allowed to!

RAGNAR: *(As if feeling his way.)* Who won't allow her?

HILDA: *(Rapidly.)* He won't either?

RAGNAR: Oh no—I understand the whole thing now. After this she would merely be—in the way.

HILDA: You understand nothing—since you can talk like that! No, *I* will tell you why he kept hold of her.

RAGNAR: Well then, why?

HILDA: In order to keep hold of *you.*

RAGNAR: Has he told you so?

HILDA: No, but it is so. It *must* be so! *(Wildly.)* I will— I *will* have it so!

RAGNAR: And at the very moment when you came—he let her go.

HILDA: It was *you—you* that he let go! What do you suppose he cares about strange women like her?

RAGNAR: *(Reflects.)* Is it possible that all this time he's been afraid of me?

HILDA: *He* afraid! I wouldn't be so conceited if I were you.

RAGNAR: Oh, he must have seen long ago that I had something in me, too. Besides—cowardly—that's just what he is, you see.

HILDA: He! Oh yes, I'm likely to believe *that.*

RAGNAR: In a certain sense he *is* cowardly—he, the great master builder. He's not afraid of robbing others of their life's happiness—as he has done both for my father and for me. But when it comes to climbing a paltry bit of scaffolding—he'll do anything rather than *that.*

HILDA: Oh, you should just have seen him high, high up—at the dizzy height where I once saw him.

RAGNAR: Did you see that?

HILDA: Yes, indeed I did. How free and great he looked as he stood and fastened the wreath to the church-vane!

RAGNAR: I know that he ventured that, *once* in his life—one solitary time. It's a tradition among us younger men. But no power on earth would induce him to do it again.

HILDA: To-day he will do it again!

RAGNAR: *(Scornfully.)* Yes, I daresay!

HILDA: We shall see it.

RAGNAR: That neither you nor I will see.

HILDA: *(With uncontrollable vehemence.)* I *will* see it! I *will* and *must* see it!

RAGNAR: But he won't do it. He simply daren't do it. For you see he can't get over this infirmity—master builder though he be.

(MRS. SOLNESS *comes from the house on to the veranda.*)

MRS. SOLNESS: *(Looks around.)* Isn't he here? Where has he gone to?

RAGNAR: Mr. Solness is down with the men.

HILDA: He took the wreath with him.

MRS. SOLNESS: *(Terrified.)* Took the wreath with him! Oh God! Oh God! Brovik—you must go down to him! Get him to come back here!

RAGNAR: Shall I say you want to speak to him, Mrs. Solness?

MRS. SOLNESS: Oh yes, do! No, no—don't say that *I* want anything! You can say that somebody is here, and that he must come at once.

RAGNAR: Good. I will do so, Mrs. Solness.

(He goes down the flight of steps and away through the garden.)

MRS. SOLNESS: Oh, Miss Wangel, you can't think how anxious I feel about him.

HILDA: Is there anything in this to be so terribly frightened about?

MRS. SOLNESS: Oh yes; surely you can understand. Just think, if he were really to do it! If he should take it into his head to climb up the scaffolding!

HILDA: *(Eagerly.)* Do you think he will?

MRS. SOLNESS: Oh, one can never tell what he might take into his head. I'm afraid there's nothing he mightn't think of doing.

HILDA: Aha! Perhaps you think that he's—well——?

MRS. SOLNESS: Oh, I don't know what to think about him now. The doctor has been telling me all sorts of things; and putting it all together with several things I've heard him say——

(DR. HERDAL looks out through the door.)

DR. HERDAL: Isn't he coming soon?

MRS. SOLNESS: Yes, I think so. I've sent for him at any rate.

DR. HERDAL: *(Coming closer.)* I'm afraid you'll have to go in, my dear lady——

MRS. SOLNESS: Oh no! Oh no! I shall stay out here and wait for Halvard.

DR. HERDAL: But some ladies have just come to call on you—

MRS. SOLNESS: Good heavens, that too! And just at this moment!

DR. HERDAL: They say they positively must see the ceremony.

MRS. SOLNESS: Well, well, I suppose I must go to them after all. It's my duty.

HILDA: Can't you ask the ladies to go away?

MRS. SOLNESS: No; that would never do. Now that they're here, it's my duty to see them. But do you stay out here in the mean time, and receive him when he comes.

DR. HERDAL: And try to occupy his attention as long as possible——

MRS. SOLNESS: Yes, do, dear Miss Wangel. Keep as firm hold of him as ever you can.

HILDA: Wouldn't it be best for you to do that?

MRS. SOLNESS: Yes; God knows that is *my* duty. But when one has duties in so many directions——

DR. HERDAL: *(Looks towards the garden.)* There he's coming!

MRS. SOLNESS: And I have to go in!

DR. HERDAL: *(To* HILDA.*)* Don't say anything about *my* being here.

HILDA: Oh no! I dare say I shall find something else to talk to Mr. Solness about.

MRS. SOLNESS: And be sure you keep firm hold of him. I believe *you* can do it best.

*(*MRS. SOLNESS *and* DR. HERDAL *go into the house.* HILDA *remains standing on the veranda.* SOLNESS *comes from the garden up the flight of steps.)*

SOLNESS: Somebody wants me, I hear.

HILDA: Yes; it's I, Mr. Solness.

SOLNESS: Oh, is it you, Hilda? I was afraid it might be Aline or the Doctor.

HILDA: You're very easily frightened, it seems!

SOLNESS: Do you think so?

HILDA: Yes; people say that you're afraid to climb about—on the scaffoldings, you know.

SOLNESS: Well, that's quite a special thing.

HILDA: Then it's true that you're afraid to do it.

SOLNESS: Yes, I am.

HILDA: Afraid of falling down and killing yourself?

SOLNESS: No, not of that.

HILDA: Of what then?

SOLNESS: I'm afraid of retribution, Hilda.

HILDA: Of retribution? *(Shakes her head.)* I don't understand that.

SOLNESS: Sit down, and I'll tell you something.

HILDA: Yes, do—at once!

(She sits on a stool by the railing, and looks expectantly at him.)

SOLNESS: *(Throws his hat on the table.)* You know that I began by building churches.

HILDA: *(Nods.)* I know that well.

SOLNESS: For, you see, I came as a boy from a pious home in the country; and so it seemed to me that this church building was the noblest task I could set myself.

HILDA: Yes, yes.

SOLNESS: And I venture to say that I built those poor little churches with such honest and warm and heart-felt devotion that—that——

HILDA: That——? Well?

SOLNESS: Well, that I think he ought to have been pleased with me.

HILDA: *He?* What *he?*

SOLNESS: He who was to have the churches, of course! He to whose honor and glory they were dedicated.

HILDA: Oh, indeed! But are you certain, then, that—that he wasn't—pleased with you?

SOLNESS: *(Scornfully.)* He pleased with *me!* How can you talk so, Hilda? He who gave the troll in me leave to lord it just as it pleased. He who bade them be at hand to serve me, both day and night—all these—all these——

HILDA: Devils——

SOLNESS: Yes, of both kinds. Oh no, he made me feel clearly enough that he wasn't pleased with me. *(Mysteriously.)* You see, that was really the reason why he made the old house burn down.

HILDA: Was that why?

SOLNESS: Yes, don't you understand? He wanted to give me the chance of becoming an accomplished master in my own sphere—so that I might build all the more glorious churches for him. At first I didn't understand what he was driving at; but all of a sudden it flashed upon me.

HILDA: When was that?

SOLNESS: It was when I was building the church-tower up at Lysanger.

HILDA: I thought so.

SOLNESS: For you see, Hilda—up there, amid those new surroundings, I used to go about musing and pondering within myself. Then I saw plainly why he had taken my little children from me. It was that I should have nothing else to attach myself to. No such thing as love and happiness, you understand. I was to be only a master builder—nothing else. And all my life long I was to go on building for him. *(Laughs.)* But I can tell you nothing came of that.

HILDA: What did you do, then?

SOLNESS: First of all, I searched and tried my own heart———

HILDA: And then?

SOLNESS: Then I did the *impossible*—I no less than *he.*

HILDA: The impossible?

SOLNESS: I had never before been able to climb up to a great, free height. But that day, I did it.

HILDA: *(Leaping up.)* Yes, yes, you did!

SOLNESS: And when I stood there, high over everything, and was hanging the wreath over the vane, I said to him: Here me now, thou Mighty One! From this day forward I will be a free builder—I too, in my sphere—just as thou in thine. I will never build any more churches for thee—only homes for human beings.

HILDA: *(With great sparkling eyes.) That* was the song that I heard through the air!

SOLNESS: But afterwards his turn came.

HILDA: What do you mean?

SOLNESS: *(Looks disconsolately at her.)* Building homes for human beings is not worth sixpence, Hilda.

HILDA: Do you say *that* now?

SOLNESS: Yes, for now I *see* it. Men have no use for these homes of theirs—to be happy in. And I shouldn't have had any use for such a home, if I'd had one. *(With a quiet, bitter laugh.)* See, that is the upshot of the whole affair, however far back I look. Nothing really built; nor anything sacrificed for the chance of building. Nothing, nothing! the whole is nothing!

HILDA: Then you will never build anything more?

SOLNESS: *(With animation.)* On the contrary, I'm just going to begin.

HILDA: What, then? What will you build? Tell me at once!

SOLNESS: I believe there's only one possible dwelling-place for human happiness—and that's what I'm going to build now.

HILDA: *(Looks firmly at him.)* Mr. Solness—you mean our castles in the air.

SOLNESS: The castles in the air—yes.

HILDA: I'm afraid you would turn dizzy before we got half-way up.

SOLNESS: Not if I can mount hand in hand with you, Hilda.

HILDA: *(With an expression of suppressed resentment.)* Only with me? Won't there be others of the party?

SOLNESS: Who else should there be?

HILDA: Oh—that girl—that Kaia at the desk. Poor thing—don't you want to take her with you too?

SOLNESS: Oho! Was it about her that Aline was talking to you?

HILDA: Is it so—yes or no?

SOLNESS: *(Vehemently.)* I won't answer such a question! You must believe in me, utterly and entirely!

HILDA: All these ten years I've believed in you so fully—so fully.

SOLNESS: You must go on believing in me!

HILDA: Then let me see you stand free and high up!

SOLNESS: *(Sadly.)* Oh, Hilda—it's not every day that I can do that.

HILDA: *(Passionately.)* I will have you do it! I will have it! *(Imploringly.)* Just once more, Mr. Solness! Do the *impossible* once again!

SOLNESS: *(Stands and looks deep into her eyes.)* If I try it, Hilda, I will stand up there and talk to him as I did that time before.

HILDA: *(In rising excitement.)* What will you say to him?

SOLNESS: I will say to him: Hear me, Mighty Lord—thou may'st judge me as seems best to thee. But hereafter I will build nothing but the loveliest thing in the world——

HILDA: *(Carried away.)* Yes—yes—yes!

SOLNESS: ——build it together with a princess, whom I love——

HILDA: Yes, tell him that! Tell him that!

SOLNESS: Yes. And then I will say to him: Now I shall go down and throw my arms round her and kiss her——

HILDA: ——many times! Say that!

SOLNESS: ——many, many times, I will say.

HILDA: And then——?

SOLNESS: Then I will wave my hat—and come down to the earth—and do as I said to him.

HILDA: *(With outstretched arms.)* Now I see you again as I did when there was song in the air!

SOLNESS: *(Looks at her with his head bowed.)* How have you become what you are, Hilda?

HILDA: How have you made me what I am?

SOLNESS: *(Shortly and firmly.)* The princess shall have her castle.

HILDA: *(Jubilant, clapping her hands.)* Oh, Mr. Solness——! My lovely, lovely castle. Our castle in the air!

SOLNESS: On a firm foundation.

(In the street a crowd of people have assembled, vaguely seen through the trees. Music of wind-instruments is heard far away behind the new house.)

(MRS. SOLNESS, with a fur collar round her neck, DOCTOR HERDAL, with her white shawl on his arm, and some ladies, come out on the veranda. RAGNAR BROVIK comes at the same time up from the garden.)

MRS. SOLNESS: *(To RAGNAR.)* Are we to have music, too?

RAGNAR: Yes. It's the band of the Masons' Union. *(To SOLNESS.)* The foreman asked me to tell you that he's ready now to go up with the wreath.

SOLNESS: *(Takes his hat.)* All right. I'll go down to him myself.

MRS. SOLNESS: *(Anxiously.)* What have you to do down there, Halvard?

SOLNESS: *(Curtly.)* I must be down below with the men.

MRS. SOLNESS: Yes, down below—only down below.

SOLNESS: That's where I always stand—on everyday occasions.

(He goes down the flight of steps and away through the garden.)

MRS. SOLNESS: *(Calls after him over the railing.)* But do beg the man to be careful when he goes up! Promise me that, Halvard!

DR. HERDAL: *(To* MRS. SOLNESS.*)* Don't you see that I was right? He's given up all thought of that folly.

MRS. SOLNESS: Oh, what a relief! Twice workmen have fallen, and each time they were killed on the spot. *(Turns to* HILDA.*)* Thank you, Miss Wangel, for having kept such a firm hold upon him. I should never have had my own way with him.

DR. HERDAL: *(Playfully.)* Yes, yes, Miss Wangel, you know how to keep firm hold on a man, when you give your mind to it.

*(*MRS. SOLNESS *and* DR. HERDAL *go up to the ladies, who are standing nearer to the steps and looking over the garden.* HILDA *remains standing beside the railing in the foreground.* RAGNER *goes up to her.)*

RAGNAR: *(With suppressed laughter, half whispering.)* Miss Wangel, do you see all those young fellows down in the street?

HILDA: Yes.

RAGNAR: They're my fellow-students come to look at the master.

HILDA: What do they want to look at *him* for?

RAGNAR: They want to see how he daren't climb to the top of his own house.

HILDA: Oh, *that's* what those boys want, is it?

RAGNAR: *(Spitefully and scornfully.)* He's kept us down so long, that man. Now we're going to see him keep quietly down below himself.

HILDA: You won't see that—not this time.

RAGNAR: *(Smiles.)* Indeed! Then where shall we see him?

HILDA: High—high up by the vane! That's where you'll see him!

RAGNAR: *(Laughs.)* Him! Oh yes, I daresay!

HILDA: His *will* is to reach the top—so at the top you shall see him.

RAGNAR: His *will* yes; that I can easily believe. But he simply *can't* do it. His head would swim round, long, long before he got half-way. He'd have to crawl down again on his hands and knees.

DR. HERDAL: *(Points across.)* Look! there goes the foreman up the ladders.

MRS. SOLNESS: And of course he's got the wreath to carry too. Oh, I do hope he'll be careful!

RAGNAR: *(Stares incredulously and shouts.)* Why, but it's——

HILDA: *(Breaking out in jubilation.)* It's the master builder himself.

MRS. SOLNESS: *(Screams with terror.)* Yes, it's Halvard! O my great God——! Halvard! Halvard!

DR. HERDAL: Hush! Don't shout to him!

MRS. SOLNESS: *(Half beside herself.)* I must go to him! I must bring him down again.

DR. HERDAL: *(Holds her.)* Don't move, any of you! Not a sound!

HILDA: *(Immovable, follows* SOLNESS *with her eyes.)* He climbs and climbs. Higher and higher! Higher and higher! Look! Just look!

RAGNAR: *(Breathless.)* He *must* turn now. He can't possibly help it.

HILDA: He climbs and climbs. He'll soon be at the top now.

MRS. SOLNESS: Oh, I shall die of terror. I can't bear to see it!

DR. HERDAL: Then don't look up at him.

HILDA: There, he's standing on the topmost planks! Right at the top!

DR. HERDAL: Nobody must move! Do you hear?

HILDA: *(Exulting, with quiet intensity.)* At last! At last! Now I see him great and free again!

RAGNAR: *(Almost voiceless.)* But this is im——

HILDA: So I have seen him all through these ten years. How secure he stands! Frightfully thrilling all the same. Look at him! Now he's hanging the wreath round the vane!

RAGNAR: I feel as if I were looking at something utterly impossible.

HILDA: Yes, it *is* the *impossible* that he's doing now! *(With the indefinable expression in her eyes.)* Can you see any one else up there with him?

RAGNAR: There is no one else.

HILDA: Yes, there is one he is striving with.

RAGNAR: You are mistaken.

HILDA: Then do you hear no song in the air, either?

RAGNAR: It must be the wind in the tree-tops.

HILDA: *I* hear a song—a mighty song! *(Shouts in wild jubilation and glee.)* Look, look! Now he's waving his hat! He's waving it to us down here! Oh, wave, wave back to him! For now it's finished! *(Tears the white shawl from the doctor, waves it, and shouts up to* SOLNESS.*)* Hurrah for Master Builder Solness!

DR. HERDAL: Stop! Stop! For God's sake——!

(The ladies on the veranda wave their pocket-handkerchiefs, and the shouts of "Hurrah" are taken up in the street below. Then they are suddenly silenced, and the crowd bursts out into a shriek of horror. A human body, with planks and fragments of wood, is vaguely perceived crashing down behind the trees.)

MRS. SOLNESS AND THE LADIES: *(At the same time.)* He's falling! He's falling! *(*MRS. SOLNESS *totters, falls backwards, swooning, and is caught, amid cries and confusion, by the ladies. The crowd in the street breaks down the fence and storms into the garden. At the same time* DR. HERDAL, *too, rushes down thither. A short pause.)*

HILDA: *(Stares fixedly upwards, and says as if petrified.)* My Master Builder.

RAGNAR: *(Supports himself, trembling, against the railing.)* He must be dashed to pieces—killed on the spot.

ONE OF THE LADIES: *(Whilst Mrs. Solness is carried into the house.)* Run down for the doctor——

RAGNAR: I can't stir a foot——

ANOTHER LADY: Then call to some one!

RAGNAR: *(Tries to call out.)* How is it? Is he alive?

A VOICE: *(Below, in the garden.)* Mr. Solness is dead!

OTHER VOICES: *(Nearer.)* The head is all crushed.—He fell right into the quarry.

HILDA: *(Turns to* RAGNAR, *and says quietly:)* I can't see him up there now.

RAGNAR: This is terrible. So, after all, he could not do it.

HILDA: *(As if in quiet spell-bound triumph.)* But he mounted right to the top. And I heard harps in the air. *(Waves her shawl in the air, and shrieks with wild intensity.)* My—my Master Builder!

THE END.

—*Translated by Edmund Gosse and William Archer*

ACTIVITIES FOR WRITING AND DISCUSSION

1. Reread any passages where **symbols** appear, such as the high towers, the empty nursery rooms, Mrs. Solness's burned belongings (enumerated in Act III), the cracked chimney in the Solness's first house. Then analyze and discuss the symbols and their multiple meanings.

2. Throughout the play Solness expresses fear of the younger generation and the threat it poses to his professional supremacy. How do you explain his immediate attraction to Hilda, herself a member of the younger generation, when she appears in Act I?

3. Would the play have ended as it did if Hilda had not appeared? What does she introduce into Solness's life? What does she represent or symbolize in his imagination?

4. When Hilda was twelve or thirteen years old Solness promised to make her his "princess" and to buy her "a kingdom." Ten years later to the day she shows up at his house to collect on the promise. It isn't clear that she has done anything during the intervening years except *wait*. Skim the play for any information about Hilda's life between ages thirteen and twenty-three. Then imagine she kept a diary during those years and invent a few entries.

5. In Act II Solness says, "That I might build homes for others, I had to forego—to forego for all time—the home that might have been my own," suggesting a potential conflict between professional ambition and personal relationships. Consider this conflict carefully.
   a. Share a story or two of your own experiences (if any) with this conflict; or
   b. *Invent* a story that has this conflict at its center.
   c. How has Solness balanced—or failed to balance—professional ambition with personal relationships in his own life? How are the two connected in his mind? To focus your answer, look at one or more of his specific relationships, e.g., with Kaia, with Mrs. Solness, or with Ragnar.

6. Drawing on biographical details provided in the play and inventing others as needed, write Solness's obituary (a) as he might have composed it in anticipation of his death or (b) as his wife or some other character in the play might have written it. Discuss and interpret the results in class.

WORK AND THE QUALITY OF LIFE: ADDITIONAL ACTIVITIES FOR WRITING AND DISCUSSION

1. Reread all or a portion of your notebook. Mark any passages, however long or short, that strike you, for whatever reason. Beside each such passage, write a note explaining its significance for you. Finally, pick a favorite passage and either:
    a. Expand it into a new piece of writing, or
    b. Make notes of how you could expand or use it at some future date, or
    c. Rewrite it in a different form, e.g., a poem, dialogue, letter, memoir.

For a list of strategies for expanding or revising, see Chapter 12.

2. What is the purpose and value of work? How does work relate to happiness? Are the two complementary, or are they antithetical in some ways? These are important questions that everyone must answer for him- or herself. Identify and list a few such "life questions" that are compelling to you. Then:
    a. Bring together various characters and speakers from this thematic section and write a dialogue in which they (and you, if you wish) discuss your questions and some possible answers; or
    b. Address these questions in an essay.

3. Though people work for pay, they also work for the inherent pleasures of working. Considering such texts as Raymond Carver's "Kindling," Gary Snyder's "Axe Handles," and Janice M. Lynch's "Sixty-Four Caprices for a Long-Distance Swimmer," discuss the qualities of work that enrich our lives physically, intellectually, and spiritually. Illustrate your essay with examples and/or stories drawn from the texts, personal experience, or outside research.

4. Explore the various meanings of "art" in Thomas Moore's "The Sacred Arts of Life" and Linda Hogan's "Waking Up the Rake." How do the two writers challenge or extend your own sense of the nature of "art"?

5. Several pieces in this thematic section are in unconventional literary forms (e.g., Jack Ridl's "Last Ditch" is a **prose poem** and Janice Lynch's "Sixty-Four Caprices" is a sequence of poetic **aphorisms**) or unusual **points of view** (both Lorrie Moore's "How to Become a Writer" and Jan Beatty's "A Waitress's Instructions on Tipping" address the reader directly, using a second-person point of view). Borrowing any of these forms or points of view (or devising another of your own choosing that is equally unconventional) write a text of your own on some work-related topic. If you write in the second person, think carefully about the identity of your intended audience (your "you") and what that audience might wish to gain or learn from your text.

6. The **speaker** in James Wright's poem, "Lying in a Hammock at William Duffy's Farm in Pine Island, Minnesota" says "I have wasted my life." Chekhov's "Gooseberries" invites us to ask whether the **protagonist** and his brother, Nikolay, have wasted their lives. Allan Gurganus's "He's at the Office" raises the issues of overwork and the well-lived life. On the other hand, in their writings

Henry David Thoreau, Thomas Moore, and Linda Hogan discuss the necessity of creating personally and spiritually meaningful work. (Thoreau says he did not want to reach the end of his life and "discover that I had not lived.") Write an essay examining the concept of a "wasted life" in any one of these works or comparing its treatment in two or more works. Wherein does the "waste" consist? How is it represented in the particular text(s), and what alternatives (if any) are suggested or implied?

7. Review your entire notebook; as you do, make a running list of memorable or striking topics, e.g., "escape," "happiness," "competition," "fear of failure," and so forth. Then make a Topic/Form Grid (see Chapter 5), choose a favorite topic, and use one of the forms on your grid to create a new notebook entry about the topic. If your chosen form does not work, do a Topic/Form Shift to a different form on your grid.

Coda: Literature, So What?

Reclaiming the Pleasures of Time and Space

For several centuries, and at a dramatically accelerating rate during the last few decades, technological innovations have enabled us to move faster and faster, to get places more quickly than our forebears could have dreamed; distances once deemed insurmountable have been spanned and the term "global village," with its connotation of all of us fitting comfortably inside one small place, has become a cliché. However, every "advance" comes at a cost.

One significant cost of the time- and space-reducing technologies is that they have *impoverished* time and space. As they scale back or eliminate the hardships associated with time and space, they also reduce or eliminate the pleasures. For instance, when travel by horse and carriage gave way to the railroad in the nineteenth century, the pleasures of a long journey by carriage—the opportunities for conversation, enjoying scenery, stopping in a picturesque spot for lunch—were erased along with the hardships of travelling muddy rutted roads, coping with bad weather, broken wheels, and tired or injured horses. Travelling by jet in the twenty-first century we experience none of the discomforts and inconveniences of a long journey on foot such as blisters, sore joints, or twisted ankles, but we also experience almost no pleasure whatsoever; we board a jet in city "A" *only* in order to get to city "B." No one, or almost no one, flies commercially for "pleasure."

Of course, speed in itself is not pleasureless. Going fast can be exhilarating and fun: driving a fast car or boat, cycling at top speed, skiing hard down a precipitous slope, or taking a fast ride at an amusement park. Even in these cases, however, the pleasure is in the moving, in the enjoyment of extreme speed—hair flying, heart pounding, adrenaline rushing—not in arriving somewhere. In fact, unless the excursion is a competitive race, the end of the drive, ride, or trip is usually experienced as a letdown. Speed itself is not antagonistic to pleasure, only the effect that it has on the space traversed; namely, of reducing that space and all it contains to a blur or near-blur, of rendering it and all that it contains invisible. The flower or bird you pass at 70 miles an hour is for all purposes nonexistent.

Ironically, speed-enhancing technologies enable us to "conquer" the obstacles of time and space but simultaneously make the reduced obstacles or bumps that remain seem more mountainous and frustrating. The mountains get larger as they get smaller because they are almost completely joyless. The "obstacle" of the eight-hundred-plus miles one must traverse by plane to get from Chicago to New York can seem interminable (though it is crossed in a few hours) because it is a "pain." By contrast, the six miles you want to travel on foot along a winding woodland path are not experienced as an obstacle because you *enjoy* them. Our experiences of time and space are a function of pleasure and are inseparable from it; for a decline in pleasure, speed seems to offer few consolations.

I think of a few steps I can take personally to reverse the impoverishment of time and space, and of ways that literature can help.

First, I will continue many things as usual. I will keep on getting places on time and carrying out my responsibilities to job, family, friends, and community. I will continue to drive my car, while trying to use it somewhat less. I will show up to teach classes on schedule because my employers and students expect me to and because I enjoy teaching.

At the same time I will look for small ways to slow down. That word "small" deserves special comment. The importance of the small is constantly underrated, equated with "insignificant" or "useless." Several years ago the words of a famous Roman Catholic saint, Thérèse of Lisieux, disabused me of this notion once and for all. Thérèse taught what she called "the little way," which I summarize as follows: the smaller a thing or an action is, the more important it is. Try changing the world in the grandiose sense that most people think of and see how far you get; mentor a child, feed a streetperson, or teach an illiterate adult to read, and your impact may be incalculable. So-called "small" actions have the added advantage that opportunities to perform them abound: you are free to do a kind or constructive deed right this minute, wherever you happen to be, in a way that you are not free to be president of the United States or Albert Einstein.

So I will find small—that is, large and inestimably important—ways of slowing down. I will pause more often to look at people and things, to use all five senses as intensively as I can. I will aspire to see more disinterestedly and self-forgetfully, in the manner prescribed by G.K. Chesterton. I will strive to reduce myself, as he advises, "to a point . . . to a thing with no size at all," so that, from my point's-eye view, I may see the "immeasurable stature" of "the cosmic things." I will recognize that "the grass is an everlasting forest, with dragons as denizens" and "the dandelions are like gigantic bonfires illuminating the lands around. . ."

I will also devote more time to pleasantly repetitive physical activities. I could bike or run, but I prefer walking, an activity favored by poets and writers for millenia. In *Wanderlust: A History of Walking*, Rebecca Solnit points out that Socrates and other philosophers in ancient Greece were peripatetic (or said to be): they philosophized on their feet, walking, shoulder to shoulder and face to face, without computer or book, in the open air, literally "outside the box" of the room or building.

To walk for pleasure, even for a few minutes between classes or appointments, is to heal the divorce between mind and body that symptomizes ordinary sedentary—or hurried—life. When walking the mind affectionately approves this old horse of a body; body and mind saunter along happily together, like horse and rider.

A Short Life Can Be a Very Long One

As I reread my notebooks, I see repeated references to the topics of time, speed, literature, and contemplation, how we experience them, and how, perhaps, we can experience them differently or better.

> An English class should be a leisure space. Teachers should do everything they can to promote easy conversation that people look forward to as an oasis in their busy day, a release from the break-neck hustle that passes for "education" in our frenetic age. We must model leisure at all times.

> The frictionlessness of contemporary life. Everything is getting almost too easy; we can accomplish more and more tasks with the tips of our fingers. Like everyone else I like my comforts and conveniences. But I also like friction. It's the experience of friction or resistance—difficulty, illness, discomfort—that puts us back inside our bodies and reminds us who we are.

> When I was a student in college I equated idleness with laziness. I began to discover the pleasures and power of idleness at precisely the time my life became more hectic: when I had a full-time job, family and social obligations, and especially children, who demanded my attention *now*. My day, once a smooth uninterrupted surface, was suddenly fractured, and I had to learn to think and write in the "cracks" between shards. I thought of these cracks as breathing spaces without which I would spiritually suffocate. The "odd" moment is the only possible transcendent one. Much as I love my job, my family, and my work, even they become oppressive without the additional element of contemplation, which fits the fragments into a larger design. Even a moment or two of reflective pause—and its ordinary or wayward thought—felt, because of the "lift" it gave me, like what Emerson called a "concentrated eternity." The idle moment was sweeter because more rare, and because I had to create it rather than simply wait for it.

> "To have leisure is to have power." (Su Tungpo, 11th century).

> "There are two ways of extending life: firstly by moving the two points 'born' and 'died' farther away from one another . . . The other method is to go more slowly and leave the two points wherever God wills they should be, and this method is for the philosophers . . ." (G.C. Lichtenberg)

> "What is time but the stuff delay is made of?" (Henry David Thoreau)

The ancient Greeks had two words to describe time, *kronos* and *kairos*. *Kronos* refers to regular, quantifiable time, or what we might call "clock" time; *kairos* refers to time as it is actually experienced, as long or short, without any necessary reference to *kronos* time. Thus five minutes, a short period of time chronologically speaking, can be experienced as interminable if the minutes are unpleasant or anxiety-ridden. While *kronos* is unchanging and uniform for everybody (24/7), *kairos* differs from person to person, and even moment to moment, according to how the person lives and the character and concentration of his or her lifestyle. Small children live primarily in *kairos* time, for better and for worse: they are not "slaves" to time, as so many adults are. They can sit on the ground for long stretches of time turning over fistfuls of grass. On the other hand, they have to be coaxed and dragged to get anywhere on time.

Kronos time dictates to us ("You must be at work by 8 A.M."; "You must arrive at the meeting punctually at 1:45 P.M."; "Your body will fail after X years"), but we can control *kairos* time. A cancer patient under a three- or four-month sentence of death cannot (barring a miracle) undo the sentence, but she can pack more living into those months than other people do into 20 years or a whole chronological lifetime: she is too busy living, renewing old friendships, achieving closure to existence, doing what she always meant to do but had never done, to regret lost time. Regret is a luxury the truly living cannot afford.

Kronos is quantitative, *kairos* is qualitative. Our technologically sophisticated societies devote enormous energies and resources to the subject of *kronos,* to extending the quantitative length of life, and for that we are grateful; but I look forward to the day when we will give comparable attention to improving the *qualitative* "length" of life. Think of John Keats, a great poet who died of tuberculosis at the age of 25. Three years before his death Keats wrote the following poem:

> When I have fears that I may cease to be
>   Before my pen has glean'd my teeming brain,
> Before high piled books, in charactry,
>   Hold like rich garners the full-ripen'd grain;
> When I behold, upon the night's starr'd face,
>   Huge cloudy symbols of a high romance,
> And think that I may never live to trace
>   Their shadows, with the magic hand of chance;
> And when I feel, fair creature of an hour,
>   That I shall never look upon thee more,
> Never have relish in the fairy power
>   Of unreflecting love;—then on the shore
> Of the wide world I stand alone, and think
> Till love and fame to nothingness do sink.

These are the words of a person who can't get enough of life. Every day, every minute is a priceless gift. Words, love, fame—all the things that have mattered most to him—pale beside the fact of mere *being* itself.

It is possible to look at Keats and say, "How sad! Only think what he could have accomplished in a normal lifespan!" A good answer to this sort of remark is to say that, in the qualitative *kairos* sense, Keats actually lived a very "long" life because he didn't just swallow anything without also tasting it. This fact surfaces repeatedly in his poetry, which is uniquely sensuous and emphasizes particularly the sense of taste. In his final days, while dying of tuberculosis in a small apartment in Rome, Keats raged against death, driven less by fear, it seems, than by a passion to live, with so little time and so much still to do. It would be thrilling—and terrifying—to live as "long" as Keats did. When you are talking of *kairos* time, a short life can be a very long one.

None of this is meant to underrate the importance and value of *kronos* time. In our earthly physical existence, *kronos* time and *kairos* time continually overlap. To experience time purely as *kairos* you would have to exist entirely outside chronological time—a physical impossibility. *Kronos* time gives *kairos* its urgency and hence its value. If the clock did not move inexorably forward, many of us would devolve from a human to a merely vegetable existence; we would have no incentive not to procrastinate and waste our lives away doing nothing. As a wise person wrote, "The more time I have, the more I sleep."

"Life . . . Too Strong to Stop, Too Sweet to Lose"

Literary scholars have devoted books and careers to defining the *differences* among writers—how this one is innovative and that one "traditional"; how this one is "romantic" and that one is "classical"; this one "postmodern" and that one something else. The terms of classification multiply along with the scholarly books and articles, and the ordinary student or teacher can come away from it all feeling dizzy.

So perhaps, for once, we can ask a different question: What *unites* writers? In what sense are Samuel Johnson and bell hooks, Joy Harjo and Eugene O'Neill, Colette and Adrienne Rich and James Thurber, traditionalists and revolutionaries, writers dead and living, writers ancient, medieval, and modern, a part of one dedicated or spiritual collective, or, as Emily Dickinson liked to call it, a great "host"? One point of commonality may be this rapt attention to *kairos*, this longing for intense being as realized in even the most ordinary moment. It would be difficult to find any writer who would disagree with this thought of Willa Cather's:

> [W]hat [is] any art but an effort to make a sheath, a mould in which to imprison for a moment the shining, elusive element which is life itself—life hurrying past us and running away, too strong to stop, too sweet to lose? (*The Song of the Lark*)

Whether "the shining, elusive element" is horrific or gentle, bitter or sweet, comic or tragic or romantic, world-changing or ephemeral, the writer yearns to preserve it as well as he or she can and share it. "Art" does not *only* mean great creations or productions, though it includes these; it means arresting the moment, "the elusive element which is life itself"—for oneself first, for friends and acquaintances, for distant readers of your own time whose faces you may never see, perhaps for people yet unborn. When you "sheathe" a passing thought or impression in words, you create "art," and if you do so daily and accurately you are an artist.

The living host of writers—and who can doubt that the great "dead" ones are as alive today as ever to those who actively read them?—is telling us today: *It's not enough to be enamoured of reality, or partial to it; you must be drunk with it.*

While a few celebrated authors have demanded stiff drinks or drugs to induce the "creative" state, most find all the alcohol they need in ordinary air and water. The assumption that drunkenness must be *artificially* induced is a failure of imagination.

Emerson said that a poet should be "tipsy on water." Walt Whitman declared that he was "mad" to be in contact with "the atmosphere." And Emily Dickinson wrote,

> Inebriate of Air—am I—
> And Debauchee of Dew . . .

The eye-stopping word here is "Debauchee," which my dictionary defines as "a person who habitually indulges in debauchery or dissipation." "Debauchery" in turn means "extreme indulgence in sensual pleasures; dissipation . . . seduction from morality, allegiance, or duty." The word conjures images of wild orgies, unseemly acts, scandal—until you note what Dickinson is debauched, orgiastic, and sensual *about*: "dew." Here, perhaps, lies one answer to the often-asked question, Why do writers seem so "different"—or, as Dickinson said, "mad"—to the rest of the world? Because a person who is debauched by dew is one person in a thousand. Whether such a person is bold, like Walt Whitman, and sounds his "barbaric yawp over the roofs of the world," or is withdrawn, like Emily Dickinson, and remains secluded in a house, she is apt to stand out. Enthusiasts are, in the eyes of most people, "weird."

Like William Faulkner, they stop in the middle of walks to stare, entranced, at a particular flower or a house (*There is a story here. If that house could talk . . .*). They find themselves, as T.S. Eliot put it, at "the still point of the turning world," the intersection of the temporal and the transcendent, both in the stream of time and outside it.

They see—truly *see*. Some 800 years ago the Italian poet Dante wrote that "no painter can portray any figure if he have not first of all made himself such as the figure ought to be. . . . He who would draw a figure cannot do so, if he cannot be it." Perfect seeing, according to Dorothy Sayers (who wrote a book on Dante), would be to see into the souls, minds, and hearts of others and thereby fully know the miracle of their being. Though we cannot do that literally (and, for that matter, might not like it much if others could see inside *us*), we can approximate this perfect seeing through *imagination*, which might be defined as the capacity, in our supernatural minds, to walk in the body of another (person, animal, plant, thing).

The supreme purpose of literature is to exercise this faculty to our utmost capacity: to see, to feel with, to contemplate.

Reflecting on this contemplative state in his great long poem, *Paterson,* William Carlos Williams spoke for many of us, the readers and writers and stewards of literature:

> I asked him, What do you do?

> . . . . What do I do? I listen, to the water falling. (No sound of it here but with the wind!) This is my entire occupation.

Appendix A:
Sample Creative Writings

The samples below are not offered as masterpieces. (Sometimes the presence of a masterpiece does more to intimidate us as writers than it does to motivate us.) You can use these samples in at least two ways:

1. Use them as prompts for your own writing. Review them periodically, particularly when your own imaginative well runs dry. Remember the words of Emerson, which appear as an epigraph at the beginning of *Reading and Writing from Literature:*

[Texts] are for nothing but to inspire.

2. Use them to help select and revise your own favorite writings for a course portfolio or other presentation. Alone or with your small group or class, you can analyze the samples to determine what makes "successful" or "unsuccessful" writing. What do you like in a particular piece? What first gets your interest, and what makes you keep reading? What specific passages, long or short, do you find yourself annotating or underlining? What ideas does the sample give you for your own writing? What does the writer try that *you* might like to try?

Samples are keyed to the "Ten Ideas for Writing" introduced in Chapter 3. Terms in **boldface** are defined and illustrated in Part IV, "An Introduction to the Major Genres," and Appendix C, "Glossary of Literary Terms."

1. Converse with Specific Points in the Text That Strike You

See sample in Chapter 3.

2. Write About Any Personal Connections You Have with the Reading

"Grandpa Jack" by Tyler (see Chapter 2) is a good example.

Both of my grandfathers died before I was born. My Dad's father was bucked off a horse which broke his neck and caused his death soon after. My Mom's father had cancer and also died before I was born. Although my grandmothers married again, I never got to know my stepgrandfathers well at all. As a young boy I yearned for the companionship of a grandpa.

I grew up in a small neighborhood set in the heart of a beautiful valley. There was so much to do as a child. Pineview dam was directly behind the house, giving us ample amount of fun swimming in it. The "Honda" trails, as we called them, were nearby, and we rode our dirt bikes up and down the steep hills. It was a choice place for a young child to grow up, and I loved every minute of it. But there was still a vacancy in my life, and that was to have a grandpa. An elderly couple lived next door, and from the time I was born our lives wound together tightly. I believe my desire for a grandpa came true because my neighbor, Jack Hislop, took upon himself the role of a grandfather. Jack has been special to me for as long as I can remember. He gave me my first motorcycle, my first and only bolo decorated with Indian turquoise, and many other gifts throughout my youth. But most importantly he gave me the friendship of a grandpa.

As a little boy I would go over to visit him almost every day after school. One day I ran over to his house and found him lounging on the patio in his back yard. "Take a seat, partner," said Jack as he pulled up a chair for me. He fed me some cold watermelon and a large glass of "sodi water," as he called it. While I was enjoying the fruit Jack told me a story about when he was a young sheepherder. "I was no older than you, partner, maybe eleven years old," said Jack. "Me and Pa and a few of my brothers were high on Durphie's Peak taking the sheep down to a nearby watering hole." His eyes were flashing as he was trying to point out where they were, since the mountain was in a broadside view. "A few sheep took off up a narrow canyon, and I got roped into chasin' after 'em. I rode up the canyon a little way and seen 'em up ahead so I galloped my horse to catch 'em. When I caught those little rascals I started herding 'em back down to the watering hole. On the way down the canyon my horse started to get jittery because some bushes started to shake up ahead, and out charged a huge brown bear." Jack was standing now giving the motions of the incident. Jack blurted "Holy shit!" then apologized to me because his wife didn't like him to cuss. "The damn horse started to buck and my two dogs went into a barking frenzy. The bear was huge, it was at least ten feet tall when it reared up on its hind legs. The dogs distracted the bear long enough allowin' me to ride up and around to safety." Jack was really into the story because he made a sigh of relief as he told about his escape from the bear. "Damn bear killed old Dodger, one of my best dogs," said Jack with a sad look on his face, as if it had just happened.

Jack was drafted into the war during World War II and had many stories to tell about those experiences. The stories he told me about the war are engraved in my mind, and I am more sensitive about what happened in the war because Jack told me so many of his firsthand experiences. "There were dead bodies piled twenty feet high; hell, it smelled bad," said Jack as he plugged his nose to emphasize his point. Jack had a very sorrowful look on his face when he told me about the concentration camps. "When those skinny Jews were released they just started eatin' the grass, 'cause they were so hungry. I carried extra rations so I could give 'em something good to eat." Jack could go on and on with his war stories, and all I had to do was ask him to tell me a story. . . .

Jack's health was never very good. He had diabetes and heart trouble which caused him to have a great deal of pain. "I've got a pig valve in my heart—oink-oink," he would joke. As time went on Jack's health got worse, but our attachment grew stronger. Three years before he died he said, "I want ya to speak at my funeral, partner." I chuckled and told him he could never die. When Jack died his wife again asked me if I would speak. I don't think I could have said no. I was fourteen years old and scared to death to speak, but my love for Jack implored me to do it. I don't even remember what I said, but I do know that I declared my love for my Grandpa Jack.

3. Write a Letter to the Author and/or a Return Letter from the Author to Yourself

See sample in Chapter 3.

4. Write an Imaginary Interview with the Author or with a Character in a Story, Novel, or Play

John read some poetry by Walt Whitman and then began writing a response to it in the form of "What I like about this poet." Soon, however, he tired of this mode of writing and yearned to meet the poet "in the flesh." The result was the following "Interview with Walt Whitman." Before writing John read and reread "I Sing the Body Electric" (p. 662) and other poems in Whitman's book *Leaves of Grass* in order to get a sense of the poet's voice and probable style of speech. Stylistic features he noticed were Whitman's outspokenness, his taste for informal and robust language, and his habit of illustrating and expanding on ideas with long lists (such as the example in the third paragraph below).

Interview with Walt Whitman

I interviewed Walter Whitman at his print-shop in Brooklyn on a hot, humid day in mid-July. Mr. Whitman was relaxed and cordial. He is a man of 36, large-framed, in amazingly robust health, with a thick, matted beard and penetrating eyes. As we spoke he sat on the edge of a desk, his sleeves rolled to the elbows and his shirt collar open, the tools of his trade scattered around him. Mr. Whitman, it might be noted in passing, is a methodical man, softspoken, thinking before he speaks—creating an impression quite unlike that of the "barbaric yawp" that he affects in his poems.

Interviewer (I): Mr. Whitman, your book *Leaves of Grass* has been on the market now for two weeks and is causing something of a stir among critics. Not all the reactions, I might add, are favorable. For instance, Mr. Samuels of the *Daily Press* calls you a "hog" and says that you have no business writing poetry. What do you make of this?

WW: I never published *Leaves* with an eye to receiving compliments, or the favor of critics. The real audience of *Leaves* is profounder than the critics, and vaster: it is the great American public itself, the ordinary men and women—bus drivers, farmers, ferriers, mechanics, blacksmiths, boatmen and -women, clam-diggers, horse-dealers, slaves and freemen and freewomen. . . . On the pulse of these will the future of *Leaves* be decided.

I: Surely this is unlike any book of poetry any of us has seen before. Can you tell us something about the composition of *Leaves?*

WW: Gladly. But I'll probably not give you the answer you're wanting— no "pat" answer that will "finish" the matter, click the box shut, if you will. *Leaves* cannot be put in a box—the making of it can't be either; it doesn't give itself to formulae. First thing I did was throw out the rule-books, the sonnet treatises, the grammars and so on. Then I wrote, and wrote, and wrote—every day. Every chance I got I wrote. On the wharves or in the street, in the smithies and the shops, in the open air of farms where I happened to be, loafing, jotting down, in my leisurely way, all unhurried, nothing forced, getting a record of it all, big and little, I didn't discriminate. Then I stuffed what I wrote—all these pictures of America, of our times— into envelopes. And I never worried over the result. I knew all along I'd get a Poem out of it.

I: Your self-assurance and optimism about your craft are admirable, Mr. Whitman. I'm sure many poets would be envious.

WW: Maybe so. These poets have to see that making a poem isn't a logic-game. You don't just take a fancy mold of a sonnet or ballad or rhyme and dump words into it, so that the ideas are all corseted and constrained and dead. That's the way our poets write, and that's the undoing of 'em. They're stuck in the eighteenth century, or the seventeenth—in Europe— trying to out-Shakespeare Shakespeare, I suppose. That's the poetry *disease* today. That's the point I make in my "Preface" to *Leaves*. The true poems don't come from here [Mr. Whitman points to his head] but from here [he inscribes an imaginary circle from his heart to his pelvis]. That's the birthing room of a thousand poems—a thousand thousand poems—already written and still to be written.

5. Compose a Prequel or a Sequel to a Story

See sample in Chapter 3.

6. Rewrite a Text from a Point of View Different from that Presented in the Original Text

Gary Soto's poem "Oranges" (p. 516) describes—from a boy's **point of view**—an awkward incident during a first date. Angela retold the story from the girl's point of view:

Chocolate

My first date came
when I was twelve.
He was coming for me
I had been ready for hours
My parents had the light on
and the dog ready
Their way of saying who's boss.
At the last minute
my mother drowned my face
with rouge.
My father told me to remember
Who I was and what I'm worth.
My brother told me
the way to impress him
was to think big.
He came for me
He looked so nervous
We went to the drugstore
to get some candy
the whole way there
I wondered what he had
in his pockets besides those two oranges.
He told me to choose
whatever I wanted.
I remembered my brother
and picked up a chocolate
hoping he had the money.
His eyes fell
but he didn't say a word.
My heart ached as
he placed a nickel

and then one of his
precious oranges
on the counter.
I cried that night
for being so stupid
I had hurt him
and he had brushed it aside
I stared at the chocolate
wrapper stained brown like my
aching soul,
yet glittering
much like my soul
filled with the hope
That he'd call again.

7. Rewrite a Work into a Different Genre

See sample in Chapter 3.

8. Borrow an Incident or Theme from a Work to Write a Piece of Your Own Based on a Similar Incident or Theme

See example in Chapter 3.

9. Borrow the Genre or Form of a Work to Create a Piece of Your Own Cast in the Same Genre or Form

Susan read Walt Whitman's poetry and followed it by writing a poem. She explains, "Whitman's 'Song of Myself,' a very emotional poem that created images in Walt's time and place, inspired me to write a piece in Whitmanian style, using contemporary images, while still maintaining the romantic tone that Whitman stressed."

Song of Ourselves

We celebrate ourselves, Walt,
you, I, all of us, grasping for perception, meaning
in this entrapment, awe inspired miracle,
from the deepest abyss of the earth,
to the empirical heights of the cosmos;
We keep watch.
A lonely doe crouches, staring at me from my hillside.
Her dark eyes reflect an eerie glow from the porch light.
She looks at me, through me,

knowing.
Hours pass.
I'm anxious, perplexed about my hillside occupant.
No movement from her perch.
The upstairs window elevates my eyes to hers;
Our gazes lock once again.
Am I in her yard?
Finally,
a gentle rain softly taps at the window pane.
I hurriedly glance up toward the sudden emptiness of the hillside.
I sigh . . . relieved?

A family waits for the subway in New York;
a group of cheap hoods attacks them for pocket change.
The family's son is stabbed through the heart
after lunging at his mother's assaulters.
The Mother,
hysterical, screaming in fear for her dying son,
rushes to a subway clerk, begging for help.
She's ignored.

A lost foreign boy knocks on a door
to ask for directions to a costume party,
but instead
gets a bullet through his chest.

The setting sun casts a soft illumination;
the shadows of things appear greater than life.
An orb weaving spider, its intricate web ablaze with sunset,
creeps up, hungrily,
seizing the unfortunate grasshopper nymph entrapped there.
The infant jerks uncontrollably as the fangs of the
venomous vampire
stab into its helpless form.
Another futile attempt at escape,
a final jerk—then stillness.
The spider's legs busily grope the lifeless body.

Survival, once again.

The infant's eyes question, search the face of the young mother.

The purple mountain crests up through the brown city haze.

The toddler giggles, attempts to gather the puppy into his small arms.

A rainforest smolders.

The children wait to talk to Santa Claus.

Men, women, children, humanity,
dash along the beach with buckets of sea water;
rush to quench the parched skin of a young, beached whale.

The kindergartener builds a tower of blocks,
all the way to the sky.

The sea surf roars, washes with a pile of garbage.
Plastic syringes leave imprints in the soft, wet sand.

The children wait to talk to Santa Claus.

The small girl, unsteady, finally balances the bicycle.

The space travelers orbit the earth,
watch the mysterious majesty of blueness.

The teenage boy flashes a grin and a driver's license.

The large and small quail hurriedly scamper;
tiny feet blur the roadway.

Humanity watches life and death each day,
from living room sofas.

The children wait to talk to Santa Claus.

Men armed with rifles
rush into the wilderness to kill,
chase a deer onto a frozen lake.
The frightened buck slips, straddling the frigid surface,
helplessly trapped.
He stares hopelessly into the eyes of the approaching men.
Rifles now discarded, they tie a rope about his fragile body,
gently pulling him along the ice to the shoreline,
then coaxing him back into the sanctuary of the brush;
they've finished hunting.

A group of Somali soldiers drags a trophy,
the body of an American killed in battle,
naked,

through the streets, laughing and cheering.
The body,
smoking from being set ablaze, causes a
jet black sunrise.

The autumn moonlight seeps softly, gently
through the nudeness of tree branches.
The dry leaves swirl about our feet.
Winter smells near, spring will follow.

Walt, we know who you were, and what you meant.
You waited for us.
You were there yesterday, here today, and tomorrow.
We searched and found you, I, ourselves.

10. Draft a Fictional Biography or Autobiography of a Character in a Story, Poem, or Play

Edith wrote an autobiography, in diary form, of Minnie Wright, the abused wife in Susan Glaspell's play *Trifles* (p. 300). The diary entries trace Minnie's development over a period of thirty years.

Dear Diary

April 7, 1886—Today was my 17th birthday. What a happy day! My parents gave me a beautiful white dress with blue hair ribbons. Mama said I was to wear them in the church choir program next Sunday. I can hardly wait, for I do love pretty things, and I do love to sing in the choir—makes me feel all warm and toasty inside. Maybe John will be there. He's new in town. I caught him staring at me last Sunday—I think he wants to walk me home. I've never had a boyfriend before, so the thought of it kinda gives me the "tingles." I wonder if he'll think I look pretty in my new dress.

May 2, 1886—Well, John finally got up the courage to walk me home from church yesterday. He seems awful quiet—didn't say much the whole way home, but I guess I talked enough for the both of us. I never did have trouble thinkin' of things to talk about, 'cause I just get so worked up over everything—the sun goin' down on the prairie, the new department store in town, the minister's sermon, the birds comin' back after winter, or just any old thing. Pa says conversation is my strong point. I don't know if John likes my white dress or not—probably he's too shy to say so. But it did make me feel so important to have a beau see me home!

June 25, 1886—Well, dear diary, you are never going to believe this, but I am gettin' married one month from today! I know it seems sudden, but John says there ain't no use in waitin'. I'm sure he must be right. Sometimes I get right dizzy when I think about bein' married. Most people seem to like it all right, so I guess I will too. John still don't say much, but he must like me or he wouldn't a decided we should get hitched. It *will* be fun to have babies and dress 'em up cute. I always did love babies. And you never know—once the babies come, maybe John will find his tongue a bit more. Then again—maybe not. Some folks just seems more bent on some things than other folks do.

July 25, 1887—Well dear diary, I haven't written much for a long time. It ain't that I don't have anything to write, but I guess it's partly two things: partly it's that bein' a wife is much more work than I ever thought it would be, and partly I guess I been puttin' off writing, hopin' I'd have something cheerful to write—hopin' maybe I'd find myself in the family way, or some-thin' like that. But now I'm thinkin' it's not likely to happen any time soon. Every time I bring up the subject, John turns his head the other way and pretends he doesn't hear me. I'm beginning to think he doesn't want any children! Could that be? I don't like to think on it, so sometimes I go for short walks. Don't dare go for long walks, 'cause John gets powerful upset if he comes home and finds me gone somewhere.

March 4, 1888—I can't write too much today—got too much to do. I been feelin' a bit sad lately. John says he don't want me singin' in the choir no more—says it's prideful and a sin to show off in such a way. It's hard to think that havin' a little happiness is a sin, but perhaps he's right. He 'most generally is.

August 12, 1890—Been bakin' my usual batch of bread today, and thinkin' a mite more than usual. It's been *so* hot this week. I think I'll 'most melt away. Got my cherries all bottled a couple weeks ago. Soon it'll be time to do up the peaches. The corn's growin' pretty good. John does work hard, and I try to be a good wife to him. The thing that's hardest is bein' down in this here hollow where I can't see the road or any other houses, or nothin' but just the work that's gotta be done, day in and day out. Just the sameness is enough to make a body tired. Maybe, if we get a good crop, John will say we can go to town. I won't ask for a new dress, but maybe a new apron would be nice.

December 22, 1890—We been havin' one of the *coldest* winters I've ever seen in these parts. I make up a fire in the stove, but the heat seems to creep out at all the cracks before it even warms the room. I can't seem to get warm no matter what I do. John says it's too cold to work outside, so he sits inside all day and seems to get ornrier and ornrier. I've decided it's no use to try to talk to him, so I try to cheer myself up by workin' on my quilt blocks. I'm sure that when I get it all pieced it will be the prettiest thing in the house, and maybe then I'll get warm. Haven't been warm in such a long time. Goodness knows I won't be allowed to hold no quiltin' bee when I get it put together, so I'll just have to settle for tyin' knots in it. Stichin' it would be prettier, but I guess the knots'll do. At least they'll get the job done.

Mar. 1, 1891—The fetchingest little bird landed in the cherry tree this morning. He sang and sang until I thought my heart would just bust.

May 9, 1894—Made bread, did the laundry, hoed three rows of potatoes. Cloudy all day—no wind.

Sept. 12, 1896—Canned two bushel of peaches, mopped the floor,
ironed the clothes. Seems cold tonight.

Dec. 24, 1898—Christmas tomorrow. Don't know if there'll be any
singin' at Church. Too cold to go.

Mar. 10, 1902—John's been gone for three days, buyin' seed in the
next county. I just seem to rattle around in here. Got to wishin' we might-a
had a child to keep me a speck o' company. But perhaps it's no kinda life
for a child.

Jan. 19, 1909—Found my piece quilt yesterday while cleanin' out the
closet. Can't seem to work up the spirit to work on it much. It's been put
away so long that it hurts me to look at it.

Dec. 26, 1912—Christmas yesterday. No one came to visit.

Apr. 7, 1916—My birthday. Almost forgot it, perhaps I should have.
Seems I'm gettin' on. Bought myself a little canary from a peddlar man. He
does sing pretty. Don't know what John will say.

Apr. 9, 1916—It should be spring, but we been havin' a blizzard for the
last two days. Don't know why it's turned so cold again. Sewed a couple o'
blocks on that quilt I started so long ago. It is right pretty.

Apr. 10, 1916—John couldn't stand for the singin' of my canary. Said it
made him nervous. I put the poor little thing in a pretty box I'd been saving for somethin' special. I'll bury him tomorrow.

Apr. 11, 1916—I don't know what to do. I've done a awful thing.
Couldn't help myself. God knows I didn't want to. Couldn't help myself.
Couldn't stand it no more. My poor little bird. Wrung his neck. Need to
finish my quilt. Going to knot it. Couldn't help myself. Gotta be free. Whatever shall I do. No one to talk to. So cold in here. Couldn't stand it no more.
Going to knot it. Wrung his neck. God knows I didn't want to. So cold in
here. . . .

Appendix B:
Sample Essays
About Literature

Essays about literature may assume a number of forms. This appendix illustrates four major kinds: explication, which is emphatically text-centered and focuses (generally) on a single literary text; the "reader-response" essay, which combines textual analysis with personal thoughts, feelings, and experience; the comparison/contrast essay, which explores similarities and/or differences between two or more literary texts; and the research essay.

Sample #1. Angie writes an explication of Gary Soto's poem "Oranges" (p. 516); that is, she does a line-by-line analysis of the poem itself and what it means. Since "Oranges" is quite short, Angie is able to explicate, or "explain," the entire poem. In an explication of a longer text, such as a short story or play, you might focus on a particular scene, incident, or other crucial passage rather than the whole work.

"Oranges": Moving from Childhood to Adolescence

The poem "Oranges," by Gary Soto, suggests a beginning as well as an end. The beginning is the start of a new chapter in the lives of the speaker and the "girl"; they are starting to feel the emotions of adolescence in which the opposite sex is no longer viewed as repellent or "gross" but as somewhat mystical. At the same time, their childhood is ending; their new

The boy's happiness at being able to give the girl what she wants is incredible. In the beginning of the poem, he is walking with "a girl." Now that he has bought her a chocolate, he feels that she is his: "I took my girl's hand/In mine for two blocks,/Then released it to let/Her unwrap the chocolate." She suddenly changes from *a* girl to "my" girl, and he now gets the courage to hold her hand for two whole blocks.

Soto's poem ends:

> I peeled my orange
> That was so bright against
> The gray of December
> That, from some distance,
> Someone might have thought
> I was making a fire in my hands.

These last six lines suggest a metaphor for the boy's happiness. The orange could be interpreted as him peeling off his childhood to reveal this new part of his life. This new time is sweet, like the juices of an orange; and, also like an orange, it is "bright" with hope. The speaker's mood at this moment is "bright" like "a fire."

The girl, too, is experiencing a new time in her life. She tries to look good for this boy by wearing "gloves" and "rouge," no doubt watching her mother or maybe a sister. In the candy store, she seems flattered to be offered anything she likes: "Light in her eyes, a smile/Starting at the corners/Of her mouth." This is most likely the first time a boy has offered to buy her anything. When she sees the boy place one of his oranges on the counter with his nickel, she probably wonders whether she has offended or embarrassed him in any way. Though it is not mentioned in the poem, she may suppose she has already failed in trying to be like a grown-up. Once the boy takes her hand, however, she probably feels much better, as if the date has been a success.

"Oranges" is a narrative about a young boy and girl's first exposure to the world of dating. Through this experience, they learn lessons for their subsequent lives. A door has been opened for them to continue to grow and mature; at the same time, however, they must leave their simple childhoods behind.

The closing paragraph reinforces Angie's thesis & casts the experience depicted in the poem as one of simultaneous gain & loss

Sample #2. Many of the professionally written essays in Part VI of *Reading and Writing from Literature* use narrative, or storytelling, as a means of illustrating ideas. For instance, Michael Dorris's "Life Stories" (p. 1059) is composed primarily of stories about his early jobs and their effects on his development. In "The Hand," Joe discusses Dorris's essay in relationship to an early job experience of his own. Unlike Angie's essay, which focuses quite exclusively on the literary text itself, Joe's essay integrates literary analysis with his own personal experience.

The Hand

At the end of "Life Stories," Michael Dorris writes that his various school vacation jobs were "not so much to be held as to be weighed, absorbed, and incorporated, and, collectively, they carried me forward into adult life like an escalator, unfolding a particular pattern at once amazing and inevitable" (1064). In this statement, Dorris implies that those jobs were important not for making money, but because they provided him with valuable personal insight and revealed to him a pattern or script that his later life might follow.

MLA-style parenthetical references show the source & page numbers of quotations

Dorris begins his essay by talking about a rite of passage of the Plains Indians in which a male teen was to venture out into the wilderness alone and subsist there until he happened upon some "thing" that might transform him or give him insight into his life. "Through this unique prism," Dorris writes, "abstractly preserved in a vivid memory or song, a boy caught foresight of both his adult persona and of his vocation, the two inextricably entwined" (1060). For Dorris, "this unique prism" was his collection of summer jobs.

The first job that Dorris describes is his position as a postal carrier, a job important for the opportunity it afforded him to do "casually sophisticated . . . work that required a uniform" (1061). Entrusted with possibly "important correspondence," Dorris learned—the hard way—about responsibility on the job (1061).

Quotations are skillfully interwoven with the text

Another one of Dorris's jobs was his stint as Coordinator of Tribal Youth Programs, where he was to "coordinate" a group of "bored, disgruntled kids . . . who had nothing better to do each day than to show up . . . and hate whatever Program I had planned for them" (1061). As that particular summer job progressed, Dorris came to understand the role that he was to play for the youths, and he came to greet each day with the "lightheadedness of anticipated exhaustion, that thrill of giddy dissociation in which nothing seems real or of great significance" (1061).

Dorris values both of these jobs for what they offer him: unexpected challenges and unique perspectives. From there, he presumably moves on to deal with the rest of the unexpected challenges and unique perspectives that life affords him.

My experiences with jobs afforded me "personal, enabling insight" (1059) in much the same way as Dorris's did. I'm not sure if my experiences were rites of passage or terms of a contract; but through my time spent as the managing editor of the *Iowa State Daily*, I came to understand certain conditions with which we must all live.

I wrote columns at the newspaper. In fact, I was the designated "fluff columnist"—the person responsible for commenting on the string found in coat pockets and combs found beneath couch cushions and which clouds looked like which president on a given day. The life of the fluff columnist on a newspaper is like that of a World War II bomber pilot: he fights the war from an infinitely high place while others slog through the trenches and do the work and report the minutes of school board meetings and take the shrapnel of barbed letters to the editor.

I became a mild hit, accepted by my peers and somehow deemed trustworthy by my readers. People began coming to me to have their stories told. A football player wanted to come out of the closet in my column, a philosophy professor wanted me to print his suicide note, and a co-ed wanted me to write a transcript of one of her sexual encounters. "I really hate sex," she told me on the Commons one afternoon, "and I think you could make that come across. I've never been in the paper before."

My life was running pleasantly out of tilt, happily imbalanced. I felt plugged into things. I got drunk most weekends and some weeknights, because that was what a writer did. I drank angostura bitters in my gin and tonic, because Hemingway drank angostura bitters in his gin and tonic. When I made clumsy, drunken passes at women, it was because Henry Miller made clumsy, drunken passes at women. I felt like I was a vital connection in the creative process and that, as such a connection, I needed to cultivate certain habits.

One Sunday morning, I was in the office filing my column when the report of an accident came over the

---

A thesis usually appears near the beginning of an essay—but not always. Joe's thesis appears several paragraphs into his essay; it states the connection between his own job experience & Dorris's

In this paragraph & others, Joe illustrates & enlivens his main point with examples & quotations

Like the simple word "Once," this phrase helps propel the writer (& his readers) into a specific longer story about his job experience

police scanner. It was early enough that no one else except the editor was in the office, so I was sent out with a camera to cover it. A train had struck a car in the middle of town. A man was dead. I was the first reporter on the scene.

Before I knew it, I was snapping pictures of the twisted wreckage of the car, which sat—still smoking—on the tracks, a sick convolution of metal and rubber enfolded back upon itself. In its midst was a hand held tentatively out toward the pavement, dripping blood in a steady patter that looked too red to be real. I circled the wreck, snapping photos; but the only evidence of there having been anything human inside the layered metal was the hand, stretched out like the one on the ceiling of the Sistine Chapel, reaching out for another. I snapped countless photos of the hand, knowing that I would get on the front page, reveling in the exaltation a trench reporter might feel at wading around in the viscera of a story. I was at the heart of the connection.

And then, the man's wife was brought to the scene. By some fluke, her mother had been listening to the police scanner that early Sunday morning as well. She was shielded from the accident by the throng of people that surrounded it, and she pushed her way up, past the police cars, past the people, up to where I was snapping photos.

She was repeating, "What happened? What happened? What happened?" and as she got closer to the wreck, as she was able to see the cataclysm of metal, the blob of car, she knew what it meant. I think she must have seen the hand. Maybe she saw me snapping pictures and composing the lead in my head. She screamed, and I felt it in my chest. Then she dropped to one knee, spattering the pavement with her vomit, and screamed once again through the thin torrent. She didn't cry; I didn't once hear her cry. She just screamed, over and over, mortally wounded; then she was guided off to the ambulance, away from the wreck. I faded into the crowd, drove back to the office, and developed the pictures of the hand. The wreck was front page news, along with my photo and story.

When the letters began coming in later that week, I laughed. People were calling me a ghoul and a sensationalist, and I couldn't have cared less. I was a vital

connection. The city editor told me that I shouldn't take
such things personally. "The fact of the matter is, you
are a ghoul. And so am I, and so is everyone else in
the newsroom," he told me at the bar later that week.
He indicated the other people in the bar with a jerk of
his head and added, "They don't understand that."

The essay does
not end in the
usual way, with a
neat conclusion,
but with a blunt &
disturbing
metaphor. What is
the effect? Does
it matter that
Joe does not re-
turn to Dorris's
"Life Stories" at
the end of his es-
say? Why or why
not?

I didn't write on the paper the next semester and
dropped out of school the semester after that. I avoided
seeing any of my friends from the paper, but wondered
in a sulking child's way if I was missed by them or by
any of the readers. None of my self-pity mattered then
or now, because I was a ghoul and still am, and only
now am I comfortable with that truth.

Beyond the angostura bitters and the clumsy,
drunken, poetic passes at women, is what Hemingway
and Miller avoided saying directly, though it is a truth
as blunt as any: a writer is a ghoul, a person who
passes his hands over dead skin and then tells others
how it feels.

Sample #3. One common type of essay about literature is the comparison/
contrast essay. In the next example, Sara compares the protagonists in two short
stories, "The Story of an Hour" (p. 221) and "The Yellow Wallpaper" (p. 224).

Free at Last

There are strong similarities between "The Story of
an Hour" and "The Yellow Wallpaper." Both stories feature women who are products of their times, confined
by the constraints of both husband and society. The
women grow in awareness of their situation and make
a deliberate decision to free themselves from it.

Sara deftly limits
her thesis: rather
than trying to
compare every-
thing about the
two stories, she
focuses on the
two women
protagonists &
their move toward
freedom

The time frame of the stories, loosely from the late
1800's through the early 1900's, implies a standard of
behavior and a conformity to male/female role models
that influences the female protagonists in "The Story
of an Hour" and "The Yellow Wallpaper." In this era,
females were raised to be the helpmates of man. The
clothes, etiquette, education, curricular activities, and
household chores functioned to transform a girl into a
young lady and to communicate her primary responsibilities as future wife and mother. Similarly, a young
boy was trained to assume his birthright as wage
earner and husband. Men and women followed closely
dictated societal roles: men were the supporters,
defenders, and rulers; women were the supported,

defended, and governed. Men led; women followed. To venture beyond the confines of the prescribed role was a breach of conduct. Often the punishment was abandonment, alienation, or banishment by family or community. Just as men were instilled with virtues, such as bravery and stoicism, that complemented their role, so women were imbued with submissiveness. <u>These narrowly defined roles form the foundation for the conflict in "The Yellow Wallpaper" and "The Story of an Hour."</u>

Long before the "hour" depicted in Chopin's story, Louise Mallard has been indoctrinated into the values and morals of her time period. She has been carefully prepared to fulfill the role of a wife. Within their marriage, she and Brently function in their prescribed roles. Louise is neither happy nor unhappy; she is comfortable. Her days pass predictably, and she feels no desire to change the pattern of her existence.

<u>The doctor's wife in "The Yellow Wallpaper" is a product of the same expectations and conformity.</u> She defers to the judgment of her husband and acquiesces in his decisions. "It is so hard to talk with John about my case," she writes, "because he is so wise, and because he loves me so" (230). Her rebellions are small and confined to his absence. The role modeling and constraints imposed by society form the background of her story and heighten her conflict as she comes into awareness of the self she has imprisoned.

<u>Just as Louise has been molded into the role of wife, so, too, has the doctor's wife.</u> Although neither is intentionally limited by her husband from achieving her potential as a woman, both are victims of a confining relationship. The tragic result is a loss of identity. Each woman can perceive herself only in terms of her husband. Because society dictated a submissive role for women, a woman seldom challenged her destiny. If she found her lot unpalatable, she kept the pain to herself. It would not occur to a woman to think in terms of her own development, needs, and expression. Only a crisis or some other catalyst could make her confront the identity she had repressed.

The crisis for Louise is the announcement of her husband's death. After the initial shock, she begins to contemplate her lack of remorse. As she gazes out the window towards the blue sky, she embarks on a

Sara places the two characters in a historical & social context but does not lose sight of her focus: this last sentence returns us to the two stories

Paragraph transitions are particularly important in comparison / contrast essays. These and other opening sentences of paragraphs keep the focus on connections between the two women rather than on either woman in isolation

process of self-discovery. She does not feel loss but a
sense of release from her confinement in an imposed
role. She is "Free, free, free!" (222). Her awareness is
sparked by her ability to confront the identity she
has repressed. Louise's excitement over her freedom
is in stark contrast to the apathy that defined her
marriage role.

    The doctor's wife's journey towards self-realization
is more tortured and lengthy than Louise's. She does
not experience a dramatic crisis that challenges her to
confront her inner self or open her eyes in sudden self-
awareness. Her conformity to the established norm ex-
acts a price—illness. Her postpartum depression is a
symptom of the repressed self. The wallpaper serves
as the catalyst for the journey into the depths of her
being. It symbolizes her overpowering illness and represents an elaborate description of her struggle. The
design in the paper illustrates her feelings. The bars
are the strings of steel in her mind that deny her the
courage and strength to move on with life and that
imprison her within her *role:*

>   The front pattern *does* move—and no wonder!
> The woman behind shakes it!
>   Sometimes I think there are a great many
> women behind, and sometimes only one, and she
> crawls around fast, and her crawling shakes it all
> over. . . .
>   And she is all the time trying to climb through.
> But nobody could climb through that pattern—it
> strangles so; I think that is why it has so many
> heads. (233)

The woman that the doctor's wife envisions in the
wallpaper, who is alternately trapped and freed, finally
lures the wife deeper into herself. As she struggles to
free the woman by ripping down the wallpaper, she is
struggling to free herself.

    Both Louise and the doctor's wife become aware of
their inner selves through a process of discovery
brought on by an incident in their life. Their previous
existence serves to contrast their former selves with
their new revelations. Unfortunately, their realizations
are dramatically extinguished: Louise dies when she
sees her husband walk through the door; the doctor's

[margin notes]

MLA-style paren-
thetical reference

Quotations of
more than four
lines are block-
indented

The conclusion re-
iterates the main
similarities & dif-
ferences between
the 2 characters
& their search for
freedom

wife joins the trapped woman in the wallpaper. Yet both endings represent a triumph. Louise's death is an alternative to returning to her submissive self. The doctor's wife's decision marks the severance of her submission to her husband. Both women are free.

Sample #4. Here is an excerpt from a research essay by Kristin. (The essay is too long to reprint in its entirety.)

"The Yellow Wallpaper": A Critical Survey

Charlotte Perkins Gilman's "The Yellow Wallpaper," written over one hundred years ago, is the narration or journal of a woman who is severely oppressed by her husband. While she is suffering from a "nervous disorder," a result of post-partum depression, he takes her to an old abandoned house and demands that she rest from all her work. He does not allow her to think or act for herself. She is afraid to speak out against him, so she records her feelings and impressions in her journal which becomes the text for the story.

"The Yellow Wallpaper" has undergone a variety of interpretational changes in its hundred year history. Its original audiences thought of it simply as a tale of horror or a depiction of mental breakdown. Consequently, it was ignored by most literary critics immediately following its publication. It was not until the latter part of the twentieth-century that the onset of the feminist movement demanded a closer look at the symbolism behind "The Yellow Wallpaper." Jean E. Kennard suggested "that the recent appearance of feminist novels has . . . led us to find in the story an exploration of women's role instead of the tale of horror . . . its original audience found" (qtd. in Shumaker 588). At a 1989 Modern Language Association convention in Washington, D.C., Elaine R. Hedges called "The Yellow Wallpaper" "the most well-known rediscovered work by a nineteenth-century American woman." At present "The Yellow Wallpaper" is firmly established in the literary canon appearing in all major literary anthologies (222).

Subsequent to its republication, "The Yellow Wallpaper" has been subject to many critical studies. Feminist critics from North America to Europe have used its text as an explicit illustration of the degrading and detrimental effects of women's life in a male dominated society.

Title of essay centered on page

Titles of short stories, poems, essays, and other kinds of short works are enclosed in quotation marks

Kristin Introduces quotations and integrates them into her own prose

Example of a parenthetical reference omitting author's last name.

Michelle A. Masse, from the department of English at Louisiana State University in Baton Rouge, wrote a critical essay on "The Yellow Wallpaper" entitling it "Gothic Repetition." She employed a variety of techniques in her interpretation. She utilized feminist criticism throughout the work, but also used psychoanalytic and formalist. Much of the essay concentrated on Gilman's use of repetition in her phrases and symbols creating a classic Gothic tale. Though this was the primary purpose of the essay, it was not as important as her explanations for the narrator's motivations and actions.

Masse begins by describing the narrator's loss of identity as a direct cause of her anxiety. Because of John's infantilizing treatment she is forced to deny her identity as an adult, mother, and intelligent human being (702). Using names such as "darling," "little goose," and "little girl" in addressing her and compelling her to stay in a room previously used as nursery or asylum forces her, according to Masse, to see herself as a child and ambiguously joins children with infantilized women (702).

Masse states that the narrator is subject to Freud's theories of displacement and repression. "At a certain pitch of intensity, she ostensibly moves away from talking about herself to discussion of safe inanimate objects . . ." (705). This is shown on page 88 of Gilman's text when the narrator states, "John says the very worst thing I can do is to think about my condition, and I confess it always makes me feel bad. So I will . . . talk about the house." Not being able to consciously deal with her submission and gradual loss of identity, she displaces and represses her feelings onto the house. She also displaces the restrictions placed upon her by her husband/doctor onto the woman she sees imprisoned behind the wallpaper (Masse 701).

Example of a paraphrase or summary

Example of a parenthetical reference using author's last name

The key symbol in this work is the yellow wallpaper. Its bulbous eyed, crawling, fungus–like pattern becomes the object of the narrator's unconscious attempts to resolve her problems. She is determined to find the pattern behind the paper because, as Masse states: "[she] believes that there must be a logical principle . . . determining the pattern of the paper, because there are supposed to be rules for such things, just as there must be comprehensible reasons for gender expectations" (707). Her attempts to find order and control within the paper are in vain. After staring at the paper for a number of hours, she writes: "just as you get well underway in following, it turns a back-somersault and there you are. It slaps you in the face, knocks you down, and tramples upon you. It is like a bad dream" (Gilman 95). Just as she cannot conquer and control the paper, she cannot conquer and control her husband. Masse says "The paper, unlikely con-cretization of authority's horror though it is, is inescap-able and aggressive when challenged" (Masse 708). The narrator becomes angry with the "everlasting-ness" of the paper (Gilman 91), symbolizing the conti-nuity of oppressiveness. Masse points out that the nar-rator believes others have been subjected to the paper and angered by it and worries that it will continue to be detrimental to women (708). The narrator spends many long hours studying the paper and eventually "sees what the cultural codes found in this story re-veal: a trapped woman" (Masse 708).

Examples of paraphrasing

Masse states that the narrator finally finds freedom, autonomy and power through her identification with the woman in the wallpaper. "[The narrator] has finally recognized her dilemma, measured the scope allowed to her, and disabused herself of belief in the benevo-lent intention behind those limits" (Masse 709). She no longer struggles to deal with her prohibited identity. Although her escape is destructive and only partial, it is nonetheless an escape to the only freedom available to her. She has finally spoken and been heard by John (Masse 709).

This essay is very detailed and specific. Masse did many close readings of "The Yellow Wallpaper," and most of her symbolisms can be traced back to certain words in the text. I am in strong agreement with her interpretation of the story's conclusion and of the wall-paper's symbolism as a representation of her sense of repression and submission. I too feel that the narrator displaced many of her feelings onto the wallpaper, re-fusing to talk or write about them. This essay, however, seemed very complex and only a few parts opened up the text and gave me a better understanding of it. Masse concentrated on too many symbols, and thus her essay was not clear and concise. Her lack of focus made it difficult to discern what was actually being discussed.

Conrad Shumaker, of the University of Central Arkansas, describes "The Yellow Wallpaper" as:

> a question that was . . . and still is—central . . . to the place of women in American culture: What happens to the imagination when it's defined as feminine (and thus weak) and has to face a society that values the useful and the practical and rejects anything else as nonsense? (590)

Block-Indented quotation (use when a quotation runs to 5 or more typed lines)

In a block-indented quotation, the terminal punctuation <u>precedes</u> the parenthetical reference

Through the use of feminist criticism, Shumaker shows how the narrator's husband tries to force her to shut out all imaginative powers and be logical. He, like most males of that day, is unable to see anything that is not practical and materialistic. Anything illogical, like his wife's problem not really being physical or her "work" helping her to improve, is unfathomable to him. He wants only to deal with physical causes and effects (Shumaker 591). By labeling his wife's imagination as a negative force, John can control her and maintain his materialistic view of the world (Shumaker 593). John represents reason to his wife, so when her feelings contradict him it is automatically her sensitivity that is at fault because she cannot question his authority (594). The narrator believes that John loves her just as John believes that she is obedient to all of his demands. Although neither is true, this shows that they both are doomed to act out these roles until the disastrous end (595). Shumaker points out the irony in the fact that the reason John fails to cure his wife is because of his deeply rooted belief and faith in materialism, "a faith that will not allow him even to consider the possibility that his wife's imagination could be a positive force" (592). The chilling conclusion of the story, as seen by Shumaker, is a very limited amount of freedom for the narrator. The most important thing accomplished is the fact that "she has discovered . . . and finally revealed to John, the wife he is attempting to create—the woman without illusions or imagination who spends all her time creeping" (598).

Kristin's essay continues for several more pages. It ends with the following "Works Cited" page, which lists all of the sources to which she referred in her essay:

Works Cited

Gilman, Charlotte Perkins. "The Yellow Wallpaper." *Literature: An Introduction to Critical Reading.* Ed. William Vesterman. New York: Harcourt, 1993: 87–100.

Golden, Catherine. "'Overwriting' the Rest Cure: Charlotte Perkins Gilman's Literary Escape from S. Weir Mitchell's Fictionalization of Women." *Critical Essays on Charlotte Perkins Gilman.* Ed. Joanne B. Karpinski. New York: G. K. Hall & Co., 1992: 144–58.

Hedges, Elaine R. "'Out at Last?' 'The Yellow Wallpaper' after Two Decades of Feminist Criticism." *Critical Essays on Charlotte Perkins Gilman.* Ed. Joanne B. Karpinski. New York: G. K. Hall & Co., 1992: 222–33.

Lane, Ann J. *The Charlotte Perkins Gilman Reader.* New York: Pantheon Books, 1980.

Masse, Michelle A. "Gothic Repetition: Husbands, Horrors and Things That Go Bump in the Night." *Signs* 15 (1990): 679–709.

Shumaker, Conrad. "Too Terribly Good to Be Printed: Charlotte Gilman's 'The Yellow Wallpaper.'" *American Literature* 57 (1985): 588–99.

Appendix C:
Glossary of Literary Terms

Most of the terms below are also discussed in Part IV, "An Introduction to the Major Genres." For additional references and examples, consult the appropriate chapter in Part IV or Part V, "An Introduction to Figurative Language."

Abstract language *See* concrete language.

Act A major structural division within a play.

Alliteration A sound effect in which consonant sounds are repeated, particularly at the beginnings of words or of stressed syllables. Examples: *"low"/"long"; "cracks"/"crazes."*

Allusion A reference to something (such as a character or event in literature, history, or mythology) outside the literary text itself.

Anapest A metrical foot composed of two lightly stressed syllables followed by a stressed syllable, e.g., in the énd. *See also* meter.

Antagonist The main opponent of the protagonist in a story, play, or other narrative or dramatic work.

Aphorism A terse statement of principle, truth, or opinion.

Argumentative essay *See* essay.

Assonance A sound effect in which identical or similar vowel sounds are repeated in two or more words in close proximity to each other. Example: *"storms"/"morning."*

Author The writer of a literary work. *Compare* persona.

Ballad A relatively short narrative poem, generally with an anonymous or impersonal narrator, that is usually written in rhymed four-line stanzas and that may include a refrain.

Blank verse Verse composed in unrhymed iambic pentameter lines.

Caesura   A strong pause within a line of poetry.

Characters   The imaginary persons who appear in fictional narratives or dramatic works. A flat character is one who remains essentially unchanged throughout the story and tends to be less an individual than a type. A round character evolves or undergoes change in the course of the story and is more individualized and complex.

Citation   A reference made, in an essay, to another text. The citation may be included for diverse purposes: to illustrate a point or idea, to add support or authority to the writer's argument or reasoning, to bolster reader trust in the persona, or to add depth to the essay by expanding its range of literary reference.

Climax   The moment in the plot of a story or play at which tensions are highest or suspense reaches its height.

Concrete language   Language that describes or portrays specific or observable persons, places, or things rather than general ideas or qualities. Concrete language appeals to the senses, as in this example from Robert Frost's "Birches": "They [Birches] click upon themselves/As the breeze rises, and turn many-colored/As the stir cracks and crazes their enamel" (ll. 7–9). In contrast, **abstract language** refers to general ideas or qualities, as in this later passage from the same poem: "Earth's the right place for love:/I don't know where it's likely to get better" (ll. 52–53).

Conflict   A struggle among opposing characters or forces in fiction, poetry, or drama.

Connotation   An associative or suggestive meaning of a word in addition to its literal dictionary meaning (or "denotation"). The word "politician" denotes "a person actively involved in politics," while it connotes (for some people) a corrupt and conniving individual motivated exclusively by self-interest.

Consonance   A sound effect in which identical or similar consonant sounds, occurring in nearby words, are repeated with different intervening vowels. Example: *"crush"/"crash."*

Couplet   A pair of lines of poetry, usually rhymed; a two-line stanza.

Dactyl   A metrical foot consisting of one stressed syllable followed by two lightly stressed syllables, e.g., "pŏndĕring."

Denotation   The dictionary definition of a word, without associative or implied meanings. *Compare* connotation.

Denouement   The moment of final resolution of the conflict in a plot.

Dialogue   The spoken conversation that occurs in a text.

Diction   Word choice. Diction can be described as formal or informal, abstract or concrete, general or specific, and literal or figurative.

End-stopped line   A line of poetry whose end coincides with the end of a phrase, clause, or sentence.

Enjambed line   A line of poetry that completes its grammatical unity and meaning by going into the next line without a pause.

Epic poem   A long narrative poem on a heroic subject.

Essay   A unified and relatively short work of nonfiction prose. An argumentative essay advances an explicit argument and supports it with evidence. An expository essay informs an audience or explains a particular subject. A personal or literary essay emphasizes elements that are ordinarily associated with "literary" texts—an engaging persona, an intellectual or emotional focus or theme that is usually implied rather than directly stated, and artful use of figurative language and other "literary" elements such as dialogue and narrative.

Exposition   The part of a plot of a short story or play that provides background information on characters, setting, and plot.

Expository essay   *See* essay.

Expressionism   A writing style or movement in which reality is exaggerated or distorted in order to render the world as we feel it rather than as we literally see it.

Falling action   The part of the plot of a short story or play, after the climax, in which action and suspense decline toward a denouement or resolution.

Feminine rhyme   *See* rhyme.

Figurative language   The term used to encompass all nonliteral uses of language.

Figure (or **trope**)   A word or phrase used in a way that significantly changes its standard or literal meaning. Some common kinds of figures are metaphor, simile, metonymy, irony, and paradox.

First-person narrator   *See* point of view.

Flashback   An interruption in the chronological presentation of a narrative or drama that presents an earlier episode.

Flat character   *See* characters.

Foot   *See* meter.

Free verse   Poetry that discards meter and usually dispenses with rhyme while keeping other poetic elements such as pronouncedly rhythmic phrasing, various types of patterned sound, and intensive use of figurative language.

Hero/Heroine   The main character in a narrative or dramatic work. Also called the "protagonist."

Hyperbole   A bold exaggeration used for rhetorical effect.

Iamb   A metrical foot consisting of a lightly stressed syllable followed by a stressed syllable, e.g., "aróund."

Irony   A type of incongruity. Dramatic irony involves an incongruity between what a character in a story or play *believes* and what we (the better-informed members of the audience) *know*. Verbal irony involves an incongruity between what is literally said and what is actually meant.

Limited point of view   *See* point of view.

Lyric poem   A poem, usually rather short, in which a speaker expresses a state of mind or feeling.

Masculine rhyme   *See* rhyme.

Metaphor   A figure or trope that makes an implicit comparison between dissimilar items in a way that evokes new or vivid ways of perceiving, knowing, and/or feeling. Example: "she is a green tree/in a forest of kindling" makes an implicit comparison between a young girl, indestructible in her zest for life, and an almost fireproof tree.

Meter   Rhythm that follows a regular repeating pattern of stressed and lightly stressed syllables. Within a poetic line, meters are measured in feet, with each repetition of the pattern comprising a separate foot. The most common meters are iambic (˘ ´), trochaic (´ ˘), anapestic (˘ ˘ ´), and dactylic (´ ˘ ˘). A line of three feet is described as trimeter, a line of four feet is tetrameter, and one of five feet is pentameter.

Metonymy   A figure or trope in which the literal term for one thing is used to stand for another with which it is closely associated. Example: "The White House says" instead of "The President says."

Monologue   A long speech by a single character.

Narrative poem   A poem that relates a story.

Narrator   The imaginary speaker, as distinct from the author him- or herself, who tells a story. *See* also point of view.

Octave   *See* stanza.

Ode   A lyric poem, composed in a lofty style, that is serious in subject and elaborate in stanza structure.

Omniscient narrator   *See* point of view.

One-act play   A relatively short play. Usually, though not always, a one-act dramatizes a single incident and includes fewer characters than multiple-act plays.

Oxymoron   A joining of two terms that are ordinarily conceived as opposites. Examples: "knowledgeable unknowing," "deafening silence."

Paradox   An apparently contradictory statement that proves, on examination, to be true. Example: "You must lose your life to gain it."

Persona   The "mask" or version of a self that an author projects in a particular text. The plural form of persona is **personae.**

Personal essay   *See* essay.

Personification   A figure or trope in which human qualities are ascribed to an abstract concept or inanimate object. Example: "Fortune smiled upon him."

Plot   The pattern of actions and events that combine to produce a total effect in readers or viewers of a narrative or dramatic work. Some critics divide plots into a rising action, which introduces the characters and establishes the conflict; a climax, in which the conflict reaches its height in the form of some decisive action or decision; a falling action, in which the conflict moves toward resolution; and a denouement or resolution, in which the conflicts are resolved.

Poem   A kind of literary text that is typically arranged in lines and composed in meter or free verse.

Point of view   The perspective from which a story is told. The two basic types are first-person and third-person. In a first-person narrative the narrator is a character within the story, while in a third-person narrative he or she is not a character in the story. Third-person narrators can be further classified (broadly) as either limited or omniscient. The limited narrator reports events and characters primarily through the consciousness of one character, while the omniscient functions as an all-knowing presence with access to the thoughts, feelings, and actions of any or all of the characters. An unreliable (or naive) narrator is a first-person narrator whose youth, naiveté, limited intelligence, or extreme subjectivity leads us to question the accuracy of his or her version of characters and events.

Prose poem   A poem that is shaped like prose (in paragraphs rather than lines) but that displays other features (such as pronouncedly rhythmic phrasing, various types of patterned sound, and intensive use of figurative language) characteristic of poetry.

Protagonist   The main character around whom a narrative or dramatic work centers. Also called the "hero" or "heroine."

Quatrain   *See* stanza.

Rhyme   An identity or similarity in sound patterns, the most familiar kind being the *end* rhyme that occurs between words at the ends of lines of poetry. When the end rhyme consists of a single stressed syllable ("sing"/"wing"), it is termed masculine; when the rhyme consists of a final stressed syllable followed by a lightly stressed ("whether"/"feather"), it is termed feminine. A slant, partial, or half rhyme occurs when the rhyming sounds are only approximately ("dizzy"/"easy"), rather than exactly, alike.

Rhythm   A distinct but variable pattern of stressed and lightly stressed sounds in poetry or prose.

Rising action   *See* plot.

Round character   *See* characters.

Scansion   The process of analyzing the metrical pattern of a poem.

Scene description   Text that describes what the stage looks like for a particular play.

Sestet   *See* stanza.

Setting   The place, time, and social context in which a story, poem, or play takes place.

Short story   A brief work of prose fiction.

Simile   A figure that makes an explicit (rather than implicit) comparison between dissimilar items in a way that evokes new or vivid ways of perceiving, knowing, and/or feeling. Example: "skin/worn, like the pages of her prayer book" makes an explicit comparison between an old woman's skin and the pages of a well-used book. *Compare* metaphor.

Slant rhyme   Also called a "half" or "partial" rhyme. *See* rhyme.

Sonnet   A fourteen-line lyric poem written in iambic pentameter and rhymed according to a preset conventional pattern. The **Italian** or **Petrarchan sonnet** is divided into an octave rhymed *abbaabba* and a sestet with a *cdecde* rhyme scheme or some variant. The **English** or **Shakespearean sonnet** falls into three quatrains rhymed *abab, cdcd, efef,* and a closing couplet rhymed *gg.*

Speaker   The "I" in a lyric poem.

Stage directions   In a play, text that describes the movements or gestures of characters onstage.

Stanza   A grouping of poetic lines arranged in a definite pattern that is repeated throughout the poem. Three-line stanzas are called tercets or triplets; stanzas of four lines, six lines, and eight lines are called (respectively) quatrains, sestets, and octaves.

Stream of consciousness   A narrative technique that tries to reproduce the exact flow of thoughts, feelings, and associations that go through a character's mind as he or she moves in the "stream" of time.

Symbol   Something that stands for something else. In literary analysis, something is said to be "symbolic" if it evokes an idea, quality, or concept larger than itself.

Synecdoche   A figure or trope in which a part of something is used to signify the whole or the whole is used to signify a part. Example: "All hands on deck" instead of "All sailors on deck."

Syntax   The arrangement of words within phrases, clauses, and sentences.

Tercet   *See* stanza.

Theme   A basic idea advanced (or implied) in a text.

Thesis   In a formal or academic essay, a sentence that articulates the main point that the text intends to address or argue.

Third-person narrator   *See* point of view.

Tone   The expression of a writer's attitudes toward a subject; the mood the writer has chosen for a piece.

Traditional verse   Poetry that employs meter and (often) rhyme. *See also* free verse.

Triplet   *See* stanza.

Trochee   A metrical foot consisting of one stressed syllable followed by a lightly stressed syllable, e.g., "dreary."

Trope   *See* figure.

Unreliable (or **naive**) **narrator**   *See* point of view.

Verbal irony   An incongruity between what a speaker says literally and the meaning that is implied in the larger context of the story, poem, or other work.

Voice   The felt authorial presence in a literary text.

Appendix D:
Notes on the Authors

Notes are included for all authors of short stories, essays, and plays and for authors represented by two or more poems.

Woody Allen (b. 1935)

Born in Brooklyn, New York, Woody Allen (real name Allen Stewart Konigsberg) attended college in New York City and began his career as a joke writer and comic. Though best known as a filmmaker (*Bananas, Sleeper, Annie Hall, Interiors, Manhattan, Bullets over Broadway*), the multitalented Allen is also an actor, short story writer, playwright, and jazz clarinetist. *Death Knocks* is reprinted from *Getting Even* (1971), a collection of Allen's comic stories, sketches, and plays.

Maya Angelou (b. 1928)

Maya Angelou has had a long and distinguished career as a poet, autobiographer, playwright, director, actress, singer, and producer for stage and screen. An African American, Angelou grew up amid racial segregation in Stamps, Arkansas, and attended public schools there and in California. Later she studied dance and drama and worked as a performing artist, director, and producer in the United States and abroad. Her first book, the autobiographical *I Know Why the Caged Bird Sings* (1970), was widely praised. Angelou has produced several additional books of autobiography, including *Gather Together in My Name, The Heart of a Woman,* and *All God's Children Need Traveling Shoes,* and numerous collections of poems, such as *Poems: Maya Angelou, I Shall Not Be Moved,* and *On the Pulse of Morning.* She read the title poem of this last work at the 1993 inauguration of President Bill Clinton.

Margaret Atwood (b. 1939)

Margaret Atwood has been influential as an author and editor who has asserted the cultural identity of Canadian literature. Born in Ottawa, Ontario, Atwood attended the University of Ontario and did graduate work in the United States at Radcliffe College and Harvard. She published her first book of poems, *Double Persephone* (1961), when she was in her twenties. Since then she has been prolific as a writer of novels, poems, short stories, and nonfiction. Among her best-known novels are *The Edible Woman, Surfacing, Life before Man, The Handmaid's Tale,* and *Alias Grace.* Her short stories are collected in *Dancing Girls and Other Stories, Bluebeard's Egg and Other Stories, Murder in the Dark,* and *Wilderness Tips.*

Toni Cade Bambara (1939–1995)

Writer and social activist, Toni Cade Bambara was born in New York City and grew up in the neighborhoods of Harlem, Bedford-Stuyvesant, and Queens. She was educated, also in New York, at Queens College (bachelor's degree in theater and English literature) and City College (master's degree in modern American literature), and subsequently studied filmmaking and other arts in Europe. During the 1960s, Bambara became prominently associated with African American writers who formed the Black Arts Movement, and much of her fiction and other work reflects and celebrates the folk-based language of African American music, poetry, and prose. Her short story collections include *Gorilla My Love* and *The Sea Birds Are Still Alive.* Bambara also published two novels, *The Salt Eaters* and *If Blessing Comes,* wrote television and film scripts, and edited several anthologies, including *The Black Woman* and *Tales and Stories for Black Folks.*

Wendell Berry (b. 1934)

Born in Henry County, Kentucky, Wendell Berry earned his bachelor's and master's degrees from the University of Kentucky. Following formal studies in creative writing and periods of living in California and Europe, he was on his way to a brilliant writing and teaching career in New York City when he decided that his proper place was back home in Kentucky. Since then, in addition to teaching at the University of Kentucky, Berry has pursued two complementary lines of work—farming his family's farm in Henry County and writing. Much of his writing has been about "homecoming," about the need to conserve land, people, and ecosystems through the nurturing of caring communities grounded in an affection for place. Berry has written many books—novels, essays, poems, and short stories—including *Jayber Crow* (novel), *Fidelity* (stories), *Life Is a Miracle* (long essay), *The Unsettling of America* (essays), and *The Selected Poems of Wendell Berry* (1998).

William Blake (1757–1827)

Poet and artist, William Blake was born in London, the son of a hosier. Lacking any formal education, he began studying drawing at age ten, served an apprenticeship to an engraver, and for the rest of his life earned a modest income as an engraver and illustrator. Blake was writing verse in his teens and published his first volume of poems (*Poetical Sketches*) in 1783. In 1789 he began engraving, illustrating, and printing his own works, including *Songs of Innocence* and *The Book of Thel* (1789), *The Marriage of Heaven & Hell* (ca. 1790), and *Songs of Experience* (1794). Visionary, iconoclastic in style and outlook, and largely indifferent to the commercial success or failure of his writings, Blake also wrote and illustrated numerous books in verse that developed his own political and cosmological mythology. He died in relative obscurity; his poems were little read during his lifetime, and what reputation he had was chiefly as an artist and engraver.

Carol Bly (b. 1930)

A Minnesota native, Carol Bly is best known for her essays and short stories about rural and small-town Minnesotans. Born in Duluth, Bly earned her B.A. degree from Wellesley College and did graduate study at the University of Minnesota. She married the poet Robert Bly and, before they were divorced, helped him produce an influential literary magazine, raised a family, and performed numerous tasks, paid and volunteer, in her community. In her forties she began writing essays ("letters," she called them) for Minnesota Public Radio that were collected and published as *Letters from the Country* in 1981. Bly has also written two volumes of short stories, *Backbone* (1985) and *The Tomcat's Wife and Other Stories* (1992). Bly's work both celebrates and critiques small-town life. As one reviewer explains, she distills "the essences of small-town life—its . . . satisfactions and impoverishments, the contradictory pleasures of community and isolation, and . . . the difficulty of coming to a full exercise of individual capacity without seeming an alien, even a threat, to one's neighbors."

Elizabeth Bowen (1899–1973)

Born in Dublin, Elizabeth Bowen grew up in County Cork and was educated in England, where she continued to live until permanently returning to Ireland in 1952. Author of several novels—including *The House in Paris, The Death of the Heart, and The Heat of the Day*—she was also a prolific writer of short stories, which were gathered in *Collected Stories of Elizabeth Bowen* (1981). "The Demon Lover" reflects Bowen's fascination with the occult.

Ray Bradbury (b. 1920)

Ray Bradbury was born in Waukegan, Illinois, and received no formal education beyond high school. From youth on, however, he aspired to write. In 1941 he published his first short story in the genre (science fiction) with which he was to become most intimately connected. Since then Bradbury has written prolifically for magazines, television, radio, theatre, and film. His many works include *The Martian Chronicles, The Golden Apples of the Sun, Fahrenheit 451, Dandelion Wine, Something Wicked This Way Comes,* and *The Stories of Ray Bradbury.*

Gwendolyn Brooks (1917–2000)

Born in Topeka, Kansas, Gwendolyn Brooks grew up in inner-city Chicago and graduated from high school and junior college there. She began writing poetry as a child, received encouragement from mentors, and published her first book of poetry, *A Street in Bronzeville,* in 1945. Her second book, *Annie Allen* (1949) was the first volume of poetry by an African American to win a Pulitzer Prize. Though always focused on the experience of African Americans, Brooks's work underwent an important evolution in the late 1960s, when she attended a conference with many new and younger black poets and began to write more exclusively to black audiences. In the late sixties and early seventies, her poetry became more self-consciously political as she championed the cause of black militants and feminists. Some of her books from this period are *Riot, Family Pictures,* and *Beckonings.* Brooks's poetry is a distinctive, energy-charged blend of many influences, including traditional Anglo-American rhymed verse, street talk, African chant, the biblical cadences of black Protestant preaching, and the improvisatory rhythms of jazz.

Katharine Brush (1902–1952)

Katharine Brush was an American journalist, novelist and short story writer whose books included *This is on Me* and *Other Women.*

Raymond Carver (1938–1988)

In a career cut short by lung cancer, Raymond Carver established himself as a contemporary master of the short story. Born in Clatskanie, Oregon, the son of a sawmill worker and a waitress, Carver produced fiction that relentlessly chronicled the lives of working-class Americans. Collections of his short stories include *Will You Please Be Quiet, Please?, What We Talk About When We Talk About Love,* and *Cathedral.* Carver also wrote essays and poems, which are collected in *Fires: Essays, Poems, Stories, In a Marine Light,* and in the posthumously published *A New Path to the Waterfall.* The lean, spare, and often bleak character of his stories earned him the label "minimalist."

Anton Chekhov (1860–1904)

Anton Chekhov, a major short story writer and playwright, was born in rural Russia and earned a medical degree at Moscow University School of Medicine. Though he was educated as a physician, literature was his passion. At nineteen he began submitting humorous sketches to newspapers and magazines, and his first published collection of stories appeared in 1884. By the end of his life he had written some six hundred stories. During the last decade of his life Chekhov also produced several dramatic works that revolutionized the modern theater: *The Sea Gull, Uncle Vanya, The Three Sisters,* and *The Cherry Orchard.* Long plagued by tuberculosis, Chekhov died at a resort in Germany in 1904. Chekhov's work is characterized by a strict economy and objectivity. As he wrote, "The artist should be, not the judge of his characters and their conversations, but only an unbiased witness." This stance is evident in "Gooseberries," in which the writer presents us with the "characters and their conversations" while leaving judgment and interpretation to his readers.

Gilbert Keith Chesterton (1874–1936)

Born in London, Gilbert Keith (G.K.) Chesterton attended school at St. Paul's School in London and studied art before embarking on a career in journalism. Chesterton wrote prolifically in many genres—article and essay, drama, poetry, literary criticism, and fiction (the popular "Father Brown" series of detective stories). After converting to Roman Catholicism in 1922 he also wrote religious polemics, notably *The Everlasting Man* (1925). Chesterton repeatedly but cheerfully attacked Victorian and modern social and intellectual orthodoxies, and his witty and highly figurative literary style earned him the title of "master of the paradox."

Kate Chopin (1850–1904)

Born Katherine ("Kate") O'Flaherty in St. Louis, Missouri, Kate Chopin was educated at Sacred Heart Academy, a St. Louis boarding school. Her father died in a railroad accident when Kate was a child, and she was subsequently raised by her mother, grandmother, and great-grandmother, all widowed and independent women. In 1870 she married Oscar Chopin, a well-to-do Louisiana man, and lived with him and their growing family in New Orleans until 1879, when they moved to the Chopin plantation in central Louisiana. After Oscar's sudden death in 1882 Kate returned with her six children to St. Louis. There, in 1889, she began writing for publication, producing her first novel, *At Fault,* in 1890, and two collections of short stories—*Bayou Folk* (1894) and *A Night in Acadie* (1897). In 1899 she published the novel for which she is best known today, *The Awakening,* about a heroine whose voyage of self-discovery causes her to defy conventional notions of wifehood, motherhood, and womanhood. This book drew largely negative reviews from across the country, especially from male critics, who were angered by its controversial subject matter. Chopin's stories are mainly set against the culturally diverse background of rural Louisiana. They explore themes of female sexuality, the often imprisoning effects of social institutions and conventions on individual development, and the roles and status of women in nineteenth-century American society, a time when most married women were considered the legal property of their husbands.

Judith Ortiz Cofer (b. 1952)

Born in Hormigueros, Puerto Rico, Judith Ortiz Cofer grew up on a "border" between cultures. Her father was a career navy man, and during Cofer's childhood the family shuttled between Puerto Rico and the mainland United States, between Spanish language and English, and between Puerto Rican culture and American. Cofer describes the impact of this experience in "Primary Lessons" and other autobiographical writings. Some of Cofer's collections of poetry and prose are *Latin Women Pray, Silent Dancing: A Partial Remembrance of a Puerto Rican Childhood, The Latin Deli: Prose and Poetry,* and *The Year of Our Revolution.* She has also written a novel, *The Line of the Sun* (1989).

Sidonie-Gabrielle Colette (1873–1954)

Born in Burgundy, France, Sidonie-Gabrielle Colette was a child prodigy who read classics by the age of eight and excelled at composition. Strongly influenced by her mother—an intellectual, passionate, and independent woman—Colette herself led an exciting life that included careers as a music hall dancer, novelist, and journalist. Colette wrote dozens of books (many of which have been translated into English), including novels, short stories, and other works that blend autobiography with fiction in a manner distinctly her own. Her biographer notes that, while "most of Colette's writing reveals her to be more interested in women than in men," she neither argues on behalf of women nor denigrates men. "[S]he remains feminine, never feminist. . . ."

Emily Dickinson (1830–1886)

Emily Dickinson was born in Amherst, Massachusetts, where her father, Edward, was a prominent lawyer and leading citizen. She attended Amherst Academy and, briefly, the nearby Mount Holyoke Female Seminary. After leaving the seminary without graduating in 1848, Dickinson seldom went beyond the grounds of the family home in Amherst until the day of her death. There, in an upstairs room of the house, she wrote over 1,700 poems. She was wary of publication, terming it "the Auction of the Mind," and fewer than twenty of her poems appeared in print during her lifetime. Others were published posthumously by family members and friends, and her complete poems did not appear in a scholarly edition until the 1950s. Dickinson's reclusive circumstances gave her the privacy and freedom she wanted for reading, thinking, and writing. Moreover, she was not completely isolated from the world. She lived among family and servants, maintained passionate friendships, and read voraciously—newspapers, contemporary poetry and fiction, and classics (especially Shakespeare). Many of Dickinson's poems are written in the simple iambic meters (see Appendix C) of hymns, but her verbal compression, suggestiveness, and astonishing metaphors make it impossible to label her poetry as "traditional." Tough-minded, irreverent, and stubbornly faithful to her own intuitions, Dickinson constantly pushed the limits of language—reinventing it, when necessary, to suit her ends. In her brother's words, "She saw things directly and just as they were. She abhorred sham."

Michael Dorris (1945–1997)

Part white and part Modoc Indian, writer/teacher Michael Dorris was a prominent contemporary advocate of Native American studies. Educated at Georgetown University (B.A., 1967) and Yale University (M.Phil., 1970), Dorris founded the Native American Studies department at Dartmouth College in the 1970s. In 1981 he married Louise Erdrich, one of his former students and a writer with whom he later collaborated. Dorris's books include the novels *A Yellow Raft on Blue Water* and *Cloud Chamber; The Broken Chord: A Family's Ongoing Struggle with Fetal Alcohol Syndrome* (winner of the 1989 National Book Critics Circle Award); *The Crown of Columbus,* a novel he coauthored with Erdrich; and several works for young adults. His essays are gathered in *Paper Trail: Collected Essays, 1967–1992.*

William Faulkner (1897–1962)

A "self-made" writer in the fullest sense, William Faulkner grew from humble beginnings to become a major American novelist and the 1950 winner of the Nobel Prize for literature. Faulkner was born in New Albany, Mississippi, and moved as a child to Oxford, Mississippi, where he spent most of his life. In 1918, without finishing high school, he enlisted in the Royal Canadian Air Force. Upon his return to the United States he attended school briefly and did odd jobs while dreaming of a life as a writer. His first published book, *The Marble Faun* (1924), was a collection of poems, but during a stay in New Orleans he met story writer Sherwood Anderson, who encouraged him to write fiction. A first novel, *Soldier's Pay,* came out in 1926, followed soon after by the novels that began to earn Faulkner a wider reputation: *Sartoris* (1929), *The Sound and the Fury* (1929), and *As I Lay Dying* (1930). In these and subsequent works Faulkner found his subject matter—his own South, the corrupt and violent South of myth and history, which he evoked obsessively in the people and landscapes of a fictional county named "Yoknapatawpha." Faulkner also developed a poetic, metaphoric, and syntactically complex prose style that is unique in American literature. "Barn Burning" is reprinted from *Collected Stories* (1950).

Robert Frost (1874–1963)

Though Robert Frost was born in San Francisco, California, his poetry is closely associated with rural New England, where he lived most of his life. While still a boy he moved there with his mother and sister following his father's death. He graduated from high school in Lawrence, Massachusetts (and eventually married a high school classmate), did some college work at Dartmouth and Harvard, and dedicated himself to becoming a poet. Success, however, came late; well into his thirties, Frost did odd jobs to keep his growing family out of poverty, and in 1912 he had to move to England to find a positive reception for his writing. Recognition came, first in England and then in America, with his first two books, *A Boy's Will* (1913) and *North of Boston* (1914). After moving back to New England in 1915 Frost saw critical acclaim for his work grow, and he soon became one of the most famous and widely honored poets in the United States, winning four Pulitzer prizes and reading a poem at the inauguration of President John F. Kennedy. In Frost's work the ordinary rhythms of New England speech play with and against the poetic strictures of blank verse (see Appendix C) and rhyme. Much of the pleasure experienced in reading a Frost poem comes from the contrast between the spontaneous-sounding speech, on the one hand, and the attention to form, on the other. Frost's life was plagued by personal suffering and tragedy, and the tragic occasionally surfaces in his poetry, as in "Out, Out—." Poems like "Stopping by Woods on a Snowy Evening" evoke the scenes and images of rustic tranquility that are another familiar strain in Frost's work.

Charlotte Perkins Gilman (1860–1935)

Charlotte Perkins Gilman was born in Hartford, Connecticut, to a distinguished family of independent thinkers but suffered an unstable and impoverished childhood. Her father abandoned the family when Charlotte was a small child, and she and her brother were raised by their mother and moved nineteen times in eighteen years. In 1884 Charlotte married Charles W. Stetson, a painter. After the birth of their child, a daughter, Charlotte fell into a deep depression and received treatments from Philadelphia physician S. Weir Mitchell, a specialist in nerve disorders. Mitchell's prescription of complete rest nearly drove Charlotte mad, and in 1888 she left her husband, fled to California, and obtained a divorce. Subsequently she devoted herself to lecturing and writing and emerged as a leading feminist theorist. Her major works include *Women and Economics* (1898) *The Man-Made World: Our Androcentric Culture* (1911), and the utopian novel *Herland* (1915). Gilman committed suicide in 1935 while dying of breast cancer. Her autobiography, *The Living of Charlotte Perkins Gilman,* was published posthumously.

Susan Glaspell (1882–1948)

Susan Glaspell was a native Midwesterner who spent much of her creative life in New England. In 1915 she and her husband, George Cram Cook, were instrumental in creating the Provincetown Players in Massachusetts, a group of amateur writers and actors who inaugurated "modern" American theater and drama. Also a short story writer and novelist, Glaspell is best remembered today for her plays, in which she explored such issues as women's experience and relations between the sexes. Major works include *Suppressed Desires* (1915), *The Verge* (1921), and *Alison's House,* which won a Pulitzer Prize in 1930.

Ellen Goodman (b. 1941)

A Pulitzer Prize–winning journalist, Ellen Goodman was born in Newton, Massachusetts, and earned her B.A. degree from Radcliffe College. After a job doing research for *Newsweek* magazine, she shifted to newspaper work in the mid-1960s and became a columnist for *The Boston Globe.* As a syndicated columnist, Goodman has been largely concerned with issues of family relationships and values, divorce, feminism, and changing lifestyles—what she once called the "life-and-death issues" of contemporary American society. In 1980, she won the Pulitzer Prize for distinguished commentary. Among her books and collections of columns are *Close to Home, Turning Points, At Large, Keeping in Touch, Making Sense,* and *Value Judgments.*

Francine du Plessix Gray (b. 1930)

The daughter of a French father and a Russian mother, Francine du Plessix Gray was born in Europe, immigrated to the United States in 1941, and became a naturalized United States citizen in 1952. After earning her B.A. degree from Barnard College in 1952, she worked as a reporter, editorial assistant, freelance writer, and book editor, before becoming a staff writer for the *New Yorker* magazine in 1968. Her books include *Divine Disobedience: Profiles in Catholic Radicalism, Hawaii: The Sugar-Coated Fortress, Adam and Eve and the City: Selected Nonfiction, At Home with the Marquis de Sade: A Life,* and several novels, among them the autobiographical *Lovers and Tyrants* (1976), which depicts Gray's own struggle, as a woman, to become a writer. In the latter novel her protagonist observes: "Every woman's life is a series of exorcisms from the spells of different oppressors: nurses, lovers, husbands, gurus, parents, children, myths of the good life. The most tyrannical despots can be the ones who love us the most."

Allan Gurganus (b. 1947)

Born in Rocky Mount, North Carolina, Allan Gurganus attended the University of Pennsylvania and studied painting at the Pennsylvania Academy of Fine Arts. Following military service in Vietnam during the late 1960s he returned to the United States and studied fiction writing at Sarah Lawrence College and the University of Iowa Writers' Workshop. His first novel, *Oldest Living Confederate Widow Tells All* (1989), won the Sue Kaufman Prize awarded by the American Academy of Arts and Letters. A recipient of numerous prizes for his short stories and novels, Gurganus has also published *White People* (stories, 1991) and *The Practical Heart: Four Novellas* (2001) and has taught at a variety of colleges and universities. He has raised more than 2 million dollars for AIDS research and hospice care through benefit readings and signings of his work and was recently awarded a certificate of lifetime achievement by Episcopal Caring Response to AIDS.

Thomas Hardy (1840–1928)

Thomas Hardy was born near Dorchester in rural Dorset, England. Though he trained as an architect, the young Hardy's passions for philosophy and poetry soon drove him to forsake architecture and become a writer. Beginning in the 1870s, he achieved widespread fame as a novelist, centering his fictional world in the countryside of his native Dorset (called "Wessex" in his novels). Among his best-known novels, published between 1874 and 1895, are *Far from the Madding Crowd, The Return of the Native, The Mayor of Casterbridge, Tess of the D'Urbervilles, and Jude the Obscure.* After 1896 he focused on writing poems, which were collected in *Wessex Poems* (1898) and two volumes, *Winter Words* and *Collected Poems,* published after his death. Like his novels, Hardy's poems reflect the traditions and rusticisms of the Dorset he knew in his youth.

Joy Harjo (b. 1951)

The work of Joy Harjo — poet, essayist, editor, children's book writer, and musician — has been closely tied to her identity as a Creek Indian. Harjo was born in Tulsa, Oklahoma, in the heart of the Creek Nation. She attended school at the Institute of American Indian Arts in Santa Fe, New Mexico, and graduated with a B.A. degree from the University of New Mexico, Albuquerque, in 1976. In 1978 she earned an M.F.A. in creative writing from the University of Iowa Writers Workshop, and since then she has continued both to write and to teach. Among her books are *She Had Some Horses* (1983), *Secrets from the Center of the World* (1989), *In Mad Love and War* (1990), and *The Woman Who Fell from the Sky: Poems* (1996). She has also co-edited an anthology of stories, *Reinventing the Enemy's Language: North American Native Women's Writing,* and recorded several albums with her band, Joy Harjo and Poetic Justice.

Nathaniel Hawthorne (1804–1864)

Nathaniel Hawthorne was born in Salem, Massachusetts, and was descended from New England Puritan stock, an influence which was to profoundly affect his novels and stories. After graduating from Bowdoin College in 1825, he spent twelve years in seclusion developing his craft as a writer. His first commercial success came with the short story collection *Twice-Told Tales* (1837), followed by *Mosses from an Old Manse* (1846) and several novels: *The Scarlet Letter* (1850, his masterpiece), *The House of the Seven Gables* (1851), and *The Blithedale Romance* (1852). Hawthorne called himself a writer of romances — stories which oppose strict realism and create their own reality.

Edward Hoagland (b. 1932)

Novelist and essayist, Edward Hoagland was born in New York City and earned a bachelor's degree from Harvard University in 1954. He served in the U.S. Army from 1955 to 1957, began writing novels and nonfiction, and published the first of several novels, *Cat Man,* in 1956; but his main career has been as an essayist, particularly of nature and travel, beginning with *Notes from the Century Before: A Journal from British Columbia* (1969). Other nonfiction collections include *The Courage of Turtles: Fifteen Essays by Edward Hoagland* (1971), *The Moose on the Wall: Field Notes from the Vermont Wilderness, African Calliope: A Journey to the*

Sudan, The Edward Hoagland Reader (1979), and *Balancing Acts.* Hoagland has also edited *The Penguin Nature Library* and published a collection of short stories, *The Final Fate of Alligators.*

Linda Hogan (b. 1947)

Born in Denver, Colorado, Linda Hogan is a member of the Chickasaw tribe, and her Native American heritage figures prominently in her poetry, essays, fiction, and plays. Hogan earned an M.A. degree from the University of Colorado at Boulder in 1978, and since then has taught at numerous schools and universities, such as the TRIBES program in Colorado Springs, the University of Minnesota, and the University of Colorado, Boulder. She has also held such jobs as dental assistant, homemaker, secretary, waitress, and volunteer worker at the Minnesota Wildlife Rehabilitation Clinic. Hogan says she has a focal interest in "studying the relationship between humans and other species, and trying to create world survival skills out of what I learn from this." Her writings include *Calling Myself Home* (poems), *The Book of Medicines: Poems, Dwellings: Reflections on the Natural World, Solar Storms,* and *Power* (novels). She is also co-editor of the anthology, *Between Species: Women and Animals* (1997).

bell hooks (b. 1952)

Writer and social critic bell hooks (real name Gloria Watkins) is a prominent figure in contemporary African American feminism. Hooks grew up in Kentucky, reading voraciously and gaining confidence in the importance of her own voice through writing and public speaking. With her first book, *Ain't I a Woman: Black Women and Feminism* (1981), hooks began articulating a vision for radical social change that she has since developed in *Talking Back: Thinking Feminist, Thinking Black, Teaching to Transgress: Education as the Practice of Freedom, Art on My Mind: Visual Politics, Reel to Real: Race, Sex, and Class at the Movies,* and other works. Though an "academic" (she has a Ph.D. and has taught at Yale and other prestigious institutions), hooks is known for her trenchant and accessible writing style. With her pen name, bell hooks honors her great-grandmother (Bell Hooks), "that figure in my childhood who . . . paved the way for me to speak."

Langston Hughes (1902–1967)

Regarded by some as the single most influential African American poet of the twentieth century, Langston Hughes was born in Joplin, Missouri, and started writing poetry as a boy. He graduated from high school in Cleveland and attended college for a year at Columbia University. Tiring of formal education, Hughes traveled to Africa and Europe in the early 1920s before returning to the United States and eventually settling in Harlem, New York. Harlem was then the scene of the "Harlem Renaissance" in black literature, theater, music, and other arts. Hughes became a literary leader of the Renaissance and a tireless champion of African American culture and writers. He went on to write over a dozen volumes of poetry, including *The Weary Blues* (1926) and *Montage of a Dream Deferred* (1951), as well as novels, stories, screenplays, plays, and histories. Strongly influenced by jazz, the blues, and spirituals, Hughes wrote, as he put it, "to explain and illuminate the Negro condition in America."

Henrik Ibsen (1828–1906)

A major figure in nineteenth-century drama, Henrik Ibsen was born in Skien, Norway. His father went bankrupt when Henrik was a child, and Ibsen left home at age fifteen to work as a druggist's apprentice in the town of Grimstad, where he made intellectual friends and wrote his first play (*Catiline,* published 1850). Holding managerial positions with the Bergen and new Norwegian Theatres, Ibsen published over half a dozen plays between 1851 and 1862. Most of these early efforts, composed in verse and romantic-historical in nature, were artistic and financial failures. Feeling stifled by Norwegian society, Ibsen moved in 1864 to Italy, and he continued to live there and in Germany for the next twenty-seven years. In the 1870s, his craft evolved to a new level as he began writing plays in the prose of everyday speech and portrayed characters who were ordinary members of the Norwegian middle class. Major dramas in this vein include *A Doll's House* (1879), *Ghosts* (1881), *An Enemy of the People* (1882), and *The Wild Duck* (1884). In these so-called "problem" plays, Ibsen dramatized defects in social institutions and explored hypocritical social attitudes towards divorce, venereal disease, and other taboo subjects. Enormously controversial at the time, these plays solidified Ibsen's reputation as a great playwright and helped launch European theater into the modern era. Ibsen consistently denied any intent to "preach" overt messages in his plays, insisting that he merely sought to portray life conflicts and leave it to readers and viewers to draw their own conclusions.

Fenton Johnson (b. 1953)

Born in New Haven, Kentucky, Fenton Johnson earned a B.A. degree from Stanford University and an M.F.A. degree from the University of Iowa Writer's Workshop in 1982. He is a contributor to *Harper's Magazine* and on the creative writing faculty at the University of Arizona. Johnson's books, praised for their sensitive portrayal of culture and family life in his native Kentucky, include two novels (*Crossing the River* and *Scissors, Paper, Rock*) and *Geography of the Heart,* a memoir about his lover, Larry Rose, who died of AIDS in 1990. His most recent book is *Keeping Faith: A Skeptic's Journey Among Christian and Buddhist Monks* (Houghton Mifflin, 2003).

Samuel Johnson (1709–1784)

Samuel Johnson was born in Litchfield, Staffordshire (England), the son of a bookseller. Though he attended grammar school in his hometown and studied for one year at Pembroke College, Oxford before poverty forced him to return home, Johnson was primarily self-educated, reading voraciously in his father's bookshop. His friend Adam Smith, the economist, later said that "Johnson knew more books than any man alive." Following a failed career as a schoolmaster, Johnson moved to London in 1737 and began to make a meager living writing journalism. He also composed poetry, notably *The Vanity of Human Wishes* (1749); several hundred "moral" essays which appeared in periodicals (*The Rambler, The Adventurer,* and *The Idler*) during the 1750s; and a philosophical novel, *Rasselas* (1759). Almost single-handedly, Johnson compiled the first great English dictionary (published in 1755) and an influential critical edition of Shakespeare (1765). Despite devastating bouts with melancholy and despair, Johnson managed to produce what has been called some of the sanest and most quotable writing in the English language, expressing, in the words of one biographer, "good sense wrung from concrete experience." During his last decades Johnson was the most important literary figure in England. *The Life of Samuel Johnson* (1791), written by his young friend, James Boswell, preserves Johnson's life and conversation in brilliant and colorful detail.

James Joyce (1882–1941)

James Joyce is a central figure in modern literature. Born and classically educated in Dublin, Joyce spent most of his working life on the European Continent—in Paris, Zurich, and other cities. Dublin, however, furnished the themes, characters, and cultural backdrop for all of his writing. Joyce's first published book, *Chamber Music* (poems, 1907), was followed in 1914 by *Dubliners,* a collection of short stories. In 1914 the autobiographical novel *A Portrait of the Artist as a Young Man* also began to appear serially in the London journal *The Egoist.* Other works include the landmark and controversial *Ulysses* (1922), a densely woven modern epic of alienated urban humanity, and *Finnegans Wake* (1939).

Claire Kemp (b. 1936)

Born in Worcester, Massachusetts, Claire Kemp is a short story writer who lives in Florida.

Barbara Kingsolver (b. 1955)

Born in Maryland, Barbara Kingsolver grew up in rural Kentucky. She graduated from De Pauw University in Greencastle, Indiana in 1977 and travelled in Europe for two years before settling in Tucson, Arizona, where she earned a Master of Science degree from the University of Arizona and subsequently worked as a scientific/technical writer and freelance journalist. Her first novel, *The Bean Trees,* was published in 1988. Other books include *Homeland and Other Stories, Animal Dreams: A Novel, Pigs in Heaven: A Novel, High Tide in Tucson: Essays from Now or Never, The Poisonwood Bible,* and *Small Wonder.* Without being "preachy," Kingsolver's fiction and other writings often address political questions and issues concerning women, race, class, community, ecology and the sense of place. A classically trained pianist, Kingsolver has also played in a rock band with fellow writers Amy Tan, Dave Barry, and Stephen King.

Theodore (Ted) Kooser (b. 1939)

Born in Ames, Iowa, Ted Kooser earned a B.S. degree from Iowa State University in 1962, an M.A. degree from the University of Nebraska in 1968, and has worked for many years as an insurance underwriter and executive in Lincoln, Nebraska. His collections of poetry include *Official Entry Blank* (his first book, published in 1969), *A Local Habitation and a Name, Sure Signs: New and Selected Poems, The Windflower Home Almanac of Poetry* (editor), *One World at a Time,* and *Weather Central.* Though he does not consider himself a regionalist writer, Kooser says that most of his poetry reflects "my interest in my surroundings here on the Great Plains."

D. H. Lawrence (1885–1930)

David Herbert Lawrence was born in Nottinghamshire, England, the son of a coal miner and a genteel and refined mother. He graduated from Nottingham University in 1908 and began writing poetry and fiction, including the major auto-biographical novel, *Sons and Lovers* (1913). In 1912 he eloped with Frieda von Richthofen, the wife of a Nottingham professor, whom he later married and with whom he shared his intense and emotionally tempestuous life. In the 1910s Lawrence grew increasingly disaffected with the mechanized, routinized life of industrial society and began to wander widely in search of alternative modes of life. His journeys took him and Frieda to southern Europe, Ceylon, Australia, the southwestern United States, Mexico, and eventually back to Europe. Throughout this period he continued to write novels (*The Rainbow* and *Women in Love* are among the best) as well as the travel essays and poems that established him as one of the finest descriptive writers in English. He died, of tuberculosis, in France. Lawrence's writings exhibit deep and lifelong obsessions: an emphasis on the elemental force of human sexuality, a faith in the life-forming power of the unconscious as opposed to the sterility and deadness of life lived from the merely conscious mind, and a passion to restore connections among human beings and between human beings and the earth—connections that modern society, in Lawrence's view, has largely lost or destroyed.

Doris Lessing (b. 1919)

Doris Lessing was born in Persia, the daughter of English parents. When she was five the family moved to a farm in southern Rhodesia (now Zimbabwe). Lessing remained in Africa until 1949, when she and her second husband and their child moved to England. Her first novel, *The Grass Is Singing* (1950), portrays the horrors of black-white relations in Africa, and injustices—racial, political, gender-based—have remained focal concerns of her work. Major writings include *The Golden Notebook* (1962), which narrates the growth of one woman's feminist consciousness; the five-novel *Children of Violence* series (1952–1969); *Canopus in Argos: Archives* (1979–1983), a multivolume sequence of nonrealistic novels; *The Good Terrorist* (1986); and *African Lands* (1992). Among Lessing's short story collections are *The Habit of Loving* (1957), *African Stories* (1964), and *Stories* (1978).

Denise Levertov (1923–1997)

Often described as a "visionary" poet, the English-born Denise Levertov was descended from religious mystics on both her mother's side (Welsh) and her father's (Russian Jewish). Privately educated in England, she worked as a nurse in London during World War II and afterward briefly taught English in Holland. In the late 1940s, Levertov moved to the United States, where her poetry, which she described until then as "British Romantic," was heavily influenced by the style and American idiom of such writers as Ezra Pound and William Carlos Williams. Author of nearly twenty books of poetry (among them *Collected Earlier Poems 1940–1960, Poems 1960–1967, The Jacob's Ladder, O Taste and See, Life in the Forest, The Poet in the World,* and *Breathing the Water*), Levertov also published several volumes of essays and translations. Her poems celebrate the beauty and mystery of daily life and reflect her deep appreciation of the natural world.

Clarice Lispector (1924–1977)

A major twentieth-century Brazilian writer of essays, novels, short stories, and children's literature, Clarice Lispector began composing stories as a child; however, she was too shy to make them public, and none of her earliest writings has survived. Lispector attended secondary school and later studied law and worked as a journalist in Rio de Janeiro, where she lived for most of the rest of her life. Her first novel, *Close to the Savage Heart,* was published in 1944. Other English translations of her works include *The Passion According to G.H., Family Ties, An Apprenticeship or the Book of Delights, The Apple in the Dark,* and *The Hour of the Star.* The English translators of *An Apprenticeship or the Book of Delights* comment on Lispector's composing habits: "Never very methodical, she finally learned at least to jot down her ideas and feelings as they came to her and before they were lost forever. Later she could piece them together as she understood them . . . [and nearly] all her works were composed in this rather unstructured manner."

Antonio Machado (1875–1939)

Regarded by many as the greatest poet of Spain since the seventeenth century, Antonio Machado was born in Seville and educated at a liberal school in Madrid. He published his first volume of verse in 1903 and obtained certification to teach in the Spanish secondary school system in 1907. For the next thirty years Machado was a writer and, as he put it, a "modest teacher" in various provincial public schools and in Madrid. Machado achieved national fame with his second book, *The Castilian Country* (1912), followed by other collections and *Complete Poems* (enlarged edition, 1928). During the 1930s, Machado became an impassioned spokesman for Spanish liberalism, publishing his views on a variety of public issues in the Madrid papers under the byline of "Juan de Mairena." A loyalist during the Spanish Civil War (1936–1939) he fled to France when the republican government of Spain fell to fascism, and there he died. Machado's poetry is known for its austerity, religious and philosophic concerns, and its vivid portrayal of the Spanish countryside. "The poet is a fisherman," he wrote, ". . . of fish capable of staying alive after being hauled out."

Naguib Mahfouz (b. 1911?)

Winner of the 1988 Nobel Prize for Literature, Naguib Mahfouz is generally regarded as Egypt's finest writer. He was born in Cairo (some sources say in 1911; others suggest 1912 or 1914), graduated from the University of Cairo, and did postgraduate study in philosophy. Many of Mahfouz's novels and stories depict the turbulence of Egypt's social and political past and the harsh lives of the Arab poor. Since the 1980s, Mahfouz's books (*Midaq Alley, The Thief and the Dogs, Miramar, Echoes of an Autobiography,* and many others) have been widely translated and become bestsellers in English-speaking countries.

Katherine Mansfield (1888–1923)

Born in New Zealand, Katherine Mansfield (born Kathleen Beauchamp) was educated in England and spent most of her working life there. Following a disastrous marriage in her twenties to a young musician, she obtained a divorce and in 1918 married the critic John Middleton Murry. Amid her family and personal problems and chronic ill health (she eventually died of tuberculosis), Mansfield devoted herself to writing. With such collections as *Bliss and Other Stories* (1920) and *The Garden Party and Other Stories* (1922), she established herself as a fiction writer of rare subtlety and as a daring experimenter with narrative technique. Today she is considered one of the major creators of the modern short story.

Guy de Maupassant (1850–1893)

A major influence on modern short story writers, Guy de Maupassant was born in Normandy, France, into a noble family. Following a restless youth, he fought in the Franco-Prussian War (1870–1871) and worked for nearly ten years as a government clerk in Paris. By then, writing had become his passion, and for seven years he apprenticed himself to the great French novelist, Gustave Flaubert, who was a family friend and who strongly influenced Maupassant's evolving style. With publication of his short story, "Boule de Suif" ("Ball of Fat"), in 1880, Maupassant gained instant fame; over the next decade he wrote and published hundreds of stories and articles and several novels. Maupassant's stories are populated by characters drawn from the French working and middle classes and are characterized by precise observation, unsentimental realism, and irony. His stories are often harsh in content and outlook, but typically objective in method, calculated to compel readers (as he put it) "to think, and to understand the deep, hidden meanings of events for themselves."

Terrence McNally (b. 1939)

Best known for his comedies and farces, playwright Terrence McNally was born in St. Petersburg, Florida, and graduated with a bachelor's degree from Columbia University. Subsequently he worked as a critic, editor, and stage manager as he was writing his first plays. His plays include *And Things That Go Bump in the Night, Bad Habits, The Ritz, Frankie and Johnny in the Claire de Lune* (which he rewrote for the Garry Marshall film *Frankie and Johnny), The Lisbon Traviata, Love! Valour! Compassion!,* and *Master Class.*

James Alan McPherson (b. 1943)

Born in Savannah, Georgia, James Alan McPherson earned his B.A. degree from Morris Brown College, a bachelor of laws degree from Harvard University, and an M.F.A. in creative writing from the University of Iowa (1969). In his early twenties he won first prize in a short story contest sponsored by the *Atlantic* magazine, and later he became a contributing editor to the *Atlantic.* Since 1981 McPherson has taught in the English Department at the University of Iowa. An African American, McPherson has published two widely praised books of short stories, *Hue and Cry* (1969) and the Pulitzer Prize–winning *Elbow Room* (1977). While many of McPherson's characters are African American, he has tried to transcend racial barriers in his work, regarding his characters less as "blacks" or "whites" than as individual people. McPherson's most recent books are *Crabcakes: A Memoir* and the anthology, *Fathering Daughters: Reflections by Men,* which he co-edited.

Lorrie Moore (b. 1957)

Born in Glen Falls, New York, Lorrie Moore graduated from St. Lawrence University and earned an M.F.A. degree from Cornell University in 1982. She has published widely in magazines (*The New Yorker, Ms., Cosmopolitan, Epoch*) and produced her first story collection, *Self-Help,* in 1985. In *Self-Help,* Moore experimented with writing several stories (including "How to Become a Writer") that mimic the "second person, mock imperative" voices of popular self-help manuals. Moore's other books include *Anagrams, Like Life,* and *Who Will Run the Frog Hospital?*

Thomas Moore (b. 1940)

Born in Detroit, Thomas Moore has been a professor of psychology and religious studies and a practicing psychotherapist. His books include *The Planets Within, Care of the Soul, Soulmates, The Re-Enchantment of Everyday Life,* and *The Soul of Sex.* Moore has also written numerous articles on Jungian and archetypal psychology for books and periodicals and has edited *A Blue Fire: Selected Writings* by archetypal psychologist James Hillman.

Cullen Murphy (b. 1952)

Cullen Murphy's books include *Rubbish!: The Archaeology of Garbage* (co-authored with William Rathje), *Just Curious: Essays,* and *The Word According to Eve: Women and the Bible in Ancient Times and Our Own.* He is managing editor of *The Atlantic.*

Gloria Naylor (b. 1950)

Born in New York City, Gloria Naylor earned her B.A. degree from Brooklyn College of the City University of New York in 1981 and an M.A. in African American Studies from Yale University in 1983. Her first novel, *The Women of Brewster Place* (1982), which won the American Book Award for best first novel, is about seven African American women living in an urban ghetto in the northern United States. Her other books include *Linden Hills,* about residents of an upper-middle-class black neighborhood, *Mama Day, Bailey's Cafe,* and *The Men of Brewster Place* (1998). "Kiswana Browne" is reprinted from *The Women of Brewster Place.*

Joyce Carol Oates (b. 1938)

Born in Lockport, New York, Joyce Carol Oates was educated at Syracuse University and the University of Wisconsin. She taught at the Universities of Detroit and Windsor (Ontario) and since 1978 has been on the faculty at Princeton University. An extraordinarily prolific writer, Oates has published dozens of books, including novels (e.g., *Black Water, Bellefleur, A Garden of Earthly Delights, My Heart Laid Bare*), short stories, literary and social criticism, and plays. *Tone Clusters,* reprinted from her 1991 collection *Twelve Plays,* admits us to familiar Oates terrain: a place of instability and fear, the brutal side of American experience, a world in which people are repeatedly threatened — often violently — by dark forces from without and within. The play also exhibits the interest in formal experimentation that is characteristic of Oates's fiction and dramas.

Flannery O'Connor (1925–1964)

Flannery O'Connor was born in Savannah, Georgia, and attended school at Georgia State College for Women and the University of Iowa, from which she received an M.F.A. degree. As an undergraduate O'Connor was already writing and publishing stories. In 1952 she published her first novel, *Wise Blood*. Diagnosed in 1950 with lupus, an autoimmune disease that eventually claimed her life, O'Connor moved home to live with her mother on the family farm in Milledgeville. There she devoted mornings to writing and afternoons to reading, letter writing, and the raising of peacocks. Though she published a second novel, *The Violent Bear It Away*, in 1960, O'Connor's greatest success was as a writer of short stories, which are collected in *A Good Man Is Hard to Find* (1955) and two volumes published after her death, *Everything That Rises Must Converge* (1965) and *The Complete Stories* (1971). O'Connor was devoutly Catholic and emphasized the pervasive influence of her Catholicism on her work. She was never, however, sentimentally religious, but more (in the words of a fellow novelist) like "an Old Testament prophet, crying out in our modern wilderness," exposing faithlessness, secularization, and human hypocrisy. "Her instruments," wrote a reviewer for *Time* magazine, "are a brutal irony, a slam-bang humor and a style of writing as balefully direct as a death sentence."

Sharon Olds (b. 1942)

Born in San Francisco, Sharon Olds graduated with a B.A. degree from Stanford University and a Ph.D. from Columbia University in 1972. Her collections of poems include *Satan Says, The Dead and the Living, The Gold Cell, The Matter of This World, The Sign of Saturn, The Father,* and *The Wellspring*.

Mary Oliver (b. 1935)

Born in Cleveland, Ohio, Mary Oliver attended Ohio State University and Vassar College. *No Voyage and Other Poems* (1963) was her first book. It was followed by *The Night Traveler, Twelve Moons, Sleeping in the Forest,* and *American Primitive,* which won the Pulitzer Prize in 1984. *New and Selected Poems* won the National Book Award in 1992. Fellow poet Maxine Kumin has called Oliver an "indefatigable guide to the natural world" who is comfortable with being "on the margins of things, on the line between earth and sky, the thin membrane that separates human from what we loosely call animal." Among Oliver's recent books is *West Wind* (1997), a collection of poems and prose poems.

Tillie Olsen (b. 1912/1913)

Tillie Olsen was born in Omaha, Nebraska. She married in her early twenties, had four children, and struggled for many years to write amid the competing demands of homemaking and earning a humble living at secretarial and other jobs. Not until the 1950s, with the help of a fellowship and a grant, was she able to concentrate on writing and finish her first short story collection, *Tell Me a Riddle* (1961). The title story of that volume won the O. Henry award for best American short story, and the book established Olsen's fame as a writer about the poor, the socially disenfranchised, and women. In a later nonfiction work, *Silences* (1978),

Olsen examined how class, gender, race, and other circumstances compel people into unnatural "silences." Olsen has also published *Yonnondio: From the Thirties* (1974), a novel set during the Great Depression, and has edited two books about mothers and daughters.

Eugene O'Neill (1888–1953)

The son of a famous actor, Eugene O'Neill grew up around theater but only began writing plays in his mid-twenties. His formal schooling was minimal (he spent a year at Princeton in 1906–1907 and took a playwriting class at Harvard in 1914). Most of his early education came through voracious and idiosyncratic reading of poets, romantic philosophers, and other iconoclasts and a series of experiences as gold prospector, seaman, and beachcomber that took him to Central and South America, Africa, and other parts of the globe. Abroad and in his native New York, O'Neill befriended down-and-outers, prostitutes, vagabonds, alcoholics, and other socially marginal persons who were to pose the themes and provide many of the characters for his dramas. O'Neill's first plays (mostly one-acts) were written in the 1910s and performed by experimental theater groups, notably the Provincetown Players in Provincetown, Cape Cod, Massachusetts, and in New York. *Beyond the Horizon* (1920) earned him his first of four Pulitzer Prizes, and with *The Emperor Jones* (1920), *The Hairy Ape* (1922), and *Desire Under the Elms* (1924), O'Neill emerged as the first American playwright of international stature. In 1936 he won the Nobel Prize for Literature. His powerful autobiographical play *Long Day's Journey into Night* was published posthumously in 1956. A fearless experimenter, O'Neill wrote plays of all lengths and in many forms and styles, including the expressionism (see Appendix C) of *The Hairy Ape*.

Edgar Allan Poe (1809–1849)

The son of actor parents, Edgar Allan Poe was orphaned as a child and suffered a turbulent and lonely personal life. After a brief formal education and an abortive stint at West Point, Poe turned to writing and became one of the foremost literary editors and critics of his day. He also wrote poetry and tales of horror and the macabre, which were published in magazines and collected in *Tales of the Grotesque and Arabesque* (1840) and other volumes. Poe's influence cuts across literary genres and types. He did more than any other individual writer to establish the genre of the horror story; he wrote highly rhythmic, musical, and symbolic poetry that was internationally influential, especially in France; and his intricate stories of mystery and intrigue, such as "The Murders in the Rue Morgue" and "The Purloined Letter," make him the creator of the modern detective story.

Adrienne Rich (b. 1929)

An influential feminist poet and thinker, Adrienne Rich was born in Baltimore and grew up in an intellectual household. She graduated from Radcliffe College in 1951; in the same year her first book of poems, *A Change of World,* was published in the prestigious Yale Series of Younger Poets. In the decades since, Rich has published numerous volumes of poetry, as well as collections of essays and speeches. Her poems are collected in *The Fact of a Doorframe: Poems Selected and New 1950–1984, Time's Power: Poems 1985–1988, An Atlas of the Difficult World: Poems 1988–1991, Dark Fields of the Republic: Poems 1991–1995,* and *Midnight Salvage: Poems 1995–1998.* For Rich, poetry never stands apart from life; it is always "political" in the broadest sense—about one's position in the world and how one is situated in relationship to history and to institutions (for instance, the institutions of patriarchy). Her major autobiographical essay, "When We Dead Awaken: Writing as Re-Vision" (reprinted in her 1979 prose collection, *On Lies, Secrets, and Silence*), tells the story of her evolution into feminist consciousness. Additional prose is collected in *Of Woman Born: Motherhood as Experience and Institution; Blood, Bread, and Poetry;* and *What Is Found There: Notebooks on Poetry and Politics.*

Christina Rossetti (1830–1894)

The daughter of an exiled Italian patriot father who wrote poetry and literary commentaries and an Anglo-Italian mother, Christina Rossetti and her two famous brothers, Dante Gabriel and William Michael, grew up in a household impassioned by politics and culture. As a young woman Rossetti became a devout member of the Anglican Church, and thereafter she devoted herself to writing, caring for her family, and charitable work. While much of her poetry is imbued with religious themes, it is also technically and thematically diverse, including ballads, love lyrics, sonnets, and fantasy verses for children. Her best known poetry collection is *Goblin Market and Other Poems* (1862).

Antoine de Saint-Exupéry (1900–1944)

A French aviator killed by enemy fire in World War II, Antoine de Saint-Exupéry is best remembered today for his classic fairy tale/novella, *The Little Prince* (1943). His other books include *Night Flight; Wind, Sand, and Stars;* and the posthumously published *Wisdom of the Sands.*

Milcha Sanchez-Scott (b. 1953)

Milcha Sanchez-Scott was born on the island of Bali, the daughter of a Colombian father and an Indonesian mother. She went to school in England and later at the University of California, San Diego, from which she graduated. Her published plays include *Latina, Dog Lady* and *The Cuban Swimmer* (both written in 1982 and produced for the first time in 1984), *Roosters,* and *Evening Star.*

Scott Russell Sanders (b. 1945)

Born in Memphis, Tennessee, Scott Russell Sanders earned his undergraduate degree at Brown University and his Ph.D. at Cambridge University. He has published work on subjects ranging from science fiction and literary criticism to biography and folklore. "In all of my work," he remarks, "regardless of period or style, I am concerned with the ways in which human beings come to terms with the practical problems of living on a small planet, in nature and in communities." Among his books, written in the 1980s and the 1990s, are *Fetching the Dead: Stories, Hear the Wind Blow: American Folksongs Retold, Secrets of the Universe, Staying Put: Making a Home in a Restless World,* and *The Country of Language.*

Annette Sanford (b. 1929)

Born in Cuevo, Texas, Annette Sanford worked for twenty-five years as a high school English teacher before deciding to devote herself full-time to writing. She has written several novels and short story collections, including *Lasting Attachments* (1989), *Crossing Shattuck Bridge: Stories,* and *Eleanor and Abel: A Romance.* Her stories have also been anthologized in *Her Work: Stories by Texas Women, Best American Short Stories, New Stories from the South,* and *Common Bonds: Stories By and About Modern Texas Women.*

Arthur Schopenhauer (1788–1860)

A major nineteenth-century German philosopher, Arthur Schopenhauer was born into a wealthy family and earned his doctorate in 1813. The following year he moved to Dresden, where he wrote the book for which he is best known, *The World as Will and Idea* (1818). In this work and others, Schopenhauer articulated a pessimistic philosophy that placed him at odds with the then dominant and more optimistic philosophy of G. W. F. Hegel. Largely ignored for many years, he became embittered and resigned a lectureship at a prestigious university to pursue, after 1831, a reclusive life as a writer. Only in the last decade of his life did he begin to receive widespread recognition. Schopenhauer's work, blending philosophies of West and East and stressing the centrality of the irrational in human behavior, influenced Freud, among others.

William Shakespeare (1564–1616)

Universally regarded as the greatest poet and dramatist in the English language, William Shakespeare was born in Stratford-upon-Avon, a market town in the heart of rural England. He was probably formally educated at the Stratford grammar school, where the curriculum emphasized Latin classics, Christian ethics, and rhetoric. Little is known about Shakespeare's early life. In 1582 he married Anne Hathaway, with whom he had three children, and by 1592 he was established in London as a playwright and actor. Between about 1590 and 1611 Shakespeare wrote and staged nearly forty plays, including histories (*Richard II, Richard III,* and several plays chronicling the reigns of Henry IV, Henry V, and Henry VI), comedies (*The Taming of the Shrew, A Midsummer Night's Dream, As You Like It, Twelfth Night*), and tragedies (*Hamlet, Othello, King Lear, Macbeth*). Most of these plays were performed by a repertory company known as the Lord Chamberlain's Men (later the King's Men) at the famous Globe Theatre, which was built in 1599 and destroyed by fire shortly after Shakespeare had retired permanently to Stratford in about 1610. Shakespeare also wrote a sequence of 154 *Sonnets* that are among the finest in the language and two major narrative poems, *Venus and Adonis* and *The Rape of Lucrece.* The first edition of Shakespeare's collected plays, known as the First Folio, was published in 1623, seven years after the playwright's death.

Sei Shōnagon (b. ca. 967)

Other than that she served as a lady-in-waiting to the Japanese Empress Sadako, little is known about the personal life of Sei Shōnagon; it is not even certain when and where she died. What is known about her is what she shares in her famous *Pillow Book,* which covers the approximately ten-year period she spent in Sadako's court. A type of notebook or commonplace book, *The Pillow Book* is is a classic of Japanese literature, filled (in Shōnagon's own words) "with odd facts, stories from the past, and all sorts of other things, often including the most trivial material. . . ." According to translator Ivan Morris, "pillow book" was most likely "a generic term to describe a type of informal book of notes which men and women composed when they retired to their rooms in the evening and which they kept near their sleeping place, possibly in the drawers of their wooden pillows, so that they might record stray impressions."

Shams-ud-din Muhammad (Hafiz; c. 1320–1389)

One of the most famous mystic poets of Persia, Hafiz (whose given name was Shams-ud-din Muhammad) is believed to have written some 5,000 poems, of which about ten percent have survived. His work became known in the West during the later eighteenth and nineteenth centuries through the admiring efforts of the German poet Johann Wolfgang von Goethe, American essayist/poet Ralph Waldo Emerson, and others. Though he rarely left his native city of Shiraz (in present-day Iran), Hafiz's wit, earthy humor, and mystical insight have spoken eloquently to readers around the world.

Leslie Marmon Silko (b. 1948)

Leslie Marmon Silko was born in Albuquerque, New Mexico, and grew up in the nearby village of Old Laguna. She is of mixed blood, including white, Laguna, and Plains Indian, and her cultural origins and traditions are at the heart of her writing. After attending Catholic schools in Albuquerque, Silko graduated with a B.A. from the University of New Mexico and briefly attended law school before deciding to be a writer and teacher. She published her first story in 1969 and since then has produced a volume of poems and several books of fiction, including *Ceremony* (1977, a novel), *Storyteller* (1981, a collection of stories and short prose interwoven with poetry and photographs), and *Almanac of the Dead* (1991, a novel). She has also published two more books of nonfiction,

Sacred Water: Narratives and Pictures (1993) and *Yellow Woman and a Beauty of the Spirit: Essays on Native American Life Today* (1996). Not just about characters, Silko's fiction is about the healing and protective powers inherent in storytelling itself. This emphasis on the functionality of storytelling is the focus of "Language and Literature from a Pueblo Indian Perspective," the Silko piece reprinted in *Reading and Writing from Literature.*

Rebecca Solnit (b. 1961)

An environmental activist and a long-time resident of San Francisco, Rebecca Solnit has written several books about art, culture, environment, and place, including *Savage Dreams: A Journey Into the Landscape Wars of the American West* (1999), *Hollow City: The Siege of San Francisco and the Crisis of American Urbanism* (2000), *As Eve Said to the Serpent: On Landscape, Gender, and Art* (2001), and *River of Shadows: Eadward Muybridge and the Technological Wild West* (2003). "The Disembodiment of Everyday Life" is excerpted from *Wanderlust: A History of Walking* (2000).

Gary Soto (b. 1952)

A noted Chicano poet, essayist, and fiction writer, Gary Soto grew up in a working-class family in Fresno, California. He was employed as a laborer during his childhood, and a strong identification with the working poor stamps much of his work. Soto graduated from California State University, Fresno, in 1974 and earned an M.F.A. in creative writing from the University of California, Irvine, in 1976. In 1977 he published his first book, *The Elements of San Joaquín,* a collection of poems depicting the Fresno of his childhood. Since then he has written several books of prose memoirs, including *Living Up the Street: Narrative Recollections* and *Lesser Evils: Ten Quartets,* and numerous volumes of poetry, including *Black Hair, Home Course in Religion,* and *New and Selected Poems* (1995).

Wole Soyinka (b. 1934)

Educated in England, Wole Soyinka is a Nigerian political activist who has had to flee his native land several times for criticizing the government. He is the author of *Swamp Dwellers, Death and the King's Horseman,* and over a dozen other plays that have made him Nigeria's leading playwright. In 1986 he was awarded the Nobel Prize for Literature. Though best known for his plays, Soyinka has also written novels, an autobiography, and several collections of poetry.

Anna Swir (1909–1984)

Anna Swir (Swirszcynska) was born in Warsaw, Poland, the daughter of an impoverished painter, in whose studio she spent much of her childhood. She put herself through university in Warsaw, studying medieval and Baroque Polish literature and publishing her first poems during the 1930s. During the World War

II Nazi occupation of Poland, Swir was a member of the Resistance and narrowly escaped execution. The experience changed her profoundly; her poetry, previously rather impersonal, assumed heightened urgency and emotion. Swir is known as a crafter of miniature poems that are at once descriptive and personal. As her compatriot, Czeslaw Milosz, remarks, "Anna Swir achieves in her sensual and fierce poetry a nearly calligraphic neatness." Milosz and Leonard Nathan have translated a selection of Swir's poems into English under the title *Talking to My Body* (1996).

Wislawa Szymborska (b. 1923)

Wislawa Szymborska was born in Poland, educated at Jagellonian University (also in Poland), and currently lives in Cracow. For many years she was a poetry editor and columnist for a Polish literary weekly magazine. She published her first collection of poems in 1952. Her poems have been translated into English in *Sounds, Feelings, Thoughts: Seventy Poems* (1981), *View with a Grain of Sand* (1995), and *Poems, New and Collected, 1957–1997* (1998). Her poems have also been translated into Arabic, Hebrew, Japanese, Chinese, and other languages. In 1996 she was awarded the Nobel Prize for Literature. Characteristically ironic and witty, Szymborska's poetry captures the experience of everyday life in deceptively simple language.

Henry David Thoreau (1817–1862)

Essayist, poet, and naturalist, Henry David Thoreau was born in Concord, Massachusetts. Though he graduated from Harvard in 1837, he was mainly self-taught, studying surveying and other practical arts and steeping himself in the literary classics of East and West. Above all Thoreau studied nature, both from a naturalist's perspective and from that of a poet who detected symbols of human experience in even the minutest natural phenomena. Thoreau matured into one of the era's great iconoclasts, a supreme example of a countercultural thinker. Disgruntled by the materialism of midcentury America, he built a small cabin at Walden Pond (near Concord) in 1845 and lived there, in simple relationship with nature, for two years. As he put it, he "chose to be rich by making his wants few." This experience furnished the material for *Walden* (1854), his most famous book. Other major writings include *A Week on the Concord and Merrimack Rivers* (1849) and the essay "Resistance to Civil Government" (1849), an argument for the sanctity of individual conscience in relation to political majorities that was to influence Mahatma Gandhi and Martin Luther King, Jr., among others. Thoreau's *Journal*, which he kept for some twenty-three years, supplied the material for his published writings.

James Thurber (1894–1961)

American humorist James Thurber was born and grew up in Columbus, Ohio, and attended (but never graduated from) Ohio State University. In the 1920s he became a newspaper writer, worked briefly in France, and eventually settled in New York City, where he joined the staff of the recently founded *New Yorker* magazine, with which he was to maintain a lifelong association. Beginning in the late 1920s, Thurber's humorous sketches, stories, and line cartoons—distinguished by their simple style and often wildly imaginative subject matter—became a *New Yorker* fixture. His work is collected in such volumes as *My Life and Hard Times, Fables for Our Time, The Thurber Carnival,* and *My World—and Welcome to It,* which includes "The Secret Life of Walter Mitty."

Kurt Vonnegut, Jr. (b. 1922)

Born in Indianapolis, Indiana, Kurt Vonnegut attended Cornell University and the Carnegie Institue of Technology (now Carnegie-Mellon University) and earned an M. A. degree from the University of Chicago. During World War II he served in the U.S. Army in Europe, became a POW of the Germans, and survived one of the worst military atrocities of the war—the Allied firebombing of Dresden (a story later addressed in his novel, *Slaughterhouse Five*). Among Vonnegut's many books are novels (*Cat's Cradle, Slaughterhouse Five, Breakfast of Champions, Jailbird, Bluebeard, Timequake*); two collections of short stories (*Canary in a Cathouse* and *Welcome to the Monkey House*); and numerous plays, screenplays, essays, and speeches. Largely ignored by critics at the start of his career, Vonnegut became a countercultural icon in the late 1960s and 1970s, before gaining widespread critical recognition as a major American novelist. His radical experiments with style and form—blending elements of fantasy, science fiction, dark humor, and fierce social satire—coalesce around such basic human themes as happiness, the future, and the need to be humane in an inhumane world.

Alice Walker (b. 1944)

Alice Walker was born in Eatonton, Georgia, the youngest of eight children of black sharecropper parents. She attended Spelman College, a black women's school in Atlanta, and graduated in 1965 from Sarah Lawrence College in New York, where she began writing what would become some of her first published works. She participated in the civil rights movement in Mississippi in 1966 and taught college before obtaining a fellowship at the Radcliffe Institute in Cambridge, Massachusetts, in 1971. Walker's books include novels (*The Third Life of Grange Copeland, Meridian,* and *Possessing the Secret of Joy,* among others), collections of short stories (*In Love & Trouble* and *You Can't Keep a Good Woman Down*), poems (such as *Revolutionary Petunias*), and essay collections (*In Search of Our Mothers' Gardens: Womanist Prose, Living by the Word: Selected Wri-tings, 1973–1987,* and *Anything We Love Can Be Saved: A Writer's Activism.*). *The Color Purple,* an epistolary novel (a novel in the form of a series of letters) that won a Pulitzer Prize in 1983, shows Walker's characteristic interest in formal experimentation. Much of Walker's work is about strong and independent-minded African American women, such as Gracie Mae Still in the short story "Nineteen Fifty-five."

Thomas S. Whitecloud (1914–1972)

Thomas St. Germain Whitecloud was born in New York City, the son of a white mother and a Chippewa father. His parents divorced when Thomas was a child; his father returned to the Lac Du Flambeau Reservation in Wisconsin, and young Thomas grew up on both the reservation and in mainstream America. Following a troubled youth, Whitecloud graduated from the University of Redlands in 1938, afterwards earning a medical degree from Tulane School of Medicine in New Orleans. Thereafter he worked as a physician, primarily in Texas and Mississippi, and also wrote and lectured. Though he left behind numerous unpublished stories, poems, and essays at his death, Whitecloud published only one significant literary work, "Blue Winds Dancing," which appeared in *Scribner's Monthly* during his senior year of college.

Walt Whitman (1819–1892)

Born near Huntington, Long Island, Walt Whitman received virtually no formal education and worked at a variety of jobs during his youth and early manhood—as a printer, schoolteacher, journalist, and carpenter. As a poet he developed relatively late, not publishing his first book until 1855, when he was thirty-six years old. Over time, however, this book, *Leaves of Grass*, revolutionized the writing of poetry in English and exerted significant impact on poets worldwide. In an impassioned "Preface" to the book Whitman rejected the constraints of traditional verse, with its meter and rhyme, and advocated a poetry that shapes itself freely out of the poet's own "beautiful blood and . . . brain." An obsessive and fastidious rewriter, Whitman revised and expanded *Leaves of Grass* for the rest of his life, taking the book through six different editions. During the Civil War he volunteered as a nurse, assisting and comforting the dying and wounded in army hospitals in and around Washington, D.C. Out of this experience he published *Drum-Taps*, a collection of vividly realistic war poems that was later absorbed into *Leaves of Grass*. In addition to being a radical innovator of poetic style, Whitman is famous for celebrating sex and the human body as focal subjects for great poetry.

August Wilson (b. 1945)

August Wilson was born in Pittsburgh, Pennsylvania, the son of a black mother and a white father. Abandoned by their father, August and his siblings were raised by their mother in the Pittsburgh slums and, later, in a largely white community where August suffered racial harassment at school. Wilson dropped out of school at age fifteen and went on to work various jobs such as short-order cook and stock clerk. He also frequented the public library, where he steeped himself in the works of Ralph Ellison, Langston Hughes, Richard Wright, and other African American writers. While books helped give Wilson confidence to write himself, he was also inspired by many other influences in his African American culture and heritage: street talk, the rhythms of ordinary speech and conversation, political movements, and especially the music and language of the blues. Wilson was already writing fiction and poetry in the 1960s when he got caught up in the Black Power movement and helped found a black activist theater in Pittsburgh. He also began writing plays. Later, moving to Minnesota, he worked with the Playwrights Center of Minneapolis and founded the Black Horizons Theatre Company. Wilson's first commercial success, *Ma Rainey's Black Bottom* (1984)—about the legendary black blues singer—was voted Best Play of the Year 1984–85 by the New York Drama Critics Circle. Wilson's aim is to write a cycle of ten plays about the experience of African Americans, one for each decade of the twentieth century. Thus far he has completed several plays in the cycle, in addition to *Ma Rainey: Fences* and *The Piano Lesson* (both Pulitzer Prize winners), *Joe Turner's Come and Gone*, *Two Trains Running*, and *Seven Guitars*.

Sloan Wilson (b. 1920)

Before turning full-time to fiction writing, Sloan Wilson led a varied life as a blacksmith, a sailing instructor, a Coast Guard officer, a newspaper reporter, a foundation executive, an English professor, a public relations person, magazine editor, and a newspaper editor. His books include *The Man in the Gray Flannel Suit* (1955), *A Summer Place: A Novel* (1958), *What Shall We Wear to the Party? The Man in the Gray Flannel Suit Twenty Years Before & After* (1976), and *Pacific Interlude* (1982).

Tobias Wolff (b. 1945)

Born in Birmingham, Alabama, Tobias Wolff served in U.S. Army Special Forces during the Vietnam War and achieved the rank of first lieutenant. Following military service, he graduated with first-class honors from Oxford University in 1972 and earned a M.A. degree from Stanford University in 1978. Wolff published his first collection of short stories, *In the Garden of the North American Martyrs*, in 1981. Other short story collections include *Back in the World, The Stories of Tobias Wolff*, and *The Night in Question*. Wolff has also published two memoirs: *This Boy's Life*, about his teen years, and *In Pharaoh's Army: Memories of the Lost War*, which recounts his experiences fighting in the Vietnam War. *This Boy's Life* was made into a film in 1993.

William Wordsworth (1770–1850)

William Wordsworth was born in Cockermouth, Cumbria, in the Lake District of England, and his nature poetry is forever associated with that region. Orphaned by the age of thirteen, Wordsworth attended grammar school in Hawkshead and graduated from St. John's College, Cambridge. A walking tour of France and Switzerland in the early 1790s fired him with zeal for the French Revolution, with which (during the infamous Reign of Terror) he later grew disenchanted. Returning to England Wordsworth lived modestly with his sister, Dorothy, formed one of the most famous literary friendships in English literature (with Samuel Taylor Coleridge), and dedicated himself to writing poetry. His volume *Lyrical Ballads* (1798), written in collaboration with Coleridge, and a famous Preface he wrote to the 1800 edition of that work, greatly influenced the course of English poetry, introducing common people and vernacular diction into English verse. Wordsworth's subsequent volumes of poetry included *Poems in Two Volumes* (1807), *The Excursion* (1814), and the long posthumously published autobiographical poem, *The Prelude*. In 1843 he was appointed Poet Laureate of England.

William Butler Yeats (1865–1939)

Irish poet, playwright, and critic, William Butler Yeats was born near Dublin, the son of the lawyer and distinguished painter John Butler Yeats. William himself studied painting as a young man but soon abandoned art for writing, producing his first books of poems in the late 1880s. Yeats's poetry interweaves personal vision with history, mythology, psychology, mysticism, and other cultural influences. While many of his contemporaries wrote in free verse, Yeats breathed new life into old poetic forms, articulating his personal and symbolic vision in rhymed lines and tightly constructed stanzas. He was a leading advocate of Irish national art and served as president of the Irish National Theatre Society and codirector of Dublin's Abbey Theatre. In 1923 Yeats was awarded the Nobel Prize for Literature. Among his major collections of poetry are *In the Seven Woods* (1903), *The Wild Swans at Coole* (1917), *The Tower* (1928), and *Collected Poems* (definitive edition, 1956).

Author/Title Index

Subject Index

Process memorandum, 155
Proofreading, backward, 102
Prose poetry, 166
Protagonist
    explanation of, 162
    in plays, 180

Quality of life. *See* Work and
    quality of life
Quick-writing, 80–81
Quotations
    collecting, 56–58
    developing essays using il-
        lustrative, 100–102
    documentation style for,
        139
    in essays, 176

*Reader's Guide to Periodical
    Literature,* 123
Reading
    four-step process for writ-
        ing from, 10–18
    graphical representations
        of, 16–17
    as springboard for writing,
        27
Reading aloud, 103, 148
Recursive thinking, 72, 75
Reflection, 185–186, 200
Relationships. *See* Gender
    and relationships
Research essays. *See also*
        Essays; Literature-based
        research essays
    citing sources for, 126–128
    examination of sources for,
        126
    example of documented,
        130–136
    identifying useful sources
        of information for, 122–
        123
    incorporating outside
        sources into, 128–129
    introductory remarks on,
        116–117
    keeping research logs for,
        117–118
    locating and keeping track
        of sources for, 124–125
    MLA style for, 138–142
    preresearch process for,
        118–122

Research logs
    excerpts from sample,
        136–137
    methods for keeping, 117–
        118
Resolution
    in plays, 180
    in short stories, 164
Revision
    checklist of activities for,
        103
    critical approaches to, 95–
        96
    explanation of, 94–95
    global, 95, 146
    "lightning," 103, 148
    local, 95, 102
    making time for, 149–150
    peer and small group input
        for, 99–100
    for portfolio entries, 154–
        155
    postdraft outlines for, 96–
        99
    strategies for, 146–151
    tasks of, 148–149
    using quotations and ex-
        amples, 100–102
    writer-initiated feedback
        for, 100
Rhyme, 168–170
Rhythm, 167
Rising action
    in plays, 180
    in short stories, 163
Round characters
    in plays, 180
    in short stories, 162

Scansion, 168
Scene descriptions, 178
Scenes, 179
Scholarly journals, 123
Secondary sources, 124
Sequencing, 81–83
Setting
    in plays, 179–180
    in short stories, 164
Short stories
    about cultural conflict and
        change, 815–856
    about experience and iden-
        tity, 452–499
    about families, 323–371

about gender and relation-
    ships, 221–268
about individual and soci-
    ety, 605–655
about work and quality of
    life, 979–1019
characters in, 161–162
dialogue in, 162–163
explanation of, 159
plot in, 163–164
point of view in, 159–161
theme and setting in, 164
Simile, 205–206
Slant rhyme, 169
Small groups. *See* Groups
Society. *See* Individual and
    society
Sound effects, 168–170
Sources
    citing one's, 126–128
    incorporating outside,
        128–129
    for literature-based re-
        search papers, 122–123
    locating and keeping track
        of, 124–125
    primary, 122, 124
    secondary, 124
Speaker, 166–167
Stage directions, 178
Stories within essays, 175–
    176
Style, 174
Symbolism, 212–214
Symbols, 212
Synecdoche, 212
Syntax, 170–171

Table of contents, 126
Technology, 1136–1137
Tetrameter, 168
Theme
    in essays, 174
    in short stories, 164
Thesis, developing working,
    78–80
Third-person limited point of
    view, 160
Third-person point of view,
    160
Throwaway drafts
    guidelines for, 88–90,
        120–121
    rough drafts from, 91–93

Credits

ALLEN, PAULA GUNN: "Pocahontas to Her English Husband, John Rolfe," copyright © 1988 by Paula Gunn Allen. Used with permission of West End Press.

ALLEN, WOODY: *Death Knocks* by Woody Allen, copyright © 1966, 1967, 1968, 1969, 1970, 1971 by Woody Allen, from *Getting Even* by Woody Allen. Used by permission of Random House, Inc.

ANGELOU, MAYA: Excerpt from "Seven Women's Blessed Assurance," copyright © 1990 by Maya Angelou, from *I Shall Not Be Moved* by Maya Angelou. Copyright © 1990 by Maya Angelou. "Graduation", copyright © 1969 and renewed 1997 By Maya Angelou from *I Know Why The Caged Bird Sings* By Maya Angelou. Used by permission of Random House, Inc.

ANIMAL WATCH: Collection of reports received by the Washington Humane Society and the D.C. Animal Control Division, published weekly in the District section of the *Washington Post.* © 2002, The Washington Post, reprinted with permission.

APPEL, CATHY: "Letters," from *Racoon,* Issue 20, 1986. Reprinted by permission of Racoon Books.

ATWOOD, MARGARET: "The City Planners" from *The Circle Game,* copyright © 1966. Reprinted with the permission of Stoddart Publishing Co. Ltd. "The Man From Mars" is reprinted with the permission of Simon & Schuster Adult Publishing Group from *Dancing Girls And Other Stories.* Copyright © 1977, 1982 by O.W. Toad, Ltd.

BAMBARA, TONI CADE: "The Lesson" copyright © 1972 by Toni Cade Bambara, from *Gorilla, My Love* by Toni Cade Bambara. Copyright © 1972 by Toni Cade Bambara. Used by permission of Random House, Inc.

BASHŌ: Excerpt from Bashō, *The Narrow Road to the Deep North and Other Travel Sketches,* translated by Nobuyuki Yuasa (Penguin Classics, 1966), copyright © Nobuyuki Yuasa. Reproduced by permission of Penguin Books Ltd.

BEATTY, JAN: This version of "A Waitress's Instructions on Tipping, or Get the Cash Up and Don't Waste My Time" first appeared in the *Pittsburgh Post-Gazette* and was revised for *Mad River,* by Jan Beatty, © 1995. Reprinted by permission of the author.

BERRY, WENDELL: "Think Little" from *The Art Of The Commonplace: The Agrarian Essays Of Wendell Berry.* Edited and introduced by Norman Wirzba, Washington, D.C.: Counterpoint, 2002. Reprinted by permission of Shoemaker & Hoard Publishers.

BLY, CAROL: "Growing Up Expressive" from *Letters from the Country* by Carol Bly. Copyright © 1973, 1974, 1975, 1977, 1978, 1979, 1981 by Carol Bly. Reprinted by Lukeman Literary Management Ltd. on behalf of the author.

BLY, ROBERT: "In Rainy September," from *Loving a Woman in Two Worlds* by Robert Bly, copyright © 1985 by Robert Bly. Used by permission of Doubleday, a division of Random House, Inc.

BOSSELAAR, LAURE-ANNE: "The Bumper Sticker" from *The Hour Between Wolf and Dog,* copyright © 1997 by Laure-Anne Bosselaar. Reprinted with the permission of BOA Editions, Ltd.

BOWEN, ELIZABETH: "The Demon Lover" from *The Collected Stories of Elizabeth Bowen* by Elizabeth Bowen, copyright © 1981 by Curtis Brown Ltd., Literary Executors of the Estate of Elizabeth Bowen. Used by permission of Alfred A. Knopf, a Division of Random House, Inc.

BRADBURY, RAY: "[A Story About Love]" from *Long After Midnight.* Reprinted by permission of Don Congdon Associates, Inc., copyright © 1976, renewed 2004 by Ray Bradbury. "The Murderer" from *The Golden Apples of the Sun.* Reprinted by permission of Don Congdon Associates, Inc. Copyright © 1953, renewed 1981 by Ray Bradbury.